Seventeenth Edition
STANDARD CATALOG OF

United States Paper Money

By Chester L. Krause and Robert F. Lemke
Robert E. Wilhite, Editor

Special Consultants:

- ★ Fredrick J. Bart
- ★ Colin R. Bruce II
- ★ George Cuhaj
- ★ Tom Denly
- ★ Kevin Foley
- ★ David Gladfelter
- ★ Len Glazer
- ★ Alan Herbert
- ★ Gene Hessler
- ★ Harry Jones

- ★ Theodore Kemm
- ★ Dean Oakes
- ★ Vernon Oswald
- ★ Bill Rindone
- ★ Russell Rulau
- ★ Fred Schwan
- ★ John Schwartz
- ★ Neil Shafer
- ★ R. B. White

Contributions by those now deceased are gratefully remembered

Carl Allenbaugh
Hy Brown
John T. Hickman
Steven J. Koelbl
Curtis Iverson
Jim Thompson

Published by

 **krause publications**

700 E. State Street • Iola, WI 54990-0001
Telephone: 715/445-2214

Please call or write for our free catalog.
Our toll-free number to place an order or obtain a free catalog is 800-258-0929
or please use our regular business telephone 715-445-2214
for editorial comment and further information.

Library of Congress Catalog Number: 81-81876

ISBN: 0-87341-653-8

Printed in the United States of America

INDEX

Paper Money Grading

Introduction

Grading is the most controversial component of paper money collecting today. Small differences in grade can mean significant differences in value.

To facilitate communication between sellers and buyers, it is essential that grading terms and their meanings be as standardized and as widely used as possible. The standardization should reflect common usage as much as practicable.

The grades and definitions as set forth below cannot reconcile all the various systems and grading terminology variants. Rather, the attempt is made here to try and diminish the controversy with some common-sense grades and definitions that aim to give more precise meaning to the grading language of paper money.

Grading Guide

Crisp Uncirculated (CU): A perfectly preserved note, never mishandled by the issuing authority, a bank teller, the public or a collector.

Paper is clean and firm, without discoloration. Corners are sharp and square, without any evidence of rounding. (Rounded corners are often a tell-tale sign of a cleaned or "doctored" note.)

An uncirculated note will have its original, natural sheen.

About Uncirculated (AU): A virtually perfect note, with some minor handling. May show evidence of bank counting folds at a corner or one light fold through the center, but not both. An AU note cannot be creased, a crease being a hard fold which has usually "broken" the surface of the note.

Paper is clean and bright with original sheen. Corners are not rounded.

Extremely Fine (XF): AL very attractive note, with light handling. May have a maximum of three light folds or one strong crease.

Paper is clean and bright with original sheen. Corners may show only the slightest evidence of rounding. There may also be the slightest sign of wear where a fold meets the edge.

Very Fine (VF): An attractive note, but with more evidence of handling and wear. May have a number of folds both vertically and horizontally.

Paper may have minimal dirt, or possible color smudging. Paper itself is still relatively crisp and not floppy.

There are no tears into the border area, although the edges do show slight wear. Corners also show wear but not full rounding.

Fine: A note which shows considerable circulation, with many folds, creases and wrinkling.

Paper is not excessively dirty but may have some softness.

Edges may show much handling, with minor tears in the border area. Tears may not extend into the design. There will be no center hole because of excessive folding.

Colors are clear but not very bright. A staple hole or two would not be considered unusual wear in a Fine note. Overall appearance is still on the desirable side.

Very Good (VG): A well-used note, abused but still intact.

Corners may have much wear and rounding, tiny nicks, tears may extend into the design, some discoloration may be present, staining may have occurred, and a small hole may be seen at center from excessive folding.

Staple and pinholes are usually present, and the note itself is quite limp but no pieces of the note are missing. A note in VG condition may still have an overall not unattractive appearance.

Good (G): A well-worn and heavily-used note. Normal damage from prolonged circulation will include strong multiple folds and creases, stains, pinholes and/or staple holes, dirt, discoloration, edge tears, center hole, rounded corners and an overall unattractive appearance. No large pieces of the note may be missing. Graffiti is commonly seen on notes in G condition.

Fair: A totally limp, dirty, and very well-used note. Large pieces may be half torn off or missing besides the defects mentioned under the Good category. Tears will be larger, obscured portions of the note will be bigger.

Poor: A "rag" with severe damage because of wear, staining, pieces missing, graffiti, larger holes. May have tape holding pieces of the note together. Trimming may have taken place to remove rough edges.

The above Introduction and Grading Guide is an adaptation work prepared under the guidance of the Grading Committee of the International Bank Note Society.

How To Look At A Banknote

In order to ascertain the grade of a note, it is essential to examine it out of a holder and under a good light. Move the note around so that light bounces off at different angles. Try holding it up obliquely so that the note is almost even with your eye as you look up at the light. Hard-to-see folds or slight creases will show up under such examination.

Cleaning, Washing, Pressing

Cleaning, washing or pressing paper money is generally harmful and reduces both the grade and the value of a note. At the very least, a washed or pressed note may lose its original sheen and its surface may become lifeless and dull. The defects a note has, such as folds and creases, may not necessarily be completely eliminated and their telltale marks can be detected under a good light. Carelessly washed notes may also have white streaks where the folds or creases were (or still are).

Processing of a note will automatically reduce it at least one full grade.

Other Defects

Glue, tape or pencil marks may sometimes be successfully removed. While such removal will leave a cleaned surface, it will improve the overall appearance of the note without concealing any of its defects. Under such circumstances, the grade of that note may also be improved.

The words "pinholes," "staple holes," "trimmed," "writing on face...... tape marks," etc., should always be added to the description of a note.

The Term "Uncirculated"

The word "Uncirculated" is used in this grading guide only as a qualitative measurement of the appearance of a note. It has nothing at all to do with whether or not an issuer has actually released the note to circulation. Either a note is uncirculated in condition or it is not, there can be no degrees of uncirculated. Defects in color, centering and the like may be included in a description but the fact that a note is or is not in uncirculated condition should not be a disputable point.

Introduction

Though paper media representing gold or other intrinsic-value stores of wealth have been issued in the United States and its predecessor colonies and territories since 1690, the widespread acceptance of paper currency by the American people is a comparatively recent development and came only grudgingly.

Paper money emissions by the British colonies in New England, the earliest paper currency within the borders of what is now the U.S.A., circulated alongside other untraditional exchange media such as Indian wampum shells and musket balls during chronic periods of shortages of "real" - coined - money.

Even though the first issues of an organized central government, the Continental Congress' currency notes, promised to pay the bearer face value in "Spanish milled dollars, or the value thereof in gold or silver," these notes circulated at a heavy discount - if they were acceptable at all. The fledgling government's final solution for the Continental Currency problem, accepting them in 1787 at 1% of face value in exchange for interest bearing bonds, did nothing to bolster public confidence in paper money.

Neither did the often larcenous "banking" practices of the various elements of the private sector to whom the note-issuing prerogative fell. With states denied the power to issue money by the Constitution of the United States, and the powers of the Federal Government to do so left unspecified; various private issues of banks, railroads, utilities, and even individual citizens, cropped up, with varying resources to guarantee their value, until the Government halted the practice in 1863.

By the late 19th Century, U.S.-issued paper money had become a viable part of the nation's commerce as people recognized that such notes were, indeed, redeemable on demand for gold or silver. By 1963, paper currency was such an ingrained part of the American economy that the Government was able to remove all specie-redemption quality from its currency issues, raising only minimal objections from strict interpretationists of the Constitution.

Now, ironically, paper money may be on the way out as a circulating medium of exchange. The growth of demand deposits (checking accounts), electronic fund transfers and the arrival of the home computer age may one day soon put an end for the need of physical symbols of wealth to pass from hand to hand.

Scope of this catalog

It is not the intention of this catalog to provide a reference to every type of official and unofficial paper currency which has circulated in the United States. Indeed, such a project between the covers of one volume represents an impossible, though intriguing, challenge.

Rather, this catalog will provide a guide to those paper money issues since 1812 of the Government of the United States of America, along with several related currency issues which are traditionally collected by paper money hobbyists in conjunction with the regular issues of the U.S.

Such a scope is intended, therefore, to provide the collector of U.S. paper money with a catalog reflective of the current state of the hobby.

Since it is not intended that this book serve as a definitive history of paper money in the United States, the reader will be provided with sufficient background information to facilitate and illuminate the building of a collection, without being subjected to fiscal, legislative or historical data that would be of interest to only a small minority of readers.

Numbering System

In using this book, you will immediately notice that KL and FR numbers are used at the beginning of each entry. What are they? The are catalog numbers. Catalog numbers were invented as a shorthand identification system for use in price lists, advertisements and auction catalogs where space is at a premium. Instead of writing a full description of a $1 Legal Tender Note, series 1923, you can write KL-28. Therefore, many more notes can be listed in an ad for the same cost. The two commonly used numbering systems are Friedberg numbers, invented by pioneer cataloger Robert Friedberg, and Krause-Lemke numbers created by Chester L. Krause and Robert F. Lemke as an improvement. Both catalog numbers are given for each listing in this book for your convenience.

History of Pre-Federal Paper Money in the U.S.

To better understand the forces which shaped the United States Government's issues of paper currency since 1861, it is necessary to look backward to the many and varied public and private currency issues which preceded them in this country. The use of paper money in the area which would become the United States actually predates its use in many parts of Western Europe and in most of the rest of the world. While paper currencies had been in use in China since the 7th Century, when it was known as "flying money" because of its light weight and ability to circulate widely with ease, it was not until the late 17th Century that the western world began experiments with non-metallic circulating currencies. Surprisingly quickly, the North American continent had its first "paper money" issues in 1685, when the Intendant of New France (Canada) issued promissory notes hand-printed on pieces of playing cards, to circulate as money until the delayed arrival of the paymaster.

The Massachusetts Bay Colony followed suit soon after, issuing in December, 1690, £7,000 worth of the first publicly authorized paper money notes in the western world to pay expenses of a border war with Canada (previous paper money issues in Europe and North America had been either issued by banks, or were emergency measures not authorized by any public body).

Following that precedent, by the turn of the 18th Century, other colonies were emitting paper currencies as needed to run their specie-short economies. By the end of the War for Independence, all 13 colonies had issued some form of paper currency. Beginning in May, 1775, the Congress of the newly unified former colonies began the issue of Continental Currency to finance its fight for freedom.

The Continental Currency was plagued, though, by increasing public distrust. The Continental paper dollar was able to hold its value at par with a specie dollar only until October, 1777, by which time widespread counterfeiting by British, Tories and opportunists conspired with the natural inflation of a printing press economy and increasing uncertainty as to the outcome of the war to push the exchange ratio of the Continental Currency to $11 in paper for $10 in specie.

After that point, the devaluation accelerated. By the next year, October, 1778, the ratio was 4.66 to 1.

The low point was reached in April, 1780, when a dollar in silver or gold was worth $40 Continental. And these were the *official* exchange ratios adopted by the Congress and many of the states, to offset the rampant inflation. In actual commerce, the Continentals were all but worthless. George Washington himself lamented that it took a wagonful of Continental Currency to purchase a wagonload of supplies for his army. A truer measure of the value of the Government paper currency could be found in the fact that by October, 1787, amid speculation that the Continental Currency might never be redeemable, it was selling at the rate of $250 paper for $1 specie. Eventually, the Government issued 6% interest bearing bonds at the rate of $1 for every $100 of Continental Currency turned in.

Issued current with the Colonial and Continental currencies were numerous privately-sponsored paper monies emitted by banks (as early as 1732 in Connecticut), utilities, merchants, individuals and even churches.

These issues continued after the Revolutionary War, and proliferated in the 19th Century. Today, lumped together under the generic, if not altogether correct, label of "broken bank notes," these colorful, historic notes and their collectible adjuncts make up a significant portion of the paper money hobby's interest.

The ten of thousands of privately-issued bank and scrip notes of the 1800s ranged in denomination from one-half cent to several thousand dollars. While today their collector value depends on a combination of rarity, condition and demand; their value when issued was solely dependent on the reputation of the issuing authority - be it bank, railroad or Main Street apothecarian. In those days, when a note, might be worth every cent of its face value or might be worth nothing more than the paper on which it was printed, an entire industry sprang up to supply banks and merchants with accurate, timely information about which notes would pass current, which should be accepted only at a discount, and those from an issuer who had gone "broken." In addition, because of the wealth of larcenous talent available for changing broken bank notes into "good" notes through the alteration of a bank or city name, or raising the denomination of a note from $1 to $10 by deft penmanship; those who handled the dizzying variety of paper money in circulation in the mid 19th Century needed books which listed and described the genuine issues of a particular bank. (It is, incidentally, from the common name of these paper money reporting services that the name *Bank Note Reporter* was derived for the monthly paper money newspaper published by the publisher of this catalog.)

The only restraints on the issue of paper money at that time were those which the individual states cared to apply, and such restraints were infrequent and ineffective.

The Federal Government put an effective end to these halycon days of currency free-for-all in 1863, by imposing a 10% tax on outstanding notes; and later through the 14th Amendment to the Constitution, forbidding the private issue of circulating media of exchange altogether.

With that the Government of the United States of America attained a monopoly on the note-issuing function which it has maintained, except in localized emergency situations, to this day.

Large Size Notes

For the convenience of the reader, brief and basically historical backgrounds have been provided for each of the major types of U.S. currency. No great amount of fiscal or legislative data has been provided, except where it might serve to clarify some aspects of the notes themselves or their collectibility.

Demand Notes

Despite two issues of interest-bearing Treasury notes in 1860-1861, the opening guns of the Civil War found the United States Government short of the necessary funds to put down the rebellion in a protracted war.

Congress moved swiftly in the national emergency to provide legislation authorizing the issue of $60,000,000 by Acts of July 17, and Aug. 5, 1861.

It is generally believed among numismatists today that the Demand Notes were backed by faith in the Government alone; but this was not entirely the case. By the terms of the authorizing legislation, the Demand Notes were not payable in gold. But, in a circular from the Secretary of the Treasury sent out before the suspension of specie payments on Dec. 21, 1861, they were declared payable in coin, and the Government redeemed them as such in order to sustain its credit. Thus, for a short time in 1861, the Demand Notes were quoted on a par with gold. However, as the war progressed, in most parts of the country the Demand Notes — and all other paper money of the U.S. Government — were acceptable only at a discount, even though they were receivable for all payments to the Government, including duties.

The Demand Notes took their famous "Greenback" nickname from the color of their back designs (back designs in themselves were scarce on paper money in the U.S. prior to the Civil War). The name was subsequently applied to virtually every other form of U.S. currency and remains current today.

Because the United States Government was not prepared to be in the note-printing business in 1861, the work of producing the Demand Notes was contracted to the American Bank Note Company and National Bank Note Company. Working with essentially stock currency elements, the private contractors turned out more than 7.25 million $5, $10 and $20 Demand Notes.

The actual "issuing" of the notes required that they be signed by the Treasurer of the United States (Francis E. Spinner) and the Register of the Treasury (Lucius E. Chittenden), or persons designated by them.

Accordingly, platoons of clerks within the Treasury Department were put to work autographing Demand Notes. However, on the very earliest specimens, the engraved blanks on the face of the notes indicated only the office of the signer, and the clerks were required to pen in the words "for the" on each note as they signed it, a most laborious process that was eliminated with the addition of "for the" on the engraved face plates themselves. The Demand Notes which survive today with the hand-signed "for the" on the face are much scarcer than the engraved version, and command a significant price premium.

Rarity and value of the Demand Notes is also affected by the engraved location on the face of the note indicating where the notes were issued and, therefore, payable.

The obligation on the notes reads: "The United States promises to pay to the bearer five dollars (or ten dollars or twenty dollars) on demand . . . payable by the Assistant Treasurer of the United States at . . ."

One of five cities was then engraved. Those notes payable at New York are far and away the most common among the survivors, with Philadelphia second and Boston third. Specimens which promise redemption in Cincinnati and, especially, St. Louis, are extremely rare and seldom encountered.

United States Notes (Legal Tender Notes)

The longest-lived type of U.S. paper money, the United States Notes (called interchangeably Legal Tender Notes because of the wording of the obligation) was first authorized in 1862 and is still current today, though none have been issued since 1969.

The subject of major Constitutional debate at the time of their issue, the notes did much to pave the way for future issues of U.S. currency backed only by the credit of the Government.

While there are five official "issues" of large size Legal Tender Notes, as well as the small size series, they are generally collected today by type (major design) and, occasionally, by signature combination.

The First Issue of United States Notes, dated March 10, 1862, was issued in denominations of $5, $10, $20, $50, $100, $500 and $1,000.

Two different varieties of notes, bearing different obligation wording on the backs, are popularly collected among the First Issue notes.

The earliest First Issues bear what is known as the First Obligation on back, reading: "This note is a legal tender for all debts, public and private, except duties on imports and interest on the public debt, and is exchangeable for U.S. six per cent twenty year bonds, redeemable at the pleasure of the United States after five years."

The Second Obligation, much rarer, reads as follows: "This note is a legal tender for all debts, public and private, except duties on imports and interest on the public debt, and is receivable in payment of all loans made to the United States."

These First Issue notes do not carry the large face inscriptions "United States Note" or "Treasury Note," which are found on later Legal Tender issues.

Dated Aug. 1, 1862, and issued only in denominations of $1 and $2, the Second Issue U.S. Notes carry the Second Obligation on back.

The Third Issue U.S. Notes, dated March 10, 1863, were issued in denominations from $5 through $1,000, again using the Second Obligation.

Fourth Issue Legal Tenders were authorized by an Act of Congress dated March 3, 1863, and issued in denomination from $1 through $10,000 in the various Series of 1869, 1874, 1878, 1880, 1907, 1917 and 1923. Those notes in Series 1869 bear the label "Treasury Notes" on face, with all later issues carrying the "United States Notes" designation.

Back obligation on all series is the same: "This note is a legal tender at its face value for all debts public and private, except duties on imports and interest on the public debt."

The Fifth Issue Legal Tenders consisted solely of the Series 1901 $10 note (the popular Bison design), issued under the authority of the Legal Tender Acts of 1862-1863. A new face obligation was introduced: "This note is a legal tender for ten dollars subject to the provisions of Section 3588 R.S.," on back, the obligation reads: "This note is a legal tender at its face value for all debts public and private except duties on imports and interest on the public debt."

Legislation remains in force requiring that the amount of Legal Tender Notes in official circulation be maintained at $346,681,016, which is done, on paper at least, through the continuing "circulation" of the small size Red Seal $100s.

Compound Interest Treasury Notes

Circulating currency notes which grew in face value each six-month period they remained in circulation were just one of the innovations to which the Federal Government turned to finance the protracted Civil War.

Authorized by Congressional Acts of March 3, 1863, and June 30, 1864, these notes were intended to circulate for three years, bearing interest at the then-attractive rate of six percent a year, compounded semi-annually. The backs of each note carry a table spelling out the actual interest earned and current face value of the note through maturity. Theoretically, a note that was acquired when issued at face value, could be spent a year later as $10.60; although little is known as to whether this theory worked in practice. It is known, though, that those persons holding the notes at maturity generally took their profit, leaving very few surviving specimens for today's collectors.

Neither should it be assumed that the surviving notes continue to earn interest. The interest payments ended at maturity (if interest had been allowed to accumulate, the $10 note, as of June, 1985, would have a "face value" in excess of $11,000 — even more than the numismatic value of the note — with corresponding denominations — $20, $50, $100, $500 and $1,000 — worth multiples thereof).

The face of each note bears a surcharge in large gold letters, reading "Compound Interest Treasury Note," along with corresponding numerals of issue value. Unfortunately, the gold ink used for these overprints contributed greatly to the demise of the notes themselves, for it is highly acidic and attacks the rather fragile paper to the point where many examples are found with this surcharge "burned" into and through the paper. Additionally, the $50 and $100 notes, the highest values which could practically be said to have circulated, were extensively counterfeited and the Treasury was forced to withdraw them in the face of such "competition."

In any denomination, the Compound Interest Treasury Notes are scarce in better than Fine condition.

Examples are known with a number of different issue dates on face. The $10-$50 notes with the June 10 or July 15, 1864, dates are the rarest, with dates from Aug. 15, 1864, through Oct. 16, 1865, being more common; while in the $100 notes, the June 10, 1864, date is most common, followed by the Aug. 15, 1864-Sept. 1, 1865, dates. No July 15, 1864-dated $100 Compound Interest Treasury Notes are known, nor are there any reported survivors among the $500 and $1,000 denominations, though the Treasury reports several examples still officially outstanding.

Interest Bearing Notes

As a group, probably the rarest type of U.S. paper money is the Interest Bearing Note issues of the Civil War era. Like the Compound Interest Treasury Notes and the Refunding Certificates (also interest

bearing), they were something of a desperation currency issue by the Federal Government to bolster the Union war chest.

The Interest Bearing Notes were issued in a trio of distinctive types, all of which are very rare, or unknown to have survived.

The first issue was a series of One-Year Notes, issued under authority of the Act of March 3, 1863, and paying interest of five percent for one year. Face designs of the one-year issue were similar to the Compound Interest Treasury Notes, without the gold surcharges. Backs were significantly different, lacking the tabular interest-figuring chart. A face inscription reads: "One year after date the United States will pay to the bearer with five per interest — dollars." On back, the obligation was worded: "This note is a legal tender at its face value, excluding interest, for all debts public and private, except duties on imports and interest on the public debt."

Denominations of the One-Year Notes ranged from $10 through $5,000, with no specimens of the $500, $1,000 or $5,000 known. Each note bears an individually stamped date of issue on the face. One year from that date, the notes were redeemable for face value plus interest.

Two-Year Notes were also authorized by the March 3, 1863 Act of Congress. Issued only in the $50, $100, $500 and $1,000 denominations, and paying five percent interest per year for a two-year term, they are naturally much scarcer because of the high return they offered the holder near the end of the Civil War. Designs were completely different from the One-Year Notes, although the face and back inscriptions are similar.

Like the Interest Bearing Notes themselves, the Three-Year Notes are comprised of three separate issues, due to three different authorizing Acts of Congress; July 17, 1861, June 30, 1864, and March 3, 1865. Again issued in the higher denominations, from $50 through $5,000, the notes paid interest at the rate of 7-3/10 percent a year; the highest rate the Government paid on circulating notes. Like the Compound Interest Treasury Notes, the actual amount of interest is spelled out on the notes, though in this case it is expressed in terms of interest per day. Thus, the $50 note expresses a promise to pay interest of one cent per day, while the $5,000 bill paid interest at the rate of $1 per day.

That the notes were not intended to circulate widely is indicated by the fact that they are payable to the order, not to the bearer. That is, there is a blank on the face of every Three-Year Interest Bearing Note for the name of the original holder, and a corresponding blank on back for endorsement at the time of maturity.

Another feature which makes the Three-Year Notes unusual among U.S. paper money issues was the original attachment of five coupons to each note. Each coupon indicated the interest payable for a six-month period, and was removed from the note when that interest was collected semi-annually. The final interest payment was made when the note itself was presented for redemption at the end of the three-year period. This arrangement is spelled out on the face of each note.

As mentioned earlier, these notes are of the greatest rarity, most of them unknown to survive, existing only in proof form or existing in a unique, or nearly so, issued example.

Refunding Certificates

More of a government security than circulating medium of exchange, the Refunding Certificates authorized by Congress in the Act of Feb. 26, 1879, brought these interest bearing instruments within the reach of more Americans in that they were denominated at $10.

The authorizing legislation intended that these notes bear interest of four percent annually in perpetuity. However, in 1907 Congress passed a law stopping interest payments as of July 1, forever fixing the "face" value of these notes at $21.30. Presumably at that time the incentive for the public to hold these notes was removed, and their redemption accelerated.

The $10 Refunding Certificates were issued in two different forms, one type payable to the bearer, the other to the order of the original purchaser. Like the Three-Year Interest Bearing Notes, the Refunding Certificates payable to order had spaces on face and back for the owner and endorser. The "pay to order" type is far rarer than the "pay to bearer" variety.

Rather than being redeemable for specie, per se, these notes, in amounts of $50 or more, were convertible into four percent bonds.

Silver Certificates

Among the most popular of U.S. notes due to their wealth of design excellence and challenging, but not impossible, rarity, the Silver Certificates of 1878-1963 comprise five major issues of large size notes, and the various series of small size notes.

Authorizing legislation for all issues were the Congressional Act of Feb. 28, 1878, and Aug. 4, 1886.

The First Issue Silver Certificates consist of Series 1878 and 1880 notes in denominations from $10-$1,000. The notes of 1878, besides bearing the engraved signatures of G.W. Scofield, Register of the Treasury, and James Gilfillan, Treasurer of the U.S., have on their face an engraved or autographed countersignature of the Assistant

Treasurers in New York, Washington, D.C., and San Francisco, attesting that the requisite amount of silver dollars had been deposited in their offices to cover the face value of the notes. In addition to the Series 1878 countersigned notes, several $20 Series 1880 Silver Certificates are known bearing the engraved countersignature of T. Hillhouse, Assistant Treasurer at New York.

The silver bills' Second Issue was made up of notes from $1 through $1,000 in the Series of 1886, 1891 and 1908, although not all denominations were issued in all series.

The "Educational" notes, $1, $2, and $5 Silver Certificates of Series 1896, are the sole component of the Third Issue.

Similarly, the Fourth Issue Silver Certificates are made up of $1, $2 and $5 notes of the Series of 1899.

The Silver Certificates of the Fifth Issue are the Series 1923 $1 and $5 notes.

The obligation on the First Issue notes reads: "This certifies that there have been deposited with the Treasurer of the U.S. at Washington, D.C. (or Assistant Treasurers at New York and San Francisco) payable at his office to the bearer on demand — silver dollars. This certificate is receivable for customs, taxes and all public dues and when so received may be reissued."

Obligation on the last four issues of silver notes was worded: "This certifies that there have been deposited in the Treasury of the United States — silver dollars payable to the bearer on demand. This certificate is receivable for customs, taxes and all public dues and when so received may be issued."

Treasury or Coin Notes

Pushed through Congress by the silver mining industry, the authorizing legislation of July 14, 1890, which created the Treasury Notes carefully did not specify that they be redeemable in silver; only that they be issued to pay for silver bullion purchased by the Treasury and that they be payable "in Coin" (hence the more commonly encountered name Coin Notes). With the co-operation of Treasury officials, silver sellers were able to turn their bullion in at artificially high official prices, receive the Coin Notes in payment, and redeem them immediately for gold coin and a tidy profit.

In denominations of $1, $2, $5, $10, $20, $100 and $1,000, the Coin Notes were issued in Series 1890 and 1891 form, the 1890 issue bearing ornately engraved green back designs that filled the print area. The $50 was issued only in Series of 1891, and the $500 note, which had been designed and a plate prepared with the portrait of Gen. William T. Sherman, was not issued at all. It was felt that even as late as 25 years after the Civil War, the use of Sherman's portrait on a currency note would inflame passions in the South. The 1890 notes are much scarcer and in greater demand than the Series 1891 issue, especially in new condition.

Face and back obligations of the Coin Notes are interesting and unique. They read: "This United States of America will pay to bearer — dollars in coin." And, "This note is a legal tender at its face value in payment of all debts public and private except when otherwise expressly stipulated in the contract."

National Gold Bank Notes

Gold and the American West have been inseparably linked as part of this nation's history since the discovery of gold at Sutter's Mill in 1848. The unique, but short-lived National Gold Bank Note series was a contemporary part of "The Golden West," and today trades on that romantic image — and the inherent rarity of the notes themselves — as one of the most sought-after types of U.S. paper money.

The National Gold Bank Notes were authorized under the provisions of the Currency Act of July 12, 1870, and are very much analogous to the regular National Currency issue.

The principal difference, besides design, is that the National Gold Bank Notes were payable — and prominently said so — in gold coin. This was a concession to the traditional mistrust of Western America in paper currency and the California area's long history of gold use as the principal medium of exchange, whether in the form of gold dust, nuggets, private-issue coinage or genuine coins of the United States Mint.

Under the general provisions of the National Bank Act of 1863, the National Gold Banks had to secure the issue of their currency with the deposit of bonds with the Treasurer of the United States. However, the conditions for the N.G.B.N. issues were a bit more stringent. The Gold Banks could issue notes only to the value of 80% of their deposited bonds, while the other National banks could issue to 90%. Additionally, the Gold Banks were required to have on hand in their vaults gold coinage equal to 25% of the value of their note issue. The responsibility of redeeming these notes in gold, lay with the issuing banks, not the Federal Government, which did not resume specie payments until 1879, nearly a decade after the N.G.B.N. issues began. The Treasury would, of course, redeem National Gold Bank Notes for other lawful currency.

This gold redemption property gave the N.G.B.Ns, the necessary credibility, and they circulated at par with the precious metal. They circulated so extensively that surviving notes are generally found in conditions which many collectors would find unacceptable in other U.S. currency types. No strictly uncirculated National Gold Bank Note is known today, and the average condition found is Good to Very Good. Specimens in Fine or better condition command attractive premiums in the infrequent times when they become available.

Though authorized in denominations from $5-$1,000, National Gold Bank Notes were issued to circulation only as high as $500. The face of each note was similar to corresponding denominations in the First Charter National Bank Note series, while the backs had as their central feature a photo-like engraving of a stack of U.S. gold pieces, representing $211.50 face value in $1 through $20 denominations.

In all, 10 National Gold Banks were chartered, nine in California and The Kidder National Gold Bank in Boston, Mass. Notes were actually printed for the Kidder N.G.B., and delivered, but the bank eventually returned them all for cancellation, never issuing them to circulation. The Kidder was the only National Gold Bank to have $1,000 notes prepared.

Because of the relatively small size of the issue, much can be determined about the issue and survivability of the National Gold Bank Notes.

In the period 1870-1878, exactly 196,849 notes, with a face value of $3,267,420, were issued. Treasury records indicate a total of 6,639 notes remain outstanding (including four $500 examples, none of which are known to collectors). A recent comprehensive survey of known notes accounted for fewer than 275 in all denominations.

Like the other National Bank Notes, National Gold Bank Notes are known in both Original Series and Series of 1875 issues, although all nine California banks did not issue all denominations in both series. Indeed, the Series 1875 notes are somewhat scarcer than the Original notes.

Federal Reserve Bank Notes

Often confused with the Federal Reserve Notes, which are currency issues of the Federal Reserve System itself, Federal Reserve Bank Notes were issued by the 12 individual Federal Reserve Banks, much like the National Bank Notes.

Indeed, Federal Reserve Bank Notes, large and small size, carry the "National Currency" inscription.

In the large size note-issuing period, the similarity of Federal Reserve Bank Notes to Federal Reserve notes extended to nearly identical back designs in the $5-$50 denominations. FRBNs were also issued in $1 and $2 denominations, while the FRNs were issued in value from $5 through $10,000.

Two separate issues of Federal Reserve Bank Notes comprise the large size issue, while there was a single issue in small size.

The Series 1915 FRBNs were authorized under the terms of the Federal Reserve Act of Dec. 23, 1913. Issued only in denominations of $5-$20, only the banks in Atlanta, Chicago, Kansas City, Dallas and San Francisco participated, with the Frisco bank issuing only $5s.

Like the National Bank Notes, the obligation to pay the bearer on the FRBNs is made by the issuing bank, rather than the Fed system or U.S. Government. The security notice on the 1915 issue reads: "Secured by United States bonds deposited with the Treasurer of the United States."

That obligation was changed for the Series 1918 FRBNs, issued under authority of a Congressional Act of April 23, 1918. The modification reads: "Secured by United States certificates of indebtedness or United States one-year gold notes, deposited with the Treasurer of the United States."

The Series 1918 FRBNs consist of all denominations from $1 through $50, though again, not all 12 banks issued all denominations. For instance, only the Atlanta and St. Louis banks issued $20 Series 1918 FRBNs, while only St. Louis issued $50s.

Spurred initially by demand for the attractive "Battleship" back design of the $2, and the defiant eagle on the $1 (symbols of America's defense posture in World War I), all large size FRBNs are actively collected today, especially in new condition. A wealth of combinations of U.S. Government signatures combined with signatures of the various Governors and Cashiers of the individual issuing banks, creates myriad varieties to keep the series challenging.

Also contributing to the challenge is the sheer scarcity of surviving specimens. Treasury sources indicate just over $2 million worth of FRBNs outstanding, from a total issue of more than $760 million.

Federal Reserve Notes

Authorized by the Federal Reserve Act of Dec. 23, 1913 and first issued in 1914, the Federal Reserve Note is the only type of U.S. paper money which continues in production today.

The large size issues of FRNs are in two series, 1914, in denominations from $5-$100, and 1918, in denominations from $500-$10,000. Additionally, two distinctive varieties of 1914 notes exist, those with

red Treasury seal and serial number, and those with the elements in blue. The Red Seal 1914 FRNs are considerably scarcer than the blue.

While they are issued to circulation through the 12 Federal Reserve Banks, the FRNs are an obligation of the United States Government, rather than bank named thereon (unlike the Federal Reserve Bank Notes). Neither are Federal Reserve Notes secured by government bonds, precious metals or other reserves. The obligation on FRNs simply states that: "The United States of America will pay to the bearer on demand — dollars."

On back, the redemption qualities of the large size FRNs was spelled out thus: "This note is receivable by all National and member banks and Federal Reserve Banks and for all taxes, customs and other public dues. It is redeemable in gold on demand at the Treasury Department of the United States in the city of Washington, District of Columbia or in gold or lawful money at any Federal Reserve Bank."

This redeemable-in-gold clause continued in use on the Series 1928 small size FRNs, but was revoked with the passage of the Gold Reserve Act of 1933. The obligation, beginning with the Series 1934 notes, was modified to read: "This note is legal tender for all debts, public and private, and is redeemable in lawful money at the United States Treasury, or at any Federal Reserve Bank."

Beginning with Series 1963, the obligation was changed to its present form: "This note is legal tender for all debts, public and private."

Wide variances in the number of notes printed for each bank in any particular series of a denomination have created many challenging issues within the Federal Reserve Note series, both large and small size.

NOTE: Three interesting, if not altogether popular among collectors, varieties exist within the large size FRNs bearing the White-Mellon Federal signature combination, and two within the Burke-McAdoo combination notes. The variations deal with the size and placement of the numeral-letter combination designating the bank through which the notes were issued, and appearing in the lower left corner of the face. The earliest variety has a large size combination, matching that in the upper right corner of the note. The second variety has the combination greatly reduced (compared to that in the upper right). The third reverts to the larger size, but the combination has been moved higher and more to the left, while the Treasury and Fed Bank seals on each end of this variety have been moved closer to center. Not all three varieties exist on every bank in every combination. While the second and third varieties command some premium from interested collectors, the demand for them is not such as to greatly influence the market for the type as a whole, and they are, therefore, not cataloged individually.

Gold Certificates

With their bright orange back designs (though some early gold notes are uniface), the large size Gold Certificates issued from 1865 through 1928 are a popular and tangible reminder of the days when U.S. paper currency was "as good as gold."

While many of the earlier Gold Certificate issues were not designed to be used in general circulation, due to their high face value, later types did enter the channels of commerce, circulating alongside the myriad other currency issues of the late 19th and early 20th Centuries.

Nine separate issues of Gold Certificates were created in the large size series, several of which were used almost exclusively in inter-bank channels to transfer and settle gold accounts.

The first issue goldbacks were authorized by the Currency Act of March 3, 1863, and consisted of notes in denominations of $20, $100, $500, $1,000, $5,000 and $10,000. While examples of the two lowest denominations survive, they are extremely rare.

No known examples of the second issue Gold Certificates are known today. Issued pursuant to the same act, and countersigned and dated by hand in the 1870-71 period, they were in denominations of $100-$10,000 only.

Third issue gold notes, bearing the impression "Series of 1875," were also issued in limited denominations: $100, $500, and $1,000. Uniface, the issue is represented today by only a few examples of the $100 note.

With the fourth issue, Gold Certificates entered general circulation, and the type begins to be known by its series designation. Ten-dollar goldbacks were issued in Series 1907 and 1922; $20 in Series 1882, 1905, 1906 and 1922; $50 in Series 1882, 1913 and 1922; $100 in Series 1882 and 1922; $500 in Series 1882; $1,000 in Series 1882, 1907 and 1922; $5,000 in Series 1882 and 1888; and, $10,000 in Series 1882, 1888 and 1900. Naturally, the notes in denominations above $100 are very rare, though not unknown.

To correspond the various issues to the series in these post-1875 notes; the fourth issue consisted of the Series 1882 notes; the fifth issue comprises the 1888 Series, the sixth is the 1900 $10,000 notes; the seventh issue Gold Certificates are the Series 1905, 1906 and 1907 $10 and $20 notes; the eighth is the $1,000 of Series 1907; and, the ninth issue of large size Gold Certificates are the Series 1913 ($50 only) and 1922 goldbacks in $10-$1,000 denominations.

U. S. Large Size Currency Valuations

Note: National Bank Notes issued between 1863-1928 will be found in a separate section, pages 61-154.

One Dollar

United States Notes

Salmon P. Chase

KL#	Fr#	Series	Signatures	Seal	Fine	XF	CU
			Numeral "1" "2" "3" vertically in center.				
1	17	1862	Chittenden-Spinner	Small red	—	Rare	—
			National Bank Note Co. American Bank Note Co., lower border. No monogram.				
2	17-A	1862	Chittenden-Spinner	Small red	275.	640.	1250.
			As above with monogram ABN Co. upper right.				
3	16	1862	Chittenden-Spinner	Small red	225.	525.	875.
			National Bank Note Co., twice in border. No monogram.				
4	16-A	1862	Chittenden-Spinner	Small red	175.	400.	800.
			As above, with monogram ABN Co. upper right.				

George Washington

KL#	Fr#	Series	Signatures	Seal	Fine	XF	CU
			Red serial numbers.				
5	18	1869	Allison-Spinner	Large red	310.	625.	1500.
			National Bank Note Co., lower portion back design.				

KL#	Fr#	Series	Signatures	Seal	Fine	XF	CU
			Red Serial numbers. Red ornamentation at right, face design.				
6	19	1874	Allison-Spinner	Small red	75.00	260.	575.
			Face, micro at right, "Engraved & Printed at the Bureau Engraving & Printing".				
			Back, Columbian Bank Note Co., twice in lower portion.				
7	20	1875	Allison-New	Small red	80.00	220.	700.
8	21	1875 Series "A"	Allison-New	Small red	175.	400.	800.
9	22	1875 Series "B"	Allison-New	Small red	100.	200.	500.
10	23	1875 Series "C"	Allison-New	Small red	425.	650.	1000.
11	24	1875 Series "D"	Allison-New	Small red	450.	700.	1200.
12	25	1875 Series "E"	Allison-New	Small red	450.	750.	1400.
13	26	1875	Allison-Wyman	Small red	65.00	175.	500.
14	27	1878	Allison-Gilfillan	Small red	68.00	165.	525.
			"Series 1878" top margin, back design.				
			"Printed by Bureau of Engraving & Printing" lower margin, back design.				

KL#	Fr#	Series	Signatures	Seal	Fine	XF	CU
			Ornamentation removed. Large seal introduced.				
15	28	1880	Scofield-Gilfillan	Large brown	100.	185.	625.
16	29	1880	Bruce-Gilfillan	Large brown	70.00	160.	425.
17	30	1880	Bruce-Wyman	Large brown	70.00	140.	425.
			Blue serial numbers				
18	31	1880	Rosecrans-Huston	Large red	465.	1100.	2350.
19	32	1880	Rosecrans-Huston	Large brown	465.	1100.	2350.
20	33	1880	Rosecrans-Nebeker	Large brown	700.	1200.	2600.
21	34	1880	Rosecrans-Nebeker	Small red	75.00	135.	535.
22	35	1880	Tillman-Morgan	Small red	60.00	100.	390.
			Serial number panel dropped.				
23	36	1917	Teehee-Burke	Small red	35.00	65.00	190.
24	37	1917	Elliott-Burke	Small red	35.00	60.00	175.
25	37-A	1917	Burke-Elliott	Small red	200.	500.	950.
26	38	1917	Elliott-White	Small red	30.00	60.00	175.
27	39	1917	Speelman-White	Small red	30.00	60.00	175.

George Washington

KL#	Fr#	Series	Signatures	Seal	Fine	XF	CU
28	40	1923	Speelman-White	Small red	50.00	100.	325.

Silver Certificates

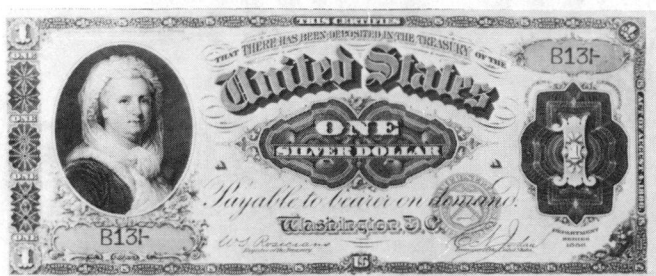

Martha Washington

KL#	Fr#	Series	Signatures	Seal	Fine	XF	CU
			Blue Serial numbers on all Silver Certificates.				
29	215	1886	Rosecrans-Jordan	Small red	230.	540.	1000.
30	216	1886	Rosecrans-Hyatt	Small red	185.	425.	900.
31	217	1886	Rosecrans-Hyatt	Large red	230.	540.	1000.
32	218	1886	Rosecrans-Huston	Large red	185.	425.	900.
33	219	1886	Rosecrans-Huston	Large brown	230.	540.	1000.
34	220	1886	Rosecrans-Nebeker	Large brown	185.	425.	900.
35	221	1886	Rosecrans-Nebeker	Small red	190.	425.	900.

KL#	Fr#	Series	Signatures	Seal	Fine	XF	CU
36	222	1891	Rosecrans-Nebeker	Small red	190.	425.	925.
37	223	1891	Tillman-Morgan	Small red	130.	325.	700.

Martha & George Washington

KL#	Fr#	Series	Signatures	Seal	Fine	XF	CU
38	224	1896	Tillman-Morgan	Small red	200.	500.	950.
39	225	1896	Bruce-Roberts	Small red	160.	450.	750.

Abraham Lincoln, U.S. Grant

KL#	Fr#	Series	Signatures	Seal	Fine	XF	CU
			Series date above serial number, upper right.				
40	226	1899	Lyons-Roberts	Small blue	62.00	100.	235.
			Series date below serial number.				
41	226-A	1899	Lyons-Roberts	Small blue	45.00	85.00	175.
42	227	1899	Lyons-Treat	Small blue	45.00	80.00	175.
43	228	1899	Vernon-Treat	Small blue	45.00	80.00	175.
44	229	1899	Vernon-Mc Clung	Small blue	45.00	80.00	175.
			Series date vertically right, on the following:				
44A	229-A	1899	Vernon-Mc Clung	Small blue	100.	225.	450.
45	230	1899	Napier-Mc Clung	Small blue	45.00	80.00	175.
46	231	1899	Napier-Thompson	Small blue	100.	175.	525.
47	232	1899	Parker-Burke	Small blue	45.00	80.00	175.
48	233	1899	Teehee-Burke	Small blue	45.00	80.00	175.
49	234	1899	Elliott-Burke	Small blue	45.00	80.00	175.
50	235	1899	Elliott-White	Small blue	45.00	85.00	175.
51	236	1899	Speelman-White	Small blue	45.00	80.00	175.

George Washington

KL#	Fr#	Series	Signatures	Seal	Fine	XF	CU
52	237	1923	Speelman-White	Small blue	22.00	35.00	75.00
53	238	1923	Woods-White	Small blue	22.00	30.00	60.00
54	239	1923	Woods-Tate	Small blue	45.00	75.00	250.

Treasury or Coin Notes

Edwin M. Stanton

KL#	Fr#	Series	Signatures	Seal	Fine	XF	CU
55	347	1890	Rosecrans-Huston	Large brown	475.	1000.	2400.

KL#	Fr#	Series	Signatures	Seal	Fine	XF	CU
56	348	1890	Rosecrans-Nebeker	Large brown	440.	900.	1750.
57	349	1890	Rosecrans-Nebeker	Small red	475.	1000.	2400.

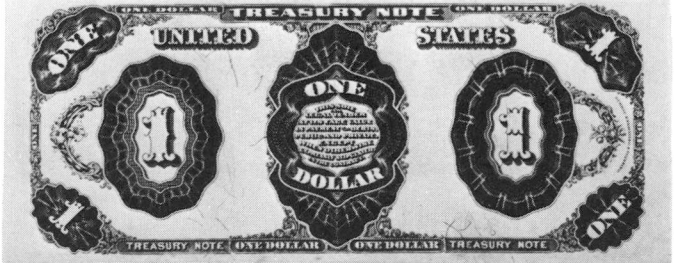

KL#	Fr#	Series	Signatures	Seal	Fine	XF	CU
58	350	1891	Rosecrans-Nebeker	Small red	125.	310.	650.
59	351	1891	Tillman-Morgan	Small red	100.	250.	500.
60	352	1891	Bruce-Roberts	Small red	85.00	250.	500.

Federal Reserve Bank Notes
Series 1918

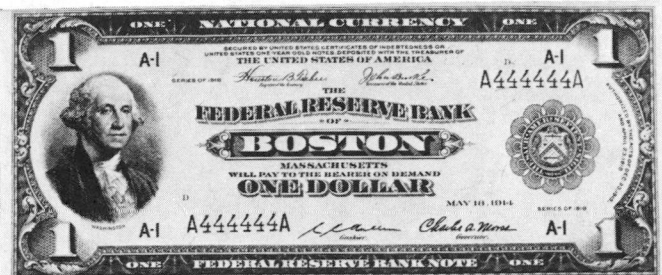

George Washington

KL#	Fr#	Bank	Federal Sigs.	Bank Sigs.	Fine	XF	CU
61	708	Boston	Teehee-Burke	Bullen-Morss	45.00	80.00	165.
62	709	Boston	Teehee-Burke	Willett-Morss	45.00	100.	350.
63	710	Boston	Elliott-Burke	Willett-Morss	45.00	80.00	165.
64	711	New York	Teehee-Burke	Sailer-Strong	45.00	80.00	165.
65	712	New York	Teehee-Burke	Hendricks-Strong	45.00	80.00	165.
66	713	New York	Elliott-Burke	Hendricks-Strong	45.00	80.00	165.
67	714	Philadelphia	Teehee-Burke	Hardt-Passmore	45.00	80.00	165.
68	715	Philadelphia	Teehee-Burke	Dyer-Passmore	45.00	80.00	165.
69	716	Philadelphia	Elliott-Burke	Dyer-Passmore	45.00	80.00	165.
70	717	Philadelphia	Elliott-Burke	Dyer-Norris	45.00	80.00	165.
71	718	Cleveland	Teehee-Burke	Baxter-Fancher	45.00	80.00	165.
72	719	Cleveland	Teehee-Burke	Davis-Fancher	45.00	80.00	165.
73	720	Cleveland	Elliott-Burke	Davis-Fancher	45.00	80.00	165.
74	721	Richmond	Teehee-Burke	Keesee-Seay	45.00	80.00	165.
75	722	Richmond	Elliott-Burke	Keesee-Seay	45.00	80.00	165.
76	723	Atlanta	Teehee-Burke	Pike-Mc Cord	45.00	80.00	165.
77	724	Atlanta	Teehee-Burke	Bell-Mc Cord	45.00	80.00	165.
78	725	Atlanta	Teehee-Burke	Bell-Wellborn	45.00	80.00	165.
79	726	Atlanta	Elliott-Burke	Bell-Wellborn	45.00	80.00	165.
80	727	Chicago	Teehee-Burke	Mc Cloud-Mc Dougall	45.00	80.00	165.
81	728	Chicago	Teehee-Burke	Cramer-Mc Dougall	45.00	80.00	165.
82	729	Chicago	Elliott-Burke	Cramer-Mc Dougall	45.00	80.00	165.
83	730	St. Louis	Teehee-Burke	Attebery-Wells	45.00	80.00	165.
84	731	St. Louis	Teehee-Burke	Attebery-Biggs	45.00	80.00	165.
85	732	St. Louis	Elliott-Burke	Attebery-Biggs	45.00	80.00	165.
86	733	St. Louis	Elliott-Burke	White-Biggs	45.00	80.00	165.
87	734	Minneapolis	Teehee-Burke	Cook-Wold	50.00	95.00	240.
88	735	Minneapolis	Teehee-Burke	Cook-Young	300.	550.	1000.
89	736	Minneapolis	Elliott-Burke	Cook-Young	50.00	95.00	240.
90	737	Kansas City	Teehee-Burke	Anderson-Miller	45.00	80.00	165.
91	738	Kansas City	Elliott-Burke	Anderson-Miller	45.00	80.00	165.
92	739	Kansas City	Elliott-Burke	Helm-Miller	45.00	80.00	165.
93	740	Dallas	Teehee-Burke	Talley-Van Zandt	55.00	100.	175.
94	741	Dallas	Elliott-Burke	Talley-Van Zandt	60.00	125.	240.

KL#	Fr#	Bank	Federal Sigs.	Bank Sigs.	Fine	XF	CU
95	742	Dallas	Elliott-Burke	Lawder-Van Zandt	45.00	95.00	175.
96	743	San Francisco	Teehee-Burke	Clerk-Lynch	45.00	80.00	165.
97	744	San Francisco	Teehee-Burke	Clerk-Calkins	45.00	80.00	165.
98	745	San Francisco	Elliott-Burke	Clerk-Calkins	45.00	80.00	165.
99	746	San Francisco	Elliott-Burke	Ambrose-Calkins	45.00	80.00	165.

Two Dollars
United States Notes

Alexander Hamilton

KL#	Fr#	Series	Signatures	Seal	Fine	XF	CU
			Red Numerals "1" "2" "3" vertically in center.				
100	41	1862	Chittenden-Spinner	Small red	400.	950.	2300.
			American Bank Note Co., vertically at left, face design.				
101	41-A	1862	Chittenden-Spinner	Small red	250.	700.	1750.
			National Bank Note Co., vertically at left, face design.				
			Patented April 23, 1860, National Bank Note Co., in lower border, on both types.				

Thomas Jefferson

KL#	Fr#	Series	Signatures	Seal	Fine	XF	CU
			Red Serial numbers				
102	42	1869	Allison-Spinner	Large red	370.	1350.	3450.
			"Engraved and printed at the Treasury Department",				
			vertically at left, face design.				
			American Bank Note Co. bottom left, face design and twice below back design.				
			Red Serial numbers. Red ornamentation at right.				
103	43	1874	Allison-Spinner	Small red	380.	750.	1350.

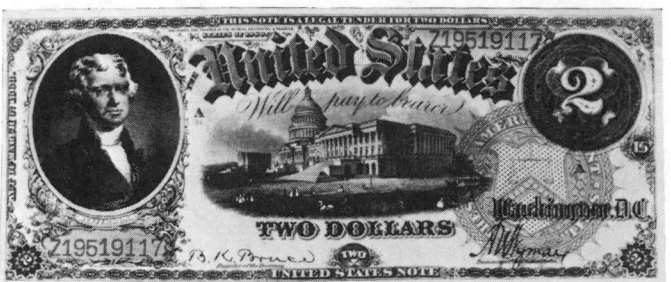

Thomas Jefferson

KL#	Fr#	Series	Signatures	Seal	Fine	XF	CU
104	44	1875	Allison-New	Small red	350.	700.	1350.
			Issued in two additional series, same design.				
105	45	1875 Series A, lower right of face design.			350.	700.	1350.
106	46	1875 Series B			350.	700.	1350.
107	47	1875	Allison-Wyman	Small red	350.	700.	1350.
108	48	1878	Allison-Gilfillan	Small red	400.	670.	1250.
109	49	1878	Scofield-Gilfillan	Small red	1900.	(Very rare)	
		Red Serial numbers. Ornamentation removed.					
110	50	1880	Scofield-Gilfillan	Large brown	90.00	300.	650.
111	51	1880	Bruce-Gilfillan	Large brown	80.00	225.	550.
112	52	1880	Bruce-Wyman	Large brown	80.00	225.	550.
		Blue serial numbers					
113	53	1880	Rosecrans-Huston	Large brown	500.	1450.	3300.
114	54	1880	Rosecrans-Huston	Large brown	475.	1375.	3100.
115	55	1880	Rosecrans-Nebeker	Small red	75.00	165.	545.
116	56	1880	Tillman-Morgan	Small red	70.00	145.	400.
		Red serial numbers					
117	57	1917	Teehee-Burke	Small red	42.00	90.00	290.
118	58	1917	Elliot-Burke	Small red	40.00	75.00	225.
119	59	1917	Elliot-White	Small red	40.00	75.00	225.
120	60	1917	Speelman-White	Small red	40.00	75.00	225.

Silver Certificates

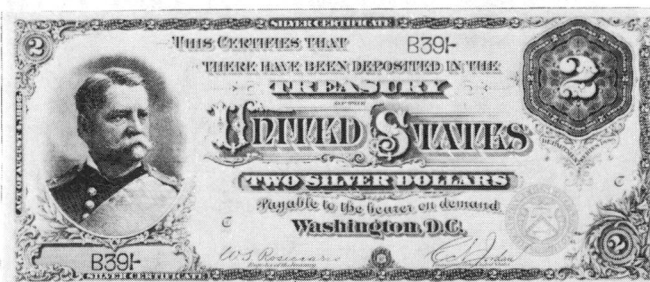

Gen. Winfield S. Hancock

KL#	Fr#	Series	Signatures	Seal	Fine	XF	CU
121	240	1886	Rosecrans-Jordan	Small red	400.	900.	1550.
122	241	1886	Rosecrans-Hyatt	Small red	350.	775.	1200.
123	242	1886	Rosecrans-Hyatt	Large red	400.	900.	1550.
124	243	1886	Rosecrans-Huston	Large red	350.	775.	1200.
125	244	1886	Rosecrans-Huston	Large brown	400.	900.	1550.

William Windom

KL#	Fr#	Series	Signatures	Seal	Fine	XF	CU
126	245	1891	Rosecrans-Nebeker	Small red	330.	1100.	2350.
127	246	1891	Tillman-Morgan	Small red	265.	925.	1950.

Robert Fulton, Samuel Morse

KL#	Fr#	Series	Signatures	Seal	Fine	XF	CU
128	247	1896	Tillman-Morgan	Small red	400.	1250.	2350.
129	248	1896	Bruce-Roberts	Small red	350.	1075.	2150.

George Washington

KL#	Fr#	Series	Signatures	Seal	Fine	XF	CU
130	249	1899	Lyons-Roberts	Small blue	100.	250.	600.
131	250	1899	Lyons-Treat	Small blue	75.00	220.	475.
132	251	1899	Vernon-Treat	Small blue	75.00	220.	475.
133	252	1899	Vernon-Mc Clung	Small blue	75.00	220.	475.
134	253	1899	Napier-Mc Clung	Small blue	75.00	220.	475.
135	254	1899	Napier-Thompson	Small blue	100.	300.	1000.
136	255	1899	Parker-Burke	Small blue	75.00	220.	475.
137	256	1899	Teehee-Burke	Small blue	75.00	220.	475.
138	257	1899	Elliott-Burke	Small blue	75.00	220.	475.
139	258	1899	Speelman-White	Small blue	100.	220.	475.

Treasury or Coin Notes

Gen. James B. McPherson

KL#	Fr#	Series	Signatures	Seal	Fine	XF	CU
140	353	1890	Rosecrans-Huston	Large brown	700.	2600.	4750.
141	354	1890	Rosecrans-Nebeker	Large brown	650.	2250.	4500.
142	355	1890	Rosecrans-Nebeker	Small red	650.	2400.	4500.

KL#	Fr#	Series	Signatures	Seal	Fine	XF	CU
143	356	1891	Rosecrans-Nebeker	Small red	265.	625.	1600.
144	357	1891	Tillman-Morgan	Small red	225.	500.	1125.
145	358	1891	Bruce-Roberts	Small red	225.	500.	1125.

Federal Reserve Bank Notes
Series 1918

Thomas Jefferson

KL#	Fr#	Bank	Federal Sigs.	Bank Sigs.	Fine	XF	CU
146	747	Boston	Teehee-Burke	Bullen-Morss	145.	290.	520.
147	748	Boston	Teehee-Burke	Willett-Morss	145.	290.	520.
148	749	Boston	Elliott-Burke	Willett-Morss	145.	290.	520.
149	750	New York	Teehee-Burke	Sailer-Strong	145.	290.	520.
150	751	New York	Teehee-Burke	Hendricks-Strong	145.	290.	520.
151	752	New York	Elliott-Burke	Hendricks-Strong	145.	290.	520.
152	753	Philadelphia	Teehee-Burke	Hardt-Passmore	145.	290.	520.
153	754	Philadelphia	Teehee-Burke	Dyer-Passmore	145.	290.	520.
154	755	Philadelphia	Elliott-Burke	Dyer-Passmore	145.	290.	520.
155	756	Philadelphia	Elliott-Burke	Dyer-Norris	145.	290.	520.
156	757	Cleveland	Teehee-Burke	Baxter-Fancher	145.	290.	520.
157	758	Cleveland	Teehee-Burke	Davis-Fancher	145.	290.	520.
158	759	Cleveland	Elliott-Burke	Davis-Fancher	145.	290.	520.

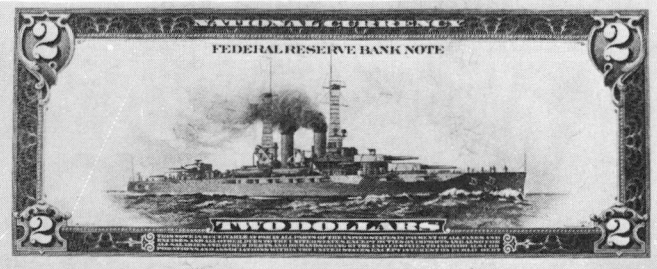

KL#	Fr#	Bank	Federal Sigs.	Bank Sigs.	Fine	XF	CU
159	760	Richmond	Teehee-Burke	Keesee-Seay	145.	290.	520.
160	761	Richmond	Elliott-Burke	Keesee-Seay	145.	290.	520.
161	762	Atlanta	Teehee-Burke	Pike-Mc Cord	145.	290.	520.
162	763	Atlanta	Teehee-Burke	Bell-Mc Cord	145.	290.	520.
163	764	Atlanta	Elliott-Burke	Bell-Wellborn	145.	290.	520.
164	765	Chicago	Teehee-Burke	Mc Cloud-Mc Dougal	145.	290.	520.
165	766	Chicago	Teehee-Burke	Cramer-Mc Dougal	145.	290.	520.
166	767	Chicago	Elliott-Burke	Cramer-Mc Dougal	145.	290.	520.
167	768	St. Louis	Teehee-Burke	Attebery-Wells	145.	290.	520.
168	769	St. Louis	Teehee-Burke	Attebery-Biggs	145.	290.	520.
169	770	St. Louis	Elliott-Burke	Attebery-Biggs	145.	290.	520.
170	771	St. Louis	Elliott-Burke	White-Biggs	145.	290.	520.
171	772	Minneapolis	Teehee-Burke	Cook-Wold	145.	290.	520.
172	773	Minneapolis	Elliott-Burke	Cook-Young	145.	290.	520.
173	774	Kansas City	Teehee-Burke	Anderson-Miller	145.	290.	520.
174	775	Kansas City	Elliott-Burke	Helm-Miller	145.	290.	520.
175	776	Dallas	Teehee-Burke	Talley-Van Zandt	145.	290.	520.
176	777	Dallas	Elliott-Burke	Talley-Van Zandt	145.	290.	520.
177	778	San Francisco	Teehee-Burke	Clerk-Lynch	145.	290.	520.
178	779	San Francisco	Elliott-Burke	Clerk-Calkins	145.	290.	520.
179	780	San Francisco	Elliott-Burke	Ambrose-Calkins	145.	290.	520.

Five Dollars
Demand Notes

Type One: "For the" autographed
Type Two: "For the" engraved

Alexander Hamilton

KL#	Fr#	Payable at:		Good	VG
180	3-A	Boston	Type One	1800.	2750.
181	3	Boston	Type Two	400.	950.
182	1-A	New York	Type One	1800.	2750.
183	1	New York	Type Two	400.	950.
184	2-A	Philadelphia	Type One	1800.	2750.
185	2	Philadelphia	Type Two	400.	950.
186	5-A	St. Louis	Type One	6000.	16,000.
187	5	St. Louis	Type Two	5000.	11,000.
188	4-A	Cincinnati	Type One	7500.	16,000.
189	4	Cincinnati	Type Two	5000.	11,000.

United States Notes

Alexander Hamilton

KL#	Fr#	Series	Signatures	Seal	Fine	XF	CU
		First Obligation inscription on back. Red Serial numbers.					
190A	61	Notes without word "Series" were the first 100,000 printed.					
190	61A	1862	Chittenden-Spinner	Small red "Series" on obverse			
					325.	725.	1150.
		American Bank Note Co. in top border face design.					
		Second Obligation inscription. Red Serial numbers.					
191	62	1862	Chittenden-Spinner	Small red	300.	700.	1125.
		American Bank Note Co. National Bank Note Co. lower border face design.					
192	63	1863	Chittenden-Spinner	Small red	325.	725.	1150.
		American Bank Note Co., twice in lower border face design. One serial number.					
193	63-A	1863	Chittenden-Spinner	Small red	300.	700.	1125.
		American Bank Note Co., twice in lower border. Two serial numbers.					
		Red serial numbers					

Andrew Jackson

KL#	Fr#	Series	Signatures	Seal	Fine	XF	CU
194	64	1869	Allison-Spinner	Large red	335.	775.	1200.
		Face: Bureau, Engraving & Printing, upper left, face design.					
		Back: American Bank Note Co., upper and lower margin.					
		Red Serial numbers. Large "V" in red ornamentation at right.					

Andrew Jackson

KL#	Fr#	Series	Signatures	Seal	Fine	XF	CU
195	65	1875	Allison-New	Small red	100.	300.	725.

KL#	Fr#	Series	Signatures	Seal	Fine	XF	CU
		Issued in two additional series, same design.					
196	66	1875 Series A in lower right of face design.			100.	300.	725.
197	67	1875 Series B			100.	350.	800.
198	68	1875	Allison-Wyman	Small red	100.	300.	725.
199	69	1878	Allison-Gilfillan	Small red	210.	390.	850.
		Red serial numbers					
200	70	1880	Scofield-Gilfillan	Large brown	150.	450.	850.
201	71	1880	Bruce-Gilfillan	Large brown	115.	400.	730.
202	72	1880	Bruce-Wyman	Large brown	115.	400.	730.
		Blue serial numbers					
203	73	1880	Bruce-Wyman	Large red	195.	550.	1650.
204	74	1880	Rosecrans-Jordan	Large red	185.	525.	1125.
205	75	1880	Rosecrans-Hyatt	Large red	185.	525.	1125.
206	76	1880	Rosecrans-Huston	Large red	250.	550.	1150.
207	77	1880	Rosecrans-Huston	Large brown	185.	525.	1125.
208	78	1880	Rosecrans-Nebeker	Large brown	195.	550.	1150.
209	79	1880	Rosecrans-Nebeker	Small red	85.00	210.	700.
210	80	1880	Tillman-Morgan	Small red	80.00	195.	675.
211	81	1880	Bruce-Roberts	Small red	95.00	195.	675.
212	82	1880	Lyons-Roberts	Small red	80.00	195.	675.

KL#	Fr#	Series	Signatures	Seal	Fine	XF	CU
		Red Serial numbers. Ornamental "V" at left.					
213	83	1907	Vernon-Treat	Small red	85.00	140.	310.
214	84	1907	Vernon-Mc Clung	Small red	80.00	130.	300.
215	85	1907	Napier-Mc Clung	Small red	80.00	130.	300.
216	86	1907	Napier-Thompson	Small red	100.	300.	650.
217	87	1907	Parker-Burke	Small red	80.00	130.	300.
218	88	1907	Teehee-Burke	Small red	80.00	130.	300.
219	89	1907	Elliott-Burke	Small red	80.00	130.	300.
220	90	1907	Elliott-White	Small red	80.00	130.	300.
221	91	1907	Speelman-White	Small red	80.00	130.	300.
222	92	1907	Woods-White	Small red	85.00	135.	400.

National Gold Bank Notes

Christopher Columbus

KL#	Fr#	Series	Issuing Bank	Location	Good	Fine
223	1136	Orig.	First Nat'l Gold Bank	San Francisco	700.	1500.
224	1137	Orig.	Nat'l Gold Bank & Trust Co.	San Francisco	700.	1500.
225	1138	Orig.	Nat'l Gold Bank of D.O. Mills	Sacramento	750.	2000.
226	1139	Orig.	First Nat'l Gold Bank	Stockton	750.	2000.
227	1140	Orig.	First Nat'l Gold Bank	Santa Barbara	750.	2500.
228	1141	Orig.	Farmers' Nat'l Gold Bank	San Jose	750.	2500.

Silver Certificates

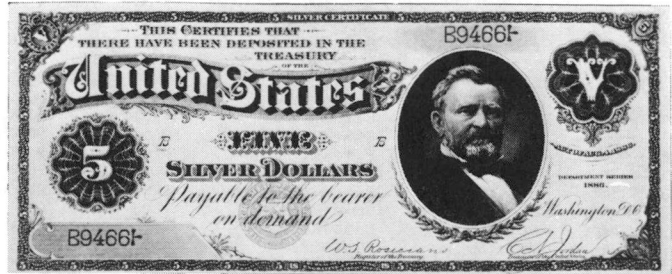

U.S. Grant

KL#	Fr#	Series	Signatures	Seal	Fine	XF	CU
			Blue serial numbers				
229	259	1886	Rosecrans-Jordan	Small red	575.	1900.	3750.
230	260	1886	Rosecrans-Hyatt	Small red	560.	1925.	3050.
231	261	1886	Rosecrans-Hyatt	Large red	560.	1925.	3050.
232	262	1886	Rosecrans-Huston	Large red	560.	1925.	3050.
233	263	1886	Rosecrans-Huston	Large brown	560.	1925.	3050.
234	264	1886	Rosecrans-Nebeker	Large brown	560.	1925.	3050.
235	265	1886	Rosecrans-Nebeker	Small red	575.	2000.	4200.

KL#	Fr#	Series	Signatures	Seal	Fine	XF	CU
236	266	1891	Rosecrans-Nebeker	Small red	450.	1200.	3200.
237	267	1891	Tillman-Morgan	Small red	425.	1150.	3100.

U.S. Grant, Philip Sheridan

KL#	Fr#	Series	Signatures	Seal	Fine	XF	CU
238	268	1896	Tillman-Morgan	Small red	850.	2250.	5750.
239	269	1896	Bruce-Roberts	Small red	850.	2250.	5750.
240	270	1896	Lyons-Roberts	Small red	850.	2250.	5750.

Sioux Chief Running Antelope

KL#	Fr#	Series	Signatures	Seal	Fine	XF	CU
241	271	1899	Lyons-Roberts	Small blue	380.	750.	1500.
242	272	1899	Lyons-Treat	Small blue	380.	750.	1500.
243	273	1899	Vernon-Treat	Small blue	380.	750.	1500.
244	274	1899	Vernon Mc Clung	Small blue	380.	750.	1500.
245	275	1899	Napier-Mc Clung	Small blue	380.	750.	1500.
246	276	1899	Napier-Thompson	Small blue	425.	800.	2300.
247	277	1899	Parker-Burke	Small blue	380.	750.	1500.
248	278	1899	Teehee-Burke	Small blue	380.	750.	1500.
249	279	1899	Elliott-Burke	Small blue	380.	750.	1500.
250	280	1899	Elliott-White	Small blue	380.	750.	1500.
251	281	1899	Speelman-White	Small blue	380.	750.	1500.

Abraham Lincoln

KL#	Fr#	Series	Signatures	Seal	Fine	XF	CU
252	282	1923	Speelman-White	Small blue	375.	1000.	1700.

Treasury or Coin Notes

Gen. George H. Thomas

KL#	Fr#	Series	Signatures	Seal	Fine	XF	CU
253	359	1890	Rosecrans-Huston	Large brown	425.	1600.	3100.
254	360	1890	Rosecrans-Nebeker	Large brown	390.	1500.	2950.
255	361	1890	Rosecrans-Nebeker	Small red	390.	1500.	2950.

KL#	Fr#	Series	Signatures	Seal	Fine	XF	CU
256	362	1891	Rosecrans-Nebeker	Small red	290.	625.	1200.
257	363	1891	Tillman-Morgan	Small red	290.	625.	1200.
258	364	1891	Bruce-Roberts	Small red	290.	625.	1200.
259	365	1891	Lyons-Roberts	Small red	290.	625.	1200.

Federal Reserve Notes
Series 1914

Abraham Lincoln

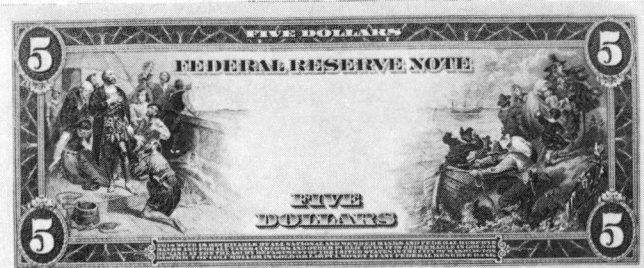

KL#	Fr#	Bank	Red Seals Signatures	Fine	XF	CU
260	832	Boston	Burke-Mc Adoo	60.00	175.	450.
261	833	New York	Burke-Mc Adoo	60.00	175.	450.
262	834	Philadelphia	Burke-Mc Adoo	65.00	200.	500.
263	835	Cleveland	Burke-Mc Adoo	65.00	200.	500.
264	836	Richmond	Burke-Mc Adoo	65.00	200.	500.
265	837	Atlanta	Burke-Mc Adoo	65.00	200.	500.
266	838	Chicago	Burke-Mc Adoo	65.00	200.	500.
267	839	St. Louis	Burke-Mc Adoo	65.00	200.	500.
268	840	Minneapolis	Burke-Mc Adoo	65.00	200.	500.
269	841	Kansas City	Burke-Mc Adoo	75.00	225.	550.
270	842	Dallas	Burke-Mc Adoo	65.00	200.	500.
271	843	San Francisco	Burke-Mc Adoo	65.00	200.	500.

KL#	Fr#	Bank	Blue Seals Signatures	Fine	XF	CU
272	844	Boston	Burke-Mc Adoo	36.00	50.00	90.00
273	845	Boston	Burke-Glass	36.00	50.00	90.00
274	846	Boston	Burke-Houston	36.00	50.00	90.00
275	847	Boston	White-Mellon	36.00	50.00	90.00
276	848	New York	Burke-Mc Adoo	36.00	50.00	90.00
277	849	New York	Burke-Glass	36.00	50.00	90.00
278	850	New York	Burke-Houston	36.00	50.00	115.
279	851	New York	White-Mellon	36.00	50.00	90.00
280	852	Philadelphia	Burke-Mc Adoo	36.00	50.00	90.00
281	853	Philadelphia	Burke-Glass	36.00	50.00	90.00
282	854	Philadelphia	Burke-Houston	36.00	50.00	90.00
283	855	Philadelphia	White-Mellon	36.00	50.00	90.00
284	856	Cleveland	Burke-Mc Adoo	36.00	50.00	90.00
285	857	Cleveland	Burke-Glass	36.00	50.00	90.00
286	858	Cleveland	Burke-Houston	36.00	50.00	90.00
287	859	Cleveland	White-Mellon	36.00	50.00	90.00
288	860	Richmond	Burke-Mc Adoo	36.00	50.00	90.00
289	861	Richmond	Burke-Glass	36.00	50.00	90.00
290	862	Richmond	Burke-Houston	36.00	50.00	90.00
291	863	Richmond	White-Mellon	36.00	52.00	95.00
292	864	Atlanta	Burke-Mc Adoo	36.00	50.00	90.00
293	865	Atlanta	Burke-Glass	36.00	50.00	90.00
294	866	Atlanta	Burke-Houston	36.00	50.00	90.00
295	867	Atlanta	White-Mellon	36.00	56.00	100.

KL#	Fr#	Bank	Blue Seals Signatures	Fine	XF	CU
296	868	Chicago	Burke-Mc Adoo	36.00	50.00	90.00
297	869	Chicago	Burke-Glass	36.00	50.00	90.00
298	870	Chicago	Burke-Houston	36.00	50.00	90.00
299	871	Chicago	White-Mellon	36.00	50.00	130.
300	872	St. Louis	Burke-Mc Adoo	36.00	50.00	90.00
301	873	St. Louis	Burke-Glass	36.00	50.00	90.00
302	874	St. Louis	Burke-Houston	36.00	50.00	90.00
303	875	St. Louis	White-Mellon	36.00	50.00	90.00
304	876	Minneapolis	Burke-Mc Adoo	36.00	50.00	90.00
305	877	Minneapolis	Burke-Glass	36.00	50.00	90.00
306	878	Minneapolis	Burke-Houston	36.00	50.00	90.00
307	879	Minneapolis	White-Mellon	36.00	50.00	90.00
308	880	Kansas City	Burke-Mc Adoo	36.00	50.00	90.00
309	881	Kansas City	Burke-Glass	36.00	50.00	90.00
310	882	Kansas City	Burke-Houston	36.00	50.00	90.00
311	883	Kansas City	White-Mellon	36.00	60.00	115.
312	884	Dallas	Burke-Mc Adoo	36.00	50.00	90.00
313	885	Dallas	Burke-Glass	36.00	50.00	90.00
314	886	Dallas	Burke-Houston	36.00	50.00	90.00
315	887	Dallas	White-Mellon	36.00	50.00	90.00
316	888	San Francisco	Burke-Mc Adoo	36.00	50.00	90.00
317	889	San Francisco	Burke-Glass	36.00	50.00	90.00
318	890	San Francisco	Burke-Houston	36.00	50.00	90.00
319	891	San Francisco	White-Mellon	36.00	60.00	115.

Federal Reserve Bank Notes
Series 1915

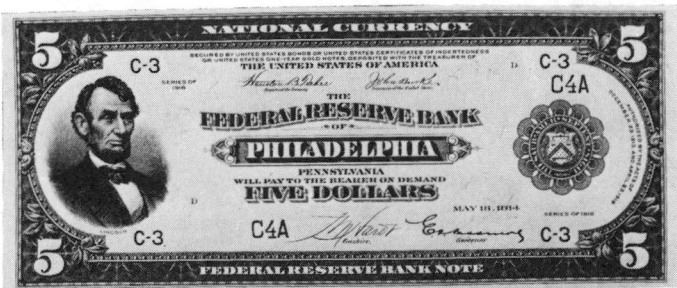

Abraham Lincoln

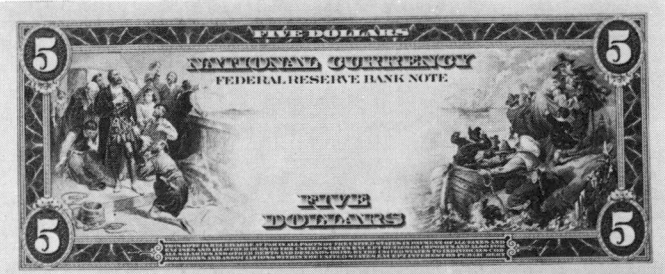

KL#	Fr#	Bank	Federal Sigs.	Bank Sigs.	Fine	XF	CU
320	788	Atlanta	Teehee-Burke	Bell-Wellborn	75.00	175.	625.
321	789	Atlanta	Teehee-Burke	Pike-Mc Cord	75.00	175.	625.
322	793	Chicago	Teehee-Burke	Mc Lallen-Mc Dougal	75.00	175.	625.
323	800	Kansas City	Teehee-Burke	Anderson-Miller	75.00	175.	625.
324	801	Kansas City	Teehee-Burke	Cross-Miller	75.00	175.	625.
325	802	Kansas City	Teehee-Burke	Helm-Miller	75.00	175.	625.
326	805	Dallas	Teehee-Burke	Hoopes-Van Zandt	75.00	175.	625.
327	806	Dallas	Teehee-Burke	Talley-Van Zandt	90.00	190.	625.
328	808	San Francisco	Teehee-Burke	Clerk-Lynch	90.00	190.	625.

Series 1918

KL#	Fr#	Bank	Federal Sigs.	Bank Sigs.	Fine	XF	CU
329	781	Boston	Teehee-Burke	Bullen-Morss	750.	1200.	1800.
330	782	New York	Teehee-Burke	Hendricks-Strong	60.00	165.	600.
331	783	Philadelphia	Teehee-Burke	Hardt-Passmore	60.00	165.	600.
332	784	Philadelphia	Teehee-Burke	Dyer-Passmore	60.00	165.	600.
333	785	Cleveland	Teehee-Burke	Baxter-Fancher	60.00	165.	600.
334	786	Cleveland	Teehee-Burke	Davis-Fancher	60.00	165.	600.
335	787	Cleveland	Elliott-Burke	Davis-Fancher	60.00	165.	600.
336	790	Atlanta	Teehee-Burke	Pike-Mc Cord	60.00	165.	600.
337	791	Atlanta	Teehee-Burke	Bell-Wellborn	60.00	165.	600.
338	792	Atlanta	Elliott-Burke	Bell-Wellborn	60.00	165.	600.
339	794	Chicago	Teehee-Burke	Mc Cloud-Mc Dougal	60.00	165.	600.
340	795	Chicago	Teehee-Burke	Cramer-Mc Dougal	60.00	165.	600.
341	796	St. Louis	Teehee-Burke	Attebery-Wells	60.00	165.	600.
342	797	St. Louis	Teehee-Burke	Attebery-Biggs	60.00	165.	600.
343	798	St. Louis	Elliott-Burke	White-Biggs	60.00	165.	600.
344	799	Minneapolis	Teehee-Burke	Cook-Wold	60.00	165.	600.
345	803	Kansas City	Teehee-Burke	Anderson-Miller	60.00	165.	600.

KL#	Fr#	Bank	Federal Sigs.	Bank Sigs.	Fine	XF	CU
346	804	Kansas City	Elliott-Burke	Helm-Miller	60.00	165.	600.
347	807	Dallas	Teehee-Burke	Talley-Van Zandt	60.00	165.	600.
348	809	San Francisco	Teehee-Burke	Clerk-Lynch	60.00	165.	600.
348A*	809A	San Francisco	Teehee-Burke	Clerk-Lynch	250.	700.	2200.

*Similar to KL348 but dated May 18, 1914. All other San Francisco notes are dated May 20, 1914.

Ten Dollars

Demand Notes

Type One: "For the" autographed
Type Two: "For the" engraved

Abraham Lincoln

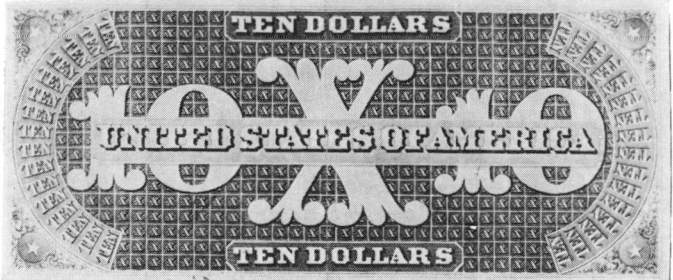

KL#	Fr#	Payable at:		Good	VG
349	8-A	Boston	Type One	1500.	7500.
350	8	Boston	Type Two	500.	1500.
351	6-A	New York	Type One	1500.	7500.
352	6	New York	Type Two	500.	1500.
353	7-A	Philadelphia	Type One	1500.	7500.
354	7	Philadelphia	Type Two	500.	1500.
355	10-A	St. Louis	Type One	Rare	—
356	10	St. Louis	Type Two	8000.	24,000.
357	9-A	Cincinnati	Type One	Rare	—
358	9	Cincinnati	Type Two	7500.	17,500.

United States Notes

Abraham Lincoln

KL#	Fr#	Series	Signatures	Seal	Fine	XF	CU
			First Obligation inscription on back. One red serial number.				
359	93	1862	Chittenden-Spinner	Small red	650.	1200.	3350.
			American Bank Note Co. upper border.				

KL#	Fr#	Series	Signatures	Seal	Fine	XF	CU
			Second Obligation on back. One red serial number.				
360	94	1862	Chittenden-Spinner	Small red	650.	1200.	3350.
			American Bank Note Co. upper border.				
			National Bank Note Co. lower border.				
			Second Obligation on back. Two red serial numbers.				
361	95-A	1863	Chittenden-Spinner	Small red	650.	1200.	3350.
			American Bank Note Co. upper and lower borders.				

Daniel Webster

KL#	Fr#	Series	Signatures	Seal	Fine	XF	CU
			Red serial numbers				
362	96	1869	Allison-Spinner	Large red	560.	1100.	3200.

Daniel Webster

KL#	Fr#	Series	Signatures	Seal	Fine	XF	CU
			Face: Bureau of Engraving and Printing. Back: National Bank Note Co.				
363	97	1875	Allison-New	Small red	525.	1100.	2900.
			Issued in one additional series, same design.				
364	98	1875 Series A in lower right of face design.			500.	1050.	2650.
365	99	1878	Allison-Gilfillan	Small red	375.	950.	2400.
			Red serial numbers				
366	100	1880	Scofield-Gilfillan	Large brown	325.	650.	1250.

KL#	Fr#	Series	Signatures	Seal	Fine	XF	CU
367	101	1880	Bruce-Gilfillan	Large brown	325.	650.	1250.
368	102	1880	Bruce-Wyman	Large brown	325.	650.	1250.
			Blue serial numbers				
369	103	1880	Bruce-Wyman	Large red	450.	875.	1650.
370	104	1880	Rosecrans-Jordan	Large red	425.	850.	1600.
371	105	1880	Rosecrans-Hyatt	Large red	425.	850.	1600.
372	106	1880	Rosecrans-Hyatt	Red spikes	425.	875.	1650.
373	107	1880	Rosecrans-Huston	Red spikes	425.	800.	1600.
374	108	1880	Rosecrans-Huston	Large brown	425.	700.	1600.
375	109	1880	Rosecrans-Nebeker	Large brown	425.	850.	1600.
376	110	1880	Rosecrans-Nebeker	Small red	335.	590.	1125.
377	111	1880	Tillman-Morgan	Small red	335.	590.	1125.
378	112	1880	Bruce-Roberts	Small red	335.	590.	1125.
379	113	1880	Lyons-Roberts	Small red	335.	590.	1125.

Meriwether Lewis, William Clark

KL#	Fr#	Series	Signatures	Seal	Fine	XF	CU
			Red Serial numbers. Large "X" at left.				
380	114	1901	Lyons-Roberts	Small red	625.	1150.	3200.
381	115	1901	Lyons-Treat	Small red	500.	1000.	2500.
382	116	1901	Vernon-Treat	Small red	500.	1000.	2500.
383	117	1901	Vernon-Mc Clung	Small red	500.	1000.	2500.
384	118	1901	Napier-Mc Clung	Small red	500.	1000.	2500.
385	119	1901	Parker-Burke	Small red	500.	1000.	2500.
386	120	1901	Teehee-Burke	Small red	500.	1000.	2500.
387	121	1901	Elliott-White	Small red	500.	1000.	2500.
388	122	1901	Speelman-White	Small red	500.	1000.	2500.

Andrew Jackson

KL#	Fr#	Series	Signatures	Seal	Fine	XF	CU
			Red Serial numbers. Large "X" at right.				
389	123	1923	Speelman-White	Small red	580.	1225.	3850.

Compound Interest Treasury Notes

Salmon P. Chase

KL#	Fr#	Act	Overprint Date	Signatures	VG	Fine	XF
390	190	1863	June 10, 1864	Chittenden-Spinner	1550.	2600.	6900.
391	190-A	1864	July 15, 1864	Chittenden-Spinner	1550.	2600.	6900.
392	190-B	1864	Aug. 15-Dec. 15,1864	Colby-Spinner	1550.	2600.	6900.

Interest Bearing Notes

Salmon P. Chase

KL#	Fr#	Act	Signatures	VG	Fine	XF
393	196	1863	Chittenden-Spinner	1350.	3900.	9200.

Refunding Certificates

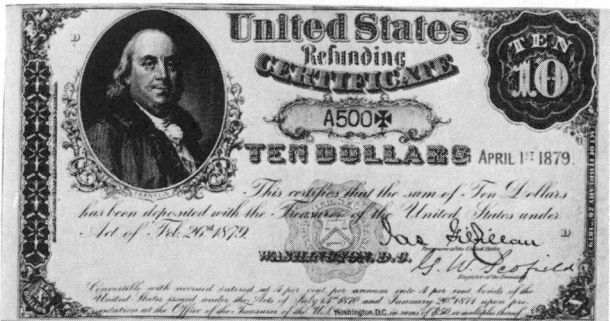

Ben Franklin

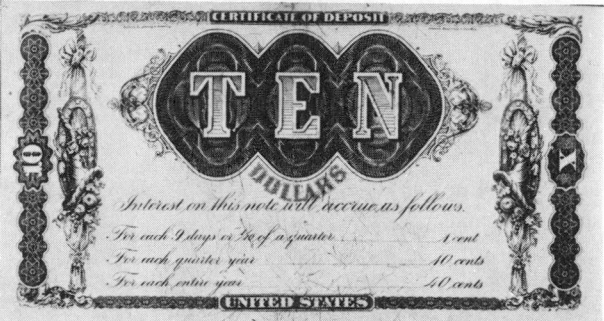

KL#	Fr#	Signatures	Payable to...	VG	Fine	XF
394	213	Scofield-Gilfillan	Order	—	—	—
395	214	Scofield-Gilfillan	Bearer	1050.	1275.	2800.

National Gold Bank Notes

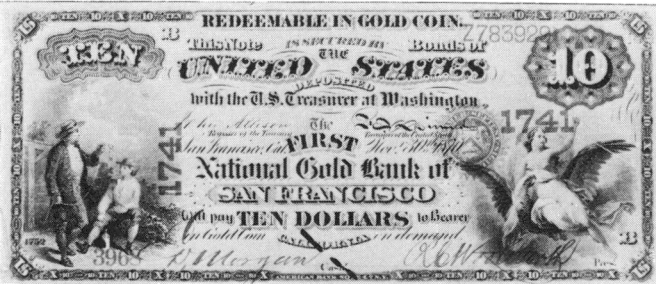

Ben Franklin

KL#	Fr#	Series	Issuing Bank	Location	Good	Fine
396	1142	Orig.	First Nat'l Gold Bank	San Francisco	850.	2900.
397	1143	1872	Nat'l Gold Bank & Trust Co.	San Francisco	850.	2900.
398	1144	Orig.	Nat'l Gold Bank of D.O. Mills	Sacramento	1000.	4000.
399	1146	Orig.	First Nat'l Gold Bank	Stockton	1000.	4000.
400	1145	Orig.	First Nat'l Gold Bank	Santa Barbara	1150.	4000.
401	1148	Orig.	Farmers' Nat'l Gold Bank	San Jose	1000.	4000.
402	1149	Orig.	First Nat'l Gold Bank	Petaluma	1000.	4000.
403	1150	1875	First Nat'l Gold Bank	Petaluma	1000.	4000.
404	1151	1875	First Nat'l Gold Bank	Oakland	1000.	4000.
405	1151-A	1875	Union Nat'l Gold Bank	Oakland	1100.	4000.
406	1147	1875	First Nat'l Gold Bank	Stockton	1000.	4000.

Silver Certificates

The Countersigned Series
Scofield-Gilfillan signatures. Blue serial numbers.
Types 1, 2 4 and 5, place of deposit: New York.
Type 3 place of deposit: Washington, D.C.
Series 1878 Large red seal and large red
''ten'' below seal.
Series 1880 Large brown seal and large
''X'' below seal.

Robert Morris

KL#	Fr#	Series	Countersigned by:	Good	Fine
407	284	1878	J.C. Hopper, Asst. U.S. Treas.	3000.	7000.
408	283	1878	W.G. White, Asst. U.S. Treas.	3000.	7000.
409	285-A	1878	A.V. Wyman, Asst. U.S. Treas.	3000.	7000.
410	284-A	1878	T. Hillhouse, Asst. U.S. Treas.	3000.	7000.
411	286	1880	T. Hillhouse, Asst. U.S. Treas.	3000.	7000.

KL#	Fr#	Series	Signatures	Seal	Fine	XF	CU
			Blue serial numbers, without large "X" below center seal.				
412	287	1880	Scofield-Gilfillan	Large brown	1200.	3000.	4700.
413	288	1880	Bruce-Gilfillan	Large brown	1200.	3000.	4700.
414	289	1880	Bruce-Wyman	Large brown	1200.	3000.	4700.
			Blue serial numbers, without large "X" below center seal.				
415	290	1880	Bruce-Wyman	Large red	1075.	2700.	4400.

Thomas A. Hendricks

KL#	Fr#	Series	Signatures	Seal	Fine	XF	CU
416	291	1886	Rosecrans-Jordan	Small red	750.	2200.	4800.
417	292	1886	Rosecrans-Hyatt	Small red	750.	2200.	4800.
418	293	1886	Rosecrans-Hyatt	Large red	750.	2200.	4800.
419	294	1886	Rosecrans-Huston	Large red	750.	2200.	4800.
420	295	1886	Rosecrans-Huston	Large brown	750.	2200.	4800.
421	296	1886	Rosecrans-Nebeker	Large brown	750.	2200.	4800.
422	297	1886	Rosecrans-Nebeker	Small red	750.	2200.	4800.
423	298	1891	Rosecrans-Nebeker	Small red	360.	1000.	2600.
424	299	1891	Tillman-Morgan	Small red	360.	1000.	2600.
425	300	1891	Bruce-Roberts	Small red	360.	1000.	2600.

KL#	Fr#	Series	Signatures	Seal	Fine	XF	CU
426	301	1891	Lyons-Roberts	Small red	360.	1000.	2600.
427	302	1908	Vernon-Treat	Small blue	350.	950.	2300.
428	303	1908	Vernon-Mc Clung	Small blue	340.	900.	2200.
429	304	1908	Parker-Burke	Small blue	340.	900.	2200.

KL#	Fr#	Series	Signatures	Fine	XF	CU
438	1169	1907	Napier-Mc Clung	65.00	160.	530.
439	1170	1907	Napier-Thompson	80.00	170.	1000.
440	1171	1907	Parker-Burke	65.00	160.	530.
441	1172	1907	Teehee-Burke	65.00	160.	530.
442	1173	1922	Speelman-White	80.00	225.	525.
442A	1173A	1922	Speelman-White, small serial #	90.00	200.	600.

Treasury or Coin Notes

Gen. Philip H. Sheridan

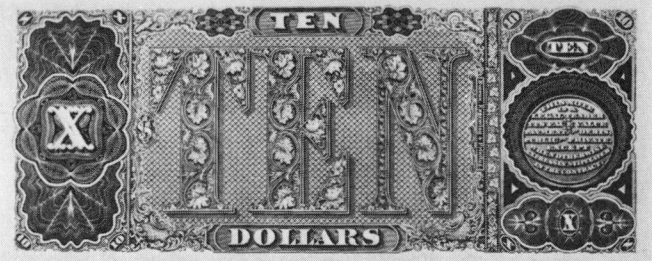

KL#	Fr#	Series	Signatures	Seal	Fine	XF	CU
430	366	1890	Rosecrans-Huston	Large brown	690.	1850.	3550.
431	367	1890	Rosecrans-Nebeker	Large brown	690.	1850.	3550.
432	368	1890	Rosecrans-Nebeker	Small red	690.	1850.	3550.

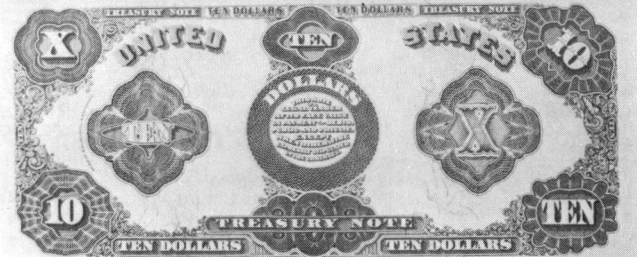

KL#	Fr#	Series	Signatures	Seal	Fine	XF	CU
433	369	1891	Rosecrans-Nebeker	Small red	440.	900.	2400.
434	370	1891	Tillman-Morgan	Small red	440.	900.	2400.
435	371	1891	Bruce-Roberts	Small red	440.	900.	2400.

Gold Certificates

Michael Hillegas

KL#	Fr#	Series	Signatures	Fine	XF	CU
436	1167	1907	Vernon-Treat	65.00	160.	530.
437	1168	1907	Vernon-Mc Clung	65.00	160.	530.

Federal Reserve Notes
Series 1914

Andrew Jackson

KL#	Fr#	Bank	Red Seals Signatures	Fine	XF	CU
443	892	Boston	Burke-Mc Adoo	70.00	185.	565.
444	893	New York	Burke-Mc Adoo	80.00	195.	600.
445	894	Philadelphia	Burke-Mc Adoo	70.00	185.	565.
446	895	Cleveland	Burke-Mc Adoo	70.00	185.	565.
447	896	Richmond	Burke-Mc Adoo	70.00	185.	565.
448	897	Atlanta	Burke-Mc Adoo	70.00	185.	565.
449	898	Chicago	Burke-Mc Adoo	70.00	185.	565.
450	899	St. Louis	Burke-Mc Adoo	85.00	200.	625.
451	900	Minneapolis	Burke-Mc Adoo	70.00	185.	565.
452	901	Kansas City	Burke-Mc Adoo	70.00	185.	565.
453	902	Dallas	Burke-Mc Adoo	70.00	185.	565.
454	903	San Francisco	Burke-Mc Adoo	70.00	185.	565.
			Blue Seals			
455	904	Boston	Burke-Mc Adoo	35.00	50.00	110.
456	905	Boston	Burke-Glass	35.00	50.00	110.
457	906	Boston	Burke-Houston	35.00	50.00	110.
458	907	Boston	White-Mellon	35.00	50.00	110.
459	908	New York	Burke-Mc Adoo	35.00	50.00	110.
460	909	New York	Burke-Glass	35.00	50.00	110.
461	910	New York	Burke-Houston	35.00	50.00	110.
462	911	New York	White-Mellon	35.00	50.00	110.
463	912	Philadelphia	Burke-Mc Adoo	35.00	50.00	110.
464	913	Philadelphia	Burke-Glass	35.00	50.00	110.
465	914	Philadelphia	Burke-Houston	35.00	50.00	110.
466	915	Philadelphia	White-Mellon	35.00	50.00	110.
467	916	Cleveland	Burke-Mc Adoo	35.00	50.00	110.
468	917	Cleveland	Burke-Glass	35.00	50.00	110.
469	918	Cleveland	Burke-Houston	35.00	50.00	110.
470	919	Cleveland	White-Mellon	35.00	50.00	110.
471	920	Richmond	Burke-Mc Adoo	35.00	50.00	110.
472	921	Richmond	Burke-Glass	35.00	50.00	110.
473	922	Richmond	Burke-Houston	35.00	50.00	110.
474	923	Richmond	White-Mellon	35.00	50.00	110.
475	924	Atlanta	Burke-Mc Adoo	35.00	50.00	110.
476	925	Atlanta	Burke-Glass	35.00	50.00	110.
477	926	Atlanta	Burke-Houston	35.00	50.00	110.
478	927	Atlanta	White-Mellon	35.00	50.00	110.
479	928	Chicago	Burke-Mc Adoo	35.00	50.00	110.
480	929	Chicago	Burke-Glass	35.00	50.00	110.
481	930	Chicago	Burke-Houston	35.00	50.00	110.
482	931	Chicago	White-Mellon	35.00	50.00	110.
483	932	St. Louis	Burke-Mc Adoo	35.00	50.00	110.
484	933	St. Louis	Burke-Glass	35.00	50.00	110.
485	934	St. Louis	Burke-Houston	35.00	50.00	110.
486	935	St. Louis	White-Mellon	35.00	50.00	110.
487	936	Minneapolis	Burke-Mc Adoo	35.00	50.00	110.
488	937	Minneapolis	Burke-Glass	35.00	50.00	110.
489	938	Minneapolis	Burke-Houston	35.00	50.00	110.
490	939	Minneapolis	White-Mellon	35.00	50.00	110.
491	940	Kansas City	Burke-Mc Adoo	35.00	50.00	110.
492	941	Kansas City	Burke-Glass	40.00	60.00	115.
493	942	Kansas City	Burke-Houston	35.00	50.00	110.
494	943	Kansas City	White-Mellon	35.00	50.00	110.
495	944	Dallas	Burke-Mc Adoo	35.00	50.00	110.
496	945	Dallas	Burke-Glass	35.00	50.00	110.

KL#	Fr#	Bank	Signatures	Fine	XF	CU
497	946	Dallas	Burke-Houston	35.00	50.00	110.
498	947	Dallas	White-Mellon	35.00	50.00	110.
499	948	San Francisco	Burke-Mc Adoo	35.00	50.00	110.
500	949	San Francisco	Burke-Glass	40.00	75.00	225.
501	950	San Francisco	Burke-Houston	35.00	50.00	110.
502	951	San Francisco	White-Mellon	35.00	50.00	110.

KL#	Fr#	Payable at:		Good	VG
517	11-A	New York	Type One	Rare	—
518	11	New York	Type Two	7000.	12,000.
519	12-A	Philadelphia	Type One	Rare	—
520	12	Philadelphia	Type Two	7000.	12,000.
521	14-A	Cincinnati	Type One	(VERY RARE)	
522	14	Cincinnati	Type Two	(VERY RARE)	

Federal Reserve Bank Notes
Series 1915

KL#	Fr#	Bank	Federal Sigs.	Bank Sigs.	Fine	XF	CU
503	811	Atlanta	Teehee-Burke	Bell-Wellborn	300.	600.	2000.
504	813	Chicago	Teehee-Burke	Mc Lallen-Mc Dougal	275.	725.	1925.
505	816	Kansas City	Teehee-Burke	Anderson-Miller	275.	725.	1925.
506	817	Kansas City	Teehee-Burke	Cross-Miller	275.	725.	1925.
507	818	Kansas City	Teehee-Burke	Helm-Miller	275.	725.	1925.
508	819	Dallas	Teehee-Burke	Hoopes-Van Zandt	275.	725.	1925.
509	820	Dallas	Teehee-Burke	Gilbert-Van Zandt	350.	700.	2000.
510	821	Dallas	Teehee-Burke	Talley-Van Zandt	275.	725.	1925.

Series 1918

KL#	Fr#	Bank	Federal Sigs.	Bank Sigs.	Fine	XF	CU
511	810	New York	Teehee-Burkee	Hendricks-Strong	275.	725.	1925.
512	812	Atlanta	Elliott-Burke	Bell-Wellborn	275.	725.	1925.
513	814	Chicago	Teehee-Burke	Mc Cloud-Mc Dougal	275.	725.	1925.
514	815	St. Louis	Teehee-Burke	Attebery-Wells	275.	725.	1925.

United States Notes

KL#	Fr#	Series	Signatures	Seal	Fine	XF	CU
		First Obligation inscription on back. One red serial number.					
523	124	1862	Chittenden-Spinner	Small red	1550.	2650.	5100.
		American Bank Note Co. lower border.					
		Second Obligation on back. One red serial number.					
524	125	1862	Chittenden-Spinner	Small red	1550.	2650.	5100.
		National Bank Note Co. American Bank Note Co.					
		Second Obligation on back. Two red serial numbers.					
525	126	1863	Chittenden-Spinner	Small red	1550.	2650.	5100.
		American Bank Note Co. lower border.					

Twenty Dollars
Demand Notes

Type One: "For the" autographed
Type Two: "For the" engraved

KL#	Fr#	Payable at:		Good	VG
515	13-A	Boston	Type One	Rare	Rare
516	13	Boston	Type Two	9000.	15,000.

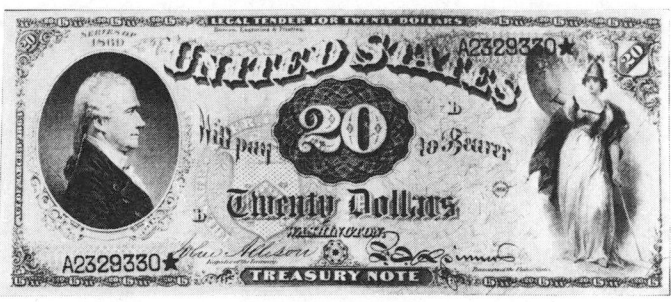

Alexander Hamilton

KL#	Fr#	Series	Signatures	Seal	Fine	XF	CU
		Blue serial numbers					
526	127	1869	Allison-Spinner	Large red	1600.	3400.	5750.
		Blue Serial numbers. "XX" twice on face of note.					
527	128	1875	Allison-New	Small red	900.	1700.	3400.

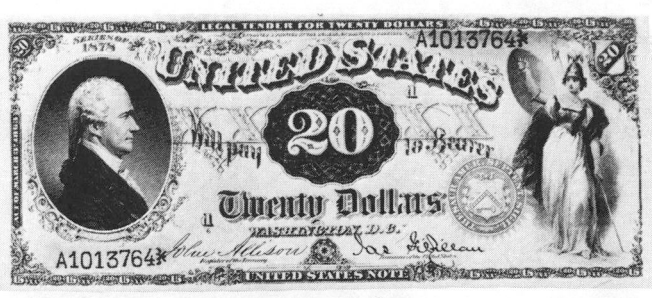

Alexander Hamilton

KL#	Fr#	Series	Signatures	Seal	Fine	XF	CU
528	129	1878	Allison-Gilfillan	Small red	650.	1100.	2900.
			Blue Serial numbers. "XX" removed.				
529	130	1880	Scofield-Gilfillan	Large brown	575.	1150.	1900.
530	131	1880	Bruce-Gilfillan	Large brown	575.	1150.	1900.
531	132	1880	Bruce-Wyman	Large brown	575.	1150.	1900.
532	133	1880	Bruce-Wyman	Large red	575.	1150.	1900.
533	134	1880	Rosecrans-Jordan	Large red	575.	1150.	1900.
534	135	1880	Rosecrans-Hyatt	Large red	575.	1150.	1900.
535	136	1880	Rosecrans-Hyatt	Red spikes	575.	1150.	1900.
536	137	1880	Rosecrans-Huston	Red spikes	575.	1150.	1900.
537	138	1880	Rosecrans-Huston	Large brown	575.	1150.	1900.
538	139	1880	Rosecrans-Nebeker	Large brown	575.	1150.	1900.
539	140	1880	Rosecrans-Nebeker	Small red	300.	750.	1500.
540	141	1880	Tillman-Morgan	Small red	300.	750.	1500.
541	142	1880	Bruce-Roberts	Small red	300.	750.	1500.
542	143	1880	Lyons-Roberts	Small red	300.	750.	1600.
543	144	1880	Vernon-Treat	Small red	325.	775.	1550.
544	145	1880	Vernon-Mc Clung	Small red	300.	750.	1500.
			Red serial numbers.				
545	146	1880	Teehee-Burke	Small red	275.	750.	1250.
546	147	1880	Elliott-White	Small red	260.	700.	1200.

Compound Interest Treasury Notes

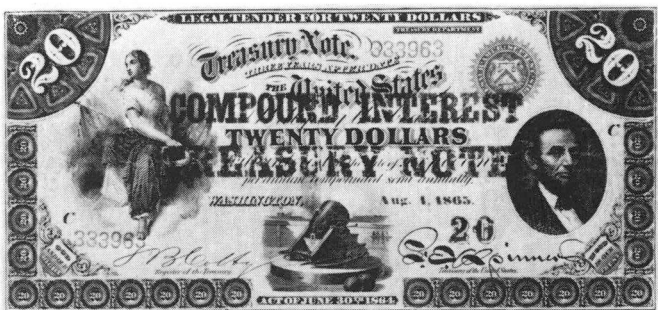

Abraham Lincoln

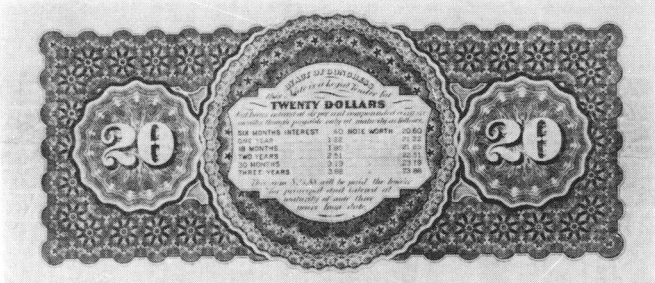

KL#	Fr#	Act	Overprint Date	Signatures	VG	Fine	XF
547	191	1864	July 14, 1864	Chittenden-Spinner	1600.	2250.	10,000.
548	191-A	1864	Aug. 15, 1864-Oct.16,1865	Colby-Spinner	1600.	2250.	10,000.

Interest Bearing Notes

Abraham Lincoln

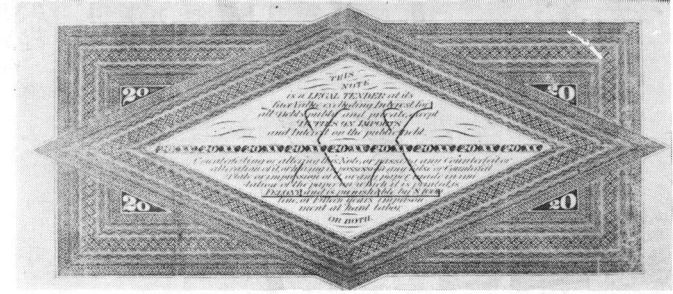

KL#	Fr#	Act	Signatures	VG	Fine	XF
549	197	1863	Chittenden-Spinner	3000.	5200.	17,000.

Gold Certificates

KL#	Fr#	Issue/Act/Series	Signatures	Fine	XF	CU
550	1166-B	First/1863	Colby-Spinner			(Two known)

Note pictured sold at auction in 1979 for $75,000.

James A. Garfield

KL#	Fr#	Series	Signatures	Seal	Fine	XF	CU
551	1175	1882	Bruce Gilfillan-(countersigned by Asst. Treas. of the U.S. Thos. C. Acton)	Brown	Rare	—	—

KL#	Fr#	Series	Signatures	Seal	Fine	XF	CU
552	1174	1882	Bruce-Gilfillan	Brown	2000.	4000.	—
553	1176	1882	Bruce-Wyman	Brown	1500.	2500.	—
554	1177	1882	Rosecrans-Huston	Large brown	750.	3000.	—
555	1178	1882	Lyons-Roberts	Small red	530.	1700.	3350.

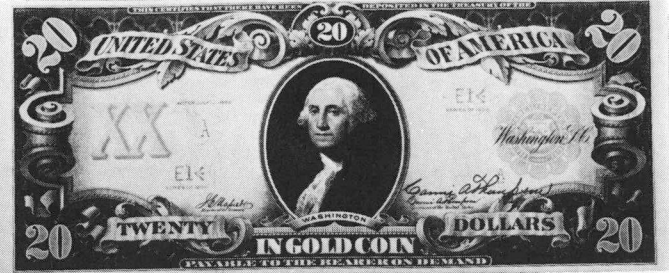

George Washington

KL#	Fr#	Series	Signatures	Seal	Fine	XF	CU
556	1179	1905	Lyons-Roberts	Small red	900.	3200.	8300.
557	1180	1905	Lyons-Treat	Small red	900.	3200.	8300.
558	1181	1906	Vernon-Treat	Gold	110.	335.	775.
559	1182	1906	Vernon-McClung	Gold	110.	335.	775.
560	1183	1906	Napier-McClung	Gold	125.	350.	800.
561	1184	1906	Napier-Thompson	Gold	125.	350.	800.
562	1185	1906	Parker-Burke	Gold	110.	335.	775.
563	1186	1906	Teehee-Burke	Gold	110.	335.	775.
564	1187	1922	Speelman-White	Gold	145.	290.	800.

National Gold Bank Notes

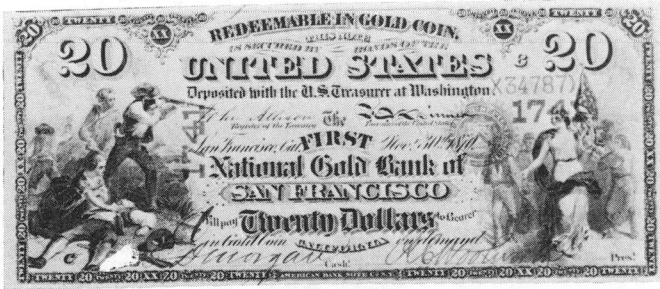

KL#	Fr#	Series	Issuing Bank	Location	Good	Fine
566	1152	Orig.	First Nat'l Gold Bank	San Francisco	1200.	5400.
567	1154	Orig.	Nat'l Gold Bank of D.O. Mills	Sacramento	1200.	5400.
568	1155	Orig.	First Nat'l Gold Bank	Stockton	1700.	5800.
569	1159-A	Orig.	First Nat'l Gold Bank	Santa Barbara	1700.	5800.
570	1156	Orig.	Farmers Nat'l Gold Bank	San Jose	1700.	5800.
571	1153	1875	Farmers' Nat'l Gold Bank	San Francisco	1300.	5500.
572	1157	1875	First Nat'l Gold Bank	Petaluma	1300.	5500.
573	1158	1875	First Nat'l Gold Bank	Oakland	1300.	5500.
574	1159	1875	Union Nat'l Gold Bank	Oakland	1300.	5500.

Silver Certificates

The Countersigned Series
Scofield-Gilfillan signatures. Blue serial numbers.
Types 1, 4 and 5: Place of deposit, New York.
Type 3: Place of deposit, Washington, D.C.

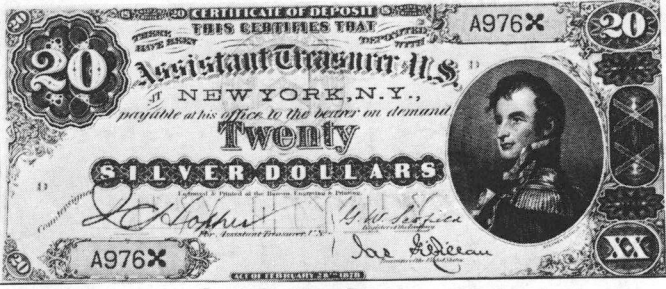

Capt. Stephen Decatur

KL#	Fr#	Series	Countersigned by:		Good	Fine
575	305	1878	J.C. Hopper, Asst. U.S. Treas.		—	—
576	307	1878	A.U. Wyman, Asst. U.S. Treas.		—	—
577	306	1878	T. Hillhouse, Asst. U.S. Treas.		—	—
578	308	1880	T. Hillhouse, Asst. U.S. Treas.		—	—

KL#	Fr#	Series	Signatures	Seal	Fine	XF	CU
579	309	1880	Scofield-Gilfillan	Large brown	2500.	5200.	10,000.
580	310	1880	Bruce-Gilfillan	Large brown	2500.	5200.	10,000.
581	311	1880	Bruce-Wyman	Large brown	2500.	5200.	10,000.
			Large "XX" removed.				
582	312	1880	Bruce-Wyman	Small red	2500.	5200.	10,000.

Daniel Manning

KL#	Fr#	Series	Signatures	Seal	Fine	XF	CU
583	313	1886	Rosecrans-Hyatt	Large red	2900.	7000.	11,000.
584	314	1886	Rosecrans-Huston	Large brown	2900.	7000.	11,000.
585	315	1886	Rosecrans-Nebeker	Large brown	2750.	6600.	11,000.
586	316	1886	Rosecrans-Nebeker	Large red	2900.	7000.	11,000.
			"Series 1891" upper right and lower left.				
587	317	1891	Rosecrans-Nebeker	Small red	900.	2000.	3850.
588	318	1891	Tillman-Morgan	Small red	900.	2000.	3850.
589	319	1891	Bruce-Roberts	Small red	900.	2000.	3850.
590	320	1891	Lyons-Roberts	Small red	900.	2000.	3850.
			Large blue "XX" at left.				
591	321	1891	Parker-Burke	Small blue	900.	2000.	3850.
592	322	1891	Teehee-Burke	Small blue	900.	2000.	3850.

NOTE: LARGE and SMALL size signatures known.

Treasury or Coin Notes

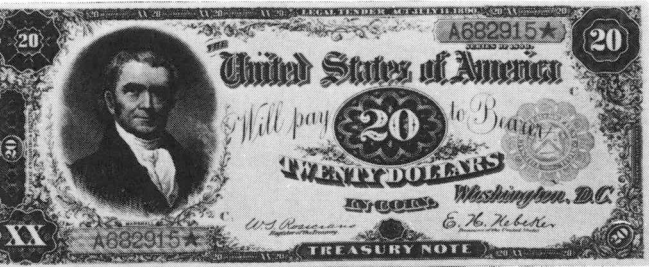

John Marshall

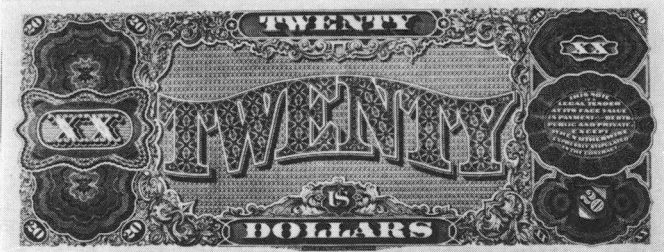

KL#	Fr#	Series	Signatures	Seal	Fine	XF	CU
593	372	1890	Rosecrans-Huston	Large brown	2500.	5750.	14,000.
594	373	1890	Rosecrans-Nebeker	Large brown	2500.	5750.	14,000.
595	374	1890	Rosecrans-Nebeker	Small red	2500.	5750.	14,000.

KL#	Fr#	Series	Signatures	Seal	Fine	XF	CU
596	375	1891	Tillman-Morgan	Small red	2750.	6900.	14,000.
597	375-A	1891	Bruce-Roberts	Small red	2750.	6900.	14,000.

Federal Reserve Notes
Series 1914

Grover Cleveland

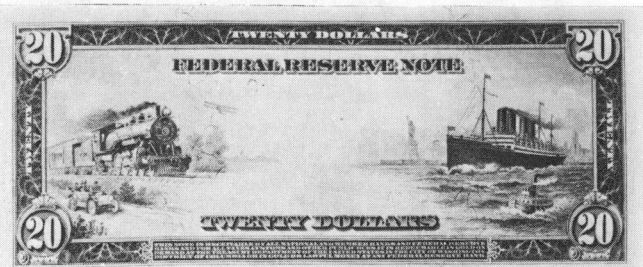

KL#	Fr#	Bank	Red Seals Signatures	Fine	XF	CU
598	952	Boston	Burke-Mc Adoo	115.	500.	1450.
599	953	New York	Burke-Mc Adoo	115.	500.	1450.
600	954	Philadelphia	Burke-Mc Adoo	115.	500.	1450.
601	955	Cleveland	Burke-Mc Adoo	115.	500.	1450.

KL#	Fr#	Bank	Signatures	Fine	XF	CU
602	956	Richmond	Burke-Mc Adoo	115.	500.	1450.
603	957	Atlanta	Burke-Mc Adoo	115.	500.	1450.
604	958	Chicago	Burke-Mc Adoo	115.	500.	1450.
605	959	St. Louis	Burke-Mc Adoo	115.	500.	1450.
606	960	Minneapolis	Burke-Mc Adoo	115.	500.	1450.
607	961	Kansas City	Burke-Mc Adoo	115.	500.	1450.
608	962	Dallas	Burke-Mc Adoo	115.	500.	1450.
609	963	San Francisco	Burke-Mc Adoo	115.	500.	1450.
			Blue Seals			
610	964	Boston	Burke-Mc Adoo	45.00	60.00	170.
611	965	Boston	Burke-Glass	45.00	60.00	170.
612	966	Boston	Burke-Houston	45.00	60.00	170.
613	967	Boston	White-Mellon	45.00	60.00	170.
614	968	New York	Burke-Mc Adoo	45.00	60.00	170.
615	969	New York	Burke-Glass	45.00	60.00	170.
616	970	New York	Burke-Houston	45.00	60.00	170.
617	971	New York	White-Mellon	45.00	60.00	170.
618	972	Philadelphia	Burke-Mc Adoo	45.00	70.00	170.
619	973	Philadelphia	Burke-Glass	45.00	70.00	170.
620	974	Philadelphia	Burke-Houston	45.00	70.00	170.
621	975	Philadelphia	White-Mellon	45.00	70.00	170.
622	976	Cleveland	Burke-Mc Adoo	45.00	70.00	170.
623	977	Cleveland	Burke-Glass	45.00	70.00	170.
624	978	Cleveland	Burke-Houston	45.00	70.00	170.
625	979	Cleveland	White-Mellon	45.00	70.00	170.
626	980	Richmond	Burke-Mc Adoo	45.00	60.00	170.
627	981	Richmond	Burke-Glass	45.00	60.00	170.
628	982	Richmond	Burke-Houston	45.00	60.00	170.
629	983	Richmond	White-Mellon	45.00	60.00	170.
630	984	Atlanta	Burke-Mc Adoo	45.00	60.00	170.
631	985	Atlanta	Burke-Glass	45.00	60.00	170.
632	986	Atlanta	Burke-Houston	45.00	60.00	170.
633	987	Atlanta	White-Mellon	45.00	60.00	170.
634	988	Chicago	Burke-Mc Adoo	50.00	70.00	180.
635	989	Chicago	Burke-Glass	50.00	70.00	180.
636	990	Chicago	Burke-Houston	50.00	70.00	180.
637	991	Chicago	White-Mellon	50.00	70.00	180.
638	992	St. Louis	Burke-Mc Adoo	45.00	60.00	170.
639	993	St. Louis	Burke-Glass	45.00	60.00	170.
640	994	St. Louis	Burke-Houston	45.00	60.00	170.
641	995	St. Louis	White-Mellon	45.00	60.00	170.
642	996	Minneapolis	Burke-Mc Adoo	45.00	60.00	170.
643	997	Minneapolis	Burke-Glass	45.00	60.00	170.
644	998	Minneapolis	Burke-Houston	45.00	60.00	170.
645	999	Minneapolis	White-Mellon	45.00	60.00	170.
646	1000	Kansas City	Burke-Mc Adoo	45.00	60.00	170.
647	1001	Kansas City	Burke-Glass	45.00	60.00	170.
648	1002	Kansas City	Burke-Houston	45.00	60.00	170.
649	1003	Kansas City	White-Mellon	45.00	60.00	170.
650	1004	Dallas	Burke-Mc Adoo	45.00	60.00	170.
651	1005	Dallas	Burke-Glass	45.00	70.00	180.
652	1006	Dallas	Burke-Houston	45.00	60.00	170.
653	1007	Dallas	White-Mellon	60.00	85.00	195.
654	1008	San Francisco	Burke-Mc Adoo	50.00	70.00	180.
655	1009	San Francisco	Burke-Glass	45.00	70.00	225.
656	1010	San Francisco	Burke-Houston	45.00	60.00	180.
657	1011	San Francisco	White-Mellon	50.00	70.00	180.

Federal Reserve Bank Notes
Series 1915

Grover Cleveland

KL#	Fr#	Bank	Federal Sigs.	Bank Sigs.	Fine	XF	CU
658	822	Atlanta	Teehee-Burke	Bell-Wellborn	540.	1100.	2500.
659	822-A	Atlanta	Teehee-Burke	Pike-Mc Cord	600.	1250.	3500.

KL#	Fr#	Bank	Federal Sigs.	Bank Sigs.	Fine	XF	CU
660	824	Chicago	Teehee-Burke	Mc Lallen-Mc Dougal	540.	1100.	2500.
661	826	Kansas City	Teehee-Burke	Anderson-Miller	540.	1100.	2500.
662	827	Kansas City	Teehee-Burke	Cross-Miller	540.	1100.	2500.
663	828	Dallas	Teehee-Burke	Hoopes-Van Zandt	540.	1100.	2500.
664	829	Dallas	Teehee-Burke	Gilbert-Van Zandt	540.	1100.	2500.
665	830	Dallas	Teehee-Burke	Talley-Van Zandt	540.	1100.	2500.

Series 1918

KL#	Fr#	Bank	Federal Sigs.	Bank Sigs.	Fine	XF	CU
666	823	Atlanta	Elliott-Burke	Bell-Wellborn	575.	1100.	2500.
667	825	St. Louis	Teehee-Burke	Attebery-Wells	700.	1250.	3500.

Fifty Dollars

United States Notes

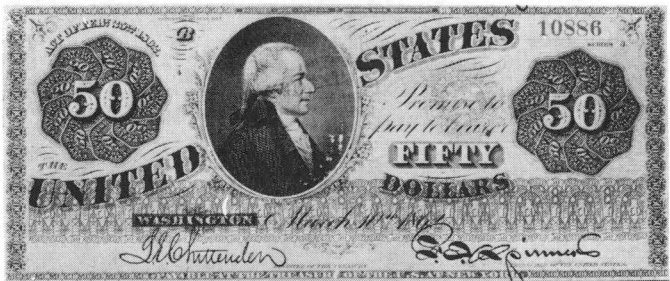

Alexander Hamilton

KL#	Fr#	Series	Signatures	Seal	Fine	XF	CU
			First Obligation inscription on back. Red Serial numbers.				
668	148	1862	Chittenden-Spinner	Small red	7000.	14,500.	—
			American Bank Note Co.				
			Second Obligation inscription on back. Red Serial numbers.				
669	149	1862	Chittenden-Spinner	Small red	6750.	14,000.	—
			National Bank Note Co.				
			Second Obligation inscription on back. Red Serial numbers.				
670	150	1863	Chittenden-Spinner	Small red	6750.	14,000.	—

Henry Clay

KL#	Fr#	Series	Signatures	Seal	Fine	XF	CU
			Blue Serial numbers. Ornate "L" twice on face.				
671	151	1869	Allison-Spinner	Large red	12,750.	30,000.	Rare

Ben Franklin

Blue Serial numbers in center, unlike any other series. Ornate "L" twice on face.

KL#	Fr#	Series	Signatures	Seal	Fine	XF	CU
672	152	1874	Allison-Spinner	Small red	4150.	5750.	10,000.
673	153	1875	Allison-Spinner	Small red	6000.	12,500.	—
674	154	1878	Allison-Gilfillan	Small red	4400.	8750.	35,000.
			Blue Serial numbers in center, unlike any other series.				
675	155	1880	Bruce-Gilfillan	Large brown	2800.	6000.	13,000.
676	156	1880	Bruce-Wyman	Large brown	2800.	6000.	13,000.
677	157	1880	Rosecrans-Jordan	Large red	2750.	5750.	11,000.
678	158	1880	Rosecrans-Hyatt	Large red	2750.	5750.	11,000.
679	159	1880	Rosecrans-Hyatt	Red spikes	2750.	5750.	11,000.
680	160	1880	Rosecrans-Huston	Red spikes	2750.	5750.	11,000.
681	161	1880	Rosecrans-Huston	Large brown	2750.	5750.	11,500.
682	162	1880	Tillman-Morgan	Small red	2600.	5200.	10,000.
683	163	1880	Bruce-Roberts	Small red	2600.	5200.	10,000.
684	164	1880	Lyons-Roberts	Small red	2600.	5200.	10,000.

Compound Interest Treasury Notes

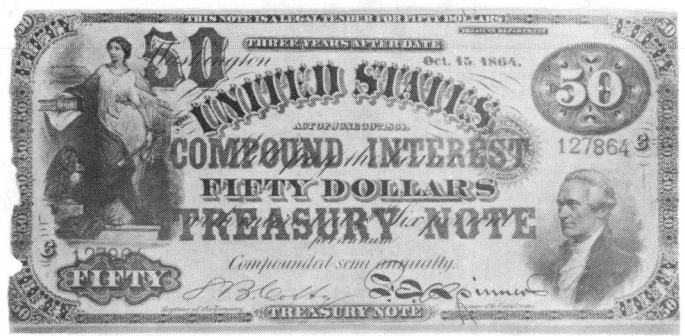

Alexander Hamilton

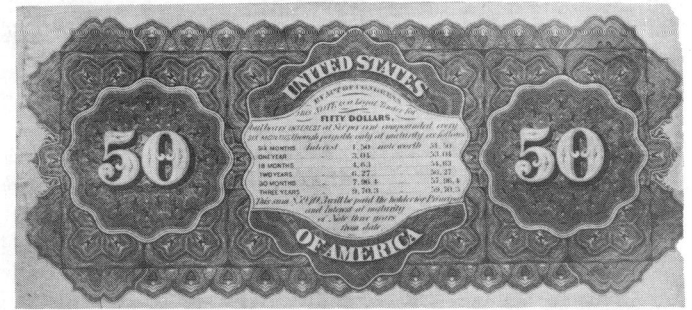

KL#	Fr#	Act	Overprint Date	Signatures	Fine	XF	CU
685	192	1863	June 10, 1864	Chittenden-Spinner			(Unique)
686	192-A	1864	July 15, 1864	Chittenden-Spinner			(Unknown)
687	192-B	1864	Aug. 15, 1864-	Colby-Spinner	14,000.	25,000.	—
			Sept. 1, 1865	Colby-Spinner			(Two known)

Interest Bearing Notes

KL#	Fr#	Act	Term	Signatures	Fine	XF	CU
688	198	1863	One year	Chittenden-Spinner			(3 known)

KL#	Fr#	Act	Term	Signatures	Fine	XF	CU
689	203	1863	Two years	Chittenden-Spinner			(Extremely rare)

KL#	Fr#	Act	Term	Signatures	Fine	XF	CU
690	207	1861	Three years	Chittenden-Spinner			(Unknown)
691	212	1864	Three years	Colby-Spinner			(Unknown)

KL#	Fr#	Act	Term	Signatures	Fine	XF	CU
692	212-D	1865	Three years	Colby-Spinner			(Extremely rare)

Gold Certificates

Silas Wright

KL#	Fr#	Series	Signatures	Seal	Fine	XF	CU
693	1189	1882	Bruce-Gilfillan (Countersigned)	Brown	—	—	Unique

KL#	Fr#	Series	Signatures	Seal	Fine	XF	CU
694	1188	1882	Bruce-Gilfillan	Brown	—	4500.	—
695	1190	1882	Bruce-Wyman	Brown	2500.	4000.	—
696	1191	1882	Rosecrans-Hyatt	Large red	1200.	3800.	—
697	1192	1882	Rosecrans-Huston	Large brown	1200.	3800.	—
698	1193	1882	Lyons-Roberts	Small red	725.	2100.	5750.
699	1194	1882	Lyons-Treat	Small red	725.	2100.	5750.
700	1195	1882	Vemon-Treat	Small red	725.	2100.	5750.
701	1196	1882	Vemon-McClung	Small red	725.	2100.	5750.
702	1197	1882	Napier-McClung	Small red	725.	2100.	5750.

U.S. Grant

KL#	Fr#	Series	Signatures	Seal	Fine	XF	CU
703	1198	1913	Parker-Burke	Gold	500.	975.	2000.
704	1199	1913	Teehee-Burke	Gold	500.	975.	2000.
705	1200	1922	Speelman-White*	Gold	450.	850.	1900.

*NOTE: Large and small serial numbers exist.

National Gold Bank Notes

KL#	Fr#	Series	Issuing Bank	Location	Good	Fine
706	1160	Orig.	First Nat'l Gold Bank	San Francisco	4000.	(Rare)
707	1161	Orig.	Nat'l Gold Bank	San Jose	4000.	(Rare)

Silver Certificates

The Countersigned Series
Scofield-Gilfillan signatures. Blue serial numbers.
Type 3 payable at Washington D.C.
Type 4 payable in New York.
Type 6 payable at San Francisco

Edward Everett

KL#	Fr#	Series	Countersigned by:	Type	Fine	XF	CU
			Large "FIFTY" below center seal.				
708	324-C	1878	A.U. Wyman, Asst. U.S. Treasurer	3	(Very Rare)	—	—
709	324	1878	T. Hillhouse, Asst. U.S. Treasurer	4	(Very Rare)	—	—
710	324-A	1878	R.M. Anthony, Asst. U.S. Treasurer	6	Possibly exists	—	—

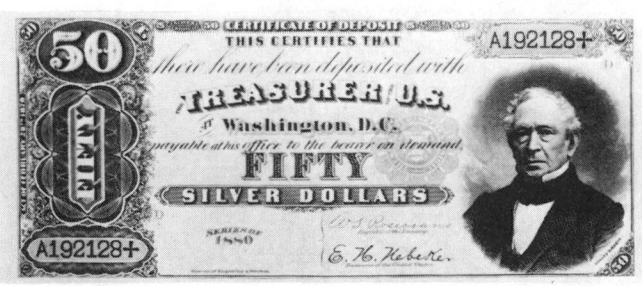

Edward Everett

KL#	Fr#	Series	Signatures	Seal	Fine	XF	CU
			Large "FIFTY" in center.				
711	325	1880	Scofield-Gilfillan	Large brown	6300.	15,500.	27,500.
712	326	1880	Bruce-Gilfillan	Large brown	6300.	15,500.	27,500.
713	327	1880	Bruce-Wyman	Large brown	6300.	15,500.	27,500.
714	328	1880	Rosecrans-Huston	Large brown	6300.	15,500.	27,500.
715	329	1880	Rosecrans-Nebeker	Small red	5200.	13,000.	24,000.
716	330	1891	Rosecrans-Nebeker	Small red	1550.	3450.	7150.
717	331	1891	Tillman-Morgan	Small red	1550.	3450.	7150.
718	332	1891	Bruce-Roberts	Small red	1550.	3450.	7150.
719	333	1891	Lyons-Roberts	Small red	1550.	3450.	7150.
720	334	1891	Vernon-Treat	Small red	1550.	3450.	7150.

Edward Everett

KL#	Fr#	Series	Signatures	Seal	Fine	XF	CU
721	335	1891	Parker-Burke	Blue	1550.	3450.	8000.

Treasury or Coin Notes

William H. Seward

KL#	Fr#	Series	Signatures	Seal	Fine	XF	CU
722	376	1891	Rosecrans-Nebeker	Small red	10,500.	22,500.	—

U.S. Grant

KL#	Fr#	Bank	Red Seals Signatures	Fine	XF	CU
723	1012	Boston	Burke-Mc Adoo	475.	1000.	2700.
724	1013	New York	Burke-Mc Adoo	475.	1000.	2700.
725	1014	Philadelphia	Burke-Mc Adoo	475.	1000.	2700.
726	1015	Cleveland	Burke-Mc Adoo	475.	1000.	2700.
727	1016	Richmond	Burke-Mc Adoo	475.	1000.	2700.
728	1017	Atlanta	Burke-Mc Adoo	475.	1000.	2700.
729	1018	Chicago	Burke-Mc Adoo	500.	1050.	2900.
730	1019	St. Louis	Burke-Mc Adoo	475.	1000.	2700.
731	1020	Minneapolis	Burke-Mc Adoo	475.	1000.	2700.
732	1021	Kansas City	Burke-Mc Adoo	475.	1000.	2700.
733	1022	Dallas	Burke-Mc Adoo	475.	1000.	2700.
734	1023	San Francisco	Burke-Mc Adoo	475.	1000.	2700.
			Blue Seals			
735	1024	Boston	Burke-Mc Adoo	130.	300.	1100.
736	1025	Boston	Burke-Glass	130.	300.	1100.
737	1026	Boston	Burke-Houston	130.	300.	1100.
738	1027	Boston	White-Mellon	130.	300.	1100.
739	1028	New York	Burke-Mc Adoo	130.	300.	1100.
740	1029	New York	Burke-Glass	130.	300.	1100.
741	1030	New York	Burke-Houston	130.	300.	1100.
742	1031	New York	White-Mellon	130.	300.	1100.
743	1032	Philadelphia	Burke-Mc Adoo	130.	300.	1100.
744	1033	Philadelphia	Burke-Glass	130.	300.	1100.
745	1034	Philadelphia	Burke-Houston	130.	300.	1100.
746	1035	Philadelphia	White-Mellon	130.	300.	1100.
747	1036	Cleveland	Burke-Mc Adoo	130.	300.	1100.
748	1037	Cleveland	Burke-Glass	130.	300.	1100.
749	1038	Cleveland	Burke-Houston	130.	300.	1100.
750	1039	Cleveland	White-Mellon	130.	300.	1100.
751	1040	Richmond	Burke-Mc Adoo	130.	300.	1100.
752	1041	Richmond	Burke-Glass	130.	300.	1100.
753	1042	Richmond	Burke-Houston	130.	300.	1100.
754	1043	Richmond	White-Mellon	130.	300.	1100.
755	1044	Atlanta	Burke-Mc Adoo	130.	300.	1100.
756	1045	Atlanta	Burke-Glass	130.	300.	1100.
757	1046	Atlanta	Burke-Houston	130.	300.	1100.
758	1047	Atlanta	White-Mellon	130.	300.	1100.
759	1048	Chicago	Burke-Mc Adoo	130.	300.	1100.
760	1049	Chicago	Burke-Glass	130.	300.	1100.
761	1050	Chicago	Burke-Houston	130.	300.	1100.
762	1051	Chicago	White-Mellon	130.	300.	1100.
763	1052	St. Louis	Burke-Mc Adoo	130.	300.	1100.
764	1053	St. Louis	Burke-Glass	130.	300.	1100.
765	1054	St. Louis	Burke-Houston	130.	300.	1100.
766	1055	St. Louis	White-Mellon	130.	300.	1100.
767	1056	Minneapolis	Burke-Mc Adoo	130.		
768	1057	Minneapolis	Burke-Glass		Not issued	
769	1058	Minneapolis	Burke-Houston	130.	300.	1100.
770	1059	Minneapolis	White-Mellon	130.	300.	1100.
771	1060	Kansas City	Burke-Mc Adoo	130.	300.	1100.
772	1061	Kansas City	Burke-Glass		Not issued	
773	1062	Kansas City	Burke-Houston		Not issued	
774	1063	Kansas City	White-Mellon	130.	300.	1100.
775	1064	Dallas	Burke-Mc Adoo	130.	300.	1100.
776	1065	Dallas	Burke-Glass	130.	300.	1100.
777	1066	Dallas	Burke-Houston	130.	300.	1100.
778	1067	Dallas	White-Mellon	130.	300.	1100.
779	1068	San Francisco	Burke-Mc Adoo	130.	300.	1100.
780	1069	San Francisco	Burke-Glass	130.	300.	1100.
781	1070	San Francisco	Burke-Houston	130.	300.	1100.
782	1071	San Francisco	White-Mellon	130.	300.	1100.

Federal Reserve Bank Notes
Series 1918

U.S. Grant

KL#	Fr#	Bank	Federal Sigs.	Bank Sigs.	Fine	XF	CU
783	831	St. Louis	Teehee-Burke	Attebery-Wells	3000.	5000.	11,000.

One Hundred Dollars
United States Notes

KL#	Fr#	Series	Signatures	Seal	Fine	XF	CU
			First Obligation inscription on back. Red serial numbers.				
784	165	1862	Chittenden-Spinner	Small red	10,000.	20,000.	45,000.
			American Bank Note Co. or National Bank Note Co.				
			Second Obligation inscription on back. Red Serial numbers.				
785	166	1862	Chittenden-Spinner	Small red	9200.	18,000.	42,000.
			Second Obligation on back. Red Serial numbers.				
786	167	1863	Chittenden-Spinner	Small red	10,000.	20,000.	45,000.

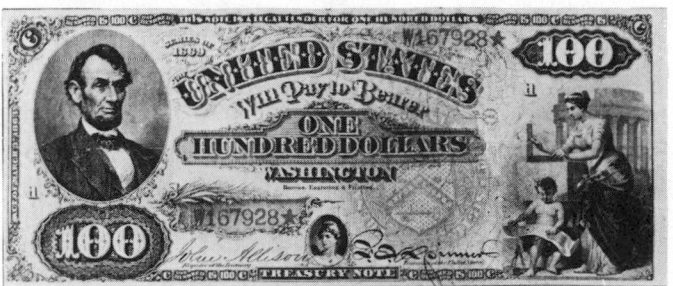

Abraham Lincoln

KL#	Fr#	Series	Signatures	Seal	Fine	XF	CU
				Blue serial numbers			
787	168	1869	Allison-Spinner	Large red	10,000.	18,000.	40,000.
788	169	1875 Series A	Allison-New	Small red	6900.	13,000.	31,000.
789	170	1875	Allison-Wyman	Small red	6900.	13,000.	31,000.
790	171	1878	Allison-Gilfillan	Small red	5200.	15,500.	—
791	172	1880	Bruce-Gilfillan	Large brown	5500.	17,000.	32,000.
792	173	1880	Bruce-Wyman	Large brown	5500.	17,000.	32,000.
793	174	1880	Rosecrans-Jordan	Large red	5500.	17,000.	32,000.
794	175	1880	Rosecrans-Hyatt	Large red	(Very Rare)		—
795	176	1880	Rosecrans-Hyatt	Red spikes	5500.	17,000.	32,000.
796	177	1880	Rosecrans-Huston	Red spikes	5500.	17,000.	32,000.
797	178	1880	Rosecrans-Huston	Large brown	5500.	17,000.	32,000.
798	179	1880	Tillman-Morgan	Small red	4000.	9000.	16,000.
799	180	1880	Bruce-Roberts	Small red	4000.	9000.	16,000.
800	181	1880	Lyons-Roberts	Small red	4000.	9000.	16,000.
801	182	1880	Napier-Mc Clung	Small red	—	—	—

Compound Interest Treasury Notes

George Washington

KL#	Fr#	Act	Overprint Date	Signatures	Fine	XF	CU
802	193	1863	June 10, 1864	Chittenden-Spinner	(Extremely rare)		
803	193-A	1864	July 15, 1864	Chittenden-Spinner	(Unknown)		
804	193-B	1864	Aug. 15, 1864- Sept. 1, 1865	Colby-Spinner	(Extremely rare)		

Interest Bearing Notes

KL#	Fr#	Act	Term	Signatures	Fine	XF	CU
805	199	1863	One year	Chittenden-Spinner			(Two known)
806	204	1863	Two years	Chittenden-Spinner			(One known)

KL#	Fr#	Act	Term	Signatures	Fine	XF	CU
807	208	1861	Three years	Chittenden-Spinner			(Extremely rare)

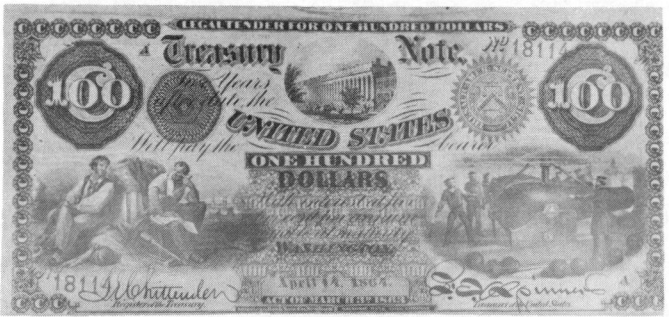

KL#	Fr#	Act	Term	Signatures	Fine	XF	CU
808	212-A	1864	Three years	Colby-Spinner			(Extremely rare)
809	212-E	1865	Three years	Colby-Spinner			(Two known)

Gold Certificates

KL#	Fr#	Issue/Act/Series	Signatures	Fine	XF	CU
810	1166-C	First/1863	Colby-Spinner			(Extremely rare)
811	1166-H	Second/1863	Allison-Spinner			(Unknown)
812	1166-M	Third/1863/1875	Allison-New			(Extremely rare)

Thomas H. Benton

KL#	Fr#	Series	Signatures	Seal	Fine	XF	CU
813	1202	1882	Bruce-Gilfillan	Brown	—		—(Unique)
			(countersigned by Thos. C. Acton, Ass't Treasurer, New York)				
814	1201	1882	Bruce-Gilfillan	Brown	3500.	7500.	17,500.
815	1203	1882	Bruce-Wyman	Brown	3500.	7500.	17,500.
816	1204	1882	Rosecrans-Hyatt	Large red	3500.	7500.	30,000.
817	1205	1882	Rosecrans-Huston	Large brown	3500.	7500.	17,500.
818	1206	1882	Lyons-Roberts	Small red	700.	1350.	3850.

KL#	Fr#	Series	Signatures	Seal	Fine	XF	CU
819	1207	1882	Lyons-Treat	Small red	700.	1350.	3850.
820	1208	1882	Vernon-Treat	Small red	700.	1350.	3850.
821	1209	1882	Vernon-McClung	Small red	700.	1350.	3850.
822	1210	1882	Napier-McClung	Small red	700.	1350.	3850.
823	1211	1882	Napier-Thompson	Small red	700.	1350.	3850.
824	1212	1882	Napier-Burke	Small red	700.	1350.	3850.
825	1213	1882	Parker-Burke	Small red	700.	1350.	3850.
826	1214	1882	Teehee-Burke	Small red	700.	1350.	3850.
827	1215	1922	Speelman-White	Small red	500.	975.	3350.

National Gold Bank Notes

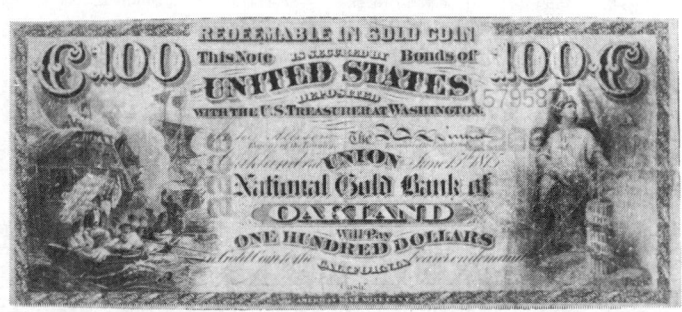

KL#	Fr#	Series	Issuing Bank	Location	Good	Fine
828	1162	Orig.	First Nat'l Gold Bank	San Francisco	11,250.	Rare
829	1163	1875	First Nat'l Gold Bank	San Francisco	11,250.	Rare
830	1164	Orig.	First Nat'l Gold Bank	Santa Barbara	11,250.	Rare
831	1165	Orig.	First Nat'l Gold Bank	Petaluma	11,250.	Rare
832	1166	1875	Union Nat'l Gold Bank	Oakland	11,250.	Rare

Silver Certificates

The Countersigned Series:
Scofield-Gilfillan signatures. Blue serial numbers.
Type 3: Place of deposit, Washington, D.C.
Type 6: Place of deposit, San Francisco
Type 7: Place of deposit, New York.

James Monroe

KL#	Fr#	Series	Countersigned by:	Type	Fine	XF	CU
833	337-B	1878	A. U. Wyman, Asst. U.S. Treas.	3	Very Rare		—

KL#	Fr#	Series	Countersigned by:	Type	Fine	XF	CU
834	337	1878	R.M. Anthony, Asst. U.S. Treas.	6	Extremely Rare		—

*NOTE: R.M. Anthony was never the Asst. U.S. Treasurer. When he signed this note he was a bookkeeper for the Asst. Treasurer.

KL#	Fr#	Series	Countersigned by:	Type	Fine	XF	CU
835	—	1878	W.G. White, Asst. U.S. Treas.	7	Possibly exists		—

All have large red "100" below center seal.

With large "C" below center seal.

KL#	Fr#	Series	Signatures	Seal	Fine	XF	CU
836	338	1880	Scofield-Gilfillan	Large brown	10,500.	20,000.	30,000.
837	339	1880	Bruce-Gilfillan	Large brown	10,500.	20,000.	30,000.
838	340	1880	Bruce-Wyman	Large brown	10,500.	20,000.	30,000.

KL#	Fr#	Series	Signatures	Seal	Fine	XF	CU
			No "C" below center seal.				
839	341	1880	Rosecrans-Huston	Large brown	10,500.	22,000.	32,000.
840	342	1880	Rosecrans-Nebeker	Small red	10,500.	22,000.	32,000.

KL#	Fr#	Series	Signatures	Seal	Fine	XF	CU
841	343	1891	Rosecrans-Nebeker	Small red	5900.	11,000.	16,000.
842	344	1891	Tillman-Morgan	Small red	5900.	11,000.	16,000.

Treasury or Coin Notes

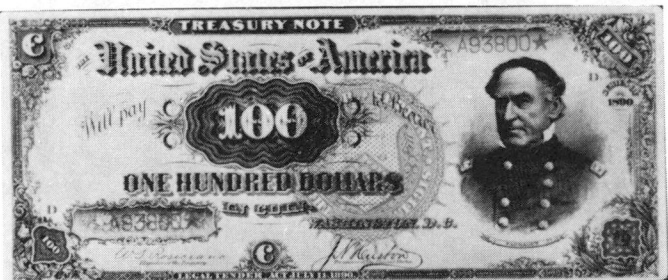

Admiral David G. Farragut

KL#	Fr#	Series	Signatures	Seal	Fine	XF	CU
843	377	1890	Rosecrans-Huston	Large brown	12,000.	22,500.	—

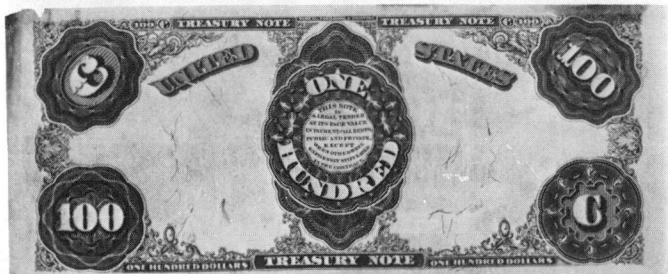

KL#	Fr#	Series	Signatures	Seal	Fine	XF	CU
844	378	1891	Rosecrans-Nebeker	Small red	22,500.	35,000.	—

Federal Reserve Notes
Series 1914

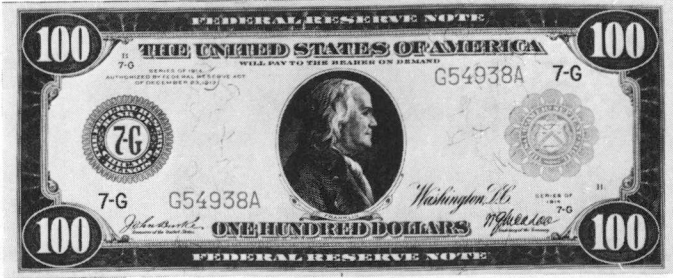

Ben Franklin

KL#	Fr#	Bank	Signatures	Fine	XF	CU
			Red Seals			
845	1072	Boston	Burke-Mc Adoo	585.	1100.	3000.
846	1073	New York	Burke-Mc Adoo	585.	1100.	3000.
847	1074	Philadelphia	Burke-Mc Adoo	585.	1100.	3000.
848	1075	Cleveland	Burke-Mc Adoo	585.	1100.	3000.
849	1076	Richmond	Burke-Mc Adoo	585.	1100.	3000.
850	1077	Atlanta	Burke-Mc Adoo	585.	1100.	3000.
851	1078	Chicago	Burke-Mc Adoo	585.	1100.	3000.
852	1079	St. Louis	Burke-Mc Adoo	585.	1100.	3000.
853	1080	Minneapolis	Burke-Mc Adoo	585.	1100.	3000.
854	1081	Kansas City	Burke-Mc Adoo	585.	1100.	3000.
855	1082	Dallas	Burke-Mc Adoo	585.	1100.	3000.
856	1083	San Francisco	Burke-Mc Adoo	585.	1100.	3000.
			Blue Seals			
857	1084	Boston	Burke-Mc Adoo	300.	450.	975.
858	1085	Boston	Burke-Glass	300.	450.	975.
859	1086	Boston	Burke-Houston		Not issued	
860	1087	Boston	White-Mellon	300.	450.	975.
861	1088	New York	Burke-Mc Adoo	300.	450.	975.
862	1089	New York	Burke-Glass	300.	450.	975.
863	1090	New York	Burke-Houston	300.	450.	975.
864	1091	New York	White-Mellon	300.	450.	975.
865	1092	Philadelphia	Burke-Mc Adoo	300.	450.	975.
866	1093	Philadelphia	Burke-Glass		Not issued	
867	1094	Philadelphia	Burke-Houston		Not issued	
868	1095	Philadelphia	White-Mellon	300.	450.	975.
869	1096	Cleveland	Burke-Mc Adoo	300.	450.	975.
870	1097	Cleveland	Burke-Glass	300.	450.	975.
871	1098	Cleveland	Burke-Huston	300.	450.	975.
872	1099	Cleveland	White-Mellon	300.	450.	975.
873	1100	Richmond	Burke-Mc Adoo	300.	450.	975.
874	1101	Richmond	Burke-Glass	300.	450.	975.
875	1102	Richmond	Burke-Houston		Not issued	
876	1103	Richmond	White-Mellon	300.	450.	975.
877	1104	Atlanta	Burke-Mc Adoo	300.	450.	975.
878	1105	Atlanta	Burke-Glass		Not issued	
879	1106	Atlanta	Burke-Houston	300.	450.	975.
880	1107	Atlanta	White-Mellon	300.	450.	975.
881	1108	Chicago	Burke-Mc Adoo	300.	450.	975.
882	1109	Chicago	Burke-Glass		Not issued	
883	1110	Chicago	Burke-Houston	300.	450.	975.
884	1111	Chicago	White-Mellon	300.	450.	975.
885	1112	St. Louis	Burke-Mc Adoo	300.	450.	975.
886	1113	St. Louis	Burke-Glass		Not issued	
887	1114	St. Louis	Burke-Houston		Not issued	
888	1115	St. Louis	White-Mellon	300.	450.	975.
889	1116	Minneapolis	Burke-Mc Adoo	300.	450.	975.
890	1117	Minneapolis	Burke-Glass		Not issued	
891	1118	Minneapolis	Burke-Houston		Not issued	
892	1119	Minneapolis	White-Mellon	300.	450.	975.
893	1120	Kansas City	Burke-Mc Adoo	300.	450.	975.
894	1121	Kansas City	Burke-Glass		Not issued	
895	1122	Kansas City	Burke-Houston		Not issued	
896	1123	Kansas City	White-Mellon	300.	450.	975.
897	1124	Dallas	Burke-Mc Adoo	300.	450.	975.
898	1125	Dallas	Burke-Glass		Not issued	
899	1126	Dallas	Burke-Houston		Not issued	
900	1127	Dallas	White-Mellon	300.	450.	975.
901	1128	San Francisco	Burke-Mc Adoo	300.	450.	975.
902	1129	San Francisco	Burke-Glass		Not issued	
903	1130	San Francisco	Burke-Houston	300.	450.	975.
904	1131	San Francisco	White-Mellon	300.	450.	975.

Five Hundred Dollars
United States Notes

Albert Gallatin

KL#	Fr#	Series	Signatures	Seal	Fine	XF	CU
		First Obligation inscription on back. Red serial numbers.					
904A	183-A	1862	Chittenden-Spinner	Small red			(Extremely rare)
		Second Obligation inscription on back. Red serial numbers.					
905	183-B	1862	Chittenden-Spinner	Small red			(Extremely rare)
906	183-C	1863	Chittenden-Spinner	Small red			(Extremely rare)
		Blue serial numbers.					
907	184	1869	Allison-Spinner	Large red			(Extremely rare)
908	185-A	1874	Allison-Spinner	Small red			(Two known)
909	185-B	1875	Allison-New	Small red			(Extremely rare)
910	185-C	1875	Allison-Wyman	Small red			(Extremely rare)

Gen. Joseph K. Mansfield

KL#	Fr#	Series	Signatures	Seal	Fine	XF	CU
911	185-D	1878	Allison-Gilfillan	Small red			(Three known)
912	185-E	1880	Scofield-Gilfillan	Large brown			(Extremely rare)
913	185-F	1880	Bruce-Wyman	Large brown			(Extremely rare)
914	185-G	1880	Rosecrans-Jordan	Large red			(Extremely rare)
915	185-H	1880	Rosecrans-Hyatt	Large red			(Extremely rare)
916	185-I	1880	Rosecrans-Huston	Large red			(Extremely rare)
917	185-J	1880	Rosecrans-Nebeker	Large brown			(Extremely rare)
918	185-K	1880	Tillman-Morgan	Small red			(Extremely rare)
919	185-L	1880	Bruce-Roberts	Small red			(Extremely rare)
920	185-M	1880	Lyons-Roberts	Small red			(Extremely rare)
921	185-N	1880	Napier-Mc Clung	Small red			(Not issued)

Compound Interest Treasury Notes

KL#	Fr#	Act	Overprint Date	Signatures	Fine	XF	CU
922	194	1863	June 10, 1864	Chittenden-Spinner			(Unknown)
923	194-A	1864	July 15, 1864	Chittenden-Spinner			(Unknown)
924	194-B	1864	Aug. 15, 1864- Oct. 1, 1865	Colby-Spinner			(Unknown)

Interest Bearing Notes

George Washington

KL#	Fr#	Act	Term	Signatures	Fine	XF	CU
925	200	1863	One year	Chittenden-Spinner			(Unknown)
925A	—	1861	Two years	Chittenden-Spinner			(Unknown)
926	205	1863	Two years	Chittenden-Spinner			(Unknown)
927	209	1861	Three years	Chittenden-Spinner			(Unknown)
928	212-B	1864	Three years	Colby-Spinner			(Extremely rare)
929	212-F	1865	Three years	Colby-Spinner			(Unknown)

Gold Certificates

KL#	Fr#	Issue/Act/Series	Signatures	Fine	XF	CU
930	1160-O	First/1863	Colby-Spinner			(Unknown)
931	1166-I	Second/1863	Allison-Spinner			(Unknown)
932	1166-N	Third/1863/1875	Allison-New			(Unknown)

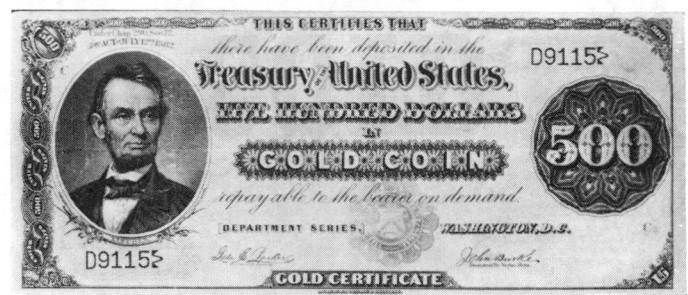

Abraham Lincoln

KL#	Fr#	Issue/Act/Series	Signatures	Fine	XF	CU
933	1215-B	1882	Bruce-Gilfillan (countersigned)	—		(Rare)
934	1215-A	1882	Bruce-Gilfillan	—		(Rare)
935	1215-C	1882	Bruce-Wyman	—		(Rare)
936	1215-D	1882	Rosecrans-Hyatt	—		(Rare)
937	1216	1882	Lyons-Roberts	11,000.		(Rare)
938	1216-A	1882	Parker-Burke	11,000.		(Rare)
939	1216-B	1882	Teehee-Burke	11,000.		(Rare)
940	1217	1922	Speelman-White	4150.	9950.	21,000.

National Gold Bank Notes

KL#	Fr#	Series	Issuing Bank	Location	Good	Fine
941	—	1875	First National Gold Bank	San Francisco		
942	—	Orig.	National Gold Bank and Trust Company	San Francisco		
943	—	Orig.	National Gold Bank of D.O. Mills and Company	Sacramento		
		(Four of the above remain unredeemed, none are known)				

Silver Certificates
The Countersigned Series
Scofield-Gilfillan signatures. Blue serial numbers.
Type 3: Place of deposit, Washington, D.C.
Type 6: Place of deposit, San Francisco
Type 7: Place of deposit, New York

KL#	Fr#	Series	Countersigned by:	Type	Fine	XF	CU
944	345-A	1878	W.G. White, Asst. Treas.	7			(Unknown)
945	345-A	1878	J.C. Hopper, Asst. Treas.	7			(Unknown)

KL#	Fr#	Series	Countersigned by:	Type	Fine	XF CU
946	345-A	1878	T. Hillhouse, Asst. Treas.	7		(Unknown)
947	345-A	1878	R.M. Anthony, Asst. Treas.	6		(Unknown)
948	345-A	1878	A.U. Wyman, Asst. Treas.	3		(Unknown)

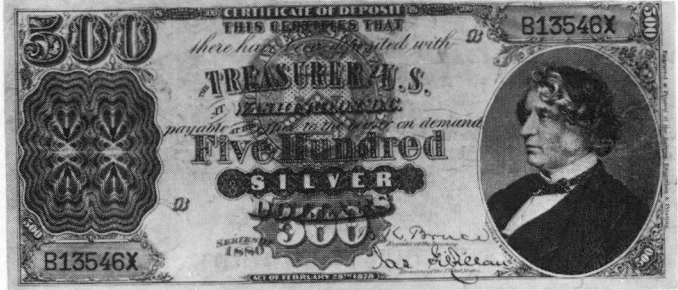

Charles Sumner

KL#	Fr#	Series	Signatures	Seal	Fine	XF CU
949	345-B	1880	Scofield-Gilfillan	Brown		(Unknown)
950	345-C	1880	Bruce-Gilfillan	Brown		(3 known)
951	345-D	1880	Bruce-Wyman	Brown		(1 known)

Federal Reserve Notes
Series 1918

John Marshall

KL#	Fr#	Bank	Signatures	VG	Fine	CU
952	1132	Boston	Burke-Glass	1600.	3800.	10,000.
953	1132	New York	Burke-Glass	1600.	3800.	10,000.
954	1132	New York	White-Mellon	—		(6 known)
955	1132	Philadelphia	Burke-Glass	—		(Rare)
956	1132	Cleveland	Burke-Glass	—		(Rare)
957	1132	Richmond		—		(Unknown)
958	1132	Atlanta	Burke-Glass	—		(Rare)
959	1132	Chicago	Burke-McAdoo	—		(Rare)
960	1132	Chicago	Burke-Glass	—		(Rare)
961	1132	St. Louis		—		(Rare)
962	1132	Minneapolis		—		(Unknown)
963	1132	Kansas City	Burke-Glass	—		(Rare)
964	1132	Dallas	Burke-Glass	—		(Rare)
965	1132	San Francisco	Burke-Glass	—		(Rare)

One Thousand Dollars
United States Notes

Robert Morris

KL#	Fr#	Series	Signatures	Seal	Fine	XF CU
			First Obligation inscription on back. Red serial numbers.			
966	186-A	1862	Chittenden-Spinner	Small red		(Extremely rare)
			Second Obligation inscription on back. Red serial numbers.			
967	186-B	1862	Chittenden-Spinner	Small red		(Extremely rare)
968	186-C	1863	Chittenden-Spinner	Small red		(Extremely rare)
			Blue serial numbers			

Christopher Columbus, DeWitt Clinton

KL#	Fr#	Series	Signatures	Seal	Fine	XF	CU
969	186-D	1869	Allison-Spinner	Large red			(Extremely rare)
970	187-A	1878	Allison-Gilfillan	Small red			(Extremely rare)
971	187-B	1880	Bruce-Wyman	Large brown			(Extremely rare)
972	187-C	1880	Rosecrans-Jordan	Large red			(Extremely rare)
973	187-D	1880	Rosecrans-Hyatt	Large red			(Extremely rare)
974	187-E	1880	Rosecrans-Huston	Large red			(Extremely rare)
975	187-F	1880	Rosecrans-Nebeker	Large brown			(Extremely rare)
976	187-G	1880	Tillman-Morgan	Small red			(Extremely rare)
977	187-H	1880	Tillman-Roberts	Small red			(Extremely rare)
978	187-I	1880	Bruce-Roberts	Small red			(Extremely rare)
979	187-J	1880	Lyons-Roberts	Small red		12,000.	18,000.
980	187-K	1880	Vernon-Treat	Small red			(Extremely rare)
981	187-L	1880	Napier-McClung	Small red			(Not issued)

Compound Interest Treasury Notes

KL#	Fr#	Act	Overprint Date	Signatures	Fine	XF CU
982	195	1864	July 15, 1864	Chittenden-Spinner		(Unknown)
983	195-A	1864	Aug. 15, 1864- Sept. 15, 1865	Colby-Spinner		(Unknown)

Interest Bearing Notes

KL#	Fr#	Act	Signatures	Fine	XF	CU
984	201	1863	Chittenden-Spinner			(Unknown)

KL#	Fr#	Act	Signatures	Fine	XF	CU
984A	—	1861	Chittenden-Spinner			(Unknown)
985	206	1863	Chittenden-Spinner			(Unknown)

KL#	Fr#	Series	Signatures	Seal	VG	Fine	CU
1002	1219	1907	Napier-McClung	Small red			(Rare)
1003	1219	1907	Parker-Burke	Small red			(Rare)
1004	1219	1907	Teehee-Burke	Small red			(Rare)
1005	1219	1907	Napier-Burke	Small red			(Rare)
1006	1220	1907	Speelman-White	Small red	2750.	5200.	21,000.

Silver Certificates

The Countersigned Series
Scofield-Gilfillan signatures. Blue serial numbers.
Type 3: Place of deposit, Washington, D.C.
Type 6: Place of deposit, San Francisco
Type 7: Place of deposit, New York

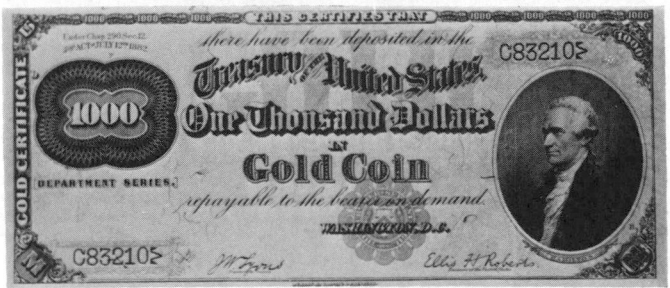

Salmon P. Chase

KL#	Fr#	Act	Signatures	Fine	XF	CU
986	210	1861	Chittenden-Spinner			(Unknown)
987	212-C	1864	Colby-Spinner			(Unknown)
988	212-G	1865	Colby-Spinner			(1 known)

Gold Certificates

KL#	Fr#	Issue/Act/Series	Signatures	Fine	XF	CU
989	1166-E	First/1863	Colby-Spinner			(Unknown)
990	1166-J	Second/1863	Allison-Spinner			(Unknown)
991	1166-O	Third/1863/1875	Allison-New			(Unknown)

KL#	Fr#	Series	Signatures	Seal	VG	Fine	CU
992	1218-A	1882	Bruce-Gilfillan (countersigned)	Large brown			(Rare)
993	1218	1882	Bruce-Gilfillan	Large brown			(Rare)
994	1218-B	1882	Bruce-Wyman	Large brown			(Rare)
995	1218-C	1882	Rosecrans-Hyatt	Large red			(Rare)
996	1218-D	1882	Rosecrans-Huston	Large brown			(Rare)
997	1218-E	1882	Rosecrans-Nebeker	Small red			(Rare)

William L. Marcy

Alexander Hamilton

KL#	Fr#	Series	Countersigned by:	Type	Fine	XF	CU
1007	346-A	1878	A.U. Wyman, Asst. Treas.	3			(Unknown)
1008	346-A	1878	R.M. Anthony, Asst. Treas.	6			(Unknown)
1009	346-A	1878	Unknown signers	7			(Unknown)

KL#	Fr#	Series	Signatures	Seal	Fine	XF	CU
1010	346-B	1880	Scofield-Gilfillan	Large brown			(Unknown)
1011	346-C	1880	Bruce-Gilfillan	Large brown			(Unknown)
1012	346-D	1880	Bruce-Wyman	Large brown			(3 known)
1013	346-E	1891	Tillman-Morgan	Small red			(1 known)

Alexander Hamilton

KL#	Fr#	Series	Signatures	Seal	VG	Fine	CU
998	1218-F	1882	Lyons-Roberts	Small red	—	15,000.	—
999	1218-G	1882	Lyons-Treat	Small red			(Rare)

Treasury or Coin Notes

Gen. George G. Meade

KL#	Fr#	Series	Signatures	Seal	VG	Fine	CU
1000	1219	1907	Vernon-Treat	Small red			(Rare)
1001	1219	1907	Vernon-McClung	Small red			(Rare)

KL#	Fr#	Series	Signatures	Seal	Fine	XF	CU
1014	379-A	1890	Rosecrans-Huston	Large brown			(3 known)
1015	379-B	1890	Rosecrans-Nebeker	Small red			(1 known)

KL#	Fr#	Series	Signatures	Seal	Fine	XF	CU
1016	379-D	1891	Rosecrans-Nebeker	Small red			(1 known)
1017	379-C	1891	Tillman-Morgan	Small red			(1 known)

Federal Reserve Notes
Series 1918

Alexander Hamilton

KL#	Fr#	Bank	Signatures	Fine	XF	CU
1018	1133	Boston	Burke-Glass	—		(Unknown)
1019	1133	New York	Burke-Glass	3100.	4500.	(Rare)
1020	1133	New York	Burke-Houston	3100.	4500.	(Rare)
1021	1133	New York	White-Mellon	3100.	4500.	(Rare)
1022	1133	Philadelphia	Burke-Glass	—		(Rare)
1023	1133	Cleveland	Burke-Glass	—		(Rare)
1024	1133	Richmond	Burke-Glass	—		(Unknown)
1025	1133	Atlanta	Burke-Glass	—		(Rare)
1026	1133	Atlanta	White-Mellon			(3 known)
1027	1133	Chicago	Burke-Glass	3900.	5100.	12,500.
1028	1133	St. Louis	Burke-Glass	3900.	5100.	12,500.
1029	1133	Minneapolis	Burke-Glass	—		(Rare)
1030	1133	Kansas City	Burke-Glass	4300.	5600.	(Rare)
1031	1133	Dallas	Burke-Glass	4300.	5600.	(Rare)
1032	1133	San Francisco	Burke-Glass	—	5600.	(Rare)
1033	1133	San Francisco	White-Mellon	—		(Unique)

Five Thousand Dollars
Interest Bearing Notes

KL#	Fr#	Act	Term	Signatures	Fine	XF	CU
1044	202	1863	One year	Chittenden-Spinner			(Unknown)
1045	211	1861	Three years	Chittenden-Spinner			(Unknown)
1045A	—	1865	Three years	Colby-Spinner			(Unknown)

Gold Certificates

KL#	Fr#	Issue/Act/Series	Signatures	Fine	XF	CU
1046	1166-F	First/1863	Colby-Spinner			(Unknown)
1047	1166-K	Second/1863	Allison-Spinner			(Unknown)
1048	—	Third/1863/1875	Allison-New			(Unknown)

KL#	Fr#	Series	Signatures	Seal	Fine	XF	CU
1049	1221-A	1882	Bruce-Gilfillan (countersigned)	Large brown			(Extremely rare)
1050	1221	1882	Bruce-Gilfillan	Large brown			(Extremely rare)
1051	1221-B	1882	Bruce-Wyman	Large brown			(Extremely rare)
1052	1221-C	1882	Rosecrans-Hyatt	Large red			(Extremely rare)
1053	1221-D	1882	Rosecrans-Nebeker	Small red			(Extremely rare)
1054	1221-E	1882	Lyons-Roberts	Small red			(Extremely rare)
1055	1221-F	1882	Vernon-Treat	Small red			(Extremely rare)
1056	1221-G	1882	Vernon-McClung	Small red			(Extremely rare)
1057	1221-H	1882	Napier-McClung	Small red			(Extremely rare)
1058	1221-I	1882	Parker-Burke	Small red			(Extremely rare)
1059	1221-J	1882	Teehee-Burke	Small red			(Extremely rare)
1059A	1222	1888	Rosecrans-Hyatt	Large red			(Extremely rare)
1059B	1222-A	1888	Rosecrans-Nebeker	Small red			(Extremely rare)
1059C	1222-B	1888	Lyons-Roberts	Small red			(Extremely rare)

Federal Reserve Notes
Series 1918

KL#	Fr#	Bank	Signatures	Fine	XF	CU
1060	1134	Boston	Burke-Glass			(Unknown)
1061	1134	New York	Burke-Glass			(Unknown)

KL#	Fr#	Bank	Signatures	Fine	XF	CU
1062	1134	Cleveland	Burke-Glass			(Unknown)
1063	1134	Richmond	Burke-Glass			(Unknown)
1064	1134	Atlanta	Burke-Glass			(Unknown)
1065	1134	Chicago	Burke-Glass			(1 known)
1066	1134	St. Louis	Burke-Glass			(Unknown)
1067	1134	San Francisco	Burke-Glass			(Unknown)

Ten Thousand Dollars
Gold Certificates

KL#	Fr#	Issue/Act/Series	Signatures	Fine	XF	CU
1068	1166-G	First/1863	Colby-Spinner			(Unknown)
1069	1166-L	Second/1863	Allison-Spinner			(Unknown)
1070	—	Third/1863/1875	Allison-New			(Unknown)

KL#	Fr#	Series	Signatures	Seal	Fine	XF	CU
1071	1223-A	1882	Bruce-Gilfillan (countersigned)	Large brown			(Extremely rare)
1072	1223	1882	Bruce-Gilfillan	Large brown			(Extremely rare)
1073	1223-B	1882	Bruce-Wyman	Large brown			(Extremely rare)
1074	1223-C	1882	Rosecrans-Hyatt	Large red			(Extremely rare)
1075	1223-D	1882	Rosecrans-Nebeker	Small red			(Extremely rare)
1076	1223-E	1882	Lyons-Roberts	Small red			(Extremely rare)
1077	1223-F	1882	Vernon-Treat	Small red			(Extremely rare)
1078	1223-G	1882	Teehee-Burke	Small red			(Extremely rare)
1078A	1224	1882	Rosecrans-Hyatt	Large red			(Extremely rare)
1078B	1224-A	1888	Rosecrans-Nebeker	Small red			(Extremely rare)
1078C	1224-B	1888	Lyons-Roberts	Small red			(Extremely rare)
1079	1225	1900	Teehee-Burke	Small red			*

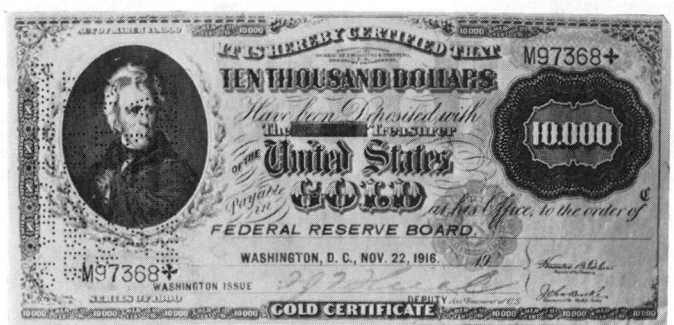

Andrew Jackson

*All outstanding 1900 $10,000 Gold Certificates are the result of a 1935 fire in a Treasury storage area in Washington, D.C. While fighting the fire, a quantity of these redeemed and cancelled notes was thrown out into the street, where the notes were picked up by passers-by. They have no redemption value, though they sometimes sell in the paper money hobby in the $400-$750 price range.

Federal Reserve Notes
Series 1918

Salmon P. Chase

KL#	Fr#	Bank	Signatures	Fine	XF	CU
1080	1135	Boston	Burke-Glass			(Unknown)
1081	1135	New York	Burke-Glass			(1 known)
1082	1135	Cleveland	Burke-Glass			(Unknown)
1083	1135	Richmond	Burke-Glass			(Unknown)
1084	1135	St. Louis	Burke-Glass			(Unknown)
1085	1135	San Francisco	Burke-Glass			(Unknown)

Small Size Notes

United States Notes

When the switch to the smaller, current size U.S. currency was made in July, 1929, the United States Notes (Legal Tender Notes), bearing red Treasury seals and serial numbers, were included, although denominations were pared back to $1, $2, $5 and $100.

The Red Seal $1 is especially popular with collectors in that it was issued only in one series (1928) and in fewer than two million notes. The 1928 $1 Legal Tenders were principally released in Puerto Rico more than 20 years after the notes had been printed. Star notes of the type are especially sought-after and command a strong premium, even in circulated grades.

The small size U.S. Note remained current in the $2 denomination until July, 1965, and in the $5 value until November, 1967. The last issue of Red Seal $100s was in 1968, though the denomination remains technically current.

The obligation for small size U.S. Notes began in Series 1928 as: "This note is a legal tender at its face value for all debts public and private except duties on imports and interest on the public debt." Under terms of the Act of May 12, 1933, the clause was amended to read: "This note is a legal tender at its face value for all debts public and private." Beginning in Series 1963, it was changed to: "This note is legal tender for all debts, public and private."

Gold Certificates

With the rest of the U.S. currency, the change to smaller notes in 1929 affected the Gold Certificates. Most noticably, the type lost its distinguishing gold-colored back design as the general configuration of the notes was standardized in all types. The seal and serial numbers continued in gold ink. Among the small size notes, Gold Certificate denominations continued from $10-$10,000, nominally intended for circulation, and even included the $100,000 Gold Certificate of Series 1934, for use in fiscal channels. Like the $100, $1,000 and $10,000 gold notes of Series 1934, the $100,000s were never released to general circulation and may not be legally held by collectors.

Likewise, Series 1928A Gold Certificates were printed in denominations of $10, $20 and $100, though never released.

The small size gold notes were a short series, cut off by the Gold Reserve Act of 1933, which required the surrender of all Gold Certificates (a restriction which was lifted in 1964). For practical purposes the collectibility of the type is thus limited to the Series 1928 notes in the $10, $20, $50 and $100 denominations, which are currently in strong demand in uncirculated condition. Star notes are especially in demand.

Silver Certificates

From the 1929 release date of the small size U.S. currency issues, until Silver Certificate legislation was abolished by a Congressional Act on June 4, 1963, small size Silver Certificates, distinguished by their blue Treasury seal and serial number, were issued in denominations of $1, $5, and $10.

The earliest small size silver notes were redeemable for "One Silver Dollar," (or the appropriate number) as had been the large size issues. A change in the redemption clause, however, was made with the Silver Purchase Act of 1934, which specified the certificates be redeemable for silver dollars or silver bullion. At that time the wording on the notes was changed to read: "One Dollar in Silver." In March, 1964, by order of the Secretary of the Treasury, redemption in silver dollars was halted, and on June 24, 1968, redemption in silver bullion was also discontinued. Like all U.S. currency issued since 1861, Silver Certificates retain their status as legal tender, though today they are convertible only into current U.S. Federal Reserve Notes.

Federal Reserve Notes

Virtually the only type of U.S. paper money encountered in circulation today is the Federal Reserve Note, in denominations of $1-$100. Beginning with the Series 1990 $100 and $50 notes new security features have been added, including a metallic strip and microprinting. A second printing plant was opened at Fort Worth, Texas in 1990, with the notes identified by a "FW" prefix on the face plate check number.

Authorization continued in the small size period for FRNs to be issued in denominations from $5-$10,000. With the demise of the Silver Certificate $1 bill in 1963, that denomination was moved into the FRN realm. The Bicentennial in 1976 led to the re-introduction of the $2 note, which had last been issued as a United States Note in 1966, in the guise of a green-seal Federal Reserve Note.

No Federal Reserve Note of denomination higher than $100 has been printed since 1945, and since 1969 all notes of $500 and higher face value have been actively retired as they are turned into the Federal Reserve System.

Federal Reserve Bank Notes

The small size Federal Reserve Bank Notes were an emergency currency issue authorized March 9, 1933, to inject cash into the economy to combat heavy withdrawals from the Federal Reserve System in the first months of that year.

FRBNs in the small size were printed on currency stock prepared for the regular Series 1929 National Currency. Changes consisted of overprinting several elements. The President (and sometimes Cashier) title at the bottom of the notes was obliterated, and replaced with Governor, and the appropriate signatures of those Federal Reserve Bank officers engraved. There are, however, three exceptions to the Cashier-Governor combination on the small size FRBNs. On the notes of the Chicago bank, the signatures are those of the Assistant Deputy Governor and Governor; for New York, the signature of the Deputy Governor replaces that of the Cashier, and in the St. Louis district, the Controller signed instead of the Cashier.

In the places where the National Bank's charter number would have been imprinted, the proper district letter of the issuing bank appears in heavy black block type. At top of the note, near the obligation, a line was added to read: "or by like deposit of other securities."

Like the regular National Bank Notes of the small size era, the Treasury seal and serial number on the Federal Reserve Bank Notes are in brown ink.

Collector demand for this type has been almost non-existant until recent years. Now, however, the true rarity of some banks and denominations ($5-$100), especially in star notes, is being appreciated.

WWII Emergency Notes

Emergency conditions during World War II brought about several interesting and collectible varieties of small size U.S. currency.

North African Invasion Notes

When U.S. armed forces hit the beaches of North Africa in 1942 to begin the advance into Axis-held Europe from the south, special currency was issued to the troops which could be easily identified and demonitized in the event of military reverses and the capture of large quantities of the cash.

The notes were normal Silver Certificates, with blue serial numbers, but with Treasury seals printed in yellow. All bearing the Julian-Morgenthau signature combination, the $1 denominations were issued in Series 1935A, the $5s in Series 1934A and $10s in Series 1934 and 1934A. The 1934 $10 notes are quite scarce, especially as star notes.

Hawaii Overprints

As an economic defense precaution against Japanese invasion and occupation of Hawaii, specially marked U.S. currency was issued there in July, 1942, to replace other types in circulation. Distinguished by brown seal and serial numbers, and by "HAWAII" overprints on face and back, such notes could have been declared worthless in the event large numbers of them were captured.

The $1 notes used as emergency currency were Silver Certificates of Series 1935A, while $5s, $10s, and $20s were overprinted examples of San Francisco-district Federal Reserve Notes; the $5s in Series 1934 and '34A, the $10s in Series 1934A only, and the $20s in Series 1934 and '34A. All notes bear the Julian-Morgenthau combination.

By late October, 1944, the emergency monetary conditions were declared ended, and normal currency returned to use in Hawaii, and the Hawaii-overprinted notes went on to do further duty during the occupation of formerly Japanese-held islands in the Pacific.

R & S Experimentals

To test different types of security paper during World War II, when it was not known whether supplies of normal U.S. bank note paper could be maintained, an experimental run of notes was produced using normal, and a new special paper.

Notes on the special paper were overprinted with a large red S in the lower right corner, while a control group on regular paper was printed with a large red R in the same location. Exactly 1,184,000 of each type were released to circulation, all Silver Certificates bearing Series 1935A designation and the Julian-Morgenthau signature combination. The tests proved to be inconclusive, so no change in bank note paper resulted, but collectors were left with an interestingly variety that is especially challenging in uncirculated condition, and truly rare in star note form.

Because unscrupulous persons have applied phony R and S overprints to regular Series 1935A $1 Silver Certificates in an effort to pass them off as the higher-value experimental issue, collectors should be aware of the serial number ranges of the genuine issues. Serial numbers for the genuine R notes run from S70884001C through S72068000C; while those for the S notes are S73884001C through S75068000C.

U. S. Small Size Currency Valuations

STAR NOTES—It is inevitable that some misprints, smudged notes, or otherwise imperfect notes will be made during note production. At the time of examination, these imperfect notes are replaced by new notes that have a star on one end of the serial number. The percentage of spoiled notes is very small, hence the number of star notes is rather limited. In the early series of our small size notes, the spoilage percentage has been accurately estimated at less than 1% of total notes. No attempt is made to replace any defective note with the same serial number star note. Star notes are also used to replace the 100 millionth note instead of a note with serial 00 000 000 as printed.

Note: National Bank Notes issued between 1929-1935 will be found in a separate section, pages 65-158.

One Dollar
United States Notes

George Washington

KL#	Fr#	Series	Signatures	Fine	VF	CU
1444	1500	1928	Woods-Woodin	20.00	—	150.
1444☆	1500☆	1928☆	Woods-Woodin	1500.	—	6000.

Silver Certificates

George Washington

KL#	Fr#	Series	Signatures	Fine	VF	CU
1445	1600	1928	Tate-Mellon	8.00	—	25.00
1445☆	1600☆	1928☆	Tate-Mellon	—	—	150.
1446	1601	1928A	Woods-Mellon	6.00	—	25.00
1446☆	1601☆	1928A☆	Woods-Mellon	—	—	150.

KL#	Fr#	Series	Signatures	Fine	VF	CU
1447	1602	1928B	Woods-Mills	6.00	—	25.00
1447☆	1602☆	1928B☆	Woods-Mills	—	—	450.
1448	1603	1928C	Woods-Woodin	50.00	—	400.
1448☆	1603☆	1928C☆	Woods-Woodin	1500.	—	5000.
1449	1604	1928D	Julian-Woodin	35.00	—	275.
1449☆	1604☆	1928D☆	Julian-Woodin	1500.	—	5000.
1450	1605	1928E	Julian-Morgenthau	300.	—	1250.
1450☆	1605☆	1928E☆	Julian-Morgenthau	2500.	—	7000.

George Washington

KL#	Fr#	Series	Signatures	Fine	VF	CU
1451	1606	1934	Julian-Morgenthau	8.00	—	45.00
1451☆	1606☆	1934☆	Julian-Morgenthau	50.00	—	400.

KL#	Fr#	Series	Signatures	Fine	VF	CU
1452	1607	1935	Julian-Morgenthau	5.00	—	10.00
1452☆	1607☆	1935☆	Julian-Morgenthau	25.00	—	150.
1453	1608	1935A	Julian-Morgenthau	3.00	—	6.00
1453☆	1608☆	1935A☆	Julian-Morgenthau	5.00	—	25.00
1454	1611	1935B	Julian-Vinson	2.00	—	7.50
1454☆	1611☆	1935B☆	Julian-Vinson	12.50	—	65.00
1455	1612	1935C	Julian-Snyder	2.50	—	5.50
1455☆	1612☆	1935C☆	Julian-Snyder	5.00	—	25.00
1456	1613	1935D	Clark-Snyder (W)	2.00	—	6.00
1456☆	1613☆	1935D☆	Clark-Snyder (W)	3.50	—	20.00
1456A	1613	1935D	Clark-Snyder (N)	2.00	—	5.50
1456A☆	1613☆	1935D☆	Clark-Snyder (N)	3.50	—	15.00
1457	1614	1935E	Priest-Humphrey	—	—	5.00
1457☆	1614☆	1935E☆	Priest-Humphrey	—	—	7.50
1458	1615	1935F	Priest-Anderson	—	—	5.00
1458☆	1615☆	1935F☆	Priest-Anderson	—	—	7.50
1459	1616	1935G	Smith-Dillon (no motto)	—	—	6.00
1459☆	1616☆	1935G☆	Smith-Dillon (no motto)	—	—	9.00

KL#	Fr#	Series	Signatures	Fine	VF	CU
1460	1617	1935G	Smith-Dillon (w/motto)..........	—		15.00
1460☆	1617☆	1935G☆	Smith-Dillon (w/motto)..........	5.00	—	35.00
1461	1618	1935H	Granahan-Dillon..........	—	—	6.50
1461☆	1618☆	1935H☆	Granahan-Dillon..........	—	—	11.00
1462	1619	1957	Priest-Anderson..........	—	—	4.50
1462☆	1619☆	1957☆	Priest-Anderson..........	—	—	15.00
1463	1620	1957A	Smith-Dillon..........	—	—	5.00
1463☆	1620☆	1957A☆	Smith-Dillon..........	—	—	6.00
1464	1621	1957B	Granahan-Dillon..........	—	—	4.50
1464☆	1621☆	1957B☆	Granahan-Dillon..........	—	—	5.50

Federal Reserve Notes

George Washington

Series 1963 Granahan-Dillon

KL#	Fr#	Bank	XF	CU
1465	1900A	Boston..........	1.50	3.00
1465☆	1900A☆	Boston☆..........	2.00	5.00
1466	1900B	New York..........	1.50	3.00
1466☆	1900B☆	New York☆..........	1.75	4.00
1467	1900C	Philadelphia..........	1.50	3.00
1467☆	1900C☆	Philadelphia☆..........	2.00	5.00
1468	1900D	Cleveland..........	1.50	3.00
1468☆	1900D☆	Cleveland☆..........	2.00	5.00
1469	1900E	Richmond..........	1.50	3.00
1469☆	1900E☆	Richmond☆..........	2.00	5.00
1470	1900F	Atlanta..........	1.50	3.00
1470☆	1900F☆	Atlanta☆..........	1.75	4.00
1471	1900G	Chicago..........	1.50	3.00
1471☆	1900G☆	Chicago☆..........	1.75	4.00
1472	1900H	St. Louis..........	1.50	3.00
1472☆	1900H☆	St. Louis☆..........	1.75	4.00
1473	1900I	Minneapolis..........	1.50	3.00
1473☆	1900I☆	Minneapolis☆..........	2.00	5.00
1474	1900J	Kansas City..........	1.50	3.00
1474☆	1900J☆	Kansas City☆..........	1.75	4.00
1475	1900K	Dallas..........	1.50	3.00
1475☆	1900K☆	Dallas☆..........	1.75	4.00
1476	1900L	San Francisco..........	1.50	3.00
1476☆	1900L☆	San Francisco☆..........	6.00	10.00

Series 1963A Granahan-Fowler

KL#	Fr#	Bank	XF	CU
1477	1901A	Boston..........	1.50	3.00
1477☆	1901A☆	Boston☆..........	1.75	4.00
1478	1901B	New York..........	1.50	3.00
1478☆	1901B☆	New York☆..........	1.75	3.50
1479	1901C	Philadelphia..........	1.50	3.00
1479☆	1901C☆	Philadelphia☆..........	1.75	3.50
1480	1901D	Cleveland..........	1.50	3.00
1480☆	1901D☆	Cleveland☆..........	1.75	3.50
1481	1901E	Richmond..........	1.50	3.00
1481☆	1901E☆	Richmond☆..........	1.75	3.50
1482	1901F	Atlanta..........	1.50	3.00
1482☆	1901F☆	Atlanta☆..........	1.75	3.50
1483	1901G	Chicago..........	1.50	3.00
1483☆	1901G☆	Chicago☆..........	1.75	3.50

Series 1963A Granahan-Fowler

KL#	Fr#	Bank	XF	CU
1484	1901H	St. Louis..........	1.50	3.00
1484☆	1901H☆	St. Louis☆..........	1.75	3.50
1485	1901I	Minneapolis..........	1.50	3.00
1485☆	1901I☆	Minneapolis☆..........	1.75	3.50
1486	1901J	Kansas City..........	1.50	3.00
1486☆	1901J☆	Kansas City☆..........	1.75	3.50
1487	1901K	Dallas..........	1.50	3.00
1487☆	1901K☆	Dallas☆..........	1.75	4.00
1488	1901L	San Francisco..........	1.50	3.00
1488☆	1901L☆	San Francisco☆..........	1.75	3.50

Series 1963B Granahan-Barr

KL#	Fr#	Bank	XF	CU
1490	1902B	New York..........	1.75	3.50
1490☆	1902B☆	New York☆..........	1.85	4.50
1493	1902E	Richmond..........	1.75	3.50
1493☆	1902E☆	Richmond☆..........	2.00	5.00
1495	1902G	Chicago..........	1.75	4.00
1495☆	1902G☆	Chicago☆..........	1.85	4.50
1498	1902J	Kansas City..........	1.75	4.00
1498☆	1902J☆	Kansas City☆..........	—	Not issued
1500	1902L	San Francisco..........	1.75	4.00
1500☆	1902L☆	San Francisco☆..........	1.85	4.50

Series 1969 Elston-Kennedy

KL#	Fr#	Bank	XF	CU
1501	1903A	Boston..........	1.25	2.50
1501☆	1903A☆	Boston☆..........	1.50	3.00
1502	1903B	New York..........	1.25	2.50
1502☆	1903B☆	New York☆..........	1.50	3.00
1503	1903C	Philadelphia..........	1.25	2.50
1503☆	1903C☆	Philadelphia☆..........	1.50	3.00
1504	1903D	Cleveland..........	1.25	2.50
1504☆	1903D☆	Cleveland☆..........	1.50	3.00
1505	1903E	Richmond..........	1.25	2.50
1505☆	1903E☆	Richmond☆..........	1.50	3.00
1506	1903F	Atlanta..........	1.25	2.50
1506☆	1903F☆	Atlanta☆..........	1.50	3.00
1507	1903G	Chicago..........	1.25	2.50
1507☆	1903G☆	Chicago☆..........	1.50	3.00
1508	1903H	St. Louis..........	1.25	2.50
1508☆	1903H☆	St. Louis☆..........	1.50	3.00
1509	1903I	Minneapolis..........	1.25	2.50
1509☆	1903I☆	Minneapolis☆..........	1.75	4.00
1510	1903J	Kansas City..........	1.25	2.50
1510☆	1903J☆	Kansas City☆..........	1.50	3.00
1511	1903K	Dallas..........	1.25	2.50
1511☆	1903K☆	Dallas☆..........	1.50	3.00
1512	1903L	San Francisco..........	1.25	2.50
1512☆	1903L☆	San Francisco☆..........	1.85	3.50

Series 1969A Kabis-Kennedy

KL#	Fr#	Bank	XF	CU
1513	1904A	Boston..........	1.25	2.50
1513☆	1904A☆	Boston☆..........	1.85	4.00
1514	1904B	New York..........	1.25	2.50
1514☆	1904B☆	New York☆..........	1.75	3.50
1515	1904C	Philadelphia..........	1.25	2.50
1515☆	1904C☆	Philadelphia☆..........	1.75	3.50
1516	1904D	Cleveland..........	1.25	2.50
1516☆	1904D☆	Cleveland☆..........	1.75	4.00
1517	1904E	Richmond..........	1.25	2.50
1517☆	1904E☆	Richmond☆..........	1.50	3.00
1518	1904F	Atlanta..........	1.25	2.50
1518☆	1904F☆	Atlanta☆..........	1.50	3.00
1519	1904G	Chicago..........	1.25	2.50
1519☆	1904G☆	Chicago☆..........	1.50	3.00
1520	1904H	St. Louis..........	1.25	2.50
1520☆	1904H☆	St. Louis☆..........	1.50	3.50
1521	1904I	Minneapolis..........	1.50	3.00
1521☆	1904I☆	Minneapolis☆..........	2.50	5.00
1522	1904J	Kansas City..........	1.25	2.50
1522☆	1904J☆	Kansas City☆..........	1.75	4.00
1523	1904K	Dallas..........	1.50	3.00
1523☆	1904K☆	Dallas☆..........	—	Not issued
1524	1904L	San Francisco..........	1.25	2.50
1524☆	1904L☆	San Francisco☆..........	1.50	3.00

Series 1969B Kabis-Connally

KL#	Fr#	Bank	XF	CU
1525	1905A	Boston..........	1.25	2.50
1525☆	1905A☆	Boston☆..........	1.75	3.50
1526	1905B	New York..........	1.25	2.50
1526☆	1905B☆	New York☆..........	1.50	3.00
1527	1905C	Philadelphia..........	1.25	2.50
1527☆	1905C☆	Philadelphia☆..........	1.50	3.00
1528	1905D	Cleveland..........	1.25	2.50
1528☆	1905D☆	Cleveland☆..........	1.50	3.00
1529	1905E	Richmond..........	1.25	2.50
1529☆	1905E☆	Richmond☆..........	1.50	3.00
1530	1905F	Atlanta..........	1.25	2.50
1530☆	1905F☆	Atlanta☆..........	1.50	3.00
1531	1905G	Chicago..........	1.25	2.50
1531☆	1905G☆	Chicago☆..........	1.50	3.00
1532	1905H	St. Louis..........	1.25	2.50
1532☆	1905H☆	St. Louis☆..........	1.50	3.00
1533	1905I	Minneapolis..........	1.25	2.50
1533☆	1905I☆	Minneapolis☆..........	1.75	3.50

Series 1969B Kabis-Connally

KL#	Fr#	Bank	XF	CU
1534	1905J	Kansas City	1.25	2.50
1534☆	1905J☆	Kansas City☆	1.50	3.00
1535	1905K	Dallas	1.25	2.50
1535☆	1905K☆	Dallas☆	1.50	3.00
1536	1905L	San Francisco	1.25	2.50
1536☆	1905L☆	San Francisco☆	1.50	3.00

Series 1969C Banuelos-Connally

KL#	Fr#	Bank	XF	CU
1538	1906B	New York	1.50	2.50
1538☆	1906B☆	New York☆	—	Not issued
1540	1906D	Cleveland	1.50	2.50
1540☆	1906D☆	Cleveland☆	2.50	5.00
1541	1906E	Richmond	1.25	2.50
1541☆	1906E☆	Richmond☆	2.50	5.00
1542	1906F	Atlanta	1.50	2.50
1542☆	1906F☆	Atlanta☆	1.75	3.50
1543	1906G	Chicago	1.25	2.50
1543☆	1906G☆	Chicago☆	2.00	4.00
1544	1906H	St. Louis	1.50	2.50
1544☆	1906H☆	St. Louis☆	2.00	4.00
1545	1906I	Minneapolis	1.50	2.50
1545☆	1906I☆	Minneapolis☆	2.25	4.50
1546	1906J	Kansas City	1.50	2.50
1546☆	1906J☆	Kansas City☆	2.00	4.00
1547	1906K	Dallas	1.50	2.50
1547☆	1906K☆	Dallas☆	2.00	4.00
1548	1906L	San Francisco	1.50	2.50
1548☆	1906L☆	San Francisco☆	7.50	20.00

Series 1969D Banuelos-Shultz

KL#	Fr#	Bank	XF	CU
1561	1907A	Boston	1.50	2.50
1561☆	1907A☆	Boston☆	1.75	3.50
1562	1907B	New York	1.50	2.50
1562☆	1907B☆	New York☆	1.50	3.00
1563	1907C	Philadelphia	1.25	2.50
1563☆	1907C☆	Philadelphia☆	1.50	3.00
1564	1907D	Cleveland	1.25	2.50
1564☆	1907D☆	Cleveland☆	1.50	3.00
1565	1907E	Richmond	1.25	2.50
1565☆	1907E☆	Richmond☆	1.50	3.00
1566	1907F	Atlanta	1.25	2.50
1566☆	1907F☆	Atlanta☆	1.50	3.00
1567	1907G	Chicago	1.25	2.50
1567☆	1907G☆	Chicago☆	1.50	3.00
1568	1907H	St. Louis	1.25	2.50
1568☆	1907H☆	St. Louis☆	1.75	3.50
1569	1907I	Minneapolis	1.25	2.50
1569☆	1907I☆	Minneapolis☆	—	Not issued
1570	1907J	Kansas City	1.25	2.50
1570☆	1907J☆	Kansas City☆	1.75	3.50
1571	1907K	Dallas	1.25	—
1571☆	1907K☆	Dallas☆	1.75	3.50
1572	1907L	San Francisco	1.25	2.50
1572☆	1907L☆	San Francisco☆	1.75	3.50

Series 1974 Neff-Simon

KL#	Fr#	Bank	XF	CU
1573	1908A	Boston	—	2.00
1573☆	1908A☆	Boston☆	1.50	3.00
1574	1908B	New York	—	2.00
1574☆	1908B☆	New York☆	1.50	3.00
1575	1908C	Philadelphia	—	2.00
1575☆	1908C☆	Philadelphia☆	1.50	3.00
1576	1908D	Cleveland	—	2.00
1576☆	1908D☆	Cleveland☆	2.00	4.00
1577	1908E	Richmond	—	2.00
1577☆	1908E☆	Richmond☆	1.50	3.00
1578	1908F	Atlanta	—	2.00
1578☆	1908F☆	Atlanta☆	1.50	3.00
1579	1908G	Chicago	—	2.00
1579☆	1908G☆	Chicago☆	1.50	3.00
1580	1908H	St. Louis	—	2.00
1580☆	1908H☆	St. Louis☆	1.50	3.00
1581	1908I	Minneapolis	—	2.00
1581☆	1908I☆	Minneapolis☆	6.00	10.00
1582	1908J	Kansas City	—	2.00
1582☆	1908J☆	Kansas City☆	1.50	3.00
1583	1908K	Dallas	—	2.00
1583☆	1908K☆	Dallas☆	1.50	3.00
1584	1908L	San Francisco	—	2.00
1584☆	1908L☆	San Francisco☆	1.75	3.50

Series 1977 Morton-Blumenthal

KL#	Fr#	Bank	XF	CU
1585	1909A	Boston	—	2.00
1585☆	1909A☆	Boston☆	1.50	3.00
1586	1909B	New York	—	2.00
1586☆	1909B☆	New York☆	1.50	3.00
1587	1909C	Philadelphia	—	2.00
1587☆	1909C☆	Philadelphia☆	1.50	3.00
1588	1909D	Cleveland	—	2.00
1588☆	1909D☆	Cleveland☆	1.50	3.00
1589	1909E	Richmond	—	2.00
1589☆	1909E☆	Richmond☆	1.50	3.00
1590	1909F	Atlanta	—	2.00
1590☆	1909F☆	Atlanta☆	1.50	3.00
1591	1909G	Chicago	—	2.00

Series 1977 Morton-Blumenthal

KL#	Fr#	Bank	XF	CU
1591☆	1909G☆	Chicago☆	1.50	3.00
1592	1909H	St. Louis	—	2.00
1592☆	1909H☆	St. Louis☆	1.50	3.00
1593	1909I	Minneapolis	—	2.00
1593☆	1909I☆	Minneapolis☆	2.50	5.00
1594	1909J	Kansas City	—	2.00
1594☆	1909J☆	Kansas City☆	1.50	3.00
1595	1909K	Dallas	—	2.00
1595☆	1909K☆	Dallas☆	1.50	3.00
1596	1909L	San Francisco	—	2.00
1596☆	1909L☆	San Francisco☆	1.50	3.00

Series 1977A Morton-Miller

KL#	Fr#	Bank	XF	CU
1597	1910A	Boston	—	2.00
1597☆	1910A☆	Boston☆	1.50	3.00
1598	1910B	New York	—	2.00
1598☆	1910B☆	New York☆	—	2.50
1599	1910C	Philadelphia	—	2.00
1599☆	1910C☆	Philadelphia☆	—	2.50
1600	1910D	Cleveland	—	2.00
1600☆	1910D☆	Cleveland☆	—	2.50
1601	1910E	Richmond	—	2.00
1601☆	1910E☆	Richmond☆	—	2.50
1602	1910F	Atlanta	—	2.00
1602☆	1910F☆	Atlanta☆	—	2.50
1603	1910G	Chicago	—	2.00
1603☆	1910G☆	Chicago☆	—	2.50
1604	1910H	St. Louis	—	2.00
1604☆	1910H☆	St. Louis☆	—	2.50
1605	1910I	Minneapolis	—	2.50
1605☆	1910I☆	Minneapolis☆	2.50	5.00
1606	1910J	Kansas City	—	2.00
1606☆	1910J☆	Kansas City☆	—	2.50
1607	1910K	Dallas	—	2.00
1607☆	1910K☆	Dallas☆	—	2.50
1608	1910L	San Francisco	—	2.00
1608☆	1910L☆	San Francisco☆	—	2.50

Series 1981 Buchanan-Regan

KL#	Fr#	Bank	XF	CU
3500	1911A	Boston	—	2.00
3500☆	1911A☆	Boston☆	1.75	3.50
3501	1911B	New York	—	2.00
3501☆	1911B☆	New York☆	1.75	3.50
3502	1911C	Philadelphia	—	2.50
3502☆	1911C☆	Philadelphia☆	1.75	3.50
3503	1911D	Cleveland	—	2.00
3503☆	1911D☆	Cleveland☆	1.75	3.50
3504	1911E	Richmond	—	2.00
3504☆	1911E☆	Richmond☆	1.75	3.50
3505	1911F	Atlanta	—	2.00
3505☆	1911F☆	Atlanta☆	1.75	3.50
3506	1911G	Chicago	—	2.00
3506☆	1911G☆	Chicago☆	1.75	3.50
3507	1911H	St. Louis	—	2.00
3507☆	1911H☆	St. Louis☆	1.75	3.50
3508	1911I	Minneapolis	1.50	3.00
3508☆	1911I☆	Minneapolis☆	1.75	3.50
3509	1911J	Kansas City	—	2.00
3509☆	1911J☆	Kansas City☆	1.75	3.50
3510	1911K	Dallas	—	2.00
3510☆	1911K☆	Dallas☆	1.75	3.50
3511	1911L	San Francisco	—	2.00
3511☆	1911L☆	San Francisco☆	1.75	3.50

Series 1981A Ortega-Regan

KL#	Fr#	Bank	XF	CU
3600	1912A	Boston	1.50	3.00
3600A	—	Boston (Back plate #129 at left)	3.00	6.00
3600☆	1912A☆	Boston☆	—	Not issued
3601	1912B	New York	1.25	2.50
3601A	—	New York (Back plate #129 at left)	4.00	8.00
3601☆	1912B☆	New York☆	1.75	3.50
3602	1912C	Philadelphia	1.50	3.00
3602A	—	Philadelphia (Back plate #129 at left)	4.00	8.00
3602☆	1912C☆	Philadelphia☆	—	Not issued
3603	1912D	Cleveland	1.25	2.50
3603A	—	Cleveland (Back plate #129 at left)	—	Not issued
3603☆	1912D☆	Cleveland☆	—	Not issued
3604	1912E	Richmond	1.50	3.00
3604A	—	Richmond (Back plate #129 at left)	4.00	8.00
3604☆	1912E☆	Richmond☆	1.75	3.50
3605	1912F	Atlanta	1.25	2.50
3605A	—	Atlanta (Back plate #129 at left)	4.00	8.00
3605☆	1912F☆	Atlanta☆	—	Not issued
3606	1912G	Chicago	1.25	2.50

Series 1981A Ortega-Regan

KL#	Fr#	Bank	XF	CU
3606A	—	Chicago (Back plate #129 at left)	4.00	8.00
3606☆	1912G☆	Chicago☆	1.75	3.50
3607	1912H	St. Louis	1.50	3.00
3607A	—	St. Louis (Back plate #129 at left)	4.00	8.00
3607☆	1912H☆	St. Louis☆	—	Not issued
3608	1912I	Minneapolis	1.50	3.00
3608A	—	Minneapolis (Back plate #129 at left)	4.00	8.00
3608☆	1912I☆	Minneapolis☆	—	Not issued
3609	1912J	Kansas City	1.50	3.00
3609A	—	Kansas City (Back plate #129 at left)	—	(Unreported)
3609☆	1912J☆	Kansas City☆	—	Not issued
3610	1912K	Dallas	1.50	3.00
3610A	—	Dallas (Back plate #129 at left)	4.00	8.00
3610☆	1912K☆	Dallas☆	18.00	35.00
3611	1912L	San Francisco	1.25	2.50
3611A	—	San Francisco (Back plate #129 at left)	4.00	8.00
3611☆	1912L☆	San Francisco☆	1.75	3.50

Series 1985 Ortega-Baker

KL#	Fr#	Bank	XF	CU
3700	1913A	Boston	—	2.00
3700A	—	Boston (Back plate #129 at left)	4.00	8.00
3700☆	1913A	Boston☆	—	Not issued
3701	1913B	New York	—	2.00
3701A	—	New York (Back plate #129 at left)	4.00	8.00
3701☆	1913B	New York☆	—	Not issued
3702	1913C	Philadelphia	—	2.00
3702A	—	Philadelphia (Back plate #129 at left)	4.00	8.00
3702☆	1913C	Philadelphia☆	—	Not issued
3703	1913D	Cleveland	—	2.00
3703A	—	Cleveland (Back plate #129 at left)	4.00	8.00
3703☆	1913D	Cleveland☆	—	Not issued
3704	1913E	Richmond	—	2.00
3704A	—	Richmond (Back plate #129 at left)	4.00	8.00
3704☆	1913E☆	Richmond☆	1.25	2.50
3705	1913F	Atlanta	—	2.00
3705A	—	Atlanta (Back plate #129 at left)	4.00	8.00
3706	1913G	Chicago	—	2.00
3706A	—	Chicago (Back plate #129 at left)	4.00	8.00
3706☆	1913G☆	Chicago☆	1.25	2.50
3707	1913H	St. Louis	—	2.00
3707A	—	St. Louis (Back plate #129 at left)	4.00	8.00
3707☆	1913H☆	St. Louis☆	7.50	15.00
3708	1913I	Minneapolis	—	2.00
3708A	—	Minneapolis (Back plate #129 at left)	—	Not issued
3708☆	1913I☆	Minneapolis☆	1.50	3.00
3709	1913J	Kansas City	—	2.00
3709A	—	Kansas City (Back plate #129 at left)	4.00	8.00
3709☆	1913J	Kansas City☆	—	Not issued
3710	1913K	Dallas	—	2.00
3710A	—	Dallas (Back plate #129 at left)	4.00	8.00
3710☆	1913K☆	Dallas☆	1.50	3.00
3711	1913L	San Francisco	—	2.00
3711A	—	San Francisco (Back plate #129 at left)	4.00	8.00
3711☆	1913L☆	San Francisco☆	1.25	2.50

Series 1988 Ortega-Brady

KL#	Fr#	Bank	XF	CU
3772	1914A	Boston	1.50	3.00
3772☆	1914A☆	Boston☆	2.50	5.00
3773	1914B	New York	1.25	2.50
3773☆	1914B☆	New York☆	1.50	3.00
3774	1914C	Philadelphia	2.00	4.00
3774☆	1914C☆	Philadelphia☆	—	Not issued
3775	1914D	Cleveland	1.75	3.50
3775☆	1914D☆	Cleveland☆	—	Not issued
3776	1914E	Richmond	1.50	3.00
3776☆	1914E☆	Richmond☆	2.25	4.50
3777	1914F	Atlanta	1.50	3.00
3777☆	1914F☆	Atlanta☆	75.00	150.
3778	1914G	Chicago	1.50	3.00
3778☆	1914G☆	Chicago☆	—	Not issued
3779	1914H	St. Louis	1.50	3.00
3779☆	1914H☆	St. Louis☆	—	Not issued
3780	1914I	Minneapolis	1.50	3.00
3780☆	1914I☆	Minneapolis☆	—	Not issued
3781	1914J	Kansas City	1.50	3.00
3781☆	1914J☆	Kansas City☆	4.25	4.50
3782	1914K	Dallas	2.00	4.00
3782☆	1914K☆	Dallas☆	3.00	6.00
3783	1914L	San Francisco	1.50	3.00
3783☆	1914L☆	San Francisco☆	3.00	6.00

Series 1988A Villalpando-Brady

KL#	Fr#	Bank	XF	CU
3844	—	Boston	—	2.00
3844☆	—	Boston☆	—	Not issued
3845	—	New York	—	2.00
3845☆	—	New York☆	—	2.50
3846	—	Philadelphia	—	2.00
3846☆	—	Philadelphia☆	—	Not issued
3847	—	Cleveland	—	2.00
3847☆	—	Cleveland☆	—	2.50
3848	—	Richmond	—	2.00
3848☆	—	Richmond☆	—	2.50
3849	—	Atlanta	—	2.00
3849☆	—	Atlanta☆	—	2.50
3850	—	Chicago	—	2.00
3850☆	—	Chicago☆	—	2.50

Fort Worth, Texas plant identifying letters.

Series 1988A Villalpando-Brady

KL#	Fr#	Bank	XF	CU
3851	—	St. Louis	—	2.00
3851☆	—	St. Louis☆	—	2.50
3852	—	Minneapolis	—	2.00
3852☆	—	Minneapolis☆	—	2.50
3853	—	Kansas City	—	2.00
3853☆	—	Kansas City☆	—	Not issued
3854	—	Dallas	—	2.00
3854☆	—	Dallas☆	—	2.50
3855	—	San Francisco	—	2.00
3855☆	—	San Francisco☆	—	2.50

Series 1988A Villalpando-Brady

(Web Press)

With an initial press run in May, 1992, the Bureau of Engraving and Printing began testing the high volume Web-Fed intaglio currency press in actual production. With this press, both sides of the note are printed in a single pass of a continuous roll of paper from a printing cylinder of 96 subjects or notes. Some obvious face design changes including the removal of the face check letters and quadrant number. Check numbers begin a new sequence on both face and back with #1. The back check number has been relocated to the right of the word "TRUST."

Face check numbers used to press time include 1,2,3,4,5,8,9,10.

Back check numbers in use include 1,2,4,5,6,7,8.

KL#	Fr#	Bank	XF	CU
3988	—	Boston	7.50	15.00
3988☆	—	Boston☆	—	Not issued
3989	—	New York	250.	500.
3989☆	—	New York☆	—	Not issued
3990	—	Philadelphia	5.00	10.00
3990☆	—	Philadelphia☆	—	Not issued
3991	—	Cleveland	—	Not issued
3991☆	—	Cleveland☆	—	Not issued
3992	—	Richmond	5.00	10.00
3992☆	—	Richmond☆	—	Not issued
3993	—	Atlanta	5.00	10.00
3993☆	—	Atlanta☆	350.	750.
3994	—	Chicago	25.00	50.00
3994☆	—	Chicago☆	—	Not issued
3995	—	St. Louis	—	Not issued
3995☆	—	St. Louis☆	—	Not issued
3996	—	Minneapolis	—	Not issued
3996☆	—	Minneapolis☆	—	Not issued
3997	—	Kansas City	—	Not issued
3997☆	—	Kansas City☆	—	Not issued
3998	—	Dallas	—	Not issued
3998☆	—	Dallas☆	—	Not issued
3999	—	San Francisco	—	Not issued
3999☆	—	San Francisco☆	—	Not issued

Series 1993 Withrow-Bentsen

KL#	Fr#	Bank	XF	CU
4012	—	Boston	—	2.00
4012☆	—	Boston☆	—	Not issued
4013	—	New York	—	2.00
4013☆	—	New York☆	—	2.50
4014	—	Philadelphia	—	2.00
4014☆	—	Philadelphia☆	2.50	5.00
4015	—	Cleveland	—	2.00
4015☆	—	Cleveland☆	—	Not issued
4016	—	Richmond	—	2.00
4016☆	—	Richmond☆	—	Not issued
4017	—	Atlanta	—	2.00
4017☆	—	Atlanta☆	—	2.50
4018	—	Chicago	—	2.00
4018☆	—	Chicago☆	—	2.50
4019	—	St. Louis	—	2.00
4019☆	—	St. Louis☆	—	Not issued
4020	—	Minneapolis	2.50	5.00
4020☆	—	Minneapolis☆	—	Not issued
4021	—	Kansas City	—	Not issued
4021☆	—	Kansas City☆	—	Not issued
4022	—	Dallas	—	2.00
4022☆	—	Dallas☆	—	2.50
4023	—	San Francisco	—	2.00
4023☆	—	San Francisco☆	—	Not issued

Series 1993 Withrow-Bentsen
(Web Press)

KL#	Fr#	Bank	XF	CU
4144	—	New York	3.00	6.00
4144☆	—	New York☆	—	Not issued
4145	—	Philadelphia	3.00	6.00
4145☆	—	Philadelphia☆	—	Not issued

Series 1995 Withrow-Rubin

KL#	Fr#	Bank	XF	CU
4084	—	Boston	—	2.00
4084☆	—	Boston☆	—	2.50
4085	—	New York	—	2.00
4085☆	—	New York☆	—	3.00
4086	—	Philadelphia	—	2.00
4086☆	—	Philadelphia☆	—	3.00
4087	—	Cleveland	—	2.00
4087☆	—	Cleveland☆	—	2.50
4088	—	Richmond	—	2.00
4088☆	—	Richmond☆	—	2.50
4089	—	Atlanta	—	2.00
4089☆	—	Atlanta☆	—	2.50
4090	—	Chicago	—	2.00
4090☆	—	Chicago☆	—	2.50
4091	—	St. Louis	—	2.50
4091☆	—	St. Louis☆	—	Not issued
4092	—	Minneapolis	—	2.50
4092☆	—	Minneapolis☆	—	3.00
4093	—	Kansas City	—	2.00
4093☆	—	Kansas City☆	—	Not issued
4094	—	Dallas	—	2.00
4094☆	—	Dallas☆	—	Not issued
4095	—	San Francisco	—	2.00
4095☆	—	San Francisco☆	—	3.00

Series 1995 Withrow-Rubin
(Web Press)

KL#	Fr#	Bank	XF	CU
4146	—	Boston	3.00	6.00
4146☆	—	Boston☆	—	Not issued
4147	—	New York	3.00	6.00
4147☆	—	New York☆	—	Not issued
4148	—	Cleveland	3.00	6.00
4148☆	—	Cleveland☆	—	Not issued
4149	—	Atlanta	3.00	6.00
4149☆	—	Atlanta☆	—	Not issued

Hawaii Emergency
Silver Certificates

George Washington

KL#	Fr#	Series	Signatures	Fine	XF	CU
1609	2300	1935A	Julian-Morgenthau	13.50	16.00	60.00
1609☆	2300☆	1935A☆	Julian-Morgenthau	60.00	175.	750.

North Africa Emergency
Silver Certificates

KL#	Fr#	Series	Signatures	Fine	XF	CU
1610	2306	1935A	Julian-Morgentau	16.00	20.00	60.00
1610☆	2306☆	1935A☆	Julian-Morgentau	60.00	175.	750.

1935A Experimental Issue
Silver Certificates

George Washington

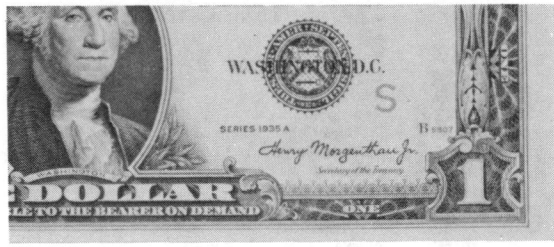

KL#	Fr#	Type	Fine	XF	CU
1611	1609	$1 Red "R"	20.00	43.00	175.
1611☆	1609☆	$1 Red "R"☆	500.	1000.	2500.
1612	1610	$1 Red "S"	20.00	36.00	150.
1612☆	1610☆	$1 Red "S"☆	500.	1000.	2350.

Two Dollars
United States Notes

Thomas Jefferson

KL#	Fr#	Series	Signatures	Fine	VF	CU
1613	1501	1928	Tate-Mellon..................	12.50	15.00	30.00

KL#	Fr#	Series	Signatures	Fine	VF	CU
1613☆	1501☆	1928☆	Tate-Mellon................	75.00	100.	300.
1614	1502	1928A	Woods-Mellon...........	35.00	45.00	150.
1614☆	1502☆	1928A☆	Woods-Mellon...........	550.	650.	2500.
1615	1503	1928B	Woods-Mills..............	45.00	55.00	375.
1615☆	1503☆	1928B☆	Woods-Mills..............	3500.	4500.	Rare
1616	1504	1928C	Julian-Morgenthau.....	15.00	18.00	75.00
1616☆	1504☆	1928C☆	Julian-Morgenthau.....	—	—	400.
1617	1505	1928D	Julian-Morgenthau.....	10.00	12.00	25.00
1617☆	1505☆	1928D☆	Julian-Morgenthau.....	—	—	175.
1618	1506	1928E	Julian-Vinson............	15.00	18.00	45.00
1618☆	1506☆	1928E☆	Julian-Vinson............	1200.	1800.	4500.
1619	1507	1928F	Julian-Snyder...........	4.50	6.50	18.00
1619☆	1507☆	1928F☆	Julian-Snyder...........	20.00	25.00	125.
1620	1508	1928G	Clark-Snyder............	5.00	6.00	12.50
1620☆	1508☆	1928G☆	Clark-Snyder............	15.00	18.00	100.

Thomas Jefferson

KL#	Fr#	Series	Signatures	Fine	VF	CU
1621	1509	1953	Priest-Humphrey................	—	—	7.50
1621☆	1509☆	1953☆	Priest-Humphrey................	—	—	24.00
1622	1510	1953A	Priest-Anderson................	—	—	5.00
1622☆	1510☆	1953A☆	Priest-Anderson................	—	—	35.00
1623	1511	1953B	Smith-Dillon.....................	—	—	5.50
1623☆	1511☆	1953B☆	Smith-Dillon.....................	—	—	18.00
1624	1512	1953C	Granahan-Dillon................	—	—	6.50
1624☆	1512☆	1953C☆	Granahan-Dillon................	—	—	30.00
1625	1513	1963	Granahan-Dillon................	—	—	5.00
1625☆	1513☆	1963☆	Granahan-Dillon................	—	—	10.00
1626	1514	1963A	Granahan-Fowler...............	—	—	7.50
1626☆	1514☆	1963A☆	Granahan-Fowler...............	—	—	17.00

Federal Reserve Notes

Series 1976 Neff-Simon

Thomas Jefferson

KL#	Fr#	Bank	XF	CU
1627	1935A	Boston................	—	4.00
1627☆	1935A☆	Boston................	—	6.00
1628	1935B	New York...........	—	4.00
1628☆	1935B☆	New York☆...........	—	5.00
1629	1935C	Philadelphia.......	—	4.00
1629☆	1935C☆	Philadelphia☆.......	—	6.00
1630	1935D	Cleveland...........	—	4.00
1630☆	1935D☆	Cleveland☆...........	—	6.00
1631	1935E	Richmond...........	—	4.00
1631☆	1935E☆	Richmond☆...........	—	6.00
1632	1935F	Atlanta..............	—	4.00
1632☆	1935F☆	Atlanta☆..............	—	6.00
1633	1935G	Chicago.............	—	4.00
1633☆	1935G☆	Chicago☆.............	—	6.00
1634	1935H	St. Louis............	—	4.00
1634☆	1935H☆	St. Louis☆............	—	6.00
1635	1935I	Minneapolis........	—	4.00
1635☆	1935I☆	Minneapolis☆........	—	6.00
1636	1935J	Kansas City........	—	4.00
1636☆	1935J☆	Kansas City☆........	—	6.00
1637	1935K	Dallas...............	—	4.00
1637☆	1935K☆	Dallas☆...............	—	6.00
1638	1935L	San Francisco.....	—	4.00
1638☆	1935L☆	San Francisco☆.....	—	6.00

Series 1995 Withrow-Rubin

KL#	Fr#	Bank	XF	CU
4150	—	Atlanta...............	—	3.50
4150☆	—	Atlanta☆...............	—	7.50

Five Dollars
United States Notes

Abraham Lincoln

KL#	Fr#	Series	Signatures	Fine	VF	CU
1639	1525	1928	Woods-Mellon................	8.00	10.00	30.00
1639☆	1525☆	1928☆	Woods-Mellon................	25.00	75.00	700.
1640	1526	1928A	Woods-Mills..................	12.00	13.00	60.00
1640☆	1526☆	1928A☆	Woods-Mills..................	700.	1250.	3000.
1641	1527	1928B	Julian-Morgenthau..........	8.00	9.00	20.00
1641☆	1527☆	1928B☆	Julian-Morgenthau..........	20.00	30.00	400.
1642	1528	1928C	Julian-Morgenthau..........	10.00	12.50	25.00
1642☆	1528☆	1928C☆	Julian-Morgenthau..........	30.00	75.00	350.
1643	1529	1928D	Julian-Vinson.................	16.00	22.00	100.
1643☆	1529☆	1928D☆	Julian-Vinson.................	500.	800.	2250.
1644	1530	1928E	Julian-Snyder................	9.50	12.50	25.00
1644☆	1530☆	1928E☆	Julian-Snyder................	50.00	65.00	300.
1645	1531	1928F	Clark-Snyder.................	9.50	12.50	25.00
1645☆	1531☆	1928F☆	Clark-Snyder.................	30.00	50.00	200.
1646	1532	1953	Priest-Humphrey............	8.50	10.00	25.00
1646☆	1532☆	1953☆	Priest-Humphrey............	15.00	20.00	75.00
1647	1533	1953A	Priest-Anderson............	7.00	8.00	22.00
1647☆	1533☆	1953A☆	Priest-Anderson............	15.00	18.00	35.00
1648	1534	1953B	Smith-Dillon.................	7.00	7.50	15.00
1648☆	1534☆	1953B☆	Smith-Dillon.................	10.00	15.00	35.00
1649	1535	1953C	Granahan-Dillon............	7.50	8.00	20.00
1649☆	1535☆	1953C☆	Granahan-Dillon............	10.00	15.00	60.00
1650	1536	1963	Granahan-Dillon............	7.00	8.00	12.00
1650☆	1536☆	1963☆	Granahan-Dillon............	7.50	9.00	15.00

Abraham Lincoln

Silver Certificates

Abraham Lincoln

KL#	Fr#	Series	Signatures	Fine	VF	CU
1651	1650	1934	Julian-Morgenthau	—	8.00	20.00
1651☆	1650☆	1934☆	Julian-Morgenthau	—	25.00	50.00
1652	1651	1934A	Julian-Morgenthau	—	8.00	15.00
1652☆	1651☆	1934A☆	Julian-Morgenthau	—	25.00	50.00
1653	1652	1934B	Julian-Vinson	10.00	12.00	35.00
1653☆	1652☆	1934B☆	Julian-Vinson	50.00	60.00	150.
1654	1653	1934C	Julian-Snyder	10.00	12.00	20.00
1654☆	1653☆	1934C☆	Julian-Snyder	17.50	20.00	75.00
1655	1654	1934D	Clark-Snyder	8.00	10.00	20.00
1655☆	1654☆	1934D☆	Clark-Snyder	15.00	20.00	35.00

Abraham Lincoln

KL#	Fr#	Series	Signatures	Fine	VF	CU
1656	1655	1953	Priest-Humphrey	—	—	17.50
1656☆	1655☆	1953☆	Priest-Humphrey	—	—	30.00
1657	1656	1953A	Priest-Anderson	—	—	12.00
1657☆	1656☆	1953A☆	Priest-Anderson	—	—	20.00
1658	1657	1953B	Smith-Dillon	—	—	15.00
1658☆	1657☆	1953B☆	Smith-Dillon	1000.	1350.	3500.

Federal Reserve Bank Notes

Abraham Lincoln

KL#	Fr#	Series	District	Fine	VF	CU
1659	1850A	1929	Boston	15.00	22.50	70.00
1659☆	1850A☆	1929☆	Boston☆	100.	200.	600.
1660	1850B	1929	New York	15.00	22.50	60.00
1660☆	1850B☆	1929☆	New York☆	100.	200.	600.
1661	1850C	1929	Philadelphia	15.00	22.50	70.00
1661☆	1850C☆	1929☆	Philadelphia☆	100.	200.	600.
1662	1850D	1929	Cleveland	15.00	22.50	60.00
1662☆	1850D☆	1929☆	Cleveland☆	100.	200.	600.
1664	1850F	1929	Atlanta	15.00	27.50	100.
1664☆	1850F☆	1929☆	Atlanta☆	100.	200.	600.
1665	1850G	1929	Chicago	12.00	20.00	75.00
1665☆	1850G☆	1929☆	Chicago☆	100.	200.	600.
1666	1850H	1929	St. Louis	90.00	150.	750.
1666☆	1850H☆	1929☆	St. Louis☆	550.	1000.	4000.
1667	1850I	1929	Minneapolis	25.00	55.00	225.
1667☆	1850I☆	1929☆	Minneapolis☆	450.	750.	2000.
1668	1850J	1929	Kansas City	12.50	25.00	85.00
1668☆	1850J☆	1929☆	Kansas City☆	100.	200.	700.
1669	1850K	1929	Dallas	20.00	30.00	85.00
1669☆	1850K☆	1929☆	Dallas☆	450.	750.	2000.
1670	1850L	1929	San Francisco	350.	500.	2000.
1670☆	1850L☆	1929☆	San Francisco☆	1250.	2500.	5000.

Federal Reserve Notes

Abraham Lincoln

KL#	Fr#	Bank	XF	CU
1671	1950A	Boston	25.00	60.00
1671☆	1950A☆	Boston☆	100.	250.
1672	1950B	New York	25.00	60.00
1672☆	1950B☆	New York☆	125.	250.
1673	1950C	Philadelphia	25.00	60.00
1673☆	1950C☆	Philadelphia☆	125.	250.
1674	1950D	Cleveland	25.00	60.00
1674☆	1950D☆	Cleveland☆	125.	250.
1675	1950E	Richmond	25.00	60.00
1675☆	1950E☆	Richmond☆	125.	250.
1676	1950F	Atlanta	25.00	50.00
1676☆	1950F☆	Atlanta☆	125.	250.
1677	1950G	Chicago	25.00	50.00
1677☆	1950G☆	Chicago☆	100.	250.
1678	1950H	St. Louis	25.00	60.00
1678☆	1950H☆	St. Louis☆	100.	250.
1679	1950I	Minneapolis	25.00	75.00
1679☆	1950I☆	Minneapolis☆	225.	500.
1680	1950J	Kansas City	25.00	60.00
1680☆	1950J☆	Kansas City☆	100.	250.
1681	1950K	Dallas	25.00	40.00
1681☆	1950K☆	Dallas☆	100.	250.
1682	1950L	San Francisco	25.00	100.
1682☆	1950L☆	San Francisco☆	225.	500.

Series 1928A Woods-Mellon

KL#	Fr#	Bank	XF	CU
1683	1951A	Boston	25.00	40.00
1683☆	1951A☆	Boston☆	125.	300.
1684	1951B	New York	25.00	40.00
1684☆	1951B☆	New York☆	125.	300.
1685	1951C	Philadelphia	25.00	40.00
1685☆	1951C☆	Philadelphia☆	125.	300.
1686	1951D	Cleveland	25.00	40.00
1686☆	1951D☆	Cleveland☆	100.	300.
1687	1951E	Richmond	40.00	75.00
1687☆	1951E☆	Richmond☆	100.	300.
1688	1951F	Atlanta	25.00	40.00
1688☆	1951F☆	Atlanta☆	125.	300.
1689	1951G	Chicago	25.00	40.00

Series 1928-A Woods-Mellon

KL#	Fr#	Bank	XF	CU
1689☆	1951G☆	Chicago☆	75.00	275.
1690	1951H	St. Louis	40.00	60.00
1690☆	1951H☆	St. Louis☆	125.	300.
1691	1951I	Minneapolis	80.00	200.
1691☆	1951I☆	Minneapolis☆	200.	450.
1692	1951J	Kansas City	40.00	60.00
1692☆	1951J☆	Kansas City☆	125.	300.
1693	1951K	Dallas	40.00	75.00
1693☆	1951K☆	Dallas☆	125.	500.
1694	1951L	San Francisco	25.00	50.00
1694☆	1951L☆	San Francisco☆	125.	300.

Series 1928B Woods-Mellon

KL#	Fr#	Bank	XF	CU
1695	1952A	Boston	20.00	40.00
1695☆	1952A☆	Boston☆	75.00	200.
1696	1952B	New York	20.00	40.00
1696☆	1952B☆	New York☆	75.00	200.
1697	1952C	Philadelphia	20.00	40.00
1697☆	1952C☆	Philadelphia☆	75.00	200.
1698	1952D	Cleveland	20.00	40.00
1698☆	1952D☆	Cleveland☆	75.00	200.
1699	1952E	Richmond	20.00	40.00
1699☆	1952E☆	Richmond☆	75.00	200.
1700	1952F	Atlanta	20.00	40.00
1700☆	1952F☆	Atlanta☆	75.00	200.
1701	1952G	Chicago	20.00	40.00
1701☆	1952G☆	Chicago☆	75.00	200.
1702	1952H	St. Louis	20.00	40.00
1702☆	1952H☆	St. Louis☆	75.00	200.
1703	1952I	Minneapolis	20.00	40.00
1703☆	1952I☆	Minneapolis☆	75.00	200.
1704	1952J	Kansas City	20.00	40.00
1704☆	1952J☆	Kansas City☆	75.00	200.
1705	1952K	Dallas	20.00	40.00
1705☆	1952K☆	Dallas☆	75.00	200.
1706	1952L	San Francisco	20.00	40.00
1706☆	1952L☆	San Francisco☆	75.00	200.

Series 1928C Woods-Mills

KL#	Fr#	Bank	XF	CU
1710	1953D	Cleveland	750.	1000.
1712	1953F	Atlanta	350.	575.
1718	1953L	San Francisco	750.	1000.

Series 1928D Woods-Woodin

KL#	Fr#	Bank	XF	CU
1724	1954F	Atlanta	600.	1000.

Series 1934 Julian-Morgenthau

KL#	Fr#	Bank	XF	CU
1731	1955A	Boston	—	37.50
1731☆	1955A☆	Boston☆	—	150.
1732	1955B	New York	—	20.00
1732☆	1955B☆	New York☆	—	150.
1733	1955C	Philadelphia	—	20.00
1733☆	1955C☆	Philadelphia☆	—	150.
1734	1955D	Cleveland	—	20.00
1734☆	1955D☆	Cleveland☆	—	150.
1735	1955E	Richmond	—	20.00
1735☆	1955E☆	Richmond☆	—	150.
1736	1955F	Atlanta	—	20.00
1736☆	1955F☆	Atlanta☆	—	150.
1737	1955G	Chicago	—	20.00
1737☆	1955G☆	Chicago☆	—	150.
1738	1955H	St. Louis	—	20.00
1738☆	1955H☆	St. Louis☆	—	150.
1739	1955I	Minneapolis	—	20.00
1739☆	1955I☆	Minneapolis☆	—	150.
1740	1955J	Kansas City	—	20.00
1740☆	1955J☆	Kansas City☆	—	150.
1741	1955K	Dallas	—	20.00
1741☆	1955K☆	Dallas☆	—	150.
1742	1955L	San Francisco	—	20.00
1742☆	1955L☆	San Francisco☆	—	150.

Series 1934-A Julian-Morgenthau

KL#	Fr#	Bank	XF	CU
1743	1957A	Boston	—	20.00
1743☆	1957A☆	Boston☆	—	100.
1744	1957B	New York	—	35.00
1744☆	1957B☆	New York☆	—	100.
1745	1957C	Philadelphia	—	20.00
1745☆	1957C☆	Philadelphia☆	—	100.
1746	1957D	Cleveland	—	50.00
1746☆	1957D☆	Cleveland☆	—	100.
1747	1957E	Richmond	—	20.00
1747☆	1957E☆	Richmond☆	—	120.
1748	1957F	Atlanta	—	20.00
1748☆	1957F☆	Atlanta☆	—	100.
1749	1957G	Chicago	—	20.00
1749☆	1957G☆	Chicago☆	—	100.
1750	1957H	St. Louis	—	20.00
1750☆	1957H☆	St. Louis☆	—	120.
1754	1957L	San Francisco	—	20.00
1754☆	1957L☆	San Francisco☆	—	100.

Series 1934-B Julian-Vinson

KL#	Fr#	Bank	XF	CU
1755	1958A	Boston	—	40.00
1755☆	1958A☆	Boston☆	—	200.
1756	1958B	New York	—	40.00
1756☆	1958B☆	New York☆	—	200.
1757	1958C	Philadelphia	—	40.00
1757☆	1958C☆	Philadelphia☆	—	200.
1758	1958D	Cleveland	—	40.00
1758☆	1958D☆	Cleveland☆	—	200.
1759	1958E	Richmond	—	30.00
1759☆	1958E☆	Richmond☆	—	250.
1760	1958F	Atlanta	—	40.00
1760☆	1958F☆	Atlanta☆	—	250.
1761	1958G	Chicago	—	40.00
1761☆	1958G☆	Chicago☆	—	250.
1762	1958H	St. Louis	—	40.00
1762☆	1958H☆	St. Louis☆	—	200.
1763	1958I	Minneapolis	—	40.00
1763☆	1958I☆	Minneapolis☆	—	250.
1764	1958J	Kansas City	—	500.
1764☆	1958J☆	Kansas City☆	—	Rare
1766	1958L	San Francisco	—	40.00
1766☆	1958L☆	San Francisco☆	—	250.

Series 1934C Julian-Snyder

KL#	Fr#	Bank	XF	CU
1767	1959A	Boston	—	45.00
1767☆	1959A☆	Boston☆	—	125.
1768	1959B	New York	—	30.00
1768☆	1959B☆	New York☆	—	85.00
1769	1959C	Philadelphia	—	30.00
1769☆	1959C☆	Philadelphia☆	—	85.00
1770	1959D	Cleveland	—	30.00
1770☆	1959D☆	Cleveland☆	—	85.00
1771	1959E	Richmond	—	30.00
1771☆	1959E☆	Richmond☆	—	85.00
1772	1959F	Atlanta	—	30.00
1772☆	1959F☆	Atlanta☆	—	125.
1773	1959G	Chicago	—	30.00
1773☆	1959G☆	Chicago☆	—	85.00
1774	1959H	St. Louis	—	30.00
1774☆	1959H☆	St. Louis☆	—	85.00
1775	1959I	Minneapolis	—	30.00
1775☆	1959I☆	Minneapolis☆	—	125.
1776	1959J	Kansas City	—	30.00
1776☆	1959J☆	Kansas City☆	—	100.
1777	1959K	Dallas	—	30.00
1777☆	1959K☆	Dallas☆	—	125.
1778	1959L	San Francisco	—	30.00
1778☆	1959L☆	San Francisco☆	—	100.

Series 1934D Clark-Snyder

KL#	Fr#	Bank	XF	CU
1779	1960A	Boston	—	30.00
1779☆	1960A☆	Boston☆	—	110.
1780	1960B	New York	—	30.00
1780☆	1960B☆	New York☆	—	110.
1781	1960C	Philadelphia	—	30.00
1781☆	1960C☆	Philadelphia☆	—	110.
1782	1960D	Cleveland	—	30.00
1782☆	1960D☆	Cleveland☆	—	200.
1783	1960E	Richmond	—	30.00
1783☆	1960E☆	Richmond☆	—	150.
1784	1960F	Atlanta	—	350.
1784☆	1960F☆	Atlanta☆	—	750.
1785	1960G	Chicago	—	30.00
1785☆	1960G☆	Chicago☆	—	110.
1786	1960H	St. Louis	—	30.00
1786☆	1960H☆	St. Louis☆	—	110.
1787	1960I	Minneapolis	—	30.00
1787☆	1960I☆	Minneapolis☆	—	150.
1788	1960J	Kansas City	—	30.00
1788☆	1960J☆	Kansas City☆	—	150.
1789	1960K	Dallas	—	30.00
1789☆	1960K☆	Dallas☆	—	150.
1790	1960L	San Francisco	—	30.00
1790☆	1960L☆	San Francisco☆	—	150.

Series 1950 Clark-Snyder

KL#	Fr#	Bank	XF	CU
1791	1961A	Boston	—	30.00
1791☆	1961A☆	Boston☆	—	110.
1792	1961B	New York	—	30.00
1792☆	1961B☆	New York☆	—	85.00
1793	1961C	Philadelphia	—	30.00
1793☆	1961C☆	Philadelphia☆	—	110.
1794	1961D	Cleveland	—	30.00
1794☆	1961D☆	Cleveland☆	—	110.
1795	1961E	Richmond	—	30.00
1795☆	1961E☆	Richmond☆	—	100.
1796	1961F	Atlanta	—	30.00
1796☆	1961F☆	Atlanta☆	—	110.
1797	1961G	Chicago	—	30.00
1797☆	1961G☆	Chicago☆	—	85.00
1798	1961H	St. Louis	—	30.00
1798☆	1961H☆	St. Louis☆	—	150.
1799	1961I	Minneapolis	—	30.00
1799☆	1961I☆	Minneapolis☆	—	150.
1800	1961J	Kansas City	—	30.00
1800☆	1961J☆	Kansas City☆	—	85.00
1801	1961K	Dallas	—	30.00
1801☆	1961K☆	Dallas☆	—	110.

Series 1950 Clark-Snyder

KL#	Fr#	Bank	XF	CU
1802	1961L	San Francisco	—	30.00
1802☆	1961L☆	San Francisco☆	—	85.00

Series 1950A Priest-Humphrey

KL#	Fr#	Bank	XF	CU
1803	1962A	Boston	—	16.00
1803☆	1962A☆	Boston☆	—	26.00
1804	1962B	New York	—	16.00
1804☆	1962B☆	New York☆	—	24.00
1805	1962C	Philadelphia	—	16.00
1805☆	1962C☆	Philadelphia☆	—	26.00
1806	1962D	Cleveland	—	16.00
1806☆	1962D☆	Cleveland☆	—	30.00
1807	1962E	Richmond	—	16.00
1807☆	1962E☆	Richmond☆	—	26.00
1808	1962F	Atlanta	—	16.00
1808☆	1962F☆	Atlanta☆	—	24.00
1809	1962G	Chicago	—	16.00
1809☆	1962G☆	Chicago☆	—	24.00
1810	1962H	St. Louis	—	16.00
1810☆	1962H☆	St. Louis☆	—	30.00
1811	1962I	Minneapolis	—	16.00
1811☆	1962I☆	Minneapolis☆	—	40.00
1812	1962J	Kansas City	—	16.00
1812☆	1962J☆	Kansas City☆	—	35.00
1813	1962K	Dallas	—	16.00
1813☆	1962K☆	Dallas☆	—	35.00
1814	1962L	San Francisco	—	16.00
1814☆	1962L☆	San Francisco☆	—	30.00

Series 1950B Priest-Anderson

KL#	Fr#	Bank	XF	CU
1815	1963A	Boston	—	15.00
1815☆	1963A☆	Boston☆	—	30.00
1816	1963B	New York	—	15.00
1816☆	1963B☆	New York☆	—	30.00
1817	1963C	Philadelphia	—	15.00
1817☆	1963C☆	Philadelphia☆	—	30.00
1818	1963D	Cleveland	—	15.00
1818☆	1963D☆	Cleveland☆	—	30.00
1819	1963E	Richmond	—	15.00
1819☆	1963E☆	Richmond☆	—	30.00
1820	1963F	Atlanta	—	15.00
1820☆	1963F☆	Atlanta☆	—	30.00
1821	1963G	Chicago	—	15.00
1821☆	1963G☆	Chicago☆	—	30.00
1822	1963H	St. Louis	—	15.00
1822☆	1963H☆	St. Louis☆	—	30.00
1823	1963I	Minneapolis	—	15.00
1823☆	1963I☆	Minneapolis☆	—	40.00
1824	1963J	Kansas City	—	15.00
1824☆	1963J☆	Kansas City☆	—	30.00
1825	1963K	Dallas	—	15.00
1825☆	1963K☆	Dallas☆	—	30.00
1826	1963L	San Francisco	—	15.00
1826☆	1963L☆	San Francisco☆	—	30.00

Series 1950C Smith-Dillon

KL#	Fr#	Bank	XF	CU
1827	1964A	Boston	—	15.00
1827☆	1964A☆	Boston☆	—	35.00
1828	1964B	New York	—	15.00
1828☆	1964B☆	New York☆	—	30.00
1829	1964C	Philadelphia	—	15.00
1829☆	1964C☆	Philadelphia☆	—	30.00
1830	1964D	Cleveland	—	15.00
1830☆	1964D☆	Cleveland☆	—	30.00
1831	1964E	Richmond	—	15.00
1831☆	1964E☆	Richmond☆	—	30.00
1832	1964F	Atlanta	—	15.00
1832☆	1964F☆	Atlanta☆	—	30.00
1833	1964G	Chicago	—	15.00
1833☆	1964G☆	Chicago☆	—	30.00
1834	1964H	St. Louis	—	15.00
1834☆	1964H☆	St. Louis☆	—	50.00
1835	1964I	Minneapolis	—	15.00
1835☆	1964I☆	Minneapolis☆	—	50.00
1836	1964J	Kansas City	—	15.00
1836☆	1964J☆	Kansas City☆	—	30.00
1837	1964K	Dallas	—	35.00
1837☆	1964K☆	Dallas☆	—	80.00
1838	1964L	San Francisco	—	15.00
1838☆	1964L☆	San Francisco☆	—	30.00

Series 1950D Granahan-Dillon

KL#	Fr#	Bank	XF	CU
1839	1965A	Boston	—	15.00
1839☆	1965A☆	Boston☆	—	30.00
1840	1965B	New York	—	15.00
1840☆	1965B☆	New York☆	—	30.00
1841	1965C	Philadelphia	—	15.00
1841☆	1965C☆	Philadelphia☆	—	30.00
1842	1965D	Cleveland	—	15.00
1842☆	1965D☆	Cleveland☆	—	30.00
1843	1965E	Richmond	—	15.00
1843☆	1965E☆	Richmond☆	—	30.00
1844	1965F	Atlanta	—	15.00
1844☆	1965F☆	Atlanta☆	—	30.00

Series 1950-D Granahan-Dillon

KL#	Fr#	Bank	XF	CU
1845	1965G	Chicago	—	15.00
1845☆	1965G☆	Chicago☆	—	30.00
1846	1965H	St. Louis	—	15.00
1846☆	1965H☆	St. Louis☆	—	35.00
1847	1965I	Minneapolis	—	15.00
1847☆	1965I☆	Minneapolis☆	—	50.00
1848	1965J	Kansas City	—	15.00
1848☆	1965J☆	Kansas City☆	—	35.00
1849	1965K	Dallas	—	15.00
1849☆	1965K☆	Dallas☆	—	40.00
1850	1965L	San Francisco	—	15.00
1850☆	1965L☆	San Francisco☆	—	30.00

Series 1950E Granahan-Fowler

KL#	Fr#	Bank	XF	CU
1852	1966B	New York	—	20.00
1852☆	1966B☆	New York☆	—	35.00
1853	1966G	Chicago	—	25.00
1853☆	1966G☆	Chicago☆	—	50.00
1854	1966L	San Francisco	—	20.00
1854☆	1966L☆	San Francisco☆	—	50.00

Series 1963 Granahan-Dillon

KL#	Fr#	Bank	XF	CU
1855	1967A	Boston	—	14.00
1855☆	1967A☆	Boston☆	—	45.00
1856	1967B	New York	—	14.00
1856☆	1967B☆	New York☆	—	20.00
1857	1967C	Philadelphia	—	14.00
1857☆	1967C☆	Philadelphia☆	—	20.00
1858	1967D	Cleveland	—	14.00
1858☆	1967D☆	Cleveland☆	—	20.00
1859	1967F	Atlanta	—	14.00
1859☆	1967F☆	Atlanta☆	—	20.00
1860	1967G	Chicago	—	14.00
1860☆	1967G☆	Chicago☆	—	16.00
1861	1967H	St. Louis	—	14.00
1861☆	1967H☆	St. Louis☆	—	20.00
1861A	1967J	Kansas City	—	14.00
1861A☆	1967J☆	Kansas City☆	—	45.00
1862	1967K	Dallas	—	14.00
1862☆	1967K☆	Dallas☆	—	20.00
1863	1967L	San Francisco	—	14.00
1863☆	1967L☆	San Francisco☆	—	20.00

Series 1963A Granahan-Fowler

KL#	Fr#	Bank	XF	CU
1864	1968A	Boston	—	12.00
1864☆	1968A☆	Boston☆	—	17.00
1865	1968B	New York	—	12.00
1865☆	1968B☆	New York☆	—	17.00
1866	1968C	Philadelphia	—	12.00
1866☆	1968C☆	Philadelphia☆	—	17.00
1867	1968D	Cleveland	—	12.00
1867☆	1968D☆	Cleveland☆	—	17.00
1868	1968E	Richmond	—	12.00
1868☆	1968E☆	Richmond☆	—	17.00
1869	1968F	Atlanta	—	12.00
1869☆	1968F☆	Atlanta☆	—	17.00
1870	1968G	Chicago	—	12.00
1870☆	1968G☆	Chicago☆	—	17.00
1871	1968H	St. Louis	—	12.00
1871☆	1968H☆	St. Louis☆	—	17.00
1872	1968I	Minneapolis	—	12.00
1872☆	1968I☆	Minneapolis☆	—	17.00
1873	1968J	Kansas City	—	12.00
1873☆	1968J☆	Kansas City☆	—	17.00
1874	1968K	Dallas	—	12.00
1874☆	1968K☆	Dallas☆	—	17.00
1875	1968L	San Francisco	—	12.00
1875☆	1968L☆	San Francisco☆	—	17.00

Series 1969 Elston-Kennedy

KL#	Fr#	Bank	XF	CU
1876	1969A	Boston	—	10.00
1876☆	1969A☆	Boston☆	—	20.00
1877	1969B	New York	—	10.00
1877☆	1969B☆	New York☆	—	20.00
1878	1969C	Philadelphia	—	10.00
1878☆	1969C☆	Philadelphia☆	—	20.00
1879	1969D	Cleveland	—	10.00
1879☆	1969D☆	Cleveland☆	—	20.00
1880	1969E	Richmond	—	10.00
1880☆	1969E☆	Richmond☆	—	20.00
1881	1969F	Atlanta	—	10.00
1881☆	1969F☆	Atlanta☆	—	20.00
1882	1969G	Chicago	—	10.00
1882☆	1969G☆	Chicago☆	—	20.00
1883	1969H	St. Louis	—	10.00
1883☆	1969H☆	St. Louis☆	—	20.00
1884	1969I	Minneapolis	—	10.00
1884☆	1969I☆	Minneapolis☆	—	20.00
1885	1969J	Kansas City	—	10.00
1885☆	1969J☆	Kansas City☆	—	20.00
1886	1969K	Dallas	—	10.00
1886☆	1969K☆	Dallas☆	—	20.00
1887	1969L	San Francisco	—	10.00
1887☆	1969L☆	San Francisco☆	—	20.00

Series 1969A Kabis-Connally

KL#	Fr#	Bank	XF	CU
1888	1970A	Boston	—	12.00
1888☆	1970A☆	Boston☆	—	30.00
1889	1970B	New York	—	12.00
1889☆	1970B☆	New York☆	—	25.00
1890	1970C	Philadelphia	—	12.00
1890☆	1970C☆	Philadelphia☆	—	25.00
1891	1970D	Cleveland	—	12.00
1891☆	1970D☆	Cleveland☆	—	35.00
1892	1970E	Richmond	—	12.00
1892☆	1970E☆	Richmond☆	—	30.00
1893	1970F	Atlanta	—	12.00
1893☆	1970F☆	Atlanta☆	—	35.00
1894	1970G	Chicago	—	12.00
1894☆	1970G☆	Chicago☆	—	25.00
1895	1970H	St. Louis	—	12.00
1895☆	1970H☆	St. Louis☆	—	35.00
1896	1970I	Minneapolis	—	12.00
1896☆	1970I☆	Minneapolis☆	—	35.00
1897	1970J	Kansas City	—	12.00
1897☆	1970J☆	Kansas City☆	—	35.00
1898	1970K	Dallas	—	12.00
1898☆	1970K☆	Dallas☆	—	35.00
1899	1970L	San Francisco	—	12.00
1899☆	1970L☆	San Francisco☆	—	25.00

Series 1969B Banuelos-Connally

KL#	Fr#	Bank	XF	CU
1900	1971A	Boston	—	20.00
1900☆	1971A☆	Boston☆	—	Not issued
1901	1971B	New York	—	14.00
1901☆	1971B☆	New York☆	—	50.00
1902	1971C	Philadelphia	—	20.00
1902☆	1971C☆	Philadelphia☆	—	Not issued
1903	1971D	Cleveland	—	20.00
1903☆	1971D☆	Cleveland☆	—	Not issued
1904	1971E	Richmond	—	20.00
1904☆	1971E☆	Richmond☆	—	50.00
1905	1971F	Atlanta	—	20.00
1905☆	1971F☆	Atlanta☆	—	50.00
1906	1971G	Chicago	—	18.00
1906☆	1971G☆	Chicago☆	—	50.00
1907	1971H	St. Louis	—	20.00
1907☆	1971H☆	St. Louis☆	—	Not issued
1908	1971I	Minneapolis	—	20.00
1908☆	1971I☆	Minneapolis☆	—	Not issued
1909	1971J	Kansas City	—	20.00
1909☆	1971J☆	Kansas City☆	—	50.00
1910	1971K	Dallas	—	20.00
1910☆	1971K☆	Dallas☆	—	Not issued
1911	1971L	San Francisco	—	20.00
1911☆	1971L☆	San Francisco☆	—	50.00

Series 1969C Banuelos-Shultz

KL#	Fr#	Bank	XF	CU
1912	1972A	Boston	—	10.00
1912☆	1972A☆	Boston☆	—	25.00
1913	1972B	New York	—	10.00
1913☆	1972B☆	New York☆	—	25.00
1914	1972C	Philadelphia	—	10.00
1914☆	1972C☆	Philadelphia☆	—	25.00
1915	1972D	Cleveland	—	10.00
1915☆	1972D☆	Cleveland☆	—	40.00
1916	1972E	Richmond	—	10.00
1916☆	1972E☆	Richmond☆	—	35.00
1917	1972F	Atlanta	—	10.00
1917☆	1972F☆	Atlanta☆	—	25.00
1918	1972G	Chicago	—	10.00
1918☆	1972G☆	Chicago☆	—	Not issued
1919	1972H	St. Louis	—	10.00
1919☆	1972H☆	St. Louis☆	—	25.00
1920	1972I	Minneapolis	—	10.00
1920☆	1972I☆	Minneapolis☆	—	Not issued
1921	1972J	Kansas City	—	10.00
1921☆	1972J☆	Kansas City☆	—	25.00
1922	1972K	Dallas	—	10.00
1922☆	1972K☆	Dallas☆	—	25.00
1923	1972L	San Francisco	—	10.00
1923☆	1972L☆	San Francisco☆	—	25.00

Series 1974 Neff-Simon

KL#	Fr#	Bank	XF	CU
1924	1973A	Boston	—	10.00
1924☆	1973A☆	Boston☆	—	20.00
1925	1973B	New York	—	10.00
1925☆	1973B☆	New York☆	—	15.00
1926	1973C	Philadelphia	—	10.00
1926☆	1973C☆	Philadelphia☆	—	15.00
1927	1973D	Cleveland	—	10.00
1927☆	1973D☆	Cleveland☆	—	20.00
1928	1973E	Richmond	—	10.00
1928☆	1973E☆	Richmond☆	—	20.00
1929	1973F	Atlanta	—	10.00
1929☆	1973F☆	Atlanta☆	—	15.00
1930	1973G	Chicago	—	10.00
1930☆	1973G☆	Chicago☆	—	15.00
1931	1973H	St. Louis	—	10.00
1931☆	1973H☆	St. Louis☆	—	25.00
1932	1973I	Minneapolis	—	10.00
1932☆	1973I☆	Minneapolis☆	—	15.00
1933	1973J	Kansas City	—	10.00
1933☆	1973J☆	Kansas City☆	—	15.00
1934	1973K	Dallas	—	10.00
1934☆	1973K☆	Dallas☆	—	20.00
1935	1973L	San Francisco	—	10.00
1935☆	1973L☆	San Francisco☆	—	15.00

Series 1977 Morton-Blumenthal

KL#	Fr#	Bank	XF	CU
1936	1974A	Boston	—	10.00
1936☆	1974A☆	Boston☆	—	25.00
1937	1974B	New York	—	10.00
1937☆	1974B☆	New York☆	—	15.00
1938	1974C	Philadelphia	—	10.00
1938☆	1974C☆	Philadelphia☆	—	15.00
1939	1974D	Cleveland	—	10.00
1939☆	1974D☆	Cleveland☆	—	20.00
1940	1974E	Richmond	—	10.00
1940☆	1974E☆	Richmond☆	—	20.00
1941	1974F	Atlanta	—	10.00
1941☆	1974F☆	Atlanta☆	—	20.00
1942	1974G	Chicago	—	10.00
1942☆	1974G☆	Chicago☆	—	20.00
1943	1974H	St. Louis	—	10.00
1943☆	1974H☆	St. Louis☆	—	30.00
1944	1974I	Minneapolis	—	10.00
1944☆	1974I☆	Minneapolis☆	—	Not issued
1945	1974J	Kansas City	—	10.00
1945☆	1974J☆	Kansas City☆	—	25.00
1946	1974K	Dallas	—	10.00
1946☆	1974K☆	Dallas☆	—	20.00
1947	1974L	San Francisco	—	10.00
1947☆	1974L☆	San Francisco☆	—	20.00

Series 1977A Morton-Miller

KL#	Fr#	Bank	XF	CU
1948	1975A	Boston	—	10.00
1948☆	1975A☆	Boston☆	—	25.00
1949	1975B	New York	—	10.00
1949☆	1975B☆	New York☆	—	15.00
1950	1975C	Philadelphia	—	10.00
1950☆	1975C☆	Philadelphia☆	—	15.00
1951	1975D	Cleveland	—	10.00
1951☆	1975D☆	Cleveland☆	—	25.00
1952	1975E	Richmond	—	10.00
1952☆	1975E☆	Richmond☆	—	25.00
1953	1975F	Atlanta	—	10.00
1953☆	1975F☆	Atlanta☆	—	15.00
1954	1975G	Chicago	—	10.00
1954☆	1975G☆	Chicago☆	—	15.00
1955	1975H	St. Louis	—	10.00
1955☆	1975H☆	St. Louis☆	—	25.00
1956	1975I	Minneapolis	—	10.00
1956☆	1975I☆	Minneapolis☆	—	25.00
1957	1975J	Kansas City	—	10.00
1957☆	1975J☆	Kansas City☆	—	25.00
1958	1975K	Dallas	—	10.00
1958☆	1975K☆	Dallas☆	—	20.00
1959	1975L	San Francisco	—	10.00
1959☆	1975L☆	San Francisco☆	—	15.00

Series 1981 Buchanan-Regan

KL#	Fr#	Bank	XF	CU
3512	1976A	Boston	—	10.00
3512☆	1976A☆	Boston☆	—	Not issued
3513	1976B	New York	—	10.00
3513☆	1976B☆	New York☆	—	20.00
3514	1976C	Philadelphia	—	10.00
3514☆	1976C☆	Philadelphia☆	—	20.00
3515	1976D	Cleveland	—	10.00
3515☆	1976D☆	Cleveland☆	—	20.00
3516	1976E	Richmond	—	10.00
3516☆	1976E☆	Richmond☆	—	20.00
3517	1976F	Atlanta	—	10.00
3517☆	1976F☆	Atlanta☆	—	20.00
3518	1976G	Chicago	—	10.00
3518☆	1976G☆	Chicago☆	—	20.00
3519	1976H	St. Louis	—	10.00
3519☆	1976H☆	St. Louis☆	—	20.00
3520	1976I	Minneapolis	—	10.00
3520☆	1976I☆	Minneapolis☆	—	20.00
3521	1976J	Kansas City	—	10.00
3521☆	1976J☆	Kansas City☆	—	20.00
3522	1976K	Dallas	—	10.00
3522☆	1976K☆	Dallas☆	—	20.00
3523	1976L	San Francisco	—	10.00
3523☆	1976L☆	San Francisco☆	—	20.00

Series 1981A Ortega-Regan

KL#	Fr#	Bank	XF	CU
3612	1977A	Boston	—	10.00
3612☆	1977A☆	Boston☆	—	Not issued
3613	1977B	New York	—	10.00
3613☆	1977B☆	New York☆	—	25.00
3614	1977C	Philadelphia	—	10.00
3614☆	1977C☆	Philadelphia☆	—	Not issued
3615	1977D	Cleveland	—	10.00
3615☆	1977D☆	Cleveland☆	—	Not issued
3616	1977E	Richmond	—	10.00
3616☆	1977E☆	Richmond☆	—	20.00
3617	1977F	Atlanta	—	10.00
3617☆	1977F☆	Atlanta☆	—	Not issued

Series 1981-A Ortega-Regan

KL#	Fr#	Bank	XF	CU
3618	1977G	Chicago	—	10.00
3618☆	1977G☆	Chicago☆	—	Not issued
3619	1977H	St. Louis	—	10.00
3619☆	1977H☆	St. Louis☆	—	Not issued
3620	1977I	Minneapolis	—	10.00
3620☆	1977I☆	Minneapolis☆	—	Not issued
3621	1977J	Kansas City	—	10.00
3621☆	1977J☆	Kansas City☆	—	Not issued
3622	1977K	Dallas	—	10.00
3622☆	1977K☆	Dallas☆	—	20.00
3623	1977L	San Francisco	—	10.00
3623☆	1977L☆	San Francisco☆	—	20.00

Series 1985 Ortega-Baker

KL#	Fr#	Bank	XF	CU
3712	1978A	Boston	—	10.00
3712☆	1978A☆	Boston☆	—	Not issued
3713	1978B	New York	—	10.00
3713☆	1978B☆	New York☆	—	20.00
3714	1978C	Philadelphia	—	10.00
3714☆	1978C☆	Philadelphia☆	—	25.00
3715	1978D	Cleveland	—	10.00
3715☆	1978D☆	Cleveland☆	—	Not issued
3716	1978E	Richmond	—	10.00
3716☆	1978E☆	Richmond☆	—	20.00
3717	1978F	Atlanta	—	10.00
3717☆	1978F☆	Atlanta☆	—	20.00
3718	1978G	Chicago	—	10.00
3718☆	1978G☆	Chicago☆	—	20.00
3719	1978H	St. Louis	—	10.00
3719☆	1978H☆	St. Louis☆	—	Not issued
3720	1978I	Minneapolis	—	10.00
3720☆	1978I☆	Minneapolis☆	—	Not issued
3721	1978J	Kansas City	—	10.00
3721☆	1978J☆	Kansas City☆	—	Not issued
3722	1978K	Dallas	—	10.00
3722☆	1978K☆	Dallas☆	—	25.00
3723	1978L	San Francisco	—	10.00
3723☆	1978L☆	San Francisco☆	—	20.00

Series 1988 Ortega-Brady

KL#	Fr#	Bank	XF	CU
3784	1979A	Boston	—	10.00
3784☆	1979A☆	Boston☆	—	20.00
3785	1979B	New York	—	10.00
3785☆	1979B☆	New York☆	—	15.00
3786	1979C	Philadelphia	—	10.00
3786☆	1979C☆	Philadelphia☆	—	Not issued
3787	1979D	Cleveland	—	10.00
3787☆	1979D☆	Cleveland☆	—	Not issued
3788	1979E	Richmond	—	10.00
3788☆	1979E☆	Richmond☆	—	Not issued
3789	1979F	Atlanta	—	10.00
3789☆	1979F☆	Atlanta☆	—	15.00
3790	1979G	Chicago	—	10.00
3790☆	1979G☆	Chicago☆	—	Not issued
3791	1979H	St. Louis	—	10.00
3791☆	1979H☆	St. Louis☆	—	Not issued
3792	1979I	Minneapolis	—	10.00
3792☆	1979I☆	Minneapolis☆	—	Not issued
3793	1979J	Kansas City	—	10.00
3793☆	1979J☆	Kansas City☆	—	Not issued
3794	1979K	Dallas	—	10.00
3794☆	1979K☆	Dallas☆	—	Not issued
3795	1979L	San Francisco	—	10.00
3795☆	1979L☆	San Francisco☆	—	Not issued

Series 1988A Villalpando-Brady

KL#	Fr#	Bank	XF	CU
3856	—	Boston	—	10.00
3856☆	—	Boston☆	—	20.00
3857	—	New York	—	10.00
3857☆	—	New York☆	—	20.00
3858	—	Philadelphia	—	10.00
3858☆	—	Philadelphia☆	—	Not issued
3859	—	Cleveland	—	10.00
3859☆	—	Cleveland☆	—	20.00
3860	—	Richmond	—	10.00
3860☆	—	Richmond☆	—	20.00
3861	—	Atlanta	—	10.00
3861☆	—	Atlanta☆	—	20.00
3862	—	Chicago	—	10.00
3862☆	—	Chicago☆	—	20.00
3863	—	St. Louis	—	10.00
3863☆	—	St. Louis☆	—	20.00
3864	—	Minneapolis	—	10.00
3864☆	—	Minneapolis☆	—	20.00
3865	—	Kansas City	—	10.00
3865☆	—	Kansas City☆	—	Not issued
3866	—	Dallas	—	10.00
3866☆	—	Dallas☆	—	Not issued
3867	—	San Francisco	—	10.00
3867☆	—	San Francisco☆	—	20.00

Series 1993 Withrow-Bentsen

KL#	Fr#	Bank	XF	CU
4024	—	Boston	—	10.00
4024☆	—	Boston☆	—	Not issued
4025	—	New York	—	10.00
4025☆	—	New York☆	—	20.00

Series 1993 Withrow-Bentsen

KL#	Fr#	Bank	XF	CU
4026	—	Philadelphia	—	10.00
4026☆	—	Philadelphia☆	—	Not issued
4027	—	Cleveland	—	Not issued
4027☆	—	Cleveland☆	—	Not issued
4028	—	Richmond	—	10.00
4028☆	—	Richmond☆	—	15.00
4029	—	Atlanta	—	10.00
4029☆	—	Atlanta☆	—	Not issued
4030	—	Chicago	—	10.00
4030☆	—	Chicago☆	—	20.00
4031	—	St. Louis	—	10.00
4031☆	—	St. Louis☆	—	20.00
4032	—	Minneapolis	—	10.00
4032☆	—	Minneapolis☆	—	Not issued
4033	—	Kansas City	—	10.00
4033☆	—	Kansas City☆	—	Not issued
4034	—	Dallas	—	10.00
4034☆	—	Dallas☆	—	Not issued
4035	—	San Francisco	—	10.00
4035☆	—	San Francisco☆	—	20.00

Series 1995 Withrow-Rubin

KL#	Fr#	Bank	XF	CU
4096	—	Boston	—	10.00
4096☆	—	Boston☆	—	25.00
4097	—	New York	—	10.00
4097☆	—	New York☆	—	20.00
4098	—	Philadelphia	—	10.00
4098☆	—	Philadelphia☆	—	Not issued
4099	—	Cleveland	—	10.00
4099☆	—	Cleveland☆	—	20.00
4100	—	Richmond	—	10.00
4100☆	—	Richmond☆	—	Not issued
4101	—	Atlanta	—	10.00
4101☆	—	Atlanta☆	—	Not issued
4102	—	Chicago	—	10.00
4102☆	—	Chicago☆	—	20.00
4103	—	St. Louis	—	10.00
4103☆	—	St. Louis☆	—	Not issued
4104	—	Minneapolis	—	10.00
4104☆	—	Minneapolis☆	—	Not issued
4105	—	Kansas City	—	10.00
4105☆	—	Kansas City☆	—	Not issued
4106	—	Dallas	—	10.00
4106☆	—	Dallas☆	—	Not issued
4107	—	San Francisco	—	10.00
4107☆	—	San Francisco☆	—	Not issued

Hawaii Emergency Federal Reserve Notes

Abraham Lincoln

KL#	Fr#	Series	Signatures	Fine	VF	CU
1960	2301	1934	Julian-Morgenthau	40.00	50.00	200.
1960☆	2301☆	1934☆	Julian-Morgenthau	500.	750.	3000.
1961	2302	1934A	Julian-Morgenthau	40.00	50.00	185.
1961☆	2302☆	1934A☆	Julian-Morgenthau	1500.	2000.	6000.

North Africa Emergency Silver Certificates

Abraham Lincoln

KL#	Fr#	Series	Signatures	Fine	VF	CU
1962	2307	1934A	Julian-Morgenthau	18.50	30.00	100.
1962☆	2307☆	1934A☆	Julian-Morgenthau	50.00	75.00	300.

Ten Dollars
Gold Certificates

Alexander Hamilton

KL#	Fr#	Series	Signatures	Fine	VF	CU
1963	2400	1928	Woods-Mellon	35.00	50.00	250.
1963☆	2400☆	1928☆	Woods-Mellon	150.	200.	750.

Silver Certificates

Alexander Hamilton

KL#	Fr#	Series	Signatures	Fine	VF	CU
1964	1700	1933	Julian-Woodin	1200.	2500.	6500.
1964☆	1700☆	1933☆	Julian-Woodin	—	—	—
1965	1700A	1933A	Julian-Morgenthau	—	—	Unique
1966	1701	1934	Julian-Morgenthau	20.00	50.00
1966☆	1701☆	1934☆	Julian-Morgenthau	—	50.00	350.
1967	1702	1934A	Julian-Morgenthau	—	22.00	80.00
1967☆	1702☆	1934A☆	Julian-Morgenthau	—	65.00	450.
1968	1703	1934B	Julian-Vinson	50.00	75.00	1250.
1968☆	1703☆	1934B☆	Julian-Vinson	—	700.	2400.
1969	1704	1934C	Julian-Snyder	25.00	30.00	80.00
1969☆	1704☆	1934C☆	Julian-Snyder	40.00	55.00	120.
1970	1705	1934D	Clark-Snyder	25.00	30.00	90.00
1970☆	1705☆	1934D☆	Clark-Snyder	50.00	95.00	500.
1971	1706	1953	Priest-Humphrey	25.00	35.00	100.
1971☆	1706☆	1953☆	Priest-Humphrey	18.00	25.00	200.
1972	1707	1953A	Priest-Anderson	20.00	30.00	125.
1972☆	1707☆	1953A☆	Priest-Anderson	—	40.00	225.
1973	1708	1953B	Smith-Dillon	12.50	25.00	75.00

Federal Reserve Bank Notes

Alexander Hamilton

KL#	Fr#	Series	District	Fine	VF	CU
1974	1860A	1929	Boston	15.00	20.00	60.00
1974☆	1860A☆	1929☆	Boston☆	250.	400.	1500.
1975	1860B	1929	New York	15.00	18.00	45.00
1975☆	1860B☆	1929☆	New York☆	90.00	150.	1000.
1976	1860C	1929	Philadelphia	15.00	20.00	55.00
1976☆	1860C☆	1929☆	Philadelphia☆	100.	200.	1250.
1977	1860D	1929	Cleveland	15.00	20.00	60.00
1977☆	1860D☆	1929☆	Cleveland☆	110.	250.	1250.
1978	1860E	1929	Richmond	15.00	22.00	85.00
1978☆	1860E☆	1929☆	Richmond☆	110.	250.	1500.
1979	1860F	1929	Atlanta	15.00	22.00	65.00
1979☆	1860F☆	1929☆	Atlanta☆	200.	400.	1500.
1980	1860G	1929	Chicago	15.00	18.00	45.00
1980☆	1860G☆	1929☆	Chicago☆	100.	250.	1500.
1981	1860H	1929	St. Louis	15.00	18.00	55.00
1981☆	1860H☆	1929☆	St. Louis☆	100.	200.	1000.
1982	1860I	1929	Minneapolis	15.00	20.00	70.00
1982☆	1860I☆	1929☆	Minneapolis☆	100.	250.	1500.
1983	1860J	1929	Kansas City	15.00	20.00	60.00
1983☆	1860J☆	1929☆	Kansas City☆	85.00	175.	750.
1984	1860K	1929	Dallas	100.	150.	1000.
1984☆	1860K☆	1929☆	Dallas☆	550.	1000.	2500.
1985	1860L	1929	San Francisco	15.00	22.00	90.00
1985☆	1860L☆	1929☆	San Francisco☆	100.	200.	1200.

Federal Reserve Notes

Alexander Hamilton

Series 1928 Tate-Mellon

KL#	Fr#	Bank	XF	CU
1986	2000A	Boston	60.00	150.
1986☆	2000A☆	Boston☆	150.	350.
1987	2000B	New York	60.00	150.
1987☆	2000B☆	New York☆	150.	350.
1988	2000C	Philadelphia	60.00	150.
1988☆	2000C☆	Philadelphia☆	150.	350.
1989	2000D	Cleveland	60.00	150.
1989☆	2000D☆	Cleveland☆	150.	350.
1990	2000E	Richmond	60.00	150.
1990☆	2000E☆	Richmond☆	150.	350.
1991	2000F	Atlanta	60.00	150.
1991☆	2000F☆	Atlanta☆	150.	375.
1992	2000G	Chicago	60.00	100.
1992☆	2000G☆	Chicago☆	150.	325.
1993	2000H	St. Louis	60.00	150.
1993☆	2000H☆	St. Louis☆	150.	350.
1994	2000I	Minneapolis	65.00	155.
1994☆	2000I☆	Minneapolis☆	160.	375.
1995	2000J	Kansas City	60.00	150.
1995☆	2000J☆	Kansas City☆	150.	375.
1996	2000K	Dallas	65.00	150.
1996☆	2000K☆	Dallas☆	150.	350.
1997	2000L	San Francisco	60.00	160.
1997☆	2000L☆	San Francisco☆	150.	475.

Series 1928A Woods-Mellon

KL#	Fr#	Bank	XF	CU
1998	2001A	Boston	60.00	190.
1998☆	2001A☆	Boston☆	250.	500.
1999	2001B	New York	60.00	190.
1999☆	2001B☆	New York☆	250.	500.
2000	2001C	Philadelphia	60.00	190.
2000☆	2001C☆	Philadelphia☆	350.	500.
2001	2001D	Cleveland	60.00	190.
2001☆	2001D☆	Cleveland☆	250.	500.
2002	2001E	Richmond	100.	250.
2002☆	2001E☆	Richmond☆	350.	500.

SMALL SIZE $10 NOTES

Series 1928-A Woods-Mellon

KL#	Fr#	Bank	XF	CU
2003	2001F	Atlanta	60.00	190.
2003☆	2001F☆	Atlanta☆	350.	500.
2004	2001G	Chicago	60.00	190.
2004☆	2001G☆	Chicago☆	350.	500.
2005	2001H	St. Louis	70.00	190.
2005☆	2001H☆	St. Louis☆	375.	500.
2006	2001J	Minneapolis	125.	300.
2006☆	2001J☆	Minneapolis☆	450.	650.
2007	2001J	Kansas City	75.00	250.
2007☆	2001J☆	Kansas City☆	350.	450.
2008	2001K	Dallas	75.00	200.
2008☆	2001K☆	Dallas☆	—	Not issued
2009	2001L	San Francisco	90.00	200.
2009☆	2001L☆	San Francisco☆	350.	400.

Series 1928B Woods-Mellon

KL#	Fr#	Bank	XF	CU
2010	2002A	Boston	30.00	75.00
2010☆	2002A☆	Boston☆	125.	450.
2011	2002B	New York	25.00	55.00
2011☆	2002B☆	New York☆	200.	450.
2012	2002C	Philadelphia	25.00	65.00
2012☆	2002C☆	Philadelphia☆	200.	450.
2013	2002D	Cleveland	25.00	65.00
2013☆	2002D☆	Cleveland☆	150.	300.
2014	2002E	Richmond	25.00	75.00
2014☆	2002E☆	Richmond☆	175.	450.
2015	2002F	Atlanta	25.00	75.00
2015☆	2002F☆	Atlanta☆	200.	450.
2016	2002G	Chicago	25.00	55.00
2016☆	2002G☆	Chicago☆	150.	300.
2017	2002H	St. Louis	25.00	50.00
2017☆	2002H☆	St. Louis☆	200.	450.
2018	2002I	Minneapolis	25.00	75.00
2018☆	2002I☆	Minneapolis☆	200.	450.
2019	2002J	Kansas City	25.00	50.00
2019☆	2002J☆	Kansas City☆	200.	450.
2020	2002K	Dallas	25.00	75.00
2020☆	2002K☆	Dallas☆	—	Not issued
2021	2002L	San Francisco	25.00	60.00
2021☆	2002L☆	San Francisco☆	175.	450.

Series 1928C Woods-Mills

KL#	Fr#	Bank	XF	CU
2022	2003B	New York	60.00	150.
2022☆	2003B☆	New York☆	—	Not issued
2023	2003D	Cleveland	150.	300.
2023☆	2003D☆	Cleveland☆	2000.	6000.
2024	2003E	Richmond	500.	1000.
2024☆	2003E☆	Richmond☆	—	Not issued
2025	2003F	Atlanta	—	Not issued
2026	2003G	Chicago	—	Not issued

Series 1934 Julian-Morgenthau

KL#	Fr#	Bank	XF	CU
2027	2004A	Boston	18.00	25.00
2027☆	2004A☆	Boston☆	75.00	150.
2028	2004B	New York	18.00	25.00
2028☆	2004B☆	New York☆	75.00	150.
2029	2004C	Philadelphia	18.00	25.00
2029☆	2004C☆	Philadelphia☆	60.00	150.
2030	2004D	Cleveland	18.00	25.00
2030☆	2004D☆	Cleveland☆	75.00	150.
2031	2004E	Richmond	18.00	25.00
2031☆	2004E☆	Richmond☆	100.	200.
2032	2004F	Atlanta	18.00	25.00
2032☆	2004F☆	Atlanta☆	75.00	150.
2033	2004G	Chicago	18.00	25.00
2033☆	2004G☆	Chicago☆	60.00	150.
2034	2004H	St. Louis	18.00	25.00
2034☆	2004H☆	St. Louis☆	75.00	150.
2035	2004I	Minneapolis	18.00	25.00
2035☆	2004I☆	Minneapolis☆	125.	200.
2036	2004J	Kansas City	18.00	25.00
2036☆	2004J☆	Kansas City☆	75.00	150.
2037	2004K	Dallas	18.00	25.00
2037☆	2004K☆	Dallas☆	100.	200.
2038	2004L	San Francisco	18.00	25.00
2038☆	2004L☆	San Francisco☆	75.00	150.

Series 1934A Julian-Morgenthau

KL#	Fr#	Bank	XF	CU
2039	2006A	Boston	15.00	25.00
2039☆	2006A☆	Boston☆	50.00	100.
2040	2006B	New York	15.00	25.00
2040☆	2006B☆	New York☆	50.00	100.
2041	2006C	Philadelphia	15.00	25.00
2041☆	2006C☆	Philadelphia☆	50.00	100.
2042	2006D	Cleveland	15.00	25.00
2042☆	2006D☆	Cleveland☆	50.00	100.
2043	2006E	Richmond	15.00	25.00
2043☆	2006E☆	Richmond☆	50.00	100.
2044	2006F	Atlanta	15.00	25.00
2044☆	2006F☆	Atlanta☆	40.00	80.00
2045	2006G	Chicago	15.00	25.00
2045☆	2006G☆	Chicago☆	50.00	100.
2046	2006H	St. Louis	15.00	25.00
2046☆	2006H☆	St. Louis☆	50.00	100.

Series 1934-A Julian-Morgenthau

KL#	Fr#	Bank	XF	CU
2047	2006I	Minneapolis	15.00	25.00
2047☆	2006I☆	Minneapolis☆	50.00	100.
2048	2006J	Kansas City	15.00	25.00
2048☆	2006J☆	Kansas City☆	50.00	100.
2049	2006K	Dallas	15.00	25.00
2049☆	2006K☆	Dallas☆	50.00	100.
2050	2006L	San Francisco	15.00	25.00
2050☆	2006L☆	San Francisco☆	50.00	100.

Series 1934B Julian-Vinson

KL#	Fr#	Bank	XF	CU
2051	2007A	Boston	25.00	35.00
2051☆	2007A☆	Boston☆	60.00	125.
2052	2007B	New York	15.00	25.00
2052☆	2007B☆	New York☆	75.00	175.
2053	2007C	Philadelphia	15.00	35.00
2053☆	2007C☆	Philadelphia☆	75.00	175.
2054	2007D	Cleveland	18.00	35.00
2054☆	2007D☆	Cleveland☆	65.00	150.
2055	2007E	Richmond	15.00	25.00
2055☆	2007E☆	Richmond☆	65.00	150.
2056	2007F	Atlanta	15.00	25.00
2056☆	2007F☆	Atlanta☆	65.00	150.
2057	2007G	Chicago	15.00	25.00
2057☆	2007G☆	Chicago☆	50.00	100.
2058	2007H	St. Louis	18.00	30.00
2058☆	2007H☆	St. Louis☆	50.00	100.
2059	2007I	Minneapolis	15.00	25.00
2059☆	2007I☆	Minneapolis☆	50.00	150.
2060	2007J	Kansas City	15.00	25.00
2060☆	2007J☆	Kansas City☆	50.00	150.
2061	2007K	Dallas	15.00	25.00
2061☆	2007K☆	Dallas☆	50.00	150.
2062	2007L	San Francisco	15.00	25.00
2062☆	2007L☆	San Francisco☆	55.00	150.

Series 1934-C Julian-Snyder

KL#	Fr#	Bank	XF	CU
2063	2008A	Boston	15.00	20.00
2063☆	2008A☆	Boston☆	45.00	125.
2064	2008B	New York	15.00	20.00
2064☆	2008B☆	New York☆	40.00	125.
2065	2008C	Philadelphia	15.00	20.00
2065☆	2008C☆	Philadelphia☆	40.00	125.
2066	2008D	Cleveland	15.00	20.00
2066☆	2008D☆	Cleveland☆	45.00	125.
2067	2008E	Richmond	15.00	20.00
2067☆	2008E☆	Richmond☆	40.00	125.
2068	2008F	Atlanta	15.00	20.00
2068☆	2008F☆	Atlanta☆	40.00	125.
2069	2008G	Chicago	15.00	20.00
2069☆	2008G☆	Chicago☆	35.00	100.
2070	2008H	St. Louis	15.00	20.00
2070☆	2008H☆	St. Louis☆	35.00	100.
2071	2008I	Minneapolis	15.00	20.00
2071☆	2008I☆	Minneapolis☆	50.00	150.
2072	2008J	Kansas City	15.00	20.00
2072☆	2008J☆	Kansas City☆	35.00	100.
2073	2008K	Dallas	15.00	20.00
2073☆	2008K☆	Dallas☆	50.00	150.
2074	2008L	San Francisco	15.00	20.00
2074☆	2008L☆	San Francisco☆	35.00	100.

Series 1934D Clark-Snyder

KL#	Fr#	Bank	XF	CU
2075	2009A	Boston	15.00	25.00
2075☆	2009A☆	Boston☆	40.00	100.
2076	2009B	New York	15.00	25.00
2076☆	2009B☆	New York☆	40.00	100.
2077	2009C	Philadelphia	15.00	25.00
2077☆	2009C☆	Philadelphia☆	40.00	100.
2078	2009D	Cleveland	15.00	25.00
2078☆	2009D☆	Cleveland☆	40.00	100.
2079	2009E	Richmond	15.00	25.00
2079☆	2009E☆	Richmond☆	50.00	150.
2080	2009F	Atlanta	15.00	25.00
2080☆	2009F☆	Atlanta☆	40.00	100.
2081	2009G	Chicago	25.00	50.00
2081☆	2009G☆	Chicago☆	45.00	125.
2082	2009H	St. Louis	25.00	50.00
2082☆	2009H☆	St. Louis☆	45.00	125.
2083	2009I	Minneapolis	25.00	50.00
2083☆	2009I☆	Minneapolis☆	45.00	125.
2084	2009J	Kansas City	25.00	50.00
2084☆	2009J☆	Kansas City☆	45.00	125.
2085	2009K	Dallas	25.00	50.00
2085☆	2009K☆	Dallas☆	65.00	175.
2086	2009L	San Francisco	25.00	50.00
2086☆	2009L☆	San Francisco☆	65.00	175.

Series 1950 Clark-Snyder

KL#	Fr#	Bank	XF	CU
2087	2010A	Boston	25.00	50.00
2087☆	2010A☆	Boston☆	50.00	150.
2088	2010B	New York	25.00	50.00
2088☆	2010B☆	New York☆	50.00	150.
2089	2010C	Philadelphia	25.00	50.00
2089☆	2010C☆	Philadelphia☆	50.00	150.
2090	2010D	Cleveland	25.00	50.00

Series 1950 Clark-Snyder

KL#	Fr#	Bank	XF	CU
2090☆	2010D☆	Cleveland☆	50.00	150.
2091	2010E	Richmond	25.00	50.00
2091☆	2010E☆	Richmond☆	50.00	150.
2092	2010F	Atlanta	25.00	50.00
2092☆	2010F☆	Atlanta☆	50.00	150.
2093	2010G	Chicago	25.00	50.00
2093☆	2010G☆	Chicago☆	50.00	150.
2094	2010H	St. Louis	25.00	50.00
2094☆	2010H☆	St. Louis☆	75.00	175.
2095	2010I	Minneapolis	25.00	50.00
2095☆	2010I☆	Minneapolis☆	50.00	150.
2096	2010J	Kansas City	35.00	60.00
2096☆	2010J☆	Kansas City☆	50.00	150.
2097	2010K	Dallas	25.00	50.00
2097☆	2010K☆	Dallas☆	50.00	150.
2098	2010L	San Francisco	25.00	50.00
2098☆	2010L☆	San Francisco☆	50.00	150.

Series 1950A Priest-Humphrey

KL#	Fr#	Bank	XF	CU
2099	2011A	Boston	20.00	35.00
2099☆	2011A☆	Boston☆	40.00	100.
2100	2011B	New York	20.00	35.00
2100☆	2011B☆	New York☆	40.00	100.
2101	2011C	Philadelphia	20.00	35.00
2101☆	2011C☆	Philadelphia☆	40.00	100.
2102	2011D	Cleveland	20.00	35.00
2102☆	2011D☆	Cleveland☆	40.00	100.
2103	2011E	Richmond	20.00	35.00
2103☆	2011E☆	Richmond☆	40.00	100.
2104	2011F	Atlanta	20.00	35.00
2104☆	2011F☆	Atlanta☆	40.00	100.
2105	2011G	Chicago	20.00	35.00
2105☆	2011G☆	Chicago☆	40.00	100.
2106	2011H	St. Louis	20.00	35.00
2106☆	2011H☆	St. Louis☆	40.00	100.
2107	2011I	Minneapolis	20.00	35.00
2107☆	2011I☆	Minneapolis☆	40.00	100.
2108	2011J	Kansas City	20.00	35.00
2108☆	2011J☆	Kansas City☆	40.00	100.
2109	2011K	Dallas	20.00	35.00
2109☆	2011K☆	Dallas☆	40.00	100.
2110	2011L	San Francisco	20.00	35.00
2110☆	2011L☆	San Francisco☆	40.00	100.

Series 1950B Priest-Anderson

KL#	Fr#	Bank	XF	CU
2111	2012A	Boston	—	30.00
2111☆	2012A☆	Boston☆	—	60.00
2112	2012B	New York	—	30.00
2112☆	2012B☆	New York☆	—	60.00
2113	2012C	Philadelphia	—	30.00
2113☆	2012C☆	Philadelphia☆	—	60.00
2114	2012D	Cleveland	—	30.00
2114☆	2012D☆	Cleveland☆	—	60.00
2115	2012E	Richmond	—	30.00
2115☆	2012E☆	Richmond☆	—	60.00
2116	2012F	Atlanta	—	30.00
2116☆	2012F☆	Atlanta☆	—	60.00
2117	2012G	Chicago	—	30.00
2117☆	2012G☆	Chicago☆	—	60.00
2118	2012H	St. Louis	—	30.00
2118☆	2012H☆	St. Louis☆	—	60.00
2119	2012I	Minneapolis	—	30.00
2119☆	2012I☆	Minneapolis☆	—	60.00
2120	2012J	Kansas City	—	30.00
2120☆	2012J☆	Kansas City☆	—	60.00
2121	2012K	Dallas	—	30.00
2121☆	2012K☆	Dallas☆	—	60.00
2122	2012L	San Francisco	—	30.00
2122☆	2102L☆	San Francisco☆	—	60.00

Series 1950C Smith-Dillon

KL#	Fr#	Bank	XF	CU
2123	2013A	Boston	—	35.00
2123☆	2013A☆	Boston☆	—	50.00
2124	2013B	New York	—	35.00
2124☆	2013B☆	New York☆	—	50.00
2125	2013C	Philadelphia	—	35.00
2125☆	2013C☆	Philadelphia☆	—	60.00
2126	2013D	Cleveland	—	35.00
2126☆	2013D☆	Cleveland☆	—	40.00
2127	2013E	Richmond	—	35.00
2127☆	2013E☆	Richmond☆	—	40.00
2128	2013F	Atlanta	—	35.00
2128☆	2013F☆	Atlanta☆	—	40.00
2129	2013G	Chicago	—	35.00
2129☆	2013G☆	Chicago☆	—	40.00
2130	2013H	St. Louis	—	35.00
2130☆	2013H☆	St. Louis☆	—	40.00
2131	2013I	Minneapolis	—	40.00
2131☆	2013I☆	Minneapolis☆	—	40.00
2132	2013J	Kansas City	—	45.00
2132☆	2013J☆	Kansas City☆	—	60.00
2133	2013K	Dallas	—	40.00
2133☆	2013K☆	Dallas☆	—	60.00
2134	2013L	San Francisco	—	35.00
2134☆	2013L☆	San Francisco☆	—	40.00

Series 1950D Granahan-Dillon

KL#	Fr#	Bank	XF	CU
2135	2014A	Boston	—	35.00
2135☆	2014A☆	Boston☆	—	40.00
2136	2014B	New York	—	35.00
2136☆	2014B☆	New York☆	—	40.00
2137	2014C	Philadelphia	—	35.00
2137☆	2014C☆	Philadelphia☆	—	40.00
2138	2014D	Cleveland	—	35.00
2138☆	2014D☆	Cleveland☆	—	60.00
2139	2014E	Richmond	—	35.00
2139☆	2014E☆	Richmond☆	—	50.00
2140	2014F	Atlanta	—	35.00
2140☆	2014F☆	Atlanta☆	—	40.00
2141	2014G	Chicago	—	35.00
2141☆	2014G☆	Chicago☆	—	40.00
2142	2014H	St. Louis	—	40.00
2142☆	2014H☆	St. Louis☆	—	50.00
2143	2014I	Minneapolis	—	Not issued
2144	2014J	Kansas City	—	35.00
2144☆	2014J☆	Kansas City☆	—	50.00
2145	2014K	Dallas	—	35.00
2145☆	2014K☆	Dallas☆	—	50.00
2146	2014L	San Francisco	—	35.00
2146☆	2014L☆	San Francisco☆	—	40.00

Series 1950E Granahan-Fowler

KL#	Fr#	Bank	XF	CU
2147	2015B	New York	—	35.00
2147☆	2015B☆	New York☆	—	60.00
2148	2015G	Chicago	—	30.00
2148☆	2015G☆	Chicago☆	—	50.00
2149	2015L	San Francisco	—	35.00
2149☆	2015L☆	San Francisco☆	—	80.00

Series 1963 Granahan-Dillon

KL#	Fr#	Bank	XF	CU
2150	2016A	Boston	—	20.00
2150☆	2016A☆	Boston☆	—	30.00
2151	2016B	New York	—	20.00
2151☆	2016B☆	New York☆	—	30.00
2152	2016C	Philadelphia	—	20.00
2152☆	2016C☆	Philadelphia☆	—	30.00
2153	2016D	Cleveland	—	20.00
2153☆	2016D☆	Cleveland☆	—	30.00
2154	2016E	Richmond	—	20.00
2154☆	2016E☆	Richmond☆	—	30.00
2155	2016F	Atlanta	—	20.00
2155☆	2016F☆	Atlanta☆	—	30.00
2156	2016G	Chicago	—	20.00
2156☆	2016G☆	Chicago☆	—	30.00
2157	2016H	St. Louis	—	20.00
2157☆	2016H☆	St. Louis☆	—	30.00
2159	2016J	Kansas City	—	20.00
2159☆	2016J☆	Kansas City☆	—	30.00
2160	2016K	Dallas	—	20.00
2160☆	2016K☆	Dallas☆	—	30.00
2161	2016L	San Francisco	—	20.00
2161☆	2016L☆	San Francisco☆	—	30.00

Series 1963A Granahan-Fowler

KL#	Fr#	Bank	XF	CU
2162	2017A	Boston	—	20.00
2162☆	2017A☆	Boston☆	—	30.00
2163	2017B	New York	—	20.00
2163☆	2017B☆	New York☆	—	30.00
2164	2017C	Philadelphia	—	20.00
2164☆	2017C☆	Philadelphia☆	—	30.00
2165	2017D	Cleveland	—	20.00
2165☆	2017D☆	Cleveland☆	—	30.00
2166	2017E	Richmond	—	20.00
2166☆	2017E☆	Richmond☆	—	30.00
2167	2017F	Atlanta	—	20.00
2167☆	2017F☆	Atlanta☆	—	30.00
2168	2017G	Chicago	—	20.00
2168☆	2017G☆	Chicago☆	—	30.00
2169	2017H	St. Louis	—	20.00
2169☆	2017H☆	St. Louis☆	—	30.00
2170	2017I	Minneapolis	—	20.00
2170☆	2017I☆	Minneapolis☆	—	30.00
2171	2017J	Kansas City	—	20.00
2171☆	2017J☆	Kansas City☆	—	30.00
2172	2017K	Dallas	—	20.00
2172☆	2017K☆	Dallas☆	—	30.00
2173	2017L	San Francisco	—	20.00
2173☆	2017L☆	San Francisco☆	—	30.00

Series 1969 Elston-Kennedy

KL#	Fr#	Bank	XF	CU
2174	2018A	Boston	—	20.00
2174☆	2018A☆	Boston☆	—	30.00
2175	2018B	New York	—	20.00
2175☆	2018B☆	New York☆	—	25.00
2176	2018C	Philadelphia	—	20.00
2176☆	2018C☆	Philadelphia☆	—	30.00
2177	2018D	Cleveland	—	20.00
2177☆	2018D☆	Cleveland☆	—	30.00
2178	2018E	Richmond	—	20.00
2178☆	2018E☆	Richmond☆	—	30.00
2179	2018F	Atlanta	—	20.00
2179☆	2018F☆	Atlanta☆	—	30.00
2180	2018G	Chicago	—	20.00
2180☆	2018G☆	Chicago☆	—	25.00

Series 1969 Elston-Kennedy

KL#	Fr#	Bank	XF	CU
2181	2018H	St. Louis	—	20.00
2181☆	2018H☆	St. Louis☆	—	30.00
2182	2018I	Minneapolis	—	20.00
2182☆	2018I☆	Minneapolis☆	—	30.00
2183	2018J	Kansas City	—	20.00
2183☆	2018J☆	Kansas City☆	—	30.00
2184	2018K	Dallas	—	20.00
2184☆	2018K☆	Dallas☆	—	30.00
2185	2018L	San Francisco	—	20.00
2185☆	2018L☆	San Francisco☆	—	25.00

Series 1969A Kabis-Connally

KL#	Fr#	Bank	XF	CU
2186	2019A	Boston	—	20.00
2186☆	2019A☆	Boston☆	—	25.00
2187	2019B	New York	—	20.00
2187☆	2019B☆	New York☆	—	25.00
2188	2019C	Philadelphia	—	20.00
2188☆	2019C☆	Philadelphia☆	—	25.00
2189	2019D	Cleveland	—	20.00
2189☆	2019D☆	Cleveland☆	—	25.00
2190	2019E	Richmond	—	20.00
2190☆	2019E☆	Richmond☆	—	30.00
2191	2019F	Atlanta	—	20.00
2191☆	2019F☆	Atlanta☆	—	30.00
2192	2019G	Chicago	—	20.00
2192☆	2019G☆	Chicago☆	—	25.00
2193	2019H	St. Louis	—	20.00
2193☆	2019H☆	St. Louis☆	—	30.00
2194	2019I	Minneapolis	—	25.00
2194☆	2019I☆	Minneapolis☆	—	Not issued
2195	2019J	Kansas City	—	20.00
2195☆	2019J☆	Kansas City☆	—	Not issued
2196	2019K	Dallas	—	20.00
2196☆	2019K☆	Dallas☆	—	30.00
2197	2019L	San Francisco	—	20.00
2197☆	2019L☆	San Francisco☆	—	25.00

Series 1969B Banuelos-Connally

KL#	Fr#	Bank	XF	CU
2198	2020A	Boston	—	30.00
2198☆	2020A☆	Boston☆	—	Not issued
2199	2020B	New York	—	25.00
2199☆	2020B☆	New York☆	—	40.00
2200	2020C	Philadelphia	—	30.00
2200☆	2020C☆	Philadelphia☆	—	Not issued
2201	2020D	Cleveland	—	30.00
2201☆	2020D☆	Cleveland☆	—	Not issued
2202	2020E	Richmond	—	30.00
2202☆	2020E☆	Richmond☆	—	50.00
2203	2020F	Atlanta	—	30.00
2203☆	2020F☆	Atlanta☆	—	50.00
2204	2020G	Chicago	—	25.00
2204☆	2020G☆	Chicago☆	—	40.00
2205	2020H	St. Louis	—	30.00
2205☆	2020H☆	St. Louis☆	—	40.00
2206	2020I	Minneapolis	—	35.00
2206☆	2020I☆	Minneapolis☆	—	Not issued
2207	2020J	Kansas City	—	35.00
2207☆	2020J☆	Kansas City☆	—	50.00
2208	2020K	Dallas	—	35.00
2208☆	2020K☆	Dallas☆	—	Not issued
2209	2020L	San Francisco	—	25.00
2209☆	2020L☆	San Francisco☆	—	50.00

Series 1969C Banuelos-Shultz

KL#	Fr#	Bank	XF	CU
2210	2021A	Boston	—	18.00
2210☆	2021A☆	Boston☆	—	30.00
2211	2021B	New York	—	18.00
2211☆	2021B☆	New York☆	—	25.00
2212	2021C	Philadelphia	—	18.00
2212☆	2021C☆	Philadelphia☆	—	30.00
2213	2021D	Cleveland	—	18.00
2213☆	2021D☆	Cleveland☆	—	25.00
2214	2021E	Richmond	—	18.00
2214☆	2021E☆	Richmond☆	—	30.00
2215	2021F	Atlanta	—	18.00
2215☆	2021F☆	Atlanta☆	—	30.00
2216	2021G	Chicago	—	18.00
2216☆	2021G☆	Chicago☆	—	30.00
2217	2021H	St. Louis	—	18.00
2217☆	2021H☆	St. Louis☆	—	30.00
2218	2021I	Minneapolis	—	20.00
2218☆	2021I☆	Minneapolis☆	—	30.00
2219	2021J	Kansas City	—	18.00
2219☆	2021J☆	Kansas City☆	—	30.00
2220	2021K	Dallas	—	18.00
2220☆	2021K☆	Dallas☆	—	30.00
2221	2021L	San Francisco	—	18.00
2221☆	2021L☆	San Francisco☆	—	35.00

Series 1974 Neff-Simon

KL#	Fr#	Bank	XF	CU
2222	2022A	Boston	—	17.00
2222☆	2022A☆	Boston☆	—	25.00
2223	2022B	New York	—	17.00
2223☆	2022B☆	New York☆	—	20.00
2224	2022C	Philadelphia	—	17.00

Series 1974 Neff-Simon

KL#	Fr#	Bank	XF	CU
2224	2022C☆	Philadelphia☆	—	25.00
2225	2022D	Cleveland	—	17.00
2225☆	2022D☆	Cleveland☆	—	30.00
2226	2022E	Richmond	—	17.00
2226☆	2022E☆	Richmond☆	—	25.00
2227	2022F	Atlanta	—	17.00
2227☆	2022F☆	Atlanta☆	—	20.00
2228	2022G	Chicago	—	17.00
2228☆	2022G☆	Chicago☆	—	20.00
2229	2022H	St. Louis	—	17.00
2229☆	2022H☆	St. Louis☆	—	25.00
2230	2022I	Minneapolis	—	17.00
2230☆	2022I☆	Minneapolis☆	—	30.00
2231	2022J	Kansas City	—	17.00
2231☆	2022J☆	Kansas City☆	—	25.00
2232	2022K	Dallas	—	17.00
2232☆	2022K☆	Dallas☆	—	25.00
2233	2022L	San Francisco	—	17.00
2233☆	2022L☆	San Francisco☆	—	25.00

Series 1977 Morton-Blumenthal

KL#	Fr#	Bank	XF	CU
2234	2023A	Boston	—	17.00
2234☆	2023A☆	Boston☆	—	25.00
2235	2023B	New York	—	17.00
2235☆	2023B☆	New York☆	—	25.00
2236	2023C	Philadelphia	—	17.00
2236☆	2023C☆	Philadelphia☆	—	25.00
2237	2023D	Cleveland	—	17.00
2237☆	2023D☆	Cleveland☆	—	25.00
2238	2023E	Richmond	—	17.00
2238☆	2023E☆	Richmond☆	—	25.00
2239	2023F	Atlanta	—	17.00
2239☆	2023F☆	Atlanta☆	—	25.00
2240	2023G	Chicago	—	17.00
2240☆	2023G☆	Chicago☆	—	20.00
2241	2023H	St. Louis	—	17.00
2241☆	2023H☆	St. Louis☆	—	25.00
2242	2023I	Minneapolis	—	20.00
2242☆	2023I☆	Minneapolis☆	—	30.00
2243	2023J	Kansas City	—	17.00
2243☆	2023J☆	Kansas City☆	—	25.00
2244	2023K	Dallas	—	17.00
2244☆	2023K☆	Dallas☆	—	25.00
2245	2023L	San Francisco	—	17.00
2245☆	2023L☆	San Francisco☆	—	20.00

Series 1977A Morton-Miller

KL#	Fr#	Bank	XF	CU
2246	2024A	Boston	—	16.00
2246☆	2024A☆	Boston☆	—	25.00
2247	2024B	New York	—	16.00
2247☆	2024B☆	New York☆	—	20.00
2248	2024C	Philadelphia	—	16.00
2248☆	2024C☆	Philadelphia☆	—	20.00
2249	2024D	Cleveland	—	16.00
2249☆	2024D☆	Cleveland☆	—	20.00
2250	2024E	Richmond	—	16.00
2250☆	2024E☆	Richmond☆	—	20.00
2251	2024F	Atlanta	—	16.00
2251☆	2024F☆	Atlanta☆	—	25.00
2252	2024G	Chicago	—	16.00
2252☆	2024G☆	Chicago☆	—	20.00
2253	2024H	St. Louis	—	16.00
2253☆	2024H☆	St. Louis☆	—	25.00
2254	2024I	Minneapolis	—	16.00
2254☆	2024I☆	Minneapolis☆	—	50.00
2255	2024J	Kansas City	—	16.00
2255☆	2024J☆	Kansas City☆	—	20.00
2256	2024K	Dallas	—	16.00
2256☆	2024K☆	Dallas☆	—	20.00
2257	2024L	San Francisco	—	16.00
2257☆	2024L☆	San Francisco☆	—	20.00

Series 1981 Buchanan-Regan

KL#	Fr#	Bank	XF	CU
3524	2025A	Boston	—	15.00
3524☆	2025A☆	Boston☆	—	30.00
3525	2025B	New York	—	15.00
3525☆	2025B☆	New York☆	—	30.00
3526	2025C	Philadelphia	—	15.00
3526☆	2025C☆	Philadelphia☆	—	35.00
3527	2025D	Cleveland	—	15.00
3527☆	2025D☆	Cleveland☆	—	30.00
3528	2025E	Richmond	—	15.00
3528☆	2025E☆	Richmond☆	—	30.00
3529	2025F	Atlanta	—	15.00
3529☆	2025F☆	Atlanta☆	—	30.00
3530	2025G	Chicago	—	15.00
3530☆	2025G☆	Chicago☆	—	30.00
3531	2025H	St. Louis	—	15.00
3531☆	2025H☆	St. Louis☆	—	Not issued
3532	2025I	Minneapolis	—	15.00
3532☆	2025I☆	Minneapolis☆	—	35.00
3533	2025J	Kansas City	—	15.00
3533☆	2025J☆	Kansas City☆	—	Not issued
3534	2025K	Dallas	—	15.00
3534☆	2025K☆	Dallas☆	—	Not issued
3535	2025L	San Francisco	—	15.00
3535☆	2025L☆	San Francisco☆	—	30.00

Series 1981A Ortega-Regan

KL#	Fr#	Bank	XF	CU
3624	2026A	Boston	—	15.00
3624☆	2026A☆	Boston☆	—	Not issued
3625	2026B	New York	—	15.00
3625☆	2026B☆	New York☆	—	30.00
3626	2026C	Philadelphia	—	15.00
3626☆	2026C☆	Philadelphia☆	—	Not issued
3627	2026D	Cleveland	—	15.00
3627☆	2026D☆	Cleveland☆	—	Not issued
3628	2026E	Richmond	—	15.00
3628☆	2026E☆	Richmond☆	—	30.00
3629	2026F	Atlanta	—	15.00
3629☆	2026F☆	Atlanta☆	—	30.00
3630	2026G	Chicago	—	15.00
3630☆	2026G☆	Chicago☆	—	Not issued
3631	2026H	St. Louis	—	15.00
3631☆	2026H☆	St. Louis☆	—	Not issued
3632	2026I	Minneapolis	—	15.00
3632☆	2026I☆	Minneapolis☆	—	Not issued
3633	2026J	Kansas City	—	15.00
3633☆	2026J☆	Kansas City☆	—	Not issued
3634	2026K	Dallas	—	15.00
3634☆	2026K☆	Dallas☆	—	Not issued
3635	2026L	San Francisco	—	15.00
3635☆	2026L☆	San Francisco☆	—	Not issued

Series 1985 Ortega-Baker

KL#	Fr#	Bank	XF	CU
3724	2027A	Boston	—	15.00
3724☆	2027A☆	Boston☆	—	20.00
3725	2027B	New York	—	15.00
3725☆	2027B☆	New York☆	—	25.00
3726	2027C	Philadelphia	—	15.00
3726☆	2027C☆	Philadelphia☆	—	Not issued
3727	2027D	Cleveland	—	15.00
3727☆	2027D☆	Cleveland☆	—	25.00
3728	2027E	Richmond	—	15.00
3728☆	2027E☆	Richmond☆	—	Not issued
3729	2027F	Atlanta	—	15.00
3729☆	2027F☆	Atlanta☆	—	30.00
3730	2027G	Chicago	—	15.00
3730☆	2027G☆	Chicago☆	—	Not issued
3731	2027H	St. Louis	—	15.00
3731☆	2027H☆	St. Louis☆	—	25.00
3732	2027I	Minneapolis	—	15.00
3732☆	2027I☆	Minneapolis☆	—	Not issued
3733	2027J	Kansas City	—	15.00
3733☆	2027J☆	Kansas City☆	—	Not issued
3734	2027K	Dallas	—	15.00
3734☆	2027K☆	Dallas☆	—	25.00
3735	2027L	San Francisco	—	15.00
3735☆	2027L☆	San Francisco☆	—	25.00

Series 1988A Villalpando-Brady

KL#	Fr#	Bank	XF	CU
3868	—	Boston	—	15.00
3868☆	—	Boston☆	—	25.00
3869	—	New York	—	15.00
3869☆	—	New York☆	—	25.00
3870	—	Philadelphia	—	15.00
3870☆	—	Philadelphia☆	—	Not issued
3871	—	Cleveland	—	15.00
3871☆	—	Cleveland☆	—	25.00
3872	—	Richmond	—	15.00
3872☆	—	Richmond☆	—	Not issued
3873	—	Atlanta	—	15.00
3873☆	—	Atlanta☆	—	Not issued
3874	—	Chicago	—	15.00
3874☆	—	Chicago☆	—	Not issued
3875	—	St. Louis	—	15.00
3875☆	—	St. Louis☆	—	Not issued
3876	—	Minneapolis	—	15.00
3876☆	—	Minneapolis☆	—	Not issued
3877	—	Kansas City	—	15.00
3877☆	—	Kansas City☆	—	Not issued
3878	—	Dallas	—	15.00
3878☆	—	Dallas☆	—	Not issued
3879	—	San Francisco	—	15.00
3879☆	—	San Francisco☆	—	25.00

Series 1990 Villalpando-Brady

KL#	Fr#	Bank	XF	CU
4000	—	Boston	—	15.00
4000☆	—	Boston☆	—	Not issued
4001	—	New York	—	15.00
4001☆	—	New York☆	—	20.00
4002	—	Philadelphia	—	15.00
4002☆	—	Philadelphia☆	—	20.00
4003	—	Cleveland	—	15.00
4003☆	—	Cleveland☆	—	Not issued
4004	—	Richmond	—	15.00
4004☆	—	Richmond☆	—	Not issued
4005	—	Atlanta	—	15.00
4005☆	—	Atlanta☆	—	Not issued
4006	—	Chicago	—	15.00
4006☆	—	Chicago☆	—	25.00
4007	—	St. Louis	—	15.00
4007☆	—	St. Louis☆	—	25.00
4008	—	Minneapolis	—	17.50
4008☆	—	Minneapolis☆	—	Not issued
4009	—	Kansas City	—	15.00

Series 1990 Villalpando-Brady

KL#	Fr#	Bank	XF	CU
4009☆	—	Kansas City☆	—	Not issued
4010	—	Dallas	—	15.00
4010☆	—	Dallas☆	—	Not issued
4011	—	San Francisco	—	15.00
4011☆	—	San Francisco☆	—	Not issued

Series 1993 Withrow-Bentsen

KL#	Fr#	Bank	XF	CU
4036	—	Boston	—	15.00
4036☆	—	Boston☆	—	Not issued
4037	—	New York	—	15.00
4037☆	—	New York☆	—	25.00
4038	—	Philadelphia	—	15.00
4038☆	—	Philadelphia☆	—	25.00
4039	—	Cleveland	—	15.00
4039☆	—	Cleveland☆	—	Not issued
4040	—	Richmond	—	Not issued
4040☆	—	Richmond☆	—	Not issued
4041	—	Atlanta	—	15.00
4041☆	—	Atlanta☆	—	Not issued
4042	—	Chicago	—	15.00
4042☆	—	Chicago☆	—	20.00
4043	—	St. Louis	—	15.00
4043☆	—	St. Louis☆	—	Not issued
4044	—	Minneapolis	—	Not issued
4044☆	—	Minneapolis☆	—	Not issued
4045	—	Kansas City	—	15.00
4045☆	—	Kansas City☆	—	Not issued
4046	—	Dallas	—	Not issued
4046☆	—	Dallas☆	—	Not issued
4047	—	San Francisco	—	15.00
4047☆	—	San Francisco☆	—	Not issued

Series 1995 Withrow-Rubin

KL#	Fr#	Bank	XF	CU
4108	—	Boston	—	20.00
4108☆	—	Boston☆	—	Not issued
4109	—	New York	—	15.00
4109☆	—	New York☆	—	20.00
4110	—	Philadelphia	—	Not issued
4110☆	—	Philadelphia☆	—	Not issued
4111	—	Cleveland	—	25.00
4111☆	—	Cleveland☆	—	35.00
4112	—	Richmond	—	15.00
4112☆	—	Richmond☆	—	Not issued
4113	—	Atlanta	—	15.00
4113☆	—	Atlanta☆	—	Not issued
4114	—	Chicago	—	15.00
4114☆	—	Chicago☆	—	20.00
4115	—	St. Louis	—	15.00
4115☆	—	St. Louis☆	—	Not issued
4116	—	Minneapolis	—	15.00
4116☆	—	Minneapolis☆	—	Not issued
4117	—	Kansas City	—	15.00
4117☆	—	Kansas City☆	—	Not issued
4118	—	Dallas	—	15.00
4118☆	—	Dallas☆	—	Not issued
4119	—	San Francisco	—	15.00
4119☆	—	San Francisco☆	—	20.00

Hawaii Emergency Federal Reserve Notes

Alexander Hamilton

KL#	Fr#	Series	Signatures	Fine	VF	CU
2258	2303	1934A	Julian-Morgenthau	40.00	42.00	210.
2258☆	2303☆	1934A☆	Julian-Morgenthau	400.	750.	5000.

North Africa
Silver Certificates

Alexander Hamilton

KL#	Fr#	Series	Signatures	Fine	VF	CU
2259	2308	1934	Julian-Morgenthau	1200.	2000.	6000.
2259☆	2308☆	1934☆	Julian-Morgenthau	—	Unique	—
2260	2309	1934A	Julian-Morgenthau	25.00	30.00	125.
2260☆	2309☆	1934A☆	Julian-Morgenthau	65.00	90.00	350.

Twenty Dollars
Gold Certificates

Andrew Jackson

KL#	Fr#	Series	Signatures	Fine	VF	CU
2261	2402	1928	Woods-Mellon	55.00	72.00	300.
2261☆	2402☆	1928☆	Woods-Mellon	150.	250.	1000.

Federal Reserve Bank Notes

Andrew Jackson

KL#	Fr#	Series	District	Fine	VF	CU
2262	1870A	1929	Boston	—	—	150.
2262☆	1870A☆	1929☆	Boston	125.	150.	1200.
2263	1870B	1929	New York	—	—	90.00
2263☆	1870B☆	1929☆	New York	125.	250.	1200.
2264	1870C	1929	Philadelphia	—	—	95.00
2264☆	1870C☆	1929☆	Philadelphia	125.	250.	1200.
2265	1870D	1929	Cleveland	—	—	120.
2265☆	1870D☆	1929☆	Cleveland	150.	200.	1200.
2266	1870E	1929	Richmond	—	—	120.
2266☆	1870E☆	1929☆	Richmond	—	150.	1200.
2267	1870F	1929	Atlanta	—	—	120.
2267☆	1870F☆	1929☆	Atlanta	175.	200.	2000.
2268	1870G	1929	Chicago	—	—	120.
2268☆	1870G☆	1929☆	Chicago	125.	150.	2000.
2269	1870H	1929	St. Louis	—	—	120.
2269☆	1870H☆	1929☆	St. Louis	50.00	75.00	700.
2270	1870I	1929	Minneapolis	—	—	120.
2270☆	1870I☆	1929☆	Minneapolis	175.	200.	1500.
2271	1870J	1929	Kansas City	—	—	120.
2271☆	1870J☆	1929☆	Kansas City	125.	150.	700.
2272	1870K	1929	Dallas	—	40.00	300.
2272☆	1870K☆	1929☆	Dallas	350.	750.	2500.
2273	1870L	1929	San Francisco	—	35.00	250.
2273☆	1870L☆	1929☆	San Francisco	350.	750.	2000.

Federal Reserve Notes

Andrew Jackson

Series 1928 Tate-Mellon

KL#	Fr#	Bank	XF	CU
2274	2050A	Boston	—	125.
2274☆	2050A☆	Boston☆	250.	500.
2275	2050B	New York	—	125.
2275☆	2050B☆	New York☆	200.	400.
2276	2050C	Philadelphia	40.00	100.
2276☆	2050C☆	Philadelphia☆	250.	500.
2277	2050D	Cleveland	110.	125.
2277☆	2050D☆	Cleveland☆	200.	400.
2278	2050E	Richmond	110.	125.
2278☆	2050E☆	Richmond☆	500.	1000.
2279	2050F	Atlanta	40.00	100.
2279☆	2050F☆	Atlanta☆	200.	500.
2280	2050G	Chicago	35.00	75.00
2280☆	2050G☆	Chicago☆	200.	400.
2281	2050H	St. Louis	35.00	75.00
2281☆	2050H☆	St. Louis☆	225.	400.
2282	2050I	Minneapolis	35.00	75.00
2282☆	2050I☆	Minneapolis☆	250.	500.
2283	2050J	Kansas City	35.00	100.
2283☆	2050J☆	Kansas City☆	250.	500.
2284	2050K	Dallas	35.00	100.
2284☆	2050K☆	Dallas☆	500.	1500.
2285	2050L	San Francisco	35.00	75.00
2285☆	2050L☆	San Francisco☆	250.	500.

Series 1928A Woods-Mellon

KL#	Fr#	Bank	XF	CU
2286	2051A	Boston	55.00	85.00
2286☆	2051A☆	Boston☆	600.	1100.
2287	2051B	New York	55.00	85.00
2287☆	2051B☆	New York☆	600.	1100.
2288	2051C	Philadelphia	55.00	75.00
2288☆	2051C☆	Philadelphia☆	600.	1100.
2289	2051D	Cleveland	65.00	100.
2289☆	2051D☆	Cleveland☆	600.	1100.
2290	2051E	Richmond	55.00	75.00
2290☆	2051E☆	Richmond☆	600.	1100.
2291	2051F	Atlanta	55.00	75.00
2291☆	2051F☆	Atlanta☆	600.	1100.
2292	2051G	Chicago	55.00	75.00
2292☆	2051G☆	Chicago☆	600.	1100.
2293	2051H	St. Louis	55.00	100.
2293☆	2051H☆	St. Louis☆	600.	1100.
2294	2051J	Kansas City	70.00	150.
2294☆	2051J☆	Kansas City☆	550.	1000.
2295	2051K	Dallas	55.00	75.00
2295☆	2051K☆	Dallas☆	550.	1000.

Series 1928B Woods-Mellon

KL#	Fr#	Bank	XF	CU
2296	2052A	Boston	40.00	65.00
2297	2052B	New York	40.00	65.00
2298	2052C	Philadelphia	40.00	65.00
2299	2052D	Cleveland	40.00	65.00
2300	2052E	Richmond	40.00	70.00
2301	2052F	Atlanta	40.00	120.
2302	2052G	Chicago	40.00	65.00
2303	2052H	St. Louis	40.00	70.00
2304	2052I	Minneapolis	40.00	75.00
2305	2052J	Kansas City	40.00	60.00
2306	2052K	Dallas	40.00	150.
2307	2052L	San Francisco	40.00	65.00

Series 1928C Woods-Mills

KL#	Fr#	Bank	XF	CU
2308	2053G	Chicago	200.	500.
2309	2053L	San Francisco	200.	600.

Series 1934 Julian-Morgenthau

KL#	Fr#	Bank	XF	CU
2310	2054A	Boston	30.00	40.00
2310☆	2054A☆	Boston☆	100.	300.
2311	2054B	New York	30.00	40.00
2311☆	2054B☆	New York☆	100.	300.
2312	2054C	Philadelphia	30.00	40.00
2312☆	2054C☆	Philadelphia☆	100.	300.
2313	2054D	Cleveland	30.00	40.00
2313☆	2054D☆	Cleveland☆	100.	300.
2314	2054E	Richmond	30.00	40.00
2314☆	2054E☆	Richmond☆	100.	300.

Series 1934-A Julian-Morgenthau

KL#	Fr#	Bank	XF	CU
2315	2054F	Atlanta	30.00	40.00
2315☆	2054F☆	Atlanta☆	100.	300.
2316	2054G	Chicago	30.00	40.00
2316☆	2054G☆	Chicago☆	100.	300.
2317	2054H	St. Louis	30.00	40.00
2317☆	2054H☆	St. Louis☆	100.	300.
2318	2054I	Minneapolis	30.00	40.00
2318☆	2054I☆	Minneapolis☆	100.	300.
2319	2054J	Kansas City	30.00	40.00
2319☆	2054J☆	Kansas City☆	100.	300.
2320	2054K	Dallas	30.00	40.00
2320☆	2054K☆	Dallas☆	—	Not issued
2321	2054L	San Francisco	30.00	40.00
2321☆	2054L☆	San Francisco☆	—	Not issued
2322	2055A	Boston	35.00	40.00
2322☆	2055A☆	Boston☆	75.00	175.
2323	2055B	New York	30.00	40.00
2323☆	2055B☆	New York☆	55.00	110.
2324	2055C	Philadelphia	30.00	40.00
2324☆	2055C☆	Philadelphia☆	60.00	125.
2325	2055D	Cleveland	30.00	40.00
2325☆	2055D☆	Cleveland☆	55.00	125.
2326	2055E	Richmond	30.00	40.00
2326☆	2055E☆	Richmond☆	60.00	125.
2327	2055F	Atlanta	35.00	40.00
2327☆	2055F☆	Atlanta☆	50.00	125.
2328	2055G	Chicago	30.00	40.00
2328☆	2055G☆	Chicago☆	55.00	110.
2329	2055H	St. Louis	35.00	40.00
2329☆	2055H☆	St. Louis☆	50.00	125.
2330	2055I	Minneapolis	45.00	60.00
2330☆	2055I☆	Minneapolis☆	75.00	175.
2331	2055J	Kansas City	35.00	40.00
2331☆	2055J☆	Kansas City☆	55.00	125.
2332	2055K	Dallas	35.00	40.00
2332☆	2055K☆	Dallas☆	75.00	175.
2333	2055L	San Francisco	30.00	40.00
2333☆	2055L☆	San Francisco☆	55.00	125.

Series 1934B Julian-Vinson

KL#	Fr#	Bank	XF	CU
2334	2056A	Boston	35.00	40.00
2334☆	2056A☆	Boston☆	125.	400.
2335	2056B	New York	32.00	40.00
2335☆	2056B☆	New York☆	100.	300.
2336	2056C	Philadelphia	35.00	40.00
2336☆	2056C☆	Philadelphia☆	125.	400.
2337	2056D	Cleveland	40.00	50.00
2337☆	2056D☆	Cleveland☆	125.	400.
2338	2056E	Richmond	32.00	40.00
2338☆	2056E☆	Richmond☆	125.	400.
2339	2056F	Atlanta	35.00	40.00
2339☆	2056F☆	Atlanta☆	125.	400.
2340	2056G	Chicago	32.00	40.00
2340☆	2056G☆	Chicago☆	100.	300.
2341	2056H	St. Louis	35.00	40.00
2341☆	2056H☆	St. Louis☆	125.	400.
2342	2056I	Minneapolis	40.00	50.00
2342☆	2056I☆	Minneapolis☆	125.	400.
2343	2056J	Kansas City	35.00	40.00
2343☆	2056J☆	Kansas City☆	100.	300.
2344	2056K	Dallas	40.00	50.00
2344☆	2056K☆	Dallas☆	125.	400.
2345	2056L	San Francisco	35.00	40.00
2345☆	2056L☆	San Francisco☆	125.	400.

Series 1934C Julian-Snyder

KL#	Fr#	Bank	XF	CU
2346	2057A	Boston	30.00	35.00
2346☆	2057A☆	Boston☆	50.00	75.00
2347	2057B	New York	30.00	35.00
2347☆	2057B☆	New York☆	50.00	75.00
2348	2057C	Philadelphia	30.00	35.00
2348☆	2057C☆	Philadelphia☆	50.00	75.00
2349	2057D	Cleveland	30.00	35.00
2349☆	2057D☆	Cleveland☆	65.00	90.00
2350	2057E	Richmond	30.00	35.00
2350☆	2057E☆	Richmond☆	45.00	75.00
2351	2057F	Atlanta	30.00	35.00
2351☆	2057F☆	Atlanta☆	65.00	95.00
2352	2057G	Chicago	30.00	35.00
2352☆	2057G☆	Chicago☆	50.00	75.00
2353	2057H	St. Louis	30.00	35.00
2353☆	2057H☆	St. Louis☆	50.00	75.00
2354	2057I	Minneapolis	40.00	50.00
2354☆	2057I☆	Minneapolis☆	65.00	90.00
2355	2057J	Kansas City	30.00	35.00
2355☆	2057J☆	Kansas City☆	50.00	75.00
2356	2057K	Dallas	30.00	35.00
2356☆	2057K☆	Dallas☆	60.00	80.00
2357	2057L	San Francisco	30.00	35.00
2357☆	2057L☆	San Francisco☆	60.00	80.00

Series 1934D Clark-Snyder

KL#	Fr#	Bank	XF	CU
2358	2058A	Boston	—	35.00
2358☆	2058A☆	Boston☆	65.00	125.
2359	2058B	New York	—	35.00
2359☆	2058B☆	New York☆	50.00	80.00
2360	2058C	Philadelphia	—	35.00
2360☆	2058C☆	Philadelphia☆	50.00	80.00

Series 1934-D Clark-Snyder

KL#	Fr#	Bank	XF	CU
2361	2058D	Cleveland	—	35.00
2361☆	2058D☆	Cleveland☆	50.00	80.00
2362	2058E	Richmond	—	35.00
2362☆	2058E☆	Richmond☆	50.00	80.00
2363	2058F	Atlanta	—	35.00
2363☆	2058F☆	Atlanta☆	50.00	80.00
2364	2058G	Chicago	—	35.00
2364☆	2058G☆	Chicago☆	50.00	80.00
2365	2058H	St. Louis	—	35.00
2365☆	2058H☆	St. Louis☆	50.00	80.00
2366	2058I	Minneapolis	30.00	40.00
2366☆	2058I☆	Minneapolis☆	60.00	125.
2367	2058J	Kansas City	—	35.00
2367☆	2058J☆	Kansas City☆	60.00	125.
2368	2058K	Dallas	—	35.00
2368☆	2058K☆	Dallas☆	60.00	125.
2369	2058L	San Francisco	—	35.00
2369☆	2058L☆	San Francisco☆	60.00	125.

Series 1950 Clark-Snyder

KL#	Fr#	Bank	XF	CU
2370	2059A	Boston	—	50.00
2370☆	2059A☆	Boston☆	95.00	200.
2371	2059B	New York	—	50.00
2371☆	2059B☆	New York☆	90.00	200.
2372	2059C	Philadelphia	—	50.00
2372☆	2059C☆	Philadelphia☆	95.00	200.
2373	2059D	Cleveland	—	50.00
2373☆	2059D☆	Cleveland☆	90.00	200.
2374	2059E	Richmond	—	50.00
2374☆	2059E☆	Richmond☆	80.00	175.
2375	2059F	Atlanta	—	50.00
2375☆	2059F☆	Atlanta☆	85.00	175.
2376	2059G	Chicago	—	50.00
2376☆	2059G☆	Chicago☆	85.00	175.
2377	2059H	St. Louis	—	50.00
2377☆	2059H☆	St. Louis☆	85.00	175.
2378	2059I	Minneapolis	—	50.00
2378☆	2059I☆	Minneapolis☆	125.	275.
2379	2059J	Kansas City	—	50.00
2379☆	2059J☆	Kansas City☆	125.	275.
2380	2059K	Dallas	—	50.00
2380☆	2059K☆	Dallas☆	125.	275.
2381	2059L	San Francisco	—	50.00
2381☆	2059L☆	San Francisco☆	80.00	175.

Series 1950A Priest-Humphrey

KL#	Fr#	Bank	XF	CU
2382	2060A	Boston	—	40.00
2382☆	2060A☆	Boston☆	—	75.00
2383	2060B	New York	—	40.00
2383☆	2060B☆	New York☆	—	75.00
2384	2060C	Philadelphia	—	40.00
2384☆	2060C☆	Philadelphia☆	—	75.00
2385	2060D	Cleveland	—	40.00
2385☆	2060D☆	Cleveland☆	—	75.00
2386	2060E	Richmond	—	40.00
2386☆	2060E☆	Richmond☆	—	70.00
2387	2060F	Atlanta	—	40.00
2387☆	2060F☆	Atlanta☆	—	75.00
2388	2060G	Chicago	—	40.00
2388☆	2060G☆	Chicago☆	—	75.00
2389	2060H	St. Louis	—	40.00
2389☆	2060H☆	St. Louis☆	—	75.00
2390	2060I	Minneapolis	—	45.00
2390☆	2060I☆	Minneapolis☆	—	75.00
2391	2060J	Kansas City	—	40.00
2391☆	2060J☆	Kansas City☆	—	75.00
2392	2060K	Dallas	—	40.00
2392☆	2060K☆	Dallas☆	—	75.00
2393	2060L	San Francisco	—	40.00
2393☆	2060L☆	San Francisco☆	—	75.00

Series 1950B Priest-Anderson

KL#	Fr#	Bank	XF	CU
2394	2061A	Boston	—	40.00
2394☆	2061A☆	Boston☆	—	100.
2395	2061B	New York	—	40.00
2395☆	2061B☆	New York☆	—	75.00
2396	2061C	Philadelphia	—	40.00
2396☆	2061C☆	Philadelphia☆	—	100.
2397	2061D	Cleveland	—	40.00
2397☆	2061D☆	Cleveland☆	—	75.00
2398	2061E	Richmond	—	40.00
2398☆	2061E☆	Richmond☆	—	75.00
2399	2061F	Atlanta	—	40.00
2399☆	2061F☆	Atlanta☆	—	75.00
2400	2061G	Chicago	—	40.00
2400☆	2061G☆	Chicago☆	—	75.00
2401	2061H	St. Louis	—	40.00
2401☆	2061H☆	St. Louis☆	—	100.
2402	2061I	Minneapolis	—	40.00
2402☆	2061I☆	Minneapolis☆	—	75.00
2403	2061J	Kansas City	—	40.00
2403☆	2061J☆	Kansas City☆	—	100.
2404	2061K	Dallas	—	40.00
2404☆	2061K☆	Dallas☆	—	75.00
2405	2061L	San Francisco	—	40.00
2405☆	2061L☆	San Francisco☆	—	75.00

Series 1950C Smith-Dillon

KL#	Fr#	Bank	XF	CU
2406	2062A	Boston	—	50.00
2406☆	2062A☆	Boston	—	100.
2407	2062B	New York	—	40.00
2407☆	2062B☆	New York☆	—	100.
2408	2062C	Philadelphia	—	50.00
2408☆	2062C☆	Philadelphia☆	—	100.
2409	2062D	Cleveland	—	40.00
2409☆	2062D☆	Cleveland☆	—	100.
2410	2062E	Richmond	—	40.00
2410☆	2062E☆	Richmond☆	—	100.
2411	2062F	Atlanta	—	40.00
2411☆	2062F☆	Atlanta☆	—	100.
2412	2062G	Chicago	—	40.00
2412☆	2062G☆	Chicago☆	—	100.
2413	2062H	St. Louis	—	40.00
2413☆	2062H☆	St. Louis☆	—	100.
2414	2062I	Minneapolis	—	40.00
2414☆	2062I☆	Minneapolis☆	—	100.
2415	2062J	Kansas City	—	40.00
2415☆	2062J☆	Kansas City☆	—	100.
2416	2062K	Dallas	—	40.00
2416☆	2062K☆	Dallas☆	—	100.
2417	2062L	San Francisco	—	40.00
2417☆	2062L☆	San Francisco☆	—	100.

Series 1950D Granahan-Dillon

KL#	Fr#	Bank	XF	CU
2418	2063A	Boston	—	40.00
2418☆	2063A☆	Boston☆	—	80.00
2419	2063B	New York	—	40.00
2419☆	2063B☆	New York☆	—	80.00
2419A	2063C	Philadelphia	—	40.00
2419A☆	2063C☆	Philadelphia☆	—	80.00
2420	2063D	Cleveland	—	40.00
2420☆	2063D☆	Cleveland☆	—	80.00
2421	2063E	Richmond	—	40.00
2421☆	2063E☆	Richmond☆	—	80.00
2422	2063F	Atlanta	—	40.00
2422☆	2063F☆	Atlanta☆	—	80.00
2423	2063G	Chicago	—	40.00
2423☆	2063G☆	Chicago☆	—	80.00
2424	2063H	St. Louis	—	40.00
2424☆	2063H☆	St. Louis☆	—	80.00
2424A	2063I	Minneapolis	—	40.00
2424A☆	2063I☆	Minneapolis☆	—	80.00
2425	2063J	Kansas City	—	40.00
2425☆	2063J☆	Kansas City☆	—	80.00
2426	2063K	Dallas	—	40.00
2426☆	2063K☆	Dallas☆	—	80.00
2427	2063L	San Francisco	—	40.00
2427☆	2063L☆	San Francisco☆	—	80.00

Series 1950E Granahan-Fowler

KL#	Fr#	Bank	XF	CU
2428	2064B	New York	—	60.00
2428☆	2064B☆	New York☆	—	175.
2429	2064G	Chicago	—	60.00
2429☆	2064G☆	Chicago☆	—	250.
2430	2064L	San Francisco	—	60.00
2430☆	2064L☆	San Francisco☆	—	200.

Series 1963 Granahan-Dillon

KL#	Fr#	Bank	XF	CU
2431	2065A	Boston	—	40.00
2431☆	2065A☆	Boston☆	—	50.00
2432	2065B	New York	—	35.00
2432☆	2065B☆	New York☆	—	40.00
2433	2065D	Cleveland	—	40.00
2433☆	2065D☆	Cleveland☆	—	45.00
2434	2065E	Richmond	—	40.00
2434☆	2065E☆	Richmond☆	—	50.00
2435	2065F	Atlanta	—	40.00
2435☆	2065F☆	Atlanta☆	—	50.00
2436	2065G	Chicago	—	40.00
2436☆	2065G☆	Chicago☆	—	60.00
2437	2065H	St. Louis	—	40.00
2437☆	2065H☆	St. Louis☆	—	60.00
2438	2065J	Kansas City	—	40.00
2438☆	2065J☆	Kansas City☆	—	50.00
2439	2065K	Dallas	—	40.00
2439☆	2065K☆	Dallas☆	—	50.00
2440	2065L	San Francisco	—	40.00
2440☆	2065L☆	San Francisco☆	—	60.00

Series 1963A Granahan-Fowler

KL#	Fr#	Bank	XF	CU
2441	2066A	Boston	—	30.00
2441☆	2066A☆	Boston☆	—	40.00
2442	2066B	New York	—	30.00
2442☆	2066B☆	New York☆	—	40.00
2443	2066C	Philadelphia	—	30.00
2443☆	2066C☆	Philadelphia☆	—	40.00
2444	2066D	Cleveland	—	30.00
2444☆	2066D☆	Cleveland☆	—	45.00
2445	2066E	Richmond	—	30.00
2445☆	2066E☆	Richmond☆	—	40.00
2446	2066F	Atlanta	—	30.00
2446☆	2066F☆	Atlanta☆	—	40.00

Series 1963A Granahan-Fowler

KL#	Fr#	Bank	XF	CU
2447	2066G	Chicago	—	30.00
2447☆	2066G☆	Chicago☆	—	40.00
2448	2066H	St. Louis	—	30.00
2448☆	2066H☆	St. Louis☆	—	40.00
2449	2066I	Minneapolis	—	30.00
2449☆	2066I☆	Minneapolis☆	—	40.00
2450	2066J	Kansas City	—	30.00
2450☆	2066J☆	Kansas City☆	—	40.00
2451	2066K	Dallas	—	30.00
2451☆	2066K☆	Dallas☆	—	40.00
2452	2066L	San Francisco	—	30.00
2452☆	2066L☆	San Francisco☆	—	40.00

Series 1969 Elston-Kennedy

KL#	Fr#	Bank	XF	CU
2453	2067A	Boston	—	30.00
2453☆	2067A☆	Boston☆	—	50.00
2454	2067B	New York	—	30.00
2454☆	2067B☆	New York☆	—	40.00
2455	2067C	Philadelphia	—	35.00
2455☆	2067C☆	Philadelphia☆	—	50.00
2456	2067D	Cleveland	—	30.00
2456☆	2067D☆	Cleveland☆	—	50.00
2457	2067E	Richmond	—	30.00
2457☆	2067E☆	Richmond☆	—	45.00
2458	2067F	Atlanta	—	30.00
2458☆	2067F☆	Atlanta☆	—	50.00
2459	2067G	Chicago	—	30.00
2459☆	2067G☆	Chicago☆	—	45.00
2460	2067H	St. Louis	—	30.00
2460☆	2067H☆	St. Louis☆	—	50.00
2461	2067I	Minneapolis	—	35.00
2461☆	2067I☆	Minneapolis☆	—	50.00
2462	2067J	Kansas City	—	30.00
2462☆	2067J☆	Kansas City☆	—	50.00
2463	2067K	Dallas	—	30.00
2463☆	2067K☆	Dallas☆	—	50.00
2464	2067L	San Francisco	—	30.00
2464☆	2067L☆	San Francisco☆	—	45.00

Series 1969A Kabis-Connally

KL#	Fr#	Bank	XF	CU
2465	2068A	Boston	—	35.00
2465☆	2068A☆	Boston☆	—	Not issued
2466	2068B	New York	—	30.00
2466☆	2068B☆	New York☆	—	50.00
2467	2068C	Philadelphia	—	35.00
2467☆	2068C☆	Philadelphia☆	—	Not issued
2468	2068D	Cleveland	—	30.00
2468☆	2068D☆	Cleveland☆	—	60.00
2469	2068E	Richmond	—	30.00
2469☆	2068E☆	Richmond☆	—	50.00
2470	2068F	Atlanta	—	35.00
2470☆	2068F☆	Atlanta☆	—	Not issued
2471	2068G	Chicago	—	30.00
2471☆	2068G☆	Chicago☆	—	50.00
2472	2068H	St. Louis	—	35.00
2472☆	2068H☆	St. Louis☆	—	50.00
2473	2068I	Minneapolis	—	35.00
2473☆	2068I☆	Minneapolis☆	—	Not issued
2474	2068J	Kansas City	—	30.00
2474☆	2068J☆	Kansas City☆	—	Not issued
2475	2068K	Dallas	—	30.00
2475☆	2068K☆	Dallas☆	—	50.00
2476	2068L	San Francisco	—	30.00
2476☆	2068L☆	San Francisco☆	—	60.00

Series 1969B Banuelos-Connally

KL#	Fr#	Bank	XF	CU
2477	2069B	New York	—	40.00
2477☆	2069B☆	New York☆	—	75.00
2478	2069D	Cleveland	—	45.00
2478☆	2069D☆	Cleveland☆	—	Not issued
2479	2069E	Richmond	—	45.00
2479☆	2069E☆	Richmond☆	—	Not issued
2480	2069F	Atlanta	—	40.00
2480☆	2069F☆	Atlanta☆	—	75.00
2481	2069G	Chicago	—	40.00
2481☆	2069G☆	Chicago☆	—	65.00
2482	2069H	St. Louis	—	45.00
2482☆	2069H☆	St. Louis☆	—	Not issued
2483	2069I	Minneapolis	—	50.00
2483☆	2069I☆	Minneapolis☆	—	Not issued
2484	2069J	Kansas City	—	45.00
2484☆	2069J☆	Kansas City☆	—	75.00
2485	2069K	Dallas	—	40.00
2485☆	2069K☆	Dallas☆	—	Not issued
2486	2069L	San Francisco	—	40.00
2486☆	2069L☆	San Francisco☆	—	75.00

Series 1969C Banuelos-Shultz

KL#	Fr#	Bank	XF	CU
2487	2070A	Boston	—	35.00
2487☆	2070A☆	Boston☆	—	50.00
2488	2070B	New York	—	30.00
2488☆	2070B☆	New York☆	—	45.00
2489	2070C	Philadelphia	—	30.00
2489☆	2070C☆	Philadelphia☆	—	50.00
2490	2070D	Cleveland	—	30.00

Series 1969-C Banuelos-Shultz

KL#	Fr#	Bank	XF	CU
2490☆	2070D☆	Cleveland	—	50.00
2491	2070E	Richmond	—	30.00
2491☆	2070E☆	Richmond☆	—	45.00
2492	2070F	Atlanta	—	30.00
2492☆	2070F☆	Atlanta☆	—	50.00
2493	2070G	Chicago	—	30.00
2493☆	2070G☆	Chicago☆	—	30.00
2494	2070H	St. Louis	—	50.00
2494☆	2070H☆	St. Louis☆	—	35.00
2495	2070I	Minneapolis	—	50.00
2495☆	2070I☆	Minneapolis☆	—	30.00
2496	2070J	Kansas City	—	50.00
2496☆	2070J☆	Kansas City☆	—	30.00
2497	2070K	Dallas	—	45.00
2497☆	2070K☆	Dallas☆	—	30.00
2498	2070L	San Francisco	—	30.00
2498☆	2070L☆	San Francisco☆	—	50.00

Series 1974 Neff-Simon

KL#	Fr#	Bank	XF	CU
2499	2071A	Boston	—	30.00
2499☆	2071A☆	Boston☆	—	40.00
2500	2071B	New York	—	30.00
2500☆	2071B☆	New York☆	—	35.00
2501	2071C	Philadelphia	—	30.00
2501☆	2071C☆	Philadelphia☆	—	40.00
2502	2071D	Cleveland	—	30.00
2502☆	2071D☆	Cleveland☆	—	40.00
2503	2071E	Richmond	—	30.00
2503☆	2071E☆	Richmond☆	—	40.00
2504	2071F	Atlanta	—	30.00
2504☆	2071F☆	Atlanta☆	—	45.00
2505	2071G	Chicago	—	30.00
2505☆	2071G☆	Chicago☆	—	40.00
2506	2071H	St. Louis	—	30.00
2506☆	2071H☆	St. Louis☆	—	45.00
2507	2071I	Minneapolis	—	30.00
2507☆	2071I☆	Minneapolis☆	—	45.00
2508	2071J	Kansas City	—	30.00
2508☆	2071J☆	Kansas City☆	—	45.00
2509	2071K	Dallas	—	30.00
2509☆	2071K☆	Dallas☆	—	45.00
2510	2071L	San Francisco	—	30.00
2510☆	2071L☆	San Francisco☆	—	40.00

Series 1977 Morton-Blumenthal

KL#	Fr#	Bank	XF	CU
2511	2072A	Boston	—	30.00
2511☆	2072A☆	Boston☆	—	40.00
2512	2072B	New York	—	30.00
2512☆	2072B☆	New York☆	—	40.00
2513	2072C	Philadelphia	—	30.00
2513☆	2072C☆	Philadelphia☆	—	40.00
2514	2072D	Cleveland	—	30.00
2514☆	2072D☆	Cleveland☆	—	40.00
2515	2072E	Richmond	—	30.00
2515☆	2072E☆	Richmond☆	—	40.00
2516	2072F	Atlanta	—	30.00
2516☆	2072F☆	Atlanta☆	—	40.00
2517	2072G	Chicago	—	30.00
2517☆	2072G☆	Chicago☆	—	40.00
2518	2072H	St. Louis	—	30.00
2518☆	2072H☆	St. Louis☆	—	40.00
2519	2072I	Minneapolis	—	30.00
2519☆	2072I☆	Minneapolis☆	—	50.00
2520	2072J	Kansas City	—	30.00
2520☆	2072J☆	Kansas City☆	—	40.00
2521	2072K	Dallas	—	30.00
2521☆	2072K☆	Dallas☆	—	40.00
2522	2072L	San Francisco	—	30.00
2522☆	2072L☆	San Francisco☆	—	40.00

Series 1981 Buchanan-Regan

KL#	Fr#	Bank	XF	CU
3536	2073A	Boston	—	30.00
3536☆	2073A☆	Boston☆	—	40.00
3537	2073B	New York	—	30.00
3537☆	2073B☆	New York☆	—	40.00
3538	2073C	Philadelphia	—	30.00
3538☆	2073C☆	Philadelphia☆	—	50.00
3539	2073D	Cleveland	—	30.00
3539☆	2073D☆	Cleveland☆	—	40.00
3540	2073E	Richmond	—	30.00
3540☆	2073E☆	Richmond☆	—	40.00
3541	2073F	Atlanta	—	30.00
3541☆	2073F☆	Atlanta☆	—	40.00
3542	2073G	Chicago	—	30.00
3542☆	2073G☆	Chicago☆	—	40.00
3543	2073H	St. Louis	—	30.00
3543☆	2073H☆	St. Louis☆	—	40.00
3544	2073I	Minneapolis	—	30.00
3544☆	2073I☆	Minneapolis☆	—	50.00
3545	2073J	Kansas City	—	30.00
3545☆	2073J☆	Kansas City☆	—	40.00
3546	2073K	Dallas	—	30.00
3546☆	2073K☆	Dallas☆	—	40.00
3547	2073L	San Francisco	—	30.00
3547☆	2073L☆	San Francisco☆	—	40.00

Series 1981A Ortega-Regan

KL#	Fr#	Bank	XF	CU
3636	2074A	Boston	—	30.00
3636☆	2074A☆	Boston☆	—	Not issued
3637	2074B	New York	—	30.00
3637☆	2074B☆	New York☆	—	Not issued
3638	2074C	Philadelphia	—	30.00
3638☆	2074C☆	Philadelphia☆	—	40.00
3639	2074D	Cleveland	—	30.00
3639☆	2074D☆	Cleveland☆	—	40.00
3640	2074E	Richmond	—	30.00
3640☆	2074E☆	Richmond☆	—	Not issued
3641	2074F	Atlanta	—	30.00
3641☆	2074F☆	Atlanta☆	—	40.00
3642	2074G	Chicago	—	30.00
3642☆	2074G☆	Chicago☆	—	Not issued
3643	2074H	St. Louis	—	30.00
3643☆	2074H☆	St. Louis☆	—	Not issued
3644	2074I	Minneapolis	—	Not issued
3644☆	2074I☆	Minneapolis☆	—	Not issued
3645	2074J	Kansas City	—	30.00
3645☆	2074J☆	Kansas City☆	—	Not issued
3646	2074K	Dallas	—	30.00
3646☆	2074K☆	Dallas☆	—	Not issued
3647	2074L	San Francisco	—	30.00
3647☆	2074L☆	San Francisco☆	—	50.00

Series 1985 Ortega-Baker

KL#	Fr#	Bank	XF	CU
3736	2075A	Boston	—	30.00
3736☆	2075A☆	Boston☆	—	40.00
3737	2075B	New York	—	30.00
3737☆	2075B☆	New York☆	—	40.00
3738	2075C	Philadelphia	—	30.00
3738☆	2075C☆	Philadelphia☆	—	40.00
3739	2075D	Cleveland	—	30.00
3739☆	2075D☆	Cleveland☆	—	40.00
3740	2075E	Richmond	—	30.00
3740☆	2075E☆	Richmond☆	—	40.00
3741	2075F	Atlanta	—	30.00
3741☆	2075F☆	Atlanta☆	—	Not issued
3742	2075G	Chicago	—	30.00
3742☆	2075G☆	Chicago☆	—	40.00
3743	2075H	St. Louis	—	30.00
3743☆	2075H☆	St. Louis☆	—	Not issued
3744	2075I	Minneapolis	—	30.00
3744☆	2075I☆	Minneapolis☆	—	Not issued
3745	2075J	Kansas City	—	30.00
3745☆	2075J☆	Kansas City☆	—	40.00
3746	2075K	Dallas	—	30.00
3746☆	2075K☆	Dallas☆	—	40.00
3747	2075L	San Francisco	—	30.00
3747☆	2075L☆	San Francisco☆	—	40.00

Series 1988A Villalpando-Brady

KL#	Fr#	Bank	XF	CU
3880	—	Boston	—	30.00
3880☆	—	Boston☆	—	Not issued
3881	—	New York	—	30.00
3881☆	—	New York☆	—	35.00
3882	—	Philadelphia	—	30.00
3882☆	—	Philadelphia☆	—	45.00
3883	—	Cleveland	—	30.00
3883☆	—	Cleveland☆	—	Not issued
3884	—	Richmond	—	30.00
3884☆	—	Richmond☆	—	Not issued
3885	—	Atlanta	—	30.00
3885☆	—	Atlanta☆	—	40.00
3886	—	Chicago	—	30.00
3886☆	—	Chicago☆	—	40.00
3887	—	St. Louis	—	30.00
3887☆	—	St. Louis☆	—	Not issued
3888	—	Minneapolis	—	30.00
3888☆	—	Minneapolis☆	—	Not issued
3889	—	Kansas City	—	30.00
3889☆	—	Kansas City☆	—	Not issued
3890	—	Dallas	—	30.00
3890☆	—	Dallas☆	—	40.00
3891	—	San Francisco	—	30.00
3891☆	—	San Francisco☆	—	Not issued

Series 1990 Villalpando-Brady

KL#	Fr#	Bank	XF	CU
3952	—	Boston	—	30.00
3952☆	—	Boston☆	—	40.00
3953	—	New York	—	30.00
3953☆	—	New York☆	—	40.00
3954	—	Philadelphia	—	30.00
3954☆	—	Philadelphia☆	—	Not issued
3955	—	Cleveland	—	30.00
3955☆	—	Cleveland☆	—	40.00
3956	—	Richmond	—	30.00
3956☆	—	Richmond☆	—	40.00
3957	—	Atlanta	—	40.00
3957☆	—	Atlanta☆	—	40.00
3958	—	Chicago	—	30.00
3958☆	—	Chicago☆	—	40.00
3959	—	St. Louis	—	30.00
3959☆	—	St. Louis☆	—	50.00
3960	—	Minneapolis	—	30.00
3960☆	—	Minneapolis☆	—	40.00
3961	—	Kansas City	—	30.00
3961☆	—	Kansas City☆	—	Not issued
3962	—	Dallas	—	30.00
3962☆	—	Dallas☆	—	Not issued
3963	—	San Francisco	—	30.00
3963☆	—	San Francisco☆	—	Not issued

Series 1993 Withrow-Bentsen

KL#	Fr#	Bank	XF	CU
4048	—	Boston	—	30.00
4048☆	—	Boston☆	—	40.00
4049	—	New York	—	30.00
4049☆	—	New York☆	—	35.00
4050	—	Philadelphia	—	30.00
4050☆	—	Philadelphia☆	—	Not issued
4051	—	Cleveland	—	30.00
4051☆	—	Cleveland☆	—	40.00
4052	—	Richmond	—	30.00
4052☆	—	Richmond☆	—	40.00
4053	—	Atlanta	—	30.00
4053☆	—	Atlanta☆	—	Not issued
4054	—	Chicago	—	30.00
4054☆	—	Chicago☆	—	Not issued
4055	—	St. Louis	—	30.00
4055☆	—	St. Louis☆	—	Not issued
4056	—	Minneapolis	—	Not issued
4056☆	—	Minneapolis☆	—	Not issued
4057	—	Kansas City	—	30.00
4057☆	—	Kansas City☆	—	Not issued
4058	—	Dallas	—	30.00
4058☆	—	Dallas☆	—	Not issued
4059	—	San Francisco	—	30.00
4059☆	—	San Francisco☆	—	35.00

Series 1995 Withrow-Rubin

KL#	Fr#	Bank	XF	CU
4120	—	Boston	—	Not issued
4120☆	—	Boston☆	—	Not issued
4121	—	New York	—	30.00
4121☆	—	New York☆	—	40.00
4122	—	Philadelphia	—	30.00
4122☆	—	Philadelphia☆	—	Not issued
4123	—	Cleveland	—	30.00
4123☆	—	Cleveland☆	—	40.00
4124	—	Richmond	—	30.00
4124☆	—	Richmond☆	—	Not issued
4125	—	Atlanta	—	30.00
4125☆	—	Atlanta☆	—	30.00
4126	—	Chicago	—	30.00
4126☆	—	Chicago☆	—	Not issued
4127	—	St. Louis	—	30.00
4127☆	—	St. Louis☆	—	Not issued
4128	—	Minneapolis	—	30.00
4128☆	—	Minneapolis☆	—	Not issued
4129	—	Kansas City	—	30.00
4129☆	—	Kansas City☆	—	Not issued
4130	—	Dallas	—	30.00
4130☆	—	Dallas☆	—	Not issued
4131	—	San Francisco	—	30.00
4131☆	—	San Francisco☆	—	Not issued

Series 1996 Withrow-Rubin

NOTE: To be issued in the Fall of 1998.

KL#	Fr#	Bank	XF	CU
4162	—	Boston	—	—
4162☆	—	Boston☆	—	—
4163	—	New York	—	—
4163☆	—	New York☆	—	—
4164	—	Philadelphia	—	—
4164☆	—	Philadelphia☆	—	—
4165	—	Cleveland	—	—
4165☆	—	Cleveland☆	—	—
4166	—	Richmond	—	—
4166☆	—	Richmond☆	—	—
4167	—	Atlanta	—	—
4167☆	—	Atlanta☆	—	—
4168	—	Chicago	—	—
4168☆	—	Chicago☆	—	—
4169	—	St. Louis	—	—
4169☆	—	St. Louis☆	—	—
4170	—	Minneapolis	—	—
4170☆	—	Minneapolis☆	—	—
4171	—	Kansas City	—	—
4171☆	—	Kansas City☆	—	—
4172	—	Dallas	—	—
4172☆	—	Dallas☆	—	—
4173	—	San Francisco	—	—
4173☆	—	San Francisco☆	—	—

Andrew Jackson

Hawaii Emergency Federal Reserve Notes

Andrew Jackson

KL#	Fr#	Series	Signatures	Fine	VF	CU
2523	2304	1934	Julian-Morgenthau	50.00	65.00	800.
2523☆	2304☆	1934☆	Julian-Morgenthau	400.	750.	6000.
2524	2305	1934A	Julian-Morgenthau	45.00	50.00	500.
2524☆	2305☆	1934A☆	Julian-Morgenthau	300.	450.	3000.

Fifty Dollars Gold Certificates

U.S. Grant

KL#	Fr#	Series	Signatures	Fine	VF	CU
2525	2404	1928	Woods-Mellon	125.	200.	1150.
2525☆	2404☆	1928☆	Woods-Mellon	750.	1000.	4000.

Federal Reserve Bank Notes

U.S. Grant

KL#	Fr#	Series	District	Fine	VF	CU
2526	1880-B	1929	New York	65.00	—	175.
2526☆	1880-B☆	1929	New York	150.	—	600.
2527	1880-D	1929	Cleveland	65.00	—	175.
2527☆	1880-D☆	1929☆	Cleveland	300.	—	1000.
2528	1880-G	1929	Chicago	65.00	—	150.
2528☆	1880-G☆	1929☆	Chicago	300.	—	1000.
2529	1880-I	1929	Minneapolis	75.00	—	175.
2529☆	1880-I☆	1929☆	Minneapolis	300.	—	1000.
2530	1880-J	1929	Kansas City	75.00	—	150.
2530☆	1880-J☆	1929☆	Kansas City	300.	—	1000.
2531	1880-K	1929	Dallas	85.00	—	200.
2531☆	1880-K☆	1929☆	Dallas	400.	—	1500.
2532	1880-L	1929	San Francisco	85.00	—	300.
2532☆	1880-L☆	1929☆	San Francisco	300.	—	1500.

Federal Reserve Notes

U.S. Grant

Series 1928 Woods-Mellon

KL#	Fr#	Bank	XF	CU
2533	2100A	Boston	125.	200.
2533☆	2100A☆	Boston☆	180.	800.
2534	2100B	New York	100.	200.
2534☆	2100B☆	New York☆	150.	600.
2535	2100C	Philadelphia	100.	200.
2535☆	2100C☆	Philadelphia☆	150.	600.
2536	2100D	Cleveland	100.	200.
2536☆	2100D☆	Cleveland☆	150.	600.
2537	2100E	Richmond	100.	200.
2537☆	2100E☆	Richmond☆	180.	500.
2538	2100F	Atlanta	100.	200.
2538☆	2100F☆	Atlanta☆	180.	600.
2539	2100G	Chicago	100.	200.
2539☆	2100G☆	Chicago☆	180.	600.
2540	2100H	St. Louis	100.	200.
2540☆	2100H☆	St. Louis☆	180.	600.
2541	2100I	Minneapolis	150.	200.
2541☆	2100I☆	Minneapolis☆	275	800.
2542	2100J	Kansas City	110.	200.
2542☆	2100J☆	Kansas City☆	180.	600.
2543	2100K	Dallas	150.	200.
2543☆	2100K☆	Dallas☆	275.	800.
2544	2100L	San Francisco	100.	200.
2544☆	2100L☆	San Francisco☆	200.	750.

Series 1928A Woods-Mellon

KL#	Fr#	Bank	XF	CU
2545	2101A	Boston	90.00	150.
2546	2101B	New York	90.00	150.
2547	2101C	Philadelphia	90.00	150.
2548	2101D	Cleveland	90.00	150.
2549	2101E	Richmond	90.00	150.
2550	2101F	Atlanta	120.	175.
2551	2101G	Chicago	90.00	150.
2552	2101H	St. Louis	110.	175.
2553	2101I	Minneapolis	110.	175.
2554	2101J	Kansas City	110.	175.
2555	2101K	Dallas	85.00	175.
2556	2101L	San Francisco	95.00	150.

Series 1934 Julian-Morgenthau

KL#	Fr#	Bank	XF	CU
2557	2102A	Boston	80.00	160.
2557☆	2102A☆	Boston☆	140.	450.
2558	2102B	New York	80.00	160.
2558☆	2102B☆	New York☆	140.	450.
2559	2102C	Philadelphia	80.00	160.
2559☆	2102C☆	Philadelphia☆	140.	450.
2560	2102D	Cleveland	80.00	160.
2560☆	2102D☆	Cleveland☆	140.	450.
2561	2102E	Richmond	80.00	160.
2561☆	2102E☆	Richmond☆	150.	550.
2562	2102F	Atlanta	80.00	160.
2562☆	2102F☆	Atlanta☆	140.	450.
2563	2102G	Chicago	80.00	160.
2563☆	2102G☆	Chicago☆	140.	450.
2564	2102H	St. Louis	85.00	160.
2564☆	2102H☆	St. Louis☆	150.	550.
2565	2102I	Minneapolis	85.00	160.
2565☆	2102I☆	Minneapolis☆	150.	550.
2566	2102J	Kansas City	85.00	160.
2566☆	2102J☆	Kansas City☆	125.	400.
2567	2102K	Dallas	85.00	160.
2567☆	2102K☆	Dallas☆	125.	400.
2568	2102L	San Francisco	80.00	160.
2568☆	2102L☆	San Francisco☆	125.	400.

Series 1934A Julian-Morgenthau

KL#	Fr#	Bank	XF	CU
2569	2103A	Boston	80.00	160.
2569☆	2103A☆	Boston☆	130.	450.
2570	2103B	New York	80.00	160.
2570☆	2103B☆	New York☆	130.	450.
2571	2103D	Cleveland	80.00	160.
2571☆	2103D☆	Cleveland☆	130.	450.
2572	2103E	Richmond	80.00	160.
2572☆	2103E☆	Richmond☆	130.	450.
2573	2103F	Atlanta	80.00	160.
2573☆	2103F☆	Atlanta☆	130.	450.
2574	2103G	Chicago	80.00	160.
2574☆	2103G☆	Chicago☆	130.	450.
2575	2103H	St. Louis	80.00	160.
2575☆	2103H☆	St. Louis☆	130.	450.
2576	2103I	Minneapolis	80.00	160.
2576☆	2103I☆	Minneapolis☆	130.	450.
2577	2103J	Kansas City	80.00	160.
2577☆	2103J☆	Kansas City☆	130.	450.
2578	2103K	Dallas	80.00	160.
2578☆	2103K☆	Dallas☆	130.	450.
2579	2103L	San Francisco	80.00	160.
2579☆	2103L☆	San Francisco☆	130.	450.

Series 1934B Julian-Vinson

KL#	Fr#	Bank	XF	CU
2580	2104C	Philadelphia	75.00	125.
2581	2104D	Cleveland	75.00	125.
2582	2104E	Richmond	—	125.
2583	2104F	Atlanta	—	125.
2584	2104G	Chicago	—	125.
2585	2104H	St. Louis	—	125.
2586	2104I	Minneapolis	—	200.
2587	2104J	Kansas City	—	175.
2588	2104K	Dallas	—	200.
2589	2104L	San Francisco	—	150.

Series 1934C Julian-Snyder

KL#	Fr#	Bank	XF	CU
2590	2105A	Boston	—	125.
2591	2105B	New York	—	85.00
2592	2105C	Philadelphia	—	125.
2593	2105D	Cleveland	—	85.00
2594	2105E	Richmond	—	85.00
2595	2105F	Atlanta	—	85.00
2596	2105G	Chicago	—	85.00
2597	2105H	St. Louis	—	85.00
2598	2105I	Minneapolis	—	125.
2599	2105J	Kansas City	—	85.00
2600	2105K	Dallas	—	85.00

Series 1934D Clark-Snyder

KL#	Fr#	Bank	XF	CU
2601	2106A	Boston	—	250.
2602	2106B	New York	—	250.
2603	2106C	Philadelphia	—	250.
2604	2106E	Richmond	—	400.
2605	2106F	Atlanta	—	400.
2606	2106G	Chicago	—	250.
2607	2106K	Dallas	—	350.
2608	2107A	Boston	—	120.
2608☆	2107A☆	Boston☆	—	300.
2609	2107B	New York	—	120.
2609☆	2107B☆	New York☆	—	300.
2610	2107C	Philadelphia	—	120.
2610☆	2107C☆	Philadelphia☆	—	300.
2611	2107D	Cleveland	—	120.
2611☆	2107D☆	Cleveland☆	—	300.
2612	2107E	Richmond	—	120.
2612☆	2107E☆	Richmond☆	—	350.
2613	2107F	Atlanta	—	120.
2613☆	2107F☆	Atlanta☆	—	350.
2614	2107G	Chicago	—	120.

SMALL SIZE $50 NOTES

Series 1934-D Clark-Snyder

KL#	Fr#	Bank	XF	CU
2614☆	2107G☆	Chicago☆	—	300.
2615	2107H	St. Louis	—	120.
2615☆	2107H☆	St. Louis☆	—	300.
2616	2107I	Minneapolis	—	120.
2616☆	2107I☆	Minneapolis☆	—	350.
2617	2107J	Kansas City	—	120.
2617☆	2107J☆	Kansas City☆	—	350.
2618	2107K	Dallas	—	120.
2618☆	2107K☆	Dallas☆	—	350.
2619	2107L	San Francisco	—	120.
2619☆	2107L☆	San Francisco☆	—	350.

Series 1950A Priest-Humphrey

KL#	Fr#	Bank	XF	CU
2620	2108A	Boston	—	120.
2620☆	2108A☆	Boston☆	—	300.
2621	2108B	New York	—	120.
2621☆	2108B☆	New York☆	—	300.
2622	2108C	Philadelphia	—	120.
2622☆	2108C☆	Philadelphia☆	—	300.
2623	2108D	Cleveland	—	120.
2623☆	2108D☆	Cleveland☆	—	300.
2624	2108E	Richmond	—	120.
2624☆	2108E☆	Richmond☆	—	300.
2625	2108F	Atlanta	—	120.
2625☆	2108F☆	Atlanta☆	—	350.
2626	2108G	Chicago	—	120.
2626☆	2108G☆	Chicago☆	—	300.
2627	2108H	St. Louis	—	120.
2627☆	2108H☆	St. Louis☆	—	300.
2628	2108J	Kansas City	—	120.
2628☆	2108J☆	Kansas City☆	—	300.
2629	2108K	Dallas	—	120.
2629☆	2108K☆	Dallas☆	—	300.
2630	2108L	San Francisco	—	120.
2630☆	2108L☆	San Francisco☆	—	300.

Series 1950B Priest-Anderson

KL#	Fr#	Bank	XF	CU
2631	2109A	Boston	—	120.
2631☆	2109A☆	Boston☆	—	300.
2632	2109B	New York	—	120.
2632☆	2109B☆	New York☆	—	300.
2633	2109C	Philadelphia	—	120.
2633☆	2109C☆	Philadelphia☆	—	300.
2634	2109D	Cleveland	—	120.
2634☆	2109D☆	Cleveland☆	—	300.
2635	2109E	Richmond	—	120.
2635☆	2109E☆	Richmond☆	—	300.
2636	2109G	Chicago	—	120.
2636☆	2109G☆	Chicago☆	—	300.
2637	2109H	St. Louis	—	120.
2637☆	2109H☆	St. Louis☆	—	300.
2638	2109J	Kansas City	—	120.
2638☆	2109J☆	Kansas City☆	—	300.
2639	2109K	Dallas	—	120.
2639☆	2109K☆	Dallas☆	—	300.
2640	2109L	San Francisco	—	120.
2640☆	2109L☆	San Francisco☆	—	300.

Series 1950C Smith-Dillon

KL#	Fr#	Bank	XF	CU
2641	2110A	Boston	—	110.
2641☆	2110A☆	Boston☆	—	250.
2642	2110B	New York	—	110.
2642☆	2110B☆	New York☆	—	200.
2643	2110C	Philadelphia	—	110.
2643☆	2110C☆	Philadelphia☆	—	250.
2644	2110D	Cleveland	—	110.
2644☆	2110D☆	Cleveland☆	—	300.
2645	2110E	Richmond	—	110.
2645☆	2110E☆	Richmond☆	—	300.
2646	2110G	Chicago	—	110.
2646☆	2110G☆	Chicago☆	—	300.
2647	2110H	St. Louis	—	110.
2647☆	2110H☆	St. Louis☆	—	300.
2648	2110I	Minneapolis	—	110.
2648☆	2110I☆	Minneapolis☆	—	300.
2649	2110J	Kansas City	—	110.
2649☆	2110J☆	Kansas City☆	—	300.
2650	2110K	Dallas	—	110.
2650☆	2110K☆	Dallas☆	—	300.
2651	2110L	San Francisco	—	110.
2651☆	2110L☆	San Francisco☆	—	300.

Series 1950D Granahan-Dillon

KL#	Fr#	Bank	XF	CU
2652	2111A	Boston	—	150.
2652☆	2111A☆	Boston☆	—	400.
2653	2111B	New York	—	150.
2653☆	2111B☆	New York☆	—	400.
2654	2111C	Philadelphia	—	150.
2654☆	2111C☆	Philadelphia☆	—	400.
2655	2111D	Cleveland	—	150.
2655☆	2111D☆	Cleveland☆	—	400.
2656	2111E	Richmond	—	150.
2656☆	2111E☆	Richmond☆	—	400.
2657	2111F	Atlanta	—	150.
2657☆	2111F☆	Atlanta☆	—	400.

Series 1969-A Kabis-Connally

KL#	Fr#	Bank	XF	CU
2658	2111G	Chicago	—	150.
2658☆	2111G☆	Chicago☆	—	400.
2659	2111H	St. Louis	—	150.
2659☆	2111H☆	St. Louis☆	—	400.
2660	2111I	Minneapolis	—	150.
2660☆	2111I☆	Minneapolis☆	—	400.
2661	2111J	Kansas City	—	150.
2661☆	2111J☆	Kansas City☆	—	400.
2662	2111K	Dallas	—	150.
2662☆	2111K☆	Dallas☆	—	400.
2663	2111L	San Francisco	—	150.
2663☆	2111L☆	San Francisco☆	—	400.

Series 1950E Granahan-Fowler

KL#	Fr#	Bank	XF	CU
2664	2112B	New York	—	150.
2664☆	2112B☆	New York☆	—	300.
2665	2112G	Chicago	—	175.
2665☆	2112G☆	Chicago☆	—	400.
2666	2112L	San Francisco	—	175.
2666☆	2112L☆	San Francisco☆	—	400.

Series 1963A Granahan-Fowler

KL#	Fr#	Bank	XF	CU
2667	2113A	Boston	—	100.
2667☆	2113A☆	Boston☆	—	200.
2668	2113B	New York	—	100.
2668☆	2113B☆	New York☆	—	175.
2669	2113C	Philadelphia	—	100.
2669☆	2113C☆	Philadelphia☆	—	175.
2670	2113D	Cleveland	—	100.
2670☆	2113D☆	Cleveland☆	—	175.
2671	2113E	Richmond	—	100.
2671☆	2113E☆	Richmond☆	—	175.
2672	2113F	Atlanta	—	100.
2672☆	2113F☆	Atlanta☆	—	175.
2673	2113G	Chicago	—	100.
2673☆	2113G☆	Chicago☆	—	175.
2674	2113H	St. Louis	—	120.
2674☆	2113H☆	St. Louis☆	—	200.
2675	2113I	Minneapolis	—	120.
2675☆	2113I☆	Minneapolis☆	—	275.
2676	2113J	Kansas City	—	100.
2676☆	2113J☆	Kansas City☆	—	200.
2677	2113K	Dallas	—	100.
2677☆	2113K☆	Dallas☆	—	200.
2678	2113L	San Francisco	—	100.
2678☆	2113L☆	San Francisco☆	—	175.

Series 1969 Elston-Kennedy

KL#	Fr#	Bank	XF	CU
2679	2114A	Boston	—	100.
2679☆	2114A☆	Boston☆	—	Not issued
2680	2114B	New York	—	100.
2680☆	2114B☆	New York☆	—	150.
2681	2114C	Philadelphia	—	100.
2681☆	2114C☆	Philadelphia☆	—	150.
2682	2114D	Cleveland	—	100.
2682☆	2114D☆	Cleveland☆	—	150.
2683	2114E	Richmond	—	100.
2683☆	2114E☆	Richmond☆	—	200.
2684	2114F	Atlanta	—	150.
2684☆	2114F☆	Atlanta☆	—	Not issued
2685	2114G	Chicago	—	100.
2685☆	2114G☆	Chicago☆	—	150.
2686	2114H	St. Louis	—	100.
2686☆	2114H☆	St. Louis☆	—	Not issued
2687	2114I	Minneapolis	—	100.
2687☆	2114I☆	Minneapolis☆	—	Not issued
2688	2114J	Kansas City	—	100.
2688☆	2114J☆	Kansas City☆	—	200.
2689	2114K	Dallas	—	100.
2689☆	2114K☆	Dallas☆	—	175.
2690	2114L	San Francisco	—	100.
2690☆	2114L☆	San Francisco☆	—	175.

Series 1969A Kabis-Connally

KL#	Fr#	Bank	XF	CU
2691	2115A	Boston	—	100.
2691☆	2115A☆	Boston☆	—	140.
2692	2115B	New York	—	90.00
2692☆	2115B☆	New York☆	—	120.
2693	2115C	Philadelphia	—	90.00
2693☆	2115C☆	Philadelphia☆	—	Not issued
2694	2115D	Cleveland	—	100.
2694☆	2115D☆	Cleveland☆	—	Not issued
2695	2115E	Richmond	—	100.
2695☆	2115E☆	Richmond☆	—	200.
2696	2115F	Atlanta	—	100.
2696☆	2115F☆	Atlanta☆	—	200.
2697	2115G	Chicago	—	100.
2697☆	2115G☆	Chicago☆	—	150.
2698	2115H	St. Louis	—	110.
2698☆	2115H☆	St. Louis☆	—	Not issued
2699	2115I	Minneapolis	—	100.
2699☆	2115I☆	Minneapolis☆	—	Not issued
2700	2115J	Kansas City	—	100.
2700☆	2115J☆	Kansas City☆	—	Not issued
2701	2115K	Dallas	—	100.
2701☆	2115K☆	Dallas☆	—	200.

Series 1969-A Kabis-Connally

KL#	Fr#	Bank	XF	CU
2702	2115L	San Francisco	—	90.00
2702☆	2115L☆	San Francisco☆	—	120.

Series 1969B Banuelos-Connally

KL#	Fr#	Bank	XF	CU
2703	2116A	Boston	—	100.
2704	2116B	New York	—	90.00
2705	2116E	Richmond	—	100.
2706	2116F	Atlanta	—	120.
2707	2116G	Chicago	—	100.
2708	2116K	Dallas	—	100.
2708☆	2116K☆	Dallas☆	—	1000.

Series 1969C Banuelos-Shultz

KL#	Fr#	Bank	XF	CU
2709	2117A	Boston	—	100.
2709☆	2117A☆	Boston☆	—	300.
2710	2117B	New York	—	100.
2710☆	2117B☆	New York☆	—	200.
2711	2117C	Philadelphia	—	100.
2711☆	2117C☆	Philadelphia☆	—	200.
2712	2117D	Cleveland	—	70.00
2712☆	2117D☆	Cleveland☆	—	100.
2713	2117E	Richmond	—	70.00
2713☆	2117E☆	Richmond☆	—	300.
2714	2117F	Atlanta	—	100.
2714☆	2117F☆	Atlanta☆	—	300.
2715	2117G	Chicago	—	70.00
2715☆	2117G☆	Chicago☆	—	85.00
2716	2117H	St. Louis	—	70.00
2716☆	2117H☆	St. Louis☆	—	300.
2717	2117I	Minneapolis	—	100.
2717☆	2117I☆	Minneapolis☆	—	300.
2718	2117J	Kansas City	—	75.00
2718☆	2117J☆	Kansas City☆	—	125.
2719	2117K	Dallas	—	70.00
2719☆	2117K☆	Dallas☆	—	300.
2720	2117L	San Francisco	—	70.00
2720☆	2117L☆	San Francisco☆	—	100.

Series 1974 Neff-Simon

KL#	Fr#	Bank	XF	CU
2721	2118A	Boston	—	100.
2721☆	2118A☆	Boston☆	—	160.
2722	2118B	New York	—	100.
2722☆	2118B☆	New York☆	—	160.
2723	2118C	Philadelphia	—	100.
2723☆	2118C☆	Philadelphia☆	—	160.
2724	2118D	Cleveland	—	100.
2724☆	2118D☆	Cleveland☆	—	160.
2725	2118E	Richmond	—	100.
2725☆	2118E☆	Richmond☆	—	160.
2726	2118F	Atlanta	—	100.
2726☆	2118F☆	Atlanta☆	—	160.
2727	2118G	Chicago	—	100.
2727☆	2118G☆	Chicago☆	—	160.
2728	2118H	St. Louis	—	100.
2728☆	2118H☆	St. Louis☆	—	160.
2729	2118I	Minneapolis	—	100.
2729☆	2118I☆	Minneapolis☆	—	160.
2730	2118J	Kansas City	—	100.
2730☆	2118J☆	Kansas City☆	—	160.
2731	2118K	Dallas	—	100.
2731☆	2118K☆	Dallas☆	—	160.
2732	2118L	San Francisco	—	100.
2732☆	2118L☆	San Francisco☆	—	160.

Series 1977 Morton-Blumenthal

KL#	Fr#	Bank	XF	CU
2733	2119A	Boston	—	95.00
2733☆	2119A☆	Boston☆	—	125.
2734	2119B	New York	—	95.00
2734☆	2119B☆	New York☆	—	125.
2735	2119C	Philadelphia	—	95.00
2735☆	2119C☆	Philadelphia☆	—	125.
2736	2119D	Cleveland	—	95.00
2736☆	2119D☆	Cleveland☆	—	125.
2737	2119E	Richmond	—	95.00
2737☆	2119E☆	Richmond☆	—	125.
2738	2119F	Atlanta	—	95.00
2738☆	2119F☆	Atlanta☆	—	125.
2739	2119G	Chicago	—	95.00
2739☆	2119G☆	Chicago☆	—	125.
2740	2119H	St. Louis	—	95.00
2740☆	2119H☆	St. Louis☆	—	125.
2741	2119I	Minneapolis	—	95.00
2741☆	2119I☆	Minneapolis☆	—	125.
2742	2119J	Kansas City	—	95.00
2742☆	2119J☆	Kansas City☆	—	125.
2743	2119K	Dallas	—	95.00
2743☆	2119K☆	Dallas☆	—	125.
2744	2119L	San Francisco	—	95.00
2744☆	2119L☆	San Francisco☆	—	125.

Series 1981 Buchanan-Regan

KL#	Fr#	Bank	XF	CU
3548	2120A	Boston	—	85.00
3548☆	2120A☆	Boston☆	—	Not issued
3549	2120B	New York	—	85.00
3549☆	2120B☆	New York☆	—	125.
3550	2120C	Philadelphia	—	85.00
3550☆	2120C☆	Philadelphia☆	—	Not issued
3551	2120D	Cleveland	—	85.00
3551☆	2120D☆	Cleveland☆	—	125.
3552	2120E	Richmond	—	85.00
3552☆	2120E☆	Richmond☆	—	Not issued
3553	2120F	Atlanta	—	85.00
3553☆	2120F☆	Atlanta☆	—	125.
3554	2120G	Chicago	—	85.00
3554☆	2120G☆	Chicago☆	—	125.
3555	2120H	St. Louis	—	85.00
3555☆	2120H☆	St. Louis☆	—	Not issued

Series 1981 Buchanan-Regan

KL#	Fr#	Bank	XF	CU
3556	2120I	Minneapolis	—	85.00
3556☆	2120I☆	Minneapolis☆	—	125.
3557	2120J	Kansas City	—	85.00
3557☆	2120J☆	Kansas City☆	—	125.
3558	2120K	Dallas	—	85.00
3558☆	2120K☆	Dallas☆	—	Not issued
3559	2120L	San Francisco	—	85.00
3559☆	2120L☆	San Francisco☆	—	125.

Series 1981A Ortega-Regan

KL#	Fr#	Bank	XF	CU
3648	2121A	Boston	—	80.00
3648☆	2121A☆	Boston☆	—	Not issued
3649	2121B	New York	—	80.00
3649☆	2121B☆	New York☆	—	125.
3650	2121C	Philadelphia	—	Not issued
3650☆	2121C☆	Philadelphia☆	—	Not issued
3651	2121D	Cleveland	—	80.00
3651☆	2121D☆	Cleveland☆	—	Not issued
3652	2121E	Richmond	—	80.00
3652☆	2121E☆	Richmond☆	—	125.
3653	2121F	Atlanta	—	80.00
3653☆	2121F☆	Atlanta☆	—	Not issued
3654	2121G	Chicago	—	80.00
3654☆	2121G☆	Chicago☆	—	Not issued
3655	2121H	St. Louis	—	80.00
3655☆	2121H☆	St. Louis☆	—	Not issued
3656	2121I	Minneapolis	—	80.00
3656☆	2121I☆	Minneapolis☆	—	Not issued
3657	2121J	Kansas City	—	Not issued
3657☆	2121J☆	Kansas City☆	—	Not issued
3658	2121K	Dallas	—	80.00
3658☆	2121K☆	Dallas☆	—	Not issued
3659	2121L	San Francisco	—	80.00
3659☆	2121L☆	San Francisco☆	—	125.

Series 1985 Ortega-Baker

KL#	Fr#	Bank	XF	CU
3748	2122A	Boston	—	75.00
3748☆	2122A☆	Boston☆	—	110.
3749	2122B	New York	—	75.00
3749☆	2122B☆	New York☆	—	110.
3750	2122C	Philadelphia	—	75.00
3750☆	2122C☆	Philadelphia☆	—	Not issued
3751	2122D	Cleveland	—	75.00
3751☆	2122D☆	Cleveland☆	—	110.
3752	2122E	Richmond	—	75.00
3752☆	2122E☆	Richmond☆	—	Not issued
3753	2122F	Atlanta	—	75.00
3753☆	2122F☆	Atlanta☆	—	Not issued
3754	2122G	Chicago	—	75.00
3754☆	2122G☆	Chicago☆	—	110.
3755	2122H	St. Louis	—	75.00
3755☆	2122H☆	St. Louis☆	—	Not issued
3756	2122I	Minneapolis	—	75.00
3756☆	2122I☆	Minneapolis☆	—	Not issued
3757	2122J	Kansas City	—	75.00
3757☆	2122J☆	Kansas City☆	—	Not issued
3758	2122K	Dallas	—	75.00
3758☆	2122K☆	Dallas☆	—	Not issued
3759	2122L	San Francisco	—	75.00
3759☆	2122L☆	San Francisco☆	—	Not issued

Series 1988 Ortega-Brady

KL#	Fr#	Bank	XF	CU
3820	2123A	Boston	—	65.00
3820☆	2123A☆	Boston☆	—	Not issued
3821	2123B	New York	—	65.00
3821☆	2123B☆	New York☆	—	100.
3822	2123C	Philadelphia	—	Not issued
3822☆	2123C☆	Philadelphia☆	—	Not issued
3823	2123D	Cleveland	—	70.00
3823☆	2123D☆	Cleveland☆	—	Not issued
3824	2123E	Richmond	—	70.00
3824☆	2123E☆	Richmond☆	—	Not issued
3825	2123F	Atlanta	—	Not issued
3825☆	2123F☆	Atlanta☆	—	Not issued
3826	2123G	Chicago	—	70.00
3826☆	2123G☆	Chicago☆	—	Not issued
3827	2123H	St Louis	—	Not issued
3827☆	2123H☆	St Louis☆	—	Not issued
3828	2123I	Minneapolis	—	Not issued
3828☆	2123I☆	Minneapolis☆	—	Not issued
3829	2123J	Kansas City	—	70.00
3829☆	2123J☆	Kansas City☆	—	Not issued
3830	2123K	Dallas	—	Not issued

Series 1988 Ortega-Brady

KL#	Fr#	Bank	XF	CU
3830☆	2123K☆	Dallas☆	—	Not issued
3831	2123L	San Francisco	—	70.00
3831☆	2123L☆	San Francisco☆	—	Not issued

Series 1990 Villalpando-Brady

KL#	Fr#	Bank	XF	CU
3964	—	Boston	—	65.00
3964☆	—	Boston☆	—	Not Issued
3965	—	New York	—	65.00
3965☆	—	New York☆	—	80.00
3966	—	Philadelphia	—	65.00
3966☆	—	Philadelphia☆	—	80.00
3967	—	Cleveland	—	65.00
3967☆	—	Cleveland☆	—	Not issued
3968	—	Richmond	—	65.00
3968☆	—	Richmond☆	—	Not issued
3969	—	Atlanta	—	Not issued
3969☆	—	Atlanta☆	—	Not issued
3970	—	Chicago	—	65.00
3970☆	—	Chicago☆	—	80.00
3971	—	St. Louis	—	65.00
3971☆	—	St. Louis☆	—	Not issued
3972	—	Minneapolis	—	65.00
3972☆	—	Minneapolis☆	—	Not issued
3973	—	Kansas City	—	65.00
3973☆	—	Kansas City☆	—	80.00
3974	—	Dallas	—	65.00
3974☆	—	Dallas☆	—	Not issued
3975	—	San Francisco	—	65.00
3975☆	—	San Francisco☆	—	Not issued

Series 1993 Withrow-Bentsen

KL#	Fr#	Bank	XF	CU
4060	—	Boston	—	65.00
4060☆	—	Boston☆	—	Not issued
4061	—	New York	—	65.00
4061☆	—	New York☆	—	75.00
4062	—	Philadelphia	—	Not issued
4062☆	—	Philadelphia☆	—	Not issued
4063	—	Cleveland	—	65.00
4063☆	—	Cleveland☆	—	75.00
4064	—	Richmond	—	65.00
4064☆	—	Richmond☆	—	Not issued
4065	—	Atlanta	—	Not issued
4065☆	—	Atlanta☆	—	Not issued
4066	—	Chicago	—	65.00
4066☆	—	Chicago☆	—	75.00
4067	—	St. Louis	—	65.00
4067☆	—	St. Louis☆	—	Not issued
4068	—	Minneapolis	—	Not issued
4068☆	—	Minneapolis☆	—	Not issued
4069	—	Kansas City	—	65.00
4069☆	—	Kansas City☆	—	Not issued
4070	—	Dallas	—	Not issued
4070☆	—	Dallas☆	—	Not issued
4071	—	San Francisco	—	65.00
4071☆	—	San Francisco☆	—	Not issued

Series 1996 Withrow-Rubin

KL#	Fr#	Bank	XF	CU
4150	—	Boston	—	60.00
4150☆	—	Boston☆	—	Not issued
4151	—	New York	—	60.00
4151☆	—	New York☆	—	70.00
4152	—	Philadelphia	—	60.00
4152☆	—	Philadelphia☆	—	Not issued
4153	—	Cleveland	—	60.00
4153☆	—	Cleveland☆	—	Not issued
4154	—	Richmond	—	Not issued
4154☆	—	Richmond☆	—	Not issued
4155	—	Atlanta	—	60.00
4155☆	—	Atlanta☆	—	Not issued
4156	—	Chicago	—	60.00
4156☆	—	Chicago☆	—	Not issued
4157	—	St. Louis	—	60.00
4157☆	—	St. Louis☆	—	Not issued
4158	—	Minneapolis	—	60.00
4158☆	—	Minneapolis☆	—	Not issued
4159	—	Kansas City	—	60.00
4159☆	—	Kansas City☆	—	70.00
4160	—	Dallas	—	Not issued
4160☆	—	Dallas☆	—	Not issued
4161	—	San Francisco	—	60.00
4161☆	—	San Francisco☆	—	Not issued

U.S. Grant

One Hundred Dollars
United States Notes

Ben Franklin

KL#	Fr#	Series	Signatures	Fine	VF	CU
2745	1550	1966	Granahan-Fowler	—	130.	300.
2745☆	1550☆	1966☆	Granahan-Fowler	175.	225.	600.
2746	1551	1966A	Elston-Kennedy	125.	225.	750.
2746A☆	—	1966A☆	Elston-Kennedy			Not issued

Gold Certificates

Ben Franklin

KL#	Fr#	Series	Signatures	Fine	VF	CU
2747	2405	1928	Woods-Mellon	275.	—	1400.
2747☆	2405☆	1928☆	Woods-Mellon	750.	—	4500.

Federal Reserve Bank Notes

Ben Franklin

KL#	Fr#	Series	District	Fine	VF	CU
2749	1890B	1929	New York	125.	—	300.
2749☆	1890B☆	1929☆	New York☆	300.	—	2000.
2751	1890D	1929	Cleveland	135.	—	250.
2751☆	1890D☆	1929☆	Cleveland☆	300.	—	1200.

KL#	Fr#	Series	District	Fine	VF	CU
2752	1890E	1929	Richmond	125.	—	500.
2752☆	1890E☆	1929☆	Richmond☆	300.	—	1200.
2754	1890G	1929	Chicago	125.	—	300.
2754☆	1890G☆	1929☆	Chicago☆	300.	—	1500.
2756	1890I	1929	Minneapolis	125.	—	300.
2756☆	1890I☆	1929☆	Minneapolis☆	300.	—	1750.
2757	1890J	1929	Kansas City	125.	—	275.
2757☆	1890J☆	1929☆	Kansas City☆	250.	—	750.
2758	1890K	1929	Dallas	150.	—	500.
2758☆	1890K☆	1929☆	Dallas☆	450.	—	2200.

Federal Reserve Notes

Ben Franklin

Series 1928 Woods-Mellon

KL#	Fr#	Bank	XF	CU
2760	2150A	Boston	200.	300.
2760☆	2150A☆	Boston☆	300.	600.
2761	2150B	New York	175.	225.
2761☆	2150B☆	New York☆	300.	450.
2762	2150C	Philadelphia	175.	250.
2762☆	2150C☆	Philadelphia☆	275.	500.
2763	2150D	Cleveland	200.	300.
2763☆	2150D☆	Cleveland☆	300.	600.
2764	2150E	Richmond	200.	300.
2764☆	2150E☆	Richmond☆	300.	600.
2765	2150F	Atlanta	200.	300.
2765☆	2150F☆	Atlanta☆	300.	600.
2766	2150G	Chicago	175.	200.
2766☆	2150G☆	Chicago☆	210.	375.
2767	2150H	St. Louis	165.	250.
2767☆	2150H☆	St. Louis☆	225.	500.
2768	2150I	Minneapolis	165.	250.
2768☆	2150I☆	Minneapolis☆	225.	500.
2769	2150J	Kansas City	175.	250.
2769☆	2150J☆	Kansas City☆	325.	600.
2770	2150K	Dallas	180.	200.
2770☆	2150K☆	Dallas☆	325.	500.
2771	2150L	San Francisco	175.	200.
2771☆	2150L☆	San Francisco☆	225.	450.

Series 1928A Woods-Mellon

KL#	Fr#	Bank	XF	CU
2772	2151A	Boston	200.	275.
2773	2151B	New York	175.	200.
2774	2151C	Philadelphia	200.	275.
2775	2151D	Cleveland	185.	250.
2776	2151D	Richmond	210.	350.
2777	2151E	Atlanta	195.	300.
2778	2151G	Chicago	175.	200.
2779	2151H	St. Louis	185.	250.
2779☆	2151H☆	St. Louis☆	850.	2000.
2780	2151I	Minneapolis	195.	300.
2781	2151J	Kansas City	210.	350.
2782	2151K	Dallas	195.	300.
2783	2151L	San Fransisco	185.	250.

Series 1934 Julian-Morgenthau

KL#	Fr#	Bank	XF	CU
2784	2152A	Boston	175.	250.
2784☆	2152A☆	Boston☆	200.	325.
2785	2152B	New York	175.	225.
2785☆	2152B☆	New York☆	200.	325.
2786	2152C	Philadelphia	175.	225.
2786☆	2152C☆	Philadelphia☆	200.	325.
2787	2152D	Cleveland	175.	225.
2787☆	2152D☆	Cleveland☆	200.	325.
2788	2152E	Richmond	175.	225.
2788☆	2152E☆	Richmond☆	200.	325.
2789	2152F	Atlanta	210.	275.
2789☆	2152F☆	Atlanta☆	250.	375.
2790	2152G	Chicago	175.	225.
2790☆	2152G☆	Chicago☆	200.	275.
2791	2152H	St. Louis	175.	225.
2791☆	2152H☆	St. Louis☆	210.	370.
2792	2152I	Minneapolis	175.	225.
2792☆	2152I☆	Minneapolis☆	200.	300.
2793	2152J	Kansas City	175.	225.
2793☆	2152J☆	Kansas City☆	200.	350.
2794	2152K	Dallas	175.	225.
2794☆	2152K☆	Dallas☆	215.	375.
2795	2152L	San Francisco	175.	225.
2795☆	2152L☆	San Francisco☆	200.	350.

Series 1934A Julian-Morgenthau

KL#	Fr#	Bank	XF	CU
2784A	2153A	Boston	175.	200.
2784A☆	2153A☆	Boston☆	200.	300.
2785A	2153B	New York	150.	200.
2785A☆	2153B☆	New York☆	250.	300.
2786A	2153C	Philadelphia	150.	200.
2786A☆	2153C☆	Philadelphia☆	200.	275.
2787A	2153D	Cleveland	150.	200.
2787A☆	2153D☆	Cleveland☆	200.	275.
2788A	2153E	Richmond	150.	200.
2788A☆	2153E☆	Richmond☆	200.	275.
2789A	2153F	Atlanta	150.	200.
2789A☆	2153F☆	Atlanta☆	175.	275.
2790A	2153G	Chicago	150.	200.
2790A☆	2153G☆	Chicago☆	175.	275.
2791A	2153H	St. Louis	150.	200.
2791A☆	2153H☆	St. Louis☆	175.	275.
2792A	2153I	Minneapolis	150.	200.
2792A☆	2153I☆	Minneapolis☆	175.	275.
2793A	2153J	Kansas City	150.	200.
2793A☆	2153J☆	Kansas City☆	175.	275.
2794A	2153K	Dallas	150.	200.
2794A☆	2153K☆	Dallas☆	175.	275.
2795A	2153L	San Francisco	150.	200.
2795A☆	2153L☆	San Francisco☆	175.	275.

Series 1934B Julian-Vinson

KL#	Fr#	Bank	XF	CU
2796	2154A	Boston	200.	250.
2796☆	2154A☆	Boston☆	—	Not issued
2797	2154C	Philadelphia	200.	250.
2797☆	2154C☆	Philadelphia☆	—	Not issued
2798	2154D	Cleveland	200.	250.
2798☆	2154D☆	Cleveland☆	—	Not issued
2799	2154E	Richmond	185.	250.
2799☆	2154E☆	Richmond☆	500.	2000.
2800	2154F	Atlanta	175.	250.
2800☆	2154F☆	Atlanta☆	500.	2000.
2801	2154G	Chicago	175.	250.
2801☆	2154G☆	Chicago☆	500.	2000.
2802	2154H	St. Louis	175.	250.
2802☆	2154H☆	St. Louis☆	500.	2000.
2803	2154I	Minneapolis	175.	250.
2803☆	2154I☆	Minneapolis☆	500.	2000.
2804	2154J	Kansas City	175.	250.
2804☆	2154J☆	Kansas City☆	500.	2000.
2805	2154K	Dallas	175.	250.
2805☆	2154K☆	Dallas☆	500.	2000.

Series 1934C Julian-Snyder

KL#	Fr#	Bank	XF	CU
2806	2155A	Boston	175.	200.
2807	2155B	New York	200.	275.
2808	2155C	Philadelphia	200.	275.
2809	2155D	Cleveland	200.	275.
2810	2155F	Atlanta	200.	275.
2811	2155G	Chicago	200.	275.
2812	2155H	St. Louis	200.	275.
2813	2155I	Minneapolis	200.	275.
2814	2155J	Kansas City	200.	275.
2815	2155K	Dallas	200.	275.
2816	2155L	San Francisco	200.	275.

Series 1934D Clark-Snyder

KL#	Fr#	Bank	XF	CU
2817	2156B	New York	1500.	2500.
2818	2156C	Philadelphia	150.	225.
2819	2156F	Atlanta	150.	225.
2820	2156G	Chicago	150.	225.
2821	2156H	St. Louis	150.	225.
2822	2156K	Dallas	150.	225.

Series 1950 Clark-Snyder

KL#	Fr#	Bank	XF	CU
2823	2157A	Boston	—	250.
2824	2157B	New York	—	250.
2825	2157C	Philadelphia	—	250.
2825☆	2157C☆	Philadelphia☆	—	500.
2826	2157D	Cleveland	—	250.
2827	2157E	Richmond	—	250.
2828	2157F	Atlanta	—	250.
2829	2157G	Chicago	—	250.
2830	2157H	St. Louis	—	250.
2831	2157I	Minneapolis	—	250.
2832	2157J	Kansas City	—	250.
2833	2157K	Dallas	—	250.
2834	2157L	San Francisco	—	250.

Series 1950A Priest-Humphrey

KL#	Fr#	Bank	XF	CU
2835	2158A	Boston	—	175.
2836	2158B	New York	—	175.
2836☆	2158B☆	New York☆	—	300.
2837	2158C	Philadelphia	—	175.
2838	2158D	Cleveland	—	175.
2839	2158E	Richmond	—	130.
2840	2158F	Atlanta	—	175.

Series 1950-A Priest-Humphrey

KL#	Fr#	Bank	XF	CU
2841	2158G	Chicago	—	175.
2842	2158H	St. Louis	—	175.
2843	2158I	Minneapolis	—	175.
2844	2158J	Kansas City	—	175.
2845	2158K	Dallas	—	175.
2846	2158L	San Francisco	—	175.

Series 1950B Priest-Anderson

KL#	Fr#	Bank	XF	CU
2847	2159A	Boston	—	250.
2848	2159B	New York	—	250.
2848☆	2159B☆	New York☆	—	375.
2849	2159C	Philadelphia	—	250.
2849☆	2159C☆	Philadelphia☆	—	375.
2850	2159D	Cleveland	—	250.
2851	2159E	Richmond	—	250.
2852	2159F	Atlanta	—	250.
2852☆	2159F☆	Atlanta☆	—	375.
2853	2159G	Chicago	—	250.
2853☆	2159G☆	Chicago☆	—	375.
2854	2159H	St. Louis	—	250.
2854☆	2159H☆	St. Louis☆	—	375.
2855	2159I	Minneapolis	—	250.
2855☆	2159I☆	Minneapolis☆	—	375.
2856	2159J	Kansas City	—	250.
2857	2159K	Dallas	—	250.
2857☆	2159K☆	Dallas☆	—	375.
2858	2159L	San Francisco	—	250.

Series 1950C Smith-Dillon

KL#	Fr#	Bank	XF	CU
2859	2160A	Boston	—	225.
2859☆	2160A☆	Boston☆	—	425.
2860	2160B	New York	—	225.
2860☆	2160B☆	New York☆	—	425.
2861	2160C	Philadelphia	—	225.
2861☆	2160C☆	Philadelphia☆	—	425.
2862	2160D	Cleveland	—	225.
2863	2160E	Richmond	—	225.
2863☆	2160E☆	Richmond☆	—	425.
2864	2160F	Atlanta	—	225.
2864☆	2160F☆	Atlanta☆	—	425.
2865	2160G	Chicago	—	225.
2865☆	2160G☆	Chicago☆	—	425.
2866	2160H	St. Louis	—	225.
2866☆	2160H☆	St. Louis☆	—	425.
2867	2160I	Minneapolis	—	225.
2867☆	2160I☆	Minneapolis☆	—	425.
2868	2160J	Kansas City	—	225.
2868☆	2160J☆	Kansas City☆	—	425.
2869	2160K	Dallas	—	225.
2869☆	2160K☆	Dallas☆	—	425.
2870	2160L	San Francisco	—	225.
2870☆	2160L☆	San Francisco☆	—	425.

Series 1950D Granahan-Dillon

KL#	Fr#	Bank	XF	CU
2871	2161A	Boston	—	250.
2871☆	2161A☆	Boston☆	—	400.
2872	2161B	New York	—	250.
2872☆	2161B☆	New York☆	—	400.
2873	2161C	Philadelphia	—	250.
2873☆	2161C☆	Philadelphia☆	—	400.
2874	2161D	Cleveland	—	250.
2874☆	2161D☆	Cleveland☆	—	400.
2875	2161E	Richmond	—	250.
2875☆	2161E☆	Richmond☆	—	400.
2876	2161F	Atlanta	—	250.
2876☆	2161F☆	Atlanta☆	—	400.
2877	2161G	Chicago	—	250.
2877☆	2161G☆	Chicago☆	—	400.
2878	2161H	St. Louis	—	250.
2878☆	2161H☆	St. Louis☆	—	400.
2879	2161I	Minneapolis	—	250.
2879☆	2161I☆	Minneapolis☆	—	400.
2880	2161J	Kansas City	—	250.
2880☆	2161J☆	Kansas City☆	—	400.
2881	2161K	Dallas	—	250.
2881☆	2161K☆	Dallas☆	—	400.
2882	2161L	San Francisco	—	250.
2882☆	2161L☆	San Francisco☆	—	400.

Series 1950E Granahan-Fowler

KL#	Fr#	Bank	XF	CU
2883	2162B	New York	—	250.
2883☆	2162B☆	New York☆	—	1250.
2884	2162G	Chicago	—	250.
2884☆	2162G☆	Chicago☆	—	1250.
2885	2162L	San Francisco	—	250.
2885☆	2162L☆	San Francisco☆	—	1250.

Series 1963A Granahan-Fowler

KL#	Fr#	Bank	XF	CU
2886	2163A	Boston	—	200.
2886☆	2163A☆	Boston☆	—	275.
2887	2163B	New York	—	200.
2887☆	2163B☆	New York☆	—	275.
2888	2163C	Philadelphia	—	200.
2888☆	2163C☆	Philadelphia☆	—	275.
2889	2163D	Cleveland	—	200.
2889☆	2163D☆	Cleveland☆	—	275.
2890	2163E	Richmond	—	200.
2890☆	2163E☆	Richmond☆	—	275.
2891	2163F	Atlanta	—	200.
2891☆	2163F☆	Atlanta☆	—	275.
2892	2163G	Chicago	—	200.
2892☆	2163G☆	Chicago☆	—	275.
2893	2163H	St. Louis	—	200.
2893☆	2163H☆	St. Louis☆	—	275.
2894	2163I	Minneapolis	—	200.
2894☆	2163I☆	Minneapolis☆	—	275.
2895	2163J	Kansas City	—	200.
2895☆	2163J☆	Kansas City☆	—	275.
2896	2163K	Dallas	—	200.
2896☆	2163K☆	Dallas☆	—	275.
2897	2163L	San Francisco	—	200.
2897☆	2163L☆	San Francisco☆	—	275.

Series 1969 Elston-Kennedy

KL#	Fr#	Bank	XF	CU
2898	2164A	Boston	—	175.
2898☆	2164A☆	Boston☆	—	250.
2899	2164B	New York	—	175.
2899☆	2164B☆	New York☆	—	250.
2900	2164C	Philadelphia	—	175.
2900☆	2164C☆	Philadelphia☆	—	250.
2901	2164D	Cleveland	—	175.
2901☆	2164D☆	Cleveland☆	—	250.
2902	2164E	Richmond	—	175.
2902☆	2164E☆	Richmond☆	—	250.
2903	2164F	Atlanta	—	175.
2903☆	2164F☆	Atlanta☆	—	250.
2904	2164G	Chicago	—	175.
2904☆	2164G☆	Chicago☆	—	250.
2905	2164H	St. Louis	—	175.
2905☆	2164H☆	St. Louis☆	—	250.
2906	2164I	Minneapolis	—	175.
2906☆	2164I☆	Minneapolis☆	—	250.

Series 1969 Elston-Kennedy

KL#	Fr#	Bank	XF	CU
2907	2164J	Kansas City	—	175.
2907☆	2164J☆	Kansas City☆	—	250.
2908	2164K	Dallas	—	175.
2908☆	2164K☆	Dallas☆	—	250.
2909	2164L	San Francisco	—	175.
2909☆	2164L☆	San Francisco☆	—	250.

Series 1969A Kabis-Connally

KL#	Fr#	Bank	XF	CU
2898A	2165A	Boston	—	175.
2898A☆	2165A☆	Boston☆	—	275.
2899A	2165B	New York	—	175.
2899A☆	2165B☆	New York☆	—	275.
2900A	2165C	Philadelphia	—	175.
2900A☆	2165C☆	Philadelphia☆	—	275.
2901A	2165D	Cleveland	—	175.
2901A☆	2165D☆	Cleveland☆	—	275.
2902A	2165E	Richmond	—	175.
2902A☆	2165E☆	Richmond☆	—	275.
2903A	2165F	Atlanta	—	175.
2903A☆	2165F☆	Atlanta☆	—	275.
2904A	2165G	Chicago	—	175.
2904A☆	2165G☆	Chicago☆	—	275.
2905A	2165H	St. Louis	—	175.
2905A☆	2165H☆	St. Louis☆	—	275.
2906A	2165I	Minneapolis	—	175.
2906A☆	2165I☆	Minneapolis☆	—	Not issued
2907A	2165J	Kansas City	—	175.
2907A☆	2165J☆	Kansas City☆	—	Not issued
2908A	2165K	Dallas	—	175.
2908A☆	2165K☆	Dallas☆	—	275.
2909A	2165L	San Francisco	—	175.
2909A☆	2165L☆	San Francisco☆	—	275.

Series 1969C Banuelos-Shultz

KL#	Fr#	Bank	XF	CU
2910	2166A	Boston	—	150.
2910☆	2166A☆	Boston☆	—	350.
2911	2166B	New York	—	150.
2911☆	2166B☆	New York☆	—	250.
2912	2166C	Philadelphia	—	150.
2912☆	2166C☆	Philadelphia☆	—	350.
2913	2166D	Cleveland	—	150.
2913☆	2166D☆	Cleveland☆	—	350.
2914	2166E	Richmond	—	150.
2914☆	2166E☆	Richmond☆	—	300.
2915	2166F	Atlanta	—	150.
2915☆	2166F☆	Atlanta☆	—	350.
2916	2166G	Chicago	—	150.
2916☆	2166G☆	Chicago☆	—	250.
2917	2166H	St. Louis	—	150.
2917☆	2166H☆	St. Louis☆	—	350.
2918	2166I	Minneapolis	—	150.
2918☆	2166I☆	Minneapolis☆	—	350.
2919	2166J	Kansas City	—	150.
2919☆	2166J☆	Kansas City☆	—	250.
2920	2166K	Dallas	—	150.
2920☆	2166K☆	Dallas☆	—	350.
2921	2166L	San Francisco	—	150.
2921☆	2166L☆	San Francisco☆	—	250.

Series 1974 Neff-Simon

KL#	Fr#	Bank	XF	CU
2922	2167A	Boston	—	150.
2922☆	2167A☆	Boston☆	—	250.
2923	2167B	New York	—	150.
2923☆	2167B☆	New York☆	—	200.
2924	2167C	Philadelphia	—	150.
2924☆	2167C☆	Philadelphia☆	—	250.
2925	2167D	Cleveland	—	150.
2925☆	2167D☆	Cleveland☆	—	250.
2926	2167E	Richmond	—	150.
2926☆	2167E☆	Richmond☆	—	250.
2927	2167F	Atlanta	—	150.
2927☆	2167F☆	Atlanta☆	—	250.
2928	2167G	Chicago	—	150.
2928☆	2167G☆	Chicago☆	—	200.
2929	2167H	St. Louis	—	150.
2929☆	2167H☆	St. Louis☆	—	250.
2930	2167I	Minneapolis	—	150.
2930☆	2167I☆	Minneapolis☆	—	250.
2931	2167J	Kansas City	—	150.
2931☆	2167J☆	Kansas City☆	—	250.
2932	2167K	Dallas	—	150.
2932☆	2167K☆	Dallas☆	—	250.
2933	2167L	San Francisco	—	150.
2933☆	2167L☆	San Francisco☆	—	200.

Series 1977 Morton-Blumenthal

KL#	Fr#	Bank	XF	CU
2934	2168A	Boston	—	150.
2934☆	2168A☆	Boston☆	—	190.
2935	2168B	New York	—	150.
2935☆	2168B☆	New York☆	—	180.
2936	2168C	Philadelphia	—	150.
2936☆	2168C☆	Philadelphia☆	—	190.
2937	2168D	Cleveland	—	150.
2937☆	2168D☆	Cleveland☆	—	180.
2938	2168E	Richmond	—	150.
2938☆	2168E☆	Richmond☆	—	180.
2939	2168F	Atlanta	—	150.
2939☆	2168F☆	Atlanta☆	—	225.
2940	2168G	Chicago	—	150.
2940☆	2168G☆	Chicago☆	—	180.
2941	2168H	St. Louis	—	150.
2941☆	2168H☆	St. Louis☆	—	180.
2942	2168I	Minneapolis	—	150.
2942☆	2168I☆	Minneapolis☆	—	190.
2943	2168J	Kansas City	—	150.
2943☆	2168J☆	Kansas City☆	—	180.
2944	2168K	Dallas	—	150.
2944☆	2168K☆	Dallas☆	—	180.
2944A	2168L	San Francisco	—	150.
2944A☆	2168L☆	San Francisco☆	—	180.

Series 1981 Buchanan-Regan

KL#	Fr#	Bank	XF	CU
3560	2169A	Boston	—	200.
3560☆	2169A☆	Boston☆	—	Not issued
3561	2169B	New York	—	200.
3561☆	2169B☆	New York☆	—	Not issued
3562	2169C	Philadelphia	—	200.
3562☆	2169C☆	Philadelphia☆	—	Not issued
3563	2169D	Cleveland	—	200.
3563☆	2169D☆	Cleveland☆	—	Not issued
3564	2169E	Richmond	—	200.
3564☆	2169E☆	Richmond☆	—	375.
3565	2169F	Atlanta	—	200.
3565☆	2169F☆	Atlanta☆	—	Not issued
3566	2169G	Chicago	—	200.
3566☆	2169G☆	Chicago☆	—	Not issued
3567	2169H	St. Louis	—	200.
3567☆	2169H☆	St. Louis☆	—	Not issued
3568	2169I	Minneapolis	—	200.
3568☆	2169I☆	Minneapolis☆	—	Not issued
3569	2169J	Kansas City	—	200.
3569☆	2169J☆	Kansas City☆	—	Not issued
3570	2169K	Dallas	—	200.
3570☆	2169K☆	Dallas☆	—	Not issued
3571	2169L	San Francisco	—	200.
3571☆	2169L☆	San Francisco☆	—	Not issued

Series 1981A Ortega-Regan

KL#	Fr#	Bank	XF	CU
3660	2170A	Boston	—	200.
3660☆	2170A☆	Boston☆	—	Not issued
3661	2170B	New York	—	200.
3661☆	2170B☆	New York☆	—	Not issued
3662	2170C	Philadelphia	—	200.
3662☆	2170C☆	Philadelphia☆	—	Not issued
3663	2170D	Cleveland	—	200.
3663☆	2170D☆	Cleveland☆	—	Not issued
3664	2170E	Richmond	—	200.
3664☆	2170E☆	Richmond☆	—	Not issued
3665	2170F	Atlanta	—	200.
3665☆	2170F☆	Atlanta☆	—	Not issued
3666	2170G	Chicago	—	200.
3666☆	2170G☆	Chicago☆	—	Not issued
3667	2170H	St. Louis	—	200.
3667☆	2170H☆	St. Louis☆	—	Not issued
3668	2170I	Minneapolis	—	200.
3668☆	2170I☆	Minneapolis☆	—	Not issued
3669	2170J	Kansas City	—	200.
3669☆	2170J☆	Kansas City☆	—	Not issued
3670	2170K	Dallas	—	200.
3670☆	2170K☆	Dallas☆	—	Not issued
3671	2170L	San Francisco	—	200.
3671☆	2170L☆	San Francisco☆	—	375.

Series 1985 Ortega-Baker

KL#	Fr#	Bank	XF	CU
3760	2171A	Boston	—	175.
3760☆	2171A☆	Boston☆	—	Not issued
3761	2171B	New York	—	175.
3761☆	2171B☆	New York☆	—	Not issued
3762	2171C	Phildelphia	—	175.
3762☆	2171C☆	Phildelphia☆	—	Not issued
3763	2171D	Cleveland	—	175.
3763☆	2171D☆	Cleveland☆	—	300.
3764	2171E	Richmond	—	175.
3764☆	2171E☆	Richmond☆	—	Not issued
3765	2171F	Atlanta	—	175.
3765☆	2171F☆	Atlanta☆	—	Not issued
3766	2171G	Chicago	—	175.
3766☆	2171G☆	Chicago☆	—	Not issued
3767	2171H	St. Louis	—	175.
3767☆	2171H☆	St. Louis☆	—	Not issued
3768	2171I	Minneapolis	—	175.
3768☆	2171I☆	Minneapolis☆	—	Not issued
3769	2171J	Kansas City	—	175.
3769☆	2171J☆	Kansas City☆	—	300.
3770	2171K	Dallas	—	175.
3770☆	2171K☆	Dallas☆	—	300.
3771	2171L	San Francisco	—	175.
3771☆	2171L☆	San Francisco☆	—	Not issued

Series 1988 Ortega-Brady

KL#	Fr#	Bank	XF	CU
3832	2172A	Boston	—	150.
3832☆	2172A☆	Boston☆	—	Not issued
3833	2172B	New York	—	150.
3833☆	2172B☆	New York☆	—	250.
3834	2172C	Philadelphia	—	150.
3834☆	2172C☆	Philadelphia☆	—	Not issued
3835	2172D	Cleveland	—	150.
3835☆	2172D☆	Cleveland☆	—	Not issued
3836	2172E	Richmond	—	150.
3836☆	2172E☆	Richmond☆	—	Not issued
3837	2172F	Atlanta	—	Not issued
3837☆	2172F☆	Atlanta☆	—	Not issued
3838	2172G	Chicago	—	150.
3838☆	2172G☆	Chicago☆	—	Not issued
3839	2172H	St. Louis	—	150.
3839☆	2172H☆	St. Louis☆	—	Not issued
3840	2172I	Minneapolis	—	Not issued
3840☆	2172I☆	Minneapolis☆	—	Not issued
3841	2172J	Kansas City	—	150.
3841☆	2172J☆	Kansas City☆	—	Not issued
3842	2172K	Dallas	—	Not issued
3842☆	2172K☆	Dallas☆	—	Not issued
3843	2172L	San Francisco	—	150.
3843☆	2172L☆	San Francisco☆	—	Not issued

Series 1990 Villalpando-Brady

KL#	Fr#	Bank	XF	CU
3976	—	Boston	—	125.
3976☆	—	Boston☆	—	Not issued
3977	—	New York	—	125.
3977☆	—	New York☆	—	145.
3978	—	Philadelphia	—	125.
3978☆	—	Philadelphia☆	—	145.
3979	—	Cleveland	—	125.
3979☆	—	Cleveland☆	—	Not issued
3980	—	Richmond	—	125.
3980☆	—	Richmond☆	—	Not issued
3981	—	Atlanta	—	125.
3981☆	—	Atlanta☆	—	Not issued
3982	—	Chicago	—	125.
3982☆	—	Chicago☆	—	145.
3983	—	St. Louis	—	125.
3983☆	—	St. Louis☆	—	Not issued
3984	—	Minneapolis	—	125.
3984☆	—	Minneapolis☆	—	Not issued
3985	—	Kansas City	—	125.
3985☆	—	Kansas City☆	—	175.
3986	—	Dallas	—	125.
3986☆	—	Dallas☆	—	145.
3987	—	San Francisco	—	125.
3987☆	—	San Francisco☆	—	145.

Series 1993 Withrow-Bentsen

KL#	Fr#	Bank	XF	CU
4072	—	Boston	—	120.
4072☆	—	Boston☆	—	Not issued
4073	—	New York	—	120.
4073☆	—	New York☆	—	130.
4074	—	Philadelphia	—	120.
4074☆	—	Philadelphia☆	—	130.
4075	—	Cleveland	—	120.
4075☆	—	Cleveland☆	—	130.
4076	—	Richmond	—	120.
4076☆	—	Richmond☆	—	Not issued
4077	—	Atlanta	—	120.

Series 1993 Withrow-Bentsen

KL#	Fr#	Bank	XF	CU
4077☆	—	Atlanta☆	—	Not issued
4078	—	Chicago	—	120.
4078☆	—	Chicago☆	—	Not issued
4079	—	St. Louis	—	120.
4079☆	—	St. Louis☆	—	135.
4080	—	Minneapolis	—	120.
4080☆	—	Minneapolis☆	—	Not issued
4081	—	Kansas City	—	120.
4081☆	—	Kansas City☆	—	Not issued
4082	—	Dallas	—	120.
4082☆	—	Dallas☆	—	Not issued
4083	—	San Francisco	—	120.
4083☆	—	San Francisco☆	—	Not issued

Series 1996 Withrow-Rubin

Note: The second prefix letter before the serial number indicates the Federal Reserve district.

Ben Franklin

KL#	Fr#	Bank	XF	CU
4132	—	Boston	—	115.
4132☆	—	Boston☆	—	125.
4133	—	New York	—	115.
4133☆	—	New York☆	—	120.
4134	—	Philadelphia	—	115.
4134☆	—	Philadelphia☆	—	Not issued
4135	—	Cleveland	—	115.
4135☆	—	Cleveland☆	—	135.
4136	—	Richmond	—	115.
4136☆	—	Richmond☆	—	Not issued
4137	—	Atlanta	—	115.
4137☆	—	Atlanta☆	—	Not issued
4138	—	Chicago	—	115.
4138☆	—	Chicago☆	—	Not issued
4139	—	St. Louis	—	115.
4139☆	—	St. Louis☆	—	Not issued
4140	—	Minneapolis	—	115.
4140☆	—	Minneapolis☆	—	Not issued
4141	—	Kansas City	—	115.
4141☆	—	Kansas City☆	—	Not issued
4142	—	Dallas	—	115.
4142☆	—	Dallas☆	—	Not issued
4143	—	San Francisco	—	115.
4143☆	—	San Francisco☆	—	120.

Five Hundred Dollars Gold Certificates

William McKinley

KL#	Fr#	Series	Signatures	Fine	VF	CU
2945	2407	1928	Woods-Mellon	1850.	2750.	7000.

Federal Reserve Notes
Series 1928 Woods-Mellon

KL#	Fr#	Bank	XF	CU
2946	2000A	Boston	750.	1000.
2946☆	2000A☆	Boston☆	900.	1500.
2947	2200B	New York	750.	1000.
2947☆	2200B☆	New York☆	900.	1500.
2948	2200C	Philadelphia	750.	1000.
2948☆	2200C☆	Philadelphia☆	900.	1500.
2949	2200D	Cleveland	750.	1000.
2949☆	2200D☆	Cleveland☆	900.	1500.
2950	2200E	Richmond	750.	1000.
2950☆	2200E☆	Richmond☆	850.	1500.
2951	2200F	Atlanta	750.	1000.
2951☆	2200F☆	Atlanta☆	850.	1600.
2952	2200G	Chicago	750.	1000.
2952☆	2200G☆	Chicago☆	850.	1500.
2953	2200H	St. Louis	750.	1000.
2953☆	2200H☆	St. Louis☆	850.	1500.
2954	2200I	Minneapolis	800.	1100.
2954☆	2200I☆	Minneapolis☆	900.	1600.
2955	2200J	Kansas City	750.	1000.
2955☆	2200J☆	Kansas City☆	800.	1500.
2956	2200K	Dallas	750.	1050.
2956☆	2200K☆	Dallas☆	800.	1500.
2957	2200L	San Francisco	750.	1050.
2957☆	2200L☆	San Francisco☆	800.	1500.

Series 1934 Julian-Morgenthau

KL#	Fr#	Bank	XF	CU
2958	2201A	Boston	650.	750.
2958☆	2201A☆	Boston☆	950.	1250.
2959	2201B	New York	650.	750.
2959☆	2201B☆	New York☆	750.	1250.
2960	2201C	Philadelphia	650.	850.
2960☆	2201C☆	Philadelphia☆	800.	1250.
2961	2201D	Cleveland	650.	850.
2961☆	2201D☆	Cleveland☆	800.	1250.
2962	2201E	Richmond	650.	850.
2962☆	2201E☆	Richmond☆	800.	1250.
2963	2201F	Atlanta	650.	850.
2963☆	2201F☆	Atlanta☆	800.	1250.
2964	2201G	Chicago	600.	800.
2964☆	2201G☆	Chicago☆	800.	1250.
2965	2201H	St. Louis	650.	850.
2965☆	2201H☆	St. Louis☆	800.	1250.
2966	2201I	Minneapolis	650.	850.
2966☆	2201I☆	Minneapolis☆	800.	1250.
2967	2201J	Kansas City	650.	850.
2967☆	2201J☆	Kansas City☆	800.	1250.
2968	2201K	Dallas	675.	900.
2968☆	2201K☆	Dallas☆	850.	1350.
2969	2201L	San Francisco	625.	850.
2969☆	2201L☆	San Francisco☆	800.	1250.

Series 1934A Julian-Morgenthau

KL#	Fr#	Bank	XF	CU
2971	2202B	New York	650.	700.
2971☆	2202B☆	New York☆	850.	1000.
2972	2202C	Philadelphia	650.	750.
2973	2202D	Cleveland	650.	750.
2974	2202E	Richmond	650.	750.
2974☆	2202E☆	Richmond☆	850.	1000.
2974A	—	Atlanta	700.	850.
2975	2202G	Chicago	600.	700.
2976	2202H	St. Louis	650.	750.
2977	2202I	Minneapolis	700.	850.
2978	2202J	Kansas City	650.	750.
2978☆	2202J☆	Kansas City☆	800.	1000.
2979	2202K	Dallas	650.	750.
2980	2202L	San Francisco	650.	750.
2980☆	2202L☆	San Francisco☆	800.	1000.

Series 1934B Julian-Vinson

KL#	Fr#	Bank	XF	CU
2981	2203F	Atlanta	—	Specimen notes only

Series 1934C Julian-Snyder

KL#	Fr#	Bank	XF	CU
2982	2204A	Boston	—	Specimen notes only
2983	2204B	New York	—	Specimen notes only

One Thousand Dollars
Gold Certificates

Grover Cleveland

KL#	Fr#	Series	Signatures	Fine	VF	CU
2984	2408	1928	Woods-Mellon	2300.	—	9000.

Federal Reserve Notes

Grover Cleveland

Series 1928 Woods-Mellon

KL#	Fr#	Bank	XF	CU
2985	2210A	Boston	1250.	1450.
2985☆	2210A☆	Boston☆	1500.	2000
2986	2210B	New York	1200.	1400.
2986☆	2210B☆	New York☆	1400.	1850.
2987	2210C	Philadelphia	1250.	1450.
2987☆	2210C☆	Philadelphia☆	1500.	2000.
2988	2210D	Cleveland	1250.	1450.
2988☆	2210D☆	Cleveland☆	1500.	2000.
2989	2210E	Richmond	1250.	1450.
2989☆	2210E☆	Richmond☆	1500.	2000.
2990	2210F	Atlanta	1250.	1450.
2990☆	2210F☆	Atlanta☆	1500.	2000.
2991	2210G	Chicago	1200.	1400.
2991☆	2210G☆	Chicago☆	1450.	1850.
2992	2210H	St. Louis	1250.	1450.
2992☆	2210H☆	St. Louis☆	1500.	2000.
2993	2210I	Minneapolis	1300.	1600.
2993☆	2210I☆	Minneapolis☆	1500.	2000.
2994	2210J	Kansas City	1250.	1450.
2994☆	2210J☆	Kansas City☆	1500.	2000.
2995	2210K	Dallas	1250.	1450.
2995☆	2210K☆	Dallas☆	1500.	2000.
2996	2210L	San Francisco	1250.	1450.
2996☆	2210L☆	San Francisco☆	1500.	2000.

Series 1934 Julian-Morgenthau

KL#	Fr#	Bank	XF	CU
2997	2211A	Boston	1200.	1400.
2997☆	2211A☆	Boston☆	1400.	1800.
2998	2211B	New York	1150.	1350.
2998☆	2211B☆	New York☆	1350.	1700.
2999	2211C	Philadelphia	1200.	1400.
2999☆	2211C☆	Philadelphia☆	1400.	1800.
3000	2211D	Cleveland	1200.	1400.
3000☆	2211D☆	Cleveland☆	1300.	1600.
3001	2211E	Richmond	1250.	1450.
3001☆	2211E☆	Richmond☆	1400.	2500.
3002	2211F	Atlanta	1200.	1400.
3002☆	2211F☆	Atlanta☆	1400.	1800.
3003	2211G	Chicago	1150.	1350.
3003☆	2211G☆	Chicago☆	1300.	1600.

KL#	Fr#	Bank	XF	CU
3004	2211H	St. Louis	1200.	1400.
3004☆	2211H☆	St. Louis☆	1400.	1800.
3005	2211I	Minneapolis	1500.	2500.
3005☆	2211I☆	Minneapolis☆	1600.	2750.
3006	2211J	Kansas City	1200.	1400.
3006☆	2211J☆	Kansas City☆	1400.	1800.
3007	2211K	Dallas	1200.	1400.
3007☆	2211K☆	Dallas☆	1400.	1800.
3008	2211L	San Francisco	1200.	1400.
3008☆	2211L☆	San Francisco☆	1400.	1800.

Series 1934A Julian-Morgenthau

KL#	Fr#	Bank	XF	CU
3009	2212A	Boston	1200.	1400.
3009☆	2212A☆	Boston☆	1500.	2000.
3010	2212B	New York	1150.	1350.
3010☆	2212B☆	New York☆	1400.	1800.
3011	2212C	Philadelphia	1200.	1400.
3011☆	2212C☆	Philadelphia☆	1500.	2000.
3012	2212D	Cleveland	1200.	1400.
3012☆	2212D☆	Cleveland☆	1500.	2000.
3013	2212E	Richmond	1250.	1500.
3013☆	2212E☆	Richmond☆	1500.	2000.
3014	2212F	Atlanta	1200.	1400.
3014☆	2212F☆	Atlanta☆	1500.	2000.
3015	2212G	Chicago	1150.	1350.
3015☆	2212G☆	Chicago☆	1400.	1800.
3016	2212H	St. Louis	1200.	1400.
3016☆	2212H☆	St. Louis☆	1500.	2000.
3017	2212I	Minneapolis	1300.	1600.
3017☆	2212I☆	Minneapolis☆	1600.	2000.
3018	2212J	Kansas City	1250.	1500.
3018☆	2212J☆	Kansas City☆	1500.	2000.
3019	2212L	San Francisco	1200.	1400.
3019☆	2212L☆	San Francisco☆	1500.	2000.

Series 1934C Julian-Snyder

KL#	Fr#	Bank	XF	CU
3020	2213A	Boston		
				Specimen notes only
3021	2213B	New York		
				Specimen notes only

Five Thousand Dollars
Gold Certificates

KL#	Fr#	Series	Signatures	Fine	VF	CU
3022	2410	1928	Woods-Mellon	—	—	—

Federal Reserve Notes

James Madison

Series 1928 Woods-Mellon

KL#	Fr#	Bank	XF	CU
3023	2220A	Boston	15,000.	22,500.
3024	2220B	New York	15,000.	22,500.
3025	2220D	Cleveland	15,000.	22,500.
3026	2220E	Richmond	15,000.	22,500.
3027	2220F	Atlanta	15,000.	22,500.
3028	2220G	Chicago	15,000.	22,500.
3029	2220J	Kansas City	15,000.	22,500.
3030	2220K	Dallas	15,000.	22,500.
3031	2220L	San Francisco	15,000.	22,500.

Series 1934 Julian-Morgenthau

KL#	Fr#	Bank	XF	CU
3032	2221A	Boston	15,000.	22,500.
3033	2221B	New York	15,000.	22,500.
3034	2221C	Philadelphia	15,000.	22,500.
3035	2221D	Cleveland	15,000.	22,500.

Series 1934 Julian-Morgenthau

KL#	Fr#	Bank	XF	CU
3036	2221E	Richmond	15,000.	22,500.
3037	2221F	Atlanta	15,000.	22,500.
3038	2221G	Chicago	15,000.	22,500.
3039	2221H	St. Louis	15,000.	22,500.
3040	2221J	Kansas City	15,000.	22,500.
3041	2221K	Dallas	15,000.	22,500.
3042	2221L	San Francisco	15,000.	22,500.

Series 1934A Julian-Morgenthau

KL#	Fr#	Bank	XF	CU
3043	2222H	St. Louis		

Specimen notes only

Series 1934B Julian-Vinson

KL#	Fr#	Bank	XF	CU
3044	2223A	Boston	—	100,000.
				Specimen notes only
3045	2223B	New York	—	100,000.
				Specimen notes only

Series 1934 Julian-Morgenthau

KL#	Fr#	Bank	XF	CU
3063	2231F	Atlanta	30,000.	45,000.
3064	2231G	Chicago	30,000.	45,000.
3065	2231H	St. Louis	30,000.	45,000.
3066	2231J	Kansas City	30,000.	45,000.
3067	2231K	Dallas	30,000.	45,000.
3068	2231L	San Francisco	30,000.	45,000.

Series 1934A Julian-Morgenthau

KL#	Fr#	Bank	XF	CU
3069	2232G	Chicago		

Specimen notes only

Series 1934B Julian-Vinson

KL#	Fr#	Bank	XF	CU
3070	2233B	New York		150,000.
				Specimen notes only

Ten Thousand Dollars
Gold Certificates

Salmon P. Chase

KL#	Fr#	Series	Signatures	Fine	VF	CU
3046	2411	1928	Woods-Mellon	—	—	—

Federal Reserve Notes

Salmon P. Chase

Series 1928 Woods-Mellon

KL#	Fr#	Bank	XF	CU
3047	2230A	Boston	30,000.	45,000.
3048	2230B	New York	30,000.	45,000.
3049	2230D	Cleveland	30,000.	45,000.
3050	2230E	Richmond	30,000.	45,000.
3051	2230F	Atlanta	30,000.	45,000.
3052	2230G	Chicago	30,000.	45,000.
3053	2230H	St. Louis	30,000.	45,000.
3054	2230I	Minneapolis	30,000.	45,000.
3055	2230J	Kansas City	30,000.	45,000.
3056	2230K	Dallas	30,000.	45,000.
3057	2230L	San Francisco	30,000.	45,000.

Series 1934 Julian-Morgenthau

KL#	Fr#	Bank	XF	CU
3058	2231A	Boston	30,000.	45,000.
3059	2231B	New York	30,000.	45,000.
3060	2231C	Philadelphia	30,000.	45,000.
3061	2231D	Cleveland	30,000.	45,000.
3062	2231E	Richmond	30,000.	45,000.

National Bank Notes

In the 72 years of their issue by more than 14,000 "home town" banks across the United States, the $17,000,000,000 ($17 billion) worth of National Bank Notes issued between December, 1863, and May, 1935, represent the most popularly collected series of United States paper money in the hobby today.

Their long and historically, as well as financially, interesting life began with the National Currency Act being signed into law by President Abraham Lincoln on Feb. 25, 1863. The dual aim of the legislation was to provide a ready and steady market for the sale of United States bonds issued to finance Federal involvement in the Civil War, and to create a sound bank currency to replace the generally insecure issues of the state banks then in circulation.

While National Bank Notes were only one of seven different types of U.S. paper money in circulation virtually simultaneously during and after the Civil War, they represent more interesting variations and types than any other. For more than half a century, from the implementation of the National Currency Act in 1863 until the creation of the Federal Reserve System in 1914, the National Bank Notes were an important part of the paper money in circulation.

The composition of these notes and the individual histories behind each of the issuing banks and its officers present unlimited fascination for the modern hobbyist.

The National Currency era came to end in May, 1935, when the Comptroller of the Currency shipped the last National Bank Notes to the issuing bank. The United States bonds which the banks had purchased to secure the value of their Nationals in circulation were called in for payment, ending nearly three-quarters of a century of an important era of "Main Street Banking."

Six distinct series make up the National Bank Note issue; four in large size, two in small size. Large size Nationals are comprised of 1) The Original Series, 2) Series of 1875, 3) Series of 1882 and 4) Series of 1902. In small size, there are the Series of 1929, Type 1 and Type 2. Within each of the large size series, there are several varieties and subtypes.

Alternatively, the Nationals are sometimes grouped according to Charter Period, thus: First Charter, Original Series and Series of 1875;

Second Charter, Series of 1882; Third Charter, Series of 1902, and Small Size.

The terms Charter Period and Charter Number are particularly important to National Bank Notes and refer to the issuing authority of each particular bank.

The original National Currency Act of 1863 provided that banks organized under its provisions be chartered as National Banks for a period of 20 years.

In anticipation of the expiration of those first charters in February, 1883, an act was passed on July 12, 1882, extending the banks' existence for another 20 years. A similar extension was granted with an Act of Congress on April 12, 1902, and just before the 1922 expiration date, the National Currency Act was amended to provide 99-year lives for all National banks. This, in turn, was amended five years later, on Feb. 25, 1927, with the endowment of perpetual succession of their corporate identity on National banks.

A better understanding of National Bank Notes as a whole can be gained by a study of the several unique component parts of the National Currency issues.

Charter Number. Upon the approval of its organization as a National Bank, the Comptroller would issue each bank a unique charter number, designating its place on the roster of all such banks. Charter No. 1 was issued to The First National Bank of Philadelphia in June, 1863. Charter No. 14320, the highest to appear on a National Bank Note, was issued in early 1935 to The Liberty National Bank & Trust Company, Louisville, Ky.

The very earliest Original Series National Bank Notes were not required to have their charter number imprinted. However, when it was discovered that notes being presented at the Treasury for redemption could not be quickly sorted, an Act of June 20, 1874, was passed, requiring the charter number be overprinted twice on the face of each note. In the 1882 revision of the National Currency Act, the printing of the charter number as part of the engraved border design in six different places on the face of the note was required; this to facilitate the redemption of partial notes. The 1882 act also required the surcharge of the number on the face, and its printing in the center of the back, giving rise to the popular Series 1882 Brown Back type notes. The

Aldrich-Vreeland Act of May 30, 1908, provided for dropping the charter number from the back of the note, thus creating the 1882 Date Back and Value Back series.

The Series of 1902 notes, authorized by the Act of April 12, 1902, again provided for the engraving of the charter number six times on the face border, and overprinting of the number twice on the face.

The small size National Bank Notes which debuted in 1929 were no longer printed from plates specially engraved for each bank. Rather, for the Type 1 notes, the charter number was overprinted twice in black on the face, along with the bank, city and state names, and the officers' signatures. On the Type 2 small size Nationals, the charter number was printed an extra two times on the face, in brown ink, matching the Treasury seal and serial numbers.

Bank Title. Each National bank's title, once approved by the Comptroller of the Currency, was engraved on the face of all currency printing plates for that bank. On large size Nationals, the title, along with city and state of the bank's location, is printed in a variety of bold and interesting type faces in the center of the note. On small size Nationals, the title is printed to the left of the portrait. Prior to May 1, 1886, it took an act of Congress to change the title of a National Bank. Legislation on that date, though, gave the banks authority to change their name upon a vote of the stockholders and with the approval of the Comptroller of the Currency.

Date. While the engraved date near the title on the face of all large size National Bank Notes remains something of an enigma, it is generally believed to have been chosen by the Comptroller of the Currency to represent the approximate date of issue for the note. This is not an absolute indicator of issue, though, and thus has little significance to the collector.

Treasury Serial Number. From the first issues of National Bank Notes of Dec. 21, 1863, to Aug. 22, 1925, all National Bank Notes carried a U.S. Treasury serial number on the face of the note. On all notes except the $1 and $2, the Treasury serial number appears somewhere in the upper right of the note. On the First Charter $1 and $2 notes, the Treasury number runs vertically at the left end of the note. After Aug. 22, 1925, the Treasury number was replaced by a second impression of the issuing bank's serial number.

Bank Serial Number. Found on all National Bank Notes, except for the small size Type 2 notes, it indicates how many impressions of a particular plate configuration had been printed for a bank. For the Type 2 small size notes, the bank serial number is an indicator of how many notes of a particular denomination had been issued by a bank.

Treasury Signatures. On all National Bank Notes, the engraved signatures of the Register of the Treasury and the Treasurer of the U.S. appear on the face, usually just above center, the Register's to the left of the bank title, and the Treasurer's to the right; though there are exceptions to this placement. The particular combination of these signatures can pinpoint the period in which a plate was engraved for a given bank.

Bank Officers' Signatures. The original National Currency Act of 1863 required that each National Bank Note be signed by the Cashier and the bank's President or Vice President. These signatures, whether pen autographed, rubber stamped, or engraved, always appear at the bottom of the face of the note, the Cashier to the left, the President (or VP) to the right. The signatures gave a local stamp of approval to this type of currency, probably an important consideration when it was first issued and at a time when paper money was often distrusted. The thousands of persons whose signatures appear on National Bank Notes help give each individual note a unique history not found in other forms of U.S. currency.

Treasury Seal. Found on the face of all National Bank Notes, the overprinted Treasury seal was the final Federal authentication of the note, giving each note its validity as circulating currency. Generally found on the right side of the note's face, it varies in color (red, brown, blue), size and embellishment (8 or 12 scallops, 34 or 40 rays).

Geographic Letters. From 1902-1924, large block letters were overprinted with and near the bank's charter number on each National Bank Note to facilitate sorting at central redemption points. Each letter stood for a particular geographic area of the country where the issuing bank was located: N for New England, E for Eastern, S for Southern, M for Midwest, W for Western and P for Pacific.

Plate Position Letters. On all large size National Bank Notes, a letter from A through D appears twice on the face of the note to indicate from which position (top, 2nd, 3rd or bottom) on a printing plate the note had been produced. Because the great variety of plate configurations used, there is little significance attached by collectors to plate letters, except perhaps in the case of bank serial number 1 notes, in which case the A-position notes might be of greater value.

Among small size Nationals, the plate position letter is part of the serial number. On Series 1929 Nationals, the prefix letter of the serial

number is the plate position. Since 1929s were printed six-up in a sheet, the plate positions letters (prefix) run from A through F.

Denominations. National Bank Notes were authorized, over the course of their history, in denominations of $1, $2, $3, $5, $10, $20, $50, $100, $500, $1,000, and $10,000. No notes of the $3 or $10,000 denomination were printed. No surviving $1,000 Nationals are known, although the Treasury still reports 21 outstanding. Only three, of a reported-outstanding 173, $500 Nationals are known in collections.

It should also be noted that not all banks issued all denominations in all series.

Circulation. While the original National Banking Act of Feb. 25, 1863, authorized state, as well as National, banks to issue circulating currency upon deposit of U.S. bonds with the Treasury as security, no state banks took advantage of this privilege before it was withdrawn from them by the Act of June 3, 1864, leaving the National banks in a monopoly position as far as bank-issued currency.

The 1863 legislation allowed National banks to issue notes to the total of 90% of the market value of specified series of United States bonds which they had deposited with the Treasurer of the United States. The revision of June 3, 1864, limited the total amount of National Bank Notes in circulation to $300 million; while a provision to apportion that total was added in March 3, 1865, legislation. That act — which also imposed a 10% tax on state bank notes in circulation, effectively killing them off — specified that half of the circulation be apportioned on the basis of population, and half on the basis of banking capital.

In 1870, additional circulation of $54 million was added to the total, and measures taken to more equitably distribute it, while a $500,000 circulation per bank limit was imposed. In 1875, the restrictions on a per bank basis, as well as total circulation, were taken off. In 1900, banks were allowed to issue notes to the full 100% market value of their bond deposits, instead of the 90%.

The circulation privilege was effectively withdrawn in favor of the Federal Reserve Bank System in July, 1935, when the last of the U.S. bonds carrying that privilege were called in. No new bonds of the type have been issued since.

Closing. A National bank could wind up its affairs in one of three manners, as specified by law.

A bank which violated provisions of the current legislation or charter, or which refused to redeem its notes, could be placed in charge of a receiver by order of the Comptroller of the Currency. It may have been allowed to reopen if it could be proved to be sound. If not, the receiver liquidated the bank's assets so as to provide for meeting the greatest amount of the bank's liabilities.

A bank could also go into voluntary liquidation on a two-thirds vote of the stockholders. Such might be done to allow the bank to be absorbed by or to absorb and consolidate with another bank, either National or state.

After Nov. 18, 1918, a National Bank could also close its corporate doors by consolidating with another bank, but not liquidating its assets.

National Bank Note Chronology

Act of Feb. 25, 1863. The original National Currency Act allowed banks with more than $50,000 capital to organize as National banks. Before starting business as such, the bank was required to deposit with the Treasurer of the United States, specified U.S. bonds to the amount of not less than one-third of its capital stock. With that deposit, the Comptroller of the Currency would issue the bank its "Certificate of Authority to Commence Business," its charter. Banks organized under this act were given a corporate life of 20 years from the date of the act.

Act of June 3, 1864. This act provided that any National bank now organized would have a 20-year charter from the date of organization. It also required that bonds deposited against note-issue be registered, interest bearing U.S. bonds.

Act of March 3, 1865. Besides provision mentioned in the earlier text, this allowed state banks with branches to convert to National status. At that time, National banks were not allowed to establish branch banks.

Act of July 12, 1870. This act provided for the organization of National Gold Banks. Subject to greater restrictions than other National Banks, the National Gold Banks could issue currency only to the total of 80% of their deposited bonds, and had to maintain in their vaults gold and silver equal to 25% of their circulation.

Act of Feb. 14, 1880. The act permitted the conversion of National Gold Banks to regular National banks, and allowed them to keep their original date of organization.

Act of July 12, 1882. This act created the Second Charter Period, allowing National banks to extend their charters for another 20 years.

Act of March 14, 1900. This act greatly increased the number of

National banks by allowing the organization of banks with a minimum of $25,000 capital in localities of fewer than 3,000 population.

Act of April 12, 1902. This act created the Third Charter Period by extending the charters of banks chartered or re-chartered under the 1882 act for another 20 years.

Act of May 30, 1908. A response to the financial panic of 1907, this act, known as the Aldrich-Vreeland Act, allowed the formation of voluntary National Currency Associations. To form such an association required at least 10 National banks with a total of at least $50 million in capital and a surplus of at least 2. After formation, such associations could deposit "other securities" against which they could circulate notes to the extent of 75% of their value. These other securities were usually short-term notes, payable within six months. Due to expire on June 30, 1914, the act was extended by the Federal Reserve Act of Dec. 23, 1913, to June 30, 1915, when it did expire.

Act of July 1, 1922. The act provided that all National banks then in existence would have a corporate life of 99 years from the date of the legislation. All National banks organized after this date would have a corporate existence of 99 years from the date of organization.

Act of Feb. 25, 1927. This act provided perpetual corporate life for all National banks then in existence or to be organized in the future. It also allowed National banks to establish branch banks and for the assumption of state banks by National banks.

First Charter Notes

Although the First Charter Period ran from Feb. 25, 1863, through July 11, 1882, notes of the First Charter type were issued until 1902, a 40-year period. This was due to the authorizing legislation which granted a National bank a charter good for 20 years from the date of reorganization, not the date of the National Bank Act (Feb. 25, 1863). Once a bank was chartered in this period, it issued the same type of notes for 20 years, despite the fact that the Second Charter Period may have come into effect (July 12, 1902) during the course of that time. When the bank's original 20-year charter expired, and it was re-chartered under the Second (or even Third) Period, it would begin issue of Second (or Third) Period notes, as appropriate to the date of its charter extension.

During the First Charter period, two different series of notes were issued, Original Series and Series of 1875.

Notes of the Original Series appeared in denominations from $1 through $1,000, and are distinguishable principally by their lack of overprinted charter numbers, although some banks did issue Original Series notes with charter numbers surcharged. The nearly identical Series 1875 notes all have red (or in rare cases, black) charter numbers imprinted, along with the notation at the left of the bank title "Series 1875."

Serial numbers of First Charter notes appear in either red or blue, with the blue variety being the scarcer.

Obligation of the face of the note reads: "This note is secured by bonds of the United States deposited with the U.S. Treasurer in Washington ... The (name and location of bank) will pay the bearer on demand — dollars." On back, there is the inscription: "This note is receivable at par in all parts of the United States, in payment of all taxes and excises and other dues to the United States, except duties on imports, and also for all salaries and other debts and demands owing by the United States to individuals, corporations and associations within the United States, except interest on the public debt."

Second Charter Notes

Three distinct note issues make up the National Currency of the Second Charter Period, July 12, 1882, through April 11, 1902. These types differ principally in their back designs for which collectors have evolved the nicknames Brown Back, Date Back and Value Back.

Like the notes of the First Charter Period, the Second Charter Period currency was issued for a span of 40 years, until 1922, when all charters had to be renewed.

The Brown Backs of Series 1882 were placed in circulation that year, and were issued until 1908. The Brown Backs take their name from the large charter number printed on the back in the center of two cartouches of geometric design in brown ink. All other printing on back was also in the brown shades which matched the predominant color of the note's face.

Called Date Backs because of the large 1882-1908 dates on their green-printed backs, the second issue of Series 1882 Nationals was a result of the previously described Aldrich-Vreeland Act. Denominations from $5-$100 were in circulation from June, 1908, to July, 1916, and the $50s and $100s continued current in this type until 1922. Date Back 1882 Nationals were issued only by banks which had issued Brown Backs, and the charters of which were still in force. Those banks whose charter expired in the 1908-1916 period were re-chartered and issued notes of the Third Charter Period.

The expiration of the Aldrich-Vreeland Act in 1915 gave rise to the third type of Series 1882 Nationals, the rare Value Backs (sometimes called Denomination Backs). As implied, the name comes from the large spelled-out indication of value in the center of the back design. As a type, they are the rarest of National Bank Notes, having been issued in the period 1916-1922 by banks which had issued the Date Back type and for which the charter was still in effect. Naturally, this number dwindled each successive year as banks were re-chartered and their note issues switched to the Third Period types.

The Date Back and Value Back notes of Series 1882 were something of emergency issues, produced at a time when it was felt an increase in the supply of currency in circulation was needed to combat hard times. Accordingly, for their issue, the Treasury accepted certain securities other than U.S. bonds on deposit against circulation. This addition is stated on the obligations of these notes.

Third Charter Notes

Passed to extend the life of those National banks whose charters were coming to expiration beginning in 1902, the Currency Act of April 12, 1902, created the Third Charter Period and the three distinct types of National Currency issued thereunder.

In 1922, Congress did away with the need for continual renewing of charters every 20 years by granting Nationals banks perpetual charters to operate.

Issued from 1902 until they were replaced by the small size National Currency in 1929, the Third Charter Nationals represented a change in design to distinguish them from the notes of the Second Charter Period.

The first issue of the Third Charter Period was the popular and often-rare Red Seals. Issued only from 1902-1908, due to the intervention of the Aldrich-Vreeland Emergency Money Act, the Red Seals were issued for a shorter period and by fewer banks than the other two Third Charter types. Their rarity, and the fact that they were issued by every U.S. state and Territory except Hawaii, make them a challenge among collectors who seek to build a state set of this type.

The latter two issues of the Third Charter Period both feature blue Treasury seals, and are principally distinguished by their backs.

The Series 1902 Date Back carries the dates 1902 and 1908 in the white space on the upper back. Like the Second Charter Date Backs, they are something of an emergency issue, having been released during the term of the Aldrich-Vreeland Act, 1908-1915, with the $50s and $100, as in Series 1882, being issued later, until 1926.

Upon expiration of that emergency currency measure, the issues of the Third Charter Period continued with the 1902 Plain Backs, named thus for their lack of the 1902-1908 dates on back. The most plentiful of all National Bank Notes, they were issued from 1915 to 1929, when they were superceded by the small size issue.

Small Size Nationals

When the rest of the currency classes were "down-sized" in July, 1929, the National Bank Notes were included. At the same time, their designs were standardized to fit in with the other types of notes in the same denominations.

Two separate types of small size Nationals were issued. Type 1, current from July, 1929-May, 1933, is distinguished chiefly by the appearance of the bank charter number only twice on the face of the note, in heavy black numerals. Serial numbers of the Type 1 notes consisted of a prefix letter A through F (corresponding to the note's position on the printing plate), six digits and the suffix A (or B, in the case of Ch. No. 2379, The Chase N.B., New York City, the only bank to issue more than six million small size notes in any denomination). The Type 2 Series 1929 Nationals had the same two charter imprints as Type 1, but had an extra pair in brown ink alongside the serial numbers. Serial numbering of the Type 2 notes was also different, being made up of a prefix letter A (B only in the case of The Bank of America National Trust and Savings Association of San Francisco) along with six digits.

The obligation was changed on the Series 1929 Nationals, to read as follows: "National Currency secured by United States bonds deposited with the Treasurer of the United Starts of America ... The (bank name and city/state) will pay to the bearer on demand — dollars." At right, across the brown Treasury seal, was the obligation: "Redeemable in lawful money of the United States at United States Treasury or at the bank of issue."

The calling in of the bonds which secured the National Currency issue ended this Golden Era for U.S. paper money in May, 1935.

Surviving National Bank Notes

Of the approximately $17 billion worth of National Currency issued between 1863-1935, it is estimated that some $50 million worth remain outstanding today, with most knowledgeable observers are in agreement that the surviving amount is about equally divided between large and small size issues, representing about 3/10s of 1% of the total issue.

National Bank Notes for Type Collectors

While it is not the most popular method of collecting National Currency, there is some demand for National Bank Notes by type and signature variety. Generally, only the highest grade notes from the most common banks are collected in this manner.

The listing below provides indication of which signature combinations were issued, and relative values for those notes on the most common banks of issue.

KL#	Fr#	Type	Denom.	Signatures	VG	VF	CU
1086	380	Orig	$1	Colby Spinner	80.00	200.	900.
1087	381	Orig	$1	Jeffries-Spinner	600.	1100.	2500.
1088	382	Orig	$1	Allison-Spinner	80.00	200.	900.
1089	383	1875	$1	Allison-New	80.00	200.	900.
1090	384	1875	$1	Allison-Wyman	80.00	200.	900.
1091	385	1875	$1	Allison-Gilfillan	80.00	200.	900.
1092	386	1875	$1	Scofield-Gilfillan	80.00	200.	900.
1093	387	Orig	$2	Colby-Spinner	300.	750.	3000.
1094	388	Orig	$2	Jeffries-Spinner	1100.	1650.	4000.
1095	389	Orig	$2	Allison-Spinner	300.	750.	3000.
1096	390	1875	$2	Allison-New	300.	750.	2500.
1097	391	1875	$2	Allison-Wyman	300.	750.	2500.
1098	392	1875	$2	Allison-Gilfillan	300.	750.	2500.
1099	393	1875	$2	Scofield-Gilfillan	300.	750.	2500.
1100	394	Orig	$5	Chittenden-Spinner	100.	225.	1200.
1101	397	Orig	$5	Colby-Spinner	100.	225.	1200.
1102	398	Orig	$5	Jeffries-Spinner	600.	1500.	3500.
1103	399	Orig	$5	Allison-Spinner	100.	225.	1200.
1104	401	1875	$5	Allison-New (Black Ch)	—	Rare	—
1105	401	1875	$5	Allison-New (Red Ch)	100.	225.	1000.
1106	402	1875	$5	Allison-Wyman	100.	225.	1000.
1107	403	1875	$5	Allison-Gilfillan	100.	225.	1000.
1108	404	1875	$5	Scofield-Gilfillan	100.	225.	1000.
1109	405	1875	$5	Bruce-Gilfillan	100.	225.	1000.
1110	406	1875	$5	Bruce-Wyman	100.	225.	1000.
1111	406-A	1875	$5	Bruce-Jordan	600.	1500.	3200.
1112	407	1875	$5	Rosecrans-Huston	100.	225.	1000.
1113	408	1875	$5	Rosecrans-Jordan	100.	225.	1000.
1114	466	'82BB	$5	Bruce-Gilfillan	65.00	150.	600.
1115	467	'82BB	$5	Bruce-Wyman	65.00	150.	600.
1116	468	'82BB	$5	Bruce-Jordan	65.00	150.	600.
1117	469	'82BB	$5	Rosecrans-Jordan	65.00	150.	600.
1118	470	'82BB	$5	Rosecrans-Hyatt	65.00	150.	600.
1119	471	'82BB	$5	Rosecrans-Houston	65.00	150.	600.
1120	472	'82BB	$5	Rosecrans-Nebeker	65.00	150.	600.
1121	473	'82BB	$5	Rosecrans-Morgan	200.	400.	1000.
1122	474	'82BB	$5	Tillman-Morgan	65.00	150.	600.
1123	475	'82BB	$5	Tillman-Roberts	65.00	150.	600.
1124	476	'82BB	$5	Bruce-Roberts	65.00	150.	600.
1125	477	'82BB	$5	Lyons-Roberts	65.00	150.	600.
1126	478	'82BB	$5	Vernon-Treat	65.00	150.	600.
1127	532	'82BB	$5	Rosecrans-Huston	70.00	125.	500.
1128	533	'82DB	$5	Rosecrans-Nebeker	70.00	100.	500.
1129	533-A	'82DB	$5	Rosecrans-Morgan	300.	750.	1800.
1130	534	'82DB	$5	Tillman-Morgan	70.00	100.	500.
1131	535	'82DB	$5	Tillman-Roberts	70.00	100.	500.
1132	536	'82DB	$5	Bruce-Roberts	70.00	100.	500.
1133	537	'82DB	$5	Lyons-Roberts	70.00	100.	500.
1134	538	'82DB	$5	Vernon-Treat	70.00	100.	500.
1135	538-B	'82DB	$5	Napier-McClung	75.00	150.	800.
1136	573	'82VB	$5	Tillman-Morgan	100.	300.	1200.
1137	573-A	'82VB	$5	Tillman-Roberts	100.	300.	1200.
1138	574	'82VB	$5	Lyons-Roberts	100.	300.	1200.
1139	574-A	'82VB	$5	Bruce-Roberts	100.	300.	1200.
1140	575	'82VB	$5	Vernon-Treat	100.	300.	1200.
1141	575-A	'82VB	$5	Napier-McClung	100.	300.	1200.
1142	575-B	'82VB	$5	Teehee-Burke	275.	450.	2500.
1143	587	'02RS	$5	Lyons-Roberts	65.00	150.	700.
1144	588	'02RS	$5	Lyons-Treat	65.00	150.	700.
1145	589	'02RS	$5	Vernon-Treat	65.00	150.	700.
1146	590	'02DB	$5	Lyons-Roberts	23.00	40.00	200.
1147	591	'02DB	$5	Lyons-Treat	23.00	40.00	200.
1148	592	'02DB	$5	Vernon-Treat	23.00	40.00	200.
1149	593	'02DB	$5	Vernon-McClung	23.00	40.00	200.
1150	594	'02DB	$5	Napier-McClung	23.00	40.00	200.
1151	595	'02DB	$5	Napier-Thompson	30.00	70.00	400.
1152	596	'02DB	$5	Napier-Burke	23.00	40.00	200.
1153	597	'02DB	$5	Parker-Burke	23.00	40.00	200.
1154	597-A	'02DB	$5	Teehee-Burke	40.00	100.	300.
1155	598	'02PB	$5	Lyons-Roberts	20.00	33.00	175.
1156	599	'02PB	$5	Lyons-Treat	20.00	33.00	175.
1157	600	'02PB	$5	Vernon-McClung	20.00	33.00	175.
1158	601	'02PB	$5	Vernon-Treat	20.00	33.00	175.
1159	602	'02PB	$5	Napier-McClung	20.00	33.00	175.
1160	603	'02PB	$5	Napier-Thompson	25.00	55.00	200.
1161	604	'02PB	$5	Napier-Burke	20.00	33.00	175.
1162	605	'02PB	$5	Parker-Burke	20.00	33.00	175.
1163	606	'02PB	$5	Teehee-Burke	20.00	33.00	175.
1164	607	'02PB	$5	Elliott-Burke	20.00	33.00	175.
1165	608	'02PB	$5	Elliott-White	20.00	33.00	175.
1166	609	'02PB	$5	Speelman-White	20.00	33.00	175.
1167	610	'02PB	$5	Woods-White	20.00	33.00	175.
1168	611	'02PB	$5	Woods-Tate	20.00	33.00	175.
1169	612	'02PB	$5	Jones-Woods	100.	175.	400.
1170	1800-1	'29TI	$5	Jones-Woods	10.00	15.00	50.00
1171	1800-2	'29T2	$5	Jones-Woods	12.00	20.00	55.00
1172	409	Orig	$10	Chittenden-Spinner	175.	350.	1800.
1173	412	Orig	$10	Colby-Spinner	175.	350.	1800.
1174	413	Orig	$10	Jeffries-Spinner	550.	1000.	2250.
1175	414	Orig	$10	Allison-Spinner	175.	350.	1800.
1176	416	1875	$10	Allison-New	175.	350.	1450.
1177	417	1875	$10	Allison-Wyman	175.	350.	1450.
1178	418	1875	$10	Allison-Gilfillan	175.	350.	1450.
1179	419	1875	$10	Scofield-Gilfillan	175.	350.	1450.
1180	420	1875	$10	Bruce-Gilfillan	175.	350.	1450.
1181	421	1875	$10	Bruce-Wyman	175.	350.	1450.
1182	422	1875	$10	Rosecrans-Huston	175.	350.	1450.
1183	423	1875	$10	Rosecrans-Nebeker	175.	350.	1450.
1184	423-A	1875	$10	Tillman-Morgan	(Reported, not confirmed)		
1185	479	'82BB	$10	Bruce-Gilfillan	75.00	150.	650.
1186	480	'82BB	$10	Bruce-Wyman	75.00	150.	650.
1187	481	'82BB	$10	Bruce-Jordan	75.00	150.	650.
1188	482	'82BB	$10	Rosecrans-Jordan	75.00	150.	650.
1189	483	'82BB	$10	Rosecrans-Hyatt	75.00	150.	650.
1190	484	'82BB	$10	Rosecrans-Huston	75.00	150.	650.
1191	485	'82BB	$10	Rosecrans-Nebeker	75.00	150.	650.
1192	486	'82BB	$10	Rosecrans-Morgan	300.	700.	1000.
1193	487	'82BB	$10	Tillman-Morgan	75.00	150.	650.
1194	488	'82BB	$10	Tillman-Roberts	75.00	150.	650.
1195	489	'82BB	$10	Bruce-Roberts	75.00	150.	650.
1196	490	'82BB	$10	Lyons-Roberts	75.00	150.	650.
1197	491	'82BB	$10	Lyons-Treat	75.00	150.	650.
1198	492	'82BB	$10	Vernon-Treat	75.00	150.	650.
1199	539	'82DB	$10	Rosecrans-Huston	80.00	140.	550.
1200	540	'82DB	$10	Rosecrans-Nebeker	80.00	140.	550.
1201	541	'82DB	$10	Rosecrans-Morgan	225.	600.	1100.
1202	542	'82DB	$10	Tillman-Morgan	80.00	140.	550.
1203	543	'82DB	$10	Tillman-Roberts	80.00	140.	550.
1204	544	'82DB	$10	Bruce-Roberts	80.00	140.	550.
1205	545	'82DB	$10	Lyons-Roberts	80.00	140.	550.
1206	546	'82DB	$10	Vernon-Treat	80.00	140.	550.
1207	547	'82DB	$10	Vernon-McClung	80.00	140.	550.
1208	548	'82DB	$10	Napier-McClung	80.00	140.	550.
1209	576	'82VB	$10	Tillman-Morgan	200.	350.	1500.
1210	576-A	'82VB	$10	Tillman-Roberts	125.	300.	2100.
1211	576-B	'82VB	$10	Bruce-Roberts	200.	350.	2500.
1212	577	'82VB	$10	Lyons-Roberts	125.	300.	2100.
1213	578	'82VB	$10	Vernon-Treat	175.	325.	2100.
1214	579	'82VB	$10	Napier-McClung	125.	300.	1500.
1215	579-B	'82VB	$10	Teehee-Burke	200.	350.	1500.
1216	613	'02RS	$10	Lyons-Roberts	70.00	175.	800.
1217	614	'02RS	$10	Lyons-Treat	70.00	175.	800.
1218	615	'02RS	$10	Vernon-Treat	85.00	225.	850.
1219	616	'02DB	$10	Lyons-Roberts	28.00	45.00	200.
1220	617	'02DB	$10	Lyons-Treat	28.00	45.00	200.
1221	618	'02DB	$10	Vernon-Treat	28.00	45.00	200.
1222	619	'02DB	$10	Vernon-McClung	28.00	45.00	200.
1223	620	'02DB	$10	Napier-McClung	28.00	45.00	200.
1224	621	'02DB	$10	Napier-Thompson	35.00	75.00	600.
1225	622	'02DB	$10	Napier-Burke	28.00	45.00	200.
1226	623	'02DB	$10	Parker-Burke	28.00	45.00	200.
1227	623-A	'02DB	$10	Teehee-Burke	40.00	80.00	225.
1228	624	'02PB	$10	Lyons-Roberts	23.00	40.00	200.
1229	625	'02PB	$10	Lyons-Treat	23.00	40.00	200.
1230	626	'02PB	$10	Vernon-Treat	23.00	40.00	200.
1231	627	'02PB	$10	Vernon-McClung	23.00	40.00	200.
1232	628	'02PB	$10	Napier-McClung	23.00	40.00	200.
1233	629	'02PB	$10	Napier-Thompson	30.00	60.00	475.
1234	630	'02PB	$10	Napier-Burke	23.00	40.00	200.
1235	631	'02PB	$10	Parker-Burke	23.00	40.00	200.
1236	632	'02PB	$10	Teehee-Burke	23.00	40.00	200.
1237	633	'02PB	$10	Elliot-Burke	23.00	40.00	200.
1238	634	'02PB	$10	Elliot-White	23.00	40.00	200.
1239	635	'02PB	$10	Speelman-White	23.00	40.00	200.
1240	636	'02PB	$10	Woods-White	23.00	40.00	200.
1241	637	'02PB	$10	Woods-Tate	23.00	40.00	200.
1242	638	'02PB	$10	Jones-Woods	100.	250.	1000.
1243	1801-1	'29T1	$10	Jones-Woods	12.00	20.00	50.00
1244	1801-2	'29T2	$10	Jones-Woods	13.00	20.00	60.00
1245	424	Orig	$20	Chittenden-Spinner	375.	650.	3100.
1246	427	Orig	$20	Colby-Spinner	325.	550.	2950.
1247	428	Orig	$20	Jeffries-Spinner	1250.	2000.	4500.
1248	429	Orig	$20	Allison-Spinner	325.	550.	2950.
1249	431	1875	$20	Allison-New	300.	500.	2750.
1250	432	1875	$20	Allison-Wyman	300.	500.	2750.
1251	433	1875	$20	Allison-Gilfillan	300.	500.	2750.
1252	434	1875	$20	Scofield-Gilfillan	300.	500.	2750.
1253	435	1875	$20	Bruce-Gilfillan	300.	500.	2750.
1254	436	1875	$20	Bruce-Wyman	350.	650.	3800.
1255	437	1875	$20	Rosecrans-Huston	300.	500.	2750.
1256	438	1875	$20	Rosecrans-Nebeker	385.	750.	4250.
1257	439	1875	$20	Tillman-Morgan	400.	800.	4300.
1258	493	'82BB	$20	Bruce-Gilfillan	100.	225.	900.
1259	494	'82BB	$20	Bruce-Wyman	100.	225.	900.
1260	495	'82BB	$20	Bruce-Jordan	100.	225.	900.
1261	496	'82BB	$20	Rosecrans-Jordan	100.	225.	900.
1262	497	'82BB	$20	Rosecrans-Hyatt	100.	225.	900.

NATIONAL BANK NOTE VALUATIONS BY TYPE $20-$1,000 NOTES 69

KL#	Fr#	Type	Denom.	Signatures	VG	VF	CU
1263	498	'82BB	$20	Rosecrans-Huston	100.	225.	900.
1264	499	'82BB	$20	Rosecrans-Nebeker	100.	225.	900.
1265	500	'82BB	$20	Rosecrans-Morgan	350.	850.	2000.
1266	501	'82BB	$20	Tillman-Morgan	100.	225.	900.
1267	502	'82BB	$20	Tillman-Roberts	100.	225.	900.
1268	503	'82BB	$20	Bruce-Roberts	100.	225.	900.
1269	504	'82BB	$20	Lyons-Roberts	100.	225.	900.
1270	505	'82BB	$20	Lyons-Treat	110.	275.	1050.
1271	506	'82BB	$20	Vernon-Treat	110.	275.	1050.
1272	549	'82DB	$20	Rosecrans-Huston	110.	225.	800.
1273	550	'82DB	$20	Rosecrans-Nebeker	110.	225.	800.
1274	551	'82DB	$20	Rosecrans-Morgan	400.	850.	1500.
1275	552	'82DB	$20	Tillman-Morgan	110.	225.	800.
1276	553	'82DB	$20	Tillman-Roberts	110.	225.	800.
1277	554	'82DB	$20	Bruce-Roberts	110.	225.	800.
1278	555	'82DB	$20	Lyons-Roberts	110.	225.	800.
1279	556	'82DB	$20	Vernon-Treat	110.	225.	800.
1280	557	'82DB	$20	Napier-McClung	135.	300.	800.
1281	580	'82VB	$20	Tillman-Morgan	200.	400.	1700.
1282	580-A	'82VB	$20	Tillman-Roberts	300.	600.	2100.
1283	580-B	'82VB	$20	Bruce-Roberts	300.	600.	2100.
1284	581	'82VB	$20	Lyons-Roberts	200.	400.	1700.
1285	582	'82VB	$20	Lyons-Treat	200.	400.	1700.
1286	583	'82VB	$20	Vernon-Treat	200.	400.	1700.
1287	584	'82VB	$20	Napier-McClung	200.	400.	1700.
1288	584-A	'82VB	$20	Parker-Burke	—	(Rare)	—
1289	585	'82VB	$20	Teehee-Burke	225.	550.	2200.
1290	639	'02RS	$20	Lyons-Roberts	100.	200.	900.
1291	640	'02RS	$20	Lyons-Treat	100.	200.	900.
1292	641	'02RS	$20	Vernon-Treat	125.	250.	1600.
1293	642	'02DB	$20	Lyons-Roberts	35.00	75.00	300.
1294	643	'02DB	$20	Lyons-Treat	35.00	75.00	300.
1295	644	'02DB	$20	Vernon-Treat	35.00	75.00	300.
1296	645	'02DB	$20	Vernon-McClung	35.00	75.00	300.
1297	646	'02DB	$20	Napier-McClung	35.00	75.00	300.
1298	647	'02DB	$20	Napier-Thompson	40.00	85.00	500.
1299	648	'02DB	$20	Napier-Burke	35.00	75.00	300.
1300	649	'02DB	$20	Parker-Burke	35.00	75.00	300.
1301	649-A	'02DB	$20	Teehee-Burke	50.00	100.	300.
1302	650	'02PB	$20	Lyons-Roberts	30.00	65.00	275.
1303	651	'02PB	$20	Lyons-Treat	30.00	65.00	275.
1304	652	'02PB	$20	Vernon-Treat	30.00	65.00	275.
1305	653	'02PB	$20	Vernon-McClung	30.00	65.00	275.
1306		'02PB	$20	Napier-McClung	30.00	65.00	275.
1307	655	'02PB	$20	Napier-Thompson	40.00	80.00	275.
1308	656	'02PB	$20	Napier-Burke	30.00	65.00	275.
1309	657	'02PB	$20	Parker-Burke	30.00	65.00	275.
1310	658	'02PB	$20	Teehee-Burke	30.00	65.00	275.
1311	659	'02PB	$20	Elliott-Burke	30.00	65.00	275.
1312	660	'02PB	$20	Elliott-White	30.00	65.00	275.
1313	661	'02PB	$20	Speelman-White	30.00	65.00	275.
1314	662	'02PB	$20	Woods-White	35.00	100.	275.
1315	663	'02PB	$20	Woods-Tate	50.00	175.	450.
1316	663-A	'02PB	$20	Jones-Woods	500.	1000.	5000.
1317	1802-1	'29T1	$20	Jones-Woods	24.00	35.00	95.00
1318	1802-2	'29T2	$20	Jones-Woods	25.00	38.00	100.
1319	440	Orig	$50	Chittenden-Spinner	2000.	3000.	—
1320	442	Orig	$50	Colby-Spinner	2000.	3000.	—
1321	443	Orig	$50	Allison-Spinner	2000.	3000.	—
1322	444	1875	$50	Allison-New	1800.	2800.	—
1323	444-A	1875	$50	Allison-Wyman	1900.	3000.	—
1324	445	1875	$50	Allison-Gilfillan	1800.	2800.	—
1325	446	1875	$50	Scofield-Gilfillan	1800.	2800.	—
1326	447	1875	$50	Bruce-Gilfillan	1800.	2800.	—
1327	448	1875	$50	Bruce-Wyman	1800.	2800.	—
1328	449	1875	$50	Rosecrans-Houston	1800.	2800.	—
1329	450	1875	$50	Rosecrans-Nebeker	1950.	2900.	—
1330	451	1875	$50	Tillman-Morgan	1800.	2800.	—
1331	507	'82BB	$50	Bruce-Gilfillan	600.	500.	3500.
1332	508	'82BB	$50	Bruce-Wyman	600.	500.	3500.
1333	509	'82BB	$50	Bruce-Jordan	600.	500.	3500.
1334	510	'82BB	$50	Rosecrans-Jordan	600.	500.	3500.
1335	511	'82BB	$50	Rosecrans-Hyatt	600.	500.	3500.
1336	512	'82BB	$50	Rosecrans-Huston	600.	500.	3500.
1337	513	'82BB	$50	Rosecrans-Nebeker	600.	500.	3500.
1338	514	'82BB	$50	Rosecrans-Morgan	900.	1300.	4000.
1339	515	'82BB	$50	Tillman-Morgan	600.	500.	3500.
1340	516	'82BB	$50	Tillman-Roberts	600.	500.	3500.
1341	517	'82BB	$50	Bruce-Roberts	600.	500.	3500.
1342	518	'82BB	$50	Lyons-Roberts	600.	500.	3500.
1343	518-A	'82BB	$50	Vernon-Treat	900.	1300.	4000.
1344	558	'82DB	$50	Rosecrans-Huston	350.	600.	2500.
1345	559	'82DB	$50	Rosecrans-Nebeker	350.	600.	2500.
1346	560	'82DB	$50	Tillman-Morgan	350.	600.	2500.
1347	561	'82DB	$50	Tillman-Roberts	350.	600.	2500.
1348	562	'82DB	$50	Bruce-Roberts	350.	600.	2500.
1349	563	'82DB	$50	Lyons-Roberts	350.	600.	2500.
1350	564	'82DB	$50	Vernon-Treat	350.	600.	2500.
1351	565	'82DB	$50	Napier-McClung	350.	600.	2500.
1352	586	'82VB	$50	Lyons-Roberts	—	(Four known)	
1353	664	'02RS	$50	Lyons-Roberts	500.	1750.	7000.
1354	665	'02RS	$50	Lyons-Treat	500.	1750.	7000.
1355	666	'02RS	$50	Vernon-Treat	500.	1750.	7000.
1356	667	'02DB	$50	Lyons-Roberts	75.00	125.	1200.
1357	668	'02DB	$50	Lyons-Roberts	75.00	125.	1200.
1358	669	'02DB	$50	Vernon-Treat	75.00	125.	1200.
1359	670	'02DB	$50	Vernon-McClung	75.00	125.	1200.
1360	671	'02DB	$50	Napier-McClung	75.00	125.	1200.
1361	672	'02DB	$50	Napier-Thompson	85.00	185.	1600.
1362	673	'02DB	$50	Napier-Burke	75.00	130.	1200.
1363	674	'02DB	$50	Parker-Burke	75.00	130.	1200.
1364	674-A	'02DB	$50	Teehee-Burke	125.	275.	1200.
1365	675	'02PB	$50	Lyons-Roberts	165.	300.	1100.
1366	676	'02PB	$50	Lyons-Treat	165.	300.	1100.
1367	677	'02PB	$50	Vernon-Treat	165.	300.	1100.
1368	678	'02PB	$50	Vernon-McClung	165.	300.	1100.
1369	679	'02PB	$50	Napier-McClung	165.	300.	1100.
1370	679-A	'02PB	$50	Napier-Thompson	200.	400.	1350.
1371	680	'02PB	$50	Napier-Burke	165.	300.	1100.
1372	681	'02PB	$50	Parker-Burke	165.	300.	1100.
1373	682	'02PB	$50	Teehee-Burke	165.	300.	1100.
1374	683	'02PB	$50	Elliott-Burke	165.	300.	1100.
1375	684	'02PB	$50	Elliott-White	165.	300.	1100.
1376	685	'02PB	$50	Speelman-White	165.	300.	1100.
1377	685-A	'02PB	$50	Woods-White	100.	250.	1000.
1378	1803-1	'29T1	$50	Jones-Woods	55.00	85.00	200.
1379	1803-2	'29T2	$50	Jones-Woods	75.00	165.	600.
1380	452	Orig	$100	Chittenden-Spinner	2100.	3500.	—
1381	454	Orig	$100	Colby-Spinner	2100.	3500.	—
1382	455	Orig	$100	Allison-Spinner	2100.	3500.	—
1383	456	1875	$100	Allison-New	1900.	3250.	—
1384	457	1875	$100	Allison-Wyman	1900.	3250.	—
1385	458	1875	$100	Allison-Gilfillan	1900.	3250.	—
1386	459	1875	$100	Scofield-Gilfillan	1900.	3250.	—
1387	460	1875	$100	Bruce-Gilfillan	1900.	3250.	—
1388	461	1875	$100	Bruce-Wyman	1900.	3250.	—
1389	462	1875	$100	Rosecrans-Huston	1900.	3250.	—
1390	462-A	1875	$100	Rosecrans-Nebeker	1900.	3250.	—
1391	463	1875	$100	Tillman-Morgan	1900.	3250.	—
1392	519	'82BB	$100	Bruce-Gilfillan	700.	1150.	4000.
1393	520	'82BB	$100	Bruce-Wyman	700.	1150.	4000.
1394	521	'82BB	$100	Bruce-Jordan	700.	1150.	4000.
1395	522	'82BB	$100	Rosecrans-Jordan	700.	1150.	4000.
1396	523	'82BB	$100	Rosecrans-Hyatt	700.	1150.	4000.
1397	524	'82BB	$100	Rosecrans-Huston	700.	1150.	4000.
1398	525	'82BB	$100	Rosecrans-Nebeker	700.	1150.	4000.
1399	526	'82BB	$100	Rosecrans-Morgan	1000.	2000.	4000.
1400	527	'82BB	$100	Tillman-Morgan	700.	1150.	4000.
1401	528	'82BB	$100	Tillman-Roberts	700.	1150.	4000.
1401A	529	'88BB	$100	Bruce-Roberts	700.	1150.	4000.
1402	530	'82BB	$100	Lyons-Roberts	700.	1150.	4000.
1403	531	'82BB	$100	Vernon-Treat	1000.	2000.	4000.
1404	566	'82DB	$100	Rosecrans-Huston	500.	850.	3250.
1405	567	'82DB	$100	Rosecrans-Nebeker	500.	850.	3250.
1406	568	'82DB	$100	Tillman-Morgan	500.	850.	3250.
1407	569	'82DB	$100	Tillman-Roberts	500.	850.	3250.
1408	570	'82DB	$100	Bruce-Roberts	500.	850.	3250.
1409	571	'82DB	$100	Lyons-Roberts	500.	850.	3250.
1410	572	'82DB	$100	Vernon-Treat	500.	850.	3250.
1411	572-A	'82DB	$100	Napier-McClung	500.	850.	3250.
1412	586-A	'82VB	$100	Lyons-Roberts	—	(One known)	
1413	686	'02RS	$100	Lyons-Roberts	600.	1800.	7200.
1414	687	'02RS	$100	Lyons-Roberts	600.	1800.	7200.
1415	688	'02RS	$100	Vernon-Treat	600.	1800.	7200.
1416	689	'02DB	$100	Lyons-Roberts	200.	350.	1300.
1417	690	'02DB	$100	Lyons-Treat	200.	350.	1300.
1418	691	'02DB	$100	Vernon-Treat	200.	350.	1300.
1419	692	'02DB	$100	Vernon-McClung	200.	350.	1300.
1420	693	'02DB	$100	Napier-McClung	200.	350.	1300.
1421	694	'02DB	$100	Napier-Thompson	250.	450.	1650.
1422	695	'02DB	$100	Napier-Burke	200.	350.	1300.
1423	696	'02DB	$100	Parker-Burke	200.	350.	1300.
1424	697	'02DB	$100	Teehee-Burke	250.	450.	1150.
1425	698	'02PB	$100	Lyons-Roberts	180.	325.	1200.
1426	699	'02PB	$100	Lyons-Treat	180.	325.	1200.
1427	700	'02PB	$100	Vernon-Treat	180.	325.	1200.
1428	701	'02PB	$100	Vernon-McClung	180.	325.	1200.
1429	702	'02PB	$100	Napier-McClung	180.	325.	1200.
1430	702-A	'02PB	$100	Napier-Thompson	225.	400.	1350.
1431	703	'02PB	$100	Parker-Burke	180.	325.	1200.
1432	704	'02PB	$100	Teehee-Burke	180.	325.	1200.
1433	705	'02PB	$100	Elliott-Burke	180.	325.	1200.
1434	706	'02PB	$100	Elliott-White	180.	325.	1200.
1435	707	'02PB	$100	Speelman-White	180.	325.	1200.
1436	707-A	'02PB	$100	Woods-White	—	(Two known)	
1437	1804-1	'29T1	$100	Jones-Woods	110.	140.	360.
1438	1804-2	'29T2	$100	Jones-Woods	130.	200.	800.
1439	464	Orig	$500	Colby-Spinner	—	(One known)	
1440	464	1875	$500	Colby-Spinner	—	(One known)	
1441	464	1875	$500	Allison-New	—	(One known)	
1442	465	Orig	$1,000	Chittenden-Spinner	—	(Unknown)	
1443	465	1875	$1,000	Allison-Wyman	—	(Unknown)	

National Bank Note Valuations By State

Original Series $1
(KL #1086-1088) (Fr #380-382)

	VG	VF	AU
Alabama	250.	750.	1250.
Arkansas		Unknown	—
Colorado Territory	750.	1500.	2500.
Connecticut	150.	350.	750.
Dakota Territory	2000.	3500.	4500.
Delaware	600.	900.	1500.
District of Columbia	350.	750.	1100.
Georgia	200.	600.	1200.
Idaho Territory			
Illinois	80.00	200.	625.
Indiana	125.	275.	600.
Iowa	110.	250.	550.
Kansas	125.	300.	650.
Kentucky	200.	450.	925.
Louisiana	250.	700.	1100.
Maine	200.	550.	1100.
Maryland	225.	475.	860.
Massachusetts	80.00	200.	450.
Michigan	250.	450.	800.
Minnesota	250.	450.	800.
Missouri	100.	250.	650.
Montana Territory	1500.	2500.	4000.
Nebraska	250.	500.	900.
Nebraska Territory	3000.	5000.	—
New Hampshire	175.	400.	800.
New Jersey	145.	315.	650.
New Mexico Territory	1000.	2000.	3500.
New York	80.00	200.	450.
North Carolina	400.	900.	1750.
Ohio	100.	225.	500.
Pennsylvania	80.00	200.	450.
Rhode Island	175.	480.	850.
South Carolina	750.	1500.	3000.
Tennessee	650.	1250.	2250.
Texas	300.	600.	1000.
Utah Territory	1250.	2500.	4500.
Vermont	150.	450.	1100.
Virginia	275.	600.	1250.
West Virginia	400.	650.	1400.
Wisconsin	145.	315.	650.
Wyoming Territory	—	—	—

Series 1875 $1
(KL# 1089-1092) (Fr #383-386)

	VG	VF	AU
Colorado Territory	750.	1500.	2500.
Connecticut	150.	350.	750.
Delaware	600.	900.	1500.
Georgia	190.	460.	920.
Idaho Territory			
Illinois	80.00	200.	500.
Indiana	125.	275.	600.
Iowa	110.	250.	550.
Kansas	125.	300.	650.
Kentucky	200.	500.	925.

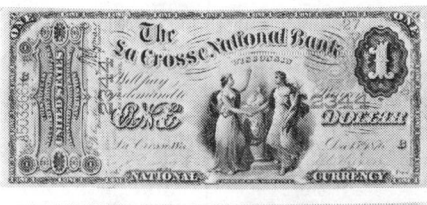

	VG	VF	AU
Maine	190.	550.	1100.
Massachusetts	80.00	200.	450.
Michigan	250.	450.	800.
Minnesota	250.	450.	800.
Missouri	100.	250.	675.
Nebraska	250.	500.	900.
Nebraska Territory	3000.	5000.	—
New Hampshire	165.	375.	800.
New Jersey	120.	315.	650.
New Mexico Territory	1000.	2000.	3500.
New York	80.00	200.	450.
North Carolina	400.	900.	1750.
Ohio	100.	225.	500.
Pennsylvania	80.00	200.	450.
Rhode Island	175.	480.	850.
South Carolina	750.	1500.	3000.
Tennessee	650.	1250.	2250.
Texas	300.	600.	1000.
Vermont	150.	450.	1100.
Wisconsin	145.	315.	650.

Original Series $2
(KL# 1093-1095) (Fr #387-389)

	VG	VF	AU
Alabama	750.	1250.	2500.
Arkansas	800.	1650.	2800.
Colorado Territory	1500.	3000.	6000.
Connecticut	400.	800.	1800.
Dakota Territory	3000.	5000.	9000.
Delaware	1000.	2200.	4000.
District of Columbia	800.	1650.	2800.
Georgia	900.	1800.	3250.
Idaho Territory	10,000.	—	—
Illinois	250.	750.	1500.
Indiana	400.	900.	1800.
Iowa	400.	850.	1700.
Kansas	350.	950.	1900.
Kentucky	500.	1100.	2450.
Louisiana	750.	1650.	2800.
Maine	650.	1650.	2800.

	VG	VF	AU
Maryland	800.	1400.	3250.
Massachusetts	250.	750.	1500.
Michigan	500.	1000.	2000.
Minnesota	500.	1000.	2000.
Missouri	375.	900.	1900.
Montana Territory	4000.	6000.	10,000.
Nebraska	500.	1125.	1900.
Nebraska Territory	5000.	—	—
New Hampshire	600.	1250.	2600.
New Jersey	450.	800.	1700.
New Mexico Territory	1500.	2500.	5000.
New York	250.	750.	1500.
North Carolina	1750.	3750.	6000.
Ohio	275.	800.	1700.
Pennsylvania	250.	750.	1500.
Rhode Island	650.	1300.	2200.
South Carolina	2000.	4000.	7000.
Tennessee	1250.	2000.	4000.
Texas	—	Rare	—
Utah Territory	5000.	10,000.	18,000.
Vermont	650.	1400.	2800.
Virginia	750.	1500.	2450.
West Virginia	—	—	—
Wisconsin	350.	1000.	1700.
Wyoming Territory	—	Rare	—

Series 1875 $2
(KL# 1096-1099) (Fr #390-393)

	VG	VF	AU
Colorado Territory	1500.	3000.	6000.
Connecticut	400.	800.	1800.
Delaware	1000.	2000.	4000.
Georgia	900.	1800.	3250.
Idaho Territory	10,000.	—	—
Illinois	250.	750.	1500.
Indiana	400.	900.	1800.
Iowa	400.	850.	1700.
Kansas	350.	900.	1900.
Kentucky	500.	1100.	2500.
Maine	650.	1700.	2900.
Massachusetts	250.	750.	1500.
Michigan	500.	1000.	2000.
Minnesota	500.	1000.	2000.
Missouri	375.	900.	1900.
Montana Territory	4000.	6000.	10,000.
Nebraska	500.	1150.	1900.
Nebraska Territory	5000.	—	—
New Hampshire	600.	1250.	2600.
New Jersey	450.	800.	1725.
New Mexico Territory	1500.	2250.	5000.
New York	250.	750.	1500.
North Carolina	1750.	3750.	6000.
Ohio	275.	800.	1700.
Pennsylvania	250.	750.	1500.
Rhode Island	650.	1300.	2200.
South Carolina	2000.	4000.	7000.
Tennessee	1250.	2000.	4000.
Texas	—	Rare	—
Vermont	650.	1400.	2800.
Wisconsin	350.	1000.	1700.

Original Series $5
(KL# 1100-1103) (Fr #394-399)

	VG	VF	AU
Alabama	250.	375.	600.
Arkansas	750.	1250.	2000.
Colorado Territory	2000.	3000.	4500.
Connecticut	135.	500.	1000.
Dakota Territory	2000.	4000.	6000.
Delaware	600.	900.	1500.
District of Columbia	350.	750.	1150.
Florida	2000.	3000.	5000.
Georgia	750.	1250.	2000.
Idaho Territory	7500.	12,500.	—
Illinois	110.	275.	650.
Indiana	125.	400.	700.
Iowa	150.	500.	900.
Kansas	225.	600.	1100.
Kentucky	300.	750.	1400.
Louisiana	550.	900.	1700.
Maine	500.	800.	1500.
Maryland	125.	475.	900.
Massachusetts	100.	250.	600.
Michigan	275.	450.	900.
Minnesota	300.	500.	1000.
Mississippi		Unknown	
Missouri	200.	350.	700.
Montana Territory	2000.	4000.	6000.
Montana	1000.	2000.	3500.
Nebraska	500.	800.	1500.
Nebraska Territory	—	Rare	—
Nevada		Unknown	
New Hampshire	200.	550.	1500.
New Jersey	125.	350.	700.
New Mexico Territory	1250.	2000.	4000.
New York	100.	225.	500.
North Carolina	900.	1500.	3000.
Ohio	110.	250.	700.
Oregon	1500.	2500.	5000.
Pennsylvania	100.	225.	500.
Rhode Island	175.	350.	900.
South Carolina	1000.	1750.	3500.
Tennessee	750.	1500.	3000.
Texas	1250.	2000.	3000.
Utah Territory	2500.	4000.	6000.
Vermont	225.	575.	1150.
Virginia	450.	750.	1500.
West Virginia	600.	900.	1750.
Wisconsin	200.	350.	700.
Wyoming Territory	1500.	2500.	4000.

Series 1875 $5
(KL# 1104-1113) (Fr #401-408)

	VG	VF	AU
Alabama	250.	375.	600.
Arizona Territory	2000.	4000.	6500.
Arkansas	750.	1250.	2000.
California	750.	1500.	3000.
Colorado Territory	2000.	3000.	4500.
Colorado	1000.	1750.	3000.
Connecticut	135.	500.	1000.
Dakota Territory	2000.	4000.	6000.
Delaware	600.	900.	1500.
District of Columbia	500.	750.	1150.
Florida	2000.	3000.	5000.

	VG	VF	AU
Georgia	750.	1250.	2000.
Idaho Territory	7500.	12,500.	—
Illinois	110.	275.	650.
Indiana	120.	400.	700.
Iowa	150.	500.	900.
Kansas	225.	600.	1100.
Kentucky	300.	750.	1400.
Louisiana	550.	900.	1700.
Maine	500.	800.	1500.
Maryland	125.	450.	900.
Massachusetts	100.	250.	600.
Michigan	275.	450.	900.
Minnesota	300.	500.	1000.
Missouri	200.	325.	650.
Montana Territory	2000.	4000.	6000.
Nebraska	500.	800.	1500.
Nebraska Territory	—	Rare	—
New Hampshire	200.	550.	1500.
New Jersey	125.	325.	650.
New Mexico Territory	1250.	2000.	4000.
New York	100.	225.	500.
North Carolina	900.	1500.	3000.
North Dakota	800.	1750.	3500.
Ohio	95.00	295.	660.
Pennsylvania	100.	300.	575.
Rhode Island	145.	475.	1000.
South Carolina	145.	475.	1000.
South Dakota	900.	1800.	3250.
Tennessee	750.	1500.	3000.
Texas	1250.	2000.	3000.
Utah Territory	2500.	4000.	6000.
Vermont	225.	550.	1100.
Virginia	450.	750.	1500.
Washington	1500.	3000.	6000.
West Virginia	600.	900.	1750.
Wisconsin	200.	350.	700.
Wyoming Territory	—	Rare	—
Wyoming	1250.	2200.	3500.

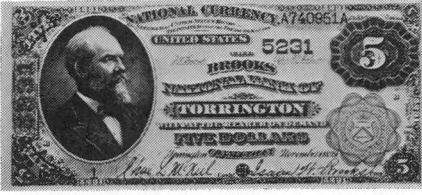

James A. Garfield

1882 Brown Back $5
(KL# 1114-1126) (Fr #466-478)

	VG	VF	AU
Alabama	175.	400.	800.
Arizona Territory	3000.	5000.	10,000.
Arkansas	250.	500.	900.
California	125.	250.	500.
Colorado	400.	750.	1500.
Connecticut	110.	300.	500.
Dakota Territory	1500.	2500.	4000.
Delaware	500.	900.	1800.
District of Columbia	150.	375.	900.
Florida	1000.	1500.	3000.
Georgia	200.	500.	1100.
Hawaii	450.	750.	1100.
Idaho Territory	5000.	7500.	—
Idaho	2000.	3500.	5500.
Illinois	70.00	200.	400.
Indian Territory	850.	1500.	2500.
Indiana	100.	275.	550.
Iowa	100.	250.	550.
Kansas	125.	275.	600.
Kentucky	90.00	300.	500.
Louisiana	250.	500.	900.
Maine	200.	450.	750.
Maryland	100.	275.	475.
Massachusetts	75.00	210.	400.
Michigan	150.	350.	600.
Minnesota	90.00	250.	450.
Mississippi	750.	1250.	2500.
Missouri	75.00	210.	450.
Montana Territory	1250.	2500.	5000.
Montana	650.	1200.	2250.
Nebraska	175.	300.	600.
Nevada	7500.	15,000.	30,000.
New Hampshire	150.	450.	900.
New Jersey	125.	250.	450.
New Mexico Territory	900.	1500.	3000.
New York	75.00	150.	300.

	VG	VF	AU
North Carolina	225.	450.	800.
North Dakota	450.	750.	1500.
Ohio	75.00	210.	325.
Oklahoma Territory	500.	800.	1500.
Oklahoma	400.	700.	1250.
Oregon	300.	700.	1500.
Pennsylvania	65.00	150.	300.
Rhode Island	175.	400.	800.
South Carolina	300.	550.	1000.
South Dakota	450.	800.	1600.
Tennessee	250.	500.	950.
Texas	200.	400.	750.
Utah Territory	3000.	5000.	8000.
Utah	400.	700.	1600.
Vermont	150.	450.	900.
Virginia	150.	375.	750.
Washington Territory	5000.	8000.	15,000.
Washington	500.	900.	2000.
West Virginia	150.	450.	800.
Wisconsin	125.	300.	500.
Wyoming Territory	—	—	—
Wyoming	900.	1500.	2500.

James A. Garfield

George Washington

1882 Date Back $5
(KL# 1127-1135) (Fr #532-538-B)

	VG	VF	AU
Alabama	125.	250.	500.
Arizona Territory	2000.	3250.	6750.
Arizona	1500.	2500.	4000.
California	115.	200.	400.
Colorado	250.	450.	900.
Connecticut	85.00	200.	415.
Delaware	400.	700.	1400.
District of Columbia	135.	300.	650.
Florida	500.	900.	1700.
Georgia	200.	400.	800.
Hawaii	300.	475.	800.
Idaho	750.	1250.	2500.
Illinois	75.00	175.	350.
Indian Territory	600.	900.	2000.
Indiana	75.00	200.	400.
Iowa	90.00	175.	350.
Kansas	110.	225.	400.
Kentucky	85.00	200.	415.
Louisiana	200.	400.	750.
Maine	175.	350.	650.
Maryland	100.	250.	500.
Massachusetts	80.00	175.	400.
Michigan	125.	250.	500.
Minnesota	110.	225.	450.
Mississippi	250.	400.	750.
Missouri	90.00	200.	400.
Montana	500.	800.	1500.
Nebraska	125.	250.	450.
New Hampshire	135.	300.	700.
New Jersey	110.	225.	400.
New Mexico Territory	500.	800.	2000.
New Mexico	400.	600.	1100.
New York	70.00	125.	250.
North Carolina	200.	400.	750.
North Dakota	250.	500.	850.
Ohio	70.00	125.	300.
Oklahoma	175.	350.	700.
Oregon	300.	600.	1000.
Pennsylvania	70.00	125.	250.
Rhode Island	200.	350.	600.
South Carolina	250.	500.	900.
South Dakota	250.	500.	850.
Tennessee	200.	400.	1250.
Texas	125.	225.	450.
Utah	350.	650.	1300.
Vermont	150.	400.	800.
Virginia	125.	250.	500.
Washington	400.	750.	1500.
West Virginia	175.	375.	700.
Wisconsin	115.	250.	400.
Wyoming	400.	700.	1400.

James A. Garfield

1882 Value Back $5
(KL# 1136-1142) (Fr #573-575-B)

	VG	VF	AU
Alabama	200.	525.	1150.
California	175.	375.	825.
Colorado	250.	500.	1000.
Connecticut	175.	350.	850.
Delaware	450.	900.	2000.
District of Columbia	300.	650.	1450.
Florida	500.	900.	1800.
Georgia	300.	525.	1150.
Hawaii	275.	700.	2000.
Idaho	450.	900.	1800.
Illinois	110.	375.	825.
Indian Territory	500.	900.	2000.
Indiana	175.	375.	850.
Iowa	150.	350.	750.
Kansas	200.	435.	950.
Kentucky	170.	550.	1250.
Maine	300.	650.	1450.
Maryland	190.	450.	900.
Massachusetts	200.	500.	1000.
Michigan	175.	350.	750.
Minnesota	190.	390.	850.
Mississippi	350.	750.	1450.
Missouri	175.	390.	850.
Nebraska	160.	375.	750.
Nevada		None issued	
New Hampshire	250.	600.	1350.
New Jersey	200.	390.	850.
New Mexico	400.	650.	1450.
New York	100.	300.	600.
North Carolina	450.	750.	1250.
North Dakota	350.	600.	1350.
Ohio	115.	390.	850.
Oklahoma	155.	525.	1150.
Oregon	375.	650.	1450.
Pennsylvania	400.	220.	600.
Rhode Island		None issued	
South Carolina	500.	900.	1750.
South Dakota	350.	600.	1350.
Tennessee	325.	560.	1250.
Texas	175.	375.	820.
Utah	400.	800.	1450.
Vermont	250.	650.	1300.
Virginia	170.	450.	950.
Washington	400.	800.	1450.
West Virginia	225.	500.	1350.
Wisconsin	150.	375.	820.
Wyoming	1000.	1600.	3000.

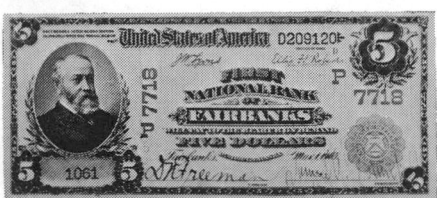

Benjamin Harrison

1902 Red Seal $5
(KL# 1143-1145) (Fr #587-589)

	VG	VF	AU
Alabama	400.	800.	1400.
Alaska	3000.	4500.	7500.
Arizona Territory	3000.	5000.	9450.
Arkansas	300.	700.	1050.
California	200.	450.	750.
Colorado	300.	600.	1250.
Connecticut	200.	450.	900.
Delaware	2000.	5000.	9000.
District of Columbia	300.	550.	1050.
Florida	900.	1500.	2750.
Georgia	400.	750.	1500.
Idaho	2000.	3500.	5000.
Illinois	80.00	290.	600.
Indian Territory	600.	1000.	1800.
Indiana	115.	350.	750.
Iowa	175.	400.	800.
Kansas	225.	500.	900.
Kentucky	275.	550.	1000.
Louisiana	350.	700.	1400.
Maine	300.	650.	1200.
Maryland	115.	420.	850.
Massachusetts	125.	300.	625.
Michigan	200.	450.	900.
Minnesota	175.	400.	750.
Mississippi	900.	1600.	2750.
Missouri	125.	300.	625.
Montana	1000.	2500.	5000.
Nebraska	200.	400.	900.
Nevada	2000.	3500.	6000.
New Hampshire	300.	600.	1100.
New Jersey	150.	300.	625.
New Mexico Territory	750.	1500.	2450.
New York	65.00	150.	350.
North Carolina	750.	1400.	2200.
North Dakota	650.	1000.	2000.
Ohio	125.	400.	625.
Oklahoma Territory	750.	1400.	3000.
Oklahoma	600.	1200.	2100.
Oregon	500.	1000.	2000.
Pennsylvania	65.00	150.	350.
Rhode Island	200.	400.	850.
South Carolina	1000.	1600.	2500.
South Dakota	750.	1500.	2500.
Tennessee	500.	1000.	1800.
Texas	250.	500.	1000.
Utah	2000.	4000.	8000.
Vermont	300.	550.	1050.
Virginia	250.	450.	900.
Washington	900.	1750.	3000.
West Virginia	200.	475.	960.
Wisconsin	150.	300.	625.
Wyoming	1250.	2200.	3500.

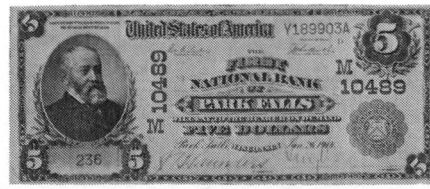

Benjamin Harrison

1902 Date Back $5
(KL# 1146-1154) (Fr #590-597-A)

	VG	VF	AU
Alabama	25.00	55.00	160.
Alaska	2250.	3500.	6000.
Arizona Territory	1250.	2500.	5000.
Arizona	250.	500.	900.
Arkansas	100.	250.	500.
California	23.00	40.00	110.
Colorado	40.00	80.00	200.
Connecticut	27.00	60.00	170.
Delaware	225.	450.	800.
District of Columbia	40.00	95.00	235.
Florida	75.00	150.	300.
Georgia	25.00	75.00	200.
Hawaii	200.	400.	700.
Idaho	150.	350.	650.
Illinois	23.00	40.00	110.
Indiana	25.00	55.00	160.
Iowa	25.00	50.00	135.
Kansas	26.00	45.00	130.
Kentucky	27.00	60.00	170.
Louisiana	50.00	95.00	235.
Maine	75.00	150.	300.
Maryland	25.00	55.00	160.
Massachusetts	25.00	45.00	115.
Michigan	30.00	50.00	130.
Minnesota	25.00	45.00	115.
Mississippi	100.	250.	500.
Missouri	25.00	45.00	115.
Montana	150.	300.	600.
Nebraska	30.00	60.00	130.
Nevada	250.	500.	900.
New Hampshire	40.00	80.00	190.
New Jersey	25.00	45.00	115.
New Mexico Territory	500.	800.	1600.
New Mexico	125.	300.	600.
New York	23.00	40.00	100.
North Carolina	50.00	100.	300.
North Dakota	100.	250.	500.
Ohio	25.00	45.00	115.
Oklahoma	25.00	55.00	160.
Oregon	75.00	200.	450.
Pennsylvania	22.50	40.00	100.
Rhode Island	40.00	80.00	190.
South Carolina	60.00	150.	300.
South Dakota	100.	250.	500.
Tennessee	40.00	90.00	225.
Texas	23.00	75.00	200.
Utah	75.00	150.	400.
Vermont	50.00	95.00	235.
Virginia	27.00	60.00	170.
Washington	50.00	125.	300.
West Virginia	40.00	80.00	190.
Wisconsin	25.00	40.00	115.
Wyoming	125.	300.	600.

Benjamin Harrison

1902 Plain Back $5
(KL# 1155-1169) (Fr #598-612)

	VG	VF	AU
Alabama	20.00	45.00	140.
Alaska	2000.	3250.	5750.
Arizona	225.	450.	800.
Arkansas	75.00	225.	450.
California	21.00	38.00	95.00
Colorado	35.00	75.00	180.
Connecticut	25.00	50.00	150.
Delaware	200.	400.	750.
District of Columbia	35.00	90.00	220.
Florida	65.00	135.	275.
Georgia	20.00	70.00	180.
Hawaii	180.	375.	650.
Idaho	135.	300.	600.
Illinois	21.00	38.00	95.00
Indiana	20.00	45.00	140.
Iowa	21.00	38.00	95.00
Kansas	25.00	40.00	115.
Kentucky	25.00	50.00	150.
Louisiana	45.00	90.00	220.
Maine	65.00	135.	275.
Maryland	20.00	45.00	140.
Massachusetts	22.00	39.00	100.
Michigan	25.00	40.00	115.
Minnesota	22.00	39.00	100.
Mississippi	90.00	225.	450.
Missouri	22.00	39.00	100.
Montana	135.	275.	550.
Nebraska	20.00	38.00	115.
Nevada	225.	450.	850.
New Hampshire	35.00	75.00	185.
New Jersey	22.00	39.00	100.
New Mexico	110.	275.	550.
New York	20.00	37.50	90.00
North Carolina	45.00	90.00	270.
North Dakota	90.00	225.	450.
Ohio	20.00	33.00	100.
Oklahoma	20.00	45.00	140.
Oregon	50.00	150.	400.
Pennsylvania	20.00	37.50	90.00
Rhode Island	35.00	75.00	185.
South Carolina	55.00	135.	275.
South Dakota	90.00	225.	450.
Tennessee	25.00	80.00	200.
Texas	21.00	70.00	180.
Utah	70.00	135.	350.
Vermont	45.00	90.00	220.
Virginia	24.00	50.00	150.

	VG	VF	AU
Washington	45.00	115.	275.
West Virginia	35.00	75.00	185.
Wisconsin	22.00	39.00	100.
Wyoming	115.	275.	550.

Abraham Lincoln
1929 Type 1 $5
(KL# 1170) (Fr #1800-1)

	VG	VF	AU
Alabama	12.00	30.00	45.00
Alaska	1500.	2000.	3000.
Arizona	75.00	175.	300.
Arkansas	50.00	75.00	125.
California	11.00	22.00	30.00
Colorado	11.00	34.00	48.00
Connecticut	13.00	25.00	40.00
Delaware	75.00	135.	195.
District of Columbia	15.00	30.00	70.00
Florida	30.00	50.00	75.00
Georgia	16.00	30.00	45.00
Hawaii	65.00	100.	175.
Idaho	75.00	150.	300.
Illinois	11.00	22.00	30.00
Indiana	12.00	25.00	40.00
Iowa	11.00	22.00	30.00
Kansas	12.00	22.00	30.00
Kentucky	17.00	34.00	48.00
Louisiana	20.00	50.00	80.00
Maine	25.00	50.00	90.00
Maryland	12.00	25.00	45.00
Massachusetts	11.00	22.00	30.00
Michigan	13.00	25.00	36.00
Minnesota	12.00	23.00	32.00
Mississippi	40.00	70.00	95.00
Missouri	12.00	23.00	32.00
Montana	75.00	175.	300.
Nebraska	13.00	25.00	36.00
Nevada	150.	300.	600.
New Hampshire	20.00	40.00	80.00
New Jersey	12.00	23.00	32.00
New Mexico	50.00	125.	225.
New York	10.00	15.00	28.00
North Carolina	25.00	45.00	75.00
North Dakota	40.00	100.	200.
Ohio	12.00	23.00	32.00
Oklahoma	13.00	25.00	60.00
Oregon	20.00	30.00	70.00
Pennsylvania	10.00	15.00	28.00
Rhode Island	20.00	40.00	65.00
South Carolina	40.00	75.00	95.00
South Dakota	60.00	125.	225.
Tennessee	17.00	34.00	48.00
Texas	11.00	22.00	30.00
Utah	25.00	75.00	125.
Vermont	20.00	40.00	80.00
Virginia	17.00	34.00	48.00
Washington	12.00	35.00	70.00
West Virginia	12.00	30.00	60.00
Wisconsin	12.00	23.00	32.00
Wyoming	75.00	150.	250.

Continuation:

	VG	VF	AU
Maine	28.00	55.00	95.00
Maryland	13.00	27.00	50.00
Massachusetts	13.00	26.00	35.00
Michigan	16.00	30.00	40.00
Minnesota	14.00	27.00	36.00
Mississippi	45.00	75.00	100.
Missouri	14.00	27.00	36.00
Montana	80.00	185.	325.
Nebraska	16.00	30.00	40.00
Nevada	160.	325.	650.
New Hampshire	23.00	45.00	85.00
New Jersey	14.00	27.00	36.00
New Mexico	60.00	140.	250.
New York	12.00	20.00	32.00
North Carolina	30.00	50.00	85.00
North Dakota	45.00	110.	225.
Ohio	14.00	27.00	36.00
Oklahoma	14.00	27.00	65.00
Oregon	22.00	32.00	75.00
Pennsylvania	12.00	20.00	32.00
Rhode Island	23.00	45.00	65.00
South Carolina	45.00	80.00	100.
South Dakota	75.00	140.	250.
Tennessee	20.00	40.00	55.00
Texas	13.00	26.00	35.00
Utah	28.00	80.00	140.
Vermont	22.00	45.00	90.00
Virginia	20.00	40.00	55.00
Washington	13.00	38.00	75.00
West Virginia	13.00	32.00	65.00
Wisconsin	14.00	27.00	36.00
Wyoming	80.00	160.	270.

Abraham Lincoln
1929 Type 2 $5
(KL# 1171) (Fr #1800-2)

	VG	VF	AU
Alabama	13.00	32.00	50.00
Alaska	1600.	2100.	3200.
Arizona	80.00	185.	325.
Arkansas	55.00	80.00	135.
California	13.00	26.00	35.00
Colorado	12.00	40.00	55.00
Connecticut	14.00	27.00	45.00
Delaware	80.00	140.	200.
District of Columbia	17.00	32.00	75.00
Florida	35.00	55.00	80.00
Georgia	19.00	36.00	50.00
Hawaii	70.00	110.	190.
Idaho	85.00	175.	325.
Illinois	13.00	26.00	35.00
Indiana	13.00	27.00	44.00
Iowa	13.00	26.00	35.00
Kansas	13.00	23.00	32.00
Kentucky	20.00	40.00	50.00
Louisiana	22.00	55.00	85.00

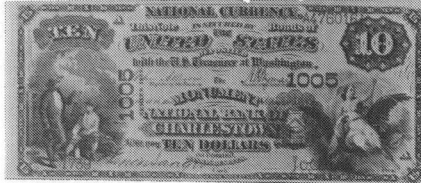

Ben Franklin

Original Series $10
(KL# 1172-1175) (Fr #409-414)

	VG	VF	AU
Alabama	500.	900.	1800.
Arkansas	900.	1500.	2250.
California		None issued	
Colorado Territory	2250.	3500.	7000.
Connecticut	200.	675.	2000.
Delaware	750.	1500.	3000.
District of Columbia	400.	900.	2250.
Florida	2250.	3500.	5500.
Georgia	850.	1400.	2250.
Idaho Territory	—	Rare	—
Illinois	175.	375.	900.
Indiana	225.	550.	1200.
Iowa	225.	550.	1200.
Kansas	275.	650.	1350.
Kentucky	350.	750.	1500.
Louisiana	650.	1000.	2250.
Maine	600.	900.	2000.
Maryland	250.	500.	1100.
Massachusetts	175.	375.	900.
Michigan	400.	750.	1500.
Minnesota	400.	750.	1350.
Mississippi		Unknown	—
Missouri	275.	550.	1350.
Montana Territory	2250.	4500.	7000.
Montana	1250.	2250.	4000.
Nebraska	600.	900.	1500.
Nebraska Territory	—	—	—
Nevada		Unknown	—
New Hampshire	275.	650.	1400.
New Jersey	225.	460.	1100.
New Mexico Territory	1750.	2750.	5000.
New York	175.	350.	800.
North Carolina	1000.	2250.	4000.
Ohio	200.	400.	900.
Pennsylvania	175.	350.	800.
Rhode Island	275.	550.	1500.
South Carolina	1500.	2500.	5000.
Tennessee	900.	1750.	3000.
Texas	1500.	2500.	4000.
Utah Territory	4000.	6000.	9000.
Vermont	300.	750.	1600.
Virginia	550.	850.	2000.
West Virginia	700.	1000.	2100.
Wisconsin	300.	600.	1350.
Wyoming Territory	—	Rare	—

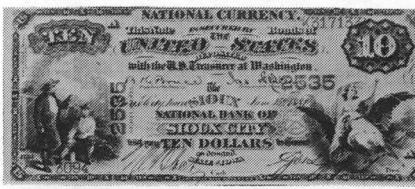

Ben Franklin

Series 1875 $10
(KL# 1176-1184) (Fr #416-423-A)

	VG	VF	AU
Alabama	500.	900.	1800.
Arkansas	900.	1500.	2250.
California	1250.	2500.	4000.
Colorado Territory	2250.	3500.	6500.
Colorado	1250.	2000.	3500.
Connecticut	200.	675.	2000.
Dakota Territory	2500.	4500.	6500.
Delaware	750.	1500.	3000.
District of Columbia	400.	900.	2250.
Florida	2250.	3500.	5500.
Georgia	850.	1400.	2250.
Idaho Territory	—	Rare	
Illinois	175.	375.	900.
Indiana	225.	550.	1200.
Iowa	225.	550.	1200.
Kansas	275.	650.	1350.
Kentucky	350.	750.	1500.
Louisiana	650.	1000.	2250.
Maine	600.	900.	2000.
Maryland	250.	500.	1100.
Massachusetts	175.	375.	900.
Michigan	400.	750.	1500.
Minnesota	400.	750.	1350.
Missouri	275.	550.	1350.
Montana Territory	2250.	4500.	7000.
Montana	1250.	2250.	4000.
Nebraska	600.	900.	1500.
Nebraska Territory	—	Rare	
New Hampshire	275.	650.	1400.
New Jersey	225.	420.	1100.
New Mexico Territory	1750.	2750.	5000.
New York	175.	350.	800.
North Carolina	1000.	2250.	4000.
North Dakota	900.	1900.	3000.
Ohio	200.	400.	900.
Oregon	1750.	2750.	5500.
Pennsylvania	175.	350.	800.
Rhode Island	275.	550.	1500.
South Carolina	1500.	2500.	5000.
South Dakota	1100.	2000.	3100.
Tennessee	900.	1750.	3000.
Texas	1500.	2500.	4000.
Utah Territory	4000.	6000.	9000.
Utah	2500.	4000.	6000.
Vermont	300.	675.	1600.
Virginia	550.	850.	2000.
West Virginia	700.	1000.	2100.
Wisconsin	300.	600.	1350.
Wyoming Territory	—	Rare	—
Wyoming	1400.	2450.	3750.

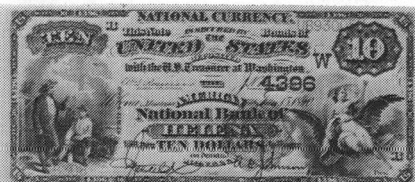

Ben Franklin

1882 Brown Back $10
(KL# 1185-1198) (Fr #479-492)

	VG	VF	AU
Alabama	200.	450.	875.
Arizona Territory	3000.	5000.	10,000.
Arkansas	275.	550.	950.
California	135.	275.	550.

	VG	VF	AU
Colorado	450.	800.	1600.
Connecticut	120.	300.	525.
Dakota Territory	1500.	2500.	4000.
Delaware	550.	950.	1825.
District of Columbia	175.	400.	950.
Florida	1100.	1600.	3200.
Georgia	250.	550.	1200.
Hawaii	500.	800.	1500.
Idaho Territory	5000.	7500.	—
Idaho	2000.	3500.	5500.
Illinois	80.00	200.	400.
Indian Territory	850.	1500.	2500.
Indiana	110.	285.	575.
Iowa	110.	275.	550.
Kansas	150.	300.	625.
Kentucky	100.	300.	525.
Louisiana	275.	550.	950.
Maine	225.	475.	800.
Maryland	110.	300.	500.
Massachusetts	85.00	210.	425.
Michigan	175.	400.	650.
Minnesota	100.	275.	500.
Mississippi	800.	1800.	2700.
Missouri	85.00	225.	475.
Montana Territory	1300.	2600.	5000.
Montana	700.	1300.	2400.
Nebraska	190.	325.	650.
Nevada	8000.	16,000.	32,000.
New Hampshire	175.	500.	950.
New Jersey	140.	275.	500.
New Mexico Territory	950.	1600.	2800.
New York	80.00	160.	325.
North Carolina	250.	475.	900.
North Dakota	475.	800.	1600.
Ohio	85.00	225.	375.
Oklahoma Territory	550.	850.	1600.
Oklahoma	450.	750.	1300.
Oregon	350.	750.	1600.
Pennsylvania	75.00	150.	325.
Rhode Island	125.	320.	550.
South Carolina	350.	600.	1100.
South Dakota	500.	850.	1700.
Tennessee	300.	550.	1000.
Texas	225.	450.	800.
Utah Territory	3000.	5000.	8250.
Utah	450.	750.	1700.
Vermont	165.	475.	950.
Virginia	175.	400.	800.
Washington Territory	5000.	8000.	15,000.
Washington	550.	950.	2100.
West Virginia	160.	475.	950.
Wisconsin	140.	325.	550.
Wyoming Territory	—	Rare	—
Wyoming	1000.	1600.	2600.

Ben Franklin

1882 Date Back $10
(KL# 1199-1208) (Fr #539-548)

	VG	VF	AU
Alabama	140.	275.	550.
Arizona Territory	2250.	3750.	7250.
Arizona	1500.	2500.	4000.
Arkansas	200.	450.	800.
California	150.	250.	450.
Colorado	275.	500.	950.
Connecticut	100.	230.	460.
Delaware	450.	750.	1500.
District of Columbia	150.	325.	700.
Florida	550.	950.	1800.
Georgia	225.	450.	850.
Hawaii	325.	500.	900.
Idaho	800.	1300.	2600.
Illinois	80.00	190.	375.
Indiana	90.00	215.	420.
Iowa	100.	190.	375.
Kansas	125.	250.	450.
Kentucky	100.	230.	460.
Louisiana	225.	450.	800.
Maine	200.	375.	700.
Maryland	110.	275.	650.
Massachusetts	90.00	190.	450.
Michigan	140.	275.	550.

	VG	VF	AU
Minnesota	125.	240.	500.
Mississippi	300.	450.	800.
Missouri	100.	225.	450.
Montana	550.	900.	1600.
Nebraska	140.	275.	500.
New Hampshire	150.	325.	750.
New Jersey	125.	250.	450.
New Mexico Territory	550.	900.	1600.
New Mexico	450.	650.	1200.
New York	80.00	140.	275.
North Carolina	250.	500.	800.
North Dakota	300.	550.	900.
Ohio	80.00	160.	315.
Oklahoma	200.	400.	750.
Oregon	325.	650.	1100.
Pennsylvania	80.00	140.	275.
Rhode Island	225.	400.	700.
South Carolina	275.	550.	900.
South Dakota	300.	550.	900.
Tennessee	225.	450.	850.
Texas	150.	250.	500.
Utah	375.	700.	1400.
Vermont	175.	450.	875.
Virginia	140.	275.	550.
Washington	450.	800.	1600.
West Virginia	200.	400.	750.
Wisconsin	125.	275.	500.
Wyoming	450.	750.	1500.

Ben Franklin

1882 Value Back $10
(KL# 1209-1215) (Fr #576-579-B)

	VG	VF	AU
Alabama	225.	575.	1200.
Arizona	1750.	2750.	4500.
Arkansas	750.	1150.	2000.
California	200.	400.	875.
Colorado	300.	500.	1100.
Connecticut	200.	450.	900.
Delaware	500.	950.	2100.
Florida	550.	1000.	2000.
Georgia	325.	550.	1200.
Hawaii	300.	750.	2000.
Idaho	500.	950.	2000.
Illinois	150.	400.	850.
Indiana	200.	460.	950.
Iowa	175.	375.	800.
Kansas	225.	450.	1000.
Kentucky	190.	600.	1300.
Louisiana	450.	800.	1500.
Maine	325.	700.	1500.
Maryland	200.	500.	950.
Massachusetts	225.	550.	1100.
Michigan	200.	380.	775.
Minnesota	200.	400.	900.
Mississippi	400.	800.	1600.
Missouri	200.	400.	900.
Montana	600.	1100.	2200.
Nebraska	175.	380.	775.
Nevada		None issued	
New Hampshire	275.	650.	1400.
New Jersey	225.	400.	900.
New Mexico	450.	700.	1500.
New York	125.	350.	650.
North Carolina	500.	800.	1400.
North Dakota	400.	650.	1300.
Ohio	125.	400.	850.
Oklahoma	300.	550.	1200.
Oregon	450.	700.	1500.
Pennsylvania	125.	300.	650.
Rhode Island		None issued	
South Carolina	550.	950.	1800.
South Dakota	400.	650.	1400.
Tennessee	350.	600.	1800.
Texas	200.	400.	850.
Utah	450.	900.	1600.
Vermont	275.	450.	1300.
Virginia	200.	500.	1000.
Washington	450.	900.	1600.
West Virginia	250.	530.	1400.
Wisconsin	175.	400.	850.
Wyoming	1100.	1700.	3200.

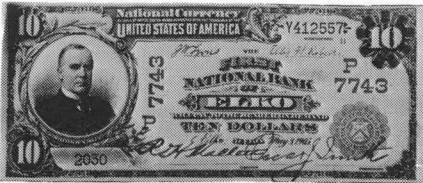

William McKinley

1902 Red Seal $10
(KL# 1216-1218) (Fr #613-615)

	VG	VF	AU
Alabama	450.	850.	1500.
Alaska	3000.	4500.	7500.
Arizona Territory	3000.	5000.	10,000.
Arkansas	350.	750.	1175.
California	250.	500.	800.
Colorado	350.	700.	1400.
Connecticut	225.	460.	1000.
Delaware	2250.	5000.	9000.
District of Columbia	350.	550.	1175.
Florida	1000.	1600.	3000.
Georgia	450.	800.	1600.
Idaho	2250.	3500.	5000.
Illinois	90.00	300.	650.
Indian Territory	650.	1100.	1900.
Indiana	140.	430.	925.
Iowa	200.	450.	900.
Kansas	250.	550.	950.
Kentucky	300.	600.	1100.
Louisiana	400.	750.	1500.
Maine	350.	700.	1300.
Maryland	120.	430.	925.
Massachusetts	135.	310.	675.
Michigan	225.	500.	1000.
Minnesota	200.	450.	800.
Mississippi	1000.	1700.	3000.
Missouri	150.	310.	675.
Montana	1100.	2600.	5000.
Nebraska	225.	450.	950.
Nevada	2000.	3500.	6000.
New Hampshire	350.	650.	1200.
New Jersey	175.	310.	675.
New Mexico Territory	800.	1600.	2500.
New York	70.00	175.	400.
North Carolina	800.	1500.	2400.
North Dakota	700.	1100.	2100.
Ohio	135.	250.	450.
Oklahoma Territory	800.	1600.	3000.
Oklahoma	700.	1300.	2200.
Oregon	550.	1100.	2100.
Pennsylvania	70.00	175.	400.
Puerto Rico	—	—	—
Rhode Island	225.	450.	900.
South Carolina	1100.	1700.	2600.
South Dakota	800.	1600.	2500.
Tennessee	550.	1100.	1900.
Texas	275.	550.	1100.
Utah	2250.	4500.	8500.
Vermont	350.	600.	1175.
Virginia	275.	460.	1000.
Washington	1000.	1800.	3200.
West Virginia	225.	500.	1075.
Wisconsin	175.	350.	675.
Wyoming	1500.	2500.	4000.

1902 Date Back $10
(KL# 1219-1227) (Fr #616-623-A)

	VG	VF	AU
Alabama	39.00	70.00	170.
Alaska	2300.	3600.	6500.
Arizona Territory	1300.	2600.	5000.
Arizona	300.	550.	1000.
Arkansas	125.	275.	550.
California	29.00	49.00	120.
Colorado	50.00	90.00	250.
Connecticut	40.00	72.00	185.
Delaware	250.	500.	900.
District of Columbia	45.00	100.	245.

	VG	VF	AU
Florida	90.00	175.	350.
Georgia	39.00	90.00	225.
Hawaii	225.	450.	750.
Idaho	175.	400.	700.
Illinois	29.00	49.00	120.
Indiana	39.00	70.00	170.
Iowa	30.00	60.00	150.
Kansas	32.00	57.00	140.
Kentucky	34.00	68.00	185.
Louisiana	70.00	135.	245.
Maine	80.00	160.	325.
Maryland	30.00	60.00	170.
Massachusetts	30.00	51.00	125.
Michigan	35.00	57.00	140.
Minnesota	30.00	51.00	125.
Mississippi	100.	250.	500.
Missouri	30.00	51.00	125.
Montana	175.	325.	650.
Nebraska	35.00	57.00	140.
Nevada	275.	525.	950.
New Hampshire	45.00	85.00	200.
New Jersey	30.00	51.00	125.
New Mexico Territory	500.	800.	1600.
New Mexico	135.	325.	650.
New York	27.50	45.00	110.
North Carolina	55.00	110.	325.
North Dakota	110.	275.	550.
Ohio	30.00	46.00	125.
Oklahoma	39.00	70.00	170.
Oregon	80.00	225.	500.
Pennsylvania	28.00	45.00	110.
Puerto Rico	—	Rare	—
Rhode Island	45.00	85.00	200.
South Carolina	70.00	175.	350.
South Dakota	110.	275.	550.
Tennessee	45.00	100.	250.
Texas	29.00	85.00	225.
Utah	80.00	175.	450.
Vermont	55.00	100.	245.
Virginia	35.00	72.00	185.
Washington	55.00	150.	350.
West Virginia	45.00	85.00	200.
Wisconsin	30.00	51.00	125.
Wyoming	140.	325.	650.

William McKinley

1902 Plain Back $10
(KL# 1228-1242) (Fr #624-638)

	VG	VF	AU
Alabama	35.00	50.00	140.
Alaska	2000.	3250.	5750.
Arizona	275.	500.	900.
Arkansas	80.00	250.	500.
California	25.00	40.00	95.00
Colorado	45.00	80.00	225.
Connecticut	35.00	60.00	150.
Delaware	225.	450.	800.
District of Columbia	35.00	90.00	220.
Florida	80.00	160.	300.
Georgia	35.00	80.00	200.
Hawaii	200.	400.	700.
Idaho	150.	350.	650.
Illinois	25.00	40.00	95.00
Indiana	35.00	50.00	140.
Iowa	25.00	55.00	135.
Kansas	30.00	45.00	115.
Kentucky	30.00	50.00	150.
Louisiana	50.00	90.00	220.
Maine	70.00	140.	300.
Maryland	25.00	55.00	140.
Massachusetts	25.00	42.00	100.
Michigan	30.00	45.00	115.
Minnesota	25.00	42.00	100.
Mississippi	90.00	225.	450.
Missouri	25.00	42.00	100.
Montana	160.	300.	600.
Nebraska	30.00	50.00	115.
Nevada	250.	500.	900.
New Hampshire	40.00	75.00	185.
New Jersey	25.00	45.00	100.
New Mexico	120.	300.	600.
New York	24.00	40.00	90.00
North Carolina	50.00	100.	300.

	VG	VF	AU
North Dakota	100.	250.	500.
Ohio	25.00	42.00	100.
Oklahoma	34.00	60.00	140.
Oregon	50.00	150.	450.
Pennsylvania	23.00	40.00	90.00
Rhode Island	40.00	75.00	185.
South Carolina	60.00	160.	300.
South Dakota	100.	250.	500.
Tennessee	40.00	90.00	225.
Texas	30.00	75.00	200.
Utah	70.00	160.	400.
Vermont	50.00	90.00	220.
Virginia	30.00	65.00	150.
Washington	40.00	90.00	220.
West Virginia	40.00	75.00	185.
Wisconsin	25.00	45.00	100.
Wyoming	125.	300.	600.

Alexander Hamilton

1929 Type 1 $10
(KL# 1243) (Fr #1801-1)

	VG	VF	AU
Alabama	15.00	28.00	40.00
Alaska	1800.	2500.	3500.
Arizona	80.00	185.	325.
Arkansas	50.00	75.00	125.
California	12.00	22.00	32.00
Colorado	18.00	28.00	40.00
Connecticut	18.00	40.00	60.00
Delaware	75.00	135.	195.
District of Columbia	16.00	40.00	60.00
Florida	25.00	35.00	60.00
Georgia	20.00	30.00	50.00
Hawaii	65.00	100.	175.
Idaho	75.00	150.	300.
Illinois	13.00	24.00	35.00
Indiana	14.00	25.00	37.00
Iowa	14.00	24.00	35.00
Kansas	15.00	24.00	35.00
Kentucky	18.00	28.00	40.00
Louisiana	19.00	37.00	80.00
Maine	35.00	50.00	90.00
Maryland	15.00	34.00	50.00
Massachusetts	14.00	22.00	32.00
Michigan	16.00	25.00	37.00
Minnesota	14.00	25.00	37.00
Mississippi	40.00	70.00	85.00
Missouri	13.00	28.00	40.00
Montana	75.00	175.	300.
Nebraska	13.00	25.00	37.00
Nevada	150.	300.	600.
New Hampshire	28.00	40.00	80.00
New Jersey	15.00	24.00	35.00
New Mexico	50.00	125.	225.
New York	12.50	22.00	32.00
North Carolina	30.00	45.00	75.00
North Dakota	40.00	100.	200.
Ohio	13.00	24.00	35.00
Oklahoma	18.00	28.00	40.00
Oregon	20.00	30.00	55.00
Pennsylvania	12.00	20.00	32.00
Rhode Island	25.00	50.00	75.00
South Carolina	40.00	75.00	90.00
South Dakota	60.00	125.	225.
Tennessee	20.00	34.00	50.00
Texas	15.00	24.00	35.00
Utah	30.00	75.00	125.
Vermont	24.00	45.00	90.00
Virginia	20.00	40.00	55.00
Washington	16.00	37.00	55.00
West Virginia	15.00	30.00	50.00
Wisconsin	13.00	24.00	35.00
Wyoming	75.00	150.	250.

Alexander Hamilton

1929 Type 2 $10
(KL# 1244) (Fr #1801-2)

	VG	VF	AU
Alabama	17.00	35.00	45.00
Alaska	1900.	2750.	4000.
Arizona	90.00	200.	350.
Arkansas	55.00	80.00	135.

	VG	VF	AU
California	13.00	25.00	40.00
Colorado	19.00	30.00	45.00
Connecticut	20.00	45.00	65.00
Delaware	75.00	135.	195.
District of Columbia	18.00	45.00	65.00
Florida	20.00	35.00	65.00
Georgia	24.00	35.00	55.00
Hawaii	70.00	110.	185.
Idaho	85.00	165.	325.
Illinois	14.00	29.00	38.00
Indiana	15.00	30.00	40.00
Iowa	15.00	30.00	40.00
Kansas	17.00	30.00	42.00
Kentucky	19.00	30.00	45.00
Louisiana	20.00	45.00	80.00
Maine	36.00	60.00	90.00
Maryland	17.00	40.00	55.00
Massachusetts	16.00	28.00	35.00
Michigan	18.00	32.00	40.00
Minnesota	16.00	30.00	40.00
Mississippi	40.00	70.00	85.00
Missouri	14.00	30.00	45.00
Montana	80.00	185.	325.
Nebraska	14.00	27.00	40.00
Nevada	160.	325.	650.
New Hampshire	25.00	50.00	80.00
New Jersey	16.00	26.00	38.00
New Mexico	55.00	135.	250.
New York	13.00	20.00	35.00
North Carolina	35.00	50.00	80.00
North Dakota	45.00	110.	215.
Ohio	14.00	26.00	38.00
Oklahoma	20.00	30.00	45.00
Oregon	22.00	35.00	60.00
Pennsylvania	13.00	21.00	35.00
Rhode Island	30.00	55.00	80.00
South Carolina	40.00	75.00	95.00
South Dakota	65.00	135.	250.
Tennessee	22.00	36.00	50.00
Texas	16.00	36.00	38.00
Utah	35.00	80.00	135.
Vermont	26.00	50.00	95.00
Virginia	22.00	45.00	60.00
Washington	18.00	40.00	60.00
West Virginia	18.00	32.00	55.00
Wisconsin	14.00	26.00	38.00
Wyoming	85.00	165.	275.

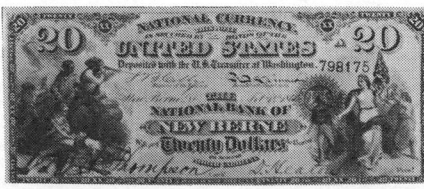

Original Series $20
(KL# 1245-1248) (Fr #424-429)

	VG	VF	AU
Alabama	800.	1500.	3000.
Arkansas	1000.	1600.	2750.
California		None issued	
Colorado Territory	3000.	4500.	6000.
Connecticut	450.	675.	2000.
Delaware	1000.	1750.	3500.
District of Columbia	750.	1000.	2250.
Georgia	1000.	1500.	2500.
Idaho Territory	—	Rare	—
Illinois	350.	600.	1300.
Indiana	400.	650.	1800.
Iowa	400.	650.	1700.
Kansas	600.	900.	2000.
Kentucky	550.	850.	2000.
Louisiana	750.	1500.	2750.
Maine	650.	1000.	2250.
Maryland	450.	700.	1800.
Massachusetts	350.	600.	1350.
Michigan	550.	800.	1500.
Minnesota	500.	750.	1450.
Mississippi		Unknown	
Missouri	450.	750.	1500.
Montana Territory	3000.	5000.	9000.
Montana	1500.	2500.	5000.
Nebraska	750.	1350.	2250.
Nebraska Territory	—	Rare	—
Nevada		Unknown	
New Hampshire	600.	950.	2100.
New Jersey	450.	800.	1800.
New Mexico Territory	2500.	4000.	7000.

NATIONAL BANK NOTE VALUATIONS BY STATE $10 AND $20 NOTES

	VG	VF	AU
New York	325.	550.	1200.
North Carolina	1500.	2500.	4500.
Ohio	350.	600.	1350.
Pennsylvania	325.	550.	1200.
Rhode Island	450.	700.	2100.
South Carolina	1500.	2500.	4500.
Tennessee	1200.	2000.	3200.
Texas	2000.	3000.	5000.
Utah Territory	4000.	6000.	9000.
Utah		None issued	
Vermont	500.	900.	2250.
Virginia	650.	1000.	2500.
West Virginia	1000.	1500.	3000.
Wisconsin	500.	900.	2100.
Wyoming Territory	—	—	—

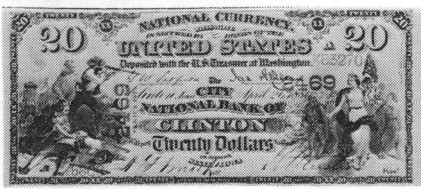

Series 1875 $20
(KL# 1249-1257) (Fr #431-439)

	VG	VF	AU
Alabama	700.	1350.	2500.
Arkansas	900.	1500.	2600.
California	1500.	2500.	4000.
Colorado Territory	2750.	4000.	6000.
Colorado	1500.	2500.	4000.
Connecticut	400.	600.	1750.
Dakota Territory	3500.	5500.	8000.
Delaware	900.	1600.	3000.
District of Columbia	600.	1000.	2000.
Georgia	900.	1350.	2250.
Hawaii		None issued	
Idaho Territory	—	Rare	—
Illinois	325.	550.	1200.
Indiana	375.	600.	1700.
Iowa	375.	600.	1650.
Kansas	550.	850.	1800.
Kentucky	500.	750.	1800.
Louisiana	700.	1400.	2100.
Maine	600.	900.	2000.
Maryland	400.	680.	1800.
Massachusetts	325.	550.	1250.
Michigan	500.	750.	1400.
Minnesota	450.	700.	1350.
Missouri	400.	700.	1350.
Montana Territory	2750.	4500.	8000.
Montana	1350.	2250.	4500.
Nebraska	700.	1250.	2000.
Nebraska Territory		None issued	
Nevada		Unknown	—
New Hampshire	550.	900.	2000.
New Jersey	400.	750.	1700.
New Mexico Territory	2250.	3500.	6000.
New York	300.	500.	1100.
North Carolina	1350.	2250.	4000.
North Dakota	1500.	2000.	4000.
Ohio	325.	550.	1250.
Oregon	2500.	3500.	5500.
Pennsylvania	300.	500.	1100.
Rhode Island	400.	650.	1900.
South Carolina	1350.	2250.	4000.
South Dakota	2000.	3000.	5000.
Tennessee	1100.	1800.	3000.
Texas	1800.	2700.	4500.
Utah Territory	3600.	5500.	8000.
Utah	2500.	4000.	6000.
Vermont	450.	800.	2000.
Virginia	600.	900.	2250.
West Virginia	900.	1350.	2750.
Wisconsin	450.	800.	1900.
Wyoming Territory	—	Rare	—
Wyoming	2000.	3000.	5000.

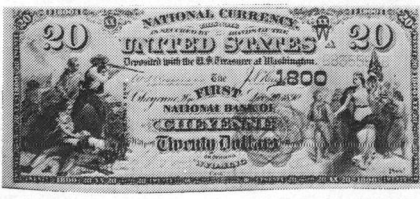

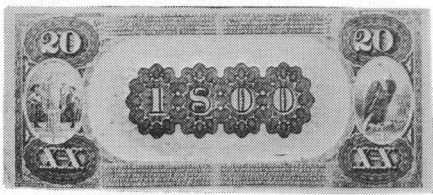

1882 Brown Back $20
(KL# 1258-1271) (Fr #493-506)

	VG	VF	AU
Alabama	300.	550.	1100.
Arizona Territory	4000.	6000.	11,000.
Arkansas	350.	600.	1100.
California	175.	350.	650.
Colorado	550.	900.	1750.
Connecticut	175.	350.	650.
Dakota Territory	1800.	3000.	5000.
Delaware	650.	1100.	2000.
District of Columbia	350.	600.	1100.
Florida	1000.	1800.	3500.
Georgia	500.	900.	1500.
Hawaii	700.	1100.	2000.
Idaho Territory	6000.	9000.	—
Idaho	2750.	4500.	7500.
Illinois	100.	250.	500.
Indian Territory	1000.	1750.	3000.
Indiana	110.	300.	600.
Iowa	125.	325.	650.
Kansas	175.	350.	750.
Kentucky	150.	350.	650.
Louisiana	350.	700.	1350.
Maine	300.	600.	1200.
Maryland	150.	350.	650.
Massachusetts	110.	250.	500.
Michigan	250.	500.	900.
Minnesota	175.	350.	600.
Mississippi	1000.	2000.	3500.
Missouri	135.	275.	550.
Montana Territory	1750.	3500.	6000.
Montana	1000.	1600.	3000.
Nebraska	250.	450.	850.
Nevada	10,000.	20,000.	40,000.
New Hampshire	250.	600.	1200.
New Jersey	200.	375.	600.
New Mexico Territory	1200.	2000.	3200.
New York	100.	225.	450.
North Carolina	500.	800.	1400.
North Dakota	600.	1000.	2000.
Ohio	110.	230.	500.
Oklahoma Territory	900.	1600.	2900.
Oklahoma	600.	900.	1600.
Oregon	500.	900.	1750.
Pennsylvania	100.	225.	450.
Rhode Island	175.	360.	615.
South Carolina	550.	900.	1500.
South Dakota	650.	1100.	2100.
Tennessee	400.	700.	1300.
Texas	300.	600.	1100.
Utah Territory	4500.	7000.	11,000.
Utah	600.	900.	2000.
Vermont	275.	550.	1200.
Virginia	250.	500.	1000.
Washington Territory	6000.	9000.	18,000.
Washington	700.	1200.	2500.
West Virginia	300.	600.	1200.
Wisconsin	200.	375.	650.
Wyoming Territory	—	Rare	—
Wyoming	1250.	2000.	3250.

1882 Date Back $20
(KL# 1272-1280) (Fr #549-557)

	VG	VF	AU
Alabama	200.	400.	750.

	VG	VF	AU
Alaska	5000.	9000.	15,000.
Arizona Territory	2750.	4250.	8000.
Arizona	1800.	3000.	5000.
Arkansas	275.	550.	1000.
California	200.	300.	550.
Colorado	350.	600.	1100.
Connecticut	150.	300.	600.
Delaware	550.	900.	1800.
District of Columbia	300.	500.	850.
Florida	650.	1100.	2000.
Georgia	275.	550.	1100.
Hawaii	400.	650.	1200.
Idaho	1000.	1500.	3000.
Illinois	125.	250.	500.
Indiana	140.	275.	550.
Iowa	150.	300.	600.
Kansas	175.	350.	650.
Kentucky	150.	300.	575.
Louisiana	300.	550.	1000.
Maine	275.	500.	900.
Maryland	175.	350.	750.
Massachusetts	125.	250.	500.
Michigan	175.	350.	650.
Minnesota	150.	300.	600.
Mississippi	450.	650.	950.
Missouri	140.	275.	575.
Montana	650.	1000.	2000.
Nebraska	175.	350.	650.
New Hampshire	200.	375.	900.
New Jersey	150.	300.	600.
New Mexico Territory	700.	1100.	1800.
New Mexico	550.	800.	1400.
New York	110.	200.	400.
North Carolina	350.	600.	1000.
North Dakota	400.	700.	1200.
Ohio	115.	225.	450.
Oklahoma	300.	500.	900.
Oregon	400.	800.	1300.
Pennsylvania	110.	225.	450.
Rhode Island	300.	500.	900.
South Carolina	400.	650.	1100.
South Dakota	400.	700.	1200.
Tennessee	300.	550.	1000.
Texas	200.	300.	600.
Utah	450.	900.	1600.
Vermont	250.	550.	1050.
Virginia	200.	350.	650.
Washington	600.	900.	1800.
West Virginia	250.	500.	900.
Wisconsin	160.	325.	600.
Wyoming	600.	900.	1800.

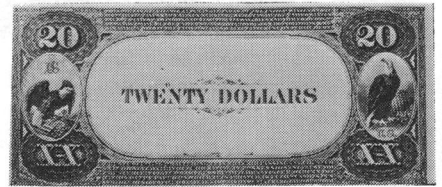

1882 Value Back $20
(KL# 1281-1289) (Fr #580-585)

	VG	VF	AU
Alabama	300.	600.	1300.
Arizona	2250.	3500.	6000.
Arkansas	400.	750.	1650.
California	300.	500.	925.
Colorado	500.	800.	1400.
Connecticut	400.	800.	1600.
Delaware	1000.	2000.	4000.
Florida	900.	1800.	3500.
Georgia	500.	1000.	2000.
Hawaii	600.	900.	1500.
Idaho	1500.	3000.	5000.
Illinois	200.	400.	925.
Indiana	250.	500.	950.
Iowa	250.	500.	925.
Kansas	300.	600.	1200.
Kentucky	350.	700.	1400.
Louisiana	500.	1000.	2000.
Maine	450.	900.	1800.
Maryland	250.	500.	1000.
Massachusetts	300.	600.	1200.
Michigan	275.	550.	1050.
Minnesota	250.	500.	975.
Mississippi	750.	1500.	3000.
Missouri	250.	500.	975.

	VG	VF	AU
Montana	1000.	1500.	2500.
Nebraska	275.	550.	1050.
Nevada	None issued		
New Hampshire	400.	720.	1500.
New Jersey	275.	550.	1100.
New Mexico	800.	1300.	2250.
New York	200.	400.	850.
North Carolina	500.	900.	1400.
North Dakota	500.	1000.	1750.
Ohio	225.	450.	975.
Oklahoma	450.	900.	1600.
Oregon	700.	1100.	2100.
Pennsylvania	200.	400.	850.
Rhode Island	None issued		
South Carolina	600.	1000.	1800.
South Dakota	500.	1000.	1750.
Tennessee	500.	900.	1600.
Texas	300.	550.	1100.
Utah	800.	1500.	2750.
Vermont	500.	1000.	2000.
Virginia	350.	700.	1400.
Washington	900.	1600.	2600.
West Virginia	450.	850.	1500.
Wisconsin	250.	500.	1000.
Wyoming	1250.	2250.	4000.

Hugh McCulloch

1902 Red Seal $20
(KL# 1290-1292) (Fr #639-641)

	VG	VF	AU
Alabama	600.	1000.	1750.
Alaska	Unknown		
Arizona Territory	3500.	5500.	12,000.
Arkansas	450.	900.	1500.
California	350.	600.	1000.
Colorado	500.	900.	1700.
Connecticut	275.	550.	1250.
Delaware	2750.	5500.	10,000.
District of Columbia	350.	750.	1500.
Florida	1250.	2000.	4000.
Georgia	600.	1000.	1800.
Idaho	2500.	5000.	9000.
Illinois	125.	250.	500.
Indian Territory	800.	1400.	2100.
Indiana	150.	300.	600.
Iowa	225.	350.	675.
Kansas	300.	600.	1100.
Kentucky	400.	750.	1250.
Louisiana	500.	900.	1800.
Maine	450.	800.	1500.
Maryland	150.	475.	1150.
Massachusetts	200.	400.	850.
Michigan	300.	600.	1200.
Minnesota	275.	550.	1000.
Mississippi	1500.	2500.	3750.
Missouri	200.	400.	850.
Montana	1500.	3000.	6000.
Nebraska	300.	600.	1100.
Nevada	2500.	4000.	7500.
New Hampshire	450.	800.	1350.
New Jersey	250.	500.	850.
New Mexico Territory	1000.	2000.	3100.
New York	100.	200.	450.
North Carolina	1000.	1800.	2700.
North Dakota	900.	1400.	2350.
Ohio	110.	300.	500.
Oklahoma Territory	1000.	1875.	3100.
Oklahoma	900.	1600.	2500.
Oregon	700.	1300.	2500.
Pennsylvania	100.	200.	450.
Puerto Rico	—	Rare	—
Rhode Island	300.	600.	1200.
South Carolina	1250.	2500.	3500.
South Dakota	900.	1400.	2400.
Tennessee	750.	1300.	2250.
Texas	400.	700.	1300.
Utah	2750.	5000.	9000.
Vermont	500.	900.	1500.
Virginia	350.	600.	1250.
Washington	1250.	2100.	3500.
West Virginia	300.	600.	1350.
Wisconsin	250.	450.	850.
Wyoming	2000.	3000.	5000.

Hugh McCulloch

1902 Date Back $20
(KL# 1293-1301) (Fr #642-649-A)

	VG	VF	AU
Alabama	75.00	150.	350.
Alaska	3000.	5000.	9000.
Arizona Territory	2000.	3000.	5000.
Arizona	400.	700.	1300.
Arkansas	175.	350.	650.
California	45.00	70.00	160.
Colorado	80.00	150.	350.
Connecticut	60.00	125.	300.
Delaware	350.	600.	1000.
District of Columbia	60.00	150.	350.
Florida	125.	275.	525.
Georgia	105.	240.	460.
Hawaii	300.	500.	900.
Idaho	250.	500.	900.
Illinois	45.00	90.00	200.
Indiana	55.00	110.	240.
Iowa	50.00	100.	225.
Kansas	60.00	125.	260.
Kentucky	55.00	110.	250.
Louisiana	90.00	175.	400.
Maine	100.	200.	400.
Maryland	45.00	95.00	225.
Massachusetts	40.00	80.00	170.
Michigan	50.00	100.	200.
Minnesota	45.00	95.00	190.
Mississippi	130.	250.	475.
Missouri	45.00	80.00	170.
Montana	225.	450.	850.
Nebraska	50.00	100.	200.
Nevada	350.	600.	1100.
New Hampshire	75.00	160.	375.
New Jersey	45.00	80.00	170.
New Mexico Territory	700.	1000.	1800.
New Mexico	190.	400.	750.
New York	35.00	75.00	150.
North Carolina	100.	180.	400.
North Dakota	150.	350.	700.
Ohio	40.00	80.00	170.
Oklahoma	60.00	110.	250.
Oregon	100.	250.	500.
Pennsylvania	35.00	75.00	150.
Puerto Rico	—	Rare	—
Rhode Island	75.00	150.	300.
South Carolina	110.	200.	450.
South Dakota	150.	350.	700.
Tennessee	70.00	140.	300.
Texas	45.00	70.00	160.
Utah	125.	250.	500.
Vermont	85.00	175.	425.
Virginia	60.00	125.	250.
Washington	80.00	200.	400.
West Virginia	75.00	150.	300.
Wisconsin	45.00	80.00	170.
Wyoming	200.	400.	800.

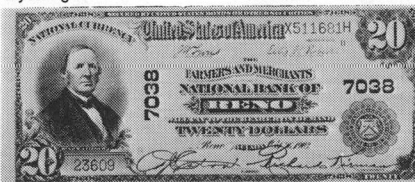

Hugh McCulloch

1902 Plain Back $20
(KL# 1302-1316) (Fr #650-663-A)

	VG	VF	AU
Alabama	65.00	130.	300.

	VG	VF	AU
Alaska	2700.	4500.	8000.
Arizona	350.	600.	1100.
Arkansas	150.	300.	550.
California	40.00	60.00	140.
Colorado	70.00	13.00	300.
Connecticut	55.00	110.	260.
Delaware	300.	525.	900.
District of Columbia	55.00	135.	300.
Florida	110.	225.	450.
Georgia	90.00	200.	400.
Hawaii	260.	450.	800.
Idaho	225.	425.	750.
Illinois	40.00	80.00	175.
Indiana	50.00	95.00	210.
Iowa	45.00	90.00	200.
Kansas	55.00	110.	225.
Kentucky	50.00	100.	220.
Louisiana	80.00	150.	325.
Maine	90.00	175.	350.
Maryland	40.00	75.00	170.
Massachusetts	35.00	70.00	150.
Michigan	45.00	90.00	175.
Minnesota	40.00	85.00	170.
Mississippi	120.	225.	425.
Missouri	40.00	75.00	150.
Montana	200.	400.	750.
Nebraska	45.00	90.00	175.
Nevada	300.	525.	950.
New Hampshire	65.00	140.	325.
New Jersey	40.00	70.00	150.
New Mexico	170.	350.	650.
New York	30.00	65.00	135.
North Carolina	90.00	160.	350.
North Dakota	135.	300.	600.
Ohio	35.00	70.00	150.
Oklahoma	55.00	100.	225.
Oregon	90.00	225.	450.
Pennsylvania	30.00	65.00	135.
Rhode Island	65.00	135.	260.
South Carolina	100.	175.	400.
South Dakota	135.	300.	600.
Tennessee	60.00	125.	260.
Texas	40.00	65.00	140.
Utah	110.	225.	450.
Vermont	75.00	160.	375.
Virginia	55.00	110.	225.
Washington	70.00	175.	350.
West Virginia	65.00	135.	270.
Wisconsin	40.00	70.00	150.
Wyoming	175.	350.	700.

Andrew Jackson

1929 Type 1 $20
(KL# 1317) (Fr #1802-1)

	VG	VF	AU
Alabama	29.00	36.00	50.00
Alaska	2000.	2800.	4000.
Arizona	100.	200.	350.
Arkansas	60.00	90.00	150.
California	24.00	35.00	55.00
Colorado	26.00	40.00	60.00
Connecticut	32.00	50.00	90.00
Delaware	85.00	150.	250.
District of Columbia	30.00	50.00	80.00
Florida	45.00	65.00	95.00
Georgia	32.00	50.00	80.00
Idaho	90.00	175.	350.
Illinois	25.00	40.00	55.00
Indiana	26.00	45.00	60.00
Iowa	25.00	42.00	58.00
Kansas	30.00	50.00	80.00
Kentucky	29.00	45.00	65.00
Louisiana	34.00	50.00	75.00
Maine	43.00	60.00	95.00
Maryland	28.00	40.00	60.00
Massachusetts	24.00	40.00	55.00
Michigan	26.00	40.00	55.00
Minnesota	26.00	40.00	55.00
Mississippi	50.00	85.00	110.
Missouri	25.00	40.00	55.00
Montana	90.00	200.	375.
Nebraska	24.00	40.00	60.00
Nevada	180.	350.	700.
New Hampshire	37.00	60.00	95.00
New Jersey	25.00	40.00	55.00
New Mexico	75.00	150.	275.
New York	24.00	35.00	55.00
North Carolina	50.00	70.00	125.
North Dakota	66.00	120.	250.
Ohio	25.00	40.00	60.00
Oklahoma	26.00	40.00	60.00
Oregon	34.00	55.00	85.00
Pennsylvania	24.00	35.00	55.00

	VG	VF	AU
Rhode Island	45.00	85.00	115.
South Carolina	55.00	75.00	125.
South Dakota	60.00	115.	250.
Tennessee	32.00	50.00	80.00
Texas	25.00	45.00	75.00
Utah	34.00	55.00	90.00
Vermont	43.00	65.00	100.
Virginia	32.00	50.00	75.00
Washington	34.00	55.00	90.00
West Virginia	30.00	45.00	70.00
Wisconsin	25.00	40.00	60.00
Wyoming	90.00	175.	300.

Andrew Jackson
1929 Type 2 $20
(KL# 1318) (Fr #1802-2)

	VG	VF	AU
Alabama	32.00	40.00	60.00
Alaska	2000.	3000.	5000.
Arizona	110.	225.	400.
Arkansas	65.00	100.	175.
California	25.00	40.00	65.00
Colorado	30.00	45.00	70.00
Connecticut	35.00	55.00	100.
Delaware	95.00	170.	300.
District of Columbia	35.00	55.00	90.00
Florida	50.00	75.00	110.
Georgia	34.00	55.00	90.00
Idaho	100.	200.	400.
Illinois	26.00	45.00	60.00
Indiana	27.00	50.00	65.00
Iowa	26.00	47.00	63.00
Kansas	33.00	55.00	90.00
Kentucky	32.00	50.00	70.00
Louisiana	36.00	55.00	85.00
Maine	45.00	65.00	100.
Maryland	30.00	45.00	65.00
Massachusetts	26.00	43.00	60.00
Michigan	30.00	45.00	60.00
Minnesota	27.00	45.00	60.00
Mississippi	55.00	95.00	125.
Missouri	28.00	45.00	60.00
Montana	100.	225.	400.
Nebraska	27.00	45.00	65.00
Nevada	200.	375.	750.
New Hampshire	40.00	65.00	100.
New Jersey	26.00	45.00	60.00
New Mexico	85.00	170.	300.
New York	25.00	38.00	60.00
North Carolina	55.00	80.00	140.
North Dakota	70.00	125.	275.
Ohio	26.00	45.00	65.00
Oklahoma	28.00	45.00	65.00
Oregon	36.00	60.00	95.00
Pennsylvania	25.00	40.00	60.00
Rhode Island	50.00	90.00	120.
South Carolina	60.00	85.00	140.
South Dakota	70.00	125.	275.
Tennessee	34.00	55.00	90.00
Texas	28.00	50.00	85.00
Utah	36.00	60.00	100.
Vermont	45.00	70.00	110.
Virginia	34.00	55.00	85.00
Washington	36.00	60.00	100.
West Virginia	33.00	50.00	80.00
Wisconsin	26.00	45.00	70.00
Wyoming	100.	200.	350.

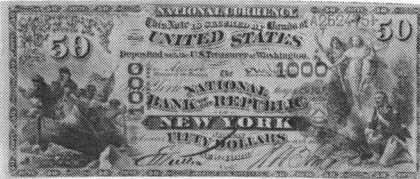

George Washington

Original Series $50
(KL# 1319-1321) (Fr #440-443)

	VG	VF	AU
Alabama	3000.	4650.	8600.

	VG	VF	AU
Colorado Territory	3750.	7500.	15,000.
Connecticut	3000.	5000.	9400.
Delaware	5000.	7500.	15,000.
District of Columbia	2900.	5700.	10,500.
Georgia	3000.	4650.	8600.
Illinois	2000.	3300.	6250.
Indiana	2300.	4650.	8600.
Iowa	2200.	3300.	6250.
Kentucky	2500.	5000.	9400.
Louisiana	3250.	5700.	10,500.
Maine	3500.	5700.	10,500.
Maryland	2600.	4650.	8600.
Massachusetts	2000.	3450.	6500.
Michigan	2300.	4000.	7000.
Minnesota	2500.	4500.	7500.
Missouri	2300.	4000.	7000.
Montana Territory	6000.	9000.	15,000.
Nebraska	2600.	4700.	9000.
New Hampshire	2650.	5300.	9850.
New Jersey	2200.	4500.	8000.
New Mexico Territory	3750.	7500.	15,000.
New York	2000.	3000.	5750.
North Carolina	3500.	6000.	9400.
Ohio	2000.	3450.	6500.
Pennsylvania	2000.	3000.	5750.
Rhode Island	3000.	5300.	9850.
South Carolina	3500.	6300.	9850.
Tennessee	3250.	5000.	9400.
Texas	2750.	5250.	9400.
Utah Territory	6000.	10,000.	20,000.
Utah	4000.	6500.	12,500.
Vermont	2900.	5700.	10,500.
Virginia	2500.	5000.	9400.

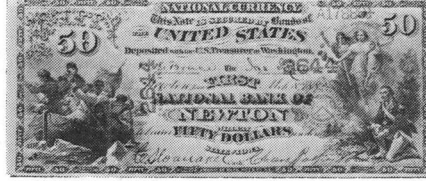

George Washington

Series 1875 $50
(KL# 1322-1330) (Fr #444-451)

	VG	VF	AU
Alabama	2600.	4200.	8000.
Arkansas	3000.	5250.	10,000.
California	4000.	6000.	9000.
Colorado Territory	3500.	7200.	14,000.
Colorado	2750.	4600.	8750.
Connecticut	2600.	4600.	8750.
Delaware	4500.	7200.	14,000.
District of Columbia	2700.	5250.	10,000.
Georgia	2700.	4200.	8000.
Illinois	1800.	3100.	6000.
Indiana	2100.	4200.	8000.
Iowa	2000.	3100.	6000.
Kansas	2750.	4000.	7500.
Kentucky	2300.	4600.	8750.
Louisiana	3000.	5250.	10,000.
Maine	3200.	5250.	10,000.
Maryland	2300.	4200.	8000.
Massachusetts	1800.	3250.	6250.
Michigan	2100.	3750.	6800.
Minnesota	2250.	4000.	7000.
Mississippi		None known	
Missouri	2100.	3600.	6500.
Montana Territory	5500.	8500.	14,000.
Nebraska	2400.	4400.	8000.
New Hampshire	2450.	4900.	9400.
New Jersey	2000.	4000.	7250.
New Mexico Territory	3500.	7200.	14,000.
New York	1800.	2800.	5500.
Ohio	1800.	3250.	6250.
Pennsylvania	1800.	2800.	5500.
Rhode Island	2750.	4900.	9400.
South Carolina	3300.	5900.	9400.
Tennessee	3000.	4600.	8750.
Texas	2500.	5000.	7500.
Utah Territory	5500.	9500.	18,000.
Vermont	2700.	5250.	10,000.
Virginia	2300.	4600.	8750.
Wisconsin	2250.	4000.	6250.

George Washington

1882 Brown Back $50
(KL# 1331-1343) (Fr #507-518-A)

	VG	VF	AU
Alabama	900.	1800.	3000.
Arizona Territory	15,000.	27,500.	45,000.
Arkansas	1250.	2500.	4500.
California	1000.	1900.	3000.
Colorado	1500.	2500.	4000.
Connecticut	900.	1700.	2900.
Dakota Territory	4000.	6000.	10,000.
Delaware	2500.	4500.	8000.
District of Columbia	1250.	2500.	4500.
Florida	2000.	3500.	5500.
Georgia	1500.	2500.	4250.
Hawaii	3000.	5500.	10,000.
Idaho	4000.	7500.	12,500.
Illinois	600.	1100.	1900.
Indian Territory	2000.	3750.	5500.
Indiana	700.	1550.	2600.
Iowa	650.	1300.	2250.
Kansas	750.	1600.	2600.
Kentucky	700.	1500.	2500.
Louisiana	1200.	1950.	3400.
Maine	1400.	2400.	4000.
Maryland	950.	1750.	3000.
Massachusetts	700.	1350.	2200.
Michigan	700.	1700.	2750.
Minnesota	1100.	2000.	3000.
Mississippi	2500.	4500.	7500.
Missouri	800.	1650.	2800.
Montana Territory	5000.	7500.	14,500.
Montana	3000.	5000.	8000.
Nebraska	1250.	2400.	4000.
New Hampshire	1000.	1800.	3100.
New Jersey	750.	1400.	2750.
New Mexico Territory	3000.	4500.	7500.
New York	600.	1000.	1750.
North Carolina	2000.	3500.	5500.
North Dakota	2250.	4000.	6000.
Ohio	600.	1150.	2000.
Oklahoma Territory	2000.	2750.	4500.
Oklahoma	1500.	2400.	3750.
Oregon	1750.	2800.	4750.
Pennsylvania	600.	1000.	1750.
Rhode Island	950.	1800.	3100.
South Carolina	2100.	3750.	5750.
South Dakota	2250.	4000.	6000.
Tennessee	1600.	2700.	4900.
Texas	1400.	2400.	3600.
Utah Territory	4500.	7000.	12,500.
Utah	3000.	4500.	9000.
Vermont	1100.	1950.	3400.
Virginia	1000.	1700.	2950.
Washington	2000.	3500.	6000.
West Virginia	1400.	2100.	4000.
Wisconsin	750.	1400.	3000.

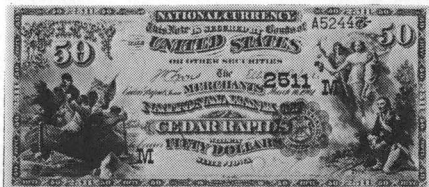

George Washington

1882 Date Back $50
(KL# 1344-1351) (Fr #558-565)

	VG	VF	AU
Alabama	800.	1600.	2500.

	VG	VF	AU
Arizona Territory	5000.	9000.	20,000.
Arkansas	900.	1750.	3100.
California	600.	1000.	1750.
Colorado	900.	1500.	2700.
Connecticut	700.	1200.	2400.
Delaware	1750.	3000.	5500.
District of Columbia	800.	1750.	3100.
Florida	1250.	2400.	4000.
Georgia	1000.	1800.	3250.
Idaho	2500.	4500.	9000.
Illinois	400.	750.	1500.
Indiana	450.	850.	1700.
Iowa	425.	800.	1600.
Kansas	550.	1150.	2100.
Kentucky	580.	1500.	2700.
Maryland	525.	1350.	2450.
Massachusetts	500.	1050.	1850.
Michigan	650.	1150.	2100.
Minnesota	750.	1250.	2250.
Missouri	450.	800.	1650.
Montana	2000.	3500.	6000.
Nebraska	750.	1300.	2400.
New Hampshire	620.	1200.	2100.
New Jersey	500.	800.	1400.
New Mexico Territory	1950.	3500.	5500.
New Mexico	1300.	2500.	3750.
New York	350.	600.	1250.
North Carolina	1000.	1500.	2700.
North Dakota	1200.	1600.	2850.
Ohio	400.	750.	1500.
Oklahoma	950.	1600.	3000.
Pennsylvania	350.	600.	1250.
South Carolina	1100.	1600.	2850.
Tennessee	1000.	1500.	2700.
Texas	800.	1600.	2600.
Utah	1800.	3000.	6000.
Vermont	700.	1750.	3100.
Virginia	800.	1500.	2700.
Washington	1250.	2400.	4400.
West Virginia	950.	1800.	3250.

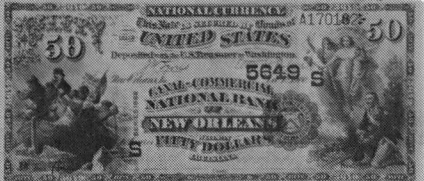

George Washington

1882 Value Back $50
(KL# 1352) (Fr #586)

	VG	VF	AU
Louisiana			(Three known)
Ohio			(One known)

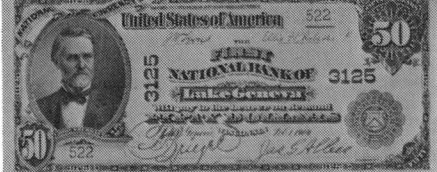

John Sherman

1902 Red Seal $50
(KL# 1353-1355) (Fr #664-666)

	VG	VF	AU
Alabama	—	Rare	—
Arkansas	2000.	4000.	7800.
California	1500.	2700.	4600.
Colorado	1750.	4000.	6800.
Connecticut	1250.	2500.	5800.
Delaware	4000.	7000.	12,000.
Florida	3000.	5500.	8500.
Idaho	4000.	6500.	9500.
Illinois	500.	1750.	3500.
Indian Territory	2500.	5000.	10,000.

	VG	VF	AU
Indiana	700.	2000.	4000.
Iowa	675.	1900.	3750.
Kansas	800.	2250.	4000.
Kentucky	900.	2500.	4250.
Louisiana	1100.	2800.	4500.
Maine	1400.	3250.	5000.
Maryland	650.	1750.	3500.
Massachusetts	750.	2000.	3800.
Michigan	700.	1800.	3600.
Minnesota	700.	1800.	3600.
Mississippi	1500.	3000.	6000.
Missouri	600.	1750.	3500.
Montana	2250.	4200.	7250.
Nebraska	900.	2500.	5300.
Nevada	2500.	5000.	10,000.
New Hampshire	1250.	3000.	4800.
New Jersey	650.	1850.	3600.
New York	600.	1750.	3500.
North Carolina	2000.	4000.	6800.
North Dakota	2250.	4200.	7250.
Ohio	625.	1800.	3600.
Oklahoma	1200.	2500.	4500.
Oregon	2000.	4000.	7800.
Pennsylvania	600.	1750.	3500.
Puerto Rico	—	Rare	—
Rhode Island	800.	2000.	4000.
South Dakota	2400.	4800.	8250.
Tennessee	1600.	3200.	5800.
Texas	900.	1900.	4000.
Vermont	1400.	3250.	5400.
Virginia	1300.	2750.	4750.
Washington	2000.	4000.	7800.
West Virginia	1500.	3000.	6000.
Wisconsin	750.	1800.	3750.

John Sherman

1902 Date Back $50
(KL# 1356-1364) (Fr #667-674-A)

	VG	VF	AU
Alabama	350.	650.	1000.
Arizona Territory	2000.	4000.	7500.
Arkansas	600.	900.	1500.
California	200.	350.	650.
Colorado	400.	750.	1250.
Connecticut	300.	600.	1100.
Delaware	800.	1400.	2750.
Florida	750.	1350.	2600.
Georgia	600.	900.	1700.
Idaho	450.	650.	1000.
Illinois	200.	350.	650.
Indiana	250.	400.	700.
Iowa	240.	375.	700.
Kansas	325.	525.	900.
Kentucky	275.	475.	800.
Louisiana	400.	650.	1050.
Maryland	250.	400.	700.
Massachusetts	250.	400.	700.
Michigan	275.	450.	750.
Minnesota	275.	450.	750.
Mississippi	900.	1800.	2250.
Missouri	200.	350.	650.
Montana	900.	1750.	3250.
Nebraska	225.	375.	650.
Nevada	750.	1400.	2750.
New Hampshire	400.	700.	1300.
New Jersey	250.	400.	700.
New York	175.	325.	600.
North Carolina	900.	1650.	2900.
North Dakota	1000.	1800.	3250.
Ohio	200.	350.	650.
Oklahoma	250.	400.	700.
Oregon	500.	900.	1750.
Pennsylvania	175.	325.	600.
Rhode Island	600.	900.	1500.
South Dakota	1100.	1900.	3500.
Tennessee	750.	1300.	2400.
Texas	225.	360.	675.
Utah	1250.	2400.	3600.
Vermont	450.	750.	1400.
Virginia	350.	650.	1200.
Washington	220.	650.	1100.
West Virginia	400.	700.	1300.
Wisconsin	225.	375.	675.

1902 Plain Back $50
(KL# 1365-1377) (Fr #675-685-A)

	VG	VF	AU
California	190.	325.	600.
Colorado	375.	700.	1100.
Connecticut	275.	550.	1000.
Delaware	700.	1800.	2500.
District of Columbia	400.	750.	1250.
Florida	700.	1250.	2500.
Idaho	400.	600.	900.
Illinois	190.	325.	600.
Indian Territory		None issued	
Indiana	225.	375.	700.
Iowa	220.	360.	675.
Kansas	300.	500.	850.
Kentucky	260.	450.	750.
Louisiana	350.	600.	950.
Maryland	225.	375.	650.
Massachusetts	225.	375.	650.
Michigan	250.	400.	700.
Minnesota	250.	400.	700.
Mississippi	850.	1700.	3100.
Missouri	190.	325.	600.
Montana	850.	1650.	3000.
Nebraska	200.	350.	600.
Nevada	650.	1300.	2500.
New Hampshire	375.	650.	1200.
New Jersey	225.	350.	650.
New York	165.	300.	550.
North Carolina	850.	1500.	2700.
North Dakota	900.	1700.	3000.
Ohio	180.	325.	600.
Oklahoma	225.	350.	650.
Oregon	450.	850.	1600.
Pennsylvania	165.	300.	550.
Rhode Island	550.	800.	1400.
South Dakota	1000.	1800.	3250.
Tennessee	700.	1200.	2200.
Texas	200.	325.	600.
Utah		None issued	
Vermont	400.	700.	1250.
Washington	200.	520.	850.
West Virginia	350.	650.	1200.
Wisconsin	200.	350.	600.

U.S. Grant

1929 Type 1 $50
(KL# 1378) (Fr #1803-1)

	VG	VF	AU
California	55.00	90.00	150.
Colorado	75.00	150.	250.
Connecticut	150.	275.	500.
Delaware	400.	750.	1400.
Florida	125.	250.	450.
Hawaii	125.	225.	400.
Idaho	175.	300.	500.
Illinois	55.00	85.00	130.
Indiana	60.00	90.00	135.
Iowa	70.00	100.	175.
Kansas	85.00	125.	225.
Kentucky	75.00	120.	190.
Louisiana	95.00	130.	200.
Maryland	90.00	120.	185.
Massachusetts	125.	190.	375.
Michigan	65.00	110.	190.
Minnesota	65.00	110.	190.
Mississippi	350.	600.	1000.
Missouri	65.00	100.	175.
Montana	250.	450.	900.
Nebraska	55.00	90.00	175.
Nevada	400.	600.	1100.
New Hampshire	225.	400.	750.
New Jersey	60.00	100.	175.
New York	55.00	85.00	140.
North Carolina	300.	500.	950.
North Dakota	350.	550.	1000.
Ohio	55.00	85.00	140.
Oklahoma	55.00	90.00	150.
Oregon	350.	650.	1050.
Pennsylvania	55.00	85.00	140.
Rhode Island	150.	300.	600.

	VG	VF	AU
South Dakota	300.	550.	850.
Tennessee	90.00	165.	250.
Texas	55.00	90.00	150.
Utah	175.	350.	600.
Vermont	250.	450.	800.
Washington	75.00	150.	250.
West Virginia	200.	400.	750.
Wisconsin	60.00	90.00	145.
Wyoming	500.	900.	1750.

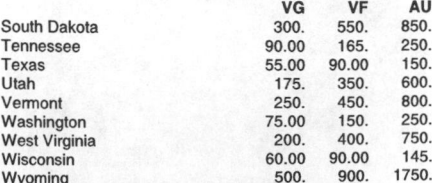

U.S. Grant
1929 Type 2 $50
(KL# 1379) (Fr #1803-2)

	VG	VF	AU
Arkansas	500.	800.	1250.
California	75.00	175.	400.
Colorado	200.	350.	700.
Hawaii	225.	375.	750.
Illinois	90.00	190.	450.
Indiana	125.	200.	475.
Kansas	175.	325.	650.
Kentucky	165.	300.	600.
Louisiana	125.	250.	500.
Maryland	175.	350.	700.
Michigan	135.	225.	475.
Minnesota	150.	250.	500.
Missouri	155.	260.	525.
Nebraska	175.	325.	625.
New Jersey	125.	225.	450.
New York	75.00	165.	300.
Ohio	100.	190.	375.
Oklahoma	155.	275.	525.
Pennsylvania	75.00	165.	300.
Rhode Island	250.	450.	850.
Tennessee	225.	400.	750.
Texas	125.	225.	450.
Virginia	250.	400.	750.
Wisconsin	125.	225.	450.

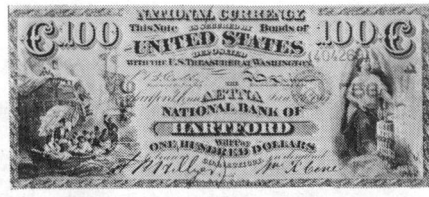

Original Series $100
(KL# 1380-1382) (Fr #452-455)

	VG	VF	AU
Alabama	3000.	5300.	10,500.
Colorado Territory	4000.	8500.	17,500.
Connecticut	3250.	5700.	10,500.
Delaware	5250.	8500.	17,500.
District of Columbia	3100.	6500.	12,000.
Georgia	3100.	5300.	10,000.
Illinois	2100.	3500.	6500.
Indiana	2200.	4850.	9000.
Iowa	2300.	3800.	6750.
Kentucky	2750.	5700.	11,000.
Louisiana	3500.	6500.	12,000.
Maine	3750.	6500.	12,000.
Maryland	2900.	4950.	9000.
Massachusetts	2100.	3750.	7000.
Michigan	2500.	4350.	7500.
Minnesota	2750.	4750.	8000.
Missouri	2500.	4500.	7400.
Montana Territory	7000.	9500.	17,500.
New Hampshire	2550.	6000.	12,000.
New Jersey	2400.	5000.	8500.
New York	2100.	3500.	6500.
North Carolina	3950.	6500.	12,000.
Ohio	2100.	3600.	7000.
Pennsylvania	2100.	3500.	6500.
Rhode Island	3500.	6000.	11,500.
South Carolina	4000.	7000.	12,500.
Tennessee	3500.	6000.	11,000.
Texas	3000.	5500.	8500.
Utah Territory	7000.	11,000.	22,500.

	VG	VF	AU
Vermont	3100.	6000.	12,000.
Virginia	2750.	5500.	11,000.
Wisconsin	2500.	5000.	9000.

Series 1875 $100
(KL# 1383-1391) (Fr #456-463)

	VG	VF	AU
Alabama	2750.	4800.	9000.
Arkansas	4000.	7500.	14,000.
California	4500.	6500.	10,000.
Colorado Territory	3600.	8000.	15,750.
Colorado	3000.	5200.	9600.
Connecticut	3000.	5200.	9600.
Delaware	5000.	8000.	15,750.
District of Columbia	3000.	6000.	11,000.
Georgia	2900.	4750.	8800.
Illinois	1900.	3250.	6000.
Indiana	2150.	4750.	8800.
Iowa	2100.	3500.	6500.
Kansas	3000.	4500.	8000.
Kentucky	2500.	5200.	9600.
Louisiana	3250.	6000.	11,000.
Maine	3400.	6000.	11,000.
Maryland	2700.	4750.	8500.
Massachusetts	1900.	3500.	6500.
Michigan	2250.	4000.	7000.
Minnesota	2500.	4500.	7500.
Mississippi		None known	
Missouri	2250.	4250.	6800.
Montana Territory	6500.	9000.	15,750.
Nebraska	2750.	4750.	8500.
New Hampshire	2300.	5500.	10,000.
New Jersey	2200.	4500.	8000.
New York	1900.	3250.	6000.
Ohio	1950.	3700.	6800.
Pennsylvania	1900.	3250.	6000.
Rhode Island	3250.	5500.	10,300.
South Carolina	3750.	6500.	10,300.
Tennessee	3250.	5200.	9600.
Texas	2700.	5200.	9600.
Utah Territory	6500.	10,000.	20,000.
Vermont	2950.	5500.	11,000.
Virginia	2500.	5200.	9600.
Wisconsin	2250.	4500.	8000.

1882 Brown Back $100
(KL# 1392-1403) (Fr #519-531)

	VG	VF	AU
Alabama	1000.	2000.	3500.
Alaska		None issued	
Arizona Territory	16,000.	27,500.	45,000.
Arkansas	1400.	2750.	4950.
California	1100.	2000.	3250.
Colorado	1600.	2750.	4250.
Connecticut	1000.	1700.	2900.
Dakota Territory	4000.	6000.	10,000.
Delaware	2750.	5000.	8500.
District of Columbia	1400.	2750.	4800.
Florida	2200.	3750.	6000.
Georgia	1600.	2750.	4500.
Hawaii	3250.	5500.	10,000.
Idaho	4500.	8000.	13,000.
Illinois	700.	1150.	2000.
Indian Territory	2000.	3750.	5500.
Indiana	800.	1550.	2100.
Iowa	750.	1400.	2300.
Kansas	800.	1700.	2800.
Kentucky	775.	1600.	2600.
Louisiana	1300.	2100.	3500.
Maine	1500.	2500.	4250.
Maryland	1000.	1800.	3200.

	VG	VF	AU
Massachusetts	800.	1500.	2500.
Michigan	1000.	1800.	3000.
Minnesota	1200.	2250.	3300.
Mississippi	3000.	8000.	8500.
Missouri	900.	1750.	3000.
Montana Territory	5500.	8000.	15,000.
Montana	3250.	5500.	9000.
Nebraska	1400.	2500.	4500.
Nebraska Territory		None issued	
New Hampshire	1100.	2000.	3500.
New Jersey	800.	1500.	3000.
New Mexico Territory	3000.	4500.	7500.
New York	700.	1150.	2000.
North Carolina	2000.	3500.	5500.
North Dakota	2400.	4500.	6500.
Ohio	700.	1150.	2000.
Oklahoma Territory	2000.	3000.	5000.
Oklahoma	1750.	2750.	4000.
Oregon	2000.	3000.	5000.
Pennsylvania	700.	1150.	2000.
Rhode Island	1000.	2000.	3500.
South Carolina	2200.	4000.	6000.
South Dakota	2400.	4500.	6500.
Tennessee	1750.	3000.	5000.
Texas	1500.	2500.	4000.
Utah Territory	5000.	8000.	14,500.
Utah	3250.	5000.	9500.
Vermont	1200.	2000.	3500.
Virginia	1100.	1800.	3000.
Washington	2500.	4000.	7000.
West Virginia	1500.	2200.	4500.
Wisconsin	800.	1500.	3200.

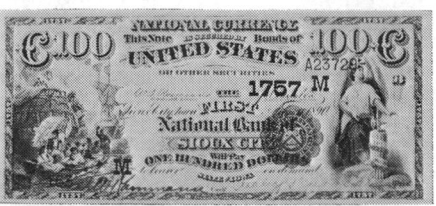

1882 Date Back $100
(KL# 1404-1411) (Fr #566-572-A)

	VG	VF	AU
Alabama	900.	1800.	3000.
Alaska		None issued	
Arizona Territory	11,500.	22,500.	35,000.
Arkansas	1200.	2500.	4400.
California	900.	1750.	2900.
Colorado	1400.	2400.	3600.
Connecticut	800.	1500.	2500.
Delaware	2400.	4500.	7500.
District of Columbia	1200.	2400.	3750.
Florida	1750.	3000.	5000.
Georgia	1400.	2400.	4000.
Hawaii	2750.	4500.	9000.
Idaho	4000.	7000.	11,500.
Illinois	500.	850.	1750.
Indiana	600.	1000.	1900.
Iowa	550.	925.	1850.
Kansas	700.	1500.	2400.
Kentucky	675.	1400.	2300.
Maryland	900.	1600.	2600.
Massachusetts	700.	1300.	2100.
Michigan	800.	1550.	2500.
Minnesota	1000.	1900.	2750.
Missouri	800.	1600.	2500.
Montana	2750.	4500.	7500.
Nebraska	1150.	2100.	4000.
New Hampshire	900.	1700.	3050.
New Jersey	700.	1300.	2500.
New Mexico Territory	2400.	3600.	6000.
New Mexico	1200.	1800.	3400.
New York	500.	850.	1700.
North Carolina	1600.	3000.	4500.
North Dakota	2000.	3600.	5500.
Ohio	500.	850.	1750.
Oklahoma	1300.	2200.	3600.
Pennsylvania	500.	850.	1700.
South Carolina	1800.	3500.	5000.
Tennessee	1400.	2500.	4250.
Texas	1200.	2000.	3000.
Utah	2500.	4000.	7500.
Vermont	1000.	1600.	3000.
Virginia	900.	1500.	2500.
Washington	2000.	3000.	6000.
West Virginia	1200.	1900.	3600.

1882 Value Back $100
(KL# 1412) (Fr #586-A)

	VG	VF	AU
Louisiana			(One known)
Ohio			(One known)

John J. Knox

1902 Red Seal $100
(KL# 1413-1415) (Fr #686-688)

	VG	VF	AU
Alabama	—	Rare	—
Arkansas	2200.	4400.	8400.
California	1500.	2850.	4800.
Colorado	1750.	4250.	7200.
Connecticut	1350.	2600.	6000.
Delaware	4500.	7500.	13,000.
Florida	3300.	6000.	9000.
Idaho	4500.	7000.	10,000.
Illinois	600.	1850.	3750.
Indian Territory	2750.	5500.	10,000.
Indiana	800.	2200.	4400.
Iowa	700.	2000.	3900.
Kansas	850.	2400.	4400.
Kentucky	950.	2600.	4500.
Louisiana	1200.	3000.	4800.
Maine	1500.	3000.	5250.
Maryland	700.	1800.	3800.
Massachusetts	800.	2200.	4000.
Michigan	750.	2000.	3900.
Minnesota	750.	2000.	3900.
Mississippi	1600.	3300.	6500.
Missouri	650.	1800.	3600.
Montana	2400.	4500.	7750.
Nebraska	950.	2600.	5500.
Nevada	2750.	5500.	11,000.
New Hampshire	1300.	2300.	5000.
New Jersey	700.	2000.	3800.
New York	600.	1800.	3600.
North Carolina	2250.	4250.	7200.
North Dakota	2400.	4500.	7750.
Ohio	675.	2000.	3900.
Oklahoma Territory	2750.	5500.	10,000.
Oklahoma	1300.	2700.	5250.
Oregon	2400.	5000.	8400.
Pennsylvania	650.	1800.	3600.
Puerto Rico	—	Rare	—
Rhode Island	900.	2200.	4400.
South Dakota	2500.	5000.	8500.
Tennessee	1700.	3400.	6200.
Texas	1000.	2000.	4400.
Vermont	1500.	3400.	5500.
Virginia	1400.	3200.	4800.
Washington	2200.	4400.	8000.
West Virginia	1600.	3200.	6200.
Wisconsin	800.	2000.	4000.

1902 Date Back $100
(KL# 1416-1424) (Fr #689-697)

	VG	VF	AU
Alabama	375.	700.	1100.
Arizona	1250.	2500.	5000.
Arkansas	650.	950.	1750.
California	225.	400.	750.
Colorado	450.	800.	1400.
Connecticut	350.	650.	1200.
Delaware	900.	1500.	3000.
Florida	850.	1450.	2900.
Georgia	650.	950.	1800.
Idaho	500.	700.	1200.
Illinois	225.	400.	700.
Indiana	275.	450.	800.
Iowa	260.	425.	750.
Kansas	350.	550.	1000.
Kentucky	280.	525.	950.
Louisiana	425.	700.	1200.
Maryland	275.	450.	750.
Massachusetts	275.	450.	750.
Michigan	300.	500.	800.
Minnesota	300.	500.	800.
Mississippi	1000.	1900.	3500.
Missouri	225.	400.	700.
Montana	1000.	1800.	3500.
Nebraska	250.	400.	700.
Nevada	800.	1500.	3000.
New Hampshire	425.	750.	1400.
New Jersey	275.	450.	750.
New York	200.	350.	650.
North Carolina	1000.	1800.	3200.
North Dakota	1100.	1900.	3400.
Ohio	225.	375.	700.
Oklahoma	275.	500.	900.
Oregon	550.	1000.	1900.
Pennsylvania	200.	350.	650.
Puerto Rico	—	Rare	
Rhode Island	650.	1000.	1750.
South Dakota	1200.	2000.	3600.
Tennessee	800.	1400.	2500.
Texas	250.	400.	750.
Utah	1300.	2500.	4000.
Vermont	500.	800.	1600.
Virginia	400.	700.	1300.
Washington	250.	700.	1200.
West Virginia	450.	750.	1400.
Wisconsin	250.	400.	750.

1902 Plain Back $100
(KL# 1425-1436) (Fr #698-707-A)

	VG	VF	AU
California	200.	350.	700.
Colorado	400.	750.	1300.
Connecticut	325.	400.	1100.
Delaware	850.	1400.	2800.
Florida	800.	1350.	2600.
Idaho	450.	650.	1100.
Illinois	200.	350.	650.
Indian Territory		None issued	
Indiana	250.	400.	750.
Iowa	240.	375.	700.
Kansas	325.	500.	900.
Kentucky	250.	450.	850.
Louisiana	400.	650.	1100.
Maryland	250.	400.	700.
Massachusetts	250.	400.	700.
Michigan	275.	450.	750.
Minnesota	275.	450.	750.
Mississippi	900.	1800.	3200.
Missouri	200.	350.	650.
Montana	900.	1700.	3200.
Nebraska	225.	350.	650.
Nevada	750.	1400.	2800.
New Hampshire	400.	700.	1300.
New Jersey	250.	400.	700.
New York	180.	325.	600.
North Carolina	900.	1700.	3000.
North Dakota	1000.	1800.	3200.
Ohio	200.	350.	650.
Oklahoma	250.	450.	800.
Oregon	500.	900.	1800.
Pennsylvania	180.	325.	600.
Rhode Island	600.	900.	1600.
South Dakota	1100.	1800.	3400.
Tennessee	750.	1300.	2200.
Texas	225.	350.	700.
Utah		None issued	
Vermont	450.	750.	1500.
Washington	225.	650.	1100.
Wisconsin	225.	375.	700.

Ben Franklin

1929 Type 1 $100
(KL# 1437) (Fr #1804-1)

	VG	VF	AU
California	110.	140.	200.
Colorado	125.	200.	300.
Connecticut	175.	300.	550.
Delaware	450.	800.	1500.
Florida	175.	300.	500.
Hawaii	175.	275.	480.
Idaho	250.	350.	550.
Illinois	110.	145.	180.
Indiana	125.	150.	190.
Iowa	120.	160.	200.
Kansas	135.	175.	275.
Kentucky	135.	165.	220.
Louisiana	165.	210.	270.
Maryland	155.	190.	250.
Massachusetts	175.	250.	400.
Michigan	125.	150.	250.
Minnesota	125.	150.	275.
Mississippi	400.	650.	1100.
Missouri	135.	165.	285.
Montana	300.	500.	1000.
Nebraska	125.	150.	250.
Nevada	400.	600.	1100.
New Hampshire	250.	450.	800.
New Jersey	120.	145.	240.
New York	115.	140.	220.
North Carolina	300.	500.	950.
North Dakota	350.	550.	1000.
Ohio	120.	145.	225.
Oklahoma	135.	165.	260.
Oregon	375.	675.	1100.
Pennsylvania	115.	140.	220.
Rhode Island	200.	300.	600.
South Dakota	300.	550.	850.
Tennessee	150.	225.	325.
Texas	120.	160.	240.
Vermont	275.	475.	850.
Washington	135.	190.	300.
West Virginia	1500.	2000.	3000.
Wisconsin	120.	160.	260.
Wyoming	1000.	2000.	4000.

Ben Franklin

1929 Type 2 $100
(KL# 1438) (Fr #1804-2)

	VG	VF	AU
Arkansas	750.	1100.	1650.
California	130.	225.	500.
Colorado	250.	400.	750.
Hawaii	350.	550.	1500.
Illinois	165.	275.	550.
Indiana	175.	300.	600.
Kentucky	200.	350.	750.
Louisiana	260.	450.	1000.
Maryland	240.	400.	800.
Michigan	175.	250.	575.
Minnesota	175.	300.	600.
New Jersey	165.	275.	525.
New York	140.	200.	400.
Pennsylvania	140.	200.	400.
Rhode Island	350.	550.	1200.
Tennessee	275.	450.	950.
Texas	165.	240.	500.
Virginia	300.	450.	950.

	VG	VF	AU
Ohio	200.	350.	650.
Oklahoma	250.	450.	800.
Oregon	500.	900.	1800.
Pennsylvania	180.	325.	600.
Rhode Island	600.	900.	1600.
South Dakota	1100.	1800.	3400.
Tennessee	750.	1300.	2200.
Texas	225.	350.	700.
Utah		None issued	
Vermont	450.	750.	1500.
Washington	225.	650.	1100.
Wisconsin	225.	375.	700.

Note-Issuing National Banks
State-City Alphabetical Listing with Bank Rarity Rating

The following pages present a complete listing of note-issuing National Banks arranged alphabetically by city within state. Only those banks which actually issued currency in the 1863-1935 period are listed.

The numerals shown after the charter number of a bank indicate the relative scarcity of known surviving notes in both Large (L) and Small (S) size issues. A dash in one of the columns indicates the bank did not issue notes in that size.

These bank and state rarity figures are based on data derived from the *Standard Catalog of National Bank Notes*, by John Hickman and Dean Oakes, the standard reference to this popularly-collected currency series.

R6 Very Rare — 0-2 notes known
R5 Rare — 3-5 notes known
R4 Very Scarce — 6-11 notes known
R3 Scarce — 12-25 notes known
R2 Common — 25-50 notes known
R1 Very Common — 50+ notes known

State/Bank Rarity Valuation Tables

The following tables provide approximate base figures for the value of any National Bank Note with a particular state/bank rarity combination. These tables may be used in conjunction with the bank rarity listings which follow to help determine a ballpark value.

While other factors, such as popularity of bank or city name, changing collector demand or the note's type/variety/denomination combination will affect value, the figures given in these tables can generally be regarded as a base value.

All valuations are for notes in Very Fine condition. Except in cases of the highest bank/state rarity combinations, notes in lesser grade will command a lower price. Notes in higher grade will command a higher price.

State Rarity Ranking — Large Size Nationals

Rarity 1
Pennsylvania
New York

Indiana
Kansas
Kentucky
Maryland

Louisiana
Connecticut
Florida

Nevada
New Mexico Terr.

Rarity 2
Iowa
Illinois
California
Texas

Rarity 3
Wisconsin
New Jersey
Missouri
Massachusetts
Minnesota
Ohio

Rarity 5
South Dakota
Virginia
Tennessee
Georgia
Oklahoma
North Carolina
Alabama

Rarity 7
North Dakota
Montana
New Hampshire
Delaware
Vermont
Wyoming
Dist. Columbia
Oregon
Arkansas
Utah
Washington
New Mexico
Mississippi

Rarity 9
Indian Terr.
Hawaii
Alaska
Oklahoma Terr.
Colorado Terr.
Montana Terr.
Arizona Terr.
Utah Terr.
Dakota Terr.

Rarity 4
Michigan
Nebraska

Rarity 6
Rhode Island
West Virginia
Colorado
South Carolina
Maine

Rarity 8
Idaho
Arizona

Rarity 10
Porto Rico
Wyoming Terr.
Washington Terr.
Idaho Terr.
Nebraska Terr.

Bank Rarity	1	2	3	4	5	6
State Rarity 1	40	50	60	85	150	300
State Rarity 2	45	55	70	95	165	330
State Rarity 3	45	60	70	100	175	345
State Rarity 4	50	65	80	110	195	390
State Rarity 5	65	80	95	135	240	540
State Rarity 6	70	90	110	155	270	610
State Rarity 7	85	110	135	190	330	770
State Rarity 8	—	250	575	660	740	1,300
State Rarity 9	—	—	3,500	3,750	4,300	4,500
State Rarity 10	—	—	—	8,000	8,750	9,500

State Rarity Ranking — Small Size Nationals

Rarity 1
Minnesota
Pennsylvania
New York
California
Massachusetts
Illinois

Michigan

Georgia
Washington
Mississippi
South Dakota
South Carolina
Wyoming
Connecticut
New Hampshire

Arkansas
Rhode Island

Rarity 8
New Mexico
Vermont

Rarity 4
Alabama
Maryland
Colorado
Kentucky
Florida
Oklahoma
Tennessee
North Carolina
Missouri

Rarity 2
Wisconsin
Iowa
Kansas
New Jersey
Texas
Ohio

Rarity 6
Louisiana
Oregon
Utah
North Dakota
Dist. Columbia

Rarity 9
Delaware
Idaho
Hawaii
Arizona
Montana
Nevada

Rarity 3
Nebraska
Indiana

Rarity 5
Virginia
West Virginia

Rarity 7
Maine

Rarity 10
Alaska

Bank Rarity	1	2	3	4	5	6
State Rarity 1	20	25	30	35	60	175
State Rarity 2	20	25	30	35	65	195
State Rarity 3	25	30	35	40	70	200
State Rarity 4	25	30	35	40	80	230
State Rarity 5	30	35	40	50	95	280
State Rarity 6	35	40	45	55	110	315
State Rarity 7	35	40	45	55	125	350
State Rarity 8	40	50	65	75	150	440
State Rarity 9	125	165	175	200	330	960
State Rarity 10	—	—	4,000	4,000	—	—

National Banks, Year of Organization

Many collectors find it desirable to learn the year in which a particular National Bank was organized. The charter number which appears on the notes can yield that information when matched with the following list.

Ch. #s	Year	Ch. #s	Year	Ch. #s	Year
1 to 179	1863	3833 to 3954	1888	10306 to 10472	1913
180 to 682	1864	3955 to 4190	1889	10473 to 10672	1914
683 to 1626	1865	4191 to 4494	1890	10673 to 10810	1915
1627 to 1665	1866	4495 to 4673	1891	10811 to 10932	1916
1666 to 1675	1867	4674 to 4832	1892	10933 to 11126	1917
1676 to 1688	1868	4833 to 4934	1893	11127 to 11282	1918
1689 to 1696	1869	4935 to 4983	1894	11283 to 11570	1919
1697 to 1759	1870	4984 to 5029	1895	11571 to 11903	1920
1760 to 1912	1871	5030 to 5054	1896	11904 to 12082	1921
1913 to 2073	1872	5055 to 5108	1897	12083 to 12287	1922
2074 to 2131	1873	5109 to 5165	1898	12288 to 12481	1923
2132 to 2214	1874	5166 to 5240	1899	12482 to 12615	1924
2215 to 2315	1875	5241 to 5662	1900	12616 to 12866	1925
2316 to 2344	1876	5663 to 6074	1901	12867 to 13022	1926
2345 to 2375	1877	6075 to 6566	1902	13023 to 13159	1927
2376 to 2405	1878	6567 to 7081	1903	13160 to 13269	1928
2406 to 2445	1879	7082 to 7541	1904	13270 to 13412	1929
2446 to 2498	1880	7542 to 8027	1905	13413 to 13516	1930
2499 to 2606	1881	8028 to 8489	1906	13517 to 13586	1931
2607 to 2849	1882	8490 to 8979	1907	13587 to 13654	1932
2850 to 3101	1883	8980 to 9302	1908	13655 to 13920	1933
3102 to 3281	1884	9303 to 9622	1909	13921 to 14317	1934
3282 to 3427	1885	9623 to 9913	1910	14318 to 14348	1935
3428 to 3612	1886	9914 to 10119	1911		
3613 to 3832	1887	10120 to 10305	1912		

Some banks and charter numbers are listed twice in the following tables. The reason is because the charter was once dissolved and later re-issued with the same number.

ALABAMA

City, Bank	Ch. No.	L	S
Abbeville			
The First National Bank Of Abbeville	5987	4	–
The Henry National Bank Of Abbeville	10959	5	–
Albany			
The Central National Bank Of Albany	10423	4	–
The Morgan County National Bank Of Albany	6380	4	–
Albertville			
The Albertville National Bank	11820	5	3
The First National Bank Of Albertville	11819	–	3
Alexander City			
The First National Bank Of Alexander City	7417	5	3
Andalusia			
The Andalusia National Bank	11955	3	3
The First National Bank Of Andalusia	5970	5	6
Anniston			
The Anniston City National Bank	4250	6	–
The Anniston National Bank	4250	6	–
The Anniston National Bank	4250	3	3
The City National Bank Of Anniston	6021	6	–
The Commercial National Bank Of Anniston	11753	3	3
The First National Bank Of Anniston	3041	4	3
Ashford			
The First National Bank Of Ashford	10102	6	6
Ashland			
The First National Bank Of Ashland	9580	6	4
Athens			
The First National Bank Of Athens	6146	6	–
Atmore			
The First National Bank Of Atmore	10697	6	4
Attalla			
The First National Bank Of Attalla	7951	6	–
Auburn			
The First National Bank Of Auburn	12455	6	6
Bessemer			
First National Bank In Bessemer	6961	5	4
The Bessemer National Bank	6961	5	–
The City National Bank Of Bessemer	11905	5	6
The First National Bank At Bessemer	13789	–	6
The First National Bank Of Bessemer	4220	6	–
Birmingham			
American-Traders National Bank Of Birmingham	7020	2	3
The Alabama National Bank Of Birmingham	3587	6	–
The American National Bank Of Birmingham	3734	6	–
The Berney National Bank Of Birmingham	3442	6	–
The Birmingham National Bank	3679	6	–
The City National Bank Of Birmingham	3993	6	–
The Ensley National Bank Of Birmingham	12906	3	4
The First National Bank Of Birmingham	3185	1	1
The National Bank Of Birmingham	2065	6	–
The Woodlawn-American National Bank Of Birmingham	13358	–	2
Traders National Bank Of Birmingham	7020	4	–
Boaz			
The First National Bank Of Boaz	10441	6	–
The National Bank Of Boaz	11870	6	4
Brantley			
The First National Bank Of Brantley	7991	6	6
Bridgeport			
The American National Bank Of Bridgeport	11168	6	5
The First National Bank Of Bridgeport	4591	6	–
Brundidge			
The First National Bank Of Brundidge	7429	5	5
Camden			
The Camden National Bank	8217	6	5
Childersburg			
The First National Bank Of Childersburg	10066	6	–
Citronelle			
The First National Bank Of Citronelle	6835	6	–
Clanton			
The First National Bank Of Clanton	11515	5	4
Coffee Springs			
The First National Bank Of Coffee Springs	11259	6	6
Collinsville			
The First National Bank Of Collinsville	11337	5	4
Columbia			
The First National Bank Of Columbia	8095	6	–
Cullman			
The First National Bank Of Cullman	7097	6	–
The Leeth National Bank Of Cullman	9614	4	2
Decatur			
First National Bank In Decatur	10336	–	3
The Central National Bank Of Decatur	10423	6	5
The City National Bank Of Decatur	10336	4	5
The First National Bank Of Decatur	3699	6	–
The Morgan County National Bank Of Decatur	6380	6	4
Demopolis			
The Commercial National Bank Of Demopolis	10035	4	3
The First National Bank Of Demopolis	4394	6	–
Dothan			
The Dothan National Bank	5909	3	–
The First National Bank Of Dothan	5249	3	3
The Houston National Bank Of Dothan	7932	4	5
The Third National Bank Of Dothan	7938	6	–
Dozier			
The First National Bank Of Dozier	9681	6	5
Elba			
The First National Bank Of Elba	6897	5	4
Ensley			
The First National Bank Of Ensley	5962	6	–
Enterprise			
The Farmers And Merchants National Bank Of Enterprise	10421	5	4
The First National Bank Of Enterprise	6319	4	6
Eufaula			
The Commercial National Bank Of Eufaula	5024	3	5
The East Alabama National Bank Of Eufaula	3622	4	–
The Eufaula National Bank	2309	6	–
Eutaw			
The First National Bank Of Eutaw	3931	4	4
Evergreen			
First National Bank Of Evergreen	7687	4	6
Fairfield			
The Fairfield American National Bank, Fairfield	11766	–	4
The First National Bank Of Fairfield	11766	–	4
Fayette			
The First National Bank Of Fayette	10377	5	4
Florala			
The First National Bank Of Florala	8910	4	6
Florence			
The First National Bank Of Florence	3981	4	3
The Florence National Bank	4135	6	–
Fort Payne			
The First National Bank In Fort Payne	11451	5	4
The First National Bank Of Fort Payne	4064	6	–
Gadsden			
The American National Bank Of Gadsden	13412	–	3
The First National Bank In Gadsden	13728	–	5
The First National Bank Of Gadsden	3663	4	3
The Gadsden National Bank	8560	4	5
Gainesville			
The Gainesville National Bank	1822	6	–
Geneva			
The Farmers National Bank Of Geneva	10307	6	6
The First National Bank Of Geneva	5714	5	–
Goodwater			
The First National Bank Of Goodwater	12960	6	5
Greensboro			
The First National Bank Of Greensboro	5693	3	5
Greenville			
The First National Bank Of Greenville	5572	4	3
Guntersville			
The First National Bank Of Guntersville	10990	6	3
Haleyville			
The First National Bank Of Haleyville	11613	–	–
Hartford			
The First National Bank Of Hartford	7592	6	5
The Hartford National Bank Of Hartford	13128	–	–
Hartselle			
The First National Bank Of Hartselle	8067	4	6
Haynesville			
The First National Bank Of Haynesville	7975	6	–
Headland			
The Farmers And Merchants National Bank Of Headland	11445	6	–
The First National Bank Of Headland	7424	4	4
The Headland National Bank	13752	–	6
Huntsville			
The Farmers And Merchants National Bank Of Huntsville	4689	6	–
The First National Bank Of Huntsville	4067	5	4
The Henderson National Bank Of Huntsville	8765	4	1
The National Bank Of Huntsville	1560	6	–
Jackson			
The First National Bank Of Jackson	5983	6	–
Jacksonville			
The First National Bank Of Jacksonville	4319	6	5
The Tredegar National Bank Of Jacksonville	4319	5	–
Jasper			
The First National Bank Of Jasper	7746	3	4
La Pine			
The First National Bank Of La Pine	10799	–	–
Leeds			
The Leeds-American National Bank	13359	–	5
The Leeds-American National Bank Of Leeds	13359	–	5
Lincoln			
The First National Bank Of Lincoln	10131	5	5
Linden			
The First National Bank Of Linden	7148	6	4
Lineville			
The Citizens National Bank Of Lineville	8856	6	–
The First National Bank Of Lineville	7516	6	–
The Lineville National Bank	7551	5	5
Luverne			
The First National Bank Of Luverne	7992	6	6
Midland City			
The First National Bank Of Midland City	8458	5	4
Mobile			
Merchants National Bank Of Mobile	13097	3	–
The Alabama National Bank Of Mobile	1817	6	–
The American National Bank & Trust Company Of Mobile	13414	–	2
The Bank Of Mobile, National Banking Assoc Of Mobile	7062	6	–
The City National Bank Of Mobile	5219	6	–
The First National Bank Of Mobile	1595	3	1
The Merchants National Bank Of Mobile	13097	–	1
The Mobile National Bank	13195	4	5
The National City Bank Of Mobile	10732	–	–
The National Commercial Bank Of Mobile	1817	6	–
Monroeville			
The First National Bank Of Monroeville	12642	6	4
Montgomery			
The Alabama National Bank Of Montgomery	12993	3	4
The American National Bank Of Montgomery	7141	6	–
The Capital National Bank Of Montgomery	8460	5	–
The Exchange National Bank Of Montgomery	8284	3	–
The Farley National Bank Of Montgomery	4180	6	–
The First National Bank Of Montgomery	1814	3	2
The Fourth National Bank Of Montgomery	5877	2	–
The Merchants & Planters Farley Natl. Bank Of Montgomery	4180	6	–
The Merchants And Planters National Bank Of Montgomery	2029	6	–
The New Farley National Bank Of Montgomery	8460	6	–
New Brockton			
The First National Bank Of New Brockton	10457	6	–
New Decatur			
The Central National Bank Of New Decatur	10423	6	–
The Morgan County National Bank Of New Decatur	6380	6	–
Newville			
The First National Bank Of Newville	9927	5	6
Oneonta			
The First National Bank Of Oneonta	12006	6	4
Opelika			
The Farmers National Bank Of Opelika	9550	4	2
The First National Bank Of Opelika	3452	3	4
The National Bank Of Opelika	11635	3	3
Opp			
The First National Bank Of Opp	7985	4	3
Oxford			
The First National Bank Of Oxford	7073	3	6
The Oxford National Bank	9925	6	–
Ozark			
The First National Bank Of Ozark	7629	5	–
Pell City			
The First National Bank Of Pell City	9506	6	–
Piedmont			
The First National Bank Of Piedmont	7464	6	4
Prattville			
The First National Bank Of Prattville	9055	6	6
Reform			
The First National Bank Of Reform	11233	6	–
Russellville			
The First National Bank Of Russellville	11846	6	4
Samson			
The First National Bank Of Samson	8028	6	6
Scottsboro			
The First National Bank Of Scottsboro	8963	6	5
Seals			
The First National Bank Of Seals	10654	–	–
Selma			
The City National Bank Of Selma	1736	1	3
The First National Bank Of Selma	1537	6	–
The Selma National Bank	7084	4	3
Sheffield			
The First National Bank Of Sheffield	3617	6	–
The Sheffield National Bank	6759	4	5
Slocomb			
The First National Bank Of Slocomb	7871	6	–
The Slocomb National Bank	7940	6	3
Stevenson			
The First National Bank Of Stevenson	9855	6	5
Sylacauga			
The City National Bank Of Sylacauga	10879	5	4
The First National Bank Of Sylacauga	7451	5	6
The Merchants And Planters National Bank Of Sylacauga	7484	4	4
Talladega			
The First National Bank Of Talladega	3899	6	–
The Isbell National Bank Of Talladega	4838	3	5
The Talladega National Bank	7558	4	3
Tallassee			
The First National Bank Of Tallassee	10766	6	6
Thomasville			
The Citizens National Bank Of Thomasville	7371	6	–
The First National Bank Of Thomasville	5664	6	–
Troy			
First Farmers & Merchants National Bank Of Troy	5593	–	2
The Farmers And Merchants National Bank Of Troy	7044	4	4
The First National Bank Of Troy	5593	4	5
Tuscaloosa			
The City National Bank Of Tuscaloosa	6173	4	3
The First National Bank Of Tuscaloosa	1853	4	4
The Merchants National Bank Of Tuscaloosa	3678	6	–
Tuscumbia			
The First National Bank Of Tuscumbia	11281	5	5
The First National Bank Of Tuscumbia	14160	–	–
Union Springs			
The American National Bank Of Union Springs	12962	6	3
The First National Bank Of Union Springs	7467	5	5
Wetumpka			
The First National Bank Of Wetumpka	7568	6	5

ALASKA

City, Bank	Ch. No.	L	S
Anchorage			
The First National Bank Of Anchorage	12072	–	–
Fairbanks			
First National Bank Of Fairbanks	7718	1	3
Juneau			
The First National Bank Of Juneau	5117	4	4
Ketchikan			
The First National Bank Of Ketchikan	12578	–	3
Seward			
The First National Bank Of Seward	10705	–	–
The Harriman National Bank Of Alaska At Seward	10705	–	–

ARIZONA TERRITORY

City, Bank	Ch. No.	L	S
Bisbee			
The First National Bank Of Bisbee	7182	6	–
Clifton			
The First National Bank Of Clifton	5821	6	–
Douglas			
The First National Bank Of Douglas	6633	6	–
Globe			
The First National Bank Of Globe	6579	6	–
The Globe National Bank	8193	6	–
Nogales			
The First National Bank Of Nogales	6591	6	–
The Sandoval National Bank Of Nogales	6591	5	–
Phoenix			
The First National Bank Of Phoenix	3054	6	–
The National Bank Of Arizona At Phoenix	3728	6	–
The Phoenix National Bank	4729	6	–
Prescott			
The First National Bank Of Prescott	3122	6	–
The Prescott National Bank	4851	5	–
Tempe			
The Tempe National Bank	5720	6	–
Tombstone			
The First National Bank Of Tombstone	6439	6	–

City, Bank	Ch. No.	L	S
Tucson			
The Arizona National Bank Of Tucson	4440	5	–
The Consolidated National Bank Of Tucson	4287	6	–
The First National Bank Of Tucson	2639	5	–
Yuma			
The First National Bank Of Yuma	7591	6	–
The Yuma National Bank	9608	6	–

ARIZONA

City, Bank	Ch. No.	L	S
Casa Grande			
The First National Bank Of Casa Grande	11663	–	–
Chandler			
The First National Bank Of Chandler	11395	–	–
Clifton			
The First National Bank Of Clifton	5821	4	–
Douglas			
The First National Bank Of Douglas	6633	4	–
Flagstaff			
The First National Bank Of Flagstaff	11120	4	6
Florence			
The First National Bank Of Florence	10998	5	–
Glendale			
The First National Bank Of Glendale	11139	–	–
Globe			
The First National Bank Of Globe	6579	4	–
Holbrook			
The First National Bank Of Holbrook	12198	4	6
Mesa			
The First National Bank Of Mesa	11130	6	3
Nogales			
The First National Bank Of Nogales	6591	5	3
The Nogales National Bank	11012	5	5
Phoenix			
First National Bank Of Arizona At Phoenix	3728	4	1
The Commercial National Bank Of Phoenix	11559	4	–
The National Bank Of Arizona At Phoenix	3728	4	–
The Phoenix National Bank	4729	3	2
The Valley National Bank Of Phoenix	14324	–	–
Prescott			
First National Bank In Prescott	13262	–	3
The Prescott National Bank	4851	6	–
Tempe			
The Tempe National Bank	5720	5	4
Tombstone			
The First National Bank Of Tombstone	6439	4	–
Tucson			
The Arizona National Bank Of Tucson	4440	4	–
The Consolidated National Bank Of Tucson	4287	2	1
The Tucson National Bank	11159	6	–
Winslow			
The First National Bank Of Winslow	12581	4	3
Yuma			
The First National Bank Of Yuma	7591	4	–
The Yuma National Bank	9608	4	–

ARKANSAS

City, Bank	Ch. No.	L	S
Arkadelphia			
The Citizens National Bank Of Arkadelphia	10087	5	4
Ashdown			
The First National Bank In Ashdown	13534	–	5
The First National Bank Of Ashdown	10486	5	6
Batesville			
The First National Bank Of Batesville	7556	2	5
The Maxfield National Bank Of Batesville	8864	6	–
The National Bank Of Batesville	8864	5	–
Belmont			
The Army National Bank Of Belmont	11214	–	–
Benton			
The Farmers And Merchants National Bank Of Benton	11225	–	–
The First National Bank Of Benton	9494	6	–
Bentonville			
The Benton County National Bank Of Bentonville	8135	4	6
The First National Bank Of Bentonville	7523	4	5
Berryville			
The First National Bank Of Berryville	10406	5	3
Black Rock			
The First National Bank Of Black Rock	11312	–	–
Blytheville			
The First National Bank Of Blytheville	11651	–	–
Camden			
The Camden National Bank	4066	6	–
The Citizens National Bank Of Camden	14096	–	5
The First National Bank Of Camden	1631	6	–
The First National Bank Of Camden	4066	5	4
Clarksville			
The Farmers National Bank Of Clarksville	11580	5	4
The First National Bank Of Clarksville	9633	5	6
Conway			
The First National Bank Of Conway	13719	–	6
Corning			
The First National Bank Of Corning	7311	6	–
Cotton Plant			
The Farmers National Bank Of Cotton Plant	12219	–	–
The First National Bank Of Cotton Plant	10723	6	–
Dardanelle			
The First National Bank Of Dardanelle	11276	6	–
De Witt			
The First National Bank Of De Witt	10178	4	4
Dequeen			
The First National Bank Of Dequeen	5929	4	5
Des Arc			
The First National Bank Of Des Arc	11221	–	–
Earle			
The First National Bank Of Earle	9324	6	–
El Dorado			
The Citizens National Bank Of El Dorado	7323	6	–
The First National Bank Of El Dorado	7046	6	3
The National Bank Of Commerce Of El Dorado	12429	–	–
The National Bank Of El Dorado	7046	–	–
Eudora			
The First National Bank Of Eudora	12813	–	5

City, Bank	Ch. No.	L	S
Eureka Springs			
The First National Bank Of Eureka Springs	8495	6	6
Fayetteville			
The Arkansas National Bank Of Fayetteville	8786	4	4
The First National Bank Of Fayetteville	7346	3	3
The National Bank Of Fayetteville	7952	6	–
Fordyce			
The First National Bank Of Fordyce	9501	6	3
Forrest City			
The First National Bank Of Forrest City	10550	5	–
The National Bank Of Eastern Arkansas Of Forrest City	13637	–	5
Fort Smith			
The American National Bank Of Fort Smith	3634	4	–
The City National Bank Of Fort Smith	10609	3	3
The First National Bank Of Fort Smith	1631	6	–
The First National Bank Of Fort Smith	1950	2	1
The Fort Smith National Bank	4995	6	–
The Merchants National Bank Of Fort Smith	7240	3	2
The National Bank Of Western Arkansas At Fort Smith	1950	6	–
Gentry			
The First National Bank Of Gentry	12340	6	6
Gravette			
The First National Bank Of Gravette	8237	5	4
Green Forest			
The First National Bank Of Green Forest	10422	6	6
The First National Bank Of Green Forest	13543	–	–
Greenwood			
First National Bank In Greenwood	10983	6	4
The Citizens National Bank Of Greenwood	10983	6	–
The First National Bank Of Greenwood	6786	6	–
Gurdon			
The First National Bank Of Gurdon	13210	5	3
Harrison			
First National Bank In Harrison	10801	5	6
The Citizens National Bank Of Harrison	12291	5	–
The First National Bank Of Harrison	5890	6	–
The Peoples National Bank Of Harrison	10801	6	–
Hartford			
First National Bank In Hartford	11830	6	6
New First National Bank Of Hartford	11830	6	–
The Farmers And Miners National Bank Of Hartford	11830	6	–
The First National Bank Of Hartford	11748	6	–
Heber Springs			
The Arkansas National Bank Of Heber Springs	11367	–	–
The First National Bank Of Heber Springs	11180	6	–
Helena			
Phillips National Bank Of Helena	13520	–	4
The First National Bank Of Helena	3662	4	–
The Interstate National Bank Of Helena	11234	–	–
Holly Grove			
The First National Bank Of Holly Grove	12296	6	6
Hope			
The Citizens National Bank Of Hope	10579	4	3
The First National Bank Of Hope	12533	–	3
The Hope National Bank	8594	6	–
Horatio			
The First National Bank Of Horatio	10447	6	–
Hot Springs			
The Arkansas National Bank Of Hot Springs	2832	5	3
The Citizens National Bank Of Hot Springs	7531	6	–
The Hot Springs National Bank	2887	6	–
Hughes			
The Planters National Bank Of Hughes	11542	–	–
Huntsville			
The First National Bank Of Huntsville	8952	6	4
Huttig			
The First National Bank Of Huttig	10060	6	5
Jonesboro			
The First National Bank Of Jonesboro	8086	6	–
Judsonia			
The First National Bank Of Judsonia	10439	6	–
Junction City			
The First National Bank Of Junction City	11046	–	–
Lake Village			
The First National Bank In Lake Village	13632	–	3
The First National Bank Of Lake Village	11262	5	5
Lamar			
The First National Bank Of Lamar	12238	5	6
Lepanto			
The First National Bank Of Lepanto	11322	–	–
Leslie			
The First National Bank Of Leslie	10138	6	–
Lewisville			
The First National Bank Of Lewisville	9354	6	4
Lincoln			
The First National Bank Of Lincoln	11825	6	–
Little Rock			
The American National Bank Of Little Rock	3318	–	–
The Commercial National Bank Of Little Rock	14000	–	3
The England National Bank Of Little Rock	9037	4	–
The Exchange National Bank Of Little Rock	3300	3	–
The First National Bank Of Little Rock	1648	6	–
The German National Bank Of Little Rock	3318	6	–
The Merchants National Bank Of Little Rock	1648	5	–
The Peoples National Bank Of Little Rock	13949	6	–
The State National Bank Of Little Rock	6902	4	–
The Union National Bank Of Little Rock	13598	–	–
The Union National Bank Of Little Rock	13958	–	–
Malvern			
The First National Bank Of Malvern	7634	6	5
The Malvern National Bank	14238	–	–
Mansfield			
The First National Bank Of Mansfield	11195	5	4
The National Bank Of Mansfield	11196	6	4
Marianna			
The First National Bank Of Marianna	14097	–	–
The Lee County National Bank Of Marianna	10854	–	–
Marked Tree			
The First National Bank Of Marked Tree	11122	5	–

City, Bank	Ch. No.	L	S
Marshall			
The Arkansas National Bank Of Marshall	10795	6	–
The First National Bank Of Marshall	10794	6	–
Mcgehee			
The First National Bank Of Mcgehee	13280	5	5
Mena			
The First National Bank Of Mena	7163	5	–
The National Bank Of Mena	7829	6	–
The Planters National Bank Of Mena	13693	–	4
Mineral Springs			
The First National Bank Of Mineral Springs	11113	–	–
The First National Bank Of Nashville	11113	–	6
Monette			
The First National Bank Of Monette	11116	–	–
Morrilton			
The First National Bank Of Morrilton	10434	6	–
Newark			
The First National Bank Of Newark	9022	4	3
Newport			
The Farmers National Bank Of Newport	10867	–	–
The First National Bank Of Newport	6758	3	4
North Little Rock			
The First National Bank Of North Little Rock	12447	–	–
Ozark			
The First National Bank Of Ozark	12985	–	–
Paragould			
National Bank Of Commerce Of Paragould	10004	4	4
The First National Bank Of Paragould	6846	6	–
The New First National Bank Of Paragould	13155	6	4
Paris			
The First National Bank Of Paris	11592	5	4
The First National Bank Of Paris	14209	–	–
Perry			
The First National Bank Of Perry	6706	6	–
Pine Bluff			
National Bank Of Commerce Of Pine Bluff	14056	–	5
The First National Bank Of Pine Bluff	2776	6	–
The Simmons National Bank Of Pine Bluff	6680	3	3
Pinebluff			
The National Bank Of Arkansas At Pine Bluff	10768	5	6
Pocahontas			
The First National Bank Of Pocahontas	11645	–	–
Prairie Grove			
The First National Bank Of Prairie Grove	8030	4	–
Rector			
The First National Bank Of Rector	10853	5	6
Rogers			
The American National Bank Of Rogers	10750	4	4
The First National Bank Of Rogers	7789	4	6
Russellville			
The First National Bank Of Russellville	4582	6	–
Siloam Springs			
The Farmers National Bank Of Siloam Springs	9871	6	–
The First National Bank In Siloam Springs	13274	3	6
The First National Bank Of Siloam Springs	9871	5	–
The Hutchings First National Bank Of Siloam Springs	13506	–	–
Springdale			
The First National Bank Of Springdale	8763	4	4
Stuttgart			
The First National Bank Of Stuttgart	10459	4	6
The Peoples National Bank Of Stuttgart	12156	–	–
Texarkana			
The Gate City National Bank Of Texarkana	4401	6	–
The State National Bank Of Texarkana	7138	3	2
Tuckerman			
The First National Bank Of Tuckerman	10484	–	–
The First National Bank Of Tuckerman	12914	–	–
Van Buren			
The First National Bank Of Van Buren	7361	3	4
Waldron			
The First National Bank Of Waldron	5849	5	6
Walnut Ridge			
The First National Bank Of Lawrence County At Walnut Ridge	11312	–	5
The First National Bank Of Walnut Ridge	9332	5	–
The Planters National Bank Of Walnut Ridge	12083	6	6
Willisville			
The First National Bank Of Ava	10911	–	5
Wynne			
The First National Bank Of Wynne	10807	–	6

CALIFORNIA GOLD

City, Bank	Ch. No.	L	S
Oakland			
The First National Gold Bank Of Oakland	2248	3	–
The Union National Gold Bank Of Oakland	2266	5	–
Petaluma			
The First National Gold Bank Of Petaluma	2193	3	–
Sacramento			
The National Gold Bank Of D. O. Mills & Co., Sacramento	2014	2	–
San Francisco			
The First National Gold Bank Of San Francisco	1741	1	–
The National Gold Bank & Trust Company, San Francisco	1994	3	–
San Jose			
The Farmers National Gold Bank Of San Jose	2158	2	–
Santa Barbara			
The First National Gold Bank Of Santa Barbara	2104	3	–
Stockton			
The First National Gold Bank Of Stockton	2077	2	–

CALIFORNIA

City, Bank	Ch. No.	L	S
Alameda			
Alameda National Bank	9220	5	–
The Citizens National Bank Of Alameda	10150	3	–
The Commercial National Bank Of Alameda	11942	3	4
The Encinal National Bank Of Alameda	12893	–	–
The First National Bank Of Alameda	2431	6	–
Alhambra			
The Alhambra National Bank, Alhambra	9966	6	–
The First National Bank Of Alhambra	8490	5	5
The National Bank Of Alhambra	9966	6	–

City, Bank	Ch. No.	L	S
Altadena			
The Altadena National Bank	12910	–	–
Alturas			
The First National Bank Of Alturas	7219	5	–
Anaheim			
Anaheim First National Bank, Anaheim	10228	–	3
The Anaheim National Bank	10228	4	5
The First National Bank Of Anaheim	6481	4	5
The Golden State National Bank Of Anaheim	11823	6	–
Antioch			
The First National Bank Of Antioch	9892	5	3
Arcadia			
The Arcadia National Bank	13335	–	–
The First National Bank Of Arcadia	11250	–	–
Arcata			
The First National Bank Of Arcata	10372	5	–
Artesia			
The First National Bank Of Artesia	8063	4	6
Atascadero			
The First National Bank Of Atascadero	12833	–	–
Auburn			
The First National Bank Of Auburn	9227	6	–
Azusa			
The First National Bank Of Azusa	8065	5	2
The United States National Bank Of Azusa	8074	6	–
Bakersfield			
First National Bank In Bakersfield	10357	6	1
First National Bank Of Bakersfield	11327	6	–
The First National Bank Of Bakersfield	6044	3	–
The National Bank Of Bakersfield	10357	5	–
The Producers National Bank Of Bakersfield	11327	–	–
Baldwin Park			
The First National Bank Of Baldwin Park	10685	–	–
Banning			
The First National Bank Of Banning	9459	4	4
Barstow			
The First National Bank Of Barstow	10843	–	–
Bay Point			
The First National Bank Of Bay Point	11561	6	–
Bell			
The First National Bank Of Bell	11421	–	–
Bellflower			
The Commercial National Bank Of Bellflower	12754	–	5
The First National Bank Of Bellflower	12328	4	6
Berkeley			
Berkeley National Bank	7849	5	–
First National Bank In Berkeley	12320	4	–
The College National Bank Of Berkeley	11495	4	–
The Commercial National Bank Of Berkeley	13010	–	–
The First National Bank Of Berkeley	5380	3	–
Beverly Hills			
The Beverly Hills National Bank	11461	–	–
The Beverly Hills National Bank And Trust Company	13348	–	–
The Beverly National Bank Of Beverly Hills	12647	–	–
The California National Bank Of Beverly Hills	13094	–	–
The First National Bank Of Beverly Hills	11461	3	3
The Liberty National Bank Of Beverly Hills	12909	5	–
Biola			
The First National Bank Of Biola	11769	6	–
Bishop			
The First National Bank Of Bishop	10999	–	–
Blythe			
The Farmers And Merchants National Bank Of Blythe	11528	–	–
The First National Bank Of Blythe	10944	–	–
Brawley			
The First National Bank Of Brawley	9673	6	–
Brea			
Oilfields National Bank In Brea	13877	–	2
The First National Bank Of Brea	11962	–	–
The Oilfields National Bank Of Brea	13001	6	5
Burbank			
First National Bank In Burbank	12435	–	–
The First National Bank Of Burbank	10099	6	–
The Magnolia Park National Bank Of Burbank	13069	–	–
The New First National Bank Of Burbank	12435	–	–
Calexico			
The Calexico National Bank	9705	6	–
The First Central National Bank Of Calexico	13054	–	–
The First National Bank Of Calexico	9686	4	–
Calipatria			
The Farmers And Merchants National Bank Of Calipatria	11240	–	–
The First National Bank Of Calipatria	10687	6	–
Calistoga			
The Calistoga National Bank	9551	6	3
The First National Bank Of Calistoga	7388	6	–
Campbell			
The Growers National Bank Of Campbell	11572	5	–
Carlsbad			
The First National Bank Of Carlsbad	13049	–	–
Caruthers			
The First National Bank Of Caruthers	11330	5	5
Centerville			
The First National Bank Of Centerville	11743	5	–
Chico			
First National Bank Of Chico	13711	–	3
First National Trust & Savings Of Chico	8798	6	3
The Butte County National Bank Of Chico	9294	6	–
The First National Bank Of Chico	8798	5	–
Chino			
The First National Bank Of Chino	10271	5	–
Chowchilla			
The Chowchilla National Bank	11151	6	–
The First National Bank Of Chowchilla	10978	–	–
Claremont			
The Citizens National Bank Of Claremont	12693	–	–
The Claremont National Bank	10208	6	–
The First National Bank Of Claremont	9467	5	3
Cloverdale			
The First National Bank Of Cloverdale	11282	5	4
Clovis			
The First National Bank Of Clovis	10213	6	–
Coachella			
The First National Bank Of Coachella	10292	6	6
The First National Bank Of Coachella	14317	–	–
Coalinga			
The First National Bank Of Coalinga	9323	6	–
The National Bank Of Coalinga	10584	–	–
Colton			
The Citizens National Bank Of Colton	13356	–	4
The Colton National Bank	8608	4	–
The First National Bank Of Colton	3573	4	–
Colusa			
The First National Bank Of Colusa	10072	6	–
Compton			
The Compton National Bank	12904	–	–
The First National Bank Of Compton	8085	5	–
Concord			
The First National Bank Of Concord	9945	6	–
Corcoran			
First National Bank In Corcoran	14230	–	6
The First National Bank Of Corcoran	9546	6	4
Corona			
The Corona National Bank	8436	6	–
The First National Bank Of Corona	7867	3	2
Covina			
The Covina National Bank	8222	6	3
The First National Bank Of Covina	5830	3	5
Crescent Heights			
The Crescent Heights National Bank	11880	–	–
West Hollywood National Bank Of Crescent Heights	11880	6	–
Crockett			
The First National Bank Of Crockett	11326	5	4
Crows Landing			
The First National Bank Of Crows Landing	9765	6	5
Cucamonga			
The First National Bank Of Cucamonga	7152	5	6
Culver City			
The First National Bank Of Culver City	11732	–	4
Cutler			
The First National Bank Of Cutler	11241	–	–
Del Rey			
The First National Bank Of Del Rey	11041	4	6
Delano			
First National Bank In Delano	10387	–	6
The First National Bank Of Delano	9195	5	–
Dinuba			
The Dinuba National Bank	12929	–	–
The First National Bank Of Dinuba	9158	6	–
The National Bank Of Dinuba	12160	–	–
The United States National Bank Of Dinuba	9156	6	–
Dixon			
The First National Bank Of Dixon	10120	6	4
Downey			
The First National Bank Of Downey	11701	6	5
Ducor			
The First National Bank Of Ducor	10301	5	6
Earlimart			
The First National Bank Of Earlimart	11806	–	–
East San Gabriel			
The First National Bank Of East San Gabriel	12253	–	–
The First National Bank Of San Gabriel	12253	–	–
El Centro			
The El Centro National Bank	9349	6	–
The First National Bank Of El Centro	9350	6	–
El Monte			
The First National Bank Of El Monte	6993	5	4
El Segundo			
The First National Bank Of El Segundo	11850	–	–
Elsinore			
The First National Bank Of Elsinore	11922	5	4
Emeryville			
The First National Bank Of Emeryville	9410	6	–
Escondido			
The Escondido National Bank	8040	5	–
The First National Bank In Escondido	13029	6	–
The First National Bank Of Escondido	7801	5	–
Eureka			
The First National Bank Of Eureka	5986	2	3
The Humboldt National Bank Of Eureka	10528	4	–
Exeter			
The Citrus National Bank Of Exeter	10490	–	–
The First National Bank Of Exeter	9370	5	–
Fairfield			
The First National Bank Of Fairfield	10984	–	4
Fallbrook			
The First National Bank Of Fallbrook	13079	–	–
Florence			
The Florence National Bank	12624	5	6
Fontana			
The First National Bank Of Fontana	12976	–	3
Fort Bragg			
Coast National Bank In Fort Bragg	13787	–	5
The Coast National Bank Of Fort Bragg	9626	5	6
The First National Bank Of Fort Bragg	9626	6	–
Fowler			
The First National Bank Of Fowler	7390	6	–
The Fowler National Bank	10312	6	–
Fresno			
First National Bank In Fresno	11473	4	4
The Farmers National Bank Of Fresno	5162	3	–
The First National Bank Of Fresno	3321	4	–
The Fresno National Bank	3870	5	–
The Growers National Bank Of Fresno	11473	4	–
The Union National Bank Of Fresno	8718	5	–
Fullerton			
First National Trust & Savings Bank Of Fullerton	12764	5	3
The Farmers And Merchants National Bank Of Fullerton	9538	6	–
The First National Bank Of Fullerton	5654	4	–
The New First National Bank Of Fullerton	12764	–	–
Garden Grove			
The First National Bank Of Garden Grove	11251	5	5
Gardena			
The First National Bank Of Gardena	10453	4	–
Geyserville			
The First National Bank Of Geyserville	11678	6	–
Gilroy			
The First National Bank Of Gilroy	10166	6	–
Glendale			
First National Bank In Glendale	10412	6	6
The American National Bank Of Glendale	13071	–	–
The First National Bank At Glendale	14298	–	–
The First National Bank Of Glendale	7987	5	–
The Glendale National Bank, Glendale	10412	6	–
Glendora			
The First National Bank Of Glendora	8652	5	3
Graham			
The Graham National Bank	12673	6	6
Grass Valley			
First National Bank In Grass Valley	12433	5	4
The First National Bank Of Grass Valley	3648	6	–
Gridley			
The First National Bank Of Gridley	11164	6	–
Half Moon Bay			
The Security Natl. Bank Of San Mateo County In Half Moon Bay	11497	–	–
Hanford			
The Farmers And Merchants National Bank Of Hanford	7658	6	–
The First National Bank Of Hanford	5863	5	3
The Hanford National Bank	6873	5	–
Hardwick			
The First National Bank Of Hardwick	10364	6	6
Hayward			
The Farmers And Merchants National Bank Of Hayward	11752	–	–
The First National Bank In Hayward	12306	–	–
The First National Bank Of Hayward	10018	6	–
Healdsburg			
The First National Bank Of Healdsburg	10184	3	6
The Healdsburg National Bank	10204	5	–
Heber			
The First National Bank Of Heber	10503	–	–
Hemet			
The First National Bank Of Hemet	10764	6	4
Hermon			
The Highland National Bank Of Hermon	8549	–	–
Hermosa Beach			
The First National Bank Of Hermosa Beach	12209	4	5
The National Bank Of Hermosa Beach	12271	4	6
Hollister			
The First National Bank Of Hollister	9378	4	–
The Hollister National Bank	13510	–	5
Hollywood			
The First National Bank Of Hollywood	7543	4	–
The Hollywood National Bank	7803	6	–
Holtville			
The First National Bank Of Holtville	9770	6	5
Huntington Beach			
The First National Bank In Huntington Beach	12345	–	–
The First National Bank Of Huntington Beach	7868	6	–
Huntington Park			
The City National Bank Of Huntington Park	12988	–	–
The First National Bank Of Huntington Park	11587	–	–
The National Bank Of Huntington Park	11925	6	–
Hynes			
The First National Bank Of Hynes	9919	5	4
Imperial			
The First National Bank Of Imperial	6027	5	–
Indio			
The First National Bank Of Indio	11787	–	–
Inglewood			
The First National Bank Of Inglewood	9093	6	–
Jamestown			
Motherlode National Bank Of Sonora	10362	–	–
The Jamestown National Bank	10362	5	–
The Union National Bank Of Jamestown	10284	6	–
Kerman			
The First National Bank Of Kerman	9234	6	–
The First National Bank Of Kerman	12584	–	–
King City			
The First National Bank Of King City	10972	–	–
Kingsburg			
The First National Bank Of Kingsburg	8409	6	–
La Habra			
The First National Bank Of La Habra	11827	6	–
La Verne			
The First National Bank Of La Verne	9599	4	5
Lamanda Park			
The First National Bank Of Lamanda Park	10894	–	–
Lankershim			
The First National Bank Of Lankershim	11991	–	–
Laton			
The First National Bank Of Laton	9818	6	–
Lemoore			
The First National Bank Of Lemoore	7779	6	3
The National Bank Of Lemoore	12127	–	–
Lindsay			
The First National Bank Of Lindsay	7965	6	–
The Lindsay National Bank	9710	6	–
Livermore			
The Farmers And Merchants National Bank Of Livermore	9914	6	–
The First National Bank Of Livermore	8002	5	–
Lodi			
The Citizens National Bank Of Lodi	12112	4	–
The First National Bank Of Lodi	7719	3	–
The Lodi National Bank	11126	4	–
Loma Linda			
The First National Bank Of Loma Linda	13332	–	3
Lompoc			
The Farmers And Merchants National Bank Of Lompoc	11756	–	–
The First National Bank Of Lompoc	10897	–	–

City, Bank	Ch. No.	L	S
Long Beach			
California First National Bank Of Long Beach	11873	–	3
The American National Bank Of Long Beach	6749	6	–
The California National Bank Of Long Beach	11873	4	–
The City National Bank In Long Beach	8870	4	–
The Exchange National Bank Of Long Beach	8510	5	–
The First National Bank Of Long Beach	5456	4	–
The Long Beach National Bank, Long Beach	8510	6	–
The National Bank Of Long Beach	6730	4	–
The Seaside National Bank Of Long Beach	12819	6	4
Lordsburg			
The First National Bank Of Lordsburg	9599	5	–
Los Altos			
The First National Bank Of Los Altos	11522	5	4
Los Angeles			
Central National Bank In Los Angeles	13187	–	6
Citizens National Trust And Savings Bank Of Los Angeles	5927	4	1
Los Angeles-First Natl. Trust & Savings Bank, Los Angeles	2491	2	–
Merchants National Trust & Savings Bank Of Los Angeles	3538	3	–
Security-first National Bank Of Los Angeles	2491	–	1
The American Marine National Bank Of Los Angeles	11729	–	–
The American National Bank Of Los Angeles	6545	4	–
The Central National Bank Of Los Angeles	8827	5	–
The Citizens National Bank Of Los Angeles	5927	1	–
The Commercial National Bank Of Los Angeles	6864	3	–
The Commercial National Trust & Sav. Bank Of Los Angeles	6864	4	–
The Continental National Bank Of Los Angeles	10656	–	–
The Farmers And Merchants National Bank Of Los Angeles	6617	1	1
The First National Bank Of Los Angeles	2491	1	–
The First National Bank Of Wilmington	9515	4	–
The Hellman Commercial Trust & Savings, Natl Assoc Of L.A.	12986	–	–
The Los Angeles National Bank	2938	5	–
The Merchants National Bank Of Los Angeles	3538	2	–
The National Bank For Savings Of Los Angeles	13187	–	–
The National Bank Of California Of Los Angeles	4096	2	–
The National Bank Of Commerce Of Los Angeles	8117	6	–
The National Bank Of Commerce Of Los Angeles	12755	4	5
The National Bank Of Hollywood	12804	–	–
The National City Bank Of Los Angeles	12410	3	–
The Pacific National Bank Of Los Angeles	12454	2	6
The Peoples National Bank Of Los Angeles	12755	5	–
The Seaboard National Bank Of Los Angeles	12545	–	1
The Security National Bank Of Los Angeles	8827	6	–
The Southern California National Bank Of Los Angeles	3538	6	–
The Southwestern National Bank Of Los Angeles	5993	6	–
The United States National Bank Of Los Angeles	7632	3	–
The Western National Bank In Los Angeles	13187	–	4
The Wilshire National Bank Of Los Angeles	12577	–	–
Los Angelos			
The Hollywood National Bank Of Los Angelos	12804	–	3
Los Banos			
The First National Bank Of Los Banos	9933	5	–
Los Gatos			
The First National Bank Of Los Gatos	10091	5	3
Lynwood			
The National Bank Of Lynwood	13135	–	–
Madera			
The Commercial National Bank Of Madera	10197	6	–
The First National Bank Of Madera	7336	6	–
The First National Bank Of Madera	14307	–	–
Manteca			
The First National Bank Of Manteca	11720	–	–
Maricopa			
The First National Bank Of Maricopa	9957	6	–
Martinez			
The First Natl. Bank Of Contra Costa County At Martinez	8692	4	–
The National Bank Of Martinez	12511	5	–
Marysville			
The First National Bank Of Marysville	11123	5	6
Mc Cloud			
The Mc Cloud National Bank	9479	5	3
Mc Farland			
The First National Bank Of Mc Farland	10387	6	4
Merced			
First National Bank In Merced	13028	–	3
The Farmers And Merchants National Bank Of Merced	10352	4	–
The First National Bank Of Merced	3733	6	–
The First National Bank Of Merced	9437	5	–
Modesto			
California National Bank Of Modesto	10988	6	–
First National Bank In Modesto	11853	–	–
The American National Bank Of Modesto	11853	–	–
The First National Bank Of Modesto	3136	4	–
Monrovia			
First National Bank In Monrovia	7705	6	–
The American National Bank Of Monrovia	7705	6	–
The First National Bank Of Monrovia	3743	5	–
The Natioanl Bank Of Monrovia	7705	6	–
Montebello			
The First National Bank Of Montebello	11273	–	–
Monterey			
The First National Bank Of Monterey	7058	5	2
Monterey Park			
The First National Bank Of Monterey Park	12061	–	6
Mountain View			
The Farmers And Merchants National Bank Of Mountain View	11532	5	–
The First National Bank Of Mountain View	10324	4	4
Napa			
The First National Bank Of Napa	7176	4	1
National City			
The Peoples National Bank Of National City	9512	6	–

City, Bank	Ch. No.	L	S
Needles			
The Needles National Bank	4873	6	–
Newman			
The First National Bank Of Newman	9760	6	–
Newport Beach			
The First National Bank Of Newport Beach	10702	–	–
Niland			
The First National Bank Of Niland	11699	–	–
Oakdale			
The First National Bank Of Oakdale	7502	4	3
Oakland			
Central National Bank Of Oakland	9502	1	1
First National Bank In Oakland	12665	3	2
The East Bay National Bank Of Oakland	12937	–	–
The First National Bank Of Oakland	2248	2	–
The New First National Bank Of Oakland	12665	5	–
The Union National Bank Of Oakland	2266	4	–
Ocean Park			
The First National Bank Of Ocean Park	7690	4	–
Oceanside			
The First National Bank Of Oceanside	8069	5	–
Olive			
The First National Bank Of Olive	10891	5	5
Ontario			
The Citizens National Bank Of Ontario	13092	5	3
The First National Bank Of Ontario	6268	3	2
The Ontario National Bank	9935	4	–
Orange			
The First National Bank Of Orange	8181	4	2
The National Bank Of Orange	9878	4	–
Orange Cove			
The First National Bank Of Orange Cove	11616	5	3
Orland			
The First National Bank Of Orland	10378	5	6
Orosi			
The First National Bank In Orosi	13465	–	–
The First National Bank Of Orosi	9167	6	–
The National Bank Of Orosi	10328	6	6
Oroville			
Rideout, Smith National Bank Of Oroville	10282	5	–
The First National Bank Of Oroville	6919	6	5
Oxnard			
The First National Bank Of Oxnard	9481	6	–
Pacific Grove			
The First National Bank Of Pacific Grove	13375	–	2
Palo Alto			
Palo Alto National Bank	13212	–	2
The First National Bank Of Palo Alto	7069	5	–
Parlier			
The First National Bank Of Parlier	10124	4	–
Pasadena			
National Bank And Trust Company Of Pasadena	11425	5	–
Pasadena National Bank	12385	4	4
Pasadena-First National Bank, Pasadena	12385	–	6
The Central National Bank Of Pasadena	11926	–	–
The Crown City National Bank Of Pasadena	9366	6	–
The First National Bank Of Pasadena	3499	3	3
The National Bank Of Commerce Of Pasadena	10082	5	–
The National Bank Of Commerce Of Pasadena	12735	–	–
The National Bank Of Pasadena	10082	4	–
The Pasadena National Bank	3568	3	–
The Security National Bank Of Pasadena	10167	3	2
The Union National Bank Of Pasadena	9121	4	–
Paso Robles			
First National Bank In Paso Robles	12172	5	4
The First National Bank Of Paso Robles	9844	6	–
The Paso Robles National Bank	12172	6	–
Pescadero			
The First National Bank Of Pescadero	11520	–	–
Petaluma			
The First National Bank Of Petaluma	2193	6	–
The Petaluma National Bank	6904	3	–
The Sonoma County National Bank Of Petaluma	9918	3	–
Pico			
The National Bank Of Pico	13179	–	–
Pittsburg			
The First National Bank Of Pittsburg	11359	6	–
Pixley			
The First National Bank Of Pixley	11371	–	–
Placentia			
The Placentia National Bank	10092	5	–
Placerville			
The Placerville National Bank	12056	5	4
Pleasanton			
The First National Bank Of Pleasanton	9897	6	3
Pomona			
The American National Bank Of Pomona	4663	4	–
The First National Bank Of Pomona	3518	2	2
The National Bank Of Pomona	4663	6	–
Porterville			
The First National Bank Of Porterville	6808	5	6
Puente			
The First National Bank Of Puente	9894	4	4
The Puente National Bank	11303	–	–
Red Bluff			
The First National Bank Of Red Bluff	10114	6	–
The Red Bluff National Bank	10114	5	–
Redding			
The Northern California National Bank Of Redding	10100	5	3
The Redding National Bank	10070	4	–
Redlands			
First National Bank In Redlands	12316	4	–
The Citizens National Bank Of Redlands	8073	5	–
The First National Bank Of Redlands	3892	3	–
The Redlands National Bank	7259	5	–
Redondo Beach			
The Farmers And Merchants National Bank Of Redondo	7895	5	–
The First National Bank Of Redondo	8143	4	3

City, Bank	Ch. No.	L	S
Redwood City			
The First Natl. Bank Of San Mateo County At Redwood City	7279	2	1
Reedley			
The First National Bank Of Reedley	8857	6	–
The Reedley National Bank	9688	6	–
Rialto			
The Citizens National Bank Of Rialto	11867	6	6
The First National Bank Of Rialto	8768	5	5
Richmond			
First National Bank In Richmond	12341	3	4
The First National Bank Of Richmond	9735	5	–
Rio Vista			
The First National Bank Of Rio Vista	10719	–	–
Ripon			
The First National Bank Of Ripon	11918	–	–
Riverbank			
The First National Bank Of Riverbank	10427	6	–
Riverdale			
The First National Bank Of Riverdale	10200	6	6
Riverside			
First National Bank In Riverside	8377	4	2
The Citizens National Bank Of Riverside	8907	4	–
The Citizens National Trust & Savings Bank Of Riverside	8907	4	1
The First National Bank Of Riverside	3348	4	–
The National Bank Of Riverside	8377	5	–
The Orange Growers National Bank Of Riverside	6833	6	–
The Riverside National Bank	4757	6	–
Rodeo			
The First National Bank Of Rodeo	11201	6	–
Roseville			
The First National Bank Of Roseville	11961	6	–
The Railroad National Bank Of Roseville	11992	5	–
The Roseville National Bank	11961	6	–
Sacramento			
The California National Bank Of Sacramento	8504	1	1
The Capital National Bank Of Sacramento	10107	2	2
The Fort Sutter National Bank Of Sacramento	7776	4	–
The Merchants National Bank Of Sacramento	11875	4	3
The National Bank Of D. O. Mills & Co., Sacramento	2014	2	–
Saint Helena			
The Carver National Bank Of Saint Helena	3757	6	–
The First National Bank Of Saint Helena	3757	6	–
Salida			
The First National Bank Of Salida	11601	5	6
Salinas			
The First National Bank Of Salinas	5074	5	–
The Salinas National Bank	13380	–	3
San Bernardino			
American National Bank Of San Bernardino	10931	4	–
The American National Bank Of San Bernardino	10931	–	2
The Farmers Exchange National Bank Of San Bernardino	8618	5	–
The First National Bank Of San Bernardino	3527	6	–
The San Bernardino National Bank	3818	4	3
San Diego			
The American National Bank Of San Diego	7418	5	–
The California National Bank Of San Diego	3828	6	–
The Consolidated National Bank Of San Diego	3056	6	–
The First National Bank Of San Diego	3050	3	–
The First National Trust & Savings Bank Of San Diego	3050	–	2
The La Jolla National Bank Of San Diego	13208	–	–
The Marine National Bank Of San Diego	9483	6	–
The Merchants National Bank Of San Diego	4886	3	–
The National Bank Of Commerce Of San Diego	6869	6	–
The San Diego National Bank	3780	6	–
The Union National Bank Of San Diego	10435	4	–
The United States National Bank Of San Diego	10391	4	3
San Dimas			
The First National Bank Of San Dimas	10068	6	3
San Fernando			
The First National Bank Of San Fernando	9575	5	–
The San Fernando National Bank	10273	6	–
San Francisco			
Bank Of America Natl. Trust & Savings Assoc., San Francisco	13044	–	1
Bank Of Italy Natl. Trust & Savings Assoc., San Francisco	13044	1	1
Brotherhood National Bank Of San Francisco	13016	3	–
City National Bank Of San Francisco	13016	–	3
Crocker First National Bank Of San Francisco	1741	1	1
Mercantile National Bank Of San Francisco	9683	2	–
Merchants National Bank Of San Francisco	9882	2	–
Pacific National Bank Of San Francisco	12579	2	1
The American National Bank Of San Francisco	6426	2	–
The Anglo & London Paris National Bank Of San Francisco	9174	1	1
The Anglo California National Bank Of San Francisco	9174	–	1
The Bank Of California, National Association, San Francisco	9655	1	1
The California National Bank Of San Francisco	3592	6	–
The Citizens National Bank Of San Francisco	7713	5	–
The Crocker National Bank Of San Francisco	3555	1	–
The Crocker-Woolworth National Bank Of San Francisco	3555	4	–
The First National Bank Of San Francisco	1741	1	–
The Germania National Bank Of San Francisco	6592	6	–
The London Paris National Bank Of San Francisco	9174	4	–
The Merchants National Bank Of San Francisco	8487	6	–
The National Bank Of The Pacific, San Francisco	7894	5	–
The Nevada National Bank Of San Francisco	5105	2	–
The San Francisco National Bank	5096	1	–
The Seaboard National Bank Of San Francisco	9141	3	–
The United States National Bank Of San Francisco	7691	5	–
The Wells-Fargo Nevada National Bank Of San Francisco	5105	1	–

City, Bank	Ch. No.	L	S
The Western Metropolis National Bank Of San Francisco	9882	5	–
The Western National Bank Of San Francisco	5688	3	–
Wells-Fargo Nevada National Bank Of San Francisco	5105	1	–
San Jacinto			
The First National Bank Of San Jacinto	7997	4	4
San Joaquin			
The First National Bank Of San Joaquin	11484	5	–
San Jose			
San Jose National Bank	13338	–	2
The First National Bank Of San Jose	2158	2	1
The Garden City National Bank Of San Jose	3715	6	–
San Juan			
The First National Bank Of San Juan	11296	–	–
San Leandro			
First National Bank In San Leandro	13217	–	3
The First National Bank Of San Leandro	9800	6	–
The San Leandro National Bank	12802	4	–
San Luis Obispo			
The First National Bank Of San Luis Obispo	3826	6	–
The Union National Bank Of San Luis Obispo	7877	4	–
San Marino			
The San Marino National Bank, San Marino	13335	–	2
San Mateo			
The National Bank Of San Mateo	9424	4	3
San Pedro			
The First National Bank Of San Pedro	7057	4	–
San Rafael			
First National Bank In San Rafael	12640	–	4
The Marin County National Bank Of San Rafael	10177	4	–
Sanger			
The First National Bank Of Sanger	9308	4	–
Santa Ana			
The American National Bank Of Santa Ana	11869	5	–
The California National Bank Of Santa Ana	9904	4	–
The Commercial National Bank Of Santa Ana	13200	5	4
The Farmers And Merchants National Bank Of Santa Ana	7980	5	–
The First National Bank In Santa Ana	14045	–	–
The First National Bank Of Santa Ana	3520	2	1
Santa Barbara			
County National Bank & Trust Company Of Santa Barbara	2456	3	3
First National Trust & Savings Bank Of Santa Barbara	2104	4	1
The First National Bank Of Santa Barbara	2104	3	–
The Santa Barbara County National Bank	2456	4	–
Santa Cruz			
County First National Bank Of Santa Cruz	9745	4	3
Santa Cruz County National Bank	9745	3	–
The Farmers And Merchants National Bank Of Santa Cruz	10571	–	3
The First National Bank Of Santa Cruz	8403	5	–
Santa Maria			
The Commercial National Bank Of Santa Maria	12913	–	–
The First National Bank Of Santa Maria	7480	4	–
Santa Monica			
The American National Bank Of Santa Monica	12787	5	3
The First National Bank In Santa Monica	6945	6	–
The First National Bank Of Santa Monica	3845	6	–
The Merchants National Bank Of Santa Monica	6945	6	–
Santa Paula			
The First National Bank & Trust Company Of Santa Paula	4120	6	–
The First National Bank Of Santa Paula	4120	4	–
The New First National Bank Of Santa Paula	12856	–	–
Santa Rosa			
The American National Bank Of Santa Rosa	12201	–	–
The First National Bank Of Santa Rosa	12201	4	–
The Santa Rosa National Bank	3558	5	–
Sausalito			
The First National Bank Of Sausalito	12453	6	–
Sawtelle			
The United States National Bank Of Sawtelle	12226	–	–
Scotia			
The First National Bank Of Scotia	9787	6	3
Sebastopol			
The First National Bank Of Sebastopol	9648	6	6
The Sebastopol National Bank	11161	5	4
Seeley			
The First National Bank Of Seeley	10462	6	–
Selma			
The First National Bank Of Selma	5395	5	–
The Selma National Bank	10293	6	–
Shafter			
The First National Bank Of Shafter	11534	–	–
Sherman			
The First National Bank Of Sherman	11025	–	–
West Hollywood First National Bank, West Hollywood	11025	–	–
Sierra Madre			
The First National Bank Of Sierra Madre	8707	6	–
Sonoma			
The First National Bank Of Sonoma	10259	6	–
The Valley National Bank Of Sonoma	12360	–	–
Sonora			
The First National Bank Of Sonora	7202	3	4
The Sonora National Bank	10461	6	–
South Gate			
The South Gate National Bank	12807	–	–
South Pasadena			
First National Bank In South Pasadena	12797	4	–
The First National Bank Of South Pasadena	8544	6	–
The South Pasadena National Bank	12852	–	–
South San Francisco			
The Citizens National Bank Of South San Francisco	12364	6	–
Stockton			
The First National Bank Of Stockton	2412	4	4
The San Joaquin Valley National Bank Of Stockton	10817	4	–
The Stockton National Bank	2794	6	–
Suisun			
Bank Of Suisun National Association, Suisun City	11684	–	4
The First National Bank Of Suisun	10149	5	–
Taft			
The First National Bank Of Taft	10088	6	–
Temecula			
The First National Bank Of Temecula	10556	–	–
Temple			
The Temple National Bank	12766	–	–
Terra Bella			
The First National Bank Of Terra Bella	9889	6	5
Torrance			
The First National Bank Of Torrance	10396	4	4
Torrance National Bank	14202	–	6
Tranquility			
The First National Bank Of Tranquility	11433	5	6
Tropico			
The First National Bank Of Tropico	10412	5	–
Tulare			
The First National Bank Of Tulare	8626	4	–
The National Bank Of Tulare	10201	6	–
Turlock			
The First National Bank In Turlock	7738	6	–
The First National Bank Of Turlock	11124	–	–
The First National Bank Of Turlock	13418	–	–
Tustin			
The First National Bank Of Tustin	10134	5	2
Ukiah			
The First National Bank Of Ukiah	10977	4	6
Upland			
The Commercial National Bank Of Upland	9570	5	–
The First National Bank Of Upland	8266	5	4
Vacaville			
The First National Bank Of Vacaville	9795	4	5
Vallejo			
Mechanics And Merchants National Bank Of Vallejo	13368	–	3
The First National Bank Of Vallejo	9573	4	–
The Vallejo Commercial National Bank	11206	4	–
Van Nuys			
The First National Bank Of Van Nuys	10168	6	–
Venice			
The First National Bank Of Venice	10233	6	6
Ventura			
National Bank Of Ventura	9685	4	–
The First National Bank Of Ventura	7210	3	5
The Union National Bank Of Ventura	12996	6	2
Verdugo City			
Crescenta-canada National Bank At Montrose	13007	–	–
The First National Bank Of La Crescenta Valley, Verdugo	13007	–	–
The First National Bank Of Verdugo City	13007	–	–
Vernon			
The First National Bank Of Vernon	11362	–	–
Victorville			
The First National Bank Of Victorville	11005	6	5
Visalia			
National Bank Of Visalia	9173	3	–
New First National Bank Of Visalia	12678	6	–
The First National Bank Of Visalia	7063	6	–
Vista			
The First National Bank Of Vista	13178	–	–
Walnut Creek			
The First National Bank Of Walnut Creek	10281	6	–
Walnut Park			
The Walnut Park National Bank	12572	–	6
Watsonville			
The Fruit Growers National Bank Of Watsonville	11560	–	–
The Pajaro Valley National Bank Of Watsonville	9621	5	4
Watts			
The First National Bank Of Watts	12210	–	–
Weed			
The First National Bank Of Weed	9873	4	3
Westwood			
The Westwood National Bank	11840	–	–
Whittier			
First National Trust & Savings Bank Of Whittier	5588	5	–
The First National Bank Of Whittier	5588	4	–
The Whittier National Bank	7999	4	4
The Whittier National Trust & Savings Bank, Whittier	7999	–	2
Willits			
The First National Bank Of Willits	11566	5	6
Willows			
The First National Bank Of Willows	9713	5	5
Winter			
The Winters National Bank, Winters	13312	–	2
Winters			
The First National Bank Of Winters	10133	5	–
Woodlake			
The First National Bank Of Woodlake	10309	5	6
Woodland			
Bank Of Woodland National Association	10878	–	2
The First National Bank Of Woodland	9493	5	–
Yorba Linda			
The First National Bank Of Yorba Linda	10905	–	–
Yreka			
The First National Bank In Yreka	13340	–	2
The First National Bank Of Yreka	10731	5	–
Yuba City			
The First National Bank Of Yuba City	10299	6	–

COLORADO TERRITORY

City, Bank	Ch. No.	L	S
Central City			
The First National Bank Of Central City	2129	3	–
The Rocky Mountain Natl Bank Of Central City	1652	6	–
Colorado Springs			
The First National Bank Of Colorado Springs	2179	6	–
Denver			
The City National Bank Of Denver	1955	6	–
The Colorado National Bank Of Denver	1651	3	–
The First National Bank Of Denver	1016	3	–
Georgetown			
The First National Bank Of Georgetown	1991	6	–
The Miners National Bank Of Georgetown	2199	6	–
Golden			
The First National Bank Of Golden	2140	6	–
Pueblo			
The First National Bank Of Pueblo	1833	4	–
The Peoples National Bank Of Pueblo	2134	6	–
The Stock Growers National Bank Of Pueblo	2310	6	–
Trinidad			
The First National Bank Of Trinidad	2300	6	–

COLORADO

City, Bank	Ch. No.	L	S
Akron			
The Citizens National Bank Of Akron	10901	5	5
The First National Bank Of Akron	8548	6	–
Alamosa			
The Alamosa National Bank	8541	6	6
The American National Bank Of Alamosa	7904	5	5
The First National Bank Of Alamosa	3114	6	–
Arvada			
The First National Bank Of Arvada	7501	6	6
Aspen			
The Aspen National Bank	4733	6	–
The First National Bank Of Aspen	3485	5	–
The Peoples National Bank Of Aspen	8815	6	–
Ault			
The Farmers National Bank Of Ault	8167	5	5
The First National Bank Of Ault	8088	6	–
Aurora			
The First National Bank Of Aurora	11682	–	–
Berthoud			
The Berthoud National Bank	7995	5	4
The First National Bank Of Berthoud	8033	6	–
Boulder			
First National Bank In Boulder	14021	–	5
The Boulder National Bank	3246	6	–
The Citizens National Bank Of Boulder	11117	–	–
The First National Bank Of Boulder	2352	3	3
The National State Bank Of Boulder	2355	5	5
Brighton			
The First National Bank Of Brighton	7577	5	5
Brush			
The First National Bank Of Brush	6437	5	4
The Stockman's National Bank Of Brush	8520	6	–
Buena Vista			
The First National Bank Of Buena Vista	8735	6	5
Burlington			
The First National Bank Of Burlington	11455	–	–
Canon City			
The First National Bank Of Canon City	3879	5	–
The Fremont County National Bank Of Canon City	8433	4	–
Carbondale			
The First National Bank Of Carbondale	9009	6	4
Castle Rock			
The First National Bank Of Douglas County At Castle Rock	6556	5	6
Cedaredge			
The First National Bank Of Cedaredge	10272	6	4
Center			
The First National Bank Of Center	9743	6	–
Central City			
The First National Bank Of Central City	2129	4	5
The Rocky Mountain National Bank Of Central City	1652	6	–
Clifton			
The First National Bank Of Clifton	9875	6	–
Colorado City			
The City National Bank Of Colorado Springs	6238	5	4
The First National Bank Of Colorado City	6238	6	–
Colorado Springs			
The Colorado Springs National Bank	8572	4	4
The El Paso National Bank Of Colorado Springs	5283	5	–
The Exchange National Bank Of Colorado Springs	3913	5	2
The First National Bank Of Colorado Springs	2179	3	2
Cortez			
The Cortez National Bank	8967	6	–
The First National Bank Of Cortez	8967	6	–
The Montezuma Valley National Bank Of Cortez	9100	5	4
Craig			
The Craig National Bank	10560	–	–
The First National Bank Of Craig	10558	6	6
Creede			
The First National Bank Of Creede	4716	6	–
Cripple Creek			
The First National Bank Of Cripple Creek	4845	5	–
Deer Trail			
The First National Bank Of Deer Trail	11574	–	–
Del Norte			
The First National Bank Of Del Norte	4264	6	–
Delta			
The Delta National Bank	8675	5	–
The First National Bank Of Delta	5467	4	–

City, Bank	Ch. No.	L	S
Denver			
The American National Bank Of Denver	4159	6	–
The American National Bank Of Denver	12517	3	2
The Broadway National Bank Of Denver	12250	–	–
The Capitol National Bank Of Denver	6355	5	–
The Central National Bank Of Denver	8774	6	–
The Colorado National Bank Of Denver	1651	6	2
The Commercial National Bank Of Denver	4113	6	–
The Continental National Bank Of Denver	6355	6	–
The Denver National Bank	3269	2	1
The Drovers National Bank Of Denver	11564	4	–
The Federal National Bank Of Denver	10064	4	–
The First National Bank Of Denver	1016	2	1
The German National Bank Of Denver	2351	5	–
The Globe National Bank Of Denver	11623	–	–
The Hamilton National Bank Of Denver	9887	4	–
The Merchants National Bank Of Denver	2523	6	–
The National Bank Of Commerce, Denver	4358	6	–
The National City Bank Of Denver	13098	–	2
The Peoples National Bank Of Denver	4084	6	–
The South Broadway National Bank Of Denver	12974	–	–
The State National Bank Of Denver	2694	6	–
The Stock Yards National Bank Of Denver	11540	6	–
The Union National Bank Of Denver	4382	6	–
The Union National Bank Of Denver	14248	–	–
The United States National Bank Of Denver	7408	2	1
The West Side National Bank Of Denver	13098	–	3
Dolores			
The First National Bank Of Dolores	10770	6	–
Durango			
The Burns National Bank Of Durango	9797	5	4
The Durango National Bank	4126	6	–
The First National Bank Of Durango	2637	4	4
The Smelter National Bank Of Durango	4776	6	–
Eads			
The First National Bank In Eads	14213	–	3
The First National Bank Of Eads	8412	5	4
Eagle			
The First National Bank Of Eagle County, Eagle	9013	6	–
Eaton			
The Eaton National Bank	8658	6	–
The First National Bank Of Eaton	6057	5	–
Elbert			
The First National Bank Of Elbert	11681	–	–
Elizabeth			
The First National Bank Of Elizabeth	8271	6	–
Englewood			
The First National Bank Of Englewood	9907	4	4
Flagler			
The First National Bank Of Flagler	11872	–	–
Fleming			
The First National Bank Of Fleming	11571	5	4
Florence			
The First National Bank Of Florence	5381	6	5
The Security National Bank Of Florence	12431	–	–
Fort Collins			
The First National Bank In Fort Collins	14146	–	5
The First National Bank Of Fort Collins	2622	3	2
The Fort Collins National Bank	5503	3	3
The Poudre Valley National Bank Of Fort Collins	7837	3	3
Fort Morgan			
The First National Bank Of Fort Morgan	7004	4	3
The Morgan County National Bank Of Fort Morgan	7832	6	–
Fountain			
The First National Bank Of Fountain	6772	6	6
Fowler			
The First National Bank Of Fowler	7637	6	5
Fruita			
The First National Bank Of Fruita	8840	5	4
Genoa			
The First National Bank Of Genoa	12716	–	–
Georgetown			
The Merchants National Bank Of Georgetown	2394	6	–
Gill			
The First National Bank Of Gill	9697	6	–
Glenwood Springs			
The Citizens National Bank Of Glenwood Springs	6957	5	–
The First National Bank Of Glenwood Springs	3661	4	–
The Glenwood National Bank Of Glenwood Springs	3722	6	–
Golden			
The Rubey National Bank Of Golden	6497	6	5
The Woods-rubey National Bank Of Golden	6497	6	–
Granada			
The First National Bank Of Granada	7809	6	–
Grand Junction			
First National Bank In Grand Junction	13902	–	5
The First National Bank Of Grand Junction	3860	6	–
The Grand Valley National Bank Of Grand Junction	6137	5	–
The Mesa County National Bank Of Grand Junction	7766	6	–
Greeley			
The City National Bank Of Greeley	10038	6	–
The First National Bank Of Greeley	3178	4	4
The Greeley National Bank	4437	4	–
The Greeley National Bank	13928	–	4
The Greeley Union National Bank, Greeley	4437	3	1
The Union National Bank Of Greeley	7604	6	–
Gunnison			
The First National Bank Of Gunnison	2686	4	4
The Iron National Bank Of Gunnison	2975	6	–
Haxtun			
The First National Bank Of Haxtun	11099	5	3
Hayden			
The First National Bank Of Hayden	10730	–	–
Holly			
The First National Bank Of Holly	7704	5	5
Holyoke			
The First National Bank Of Holyoke	9278	6	5
Hotchkiss			
The First National Bank Of Hotchkiss	5976	6	6
Hugo			
The First National Bank Of Hugo	8489	4	4
The Hugo National Bank	10786	6	–
Idaho Springs			
The First National Bank Of Idaho Springs	2962	5	–
The Merchants And Miners National Bank Of Idaho Springs	5989	6	–
Johnstown			
The First National Bank Of Johnstown	8636	6	4
Julesburg			
The Citizens National Bank Of Julesburg	9603	6	–
The First National Bank Of Julesburg	8205	5	4
Keenesburg			
The First National Bank Of Keenesburg	11530	–	–
La Jara			
The First National Bank Of La Jara	9840	5	5
La Junta			
The First National Bank Of La Junta	4507	4	5
La Veta			
The First National Bank Of La Veta	12531	–	–
Lafayette			
The First National Bank Of Lafayette	8909	5	5
Lake City			
The First National Bank Of Lake City	2354	6	–
Lamar			
The First National Bank Of Lamar	3749	6	5
The Lamar National Bank	9036	6	3
The Lamar National Bank	14254	–	–
Las Animas			
The First National Bank Of Las Animas	6030	5	4
Leadville			
The American National Bank Of Leadville	3949	5	–
The Carbonate American National Bank Of Leadville	3746	–	–
The Carbonate National Bank Of Leadville	3746	4	–
The First National Bank Of Leadville	2420	5	–
Limon			
The First National Bank Of Limon	11504	6	5
The Limon National Bank	11619	–	–
Littleton			
The First National Bank Of Littleton	7533	6	5
The Littleton National Bank	11949	6	6
Longmont			
The American National Bank Of Longmont	11253	6	–
The Farmers National Bank Of Longmont	4653	6	–
The First National Bank Of Longmont	3354	6	–
The First National Bank Of Longmont	11253	–	3
The Longmont National Bank	7839	5	3
Loveland			
First National Bank In Loveland	13624	–	4
The First National Bank Of Loveland	7648	4	4
The Loveland National Bank	8116	4	–
Mancos			
The First National Bank Of Mancos	9674	5	5
Mead			
The First National Bank Of Mead	11321	–	–
Meeker			
The First National Bank Of Meeker	7435	6	–
Monte Vista			
The First National Bank Of Monte Vista	7228	4	6
Montrose			
The First National Bank Of Montrose	4007	4	6
The Montrose National Bank	7288	6	6
Olathe			
The First National Bank Of Olathe	9719	6	5
Ordway			
The First National Bank Of Ordway	8695	6	6
Otis			
The First National Bank Of Otis	10852	6	5
Ouray			
The First National Bank Of Ouray	4109	6	–
Pagosa Springs			
The First National Bank Of Pagosa Springs	11871	–	–
Palisades			
The Palisades National Bank	8004	5	4
Paonia			
The First National Bank Of Paonia	6671	5	2
Peetz			
The First National Bank Of Peetz	11523	–	–
Platteville			
The First National Bank Of Platteville	8755	6	–
The Platteville National Bank	9451	6	–
Pueblo			
The American National Bank Of Pueblo	4108	6	–
The Central National Bank Of Pueblo	2541	6	–
The First National Bank Of Pueblo	1833	4	2
The Mercantile National Bank Of Pueblo	4108	5	–
The Pueblo National Bank	4498	6	–
The Stock Growers National Bank Of Pueblo	2310	6	–
The Western National Bank Of Pueblo	2546	4	3
Rico			
The First National Bank Of Rico	4334	6	–
Rifle			
The First National Bank Of Rifle	6178	6	–
The Rifle National Bank	13536	–	–
Rocky Ford			
The First National Bank Of Rocky Ford	7082	6	–
The Rocky Ford National Bank	9117	5	4
Saguache			
Saguache County National Bank Of Saguache	9997	6	3
The First National Bank Of Saguache	9997	6	–
Salida			
The Commercial National Bank Of Salida	7888	6	6
The First National Bank Of Salida	4172	5	3
The Merchants National Bank Of Salida	8951	6	–
Sedgwick			
The First National Bank Of Sedgwick	9045	6	4
Silverton			
The First National Bank Of Silverton	2930	6	6
The Silverton National Bank	7784	6	–
Simla			
The First National Bank Of Simla	11354	–	–
South Pueblo			
The South Pueblo National Bank	2541	6	–
The Western National Bank Of South Pueblo	2546	6	–
Springfield			
The First National Bank Of Springfield	11660	–	–
Steamboat Springs			
The First National Bank Of Steamboat Springs	6454	6	6
Sterling			
The Farmers National Bank Of Sterling	9454	6	–
The First National Bank Of Sterling	5624	4	–
The Logan County National Bank Of Sterling	7973	5	–
The Sterling National Bank	11972	–	–
Strasburg			
The First National Bank Of Strasburg	11640	–	–
Stratton			
The First National Bank Of Stratton	11197	–	–
Sugar City			
The Citizens National Bank Of Sugar City	6472	6	–
Telluride			
The First National Bank Of Telluride	4417	4	–
Trinidad			
The First National Bank Of Trinidad	2300	4	3
The First National Bank Of Trinidad	14222	–	–
The Trinidad National Bank	3450	3	4
The Trinidad National Bank	14148	–	–
Victor			
The First National Bank Of Victor	5586	6	–
Walden			
The First National Bank Of Walden	11248	–	–
Walsenburg			
The First National Bank Of Walsenburg	7022	6	–
Wellington			
The First National Bank Of Wellington	7793	5	5
Windsor			
The Farmers National Bank Of Windsor	9120	6	–
The First National Bank Of Windsor	8296	6	–
Wray			
The First National Bank Of Wray	8752	6	3
The National Bank Of Wray	9676	6	5
Yuma			
The First National Bank Of Yuma	10093	5	5

CONNECTICUT

City, Bank	Ch. No.	L	S
Ansonia			
The Ansonia National Bank	1093	4	5
Bethel			
The Bethel National Bank	10289	5	4
The First National Bank Of Bethel	1141	6	–
Birmingham			
The Birmingham National Bank, Birmingham	1098	4	–
The Birmingham National Bank, Derby	1098	3	3
Bridgeport			
The Bridgeport National Bank	910	5	–
The City National Bank And Trust Company Of Bridgeport	921	–	–
The City National Bank Of Bridgeport	921	4	–
The Connecticut National Bank Of Bridgeport	927	3	–
The First National Bank & Trust Company Of Bridgeport	335	–	2
The First National Bank Of Bridgeport	335	4	–
The First National Bank Of Bridgeport	335	3	5
The First-Bridgeport National Bank, Bridgeport	335	3	–
The Pequonnock National Bank Of Bridgeport	928	4	–
Bristol			
The Bristol National Bank	2250	3	–
Brooklyn			
The Windham County National Bank Of Brooklyn	1360	4	–
Canaan			
The Canaan National Bank	8511	6	5
Clinton			
The Clinton National Bank	1314	3	4
Danbury			
City National Bank & Trust Company Of Danbury	1132	6	5
The City National Bank Of Danbury	1132	4	–
The Danbury National Bank	943	2	3
The National Pahquioque Bank Of Danbury	1132	6	–
Danielson			
The Windham County National Bank Of Danielson	1360	4	2
Danielsonville			
The Windham County National Bank Of Danielsonville	1360	6	–
Deep River			
The Deep River National Bank	1139	3	3
East Haddam			
The National Bank Of New England Of East Haddam	1480	6	–
The National Bank Of New England Of East Haddam	7812	5	–
East Port Chester			
The Byram National Bank Of East Port Chester	12973	6	5
Essex			
The Essex National Bank	8936	6	4
The Saybrook National Bank Of Essex	1084	6	–
Falls Village			
The National Iron Bank Of Falls Village	1214	5	4
Greenwich			
The First National Bank Of Greenwich	13042	–	–
The Greenwich National Bank	8243	6	–
Guilford			
The Guilford National Bank	5358	5	–

City, Bank	Ch. No.	L	S
Hartford			
Hartford National Bank & Trust Company	1338	3	1
The Aetna National Bank Of Hartford	756	4	–
The American National Bank Of Hartford	1165	5	–
The Capitol National Bank & Trust Company Of Hartford	13038	–	2
The Capitol National Bank Of Hartford	13038	3	–
The Charter Oak National Bank Of Hartford	486	4	–
The City National Bank Of Hartford	1377	4	–
The Colonial National Bank Of Hartford	10796	5	–
The Farmers And Mechanics National Bank Of Hartford	1321	3	–
The First National Bank Of Hartford	121	2	1
The Hartford National Bank	1338	2	–
The Hartford-Aetna National Bank	1338	2	–
The Mercantile National Bank Of Hartford	1300	6	–
The National Exchange Bank Of Hartford	361	2	–
The Phoenix National Bank Of Hartford	670	2	–
Jewett City			
The Jewett City National Bank	1478	6	–
Killingly			
The First National Bank Of Killingly	450	5	–
The First National Bank Of Killingly, West Killingly	450	4	–
Litchfield			
The First National Bank Of Litchfield	709	3	3
Meridan			
The First National Bank Of Meridan	250	3	3
Meriden			
The Home National Bank Of Meriden	720	3	2
The Meriden National Bank	1382	3	3
Middletown			
The Central National Bank Of Middletown	1340	3	3
The First National Bank Of Middletown	397	5	5
The Middlesex County National Bank Of Middletown	845	5	–
The Middletown National Bank	1216	2	–
The Middletown National Bank & Trust Company, Middlwtown	1216	–	–
The Middletown National Bank, Middletown	1216	–	3
Moosup			
The Plainfield National Bank Of Moosup	10145	–	6
Mystic			
The Mystic National Bank	1268	6	–
Mystic Bridge			
The First National Bank Of Mystic Bridge	251	6	–
Mystic River			
The Mystic River National Bank	645	4	3
Naugatuck			
The Naugatuck National Bank	3020	5	5
New Britain			
The City National Bank Of New Britain	12846	5	4
The Mechanics National Bank Of New Britain	3668	6	–
The New Britain National Bank	1184	5	4
New Canaan			
The First National Bank & Trust Of New Canaan	1249	–	4
The First National Bank Of New Canaan	1249	3	–
New Haven			
The First National Bank And Trust Company Of New Haven	2	3	1
The First National Bank Of New Haven	2	6	–
The First National Bank Of New Haven	2	2	–
The First National Bank Of New Haven	2682	6	–
The Merchants National Bank Of New Haven	1128	3	2
The National New Haven Bank	1243	5	–
The National Tradesmen's Bank & Trust Company, New Haven	1202	6	3
The National Tradesmen's Bank Of New Haven	1202	3	–
The New Haven Bank National Banking Association, New Haven	1243	3	3
The New Haven County National Bank, New Haven	1245	4	–
The Second National Bank Of New Haven	227	2	–
The Tradesmen's National Bank Of New Haven	13704	–	3
The Yale National Bank Of New Haven	796	4	–
New London			
The First National Bank Of New London	196	6	–
The National Bank Of Commerce Of New London	666	2	1
The National Union Bank Of New London	1175	6	–
The National Whaling Bank Of New London	978	4	1
The New London City National Bank	1037	2	2
New Milford			
The First National Bank Of New Milford	1193	4	3
Norwalk			
The Central National Bank Of Norwalk	2342	5	–
The Fairfield County National Bank Of Norwalk	754	3	–
The National Bank Of Norwalk	942	4	3
Norwich			
The First National Bank Of Norwich	65	6	–
The First National Bank Of Norwich	458	4	–
The Merchants National Bank Of Norwich	1481	5	–
The Norwich National Bank	1358	6	–
The Second National Bank Of Norwich	224	6	–
The Shetucket National Bank Of Norwich	1379	6	–
The Thames National Bank Of Norwich	657	1	–
The Uncas National Bank Of Norwich	1187	3	–
The Uncas-merchants National Bank Of Norwich	1187	–	–
Pawcatuck			
The Pawcatuck National Bank	919	5	–
Plainfield			
The First National Bank Of Plainfield	10145	5	6
Plainville			
The First National Bank Of Plainville	9313	6	–
Plantsville			
The Plantsville National Bank	12637	6	5
Portland			
The First National Bank Of Portland	1013	3	–
Putnam			
The Citizens National Bank Of Putnam	12594	–	–
The First National Bank Of Putnam	448	5	–
The Thompson National Bank Of Putnam	1477	6	–
Ridgefield			
The First National Bank & Trust Company Of Ridgefield	5309	5	4
The First National Bank Of Ridgefield	5309	4	–
Rockville			
The First National Bank Of Rockville	186	4	5
The Rockville National Bank	509	5	4
Seymour			
The Valley National Bank Of Seymour	5499	6	–
Sharon			
The Sharon National Bank	13245	–	–
South Norwalk			
The City National Bank Of South Norwalk	2643	3	4
The First National Bank Of South Norwalk	502	5	–
Southington			
The Southington National Bank	2814	6	–
Southport			
The Southport National Bank	660	4	–
Stafford Springs			
The First National Bank Of Stafford Springs	3914	4	6
The Stafford National Bank Of Stafford Springs	686	5	–
Stamford			
The First National Bank Of Stamford	4	2	–
The First-Stamford National Bank & Trust Co. Of Stamford	4	–	1
The First-Stamford National Bank, Stamford	4	3	3
The Peoples National Bank Of Stamford	12400	5	4
The Stamford National Bank	1038	4	–
Stonington			
The First National Bank Of Stonington	735	3	4
Suffield			
The First National Bank Of Suffield	497	4	3
Thomaston			
The Thomaston National Bank	3964	6	5
Thompson			
The Thompson National Bank	1477	6	–
Tolland			
The Tolland County National Bank Of Tolland	1385	4	–
Torrington			
The Brooks National Bank Of Torrington	5231	6	–
The Torrington National Bank	5235	3	4
The Torrington National Bank And Trust Company	5235	–	2
Wallingford			
The First National Bank Of Wallingford	2599	3	3
Waterbury			
The Citizens & Manufacturers National Bank Of Waterbury	2494	–	3
The Citizens National Bank Of Waterbury	791	4	–
The Fourth National Bank Of Waterbury	3768	6	–
The Manufacturers National Bank Of Waterbury	2494	5	–
The Waterbury National Bank	780	4	2
West Meriden			
The First National Bank Of West Meriden	250	4	–
Westport			
The First National Bank Of Westport	394	4	–
Willimantic			
The First National Bank Of Willimantic	2388	6	–
Windham			
The Windham National Bank, Willmantic	1614	3	3
The Windham National Bank, Windham	1614	6	–
Winsted			
The First National Bank Of Winsted	2414	4	4
The Hurlbut National Bank Of Winsted	1494	3	2
The Winsted National Bank	2419	6	–

DELAWARE

City, Bank	Ch. No.	L	S
Dagsboro			
The First National Bank Of Dagsboro	8972	5	2
Delaware City			
The Delaware City National Bank	1332	3	5
Delmar			
The First National Bank Of Delmar	7211	6	5
Dover			
The First National Bank Of Dover	1567	4	1
Felton			
The First National Bank Of Felton	9132	5	–
Frankford			
The First National Bank Of Frankford	8918	6	5
Frederica			
The First National Bank Of Frederica	5421	6	–
Georgetown			
The First National Bank In Georgetown	13278	–	–
The First National Bank Of Georgetown	5930	6	–
Harrington			
The First National Bank Of Harrington	3883	6	6
Laurel			
The Peoples National Bank Of Laurel	6726	5	4
Lewes			
The Lewes National Bank	5148	4	–
Middletown			
The Citizens National Bank Of Middletown	1181	4	–
The Peoples National Bank Of Middletown	3019	5	–
Milford			
The First National Bank And Trust Company Of Milford	2340	6	3
The First National Bank Of Milford	2340	3	–
Milton			
The First National Bank Of Milton	12882	–	–
Newark			
The National Bank Of Newark	1536	6	–
Newport			
The Newport National Bank	997	4	–
Odessa			
The New Castle County National Bank Of Odessa	1281	3	3
Seaford			
The First National Bank Of Seaford	795	6	3
The Sussex National Bank Of Seaford	3693	6	–
Selbyville			
The Selbyville National Bank	6718	6	–
Smyrna			
The Fruit Growers National Bank & Trust Company Of Smyrna	2336	5	5
The Fruit Growers National Bank Of Smyrna	2336	6	–
The National Bank Of Smyrna	2381	4	4
Wilmington			
The Central National Bank Of Wilmington	3395	3	2
The First National Bank Of Wilmington	473	6	–
The National Bank Of Delaware At Willmington	1420	4	6
The National Bank Of Wilmington And Brandywine	1190	4	–
The Union National Bank Of Wilmington	1390	4	3
Wyoming			
The First National Bank Of Wyoming	9428	6	5

DIST OF COLUMBIA

City, Bank	Ch. No.	L	S
Georgetown			
The Farmers And Mechanics National Bank Of Georgetown	1928	2	–
The National Bank Of Commerce Of Georgetown	682	6	–
Hagertown, Md			
The Citizens National Bank Of Washington City, DC	1893	4	–
Washington			
American National Bank Of Washington	6716	3	–
District National Bank Of Washington	9545	–	2
Federal National Bank Of Washington	10316	3	–
Federal-American National Bank & Trust Company Of Washington	10316	–	–
Federal-American National Bank Of Washington	10316	4	6
Hamilton National Bank Of Washington	13782	–	2
The Central National Bank Of Washington City	2382	3	–
The Citizens National Bank Of Hagerstown, Md	1893	5	–
The Columbia National Bank Of Washington	3625	2	2
The Commercial National Bank Of Washington	7446	1	2
The District National Bank Of Washington	9545	2	–
The Dupont National Bank Of Washington	10825	5	–
The Farmers & Mechanics National Bank Of Washington	1928	4	–
The First National Bank Of Washington	26	5	–
The Franklin National Bank Of Washington	10504	3	3
The German-American National Bank Of Washington	2358	6	–
The Hamilton National Bank Of Washington	12194	–	–
The Liberty National Bank Of Washington	11633	–	–
The Lincoln National Bank Of Washington	4247	4	1
The Merchants National Bank Of Washington	627	6	–
The National Bank Of The Metropolis Of Washington	526	5	–
The National Bank Of The Republic Of Washington	875	5	–
The National Bank Of Washington	3425	2	1
The National Capital Bank Of Washington	4107	4	–
The National City Bank Of Washington	7936	6	–
The National Metropolitan Bank Of Washington	1069	5	–
The National Metropolitan Bank Of Washington	1069	1	1
The National Metropolitan Citizens Bank Of Washington	1069	4	–
The Northwest National Bank Of Washington	12721	–	–
The Ohio National Bank Of Washington	4522	6	–
The Riggs National Bank Of Washington	5046	1	1
The Second National Bank Of Washington	2038	2	3
The Standard National Bank Of Washington	12139	–	–
The Traders National Bank Of Washington	4244	4	–
The West End National Bank Of Washington	4195	6	–

FLORIDA

City, Bank	Ch. No.	L	S
Alachua			
The First National Bank Of Alachua	8980	5	6
Apalachicola			
The First National Bank Of Apalachicola	6274	5	–
Arcadia			
The De Soto National Bank Of Arcadia	8728	4	3
The First National Bank Of Arcadia	5534	5	5
Auburndale			
The First National Bank Of Auburndale	12983	–	–
Avon Park			
The Barnett National Bank Of Avon Park	13421	–	–
The First National Bank Of Avon Park	10826	6	–
Bartow			
The Florida National Bank At Bartow	13389	–	3
The Polk County National Bank Of Bartow	4627	6	–
The Polk County National Bank Of Bartow	13309	–	–
Boynton			
The First National Bank Of Boynton	12841	–	–
Bradenton			
The American National Bank Of Bradenton	12880	–	–
The First National Bank Of Bradenton	10245	–	3
The First National Bank Of Bradentown	10245	5	–
Brooksville			
The First National Bank In Brooksville	13320	–	3
The First National Bank Of Brooksville	9891	4	–
Chipley			
The First National Bank Of Chipley	7778	4	6
Clearwater			
The First National Bank Of Clearwater	12905	5	3
Clermont			
The First National Bank Of Clermont	11921	6	–
Cocoa			
The Barnett National Bank Of Cocoa	13390	–	–
Coral Gables			
The Coral Gables First National Bank	13008	–	4
Daytona			
The First National Bank Of Daytona	10545	5	–
De Funiak Springs			
The First National Bank Of De Funiak Springs	7404	4	4
Deland			
The Barnett National Bank Of Deland	13388	–	3
The First National Bank Of Deland	9657	3	–
Fernandina			
The Citizens National Bank Of Fernandina	10024	6	–
The First National Bank Of Fernandina	4558	4	3
Fort Lauderdale			
The First National Bank Of Fort Lauderdale	12020	6	–
Fort Meade			
The First National Bank Of Fort Meade	10386	6	–

City, Bank	Ch. No.	L	S
Fort Myers			
The First National Bank In Fort Myers	14195	–	6
The First National Bank Of Fort Myers	9035	5	4
Gainesville			
The First National Bank Of Gainesville	3894	3	2
The Florida National Bank Of Gainesville	10310	4	–
The Gainesville National Bank	8802	5	–
Graceville			
The First National Bank Of Graceville	7423	4	6
Homestead			
The First National Bank Of Homestead	13641	–	2
Jacksonville			
The Ambler National Bank Of Jacksonville	2194	–	–
The Atlantic National Bank Of Jacksonville	6888	2	1
The Barnett National Bank Of Jacksonville	9049	3	2
The First National Bank Of Florida, Jacksonville	2174	6	–
The Florida National Bank Of Jacksonville	8321	2	1
The Fourth National Bank Of Jacksonville	9628	6	–
The Heard National Bank Of Jacksonville	10136	3	–
The Merchants National Bank Of Jacksonville	4332	6	–
The National Bank Of Jacksonville	3869	6	–
The National Bank Of The State Of Florida, Jacksonville	3327	6	–
Jasper			
The First National Bank Of Jasper	7757	5	6
Key West			
The First National Bank Of Key West	4672	3	3
The Island City National Bank Of Key West	7942	6	–
Kissimmee			
The First National Bank Of Kissimmee	12871	–	–
Lake City			
The First National Bank Of Lake City	7540	6	2
Lake Hamilton			
The First National Bank Of Lake Hamilton	11703	6	–
Lake Worth			
The First National Bank Of Lake Worth	11716	6	–
Lakeland			
The First National Bank Of Lakeland	9811	5	–
The Florida National Bank At Lakeland	13370	–	2
Leesburg			
The First National Bank Of Leesburg	11038	4	4
Live Oak			
The First National Bank Of Live Oak	6055	4	3
Madison			
The First National Bank Of Madison	7190	4	–
Marianna			
The First National Bank Of Marianna	6110	5	4
Miami			
The City National Bank & Trust Company Of Miami	12868	–	–
The City National Bank Of Miami	12868	–	–
The City National Bank Of Miami	13159	–	–
The First National Bank Of Miami	6370	4	1
The Florida National Bank And Trust Company At Miami	13570	–	2
The Fort Dallas National Bank Of Miami	6774	6	–
The Miami National Bank	12011	–	–
The Third National Bank Of Miami	12887	–	–
Miami Beach			
Mercantile National Bank Of Miami Beach	13828	–	5
The Miami Beach First National Bank	12047	–	2
Milton			
First National Bank In Milton	13968	–	6
The First National Bank Of Milton	7034	5	5
Mount Dora			
The First National Bank Of Mount Dora	13102	–	–
Ocala			
The Central National Bank Of Ocala	6825	6	–
The First National Bank Of Ocala	3470	6	–
The Merchants National Bank Of Ocala	3815	6	–
The Munroe And Chambliss National Bank Of Ocala	10578	5	3
The Ocala National Bank	9926	3	3
Orlando			
First National Bank & Trust Company In Orlando	10069	6	4
First National Bank In Orlando	10069	5	–
The Citizens National Bank Of Orlando	3802	6	–
The First National Bank Of Orlando	3469	5	–
The First National Bank Of Orlando	14003	–	–
The Peoples National Bank Of Orlando	10069	6	–
Palatka			
The First National Bank Of Palatka	3223	6	–
The Palatka Atlantic National Bank	13214	–	3
The Palatka National Bank	3266	6	–
The Putnam National Bank Of Palatka	4813	5	6
Palm Beach			
The First National Bank Of Palm Beach	12275	6	–
The First National Bank Of Palm Beach	13090	–	–
The Palm Beach National Bank	12600	–	–
Panama City			
The Bay National Bank Of Panama City	14338	–	–
The First National Bank Of Panama City	10346	4	5
Pensacola			
The American National Bank Of Pensacola	5603	2	1
The Citizens & Peoples Bank Of Pensacola	9007	3	2
The Citizens National Bank Of Pensacola	4837	5	–
The First National Bank Of Pensacola	2490	2	–
The National Bank Of Commerce Of Pensacola	10535	4	–
The Peoples National Bank Of Pensacola	9007	6	–
Perry			
The First National Bank Of Perry	7865	4	6
Plant City			
The First National Bank Of Plant City	10236	6	–
Punta Gorda			
The First National Bank Of Punta Gorda	10512	5	–
Quincy			
The First National Bank Of Quincy	7253	4	–
Saint Augustine			
The First National Bank Of St. Augustine	3462	3	–
The St. Augustine National Bank	11420	4	5
Saint Cloud			
The First National Bank Of St. Cloud	9707	5	–
Saint Petersburg			
The Alexander National Bank Of St. Petersburg	12623	5	–
The Central National Bank & Trust Co Of St. Petersburg	7796	5	–
The Central National Bank Of St. Petersburg	7796	5	–
The First National Bank Of St. Petersburg	7730	4	–
The Florida National Bank Of Saint Petersburg	13498	–	–
The National Bank Of St. Petersburg	7796	6	–
Sanford			
The First National Bank Of Sanford	3798	5	–
The Sanford Atlantic National Bank	13157	–	3
Sarasota			
The American National Bank Of Sarasota	12751	6	–
The First National Bank Of Sarasota	10414	6	–
The Palmer National Bank And Trust Company Of Sarasota	13352	–	1
Seabreeze			
First Atlantic National Bank Of Daytona Beach	12546	–	3
The First National Bank Of Seabreeze	12546	–	–
Sebring			
The First National Bank Of Sebring	12090	–	–
Tallahassee			
The First National Bank Of Tallahassee	4132	5	–
Tampa			
The American National Bank Of Tampa	7153	5	–
The Exchange National Bank Of Tampa	4949	3	2
The First National Bank Of Tampa	3497	3	1
The Gulf National Bank Of Tampa	4478	6	–
The National Bank Of Commerce	12842	–	–
The National City Bank Of Tampa	10958	3	–
The Tampa National Bank	4539	6	–
Tarpon Springs			
The First National Bank Of Commerce Of Tarpon Springs	12274	–	–
The First National Bank Of Tarpon Springs	12274	6	–
The First National Bank Of Tarpon Springs	13961	–	–
Vero			
The First National Bank Of Vero	11156	6	–
Wauchula			
The Carlton National Bank Of Wauchula	10691	–	–
West Palm Beach			
The American National Bank Of West Palm Beach	12057	6	–
The First National Bank Of West Palm Beach	11073	6	–
The National Bank Of West Palm Beach	12930	–	–
The West Palm Beach Atlantic National Bank	13300	–	4
Winter Garden			
The First National Bank Of Winter Garden	11389	5	5
Winter Haven			
Exchange National Bank Of Winter Haven	13437	–	3
The American National Bank In Winter Haven	13383	–	3
The American National Bank Of Winter Haven	12100	4	6
The National Bank Of Winter Haven	12100	5	–
The Snell National Bank In Winter Haven	13437	–	3
The Snell National Bank Of Winter Haven	10379	6	6

GEORGIA

City, Bank	Ch. No.	L	S
Adel			
The First National Bank Of Adel	9777	6	–
Albany			
Albany Exchange National Bank	5512	5	3
New Georgia National Bank Of Albany	12863	5	–
The Albany National Bank	5512	6	–
The Citizens First National Bank Of Albany	3872	6	–
The Citizens National Bank Of Albany	7777	6	–
The City National Bank Of Albany	13223	4	3
The First National Bank Of Albany, Georgia	3872	6	–
The Georgia National Bank Of Albany	9729	5	–
The Third National Bank Of Albany	6336	6	–
Americus			
The Americus National Bank	8305	6	–
The First National Bank Of Americus	2009	6	–
The Peoples National Bank Of Americus	2839	6	–
Arlington			
The First National Bank Of Arlington	8314	5	6
Athens			
The Georgia National Bank Of Athens	6525	3	–
The National Bank Of Athens	1639	3	3
Atlanta			
The American National Bank Of Atlanta	9105	3	–
The Atlanta & Lowry National Bank	1559	2	4
The Atlanta National Bank	1559	2	–
The Capital City National Bank Of Atlanta	5490	6	–
The City National Bank Of Atlanta	12492	–	–
The First National Bank Of Atlanta	1559	–	1
The Fourth National Bank Of Atlanta	5045	2	4
The Fulton National Bank Of Atlanta	9617	3	3
The Gate City National Bank Of Atlanta	2424	6	–
The Georgia National Bank Of Atlanta	1605	6	–
The Lowry National Bank Of Atlanta	5318	2	–
The Ninth National Bank Of Atlanta	12249	–	–
The State National Bank Of Atlanta	2064	6	–
The Third National Bank Of Atlanta	5030	3	–
Augusta			
The Merchants And Planters National Bank Of Augusta	1703	6	–
The National Bank Of Augusta	1613	4	–
The National Exchange Bank Of Augusta	1860	2	3
Ava			
The First National Bank Of Ava	10911	–	5
Bainbridge			
First National Bank Of Bainbridge	6004	4	4
First State Bank Of Bainbridge	6004	–	–
The First National Bank Of Bainbridge	6004	4	–
Barnesville			
The Citizens National Bank Of Barnesville	12404	6	6
The First National Bank Of Barnesville	6243	4	5
Blakely			
The First National Bank Of Blakely	7018	5	4
Blue Ridge			
The North Georgia National Bank Of Blue Ridge	6079	5	–
Brunswick			
The National Bank Of Brunswick	4944	2	3
The Oglethorpe National Bank Of Brunswick	3753	6	–
Buena Vista			
First National Bank Of Buena Vista	7963	6	–
Byromville			
The Byrom National Bank Of Byromville	9607	6	–
Calhoun			
The Calhoun National Bank	7549	6	5
Carrollton			
The First National Bank Of Carrollton	5264	4	6
Cartersville			
The Cartersville National Bank	12635	4	–
The First National Bank Of Cartersville	4012	5	3
Cedartown			
The First National Bank Of Cedartown	4075	6	–
The Liberty National Bank Of Cedartown	11833	6	3
Claxton			
The Claxton National Bank	14243	–	–
The First National Bank Of Claxton	10333	6	6
Cochran			
The First National Bank Of Cochran	7567	6	–
Colquitt			
The Colquitt National Bank, Colquitt	9254	6	–
The First National Bank Of Colquitt	6498	6	–
Columbus			
The Chattahoochee National Bank Of Columbus	1630	6	–
The First National Bank Of Columbus	2338	3	4
The Fourth National Bank Of Columbus	4691	4	4
The National Bank Of Columbus	2338	3	–
The Third National Bank Of Columbus	3937	4	–
Commerce			
The First National Bank Of Commerce	7431	5	5
Conyers			
The First National Bank Of Conyers	11255	6	–
Cordele			
The American National Bank Of Cordele	9074	6	–
The Cordele National Bank	5975	4	–
The First National Bank In Cordele	14257	–	6
The First National Bank Of Cordele	4554	6	–
Cornelia			
The First National Bank Of Cornelia	9613	4	4
Covington			
The First National Bank Of Covington	8945	6	–
Cuthbert			
The First National Bank Of Cuthbert	10279	6	–
Dallas			
The First National Bank Of Dallas	12105	–	–
Dalton			
The First National Bank Of Dalton	3907	4	4
Dawson			
The City National Bank Of Dawson	6496	4	5
The Dawson City National Bank, Dawson	6496	–	–
The Dawson National Bank	4115	4	4
Douglasville			
The First National Bank Of Douglasville	13227	–	–
Dublin			
The City National Bank Of Dublin	8128	6	–
The First National Bank Of Dublin	6374	3	–
East Point			
The First National Bank Of East Point	10756	–	–
Eastman			
The First National Bank Of Eastman	9593	6	–
Elberton			
The First National Bank In Elberton	14061	–	6
The First National Bank Of Elberton	9252	3	3
Fitzgerald			
Ben Hill National Bank Of Fitzgerald	8966	–	–
The Exchange National Bank Of Fitzgerald	8250	4	6
The First National Bank Of Fitzgerald	6082	3	6
The National Bank Of Fitzgerald	13550	–	6
The Third National Bank Of Fitzgerald	8966	6	–
Forsyth			
The First National Bank Of Forsyth	5644	6	–
Fort Gaines			
The First National Bank Of Fort Gaines	6002	6	6
Fort Valley			
The First National Bank Of Fort Valley	7459	6	–
Gainesville			
The First National Bank Of Gainesville	3983	5	3
The Gainesville National Bank	7616	4	5
Greensboro			
Greensboro National Bank	6967	4	–
The Copelan National Bank Of Greensboro	8452	5	–
The First National Bank Of Greensboro	6967	–	–
Griffin			
The City National Bank Of Griffin	2075	5	–
The First National Bank Of Griffin	2075	6	6
The Second National Bank Of Griffin	11597	4	–
Hampton			
The First National Bank Of Hampton	10089	6	–
Hartwell			
The First National Bank Of Hartwell	11695	4	5
Hawkinsville			
The First National Bank Of Hawkinsville	7580	5	–
Jackson			
Jackson National Bank	13897	–	3
The First National Bank Of Jackson	5709	6	–
The Jackson National Bank	9186	4	5
Jefferson			
The First National Bank Of Jefferson	9039	3	4
La Fayette			
The First National Bank Of La Fayette	7247	6	–
La Grange			
The First National Bank Of La Grange	3093	6	–
The La Grange National Bank	7762	3	3
Lavonia			
The First National Bank Of Lavonia	8470	4	3
The Vickery National Bank Of Lavonia	8470	6	–
Lawrenceville			
First National Bank Of Lawrenceville	11936	–	5

City, Bank	Ch. No.	L	S
Louisville			
The First National Bank Of Louisville	6207	5	6
Lumpkin			
The National Bank Of Lumpkin	12254	–	–
Lyons			
First National Bank Of Lyons	7979	6	–
Macon			
The American National Bank Of Macon	4547	4	–
The Bibb National Bank Of Macon	10945	5	–
The Citizens National Bank Of Macon	8990	5	–
The Commercial National Bank Of Macon	9212	5	–
The First National Bank & Trust Company In Macon	10270	–	3
The First National Bank Of Macon	1617	5	–
The Fourth National Bank Of Macon	8365	4	–
The Macon National Bank	10270	4	5
The Merchants National Bank Of Macon	3740	6	–
Madison			
The First National Bank Of Madison	7300	4	3
Marietta			
The Citizens National Bank Of Marietta	12232	–	–
The Citizens National Bank Of Marietta	13469	–	–
The First National Bank Of Marietta	3830	4	5
Maysville			
The Atkins National Bank Of Maysville	7986	6	–
Mcdonough			
First National Bank Of Mcdonough	7969	4	5
Milledgeville			
The First National Bank Of Milledgeville	9672	3	4
Millen			
The First National Bank Of Millen	9088	6	6
Monroe			
The National Bank Of Monroe	14046	–	–
Montezuma			
The Citizens National Bank Of Montezuma	11939	–	–
The First National Bank Of Montezuma	6576	6	–
Monticello			
The Farmers National Bank Of Monticello	9329	4	4
The First National Bank Of Monticello	9346	4	3
Moultrie			
Moultrie National Bank	13161	–	–
Moultrie National Bank, Moultrie	13161	–	4
The First National Bank Of Moultrie	7565	6	–
Nashville			
The First National Bank Of Nashville	9106	6	–
New Brunswick			
The First National Bank Of New Brunswick	3116	6	–
Newnan			
The Coweta National Bank Of Newnan	6047	6	–
The First National Bank Of Newnan	1861	3	4
The Manufacturers National Bank Of Newnan	8477	6	6
The Newnan National Bank	3382	6	–
Ocilla			
The First National Bank Of Ocilla	8580	6	4
Pelham			
The First National Bank Of Pelham	9870	6	5
Pembroke			
The Pembroke National Bank	8680	4	6
Quitman			
Peoples-First National Bank Of Quitman	7994	–	5
The Citizens National Bank Of Quitman	14255	–	–
The First National Bank Of Quitman	7994	3	5
The Peoples National Bank Of Quitman	11290	6	6
Reynolds			
The First National Bank Of Reynolds	9615	6	2
Rockmart			
The Citizens National Bank Of Rockmart	8628	6	–
The Farmers And Merchants National Bank Of Rockmart	10900	–	–
Rome			
The Cherokee National Bank Of Rome	9636	6	–
The Exchange National Bank Of Rome	10303	4	–
The First National Bank Of Rome	2368	4	5
The Merchants National Bank Of Rome	3670	5	–
The National City Bank Of Rome	10302	4	3
The Rome National Bank	4369	6	–
Sandersville			
The Cohen National Bank Of Sandersville	9641	6	–
The First National Bank Of Sandersville	7934	4	–
The George D Warthen National Bank Of Sandersville	13725	–	4
Savannah			
The Citizens And Southern National Bank, Savannah	13068	–	1
The City National Bank Of Savannah	1586	–	–
The Liberty National Bank And Trust Company Of Savannah	13472	–	4
The Mercantile National Bank Of Savannah	12030	–	–
The Merchants National Bank Of Savannah	1640	4	–
The National Bank Of Savannah	3406	4	–
The Savannah National Bank	1255	6	–
Senoia			
The First National Bank Of Senoia	8527	6	–
Shellman			
The First National Bank Of Shellman	8417	6	6
Sparta			
The First National Bank Of Sparta	7067	6	–
The Hancock National Bank Of Sparta	12317	4	6
Statesboro			
The First National Bank Of Statesboro	7468	5	6
Sylvania			
The National Bank Of Sylvania	10829	6	6
Sylvester			
The First National Bank Of Sylvester	6180	6	–
Tallapoosa			
The First National Bank Of Tallapoosa	7220	6	–
Thomasville			
The First National Bank Of Thomasville	3767	6	6
The Thomasville National Bank	3767	6	–
Thomson			
The First National Bank Of Thomson	9302	5	5
Tifton			
The First National Bank Of Tifton	6542	6	–
The National Bank Of Tifton	8350	4	4
Toccoa			
The First National Bank Of Toccoa	6687	6	–
Union Point			
The National Bank Of Union Point	7330	6	–
Valdosta			
The First National Bank Of Valdosta	4429	4	4
Vidalia			
The First National Bank Of Vidalia	9879	5	6
Vienna			
The First National Bank Of Vienna	9618	5	–
Washington			
The Citizens National Bank Of Washington	8894	5	–
The National Bank Of Wilkes At Washington	8848	4	6
Waycross			
The First National Bank Of Waycross	4963	5	5
The First National Bank Of Waycross	14193	–	–
Waynesboro			
The First National Bank Of Waynesboro	7899	6	4
West Point			
The First National Bank Of West Point	8046	5	–
Winder			
The First National Bank Of Winder	9051	6	–
Winder National Bank	10805	4	4
Wrightsville			
The First National Bank Of Wrightsville	8023	6	–

HAWAII

City, Bank	Ch. No.	L	S
Honolulu			
Bishop First National Bank Of Honolulu	5550	–	1
Bishop National Bank Of Hawaii At Honolulu	5550	–	2
The Army National Bank Of Schofield Barracks	11050	–	–
The First National Bank Of Hawaii	5550	1	–
Kahului			
The Baldwin National Bank Of Kahului	8207	5	–
Lahaina			
The Lahaina National Bank	8101	6	–
Paia			
The First National Bank Of Paia	10451	6	–
Wailuku			
The First National Bank Of Wailuku	5994	6	–

IDAHO TERRITORY

City, Bank	Ch. No.	L	S
Boise City			
The Boise City National Bank	3471	6	–
The First National Bank Of Idaho, Boise City	1668	6	–
Hailey			
The First National Bank Of Hailey	3895	6	–
Ketchum			
The First National Bank Of Ketchum	3142	6	–
Lewiston			
The First National Bank Of Lewiston	2972	6	–
The Lewiston National Bank	3023	6	–
Moscow			
The First National Bank Of Moscow	3408	6	–
Pocatello			
The First National Bank Of Pacatello	4023	6	–

IDAHO

City, Bank	Ch. No.	L	S
American Falls			
The First National Bank Of American Falls	8869	5	–
Arco			
The First National Bank Of Arco	11794	–	–
Ashton			
The First National Bank Of Ashton	10269	5	–
Bancroft			
The First National Bank Of Bancroft	11183	–	–
Blackfoot			
The First National Bank Of Blackfoot	7419	4	4
Boise			
The Idaho National Bank Of Boise	8346	4	–
The Overland National Bank Of Boise	10751	5	–
The Pacific National Bank Of Boise	10083	3	–
Boise City			
The Boise City National Bank	3471	3	2
The First National Bank Of Idaho, Boise City	1668	3	2
Bonners Ferry			
The First National Bank Of Bonners Ferry	10727	5	3
Buhl			
The Farmers National Bank Of Buhl	11076	–	–
The First National Bank Of Buhl	11065	6	–
Burley			
The Burley National Bank	11438	–	–
The Cassia National Bank Of Burley	12256	–	5
The First National Bank Of Burley	10341	5	–
Caldwell			
The American National Bank Of Caldwell	9333	6	–
The First National Bank Of Caldwell	4690	4	4
The Western National Bank Of Caldwell	8225	3	–
Challis			
The First National Bank Of Challis	9477	6	–
Coeur D' Alene			
First National Bank In Coeur D' Alene	13288	–	3
The First National Bank Of Coeur D' Alene	6793	6	–
Coeur D'Alene			
The Exchange National Bank Of Coeur D' Alene	7120	6	–
The First Exchange National Bank Of Coeur D'Alene	7120	5	–
Cottonwood			
The First National Bank Of Cottonwood	7923	6	4
Driggs			
The First National Bank Of Driggs	10278	4	–
The First National Bank Of Driggs	13267	–	–
The Teton National Bank Of Driggs	11471	–	–
Dubois			
The First National Bank Of Dubois	11508	6	–
Emmett			
The First National Bank Of Emmett	6145	5	–
Fairfield			
The First National Bank Of Fairfield	10162	6	–
The Security National Bank Of Fairfield	11884	–	–
Filer			
The Fidelity National Bank Of Twin Falls	11100	–	–
The First National Bank Of Filer	11100	–	–
Firth			
The First National Bank Of Firth	11198	6	–
Genessee			
The First National Bank Of Genessee	4808	6	–
Gooding			
The First National Bank Of Gooding	9371	4	–
Grace			
The First National Bank Of Grace	11179	–	–
Grangeville			
The First National Bank Of Grangeville	6927	5	4
Hagerman			
The First National Bank Of Hagerman	10294	6	–
Hailey			
The Blaine County National Bank Of Hailey	11053	5	–
The First National Bank Of Hailey	3895	6	–
The First National Bank Of Hailey	12832	–	–
The Hailey National Bank	9145	5	6
Idaho Falls			
American National Bank Of Idaho Falls	6982	4	3
The First National Bank Of Idaho Falls	5820	6	–
The Idaho Falls National Bank	11278	4	–
Jerome			
The City National Bank Of Jerome	11578	–	–
The First National Bank Of Jerome	9680	4	–
The Jerome National Bank	11135	–	–
Kellogg			
The First National Bank Of Kellogg	9566	6	6
Kendrick			
The First National Bank Of Kendrick	4790	6	–
Kimberly			
The Farmers And Merchants National Bank Of Kimberly	10969	–	–
Lewiston			
Lewiston National Bank	13819	–	4
The American National Bank Of Lewiston	11745	5	–
The Empire National Bank Of Lewiston	10212	5	–
The First National Bank Of Lewiston	2972	4	3
The Idaho National Bank Of Lewiston	5600	6	–
The Lewiston National Bank	3023	4	4
Mackay			
The First National Bank Of Mackay	11636	–	–
Malad City			
The First National Bank Of Malad City	8822	4	4
Meridian			
The First National Bank Of Meridian	10221	6	–
Minidoka			
The First National Bank Of Minidoka	11736	–	–
Montpelier			
The First National Bank Of Montpelier	7381	5	–
Moscow			
The First National Bank Of Moscow	3408	6	4
The Moscow National Bank	4584	6	–
Mountain Home			
The First National Bank Of Mountain Home	6521	5	–
Mullan			
The First National Bank Of Mullan	8906	6	5
Nampa			
The Citizens National Bank Of Nampa	10693	6	–
The Farmers And Merchants National Bank Of Nampa	10916	5	–
The First National Bank Of Nampa	8370	5	–
The Nampa National Bank	11821	–	–
The Stockmens National Bank Of Nampa	11609	–	–
Newdale			
The First National Bank Of Newdale	10975	6	–
Nezperce			
The First National Bank Of Nezperce	6697	6	–
Parma			
The First National Bank Of Parma	11496	4	5
The Parma National Bank	11556	–	–
Payette			
The First National Bank Of Payette	5906	4	–
The Payette National Bank	8075	5	–
Pocatello			
The Bannock National Bank Of Pocatello	6347	6	–
The First National Bank Of Pocatello	4023	6	–
The Idaho National Bank Of Pocatello	4827	6	–
The National Bank Of Idaho	11721	–	–
Preston			
The First National Bank Of Preston	7526	4	6
Rexburg			
The First National Bank Of Rexburg	7133	3	–
Rigby			
The First National Bank Of Rigby	11385	–	–
The Jefferson County National Bank Of Rigby	11458	6	–
Ririe			
First National Bank Of Ririe	10920	6	–
Roberts			
The First National Bank Of Roberts	11600	–	–
The Rigby National Bank Of Rigby	11600	–	–
Rupert			
The First National Bank Of Rupert	10429	6	–
The Rupert National Bank	10517	6	–
Saint Anthony			
The Commercial National Bank Of Saint Anthony	7230	6	4
The First National Bank Of Saint Anthony	5764	4	–
Saint Maries			
The First National Bank Of Saint Maries	10771	5	6
Salmon			
The Citizens National Bank Of Salmon	9432	4	4
The First National Bank Of Salmon	8080	6	–
Sandpoint			
The Bonner County National Bank Of Sandpoint	9263	5	4
The First National Bank Of Sandpoint	8341	5	4
Shelley			
The First National Bank Of Shelley	11434	6	–
Shoshone			
The First National Bank Of Shoshone	6577	6	–
The Lincoln County National Bank Of Shoshone	9272	5	5
Soldier			
The First National Bank Of Soldier	10162	6	–

City, Bank	Ch. No.	L	S
Twin Falls			
The First National Bank Of Twin Falls	7608	5	–
The Twin Falls National Bank	11274	6	6
Wallace			
The First National Bank Of Wallace	4773	4	3
The Wallace National Bank	9134	6	–
Weiser			
The First National Bank Of Weiser	6754	4	–
The Weiser National Bank	8139	5	–
Wendell			
The First National Bank Of Wendell	9491	6	–
The Wendell National Bank	12432	–	–
Wilder			
The First National Bank Of Wilder	10909	–	–

ILLINOIS

City, Bank	Ch. No.	L	S
Abingdon			
The First National Bank Of Abingdon	3377	4	–
Albany			
The First National Bank Of Albany	6089	6	–
Albion			
The Albion National Bank	9025	6	6
The First National Bank Of Albion	8429	4	6
The National Bank Of Albion	13449	–	–
Aledo			
The Farmers National Bank Of Aledo	9649	6	4
The First National Bank Of Aledo	7145	4	–
The National Bank Of Aledo	14331	–	–
Alexis			
The First National Bank Of Alexis	4967	6	6
Allendale			
The Farmers National Bank Of Allendale	10318	6	–
The First National Bank Of Allendale	8293	5	4
Altamont			
The First National Bank In Altamont	13993	–	6
The First National Bank Of Altamont	8733	6	5
Alton			
The Alton National Bank	1428	1	6
The Citizens National Bank Of Alton	5188	3	5
The First National Bank And Trust Company Of Alton	13464	–	–
The First National Bank Of Alton	1445	5	–
Altona			
The Altona National Bank	13625	–	4
The First National Bank Of Altona	11331	5	5
Amboy			
The First National Bank Of Amboy	5223	3	5
The First National Bank Of Amboy	14244	–	–
Anna			
The Anna National Bank	5525	6	5
The First National Bank Of Anna	4449	3	5
Annapolis			
The First National Bank Of Annapolis	10257	5	5
Antioch			
The First National Bank Of Antioch	12870	–	–
Arcola			
The First National Bank Of Arcola	2204	5	4
Arenzville			
The First National Bank Of Arenzville	9183	4	3
Arthur			
The First National Bank Of Arthur	5233	4	4
Assumption			
The First National Bank Of Assumption	5316	4	4
Atlanta			
The Atlanta National Bank	3711	5	4
The First National Bank Of Atlanta	2283	5	–
Atwood			
The First National Bank Of Atwood	6359	6	5
Augusta			
The First National Bank Of Augusta	6751	4	6
Aurora			
The American National Bank Of Aurora	4469	4	5
The Aurora National Bank	2945	4	3
The Aurora National Bank	14161	–	–
The First National Bank In Aurora	13565	–	5
The First National Bank Of Aurora	38	3	3
The German American National Bank Of Aurora	4469	5	–
The Merchants National Bank Of Aurora	3854	2	3
The Old Second National Bank Of Aurora	4596	2	2
The Second National Bank Of Aurora	1909	5	–
The Union National Bank Of Aurora	1792	5	–
Austin			
The Austin National Bank, Austin	10337	6	–
Ava			
The First National Bank Of Ava	10911	–	4
Barrington			
The First National Bank Of Barrington	11283	4	4
Barry			
The First National Bank Of Barry	5771	3	5
Batavia			
The Batavia National Bank	9500	4	3
The First National Bank Of Batavia	339	5	–
The First National Bank Of Batavia	4646	4	4
Beardstown			
The First National Bank Of Beardstown	3640	3	3
Beason			
The First National Bank Of Beason	10572	–	–
Beecher			
The First National Bank Of Beecher	7726	6	–
Belleville			
The Belleville National Bank	13236	–	3
The First National Bank Of Belleville	2154	3	4
The St. Clair National Bank Of Belleville	11478	5	3
Belvidere			
The First National Bank Of Belvidere	1097	4	5
The Second National Bank Of Belvidere	3190	5	3
Bement			
The First National Bank Of Bement	4829	6	–
Benld			
The First National Bank Of Benld	7728	6	5
The National Bank Of Benld	7728	6	–
Benton			
The Coal Belt National Bank Of Benton	8234	6	–
The First National Bank Of Benton	6136	4	5
Berwyn			
The First American National Bank & Trust Co. Of Berwyn	12426	–	6
The First National Bank Of Berwyn	12426	5	5
Biggsville			
The First National Bank Of Biggsville	3003	4	–
Blandinsville			
The First National Bank In Blandinsville	13597	–	6
The First National Bank Of Blandinsville	8908	6	6
Bloomington			
The First National Bank & Trust Company Of Bloomington	13499	–	–
The First National Bank And Trust Company, Bloomington	13499	–	–
The First National Bank Of Bloomington	819	4	4
The National Bank Of Bloomington	819	6	–
The National Bank Of Bloomington	14178	–	–
The National State Bank Of Bloomington	2386	6	–
The State National Bank Of Bloomington	5119	6	–
The Third National Bank Of Bloomington	2676	6	–
Blue Island			
The First National Bank Of Blue Island	12779	–	–
Blue Mound			
The First National Bank Of Blue Mound	9530	6	–
Bowmanville			
The Bowmanville National Bank, Bowmanville	10237	6	–
Braidwood			
First National Bank In Braidwood	11895	6	–
The Miners National Bank Of Braidwood	1964	5	–
Breese			
The First National Bank Of Breese	9893	5	4
Bridgeport			
The First National Bank Of Bridgeport	8347	6	3
Brighton			
The First National Bank Of Brighton	9397	4	4
Brookport			
The Brookport National Bank	6713	6	4
Brownstown			
The First National Bank Of Brownstown	10397	6	6
Bunker Hill			
The First National Bank Of Bunker Hill	10516	–	–
Bushnell			
The Farmers National Bank Of Bushnell	1791	6	–
The First National Bank Of Bushnell	4709	3	4
Cairo			
The Alexander County National Bank Of Cairo	3735	4	–
The Cairo National Bank	6815	4	–
The City National Bank Of Cairo	785	6	–
The First National Bank Of Cairo	33	6	–
The Security National Bank Of Cairo	13804	–	4
Caledonia			
The Caledonia National Bank	10567	6	5
Cambridge			
The Farmers National Bank Of Cambridge	2572	4	4
The First National Bank Of Cambridge	2540	4	4
The Peoples National Bank Of Cambridge	14237	–	–
Canton			
The Canton National Bank	3593	4	4
The First National Bank Of Canton	415	4	4
The National Bank Of Canton	13838	–	–
Carbondale			
First National Bank In Carbondale	12596	5	4
The Carbondale National Bank	7598	5	4
The First National Bank Of Carbondale	4904	4	–
Carlinville			
The Carlinville National Bank	4299	6	5
The Farmers And Merchants National Bank Of Carlinville	13966	–	–
The First National Bank Of Carlinville	2042	6	–
Carlyle			
The First National Bank Of Carlyle	5548	4	4
The First National Bank Of Carlyle	14268	–	–
Carmi			
The First National Bank Of Carmi	4934	3	3
The National Bank Of Carmi	5357	4	3
Carrier Mills			
The First National Bank Of Carrier Mills	8015	5	5
Carrollton			
The Greene County National Bank Of Carrollton	2390	2	–
The Greene County National Bank Of Carrollton	14347	–	–
Carterville			
The First National Bank Of Carterville	7889	5	4
Carthage			
The First National Bank Of Carthage	14134	–	–
The Hancock County National Bank Of Carthage	1167	3	5
Casey			
The Casey National Bank	8043	5	6
The First National Bank In Casey	13673	–	6
The First National Bank Of Casey	6026	5	4
Catlin			
The First National Bank Of Catlin	7276	6	5
Centralia			
The Centralia National Bank	11904	5	–
The City National Bank Of Centralia	11923	6	4
The First National Bank Of Centralia	1001	6	–
The Old National Bank Of Centralia	3303	5	5
Chadwick			
The First National Bank Of Chadwick	5619	4	4
Champaign			
The Champaign National Bank	2829	5	5
The First National Bank Of Champaign	913	5	4
The First National Bank Of Champaign	13630	–	–
Charleston			
The Charleston National Bank	14024	–	5
The First National Bank Of Charleston	763	3	6
The National Trust Bank Of Charleston	11358	4	4
The Second National Bank Of Charleston	1851	4	–
Chatsworth			
The Commercial National Bank Of Chatsworth	5519	4	6
Chester			
The First National Bank Of Chester	4187	6	–
Chicago			
Addison National Bank Of Chicago	13119	4	–
Albany Park National Bank & Trust Company Of Chicago	11737	6	4
Alliance National Bank Of Chicago	12001	3	3
American National Bank & Trust Company Of Chicago	13216	–	3
Chicago National Bank And Trust Company	13639	–	–
Columbia National Bank Of Chicago	3677	6	–
Continental National Bank & Trust Company Of Chicago	2894	–	–
Inland-Irving National Bank Of Chicago	10179	–	6
Inland-Irving National Bank Of Chicago	10179	–	5
Jackson Park National Bank Of Chicago	12391	4	5
Liberty National Bank Of Chicago	14246	–	3
National Builders Bank Of Chicago	13146	3	3
South Ashland National Bank Of Chicago	13253	–	–
Straus National Bank And Trust Company Of Chicago	13216	–	3
The Albany Park National Bank Of Chicago	11737	4	–
The American Exchange National Bank Of Chicago	3500	6	–
The American National Bank Of Chicago	5111	6	–
The Ashland-69th National Bank Of Chicago	13253	–	–
The Atlas Exchange National Bank Of Chicago	10763	5	–
The Atlas National Bank Of Chicago	3503	5	–
The Austin National Bank Of Chicago	10337	3	6
The Bankers National Bank Of Chicago	4787	3	–
The Bowmanville National Bank Of Chicago	10237	6	4
The Broadway National Bank Of Chicago	12323	–	–
The Calumet National Bank Of Chicago	3102	4	5
The Central National Bank Of Chicago	2047	5	–
The Chemical National Bank Of Chicago	4666	6	–
The Chicago Heights National Bank Of Chicago	14343	–	–
The Chicago National Bank	2601	5	–
The City National Bank And Trust Company Of Chicago	13638	–	–
The City National Bank Of Chicago	818	6	–
The Commercial National Bank Of Chicago	713	3	–
The Continental And Commercial National Bank Of Chicago	2894	1	–
The Continental National Bank Of Chicago	2894	2	–
The Cook County National Bank Of Chicago	1845	6	–
The Corn Exchange National Bank Of Chicago	1709	5	–
The Corn Exchange National Bank Of Chicago	3036	–	–
The Corn Exchange National Bank Of Chicago	5106	2	–
The District National Bank Of Chicago	14110	–	4
The Douglass National Bank Of Chicago	12227	2	4
The Drovers Deposit National Bank Of Chicago	6535	5	–
The Drovers National Bank Of Chicago	6535	6	2
The Federal National Bank Of Chicago	7926	5	–
The Fifth National Bank Of Chicago	320	5	–
The First National Bank Of Chicago	8	6	–
The First National Bank Of Chicago	8	2	–
The First National Bank Of Chicago	2670	2	–
The First National Bank Of Englewood	4073	5	–
The First National Bank Of Englewood, Chicago	4073	6	–
The Foreman National Bank Of Chicago	12403	–	–
The Foreman-State National Bank, Chicago	12403	–	–
The Fort Dearborn National Bank Of Chicago	3698	3	–
The Fourth National Bank Of Chicago	276	5	–
The German National Bank Of Chicago	1734	6	–
The Globe National Bank Of Chicago	4489	6	–
The Guardian National Bank Of Chicago	12615	–	–
The Halsted Exchange National Bank Of Chicago	12945	–	5
The Hamilton National Bank Of Chicago	6723	5	–
The Hide And Leather National Bank Of Chicago	2450	6	–
The Home National Bank Of Chicago	2048	5	–
The Hyde Park National Bank Of Chicago	13235	–	–
The Hyde Park-Kenwood National Bank Of Chicago	13235	–	–
The Kenwood National Bank Of Chicago	11999	4	–
The La Salle Street National Bank Of Chicago	9750	5	–
The Lawndale National Bank Of Chicago	10247	3	2
The Lawrence Avenue National Bank Of Chicago	12873	5	6
The Lincoln National Bank Of Chicago	3647	6	–
The Live Stock Exchange National Bank Of Chicago	9010	4	–
The Live Stock National Bank Of Chicago	13674	–	2
The Manufacturers National Bank Of Chicago	724	6	–
The Mechanics National Bank Of Chicago	466	6	–
The Merchants National Bank Of Chicago	642	6	–
The Merchants National Bank Of Chicago	14313	–	–
The Metropolitan National Bank Of Chicago	3179	6	–
The Mid-City National Bank Of Chicago	13684	–	3
The Midland National Bank Of Chicago	13036	–	–
The Milwaukee Avenue National Bank Of Chicago	14245	–	4
The Monroe National Bank Of Chicago	8121	5	–
The Mutual National Bank Of Chicago	11092	3	3
The National Bank Of America, Chicago	2826	6	–
The National Bank Of Commerce In Chicago	8842	5	–
The National Bank Of Commerce Of Chicago	1693	6	–
The National Bank Of Illinois, Chicago	1867	4	–
The National Bank Of North American, Chicago	6290	5	–
The National Bank Of The Republic Of Chicago	4605	1	1
The National Bank Of Woodlawn	11980	–	–
The National Boulevard Bank Of Chicago	13672	–	–
The National City Bank Of Chicago	8532	3	–
The National Live Stock Bank Of Chicago	3847	6	–
The National Produce Bank Of Chicago	8842	4	–
The National Security Bank Of Chicago	13691	–	–
The Northwestern National Bank Of Chicago	508	5	–
The Oakland National Bank, Hyde Park	3916	5	–
The Ogden National Bank Of Chicago	12480	–	–
The Park National Bank Of Chicago	3502	6	–
The Peoples National Bank And Trust Company Of Chicago	13311	–	–
The Portage Park National Bank Of Chicago	12285	5	4
The Prairie National Bank Of Chicago	7358	5	–
The Prairie State National Bank Of Chicago	3882	6	–
The Rogers Park National Bank, Rogers Park	10305	5	6
The Roseland National Bank Of Chicago	12605	5	5
The Scandinavian National Bank Of Chicago	1978	6	–
The Second National Bank Of Chicago	225	6	–

City, Bank	Ch. No.	L	S
The South East National Bank Of Chicago	14327	–	–
The Standard National Bank Of Chicago	13372	–	–
The Stock Yards National Bank Of Chicago	12493	–	–
The Terminal National Bank Of Chicago	13382	–	–
The Terminal National Bank Of Chicago	13659	–	–
The Terminus National Bank Of Chicago	13659	–	–
The Third National Bank Of Chicago	236	4	–
The Traders National Bank Of Chicago	966	6	–
The Union National Bank Of Chicago	698	5	–
The Union National Bank Of Chicago	3278	6	–
The Union Stock Yards National Bank Of Chicago, Lake	1678	6	–
The United States National Bank Of Chicago	3677	6	–
The Washington Park National Bank Of Chicago	3916	4	4
The West Englewood National Bank Of Chicago	12004	6	–
The West Side National Bank Of Chicago	11009	4	5
The West Side-Atlas National Bank Of Chicago	11009	–	5
Chicago Heights			
The Citizens National Bank Of Chicago Heights	13373	–	5
The First National Bank & Trust Company Of Chicago Heights	5876	6	5
The First National Bank Of Chicago Heights	5876	4	–
Chillicothe			
The First National Bank Of Chillicothe	5584	4	4
Chrisman			
The First National Bank Of Chrisman	7111	5	5
Christopher			
The First National Bank Of Christopher	8260	6	4
Cicero			
First National Bank Of Cicero	11662	3	4
Clifton			
The First National Bank Of Clifton	6318	6	4
Clinton			
The Dewitt County National Bank Of Clinton	1926	3	5
Coal City			
The First National Bank Of Coal City	10132	6	6
Cobden			
The First National Bank Of Cobden	5630	5	5
Coffeen			
The Coffeen National Bank	7579	5	6
Colchester			
The National Bank Of Colchester	8485	4	6
Collinsville			
The First National Bank Of Collinsville	6125	4	3
Columbia			
The First National Bank In Columbia	13805	–	3
The First National Bank Of Columbia	7717	5	4
Compton			
The First National Bank Of Compton	7031	6	5
Coulterville			
The First National Bank Of Coulterville	12000	4	3
Cowden			
The First National Bank Of Cowden	9700	6	–
Crescent City			
The First National Bank Of Crescent City	6598	4	6
Crossville			
The First National Bank Of Crossville	8801	5	4
Cuba			
The First National Bank Of Cuba	11144	5	6
Cullom			
The First National Bank Of Cullom	8684	5	4
Dahgren			
The Farmers National Bank Of Dahgren	13451	–	–
Dahlgren			
The First National Bank Of Dahlgren	7750	6	–
Dallas City			
The First National Bank Of Dallas City	5609	3	4
Danvers			
The First National Bank Of Danvers	6740	6	5
Danville			
The Danville National Bank	5812	4	–
The First National Bank Of Danville	113	4	3
The Palmer National Bank Of Danville	4731	4	4
The Palmer-American National Bank Of Danville	4731	–	6
The Second National Bank Of Danville	2584	3	3
De Kalb			
First National Bank In De Kalb	14008	–	5
The De Kalb National Bank	2702	5	–
The First National Bank Of De Kalb	2702	5	4
Decatur			
The Citizens National Bank Of Decatur	4576	3	4
The Decatur National Bank	2124	5	–
The First National Bank Of Decatur	477	6	–
The Millikin National Bank Of Decatur	5089	2	2
The National Bank Of Decatur	4920	3	3
Deland			
The First National Bank Of Deland	5699	4	4
Delavan			
The Tazewell County National Bank Of Delavan	3781	3	4
Des Plaines			
The First National Bank Of Des Plaines	10319	4	5
Dieterich			
The First National Bank Of Dieterich	9582	4	4
Divernon			
The First National Bank Of Divernon	10296	5	–
Dixon			
The City National Bank In Dixon	13856	–	4
The City National Bank Of Dixon	3294	5	4
The Dixon National Bank	1881	4	4
The Lee County National Bank Of Dixon	902	6	–
Dolton			
The First National Bank Of Dolton	8679	5	4
The First National Bank Of Dolton	14319	–	–
Dongola			
The First National Bank Of Dongola	10086	6	–
Downers Grove			
The First National Bank Of Downers Grove	9725	5	6
The Security National Bank Of Downers Grove	13258	–	–
Dundee			
The First National Bank Of Dundee	5638	4	4
Duquoin			
The First National Bank Of Duquoin	4737	5	4

City, Bank	Ch. No.	L	S
Dwight			
The First National Bank Of Dwight	8044	5	3
Earlville			
The Earlville National Bank	7555	5	–
The First National Bank Of Earlville	3323	4	4
East Peoria			
First National Bank Of East Peoria	6724	5	5
The First National Bank In East Peoria	14010	–	6
East Saint Louis			
First National Bank In East St. Louis	11596	4	3
The City National Bank Of East St. Louis	8932	6	–
The Drovers National Bank Of East St. Louis	10399	4	–
The First National Bank Of East St. Louis	4328	4	–
The First National Bank Of East St. Louis	14127	–	–
The Security National Bank Of East St. Louis	12178	5	–
The Southern Illinois National Bank Of East St. Louis	5070	3	4
Edwardsville			
The Edwardsville National Bank	11039	4	–
The Edwardsville National Bank & Trust Company	11039	–	2
The First National Bank Of Edwardsville	5062	3	–
Effingham			
The First National Bank Of Effingham	4233	4	5
El Paso			
The El Paso National Bank	13631	–	–
The First National Bank Of El Paso	2997	4	–
The National Bank Of El Paso	2997	6	–
The Woodford County National Bank Of El Paso	5510	4	–
Eldorado			
The First National Bank Of Eldorado	7539	4	–
Elgin			
The Elgin National Bank	4735	5	5
The First National Bank Of Elgin	1365	4	5
The Home National Bank Of Elgin	2016	3	5
The Union National Bank Of Elgin	7236	3	4
Elmhurst			
The First National Bank Of Elmhurst	9836	4	5
Enfield			
The First National Bank Of Enfield	7948	4	4
Equality			
The First National Bank Of Equality	6978	5	–
Erie			
The First National Bank Of Erie	6951	4	5
Eureka			
The First National Bank Of Eureka	10591	–	–
Evanston			
City National Bank & Trust Company Of Evanston	5279	6	3
First National Bank And Trust Company Of Evanston	13709	–	6
The City National Bank Of Evanston	5279	5	–
The Evanston National Bank	4767	6	–
Fairbury			
The First National Bank Of Fairbury	1987	6	–
Fairfield			
The Fairfield National Bank	6609	3	2
The First National Bank Of Fairfield	5009	4	5
Fairmount			
The First National Bank Of Fairmount	11443	6	5
Farmer City			
The First National Bank Of Farmer City	2156	4	–
The John Weedman National Bank Of Farmer City	3407	4	5
The Old First National Bank Of Farmer City	4958	4	6
Farmersville			
The First National Bank Of Farmersville	10057	5	–
Findlay			
The Findlay National Bank, Findlay	8212	6	–
The First National Bank Of Findlay	6861	5	–
Flora			
The First National Bank Of Flora	1961	3	3
The Flora National Bank	11509	4	4
Foosland			
The First National Bank Of Foosland	11299	–	–
Forrest			
The First National Bank Of Forrest	7680	6	–
Freeburg			
The First National Bank Of Freeburg	7941	4	5
Freeport			
First National Bank Of Freeport	13695	–	3
The First National Bank Of Freeport	319	6	–
The First National Bank Of Freeport	2875	3	3
The Freeport National Bank	2875	6	–
The Second National Bank Of Freeport	385	4	5
Galena			
The First National Bank Of Galena	13714	–	–
The Galena National Bank	3279	5	5
The Merchants National Bank Of Galena	979	2	6
The National Bank Of Galena	831	4	–
Galesburg			
First Galesburg National Bank & Trust Company	241	4	2
The First National Bank Of Galesburg	241	4	–
The Galesburg National Bank	3138	4	–
The Second National Bank Of Galesburg	491	6	–
Galva			
The Farmers And Merchants National Bank Of Galva	2793	6	–
The First National Bank Of Galva	827	6	–
The First National Bank Of Galva	14159	–	–
The Galva First National Bank, Galva	2793	5	5
Gardner			
The First National Bank Of Gardner	9406	5	5
Garrett			
The First National Bank Of Garrett	6192	6	–
Geneseo			
The Farmers National Bank Of Geneseo	2332	3	4
Genesso			
The First National Bank Of Geneseo	534	4	3
Geneva			
The First National Bank Of Geneva	8740	5	5
Georgetown			
The First National Bank In Georgetown	13448	–	6
The First National Bank Of Georgetown	5285	5	6
The Georgetown National Bank	7365	6	–

City, Bank	Ch. No.	L	S
Gibson City			
The First National Bank Of Gibson	8174	4	3
Gillespie			
The American National Bank Of Gillespie	12314	5	6
The Gillespie National Bank	7903	5	4
Gilman			
The First National Bank Of Gilman	5856	4	4
Golconda			
First National Bank In Golconda	14173	–	6
The First National Bank Of Golconda	7385	5	6
Goreville			
The First National Bank Of Goreville	7606	6	6
Gorham			
The First National Bank Of Gorham	10690	–	5
Grand Ridge			
The First National Bank Of Grand Ridge	6684	5	6
Grand Tower			
The First National Bank Of Grand Tower	7712	6	4
Granite City			
First Granite City National Bank	6564	–	2
The First National Bank Of Granite City	5433	4	4
The Granite City National Bank	6564	4	4
Grant Park			
The First National Bank Of Grant Park	11952	6	3
The Grant Park National Bank	5124	6	–
Granville			
The First National Bank Of Granville	10458	6	–
The Granville National Bank	14035	–	4
Grayville			
The Farmers National Bank Of Grayville	6460	5	5
The First National Bank Of Grayville	4999	5	4
Greenfield			
The First National Bank Of Greenfield	8473	6	5
Greenup			
The First National Bank Of Greenup	6191	6	–
The Greenup National Bank	8115	4	4
Greenville			
The Bradford National Bank Of Greenville	9734	4	4
The First National Bank Of Greenville	1841	5	–
Gridley			
The First National Bank Of Gridley	11208	5	–
Griggsville			
The Griggsville National Bank	2116	5	5
Hamilton			
The First National Bank Of Hamilton	9883	4	5
Hampshire			
The First National Bank Of Hampshire	11602	–	–
Harrisburg			
The City National Bank Of Harrisburg	5153	4	3
The First National Bank Of Harrisburg	4003	4	4
Harvey			
The First National Bank Of Harvey	8667	4	4
Havana			
The Havana National Bank	2242	5	4
Hegewisch			
The Inter State National Bank Of Hegewisch	8605	3	–
Henry			
The First National Bank Of Henry	1482	4	–
The First-Henry National Bank	1482	–	–
The Henry National Bank	7049	5	6
Herrin			
The City National Bank Of Herrin	8670	5	5
The First National Bank Of Herrin	5303	3	6
Highland			
The First National Bank Of Highland	6653	3	4
Hillsboro			
The Hillsboro National Bank Of Hillsboro	2789	5	3
The Peoples National Bank Of Hillsboro	8006	6	5
Hinckley			
The First National Bank Of Hinckley	11170	–	–
Hindsboro			
The First National Bank Of Hindsboro	5538	4	6
Hinsdale			
The First National Bank Of Hinsdale	11308	–	3
Homer			
The First National Bank In Homer	11882	6	5
The First National Bank Of Homer	2965	6	–
Hoopeston			
Hoopeston National Bank	9425	3	4
The City National Bank Of Hoopeston	13744	–	3
The First National Bank Of Hoopeston	2808	4	5
Hopedale			
The Hopedale National Bank	9398	5	5
Humboldt			
The First National Bank Of Humboldt	7168	6	5
Hume			
The First National Bank Of Hume	11108	4	6
Irving			
The Irving National Bank	8647	5	6
Irving Park			
The Irving Park National Bank, Irving Park	10179	5	4
Ivesdale			
First National Bank Of Ivesdale	6133	6	5
Jacksonville			
The Ayers National Bank Of Jacksonville	5763	2	2
The First National Bank Of Jacksonville	511	3	–
The Jacksonville National Bank	1719	4	–
Jefferson Park			
The Jefferson Park National Bank Of Chicago	10108	6	5
The Jefferson Park National Bank, Jefferson Park	10108	6	–
Jerseyville			
The First National Bank Of Jerseyville	2328	6	–
The National Bank Of Jerseyville	4952	2	–
Johnston City			
The First National Bank Of Johnston City	7458	6	–
Joliet			
The Citizens National Bank Of Joliet	6423	6	–
The First National Bank In Joliet	13705	–	–
The First National Bank Of Joliet	512	3	–
The Joliet National Bank, Joliet	4520	3	4
The Will County National Bank Of Joliet	1882	3	4

City, Bank	Ch. No.	L	S
Jonesboro			
The First National Bank Of Jonesboro	12373	6	6
Kankakee			
The City National Bank Of Kankakee	4342	4	1
The First National Bank Of Kankakee	1793	6	–
Kansas			
The Farmers National Bank Of Kansas	9293	5	–
The First National Bank Of Kansas	2011	2	–
The Kansas National Bank	9293	4	6
Keithsburg			
The Farmers National Bank Of Keithsburg	1805	6	–
Kewanee			
The First National Bank Of Kewanee	1785	3	3
The Kewanee National Bank	4854	6	–
The Union National Bank Of Kewanee	2501	6	–
Kinmundy			
The First National Bank Of Kinmundy	6143	4	3
Kirkwood			
The First National Bank Of Kirkwood	2313	4	4
Knoxville			
The Farmers National Bank Of Knoxville	3287	5	4
The First National Bank Of Knoxville	759	6	–
La Grange			
The First National Bank Of La Grange	12653	–	–
The La Grange National Bank	13941	–	–
La Harpe			
The First National Bank Of La Harpe	8468	6	6
La Rose			
The La Rose National Bank	10514	–	–
La Salle			
La Salle National Bank & Trust Company	2503	–	4
The City National Bank Of La Salle	2804	6	–
The First National Bank Of La Salle	114	6	–
The La Salle National Bank	2503	1	5
Lacon			
The First National Bank Of Lacon	347	6	4
Lake			
The Drovers National Bank Of Union Stock Yards, Lake	2858	5	–
Lake Forest			
The First National Bank Of Lake Forest	8937	5	4
Lanark			
The First National Bank Of Lanark	1755	4	4
The National Bank Of Lanark	14297	–	5
Lawrenceville			
The First National Bank Of Lawrenceville	5385	4	4
Le Roy			
The First National Bank Of Le Roy	6586	6	5
Lebanon			
The First National Bank Of Lebanon	12366	–	–
Leland			
The First National Bank Of Leland	7864	5	–
Lemont			
The First National Bank Of Lemont	11422	–	–
The Lemont National Bank	11715	–	–
Lerna			
The First National Bank Of Lerna	8224	5	6
Lewiston			
The First National Bank Of Lewiston	1808	6	–
Lewistown			
The Lewistown National Bank	4941	5	4
Lexington			
The First National Bank Of Lexington	2824	6	–
Libertyville			
The First Lake County National Bank Of Libertyville	6514	–	6
The First Lake County National Bank Of Libertyville	13718	–	–
The First National Bank Of Libertyville	6514	6	6
The Lake County National Bank Of Libertyville	6670	5	5
Lincoln			
First National Bank In Lincoln	14118	–	4
The American National Bank Of Lincoln	3613	5	5
The First National Bank Of Lincoln	2126	1	–
The German-American National Bank Of Lincoln	3613	4	–
The Lincoln National Bank	3369	4	3
Litchfield			
The First National Bank Of Litchfield	3962	4	4
The Litchfield National Bank	10079	4	5
Little York			
The First National Bank Of Little York	6065	6	–
Livingston			
The First National Bank Of Livingston	11845	6	5
Lockport			
The First National Bank Of Lockport	8933	5	4
Lovington			
The First National Bank Of Lovington	5494	6	–
The Shepherd National Bank Of Lovington	5494	6	–
Mackinaw			
The First National Bank Of Mackinaw	8732	4	4
Macomb			
The First National Bank Of Macomb	967	4	–
The Macomb National Bank	9169	4	3
The Union National Bank Of Macomb	1872	4	4
Madison			
The First National Bank Of Madison	8457	5	5
The First National Bank Of Madison	14235	–	–
Malta			
The First National Bank Of Malta	5815	6	5
Manhattan			
The First National Bank Of Manhattan	8713	6	5
Manlius			
The First National Bank Of Manlius	8648	4	4
Mansfield			
The First National Bank Of Mansfield	6096	5	–
Maquon			
The First National Bank Of Maquon	8482	5	–
Marengo			
The First National Bank Of Marengo	1870	5	6
Marine			
The First National Bank Of Marine	10582	–	4
Marion			
The First National Bank Of Marion	4502	4	4
Marissa			
The First National Bank Of Marissa	6691	4	4
The First National Bank Of Marissa	13735	–	3
Maroa			
The First National Bank Of Maroa	11886	–	–
Marseilles			
The First National Bank Of Marseilles	1852	4	–
Marshall			
The Dulaney National Bank Of Marshall	4759	4	4
Martinsville			
The First National Bank Of Martinsville	6721	5	6
Mascoutah			
The First National Bank In Mascoutah	13795	–	5
The First National Bank Of Mascoutah	9736	4	5
Mason City			
The First National Bank Of Mason City	1850	5	–
Mattoon			
The First National Bank Of Mattoon	1024	6	–
The Mattoon National Bank	2147	6	–
The National Bank Of Mattoon	10045	5	5
The State National Bank Of Mattoon	10144	5	–
Mazon			
The First National Bank Of Mazon	10186	4	5
Mcleansboro			
The First National Bank Of Mcleansboro	6649	5	6
The Peoples National Bank Of Mcleansboro	9408	5	5
Mendota			
The First National Bank Of Mendota	1177	4	4
The Mendota National Bank	5086	5	5
The National Bank Of Mendota	13611	–	6
Metcalf			
The First National Bank Of Metcalf	7954	5	5
Metropolis			
The City National Bank Of Metropolis	8745	5	4
The First National Bank Of Metropolis	3156	6	5
The National State Bank Of Metropolis	5254	5	5
Middletown			
The First National Bank Of Middletown	7791	6	–
Milford			
The First National Bank Of Milford	5149	4	6
Millstadt			
The First National Bank Of Millstadt	8425	5	4
Minonk			
The First National Bank Of Minonk	9601	6	–
The Minonk National Bank	11118	–	–
Minooka			
The Farmers First National Bank Of Minooka	9208	6	4
Moline			
The First National Bank Of Moline	160	6	–
The Moline National Bank	1941	6	–
The Moline National Bank	13660	–	–
Momence			
The First National Bank Of Momence	7079	5	6
Monmouth			
The First National Bank Of Monmouth	85	6	–
The First National Bank Of Monmouth	2751	6	–
The Monmouth National Bank	1706	6	–
The National Bank Of Monmouth	4400	3	4
The Peoples National Bank Of Monmouth	4313	6	5
The Second National Bank Of Monmouth	2205	5	5
Monticello			
The First National Bank Of Monticello	4826	3	4
The National Bank Of Monticello	13865	–	5
Morris			
The Farmers And Merchants National Bank Of Morris	8163	4	5
The First National Bank Of Morris	1773	3	4
The Grundy County National Bank Of Morris	531	3	4
Morrison			
The First National Bank Of Morrison	1033	4	5
Morrisonville			
The First National Bank Of Morrisonville	6745	5	5
Mound City			
The First National Bank Of Mound City	7443	6	6
Mounds			
The First National Bank Of Mounds	10445	6	6
Mount Auburn			
The First National Bank Of Mt. Auburn	9922	5	4
Mount Carmel			
American-First National Bank Of Mount Carmel	5782	–	5
The American National Bank Of Mt. Carmel	5782	4	4
The First National Bank Of Mount Carmel	4480	5	4
Mount Carroll			
The First National Bank Of Mount Carroll	409	5	–
The Mount Carroll National Bank	14247	–	–
Mount Olive			
The First National Bank In Mount Olive	13452	–	5
The First National Bank Of Mount Olive	7350	5	5
The Mount Olive National Bank	14285	–	6
Mount Prospect			
The Mount Prospect National Bank	10048	5	–
Mount Pulaski			
The First National Bank Of Mt. Pulaski	3839	3	5
Mount Sterling			
The First National Bank Of Mount Sterling	2402	3	–
The First National Bank Of Mount Sterling	13213	–	–
Mount Vernon			
The First National Bank Of Mount Vernon	13864	–	–
The Ham National Bank Of Mount Vernon	5057	4	5
The Mount Vernon National Bank	1996	6	–
The Third National Bank Of Mt. Vernon	5689	4	3
Moweaqua			
The First National Bank Of Moweaqua	7739	4	–
Mulberry Grove			
The First National Bank Of Mulberry Grove	7379	4	4
Murphysboro			
The City National Bank Of Murphysboro	4804	4	4
The First National Bank Of Murphysboro	4019	6	5
Naperville			
The First National Bank Of Naperville	4551	5	–
The Naperville National Bank	14115	–	–
Nashville			
The Farmers And Merchants National Bank Of Nashville	8221	6	4
The First National Bank Of Nashville	6524	3	4
National City			
The National Stock Yards National Bank Of National City	12991	–	2
The National Stock Yards National Bank, National Stock Yards	9118	5	–
Nauvoo			
The First National Bank Of Nauvoo	8898	6	–
Nebo			
The First National Bank Of Nebo	10492	5	5
Neoga			
The Cumberland County National Bank In Neoga	13892	–	6
The Cumberland County National Bank Of Neoga	5426	4	5
The Neoga National Bank	7841	6	–
New Bedford			
The Farmers National Bank Of New Bedford	11088	–	–
New Douglas			
The Prange National Bank Of New Douglas	13696	–	4
New Haven			
The First National Bank Of New Haven	8053	6	–
Newman			
The Newman National Bank	7575	5	5
Newton			
The First National Bank Of Newton	5869	5	5
The First National Bank Of Newton	14074	–	–
Niles Center			
The National Bank Of Niles Center	13218	–	–
Noble			
The First National Bank Of Noble	9527	5	6
Nokomis			
The Farmers National Bank Of Nokomis	7547	4	–
The Nokomis National Bank	1934	5	5
Normal			
The First National Bank Of Normal	4930	6	6
Norris City			
The First National Bank Of Norris City	7971	5	5
O'fallon			
The First National Bank Of O'fallon	6924	3	3
Oak Park			
The First National Bank Of Oak Park	11507	5	–
Oakford			
The First National Bank Of Oakford	8256	5	5
Oakland			
The Oakland National Bank	2212	4	4
Oblong			
The First National Bank Of Oblong	8607	5	3
The Oil Belt National Bank Of Oblong	8696	5	5
Odell			
The Farmers National Bank Of Odell	9624	5	–
Odin			
The First National Bank Of Odin	9525	6	5
Ogden			
The First National Bank Of Ogden	5304	5	5
Okawville			
The First National Bank Of Okawville	11754	5	4
The Old Exchange National Bank Of Okawville	11780	5	4
Olney			
The First National Bank Of Olney	1641	4	4
The First National Bank Of Olney	14217	–	–
The Olney National Bank	2629	6	–
Omaha			
The First National Bank Of Omaha	10291	6	–
Oneida			
The First National Bank Of Oneida	10752	6	5
Oquawka			
The First National Bank Of Oquawka	6086	5	–
Oregon			
The First National Bank Of Oregon	1969	5	–
The Ogle County National Bank Of Oregon	14346	–	–
Ottawa			
The First National Bank Of Ottawa	1154	4	3
The National City Bank Of Ottawa	1465	4	–
Palatine			
The First National Bank Of Palatine	11934	6	6
Palestine			
The First National Bank Of Palestine	8892	5	6
Pana			
The First National Bank Of Pana	4038	6	–
The First National Bank Of Pana	13478	–	–
The Pana National Bank	6734	4	5
Paris			
First National Bank & Trust Company Of Paris	3376	6	5
The Citizens National Bank Of Paris	6451	5	4
The Edgar County National Bank Of Paris	2100	3	4
The First National Bank Of Paris	1555	3	–
The First National Bank Of Paris	3376	5	–
Pawnee			
The National Bank Of Pawnee	7440	5	–
Pawpaw			
The First National Bank Of Pawpaw	6228	6	–
Paxton			
The First National Bank Of Paxton	1876	4	–
The First National Bank Of Paxton	2926	5	4
The First National Bank Of Paxton	13809	–	–
Pekin			
The American National Bank Of Pekin	3770	5	3
The Farmers National Bank Of Pekin	2287	3	4
The First National Bank Of Pekin	1637	6	–
The German-american National Bank Of Pekin	3770	4	–
The Herget National Bank Of Pekin	9788	3	3

City, Bank	Ch. No.	L	S
Peoria			
Commercial Merchants National Bank & Trust Co Of Peoria	3296	–	4
Merchants And Illinois National Bank Of Peoria	3254	3	5
The Central National Bank & Trust Company Of Peoria	3214	4	2
The Central National Bank Of Peoria	3214	3	–
The Commercial German National Bank Of Peoria	3296	3	–
The Commercial National Bank Of Peoria	3296	6	–
The Commercial National Bank Of Peoria	3296	3	5
The First National Bank Of Peoria	176	2	2
The German-american National Bank Of Peoria	3070	5	–
The Illinois National Bank Of Peoria	5361	6	–
The Mechanics National Bank Of Peoria	1117	6	–
The Merchants National Bank Of Peoria	3254	5	–
The Peoria National Bank	2878	6	–
The Second National Bank Of Peoria	207	6	–
Percy			
The First National Bank Of Percy	7627	5	4
Peru			
State National Bank Of Peru	13577	–	4
The First National Bank Of Peru	441	6	–
The First National Bank Of Peru	13903	–	–
The Peru National Bank	2951	4	5
The State-national Bank Of Peru, Illinois	13577	–	5
Petersburg			
The First National Bank Of Petersburg	3043	3	–
The State National Bank Of Petersburg	3043	–	5
Philo			
The First National Bank Of Philo	6211	6	–
Pinckneyville			
The First National Bank Of Pinckneyville	6025	3	4
The First National Bank Of Pinckneyville	13975	–	–
Piper City			
The First National Bank Of Piper City	5322	4	4
Pittsfield			
The First National Bank Of Pittsfield	1042	5	3
Plymouth			
The First National Bank Of Plymouth	12658	4	6
Polo			
The Exchange National Bank Of Polo	1806	4	6
The First National Bank Of Polo	13497	–	–
The Polo National Bank	14342	–	–
Pontiac			
The Livingston County National Bank Of Pontiac	1837	5	6
The National Bank Of Pontiac	2141	5	5
The Pontiac National Bank	14260	–	–
Potomac			
The Potomac National Bank	6824	5	–
Prairie City			
The First National Bank Of Prairie City	2254	6	–
Princeton			
Citizens First National Bank Of Princeton	2413	–	3
The Citizens National Bank Of Princeton	2413	3	4
The Farmers National Bank Of Princeton	2165	3	5
The First National Bank Of Princeton	903	3	4
Prophetstown			
The Farmers National Bank Of Prophetstown	6375	4	3
The First National Bank Of Prophetstown	1968	6	–
Quincy			
The First National Bank Of Quincy	424	6	–
The Merchants And Farmers National Bank Of Quincy	703	6	–
The Quincy National Bank	3752	5	–
The Quincy-Ricker National Bank & Trust Company	3752	3	4
The Ricker National Bank Of Quincy	2519	2	–
Ramsey			
The Ramsey National Bank	9895	5	4
Ransom			
The First National Bank Of Ransom	8289	6	4
Rantoul			
The First National Bank Of Rantoul	5193	5	4
Ravenswood			
The Ravenswood National Bank	10215	5	–
Raymond			
The First National Bank Of Raymond	6910	5	5
Ridge Farm			
The City National Bank Of Ridge Farm	8630	4	5
The First National Bank Of Ridge Farm	5313	5	5
Ridgway			
The First National Bank Of Ridgway	9439	6	6
Riverside			
The First National Bank Of Riverside	12386	5	4
Robinson			
The First National Bank Of Robinson	5049	5	6
The Second National Bank Of Robinson	13605	–	4
Rochelle			
The First National Bank Of Rochelle	1922	6	–
The National Bank Of Rochelle	14221	–	–
The Rochelle National Bank	1907	4	6
Rock Falls			
The First National Bank Of Rock Falls	6998	4	4
Rock Island			
The First National Bank Of Rock Island	108	6	–
The Peoples National Bank Of Rock Island	2155	3	–
The Rock Island National Bank	1889	5	–
Rockford			
The Commercial National Bank Of Rockford	11679	5	3
The First National Bank Of Rockford	429	6	–
The Forest City National Bank Of Rockford	4325	4	4
The Illinois National Bank And Trust Company Of Rockford	13652	–	3
The Manufacturers National Bank & Trust Co. Of Rockford	3952	6	4
The Manufacturers National Bank Of Rockford	3952	4	–
The Rockford National Bank	1816	3	3
The Second National Bank Of Rockford	482	6	–
The Security National Bank Of Rockford	11731	5	4
The Swedish-American National Bank Of Rockford	9823	4	4
The Third National Bank Of Rockford	479	5	4
The Winnebago National Bank Of Rockford	883	5	–
Roodhouse			
The First National Bank Of Roodhouse	8637	5	5
The Roodhouse National Bank	14348	–	–
Roseville			
The Farmers And Merchants National Bank Of Roseville	12926	–	–
The First National Bank Of Roseville	5883	5	–
Rossville			
The Farmers National Bank Of Rossville	9877	5	–
The First National Bank Of Rossville	5398	6	5
Rushville			
The First National Bank Of Rushville	1453	5	–
Saint Anne			
The First National Bank Of Saint Anne	5470	6	–
Saint Charles			
The Kane County National Bank Of Saint Charles	2021	6	–
The St. Charles National Bank, St. Charles	6219	4	4
Saint Francisville			
The First National Bank Of St. Francisville	8846	6	–
The Peoples National Bank Of St. Francisville	8846	6	4
Saint Peter			
The First National Bank Of Saint Peter	9896	4	4
Salem			
The Salem National Bank	1715	4	4
Sandoval			
The First National Bank Of Sandoval	9786	6	4
Savanna			
The First National Bank Of Savanna	8540	4	3
The National Bank Of Savanna	13886	–	4
Secor			
The First National Bank Of Secor	6007	6	5
Seneca			
The First National Bank Of Seneca	1773	6	–
Sesser			
The First National Bank Of Sesser	8758	6	6
Shawneetown			
The City National Bank Of Shawneetown	9435	5	6
The First National Bank Of Shawneetown	915	6	–
The First National Bank Of Shawneetown	14265	–	–
The Gallatin National Bank Of Shawneetown	1775	5	–
The National Bank Of Shawneetown	7752	5	5
Shelbyville			
The Citizens National Bank Of Shelbyville	7396	4	–
The First National Bank Of Shelbyville	2128	2	6
Sheridan			
The First National Bank Of Sheridan	10760	–	–
Sidell			
The First National Bank Of Sidell	8374	5	5
Smithton			
The First National Bank Of Smithton	13525	–	3
Sorento			
The Sorento National Bank	10505	–	–
South Chicago			
The Calumet National Bank Of South Chicago	3102	6	–
Sparta			
The First National Bank Of Sparta	7015	3	4
Spring Valley			
The Spring Valley National Bank	3465	6	–
Springfield			
The Farmers National Bank Of Springfield	2688	5	–
The First National Bank Of Springfield	205	3	3
The Illinois National Bank Of Springfield	3548	3	3
The Ridgely National Bank Of Springfield	1662	3	–
The State National Bank Of Springfield	1733	3	–
St Elmo			
The First National Bank Of St Elmo	9388	5	4
Staunton			
The First National Bank Of Staunton	10173	5	3
The First National Bank Of Staunton	14310	–	–
The Staunton National Bank	10777	4	4
Sterling			
First Sterling National Bank	1717	–	4
The First National Bank Of Sterling	1717	4	6
The National Bank Of Sterling	13963	–	–
The Sterling National Bank	2709	4	6
Steward			
The First National Bank Of Steward	6543	5	4
Stewardson			
The First National Bank Of Stewardson	9438	6	–
The Stewardson National Bank	13226	–	–
Stockton			
The First National Bank Of Stockton	13666	–	5
Stonington			
The First National Bank Of Stonington	5291	5	5
Strawn			
The Farmers National Bank Of Strawn	7151	5	5
Streator			
The City National Bank Of Streator	4476	6	–
The First National Bank Of Streator	2170	6	–
The Streator National Bank	2681	3	4
The Union National Bank Of Streator	2176	4	5
Stronghurst			
The First National Bank Of Stronghurst	5813	4	–
Sullivan			
The First National Bank Of Sullivan	7692	4	5
Sumner			
The First National Bank Of Sumner	6907	5	4
Sycamore			
The Citizens National Bank Of Sycamore	9572	6	–
The First National Bank Of Sycamore	1896	5	4
The National Bank And Trust Company Of Sycamore	13872	–	–
The Sycamore National Bank	1896	5	–
Tamaroa			
The First National Bank Of Tamaroa	8629	5	5
Tampico			
The First National Bank Of Tampico	9230	4	3
Taylorville			
Farmers National Bank Of Taylorville	5410	4	3
Taylorville National Bank	8940	2	5
The Farmers National Bank Of Taylorville	5410	4	–
The First National Bank Of Taylorville	3579	4	6
Thomasboro			
The First National Bank Of Thomasboro	8155	5	5
Toledo			
The First National Bank In Toledo	13682	–	5
The First National Bank Of Toledo	5273	4	5
Toluca			
The Citizens National Bank Of Toluca	11333	5	5
The First National Bank Of Toluca	4871	5	–
Tremont			
The First National Bank Of Tremont	6421	4	5
The First National Bank Of Tremont	13579	–	–
The Tremont National Bank	9325	5	–
Trenton			
The First National Bank Of Trenton	10125	5	6
Triumph			
The First National Bank Of Triumph	7660	6	5
Tuscola			
The First National Bank Of Tuscola	1723	6	4
Ullin			
The First National Bank Of Ullin	8180	6	6
Urbana			
The First National Bank Of Urbana	2915	6	5
Valier			
The First National Bank Of Valier	12479	–	–
Vandalia			
The Farmers And Merchants National Bank Of Vandalia	1779	6	–
The First National Bank Of Vandalia	4994	5	4
The National Bank Of Vandalia	1517	6	–
Vermilion			
The First National Bank Of Vermilion	10365	5	5
Vienna			
The First National Bank Of Vienna	4433	4	4
Villa Grove			
The First National Bank Of Villa Grove	7088	5	4
Viola			
The Farmers National Bank Of Viola	11779	–	–
Virginia			
The Centennial National Bank Of Virginia	2330	4	5
The Farmers National Bank Of Virginia	1471	4	–
Waddams Grove			
The First National Bank Of Waddams Grove	11675	5	–
Walnut			
The First National Bank Of Walnut	2684	6	–
Waltonville			
The First National Bank Of Waltonville	11516	6	–
Warren			
First National Bank In Warren	9096	6	–
The Farmers National Bank Of Warren	849	6	–
The National Farmers Bank Of Warren	9096	5	–
Warsaw			
The Farmers National Bank Of Warsaw	9929	6	–
The First National Bank Of Warsaw	495	6	–
Waterloo			
The First National Bank Of Waterloo	10180	4	3
Watseka			
The First National Bank Of Watseka	1721	4	5
Waukegan			
The First National Bank Of Waukegan	945	5	3
The Waukegan National Bank	10355	4	4
Waverly			
The First National Bank Of Waverly	6116	3	4
Wayne City			
The First National Bank Of Wayne City	10460	4	4
Wenona			
The First National Bank Of Wenona	3620	6	–
West Frankfort			
The First National Bank Of West Frankfort	7673	6	5
West Salem			
The First National Bank Of West Salem	9338	5	5
Westervelt			
The Farmers National Bank Of Westervelt	10641	5	6
Westfield			
The First National Bank Of Westfield	8216	3	6
Westville			
The First National Bank Of Westville	7500	6	5
Wheaton			
The First National Bank Of Wheaton	9368	4	5
White Hall			
Peoples-First National Bank Of White Hall	7121	5	6
The First National Bank Of White Hall	7121	5	–
The White Hall National Bank, White Hall	7077	4	4
Willisville			
The First National Bank Of Willisville	10911	–	–
Wilmette			
The First National Bank Of Wilmette	10828	–	3
Wilmington			
The Commercial National Bank Of Wilmington	1964	5	4
The First National Bank Of Wilmington	177	5	–
Wilsonville			
The First National Bank Of Wilsonville	12630	6	5
Winchester			
The First National Bank Of Winchester	1484	6	–
The Neat, Condit And Grout National Bank Of Winchester	14140	–	–
The Peoples National Bank Of Winchester	1821	4	–
Windsor			
The First National Bank Of Windsor	7339	6	–
Witt			
First National Bank Of Witt	7538	6	–
The National Bank Of Witt	13144	5	5
The Oland National Bank Of Witt	7538	6	–
The Security National Bank Of Witt	13650	–	4
The Witt National Bank	10264	5	–
Wood River			
The First National Bank Of Wood River	11876	4	3
The Wood River National Bank	12528	–	–
Woodhull			
The First National Bank In Woodhull	12525	6	–
The First National Bank Of Woodhull	10716	6	–
Woodlawn			
The First National Bank Of Woodlawn	11774	5	4

City, Bank	Ch. No.	L	S
Woodstock			
First National Bank Of Woodstock	14137	–	6
The American National Bank Of Woodstock	6811	6	5
The First National Bank Of Woodstock	372	6	–
The First National Bank Of Woodstock	2675	6	–
The Woodstock National Bank	11610	–	–
Worden			
The First National Bank Of Worden	10669	5	5
The Wall National Bank Of Worden	10669	6	–
Wyanet			
The First National Bank Of Wyanet	9277	4	5
Wyoming			
The First National Bank Of Wyoming	2815	6	–
The First National Bank Of Wyoming	14332	–	–
The National Bank Of Wyoming	6629	4	4
Xenia			
The First National Bank Of Xenia	12096	5	5
Yorkville			
The Yorkville National Bank	6239	6	5
Zeigler			
The First National Bank Of Zeigler	12097	5	4
INDIANA			
Albion			
The Albion National Bank	8912	6	6
Alexandria			
The Alexandria National Bank	4835	6	–
Ambia			
The First National Bank Of Ambia	9510	6	–
Amo			
The First National Bank Of Amo	8154	5	6
Anderson			
The First National Bank Of Anderson	44	6	–
The Madison County National Bank Of Anderson	2346	6	–
The National Exchange Bank Of Anderson	4685	5	6
The Peoples State National Bank Of Anderson	10290	6	–
Angola			
The First National Bank Of Angola	7023	6	6
Arcadia			
The First National Bank Of Arcadia	9488	6	–
Argos			
The First National Bank Of Argos	9726	6	–
Attica			
The Central National Bank And Trust Company Of Attica	3755	–	3
The Central National Bank Of Attica	3755	5	–
The Citizens National Bank Of Attica	3755	6	–
The First National Bank Of Attica	577	6	–
Auburn			
The City National Bank Of Auburn	6509	6	5
The First National Bank Of Auburn	2238	6	–
Aurora			
The Aurora National Bank	2963	6	–
The First National Bank Of Aurora	699	3	4
Batesville			
The First National Bank Of Batesville	7824	6	5
Bedford			
The Bedford National Bank	1892	6	–
The Bedford National Bank	5187	4	4
The Citizens National Bank Of Bedford	5173	5	4
The Indiana National Bank Of Bedford	3013	6	–
The Stone City National Bank Of Bedford	13788	–	4
Bicknell			
The First National Bank Of Bicknell	7155	6	5
Birdseye			
The Birdseye National Bank	8835	5	6
Bloomington			
The Bloomington National Bank	8415	5	4
The First National Bank Of Bloomington	1888	3	4
Bluffton			
Old-first National Bank In Bluffton	13305	–	5
The First National Bank Of Bluffton	58	6	–
The Old National Bank Of Bluffton	13305	–	3
Blufton			
First National Bank In Blufton	13317	–	3
Boonville			
First National Bank Of Boonville	10613	6	5
The Boonville National Bank	2207	5	–
The Boonville National Bank	14218	–	–
The City National Bank Of Boonville	10613	6	–
The Farmers And Merchants National Bank Of Boonville	9266	5	–
Boswell			
The First National Bank Of Boswell	5476	6	6
Brazil			
The Citizens National Bank Of Brazil	8620	4	4
The First National Bank Of Brazil	3583	5	5
The Riddell National Bank Of Brazil	5267	4	3
Brookville			
The Brookville National Bank	1619	6	–
The Franklin County National Bank Of Brookville	5629	5	5
The National Brookville Bank, Brookville	7805	5	4
Brownstown			
The First National Bank Of Brownstown	9143	6	4
Butler			
The First National Bank Of Butler	9286	6	6
The Knisely National Bank Of Butler	14226	–	–
Cambridge City			
The First National Bank & Trust Company Of Cambridge City	2734	6	5
The First National Bank Of Cambridge City	70	6	–
The First National Bank Of Cambridge City	2734	6	–
The Wayne National Bank Of Cambridge City	8871	5	–
Cannelton			
Cannelton National Bank	9682	6	4
First Cannelton National Bank	9682	–	4
The First National Bank Of Cannelton	9401	5	5
Carlisle			
The First National Bank Of Carlisle	8805	5	–
Cayuga			
The First National Bank Of Cayuga	9189	6	5
Cedar Grove			
The Cedar Grove National Bank	11424	–	–
Center Point			
The First National Bank Of Center Point	9250	4	5
Centerville			
The First National Bank Of Centerville	2696	6	–
The First National Bank Of Centreville	37	4	–
Charlestown			
The First National Bank Of Charlestown	6952	6	6
Cicero			
The Citizens National Bank Of Cicero	10720	5	5
Clay City			
The First National Bank Of Clay City	9540	5	5
Clinton			
The First National Bank Of Clinton	6480	5	6
Cloverdale			
The First National Bank Of Cloverdale	10465	6	6
Coatesville			
The First National Bank Of Coatesville	8447	6	6
Columbia City			
The Columbia City National Bank, Columbia City	7175	6	–
The First National Bank Of Columbia City	7132	5	–
Columbus			
The First National Bank Of Columbus	1066	6	6
Connersville			
The Fayette National Bank Of Connersville	6265	3	–
The First National Bank Of Connersville	1034	4	4
Converse			
The First National Bank Of Converse	11671	–	6
Corydon			
The Corydon National Bank	7760	5	–
The First National Bank Of Corydon	6625	6	–
Covington			
The First National Bank Of Covington	9860	5	–
The National Bank Of Covington	13082	–	–
Crawfordsville			
The Citizens National Bank Of Crawfordsville	2533	4	5
The Elston National Bank Of Crawfordsville	7773	5	–
The First National Bank Of Crawfordsville	571	5	4
Crown Point			
The First National Bank Of Crown Point	2183	5	5
Dana			
The First National Bank Of Dana	5997	6	5
Danville			
The First National Bank Of Danville	152	4	5
Decatur			
The Decatur National Bank	3028	4	–
The First National Bank Of Decatur	3028	4	6
Delphi			
The Citizens National Bank Of Delphi	6986	5	6
The First National Bank Of Delphi	1949	6	–
Dillsboro			
The First National Bank Of Dillsboro	6882	4	5
Dublin			
The First National Bank Of Dublin	8804	6	6
Dunkirk			
The First National Bank Of Dunkirk	4888	6	–
Dyer			
The First National Bank Of Dyer	6909	5	5
East Chicago			
The First National Bank And Trust Company Of East Chicago	7601	5	5
The First National Bank In East Chicago	13531	–	3
The First National Bank Of East Chicago	7601	5	–
The Indiana Harbor National Bank Of East Chicago	10171	6	–
The Union National Bank Of Indiana Harbor At East Chicago	13532	–	3
The United States National Bank Of Indiana Harbor	12058	5	4
Edinburg			
The Farmers National Bank Of Edinburg	6905	5	6
Elkhart			
The Elkhart National Bank	2502	6	–
The First National Bank Of Elkhart	206	5	4
The Indiana National Bank Of Elkhart	4841	6	–
Elwood			
The First National Bank Of Elwood	4675	5	5
Evansville			
Old National Bank In Evansville	12444	4	3
The Bankers National Bank Of Evansville	8832	6	–
The Citizens National Bank Of Evansville	2188	3	1
The City National Bank Of Evansville	6200	5	–
The Evansville National Bank	730	6	–
The First National Bank Of Evansville	28	6	–
The First National Bankof Evansville	2692	6	–
The German National Bank Of Evansville	1772	6	–
The Mercantile National Bank Of Evansville	8492	6	–
The Merchants National Bank Of Evansville	989	5	–
The National City Bank Of Evansville	12132	5	2
The Old National Bank Of Evansville	3281	5	–
The Old State National Bank Of Evansville	7478	5	–
Fairland			
The Fairland National Bank	8337	5	5
Farmersburg			
The First National Bank Of Farmersburg	11035	6	–
Farmland			
The First National Bank Of Farmland	6504	5	–
The New-First National Bank Of Farmland	12866	–	–
Ferdinand			
The Ferdinand National Bank	7830	6	–
Fishers			
The Fishers National Bank	10419	6	6
Flora			
The Bright National Bank Of Flora	8014	6	5
The Bright National Bank Of Flora	13977	–	–
The First National Bank Of Flora	7802	6	–
Fort Branch			
The Farmers And Merchants National Bank Of Fort Branch	9077	6	5
The First National Bank Of Fort Branch	9073	6	5
The First National Bank Of Owensville, Owensville	9073	–	–
Fort Wayne			
First & Tri State National Bank & Trust Co Of Fort Wayne	2701	–	3
First National Bank Of Fort Wayne	2701	3	4
Fort Wayne National Bank	13818	–	4
Lincoln National Bank & Trust Company Of Fort Wayne	7725	6	2
Old-first National Bank And Trust Company Of Fort Wayne	3285	–	2
The First And Hamilton National Bank Of Fort Wayne	2701	4	–
The First National Bank Of Fort Wayne	11	6	–
The First National Bank Of Fort Wayne	2701	3	–
The Fort Wayne National Bank	865	6	–
The German-American National Bank Of Fort Wayne	7725	6	–
The Hamilton National Bank Of Fort Wayne	2439	3	–
The Lincoln National Bank Of Fort Wayne	7725	4	–
The Merchants National Bank Of Fort Wayne	1100	6	–
The Old National Bank Of Fort Wayne	3285	4	4
The White National Bank Of Fort Wayne	4725	6	–
Fortville			
The First National Bank Of Fortville	9299	5	5
Fowler			
The First National Bank Of Fowler	5430	4	6
Frankfort			
The American National Bank Of Frankfort	6217	4	–
The First National Bank Of Frankfort	1854	4	4
Franklin			
Franklin National Bank	13378	–	5
The Citizens National Bank Of Franklin	3967	5	4
The First National Bank Of Franklin	50	6	–
The Franklin National Bank	3338	4	6
The Johnson County National Bank Of Franklin	14075	–	6
The National Bank Of Franklin	2769	6	–
The Second National Bank Of Franklin	78	6	–
Freeland Park			
The First National Bank Of Freeland Park	7437	6	–
Fremont			
The First National Bank Of Fremont	10718	6	5
Gary			
The First National Bank Of Gary	8426	5	4
The National Bank Of America At Gary	11094	5	4
Gas City			
The First National Bank Of Gas City	4825	6	–
Goodland			
The First National Bank Of Goodland	7863	5	5
Goshen			
First National Bank Of Goshen	14113	–	6
The City National Bank Of Goshen	2067	4	1
The First National Bank Of Goshen	146	6	–
Greencastle			
The Central National Bank Of Greencastle	2896	4	3
The Citizens National Bank Of Greencastle	10409	6	–
The First National Bank Of Greencastle	219	4	4
Greens Fork			
The First National Bank Of Greens Fork	7124	5	4
Greensburg			
Citizens Third National Bank & Trust Company Of Greensbrg	2844	–	6
The Citizens National Bank Of Greensburg	1890	4	3
The Decatur County National Bank Of Greensburg	13988	–	–
The First National Bank Of Greensburg	356	6	–
The Greensburg National Bank	5435	5	5
The Third National Bank Of Greensburg	2844	5	–
Third National Bank And Trust Company Of Greensburg	2844	6	4
Greenwood			
The Citizens National Bank Of Greenwood	8461	6	6
The First National Bank Of Greenwood	8422	6	6
The National Bank Of Greenwood	14292	–	–
Hagerstown			
The First National Bank Of Hagerstown	7902	6	–
Hammond			
Citizens National Bank Of Hammond	8199	5	–
Hammond National Bank And Trust Company, Hammond	8199	6	4
The Citizens German National Bank Of Hammond	8199	6	–
The First National Bank Of Hammond	3478	3	–
Hartford City			
The First National Bank Of Hartford City	6959	6	5
Hartsville			
The First National Bank Of Hartsville	7354	6	6
Holland			
The Holland National Bank	9090	5	4
Hope			
The Citizens National Bank Of Hope	5726	6	–
Huntingburg			
The First National Bank Of Huntingburg	8929	6	5
Huntington			
The First National Bank Of Huntington	145	6	–
The First National Bank Of Huntington	2508	5	6

City, Bank	Ch. No.	L	S
Indianapolis			
American National Bank At Indianapolis	13759	–	3
American National Bank Of Indianapolis	13759	–	3
National City Bank Of Indianapolis	10121	3	–
The American National Bank Of Indianapolis	5672	3	–
The Capital National Bank Of Indianapolis	4158	5	–
The Citizens National Bank Of Indianapolis	617	5	–
The Columbia National Bank Of Indianapolis	5845	6	–
The Commercial National Bank Of Indianapolis	10671	6	–
The Continental National Bank Of Indianapolis	9537	5	5
The First National Bank Of Indianapolis	55	4	–
The First National Bank Of Indianapolis	2556	6	–
The Fletcher American National Bank Of Indianapolis	9829	2	1
The Fletcher National Bank Of Indianapolis	5116	5	–
The Fourth National Bank Of Indianapolis	783	6	–
The Indiana National Bank Of Indianapolis	984	2	1
The Indianapolis National Bank	581	5	–
The Merchants National Bank Of Indianapolis	869	2	3
The Meridian National Bank Of Indianapolis	1878	6	–
The Union National Bank Of Indianapolis	6513	6	–
Jasonville			
The First National Bank Of Jasonville	7342	6	5
Jeffersonville			
The Citizens National Bank Of Jeffersonville	1466	6	–
The First National Bank Of Jeffersonville	956	5	3
Kendallville			
The Citizens National Bank Of Kendallville	12532	6	6
The First National Bank Of Kendallville	41	6	–
The First National Bank Of Kendallville	2687	6	–
Kewanna			
The American National Bank Of Kewanna	10616	6	6
The First National Bank Of Kewanna	8192	6	–
Kirklin			
The First National Bank Of Kirklin	9115	6	–
Knightstown			
The Citizens National Bank Of Knightstown	9152	5	4
The First National Bank Of Knightstown	872	5	3
Knox			
The First National Bank Of Knox	5919	6	–
Kokomo			
The Citizens National Bank Of Kokomo	4121	5	4
The First National Bank Of Kokomo	894	6	–
The Howard National Bank Of Kokomo	2375	4	5
The Kokomo National Bank	6261	6	–
La Fayette			
American National Bank Of La Fayette	7415	6	–
The City National Bank Of La Fayette	5940	4	–
The First National Bank Of La Fayette	23	6	–
The First National Bank Of La Fayette	2717	5	–
The First-merchants National Bank Of La Fayette	11148	5	3
The Fowler National Bank Of La Fayette	3280	6	–
The Indiana National Bank Of La Fayette	1967	6	–
The La Fayette National Bank	2213	5	–
The La Fayette National Bank	14175	–	–
The Merchants National Bank Of La Fayette	4468	4	–
The National Fowler Bank Of La Fayette	5889	5	4
The National State Bank Of La Fayette	930	3	–
The Perrin National Bank Of La Fayette	4656	6	–
The Second National Bank Of La Fayette	417	5	–
The Union National Bank Of La Fayette	882	6	–
La Grange			
The First National Bank Of La Grange	2184	6	–
The National Bank Of La Grange	4972	5	–
La Porte			
First National Bank & Trust Company Of La Porte	377	6	4
The First National Bank Of La Porte	377	5	–
Lawrenceburg			
The Citizens National Bank Of Lawrenceburg	4281	6	–
The City National Bank Of Lawrenceburg	2889	6	–
The Dearborn National Bank Of Lawrenceburg	7909	5	5
The First National Bank Of Lawrenceburg	82	5	–
The Lawrenceburg National Bank	1418	6	–
The Peoples National Bank Of Lawrenceburg	2612	–	–
Lawrenceburgh			
The Peoples National Bank Of Lawrenceburgh	2612	3	5
The Peoples National Bank, Lawrenceburgh	2612	–	5
Lebanon			
The First National Bank Of Lebanon	2057	2	5
The Lebanon National Bank	2660	6	–
Lewisville			
The First National Bank Of Lewisville	5526	6	6
Liberty			
The First National Bank Of Liberty	1925	6	–
The Union County National Bank Of Liberty	2007	5	4
Lima			
The National State Bank Of Lima	1234	6	–
Linton			
Citizens National Bank Of Linton	14258	–	4
The First National Bank Of Linton	7411	4	4
Logansport			
The City And State National Bank & Trust Co Of Logansport	5076	–	6
The City National Bank Of Logansport	5076	4	3
The First National Bank Of Logansport	3084	4	3
The Logansport National Bank	1031	6	–
The National Bank Of Logansport	13580	–	3
The State National Bank Of Logansport	2596	5	–
Loogootee			
The First National Bank Of Loogootee	7241	6	–
Lowell			
First National Bank In Lowell	5931	5	6
The First National Bank Of Lowell	5369	6	–
The Lowell National Bank	6765	6	6
The State National Bank Of Lowell	5931	6	–
Lynnville			
The Lynnville National Bank	8868	6	6
Madison			
The First National Bank Of Madison	111	4	3
The National Branch Bank Of Madison	1457	4	4
Marion			
First National Bank In Marion	13717	–	4
The First National Bank Of Marion	4189	4	3
The Marion National Bank	7758	3	4
The Marion National Bank	13729	–	–
Martinsville			
The Citizens National Bank Of Martinsville	4964	5	–
The First National Bank Of Martinsville	794	4	5
The National Bank Of Martinsville	13643	–	5
Matthews			
The First National Bank Of Matthews	5998	6	–
Mays			
The First National Bank Of Mays	8700	5	6
Medaryville			
The First National Bank Of Medaryville	8537	6	–
Mentone			
The First National Bank Of Mentone	8368	6	–
Michigan City			
The First National Bank Of Michigan City	2101	6	–
The First National Bank Of Michigan City	2747	5	6
The Merchants National Bank Of Michigan City	9381	5	4
Milltown			
The First National Bank Of Milltown	8650	6	6
Milroy			
The First National Bank Of Milroy	11782	5	5
Mishawaka			
The First National Bank Of Mishawaka	5167	4	5
Mitchell			
The First National Bank Of Mitchell	6433	6	5
Monrovia			
The First National Bank Of Monrovia	6354	6	6
Monterey			
The First National Bank Of Monterey	9784	6	5
Montezuma			
The First National Bank Of Montezuma	7463	5	6
Montgomery			
The First National Bank Of Montgomery	5734	6	–
Monticello			
The First National Bank Of Monticello	2208	6	–
The Monticello National Bank	6172	6	–
The National Bank Of Monticello	12952	–	–
Montpelier			
The First National Bank Of Montpelier	5278	5	5
Mooresville			
The First National Bank Of Mooresville	6876	5	–
Morgantown			
The First National Bank Of Morgantown	7652	3	–
Mount Vernon			
The First National Bank Of Mount Vernon	366	4	–
The Mount Vernon National Bank	7786	6	–
The Mount Vernon National Bank And Trust Company	12780	6	6
The Old First National Bank Of Mount Vernon	12466	6	5
Mulberry			
The Citizens National Bank Of Mulberry	10234	6	4
The Farmers National Bank Of Mulberry	4801	6	–
Muncie			
The Citizens National Bank Of Muncie	2234	6	–
The Delaware County National Bank Of Muncie	4809	4	1
The Farmers National Bank Of Muncie	4674	6	–
The Merchants National Bank Of Muncie	2234	4	2
The Merchants National Bank Of Muncie	4852	4	–
The Muncie National Bank	793	5	–
The Peoples National Bank Of Muncie	7454	6	–
The Union National Bank Of Muncie	2234	5	–
Nappanee			
The First National Bank Of Nappanee	8785	6	6
New Albany			
The First National Bank Of New Albany	701	6	–
The Merchants National Bank Of New Albany	965	5	–
The New Albany National Bank	775	5	5
The Second National Bank Of New Albany	2166	4	3
The Union National Bank Of New Albany	14047	–	–
New Carlisle			
The First National Bank Of New Carlisle	5639	6	5
New Castle			
The Bundy National Bank Of New Castle	2202	6	–
The Farmers And First National Bank Of New Castle	9852	5	5
The Farmers National Bank Of New Castle	9852	5	–
The First National Bank Of New Castle	804	4	–
The First National Bank Of New Castle	13816	–	–
New Harmony			
New Harmony National Bank	13542	–	5
The First National Bank Of New Harmony	6699	6	6
New Point			
The First National Bank Of New Point	8408	6	–
Newport			
The First National Bank Of Newport	1897	6	–
Noblesville			
The American National Bank Of Noblesville	9756	5	4
The First National Bank Of Noblesville	4882	5	–
North Manchester			
The First National Bank Of North Manchester	2903	6	–
The Lawrence National Bank Of North Manchester	3474	5	–
North Vernon			
The First National Bank Of North Vernon	4678	5	4
The North Vernon National Bank	9122	5	6
Oakland City			
The First National Bank Of Oakland City	9562	6	4
Odon			
The First National Bank Of Odon	7260	6	4
Orleans			
The National Bank Of Orleans	5558	5	6
Owensville			
The First National Bank Of Owensville	5432	6	–
Patoka			
The Patoka National Bank	9352	6	5
Peru			
The Citizens National Bank Of Peru	1879	4	5
The First National Bank Of Peru	363	5	5
Petersburg			
The First National Bank Of Petersburg	5300	6	5
Plainfield			
The First National Bank And Trust Company Of Plainfield	7011	6	6
The First National Bank Of Plainfield	7011	6	–
Plymouth			
The First National Bank Of Marshall County At Plymouth	2119	2	4
Portland			
The First National Bank Of Portland	7180	5	4
Poseyville			
The Bozeman Waters First National Bank Of Poseyville	13503	–	4
The Bozeman Waters National Bank Of Poseyville	8149	5	4
The First National Bank Of Poseyville	7036	6	6
Princeton			
The American National Bank Of Princeton	8166	6	–
The Farmers National Bank Of Princeton	9463	4	3
The Gibson County National Bank Of Princeton	2066	6	–
The Peoples National Bank Of Princeton	2180	5	–
The Peoples-American National Bank Of Princeton	10551	6	5
Redkey			
The Farmers And Merchants National Bank Of Redkey	9670	6	–
Remington			
The Farmers National Bank Of Remington	11355	4	4
The First National Bank Of Remington	8060	6	–
Renesslaer			
The Farmers And Merchants National Bank Of Renesslaer	14288	–	–
Rensselaer			
The Farmers And Merchants National Bank Of Rensselaer	11470	–	–
The First National Bank Of Rensselaer	6651	6	–
Richmond			
The First National Bank Of Richmond	17	5	–
The First National Bank Of Richmond	17	4	–
The First National Bank Of Richmond	2680	4	3
The Richmond National Bank	1102	6	–
The Richmond National Bank	2090	4	–
The Second National Bank Of Richmond	1988	4	3
The Union National Bank Of Richmond	3413	4	–
Ridgeville			
The First National Bank Of Ridgeville	8351	6	6
Rising Sun			
The National Bank Of Rising Sun	1959	4	4
Roanoke			
The First National Bank Of Roanoke	11427	–	–
Rochester			
The First National Bank Of Rochester	1952	5	–
The First National Bank Of Rochester	7655	5	5
Rockport			
The First National Bank Of Rockport	6194	6	6
Rockville			
The First National Bank Of Rockville	63	6	–
The National Bank Of Rockville	2361	6	–
The Rockville National Bank	5067	4	6
Rosedale			
The Harrison National Bank Of Rosedale	9006	6	–
The Rosedale National Bank	9006	6	5
Rushville			
The American National Bank Of Rushville	12420	6	4
The Peoples National Bank Of Rushville	7374	6	–
The Rush County National Bank Of Rushville	1869	5	4
The Rushville National Bank	1456	5	4
Russiaville			
The First National Bank Of Russiaville	5524	6	6
Salem			
The National Bank Of Salem	2173	6	–
Seymour			
The First National Bank Of Seymour	1032	6	4
The Seymour National Bank	4652	6	4
Shelburn			
The First National Bank Of Shelburn	7513	6	–
Shelbyville			
The Farmers National Bank Of Shelbyville	4800	5	5
The First National Bank Of Shelbyville	1263	4	5
The Shelby National Bank Of Shelbyville	7946	6	4
Sheridan			
The Farmers And Merchants National Bank Of Sheridan	13050	–	–
The Farmers National Bank Of Sheridan	6070	5	–
The First National Bank Of Sheridan	5296	5	–
The First National State Bank Of Sheridan	5296	6	–
The Sheridan National Bank	13050	–	–
Shirley			
The First National Bank Of Shirley	9209	6	–
South Bend			
The Citizens National Bank Of South Bend	4764	4	3
The City National Bank Of South Bend	13987	–	–
The First National Bank Of South Bend	126	4	2
The Merchants National Bank Of South Bend	6334	5	3
The South Bend National Bank	1739	6	–
Spencer			
The First National Bank Of Spencer	2178	6	–
The Spencer National Bank	9715	4	5
Spurgeon			
The First National Bank Of Spurgeon	12028	6	6
Sullivan			
Peoples National Bank And Trust Company Of Sullivan	5392	6	5
The Farmers National Bank Of Sullivan	2369	6	–
The First National Bank Of Sullivan	1932	6	–
The National Bank Of Sullivan	5392	4	–
Sunman			
The Farmers National Bank Of Sunman	8878	6	6
Swayzee			
The First National Bank At Swayzee	13862	–	4
The First National Bank Of Swayzee	8820	5	5
Tell City			
The Citizens National Bank Of Tell City	7375	5	4
The First National Bank Of Tell City	2201	6	–
The Tell City National Bank	5756	4	3

City, Bank	Ch. No.	L	S
Tennyson			
The Tennyson National Bank	8956	6	4
Terre Haute			
First-mckeen National Bank & Trust Company Of Terre Haute	47	6	2
Terre Haute First National Bank	2742	–	6
Terre Haute National Bank & Trust Co., Terre Haute	7562	4	2
The Citizens National Bank And Trust Company Of Terre Haute	13224	–	–
The First National Bank Of Terre Haute	47	3	–
The First National Bank Of Terre Haute	47	6	–
The First National Bank Of Terre Haute	2742	3	–
The Mckeen National Bank Of Terre Haute	7922	2	–
The Merchants National Bank Of Terre Haute	13938	–	4
The National State Bank Of Terre Haute	1103	5	–
The Terre Haute National Bank	7562	5	–
The Vigo County National Bank Of Terre Haute	3929	6	–
Thorntown			
The First National Bank Of Thorntown	1046	6	–
The Home National Bank Of Thorntown	5842	6	5
Tipton			
The Citizens National Bank Of Tipton	7496	5	5
The First National Bank Of Tipton	6251	5	–
Trafalgar			
The Farmers National Bank Of Trafalgar	7491	6	6
Union City			
The Commercial National Bank Of Union City	5094	5	–
The First National Bank Of Union City	815	6	–
Valparaiso			
The Farmers National Bank Of Valparaiso	2403	6	–
The First National Bank Of Porter County, Valparaiso	2704	5	–
The First National Bank Of Valparaiso	105	6	–
The Valparaiso National Bank	6215	3	5
Veedersburg			
The First National Bank Of Veedersburg	11044	5	5
Vernon			
The First National Bank Of Vernon	4688	6	6
Vevay			
The First National Bank Of Vevay	346	5	5
Vincennes			
The American National Bank Of Vincennes	3864	6	–
The First National Bank Of Vincennes	1873	2	5
The German National Bank Of Vincennes	3864	6	–
The Second National Bank Of Vincennes	4901	6	–
The Vincennes National Bank	1454	6	–
Wabash			
The Farmers & Wabash National Bank Of Wabash	6309	6	4
The Farmers And Merchants National Bank Of Wabash	6309	4	–
The First National Bank Of Wabash	129	6	–
The First National Bank Of Wabash	13888	–	–
The Wabash National Bank	3935	5	–
Wadesville			
The Farmers National Bank Of Wadesville	8927	5	5
Wakarusa			
The First National Bank Of Wakarusa	11043	6	5
Warren			
The First National Bank Of Warren	7930	6	–
Warsaw			
The First National Bank Of Warsaw	88	6	–
Washington			
The Peoples National Bank & Trust Company Of Washington	3842	6	4
The Peoples National Bank Of Washington	3842	4	–
The Washington National Bank	2043	5	5
West Baden			
The West Baden National Bank	6388	5	6
Westport			
The First National Bank Of Westport	9175	6	–
Whiteland			
The Whiteland National Bank	9492	6	–
Whiting			
The First National Bank Of Whiting	6526	4	–
Wilkinson			
The Farmers National Bank Of Wilkinson	9279	6	6
Williamsburg			
The First National Bank Of Williamsburg	8625	6	6
Winamac			
The Citizens National Bank Of Winamac	8747	6	–
The First National Bank Of Winamac	7761	6	5
Winchester			
The Citizens National Bank Of Winchester	10989	–	–
The First National Bank Of Winchester	889	5	–
Winslow			
The First National Bank Of Winslow	9159	6	5

IOWA

City, Bank	Ch. No.	L	S
Ackley			
The First National Bank Of Ackley	8762	3	4
Adair			
The First National Bank Of Adair	8699	6	–
Adel			
The First National Bank Of Adel	8981	3	–
Afton			
The First National Bank Of Afton	2326	6	–
Akron			
The First National Bank Of Akron	7322	4	5
Albia			
The Albia National Bank	3012	6	–
The First National Bank Of Albia	1799	4	6
The Peoples National Bank Of Albia	8603	4	4
Algona			
The First National Bank Of Algona	3197	4	–
Allerton			
The Farmers National Bank Of Allerton	9231	5	–
The First National Bank Of Allerton	2191	6	–
Alta			
The First National Bank Of Alta	7126	4	–
Ames			
The Ames National Bank	10408	4	4
The Union National Bank Of Ames	3017	4	4
Anamosa			
The Anamosa National Bank	4696	3	3
The First National Bank Of Anamosa	1813	6	–
Arlington			
The American National Bank Of Arlington	9664	4	3
The German-American National Bank Of Arlington	9664	5	–
Armstrong			
The First National Bank Of Armstrong	5442	4	–
Ashton			
The First National Bank Of Ashton	11644	–	–
The First National Bank Of Ashton	12883	–	–
Atlantic			
The Atlantic National Bank	2762	3	4
The First National Bank Of Atlantic	1836	6	–
Audubon			
The First National Bank Of Audubon	4891	4	4
Aurelia			
The Farmers National Bank Of Aurelia	9724	4	4
The First National Bank Of Aurelia	7108	5	4
Ayrshire			
The First National Bank Of Ayrshire	5479	4	6
Bagley			
The First National Bank Of Bagley	6995	4	4
Bancroft			
The First National Bank Of Bancroft	5643	4	–
Bedford			
The Bedford National Bank	5165	3	4
The First National Bank Of Bedford	2298	5	–
Belle Plaine			
The Citizens National Bank Of Belle Plaine	4754	3	4
The Citizens National Bank Of Belle Plaine	14069	–	–
The First National Bank Of Belle Plaine	2012	4	–
Bellevue			
The First National Bank Of Bellevue	12303	–	–
The First National Bank Of Bellevue	14158	–	–
Belmond			
The First National Bank Of Belmond	8478	6	–
Blanchard			
The First National Bank Of Blanchard	4902	6	–
Blockton			
The First National Bank Of Blockton	8211	5	5
Bloomfield			
The First National Bank Of Bloomfield	1299	6	–
The National Bank Of Bloomfield	9303	3	5
Bode			
The First National Bank Of Bode	10371	5	5
Boone			
The Boone National Bank	6838	4	–
The Citizens National Bank Of Boone	13817	–	3
The First National Bank Of Boone	2051	6	–
The First National Bank Of Boone	3273	3	2
The National Bank Of Boone	3273	5	–
Brighton			
The Brighton National Bank	2033	6	–
The National Bank Of Brighton	5554	6	–
Britt			
The First National Bank Of Britt	5020	5	–
Brooklyn			
The First National Bank Of Brooklyn	3284	6	–
Buffalo Center			
The First National Bank Of Buffalo Center	5154	3	3
Burlington			
First National Bank Of Burlington	351	6	–
The First National Bank Of Burlington	351	3	–
The First National Bank Of Burlington	13694	–	–
The Merchants National Bank Of Burlington	1744	2	6
The National State Bank Of Burlington	751	4	–
Burt			
The Burt National Bank	5703	5	–
The First National Bank Of Burt	5685	3	5
Cambridge			
The First National Bank Of Cambridge	9014	3	–
Carroll			
The First National Bank Of Carroll	3969	4	–
Casey			
The Abram Rutt National Bank Of Casey	8099	3	6
Cedar Falls			
The Cedar Falls National Bank	3871	3	5
The Citizens National Bank Of Cedar Falls	5507	6	–
The First National Bank Of Cedar Falls	2177	5	–
Cedar Rapids			
The Cedar Rapids National Bank	3643	1	2
The Citizens National Bank Of Cedar Rapids	5113	6	–
The City National Bank Of Cedar Rapids	483	5	–
The Commercial National Bank Of Cedar Rapids	9168	5	–
The First National Bank Of Cedar Rapids	500	6	–
The Merchants National Bank Of Cedar Rapids	2511	2	1
Centerville			
The Centerville National Bank	2841	4	5
The Farmers National Bank Of Centerville	2197	6	–
The First National Bank Of Centreville, Centerville	337	4	3
Chariton			
National Bank And Trust Company Of Chariton	13458	–	3
The Chariton And Lucas County National Bank Of Chariton	9024	1	5
The Chariton National Bank	6014	4	–
The First National Bank Of Chariton	1724	5	–
The Lucas County National Bank Of Chariton	9024	3	–
Charles City			
The Charles City National Bank	2579	5	–
The Citizens National Bank Of Charles City	4677	4	3
The Commercial National Bank Of Charles City	5979	3	3
The First National Bank Of Charles City	1810	2	–
Charter Oak			
The First National Bank Of Charter Oak	4376	3	4
Chelsea			
The First National Bank Of Chelsea	5412	5	3
Cherokee			
The First National Bank Of Cherokee	3049	4	4
The Security National Bank Of Cherokee	10711	4	5
Churdan			
The First National Bank Of Churdan	6737	5	4
Clarence			
The First National Bank Of Clarence	7682	4	6
Clarinda			
The Clarinda National Bank	3112	5	–
The First National Bank Of Clarinda	2028	5	–
Clarion			
The First National Bank Of Clarion	3796	4	3
The Wright County National Bank Of Clarion	3788	6	–
Clear Lake			
The First National Bank In Clear Lake	14085	–	–
The First National Bank Of Clear Lake	7869	5	3
Clearfield			
The First National Bank Of Clearfield	9549	4	6
Clinton			
First National Bank Of Lyons At Clinton	2733	6	–
The City National Bank Of Clinton	2469	2	1
The Clinton National Bank	994	3	3
The Merchants National Bank Of Clinton	3736	2	4
Clutier			
The First National Bank Of Clutier	5366	6	–
Coin			
The First National Bank Of Coin	7309	6	6
Colfax			
The First National Bank In Colfax	13686	–	4
The First National Bank Of Colfax	7114	5	4
College Springs			
The First National Bank Of College Springs	11295	6	–
Columbus Junction			
The Louisa County National Bank Of Columbus Junction	2032	3	3
Conrad			
The First National Bank Of Conrad	9447	5	6
Coon Rapids			
The Coon Rapids National Bank	6080	6	–
The First National Bank Of Coon Rapids	5514	3	5
Corning			
The Farmers National Bank Of Corning	8100	4	–
The First National Bank Of Corning	2936	6	–
The National Bank Of Corning	4268	6	–
The Okey - Vernon National Bank Of Corning	8725	3	1
Corwith			
The First National Bank Of Corwith	5775	6	–
Corydon			
The Commercial National Bank Of Corydon	13109	–	–
The First National Bank Of Corydon	10146	4	–
Council Bluffs			
First National Bank In Council Bluffs	14028	–	4
The City National Bank Of Council Bluffs	9306	3	3
The Commercial National Bank Of Council Bluffs	5838	3	–
The Council Bluffs National Bank	3427	6	–
The First National Bank Of Council Bluffs	1479	2	3
The Pacific National Bank Of Council Bluffs	1684	5	–
Cresco			
The First National Bank Of Cresco	4897	4	4
Creston			
The Creston National Bank	2833	4	6
The First National Bank In Creston	12636	–	2
The First National Bank Of Creston	2586	6	–
Crystal Lake			
The Farmers National Bank Of Crystal Lake	9853	4	5
The First National Bank Of Crystal Lake	5305	5	–
Cumberland			
The First National Bank Of Cumberland	7326	6	–
Davenport			
The Citizens National Bank Of Davenport	1671	3	–
The Davenport National Bank	848	6	–
The First National Bank Of Davenport	15	6	–
The First National Bank Of Davenport	15	1	–
The First National Bank Of Davenport	2695	1	1
The Iowa National Bank Of Davenport	4022	2	–
Dayton			
The First National Bank Of Dayton	5302	4	3
De Witt			
The First National Bank Of De Witt	3182	2	3
Decorah			
The First National Bank Of Decorah	493	6	–
The National Bank Of Decorah	5081	4	5
Deep River			
The First National Bank Of Deep River	6705	5	–
Denison			
The First National Bank Of Denison	4784	3	2
Derby			
The First National Bank Of Derby	10848	–	–
Des Moines			
Central National Bank & Trust Company Of Des Moines	13321	–	1
Iowa-des Moines National Bank & Trust Company, Des Moines	2307	–	1
The Citizens National Bank Of Des Moines	1970	4	–
The Des Moines National Bank	2583	1	–
The First National Bank Of Des Moines	389	6	–
The Iowa National Bank Of Des Moines	2307	2	–
The Merchants National Bank Of Des Moines	2631	6	–
The National State Bank Of Des Moines	950	6	–
The Second National Bank Of Des Moines	485	6	–
The Valley National Bank Of Des Moines	2886	1	3
Dexter			
The First National Bank Of Dexter	10030	5	–
Diagonal			
The First National Bank Of Diagonal	9125	4	4
Dike			
The First National Bank Of Dike	5372	6	–
Doon			
The First National Bank Of Doon	6764	4	4
Dougherty			
The First National Bank Of Dougherty	5576	6	5

City, Bank	Ch. No.	L	S
Dubuque			
The Commercial National Bank Of Dubuque	1801	6	–
The Consolidated National Bank Of Dubuque	2327	3	5
The Dubuque National Bank	3140	4	–
The First National Bank Of Dubuque	317	2	2
The Merchants National Bank Of Dubuque	846	6	–
The National State Bank Of Dubuque	1540	6	–
The Second National Bank Of Dubuque	2327	4	–
Dunkerton			
The First National Bank Of Dunkerton	6722	4	4
Dunlap			
The First National Bank Of Dunlap	4139	5	–
Dyersville			
The Dyersville National Bank	13508	–	–
The Dyersville National Bank, Dyersville	13508	–	–
The First National Bank Of Dyersville	9555	5	5
Dysart			
Dysart National Bank, Dysart	5934	–	–
The First National Bank Of Dysart	5934	4	–
Eagle Grove			
First National Bank In Eagle Grove	4694	6	–
The First National Bank Of Eagle Grove	3439	6	–
The Merchants National Bank Of Eagle Grove	4694	6	–
Eldon			
The First National Bank Of Eldon	5342	4	3
Eldora			
The First National Bank Of Eldora	5140	4	4
The Hardin County National Bank In Eldora	14286	–	–
The Hardin County National Bank Of Eldora	9233	3	4
Elkader			
The First National Bank Of Elkader	1815	3	4
Elliott			
The First National Bank Of Elliott	6857	5	5
Emmetsburg			
The Emmetsburg National Bank	8035	5	–
The First National Bank Of Emmetsburg	3337	4	–
The National Bank Of Emmetsburg	13059	–	–
Essex			
The Commercial National Bank Of Essex	5803	4	5
The First National Bank Of Essex	5738	4	3
Estherville			
The First National Bank Of Estherville	4700	5	–
Everly			
The First National Bank Of Everly	7828	3	5
Exira			
The First National Bank Of Exira	6870	4	5
Fairfield			
The Fairfield National Bank	8986	6	–
The First National Bank In Fairfield	13991	–	–
The First National Bank Of Fairfield	1475	3	2
Farmington			
The First National Bank Of Farmington	5579	4	–
Farnhamville			
The First National Bank Of Farnhamville	11907	4	4
Farragut			
The First National Bank Of Farragut	6700	5	6
Fayette			
The First National Bank Of Fayette	9592	5	–
Floyd			
The First National Bank Of Floyd	9821	5	6
Fonda			
The First National Bank Of Fonda	6550	5	3
Fontanelle			
The First National Bank Of Fontanelle	7061	4	5
Forest City			
The First National Bank Of Forest City	4889	4	–
The Forest City National Bank	5011	4	4
Fort Dodge			
The Commercial National Bank Of Fort Dodge	4566	2	4
The First National Bank Of Fort Dodge	1661	2	3
The Fort Dodge National Bank	2763	2	2
The Merchants National Bank Of Fort Dodge	1947	6	–
The Webster County National Bank Of Fort Dodge	11304	4	–
Fort Madison			
The First National Bank Of Fort Madison	3974	6	–
The Fort Madison National Bank	1611	6	–
Fredericksburg			
The First National Bank Of Fredericksburg	10541	2	6
Galva			
The First National Bank Of Galva	10501	4	–
Garden Grove			
The First National Bank Of Garden Grove	5464	6	–
Garner			
The Farmers National Bank Of Garner	8367	5	5
The First National Bank Of Garner	4810	4	–
The Hancock County National Bank Of Garner	14036	–	–
George			
The First National Bank Of George	9910	4	4
Gilmore City			
The First National Bank Of Gilmore	6611	6	–
Gladbrook			
The First National Bank Of Gladbrook	5461	4	4
Glenwood			
The Mills County National Bank Of Glenwood	1862	4	5
Glidden			
The First National Bank In Glidden	14326	–	–
The First National Bank Of Glidden	4814	3	4
Goldfield			
The First National Bank Of Goldfield	5373	6	–
Gowrie			
The First National Bank Of Gowrie	5707	4	4
Graettinger			
The First National Bank Of Graettinger	5571	5	5
Grafton			
The First National Bank Of Grafton	6610	6	–
Grand River			
The First National Bank Of Grand River	9737	4	5
Greene			
The First National Bank Of Greene	3071	6	–
The Merchants National Bank Of Greene	6880	5	–
Greenfield			
The First National Bank Of Greenfield	5334	3	–
Grinnel			
The Poweshiek County National Bank Of Grinnell	13473	–	2
Grinnell			
The Citizens National Bank Of Grinnell	7439	5	6
The First National Bank Of Grinnell	1629	5	–
The Merchants National Bank Of Grinnell	2953	5	–
Griswold			
The First National Bank Of Griswold	3048	6	–
The Griswold National Bank	8915	4	6
Grundy Center			
The First National Bank Of Grundy Center	3225	4	–
The Grundy County National Bank Of Grundy Center	3396	4	4
The Grundy National Bank Of Grundy Center	14066	–	–
Guthrie			
The Citizens National Bank Of Guthrie Center	7736	6	–
Guthrie Center			
The First National Bank Of Guthrie Center	5424	3	5
Hamburg			
The Farmers National Bank Of Hamburg	6017	5	–
The First National Bank In Hamburg	12610	–	–
The First National Bank Of Hamburg	2364	6	–
Hampton			
First National Bank Of Hampton	13842	–	2
The Citizens National Bank Of Hampton	7843	3	3
The First National Bank Of Hampton	2573	6	–
Harlan			
The First National Bank Of Harlan	5207	6	–
The Harlan National Bank	10354	4	–
Harris			
The First National Bank Of Harris	6949	6	–
Hartley			
The First National Bank Of Hartley	4881	4	–
Harvey			
The First National Bank Of Harvey	6936	4	4
Havelock			
The First National Bank Of Havelock	7294	4	–
Hawarden			
First National Bank In Hawarden	13939	–	4
The First National Bank Of Hawarden	4594	5	4
Hawkeye			
The First National Bank Of Hawkeye	8900	4	4
Hedrick			
The First National Bank Of Hedrick	5540	5	–
The Hedrick National Bank	12656	5	5
Henderson			
The Farmers National Bank Of Henderson	7382	4	4
Holstein			
The First National Bank Of Holstein	4553	6	–
Hubbard			
The First National Bank Of Hubbard	8970	4	5
Hudson			
The First National Bank Of Hudson	5659	6	–
Hull			
The First National Bank Of Hull	6953	4	4
Humboldt			
The First National Bank In Humboldt	13766	–	4
The First National Bank Of Humboldt	8277	4	4
Ida Grove			
The First National Bank Of Ida Grove	3930	6	–
Imogene			
The First National Bank Of Imogene	8295	6	5
Independence			
The Buchanan County National Bank Of Independence	13188	–	–
The First National Bank Of Independence	1581	6	–
The First National Bank Of Independence	3263	2	–
The First National Bank Of The City Of Independence	3263	6	–
The Peoples National Bank Of Independence	2187	2	–
Indianola			
The First National Bank Of Indianola	1811	3	–
Inwood			
The Farmers National Bank Of Inwood	8257	4	5
The First National Bank Of Inwood	7304	5	–
Iowa City			
The First Capital National Bank Of Iowa City	13697	–	–
The First National Bank Of Iowa City	18	6	–
The First National Bank Of Iowa City	18	3	3
The First National Bank Of Iowa City	2738	3	–
The Iowa City National Bank	977	6	–
The Iowa City National Bank	2821	6	–
Iowa Falls			
The First National Bank Of Iowa Falls	3252	4	4
The State National Bank Of Iowa Falls	7521	4	4
Irston			
The First National Bank Of Ireton	4794	6	–
Jefferson			
The Farmers And Merchants National Bank Of Jefferson	10123	6	–
The First National Bank Of Jefferson	8262	5	–
Jesup			
The First National Bank Of Jesup	2856	6	–
Jewell			
The First National Bank Of Jewell Junction	5743	5	4
Kanawha			
The First National Bank Of Kanawha	9018	5	4
Keokuk			
Keokuk National Bank	14309	–	6
The First National Bank Of Keokuk	80	6	–
The Keokuk National Bank	1992	3	4
The State National Bank Of Keokuk	1441	6	–
Kimballton			
The Landmands National Bank Of Kimballton	9619	4	5
Kingsley			
The Farmers National Bank Of Kingsley	9116	6	4
Klemme			
The First National Bank Of Klemme	6659	5	4
Knoxville			
Knoxville-Citizens National Bank & Trust Co Of Knoxville	12849	–	6
The Citizens National Bank Of Knoxville	4633	4	3
The Community National Bank And Trust Company	13707	–	4
The Knoxville National Bank	1871	2	–
The Knoxville National Bank And Trust Company	12849	–	6
The Marion County National Bank Of Knoxville	1986	3	–
La Porte City			
The First National Bank Of La Porte City	4114	4	–
Lake City			
The First National Bank Of Lake City	4966	4	5
Lake Mills			
The First National Bank Of Lake Mills	5123	5	–
Lake Park			
The First National Bank Of Lake Park	12645	–	–
Lansing			
The First National Bank Of Lansing	405	6	–
Laurens			
The First National Bank Of Laurens	4795	4	6
Lawler			
The First National Bank Of Lawler	10599	3	–
Le Mars			
The First National Bank Of Le Mars	14253	–	–
Lehigh			
The First National Bank Of Lehigh	5868	5	5
Lemars			
The First National Bank Of Lemars	2728	3	4
The Lemars National Bank	2818	6	–
Lenox			
First National Bank In Lenox	14040	–	5
The First National Bank Of Lenox	5517	3	4
Leon			
The Exchange National Bank Of Leon	5489	3	–
The First National Bank Of Leon	1696	6	–
Lime Springs			
The First National Bank Of Lime Springs	6750	5	3
Lineville			
The First National Bank Of Lineville	7261	6	–
Linn Grove			
The First National Bank Of Linn Grove	7137	5	4
Lisbon			
The First National Bank Of Lisbon	2182	6	–
Little Rock			
The First National Bank Of Little Rock	8119	5	5
Logan			
The First National Bank Of Logan	6771	4	4
Lorimor			
The First National Bank Of Lorimor	12248	5	4
Lost Nation			
The First National Bank Of Lost Nation	5402	5	5
Lyons			
The Citizens National Bank Of Lyons	4536	6	–
The First National Bank Of Lyons	66	6	–
The First National Bank Of Lyons	66	4	–
The First National Bank Of Lyons	2733	4	–
Macksburg			
The Macksburg National Bank	6852	6	6
Mallard			
The First National Bank Of Mallard	10562	–	–
Malvern			
The Farmers National Bank Of Malvern	4834	6	–
The First National Bank Of Malvern	2247	5	–
The Malvern National Bank	8057	6	6
Manchester			
The First National Bank Of Manchester	4221	4	–
Manilla			
The First National Bank Of Manilla	5873	4	4
The Manilla National Bank	6041	5	–
Manning			
The First National Bank Of Manning	3455	4	3
Mapleton			
The First National Bank Of Mapleton	10701	–	–
Maquoketa			
The First National Bank Of Maquoketa	999	5	5
Marathon			
The First National Bank Of Marathon	4789	6	5
Marcus			
The First National Bank Of Marcus	9819	6	–
Marengo			
The First National Bank Of Marengo	2484	3	–
Marion			
The First National Bank Of Marion	117	6	–
The First National Bank Of Marion	117	4	–
The First National Bank Of Marion	2753	4	4
Marshalltown			
The City National Bank Of Marshalltown	4359	6	–
The Commercial National Bank Of Marshalltown	2971	6	–
The Farmers National Bank Of Marshalltown	2115	6	–
The First National Bank Of Marshalltown	411	5	–
Mason City			
The City National Bank Of Mason City	4587	5	–
The First National Bank Of Mason City	2574	2	2
The Security National Bank Of Mason City	10428	4	–
Mcgregor			
The First National Bank Of Mcgregor	323	3	3
Melvin			
The First National Bank Of Melvin	5616	5	–
Merrill			
The First National Bank Of Merrill	10889	–	–
Milford			
The First National Bank Of Milford	5539	4	–
The Milford National Bank	9298	5	–
The Security National Bank Of Milford	9298	6	5
Milton			
The National Bank Of Milton	10243	6	5
Missouri Valley			
The First National Bank Of Missouri Valley	3189	4	4

City, Bank	Ch. No.	L	S
Monroe			
The First National Bank Of Monroe	2215	6	–
The Monroe National Bank	7357	6	6
Montezuma			
The First National Bank Of Montezuma	2961	5	6
Monticello			
The Monticello National Bank	2080	6	–
Montour			
The First National Bank Of Montour	7469	4	3
Moulton			
The First National Bank Of Moulton	5319	5	–
Mount Pleasant			
The First National Bank Of Mt. Pleasant	299	3	4
The National State Bank Of Mt. Pleasant	922	4	–
Muscatine			
The First National Bank Of Muscatine	1577	4	2
The Merchants Exchange National Bank Of Muscatine	1577	6	–
The Muscatine National Bank	692	6	–
Nashua			
The First National Bank Of Nashua	2411	6	–
Nevada			
Nevada National Bank	14065	–	5
The First National Bank Of Nevada	2555	3	–
The Nevada National Bank	13083	–	–
New Hampton			
The First National Bank Of New Hampton	2588	4	–
The New First National Bank In New Hampton	12998	–	–
The Second National Bank Of New Hampton	7607	3	4
New London			
The First National Bank Of New London	5420	6	–
The New London National Bank	8352	5	6
New Sharon			
The First National Bank Of New Sharon	8950	5	–
Newell			
The First National Bank Of Newell	10191	4	4
Newton			
The Clark National Bank Of Newton	10726	–	–
The First National Bank Of Newton	650	6	–
The First National Bank Of Newton	2644	4	5
The Newton National Bank	13609	–	3
Nora Springs			
The First National Bank Of Nora Springs	4761	5	5
Northboro			
The First National Bank Of Northboro	9015	4	6
Northwood			
The First National Bank Of Northwood	8373	5	4
Norway			
The First National Bank Of Norway	7287	5	–
Odebolt			
The Farmers National Bank Of Odebolt	5817	6	–
The First National Bank Of Odebolt	4511	3	3
Oelwein			
The First National Bank On Oelwein	5778	2	3
Ogden			
The First National Bank Of Ogden	11604	–	–
Olin			
The First National Bank Of Olin	7585	5	–
Orange City			
The First National Bank Of Orange City	6132	6	–
The Orange City National Bank	10877	–	–
Osage			
Osage Farmers National Bank, Osage	4885	–	4
The Farmers National Bank Of Osage	4885	5	–
The Osage National Bank	1618	4	–
Osceola			
The First National Bank Of Osceola	1776	6	–
The Osceola National Bank	6033	5	–
Oskaloosa			
The Farmers And Traders National Bank Of Oskaloosa	2895	6	–
The Farmers National Bank Of Oskaloosa	8076	4	–
The First National Bank Of Oskaloosa	147	6	–
The National State Bank Of Oskaloosa	1101	6	–
The Oskaloosa National Bank	2417	4	–
Ottumwa			
The First National Bank Of Ottumwa	107	4	4
The Iowa National Bank Of Ottumwa	1726	5	5
The Ottumwa National Bank	2621	3	5
The Second National Bank Of Ottumwa	195	–	–
Panora			
The Guthrie County National Bank Of Panora	3226	3	–
Parkersburg			
The First National Bank Of Parkersburg	9846	5	–
Paullina			
The First National Bank Of Paullina	10812	–	–
Pella			
The Citizens National Bank Of Pella	8047	5	–
The Farmers National Bank Of Pella	8047	–	–
The First National Bank Of Pella	1891	6	–
The Pella National Bank	2063	3	3
Perry			
The First National Bank Of Perry	3026	4	–
The Peoples National Bank Of Perry	10130	5	–
The Perry National Bank, Perry	10130	4	–
Peterson			
The First National Bank Of Peterson	4601	5	4
Pleasantville			
The First National Bank Of Pleasantville	5564	5	–
Pocahontas			
The First National Bank In Pocahontas	12544	5	–
The First National Bank Of Pocahontas	6303	4	–
Pomeroy			
The First National Bank Of Pomeroy	6063	4	6
Prairie City			
The First National Bank Of Prairie City	6755	5	5
Prescott			
The First National Bank Of Prescott	5912	4	4
Preston			
The First National Bank Of Preston	8273	5	5
Primghar			
The Farmers National Bank Of Primghar	6650	6	–
The First National Bank Of Primghar	4155	4	4

City, Bank	Ch. No.	L	S
Radcliffe			
The First National Bank Of Radcliffe	6435	5	4
Rake			
The Farmers First National Bank Of Rake	11735	–	3
Randolph			
The First National Bank Of Randolph	7833	5	5
Red Oak			
The Farmers National Bank Of Red Oak	6056	4	6
The First National Bank Of Red Oak	2130	3	3
The Montgomery County National Bank Of Red Oak	13785	–	–
The Red Oak National Bank	3055	4	4
The Valley National Bank Of Red Oak	2230	6	–
Rembrandt			
The First National Bank Of Rembrandt	10729	–	–
Remsen			
The First National Bank Of Remsen	6975	4	3
Renwick			
The First National Bank Of Renwick	7988	6	–
Riceville			
The First National Bank Of Riceville	8442	5	4
Richland			
The First National Bank Of Richland	5611	6	–
Rippey			
The First National Bank Of Rippey	7609	4	4
Rock Rapids			
The First National Bank Of Rock Rapids	3153	3	5
The Lyon County National Bank Of Rock Rapids	7089	4	4
Rock Valley			
The First National Bank Of Rock Valley	5200	3	4
Rockford			
The First National Bank Of Rockford	3053	4	–
Rockwell			
The First National Bank Of Rockwell	10217	5	6
Rockwell City			
The First National Bank Of Rockwell City	5185	3	–
The National Bank Of Rockwell City	13890	–	–
The Rockwell City National Bank	11582	6	4
Roland			
The First National Bank Of Roland	11249	5	2
Rolfe			
The First National Bank Of Rolfe	4954	5	–
Royal			
The Citizens National Bank Of Royal	10395	5	–
Ruthven			
The First National Bank Of Ruthven	5541	4	–
Sac City			
The First National Bank Of Sac City	4450	3	–
Saint Ansgar			
The First National Bank Of Saint Ansgar	10684	4	4
Sanborn			
The First National Bank Of Sanborn	4824	6	–
Seymour			
The First National Bank Of Seymour	8247	4	6
The National Bank Of Seymour	13495	–	–
The Seymour National Bank	11210	6	–
Shannon City			
The First National Bank Of Shannon City	9723	4	5
Sheffield			
The First National Bank Of Sheffield	12430	6	4
Sheldon			
The First National Bank Of Sheldon	3848	3	–
The Sheldon National Bank	7880	4	3
Shenandoah			
Shenandoah National Bank	12950	6	3
The City National Bank Of Shenandoah	14057	–	–
The Commercial National Bank Of Shenandoah	8971	6	–
The Farmers National Bank Of Shenandoah	11588	6	–
The First National Bank Of Shenandoah	2363	5	–
The Shenandoah National Bank	2679	5	–
Sibley			
The First National Bank Of Sibley	3320	5	4
Sidney			
The National Bank Of Sidney	5145	3	4
Sigourney			
The First National Bank Of Sigourney	1786	3	6
Sioux Center			
The First National Bank Of Sioux Center	7369	6	4
Sioux City			
Sioux National Bank In Sioux City	4510	3	4
The American National Bank Of Sioux City	3940	6	–
The Citizens National Bank Of Sioux City	1976	6	–
The City National Bank Of Sioux City	7401	6	–
The Commercial National Bank Of Sioux City	4630	6	–
The Continental National Bank Of Sioux City	10518	–	–
The Corn Exchange National Bank Of Sioux City	4235	6	–
The First National Bank Of Sioux City	1757	1	3
The First National Bank Of Sioux City	13538	–	–
The Iowa State National Bank Of Sioux City	3968	4	–
The Live Stock National Bank Of Sioux City	5022	2	1
The Merchants National Bank Of Sioux City	4209	6	–
The National Bank Of Commerce Of Sioux City	10139	5	–
The National Bank Of Sioux City	4431	6	–
The Northwestern National Bank Of Sioux City	4510	4	–
The Security National Bank Of Sioux City	3124	2	2
The Sioux National Bank Of Sioux City	2535	5	–
The Toy National Bank Of Sioux City	10139	3	2
Sioux Rapids			
First National Bank, Sioux Rapids	7189	6	–
The First National Bank In Sioux Rapids	13400	–	5
The First National Bank Of Sioux Rapids	9585	4	–
Spencer			
The Citizens National Bank Of Spencer	6941	3	–
The Clay County National Bank Of Spencer	13112	–	–
The First National Bank Of Spencer	3898	5	–
Spirit Lake			
First National Bank In Spirit Lake	13020	4	3
The First National Bank Of Spirit Lake	4758	3	–
The Spirit Lake National Bank	8032	3	–
Stanton			
The First National Bank Of Stanton	6434	6	6
State Center			
The First National Bank Of State Centre	8931	6	4

City, Bank	Ch. No.	L	S
Storm Lake			
Commercial National Bank Of Storm Lake	10223	6	–
The Citizens First National Bank Of Storm Lake	10034	5	5
The Citizens National Bank Of Storm Lake	10034	5	–
The First National Bank Of Storm Lake	2595	5	–
Story City			
The First National Bank Of Story City	9017	3	3
The Story City National Bank	10222	5	–
Strawberry Point			
The First National Bank Of Strawberry Point	9069	5	–
Stuart			
The First National Bank Of Stuart	2721	4	5
Sumner			
The First National Bank Of Sumner	8198	3	2
Sutherland			
The First National Bank Of Sutherland	3618	6	–
Swea City			
The First National Bank Of Swea City	5637	5	–
Tabor			
The First National Bank Of Tabor	4609	5	–
Tama City			
The First National Bank Of Tama	1880	4	–
The First National Bank Of Tama City	1880	5	–
Terril			
The First National Bank Of Terril	10238	1	–
Thompson			
The First National Bank Of Thompson	5054	5	4
Thornton			
The First National Bank Of Thornton	8340	6	3
Tipton			
The City National Bank Of Tipton	6760	3	–
The First National Bank Of Tipton	2983	5	–
Tipton National Bank	13232	–	4
Titonka			
The First National Bank Of Titonka	5597	5	6
Toledo			
The First National Bank Of Toledo	6432	3	–
The National Bank Of Toledo	13073	–	3
Traer			
The First National Bank In Traer	14172	–	–
The First National Bank Of Traer	5135	4	3
Valley Junction			
The First National Bank Of Valley Junction	5891	6	4
Villisca			
The First National Bank Of Villisca	2766	3	5
The Nodaway Valley National Bank Of Villisca	14041	–	3
The Villisca National Bank	7506	4	4
Vinton			
The Farmers National Bank In Vinton	13263	–	–
The Farmers National Bank Of Vinton	5088	4	–
The First National Bank Of Vinton	1593	6	–
Washington			
The Citizens National Bank Of Washington	6122	6	–
The First National Bank Of Washington	398	6	–
The First National Bank Of Washington	2656	6	–
The National Bank Of Washington	13849	–	–
The Washington National Bank	1762	3	3
Waterloo			
The Black Hawk National Bank Of Waterloo	6854	3	–
The Commercial National Bank Of Waterloo	2910	3	–
The First National Bank Of Waterloo	792	4	–
The Leavitt And Johnson National Bank Of Waterloo	5120	2	–
The National Bank Of Waterloo	13702	–	4
The Pioneer National Bank Of Waterloo	5120	4	3
The Waterloo National Bank	5700	5	–
Waukon			
The First National Bank Of Waukon	4921	3	–
The Peoples National Bank Of Waukon	10207	3	–
Waverly			
The First National Bank Of Waverly	3105	3	3
Webb			
The Citizens National Bank Of Webb	11162	–	–
Webster City			
The Farmers National Bank Of Webster City	3420	5	4
The First National Bank Of Webster City	1874	2	3
The Hamilton County National Bank Of Webster City	2984	6	–
Wesley			
The First National Bank Of Wesley	5457	6	–
West Union			
The Fayette County National Bank Of West Union	2015	2	4
The First National Bank Of West Union	13978	–	–
What Cheer			
The First National Bank Of What Cheer	3192	4	3
The First National Bank Of What Cheer	14143	–	–
Whiting			
First National Bank Of Whiting	10861	4	4
Williams			
The First National Bank Of Williams	5585	5	6
Winfield			
The Farmers National Bank Of Winfield	10640	4	5
Winterset			
The Citizens National Bank Of Winterset	2002	4	2
The Farmers And Merchants National Bank Of Winterset	14129	–	–
The First National Bank Of Winterset	1403	5	6
The National Bank Of Winterset	1403	6	–
Woodbine			
The First National Bank Of Woodbine	4745	3	3
Wyoming			
The First National Bank Of Wyoming	1943	4	6

KANSAS

City, Bank	Ch. No.	L	S
Abilene			
The Abilene National Bank	3777	3	4
The Farmers National Bank Of Abilene	8379	4	4
The First National Bank Of Abilene	2427	6	–
Agra			
The Farmers National Bank Of Agra	11933	–	–

City, Bank	Ch. No.	L	S
Alma			
First National Bank In Alma	13601	–	4
The Alma National Bank	5104	5	5
The Commercial National Bank Of Alma	8357	6	–
The Farmers National Bank Of Alma	10195	5	6
The First National Bank Of Alma	3769	6	–
Almena			
The First National Bank Of Almena	8255	4	4
Americus			
The Farmers National Bank Of Americus	10902	6	–
Anthony			
The Anthony National Bank	3394	6	–
The Citizens National Bank Of Anthony	6752	4	4
The First National Bank Of Anthony	3385	5	4
The Harper County National Bank Of Anthony	3384	6	–
Arkansas City			
The American National Bank Of Arkansas City	3992	6	–
The Farmers National Bank Of Arkansas City	4640	6	–
The First National Bank Of Arkansas City	3360	6	–
The Home National Bank Of Arkansas City	4487	5	4
The Security National Bank Of Arkansas City	10746	4	3
Ashland			
The First National Bank Of Ashland	3710	6	–
The Stockgrowers National Bank Of Ashland	5386	6	6
Atchison			
The Atchison National Bank	2082	5	–
The City National Bank Of Atchison	11405	5	3
The Exchange National Bank Of Atchison	2758	3	–
The First National Bank Of Atchison	1672	3	–
The United States National Bank Of Atchison	3612	6	–
Attica			
The First National Bank Of Attica	10359	6	5
Atwood			
The Farmers National Bank Of Atwood	10644	–	5
Augusta			
The American National Bank Of Augusta	10888	–	–
The First National Bank Of Augusta	6643	5	4
Axtell			
The First National Bank Of Axtell	11310	–	–
Barnard			
The First National Bank Of Barnard	8396	5	4
Baxter Springs			
The American National Bank Of Baxter Springs	11056	5	3
The Baxter National Bank Of Baxter Springs	5952	5	5
The First National Bank Of Baxter Springs	1838	6	–
Beattie			
The First National Bank Of Beattie	10587	–	–
Beaver			
The Farmers National Bank Of Beaver	11177	–	5
Belleville			
The First National Bank Of Belleville	3386	6	–
The Peoples National Bank Of Belleville	9559	4	4
Beloit			
The First National Bank Of Beloit	3231	4	3
The German National Bank Of Northern Kansas At Beloit	6701	6	–
The Union National Bank Of Beloit	6701	6	–
Bendena			
The Farmers National Bank Of Bendena	11945	–	–
Bonner Springs			
The First National Bank Of Bonner Springs	9197	5	6
Burlingame			
The Burlingame National Bank	9157	6	–
The First National Bank Of Burlingame	4040	6	5
Burlington			
The Burlington National Bank	1979	4	–
The Farmers National Bank Of Burlington	6955	5	–
The Peoples National Bank Of Burlington	3170	4	4
Burr Oak			
The First National Bank Of Burr Oak	3880	6	–
The Jewell County National Bank Of Burr Oak	7302	5	4
Caldwell			
The Caldwell National Bank	6333	6	–
The First National Bank Of Caldwell	3658	6	–
The Home National Bank Of Caldwell	11145	–	–
Caney			
The Caney Valley National Bank Of Caney	5349	4	3
The Home National Bank Of Caney	5516	5	5
Cawker City			
The Farmers And Merchants National Bank Of Cawker City	4618	6	–
The First National Bank Of Cawker City	2640	6	–
Cedar Vale			
The Cedar Vale National Bank	5608	6	5
The Citizens National Bank Of Cedar Vale	6530	4	3
The Dosbaugh National Bank Of Cedar Vale	6530	6	–
Centralia			
The First National Bank Of Centralia	3824	5	4
Chanute			
The Chanute National Bank	4036	6	–
The First National Bank Of Chanute	3819	4	2
The National Bank Of Chanute	6072	6	–
Cherokee			
The First National Bank Of Cherokee	5447	6	4
Cherryvale			
The Cherryvale National Bank	4288	6	–
The First National Bank Of Cherryvale	3277	6	–
The Montgomery County National Bank Of Cherryvale	4749	5	5
The Peoples National Bank Of Cherryvale	7383	6	–
Chetopa			
The First National Bank Of Chetopa	1902	5	–
The National Bank Of Chetopa	11374	5	6
Cimarron			
The First National Bank In Cimarron	13329	–	4
The First National Bank Of Cimarron	3751	6	–
Clay Center			
The First National Bank Of Clay Center	3072	4	4
The Peoples National Bank Of Clay Center	3345	4	3
Clifton			
The First National Bank Of Clifton	7178	3	5
Clyde			
The Exchange National Bank Of Clyde	11775	–	4
The First National Bank Of Clyde	3115	6	–
Coats			
The First National Bank Of Coats	11488	–	–
Coffeyville			
The Condon National Bank Of Coffeyville	6797	3	3
The First National Bank Of Coffeyville	3324	4	3
Colby			
The Citizens National Bank Of Colby	11047	6	–
The First National Bank Of Colby	3512	6	–
The Thomas County National Bank Of Colby	13076	3	3
Coldwater			
The Coldwater National Bank	6767	5	3
The First National Bank Of Coldwater	3703	6	–
Collyer			
The First National Bank Of Collyer	11855	–	4
Colony			
The First National Bank Of Colony	11531	5	5
Columbus			
The First National Bank Of Columbus	6103	6	4
Concordia			
The Citizens National Bank Of Concordia	3748	6	–
The Concordia National Bank	3090	6	–
The First National Bank Of Concordia	3066	6	–
Conway Springs			
The First National Bank Of Conway Springs	8467	4	4
Cottonwood Falls			
The Chase County National Bank Of Cottonwood Falls	2764	4	–
The Exchange National Bank Of Cottonwood Falls	6590	4	3
Council Grove			
The Council Grove National Bank	5757	4	4
The First National Bank Of Council Grove	2001	6	–
Cunningham			
The First National Bank Of Cunningham	12791	–	–
Delphos			
The First National Bank Of Delphos	7532	3	4
Dexter			
The First National Bank Of Dexter	9225	3	–
Dighton			
The First National Bank Of Dighton	3888	6	–
The First National Bank Of Dighton	9773	5	2
Dodge City			
First National Bank In Dodge City	7285	5	4
The First National Bank Of Dodge City	3596	6	–
The National Bank Of Commerce Of Dodge City	7285	6	–
The Southwest National Bank Of Dodge City	10918	–	–
Downs			
The Downs National Bank	11318	6	4
The Exchange National Bank Of Downs	3563	6	–
The First National Bank Of Downs	3569	6	–
Edmond			
The First National Bank Of Edmond	9160	5	–
Edna			
The First National Bank Of Edna	7590	4	4
El Dorado			
The El Dorado National Bank	6494	4	4
The Exchange National Bank Of El Dorado	3213	6	–
The Farmers And Merchants National Bank Of El Dorado	4981	4	4
The First National Bank Of El Dorado	1957	6	–
The Merchants National Bank Of El Dorado	3833	6	–
The National Bank Of El Dorado	3035	6	–
Elk City			
The First National Bank Of Elk City	8145	5	4
The Peoples National Bank Of Elk City	8708	6	–
Elkhart			
The First National Bank Of Elkhart	11187	–	–
Ellis			
The First National Bank Of Ellis	10987	–	–
Ellsworth			
The Central National Bank Of Ellsworth	3447	5	6
The First National Bank Of Ellsworth	3249	6	–
Emporia			
The Citizens National Bank Of Emporia	5498	4	4
The Commercial National Bank And Trust Company Of Emporia	11781	4	3
The Emporia National Bank	1983	3	–
The First National Bank Of Emporia	1915	1	–
Englewood			
The First National Bank Of Englewood	9097	6	–
Erie			
The First National Bank Of Erie	3963	4	–
Eureka			
The Citizens National Bank Of Eureka	5655	4	4
The Citizens National Bank Of Eureka	14329	–	–
The First National Bank Of Eureka	3148	6	–
The First National Bank Of Eureka	12457	6	–
The Home National Bank Of Eureka	7303	6	4
Fairview			
The Farmers National Bank Of Fairview	11107	–	–
Florence			
The First National Bank Of Florence	11773	–	–
Formoso			
The First National Bank Of Formoso	8596	5	5
Fort Leavenworth			
The Army National Bank Of Fort Leavenworth	8796	4	3
Fort Scott			
The Citizens National Bank Of Fort Scott	3175	3	2
The First National Bank Of Fort Scott	1763	6	–
The Fort Scott National Bank	12442	–	–
The Merchants National Bank Of Fort Scott	1927	6	–
Fowler			
The First National Bank Of Fowler	9595	5	5
Frankfort			
The Citizens National Bank Of Frankfort	11738	–	–
The First National Bank Of Frankfort	2809	6	–
The First National Bank Of Frankfort	11916	–	–
Fredonia			
The First National Bank Of Fredonia	3835	6	–
The Fredonia National Bank	7218	6	–
Galena			
The Galena National Bank	4798	5	5
Garden City			
The Finney County National Bank Of Garden City	3900	6	–
The First National Bank Of Garden City	3448	6	4
The Garden City National Bank	7646	6	4
The Garden National Bank Of Garden City	13990	–	–
Garnett			
The Anderson County National Bank Of Garnett	4032	6	–
The First National Bank Of Garnett	2973	6	–
The National Bank Of Commerce Of Garnett	5292	5	5
Gaylord			
The First National Bank Of Gaylord	6970	6	5
Girard			
The First National Bank Of Girard	3216	5	4
The Girard National Bank	13347	–	–
Glasco			
The First National Bank Of Glasco	7683	3	4
Goff			
The First National Bank Of Goff	7416	6	5
Goodland			
First National Bank In Goodland	14163	–	6
The Farmers National Bank Of Goodland	7882	5	–
The First National Bank Of Goodland	6039	5	4
Great Bend			
The Citizens National Bank Of Great Bend	5705	4	5
The Farmers National Bank Of Great Bend	11707	4	3
The First National Bank Of Great Bend	3363	4	3
Green			
The First National Bank Of Green	11222	–	–
Greenleaf			
The Citizens National Bank Of Greenleaf	10789	–	–
The First National Bank Of Greenleaf	3567	6	–
Greensburg			
The Farmers National Bank Of Greensburg	10557	6	6
The First National Bank In Greensburg	10557	–	6
The First National Bank Of Greensburg	3667	6	–
Gypsum			
The Gypsum Valley National Bank Of Gypsum	9695	4	4
Halstead			
The Halstead National Bank	3443	6	–
Hamilton			
The First National Bank Of Hamilton	6932	5	5
Hanover			
The First National Bank Of Hanover	11811	–	–
Harper			
First National Bank In Harper	8307	6	4
The First National Bank Of Harper	3265	6	–
The Harper National Bank	3431	6	–
The National Bank Of Harper	8307	6	–
The Security National Bank Of Harper	8308	6	–
Hartford			
The Hartford National Bank	8197	5	6
Harveyville			
The First National Bank Of Harveyville	11822	–	–
Havensville			
The First National Bank Of Havensville	5506	5	4
Haviland			
The First National Bank Of Haviland	11464	–	–
Hays City			
The First National Bank Of Hays City	3885	6	–
Herington			
The First National Bank Of Herington	4058	6	5
Hiawatha			
The First National Bank Of Hiawatha	2589	3	5
Highland			
The First National Bank Of Highland	9136	5	6
Hill City			
The First National Bank Of Hill City	3758	6	–
Hillsboro			
The First National Bank Of Hillsboro	6120	6	4
Hoisington			
The First National Bank Of Hoisington	9232	5	4
The Hoisington National Bank	12694	–	4
Holton			
The First National Bank Of Holton	3061	4	–
The National Bank Of Holton	5041	4	–
Holyrood			
The First National Bank Of Holyrood	11796	–	–
Hope			
The First National Bank Of Hope	12384	–	–
Horton			
The First National Bank Of Horton	3810	4	4
Howard			
The First National Bank Of Howard	3242	4	5
The Howard National Bank	3794	4	4
Hoxie			
The First National Bank Of Hoxie	5687	4	4
Hugoton			
The First National Bank Of Hugoton	11300	–	5
Humboldt			
The Humboldt First National Bank, Humboldt	3807	6	–
The Humboldt National Bank	6963	5	5
Hutchinson			
The American National Bank Of Hutchinson	10765	6	4
The Commercial National Bank Of Hutchinson	8430	4	–
The Exchange National Bank Of Hutchinson	13106	–	4
The Farmers National Bank Of Hutchinson	10765	6	–
The First National Bank Of Hutchinson	3180	2	–
The Hutchinson National Bank	3199	6	–
The National Bank Of Commerce Of Hutchinson	3861	6	–
Independence			
Citizens-First National Bank Of Independence	4592	4	3
First National Bank In Independence	4592	–	5
The Citizens National Bank Of Independence	4592	3	–
The Citizens National Bank Of Independence	13924	–	–
The Commercial National Bank Of Independence	4499	4	5
The First National Bank Of Independence	3021	5	–
The Security National Bank Of Independence	13492	–	3
Iola			
First National Bank Of Iola	5287	4	–
The Northrup National Bank Of Iola	5287	4	–

City, Bank	Ch. No.	L	S
Jetmore			
The First National Bank Of Jetmore	3805	6	–
Jewell City			
The First National Bank Of Jewell City	3591	4	5
Junction City			
The Central National Bank Of Junction City	4284	4	3
The First National Bank Of Junction City	1977	6	–
The First National Bank Of Junction City, Kansas	3543	4	4
Kanorado			
The First National Bank Of Kanorado	11860	–	5
Kansas City			
Security National Bank Of Kansas City	13801	–	1
The Bankers National Bank Of Kansas City	8602	6	–
The Commercial National Bank Of Kansas City	6311	2	2
The First National Bank Of Kansas City	3706	6	–
The Inter-State National Bank Of Kansas City, Kansas	4381	4	–
The Peoples National Bank Of Kansas City	9309	3	3
The Wyandotte National Bank Of Kansas City	3726	6	–
Kensington			
The First National Bank Of Kensington	7493	6	5
Kingman			
The Citizens National Bank Of Kingman	3737	6	–
The Farmers National Bank Of Kingman	7412	6	–
The First National Bank Of Kingman	3509	6	–
The Kingman National Bank	3559	6	–
Kinsley			
The First National Bank Of Kinsley	3759	6	–
The National Bank Of Kinsley	5810	6	–
Kiowa			
The First National Bank Of Kiowa	8220	5	4
Kirwin			
The First National Bank Of Kirwin	3454	6	–
La Harpe			
The First National Bank Of La Harpe	7226	4	5
Lacrosse			
The First National Bank Of Lacrosse	3970	6	–
Larned			
First National Bank In Larned	7125	5	4
The First National Bank Of Larned	2666	6	–
The Moffet Brothers National Bank Of Larned	7125	5	–
Lawrence			
The Douglas County National Bank Of Lawrence	3849	6	–
The First National Bank Of Lawrence	3584	–	2
The Lawrence National Bank	3849	3	2
The Merchants National Bank Of Lawrence	3584	3	3
The National Bank Of Lawrence	1590	6	–
The Second National Bank Of Lawrence	1732	6	–
The Watkins National Bank Of Lawrence	3881	3	–
Leavenworth			
The First National Bank Of Leavenworth	182	3	3
The Leavenworth National Bank	3033	2	3
The Manufacturers National Bank Of Leavenworth	3908	4	–
The Metropolitan National Bank Of Leavenworth	3194	6	–
The Second National Bank Of Leavenworth	1448	6	–
Lebanon			
The First National Bank Of Lebanon	5799	6	4
Leoti City			
The First National Bank Of Leoti City	3844	6	–
Leroy			
The First National Bank Of Leroy	6149	4	5
Lewis			
The First National Bank Of Lewis	10863	5	–
Liberal			
The First National Bank Of Liberal	6720	5	5
The Peoples National Bank Of Liberal	13406	–	3
Lincoln			
The Farmers National Bank Of Lincoln	6672	5	4
The First National Bank Of Lincoln	3464	6	–
Lindsborg			
The First National Bank Of Lindsborg	3589	5	5
Logan			
The First National Bank Of Logan	6841	5	4
Longton			
The First National Bank Of Longton	8525	6	–
The Home National Bank Of Longton	9911	6	4
Louisburg			
The First National Bank Of Louisburg	11798	6	5
Lucas			
The First National Bank Of Lucas	7561	5	5
Luray			
The First National Bank Of Luray	10065	6	5
Lyndon			
The First National Bank Of Lyndon	7222	5	4
Lyons			
The Chandler National Bank Of Lyons	14048	–	2
The First National Bank Of Lyons	3577	6	–
The Lyons National Bank	5353	5	5
Madison			
The First National Bank Of Madison	5529	5	5
Manhattan			
The First National Bank Of Manhattan	2094	4	–
The First National Bank Of Manhattan	3782	4	3
The Union National Bank Of Manhattan	4008	3	3
Mankato			
First National Bank In Mankato	6817	5	2
The Farmers National Bank Of Mankato	11536	–	–
The First National Bank Of Mankato	3745	6	–
The Jewell County National Bank Of Mankato	3812	6	–
The Mankato National Bank	6817	5	–
Marion			
The Cottonwood Valley National Bank Of Marion	3928	6	–
The Farmers And Drovers National Bank Of Marion	10980	–	5
The First National Bank Of Marion	3018	6	–
The Marion National Bank	7911	6	4
Marysville			
The First National Bank Of Marysville	2791	4	–
Mayetta			
The First National Bank Of Mayetta	9934	6	5
Mc Cune			
The First National Bank Of Mc Cune	12191	6	5
Mcpherson			
The First National Bank Of Mcpherson	3521	6	–
The Mcpherson National Bank	3803	6	–
The Second National Bank Of Mcpherson	3791	6	–
Meade			
The First National Bank Of Meade	7192	5	5
Meade Center			
The First National Bank Of Meade Center	3695	6	–
The Meade County National Bank Of Meade Center	3853	6	–
Medicine Lodge			
The Citizens National Bank Of Medicine Lodge	3594	6	–
The First National Bank Of Medicine Lodge	3253	6	–
The First National Bank Of Medicine Lodge	10575	–	–
Millbrook			
The First National Bank Of Millbrook	3758	6	–
Minneapolis			
The Citizens National Bank Of Minneapolis	4931	4	4
The First National Bank Of Minneapolis	3353	6	–
The Minneapolis National Bank	3731	5	–
Moline			
The First National Bank Of Moline	7318	5	6
The Moline National Bank	8369	5	–
Mound Valley			
The First National Bank Of Mound Valley	8107	6	–
Mount Hope			
The First National Bank Of Mt. Hope	5559	5	6
Natoma			
The First National Bank Of Natoma	9384	5	5
Neodesha			
The First National Bank Of Neodesha	6914	5	4
The Neodesha National Bank	6895	4	5
The Union National Bank Of Neodesha	13033	–	–
Ness City			
First National Bank In Ness City	8142	–	6
The Citizens National Bank Of Ness City	8081	5	–
The First National Bank Of Ness City	3542	6	–
The National Bank Of Ness City	8142	5	6
Newton			
The First National Bank Of Newton	2777	5	5
The German National Bank Of Newton	3473	6	–
The Midland National Bank Of Newton	4860	5	4
The Newton National Bank	3297	5	–
Norcatur			
Decatur County National Bank Of Oberlin	8290	–	6
The First National Bank Of Norcatur	8290	5	5
Norton			
The First National Bank Of Norton	3687	4	3
The National Bank Of Norton	8339	6	–
Nortonville			
The First National Bank Of Nortonville	5359	4	5
Oakley			
The First National Bank Of Oakley	10041	6	4
Oberlin			
The Farmers National Bank Of Oberlin	7298	5	4
The First National Bank Of Oberlin	3511	6	–
The Oberlin National Bank	4642	5	3
Olathe			
The First National Bank Of Olathe	1828	6	–
The First National Bank Of Olathe	3720	4	3
Onaga			
The First National Bank Of Onaga	12353	5	5
Osage City			
The First National Bank Of Osage City	3813	6	–
Osawatomie			
The First National Bank Of Osawatomie	12439	–	–
Osborne			
The Exchange National Bank Of Osborne	3472	5	3
The Farmers National Bank Of Osborne	5834	5	5
The First National Bank Of Osborne	3319	4	–
Oswego			
First National Bank At Oswego	11576	6	5
The First National Bank Of Oswego	3038	5	–
Ottawa			
The First National Bank Of Ottawa	1718	4	3
The Peoples National Bank Of Ottawa	1910	3	3
Overbrook			
The First National Bank Of Overbrook	7195	5	5
Palco			
The First National Bank Of Palco	11968	–	–
Paola			
The First National Bank Of Paola	1864	5	–
The Miami County National Bank Of Paola	3350	4	3
The National Bank Of Paola	3795	6	–
The Peoples National Bank Of Paola	3991	5	–
Parsons			
The Farmers National Bank Of Parsons	11537	5	–
The First National Bank Of Parsons	1951	3	4
Peabody			
The First National Bank Of Peabody	3134	6	6
Penalosa			
The Farmers National Bank Of Penalosa	11828	–	–
Phillipsburg			
The Farmers National Bank Of Phillipsburg	10776	–	–
The First National Bank Of Phillipsburg	3601	4	4
Pittsburg			
American Exchange National Bank Of Commerce In Pittsburg	8418	6	–
The First National Bank Of Pittsburg	3463	3	3
The Manufacturers National Bank Of Pittsburg	4136	6	–
The National Bank Of Commerce In Pittsburg	8418	5	–
The National Bank Of Pittsburg	3475	4	4
Plainville			
The First National Bank Of Plainville	7313	5	–
Pleasanton			
The First National Bank Of Pleasanton	8803	6	5
Potwin			
The First National Bank Of Potwin	10994	–	–
Prairie View			
The First National Bank Of Prairie View	9373	5	5
Pratt			
First National Bank In Pratt	6229	5	5
The First National Bank Of Pratt	3649	6	–
The National Bank Of Pratt	6229	6	–
The Pratt County National Bank Of Pratt	3787	6	–
Pretty Prairie			
The Farmers National Bank Of Pretty Prairie	11316	–	–
The First National Bank Of Pretty Prairie	11316	–	–
Quinter			
The First National Bank Of Quinter	10982	–	–
Randall			
The Randall National Bank	11887	6	–
Richmond			
The First National Bank Of Richmond	11728	6	–
The Peoples National Bank Of Richmond	11728	–	4
Russell			
The First National Bank Of Russell	3657	6	–
Russell Springs			
The First National Bank Of Russell Springs	3775	6	–
Sabetha			
The Citizens National Bank Of Sabetha	2990	6	–
The First National Bank Of Sabetha	2954	6	–
The National Bank Of Sabetha	4626	4	5
Saint Francis			
The First National Bank Of Saint Francis	11857	–	–
Saint John			
The First National Bank Of Saint John	3467	6	4
The St. John National Bank	7844	5	5
Saint Marys			
The Farmers National Bank Of Saint Marys	11186	–	–
The First National Bank Of St. Marys	3374	3	4
The National Bank Of Saint Marys	4619	6	–
Salina			
The American National Bank Of Salina	4317	6	–
The Farmers National Bank Of Salina	4742	4	3
The First National Bank Of Salina	2538	6	–
The National Bank Of America At Salina	4945	3	3
The Salina National Bank	3531	6	–
Scandia			
First National Bank In Belleville	3779	4	3
The First National Bank Of Scandia	3779	6	–
The National Bank Of Belleville	3779	5	–
Scott City			
The First National Bank Of Scott City	8808	5	4
Sedan			
The First National Bank Of Sedan	3855	4	4
The Peoples National Bank Of Sedan	7535	6	–
The Sedan National Bank	4150	6	–
Seneca			
The First National Bank Of Seneca	2952	5	–
The National Bank Of Seneca	5101	5	4
Smith Center			
The Smith County National Bank Of Smith Center	3630	6	–
Smith Centre			
The First National Bank Of Smith Centre	3546	5	4
Solomon			
The Solomon National Bank	9794	5	4
Spearville			
The First National Bank Of Spearville	10161	5	5
Stafford			
The Farmers National Bank Of Stafford	8883	6	5
The First National Bank Of Stafford	3852	6	–
Sterling			
The First National Bank Of Sterling	3207	5	4
Stockton			
The First National Bank Of Stockton	3440	6	–
The National State Bank Of Stockton	8274	5	–
The Stockton National Bank	7815	5	4
Strong City			
The Strong City National Bank	3002	6	–
Summerfield			
The First National Bank Of Summerfield	10971	–	–
Syracuse			
The First National Bank Of Syracuse	8114	5	4
Thayer			
The First National Bank Of Thayer	9465	5	3
Tonganoxie			
The First National Bank Of Tonganoxie	12821	–	–
Topeka			
National Bank Of Topeka	12740	–	3
The Capital National Bank Of Topeka	7907	5	–
The Central National Bank Of Topeka	3078	2	1
The Farmers National Bank Of Topeka	10390	4	4
The First National Bank Of Topeka	1660	6	–
The First National Bank Of Topeka	2646	4	–
The Kansas National Bank Of Topeka	3790	6	–
The Kansas Valley National Bank Of Topeka	1660	6	–
The Kaw Valley National Bank Of Topeka	11398	3	5
The Merchants National Bank Of Topeka	3909	3	3
The State National Bank Of Topeka	2192	6	–
The Topeka National Bank	1945	5	–
Toronto			
The First National Bank Of Toronto	6819	6	3
Towanda			
The First National Bank Of Towanda	11154	6	–
The Towanda National Bank	12935	6	3
Tribune			
The First National Bank Of Tribune	12168	–	–
Troy			
The First National Bank Of Troy	8162	5	4
Union Stockyards			
The Union Stockyards National Bank, Union Stockyards	9758	6	4
Valley Falls			
The First National Bank Of Valley Falls	11816	6	6
Victoria			
The Farmers National Bank Of Victoria	10749	–	–
The First National Bank Of Victoria	10749	–	–
The German National Bank Of Victoria	10749	–	–
Wakeney			
The First National Bank Of Wakeeney	3776	6	–
Wamego			
The First National Bank Of Wamego	3434	2	4

City, Bank	Ch. No.	L	S
Washington			
The First National Bank Of Washington	2912	4	–
The Washington National Bank	3167	5	–
Waverly			
The First National Bank Of Waverly	6101	5	5
Wellington			
First National Bank In Wellington	3091	6	5
The Farmers National Bank Of Wellington	11889	–	–
The First National Bank Of Wellington	2879	6	–
The National Bank Of Commerce Of Wellington	8399	5	4
The State National Bank Of Wellington	3564	6	–
The Sumner National Bank Of Wellington	3865	6	–
The Wellington National Bank	3091	6	–
West Moreland			
The First National Bank Of West Moreland	3304	6	–
Wetmore			
The First National Bank Of Wetmore	8974	5	6
White City			
The First National Bank Of White City	7970	5	5
Wichita			
First National Bank In Wichita	2782	–	1
The First National Bank Of Wichita	1913	6	–
The Fourth National Bank Of Wichita	3683	4	–
The Fourth National Bank Of Wichita	12490	–	–
The Kansas National Bank Of Wichita	2782	6	–
The National Bank Of Commerce Of Wichita	5169	4	–
The National Bank Of Wichita	6392	6	–
The Southwest National Bank Of Wichita	12346	–	3
The State National Bank Of Wichita	3524	6	–
The Union National Bank Of Wichita	11010	–	5
The West Side National Bank Of Wichita	3756	6	–
The Wichita National Bank	2786	6	–
Winfield			
The Cowley County National Bank Of Winfield	4556	5	–
The First National Bank Of Winfield	3218	3	2
The Winfield National Bank	3351	5	5
Wyandotte			
The First National Bank Of Wyandotte	1840	5	–
Yates Center			
The Woodson National Bank Of Yates Center	3108	6	–
The Yates Center National Bank	6326	6	–

KENTUCKY

City, Bank	Ch. No.	L	S
Adairville			
The First National Bank Of Adairville	8814	5	6
Ashland			
The Ashland National Bank	2010	3	4
The Merchants National Bank Of Ashland	4559	6	–
The Second National Bank Of Ashland	3944	6	3
The Third National Bank Of Ashland	12293	6	4
Augusta			
The Farmers National Bank Of Augusta	4612	5	–
The First National Bank Of Augusta	4616	6	–
Barbourville			
The First National Bank Of Barbourville	6262	6	6
The National Bank Of John A Black Of Barbourville	7284	5	6
The Union National Bank Of Barbourville	13906	–	4
Bardwell			
The First National Bank Of Bardwell	8331	5	5
Beattyville			
The National Bank Of Beattyville	7751	6	–
Berea			
The Berea National Bank	8435	5	4
Bowling Green			
The American National Bank Of Bowling Green	9365	3	4
The Bowling Green National Bank	7804	5	–
The Citizens National Bank Of Bowling Green	5900	3	3
The Liberty National Bank Of Bowling Green	11589	6	–
The National Southern Kentucky Bank Of Bowling Green	2149	6	–
The Warren National Bank Of Bowling Green	10448	6	–
Brooksville			
The First National Bank Of Brooksville	8830	5	5
Buffalo			
The First National Bank Of Buffalo	11538	6	6
Burnside			
The First National Bank Of Burnside	8903	6	6
Campbellsville			
The Taylor National Bank Of Campbellsville	6342	6	4
Cannel City			
The Morgan County National Bank Of Cannel City	7891	5	5
Carlisle			
The First National Bank Of Carlisle	5959	4	–
Carrollton			
The Carrollton National Bank	3074	4	4
The First National Bank Of Carrollton	2592	4	4
Catlettsburg			
The Big Sandy National Bank Of Catlettsburg	4200	5	–
The Catlettsburg National Bank	2740	5	–
The Kentucky National Bank Of Catlettsburg	9602	4	6
Cave City			
The H. Y. Davis National Bank Of Cave City	7919	5	–
Caverna			
The Caverna National Bank	2206	6	–
Central City			
The First National Bank Of Central City	8229	6	4
Clay			
The Farmers National Bank Of Clay	8943	6	5
Clay City			
The Clay City National Bank	4217	5	5
Clinton			
The First National Bank Of Clinton	9098	4	5
The First National Bank Of Clinton	14259	–	–
Columbia			
The First National Bank And Trust Company Of Columbia	6769	6	5
The First National Bank Of Columbia	6769	6	–
Corbin			
The First National Bank Of Corbin	7544	6	5
The Whitley National Bank Of Corbin	9634	6	5
Covington			
The Citizens National Bank Of Covington	4260	4	5
The Commercial National Bank Of Covington	8564	5	–
The Covington City National Bank	1859	5	–
The Farmers And Traders National Bank Of Covington	2722	5	–
The First National Bank And Trust Company Of Covington	718	5	3
The First National Bank Of Covington	718	3	–
The German National Bank Of Covington	1847	2	–
The Liberty National Bank Of Covington	1847	4	–
The Merchants National Bank Of Covington	8110	6	–
Cynthiana			
The Farmers National Bank Of Cynthiana	2560	4	4
The National Bank Of Cynthiana	1900	5	4
Danville			
The Boyle National Bank Of Danville	3317	6	–
The Central National Bank Of Danville	1600	6	–
The Citizens National Bank Of Danville	3381	5	4
The Farmers National Bank Of Danville	2409	4	4
The First National Bank Of Danville	1601	6	–
Dawson Springs			
The First National Bank Of Dawson Springs	11548	6	5
Dry Ridge			
The First National Bank Of Dry Ridge	7012	5	6
East Bernstadt			
The First National Bank Of East Bernstadt	10254	6	5
Eddyville			
The First National Bank Of Eddyville	7492	6	–
Elizabethtown			
The First National Bank Of Elizabethtown	3042	5	–
The First-hardin National Bank Of Elizabethtown	6028	3	4
The Hardin National Bank Of Elizabethtown	6028	6	–
The Union National Bank Of Elizabethtown	13024	–	–
Falmouth			
The First National Bank Of Falmouth	11947	5	5
Fleming			
The First National Bank Of Fleming	11988	6	4
Flemingsburg			
The Fleming County National Bank Of Flemingsburg	2323	6	–
Frankfort			
The Frankfort National Bank	4091	6	–
The National Branch Bank Of Kentucky, Frankfort	5376	5	5
The State National Bank Of Frankfort	4090	3	4
Franklin			
The Farmers And Merchants National Bank Of Franklin	7402	6	–
The First National Bank Of Franklin	1760	6	–
Fulton			
The City National Bank Of Fulton	6167	6	4
The First National Bank Of Fulton	4563	6	6
Georgetown			
The First National Bank Of Georgetown	2927	6	5
The Georgetown National Bank	8579	5	5
Glasgow			
The Citizens National Bank Of Glasgow	8439	5	5
The Farmers National Bank Of Glasgow	9722	6	5
The First National Bank Of Glasgow	4819	5	6
The New Farmers National Bank Of Glasgow	13651	–	4
The Third National Bank Of Glasgow	6872	6	–
The Trigg National Bank Of Glasgow	5486	3	5
Grayson			
The First National Bank Of Grayson	12982	–	5
Greenup			
The First National Bank Of Greenup	7037	5	5
Greenville			
The First National Bank Of Greenville	4356	5	5
Harlan			
The Citizens National Bank Of Harlan	12243	5	5
The First National Bank Of Harlan	9791	6	–
The Harlan National Bank	12295	6	4
Harrodsburg			
First-Mercer National Bank Of Harrodsburg	2531	–	6
Mercer County National Bank Of Harrodsburg	13612	–	3
The First National Bank Of Harrodsburg	1807	6	–
The Mercer National Bank Of Harrodsburg	2531	4	5
Hartford			
The First National Bank Of Hartford	5792	6	–
Hazard			
The First National Bank Of Hazard	8258	5	–
The First National Bank Of Hazard	13248	–	–
Henderson			
Ohio Valley National Bank Of Henderson	13983	–	5
The First National Bank Of Henderson	13757	–	5
The Henderson National Bank	1615	4	–
The Planters National Bank Of Henderson	2931	6	–
Hickman			
The Farmers And Merchants National Bank Of Hickman	4465	6	–
Hodgenville			
Farmers National Bank Of Hodgenville	6894	4	5
The Farmers National Bank Of Hodgenville	6894	5	–
The La Rue National Bank Of Hodgenville	9843	6	–
The Lincoln National Bank Of Hodgenville	13479	–	5
Hopkinsville			
The First National Bank Of Hopkinsville	3856	4	6
Horse Cave			
The First National Bank Of Horse Cave	7602	5	6
Hustonville			
The National Bank Of Hustonville	2917	6	4
Jackson			
The First National Bank Of Jackson	9320	5	3
Jenkins			
The First National Bank Of Jenkins	10062	5	6
The Jenkins National Bank	10062	6	–
Lancaster			
The Citizens National Bank Of Lancaster	2888	5	5
The National Bank Of Lancaster	1493	5	6
Latonia			
The First National Bank Of Latonia	6248	5	6
Lawrenceburg			
The Anderson County National Bank Of Lawrenceburg	2190	6	–
The Anderson National Bank Of Lawrenceburg	8604	4	4
The Lawrenceburg National Bank	7497	4	4
The Witherspoon National Bank Of Lawrenceburg	8862	6	–
Lebanon			
The Citizens National Bank Of Lebanon	3988	4	4
The Farmers National Bank Of Lebanon	4271	5	4
The Marion National Bank Of Lebanon	2150	4	3
The National Bank Of Lebanon	1694	6	–
Lexington			
First National Bank & Trust Company Of Lexington	906	–	1
Phoenix National Bank And Trust Company Of Lexington	3052	3	–
The Fayette National Bank Of Lexington	1720	3	4
The First And City National Bank Of Lexington	906	2	–
The First National Bank Of Lexington	760	5	–
The Lexington City National Bank	906	4	–
The National Exchange Bank Of Lexington	2393	5	–
The Phoenix And Third National Bank Of Lexington	3052	3	–
The Phoenix National Bank Of Lexington	3942	5	–
The Second National Bank Of Lexington	2901	4	4
The Third National Bank Of Lexington	3052	6	–
Litchfield			
The Grayson County National Bank Of Litchfield	5314	6	–
London			
The First National Bank Of London	3943	6	–
The National Bank Of London	7890	6	6
Louisa			
The First National Bank Of Louisa	7110	5	4
The Louisa National Bank	7122	6	5
Louisville			
Liberty National Bank And Trust Company Of Louisville	14320	–	2
National Bank Of Commerce Of Louisville	9241	4	–
The American National Bank Of Louisville	4956	4	–
The American-Southern National Bank Of Louisville	4956	6	–
The Citizens National Bank Of Louisville	2164	3	–
The Citizens Union National Bank Of Louisville	2164	4	2
The Continental National Bank Of Louisville	7457	6	–
The First National Bank Of Louisville	109	3	2
The Fourth National Bank Of Louisville	2784	6	–
The German National Bank Of Louisville	2062	4	–
The Kentucky National Bank Of Louisville	1908	6	–
The Louisville City National Bank	788	6	–
The Louisville National Bank & Trust Company, Louisville	5161	6	–
The Louisville National Bank, Louisville	5161	6	–
The Louisville National Banking Company	5161	4	–
The Merchants National Bank Of Louisville	2161	6	–
The National Bank Of Kentucky Of Louisville	5312	1	3
The Planters National Bank Of Louisville	790	5	–
The Second National Bank Of Louisville	777	5	–
The Southern National Bank Of Louisville	5195	4	–
The Third National Bank Of Louisville	2171	4	–
The Union National Bank Of Louisville	4145	4	–
The Western National Bank Of Louisville	7457	6	–
Ludlow			
The First National Bank Of Ludlow	5323	6	5
Lynch			
The Lynch National Bank	12649	–	–
Madisonville			
The Farmers National Bank Of Madisonville	8451	5	5
The Morton National Bank Of Madisonville	8386	6	–
Manchester			
The First National Bank Of Manchester	7605	4	5
Mayfield			
The City National Bank Of Mayfield	5033	5	–
The Farmers National Bank Of Mayfield	6834	6	–
The First National Bank Of Mayfield	2245	3	3
Maysville			
The Bank Of Maysville, National Banking Association	9561	6	–
The First National Bank Of Maysville	2467	4	–
The National Bank Of Maysville	1702	6	–
The State National Bank Of Maysville	2663	3	4
Middleborough			
The National Bank Of Middleborough	7086	6	4
Middlesborough			
The First National Bank Of Middlesborough	4201	6	–
Monticello			
The Citizens National Bank Of Monticello	6419	6	5
The National Bank Of Monticello	1931	6	–
Morehead			
The Lenora National Bank Of Morehead	7593	6	–
Morganfield			
The Morganfield National Bank	7490	5	4
The National Bank Of Union County, Morganfield	2209	5	–
Mount Sterling			
The Farmers National Bank Of Mount Sterling	2216	6	–
The Montgomery National Bank Of Mt. Sterling	6160	4	5
The Mt. Sterling National Bank	2185	4	4
The Traders National Bank Of Mt. Sterling	6129	5	4
Munfordville			
The National Bank Of Munfordville	11336	6	–
Murray			
The First National Bank Of Murray	10779	6	5
New Castle			
The National Bank Of New Castle	2196	6	–
Newport			
The American National Bank Of Newport	2726	5	4
The First National Bank Of Newport	2276	6	–
The German National Bank Of Newport	2726	5	–
The Newport National Bank	4765	5	4
Nicholasville			
The First National Bank Of Nicholasville	1831	5	4
Olive Hill			
The Olive Hill National Bank	7281	6	–

City, Bank	Ch. No.	L	S
Owensboro			
First National Bank And Trust Company Of Owensboro	2576	6	6
The First National Bank Of Owensboro	2576	4	–
The National Deposit Bank Of Owensboro	4006	3	3
The National Deposit Bank Of Owensboro	14138	–	–
The Owensboro National Bank	4006	6	–
The United States National Bank Of Owensboro	9456	4	–
Owenton			
The Farmers National Bank Of Owenton	2968	6	4
The First National Bank In Owenton	14026	–	6
The First National Bank Of Owenton	2868	5	5
The National Bank Of Owen At Owenton	1963	6	–
Paducah			
The American German National Bank Of Paducah	2070	5	–
The City National Bank Of Paducah	2093	3	4
The First National Bank Of Paducah	1599	5	5
The Peoples National Bank Of Paducah	12961	6	4
Paintsville			
The Citizens National Bank Of Paintsville	7164	6	–
The First National Bank Of Paintsville	13763	–	5
The Paintsville National Bank	6100	4	4
The Second National Bank Of Paintsville	13023	–	5
Paris			
The First National Bank Of Paris	6323	4	4
The National Bank And Trust Company Of Paris	14076	–	6
Pikeville			
The Day And Night National Bank Of Pikeville	11944	4	6
The First National Bank Of Pikeville	6622	4	1
The Pikeville National Bank	7030	5	3
Pineville			
The Bell National Bank Of Pineville	7215	5	5
The First National Bank Of Pineville	4598	6	–
Prestonsburg			
The First National Bank Of Prestonsburg	7254	6	6
Princeton			
The Farmers National Bank Of Princeton	5257	4	4
The First National Bank Of Princeton	3064	4	3
Providence			
The Union National Bank Of Providence	9708	6	4
Richmond			
Madison-southern National Bank & Trust Co. Of Richmond	1790	–	4
The Citizens National Bank Of Richmond	7653	5	5
The Farmers National Bank Of Richmond	1309	5	–
The First National Bank Of Richmond	1728	6	–
The Madison National Bank & Trust Company Of Richmond	1790	6	5
The Madison National Bank Of Richmond	1790	5	–
The Richmond National Bank	4430	6	–
The Second National Bank Of Richmond	2374	6	–
The Southern National Bank Of Richmond	9832	3	6
Russell			
The First National Bank Of Russell	8792	6	6
Russell Springs			
The First National Bank Of Russell Springs	11348	6	5
Russellville			
The Citizens National Bank Of Russellville	6546	5	6
The Logan County National Bank Of Russellville	2169	6	–
The National Deposit Bank Of Russellville	9842	6	–
Salyersville			
The Salyersville National Bank	8905	6	6
Scottsville			
The Allen County National Bank Of Scottsville	9356	6	–
The Farmers National Bank Of Scottsville	12456	–	–
The First National Bank Of Scottsville	8599	6	–
Sebree			
The First National Bank Of Sebree	7242	5	5
Somerset			
The Citizens National Bank Of Somerset	11544	5	4
The Farmers National Bank Of Somerset	5881	5	4
The First National Bank Of Somerset	3832	6	4
The National Bank Of Somerset	1748	6	–
The Somerset National Banking Company	5468	–	–
Springfield			
The First National Bank Of Springfield	1767	5	5
Stanford			
First National Bank In Stanford	14039	–	6
The Farmers National Bank Of Stanford	1705	6	–
The First National Bank Of Stanford	2788	6	5
The Lincoln County National Bank Of Stanford	5132	4	4
The Lincoln National Bank Of Stanford	3954	6	–
The National Bank Of Stanford	1204	5	–
Stone			
The First National Bank Of Stone	11890	6	6
Sturgis			
The First National Bank Of Sturgis	6244	6	–
Uniontown			
The First National Bank Of Uniontown	8622	6	–
Versailles			
The Commercial National Bank Of Versailles	1835	6	–
Wallins Creek			
The Wallins National Bank Of Wallins Creek	12202	6	6
West Liberty			
The First National Bank Of West Liberty	7916	6	–
Whitesburg			
The First National Bank Of Whitesburg	10433	6	5
Wickliffe			
The First National Bank Of Wickliffe	5443	6	–
Williamsburg			
The First National Bank Of Williamsburg	7174	6	5
Wilmore			
The First National Bank Of Wilmore	9880	6	4
Winchester			
The Citizens National Bank Of Winchester	2148	4	6
The Clark County National Bank Of Winchester	995	3	3
The Winchester National Bank	3290	6	–

LOUISIANA

City, Bank	Ch. No.	L	S
Abbeville			
The First National Bank Of Abbeville	5807	6	5
Alexandria			
The First National Bank Of Alexandria	5021	5	–
Arcadia			
The First National Bank Of Arcadia	7476	5	5
The First National Bank Of Arcadia	14328	–	–
Baton Rouge			
City National Bank Of Baton Rouge	13737	–	4
Louisiana National Bank Of Baton Rouge	9834	–	2
The First National Bank Of Baton Rouge	2633	5	–
The Louisiana National Bank Of Baton Rouge	9834	3	–
Bogalusa			
The First National Bank Of Bogalusa	8959	6	–
Crowley			
First National Bank Of Crowley	12523	3	4
The First National Bank Of Arcadia Parish At Crowley	10700	5	–
The First National Bank Of Crowley	5520	4	–
De Ridder			
First National Bank In De Ridder	14168	–	4
The First National Bank Of De Ridder	9237	5	4
Delhi			
The First National Bank Of Delhi	14225	–	6
The Macon Ridge National Bank Of Delhi	10912	6	5
Donaldson			
The First National Bank Of Donaldson	14281	–	–
Elton			
The First National Bank Of Elton	11541	–	–
Eunice			
The First National Bank Of Eunice	8677	6	–
Franklin			
The First National Bank Of Franklin	4555	4	–
Gibsland			
The First National Bank In Gibsland	13169	–	–
The First National Bank Of Gibsland	10049	6	–
Gretna			
The First National Bank Of Jefferson Parrish At Gretna	13732	–	4
Hammond			
The Citizens National Bank In Hammond	14086	–	–
The Citizens National Bank Of Hammond	11977	4	4
Homer			
The American National Bank Of Homer	11621	–	–
The Commercial National Bank Of Homer	11638	5	–
The Homer National Bank	4216	5	5
Jeanerette			
The First National Bank Of Jeanerette	7768	4	4
Jennings			
The First National Bank Of Jennings	5966	6	–
The Jennings National Bank	11450	4	–
The State National Bank Of Jennings	7765	6	–
Lafayette			
The Commercial National Bank Of Lafayette	13209	6	5
The First National Bank Of Lafayette	5023	4	4
Lake Arthur			
The First National Bank Of Lake Arthur	7047	6	–
Lake Charles			
Calcasieu National Bank In Lake Charles	13573	–	4
The Calcasieu N.B. Of Southwest Louisiana At Lake Charles	10836	4	6
The Calcasieu National Bank Of Lake Charles	5157	5	–
The Calcasieu National Bank Of Lake Charles	10836	–	6
The Calcasieu-Marine National Bank Of Lake Charles	14228	–	–
The First National Bank Of Lake Charles	4154	4	3
The Lake Charles National Bank	6088	6	–
Lake Providence			
The First Natl Bank Of Lake Providence At Providence	6291	5	2
Leesville			
The First National Bank Of Leesville	6264	6	–
Longville			
The First National Bank Of Longville	11254	–	–
Mansfield			
The American National Bank Of Mansfield	11669	–	4
The First National Bank Of Mansfield	7232	6	–
Minden			
The First National Bank Of Minden	10544	5	6
Monroe			
The Citizens National Bank Of Monroe	11242	6	–
The Monroe National Bank	4082	6	–
The Quachita National Bank In Monroe	13655	–	3
The Quachita National Bank Of Monroe	3692	6	–
The Quachita National Bank Of Monroe	8654	5	5
The Union National Bank Of Monroe	10153	6	–
Morgan City			
The Citizens National Bank Of Morgan City	13851	4	–
The First National Bank Of Morgan City	6801	4	–
New Iberia			
The New Iberia National Bank	3671	6	4
The Peoples National Bank Of New Iberia	4524	4	4
The State National Bank Of New Iberia	6858	5	4
New Orleans			
Canal-Commercial National Bank Of New Orleans	5649	4	–
Hibernia National Bank Of New Orleans	8734	4	–
The American National Bank Of New Orleans	3978	6	–
The City National Bank Of New Orleans	1591	6	–
The Commercial National Bank Of New Orleans	5649	2	–
The Crescent City National Bank Of New Orleans	1937	6	–
The First National Bank Of New Orleans	162	6	–
The German-American National Bank Of New Orleans	7876	4	–
The Germania National Bank Of New Orleans	1591	5	–
The Hibernia National Bank In New Orleans	13688	–	2
The Hibernia National Bank Of New Orleans	2086	6	–
The Louisiana National Bank Of New Orleans	1626	3	–
The Merchants National Bank Of New Orleans	7498	6	–
The Mutual National Bank Of New Orleans	1898	6	–
The National Bank Of Commerce In New Orleans	13689	–	2
The New Hibernia National Bank Of New Orleans	8734	6	–
The New Orleans National Bank	1778	3	–
The New Orleans National Banking Association	1825	6	–
The Peoples National Bank Of New Orleans	7498	6	–
The Southern National Bank Of New Orleans	4337	6	–
The State National Bank Of New Orleans	1774	3	–
The Teutonia National Bank Of New Orleans	1747	6	–
The Union National Bank Of New Orleans	1796	4	–
The Whitney National Bank Of New Orleans	3069	6	–
The Whitney-Central National Bank, New Orleans	3069	1	–
Whitney National Bank Of New Orleans	3069	–	1
New Roads			
The First National Bank Of New Roads	7169	6	–
Norco			
The St. Charles National Bank Of Norco	13839	–	5
Oak Grove			
The First National Bank Of Oak Grove	11650	–	–
Oberlin			
The First National Bank Of Oberlin	11324	–	–
Opelousas			
The First National Bank Of Opelousas	4340	6	–
The Opelousas National Bank	6920	6	–
The Planters National Bank Of Opelousas	9872	6	–
Patterson			
The First National Bank Of Patterson	5843	6	–
Pineville			
The First National Bank Of Pineville	12527	–	–
Ruston			
The First National Bank Of Ruston	11795	6	6
Shreveport			
Commercial National Bank In Shreveport	13648	–	1
The American National Bank Of Shreveport	8440	4	6
The Citizens National Bank Of Shreveport	5752	6	–
The City National Bank Of Shreveport	10870	6	–
The Commercial National Bank Of Shreveport	3600	2	2
The Exchange National Bank Of Shreveport	11521	5	6
The First National Bank Of Shreveport	3595	2	1
The Shreveport National Bank	5844	6	–
Tallulah			
The Madison National Bank Of Tallulah	12923	5	5
Thibodaux			
The La Fourche National Bank Of Thibodaux	13345	–	–
Ville Platte			
The First National Bank Of Ville Platte	10588	6	5
Welsh			
The First National Bank Of Welsh	6360	6	–
The Welsh National Bank	6418	6	–
Winnfield			
The First National Bank Of Winnfield	10761	–	–

MAINE

City, Bank	Ch. No.	L	S
Auburn			
The First National Bank Of Auburn	154	6	–
The National Shoe And Leather Bank Of Auburn	2270	6	4
Augusta			
First National Granite Bank Of Augusta	498	4	1
The Augusta National Bank	3271	6	–
The First National Bank Of Augusta	367	4	–
The Freeman's National Bank Of Augusta	406	6	–
The Granite National Bank Of Augusta	498	5	–
Bangor			
The Farmers National Bank Of Bangor	1687	6	–
The First National Bank Of Bangor	112	3	–
The Kenduskeag National Bank Of Bangor	518	5	–
The Merchants National Bank Of Bangor	1437	4	5
The Second National Bank Of Bangor	306	6	–
The Traders National Bank Of Bangor	1095	6	–
The Veazie National Bank Of Bangor	2089	6	–
Bath			
The Bath National Bank	494	3	3
The First National Bank Of Bath	61	5	–
The First National Bank Of Bath	2743	3	3
The Lincoln National Bank Of Bath	761	4	–
The Marine National Bank Of Bath	782	5	–
The Sagadahock National Bank Of Bath	1041	6	–
Belfast			
The Belfast National Bank	840	3	–
The City National Bank Of Belfast	7586	5	4
The First National Bank Of Belfast	13762	–	–
The Peoples National Bank Of Belfast	4806	6	–
Bethel			
The Bethel National Bank	7613	6	6
Biddeford			
The Biddeford National Bank	1575	4	–
The First National Bank Of Biddeford	1089	4	4
Boothbay Harbor			
The First National Bank Of Boothbay Harbor	5598	6	–
Bowdoinham			
The National Village Bank Of Bowdoinham	944	6	–
Bridgton			
The Bridgton National Bank	9181	5	–
Brunswick			
Brunswick National Bank, Brunswick	1315	–	6
The First National Bank Of Brunswick	192	5	3
The Pejepscot National Bank Of Brunswick	1315	5	6
The Union National Bank Of Brunswick	1118	5	6

City, Bank	Ch. No.	L	S
Bucksport			
The Bucksport National Bank	1079	5	–
Calais			
The Calais National Bank	1425	5	5
The National Bank Of Calais	13786	–	–
Camden			
The Camden National Bank	2311	4	4
The Megunticook National Bank Of Camden	6231	6	–
Caribou			
The Caribou National Bank	6190	6	6
Damariscotta			
The First National Bank Of Damariscotta	446	6	5
The New Castle National Bank Of Damariscotta	953	6	6
Dexter			
The First National Bank Of Dexter	2259	6	–
Dover			
The Kineo National Bank Of Dover	3690	6	–
Eastport			
The Frontier National Bank Of Eastport	1495	5	5
Eden			
The First National Bank Of Bar Harbor	3941	6	4
Ellsworth			
The Burrill National Bank Of Ellsworth	3804	5	–
The First National Bank Of Ellsworth	3814	6	–
The Liberty National Bank Of Ellsworth	3804	4	4
The Liberty National Bank Of Ellsworth	14303	–	–
Fairfield			
The First National Bank Of Fairfield	2175	6	–
The National Bank Of Fairfield	4973	6	–
Farmington			
The First National Bank Of Farmington	4459	5	5
The Peoples National Bank Of Farmington	5861	5	5
The Sandy River National Bank Of Farmington	901	6	–
Fort Fairfield			
The First National Bank Of Fort Fairfield	13843	–	6
The Fort Fairfield National Bank	4781	6	6
Fort Kent			
The First National Bank In Fort Kent	14224	–	6
The First National Bank Of Fort Kent	11403	6	4
Gardiner			
The Cobbossee National Bank Of Gardiner	939	6	–
The Gardiner National Bank	1174	5	–
The Merchants National Bank Of Gardiner	3219	6	–
The National Bank Of Gardiner	9609	6	6
The Oakland National Bank Of Gardiner	740	6	–
Guilford			
The First National Bank Of Guilford	4780	6	–
Hallowell			
The American National Bank Of Hallowell	624	6	–
The First National Bank Of Hallowell	310	6	–
The Hallowell National Bank	3247	6	–
The Northern National Bank Of Hallowell	532	6	–
Houlton			
The Farmers National Bank Of Houlton	4252	6	5
The Farmers National Bank Of Houlton	13827	–	–
The First National Bank Of Houlton	2749	5	4
Kennebunk			
The Ocean National Bank Of Kennebunk	1254	6	–
Kezar Falls			
The Kezar Falls National Bank	9826	6	5
Lewiston			
The First National Bank Of Lewiston	330	2	2
The Manufacturers National Bank Of Lewiston	2260	4	3
Limerick			
The Limerick National Bank	2785	3	5
Machias			
The Machias National Bank	11462	6	–
Madison			
The First National Bank Of Madison	4647	6	–
New Castle			
The New Castle National Bank	953	6	–
North Berwick			
The North Berwick National Bank	1523	5	4
Norway			
Norway National Bank	13750	–	5
The Norway National Bank	1956	5	6
Oakland			
The Messalonskee National Bank Of Oakland	2231	6	–
The West Waterville National Bank Of Oakland	2231	6	–
Orono			
The Orono National Bank	1134	6	–
Phillips			
The Phillips National Bank	4957	6	5
The Union National Bank Of Phillips	2267	6	–
Pittsfield			
The First National Bank Of Pittsfield	13777	–	5
The Pittsfield National Bank	4188	5	5
Portland			
First National Bank At Portland	13716	–	4
National Bank Of Commerce Of Portland	13710	–	5
The Canal National Bank Of Portland	941	3	2
The Casco National Bank Of Portland	1060	4	–
The Chapman National Bank Of Portland	4868	3	–
The Cumberland National Bank Of Portland	1511	5	–
The First National Bank Of Portland	221	2	3
The Merchants National Bank Of Portland	1023	4	–
The National Traders Bank Of Portland	1451	4	–
The Portland National Bank	4128	3	3
The Second National Bank Of Portland	878	6	–
Presque Isle			
Northern National Bank Of Presque Isle	13768	–	5
The Presque Isle National Bank	3827	6	5
Richmond			
The First National Bank Of Richmond	662	6	–
The Richmond National Bank	909	6	–
Rockland			
The First National Bank Of Rockland	13734	–	–
The Lime Rock National Bank Of Rockland	2097	5	–
The North National Bank Of Rockland	2371	3	5
The Rockland National Bank	1446	3	5
Rumford			
The Rumford National Bank	6287	6	5
Saco			
The Saco National Bank	1535	5	–
The York National Bank Of Saco	1528	4	3
Sanford			
The Sanford National Bank	5050	5	–
Searsport			
The Searsport National Bank	2642	5	6
Skowhegan			
The First National Bank Of Skowhegan	239	4	3
The Second National Bank Of Skowhegan	298	6	–
South Berwick			
The South Berwick National Bank	959	4	–
Springvale			
The Springvale National Bank	7835	6	6
The Springvale National Bank	13730	–	–
Thomaston			
The Georges National Bank Of Thomaston	1142	4	6
The Thomaston National Bank	890	4	5
The Thomaston National Bank, Thomaston	1142	–	4
Van Buren			
The First National Bank Of Van Buren	10628	6	6
Waldoboro			
The Medomak National Bank Of Waldoboro	1108	3	5
The Waldoboro National Bank	744	6	–
Waterville			
Peoples-Ticonic National Bank Of Waterville	880	–	4
The First National Bank Of Waterville	13769	–	–
The Merchants National Bank Of Waterville	2306	6	–
The Peoples National Bank Of Waterville	880	4	6
The Ticonic National Bank Of Waterville	762	4	5
The Waterville National Bank	798	5	–
Winthrop			
The National Bank Of Winthrop	553	6	–
Wiscasset			
The First National Bank Of Wiscasset	1549	4	–
York Village			
The York County National Bank Of York Village	4844	6	–

MARYLAND

City, Bank	Ch. No.	L	S
Aberdeen			
The First National Bank Of Aberdeen	4634	6	4
Annapolis			
The Farmers National Bank Of Annapolis	1244	3	–
The First National Bank Of Annapolis	826	6	–
The Traders National Bank Of Baltimore	826	5	–
Baltimore			
Baltimore National Bank	13745	–	3
Maryland National Bank Of Baltimore	5776	4	–
National Central Bank Of Baltimore	11207	–	2
The American National Bank Of Baltimore	4518	6	–
The Central National Bank Of Baltimore	1797	5	–
The Citizens National Bank Of Baltimore	1384	2	–
The Commercial And Farmers National Bank Of Baltimore	1303	3	–
The Continental National Bank Of Baltimore	4533	6	–
The Drovers And Mechanics National Bank Of Baltimore	2499	3	4
The Equitable National Bank Of Baltimore	4530	6	–
The Farmers And Merchants National Bank Of Baltimore	1337	2	3
The First National Bank Of Baltimore	204	3	–
The First National Bank Of Baltimore	1413	3	1
The Manufacturers National Bank Of Baltimore	2623	4	–
The Merchants National Bank Of Baltimore	1336	3	–
The Merchants National Bank Of Baltimore	1413	2	–
The Merchants-Mechanics Bank Of Baltimore	1413	4	–
The Merchants-Mechanics First National Bank Of Baltimore	1413	4	–
The National Bank Of Baltimore	1432	2	5
The National Bank Of Commerce Of Baltimore	4285	3	–
The National City Bank Of Baltimore	9639	6	–
The National Exchange Bank Of Baltimore	1109	2	–
The National Farmers And Planters Bank Of Baltimore	1252	4	–
The National Howard Bank Of Baltimore	4218	6	–
The National Marine Bank Of Baltimore	2453	3	3
The National Mechanics Bank Of Baltimore	1413	4	–
The National Union Bank Of Maryland At Baltimore	1489	2	–
The Old Town National Bank Of Baltimore	5984	2	–
The Second National Bank Of Baltimore	414	2	–
The Third National Bank Of Baltimore	814	3	–
The Western National Bank Of Baltimore	1325	3	2
Barton			
The First National Bank Of Barton	6399	5	4
Bel Air			
The Farmers And Merchants National Bank Of Bel Air	9474	6	5
The First National Bank Of Bel Air	13680	–	4
The Harford National Bank Of Bel Air	2797	6	–
The Second National Bank Of Bel Air	3933	4	4
Berlin			
The First National Bank Of Berlin	8319	6	–
Brunswick			
Peoples National Bank Of Brunswick	8244	4	3
The Peoples National Bank In Brunswick	14044	–	2
Cambridge			
The Dorchester National Bank Of Cambridge	4085	5	–
The Farmers And Merchants National Bank Of Cambridge	5880	5	4
The National Bank Of Cambridge	2498	3	4
Canton			
The Canton National Bank	4799	4	5
Catonsville			
The Catonsville National Bank	13147	–	–
The First National Bank Of Catonsville	5093	4	–
Centreville			
The Centreville National Bank Of Maryland, Centreville	2341	4	4
The Queen Anne's National Bank Of Centreville	3205	6	6
Chesapeake City			
The National Bank Of Chesapeake City	6845	6	–
Chestertown			
The Chestertown National Bank	3305	–	–
The First National Bank Of Chestertown	13798	–	6
The Kent National Bank Of Chestertown	1500	6	–
The Second National Bank Of Chestertown	4327	6	–
The Third National Bank Of Chestertown	9744	6	6
Clear Spring			
The Clear Spring National Bank	9699	5	4
Cockeysville			
The National Bank Of Cockeysville	4496	5	4
Cumberland			
The Citizens National Bank Of Cumberland	5332	5	–
The First National Bank Of Cumberland	381	3	3
The Second National Bank Of Cumberland	1519	3	1
The Third National Bank Of Cumberland	2416	4	–
Denton			
The Denton National Bank	2547	3	3
The Peoples National Bank Of Denton	5122	5	–
Easton			
The Easton National Bank Of Maryland	1434	3	3
The Farmers And Merchants National Bank Of Easton	4046	6	–
Elkton			
The National Bank Of Elkton	1236	5	6
The Second National Bank Of Elkton	4162	6	–
Ellicott City			
Patapsco National Bank In Ellicott City	13773	–	4
The Patapsco National Bank Of Ellicott City	3585	4	3
Federalsburg			
The First National Bank Of Federalsburg	10210	5	4
Frederick			
Frederick County National Bank, Frederick	13747	–	6
The Central National Bank Of Frederick	1138	4	–
The Citizens National Bank Of Frederick	3476	4	3
The Farmers And Mechanics National Bank Of Frederick	1267	4	3
The First National Bank Of Frederick	1589	5	–
The Frederick County National Bank Of Frederick	1449	4	3
Friendsville			
The First National Bank Of Friendsville	6196	5	4
Frostburg			
Frostburg National Bank	13979	–	4
The Citizens National Bank Of Frostburg	4926	4	3
The First National Bank Of Frostburg	1412	6	–
The First National Bank Of Frostburg	4149	4	3
Gaithersburg			
The First National Bank Of Gaithersburg	4608	4	3
Grantsville			
The First National Bank Of Grantsville	5943	5	4
Hagerstown			
The Citizens National Bank Of Hagerstown	1893	6	–
The First National Bank Of Hagerstown	1431	3	4
The Nicodemus National Bank Of Hagerstown	12590	4	2
The Peoples National Bank Of Hagerstown	4856	4	–
The Second National Bank Of Hagerstown	4049	3	3
Hampstead			
The First National Bank Of Hampstead	9755	6	5
Hancock			
The First National Bank Of Hancock	7859	6	4
The Peoples National Bank Of Hancock	13853	–	4
Havre De Grace			
The Citizens National Bank Of Havre De Grace	5445	4	2
The First National Bank Of Havre De Grace	3010	4	5
Hyattsville			
The First National Bank Of Hyattsville	7519	4	6
Kitzmillerville			
The Blaine National Bank Of Kitzmillerville	8272	–	–
The First National Bank Of Kitzmillerville	8302	6	4
La Plata			
The Southern Maryland National Bank Of La Plata	8456	6	3
Laurel			
The Citizens National Bank Of Laurel	4364	6	6
Leonardtown			
The First National Bank Of St. Mary's, Leonardtown	6606	4	1
Lonaconing			
The First National Bank Of Lonaconing	7732	6	4
Mechanicsville			
The National Bank Of Mechanicsville	9429	6	–
Midland			
The First National Bank Of Midland	5331	5	5
Monrovia			
The First National Bank Of Monrovia	9238	6	–
Mount Airy			
The First National Bank Of Mount Airy	7160	5	5
Mount Rainier			
The First National Bank Of Mt. Rainier	12443	5	6
Mount Savage			
The First National Bank Of Mount Savage	6144	5	3
New Windsor			
The First National Bank Of New Windsor	747	5	5
North East			
The First National Bank Of North East	7064	6	5
Oakland			
The First National Bank Of Oakland	5623	4	3
The Garrett National Bank In Oakland	13776	–	4
The Garrett National Bank Of Oakland	6588	4	3
Parkton			
The First National Bank In Parkton	13867	–	4
The First National Bank Of Parkton	9444	5	4
Perryville			
The National Bank Of Perryville	11193	5	2
Pikesville			
The Pikesville National Bank	8867	5	6
Pocomoke City			
Citizens National Bank In Pocomoke City	14106	–	5
The Citizens National Bank Of Pocomoke City	6202	6	6
The Pocomoke City National Bank	4191	6	4
Poolesville			
The Poolesville National Bank	8860	6	6

City, Bank	Ch. No.	L	S
Port Deposit			
The Cecil National Bank At Port Deposit	13840	–	4
The Cecil National Bank Of Port Deposit	1211	3	4
The National Bank Of Port Deposit	5610	6	–
Rising Sun			
The National Bank Of Rising Sun	2481	4	3
Rockville			
The Montgomery County National Bank Of Rockville	3187	3	3
Salisbury			
The Peoples National Bank Of Salisbury	6761	5	–
The Salisbury National Bank	3250	6	4
Sandy Spring			
The First National Bank Of Sandy Spring	5561	6	4
Silver Spring			
The Silver Spring National Bank	9830	5	4
Snow Hill			
The Commercial National Bank Of Snow Hill	6297	5	3
The First National Bank Of Snow Hill	3783	5	3
Sykesville			
The First National Bank Of Sykesville	8578	6	–
The Sykesville National Bank	8587	4	4
Thurmont			
The Thurmont National Bank	5829	6	–
Towson			
The Second National Bank Of Towson	8381	5	4
The Towson National Bank	3588	3	3
Union Bridge			
The First National Bank Of Union Bridge	9066	5	–
Upper Marlboro			
The First National Bank Of So. Maryland Of Upper Marlboro	5471	4	5
Westernport			
The Citizens National Bank Of Westernport	5831	5	3
Westminster			
The Farmers And Mechanics National Bank Of Westminster	1526	5	4
The First National Bank Of Westminster	742	3	3
The Union National Bank Of Westminster	1596	4	3
White Hall			
The White Hall National Bank	9469	6	–
Williamsport			
The Washington County National Bank Of Williamsport	1551	4	–
Woodbine			
The Woodbine National Bank	8799	6	6

MASSACHUSETTS

City, Bank	Ch. No.	L	S
Abington			
The Abington National Bank	1386	6	6
Adams			
The Berkshire National Bank Of Adams	1439	–	–
The First National Bank Of Adams	462	4	5
The Greylock National Bank Of Adams	4562	4	4
Amesbury			
The Amesbury National Bank	2929	5	–
The Powow River National Bank Of Amesbury	1049	4	6
Amherst			
The First National Bank Of Amherst	393	4	4
Andover			
The Andover National Bank	1129	5	–
Arlington			
The Arlington National Bank	11868	6	6
The First National Bank Of Arlington	4664	6	–
Ashburnham			
The First National Bank Of Ashburnham	2113	5	–
Athol			
The Athol National Bank	2172	5	5
The First National Bank Of Athol	13733	–	5
The Millers River National Bank Of Athol	708	4	4
Attleboro			
The First National Bank Of Attleboro	2232	2	3
Ayer			
The First National Bank Of Ayer	3073	6	6
Barre			
The First National Bank Of Barre	96	5	–
The First National Bank Of Barre	2685	5	–
The Second National Bank Of Barre	10165	5	–
The Second National Bank Of Barre	13386	–	–
Beverly			
The Beverly National Bank	969	4	3
Blackstone			
The Worcester County National Bank Of Blackstone	1207	6	–
Boston			
Boston-Continental National Bank, Boston	11903	–	5
Continental National Bank Of Boston	12540	–	6
Engineers National Bank Of Boston	12540	5	4
Federal National Bank Of Boston	12336	2	3
National Rockland Bank Of Boston	615	–	–
The American National Bank Of Boston	5840	6	–
The Atlantic National Bank Of Boston	643	3	–
The Atlantic National Bank Of Boston	643	6	3
The Atlas National Bank Of Boston	654	6	–
The Back Bay National Bank Of Boston	11068	–	–
The Blackstone National Bank Of Boston	514	4	–
The Blue Hill National Bank Of Dorchester (Boston)	684	5	–
The Boston National Bank	408	3	–
The Boston National Bank	11903	3	4
The Boylston National Bank Of Boston	545	3	–
The Broadway National Bank Of Boston	551	4	–
The Brotherhood Of Locomotive Engineers N.B. Of Boston	12540	5	–
The Central National Bank Of Boston	2103	4	–
The Citizens National Bank Of Boston	11339	4	–
The Colonial National Bank Of Boston	5163	6	–
The Columbian National Bank Of Boston	1029	3	–
The Commercial National Bank Of Boston	3923	4	–
The Commercial Security National Bank Of Boston	3923	6	–
The Commonwealth National Bank Of Boston	12377	–	–
The Commonwealth-Atlantic National Bank Of Boston	643	4	–
The Continental National Bank Of Boston	524	3	–
The Eleventh Ward National Bank Of Boston	1993	6	–
The Eliot National Bank Of Boston	536	4	–
The Everett National Bank Of Boston	1469	6	–
The Faneuil Hall National Bank Of Boston	847	3	–
The First National Bank Of Boston	200	2	2
The First Ward National Bank Of Boston	2112	3	–
The Fourth National Bank Of Boston	2277	4	–
The Fourth-Atlantic National Bank Of Boston	643	4	–
The Freeman's National Bank Of Boston	665	6	–
The Globe National Bank Of Boston	936	5	–
The Hamilton National Bank Of Boston	778	6	–
The Hancock National Bank Of Boston	1442	–	–
The Haymarket National Bank Of Boston	11790	–	–
The Howard National Bank Of Boston	578	3	–
The International National Bank Of Boston	12396	–	–
The Kidder National Gold Bank Of Boston	1699	6	–
The Lincoln National Bank Of Boston	2846	5	–
The Manufacturers National Bank Of Boston	2111	4	–
The Market National Bank Of Boston	505	4	–
The Massachusetts National Bank Of Boston	974	4	–
The Massachusetts National Bank Of Boston	12862	–	–
The Mattapan National Bank Of Boston	11137	5	–
The Maverick National Bank Of Boston	677	4	–
The Mechanics National Bank Of Boston	932	5	–
The Merchandise National Bank Of Boston	2304	3	–
The Merchants National Bank Of Boston	475	2	–
The Metropolitan National Bank Of Boston	2289	5	–
The Monument National Bank Of Boston	1005	6	–
The Mount Vernon National Bank Of Boston	716	6	–
The Mutual National Bank Of Boston	9579	6	–
The National Bank Of Brighton, Boston	1099	5	–
The National Bank Of Commerce, Boston	554	4	–
The National Bank Of North America, Boston	672	3	–
The National Bank Of Redemption Of Boston	515	4	–
The National Bank Of The Commonwealth Of Boston	1827	4	–
The National Bank Of The Republic, Boston	379	4	–
The National City Bank Of Boston	609	4	–
The National Eagle Bank Of Boston	993	4	–
The National Exchange Bank Of Boston	529	5	–
The National Hamilton Bank Of Boston	5158	6	–
The National Hide And Leather Bank Of Boston	460	3	–
The National Market Bank Of Brighton, Boston	806	4	–
The National Revere Bank Of Boston	1295	3	–
The National Rockland Bank Of Roxbury At Boston	615	4	–
The National Rockland Bank Of Roxbury, Boston	615	6	–
The National Security Bank Of Boston	1675	3	–
The National Shawmut Bank Of Boston	5155	1	–
The National Suffolk Bank Of Boston	6104	6	–
The National Union Bank Of Boston	985	2	–
The National Webster Bank Of Boston	1527	5	–
The New England National Bank Of Boston	603	3	–
The North National Bank Of Boston	525	3	–
The Oceanic National Bank Of Boston	11859	–	–
The Old Boston National Bank Of Boston	1015	5	–
The Old Colony National Bank Of Boston	13391	–	–
The Pacific National Bank Of Boston	2373	5	–
The Peoples National Bank Of Boston	595	–	–
The Peoples National Bank Of Roxbury At Boston	595	4	–
The Roxbury National Bank Of Boston	10924	–	–
The Second National Bank Of Boston	322	4	–
The Shawmut National Bank Of Boston	582	3	–
The Shoe And Leather National Bank Of Boston	646	3	–
The South Boston National Bank	12359	–	–
The South End National Bank Of Boston	4202	5	–
The State National Bank Of Boston	1028	3	–
The Suffolk National Bank Of Boston	629	5	–
The Third National Bank Of Boston	359	3	–
The Traders National Bank Of Boston	1442	6	–
The Tremont National Bank Of Boston	625	3	–
The Washington National Bank Of Boston	601	4	–
The Winthrop National Bank Of Boston	2304	3	–
Webster And Atlas National Bank Of Boston	1527	3	2
Braintree			
The Braintree National Bank	11347	5	5
Brockton			
The Brockton National Bank	2504	6	–
The Home National Bank Of Brockton	2152	6	–
Brookline			
The Brookline National Bank	3553	5	–
Buzzards Bay			
The Buzzards Bay National Bank	13222	–	3
Cambridge			
Manufacturers National Bank Of Cambridge	11152	4	–
The Cambridge National Bank	13060	–	–
The Cambridgeport National Bank Of Cambridge	1228	6	–
The Charles River National Bank Of Cambridge	731	6	–
The First National Bank Of Cambridge	433	6	–
The Lechmere National Bank Of Cambridge	614	–	5
The National City Bank Of Cambridge	770	6	–
Canton			
The Neponset National Bank Of Canton	663	4	–
Charlestown			
The Bunker Hill National Bank Of Charlestown	635	5	–
The Monument National Bank Of Charlestown	1005	5	–
Chelsea			
The Broadway National Bank Of Chelsea	9651	5	5
The First National Bank Of Chelsea	533	6	–
The Lincoln National Bank Of Chelsea	14087	–	6
The National City Bank Of Chelsea	11270	5	6
The Winnisimmet National Bank Of Chelsea	4074	6	–
Chicopee			
The First National Bank Of Chicopee	1056	4	–
Clinton			
The First National Bank Of Clinton	440	4	–
Cohasset			
The Cohasset National Bank	13283	–	–
Concord			
The Concord National Bank	833	5	4
Conway			
The Conway National Bank	895	6	4
Danvers			
The Danvers National Bank	7452	4	6
The First National Bank Of Danvers	594	5	–
Dedham			
The Dedham National Bank	669	4	–
The Dedham National Bank	12567	6	4
Dorchester			
The First National Bank Of Dorchester	156	6	–
East Cambridge			
The Cambridge National Bank, East Cambridge	449	6	–
The Lechmere National Bank Of East Cambridge	614	4	4
Easthampton			
The First National Bank Of Easthampton	428	4	1
Edgartown			
The Edgartown National Bank	7957	5	6
The Marthas Vineyard National Bank Of Edgartown	1274	5	–
Everett			
The Everett National Bank	11510	–	–
Fairhaven			
The National Bank Of Fairhaven	490	4	3
Fall River			
The Fall River National Bank	590	3	3
The First National Bank Of Fall River	256	2	–
The Massasoit National Bank Of Fall River	612	6	–
The Massasoit-Pocasset National Bank Of Fall River	6821	5	–
The Metacomet National Bank Of Fall River	924	3	–
The National Union Bank Of Fall River	1288	6	–
The Pocasset National Bank Of Fall River	679	4	–
The Second National Bank Of Fall River	439	4	–
Falmouth			
The Falmouth National Bank	1320	5	4
Fitchburg			
The Fitchburg National Bank	1077	5	–
The Rollstone National Bank Of Fitchburg	702	5	–
The Safety Fund National Bank Of Fitchburg	2153	3	3
The Wachusett National Bank Of Fitchburg	2265	4	–
Foxboro			
The Foxboro National Bank Of Foxborough	9426	5	5
Framingham			
The Framingham National Bank	528	5	3
Franklin			
The Franklin National Bank, Franklin	1207	4	4
Gardner			
The First National Bank Of Gardner	884	3	4
Georgetown			
The Georgetown National Bank	2297	5	–
Gloucester			
Gloucester National Bank Of Gloucester	13604	–	4
The Cape Ann National Bank Of Gloucester	899	3	4
The City National Bank Of Gloucester	2292	4	–
The First National Bank Of Gloucester	549	5	–
The Gloucester National Bank	1162	5	5
Grafton			
The First National Bank Of Grafton	188	6	–
The Grafton National Bank	824	4	–
Great Barrington			
The National Mahaiwe Bank Of Great Barrington	1203	4	4
Greenfield			
First National Bank & Trust Company Of Greenfield	474	–	4
The First National Bank Of Greenfield	474	3	5
The Franklin County National Bank Of Greenfield	920	5	–
The Packard National Bank Of Greenfield	2264	6	–
Harwich			
The Cape Cod National Bank Of Harwich	712	4	–
Haverhill			
Merrimack National Bank Of Haverhill	14266	–	6
The Essex National Bank Of Haverhill	589	5	5
The First National Bank Of Haverhill	481	3	4
The Haverhill National Bank	484	4	3
The Merchants National Bank Of Haverhill	4833	6	–
The Merrimack National Bank Of Haverhill	633	3	4
The Northern National Bank Of Haverhill	14266	–	6
The Second National Bank Of Haverhill	3510	5	–
Hingham			
The Hingham National Bank	1119	5	–
Holliston			
The Holliston National Bank	802	6	–
Holyoke			
Holyoke National Bank	1939	5	3
The City National Bank Of Holyoke	2430	3	–
The Hadley Falls National Bank Of Holyoke	1246	4	–
The Home National Bank Of Holyoke	3128	5	–
The Park National Bank Of Holyoke	4703	6	4
Hopkinton			
The Hopkinton National Bank	626	4	6
Hudson			
The Hudson National Bank	2618	3	4
Hyannis			
The Barnstable County National Bank Of Hyannis	13395	–	5
The First National Bank Of Hyannis	1107	3	–
Hyde Park			
The Hyde Park National Bank	7920	5	–
Ipswich			
The First National Bank Of Ipswich	4774	6	4
Lancaster			
The Lancaster National Bank	583	5	–
The Lancaster National Bank Of Clinton	583	6	–
Lawrence			
Bay State Merchants National Bank Of Lawrence	1014	–	5
The Arlington National Bank Of Lawrence	4300	6	–
The Bay State National Bank Of Lawrence	1014	3	2
The Lawrence National Bank	1962	5	–
The Merchants National Bank Of Lawrence	3977	5	–
The National Pemberton Bank Of Lawrence	1048	6	–
The Pacific National Bank Of Lawrence	2347	5	–
Lee			
The Lee National Bank	885	4	5
Leicester			
The Leicester National Bank	918	5	–
Lenox			
The Lenox National Bank	4013	3	4

City, Bank	Ch. No.	L	S
Leominster			
The First National Bank Of Leominster	513	6	–
The Leominster National Bank	3204	5	5
The Merchants National Bank Of Leominster	10059	5	1
Lowell			
The Appleton National Bank Of Lowell	986	3	3
The First National Bank Of Lowell	331	5	–
The Merchants National Bank Of Lowell	506	6	–
The Middlesex National Bank Of Lowell	12343	–	5
The Old Lowell National Bank Of Lowell	1329	5	5
The Prescott National Bank Of Lowell	960	5	–
The Railroad National Bank Of Lowell	753	4	–
The Traders National Bank Of Lowell	4753	5	–
The Union National Bank Of Lowell	6077	3	6
The Wamesit National Bank Of Lowell	781	5	–
Union Old Lowell National Bank, Lowell	6077	–	3
Lynn			
State National Bank In Lynn	12362	5	–
The Central National Bank Of Lynn	1201	4	5
The First National Bank Of Lynn	638	4	–
The Lynn National Bank	3429	6	–
The Manufacturers National Bank Of Lynn	4580	6	5
The National City Bank Of Lynn	697	5	4
The National Security Bank Of Lynn	2563	5	–
The State National Bank Of Lynn	11169	6	–
Malden			
The First National Bank Of Malden	588	3	2
The Second National Bank Of Malden	11014	–	3
Mansfield			
The First National Bank Of Mansfield	5944	4	4
Marblehead			
The Marblehead National Bank	767	5	–
The National Grand Bank Of Marblehead	676	5	5
Marlboro			
The First National Bank Of Marlboro	158	6	–
The First National Bank Of Marlboro	2770	4	3
Marlborough			
The Peoples National Bank Of Marlborough	2404	3	5
Medford			
First National Bank In Medford	12979	6	4
The Medford National Bank	5247	6	–
Melrose			
The Melrose National Bank	4769	5	–
Merrimac			
The First National Bank Of Amesbury, Merrimac	268	6	–
The First National Bank Of Merrimac	268	5	6
Methuen			
The Methuen National Bank	12800	4	4
The National Bank Of Methuen	1485	5	–
Middleborough			
The Middleborough National Bank	3994	5	–
Milford			
The Home National Bank Of Milford	2275	1	4
The Milford National Bank	866	4	–
The Milford National Bank & Trust Company	866	6	5
Millbury			
Millbury National Bank	13835	–	5
The Millbury National Bank	572	5	5
Milton			
The Blue Hill National Bank Of Milton	684	4	6
Monson			
The Monson National Bank	503	5	5
Nantucket			
The Pacific National Bank Of Nantucket	714	2	4
Natick			
The Natick National Bank	2107	5	–
Needham			
Needham National Bank, Needham	13241	–	–
The Needham National Bank For Savings And Trusts	13241	–	–
New Bedford			
The Citizens National Bank Of New Bedford	2262	6	–
The First National Bank Of New Bedford	261	2	3
The Mechanics National Bank Of New Bedford	743	4	–
The Merchants National Bank Of New Bedford	799	3	2
The National Bank Of Commerce, New Bedford	690	4	–
The Safe Deposit National Bank Of New Bedford	12405	4	3
Newburyport			
First And Ocean National Bank Of Newburyport	1011	6	4
The First National Bank Of Newburyport	279	5	–
The Mechanicks National Bank Of Newburyport	584	5	–
The Merchants National Bank Of Newburyport	1047	4	4
The Ocean National Bank Of Newburyport	1011	5	–
Newton			
Newton National Bank	13252	3	3
The First National Bank Of Newton	3598	–	5
The Newton National Bank	789	6	–
Newtonville			
The First National Bank Of Newton, Newtonville	488	6	–
North Adams			
North Adams National Bank, North Adams	1210	–	3
The Adams National Bank Of North Adams	1210	5	–
The Berkshire National Bank Of North Adams	2396	4	–
The North Adams National Bank, North Adams	1210	4	–
North Attleborough			
The Attleborough National Bank	1604	5	–
The Jewelers National Bank Of North Attleborough	7675	6	–
The Manufacturers National Bank Of North Attleborough	9086	5	5
The North Attleborough National Bank	3365	6	–
North Brookfield			
The North Brookfield National Bank	10955	–	–
The North Brookfield National Bank	13387	–	–
North Easton			
The First National Bank Of Easton	416	3	4
Northampton			
Northampton National Bank And Trust Company	1018	–	5
The First National Bank Of Northampton	383	3	5
The Hampshire County National Bank Of Northampton	418	5	–
The Northampton National Bank Of Northampton	1018	3	4
Northborough			
The Northborough National Bank	1279	4	5
Northfield			
The Northfield National Bank	13172	–	–
Norwood			
The Norwood National Bank	8474	6	–
Orange			
The Orange National Bank	2255	4	5
Oxford			
The Oxford National Bank	764	5	–
Palmer			
The Palmer National Bank	2324	3	5
Peabody			
The South Danvers National Bank Of Peabody	958	4	–
The Warren National Bank Of Peabody	616	4	4
Pepperell			
The First National Bank Of Pepperell	5964	6	6
The First National Bank Of Pepperell	13933	–	–
Pittsfield			
The Agricultural National Bank Of Pittsfield	1082	3	–
The Pittsfield National Bank & Trust Company, Pittsfield	1260	–	–
The Pittsfield National Bank Of Pittsfield	1260	4	–
The Pittsfield-Third National Bank & Trust Co, Pittsfield	1260	–	4
The Third National Bank Of Pittsfield	2525	4	–
Plymouth			
The Old Colony National Bank Of Plymouth	996	4	4
The Plymouth National Bank	779	4	4
Provincetown			
The First National Bank Of Provincetown	736	5	5
Quincy			
The National Granite Bank Of Quincy	832	6	–
The National Mount Wollaston Bank Of Quincy	517	3	3
Randolph			
The Randolph National Bank	558	5	–
Reading			
The First National Bank In Reading	13558	–	4
The First National Bank Of Reading	4488	5	6
The First National Bank Of Reading	13796	–	–
Revere			
The First National Bank Of Revere	13152	–	–
The First National Bank Of Revere	14152	–	–
Rockland			
The First National Bank Of Rockland, Massachusetts	3868	6	–
Rockport			
The Rockport National Bank	1194	5	–
Roxbury			
The Peoples National Bank Of Roxbury	595	5	–
Salem			
The Asiatic National Bank Of Salem	634	5	–
The First National Bank Of Salem	407	5	–
The Mercantile National Bank Of Salem	691	4	–
The Merchants National Bank Of Salem	726	4	–
The National Exchange Bank Of Salem	817	6	–
The Naumkeag National Bank Of Salem	647	5	–
The Salem National Bank	704	6	–
Salisbury			
The Powow River National Bank Of Salisbury	1049	5	–
Shelburne Falls			
The Shelburne Falls National Bank, Shelburne	1144	3	3
Somerville			
The Somerville National Bank	4771	4	4
South Danvers			
The Warren National Bank Of South Danvers	616	5	–
South Deerfield			
The Produce National Bank Of South Deerfield	8150	4	4
South Framingham			
The South Framingham National Bank	2485	6	–
South Weymouth			
The First National Bank Of South Weymouth	618	5	–
Southbridge			
The Peoples National Bank Of Southbridge	11388	5	5
The Southbridge National Bank	934	3	4
Spencer			
Spencer National Bank	13394	–	4
The Spencer National Bank	2288	4	6
Springfield			
Springfield National Bank, Springfield	4907	–	2
The Agawam National Bank Of Springfield	1055	4	–
The Atlas National Bank Of Springfield	12481	–	–
The Chapin National Bank Of Springfield	2435	3	3
The Chicopee National Bank Of Springfield	988	4	–
The City National Bank Of Springfield	2433	5	–
The First National Bank Of Springfield	14	4	–
The John Hancock National Bank Of Springfield	982	5	–
The Pynchon National Bank Of Springfield	987	5	–
The Second National Bank Of Springfield	181	4	–
The Springfield Chapin Natl Bank & Trust Co, Springfield	4907	–	3
The Springfield National Bank	4907	3	–
The Third National Bank & Trust Company Of Springfield	308	–	2
The Third National Bank Of Springfield	308	3	–
Stockbridge			
The Housatonic National Bank Of Stockbridge	1170	4	5
Stoneham			
The Stoneham National Bank	4240	6	–
Taunton			
The Bristol County National Bank Of Taunton	766	5	–
The Machinists National Bank Of Taunton	947	4	4
The Taunton National Bank Of Taunton	957	4	–
Tisbury			
The Marthas Vineyard National Bank Of Tisbury	1274	3	5
Townsend			
The Townsend National Bank	805	4	4
Turners Falls			
The Crocker National Bank Of Turners Falls	2058	4	5
Uxbridge			
The Blackstone National Bank Of Uxbridge	1022	4	4
Wakefield			
The National Bank Of South Reading, Wakefield	1455	6	–
The Wakefield National Bank, Wakefield	1455	5	–
Waltham			
The Waltham National Bank	688	4	4
Ware			
The Ware National Bank	628	5	–
Warren			
The First National Bank Of Warren	11567	–	–
Warsham			
The National Bank Of Wareham	1440	6	4
Watertown			
The Union Market National Bank Of Watertown	2108	4	3
Webster			
First National Bank Of Webster	13411	–	4
The First National Bank Of Webster	2312	3	6
The Webster National Bank	11236	4	5
Webster National Bank	13780	–	5
Wellesley			
The Wellesley National Bank	7297	5	3
West Newton			
The First National Bank Of West Newton, Newton	3598	5	–
Westboro			
The First National Bank Of Westboro	421	5	3
Westfield			
Hampden National Bank And Trust Company Of Westfield	1367	–	5
The First National Bank Of Westfield	190	3	3
The Hampden National Bank Of Westfield	1367	4	6
Westminster			
The Westminster National Bank	2284	6	–
The Westminster National Bank Of Gardner	2284	5	–
Weymouth			
The Union National Bank Of Weymouth	510	5	–
Whitinsville			
The Whitinsville National Bank	769	4	3
Whitman			
The Whitman National Bank	4660	6	6
Williamstown			
The Williamstown National Bank	3092	5	4
Winchendon			
The First National Bank Of Winchendon	327	4	4
Winchester			
The Middlesex County National Bank Of Winchester	5071	6	–
The Winchester National Bank	11103	5	4
Woburn			
Tanners National Bank In Woburn	14033	–	6
The First National Bank Of Woburn	746	6	–
The Tanners National Bank Of Woburn	11067	5	5
Woburn National Bank	7550	6	4
Worcester			
The Central National Bank Of Worcester	455	6	–
The Citizens National Bank Of Worcester	765	6	–
The City National Bank Of Worcester	476	5	–
The First National Bank Of Worcester	79	4	–
The Mechanics National Bank Of Worcester	1135	4	4
The Merchants National Bank Of Worcester	7595	3	–
The Quinsigamond National Bank Of Worcester	1073	6	–
The Security National Bank Of Worcester	2273	6	–
The Worcester National Bank	442	4	–
Worcester County National Bank Of Worcester	7595	3	2
Worchester			
The First National Bank Of Worchester	2699	5	–
Wrentham			
The National Bank Of Wrentham	1085	5	4
Yarmouth			
The First National Bank Of Yarmouth	516	3	4

MICHIGAN

City, Bank	Ch. No.	L	S
Adrian			
The First National Bank Of Adrian	1973	5	–
The National Bank Of Adrian	13821	–	–
The National Bank Of Commerce Of Adrian	9421	5	4
Albion			
The Albion National Bank	7552	6	–
The First National Bank Of Albion	3316	6	–
The National Exchange Bank Of Albion	1544	6	–
Algonac			
The First National Bank Of Algonac	12944	6	6
Allegan			
The First National Bank Of Allegan	1829	4	–
Almont			
The First National Bank Of Almont	12793	–	6
Alpena			
The Alpena National Bank	2847	5	5
Alpha			
The First National Bank Of Alpha	10601	5	5
Ann Arbor			
The First National Bank And Trust Company Of Ann Arbor	2714	–	3
The First National Bank Of Ann Arbor	22	5	–
The First National Bank Of Ann Arbor	2714	4	–
Avoca			
The First National Bank Of Avoca	10790	–	–

City, Bank	Ch. No.	L	S
Battle Creek			
Central National Bank & Trust Company Of Battle Creek	7013	–	4
Central National Bank Of Battle Creek	7013	3	3
Old Merchants National Bank & Trust Company Of Battle Creek	7589	–	1
The Central National Bank At Battle Creek	13858	–	5
The City National Bank & Trust Company Of Battle Creek	11852	6	2
The City National Bank Of Battle Creek	11852	4	–
The First National Bank Of The City Of Battle Creek	1205	6	–
The Merchants National Bank Of Battle Creek	3896	6	–
The National Bank Of Battle Creek	3314	5	–
The Old National Bank & Trust Company Of Battle Creek	7589	5	–
The Old National Bank Of Battle Creek	7589	4	–
The Security National Bank Of Battle Creek	14185	–	–
Bay City			
The Bay National Bank Of Bay City	2853	6	–
The First National Bank Of Bay City	410	6	–
The First National Bank Of Bay City	2853	5	4
The National Bank Of Bay City	13622	–	3
The Old Second National Bank Of Bay City	4953	6	–
The Second National Bank Of Bay City	2145	4	–
Benton Harbor			
Farmers & Merchants Natl Bank & Trust Co Of Benton Harbor	10529	5	3
The American National Bank Of Benton Harbor	10143	4	–
The American Natl Bank & Trust Company Of Benton Harbor	10143	6	3
The Farmers And Merchants National Bank Of Benton Harbor	10529	5	–
The Farmers And Merchants National Bank Of Benton Harbor	13833	–	–
The First National Bank Of Benton Harbor	4261	6	–
Bessemer			
The Bessemer National Bank	13607	–	4
The First National Bank Of Bessemer	3947	6	–
Big Rapids			
The Big Rapids National Bank	2944	6	–
The Northern National Bank Of Big Rapids	1832	6	–
Birmingham			
The Birmingham National Bank	13703	–	4
The First National Bank Of Birmingham	9874	5	4
Blissfield			
The First National Bank Of Blissfield	11813	6	6
Boyne City			
The First National Bank Of Boyne City	9020	4	5
Brighton			
The First National Bank Of Brighton	12869	–	–
Bronson			
The Peoples National Bank Of Bronson	9704	6	5
Buchanan			
The First National Bank Of Buchanan	2046	6	–
The First National Bank Of Buchanan	3925	5	6
Burr Oak			
The First National Bank Of Burr Oak	9497	5	4
Calumet			
The First National Bank Of Calumet	3457	3	4
Capac			
The First National Bank Of Capac	10631	5	6
Carsonville			
The First National Bank Of Carsonville	10753	–	–
Caspian			
The Caspian National Bank	11802	6	4
Cassopolis			
The First National Bank Of Cassopolis	1812	4	1
Centerline			
The First National Bank Of Centerline	13240	–	–
Centreville			
The First National Bank Of Centreville	2095	5	–
Charlotte			
The First National Bank Of Charlotte	1758	4	5
The Merchants National Bank Of Charlotte	3034	6	–
Cheboygan			
The Citizens National Bank Of Cheboygan	13522	–	–
The First National Bank Of Cheboygan	3235	4	6
Chesaning			
The First National Bank Of Chesaning	11454	6	–
Coldwater			
The Coldwater National Bank	1235	4	3
The Coldwater National Bank	14116	–	–
The Southern Michigan National Bank Of Coldwater	1924	3	3
Concord			
The First National Bank Of Concord	3251	6	–
Constantine			
The Farmers National Bank Of Constantine	2211	6	–
The First National Bank Of Constantine	813	6	–
Corunna			
The First National Bank Of Corunna	1256	5	–
Croswell			
The First National Bank Of Croswell	9792	6	–
Crystal Falls			
The Crystal Falls National Bank	11547	4	2
The First National Bank Of Crystal Falls	14269	–	–
The Iron County National Bank Of Crystal Falls	7525	4	4
Dearborn			
The First National Bank Of Dearborn	12989	–	3
Decatur			
The First National Bank Of Decatur	1722	4	–

City, Bank	Ch. No.	L	S
Detroit			
First And Old National Bank Of Detroit	10527	3	–
First National Bank In Detroit	10527	2	1
First National Bank, Detroit	10527	–	2
First Wayne National Bank Of Detriot	10527	–	1
Guardian National Bank Of Commerce Of Detroit	8703	–	1
Old Detroit National Bank	6492	5	–
The American Exchange National Bank Of Detroit	3357	5	–
The American National Bank Of Detroit	1542	5	–
The Commercial National Bank Of Detroit	2591	3	–
The Detroit National Bank	2870	6	–
The First National Bank Of Detroit	97	4	–
The First National Bank Of Detroit	2707	4	–
The Griswold National Bank Of Detroit	12847	4	–
The Manufacturers National Bank Of Detroit	13738	–	–
The Merchants And Manufacturers National Bank Of Detroit	2365	5	–
The Merchants National Bank Of Detroit	10600	3	–
The National Bank Of Commerce Of Detroit	8703	4	–
The National Bank Of Detroit	13671	–	–
The National Insurance Bank Of Detroit	1433	6	–
The Preston National Bank Of Detroit	3730	5	–
The Second National Bank Of Detroit	116	4	–
The Third National Bank Of Detroit	3514	6	–
The Union National Bank Of Detroit	3487	6	–
Dowagiac			
The Dowagiac National Bank	10073	5	4
The First National Bank Of Dowagiac	1625	6	–
Durand			
The First National Bank Of Durand	5415	6	–
East Saginaw			
The East Saginaw National Bank	3123	6	–
The First National Bank Of East Saginaw	637	6	–
The Home National Bank Of East Saginaw	2761	6	–
The Merchants National Bank Of East Saginaw	1550	5	–
The Second National Bank Of East Saginaw	1918	6	–
Eaton Rapids			
The First National Bank Of Eaton Rapids	2367	5	6
The National Bank Of Eaton Rapids	13995	–	–
Escanaba			
The Escanaba National Bank	8496	3	4
The First National Bank Of Escanaba	3761	3	4
Evart			
The First National Bank Of Evart	12561	–	3
Fenton			
The First National Bank Of Fenton	81	6	–
Flint			
First National Bank & Trust Company At Flint	10997	–	4
First National Bank At Flint	10997	6	5
The Citizens National Bank Of Flint	1780	6	–
The First National Bank Of Flint	1588	5	–
The First National Bank Of Flint	3361	4	–
The Flint National Bank	3361	6	–
The National Bank Of Flint	7664	5	–
The National Bank Of Flint	13976	–	–
Flushing			
The First National Bank Of Flushing	2708	6	–
Gladstone			
First National Bank In Gladstone	14111	–	6
The First National Bank Of Gladstone	10886	5	4
Gladwin			
The First National Bank Of Gladwin	10673	–	–
Grand Haven			
The First National Bank Of Grand Haven	1849	6	–
The National Bank Of Grand Haven	4578	6	–
Grand Rapids			
Grand Rapids National Bank	3293	2	2
Grand Rapids National City Bank	3293	4	–
Peoples National Bank Of Grand Rapids	13799	–	3
The American National Bank Of Grand Rapids	13328	–	2
The City National Bank Of Grand Rapids	812	6	–
The City National Bank Of Grand Rapids	12108	–	–
The Fifth National Bank Of Grand Rapids	3488	5	–
The First National Bank Of Grand Rapids	294	5	–
The Fourth National Bank Of Grand Rapids	2611	2	–
The Grand Rapids National Bank	2460	2	–
The National Bank Of Grand Rapids	13758	–	1
The National City Bank Of Grand Rapids	3293	4	–
The Old National Bank Of Grand Rapids	2890	2	–
The Security National Bank Of Grand Rapids	13434	–	–
Greenville			
The City National Bank Of Greenville	3243	6	–
The First National Bank Of Greenville	2054	5	–
The Greenville National Bank	11843	5	5
Hamtramck			
The First National Bank Of Hamtramck	11082	–	–
The Peoples National Bank Of Hamtramck	11082	6	–
Hancock			
The First National Bank Of Hancock	2143	3	3
The National Metals Bank Of Hancock	14249	–	5
The Superior National Bank Of Hancock	9087	4	3
Hart			
The First National Bank Of Hart	6727	3	4
Hartford			
The Olney National Bank Of Hartford	9854	3	5
Hastings			
National Bank Of Hastings	13857	–	5
The Hastings National Bank	1745	4	4
Hermansville			
The First National Bank Of Hermansville	11954	6	4
Hillsdale			
The First National Bank Of Hillsdale	168	4	4
The Hillsdale County National Bank Of Hillsdale	14062	–	5
The Second National Bank Of Hillsdale	1470	5	–
Holly			
The First National Bank Of Holly	1752	5	–
The Merchants National Bank Of Holly	1965	6	–
Houghton			
The Citizens National Bank Of Houghton	5896	3	4
The First National Bank Of Houghton	1247	5	–
The Houghton National Bank	7676	3	3
The National Bank Of Houghton	3334	5	–

City, Bank	Ch. No.	L	S
Howell			
First National Bank In Howell	14144	–	6
The First National Bank Of Howell	11586	5	3
Hubbell			
The First National Bank At Hubbell	13824	–	6
The First National Bank Of Hubbell	9359	6	5
Inkster			
The Inkster National Bank	12878	–	–
Ionia			
The First National Bank Of Ionia	275	5	–
The Ionia County National Bank Of Ionia	14187	–	5
The National Bank Of Ionia	5789	4	4
The Second National Bank Of Ionia	2008	6	–
Iron Mountain			
The First National Bank Of Iron Mountain	3806	4	3
The National Bank Of Iron Mountain	11929	5	–
The United States National Bank Of Iron Mountain	11929	4	2
Iron River			
The First National Bank Of Iron River	8545	4	3
The Iron River National Bank	14102	–	4
Ironwood			
The First National Bank Of Ironwood	3971	6	–
The Gogebic National Bank Of Ironwood	9517	5	4
The Iron National Bank Of Ironwood	11469	4	5
The Merchants And Miners National Bank Of Ironwood	12387	5	3
Ishpeming			
The First National Bank Of Ishpeming	2084	6	–
The Ishpeming National Bank	3095	6	–
The Miners First National Bank Of Ishpeming	13931	–	4
The Miners National Bank Of Ishpeming	5668	3	3
Ithaca			
The Commercial National Bank Of Ithaca	9654	4	5
The First National Bank Of Ithaca	3217	6	–
The Ithaca National Bank	6485	6	5
Jackson			
National Union Bank & Trust Company Of Jackson	11289	5	5
The East Side National Union Bank Of Jackson	13072	–	–
The First National Bank Of Jackson	1065	6	–
The National Bank Of Jackson	13741	–	4
The National Union Bank Of Jackson	11289	3	–
The Peoples National Bank Of Jackson	1533	4	5
Union & Peoples National Bank Of Jackson	1533	–	3
Kalamazoo			
Kalamazoo National Bank & Trust Company, Kalamazoo	3211	6	5
The American National Bank Of Kalamazoo	13820	–	–
The City National Bank Of Kalamazoo	3210	5	–
The First National Bank And Trust Company Of Kalamazoo	191	6	2
The First National Bank Of Kalamazoo	191	4	–
The Kalamazoo National Bank	3211	4	–
The Michigan National Bank Of Kalamazoo	1359	5	–
L'anse			
The Baraga County National Bank Of L'anse	9509	6	6
L'anse Creuse			
The First National Bank Of L'anse Creuse	12661	6	–
Lake Linden			
The First National Bank Of Lake Linden	3948	4	3
Lansing			
Lansing National Bank	14032	–	4
The Capital National Bank Of Lansing	8148	4	2
The City National Bank Of Lansing	3513	4	3
The First National Bank Of Lansing	232	–	–
The Lansing National Bank	1953	6	–
The Second National Bank Of Lansing	264	5	–
Lapeer			
The First National Bank Of Lapeer	1731	4	5
Laurium			
The First National Bank Of Laurium	8598	4	3
Lawton			
The First National Bank Of Lawton	12084	5	6
Leslie			
The First National Bank Of Leslie	2162	6	–
Lincoln Park			
The Lincoln Park National Bank	12999	–	4
Lowell			
The Lowell National Bank	1280	6	–
Ludington			
The First National Bank & Trust Company Of Ludington	2773	6	4
The First National Bank Of Ludington	2773	6	–
The National Bank Of Ludington	14016	–	–
Lyons			
The National Bank Of Lyons	2008	6	–
Manistee			
The First National Bank Of Manistee	2539	4	4
The Manistee National Bank	2606	6	–
Manistique			
The First National Bank In Manistique	13513	–	5
The First National Bank Of Manistique	5348	5	6
The First National Bank Of Manistique	14280	–	–
Marine City			
The Liberty National Bank Of Marine City	11260	5	6
Marquette			
The First National Bank & Trust Company Of Marquette	390	4	3
The First National Bank Of Marquette	390	2	–
The Marquette National Bank	6003	4	–
The Union National Bank Of Marquette	12027	4	3
Marshall			
The First National Bank Of Marshall	1515	4	4
The First National Bank Of Marshall	14009	–	–
The National Bank Of Michigan Of Marshall	1518	6	–
The National City Bank Of Marshall	2023	6	–
Mason			
The Dart National Bank Of Mason	12697	5	5
The First National Bank Of Mason	1764	6	–
Menominee			
The First National Bank Of Menominee	3256	3	2
The Lumbermen's National Bank Of Menominee	4454	4	4
Midland City			
The First National Bank Of Midland City	2855	–	–

City, Bank	Ch. No.	L	S
Milford			
The First National Bank Of Milford	2379	5	–
Monroe			
The First National Bank Of Monroe	1587	4	4
Morenci			
The First National Bank Of Morenci	5669	6	–
Mount Clemens			
First National Bank In Mount Clemens	12971	3	4
The First National Bank Of Mount Clemens	2214	6	–
Mount Pleasant			
The First National Bank Of Mount Pleasant	3215	6	–
Muir			
The First National Bank Of Muir	2017	6	–
Munising			
The First National Bank Of Alger County At Munising	9000	4	5
Muskegon			
The Hackley National Bank Of Muskegon	4398	5	–
The Hackley Union National Bank Of Muskegon	4398	–	3
The Lumbermans National Bank Of Muskegon	2081	6	–
The Merchants National Bank Of Muskegon	3088	6	–
The Muskegon National Bank	1730	5	–
The National Lumbermans Bank Of Muskegon	4840	5	4
The Union National Bank Of Muskegon	4125	4	–
Negaunee			
The First National Bank Of Negaunee	2085	6	–
The First National Bank Of Negaunee	3717	4	3
The Negaunee National Bank	9556	4	4
Niles			
The Citizens National Bank Of Niles	1886	6	–
The City National Bank & Trust Company Of Niles	13307	5	3
The City National Bank And Trust Company Of Niles	13307	–	–
The First National Bank Of Niles	1761	6	–
The First National Bank Of Niles	13753	–	–
Norway			
The First National Bank Of Norway	6863	4	1
Ontonagon			
The First National Bank In Ontonagon	13929	–	6
The First National Bank Of Ontonagon	6820	6	4
Ovid			
The First National Bank Of Ovid	3264	6	–
Owosso			
The First National Bank Of Owosso	1573	5	–
The Second National Bank Of Owosso	3410	6	–
Paw Paw			
The First National Bank Of Paw Paw	1521	5	5
Petoskey			
The First National Bank Of Petoskey	5607	4	4
Plymouth			
First National Bank In Plymouth	12953	5	4
The First National Bank Of Plymouth	1916	6	–
The First National Exchange Bank Of Plymouth	4649	3	–
The Plymouth National Bank	3109	6	–
Pontiac			
Community National Bank Of Pontiac	13739	–	4
First National Bank & Trust Company In Pontiac	12288	4	4
First National Bank In Pontiac	12288	4	–
The American National Bank Of Pontiac	12288	6	–
The First National Bank At Pontiac	13600	–	4
The First National Bank Of Pontiac	434	6	–
The First National Bank Of Pontiac	2607	6	–
The National Bank Of Pontiac	11549	6	–
The Pontiac National Bank	3388	6	–
The Second National Bank Of Pontiac	1574	6	–
Port Huron			
First National Bank & Trust Company Of Port Huron	4446	5	4
First National Bank In Port Huron	4446	6	–
First National Trust & Savings Bank Of Port Huron	4446	–	4
The First National Bank Of Port Huron	1857	6	–
The First National Exchange Bank Of Port Huron	4446	5	–
Quincy			
The First National Bank Of Quincy	2550	5	5
Reed City			
The First National Bank Of Reed City	4413	5	5
The Reed City National Bank	12474	–	–
Richland			
The Farmers National Bank Of Richland	9099	6	–
Richmond			
The First National Bank Of Richmond	10742	6	5
The National Bank Of Richmond	13793	–	–
Rochester			
The First National Bank Of Rochester	9218	5	5
The Rochester National Bank	13841	–	6
Rockland			
The First National Bank Of Rockland	5199	5	5
The Ontonagon County National Bank Of Rockland	5199	6	–
Romeo			
The Citizens National Bank Of Romeo	2186	4	2
The First National Bank Of Romeo	354	5	–
Royal Oak			
The First National Bank Of Royal Oak	12657	5	6
Saginaw			
Second National Bank & Trust Company Of Saginaw	1918	–	2
The Citizens National Bank Of Saginaw	2492	6	–
The Commercial National Bank Of Saginaw	3911	5	–
The First National Bank Of Saginaw	1768	6	–
The Second National Bank Of Saginaw	1918	3	4
Saint Clair			
The First National Bank Of St. Clair	1789	5	–
Saint Clair Heights			
The Michigan National Bank Of Saint Clair Heights	10632	6	–
Saint Clair Shores			
The First National Bank Of Saint Clair Shores	12661	6	6
Saint Ignace			
The First National Bank Of St. Ignace	3886	5	3
Saint Johns			
The First National Bank Of Saint Johns	1539	6	–
The St. Johns National Bank	3378	3	6
Saint Joseph			
The Commercial National Bank & Trust Co Of St. Joseph	5594	6	5
The Commercial National Bank Of St. Joseph	5594	4	–
The First National Bank Of St. Joseph	1866	5	–
Saint Louis			
The First National Bank Of Saint Louis	3239	6	–
Sault Ste Marie			
The First National Bank Of Sault Ste Marie	3547	4	3
The Sault Ste Marie National Bank	3747	6	–
Schoolcraft			
The First National Bank Of Schoolcraft	1725	6	–
South Haven			
The First National Bank Of South Haven	1823	5	–
Stanton			
The First National Bank Of Stanton	2914	6	–
Sturgis			
The First National Bank Of Sturgis	825	6	–
The National Bank Of Sturgis	3276	6	–
The Sturgis National Bank	3276	5	4
Tecumseh			
The National Bank Of Tecumseh	1063	6	–
Three Rivers			
The First National Bank Of Three Rivers	600	5	3
The Manufacturers National Bank Of Three Rivers	1919	6	–
The Three Rivers National Bank	3133	6	–
Traverse City			
The First National Bank Of Traverse City	3325	6	4
Union City			
The Farmers National Bank Of Union City	2372	5	–
The Union City National Bank	1826	5	5
Utica			
The First National Bank Of Utica	12826	–	6
The Utica National Bank	14022	–	–
Vassar			
Millington National Bank, Millington	8723	4	6
The First National Bank Of Vassar	2987	6	–
The Vassar National Bank	8723	5	–
Wakefield			
The First National Bank Of Wakefield	11305	5	3
Watervliet			
The First National Bank Of Watervliet	10498	6	5
White Pigeon			
The First National Bank Of White Pigeon	4527	6	–
Whitehall			
The First National Bank Of Whitehall	2429	6	–
Wyandotte			
The First National Bank Of Wyandotte	12616	–	4
The National Bank Of Wyandotte	13874	–	–
Yale			
The First National Bank Of Yale	5482	5	5
Ypsilanti			
The First National Bank Of Ypsilanti	155	4	4
The National Bank Of Ypsilanti	13807	–	–
The Peoples National Bank Of Ypsilanti	12436	–	–

MINNESOTA

City, Bank	Ch. No.	L	S
Ada			
The Ada National Bank	10665	4	5
The First National Bank Of Ada	5433	5	–
Adams			
The First National Bank Of Adams	8059	4	2
Adrian			
The First National Bank Of Adrian	7960	6	–
The National Bank Of Adrian	9033	4	5
Aitkin			
The Farmers National Bank Of Aitkin	10783	–	5
The First National Bank Of Aitkin	6803	5	4
The National Bank Of Aitkin	10841	–	–
Albert Lea			
The Albert Lea National Bank	4702	6	–
The Citizens National Bank Of Albert Lea	6128	4	–
The First National Bank Of Albert Lea	3560	4	3
The Freeborn County National Bank & Trust Co. Of Albert Lea	13422	–	–
The Security National Bank Of Albert Lea	6431	6	–
Alden			
The First National Bank Of Alden	6631	5	4
Alexandria			
The Farmers National Bank Of Alexandria	5859	3	–
The Farmers National Bank Of Alexandria	12864	3	–
The First National Bank Of Alexandria	2995	4	–
Amboy			
The First National Bank Of Amboy	9775	4	–
The First National Bank Of Amboy	13342	–	–
The Security National Bank Of Amboy	14068	–	–
Anoka			
First National Bank In Anoka	13547	–	6
The Anoka National Bank	3000	6	3
The First National Bank Of Anoka	2800	6	–
Appleton			
The First National Bank Of Appleton	4831	6	–
The First National Bank Of Appleton	8813	6	3
Argyle			
The First National Bank Of Argyle	5907	4	–
Atwater			
The First National Bank Of Atwater	10570	6	–
Aurora			
The First National Bank Of Aurora	11345	6	–
Austin			
The Austin National Bank	4131	3	4
The Citizens National Bank Of Austin	4847	6	–
The First National Bank Of Austin	1690	4	2
Avoca			
The First National Bank Of Avoca	11224	5	–
Bagley			
The First National Bank Of Bagley	6813	5	5
Balaton			
The First National Bank Of Balaton	6840	5	–
Barnesville			
The Barnesville National Bank	6098	6	–
The Farmers National Bank Of Barnesville	11261	–	–
The First National Bank Of Barnesville	4959	3	3
Barnum			
The First National Bank Of Barnum	11761	5	5
Battle Lake			
The First National Bank Of Battle Lake	8756	5	5
Baudette			
The First National Bank Of Baudette	10710	6	3
Beardsley			
The First National Bank Of Beardsley	7438	4	–
Beaver Creek			
The First National Bank Of Beaver Creek	9321	5	–
Belle Plaine			
The First National Bank Of Belle Plaine	7273	6	4
Bemidji			
The First National Bank Of Bemidji	5582	4	5
The Lumbermens National Bank Of Bemidji	8241	6	–
The Northern Bank Of Bemidji	8241	4	4
Benson			
The First National Bank Of Benson	6154	4	–
The National Bank Of Benson	13397	–	–
Bertha			
The First National Bank Of Bertha	7373	5	4
Big Lake			
The First National Bank Of Big Lake	11611	6	–
Biwabik			
The First National Bank Of Biwabik	8697	5	–
Blackduck			
The First National Bank Of Blackduck	9147	5	–
Blooming Prairie			
The First National Bank Of Blooming Prairie	6775	5	3
Blue Earth			
First & Farmers National Bank Of Blue Earth	5393	–	4
The Farmers National Bank Of Blue Earth	7641	4	5
The First National Bank Of Blue Earth	5393	6	5
Bovey			
The First National Bank Of Bovey	11054	6	3
Boyd			
The Boyd National Bank	6571	6	–
Braham			
The First National Bank Of Braham	7387	5	4
Brainerd			
The First National Bank Of Brainerd	2590	4	4
Brandon			
The First National Bank Of Brandon	10862	6	–
Breckenridge			
The Breckenridge National Bank	6335	5	–
The First National Bank Of Breckenridge	4644	6	5
Brewster			
The First National Bank Of Brewster	10946	6	4
Bricelyn			
The First National Bank Of Bricelyn	6478	5	–
Browerville			
The First National Bank Of Browerville	7227	5	4
Browns Valley			
The First National Bank Of Browns Valley	7341	5	–
Buffalo			
The Buffalo National Bank	12959	–	5
The First National Bank Of Buffalo	11023	6	–
The Oakley National Bank Of Buffalo	14311	–	–
Buhl			
The First National Bank Of Buhl	11622	–	–
Caledonia			
The First National Bank Of Caledonia	7508	6	4
Camb			
The First National Bank Of Cambridge	7428	5	4
Campbell			
The First National Bank Of Campbell	6259	6	–
Canby			
The First National Bank Of Canby	6366	5	6
The National Citizens Bank Of Canby	7427	5	4
Cannon Falls			
The Farmers And Merchants National Bank Of Cannon Falls	6704	5	–
The First National Bank In Cannon Falls	13713	–	4
The First National Bank Of Cannon Falls	2387	6	–
Carlton			
The First National Bank Of Carlton	6973	6	4
Cass Lake			
The First National Bank Of Cass Lake	6352	6	3
Ceylon			
The First National Bank Of Ceylon	6029	4	5
Chaska			
The First National Bank Of Chaska	8378	4	5
Chatfield			
The First National Bank Of Chatfield	6608	5	3
Chisholm			
The First National Bank Of Chisholm	7647	3	4
Chokio			
The First National Bank Of Chokio	5969	6	–
Clarkfield			
The First National Bank Of Clarkfield	6448	6	–
Clearbrook			
The First National Bank Of Clearbrook	11392	6	–
Clinton			
The First National Bank Of Clinton	7161	6	–
Cloquet			
The First National Bank Of Cloquet	5405	3	2
Cokato			
The First National Bank Of Cokato	12395	6	4
Cold Spring			
The First National Bank Of Cold Spring	8051	5	5
Coleraine			
The First National Bank Of Coleraine	8322	5	4
Columbia Heights			
The Columbia National Bank Of Columbia Heights	13114	–	–
Cottonwood			
The First National Bank Of Cottonwood	6584	4	6

City, Bank	Ch. No.	L	S
Crookston			
The First National Bank Of Crookston	2567	3	4
The Merchants National Bank Of Crookston	3262	4	–
Crosby			
The First National Bank Of Crosby	9838	5	3
Dawson			
The First National Bank Of Dawson	6321	4	5
The Northwestern National Bank Of Dawson	13564	–	5
Deer Creek			
First National Bank In Deer Creek	13303	–	5
The First National Bank Of Deer Creek	7268	6	–
Deer River			
The First National Bank Of Deer River	9131	5	5
Deerwood			
The First National Bank Of Deerwood	9703	4	4
Delano			
The First National Bank Of Delano	9903	6	–
Detroit			
The First National Bank Of Detroit	3426	4	–
The Merchants National Bank Of Detroit	8122	5	–
Detroit Lakes			
Becker County National Bank Of Detroit Lakes	13075	–	4
Dodge Center			
The Farmers National Bank Of Dodge Center	6623	6	–
The First National Bank Of Dodge Center	6682	5	–
Duluth			
American Exchange National Bank Of Duluth	9374	3	–
Duluth National Bank	12140	4	3
First & American National Bank Of Duluth	3626	–	1
The City National Bank Of Duluth	6520	2	1
The Duluth National Bank	2768	6	–
The Duluth Union National Bank, Duluth	3626	6	–
The First National Bank Of Duluth	1954	6	–
The First National Bank Of Duluth	3626	2	–
The Marine National Bank Of Duluth	4421	6	–
The Merchants National Bank Of Duluth	3453	6	–
The Minnesota National Bank Of Duluth	11810	3	2
The National Bank Of Commerce Of Duluth	4001	6	–
The Northern National Bank Of Duluth	9327	2	2
The Pioneer National Bank Of Duluth	13078	5	3
The Union National Bank Of Duluth	3626	6	–
Western National Bank Of Duluth	13116	5	4
Dunnell			
The First National Bank Of Dunnell	6738	5	5
Eagle Bend			
The First National Bank Of Eagle Bend	6266	5	4
East Grand Forks			
The First National Bank Of East Grand Forks	4638	5	–
The Minnesota National Bank Of East Grand Forks	13405	–	–
Elbow Lake			
The First National Bank Of Elbow Lake	4617	5	4
Elgin			
The First National Bank Of Elgin	7184	6	–
Elk River			
The First National Bank Of Elk River	8757	4	5
Ellsworth			
The First National Bank Of Ellsworth	5570	5	–
Elmore			
The First National Bank Of Elmore	5377	4	4
Ely			
The First National Bank Of Ely	8592	5	4
Emmons			
The First National Bank Of Emmons	6784	5	4
Erskine			
The First National Bank Of Erskine	11173	5	–
Eveleth			
The First National Bank Of Eveleth	5553	5	4
The Miners National Bank Of Eveleth	6991	5	4
Eyota			
The First National Bank Of Eyota	5374	5	–
Fairfax			
The First National Bank Of Fairfax	9771	5	5
Fairmont			
The Citizens National Bank Of Fairmont	11090	–	–
The Fairmont National Bank	8551	5	5
The First National Bank Of Fairmont	4936	5	3
The Martin County National Bank Of Fairmont	5423	3	3
Faribault			
The Citizens National Bank Of Faribault	1863	3	–
The First National Bank Of Faribault	1686	4	–
The Security National Bank & Trust Company Of Faribault	11668	–	4
The Security National Bank Of Faribault	11668	3	–
Farmington			
The First National Bank Of Farmington	11687	–	4
Farwell			
The First National Bank Of Farwell	12032	–	–
Fergus Falls			
Fergus Falls Natl Bank & Trust Company, Fergus Falls	2648	–	4
The Citizens National Bank Of Fergus Falls	2934	6	–
The Fergus Falls National Bank	2648	4	4
The First National Bank Of Fergus Falls	2030	4	3
Fertile			
The Citizens National Bank Of Fertile	6693	6	–
The First National Bank Of Fertile	5988	6	–
Foley			
The First National Bank Of Foley	7933	5	4
Forest Lake			
The First National Bank Of Forest Lake	11652	5	6
Fosston			
The First National Bank Of Fosston	6889	4	5
Frazee			
The First National Bank Of Frazee	7024	5	4
Fulda			
The First National Bank Of Fulda	6054	6	–
Gilbert			
The First National Bank Of Gilbert	9262	4	3
Glencoe			
The First National Bank Of Glencoe	2571	4	4
Glenwood			
The First National Bank Of Glenwood	7742	5	–
Gonvick			
The First National Bank Of Gonvick	10830	6	–
Good Thunder			
The First National Bank Of Good Thunder	11552	3	3
Goodhue			
The First National Bank Of Goodhue	7603	4	–
Graceville			
The First National Bank Of Graceville	7213	4	3
Granada			
The First National Bank Of Granada	11606	–	–
Grand Meadow			
The First National Bank Of Grand Meadow	6933	6	6
Grand Rapids			
The First National Bank Of Grand Rapids	6563	4	4
Granite Falls			
The First National Bank Of Granite Falls	8416	5	–
Grey Eagle			
The First National Bank Of Grey Eagle	8729	6	–
The National Bank Of Grey Eagle	12607	5	4
Hallock			
The First National Bank Of Hallock	6934	5	–
Halstad			
The First National Bank Of Halstad	7196	6	4
Hancock			
The First National Bank Of Hancock	6996	3	4
The Hancock National Bank	7033	3	5
Hanley Falls			
The First National Bank Of Hanley Falls	6285	6	–
Hanska			
The First National Bank Of Hanska	11288	4	–
Harmony			
The First National Bank Of Harmony	8683	6	4
Hastings			
The First National Bank Of Hastings	496	5	5
The Hastings National Bank	11212	–	4
The Merchants National Bank Of Hastings	1538	6	–
Hawley			
The First National Bank Of Hawley	7772	6	5
Hendricks			
The Farmers National Bank Of Hendricks	9457	4	5
The First National Bank Of Hendricks	6468	6	5
Henning			
The First National Bank Of Henning	6906	5	5
Herman			
The First National Bank Of Herman	8049	4	5
Heron Lake			
The First National Bank Of Heron Lake	5383	4	4
Hibbing			
The First National Bank Of Hibbing	5745	4	2
The Hibbing National Bank	12568	5	–
Hills			
The First National Bank Of Hills	6199	6	–
Holland			
The First National Bank Of Holland	11724	–	–
Hutchinson			
The Farmers National Bank Of Hutchinson	10147	4	5
The First National Bank Of Hutchinson	14216	–	–
International Falls			
The First National Bank Of International Falls	7380	4	4
Iona			
The First National Bank Of Iona	7128	5	–
Ironton			
The First National Bank Of Ironton	10382	5	5
Isanti			
The First National Bank Of Isanti	10554	6	6
Ivanhoe			
The Farmers And Merchants National Bank Of Ivanhoe	11627	4	4
The Farmers And Merchants National Bank Of Ivanhoe	13468	–	–
The First National Bank Of Ivanhoe	6467	5	5
The Ivanhoe National Bank	6637	6	–
Jackson			
The Brown National Bank Of Jackson	7797	5	5
The First National Bank Of Jackson	5852	4	–
The First National Bank Of Jackson	13095	–	–
The Jackson National Bank	6992	5	–
The Jackson National Bank	13269	–	–
Jasper			
The First National Bank Of Jasper	6523	5	–
Jordan			
The First National Bank Of Jordan	11218	3	5
Kasson			
National Farmers Bank Of Kasson	11042	5	3
The First National Bank Of Kasson	2159	6	–
The National Bank Of Dodge County At Kasson	10580	4	3
The National Bank Of Kasson	4969	6	–
Keewatin			
The First National Bank Of Keewatin	10903	5	4
Kerkhoven			
The First National Bank Of Kerkhoven	11365	5	6
Kiester			
The First National Bank Of Kiester	10603	6	3
Kilkenny			
The Farmers National Bank Of Kilkenny	11575	–	–
The First National Bank Of Kilkenny	11575	–	–
Lake Benton			
The First National Bank Of Lake Benton	4509	5	–
The National Citizens Bank Of Lake Benton	6696	5	5
Lake City			
The First National Bank Of Lake City	1740	6	–
Lake Crystal			
The American National Bank Of Lake Crystal	11401	5	6
The First National Bank Of Lake Crystal	6918	5	4
The Lake Crystal National Bank	13972	–	–
Lake Park			
The First National Bank Of Lake Park	7143	6	–
Lake Wilson			
The First National Bank Of Lake Wilson	11293	5	5
Lakefield			
The First National Bank Of Lakefield	6537	5	–
The First National Bank Of Lakefield	13204	–	–
Lakeville			
The First National Bank Of Lakeville	10740	–	–
Lamberton			
The First National Bank Of Lamberton	7221	5	–
The New First National Bank Of Lamberton	12844	–	–
Lancaster			
The First National Bank Of Lancaster	11356	6	–
Lanesboro			
The First National Bank Of Lanesboro	10507	3	6
Le Roy			
The First National Bank Of Le Roy	7109	6	4
Le Sueur			
The First National Bank Of Le Sueur	7199	6	6
Le Sueur Center			
The First National Bank Of Le Sueur Center	6921	5	5
The First Natoinal Bank Of Le Center	6921	–	–
Litchfield			
The First National Bank Of Litchfield	6118	2	–
The First National Bank Of Litchfield	12859	–	–
The Northwestern National Bank Of Litchfield	13486	–	2
Little Falls			
The American National Bank In Little Falls	13353	–	3
The American National Bank Of Little Falls	4655	4	–
The First National Bank Of Little Falls	4034	4	3
The German American National Bank Of Little Falls	4655	4	–
Littlefork			
The First National Bank Of Littlefork	11863	6	–
Long Prairie			
The First National Bank Of Long Prairie	6208	6	–
The Peoples National Bank Of Long Prairie	7080	5	3
Luverne			
First And Farmers National Bank In Luverne	12634	4	5
The Farmers National Bank Of Luverne	7770	6	–
The First National Bank Of Luverne	3428	4	–
The Luverne National Bank	13544	–	–
The National Bank Of Luverne	8977	6	–
Lyle			
The First National Bank Of Lyle	5706	6	3
Mabel			
The First National Bank Of Mabel	9031	5	3
Madelia			
The Citizens National Bank Of Madelia	13784	–	4
The First National Bank Of Madelia	7100	5	–
Madison			
The First National Bank Of Madison	6795	5	6
The Klein National Bank Of Madison	13561	–	4
Mahnomen			
First National Bank In Mahnomen	12941	–	4
The Farmers National Bank Of Mahnomen	11717	–	–
The First National Bank Of Mahnomen	8726	6	–
Mankato			
First National Bank & Trust Company Of Mankato	1683	–	5
First National Bank Of Mankato	1683	–	6
National Bank Of Commerce In Mankato	14220	–	5
The Citizens National Bank Of Mankato	2005	6	–
The First National Bank Of Mankato	1683	3	4
The Mankato National Bank	3562	6	–
The National Bank Of Commerce Of Mankato	6519	4	6
The National Citizens Bank Of Mankato	4727	3	2
Mapleton			
The First National Bank Of Mapleton	6787	5	5
Marble			
The First National Bank Of Marble	11608	5	4
Marshall			
The First National Bank Of Marshall	4614	4	3
The Lyon County National Bank Of Marshall	4595	5	–
Mc Intosh			
The First National Bank Of Mc Intosh	6488	5	5
Melrose			
The First National Bank Of Melrose	7566	6	–
Menahga			
The First National Bank Of Menahga	11740	6	3
Milaca			
The First National Bank Of Milaca	9050	5	4
Minneapolis			
Bloomington-Lake National Bank Of Minneapolis	12972	4	3
First National Bank & Trust Company Of Minneapolis	710	–	2
First National Bank In Minneapolis	710	1	1
Midland National Bank & Trust Company Of Minneapolis	9409	4	1
Minnehaha National Bank Of Minneapolis	13096	4	4
Northwestern National Bank & Trust Company Of Minneapolis	2006	–	–
The Bankers National Bank Of Minneapolis	11167	–	–
The Central National Bank Of Minneapolis	13108	6	3
The Clarke National Bank Of Minneapolis	6449	6	–
The Columbia National Bank Of Minneapolis	4739	6	–
The Commercial National Bank Of Minneapolis	10261	6	–
The Fifth Northwestern National Bank Of Minneapolis	13140	–	–
The First & Security National Bank Of Minneapolis	710	3	–
The First National Bank Of Minneapolis	710	2	–
The Flour City National Bank Of Minneapolis	3784	6	–
The Fourth Northwestern National Bank Of Minneapolis	13066	–	–
The Lincoln National Bank Of Minneapolis	11178	5	–
The Manufacturers National Bank Of Minneapolis	3098	6	–
The Marquette National Bank Of Minneapolis	11861	4	3
The Merchants National Bank Of Minneapolis	1830	6	–
The Metropolitan National Bank Of Minneapolis	9442	2	5
The Midland National Bank Of Minneapolis	9409	4	–
The Minneapolis National Bank	11778	6	–
The Minnesota National Bank Of Minneapolis	6449	6	–
The National Bank Of Commerce Of Minneapolis	3206	6	–
The National City Bank Of Minneapolis	10261	6	–
The National Exchange Bank Of Minneapolis	719	6	–
The Nicollet National Bank Of Minneapolis	3145	6	–
The North Western National Bank Of Minneapolis	2006	1	1
The Payday National Bank Of Minneapolis	11861	–	–
The Richfield National Bank Of Minneapolis	12115	6	5
The Scandinavian-american National Bank Of Minneapolis	9409	5	–
The Security National Bank Of Minneapolis	8720	3	–

City, Bank	Ch. No.	L	S
The State National Bank Of Minneapolis	1623	5	–
The Swedish-American National Bank Of Minneapolis	4951	5	–
The Third Northwestern National Bank Of Minneapolis	13127	–	–
The Transportation Brotherhoods National Bank Of Minneapolis	12282	5	6
The Union National Bank Of Minneapolis	2795	6	–
Minneota			
The Farmers And Merchants National Bank Of Minneota	6917	4	5
The First National Bank Of Minneota	6413	5	5
Minnesota Lake			
The Farmers National Bank Of Minnesota Lake	6532	5	5
The First National Bank Of Minnesota Lake	6204	5	–
Montevideo			
The First National Bank Of Montevideo	6860	4	–
The Security National Bank Of Montevideo	13086	–	–
Montgomery			
The First National Bank Of Montgomery	11215	5	4
Moorhead			
First National Bank In Moorhead	13297	–	3
The First & Moorhead National Bank, Moorhead	2569	6	–
The First National Bank Of Moorhead	2569	4	–
The Moorhead National Bank	4713	5	–
Moose Lake			
The First National Bank Of Moose Lake	12947	6	4
Mora			
The First National Bank Of Mora	7292	4	5
Morris			
The First National Bank Of Morris	2933	6	–
The Morris National Bank	6310	3	4
Motley			
The First National Bank Of Motley	7764	5	4
Motordale			
The First National Bank Of Motordale	11550	6	–
Mountain Lake			
The First National Bank Of Mountain Lake	9267	5	4
Nashwauk			
The American National Bank Of Nashwauk	11579	5	3
The First National Bank Of Nashwauk	10736	5	3
New Brighton			
The Twin City National Bank Of New Brighton	4302	6	–
New Duluth			
The New Duluth National Bank	4750	6	–
New Germany			
First National Bank Of New Germany	11550	4	–
New Prague			
The First National Bank Of New Prague	7092	5	3
New Richland			
The Farmers National Bank Of New Richland	10642	–	–
The First National Bank Of New Richland	10642	–	–
New Ulm			
The Citizens National Bank Of New Ulm	2318	6	–
The First National Bank Of New Ulm	631	6	–
Northfield			
Northfield National Bank And Trust Company	13350	–	3
The First National Bank Of Northfield	2073	4	3
The Northfield National Bank	5895	4	–
Olivia			
The Citizens National Bank Of Olivia	13081	–	3
The Peoples First National Bank Of Olivia	9063	6	–
Ortonville			
The Citizens National Bank Of Ortonville	6747	5	–
The First National Bank Of Ortonville	6459	4	5
Osakis			
The First National Bank Of Osakis	6837	4	5
Owatonna			
The Farmers National Bank Of Owatonna	2122	4	–
The First National Bank Of Owatonna	1911	4	3
The National Farmers Bank Of Owatonna	4928	4	–
Park Rapids			
The Citizens National Bank Of Park Rapids	13692	–	5
The First National Bank Of Park Rapids	5542	4	3
Parkers Prairie			
The First National Bank Of Parkers Prairie	6661	4	4
Paynesville			
The First National Bank Of Paynesville	11332	3	–
The First National Bank Of Paynesville	13518	–	–
Pelican Rapids			
The First National Bank Of Pelican Rapids	6349	5	–
Pequot			
The First National Bank Of Pequot	11267	6	–
Perham			
The First National Bank Of Perham	6276	5	–
Pine City			
The First National Bank Of Pine City	11581	5	5
Pine River			
The First National Bank Of Pine River	11563	–	–
Pipestone			
Pipestone National Bank	10936	6	6
The First National Bank Of Pipestone	3982	4	4
The Pipestone National Bank	13399	–	–
Plainview			
The First National Bank Of Plainview	6293	4	3
Preston			
National Bank Of Preston	9059	6	–
The First National Bank Of Preston	6279	3	4
Princeton			
The First National Bank Of Princeton	4807	6	–
The First National Bank Of Princeton	7708	3	4
Proctor			
The First National Bank Of Proctor	11125	5	4
The Peoples National Bank Of Proctor	11974	6	–
Raymond			
The First National Bank Of Raymond	8050	4	–
Red Lake Falls			
The Farmers National Bank Of Red Lake Falls	9837	5	–
The First National Bank Of Red Lake Falls	3659	6	–
Red Wing			
The First National Bank Of Red Wing	1487	3	3
The Goodhue County National Bank Of Red Wing	7307	3	4
The Red Wing National Bank And Trust Company, Red Wing	13396	–	2
Redwood Falls			
The First National Bank Of Redwood Falls	5826	5	–
Renville			
The First National Bank Of Renville	6583	5	–
Rice			
The First National Bank Of Rice	11709	–	–
The Rice National Bank	11710	–	–
Richfield			
The Richfield National Bank	12115	5	–
Rochester			
The First National Bank Of Rochester	579	3	2
The Rochester National Bank	2316	6	–
The Union National Bank Of Rochester	2088	4	4
Roseau			
The First National Bank Of Roseau	6783	5	3
The Roseau County National Bank Of Roseau	11848	6	6
Rosemount			
The First National Bank Of Rosemount	11776	5	–
Royalton			
The First National Bank Of Royalton	6731	6	–
Rush City			
The First National Bank Of Rush City	6954	5	–
Rushford			
The First National Bank Of Rushford	6436	5	3
Rushmore			
The First National Bank Of Rushmore	6862	6	–
Ruthton			
The First National Bank Of Ruthton	5892	6	–
Saint Anthony			
The First National Bank Of Saint Anthony	1830	6	–
Saint Charles			
The First National Bank Of Saint Charles	6237	6	–
The First National Bank Of Saint Charles	13973	–	–
Saint Cloud			
The American National Bank Of Saint Cloud	11818	5	3
The First National Bank Of Saint Cloud	2790	4	–
The German-American National Bank Of Saint Cloud	3009	6	–
The Merchants National Bank Of St. Cloud	4797	3	–
Saint James			
The Citizens & Security National Bank Of St. James	7021	5	4
The Citizens National Bank Of St. James	7021	5	–
The First National Bank Of Saint James	4859	4	–
The First National Bank Of Saint James	14296	–	–
Saint Paul			
National Exchange Bank Of St. Paul	10940	4	–
The American National Bank Of Saint Paul	6828	3	2
The Capital National Bank Of Saint Paul	8108	2	–
The Commercial National Bank Of Saint Paul	3689	6	–
The Empire National Bank & Trust Company Of St. Paul	12922	–	2
The Empire National Bank Of St. Paul	12922	–	–
The First National Bank Of Saint Paul	203	3	1
The Merchants National Bank Of Saint Paul	2020	1	–
The Midway National Bank Of St. Paul	13131	4	3
The National Bank Of Commerce In St Paul	10475	6	–
The National Exchange Bank Of Saint Paul	12922	–	–
The National German-American Bank Of Saint Paul	2943	5	–
The National Marine Bank Of Saint Paul	1258	6	–
The Saint Paul National Bank	13167	–	–
The Second National Bank Of Saint Paul	725	4	–
The St. Paul National Bank	2959	3	–
The Third National Bank Of Saint Paul	3233	6	–
The Twin Cities National Bank Of St. Paul	11741	3	3
The Wabash National Bank Of Saint Paul	11770	–	–
Saint Peter			
The First National Bank Of Saint Peter	1794	4	5
Sandstone			
The First National Bank Of Sandstone	9464	5	5
Sauk Centre			
The First National Bank Of Sauk Centre	3155	6	6
The Merchants National Bank Of Sauk Centre	6417	4	5
Shakopee			
The First National Bank Of Shakopee	1597	6	–
The First National Bank Of Shakopee	3039	5	4
The Merchants And Farmers National Bank Of Shakopee	3127	6	–
The Peoples National Bank Of Shakopee	11685	–	–
Sherburn			
The Sherburn National Bank	6348	5	4
Slayton			
The First National Bank Of Slayton	5256	5	–
Sleepy Eye			
The First National Bank Of Sleepy Eye	6387	3	3
The First National Bank Of Sleepy Eye Lake	6387	6	–
South Saint Paul			
Stockyards National Bank Of South Saint Paul	6732	3	3
Spring Valley			
The First National Bank Of Spring Valley	6316	4	3
Springfield			
The First National Bank Of Springfield	8269	6	–
Staples			
The City National Bank Of Staples	8523	5	4
The First National Bank Of Staples	5568	4	4
Starbuck			
The First National Bank Of Starbuck	9596	1	3
Stephen			
The First National Bank Of Stephen	9064	4	5
Stewartville			
The First National Bank Of Stewartville	5330	6	5
The Stewartville National Bank	13615	–	3
Stillwater			
The First National Bank Of Stillwater	1514	6	–
The First National Bank Of Stillwater	2674	4	2
The Lumbermans National Bank Of Stillwater	1783	5	–
Swanville			
The First National Bank Of Swanville	10824	6	5
Thief River Falls			
The First National Bank Of Thief River Falls	5894	3	4
Tower			
The First National Bank Of Tower	3924	6	–
Tracy			
The First National Bank Of Tracy	4992	6	–
Truman			
The Truman National Bank	6364	4	4
Twin Valley			
The First National Bank Of Twin Valley	6401	4	4
Two Harbors			
First National Bank In Two Harbors	12357	4	3
The First National Bank Of Two Harbors	6304	6	–
Tyler			
The First National Bank Of Tyler	6203	5	5
Ulen			
The First National Bank Of Ulen	7081	6	–
Verndale			
The First National Bank Of Verndale	6022	4	5
Virginia			
The American Exchange National Bank Of Virginia	11500	–	–
The First National Bank Of Virginia	6527	5	2
Wabasha			
The First National Bank Of Wabasha	3100	4	2
Waconia			
The First National Bank Of Waconia	11410	5	3
Wadena			
The First National Bank In Wadena	12507	5	3
The First National Bank Of Wadena	4821	3	–
The Merchants National Bank Of Wadena	4916	4	4
The National Bank Of Wadena	12507	6	–
Walker			
The First National Bank Of Walker	8476	3	4
Warren			
The First National Bank Of Warren	5866	5	–
The Warren National Bank	11286	5	–
Warroad			
The First National Bank Of Warroad	11815	–	–
Waseca			
The Farmers National Bank Of Waseca	9253	5	3
The First National Bank Of Waseca	6544	3	3
Watertown			
The First National Bank Of Watertown	11777	–	–
Waterville			
The First National Bank Of Waterville	7283	4	5
Welcome			
The Welcome National Bank	6331	4	4
Wells			
The First National Bank Of Wells	4669	4	–
The Wells National Bank	6788	5	–
Wendell			
The First National Bank Of Wendell	10898	4	5
West Concord			
First National Bank In West Concord	14167	–	5
The First National Bank Of West Concord	5362	4	1
West Minneapolis			
First National Bank Of Hopkins	7958	–	3
Security National Bank Of Hopkins	12518	–	4
The First National Bank Of West Minneapolis	7958	4	–
The Security National Bank Of West Minneapolis	12518	5	–
Westbrook			
The First National Bank Of Westbrook	6412	4	5
Wheaton			
The First National Bank Of Wheaton	6035	4	5
The First National Bank Of Wheaton	13556	–	–
The National Bank Of Wheaton	8993	6	–
White Bear Lake			
The First National Bank Of White Bear Lake	11987	–	–
Willmar			
The First National Bank Of Willmar	6151	3	–
The Security National Bank Of Willmar	13401	–	–
Wilmont			
The First National Bank Of Wilmont	5301	6	–
Windom			
The First National Bank Of Windom	5063	5	3
The Windom National Bank	6396	5	4
Winnebago			
The Blue Earth Valley National Bank Of Winnebago	10393	4	5
The First National Bank Of Winnebago City	5406	5	–
The First National Bank Of Winnebago City	13255	5	–
Winona			
The First National Bank Of Winona	550	5	–
The First National Bank Of Winona	3224	2	1
The Merchants National Bank Of Winona	2268	3	–
The National Bank Of Winona	3224	5	–
The Second National Bank Of Winona	1842	4	–
The United National Bank Of Winona	1643	6	
The Winona Deposit National Bank	1782	6	–
The Winona National And Savings Bank, Winona	10865	–	2
The Winona National Bank	10865	–	–
Winthrop			
First National Bank In Winthrop	14042	–	4
The First National Bank Of Winthrop	7014	5	4
Woodstock			
The First National Bank Of Woodstock	7625	4	4
Worthington			
The Citizens National Bank Of Worthington	5910	5	–
The First National Bank Of Worthington	3550	6	–
The Worthington National Bank	8989	4	3

MISSISSIPPI

City, Bank	Ch. No.	L	S
Aberdeen			
The Aberdeen National Bank	10555	–	–
The First National Bank Of Aberdeen	3656	3	4
Ackerman			
The First National Bank Of Ackerman	9251	6	–
Biloxi			
The First National Bank Of Biloxi	10576	4	3
Brookhaven			
The First National Bank Of Brookhaven	10494	5	5

City, Bank	Ch. No.	L	S
Canton			
The First National Bank Of Canton	6847	5	3
Clarksdale			
The First National Bank Of Clarksdale	6595	6	–
The Planters National Bank Of Clarksdale	12222	5	5
Collins			
The First National Bank Of Collins	9728	6	–
Columbia			
The Citizens National Bank Of Columbia	10326	6	–
Columbus			
First-columbus National Bank, Columbus	10738	–	1
The Columbus National Bank	10738	5	6
The First National Bank In Columbus	12822	–	–
The First National Bank Of Columbus	2638	6	–
The National Bank Of Commerce Of Columbus	10361	4	2
Corinth			
The Citizens National Bank Of Corinth	9751	4	–
The First National Bank Of Corinth	9094	3	5
Greenville			
The Commercial National Bank Of Greenville	13403	–	–
The First National Bank Of Greenville	3765	5	4
Greenwood			
The First National Bank Of Greenwood	7216	3	3
Gulfport			
First National Bank In Gulfport	13553	–	6
The First National Bank Of Gulfport	6188	3	3
The National Bank Of Gulfport	13156	–	–
Hattiesburg			
First National Bank Of Commerce Of Hattiesburg	5176	4	–
First National Bank Of Hattiesburg	5176	3	4
The Commercial National Bank Of Hattiesburg	12478	5	5
The First National Bank Of Hattiesburg	5177	5	–
The National Bank Of Commerce Of Hattiesburg	5176	6	–
Holly Springs			
The First National Bank Of Holly Springs	10873	–	–
Itta Bena			
The First National Bank Of Itta Bena	10688	4	5
Iuka			
The First National Bank Of Iuka	10154	6	–
Jackson			
Capital National Bank In Jackson	13708	–	5
The Capital National Bank Of Jackson	6646	4	4
The First National Bank Of Jackson	1610	6	–
The First National Bank Of Jackson	3332	4	6
The Jackson National Bank	10523	–	–
The Jackson-state National Bank	10523	6	–
The State National Bank Of Jackson	10463	6	–
Laurel			
The Commercial National Bank And Trust Company Of Laurel	11898	4	4
The First National Bank Of Laurel	6681	4	1
The Laurel National Bank	6923	6	–
Lexington			
The First National Bank Of Lexington	13313	–	–
Lumberton			
The First National Bank Of Lumberton	5613	5	5
Mc Comb City			
The First National Bank Of Mc Comb City	7461	5	4
Meridian			
First National Bank In Meridian	13551	–	3
The Citizens National Bank Of Meridian	7266	3	3
The First National Bank Of Meridian	2957	3	5
The Meridian National Bank	3176	6	–
Moss Point			
The Pascagoula National Bank Of Moss Point	8593	5	3
Natchez			
Britton And Koontz National Bank In Natchez	13722	–	4
The Britton And Koontz National Bank Of Natchez	12537	5	3
The First National Bank Of Natchez	3701	6	–
The National Bank Of Commerce Of Natchez	6305	6	–
New Albany			
The First National Bank Of New Albany	8514	5	–
Okolona			
The First National Bank Of Okolona	9196	6	–
Oxford			
The First National Bank Of Oxford	9865	4	5
Philadelphia			
The First National Bank Of Philadelphia	9041	5	–
Pontotoc			
The First National Bank Of Pontotoc	9040	4	4
Poplarville			
The National Bank Of Poplarville	8719	6	–
Port Gibson			
The Mississippi National Bank Of Port Gibson	5715	6	–
Ripley			
The First National Bank Of Ripley	9204	6	–
Rosedale			
The First National Bank Of Rosedale	10745	6	–
The Rosedale National Bank	12073	6	–
Shaw			
The First National Bank Of Shaw	7200	6	–
Starkville			
The First National Bank Of Starkville	3688	6	–
Summit			
The National Bank Of Summit	9753	6	–
The Progressive National Bank Of Summit	10338	6	–
Tupelo			
The First National Bank Of Tupelo	4521	6	–
Vicksburg			
Citizens National Bank Of Vicksburg	7507	4	–
The American National Bank Of Vicksburg	6121	5	–
The First National Bank And Trust Company Of Vicksburg	3258	–	3
The First National Bank Of Vicksburg	3258	3	6
The Merchants National Bank & Trust Company Of Vicksburg	3430	–	2
The Merchants National Bank Of Vicksburg	3430	5	–
The National Bank Of Vicksburg	803	6	–
The National City Savings Bank & Trust Company Of Vicksburg	12501	–	–
The National Peoples Savings Bank & Trust Co. Of Vicksburg	12499	–	–
Waynesboro			
The First National Bank Of Waynesboro	13413	–	–
The First National Bank Of Waynesboro	14176	–	–
West Point			
The First National Bank Of West Point	2891	4	3
Yazoo City			
The Delta National Bank Of Yazoo City	12587	5	1
The First National Bank Of Yazoo City	3566	6–	M

MISSOURI

City, Bank	Ch. No.	L	S
Adrian			
The First National Bank Of Adrian	10375	6	–
The National Bank Of Adrian	12413	–	–
Albany			
The First National Bank Of Albany	7205	5	4
Appleton City			
The First National Bank Of Appleton City	2636	4	6
Aurora			
The First National Bank Of Aurora	4409	6	–
Bethany			
The First National Bank Of Bethany	8009	4	5
Bolivar			
The First National Bank Of Bolivar	7271	5	6
Boonville			
The Boonville National Bank	10915	5	3
The Central National Bank Of Boonville	1584	3	–
Bosworth			
The First National Bank Of Bosworth	7573	4	3
Braymer			
The First National Bank Of Braymer	7351	3	2
Brookfield			
The First National Bank Of Brookfield	12820	6	6
Brunswick			
The First National Bank Of Brunswick	4083	5	5
Burlington Junction			
The First National Bank Of Burlington Junction	6242	6	6
Butler			
The Bates County National Bank Of Butler	1843	5	–
The Bates National Bank Of Butler	6405	6	–
The Butler National Bank	2561	6	–
The First National Bank Of Butler	14119	–	–
Cabool			
The Cabool National Bank	8877	6	–
The First National Bank Of Cabool	8877	5	–
Cainesville			
The First National Bank Of Cainesville	8407	4	4
California			
The Moniteau National Bank Of California	1712	1	4
Cameron			
The First National Bank Of Cameron	4259	4	4
Campbell			
The First National Bank Of Campbell	6885	6	6
Canton			
The First National Bank Of Canton	7729	6	–
Cape Girardeau			
The First National Bank Of Cape Girardeau	4611	4	3
Cardwell			
The First National Bank Of Cardwell	11919	–	–
Carondelet			
The First National Bank Of Carondelet	454	6	–
Carrollton			
The First National Bank Of Carrollton	4079	3	3
Carterville			
The First National Bank Of Carterville	4475	3	–
Carthage			
The Carthage National Bank	4815	6	–
The Central National Bank Of Carthage	4441	4	4
The First National Bank Of Carthage	2013	6	–
The First National Bank Of Carthage	3005	4	5
Caruthersville			
The First National Bank Of Caruthersville	10784	5	6
The National Bank Of Caruthersville	14092	–	4
Cassville			
The First National Bank Of Cassville	8979	5	6
Centralia			
The First National Bank Of Centralia	6875	4	3
Chaffee			
The First National Bank Of Chaffee	9928	5	5
Chillicothe			
The Citizens National Bank Of Chillicothe	4111	3	4
The First National Bank Of Chillicothe	3686	3	3
Clayton			
Clayton National Bank	13481	–	5
The Clayton National Bank	12329	5	5
The First National Bank Of Clayton	12333	5	3
Clinton			
The Clinton National Bank	7806	4	6
The First National Bank Of Clinton	1940	6	–
The Peoples National Bank Of Clinton	8509	4	3
Columbia			
The Boone County National Bank Of Columbia	1770	3	3
The Exchange National Bank Of Columbia	1467	2	2
The First National Bank Of Columbia	67	6	–
Cowgill			
The First National Bank Of Cowgill	6926	4	6
The First National Bank Of Cowgill	13546	–	–
Dexter			
The First National Bank Of Dexter	11320	4	5
Edina			
The First National Bank Of Edina	9490	6	–
Eldorado Springs			
The First National Bank Of Eldorado Springs	10055	4	–
Excelsior Springs			
The First National Bank Of Excelsior Springs	7741	6	–
Fairview			
The First National Bank Of Fairview	8916	5	6
Fulton			
The Farmers First National Bank Of Fulton	8358	6	–
The First National Bank Of Fulton	8358	4	–
Gallatin			
The First National Bank Of Gallatin	5827	4	4
Golden City			
The Citizens National Bank Of Golden City	10633	6	–
The First National Bank Of Golden City	7684	5	5
Grant City			
The First National Bank Of Grant City	3380	6	–
Green City			
American National Bank Of Green City	8570	5	–
The City National Bank Of Green City	9029	5	–
Hamilton			
The First National Bank Of Hamilton	4151	4	6
Hannibal			
The First National Bank Of Hannibal	1571	6	–
The First National Bank Of Hannibal	4010	6	–
The Hannibal National Bank	6635	3	3
Harrisonville			
The Citizens National Bank Of Harrisonville	6343	6	6
The First National Bank Of Harrisonville	3754	6	–
Holden			
The First National Bank Of Holden	10384	5	5
Hopkins			
The First National Bank Of Hopkins	4174	6	–
Independence			
The First National Bank Of Independence	1529	6	–
The First National Bank Of Independence	4157	4	3
Jackson			
The Peoples National Bank Of Jackson	7494	6	–
Jamesport			
The First National Bank Of Jamesport	7460	6	–
The National Bank Of Jamesport	7460	–	–
Jasper			
The First National Bank Of Jasper	6369	6	5
Jefferson City			
The Exchange National Bank Of Jefferson City	13142	5	3
The First National Bank Of Jefferson City	1809	3	4
The National Exchange Bank Of Jefferson City	2055	6	–
Joplin			
Conqueror First National Bank Of Joplin	13162	5	3
First National Bank Of Joplin	13162	–	–
The Cunningham National Bank Of Joplin	8947	5	–
The First National Bank Of Joplin	3841	5	–
The Joplin National Bank	4425	4	–
The Joplin National Bank & Trust Company, Joplin	4425	6	4
Kansas City			
Drovers National Bank In Kansas City	12794	–	4
Fidelity National Bank & Trust Company Of Kansas City	11344	3	2
National Bank Of Commerce Of Kansas City	10231	4	–
The Aetna National Bank Of Kansas City	4251	6	–
The American National Bank Of Kansas City	3544	4	–
The Central Exchange National Bank Of Kansas City	11491	5	–
The Central National Bank Of Kansas City	8660	6	–
The Citizens National Bank Of Kansas City	2613	5	–
The City National Bank And Trust Company Of Kansas City	13936	–	–
The City National Bank Of Kansas City	5250	6	–
The Columbia National Bank Of Kansas City	11472	–	3
The Commercial National Bank Of Kansas City	1995	6	–
The Commonwealth National Bank Of Kansas City	10039	5	–
The Continental National Bank & Trust Company Of Kansas City	12260	6	–
The Continental National Bank Of Kansas City	4786	6	–
The Continental Natl Bank Of Jackson County At Kansas City	11377	6	–
The Drovers National Bank Of Kansas City	9560	5	–
The First National Bank Of Kansas City	1612	6	–
The First National Bank Of Kansas City	3456	3	3
The Gate City National Bank Of Kansas City	9404	3	–
The German American National Bank Of Kansas City	3793	6	–
The Inter-State National Bank Of Kansas City, Missouri	4381	4	4
The Kansas City National Bank	1901	6	–
The Liberty National Bank Of Kansas City	10039	3	5
The Merchants National Bank Of Kansas City	2440	6	–
The Metropolitan National Bank Of Kansas City	4464	6	–
The Midland National Bank Of Kansas City	3904	6	–
The Midwest National Bank & Trust Company Of Kansas City	10892	6	–
The Midwest National Bank Of Kansas City	10892	5	–
The Missouri National Bank Of Kansas City	4494	6	–
The National Bank Of Commerce Of Kansas City, Missouri	3760	2	–
The National Bank Of Kansas City	3489	6	–
The National Bank Of The Republic Of Kansas City	8738	4	–
The National City Bank Of Kansas City	11037	4	–
The National Exchange Bank Of Kansas City	3863	6	–
The National Reserve Bank Of Kansas City	9677	4	–
The New England National Bank And Trust Company Of Kansas	12686	–	–
The New England National Bank Of Kansas City	5138	2	–
The Park National Bank Of Kansas City	9383	6	4
The Security National Bank Of Kansas City	9172	5	–
The Southwest National Bank Of Commerce Of Kansas City	10231	3	–
The Southwest National Bank Of Kansas City	9311	5	–
The Stock Yards National Bank Of Kansas City	10413	5	4
The Union National Bank Of Kansas City	3637	5	–
The Union National Bank Of Kansas City	13736	–	–
Traders Gate City National Bank Of Kansas City	9236	–	–
Traders National Bank Of Kansas City	9236	4	–
King City			
The Citizens National Bank Of King City	6383	3	3
The First National Bank & Trust Company Of King City	4373	5	–
The First National Bank Of King City	4373	2	–
Kirksville			
The Baird National Bank Of Kirksville	5871	6	–
The Citizens National Bank Of Kirksville	8276	5	3
The First National Bank Of Kirksville	2713	6	–
The National Bank Of Kirksville	5107	5	4
Knob Noster			
The First National Bank Of Knob Noster	1877	6	–

City, Bank	Ch. No.	L	S
La Grange			
The First National Bank Of La Grange	1839	6	–
Lamar			
The First National Bank Of Lamar	4057	4	5
The First National Bank Of Lamar	14196	–	–
Lancaster			
The First National Bank Of Lancaster	2218	6	–
Lathrop			
The First National Bank Of Lathrop	5544	6	–
Lebanon			
The First National Bank Of Lebanon	10695	–	–
Leeds			
The Leeds National Bank	9383	6	–
Liberal			
The First National Bank Of Liberal	7094	6	–
Liberty			
The First National Bank Of Liberty	3712	5	4
The National Commercial Bank Of Liberty	13875	–	–
Linn Creek			
The First National Bank Of Linn Creek	7853	6	6
Louisiana			
The Exchange National Bank Of Louisiana	3103	6	–
The Mercantile National Bank Of Louisiana	3111	6	–
Ludlow			
The Farmers National Bank Of Ludlow	8657	3	–
The First National Bank Of Ludlow	7900	6	6
The Ludlow National Bank	13293	–	4
Luxemburg			
Lafayette National Bank And Trust Company Of Luxemburg	13514	–	3
Macon			
The First National Bank Of Macon	2862	5	–
Manchester			
The First National Bank Of Manchester	7643	5	–
Maplewood			
The Citizens National Bank Of Maplewood	12955	5	3
Marceline			
The First National Bank Of Marceline	7066	5	3
Marshall			
The First National Bank Of Marshall	2884	6	–
Marshfield			
The First National Bank Of Marshfield	10009	6	–
Maryville			
The First National Bank Of Maryville	3268	3	5
The Maryville National Bank	4243	6	–
Memphis			
The Scotland County National Bank Of Memphis	2432	4	6
Mexico			
The First National Bank Of Mexico	2881	4	3
Milan			
The First National Bank Of Milan	3110	5	–
Moberly			
The First National Bank Of Moberly	4000	6	–
Monett			
The First National Bank Of Monett	5973	4	3
Montgomery City			
The First National Bank Of Montgomery City	11235	–	–
Mount Vernon			
The First National Bank Of Mount Vernon	13504	–	5
Mountain Grove			
The First National Bank Of Mountain Grove	7282	5	5
Neosho			
The First National Bank Of Neosho	6382	5	4
Nevada			
The First National Bank Of Nevada, Missouri	3959	4	4
The Thornton National Bank Of Nevada	9382	4	3
North Kansas City			
The National Bank & Trust Company Of North Kansas City	10367	–	6
The National Bank In North Kansas City	13690	–	6
The National Bank Of North Kansas City	10367	6	6
Odessa			
The National Bank Of Odessa	4141	6	–
Oran			
The First National Bank Of Oran	12907	–	–
Palmyra			
The First National Bank Of Palmyra	1735	6	–
The First National Bank Of Palmyra	2979	5	–
Paris			
The First National Bank Of Paris	1803	5	–
The National Bank Of Paris	3322	6	–
The Paris National Bank	5794	2	3
Parkville			
The First National Bank Of Parkville	12815	–	–
Peirce City			
The First National Bank Of Peirce City	4225	4	1
The Peirce City National Bank	4225	6	–
Perryville			
The First National Bank Of Perryville	11402	–	4
Platte City			
The Farmers National Bank Of Platte City	2356	6	–
The First National Bank Of Platte City	4329	6	–
Plattsburg			
The First National Bank Of Plattsburg	4215	3	4
Pleasant Hill			
The Farmers National Bank Of Pleasant Hill	7154	6	–
The First National Bank Of Pleasant Hill	1751	6	–
Polo			
The First National Bank Of Polo	7884	5	–
Purdy			
The First National Bank Of Purdy	10122	6	4
The Purdy National Bank	12010	–	–
Ridgeway			
The Farmers National Bank Of Ridgeway	12674	–	–
The First National Bank Of Ridgeway	6549	3	–
Rolla			
The National Bank Of Rolla	1865	4	5
Saint Charles			
The First National Bank Of Saint Charles	260	4	2
Saint Joseph			
The American National Bank Of St. Joseph	9042	3	4
The Burnes National Bank Of St. Joseph	8021	2	4
The First National Bank Of Buchanan County, St Joseph	4939	3	–
The First National Bank Of Saint Joseph	1580	5	–
The First National Bank Of St. Joseph	4939	3	5
The German American National Bank Of St. Joseph	9042	4	–
The National Bank Of St. Joseph	2970	5	–
The Saxton National Bank Of Saint Joseph	2898	6	–
The Schuster-Hax National Bank Of St. Joseph	4053	6	–
The State National Bank Of Saint Joseph	1667	5	–
The State National Bank Of Saint Joseph	4228	6	–
The Tootle-Lacy National Bank Of Saint Joseph	6272	4	–
The Tootle-Lemon National Bank Of St. Joseph	6272	3	–
Saint Louis			
Mercantile Commerce National Bank In St. Louis	4178	–	2
South Side National Bank Of St. Louis	13264	5	4
The American Exchange National Bank In St. Louis	13726	–	4
The American Exchange National Bank Of Saint Louis	7570	6	–
The American Exchange National Bank Of St. Louis	12506	4	4
The Bankers Worlds Fair National Bank Of St. Louis	7179	6	–
The Boatmen's National Bank Of St. Louis	12916	–	1
The Broadway National Bank Of St. Louis	9460	6	–
The Central National Bank Of St. Louis	8455	2	–
The Chemical National Bank Of St. Louis	4575	6	–
The Cherokee National Bank Of Saint Louis	12643	–	–
The City National Bank Of St. Louis	7808	4	–
The Continental National Bank Of St. Louis	4048	3	–
The Fifth National Bank Of St. Louis	2835	6	–
The First National Bank Of St. Louis	89	6	–
The Fourth National Bank Of St. Louis	283	4	–
The Grand Ave. National Bank Of St. Louis	12220	4	–
The Grand National Bank Of St. Louis	12220	3	2
The Laclede National Bank Of St. Louis	4262	6	–
The Mechanics National Bank Of Saint Louis	5788	4	–
The Mechanics-American National Bank Of St. Louis	7715	2	–
The Mercantile National Bank Of St. Louis	9297	3	–
The Merchants National Bank Of St. Louis	1501	5	–
The Merchants-Laclede National Bank Of Saint Louis	5002	1	–
The Missouri National Bank Of St. Louis	12220	5	–
The National Bank Of Commerce In St. Louis	4178	1	–
The National Bank Of The Republic Of St. Louis	4232	6	–
The National Bank Of The State Of Missouri, Saint Louis	1665	4	–
The National City Bank Of St. Louis	11989	2	4
The Plaza National Bank Of Saint Louis	13376	–	–
The Republic National Bank Of St. Louis	11973	3	–
The Saint Louis Union National Bank	11366	–	–
The Second National Bank Of Saint Louis	139	5	–
The Security Natl Bank Savings & Trust Co Of St Louis	12066	5	3
The State National Bank Of St. Louis	5172	1	–
The Telegraphers National Bank Of St. Louis	12389	3	2
The Third National Bank Of Saint Louis	170	1	–
The Twelfth Street National Bank Of St. Louis	12491	4	3
The Union National Bank Of St. Louis	1381	6	–
The Valley National Bank Of St. Louis	1858	6	–
The Vandeventer National Bank Of Saint Louis	13270	–	–
The Washington National Bank Of St. Louis	6773	4	–
Salem			
The First National Bank Of Salem	7921	6	3
Salisbury			
The Farmers And Merchants National Bank Of Salisbury	8359	6	–
The First National Bank Of Salisbury	8363	–	–
Sarcoxie			
The First National Bank Of Sarcoxie	5515	6	4
Savannah			
The First National Bank Of Savannah	5780	4	–
Sedalia			
The Citizens National Bank Of Sedalia	1971	3	5
The First National Bank Of Sedalia	1627	6	–
The Sedalia National Bank	4392	4	5
The Third National Bank Of Sedalia	2919	3	3
Seneca			
The First National Bank Of Seneca	7656	6	–
Seymour			
The Peoples National Bank Of Seymour	9932	5	5
Shelbina			
The First National Bank Of Shelbina	1711	6	–
The Shelbina National Bank	9137	6	–
Springfield			
The American National Bank Of Springfield	4360	6	–
The Central National Bank Of Springfield	3718	6	–
The First National Bank Of Springfield	1701	6	–
The Greene County National Bank Of Springfield	1677	5	–
The Mcdaniel National Bank Of Springfield	10074	5	5
The Merchants National Bank Of Springfield	9315	6	–
The National Bank Of Springfield	1701	6	–
The National Exchange Bank Of Springfield	5082	5	–
The New First National Bank Of Springfield	12770	–	–
The Union National Bank Of Springfield	5209	4	3
St. Louis			
First National Bank In St. Louis	170	3	1
St. Louis National Bank	12216	4	4
The American Exchange National Bank Of Saint Louis	12506	–	5
The St. Louis National Bank	1112	3	–
Steele			
The First National Bank Of Steele	12452	6	5
Steelville			
The First National Bank Of Steelville	8914	6	6
Stewartsville			
The First National Bank Of Stewartsville	4160	3	5
Stoutland			
The First National Bank Of Stoutland	11467	–	–
Sweet Springs			
The First National Bank Of Sweet Springs	11372	6	–
Tarkio			
The First National Bank Of Tarkio	3079	4	5
Trenton			
The First National Bank Of Trenton	1966	6	–
The First National Bank Of Trenton	3957	6	–
The Grundy County National Bank Of Trenton	3946	6	–
The Trenton National Bank	4933	4	4
Unionville			
National Bank Of Unionville	13268	6	6
The Marshall National Bank Of Unionville	3068	4	4
The National Bank Of Unionville	3137	4	–
Versailles			
The First National Bank In Versailles	13367	–	5
The First National Bank Of Versailles	7256	5	–
Warrensburg			
The First National Bank Of Warrensburg	1856	6	–
The Peoples National Bank Of Warrensburg	5156	4	5
Washington			
The First National Bank Of Washington	5388	5	–
Webb City			
The First National Bank Of Webb City	4475	6	–
The National Bank Of Webb City	8016	4	–
Webster Groves			
The First National Bank Of Webster Groves	12781	–	–
Wellston			
The First National Bank Of Wellston	8011	4	3
West Plains			
The First National Bank Of West Plains	5036	4	6
Windsor			
The First National Bank Of Windsor	9519	5	4
MONTANA TERRITORY			
Anaconda			
The First National Bank Of Anaconda	3965	6	–
Billings			
The First National Bank Of Billings	3097	5	–
Bozeman			
The Bozeman National Bank	2803	6	–
The First National Bank Of Bozeman	2027	6	–
The Gallatin Valley National Bank Of Bozeman	3075	6	–
Butte			
The First National Bank Of Butte	2566	5	–
Deer Lodge			
The First National Bank Of Deer Lodge	1975	6	–
Dillon			
The Dillon National Bank	3173	6	–
The First National Bank Of Dillon	3120	6	–
Fort Benton			
The First National Bank Of Fort Benton	2476	5	–
Great Falls			
The First National Bank Of Great Falls	3525	6	–
Helena			
The First National Bank Of Helena	1649	4	–
The Merchants National Bank Of Helena	2732	6	–
The Montana National Bank Of Helena	1960	6	–
The Montana National Bank Of Helena	2813	6	–
The Peoples National Bank Of Helena	2105	6	–
The Second National Bank Of Helena	2757	6	–
Livingston			
The First National Bank Of Livingston	3006	6	–
The Livington National Bank	4117	6	–
The National Park Bank Of Livingston	3605	6	–
Miles City			
The First National Bank Of Miles City	2752	6	–
The Stock Growers National Bank Of Miles City	3275	6	–
Missoula			
The First National Bank Of Missoula	2106	6	–
The Missoula National Bank	2106	4	–
The Western Montana National Bank Of Missoula	3995	6	–
Sulphur Springs			
The First National Bank Of White Sulphur Springs	3375	6	–
MONTANA			
Absarokee			
The Stillwater National Bank Of Absarokee	11066	–	–
Anaconda			
The Anaconda National Bank	9583	6	–
The First National Bank Of Anaconda	3965	6	–
The National Bank Of Anaconda	12542	5	3
Antelope			
The First National Bank Of Antelope	11350	6	–
Bainville			
The First National Bank Of Bainville	10985	–	–
Baker			
The First National Bank Of Baker	10443	6	–
Baylor			
The First National Bank Of Baylor	10917	–	–
Belt			
The First National Bank Of Belt	11673	–	–
Benton			
The Northwestern National Bank Of Great Falls	2476	6	–
Big Sandy			
The Farmers National Bank Of Big Sandy	11063	–	–
The First National Bank Of Big Sandy	11004	–	–
Big Timber			
The Big Timber National Bank	4932	6	–
Big Timer			
The First National Bank Of Big Timber	4590	6	–
Billings			
The American National Bank Of Billings	11696	–	–
The First National Bank Of Billings	3097	6	–
The Merchants National Bank Of Billings	9355	5	–
The Midland National Bank Of Billings	12407	4	1
The Montana National Bank Of Billings	10933	–	–
The Yellowstone National Bank Of Billings	4593	5	–
The Yellowstone-Merchants National Bank Of Billings	4593	6	–
Boulder Valley			
The First National Bank Of Boulder Valley	4323	6	–

City, Bank	Ch. No.	L	S
Bozeman			
The Bozeman National Bank	2803	6	–
The Commercial National Bank Of Bozeman	4968	4	3
The Gallatin Valley National Bank Of Bozeman	3075	6	–
The National Bank Of Gallatin Valley At Bozeman	7441	6	–
Brady			
The First National Bank Of Brady	11030	–	–
Bridger			
The American National Bank Of Bridger	11298	–	–
The First National Bank Of Bridger	10769	–	–
Broadus			
The First National Bank Of Broadus	11418	–	–
The Powder River National Bank Of Broadus	11418	–	–
Broadview			
The First National Bank Of Broadview	10809	–	–
Brockton			
The First National Bank Of Brockton	11027	–	–
The Stockmen's National Bank Of Poplar	11027	–	–
Browning			
The First National Bank Of Browning	10883	–	–
Butte			
The Miners National Bank Of Butte	14334	–	–
The Silver Bow National Bank Of Butte City	4283	4	–
Butte City			
The First National Bank Of Butte	2566	3	4
Carlyle			
The First National Bank Of Carlyle	10934	–	–
Carter			
The First National Bank Of Carter	10995	6	–
Castle			
The First National Bank Of Castle	4572	6	–
Charlo			
The First National Bank Of Charlo	11165	–	–
Chester			
The First National Bank Of Chester	11105	6	–
Chinook			
The Farmers National Bank In Chinook	13837	–	5
The Farmers National Bank Of Chinook	10053	6	4
The First National Bank Of Chinook	6097	5	6
Choteau			
The First National Bank Of Choteau	10937	–	–
Circle			
The First National Bank Of Circle	11101	–	4
Columbus			
The First National Bank Of Columbus	9396	5	4
The Stockmans National Bank Of Columbus	11220	–	–
Conrad			
The First National Bank Of Conrad	9759	5	3
Culbertson			
The First National Bank Of Culbertson	8168	6	–
Cut Bank			
The First National Bank Of Cut Bank	9574	6	–
Deer Lodge			
The United States National Bank Of Deer Lodge	9899	6	5
Denton			
The First National Bank Of Denton	10819	5	–
Dillon			
The Dillon National Bank	3173	6	–
The First National Bank Of Dillon	3120	4	4
Dodson			
The First National Bank Of Dodson	11086	–	–
Ekalaka			
The First National Bank Of Ekalaka	11382	–	–
Fairfield			
The First National Bank Of Fairfield	11307	6	–
Fairview			
The First National Bank Of Fairview	12015	6	–
Forsyth			
The American National Bank Of Forsyth	10942	–	–
The First National Bank Of Forsyth	7320	6	–
Fort Benton			
The First National Bank Of Fort Benton	2476	6	–
The Stockmens National Bank Of Fort Benton	4194	4	–
Fresno			
The First National Bank Of Fresno	11096	6	–
Froid			
The First National Bank Of Froid	11061	–	–
Galata			
The First National Bank Of Galata	11089	–	–
Geraldine			
The First National Bank Of Geraldine	10803	5	4
Geyser			
The First National Bank Of Geyser	10952	3	–
Glasgow			
The First National Bank Of Glasgow	7990	4	3
The Glasgow National Bank	8655	4	–
Glendive			
The First National Bank Of Glendive	7101	6	4
The Merchants National Bank Of Glendive	8055	6	–
Grass Range			
The First National Bank Of Grass Range	10939	4	6
Great Falls			
The Commercial National Bank Of Great Falls	10530	6	–
The First National Bank Of Great Falls	3525	3	2
The Great Falls National Bank	4541	4	3
The Merchants National Bank Of Great Falls	4434	6	–
The Northern National Bank Of Great Falls	11429	–	–
Hamilton			
The First National Bank Of Hamilton	9486	5	4
Hardin			
The First National Bank Of Hardin	9215	6	4
The Stockmens National Bank Of Hardin	11070	–	–
Harlem			
The First National Bank Of Harlem	7644	6	6
Harlowton			
The Continental National Bank Of Harlowton	13417	–	–
The Farmers National Bank Of Harlowton	11085	5	6
The First National Bank Of Harlowton	9270	6	–
The Musselshell Valley National Bank Of Harlowton	9270	6	–
Havre			
The Citizens National Bank Of Havre	9440	6	–
The First National Bank Of Havre	5676	6	–
The Havre National Bank	9782	6	–
The Montana National Bank Of Havre	11077	–	–
Helena			
First National Bank And Trust Company Of Helena	4396	–	2
The American National Bank Of Helena	4396	3	3
The First National Bank Of Helena	1649	6	–
The Helena National Bank	4406	6	–
The Merchants National Bank Of Helena	2732	6	–
The Montana National Bank Of Helena	2813	6	–
The National Bank Of Montana, Helena	5671	2	4
The Second National Bank Of Helena	2757	6	–
Highwood			
The First National Bank Of Highwood	11131	6	–
Hinsdale			
The First National Bank Of Hinsdale	10910	–	–
Hobson			
The First National Bank Of Hobson	10715	4	6
Hysham			
The First National Bank Of Hysham	11026	–	–
The First National Bank Of Hysham	12585	–	–
Ingomar			
The First National Bank Of Ingomar	11465	–	–
Intake			
The First National Bank Of Intake	10928	–	–
Ismay			
The First National Bank Of Ismay	9103	6	5
Joplin			
The First National Bank Of Joplin	10929	–	–
Jordan			
The First National Bank Of Jordan	11493	–	–
Judith Gap			
The First National Bank Of Judith Gap	10907	–	–
Kalispell			
The Conrad National Bank Of Kalispell	4803	2	1
The First National Bank Of Kalispell	4586	3	2
The Globe National Bank Of Kalispell	4651	6	–
The Kalispell National Bank	8635	6	–
Lambert			
The First National Bank Of Lambert	11176	–	–
Laurel			
The Citizens National Bank Of Laurel	8716	6	–
The First National Bank Of Laurel	8669	6	–
Lewistown			
The First National Bank Of Fergus County In Lewistown	7274	6	–
The First National Bank Of Lewistown	7274	3	–
The National Bank Of Lewistown	12608	–	3
Libby			
The First National Bank Of Libby	9594	5	–
Lima			
The First National Bank Of Lima	11492	3	3
The Security National Bank Of Lima	11492	5	–
Livingston			
The Livingston National Bank	4117	6	–
The National Park Bank Of Livingston	3605	4	6
The National Park Bank Of Livingston	13384	–	–
The Northwestern National Bank Of Livingston	11000	–	–
Lodge Grass			
The First National Bank Of Lodge Grass	11160	–	–
Malta			
The First National Bank Of Malta	9738	6	–
The Malta National Bank	11040	–	–
Mc Cabe			
The First National Bank Of Mc Cabe	11475	–	–
Miles City			
The Commercial National Bank Of Miles City	5015	5	–
The First National Bank In Miles City	12536	6	3
The First National Bank Of Miles City	2752	3	–
The Miles City National Bank	10884	–	–
The State National Bank Of Miles City	5015	5	–
The Stock Growers National Bank Of Miles City	3275	6	–
Missoula			
The First National Bank Of Missoula	2106	3	1
The Western Montana National Bank Of Missoula	3995	3	2
Molt			
The First National Bank Of Molt	11013	–	–
Moore			
The First National Bank Of Moore	8539	6	–
Musselshell			
The First National Bank Of Musselshell	11269	–	–
Nashua			
The First National Bank Of Nashua	11048	–	–
Neihart			
The First National Bank Of Neihart	4600	6	–
Opheim			
The Farmers And Merchants National Bank Of Opheim	11097	6	–
The First National Bank Of Opheim	11097	6	–
Oswego			
The First National Bank Of Oswego	11134	–	–
Phillipsburg			
The First National Bank Of Phillipsburg	4658	6	–
The Merchants And Miners National Bank Of Phillipsburg	4843	6	–
Plains			
The First National Bank Of Plains	7172	4	3
Plentywood			
The First National Bank Of Plentywood	10438	6	–
Plevna			
Baker National Bank, Baker	11074	–	4
The First National Bank Of Plevna	11074	–	5
Polson			
The First National Bank Of Polson	9449	6	–
Pompeys Pillar			
The First National Bank Of Pompeys Pillar	10922	–	–
Poplar			
The First National Bank Of Poplar	10885	–	–
Rapelje			
The First National Bank Of Rapelje	11017	–	–
The Stillwater National Bank Of Columbus	11017	–	–
Raymond			
The First National Bank Of Raymond	11078	5	–
Raynesford			
The Stockmens National Bank Of Raynesford	11095	–	–
Red Lodge			
The United States National Bank Of Red Lodge	9841	6	3
Reed Point			
The First National Bank Of Reed Point	11334	–	–
Reserve			
The First National Bank Of Reserve	10986	6	4
Richey			
The First National Bank Of Richey	10881	–	–
Ronan			
The First National Bank Of Ronan	9864	6	–
Rosebud			
The First National Bank Of Rosebud	11437	6	–
Roundup			
The First National Bank Of Roundup	9165	6	–
The Roundup National Bank	10675	–	–
Roy			
The First National Bank Of Roy	10991	5	–
Rudyard			
The First National Bank Of Rudyard	11203	–	–
Saco			
The First National Bank Of Saco	9789	6	–
Savage			
The First National Bank Of Savage	11032	–	–
Savoy			
The First National Bank Of Savoy	11199	–	–
Scobey			
The First National Bank Of Scobey	10838	5	5
The Merchants National Bank Of Scobey	11098	6	–
Shelby			
The First National Bank Of Shelby	10953	–	–
Sidney			
The Farmers National Bank Of Sidney	10552	6	–
The First National Bank Of Sidney	9004	5	–
The Richland National Bank Of Sidney	12679	–	–
The Sidney National Bank	10926	–	–
The Yellowstone Valley National Bank Of Sidney	10539	–	–
Stanford			
The First National Bank Of Stanford	10625	–	–
Stevensville			
The First National Bank Of Stevensville	10709	6	–
Three Forks			
The American National Bank Of Three Forks	10996	–	–
The First National Bank Of Three Forks	9337	6	–
The Labor National Bank Of Montana	12361	–	–
Townsend			
The First National Bank Of Townsend	9982	6	–
Twin Bridges			
The First National Bank Of Twin Bridges	11008	4	–
Valier			
The First National Bank Of Valier	9520	6	5
Westby			
The First National Bank Of Westby	11209	–	–
White Sulphur Springs			
The First National Bank Of White Sulphur Springs	3375	4	3
Whitefish			
The First National Bank Of Whitefish	8589	5	2
Whitehall			
The First National Bank Of Whitehall	11024	5	–
Wibaux			
The First National Bank Of Wibaux	8259	5	3
Wilsall			
The First National Bank Of Wilsall	11335	–	–
Winifred			
The First National Bank Of Winifred	11006	6	–
Winnett			
The First National Bank Of Winnett	11391	–	–
Wolf Point			
The Citizens National Bank Of Wolf Point	11075	–	–
The First National Bank Of Wolf Point	11036	–	4

NEBRASKA

City, Bank	Ch. No.	L	S
Adams			
The First National Bank Of Adams	9223	5	6
Ainsworth			
The Commercial National Bank Of Ainsworth	13139	–	–
The First National Bank Of Ainsworth	4089	6	–
The National Bank Of Ainsworth	8992	4	3
Albion			
The Albion National Bank	4173	3	1
The First National Bank Of Albion	3960	2	3
Allen			
The First National Bank Of Allen	8372	6	–
Alliance			
Alliance National Bank	5657	4	3
The Alliance National Bank	5657	6	–
The First National Bank Of Alliance	4226	5	4
The Nebraska National Bank Of Alliance	13617	–	3
Alma			
The First National Bank Of Alma	3580	6	–
Amherst			
The First National Bank Of Amherst	9092	6	4
Anoka			
The Anoka National Bank	6464	6	–
Ansley			
The First National Bank Of Ansley	7393	6	–
Arapahoe			
The First National Bank Of Arapahoe	3302	6	–
Arcadia			
The First National Bank Of Arcadia	13158	–	–
Arlington			
The First National Bank Of Arlington	4583	4	5

City, Bank	Ch. No.	L	S
Ashland			
The Citizens National Bank Of Ashland	14174	–	–
The Farmers And Merchants National Bank Of Ashland	13435	–	2
The First National Bank Of Ashland	2121	6	–
The National Bank Of Ashland	2921	4	3
Atkinson			
The Atkinson National Bank	7881	6	–
The First National Bank Of Atkinson	6489	5	4
Auburn			
The Farmers And Merchants National Bank Of Auburn	4588	6	–
The First National Bank Of Auburn	3343	3	4
Aurora			
The Aurora National Bank	9056	6	–
The Fidelity National Bank Of Aurora	8246	5	–
The First National Bank Of Aurora	2897	5	5
The First National Bank Of Aurora	14017	–	–
Bancroft			
The First National Bank Of Bancroft	8863	5	4
Bassett			
The First National Bank Of Bassett	11426	–	–
Bayard			
The First National Bank Of Bayard	9666	5	4
Bazile Mills			
The First National Bank Of Bazile Mills	8469	6	–
Beatrice			
The Beatrice National Bank	3081	3	2
The First National Bank Of Beatrice	2357	3	2
The German National Bank Of Beatrice	4148	6	–
The Nebraska National Bank Of Beatrice	4185	6	–
Beaver City			
The First National Bank Of Beaver City	3619	6	–
Beemer			
The First National Bank Of Beemer	6818	4	4
Belden			
The First National Bank Of Belden	10025	4	3
Benedict			
The First National Bank Of Benedict	8105	5	3
Bertrand			
The First National Bank Of Bertrand	8466	6	–
Blair			
The Blair National Bank	8027	6	–
The First National Bank Of Blair	2724	6	–
Bloomfield			
The First National Bank Of Bloomfield	6503	6	–
Blue Hill			
The First National Bank Of Blue Hill	3419	5	6
Bradshaw			
The First National Bank Of Bradshaw	8097	5	3
Bridgeport			
The First National Bank Of Bridgeport	9711	6	–
Bristow			
The First National Bank Of Bristow	9448	5	–
Broken Bow			
The Central Nebraska National Bank Of Broken Bow	3927	6	–
The Custer County National Bank Of Broken Bow	3445	6	–
The Custer National Bank Of Broken Bow	5995	5	–
The First National Bank Of Broken Bow	3449	5	–
Brownville			
The First National Bank Of Brownville	1846	5	–
Brunswick			
The First National Bank Of Brunswick	10033	6	–
Burwell			
The First National Bank Of Burwell	7340	6	–
Bushnell			
The First National Bank Of Bushnell	13429	–	–
Butte			
The First National Bank Of Butte	9623	3	3
Callaway			
The First National Bank Of Callaway	9258	6	–
Cambridge			
The First National Bank Of Cambridge	6506	6	2
Campbell			
The First National Bank Of Campbell	8975	6	–
Carroll			
The First National Bank Of Carroll	5957	5	–
Cedar Rapids			
The First National Bank Of Cedar Rapids	8282	6	–
Central City			
The Central City National Bank	8385	4	5
The Farmers National Bank Of Central City	13148	–	–
The First National Bank Of Central City	2871	6	–
Chadron			
The First National Bank Of Chadron	3823	5	3
Chappell			
The First National Bank Of Chappell	9790	5	–
Clarks			
The First National Bank Of Clarks	6939	6	–
Clay Center			
The First National Bank Of Clay Center	3574	6	–
Coleridge			
The Coleridge National Bank, Coleridge	10023	4	3
The First National Bank Of Coleridge	9796	4	–
Columbus			
The Central National Bank Of Columbus	8328	3	2
The Commercial National Bank Of Columbus	5180	3	4
The First National Bank Of Columbus	2807	4	5
The German National Bank Of Columbus	8328	6	–
Cozad			
First National Bank In Cozad	13426	–	3
The First National Bank Of Cozad	4165	6	–
Craig			
The First National Bank Of Craig	9591	5	5
Crawford			
The First National Bank Of Crawford	6900	6	–
Creighton			
The American National Bank Of Creighton	13591	–	–
The Creighton National Bank	8797	4	6
The First National Bank Of Creighton	4242	6	–
Crete			
The City National Bank Of Crete	9731	4	3
The Crete National Bank	4820	6	–
The First National Bank Of Crete	2706	4	–
Crofton			
The First National Bank Of Crofton	8186	4	1
Curtis			
The First National Bank Of Curtis	8812	6	–
David City			
The Central Nebraska National Bank Of David City	3801	3	3
The City National Bank Of David City	3934	4	3
The City National Bank Of David City	14194	–	–
The First National Bank Of David City	2902	4	3
De Witt			
The First National Bank Of De Witt	4895	6	–
Decatur			
The First National Bank Of Decatur	8988	4	3
Diller			
The First National Bank Of Diller	7355	6	–
Dodge			
The First National Bank Of Dodge	7333	6	–
Doniphan			
The National Bank Of Doniphan	13456	–	–
Dorchester			
The First National Bank Of Dorchester	3390	4	–
Elgin			
The First National Bank Of Elgin	5440	5	4
Elm Creek			
The First National Bank Of Elm Creek	3999	6	–
Elmwood			
The First National Bank Of Elmwood	5787	6	–
Elwood			
The First National Bank Of Elwood	7204	5	4
Emerson			
The First National Bank Of Emerson	7425	4	3
Exeter			
The Exeter National Bank	3117	6	–
The Exeter National Bank	13243	–	–
The First National Bank Of Exeter	3121	6	–
The First National Bank Of Exeter	14073	–	–
The Wallace National Bank Of Exeter	13189	–	–
Fairbury			
The Bonham National Bank Of Fairbury	8995	6	–
The Farmers And Merchants National Bank Of Fairbury	10340	5	–
The First National Bank Of Fairbury	2994	3	2
Fairfield			
The First National Bank Of Fairfield	3493	6	–
Fairmont			
The First National Bank Of Fairmont	3230	6	–
Falls City			
The First National Bank Of Falls City	2746	3	3
Franklin			
The First National Bank Of Franklin	3549	6	–
Fremont			
The Commercial National Bank Of Fremont	4504	4	–
The Farmers And Merchants National Bank Of Fremont	3188	5	–
The First National Bank Of Fremont	1974	3	–
The Fremont National Bank	2848	3	2
The Stephens National Bank Of Fremont	13408	–	2
The Union National Bank Of Fremont	3188	2	3
Friend			
The First National Bank Of Friend	2960	4	3
Fullerton			
The First National Bank Of Fullerton	2964	4	3
The Fullerton National Bank	5384	4	3
Geneva			
The First National Bank Of Geneva	4052	6	–
The Geneva National Bank	4484	6	–
Genoa			
The First National Bank Of Genoa	5189	4	3
The Genoa National Bank	6805	6	2
Gering			
The First National Bank Of Gering	8062	6	–
The Gering National Bank	9694	5	3
Gibbon			
The First National Bank Of Gibbon	3921	6	–
Glenvil			
The First National Bank Of Glenvil	13433	–	–
Gordon			
The First National Bank Of Gordon	8521	5	4
Gothenburg			
The Citizens National Bank Of Gothenburg	8113	6	–
The First National Bank Of Gothenburg	4890	6	–
The Gothenburg National Bank	6282	5	–
Grand Island			
The Citizens National Bank Of Grand Island	3101	6	–
The Commercial National Bank Of Grand Island	14340	–	–
The First National Bank Of Grand Island	2779	3	2
The Grand Island National Bank	9395	2	2
The Nebraska National Bank Of Grand Island	13424	–	–
The Overland National Bank Of Grand Island	14018	–	–
The Security National Bank Of Grand Island	4357	6	–
Grant			
The Farmers National Bank Of Grant	13419	–	–
The First National Bank Of Grant	4170	6	–
Greeley			
The City National Bank Of Greeley	13461	–	–
The First National Bank Of Greeley	7622	6	6
Greenwood			
The First National Bank Of Greenwood	3403	6	–
Gresham			
The First National Bank Of Gresham	8172	5	4
Hampton			
The First National Bank Of Hampton	8285	5	4
Harrison			
The First National Bank Of Harrison	8888	6	–
The Sioux National Bank Of Harrison	12552	6	4
Hartington			
The First National Bank Of Hartington	4528	4	4
The Hartington National Bank	5400	4	–
Harvard			
The First National Bank Of Harvard	4129	6	–
Hastings			
The City National Bank Of Hastings	3099	6	–
The City National Bank Of Hastings	13953	–	–
The Exchange National Bank Of Hastings	3086	4	–
The First National Bank Of Hastings	2528	2	3
The German National Bank Of Hastings	3732	5	–
The Hastings National Bank	13515	–	2
The Nebraska National Bank Of Hastings	3732	4	2
Havelock			
The First National Bank Of Havelock	9772	6	3
Hay Springs			
The First National Bank Of Hay Springs	8760	6	5
Hayes Center			
The First National Bank Of Hayes Center	8031	6	4
Hebron			
The First National Bank Of Hebron	2756	6	–
Hemingford			
The Citizens National Bank Of Hemingford	12495	–	–
The First National Bank Of Hemingford	10242	6	–
Henderson			
The First National Bank Of Henderson	8183	6	–
Hershey			
The First National Bank Of Hershey	10970	–	–
Holdrege			
The City National Bank Of Holdrege	4345	6	–
The First National Bank Of Holdrege	3208	4	4
The Holdrege National Bank	3875	6	–
The United States National Bank Of Holdrege	4345	6	–
Hooper			
The First National Bank Of Hooper	5297	3	5
Humboldt			
The First National Bank Of Humboldt	3238	6	–
The National Bank Of Humboldt	7065	6	–
Humphrey			
The First National Bank Of Humphrey	5337	6	6
Imperial			
The First National Bank Of Imperial	9762	5	5
Indianola			
The First National Bank Of Indianola	3483	6	–
Johnson			
The First National Bank Of Johnson	8161	4	4
The German National Bank Of Johnson	8383	6	–
Kearney			
The Buffalo County National Bank Of Kearney	3526	6	–
The Central National Bank Of Kearney	6600	5	–
The City National Bank Of Kearney	3958	4	–
The City National Bank Of Kearney	13013	–	–
The Commercial National Bank Of Kearney	8651	6	–
The First National Bank Of Kearney	2806	6	–
The Kearney National Bank	3201	6	–
Kimball			
The American National Bank Of Kimball	13420	–	1
The Kimball National Bank	13440	–	–
Laurel			
The First National Bank Of Laurel	9793	4	–
The Laurel National Bank	9979	5	–
The Security National Bank Of Laurel	13182	–	–
Lawrence			
The First National Bank Of Lawrence	8851	6	–
Leigh			
The First National Bank Of Leigh	9831	4	3
Lewellen			
The First National Bank Of Lewellen	13423	–	–
Lexington			
The Dawson County National Bank Of Lexington	4161	5	–
Liberty			
The First National Bank Of Liberty	4080	6	–
Lincoln			
City National Bank In Lincoln	13017	5	–
Lincoln National Bank And Trust Company, Lincoln	12342	–	–
National Bank Of Commerce Of Lincoln	7239	2	1
The American Exchange National Bank Of Lincoln	4606	6	–
The Capital National Bank Of Lincoln	2988	6	–
The Central National Bank Of Lincoln	8885	3	–
The City National Bank Of Lincoln	5213	2	–
The Columbia National Bank Of Lincoln	4435	6	–
The Continental National Bank Of Lincoln	13333	–	2
The First National Bank Of Lincoln	1798	2	1
The German National Bank Of Lincoln	3571	6	–
The Lincoln National Bank	2750	5	–
The Lincoln State National Bank	12342	–	–
The Marsh National Bank Of Lincoln	2988	6	–
The State National Bank Of Lincoln	1899	6	–
Litchfield			
The First National Bank Of Litchfield	8093	5	6
Lodgepole			
The First National Bank Of Lodgepole	9741	6	–
Loomis			
The First National Bank Of Loomis	5419	4	6
Loup City			
First National Bank In Loup City	13620	–	4
The First National Bank Of Loup City	3373	6	–
The First National Bank Of Loup City	7277	6	6
Lyman			
The First National Bank Of Lyman	13271	–	–
Lynch			
The First National Bank Of Lynch	9785	6	–
Lyons			
The First National Bank Of Lyons	6221	6	4
Madison			
The Farmers National Bank Of Madison	8317	5	5
The First National Bank Of Madison	3773	4	3
The Madison National Bank	10021	6	–
Marquette			
The First National Bank Of Marquette	8400	5	6
Mc Cook			
The Citizens National Bank Of Mc Cook	9436	6	–
The First National Bank Of Mc Cook	3379	5	2
The Mc Cook National Bank	8823	5	2

City, Bank	Ch. No.	L	S
Minatare			
The First National Bank Of Minatare	13316	–	5
Minden			
The First National Bank Of Minden	3057	6	6
The Minden Exchange National Bank	9400	5	3
The Nebraska National Bank Of Minden	13322	–	–
Mitchell			
The First National Bank Of Mitchell	7026	6	–
The First National Bank Of Mitchell	12626	–	–
Morrill			
The First National Bank Of Morrill	9653	6	–
The First National Bank Of Morrill	12625	–	–
Naper			
The First National Bank Of Naper	9665	6	6
Nebraska City			
The James Sweet National Bank Of Nebraska City	2536	6	–
The Merchants National Bank Of Nebraska City	2536	4	4
The Nebraska City National Bank	1855	3	2
The Otoe County National Bank Of Nebraska City	1417	1	3
Neligh			
The First National Bank Of Neligh	4110	6	–
The National Bank Of Neligh	13568	–	4
The Neligh National Bank	5690	5	–
Nelson			
The First National Bank Of Nelson	3495	6	–
Newman Grove			
The First National Bank Of Newman Grove	5282	5	4
Norfolk			
The Citizens National Bank Of Norfolk	3741	5	–
The Delay National Bank Of Norfolk	13582	–	–
The First National Bank Of Norfolk	2774	6	–
The National Bank Of Norfolk	14339	–	–
The Nebraska National Bank Of Norfolk	7329	6	–
The Norfolk National Bank	3347	4	5
North Auburn			
The First National Bank Of Auburn, North Auburn	3343	6	–
North Bend			
The First National Bank Of North Bend	3059	4	4
The National Bank Of North Bend	7449	6	–
North Platte			
The First National Bank Of North Platte	3496	4	2
The North Platte National Bank	4024	6	–
O'Neill			
The First National Bank Of O'Neill	3424	3	5
The O'Neill National Bank	5770	3	3
Oakdale			
The First National Bank Of Oakdale	13339	–	3
Oakland			
The Farmers And Merchants National Bank Of Oakland	10022	4	4
The First National Bank Of Oakland	4610	4	4
Ogalalla			
The First National Bank Of Ogalalla	3652	6	–
Omaha			
Corn Exchange National Bank Of Omaha	9730	4	–
The American National Bank Of Omaha	4087	5	–
The Central National Bank Of Omaha	1679	–	–
The City National Bank Of Omaha	9466	6	–
The Commercial National Bank Of Omaha	3163	6	–
The First National Bank Of Omaha	209	3	–
The Merchants National Bank Of Omaha	2775	4	–
The National Bank Of Commerce Of Omaha	4270	6	–
The Nebraska National Bank Of Omaha	2665	3	–
The Omaha National Bank	1633	1	1
The Packers National Bank Of Omaha	14004	–	–
The Peters National Bank Of Omaha	11829	–	–
The State National Bank Of Omaha	3603	6	–
The Union National Bank Of Omaha	3516	6	–
The United States National Bank Of Omaha	2978	3	1
Ord			
The First National Bank Of Ord	3339	3	3
The First National Bank Of Ord	13557	–	–
The Ord National Bank	3481	6	–
Orleans			
The Citizens National Bank Of Orleans	8567	6	–
The First National Bank Of Orleans	3342	6	–
Osceola			
The First National Bank Of Osceola	6493	3	4
Oshkosh			
The First National Bank Of Oshkosh	10081	6	–
Osmond			
The First National Bank Of Osmond	13101	–	–
Overton			
The First National Bank Of Overton	7925	6	–
The Overton National Bank	13446	–	2
Oxford			
The First National Bank Of Oxford	7520	6	–
Pawnee City			
The Farmers National Bank Of Pawnee City	4078	4	–
The First National Bank Of Pawnee City	2825	6	–
The National Bank Of Pawnee City	6541	6	–
Pender			
The First National Bank Of Pender	4791	5	4
The Pender National Bank	5308	6	–
Pierce			
The First National Bank Of Pierce	4280	6	–
Pilger			
The Farmers National Bank In Pilger	13453	–	2
The Farmers National Bank Of Pilger	5941	3	–
The First National Bank Of Pilger	5937	4	–
Plainview			
The First National Bank Of Plainview	9504	5	–
Plattsmouth			
The First National Bank Of Plattsmouth	1914	4	–
Plum Creek			
The First National Bank Of Lexington	3292	6	–
The First National Bank Of Plum Creek	3292	6	–
Polk			
The First National Bank Of Polk	8533	6	–
Ponca			
The First National Bank Of Ponca	3627	6	–
Primrose			
The First National Bank Of Primrose	13244	–	–
Randolph			
The First National Bank Of Randolph	7421	4	4
The Security National Bank Of Randolph	7477	4	4
Ravenna			
The First National Bank Of Ravenna	4043	6	–
Red Cloud			
The First National Bank Of Red Cloud	2811	6	–
The Red Cloud National Bank	3181	6	–
Rulo			
The First National Bank Of Rulo	3674	6	–
Rushville			
The First National Bank Of Rushville	4176	6	–
The Stockmen's National Bank Of Rushville	9191	5	4
Saint Edward			
The First National Bank Of St. Edward	5346	5	–
The Smith National Bank Of Saint Edward	5793	5	5
Saint James			
The First National Bank Of St. James	8335	6	–
The First National Bank Of Wynot	8335	6	–
Saint Paul			
Saint Paul National Bank	13463	–	–
The Citizens National Bank Of Saint Paul	13462	–	–
The Citizens National Bank Of St. Paul	3891	6	–
The First National Bank Of St. Paul	3126	6	–
The Saint Paul National Bank	3129	1	–
The Saint Paul National Bank	13463	–	–
Sargent			
The First National Bank Of Sargent	7384	6	–
Schuyler			
The First National Bank Of Schuyler	2778	4	–
The Schuyler National Bank	3152	5	–
Scottsbluff			
The First National Bank Of Scottsbluff	6240	5	–
The Scottsbluff National Bank	9581	3	2
Scribner			
The First National Bank Of Scribner	6901	5	5
The First National Bank Of Scribner	14256	–	–
Seward			
The Cattle National Bank Of Seward	13431	–	–
The First National Bank Of Seward	2771	4	6
The Jones National Bank Of Seward	3060	4	3
Shelby			
The First National Bank Of Shelby	7949	2	3
Shelton			
The First National Bank Of Shelton	4042	6	–
The First National Bank Of Shelton	13176	–	–
The Shelton National Bank	9200	6	–
Sidney			
The American National Bank Of Sidney	13425	–	2
The First National Bank Of Sidney	6201	5	–
South Auburn			
The Carson National Bank Of Auburn	3628	3	2
The Carson National Bank Of South Auburn	3628	6	–
South Omaha			
Stock Yards National Bank Of South Omaha	9908	3	1
The Live Stock National Bank Of South Omaha	8949	3	1
The Packers National Bank Of South Omaha	4589	3	–
The South Omaha National Bank	3611	5	–
The Union Stock Yards National Bank Of South Omaha	4632	6	–
South Sioux City			
The First National Bank Of South Sioux City	4557	6	–
The First National Bank Of South Sioux City	11835	–	–
Spalding			
The First National Bank Of Spalding	7574	6	–
Spencer			
The First National Bank Of Spencer	7325	5	–
Springview			
The First National Bank Of Springview	13138	–	–
Stanton			
The First National Bank Of Stanton	3364	3	3
The Stanton National Bank	7836	4	2
Sterling			
The First National Bank Of Sterling	4163	6	–
Stromsburg			
The First National Bank Of Stromsburg	8286	4	2
Stuart			
The First National Bank Of Stuart	6947	4	3
Superior			
Security National Bank Of Superior	14083	–	3
The First National Bank Of Superior	3529	6	–
The Superior National Bank	5397	6	–
Sutton			
The First National Bank Of Sutton	3240	6	–
The Sutton National Bank	3653	5	–
Syracuse			
The First National Bank Of Syracuse	3083	3	3
Tecumseh			
The Citizens National Bank Of Tecumseh	6166	6	–
The First National Bank Of Tecumseh	2955	6	–
The Tecumseh National Bank	4276	6	–
Tekamah			
The First National Bank Of Tekamah	4324	3	2
Tilden			
The First National Bank Of Tilden	9217	5	3
The Tilden National Bank	10011	5	3
Tobias			
The Citizens National Bank Of Tobias	13474	–	–
The First National Bank Of Tobias	3725	6	–
The Tobias National Bank	7578	6	–
Trenton			
The First National Bank Of Trenton	8218	6	–
Unadilla			
The First National Bank Of Unadilla	12225	–	–
University Place			
The First National Bank Of University Place	7737	5	–
Utica			
The First National Bank Of Utica	8811	4	4
Valentine			
The Farmers National Bank Of Valentine	11071	–	–
The First National Bank Of Valentine	6378	4	4
Wahoo			
The First National Bank Of Wahoo	2780	3	1
The Saunders County National Bank Of Wahoo	3118	5	5
Wakefield			
The Farmers National Bank Of Wakefield	9984	3	–
The First National Bank Of Wakefield	5368	5	–
The Wakefield National Bank	13281	–	–
Walthill			
The First National Bank, Walthill	8685	5	3
The Walthill National Bank	9816	6	6
Wausa			
The Commercial National Bank Of Wausa	10017	6	–
The First National Bank Of Wausa	9994	3	–
Wayne			
The Citizens National Bank Of Wayne	9244	5	–
The First National Bank Of Wayne	3392	6	3
The State National Bank Of Wayne	13415	–	–
The Wayne National Bank	4354	6	–
Weeping Water			
The City National Bank Of Weeping Water	5281	5	–
The First National Bank Of Weeping Water	3523	3	2
West Point			
The Farmers And Merchants National Bank Of West Point	14308	–	–
The First National Bank Of West Point	3370	6	3
The West Point National Bank	3340	3	4
Wilber			
The First National Bank Of Wilber	2991	6	–
The National Bank Of Wilber	6415	6	–
Wilcox			
The First National Bank Of Wilcox	7861	5	3
Winnebago			
The First National Bank Of Winnebago	9671	5	–
Wisner			
The Citizens National Bank Of Wisner	6866	4	3
The First National Bank Of Wisner	4029	3	3
Wolbach			
The First National Bank Of Wolbach	8413	6	–
Wood River			
The First National Bank Of Wood River	3939	1	5
Wymore			
The City National Bank Of Wymore	9138	6	–
The First National Bank Of Wymore	4210	4	3
The Wymore National Bank	14282	–	4
York			
Farmers National Bank Of York	7821	5	–
The City National Bank Of York	4935	3	3
The First National Bank Of York	2683	2	2
The Nebraska National Bank Of York	4245	6	–
The York National Bank	3162	6	–

NEVADA

City, Bank	Ch. No.	L	S
Austin			
The First National Bank Of Nevada, Austin	1331	6	–
Carson City			
The First National Bank Of Carson City	9242	6	–
East Ely			
The Copper National Bank Of East Ely	9578	5	–
Elka			
The First National Bank Of Elko	7743	3	3
Ely			
The Ely National Bank	9310	6	3
The First National Bank Of Ely	8561	4	3
Eureka			
The Farmers And Merchants National Bank Of Eureka	11784	–	3
Goldfield			
The First National Bank Of Goldfield	9078	6	–
Lovelock			
The First National Bank Of Lovelock	7654	5	4
Mc Gill			
The Mc Gill National Bank	9452	5	3
Reno			
First National Bank In Reno	7038	–	1
The Farmers And Merchants National Bank Of Reno	7038	2	–
The First National Bank Of Reno	2478	6	–
The Nixon National Bank Of Reno	8424	4	–
The Reno National Bank, Reno	8424	1	1
Rhyolite			
The First National Bank Of Rhyolite	8686	6	–
Tonopah			
The Nevada First National Bank Of Tonopah	8530	5	5
Winnemucca			
The First National Bank Of Winnemucca	3575	4	2

NEW HAMPSHIRE

City, Bank	Ch. No.	L	S
Berlin			
Berlin City National Bank, Berlin	14100	–	4
Berlin National Bank	14100	–	–
The Berlin National Bank	4523	4	3
The City National Bank Of Berlin	5622	6	5
Bristol			
The First National Bank Of Bristol	5151	5	5
Charlestown			
The Connecticut River National Bank Of Charlestown	537	5	6
Claremont			
Claremont National Bank	13829	–	5
The Claremont National Bank	596	4	4
The Peoples National Bank Of Claremont	4793	5	4
Colebrook			
The Colebrook National Bank	4041	4	5
The Farmers And Traders National Bank Of Colebrook	5183	6	5
Concord			
The First National Bank Of Concord	318	3	5
The Mechanic's National Bank Of Concord	2447	2	4
The National State Capital Bank Of Concord	758	3	3
Conway			
The Conway National Bank	9476	6	–
Derry			
The Derry National Bank	499	5	5

City, Bank	Ch. No.	L	S
Dover			
The Cochecho National Bank Of Dover	1087	6	–
The Dover National Bank	1043	6	–
The Merchants National Bank Of Dover	5274	6	4
The Strafford National Bank Of Dover	1353	5	–
East Jaffrey			
The Monadnock National Bank Of East Jaffrey	1242	4	4
Exeter			
The National Granite State Bank Of Exeter	1147	5	–
The Rockingham National Bank Of Exeter	12889	5	3
Farmington			
Farmington National Bank	13764	–	5
The Farmington National Bank	2022	4	6
Francestown			
The First National Bank Of Francestown	576	5	–
Franklin			
The Franklin National Bank	2443	3	5
Gonic			
The First National Bank Of Gonic	838	6	–
Gorham			
The White Mountain National Bank Of Gorham	9001	6	3
Groveton			
The Coos County National Bank Of Groveton	5317	6	6
The Gorham National Bank, Gorham	5258	6	–
The Groveton National Bank	5258	6	–
The Groveton National Bank	13808	–	–
Hanover			
The Dartmouth National Bank Of Hanover	1145	4	4
Hillsborough			
The First National Bank Of Hillsborough	1688	4	6
Keene			
The Ashuelot National Bank Of Keene	946	4	–
The Ashuelot-Citizens National Bank Of Keene	946	5	4
The Cheshire National Bank Of Keene	559	4	3
The Citizens National Bank Of Keene	2299	3	–
The Keene National Bank	877	3	4
Laconia			
The Laconia National Bank	1645	4	4
The Peoples National Bank Of Laconia	4037	5	5
Lakeport			
The Lakeport National Bank Of Laconia	4740	6	4
The National Bank Of Lakeport	4740	5	–
Lancaster			
The Lancaster National Bank	2600	4	5
Lebanon			
The National Bank Of Lebanon	808	4	4
Littleton			
The Littleton National Bank	1885	5	5
Manchester			
The Amoskeag National Bank Of Manchester	574	4	4
The Amoskeag National Bank, Manchester	574	6	–
The City National Bank Of Manchester	1520	6	–
The First National Bank Of Manchester	1153	4	5
The Manchester National Bank	1059	4	4
The Merchants National Bank Of Manchester	1520	4	4
The National Bank Of The Commonwealth Of Manchester	4693	6	–
The Second National Bank Of Manchester	2362	5	–
Milford			
The Souhegan National Bank Of Milford	1070	4	3
Nashua			
The First National Bank Of Nashua	84	6	–
The First National Bank Of Nashua	2741	5	–
The Indian Head National Bank Of Nashua	1310	3	4
The Second National Bank Of Nashua	2240	3	2
New Market			
The New Market National Bank	1330	5	5
Newport			
The Citizens National Bank Of Newport	3404	3	6
The First National Bank Of Newport	888	2	4
Peterborough			
The First National Bank Of Peterborough	1179	3	1
Pittsfield			
The Pittsfield National Bank	1020	6	–
Plymouth			
The Pemigewasset National Bank Of Plymouth	2587	4	4
Portsmouth			
The First National Bank Of Portsmouth	19	3	–
The First National Bank Of Portsmouth	19	4	3
The First National Bank Of Portsmouth	2672	5	–
The National Mechanics And Traders Bank Of Portsmouth	401	4	4
The New Hampshire National Bank Of Portsmouth	1052	5	5
The Rockingham National Bank Of Portsmouth	1025	5	–
Rochester			
The New Public National Bank Of Rochester	13861	–	6
The Public National Bank Of Rochester	11893	6	4
The Rochester National Bank	2138	4	–
Sanbornton			
The Citizens National Bank Of Sanbornton	1333	6	–
The Citizens National Bank Of Tilton	1333	4	5
Sandwich			
The Carroll County National Bank Of Sandwich	1071	6	–
Somersworth			
The First National Bank Of Somersworth	1180	4	5
The Great Falls National Bank	1180	6	–
The Somersworth National Bank Of Great Falls	1183	6	–
The Somersworth National Bank, Somersworth	1183	4	4
Warner			
The Kearsarge National Bank Of Warner	1674	6	–
West Derry			
The First National Bank Of West Derry	8038	6	5
Wilton			
The Wilton National Bank	13247	–	3
Winchester			
The Winchester National Bank	887	3	4
Wolfborough			
The Lake National Bank Of Wolfborough	1486	5	–
Wolfeboro			
The Wolfeboro National Bank	8147	4	4
Woodsville			
The Woodsville National Bank	5092	5	5

NEW JERSEY

City, Bank	Ch. No.	L	S
Absecon			
The First National Bank Of Absecon	10823	–	3
Allendale			
The First National Bank Of Allendale	12706	–	4
Allenhurst			
Allenhurst National Bank & Trust Company, Allenhurst	12891	–	3
The Allenhurst National Bank	12891	–	–
Allentown			
The Farmers National Bank Of Allentown	3501	3	5
Alpha			
The Alpha National Bank	12823	5	5
Arlington			
The First National Bank & Trust Company Of Kearney	8627	5	4
The First National Bank Of Arlington	8627	4	–
Asbury Park			
The Asbury Park National Bank	3792	6	–
The Asbury Park National Bank And Trust Company	13363	–	1
The First National Bank Of Asbury Park	3451	6	–
The Merchants National Bank Of Asbury Park	10932	–	–
The Seacoast National Bank Of Asbury Park	6673	6	–
Atco			
The Atco National Bank	12617	–	–
Atlantic City			
Chelsea Second Natl Bank & Trust Co Of Atlantic City	5884	–	3
The Atlantic City National Bank	2527	3	3
The Boardwalk National Bank Of Atlantic City	8800	3	1
The Chelsea National Bank Of Atlantic City	5884	3	4
The Pacific Avenue National Bank Of Atlantic City	12886	–	–
The Second National Bank Of Atlantic City	3621	2	4
The Union National Bank Of Atlantic City	4420	5	4
Atlantic Highlands			
The Atlantic Highlands National Bank	4119	4	5
Audubon			
The Audubon National Bank	11446	–	–
Avon By The Sea			
The First National Bank Of Avon By The Sea	12422	–	–
The First National Bank Of Avon By The Sea	13560	–	–
Barnegat			
The First National Bank Of Barnegat	8497	6	3
Bay Head			
The Bay Head National Bank	13065	–	–
Bayonne			
The Bayonne National Bank	12367	–	–
The Broadway National Bank Of Bayonne	12990	–	–
The First National Bank Of Bayonne	8454	5	–
The Mechanics National Bank Of Bayonne	12990	–	–
Beach Haven			
Beach Haven National Bank & Trust Company	11658	–	1
The Beach Haven National Bank	11658	–	–
Belleville			
Peoples National Bank & Trust Company Of Belleville	12019	3	3
The First National Bank Of Belleville	8382	6	3
The Peoples National Bank Of Belleville	12019	–	–
Belmar			
The Belmar National Bank	13848	–	5
The First National Bank Of Belmar	5363	6	5
Belvidere			
The Belvidere National Bank	1096	3	–
The First National Bank Of Belvidere	13628	–	3
The Warren County National Bank Of Belvidere	4980	5	–
Bergenfield			
The Bergenfield National Bank	11368	5	–
The Bergenfield National Bank & Trust Co., Bergenfield	11368	5	5
Berlin			
The Berlin National Bank, Berlin	9779	6	2
The United Towns National Bank Of Berlin	9779	–	–
Bernardsville			
The Bernardsville National Bank	6960	3	4
Beverly			
The First National Bank & Trust Company Of Beverly	8704	6	4
The First National Bank Of Beverly	8704	4	–
Blackwood			
The First National Bank & Trust Company Of Blackwood	9597	6	6
The First National Bank Of Blackwood	9597	6	–
Blairstown			
The First National Bank Of Blairstown	5621	6	4
The Peoples National Bank Of Blairstown	9833	5	5
Bloomfield			
The Bloomfield National Bank	4056	4	–
Bloomingdale			
The First National Bank Of Bloomingdale	12660	–	–
Bloomsbury			
The Bloomsbury National Bank	2271	4	–
The Citizens National Bank Of Bloomsbury	10712	3	4
Bogota			
The Bogota National Bank	11543	5	4
Boonton			
The Boonton National Bank	4274	6	6
Bordentown			
The First National Bank Of Bordentown	9268	4	4
Bound Brook			
The Bound Brook National Bank	8512	6	–
The First National Bank Of Bound Brook	3866	4	4
Bradley Beach			
The First National Bank Of Bradley Beach	10224	6	5
Branchville			
The Branchville National Bank	13855	–	4
The First National Bank Of Branchville	7364	6	6
Bridgeton			
The Bridgeton National Bank	2999	3	3
The Cumberland National Bank Of Bridgeton	1346	3	3
The Farmers And Merchants National Bank Of Bridgeton	9498	4	–
Burlington			
The Mechanics National Bank Of Burlington	1222	2	2
Butler			
The First National Bank Of Butler	6912	4	4
Caldwell			
The Caldwell National Bank	7131	6	3
The Citizens National Bank & Trust Company Of Caldwell	9612	6	5
The Citizens National Bank Of Caldwell	9612	5	–
Califon			
The Califon National Bank	9260	6	–
Camden			
First Camden National Bank & Trust Company, Camden	1209	2	1
The American National Bank Of Camden	13120	–	5
The Camden National Bank	3372	4	–
The First National Bank Of Camden	431	3	–
The First National State Bank Of Camden	1209	3	–
The National State Bank Of Camden	1209	4	–
The Third National Bank And Trust Company Of Camden	13203	–	3
Cape May			
The First National Bank Of Cape May	5839	6	–
The Merchants National Bank Of Cape May	9285	4	4
Cape May Court House			
The First National Bank Of Cape May Court House	7945	4	4
Carlstadt			
The Carlstadt National Bank	5416	4	1
Carteret			
First National Bank In Carteret	14153	–	6
Cedar Grove			
The First National Bank Of Cedar Grove	13136	–	4
Chatham			
The First National Bank Of Chatham	11943	–	–
Clayton			
The Clayton National Bank	10471	6	5
Clementon			
National Bank Of Clementon	14006	–	5
The Clementon National Bank	11147	–	–
Cliffside Park			
The Cliffside Park National Bank	11618	4	5
The United National Bank Of Cliffside Park	14162	–	4
Clifton			
The Clifton National Bank	12690	–	4
The First National Bank Of Clifton	11983	3	4
Clinton			
The Clinton National Bank	1114	5	6
The First National Bank Of Clinton	2246	3	3
Closter			
The Closter National Bank	8394	5	–
The Closter National Bank & Trust Company, Closter	8394	6	4
Collingswood			
The Citizens National Bank Of Collingswood	13969	–	4
The Collingswood National Bank	7983	5	3
Columbus			
The First National Bank Of Columbus	13166	–	–
Cranbury			
The First National Bank Of Cranbury	3168	4	3
Cranford			
The Cranford National Bank	7171	6	–
The First National Bank Of Cranford	12263	3	4
Deckertown			
The Farmers National Bank Of Deckertown	1221	5	–
The Farmers National Bank Of Sussex	1221	3	1
Dover			
The National Union Bank Of Dover	2076	3	5
The Peoples National Bank Of Dover	5136	6	–
Dumont			
The Dumont National Bank	11361	4	5
Dunellen			
The First National Bank Of Dunellen	8501	5	6
East Newark			
The First National Bank Of East Newark	9661	5	–
The Kearny National Bank, Kearny	9661	4	6
East Orange			
The East Orange National Bank	4766	4	–
East Rutherford			
The First National Bank Of East Rutherford	12228	–	–
Eatontown			
The First National Bank Of Eatontown	10110	3	2
Edgewater			
The Edgewater National Bank	13893	–	5
The First National Bank Of Edgewater	8401	5	5
Elizabeth			
The First National Bank Of Elizabeth	487	5	–
The National State Bank Of Elizabeth	1436	3	3
The Peoples National Bank Of Elizabeth	11744	3	3
Elmer			
The First National Bank Of Elmer	6707	5	3
Englewood			
The Citizens National Bank & Trust Company Of Englewood	4365	6	3
The Citizens National Bank Of Englewood	4365	5	–
Englishtown			
The First National Bank Of Englishtown	7223	5	6
Fairview			
The First National Bank Of Fairview	12465	3	3
Farmingdale			
The First National Bank Of Farmingdale	10840	–	–
Flemington			
The Flemington National Bank	2331	3	5
The Flemington National Bank & Trust Company, Flemington	2331	–	3
The Hunterdon County National Bank Of Flemington	892	2	2
Florence			
The First National Bank Of Florence	10831	–	–

City, Bank	Ch. No.	L	S
Fords			
The Fords National Bank	11428	6	6
Fort Lee			
The First National Bank Of Fort Lee	8874	4	5
The First National Bank Of Fort Lee	14287	–	–
The Palisade National Bank Of Fort Lee	12497	5	5
Freehold			
The Central National Bank Of Freehold	4182	6	5
The First National Bank Of Freehold	452	4	5
The Freehold National Banking Company, Freehold	951	4	–
The National Freehold Banking Company	7436	5	–
Frenchtown			
The Union National Bank Of Frenchtown	1459	2	4
Garfield			
First National Bank In Garfield	13946	–	4
The First National Bank Of Garfield	8462	4	4
Garwood			
The First National Bank Of Garwood	12297	–	–
Glassboro			
The First National Bank Of Glassboro	3843	4	3
Glen Rock			
Glen Rock National Bank, Glen Rock	12609	–	3
The First National Bank Of Glen Rock	12609	–	–
Gloucester City			
The Gloucester City National Bank	3936	6	–
Guttenberg			
Liberty National Bank In Guttenberg	14014	–	5
The First National Bank Of Guttenberg	8390	3	–
The Liberty National Bank Of Guttenberg	12806	4	4
Hackensack			
The Bergen County National Bank Of Hackensack	13364	–	3
The City National Bank & Trust Company Of Hackensack	12014	–	3
The City National Bank Of Hackensack	12014	3	–
The First National Bank Of Hackensack	1905	6	–
The Hackensack National Bank	5921	4	–
The Peoples National Bank Of Hackensack	7799	4	–
Hackettstown			
The Hackettstown National Bank	1259	2	4
The Peoples National Bank Of Hackettstown	8267	4	3
Haddon Heights			
Haddon Heights National Bank	9413	5	–
The First National Bank Of Haddon Heights	13530	–	3
Haddonfield			
The Haddonfield National Bank	3996	4	–
Haledon			
The Haledon National Bank	12854	–	4
Hamburg			
The Hardyston National Bank Of Hamburg	8227	5	5
Hamilton Square			
The First National Bank Of Hamilton Square	12646	–	5
Harrison			
The Harrison National Bank	13034	6	3
Hawthorne			
The First National Bank Of Hawthorne	12663	–	4
High Bridge			
The First National Bank Of High Bridge	5333	3	3
Highland Park			
The First National Bank Of Highland Park	12598	5	3
Hightstown			
The Central National Bank Of Hightstown	1759	6	–
The First National Bank Of Hightstown	1737	3	3
Hillsdale			
The Hillsdale National Bank	12902	2	2
Hillside			
The Hillside National Bank	11727	4	5
Hoboken			
The First National Bank Of Hoboken	1444	2	2
The Second National Bank Of Hoboken	3744	3	–
Hope			
The First National Bank Of Hope	10118	5	4
Hopewell			
The Hopewell National Bank	4254	5	3
Irvington			
The Irvington National Bank	7981	3	3
The Peoples National Bank & Trust Company Of Irvington	12876	–	–
The Peoples National Bank Of Irvington	12876	–	–
Jamesburg			
The First National Bank Of Jamesburg	288	5	6
Jersey City			
Bergen National Bank Of Jersey City	12255	4	–
Hudson County National Bank, Jersey City	1182	3	1
Journal Square National Bank Of Jersey City	12255	3	2
The First National Bank Of Jersey City	374	1	1
The Franklin National Bank Of Jersey City	12397	3	3
The Hudson County National Bank Of Jersey City	1182	3	–
The Labor National Bank Of Jersey City	12939	3	6
The Merchants National Bank Of Jersey City	9229	3	–
The Second National Bank Of Jersey City	695	3	–
The Third National Bank Of Jersey City	3680	3	–
The Union Trust And National Bank Of Hudson County	12301	–	–
Union Trust & Hudson County National Bank, Jersey City	1182	2	–
Keansburg			
The Keansburg National Bank	10376	6	5
Kearny			
Kearny National Bank	13537	–	2
Keyport			
The First National Bank Of Keyport	3164	6	–
The Peoples National Bank Of Keyport	4147	6	4
Lakehurst			
The First National Bank Of Lakehurst	12571	–	5
Lakewood			
The First National Bank Of Lakewood	5232	4	–
The Peoples National Bank Of Lakewood	7291	6	3
The Peoples National Bank Of Lakewood	14084	–	–
Lambertville			
The Amwell National Bank Of Lambertville	2339	5	3
The Lambertville National Bank	1272	3	2
Laurel Springs			
The Laurel Springs National Bank	12022	–	4
Leonia			
The Central National Bank Of Leonia	13337	–	–
The First National Bank Of Leonia	11950	5	–
Linden			
Linden National Bank	13540	–	5
The Linden National Bank	11545	4	–
The Linden National Bank & Trust Company, Linden	11545	5	5
Little Falls			
The Little Falls National Bank	8829	6	6
Little Ferry			
The Little Ferry National Bank	12378	6	5
Livingston			
Livingston National Bank	13129	–	4
Lodi			
The First National Bank Of Lodi	9420	4	–
The First National Bank Of Lodi	13164	–	–
Long Branch			
The Citizens National Bank Of Long Branch	6038	3	–
The First National Bank Of Long Branch	4138	6	–
Lyndhurst			
The First National Bank Of Lyndhurst	10417	6	4
Madison			
The First National Bank Of Madison	2551	3	3
Manasquan			
Manasquan National Bank	9213	5	3
The First National Bank Of Manasquan	3040	4	–
Mantua			
The National Bank Of Mantua	12917	–	–
Manville			
The Manville National Bank	12942	–	–
Maple Shade			
The Maple Shade National Bank	12428	–	–
Marlton			
The First National Bank Of Marlton	13125	–	–
Matawan			
The Farmers And Merchants National Bank Of Matawan	6440	4	4
Mays Landing			
The First National Bank Of Mays Landing	8582	6	5
Medford			
The Burlington County National Bank Of Medford	1191	4	3
Merchantville			
Merchantville National Bank & Trust Co, Merchantville	8323	–	3
The First National Bank & Trust Company Of Merchantville	8323	5	6
The First National Bank Of Merchantville	8323	6	–
Metuchen			
Metuchen National Bank	13916	–	6
The Metuchen National Bank	7754	3	4
Midland Park			
The First National Bank Of Midland Park	12603	–	–
Milford			
The First National Bank Of Milford	8779	4	4
Millburn			
The First National Bank Of Millburn	8661	6	6
Milltown			
The First National Bank Of Milltown	10935	–	3
Millville			
The Mechanics National Bank & Trust Company Of Millville	5208	–	5
The Mechanics National Bank Of Millville	5208	3	3
The Millville National Bank	1270	4	3
Minotola			
The First National Bank Of Minotola	10440	6	4
Montclair			
The Essex National Bank Of Montclair	9577	4	–
The First National Bank & Trust Company Of Montclair	9339	4	2
The First National Bank Of Montclair	9339	5	–
The Montclair National Bank	12268	6	3
The Peoples National Bank Of Montclair	12675	–	6
Moorestown			
The Moorestown National Bank	3387	4	–
Morristown			
The First National Bank Of Morristown	1188	3	2
The National Iron Bank Of Morristown	1113	4	–
Mount Ephraim			
The Mount Ephraim National Bank	12618	–	–
Mount Holly			
The Farmers National Bank Of New Jersey At Mount Holly	1168	4	–
The Mount Holly National Bank	1356	3	4
The Union National Bank At Mount Holly	2343	5	–
The Union Natl Bank & Trust Co At Mount Holly	2343	6	2
Mullica Hill			
The Farmers National Bank Of Mullica Hill	6728	4	3
Netcong			
The Citizens National Bank Of Netcong	6692	5	5
New Brunswick			
The Citizens National Bank Of New Brunswick	12468	–	–
The First National Bank Of New Brunswick	208	6	–
The National Bank Of New Jersey, New Brunswick	587	3	1
The Peoples National Bank Of New Brunswick	3697	4	3
New Egypt			
First National Bank In New Egypt	13910	–	5
The First National Bank & Trust Comapny Of New Egypt	8254	–	–
The First National Bank Of New Egypt	8254	6	–
Newark			
Lincoln National Bank Of Newark	12570	2	2
New Jersey Natl Bank & Trust Company Of Newark	9912	5	3
The American National Bank Of Newark	9605	3	–
The Broad & Market National Bank & Trust Co. Of Newark	9912	3	–
The Broad And Market National Bank Of Newark	9912	3	–
The Citizens National Bank And Trust Company Of Newark	12576	–	–
The Essex County National Bank Of Newark	1217	3	–
The First National Bank Of Newark	52	4	–
The Forest Hill National Bank Of Newark	12604	5	–
The German National Bank Of The City Of Newark	2045	5	–
The Hayes Circle National Bank And Trust Company Of Newar	13043	–	–
The Labor Cooperative National Bank Of Newark	12771	–	–
The Labor National Bank Of Newark	12771	6	–
The Manufacturers National Bank Of Newark	2040	2	–
The Mechanics National Bank Of Newark	1251	4	–
The Merchants & Manufacturers National Bank Of Newark	1818	2	–
The Merchants National Bank Of Newark	1818	2	–
The Mount Prospect National Bank Of Newark	13058	–	–
The National Newark Banking Company	1316	3	–
The National State Bank Of Newark	1452	2	3
The Natl Newark & Essex Banking Company Of Newark	1316	–	–
The Newark City National Bank	1220	4	–
The North Ward National Bank Of Newark	2083	2	6
The Peoples National Bank Of Newark	12964	–	–
The Port Newark National Bank	12946	–	–
The Second National Bank Of Newark	362	6	–
The South Side National Bank And Trust Company Of Newark	12631	–	–
Union National Bank In Newark	12771	–	3
Union National Bank Of Newark	2045	2	–
Newfield			
The First National Bank Of Newfield	12145	–	–
The First National Bank Of Newfield	14240	–	–
Newton			
The Merchants National Bank Of Newton	876	3	–
The Sussex And Merchants National Bank Of Newton	925	4	2
The Sussex National Bank Of Newton	925	3	–
North Arlington			
The North Arlington National Bank	12033	6	5
North Bergen			
The First National Bank Of North Bergen	12732	4	3
North Hudson			
The National Bank Of North Hudson At Union City	9867	3	3
North Merchantville			
The Pennsauken Township National Bank Of North Merchantville	12903	–	6
North Plainfield			
The Borough National Bank Of North Plainfield	9391	6	–
Nutley			
The First National Bank Of Nutley	11409	–	5
The Franklin National Bank Of Nutley	12750	–	3
Oaklyn			
The Oaklyn National Bank	12621	–	4
Ocean City			
The First National Bank Of Ocean City	6060	3	2
The National Bank Of Ocean City	14145	–	–
The Ocean City National Bank	12521	6	3
Ocean Grove			
The Ocean Grove National Bank	5403	5	6
Oradel			
The First National Bank Of Oradel	13117	–	–
Orange			
The Brick Church National Bank Of Orange	12338	–	–
The First National Bank Of East Orange	12338	–	–
The Orange First National Bank	13834	–	–
The Orange National Bank	1317	6	–
The Second National Bank Of Orange	4724	3	2
Palasades Park			
The Palasades Park National Bank & Trust Company	11909	–	3
Palisades Park			
The National Bank Of Palisades Park	14088	–	6
The Palisades Park National Bank	11909	3	–
Palmyra			
The Palmyra National Bank	11793	6	5
Park Ridge			
The First National Bank Of Park Ridge	12195	–	–
Passaic			
Passaic National Bank And Trust Company	12205	1	1
The American National Bank Of Passaic	12834	3	5
The Lincoln National Bank Of Passaic	13123	3	4
The Passaic National Bank	3572	4	–
Paterson			
Labor Co-operative National Bank Of Paterson	12560	5	–
National Bank Of America In Paterson	12383	3	2
The Broadway National Bank Of Paterson	12726	3	–
The Columbus National Bank Of Paterson	12895	–	–
The Eastside National Bank Of Paterson	12901	–	–
The First National Bank Of Paterson	329	2	2
The Labor National Bank Of Paterson	12560	–	–
The National Trust Bank Of Paterson	11979	–	–
The National Union Bank Of Paterson	14321	–	–
The Passaic County National Bank Of Paterson	810	6	–
The Paterson National Bank	4072	2	2
The Second National Bank Of Paterson	810	3	2
The Totowa National Bank Of Paterson	12167	–	–
Paulsboro			
The First National Bank & Trust Company Of Paulsboro	5981	6	3
The First National Bank Of Paulsboro	5981	4	–
Peapack-gladstone			
The Peapack-Gladstone National Bank	12002	4	–

City, Bank	Ch. No.	L	S
Pedricktown			
The First National Bank Of Pedricktown	8007	5	5
Pemberton			
The Peoples National Bank & Trust Company Of Pemberton	8129	6	5
The Peoples National Bank Of Pemberton	8129	6	–
Penn's Grove			
The Penn's Grove National Bank	5387	5	–
Pennington			
The First National Bank Of Pennington	5718	5	4
Penns Grove			
The Penns Grove National Bank & Trust Company	5387	6	3
Perth Amboy			
The City National Bank Of Perth Amboy	11351	5	–
The First National Bank Of Perth Amboy	5215	3	3
The Perth Amboy National Bank	12524	5	1
Phillipsburg			
The Phillipsburg National Bank	1239	2	–
The Phillipsburg National Bank & Trust Company	1239	5	2
The Second National Bank Of Phillipsburg	5556	2	3
Pitman			
Pitman National Bank	8500	6	–
Pitman National Bank & Trust Company, Pitman	8500	6	3
Plainfield			
The City National Bank Of Plainfield	2243	2	–
The First National Bank Of Plainfield	447	2	2
The First National Bank Of Plainfield	13629	–	3
The Fourth National Bank Of Plainfield	13629	–	–
The Plainfield National Bank	13174	–	2
Pleasantville			
The First National Bank Of Pleasantville	6508	5	1
The Mainland National Bank Of Pleasantville	14289	–	–
The Pleasantville National Bank	12510	5	3
Point Pleasant			
The Ocean County National Bank Of Point Pleasant Beach	5712	4	4
Point Pleasant Beach			
The Point Pleasant Beach National Bank	13215	–	–
Point Pleasent Beach			
Point Pleasent Beach National Bank & Trust Company	13215	–	5
Pompton Lakes			
The First National Bank & Trust Company Of Pompton Lakes	10787	–	–
The First National Bank Of Pompton Lakes	10787	–	–
Port Norris			
The First National Bank Of Port Norris	10036	5	5
Princeton			
The First National Bank Of Princeton	4872	3	2
The Princeton National Bank	1681	6	–
Prospect Park			
The Prospect Park National Bank	12861	6	4
Rahway			
The Citizens National Bank Of Rahway	12828	4	5
The National Bank Of Rahway	896	6	–
The Rahway National Bank	5260	3	3
The Union National Bank Of Rahway	881	5	–
Ramsey			
The First National Bank & Trust Company Of Ramsey	9367	–	2
The First National Bank Of Ramsey	9367	6	–
Red Bank			
The Broad Street National Bank Of Red Bank	11553	4	–
The First National Bank Of Red Bank	445	3	–
The National Bank And Trust Company Of Red Bank	12520	–	–
The Navesink National Bank Of Red Bank	4535	6	–
The Second National Bank & Trust Company Of Red Bank	2257	5	3
The Second National Bank Of Red Bank	2257	2	–
Ridgefield			
The Ridgefield National Bank	12037	–	–
Ridgefield Park			
The First National Bank Of Ridgefield Park	9780	5	–
Ridgewood			
Citizens First Natl Bank & Trust Company Of Ridgewood	11759	–	–
Citizens National Bank & Trust Company Of Ridgewood	11759	6	2
First National Bank & Trust Company Of Ridgewood	5205	–	5
The Citizens National Bank Of Ridgewood	11759	6	–
The First National Bank Of Ridgewood	5205	3	–
Riverside			
The First National Bank Of Riverside	12984	–	2
The Riverside National Bank	6823	6	–
Riverton			
The Cinnaminson National Bank Of Riverton	8484	6	–
Rockaway			
The First National Bank Of Rockaway	8566	6	–
The First National Bank Of Rockaway	13574	–	–
Roebling			
The First National Bank & Trust Company Of Roebling	11620	–	3
The First National Bank Of Roebling	11620	4	4
Roosevelt			
The First National Bank Of Carteret	8437	6	5
The First National Bank Of Roosevelt	8437	6	–
Roselle			
The First National Bank Of Roselle	8483	6	5
Rutherford			
The Rutherford National Bank, Rutherford	5005	3	2
Salem			
The City National Bank & Trust Company Of Salem	3922	4	2
The City National Bank Of Salem	3922	4	–
The Salem National Bank & Trust Company, Salem	1326	4	3
The Salem National Banking Company	1326	5	–
Sayreville			
The First National Bank Of Sayreville	13369	–	–
Sea Bright			
The First National Bank Of Sea Bright	13552	–	–
The Sea Bright National Bank	14177	–	6
Sea Isle City			
The First National Bank Of Sea Isle City	12279	5	5
Seabright			
The First National Bank Of Seabright	5926	5	5
Seaside Heights			
The Coast National Bank Of Seaside Heights	12354	–	–
Secaucus			
The First National Bank Of Secaucus	9380	6	4
The Peoples National Bank Of Secaucus	14151	–	–
Somers Point			
The First National Bank Of Somers Point	12559	–	6
Somerville			
The First National Bank Of Somerville	395	3	–
The Second National Bank Of Somerville	4942	4	3
South Amboy			
The First National Bank Of South Amboy	3878	3	4
South Plainfield			
The First National Bank Of South Plainfield	11847	6	–
South River			
The First National Bank Of South River	6179	6	6
Spring Lake			
The First National Bank Of Spring Lake	5730	5	6
The First National Bank Of Spring Lake	13898	–	–
Springfield			
The First National Bank Of Springfield	12830	–	–
Stone Harbor			
The First National Bank Of Stone Harbor	12978	–	–
Summit			
The First National Bank & Trust Company Of Summit	5061	5	3
The First National Bank Of Summit	5061	5	–
Swedesboro			
The Swedesboro National Bank	2923	4	2
Teaneck			
The Teaneck National Bank	12981	–	–
Tenafly			
The First National Bank Of Tenafly	8614	4	–
The Northern Valley National Bank Of Tenafly	13012	–	–
The Town Of Union			
The Union City National Bank, Union City	12749	–	–
Toms River			
The First National Bank Of Toms River	2509	2	2
The Ocean County National Bank Of Toms River	1400	6	–
Town Of Union			
The First National Bank Of Town Of Union	9544	5	–
The First National Bank Of Union City	9544	3	3
Trenton			
The Broad Street National Bank Of Trenton	3709	3	3
The First National Bank Of Trenton	281	1	–
The First-Mechanics National Bank Of Trenton	1327	4	1
The Mechanics National Bank Of Trenton	1327	1	–
The Prospect National Bank Of Trenton	12949	–	5
The Security National Bank Of Trenton	13039	–	3
Tuckahoe			
The First National Bank Of Tuckahoe	14189	–	3
The Tuckahoe National Bank	8681	6	6
Union Center			
The Union Center National Bank	12425	–	–
Union City			
The Hamilton National Bank Of The Town Of Union	12749	–	–
Ventnor City			
The Ventnor City National Bank	10248	6	2
Verona			
The Verona National Bank	10919	–	–
Vincentown			
The First National Bank Of Vincentown	370	4	3
Vineland			
The Vineland National Bank	2399	5	–
The Vineland National Bank	2918	4	–
The Vineland National Bank & Trust Company, Vineland	2918	–	–
Washington			
The First National Bank Of Washington	860	2	3
The Washington National Bank	5121	5	–
Weehawken			
The Hamilton National Bank Of Weehawken	12829	4	3
West Collingswood			
The Memorial National Bank Of Collingswood	11607	–	–
West Englewood			
The West Englewood National Bank	12402	4	3
West Hoboken			
The National Bank Of North Hudson At West Hoboken	9867	4	–
West New York			
National Bank Of West New York	14305	–	6
The First National Bank Of West New York	12064	4	3
West Orange			
The First National Bank Of West Orange	9542	4	4
West Paterson			
The Westside National Bank Of West Paterson	12848	5	5
Westfield			
The First National Bank Of Westfield	4719	6	–
The National Bank Of Westfield	10142	4	4
The Peoples National Bank Of Westfield	8623	6	–
Westmont			
The Westmont National Bank	12519	–	–
Westville			
The First National Bank Of Westville	10430	6	6
Westwood			
The First National Bank Of Westwood	8777	5	3
Wharton			
The First National Bank Of Wharton	13047	6	5
Whippany			
The First National Bank Of Whippany	13173	–	–
White House Station			
The First National Bank Of White House Station	9061	5	6
Wildwood			
The Marine National Bank Of Wildwood	6278	4	5
Williamstown			
The First National Bank Of Williamstown	7265	6	4
Woodbine			
The Woodbine National Bank	12977	–	1
Woodbridge			
The First National Bank & Trust Company Of Woodbridge	8299	–	4
The First National Bank Of Woodbridge	8299	2	6
The Woodbridge National Bank	11888	–	–
Woodbury			
The Farmers And Mechanics National Bank Of Woodbury	3716	4	3
The First National Bank & Trust Company Of Woodbury	1199	4	3
The First National Bank Of Woodbury	1199	4	–
Woodlynn			
The Woodlynn National Bank	12894	–	–
Woodridge			
The Woodridge National Bank	13265	–	–
Woodstown			
The First National Bank Of Woodstown	399	3	3
The Woodstown National Bank	11734	6	–
The Woodstown National Bank & Trust Company, Woodstown	11734	6	3
Wrightstown			
The First National Bank Of Wrightstown	11081	–	–
Wyckoff			
The First National Bank Of Wyckoff	12272	–	4
Yardville			
The Yardville National Bank	12606	–	5

NEW MEXICO TERR

City, Bank	Ch. No.	L	S
Alamogordo			
The Citizens National Bank Of Alamogordo	8315	6	–
The First National Bank Of Alamogordo	5244	6	–
Albuquerque			
The Albuquerque National Bank	3222	6	–
The First National Bank Of Albuquerque	2614	3	–
The State National Bank Of Albuquerque	7186	5	–
Artesia			
The First National Bank Of Artesia	7043	6	–
The State National Bank Of Artesia	9468	6	–
Belen			
The First National Bank Of Belen	6597	6	–
Carlsbad			
The First National Bank Of Carlsbad	5487	6	–
The National Bank Of Carlsbad	6884	6	–
Cimarron			
The First National Bank Of Cimarron	9292	6	–
Clayton			
The First National Bank Of Clayton	5713	5	–
Clovis			
The Clovis National Bank	8767	6	–
The First National Bank Of Clovis	8784	6	–
Deming			
The Deming National Bank	6974	6	–
The First National Bank Of Deming	3160	6	–
The National Bank Of Deming	4746	6	–
Eddy			
The First National Bank Of Eddy	4455	6	–
Elida			
The First National Bank Of Elida	8348	6	–
Engle			
The First National Bank Of Cutter	8662	6	–
The First National Bank Of Engle	8662	–	–
Farmington			
The First National Bank Of Farmington	6183	6	–
The San Juan County National Bank Of Farmington	9151	6	–
Gallup			
The First National Bank Of Gallup	9988	6	–
Hagerman			
The First National Bank Of Hagerman	7503	6	–
The Hagerman National Bank	7503	6	–
Hope			
The First National Bank Of Hope	9441	6	–
Lake Arthur			
The First National Bank Of Lake Arthur	8584	5	–
Lakewood			
The Lakewood National Bank	8782	6	–
Las Cruces			
The First National Bank Of Las Cruces	7720	6	–
Las Vegas			
The First National Bank Of Las Vegas	2436	4	–
The San Miguel National Bank Of Las Vegas	2454	4	–
Lordsburg			
The First National Bank Of Lordsburg	8880	6	–
Melrose			
The First National Bank Of Melrose	8397	6	–
Nara Visa			
The First National Bank Of Nara Visa	8663	5	–
Portales			
The Citizens National Bank Of Portales	8364	6	–
The First National Bank Of Portales	6187	6	–
Raton			
The Citizens National Bank Of Raton	6363	6	–
The First National Bank Of Raton	4734	3	–
The National Bank Of New Mexico Of Raton	8098	6	–
The Raton National Bank	8120	5	–
Roswell			
The American National Bank Of Roswell	6714	6	–
The Citizens National Bank Of Roswell	6777	5	–
The First National Bank Of Roswell	5220	6	–
The Roswell National Bank	6714	6	–
Santa Fe			
The First National Bank Of Santa Fe	1750	3	–
The Second National Bank Of Santa Fe	2024	4	–
Santa Rosa			
The First National Bank Of Santa Rosa	6081	6	–
Silver City			
The American National Bank Of Silver City	8132	5	–
The First National Bank Of Silver City	3554	6	–
The Silver City National Bank	3539	6	–

City, Bank	Ch. No.	L	S
Socorro			
The First National Bank Of Socorro	2627	6	–
The New Mexico National Bank Of Socorro	4485	6	–
The Socorro National Bank	4574	6	–
Sunnyside			
The First National Bank Of Fort Sumner	8617	6	–
The First National Bank Of Sunnyside	8617	–	–
Texico			
The First National Bank Of Texico	8173	6	–
The Texico National Bank	8391	6	–
Tucumcari			
The First National Bank Of Tucumcari	6288	6	–

NEW MEXICO

City, Bank	Ch. No.	L	S
Alamogordo			
The First National Bank Of Alamogordo	5244	6	–
Albuquerque			
Albuquerque National Bank	12485	2	–
Albuquerque National Trust And Savings Bank	12485	4	1
First National Bank In Albuquerque	13814	–	3
The Citizens National Bank Of Albuquerque	11442	5	–
The First National Bank Of Albuquerque	2614	1	1
The State National Bank Of Albuquerque	7186	4	–
Artesia			
The First National Bank Of Artesia	7043	4	3
The State National Bank Of Artesia	9468	6	–
Belen			
The First National Bank Of Belen	6597	4	2
Carlsbad			
The Carlsbad National Bank	12569	–	4
The First National Bank Of Carlsbad	5487	5	–
The National Bank Of Carlsbad	6884	6	–
The State National Bank Of Carlsbad	10962	–	–
Carrizozo			
The First National Bank Of Carrizozo	10963	–	–
Cimarron			
The First National Bank Of Cimarron	9292	6	–
Clayton			
The Clayton National Bank	11136	–	–
The First National Bank Of Clayton	5713	5	–
Clovis			
The Clovis National Bank	8767	5	4
The First National Bank Of Clovis	8784	5	–
The First National Bank Of Clovis	12522	–	–
Columbus			
The First National Bank Of Columbus	11449	–	–
Deming			
The Deming National Bank	6974	6	–
The First National Bank In Deming	6974	6	–
Elida			
The First National Bank Of Elida	8348	6	4
The Portales National Bank, Portales	8348	–	–
Farmington			
The First National Bank Of Farmington	6183	6	4
The Peoples National Bank Of Farmington	12514	–	–
The San Juan County National Bank Of Farmington	9151	6	–
Gallup			
The First National Bank In Gallup	11900	3	4
The First National Bank Of Gallup	9988	6	–
The National Bank Of Gallup	11900	6	–
Grady			
The First National Bank Of Grady	11746	–	–
Hagerman			
The First National Bank Of Hagerman	7503	5	4
Hatch			
The First National Bank Of Hatch	12879	–	–
Hope			
The First National Bank Of Hope	9441	5	–
Hot Springs			
The First National Bank Of Hot Springs	11011	–	–
The Hot Springs National Bank	13438	–	–
Lake Arthur			
The First National Bank Of Lake Arthur	8584	6	–
Lakewood			
The Lakewood National Bank	8782	6	–
Las Cruces			
The First National Bank Of Las Cruces	7720	5	5
Las Vegas			
The First National Bank Of Las Vegas	2436	3	–
The San Miguel National Bank Of Las Vegas	2454	5	–
Lordsburg			
The First National Bank Of Lordsburg	8880	6	–
Loving			
The First National Bank Of Loving	11711	–	–
Lovington			
The First National Bank Of Lovington	11029	–	–
Magdalena			
The First National Bank Of Magdalena	10268	4	–
Melrose			
The First National Bank Of Melrose	8397	4	4
Nara Visa			
The First National Bank Of Nara Visa	8663	5	5
New Hobbs			
The First National Bank Of New Hobbs	13488	–	–
Portales			
The First National Bank Of Portales	6187	5	4
Raton			
First National Bank In Raton	12924	–	1
The First National Bank Of Raton	4734	3	–
The National Bank Of New Mexico Of Raton	8098	5	5
Roswell			
The American National Bank Of Roswell	6714	5	–
The Citizens National Bank Of Roswell	6777	4	–
The First National Bank Of Roswell	5220	3	3
Roy			
The First National Bank Of Roy	11958	–	–
Santa Fe			
The First National Bank Of Santa Fe	1750	3	1
Santa Rosa			
The First National Bank Of Santa Rosa	6081	4	3
Silver City			
The American National Bank Of Silver City	8132	2	3
The New First National Bank Of Silver City	12710	–	–
The Silver City National Bank	3539	6	–
Springer			
The First National Bank Of Springer	11565	–	–
Sunnyside			
The First National Bank Of Fort Sumner	8617	6	–
Taos			
The First National Bank Of Taos	11102	–	–
Tucumcari			
The American National Bank Of Tucumcari	10594	–	–
The First National Bank Of Tucumcari	6288	5	5
The First-American National Bank Of Tucumcari	14081	–	5
Willard			
The First National Bank Of Mountainair	11329	–	–
The First National Bank Of Willard	11329	–	–

NEW YORK

City, Bank	Ch. No.	L	S
Adams			
The Adams National Bank	2845	6	–
The Citizens National Bank Of Adams	4103	6	–
The Farmers National Bank Of Adams	4061	4	4
The First National Bank Of Adams	71	6	–
The Hungerford National Bank Of Adams	1531	5	–
Addison			
The First National Bank Of Addison	5178	4	5
Afton			
First National Bank Of Afton	11513	6	5
The Afton National Bank	11514	–	–
Akron			
The Wickware National Bank Of Akron	5631	5	–
Albany			
The Albany City National Bank, Albany	1291	6	–
The First National Bank Of Albany	267	3	–
The Merchants National Bank Of Albany	1045	6	–
The National Albany Exchange Bank	739	6	–
The National Commercial Bank And Trust Company Of Albany	1301	3	2
The National Commercial Bank Of Albany	1301	3	–
The National Exchange Bank Of Albany	3282	5	–
The National Mechanics And Farmers Bank Of Albany	1289	6	–
The New York State National Bank Of Albany	1262	3	2
The Union National Bank And Trust Company Of Albany	11626	–	–
The Union National Bank Of Albany	1123	6	–
Albion			
The Citizens National Bank Of Albion	4998	3	6
The First National Bank Of Albion	166	5	–
The Orleans County National Bank Of Albion	1509	4	–
Alexandria Bay			
The First Natl. Bank Of The Thousand Islands, Alexandria Bay	5284	5	5
Allegany			
The First National Bank Of Allegany	7009	4	5
Altamont			
The First National Bank Of Altamont	9866	5	5
Amenia			
The First National Bank Of Amenia	706	3	4
Amityville			
First National Bank And Trust Company Of Amityville	8873	6	5
The First National Bank Of Amityville	8873	6	–
Amsterdam			
The Amsterdam City National Bank, Amsterdam	4211	4	3
The Farmers National Bank Of Amsterdam	1335	4	4
The First National Bank Of Amsterdam	1307	4	4
The Manufacturers National Bank Of Amsterdam	2239	6	–
The Merchants National Bank Of Amsterdam	2920	6	–
Andes			
The First National Bank Of Andes	302	6	–
The National Bank Of Andes	11243	5	4
Andover			
The Andover National Bank	13909	–	6
The Burrows National Bank Of Andover	8146	6	6
Angelica			
The First National Bank Of Angelica	564	6	–
Angola			
The Evans National Bank Of Angola	11583	–	–
Arcade			
The First National Bank Of Arcade	10410	6	3
Ardsley			
The First National Bank Of Ardsley	12992	–	5
Argyle			
The First National Bank Of Argyle	8343	6	6
The National Bank Of Argyle	13521	–	3
Athens			
The Athens National Bank	10856	5	5
Atlanta			
The Atlanta National Bank	12071	5	5
Attica			
The Attica National Bank	2437	6	–
The First National Bank Of Attica	199	6	–
Auburn			
The Auburn City National Bank	1285	6	–
The Auburn-Cayuga National Bank & Trust Company, Auburn	1345	–	4
The Cayuga County National Bank Of Auburn	1345	3	5
The First National Bank Of Auburn	231	6	–
The National Bank Of Auburn	1345	–	5
The National Bank Of Auburn	1350	4	5
The National Exchange Bank Of Auburn	1351	6	–
Aurora			
The First National Bank Of Aurora	412	5	5
Babylon			
The Babylon National Bank	4906	6	–
The Babylon National Bank	10358	6	–
The Babylon National Bank And Trust Company, Babylon	10358	–	3
Bainbridge			
The First National Bank Of Bainbridge	2543	4	5
Baldwin			
The Baldwin National Bank	11474	4	5
The Baldwin National Bank And Trust Company, Baldwin	11474	–	5
The Sunrise National Bank And Trust Company Of Baldwin	13062	–	–
The Sunrise National Bank Of Baldwin	13062	–	–
Baldwinsville			
The First National Bank & Trust Company Of Baldwinsville	292	–	6
The First National Bank Of Baldwinsville	292	5	6
Ballston Spa			
The Ballston Spa National Bank	1253	3	2
The First National Bank Of Ballston Spa	954	4	5
Barker			
The Somerset National Bank Of Barker	10126	6	5
Batavia			
The First National Bank Of Batavia	340	3	2
The Genesee County National Bank Of Batavia	2421	6	–
The National Bank Of Genesee Of Batavia	1074	6	–
Bath			
The Bath National Bank	10235	4	5
The First National Bank Of Bath	165	6	–
Bay Shore			
The First National Bank & Trust Company Of Bay Shore	10029	6	6
The First National Bank Of Bay Shore	10029	6	–
Bayside			
The Bayside National Bank	7939	6	–
Belfast			
The First National Bank Of Belfast	9644	6	5
Bellerose			
The First National Bank Of Bellerose	13234	–	3
Bellmore			
The First National Bank Of Bellmore	11072	6	4
Bellport			
The Bellport National Bank	12473	6	5
Binghamton			
The City National Bank Of Binghamton	1189	4	5
The First National Bank Of Binghamton	202	3	4
The Merchants National Bank Of Binghamton	2136	5	–
The National Broome County Bank Of Binghamton	1513	5	–
Bliss			
The Bliss National Bank	10754	5	5
Bolivar			
The First National Bank Of Bolivar	13246	–	6
Bolton Landing			
The Bolton National Bank Of Bolton Landing	13089	6	6
Boonville			
The First National Bank Of Boonville	2320	5	4
The National Exchange Bank Of Boonville	8022	6	5
Brasher Falls			
The Brasher Falls National Bank	10943	5	5
Brewster			
The First National Bank Of Brewsters	2225	4	5
Bridgehampton			
The Bridgehampton National Bank	9669	5	6
Brockport			
Brockport National Bank	13965	–	4
The First National Bank Of Brockport	382	4	4
Bronxville			
The Gramatan National Bank & Trust Company Of Bronxville	8240	6	3
The Gramatan National Bank Of Bronxville	8240	4	–
Brooklyn			
First National Bank Of Brooklyn	923	4	–
The Atlantic National Bank Of Brooklyn	1491	6	–
The Farmers And Citizens National Bank Of Brooklyn	1223	6	–
The First National Bank Of The City Of Brooklyn	923	3	–
The Greenpoint National Bank Of Brooklyn	10054	6	–
The Nassau National Bank Of Brooklyn	658	3	–
The Nassau National Bank Of Brooklyn In New York	658	–	–
The National City Bank Of Brooklyn	1543	6	–
The Sprague National Bank Of Brooklyn	2976	4	–
The Sprague National Bank Of New York	2976	6	–
Brown Station			
The Ashokan National Bank Of Brown Station	9482	5	–
Brushton			
The First National Bank Of Brushton	9643	5	6
Buffalo			
Community-South Side National Bank Of Buffalo	11768	5	–
Lafayette National Bank Of Buffalo	11435	4	–
The Amherst National Bank Of Buffalo	11883	6	–
The Broadway National Bank Of Buffalo	11319	5	–
The Central National Bank Of Buffalo	7823	4	–
The City National Bank Of Buffalo	5174	5	–
The Columbia National Bank Of Buffalo	4741	2	–
The Community National Bank Of Buffalo	11768	6	–
The Community National Bank Of Buffalo	11768	3	–
The East Side National Bank Of Buffalo	13220	5	3
The Farmers And Mechanics National Bank Of Buffalo	453	3	–
The First National Bank Of Buffalo	235	6	–
The Frontier National Bank Of Buffalo	13085	–	–
The Genesee National Bank Of Buffalo	12337	4	4
The Lincoln National Bank Of Buffalo	13219	–	2
The Lincoln-East Side National Bank Of Buffalo	13952	–	6
The Manufacturers And Traders National Bank Of Buffalo	6186	2	–
The Marine National Bank Of Buffalo	6184	2	–
The Merchants National Bank Of Buffalo	11836	5	–
The Niagara National Bank Of Buffalo	13441	–	2
The Riverside National Bank Of Buffalo	12445	5	–
The South Side National Bank Of Buffalo	12313	5	–
The Third National Bank Of Buffalo	850	4	–
Cairo			
The First National Bank Of Cairo	12586	–	–
Caledonia			
The First National Bank Of Caledonia	5648	5	5

City, Bank	Ch. No.	L	S
Callicoon			
First National Bank In Callicoon	13590	–	3
The Callicoon National Bank	9427	4	6
Cambridge			
The Cambridge Valley National Bank Of North White Creek	1275	5	–
The Cambridge Valley National Bank, Cambridge	1275	4	6
Camden			
The First National Bank And Trust Company Of Camden	2448	5	5
The First National Bank Of Camden	2448	3	–
Canajoharie			
National Spraker Bank In Canajoharie	13876	–	4
The Canajoharie National Bank	1122	4	5
The National Spraker Bank Of Canajoharie	1257	3	4
Canandaigua			
The Canandaigua National Bank	3817	4	–
The Canandaigua National Bank And Trust Company	3817	6	4
The County National Bank Of Canandaigua	10047	6	–
The First National Bank Of Canandaigua	259	6	–
The Ontario County National Bank Of Canandaigua	2765	6	–
Canastota			
The Canastota National Bank	1525	6	–
The First National Bank Of Canastota	4419	5	5
Candor			
The First National Bank Of Candor	353	6	2
Canton			
The First National Bank Of Canton	3696	4	4
The St. Lawrence County National Bank Of Canton	8531	4	4
Carmel			
The Putnam County National Bank Of Carmel	976	4	4
Carthage			
Carthage National Exchange Bank, Carthage	13584	–	4
The Carthage National Bank	3672	4	5
The First National Bank Of Carthage	2442	6	–
The National Exchange Bank & Trust Company Of Carthage	6094	–	5
The National Exchange Bank Of Carthage	6094	3	–
Castleton			
The National Bank Of Castleton	842	4	–
The National Exchange Bank Of Castleton	5816	4	–
The National Exchange Bank Of Castleton On Hudson	5816	5	4
Cato			
The First National Bank Of Cato	9857	6	5
Catskill			
Catskill National Bank And Trust Company, Catskill	1294	–	5
The Catskill National Bank	1294	3	5
The Tanners National Bank Of Catskill	1198	3	3
Cazenovia			
The Cazenovia National Bank	5675	6	–
The National Bank Of Cazenovia	1271	6	–
Cedarhurst			
Peninsula National Bank Of Cedarhurst	11854	4	4
Central Islip			
The Central Islip National Bank	12379	–	–
Central Park			
The Central Park National Bank	12951	–	6
Central Square			
The First National Bank Of Central Square	10109	6	6
Central Valley			
The Central Valley National Bank	9990	6	4
Champlain			
The First National Bank Of Champlain	316	4	3
Chappaqua			
The Chappaqua National Bank	12746	–	3
Chateaugay			
The First National Bank Of Chateaugay	8893	6	4
Cherry Creek			
Cherry Creek National Bank	14078	–	6
The Cherry Creek National Bank	10481	2	2
Cherry Valley			
Otsego County National Bank Of Cherry Valley	13748	–	3
The National Central Bank Of Cherry Valley	1136	4	4
Chester			
The Chester National Bank	1349	4	5
Chittenango			
The First National Bank Of Chittenango	179	5	–
Clayton			
The First National Bank Of Clayton	3797	4	6
The First National Exchange Bank Of Clayton	5108	–	5
The National Exchange Bank Of Clayton	5108	4	5
Clayville			
The National Bank Of Clayville	11277	–	–
Clifton Springs			
The Ontario National Bank Of Clifton Springs	8717	6	6
Clinton			
The Hayes National Bank Of Clinton	10295	6	5
Clyde			
The Briggs National Bank And Trust Company Of Clyde	2468	–	–
The Briggs National Bank Of Clyde	2468	3	–
The First National Bank Of Clyde	304	6	–
Cobleskill			
The First National Bank Of Cobleskill	461	2	2
Cohoes			
The National Bank Of Cohoes	1347	3	3
Cold Spring			
The National Bank Of Cold Spring On Hudson	4416	5	5
Conewango Valley			
The Conewango Valley National Bank	10930	5	6
Cooperstown			
The Cooperstown National Bank	7305	6	5
The First National Bank Of Cooperstown	280	3	1
The Second National Bank Of Cooperstown	223	3	2
The Worthington National Bank Of Cooperstown	420	6	–
Copenhagen			
The Copenhagen National Bank	10077	6	6
Corinth			
The Corinth National Bank	6479	6	6
Corning			
First National Bank & Trust Company Of Corning	2655	4	5
The First National Bank Of Corning	2655	4	–
Cornwall			
The Cornwall National Bank	10084	5	5
The First National Bank Of Cornwall	7344	6	–
Corona			
The First National Bank Of Corona	8853	6	–
Cortland			
Second National Bank And Trust Company Of Cortland	2827	6	4
The First National Bank Of Cortland	226	5	–
The National Bank Of Cortland	2272	3	3
The Second National Bank Of Cortland	2827	4	–
Coxsackie			
The National Bank Of Coxsackie	1398	4	–
Croghan			
The Croghan National Bank	10948	5	5
Croton On Hudson			
The First National Bank Of Croton On Hudson	9171	5	5
Cuba			
The Cuba National Bank	1143	4	3
The First National Bank Of Cuba	2451	3	5
Cutchogue			
The First National Bank Of Cutchogue	12551	5	6
Dansville			
The First National Bank Of Dansville	75	6	–
The Merchants And Farmers National Bank Of Dansville	4482	5	5
Delhi			
The Delaware National Bank Of Delhi	1323	3	4
The First National Bank Of Delhi	94	6	–
The First National Bank Of Port Jervis	94	3	3
Deposit			
The Deposit National Bank	472	5	–
The Farmers National Bank Of Deposit	9434	3	4
Dexter			
The First National Bank Of Dexter	8463	5	5
Dolgeville			
The First National Bank Of Dolgeville	6447	4	4
Dover Plains			
The Dover Plains National Bank	822	4	5
Downsville			
The First National Bank Of Downsville	7878	5	4
Dryden			
The First National Bank Of Dryden	6487	6	5
Dundee			
The Dundee National Bank	2463	6	6
Dunkirk			
The Lake Shore National Bank Of Dunkirk	2916	4	4
The Merchants National Bank Of Dunkirk	2619	2	3
Earlville			
The First National Bank Of Earlville	4493	5	5
East Aurora			
The First National Bank Of East Aurora	9950	6	–
East Hampton			
The East Hampton National Bank	7763	6	6
East Islip			
The First National Bank Of East Islip	9322	6	4
East Northport			
The Citizens National Bank Of East Northport	12593	6	5
East Rochester			
The First National Bank Of East Rochester	10141	5	3
East Rockaway			
East Rockaway National Bank & Trust Company, East Rockaway	12818	–	5
The East Rockaway National Bank	12818	5	6
East Setauket			
The Tinker National Bank Of East Setauket	11511	6	–
East Worcester			
The East Worcester National Bank	9060	6	–
Eastport			
The Eastport National Bank	13228	–	–
Edmeston			
The First National Bank Of Edmeston	3681	5	5
Edwards			
The Edwards National Bank	10569	6	5
Ellenville			
The First National Bank And Trust Company Of Ellensville	45	–	–
The First National Bank Of Ellenville	45	4	–
The Home National Bank Of Ellenville	2117	4	5
Elmira			
First National Bank & Trust Company Of Elmira	149	–	2
The Chemung Canal National Bank Of Elmira	811	6	–
The Elmira National Bank	4105	6	–
The First National Bank Of Elmira	119	6	–
The Merchants National Bank And Trust Company Of Elmira	5137	–	–
The Merchants National Bank Of Elmira	5137	4	–
The National Bank Of Chemung, Elmira	1391	6	–
The Second National Bank Of Elmira	149	4	5
The Southside National Bank Of Elmira	13377	–	–
Elmsford			
The First National Bank Of Elmsford	12956	5	4
Endicott			
The Endicott National Bank	13004	–	–
Fair Haven			
The Fair Haven National Bank	12958	–	–
Fairport			
Fairport National Bank And Trust Company, Fairport	10869	4	4
The Fairport National Bank	10869	6	–
Falconer			
The First National Bank Of Falconer	5407	4	4
Far Rockaway			
The National Bank Of Far Rockaway	9271	6	3
Farmingdale			
The First National Bank Of Farmingdale	8882	5	4
Fayetteville			
The National Bank Of Fayetteville	1110	6	–
Fishkill			
The Fishkill National Bank Of Beacon	35	5	5
The National Bank Of Fishkill	971	5	–
Fishkill Landing			
The First National Bank Of Fishkill Landing	35	4	–
Fleischmann			
The First National Bank Of Fleischmanns	8847	–	5
Fleischmanns			
The First National Bank Of Griffin Corners	8847	5	–
Floral Park			
The First National Bank And Trust Company Of Floral Park	12449	–	2
The First National Bank Of Floral Park	12449	–	–
Florida			
The Florida National Bank	9956	6	6
The National Bank Of Florida	13825	–	6
Flushing			
The Flushing National Bank	9691	4	–
Fond			
The National Mohawk River Bank Of Fonda	1212	3	4
Forestville			
The First National Bank Of Forestville	10444	3	3
Fort Edward			
The Farmers National Bank Of Fort Edward	1348	6	–
The First National Bank Of Fort Edward	3330	6	–
The Fort Edward National Bank	7630	6	5
The National Bank Of Fort Edward	1218	6	–
The North Granville National Bank, North Granville	1348	6	–
Fort Plain			
The Fort Plain National Bank	2860	4	6
The National Fort Plain Bank	467	6	–
Frankfort			
Citizens First National Bank Of Frankfort	10351	5	3
The Citizens National Bank Of Frankfort	10351	5	–
The First National Bank Of Frankfort	3582	6	–
Franklin			
The First National Bank Of Franklin	282	4	5
Franklin Square			
The Franklin Square National Bank	12997	–	5
Franklinville			
The Farmers National Bank Of Franklinville	2755	6	–
The First National Bank Of Franklinville	2345	6	–
The Peoples National Bank Of Franklinville	8157	6	–
The Union National Bank Of Franklinville	2755	4	4
Fredonia			
The Fredonia National Bank	841	5	–
The National Bank Of Fredonia	9019	3	2
Freeport			
The Citizens National Bank Of Freeport	11518	6	6
The First National Bank And Trust Company Of Freeport	7703	5	3
The First National Bank Of Freeport	7703	3	–
Friendship			
The Citizens National Bank Of Friendship	2632	5	–
The First National Bank Of Friendship	265	5	–
The Union National Bank Of Friendship	11055	4	4
Fulton			
Citizens National Bank And Trust Company Of Fulton	1178	–	5
The Citizens National Bank Of Fulton	1178	4	–
The First National Bank Of Fulton	968	4	–
Fultonville			
The Fultonville National Bank	2869	6	6
Gainesville			
The Gainesville National Bank	5867	4	6
Gasport			
The First National Bank Of Gasport	10623	6	6
Geneseo			
Genesee Valley National Bank And Trust Company Of Geneseo	886	–	5
Genesso			
The Genessee Valley National Bank, Geneseo	886	3	3
Geneva			
The First National Bank Of Geneva	167	5	–
The Geneva National Bank	949	5	–
The National Bank Of Geneva	12450	–	–
Genoa			
The First National Bank Of Genoa	9921	6	5
Germantown			
The Germantown National Bank	12242	5	6
Glen Cove			
The First National Bank Of Glen Cove	13143	–	–
Glen Head			
The First National Bank Of Glen Head	13126	–	2
Glens Falls			
Glens Falls National Bank And Trust Company	7699	–	6
The First National Bank Of Glens Falls	980	4	4
The Glens Falls National Bank	1293	6	–
The Merchants National Bank Of Glens Falls	4846	6	–
The National Bank Of Glens Falls	7699	4	5
Gloversville			
City National Bank And Trust Company Of Gloversville	9305	–	3
The City National Bank Of Gloversville	9305	3	–
The Fulton County National Bank Of Gloversville	3312	4	–
The Fulton County Natl Bank & Trust Co Of Gloversville	3312	–	3
The National Bank Of Gloversville	1938	6	–
The National Fulton County Bank Of Gloversville	1474	5	–
Goshen			
The Goshen National Bank	1408	5	5
The National Bank Of Orange County Of Goshen	1399	4	4
Gouverneur			
First National Bank In Gouverneur	13911	–	6
The First National Bank Of Gouverneur	2510	4	4
Grand Gorge			
The First National Bank Of Grand Gorge	7618	6	4

City, Bank	Ch. No.	L	S
Granville			
The Farmers National Bank Of Granville	3154	5	4
The Granville National Bank	4985	4	6
The National Bank Of Granville	2294	6	–
The Washington County National Bank Of Granville	7255	5	3
Great Neck Station			
The First Natl. Bank Of Great Neck At Great Neck Station	12659	5	6
Greene			
The First National Bank Of Greene	12174	–	–
The First National Bank Of Greene	13575	–	–
Greenport			
The First National Bank Of Greenport	334	5	5
The Peoples National Bank Of Greenport	3232	6	6
Greenwich			
The First National Bank Of Greenwich	2517	4	–
The Washington County National Bank Of Greenwich	1266	5	–
Greenwood			
The First National Bank Of Greenwood	8058	6	6
Groton			
The First National Bank Of Groton	1083	4	5
Hamden			
The First National Bank Of Hamden	12017	5	4
Hamilton			
The National Hamilton Bank, Hamilton	1334	3	4
Hammond			
The Citizens National Bank Of Hammond	10216	6	6
Hampton Bays			
The Hampton Bays National Bank	12987	4	4
Hancock			
The First National Bank Of Hancock	8613	3	4
Hankins			
The First National Bank Of Hankins	12549	–	–
Harrison			
The First National Bank Of Harrison	12601	6	4
Harrisville			
The First National Bank Of Harrisville	10767	6	4
Hartsdale			
The Hartsdale National Bank	12705	–	4
Hartwick			
The Hartwick National Bank	11657	6	4
Hastings Upon Hudson			
The First National Bank Of Hastings Upon Hudson	8586	5	6
Havana			
The First National Bank Of Havana	301	6	–
The Havana National Bank	343	6	–
The Second National Bank Of Havana	343	6	–
Haverstraw			
The National Bank Of Haverstraw	2229	4	–
The National Bank Of Haverstraw And Trust Company	2229	5	6
Hempstead			
The First National Bank Of Hempstead	4880	4	4
The Second National Bank Of Hempstead	11375	5	–
Herkimer			
The First National Bank Of Herkimer	3183	4	4
The Herkimer National Bank	5141	3	4
Hermon			
The First National Bank Of Hermon	5605	6	–
Heuvelton			
The First National Bank Of Heuvelton	10446	5	5
Hicksville			
The Long Island National Bank Of Hicksville	11087	4	5
Highland			
The First National Bank Of Highland	5336	5	6
Highland Falls			
The Citizens National Bank Of Highland Falls	8838	6	–
The First National Bank & Trust Company Of Highland Falls	8850	–	6
The First National Bank Of Highland Falls	8850	5	5
The First National Bank Of Highland Falls	13567	–	–
Hobart			
The First National Bank Of Hobart	193	6	–
The National Bank Of Hobart	4497	4	4
Holcomb			
The Hamlin National Bank Of Holcomb	10046	6	5
Holland Patent			
The First National Bank Of Holland Patent	5299	4	5
Homer			
The First National Bank Of Homer	2398	4	–
The Homer National Bank	3186	6	4
Hoosick Falls			
The First National Bank Of Hoosick Falls	2471	3	5
The Peoples National Bank Of Hoosick Falls	5874	3	5
The Peoples-first National Bank Of Hoosick Falls	2471	–	3
Hornellsville			
Citizens National Bank And Trust Company Of Hornell	2522	6	5
The Citizens National Bank Of Hornell	2522	4	–
The Citizens National Bank Of Hornellsville	2522	6	–
The First National Bank Of Hornell	262	5	5
The First National Bank Of Hornellsville	262	5	–
Horseheads			
The First National Bank Of Horseheads	8301	5	4
Hudson			
The Farmers National Bank Of Hudson	990	4	4
The First National Bank And Trust Company Of Hudson	396	6	3
The First National Bank Of Hudson	396	3	–
The National Hudson River Bank Of Hudson	1091	5	–
Hunter			
The Greene County National Bank Of Hunter	7485	6	–
Huntington			
First National Bank And Trust Company Of Huntington	6587	–	4
The First National Bank Of Huntington	6587	4	–
Ilion			
Ilion National Bank And Trust Company, Ilion	1670	5	4
The Ilion National Bank	1670	4	–
The Manufacturers National Bank Of Ilion	9109	4	4

City, Bank	Ch. No.	L	S
Interlaken			
The Wheeler National Bank Of Interlaken	13037	6	4
Inwood			
The First National Bank Of Inwood	12460	–	4
Irvington			
The Irvington National Bank	6371	5	5
The Irvington National Bank And Trust Company, Irvington	6371	–	5
Islip			
The First National Bank Of Islip	8794	6	3
Ithaca			
The First National Bank Of Ithaca	222	3	4
The Merchants And Farmers National Bank Of Ithaca	729	6	–
The Tompkins County National Bank Of Ithaca	1561	4	5
Jamaica			
The First National Bank Of Jamaica	8268	4	–
Jamestown			
American National Bank Of Jamestown	9748	3	2
Swedish American National Bank Of Jamestown	9748	6	–
The Chautauqua County National Bank Of Jamestown	1563	6	–
The City National Bank Of Jamestown	938	6	–
The First National Bank Of Jamestown	548	3	4
The Jamestown National Bank	3846	6	–
The Liberty National Bank Of Jamestown	11360	4	–
The National Chautauqua County Bank Of Jamestown	8453	3	3
The Second National Bank Of Jamestown	938	6	–
Jeffersonville			
The First National Bank Of Jeffersonville	10456	6	5
Johnstown			
The First National Bank Of Johnstown	2418	6	–
Jordan			
The Jordan National Bank	12375	5	5
Keeseville			
The Keeseville National Bank	1753	3	4
Kenmore			
The First National Bank Of Kenmore	12208	4	4
Kerhonkson			
The Kerhonkson National Bank	10855	–	–
Kinderhook			
The National Bank Of Kinderhook	1026	4	–
The National Union Bank Of Kinderhook	929	2	3
Kings Park			
Kings Park National Bank	12489	5	6
The National Bank Of Kings Park	14019	–	4
Kingston			
National Ulster County Bank & Trust Company Of Kingston	1050	6	4
The First National Bank Of Kingston	451	6	–
The First National Bank Of Rondout	2493	2	–
The Kingston National Bank	1149	6	–
The National Ulster County Bank Of Kingston	1050	3	–
The National Ulster County Bank Of Kingston	13822	–	5
The State Of New York National Bank Of Kingston	955	3	5
La Fargeville			
The First National Bank Of La Fargeville	13365	–	6
Lacona			
The First National Bank Of Lacona	10175	6	4
Lake George			
First National Bank Of Lake George	8793	5	3
Lake Placid			
The Lake Placid National Bank	10755	–	–
Lake Ronkonkoma			
The National Bank Of Lake Ronkonkoma	13130	–	6
Lancaster			
The Citizens National Bank Of Lancaster	11912	3	4
Lansingburgh			
The National Bank Of Lansingburgh	1426	6	–
The National Exchange Bank Of Lansingburgh	1534	6	–
Larchmont			
The Larchmont National Bank	6019	4	–
The Larchmont National Bank And Trust Company, Larchmont	6019	3	3
Le Roy			
The First National Bank Of Le Roy	937	6	–
The Le Roy National Bank	6087	4	6
The National Bank Of Le Roy	3283	6	–
Leonardsville			
The First National Bank Of Leonardsville	217	6	–
Lestershire			
The First National Bank Of Lestershire	7813	6	–
Liberty			
The National Bank Of Liberty	10037	4	3
The Sullivan County National Bank Of Liberty	4925	4	4
Lindenhurst			
The First National Bank Of Lindenhurst	8833	4	6
Lisbon			
The First National Bank Of Lisbon	12018	6	6
Lisle			
The First National Bank Of Lisle	10816	5	5
Little Falls			
The Herkimer County National Bank Of Little Falls	1344	5	–
The Little Falls National Bank	2406	3	3
The National Herkimer County Bank Of Little Falls	2400	3	–
Little Neck			
The Little Neck National Bank	12512	–	–
The Little Neck National Bank Of New York	12512	–	–
Livingston Manor			
The Livingston Manor National Bank	10043	5	3
Livonia			
The Stewart National Bank And Trust Company Of Livonia	13006	–	6
The Stewart National Bank Of Livonia	13006	5	6
The Stewart National Bank Of Livonia	13006	–	6

City, Bank	Ch. No.	L	S
Lockport			
Niagara County National Bank & Trust Company, Lockport	639	5	1
The First National Bank Of Lockport	211	5	–
The National Exchange Bank Of Lockport	1039	3	–
The Niagara County National Bank Of Lockport	639	3	–
Long Beach			
The National Bank Of Long Beach	11755	5	–
The National City Bank Of Long Beach	13074	3	5
Long Island City			
The Commercial National Bank Of Long Island City	10329	6	–
Lowville			
The Black River National Bank Of Lowville	2426	5	5
The First National Bank Of Lowville	348	5	–
Lynbrook			
The Lynbrook National Bank	8923	6	–
The Lynbrook National Bank And Trust Company	8923	–	1
The Peoples National Bank And Trust Company Of Lynbrook	11603	3	4
The Peoples National Bank Of Lynbrook	11603	5	–
Lyons			
The Gavitt National Bank Of Lyons	7479	4	–
The Lyons National Bank	1027	4	2
Lyons Falls			
The Lyons Falls National Bank	12836	5	4
Macedon			
The First National Bank Of Macedon	12494	5	6
Mahopac			
The Mahopac National Bank	13121	–	5
Malone			
The Citizens National Bank Of Malone	11897	–	4
The Farmers National Bank Of Malone	598	5	5
The National Bank Of Malone	914	6	–
The Peoples National Bank Of Malone	3307	6	–
The Third National Bank Of Malone	3366	6	–
Mamaroneck			
First National Bank In Mamaroneck	13592	–	3
The First National Bank And Trust Company Of Mamaroneck	5411	6	5
The First National Bank Of Mamaroneck	5411	4	–
Manhasset			
First National Bank And Trust Company Of Manhasset	11924	–	4
The First National Bank Of Manhasset	11924	5	–
Marathon			
The First National Bank Of Marathon	3193	4	6
Marcellus			
The First National Bank Of Marcellus	9869	5	4
Margaretville			
The Peoples National Bank Of Margaretville	5924	5	5
Mariner Harbor			
The Mariner Harbor National Bank	8194	6	5
Marion			
The First National Bank Of Marion	10546	6	6
Marlboro			
The First National Bank Of Marlboro	8834	6	4
Massena			
The First National Bank And Trust Company Of Massena	6694	6	5
The First National Bank Of Massena	6694	6	–
Matteawan			
The Matteawan National Bank	4914	6	–
The Matteawan National Bank Of Beacon	4914	4	4
Mattituck			
The Mattituck National Bank And Trust Company	13445	–	4
Maybrook			
The Maybrook National Bank	11927	4	5
Mechanicsville			
The First National Bank Of Mechanicsville	3171	5	6
Mechanicville			
The Manufacturers National Bank Of Mechanicville	5037	4	5
Medina			
The First National Bank Of Medina	229	6	–
The Medina National Bank	4986	6	–
Merrick			
The First National Bank Of Merrick	12503	6	5
Mexico			
The First National Bank Of Mexico	5293	5	5
Middleburgh			
The First National Bank Of Middleburgh	2487	4	5
Middleport			
The First National Bank Of Middleport	9206	5	6
Middleton			
The Merchants National Bank Of Middletown	3333	4	6
Middletown			
First National Bank And Trust Company Of Middletown	523	–	–
The First Merchants National Bank & Trust Co Of Middletown	13528	–	–
The First National Bank Of Middletown	523	5	–
The Merchants And Manufacturers National Bank Of Middletown	3333	6	–
The Middletown National Bank	1276	5	–
The National Bank Of Middletown	13956	–	5
The Wallkill National Bank Of Middletown	1473	6	–
Middleville			
The Middleville National Bank Of Middleville	11656	5	–
The Middleville National Bank, Middleville	11656	–	5
Milford			
The Milford National Bank	5210	4	5
Millerton			
The Millerton National Bank	2661	5	3
Milton			
The First National Bank Of Milton	11649	–	–
Mineola			
The Central National Bank Of Mineola	13404	–	4
The First National Bank Of Mineola	9187	5	4
Minoa			
First National Bank Of Minoa	13476	–	5

City, Bank	Ch. No.	L	S
Mohawk			
The National Mohawk Valley Bank Of Mohawk	1130	3	4
Monroe			
The Monroe National Bank	7563	5	–
Montgomery			
First National Bank In Montgomery	13559	–	4
The National Bank Of Montgomery	7982	6	5
Monticello			
The National Union Bank Of Monticello	1503	3	3
Montour Falls			
Montour National Bank In Montour Falls	13583	–	3
Montour National Bank Of Montour Falls	10497	5	5
Moravia			
The First National Bank Of Moravia	99	3	4
The Moravia National Bank	2353	5	–
Morris			
The First National Bank Of Morris	4870	3	4
Morristown			
The Frontier National Bank Of Morristown	8371	5	5
Morrisville			
The First National Bank Of Morrisville	245	4	5
Mount Kisco			
The Mount Kisco National Bank	5026	4	–
The Mount Kisco Natl Bank & Trust Company, Mount Kisco	5026	4	5
Mount Morris			
Genesee River National Bank & Trust Co Of Mt. Morris	1416	–	6
Genesee River National Bank Of Mt. Morris	1416	–	6
The Genesee River National Bank Of Mount Morris	1416	4	–
The Genesee River National Bank Of Mt. Morris	1416	4	–
The Genesee River National Bank, Mount Morris	1416	–	5
Mount Vernon			
The American National Bank And Trust Co Of Mount Vernon	11747	–	–
The American National Bank Of Mount Vernon	11747	–	–
The East Chester National Bank Of Mount Vernon	1772	4	–
The First National Bank Of Mount Vernon	5271	3	3
The Mount Vernon National Bank	8516	6	–
Nanuet			
Nanuet National Bank	13314	–	5
Narrowsburg			
The First National Bank Of Narrowsburg	12496	–	5
New Berlin			
The First National Bank Of New Berlin	151	4	–
The National Bank Of New Berlin	10199	6	4
New Brighton			
The First National Bank Of Staten Island At New Brighton	3444	5	–
New Hartford			
The First National Bank Of New Hartford	11785	6	5
New Paltz			
The Huguenot National Bank Of New Paltz	1186	3	4
New Rochelle			
The Central National Bank Of New Rochelle	12548	–	–
The First National Bank Of New Rochelle	13955	–	–
The National City Bank Of New Rochelle	6427	3	–
New York			
Atlantic National Bank Of The City Of New York	1080	5	–
Bowery And East River National Bank Of New York	1105	2	–
Chatham & Phenix Natl Bank & Trust Company, New York	10778	1	2
College Point National Bank Of New York	13105	–	3
Flushing National Bank In New York	13296	–	4
Grace National Bank Of New York	12553	3	2
Irving National Bank Of New York	345	3	–
Irving National Exchange Bank Of New York	345	3	–
Lafayette National Bank Of Brooklyn In New York	12892	–	3
Liberty National Bank And Trust Company In New York	12352	4	3
Liberty National Bank In New York	12352	3	–
National Bank Of Commerce In New York	733	1	–
National Bank Of Ridgewood In New York	12897	3	–
National Bank Of Yorkville In New York	12965	4	3
National Copper Bank Of New York	8665	4	–
Seventh Avenue National Bank Of New York	11844	4	–
Seventh National Bank Of New York	11844	4	–
Sterling National Bank And Trust Company Of New York	13295	–	3
Straus National Bank And Trust Company Of New York	13254	–	4
The Aetna National Bank Of New York	7450	5	–
The American Exchange National Bank Of New York City	1394	1	–
The American Exchange Pacific Natl Bank, New York	1394	3	–
The American National Bank Of New York	750	6	–
The Astor National Bank Of New York	5112	4	–
The Atlantic National Bank Of New York	1388	6	–
The Audubon National Bank Of New York	9569	6	–
The Bank Of America National Association, New York	13193	3	3
The Bank Of New York National Banking Association	1393	2	–
The Battery Park National Bank Of New York	7447	4	–
The Bay Parkway National Bank Of Brooklyn	13088	–	–
The Bayside National Bank Of New York	13334	–	1
The Beaver National Bank Of New York	8634	6	–
The Bedford National Bank Of Brooklyn	13063	–	–
The Bensonhurst National Bank Of Brooklyn	13080	–	–
The Blair National Bank Of New York	13301	–	–
The Bowery National Bank Of New York	1297	5	–
The Bowery National Bank Of New York	12837	–	–
The Broadway National Bank And Trust Company Of New York	13327	–	–
The Bronx National Bank Of The City Of New York	8926	3	–
The Brooklyn National Bank Of New York	13292	3	3
The Bushwick National Bank Of New York	12419	6	–
The Capitol National Bank & Trust Company Of New York	12213	–	–
The Capitol National Bank Of New York	12213	–	–
The Central National Bank Of The City Of New York	376	2	–
The Central National Bank Of The City Of New York	12874	4	6
The Century National Bank Of New York	10778	–	–
The Chase National Bank Of The City Of New York	2370	1	1
The Chatham & Phenix National Bank Of New York	1375	5	–
The Chatham & Phenix Natl Bank Of The City Of New York	10778	1	–
The Chatham National Bank Of New York	1375	3	–
The Chemical National Bank Of New York	1499	3	–
The Citizens Central National Bank Of New York.	1290	3	–
The Citizens National Bank Of New York	1290	6	–
The Claremont National Bank Of New York	13027	6	–
The Coal And Iron National Bank Of The City Of New York	7203	3	–
The Columbus National Bank Of New York	4512	6	–
The Commercial Exchange National Bank Of New York	11965	–	–
The Commercial Exchange National Bank Of New York	13194	–	–
The Commercial National Bank And Trust Company Of New York	13250	–	–
The Commercial National Bank Of New York	3359	6	–
The Commercial National Bank Of New York	12516	–	–
The Consolidated National Bank Of New York	6425	5	–
The Continental National Bank Of New York	1389	2	–
The Croton National Bank Of New York	1556	6	–
The Discount National Bank Of New York	13025	–	–
The Domestic Exchange National Bank Of New York	5237	6	–
The Douglaston National Bank Of New York	13115	–	–
The Dunbar National Bank Of New York	13237	2	2
The East River National Bank Of The City Of New York	1105	4	–
The Eighth National Bank Of New York	384	6	–
The Elmhurst National Bank Of New York	13035	4	4
The Equitable National Bank Of New York	6284	5	–
The Fidelity National Bank In New York	13959	–	5
The Fifth National Bank Of The City Of New York	341	3	–
The First National Bank Of The City Of New York	29	1	1
The Flatbush National Bank Of Brooklyn	13000	–	–
The Fordham National Bank In New York	12825	4	–
The Forest Hills National Bank Of New York	13242	–	–
The Fort Greene National Bank In New York	13336	–	3
The Fourth National Bank Of The City Of New York	290	2	–
The Franklin National Bank Of New York	4855	6	–
The Franklin National Bank Of New York	12370	–	–
The Fulton National Bank Of New York	1497	6	–
The Gallatin National Bank Of The City Of New York	1324	3	–
The Garfield National Bank Of The City Of New York	2598	3	–
The Gotham National Bank Of New York	9717	3	–
The Granite National Bank Of Brooklyn	12980	–	–
The Greenwich National Bank Of New York	13051	–	–
The Grocers National Bank Of New York	1371	6	–
The Guardian National Bank Of New York	13122	–	–
The Hamilton National Bank Of New York	12300	3	–
The Hanover National Bank Of The City Of New York	1352	2	–
The Harriman National Bank Of The City Of New York	9955	4	–
The Hide And Leather National Bank Of New York	4567	5	–
The Importers And Traders National Bank Of New York	1231	3	–
The Industrial National Bank Of New York	13207	–	–
The Inter-State National Bank Of New York	4152	6	–
The Irving National Bank Of New York	1357	3	–
The Jamaica National Bank, New York	12550	4	3
The Kingsboro National Bank Of Brooklyn In New York	13304	5	6
The Leather Manufacturers National Bank Of New York	1196	3	–
The Lebanon National Bank Of New York	12214	3	5
The Lefcourt National Bank & Trust Company Of New York	13260	–	–
The Lefcourt Normandie National Bank Of New York	13260	–	–
The Liberty National Bank Of New York	4645	2	–
The Lincoln National Bank Of New York	12224	–	–
The Lincoln National Bank Of The City Of New York	2608	2	–
The Long Island National Bank Of New York	12885	4	–
The Longacre National Bank Of New York	13163	–	–
The Maiden Lane National Bank Of New York	7107	4	–
The Manufacturers National Bank Of Brooklyn	1443	4	–
The Manufacturers National Bank Of New York	1443	4	–
The Marine National Bank Of The City Of New York	1215	3	–
The Market And Fulton National Bank Of New York	964	4	–
The Market National Bank Of New York	964	4	–
The Mechanics & Metals Natl Bank Of The City Of New York	1250	2	–
The Mechanics And Traders National Bank Of New York	1624	6	–
The Mechanics National Bank Of The City Of New York	1250	2	–
The Melrose National Bank Of New York	12900	5	6
The Mercantile National Bank Of New York	12123	–	–
The Mercantile National Bank Of The City Of New York	1067	2	–
The Merchants Exchange National Bank Of The City Of New York	1080	3	–
The Merchants National Bank Of The City Of New York	1370	2	–
The Metropolitan National Bank & Trust Company Of New York	12632	–	–
The Metropolitan National Bank Of New York	1121	4	–
The Metropolitan National Bank Of The City Of New York	12021	–	–
The Mutual National Bank Of New York	13132	–	–
The National American Bank Of New York	11686	–	–
The National Bank Of Bay Ridge In New York	12344	6	–
The National Bank Of Bayside In New York, Bayside	13334	–	4
The National Bank Of Commerce In New York	733	1	–
The National Bank Of Deposit Of The City Of New York	3771	6	–
The National Bank Of North America In New York	4581	3	–
The National Bank Of North America Of New York	1373	6	–
The National Bank Of Queens County In New York	13296	–	4
The National Bank Of The Commonwealth, New York	1372	6	–
The National Bank Of The Republic Of New York	1000	2	–
The National Bank Of The State Of New York, New York	1476	5	–
The National Bank Of The United States In New York	4567	5	–
The National Broadway Bank Of New York	687	5	–
The National Bronx Bank Of New York	12900	–	4
The National Citizens Bank Of The City New York	1290	5	–
The National City Bank Of New York	1461	1	1
The National Commercial Bank Of New York	5237	6	–
The National Currency Bank Of New York	444	6	–
The National Exchange Bank And Trust Company Of New York	13442	–	–
The National Mechanics Banking Association Of New York	1075	3	–
The National Nassau Bank Of New York	9939	6	–
The National Park Bank Of New York	891	1	3
The National Reserve Bank Of The City Of New York	6425	6	–
The National Safety Bank & Trust Company Of New York	13260	–	3
The National Shoe And Leather Bank Of The City Of New York	917	3	–
The National Union Bank Of New York	4898	4	–
The Natl. Butchers And Drovers Bank Of The City Of New York	1261	3	–
The New Amsterdam National Bank Of New York	5783	4	–
The New York County National Bank, New York	1116	4	–
The New York National Exchange Bank, New York	345	4	–
The New York National Irving Bank Of New York	11639	–	–
The New York Produce Exchange Bank Of New York	11713	–	–
The Newtown National Bank Of New York	13379	–	–
The Ninth National Bank Of The City Of New York	387	5	–
The Northern National Bank Of New York	6253	6	–
The Ocean National Bank Of The City Of New York	1232	6	–
The Ozone Park National Bank Of New York	12280	4	4
The Pacific National Bank Of New York	12757	–	–
The Pacific National Bank Of New York City	1224	6	–
The Peoples National Bank Of Brooklyn In New York	9219	4	3
The Peoples Trust Co Of Brooklyn Natl Banking Assoc. Of N.Y.	12932	–	–
The Phenix National Bank Of The City Of New York	1374	3	–
The Progress National Bank Of New York	11844	6	–
The Prospect National Bank Of Brooklyn	13055	–	–
The Prospect Natl Bank & Trust Co Of Brooklyn In New York	13055	–	–
The Public National Bank And Trust Company Of New York	11034	2	1
The Public National Bank Of New York	11034	2	–
The Queensboro National Bank Of The City Of New York	12398	4	6
The Richmond Hill National Bank Of New York	11655	5	–
The Richmond National Bank Of New York	11655	–	4
The Rockaway Beach National Bank Of New York	12252	6	–
The Rugby National Bank Of Brooklyn Of New York	12948	–	–
The Saint Nicholas National Bank Of New York	972	2	–
The Seaboard National Bank Of The City Of New York	3415	3	–
The Seaboard National Bank Of The City Of New York	12123	4	–
The Second National Bank Of New York	62	6	–
The Second National Bank Of The City Of New York	62	4	–
The Second National Bank Of The City Of New York	2668	3	–
The Seventh National Bank Of New York	998	5	–
The Seventh Ward National Bank Of New York	998	3	–
The Seward National Bank & Trust Company Of New York	13045	3	4
The Seward National Bank Of New York	13045	5	–
The Sherman National Bank Of New York	8922	5	–
The Sixth National Bank Of New York City	254	4	–
The Southern National Bank Of New York	3359	6	–
The Springfield Gardens National Bank Of New York	13149	–	3
The Standard National Bank Of New York	5003	6	–
The Tenth National Bank Of The City Of New York	307	4	–
The Third National Bank Of New York	87	3	–
The Thirty-fourth Street National Bank Of New York	6441	6	–
The Traders National Bank Of Brooklyn	12970	–	–
The Tradesmen's National Bank Of The City Of New York	905	2	–
The Union National Bank Of New York	1278	5	–
The Union Square National Bank Of New York	1691	6	–
The United National Bank Of New York City	5990	4	–
The United States National Bank Of New York	2507	5	–
The Wall Street National Bank Of New York	1075	–	–
The Washington National Bank Of The City Of New York	4335	6	–
The Washington Square National Bank Of New York	13360	–	6
The Western National Bank Of New York	3700	4	–

City, Bank	Ch. No.	L	S
The Western National Bank Of The United States In New York	4567	4	–
The Woodside National Bank Of New York	12957	–	–
Union Exchange National Bank Of New York	9360	4	–
United Capitol National Bank & Trust Company Of New York	12406	–	–
United National Bank In New York	12406	6	–
United National Bank Of Long Island In New York	13242	–	–
Washington National Bank Of New York	13360	–	5
New York City			
The Harriman Natl. Bank & Trust Co. Of The City Of New York	9955	4	3
Newark			
Arcadia National Bank & Trust Company Of Newark	6802	5	–
Arcadia National Bank Of Newark	6802	3	–
The First National Bank Of Newark	349	3	4
Newark Valley			
The First National Bank Of Newark Valley	10111	6	5
Newburgh			
Highland-Quassaick National Bank & Trust Co Of Newburgh	1106	6	3
The Broadway National Bank Of Newburgh	12785	–	–
The Highland National Bank & Trust Company Of Newburgh	1106	5	–
The Highland National Bank Of Newburgh	1106	4	–
The National Bank Of Newburgh	468	3	3
The Quassaick National Bank Of Newburgh	1213	3	–
Newport			
The National Bank Of Newport	1655	5	4
Niagara Falls			
National Bank Of Niagara & Trust Co Of Niagara Falls	12284	4	–
The Cataract National Bank Of Niagara Falls	12284	4	–
The Falls National Bank Of Niagara Falls	11489	6	5
The First National Bank Of Niagara Falls	4899	6	–
Nichols			
The Nichols National Bank	9399	5	5
Norfolk			
The First National Bank Of Norfolk	10895	–	–
North Creek			
The North Creek National Bank	9716	5	5
North Rose			
The First National Bank Of North Rose	10016	5	6
North Syracuse			
The North Syracuse National Bank	12938	–	–
North Tarrytown			
The First National Bank Of North Tarrytown	12515	–	–
North Tonawanda			
The State National Bank Of North Tonawanda	6809	3	–
Northport			
The First National Bank & Trust Company Of Northport	5936	6	5
The First National Bank Of Northport	5936	5	–
Norwich			
The Chenango County Natl Bank & Trust Company Of Norwich	3011	6	4
The Chenango National Bank Of Norwich	3011	4	–
The National Bank And Trust Company Of Norwich	1354	5	3
The National Bank Of Norwich	1354	3	–
Nunda			
The First National Bank Of Nunda	2224	5	–
Nyack			
The Nyack National Bank	2378	3	4
The Nyack National Bank And Trust Company	2378	–	3
The Rockland County National Bank Of Nyack	1286	6	–
Oceanside			
The Oceanside National Bank	12458	–	–
Odessa			
The First National Bank Of Odessa	13493	–	2
Ogdensburg			
The National Bank Of Ogdensburg	2446	3	–
Old Forge			
The First National Bank Of Old Forge	10964	4	5
Olean			
The Citizens National Bank Of Olean	7102	6	–
The Exchange National Bank Of Olean	2376	2	1
The First National Bank Of Olean	1887	3	3
The Olean National Bank	9822	5	–
Oneida			
The First National Bank Of Oneida	519	6	–
The National State Bank Of Oneida	2401	4	–
The Oneida Valley National Bank Of Oneida	1090	4	5
Oneonta			
The Citizens National Bank And Trust Company Of Oneonta	8920	4	4
The Citizens National Bank Of Oneonta	8920	4	–
The First National Bank Of Oneonta	420	6	–
The Wilber National Bank Of Oneonta	2151	2	3
Oriskany Falls			
The First National Bank Of Oriskany Falls	6630	6	–
Ossining			
The Ossining National Bank	6552	4	–
Oswego			
First & Second National Bank & Trust Company Of Oswego	255	–	3
Second National Bank And Trust Company Of Oswego	296	5	6
The First National Bank Of Oswego	255	3	5
The Lake Ontario National Bank Of Oswego	1355	6	–
The National Marine Bank Of Oswego	821	5	–
The Second National Bank Of Oswego	296	4	–
Ovid			
The First National Bank Of Ovid	7840	5	6
Owego			
The First National Bank Of Owego	1019	4	5
The National Union Bank Of Owego	1311	6	–
The Owego National Bank	2996	4	5
The Tioga National Bank Of Owego	862	5	–
Oxford			
The First National Bank Of Oxford	273	4	5
The National Bank Of Oxford	14025	–	4
Ozone Park			
The First National Bank Of Ozone Park	8865	6	–
Painted Post			
The Bronson National Bank Of Painted Post	3800	6	–
The First National Bank Of Painted Post	13664	–	3
The Painted Post National Bank	11956	5	6
Palmyra			
The First National Bank Of Palmyra	295	2	6
Patchogue			
The Citizens National Bank Of Patchogue	6785	6	–
The Peoples National Bank Of Patchogue	12788	–	5
Pawling			
The National Bank Of Pawling	1269	5	4
Pearl River			
First National Bank And Trust Company Of Pearl River	10526	6	5
The First National Bank Of Pearl River	10526	5	–
Peekskill			
The Peekskill National Bank	8398	4	5
The Peekskill National Bank And Trust Company, Peekskill	8398	–	5
The Westchester County National Bank Of Peekskill	1422	3	5
Pelham			
The Pelham National Bank	11951	6	–
Penn Yan			
The First National Bank Of Penn Yan	169	6	–
The Yates County National Bank Of Penn Yan	2405	6	–
Perry			
The First National Bank Of Perry	4519	4	4
Phelps			
The National Bank Of Phelps	14267	–	–
The Phelps National Bank	9839	4	4
Philmont			
Philmont National Bank	13945	–	6
The First National Bank Of Philmont	7233	5	6
Pine Bush			
The National Bank Of Pine Bush	13960	–	6
The Pine Bush National Bank	9940	4	4
Pine Plains			
The Stissing National Bank Of Pine Plains	981	5	6
Pittsford			
The Pittsford National Bank	12535	–	–
Plattsburg			
Merchants National Bank In Plattsburg	13548	–	4
Plattsburg National Bank And Trust Company, Plattsburg	5785	3	3
The City National Bank Of Plattsburg	6613	5	–
The Plattsburg National Bank	5785	4	–
Plattsburgh			
The First National Bank Of Plattsburgh	266	5	6
The Iron National Bank Of Plattsburgh	2534	5	–
The Merchants National Bank Of Plattsburgh	3174	4	5
The Second National Bank Of Plattsburgh	321	6	–
The Vilas National Bank Of Plattsburgh	321	6	–
Pleasantville			
The First National Bank Of Pleasantville	12811	–	–
Poland			
The Citizens National Bank Of Poland	9804	5	4
The National Bank Of Poland	4223	5	–
The Poland National Bank	2441	6	–
Port Byron			
The National Bank Of Port Byron	12592	–	–
Port Chester			
The First National Bank & Trust Company Of Port Chester	402	5	3
The First National Bank Of Port Chester	402	3	–
Port Henry			
The Citizens National Bank Of Port Henry	4858	4	4
The First National Bank Of Port Henry	1697	4	–
Port Jefferson			
The First National Bank Of Port Jefferson	5068	4	4
Port Jervis			
The National Bank And Trust Company Of Port Jervis	1363	4	4
The National Bank Of Port Jervis	1363	3	–
Port Leyden			
The Port Leyden National Bank	11742	6	6
Port Richmond			
Staten Island Natl Bank & Trust Company Of New York	6198	5	4
The Port Richmond National Bank	6198	5	–
Port Washington			
The Harbor National Bank Of Port Washington	13310	–	–
The Port Washington National Bank	11292	–	–
The Port Washington Natl Bank & Trust Co, Port Washington	11292	–	–
Potsdam			
The Citizens National Bank Of Potsdam	5228	4	5
The National Bank Of Potsdam	868	4	–
Poughkeepsie			
Merchants National Bank & Trust Company Of Poughkeepsie	1380	–	4
The City National Bank Of Poughkeepsie	1305	5	–
The Fallkill National Bank Of Poughkeepsie	659	3	–
The Fallkill Natl Bank & Trust Company Of Poughkeepsie	659	–	–
The Farmers And Manufacturers National Bank Of Poughkeepsie	1312	2	4
The First National Bank Of Poughkeepsie	465	4	4
The Merchants National Bank Of Poughkeepsie	1380	4	–
The Poughkeepsie National Bank	1306	6	–
Pulaski			
The Peoples National Bank Of Pulaski	10788	–	–
The Pulaski National Bank	1496	5	–
Ravena			
The First National Bank Of Ravena	9529	6	5
Red Creek			
The Red Creek National Bank	10781	5	5
Red Hook			
The First National Bank Of Red Hook	752	3	4
Redwood			
The Redwood National Bank	10374	5	6
Remsen			
The First National Bank Of Remsen	6482	6	4
Rensselaer			
The National Bank Of Rensselaer	12773	–	–
Rhinebeck			
The First National Bank Of Rhinebeck	1157	3	5
Richburg			
The First National Bank Of Richburg	2553	6	–
Richfield Springs			
The First National Bank Of Richfield Springs	2651	4	5
Ridgewood			
The Ridgewood National Bank	9414	6	–
Ripley			
The First National Bank Of Ripley	6386	5	6
Riverhead			
The Suffolk County National Bank Of Riverhead	4230	5	4
Rochester			
Lincoln National Bank Of Rochester	8026	3	–
The Clarke National Bank Of Rochester	1397	5	–
The Commercial National Bank Of Rochester	2383	6	–
The Farmers And Mechanics National Bank Of Rochester	1072	6	–
The First National Bank And Trust Company Of Rochester	13330	–	3
The First National Bank Of Rochester	527	6	–
The Flour City National Bank Of Rochester	1362	3	–
The National Bank Of Commerce Of Rochester	8111	3	–
The National Bank Of Rochester	8026	3	–
The National Bank Of Rochester	12538	3	–
The National Union Bank Of Rochester	1282	6	–
The Traders National Bank Of Rochester	1104	2	–
Rockville Center			
The Nassau County National Bank Of Rockville Center	11033	–	–
Rockville Centre			
The First National Bank Of Rockville Centre	8872	6	6
Rome			
The Central National Bank Of Rome	1376	5	–
The Farmers National Bank And Trust Company Of Rome	2410	–	4
The Farmers National Bank Of Rome	2410	3	–
The First National Bank Of Rome	1414	5	–
The Fort Stanwix National Bank Of Rome	1410	4	–
Romulus			
The Romulus National Bank	11739	6	6
Rondout			
The First National Bank Of Rondout	34	5	–
The First National Bank Of Rondout, Kingston	2493	4	4
The National Bank Of Rondout	1120	6	–
The Rondout National Bank Of Kingston	1120	5	3
Roosevelt			
The First National Bank Of Roosevelt	11953	5	6
Roscoe			
The First National Bank & Trust Company Of Roscoe	8191	–	3
The First National Bank Of Roscoe	8191	4	–
Roslyn			
The Roslyn National Bank And Trust Company	13326	–	3
Rouses Point			
The First National Bank Of Rouses Point	11969	6	6
Roxbury			
The National Bank Of Roxbury	7678	6	4
Rye			
The Rye National Bank	5662	4	5
Saint Johnsville			
The First National Bank Of St. Johnsville	375	5	3
Saint Regis Falls			
The St. Regis Falls National Bank	7733	5	5
Salamanca			
The First National Bank Of Salamanca	2472	3	4
The Salamanca National Bank	2610	5	–
Salem			
The First National Bank Of Salem	3309	6	–
The National Bank Of Salem	1127	6	–
The Peoples National Bank Of Salem	3245	5	6
The Salem National Bank	7588	5	4
Sandy Hill			
The Commercial National Bank Of Sandy Hill	8297	6	–
The First National Bank Of Sandy Hill	184	6	–
The Hudson Falls National Bank, Hudson Falls	8297	6	6
The National Bank Of Sandy Hill	2838	6	–
The Peoples National Bank Of Hudson Falls	3244	6	–
The Peoples National Bank Of Sandy Hill	3244	5	–
The Sandy Hill National Bank	6470	6	–
The Sandy Hill National Bank Of Hudson Falls	6470	5	3
Saranac Lake			
Adirondack National Bank & Trust Company Of Saranac Lake	5072	6	4
The Adirondack National Bank Of Saranac Lake	5072	6	–
The Saranac Lake National Bank	8935	6	5
Saratoga Springs			
Saratoga National Bank Of Saratoga Springs	893	6	5
The Citizens National Bank Of Saratoga Springs	2615	4	–
The Commercial National Bank Of Saratoga Springs	1227	5	–
The First National Bank Of Saratoga Springs	893	4	–
Saugerties			
The First National Bank & Trust Company Of Saugerties	1040	6	4
The First National Bank Of Saugerties	1040	4	–
The Saugerties National Bank	1208	4	–
Savannah			
The National Bank Of Savannah	12810	–	–
Savona			
The Savona National Bank	11349	6	5
Sayville			
The Oystermen's National Bank Of Sayville	5186	4	4
Scarsdale			
Scarsdale National Bank And Trust Company, Scarsdale	11708	4	3
The Scarsdale National Bank	11708	4	–

City, Bank	Ch. No.	L	S
Schenectady			
The Mohawk National Bank Of Schenectady	1226	3	3
The Union National Bank Of Schenectady	4711	4	4
Schenevus			
The Schenevus National Bank	4962	4	5
Schoharie			
The Schoharie County National Bank Of Schoharie	1510	6	–
Schuylerville			
The National Bank Of Schuylerville	1298	5	6
Seaford			
The Seaford National Bank	12963	–	–
Seneca Falls			
The Exchange National Bank Of Seneca Falls	3329	3	–
The First National Bank Of Seneca Falls	102	6	–
The National Exchange Bank Of Seneca Falls	1240	5	–
Sharon Springs			
The First National Bank Of Sharon Springs	7512	6	3
Sherburne			
The Sherburne National Bank	1166	3	3
Sherrill			
The First National Bank Of Sherrill	12884	–	–
Sidney			
First National Bank In Sidney	13563	–	4
The Peoples National Bank Of Sidney	8513	5	–
The Sidney National Bank	3822	3	6
Silver Creek			
The First National Bank Of Silver Creek	10159	4	3
The Silver Creek National Bank	10258	3	3
Silver Springs			
The Silver Springs National Bank	6148	4	6
Sing Sing			
The First National Bank & Trust Company Of Ossining	471	4	3
The First National Bank Of Ossining	471	4	–
The First National Bank Of Sing Sing	471	6	–
Skaneateles			
National Bank And Trust Company Of Skaneateles	5360	6	4
The First National Bank Of Skaneateles	303	6	–
The National Bank Of Skaneateles	5360	3	–
Smithtown Branch			
The National Bank Of Smithtown Branch	9820	5	–
Sodus			
The First National Bank Of Sodus	9418	6	4
Somers			
The Farmers And Drovers National Bank Of Somers	1304	5	–
South East			
The Croton River National Bank Of South East	830	5	–
South Fallsburg			
The South Fallsburg National Bank	11809	4	5
South Glens Falls			
The First National Bank Of South Glens Falls	5851	6	5
South Otselic			
The Otselic Valley National Bank Of South Otselic	7774	5	3
South Worcester			
The First National Bank Of South Worcester	103	6	–
Southampton			
The First National Bank Of Southampton	10185	4	4
Sparkill			
The First National Bank Of Sparkill	10477	–	–
Spring Valley			
The First National Bank Of Spring Valley	5390	6	5
Springville			
The Citizens National Bank Of Springville	6330	4	3
The First National Bank Of Springville	2892	6	–
Stamford			
The National Bank Of Stamford	2602	4	4
Stapleton			
The Richmond Borough National Bank Of Stapleton	7290	6	–
The Stapleton National Bank	6562	4	–
Suffern			
The Suffern National Bank	5846	3	–
The Suffern National Bank & Trust Company, Suffern	5846	–	3
Syracuse			
Commercial National Bank Of Syracuse	6965	5	–
Lincoln National Bank & Trust Company Of Syracuse	13393	–	1
The American Exchange National Bank Of Syracuse	5286	6	–
The First National Bank Of Syracuse	6	3	–
The Fourth National Bank Of Syracuse	1569	6	–
The Liberty National Bank & Trust Company Of Syracuse	12122	–	–
The Liberty National Bank Of Syracuse	12122	6	–
The Lincoln National Bank And Trust Company Of Syracuse	13393	–	–
The Mechanics National Bank Of Syracuse	1401	6	–
The Merchants National Bank & Trust Company Of Syracuse	1342	4	4
The Merchants National Bank Of Syracuse	1342	4	–
The National Bank Of Syracuse	5465	4	–
The Salt Springs National Bank Of Syracuse	1287	4	–
The Second National Bank Of Syracuse	140	6	–
The Syracuse National Bank	1341	6	–
The Third National Bank Of Syracuse	159	3	–
Tannersville			
The Mountains National Bank Of Tannersville	11057	4	4
Tarrytown			
The First National Bank Of Tarrytown	364	6	–
The Tarrytown National Bank	2626	4	–
The Tarrytown National Bank & Trust Company, Tarrytown	2626	–	–
Theresa			
The Farmers National Bank Of Theresa	8158	6	4
Ticonderoga			
The First National Bank Of Ticonderoga	4491	6	–
The Ticonderoga National Bank	9900	6	4
Tonawanda			
The First National Bank Of Tonawanda	4869	3	–
Tottenville			
The Tottenville National Bank	8334	5	6
Trenton			
The First National Bank Of Trenton	11238	–	–
Troy			
The Central National Bank Of Troy	1012	5	–
The First National Bank Of Troy	163	5	–
The Manufacturers National Bank Of Troy	721	3	2
The Merchants And Mechanics National Bank Of Troy	904	6	–
The Mutual National Bank Of Troy	992	3	–
The National Bank Of Troy	2873	6	–
The National City Bank Of Troy	7612	3	3
The National Exchange Bank Of Troy	621	6	–
The National State Bank Of Troy	991	3	–
The Troy City National Bank	640	4	–
The Union National Bank Of Troy	963	4	3
The United National Bank Of Troy	940	3	5
Trumansburg			
The First National Bank Of Trumansburg	7541	4	5
The State National Bank Of Trumansburg	12417	–	–
Tuckahoe			
The Crestwood National Bank In Tuckahoe	13889	–	6
The Crestwood National Bank Of Tuckahoe	12940	–	–
The First National Bank & Trust Company Of Tuckahoe	10525	5	3
The First National Bank Of Tuckahoe	10525	5	–
Tully			
The First National Bank Of Tully	5746	5	6
Tupper Lake			
The Tupper Lake National Bank	8153	5	5
Tuxedo			
The National Bank Of Tuxedo	13895	–	–
The Tuxedo National Bank	11404	5	6
Unadilla			
The National Unadilla Bank Of Unadilla	1463	6	–
The Unadilla National Bank	9516	2	4
Union			
The Farmers National Bank Of Union	9276	6	–
Union Springs			
The First National Bank Of Union Springs	342	6	–
Unionville			
The First National Bank Of Unionville	11448	6	5
Utica			
First National Bank And Trust Company Of Utica	1395	4	–
The First National Bank Of Utica	120	6	–
The First National Bank Of Utica	1395	2	–
The Oneida National Bank And Trust Company Of Utica	1392	–	2
The Oneida National Bank Of Utica	1392	2	–
The Second National Bank Of Utica	185	3	–
The Utica City National Bank Of Utica	1308	3	–
Utica National Bank And Trust Company, Utica	1308	4	5
Valley Stream			
The Valley Stream National Bank	11881	5	–
Valley Stream Natl Bank & Trust Company, Valley Stream	11881	6	4
Vernon			
The National Bank Of Vernon	1264	3	5
Walden			
The First National Bank & Trust Company Of Walden	10923	–	4
The National Bank Of Walden	5053	5	–
The Third National Bank Of Walden	10923	5	–
The Walden National Bank	2348	5	–
Wallkill			
The Wallkill National Bank	10155	6	3
Walton			
The First National Bank & Trust Company Of Walton	4495	–	4
The First National Bank Of Walton	4495	3	–
Wappingers Falls			
The National Bank Of Wappingers Falls	9326	6	6
Warrensburgh			
The Emerson National Bank Of Warrensburgh	9135	5	5
Warsaw			
The Wyoming County National Bank Of Warsaw	737	4	3
Warwick			
The First National Bank Of Warwick	314	5	4
Washingtonville			
The Central National Bank Of Washingtonville	13913	–	–
The First National Bank Of Washingtonville	9065	6	6
The First National Bank Of Washingtonville	13545	–	–
Waterford			
The Saratoga County National Bank Of Waterford	1229	6	–
Waterloo			
The First National Bank Of Waterloo	368	5	3
Watertown			
The City National Bank Of Watertown	4296	6	–
The First National Bank Of Watertown	73	6	–
The Jefferson County National Bank Of Watertown	1490	4	3
The National Bank And Loan Company Of Watertown	1508	4	–
The National Union Bank Of Watertown	1507	4	–
The Second National Bank Of Watertown	671	6	–
The Watertown National Bank	2657	4	3
Waterville			
The National Bank Of Waterville	1361	5	4
Watkins			
Glen National Bank Of Watkins	9977	5	5
The First National Bank Of Penn Yan	358	6	–
The First National Bank Of Watkins	358	6	–
The First National Bank Of Watkins	3047	6	–
The Second National Bank Of Watkins	456	4	–
The Watkins National Bank, Watkins	456	6	–
Waverly			
The Citizens National Bank Of Waverly	12954	5	4
The First National Bank Of Waverly	297	4	4
The Waverly National Bank	1192	5	–
Wayland			
The First National Bank Of Wayland	5196	4	4
Webster			
Webster National Bank	13145	6	5
Weedsport			
The First National Bank Of Weedsport	11020	5	4
Wells			
The Hamilton County National Bank Of Wells	13289	–	6
Wellsville			
The Citizens National Bank Of Wellsville	4988	4	4
The First National Bank Of Wellsville	2850	5	–
West Hempstead			
The West Hempstead National Bank, Hempstead	13104	–	6
West Seneca			
Lackawanna National Bank, Lackawanna	6964	–	3
The Lackawanna National Bank Of West Seneca	6964	6	–
The Lackawanna National Bank, Lackawanna	6964	4	–
The Seneca National Bank Of West Seneca	12925	5	6
West Troy			
The National Bank Of Watervliet	1265	3	4
The National Bank Of West Troy	1265	5	–
West Winfield			
The First National Bank Of West Winfield	801	4	–
The West Winfield National Bank	7483	5	5
Westbury			
The Wheatley Hills National Bank Of Westbury	11730	6	5
Westfield			
The First National Bank Of Westfield	504	6	–
The Grape Belt National Bank Of Westfield	12476	4	6
The National Bank Of Westfield	3166	3	4
Westport			
The Lake Champlain National Bank Of Westport	9405	5	6
White Plains			
The First National Bank Of White Plains	6351	5	–
The Peoples National Bank & Trust Company Of White Plains	12574	5	5
The Peoples National Bank Of White Plains	12574	5	–
The Plaza National Bank Of White Plains	13409	–	–
Whitehall			
The First National Bank Of Whitehall	285	6	–
The Merchants National Bank Of Whitehall	2233	4	3
The National Bank Of Whitehall	8388	5	6
The Old National Bank Of Whitehall	1160	5	–
Whitesboro			
The Whitestown National Bank Of Whitesboro	11284	5	–
Whitestone			
The First National Bank Of Whitestone	8957	5	–
Whitestown			
The National Bank Of Whitestown	1458	6	–
Whitesville			
The First National Bank Of Whitesville	7850	6	6
Whitney Point			
The First National Bank Of Whitney Point	7679	6	4
Williston Park			
The Williston National Bank Of Williston Park	13124	–	–
Willsboro			
The Essex County National Bank Of Willsboro	11971	6	6
Windham			
The First National Bank Of Windham	12164	–	4
The National Bank Of Windham	13962	–	2
Windsor			
The Windsor National Bank	9415	5	4
Winthrop			
The First National Bank Of Winthrop	10747	5	5
Wolcott			
The First National Bank Of Wolcott	5928	5	4
Woodmere			
The Hewlett-Woodmere National Bank Of Woodmere	12294	6	6
Woodridge			
The First National Bank Of Woodridge	11059	4	5
Wyoming			
The National Bank Of Wyoming	13229	–	4
Yonkers			
Central National Bank Of Yonkers	13319	–	3
The Bryn Mawr-Nepperhan National Bank Of Yonkers	13239	–	–
The Citizens National Bank Of The City Of Yonkers	2074	5	–
The First National Bank & Trust Company Of Yonkers	653	–	3
The First National Bank Of Yonkers	653	2	6
The First National Bank Of Yonkers	13882	–	–
The Yonkers National Bank	9825	5	–
The Yonkers National Bank And Trust Company, Yonkers	9825	5	3

NORTH CAROLINA

City, Bank	Ch. No.	L	S
Albemarle			
The First National Bank Of Albemarle	11091	6	2
Asheboro			
The First National Bank Of Asheboro	8953	6	5
Asheville			
First National Bank And Trust Company Of Asheville	12244	–	3
The American National Bank Of Asheville	8772	4	5
The Blue Ridge National Bank Of Asheville	5110	5	–
The First National Bank And Trust Company Of Asheville	13721	–	–
The First National Bank Of Asheville	3418	6	–
The National Bank Of Asheville	4094	6	–
The National Bank Of Commerce Of Asheville	12244	5	5
Ayden			
First National Bank In Ayden	13554	–	5
The Farmers And Merchants National Bank Of Ayden	10792	–	–
The First National Bank Of Ayden	10792	–	–
Benson			
The First National Bank Of Benson	12614	3	–
Burlington			
The First National Bank Of Burlington	8649	4	6
The National Bank Of Burlington	13613	–	3

City, Bank	Ch. No.	L	S
Charlotte			
The Charlotte National Bank	5055	3	1
The Commercial National Bank Of Charlotte	2135	1	2
The First National Bank Of Charlotte	1547	3	3
The Merchants And Farmers National Bank Of Charlotte	1781	3	3
The Traders National Bank Of Charlotte	2314	6	–
The Union National Bank Of Charlotte	9164	3	3
Cherryville			
The Cherryville National Bank	12896	–	–
The Cherryville National Bank	14229	–	–
The First National Bank Of Cherryville	9548	4	–
Concord			
The Concord National Bank	3903	3	4
Creedmoor			
The First National Bank Of Creedmoor	8902	5	–
Dunn			
The First National Bank Of Dunn	7188	1	–
Durham			
The Citizens National Bank Of Durham	7698	4	4
The Depositors National Bank Of Durham	13657	–	3
The First National Bank Of Durham	3811	2	2
Elizabeth City			
The First And Citizens National Bank Of Elizabeth City	4628	2	3
The First National Bank Of Elizabeth City	4628	5	–
Elkin			
The Elkin National Bank	5673	5	6
Fairmont			
The First National Bank Of Fairmont	12009	–	–
Fayetteville			
Fourth National Bank Of Fayetteville	8682	5	–
The Cumberland National Bank Of Fayetteville	13168	–	–
The Fayetteville National Bank	1756	4	–
The National Bank Of Fayetteville	5677	3	–
The Peoples National Bank Of Fayetteville	2003	5	–
Forest City			
The First National Bank Of Forest City	9203	6	–
The First National Bank Of Forest City	13500	–	–
The National Bank Of Forest City	12461	5	–
Gastonia			
The Citizens National Bank Of Gastonia	7536	2	2
The Citizens National Bank Of Gastonia	13779	–	–
The First National Bank Of Gastonia	4377	3	2
The National Bank Of Commerce	14291	–	–
The Third National Bank Of Gastonia	11477	5	–
Goldsboro			
The National Bank Of Goldsboro	5048	4	5
The Wayne National Bank Of Goldsboro	10614	3	4
Graham			
The National Bank Of Alamance Of Graham	8844	4	4
Greensboro			
American Exchange National Bank Of Greensboro	10112	3	–
American National Bank And Trust Company Of Greensboro	10112	5	–
Security National Bank Of Greensboro	13761	–	3
The American Exchange National Bank Of Greensboro	10112	4	–
The City National Bank Of Greensboro	5168	6	–
The Commercial National Bank Of Greensboro	9123	6	–
The Greensboro National Bank	5031	3	–
The Guilford National Bank Of Greensboro	13985	–	–
The National Bank Of Greensboro	2322	4	–
Greenville			
The National Bank Of Greenville	8160	5	6
Hamlet			
The First National Bank Of Hamlet	10851	6	–
Henderson			
First National Bank In Henderson	13636	–	3
The First National Bank Of Henderson	7564	3	4
Hendersonville			
The Citizens National Bank Of Hendersonville	10734	4	6
The First National Bank Of Hendersonville	8837	6	–
The Peoples National Bank Of Hendersonville	9571	6	–
Hertford			
The Farmers National Bank Of Hertford	10876	–	–
Hickory			
The First National Bank Of Hickory	4597	4	2
High Point			
The Commercial National Bank Of High Point	4568	2	3
The First National Bank Of High Point	3490	6	–
The National Bank Of High Point	3490	6	–
Jefferson			
The First National Bank Of Jefferson	8571	6	–
Kings Mountain			
The First National Bank Of Kings Mountain	5451	4	3
Kinston			
The First National Bank Of Kinston	9085	4	6
The National Bank Of Kinston	9044	5	6
La Grange			
The National Bank Of La Grange	12633	–	–
Laurinburg			
The First National Bank Of Laurinburg	5651	6	6
Leaksville			
The First National Bank Of Leaksville	12259	5	5
Lenoir			
The First National Bank Of Lenoir	8445	5	6
The Union National Bank Of Lenoir	13523	–	6
Lexington			
The First National Bank Of Lexington	5698	6	–
The National Bank Of Lexington	5698	6	–
Lincolnton			
The County National Bank Of Lincolnton	8184	6	–
The First National Bank Of Lincolnton	6744	3	1
Louisburg			
The Farmers National Bank Of Louisburg	10260	4	–
The First National Bank Of Louisburg	7554	4	5
Lumberton			
The First National Bank Of Lumberton	7398	4	–
The National Bank Of Lumberton	10610	6	–
Marion			
The First National Bank Of Marion	6095	4	3

City, Bank	Ch. No.	L	S
Mebane			
The First National Bank Of Mebane	11697	5	3
Monroe			
The First National Bank Of Monroe	8712	4	4
Mooresville			
The First National Bank Of Mooresville	9531	5	4
Morganton			
The First National Bank Of Morganton	5450	5	4
Mount Airy			
The First National Bank Of Mount Airy	4896	5	–
Mount Olive			
The First National Bank Of Mount Olive	10629	6	5
Murfreesboro			
The First National Bank Of Murfreesboro	11557	6	–
Murphy			
The First National Bank Of Murphy	9458	6	–
New Bern			
The First National Bank Of New Bern	13298	–	5
New Berne			
The National Bank Of New Berne	1632	4	–
Newton			
The Shuford National Bank Of Newton	6075	6	4
Oxford			
The First National Bank Of Oxford	5885	4	–
The National Bank Of Granville At Oxford	8996	5	–
The Oxford National Bank	13896	–	–
The Union National Bank Of Oxford	13859	–	–
Raleigh			
The Citizens National Bank Of Raleigh	1766	3	–
The Commercial National Bank Of Raleigh	9067	2	4
The Merchants National Bank Of Raleigh	9471	4	–
The National Bank Of Raleigh	3389	6	–
The Raleigh National Bank Of North Carolina	1557	4	–
The State National Bank Of Raleigh	1682	6	–
Reidsville			
First National Bank Of Reidsville	11229	6	4
Rocky Mount			
The First National Bank Of Rocky Mount	7362	6	–
The First National Bank Of Rocky Mount	10630	6	–
The National Bank Of Rocky Mount	10630	6	–
The Planters National Bank & Trust Company Of Rocky Mount	10608	–	5
The Planters National Bank Of Rocky Mount	10608	5	6
Roxboro			
The First National Bank Of Roxboro	11211	–	–
Salem			
The First National Bank Of Salem	1659	6	–
Salisbury			
The First National Bank Of Salisbury	2981	2	3
The Peoples National Bank Of Salisbury	9076	4	–
Sanford			
The First National Bank Of Sanford	6616	6	–
The National Bank Of Lillington	6616	6	–
The National Bank Of Sanford	13791	–	6
Selma			
The First National Bank Of Selma	10739	5	–
Shelby			
Shelby National Bank	7959	5	–
The First National Bank Of Shelby	6776	3	2
Smithfield			
The Citizens National Bank Of Smithfield	11440	6	–
The First & Citizens National Bank Of Smithfield	10502	4	–
The First National Bank Of Smithfield	10502	5	–
Snow Hill			
The First National Bank Of Snow Hill	10887	5	–
The National Bank Of Snow Hill	12772	–	–
Spencer			
The First National Bank Of Spencer	10662	–	–
Spring Hope			
The First National Bank Of Spring Hope	11431	–	–
Statesville			
The Commercial National Bank Of Statesville	9335	5	–
The First National Bank Of Statesville	3682	5	5
Tarboro			
The Edgecombe National Bank Of Tarboro	13306	–	–
The First National Bank Of Tarboro	8356	5	–
Thomasville			
The First National Bank Of Thomasville	8788	3	2
Wadesboro			
The First National Bank Of Wadesboro	4947	4	3
Warsaw			
The First National Bank Of Warsaw	11767	6	–
Washington			
The First National Bank Of Washington	4997	4	4
Waynesville			
The First National Bank Of Waynesville	6554	6	4
Weldon			
The First National Bank Of Roanoke Rapids	5767	3	–
The First National Bank Of Weldon	5767	6	–
West Jefferson			
The First National Bank Of West Jefferson	8571	6	5
Wilmington			
The American National Bank Of Wilmington	9124	5	–
The Atlantic National Bank Of Wilmington	4726	5	–
The Commercial National Bank Of Wilmington	12176	6	–
The First National Bank Of Wilmington	1656	6	–
The Murchison National Bank Of Wilmington	5182	1	–
The National Bank Of Wilmington	4960	6	–
The Southern National Bank Of Wilmington	7913	6	–
Wilson			
National Bank Of Wilson	13626	–	5
The First National Bank Of Wilson	2321	4	6
Winston			
The First National Bank Of Winston	2319	6	–
The Merchants National Bank Of Winston	9916	5	–
The Peoples National Bank Of Winston	4292	3	5
The Wachovia National Bank Of Winston	2425	6	–
Winston-Salem			
The Farmers National Bank And Trust Company Of Winston-Salem	12278	3	2
The First National Bank Of Winston-Salem	14147	–	–

NORTH DAKOTA

City, Bank	Ch. No.	L	S
Abercrombie			
The First National Bank Of Abercrombie	8419	6	–
Alexander			
The First National Bank Of Alexander	11297	5	–
Ambrose			
The First National Bank Of Ambrose	9386	6	6
Anamoose			
The Anamoose National Bank	9390	5	–
The First National Bank Of Anamoose	9412	6	–
Aneta			
The First National Bank Of Aneta	11311	–	–
Antler			
The First National Bank Of Antler	7855	6	–
Ashley			
The First National Bank Of Ashley	10864	4	6
Bathgate			
The Bathgate National Bank	11112	5	6
The First National Bank Of Bathgate	4537	6	–
Beach			
The First National Bank Of Beach	9484	5	–
Belfield			
The First National Bank Of Belfield	9539	4	4
Binford			
The First National Bank Of Binford	8265	6	4
Bisbee			
The First National Bank Of Bisbee	6733	5	–
Bismarck			
The Capital National Bank Of Bismarck	2986	6	–
The City National Bank Of Bismarck	9622	5	–
The Dakota National Bank And Trust Company Of Bismarck	13398	–	3
The First National Bank Of Bismarck	2434	3	3
Bottineau			
The Bottineau National Bank	7879	6	6
The First National Bank Of Bottineau	6085	5	–
Bowbells			
The First National Bank Of Bowbells	7116	6	4
Bowman			
The First National Bank Of Bowman	8976	6	4
Brinsmade			
The First National Bank Of Brinsmade	8502	6	–
Buffalo			
The First National Bank Of Buffalo	6559	5	4
Buxton			
The First National Bank Of Buxton	10814	6	3
Cando			
The Cando National Bank	7377	6	–
The First National Bank Of Cando	5798	6	4
Carpio			
The First National Bank Of Carpio	7315	5	4
Carrington			
The First National Bank Of Carrington	5551	5	–
Carson			
The First National Bank Of Carson	13454	–	3
Casselton			
The Cass County National Bank Of Casselton	7142	5	–
The First National Bank Of Casselton	2792	4	5
Cavalier			
The First National Bank Of Cavalier	10116	6	–
The Merchants National Bank Of Cavalier	12046	–	–
Churchs Ferry			
The First National Bank Of Churchs Ferry	6337	6	4
Cooperstown			
The First National Bank In Cooperstown	13362	–	3
The First National Bank Of Cooperstown	5375	5	–
Courtenay			
The First National Bank Of Courtenay	6210	6	6
Crary			
The First National Bank Of Crary	6407	5	5
Crosby			
The Citizens National Bank Of Crosby	10519	–	–
The First National Bank Of Crosby	10596	5	5
Crystal			
The First National Bank Of Crystal	7918	6	–
Devil's Lake			
The First National Bank Of Devil's Lake	3397	3	4
The Merchants National Bank Of Devil's Lake	3714	6	–
The Ramsey County National Bank Of Devil's Lake	5886	5	3
Dickinson			
The Dakota National Bank Of Dickinson	7663	5	–
The First National Bank Of Dickinson	4384	5	2
The Liberty National Bank Of Dickinson	12401	6	5
The Merchants National Bank Of Dickinson	8201	4	–
Donnybrook			
The First National Bank Of Donnybrook	12258	–	–
Drake			
First National Bank In Drake	12393	6	3
The First National Bank Of Drake	9524	6	–
Drayton			
The First National Bank Of Drayton	6225	4	–
East Fairview			
The First National Bank Of East Fairview	10425	6	–
Edgeley			
The First National Bank Of Edgeley	7914	4	–
The Security National Bank Of Edgeley	12003	–	–
Edmore			
The First National Bank Of Edmore	6601	6	6
Egeland			
The First National Bank Of Egeland	7872	6	6
Ellendale			
The Ellendale National Bank	9631	6	–
The Farmers National Bank Of Ellendale	9521	5	–
The First National Bank Of Ellendale	6398	4	4
Enderlin			
The First National Bank Of Enderlin	6486	6	–
Fairmount			
The First National Bank Of Fairmount	6255	5	–
The National Bank Of Fairmount	11641	–	–

City, Bank	Ch. No.	L	S
Fargo			
The Citizens National Bank Of Fargo	3602	6	–
The Dakota National Bank Of Fargo	12026	4	3
The Fargo National Bank	5087	4	3
The First National Bank & Trust Company Of Fargo	2377	–	2
The First National Bank Of Fargo	2377	3	–
The Merchants National Bank And Trust Company Of Fargo	13323	–	3
The Merchants National Bank Of Fargo	8170	3	–
The National Bank Of North Dakota, Fargo	4256	6	–
The Northern National Bank Of Fargo	11786	–	–
The Red River Valley National Bank Of Fargo	2514	5	–
The Security National Bank Of Fargo	11555	4	–
Fessenden			
The First National Bank Of Fessenden	5408	5	4
Fingal			
The First National Bank Of Fingal	7295	6	5
Finley			
The First National Bank Of Finley	7324	5	–
The Steele County National Bank Of Finley	13190	–	–
Forman			
The First National Bank Of Forman	6474	6	6
Fullerton			
The First National Bank Of Fullerton	11217	–	–
Gackle			
The First National Bank Of Gackle	12853	–	–
Garrison			
First National Bank In Garrison	13501	–	6
The First National Bank Of Garrison	9778	6	6
Glen Ullin			
First National Bank In Glen Ullin	13410	–	3
The First National Bank Of Glen Ullin	9016	6	–
Golva			
The First National Bank Of Golva	11346	–	–
Goodrich			
The First National Bank Of Goodrich	8077	6	5
Grafton			
The First National Bank Of Grafton	2840	4	–
The Grafton National Bank	3096	4	1
Grand Forks			
First National Bank In Grand Forks	13790	–	3
First National Bank Of Grand Forks	2570	–	1
The First National Bank Of Grand Forks	2570	3	–
The Grand Forks National Bank	3301	6	–
The Merchants National Bank Of Grand Forks	4812	6	–
The Northwestern National Bank Of Grand Forks	11142	3	–
The Red River National Bank & Trust Company Of Grand Forks	13357	–	–
The Second National Bank Of Grand Forks	3504	6	–
The Union National Bank Of Grand Forks	4372	6	–
Hampden			
The First National Bank Of Hampden	7650	6	5
Hankinson			
The Citizens National Bank Of Hankinson	8084	6	–
The First National Bank Of Hankinson	6218	4	5
Hannaford			
The First National Bank Of Hannaford	7727	6	–
Harvey			
The First National Bank Of Harvey	5488	4	4
Hatton			
The Farmers And Merchants National Bank Of Hatton	7905	6	4
The First National Bank Of Hatton	6743	6	6
Hebron			
The First National Bank Of Hebron	10741	5	4
Hettinger			
The First National Bank Of Hettinger	8991	5	5
The Livestock National Bank Of Hettinger	11677	6	–
Hillsboro			
First National Bank Of Hillsboro	3400	–	4
The First National Bank Of Hillsboro	3400	5	–
The Hillsboro National Bank	3411	4	–
Hope			
The First National Bank Of Hope	5893	4	–
The Hope National Bank	8395	4	–
The Security National Bank Of Hope	13041	–	–
Hunter			
The First National Bank Of Hunter	6985	6	6
Jamestown			
Citizens National Bank Of Jamestown	7820	6	–
The Farmers And Merchants National Bank Of Jamestown	10495	–	–
The James River National Bank Of Jamestown	2580	6	6
The James River National Bank Of Jamestown	2580	–	–
The James River Natl Bank & Trust Co. Of Jamestown	2580	–	4
The Lloyds National Bank Of Jamestown	4561	6	–
The National Bank And Trust Company Of Jamestown	13344	–	–
The National Bank Of Jamestown	13344	–	–
Kenmare			
First-kenmare National Bank	6555	–	6
The First National Bank Of Kenmare	6064	5	6
The Kenmare National Bank	6555	6	5
Kensal			
The First National Bank Of Kensal	7943	6	–
Killdeer			
The First National Bank Of Killdeer	10820	–	–
Knox			
The First National Bank Of Knox	6898	6	–
Kramer			
First National Bank In Bottineau	8029	–	–
The First National Bank Of Kramer	8029	5	5
Kulm			
First National Bank Of Kulm	11069	5	6
La Moure County First National Bank Of Kulm	11069	–	–
The First National Bank Of Kulm	11069	–	–
La Moure			
The Farmers National Bank Of La Moure	9714	5	–
The First National Bank Of La Moure	6690	4	5
Lakota			
The First National Bank Of Lakota	4143	6	–
The National Bank Of Lakota	5455	6	6
Langdon			
The Cavalier County National Bank Of Langdon	9075	5	–
The First National Bank Of Langdon	4802	5	–
The First National Bank Of Langdon	13053	–	–
Lansford			
The First National Bank Of Lansford	8187	6	–
Larimore			
The First National Bank Of Larimore	2854	6	–
The National Bank Of Larimore	6286	5	–
Leeds			
The First National Bank Of Leeds	6312	5	–
Lidgerwood			
Farmers National Bank Of Lidgerwood	8230	6	–
First National Bank In Lidgerwood	12776	6	4
The Farmers National Bank Of Lidgerwood	12743	–	–
The First National Bank Of Lidgerwood	5772	4	–
The Lidgerwood National Bank	8230	6	–
Linton			
The City National Bank Of Linton	11665	–	–
The First National Bank Of Linton	9590	6	5
Lisbon			
The First National Bank Of Lisbon	3669	5	–
Litchville			
The First National Bank Of Litchville	8298	4	6
Maddock			
The First National Bank Of Maddock	8226	6	–
Makoti			
The First National Bank Of Makoti	11184	6	6
Mandan			
The First National Bank Of Mandan	2585	4	4
The Merchants National Bank Of Mandan	10604	5	–
Marion			
The First National Bank Of Marion	9161	6	–
Marmarth			
The First National Bank Of Marmarth	9082	5	4
Max			
The First National Bank Of Max	11719	–	–
Mayville			
The First National Bank Of Mayville	3673	6	–
Mcclusky			
The First National Bank Of Mcclusky	8881	6	6
Mccumber			
The First National Bank Of Mccumber	7846	6	–
Mchenry			
The First National Bank Of Mchenry	8124	6	–
Mcville			
The First National Bank Of Mcville	10721	5	6
Medina			
The First National Bank Of Medina	10581	–	–
Michigan City			
The Lambs National Bank Of Michigan City	12023	–	–
Milnor			
The First National Bank Of Milnor	8280	6	4
The Milnor National Bank	8264	5	–
Milton			
The First National Bank Of Milton	6518	5	–
Minnewaukan			
The First National Bank Of Minnewaukan	5500	6	–
Minot			
First National Bank & Trust Company In Minot	6429	–	3
First National Bank In Minot	6429	6	6
First National Bank In Minot	6429	–	6
The First National Bank Of Minot	4009	6	–
The Minot National Bank	6315	6	–
The Second National Bank Of Minot	6429	4	–
The Union National Bank And Trust Company Of Minot	13455	–	–
The Union National Bank In Minot	13455	–	–
The Union National Bank Of Minot	7689	4	6
Mohall			
First National Bank Of Mohall	7008	5	–
Montpelier			
The First National Bank Of Montpelier	11494	–	–
Mooreton			
The First National Bank Of Mooreton	11605	–	–
Mott			
The First National Bank Of Mott	9489	6	3
The First National Bank Of Mott	14080	–	–
Munich			
The First National Bank Of Munich	7569	6	5
Mylo			
The First National Bank Of Mylo	7857	6	–
Napoleon			
The First National Bank Of Napoleon	11378	–	4
Neche			
The First National Bank Of Neche	11110	6	6
The First National Bank Of Neche	13436	–	–
New England			
The First National Bank Of New England	9776	5	3
New Rockford			
The First National Bank Of New Rockford	6393	5	4
New Salem			
The First National Bank Of New Salem	6428	6	–
Nome			
The First National Bank Of Nome	9287	6	–
Northwood			
The Citizens National Bank Of Northwood	9754	5	5
The First National Bank Of Northwood	5980	5	6
Oakes			
The First National Bank Of Oakes	6457	6	3
The Oakes National Bank	6988	5	–
Omemee			
The First National Bank Of Omemee	6475	6	6
Osnabrock			
The First National Bank Of Osnabrock	7234	4	5
Overly			
The First National Bank Of Overly	8096	6	–
Page			
The First National Bank Of Page	6463	6	4
Park River			
The First National Bank Of Park River	3436	5	5
Parshall			
The First National Bank Of Parshall	11226	6	6
Pembina			
The First National Bank Of Pembina	3438	6	–
Petersburg			
The First National Bank Of Petersburg	11185	5	6
Plaza			
The First National Bank Of Plaza	9689	6	5
Portland			
The Farmers National Bank Of Portland	10896	–	–
The First And Farmers National Bank Of Portland	13594	–	5
The First National Bank Of Portland	7693	6	6
Reeder			
The First National Bank Of Reeder	9684	5	6
Reynolds			
The First National Bank Of Reynolds	10496	5	5
Rock Lake			
The First National Bank Of Rock Lake	8019	5	5
Rolette			
The First National Bank Of Rolette	7866	5	–
Rolla			
The First National Bank Of Rolla	6157	6	5
Rugby			
The First National Bank Of Rugby	6341	6	–
Ryder			
The First National Bank Of Ryder	9214	5	5
Saint Thomas			
The First National Bank Of Saint Thomas	4550	5	6
Sanborn			
The First National Bank Of Sanborn	8448	4	–
Sarles			
The First National Bank Of Adams	7852	6	–
The First National Bank Of Sarles	7852	–	–
Scranton			
The First National Bank Of Scranton	10405	6	6
Sentinel Butte			
The First National Bank Of Sentinel Butte	10706	–	–
Sharon			
The First National Bank Of Sharon	9005	4	4
Sheldon			
The First National Bank Of Sheldon	6977	5	–
Sheyenne			
The First National Bank Of Sheyenne	8886	4	–
Stanley			
The First National Bank Of Stanley	9472	6	–
Starkweather			
The First National Bank Of Starkweather	6397	6	5
Steele			
The First National Bank Of Steele	8997	6	5
Streeter			
The Citizens National Bank Of Streeter	11166	–	–
The First National Bank Of Streeter	10724	6	–
Taylor			
The First National Bank Of Taylor	10921	–	–
The Security National Bank Of Taylor	12502	–	4
Thompson			
The First National Bank Of Thompson	11599	–	3
Tolley			
The First National Bank Of Tolley	7810	6	–
Tower City			
The First National Bank Of Tower City	6557	5	6
Towner			
The First National Bank Of Towner	7955	6	–
Turtle Lake			
The First National Bank Of Turtle Lake	8821	6	–
Tuttle			
The First National Bank Of Tuttle	11338	6	–
Underwood			
The First National Bank Of Underwood	11272	–	–
Valley City			
First National Bank Of Valley City	13324	–	6
The American National Bank And Trust Company Of Valley City	13385	–	2
The American National Bank Of Valley City	5364	4	–
The American National Bank Of Valley City	13385	–	6
The First & Security National Bank Of Valley City	11417	6	–
The First National Bank Of Valley City	2548	4	–
The First National Bank Of Valley City	12817	–	–
The National Bank Of Valley City	13324	–	3
The Security National Bank Of Valley City	11417	4	–
Van Hook			
The First National Bank Of Van Hook	10966	4	5
Wahpeton			
The Citizens National Bank Of Wahpeton	4552	4	2
The German-American National Bank Of Wahpeton	7695	6	–
The National Bank In Wahpeton	12875	–	5
The National Bank Of Wahpeton	4106	4	–
Walhalla			
The First National Bank Of Walhalla	9133	4	4
Washburn			
The First National Bank Of Washburn	6327	5	5
Westhope			
The First National Bank Of Westhope	7162	6	–
Whitman			
The First National Bank Of Whitman	12464	–	–
Williston			
The Citizens National Bank Of Williston	8324	6	–
The First And Commercial National Bank Of Williston	14275	–	–
The First National Bank Of Williston	5567	6	5
Willow City			
The First National Bank Of Willow City	6766	6	–
The Merchants National Bank Of Willow City	7332	6	5
Wilton			
The First National Bank Of Wilton	11712	5	5
Wimbledon			
The First National Bank Of Wimbledon	6712	6	–
The Merchants National Bank Of Wimbledon	8917	6	–
Woodworth			
The First National Bank Of Woodworth	11353	–	–
Wyndmere			
The First National Bank Of Wyndmere	7166	5	–

City, Bank	Ch. No.	L	S
Yates			
The First National Bank Of Yates	9698	6	–
OHIO			
Ada			
The First National Bank Of Ada	5425	4	5
Adena			
The Peoples National Bank Of Adena	6016	6	–
Akron			
The Citizens National Bank Of Akron	4961	6	–
The City National Bank Of Akron	2946	6	–
The First National Bank Of Akron	27	5	–
The First National Bank Of Akron	2698	6	–
The First-Second National Bank Of Akron	9953	6	–
The National City Bank Of Akron	6763	6	–
The Second National Bank Of Akron	40	6	–
The Second National Bank Of Akron	2716	5	–
Alliance			
Alliance First National Bank, Alliance	3421	4	4
The Alliance National Bank	12034	–	–
The First National Bank Of Alliance	2041	6	–
The First National Bank Of Alliance	3721	6	–
Amesville			
The First National Bank Of Amesville	7235	6	5
Ansonia			
The First National Bank Of Ansonia	9194	6	6
Antwerp			
The First National Bank Of Antwerp	11723	–	–
Arcanum			
The Arcanum National Bank	14188	–	–
The Farmers National Bank Of Arcanum	9255	6	–
The First National Bank Of Arcanum	4839	5	–
The First-Farmers National Bank Of Arcanum	4839	6	4
Arnettsville			
The First National Bank Of Arnettsville	9563	–	–
The First National Bank Of Pitsburg	9563	6	6
Ashland			
The First National Bank Of Ashland	183	5	5
Ashtabula			
The Ashtabula National Bank	2031	5	–
The Farmers National Bank And Trust Company Of Ashtabula	975	–	4
The Farmers National Bank Of Ashtabula	975	6	6
The Marine National Bank Of Ashtabula	4506	5	4
The Marine National Bank Of Sweden Of Ashtabula	4506	6	–
The National Bank Of Ashtabula	5075	4	4
Athens			
The Athens National Bank	7744	5	4
The Bank Of Athens National Banking Association	10479	6	5
The First National Bank Of Athens	233	6	–
Baltimore			
The First National Bank Of Baltimore	7639	6	6
Barberton			
The American National Bank Of Barberton	5819	6	–
The First National Bank Of Barberton	5230	6	–
Barnesville			
The First National Bank Of Barnesville	911	4	5
The National Bank Of Barnesville	6621	6	–
The Peoples National Bank Of Barnesville	2908	6	–
Batavia			
The First National Bank Of Batavia	715	4	5
Batesville			
The First National Bank Of Batesville	2219	6	–
Beallsville			
The First National Bank Of Beallsville	7025	6	6
Bellaire			
Farmers And Merchants National Bank In Bellaire	13996	–	5
First National Bank In Bellaire	13914	–	5
The Farmers And Merchants National Bank Of Bellaire	7327	5	4
The First National Bank Of Bellaire	1944	4	4
Bellefontaine			
Bellefontaine National Bank	13749	–	–
The Bellefontaine National Bank	1784	4	4
The Peoples National Bank In Bellefontaine	11726	6	–
The Peoples National Bank Of Bellefontaine	2480	6	–
Bellevue			
The First National Bank Of Bellevue	2302	5	5
Belmont			
The Belmont National Bank	6391	5	6
The First National Bank Of Belmont	4864	6	–
Belpre			
The First National Bank Of Belpre	8420	6	–
Berea			
The First National Bank Of Berea	2004	6	–
Bethel			
The First National Bank Of Bethel	5627	6	4
Bethesda			
The First National Bank Of Bethesda	5602	6	5
The Goshen National Bank Of Bethesda	14261	–	6
Beverly			
The First National Bank Of Beverly	133	5	–
Blanchester			
The First National Bank Of Blanchester	8588	6	6
Bluffton			
The Citizens National Bank Of Bluffton	11573	6	4
The First National Bank Of Bluffton	5626	6	–
Bowerston			
The First National Bank Of Bowerston	7486	5	6
Bowling Green			
The First National Bank Of Bowling Green	4045	6	–
Bradford			
The Bradford National Bank	14077	–	5
The First National Bank Of Bradford	9163	6	4
Bremen			
The First National Bank Of Bremen	9768	5	–
Bridgeport			
Bridgeport National Bank	6624	4	5
The Bridgeport National Bank	14050	–	6
The First National Bank Of Bridgeport	214	5	–
Brookville			
The Brookville National Bank	14141	–	–
The First National Bank Of Brookville	9553	6	–
Bryan			
The Citizens National Bank Of Bryan	13740	–	6
The Farmers National Bank Of Bryan	2474	3	4
The First National Bank In Bryan	13899	–	5
The First National Bank Of Bryan	237	4	4
Buckeye City			
The First National Bank Of Buckeye City	7631	6	–
Bucyrus			
The First National Bank Of Bucyrus	443	4	3
The Second National Bank Of Bucyrus	3274	2	5
Burton			
The First National Bank Of Burton	6249	6	4
Butler			
The First National Bank Of Butler	6515	6	–
Byesville			
The First National Bank Of Byesville	5641	6	6
Cadiz			
The Farmers And Mechanics National Bank Of Cadiz	2444	5	–
The First National Bank Of Cadiz	100	5	6
The Fourth National Bank Of Cadiz	4853	6	5
The Harrison National Bank Of Cadiz	1447	4	5
The Union National Bank And Trust Company Of Cadiz	100	–	5
The Union National Bank Of Cadiz	100	–	4
Caldwell			
The Citizens National Bank Of Caldwell	6458	6	5
The First National Bank Of Caldwell	13844	–	6
The Noble County National Bank In Caldwell	13154	6	6
The Noble County National Bank Of Caldwell	2102	6	–
Cambridge			
The Central National Bank At Cambridge	13905	–	6
The Central National Bank Of Cambridge	2872	5	5
The First National Bank Of Cambridge	141	6	–
The Guernsey National Bank Of Cambridge	1942	4	6
The National Bank Of Cambridge	6566	5	3
The Old National Bank Of Cambridge	2861	6	–
Camden			
The First National Bank Of Camden	8300	5	5
The First National Bank Of Camden	14316	–	–
Canal Dover			
The Exchange National Bank Of Canal Dover	4293	6	–
The Exchange National Bank Of Dover	4293	5	5
The First National Bank Of Canal Dover	4331	6	–
The First National Bank Of Dover	4331	6	4
Canfield			
The Farmers' National Bank Of Canfield	3654	6	4
Canton			
The City National Bank Of Canton	2489	3	–
The First National Bank Of Canton	76	3	3
The Second National Bank Of Canton	463	–	–
Cardington			
The First National Bank Of Cardington	127	5	6
Carey			
The First National Bank Of Carey	6119	6	5
Carrollton			
First National Bank In Carrollton	11714	5	5
The First National Bank At Carrollton	13883	–	5
The First National Bank Of Carrollton	5396	6	–
Carthage			
The First National Bank Of Carthage	8488	6	–
Celina			
The First National Bank Of Celina	5523	4	4
Centerburg			
The First National Bank Of Centerburg	8182	6	–
Centreville			
The Centreville National Bank Of Thurman, Centreville	2181	5	–
Chagrin Falls			
The First National Bank Of Chagrin Falls	11252	–	–
Chardon			
Central National Bank Of Chardon	13569	–	4
The Central National Bank Of Chardon	13569	–	6
The First National Bank Of Chardon	4671	4	5
Chesterhill			
The First National Bank Of Chesterhill	5552	6	5
Cheviot			
The First National Bank Of Cheviot	8478	6	–
Chillicothe			
The Central National Bank Of Chillicothe	2993	5	5
The Chillicothe National Bank	1277	6	–
The Citizens National Bank Of Chillicothe	5634	6	6
The First National Bank Of Chillicothe	128	4	3
The Ross County National Bank Of Chillicothe	1172	5	5
Cincinnati			
The American National Bank Of Cincinnati	8438	6	–
The Atlas National Bank Of Cincinnati	3639	4	4
The Brotherhood Of Railway Clerks National Bank Of Cincinnati	12446	3	5
The Central National Bank Of Cincinnati	620	6	–
The Cincinnati National Bank	2922	6	–
The Citizens National Bank & Trust Company Of Cincinnati	2495	3	–
The Citizens National Bank Of Cincinnati	2495	1	–
The Commercial National Bank Of Cincinnati	1185	6	–
The Equitable National Bank Of Cincinnati	3707	6	–
The Exchange National Bank Of Cincinnati	2616	6	–
The Fidelity National Bank Of Cincinnati	3461	6	–
The Fifth National Bank Of Cincinnati	2798	3	–
The Fifth-Third National Bank Of Cincinnati	20	2	–
The Fifth-Third National Bank Of Cincinnati	2798	2	–
The First National Bank Of Cincinnati	24	1	3
The Fourth National Bank Of Cincinnati	93	2	–
The German National Bank Of Cincinnati	2524	3	–
The Lincoln National Bank Of Cincinnati	2524	3	2
The Market National Bank Of Cincinnati	3642	4	–
The Merchants National Bank Of Cincinnati	844	4	–
The Metropolitan National Bank Of Cincinnati	2542	4	–
The National Bank Of Commerce Of Cincinnati	2315	6	–
The National Lafayette Bank Of Cincinnati	2315	5	–
The Ohio National Bank Of Cincinnati	630	6	–
The Ohio Valley National Bank Of Cincinnati	3606	5	–
The Queen City National Bank Of Cincinnati	2798	6	–
The Second National Bank Of Cincinnati	32	6	–
The Second National Bank Of Cincinnati	32	3	–
The Second National Bank Of Cincinnati	2664	3	3
The Third National Bank Of Cincinnati	20	6	–
The Third National Bank Of Cincinnati	2730	3	–
The Union National Bank Of Cincinnati	2549	6	–
Circleville			
The First National Bank Of Circleville	118	4	4
The Second National Bank Of Circleville	172	5	5
The Third National Bank Of Circleville	2817	6	6
Clarington			
The First National Bank Of Clarington	5762	6	5
Clarksville			
The Farmers National Bank Of Clarksville	7370	6	6
Cleveland			
Brotherhood Of Locomotive Engineers Co-op N.B. Of Cleveland	11862	2	–
Central National Bank Of Cleveland	4318	5	5
Central National Bank Savings & Trust Co Of Cleveland	4318	4	–
Central United National Bank Of Cleveland	4318	–	1
Engineers National Bank Of Cleveland	11862	3	5
The American Exchange National Bank Of Cleveland	5090	6	–
The Bank Of Commerce National Association Of Cleveland	5194	3	–
The Bankers National Bank Of Cleveland	5805	6	–
The Central National Bank Of Cleveland	4318	4	–
The Century National Bank Of Cleveland	5350	6	–
The Cleveland National Bank	2956	5	–
The Coal And Iron National Bank Of Cleveland	5191	6	–
The Colonial National Bank Of Cleveland	5152	6	–
The Commercial National Bank Of Cleveland	807	6	–
The Euclid Avenue National Bank Of Cleveland	3545	5	–
The Euclid-park National Bank Of Cleveland	3545	6	–
The First National Bank Of Cleveland	7	5	–
The First National Bank Of Cleveland	2690	2	–
The Market National Bank Of Cleveland	5678	6	–
The Mercantile National Bank Of Cleveland	3272	6	–
The Merchants National Bank Of Cleveland	773	4	–
The Metropolitan National Bank Of Cleveland	5653	6	–
The National Bank Of Commerce Of Cleveland	2662	5	–
The National City Bank Of Cleveland	786	4	2
The National Commercial Bank Of Cleveland	7487	3	–
The Northern National Bank Of Cleveland	11376	6	–
The Northern Natl Bank Savings & Trust Co Of Cleveland	11376	–	–
The Ohio National Bank Of Cleveland	1689	6	–
The Park National Bank Of Cleveland	5006	5	–
The Second National Bank Of Cleveland	13	6	–
The State National Bank Of Cleveland	3950	5	–
The Superior National Bank And Trust Company Of Cleveland	11878	–	–
The Union National Bank Of Cleveland	3202	4	–
The Western Reserve National Bank Of Cleveland	4782	6	–
Union Commerce National Bank Of Cleveland	11141	6	–
Cleves			
The Cleves National Bank	13774	–	5
The Hamilton County National Bank Of Cleves	7456	6	5
Clyde			
The First National Bank Of Clyde	4197	6	–
College Corner			
The First National Bank Of College Corner	5277	6	–
Columbiana			
The First National Bank Of Columbiana	6296	6	–
Columbus			
First National Bank In Columbus	4443	5	–
The Central National Bank Of Columbus	9282	6	–
The City National Bank & Trust Company Of Columbus	7621	–	2
The City National Bank Of Columbus	7818	4	–
The City National Bank Of Commerce Of Columbus	7621	6	6
The Clinton National Bank Of Columbus	3610	6	–
The Columbus National Bank	12350	–	–
The Commercial National Bank Of Columbus	2605	3	5
The Deshler National Bank Of Columbus	4579	5	–
The First National Bank Of Columbus	123	6	–
The Fourth National Bank Of Columbus	2423	4	–
The Franklin National Bank Of Columbus	599	6	–
The Hayden National Bank Of Columbus	4697	6	–
The Hayden-Clinton National Bank Of Columbus	4697	4	–
The Huntington National Bank Of Columbus	7745	3	2
The Merchants And Manufacturers National Bank OfColumbus	5029	6	–
The National Bank Of Commerce Of Columbus	4443	6	–
The National Bank Of Commerce Of Columbus	7621	5	–
The National Exchange Bank Of Columbus	591	6	–
The New First National Bank Of Columbus	4443	4	–
The Ohio National Bank Of Columbus	5065	3	1
The Union National Bank Of Columbus	7584	6	–
Conneaut			
The First National Bank Of Conneaut	3492	6	–
Convoy			
The First National Bank Of Convoy	8017	6	6

City, Bank	Ch. No.	L	S
Coolville			
The Coolville National Bank	8175	6	6
Cortland			
The First National Bank Of Cortland	4772	6	–
Coshocton			
Coshocton National Bank	13923	–	–
The Commercial National Bank Of Coshocton	6892	4	4
The Coshocton National Bank	5103	5	4
The First National Bank Of Coshocton	1920	6	–
Covington			
The Citizens National Bank Of Covington	5530	6	5
Crestline			
First National Bank In Crestline	13273	–	4
The First National Bank Of Crestline	5099	4	–
Cumberland			
The First National Bank Of Cumberland	11363	–	–
Cuyahoga Falls			
The First National Bank Of Cuyahoga Falls	378	6	–
Dalton			
The First National Bank Of Dalton	6372	5	6
Dayton			
The American National Bank & Trust Company Of Dayton	4054	6	–
The American National Bank Of Dayton	4054	6	–
The City National Bank And Trust Company Of Dayton	2874	6	5
The City National Bank Of Dayton	2874	5	–
The Dayton National Bank	898	4	–
The First National Bank Of Dayton	9	6	–
The Fourth National Bank Of Dayton	3821	4	–
The Merchants National Bank And Trust Company Of Dayton	1788	6	5
The Merchants National Bank Of Dayton	1788	4	–
The Second National Bank Of Dayton	10	6	–
The Teutonia National Bank Of Dayton	4054	5	–
The Third National Bank And Trust Company Of Dayton	2678	4	4
The Third National Bank Of Dayton	2678	3	–
The Winters National Bank And Trust Company Of Dayton	2604	4	3
The Winters National Bank Of Dayton	2604	2	–
Defiance			
The Defiance National Bank	1906	6	–
The First National Bank Of Defiance	4661	3	5
The Merchants National Bank Of Defiance	2516	5	6
The National Bank Of Defiance	13457	–	3
Delaware			
The Delaware County National Bank Of Delaware	853	5	–
The Delaware County National Bank, Delaware	13535	–	–
The Delaware National Bank	7505	5	5
The First National Bank Of Delaware	243	4	4
Delphos			
The Delphos National Bank	2885	6	–
The First National Bank Of Delphos	274	6	–
The National Bank Of Delphos	6280	6	–
The Old National Bank Of Delphos	12196	6	5
Delta			
The Farmers National Bank Of Delta	5577	6	–
Delware			
The Delaware County National Bank Of Delaware	13535	–	3
Dennison			
The Dennison National Bank	6843	5	4
The First National Bank Of Dennison	13802	–	6
The Twin City National Bank Of Dennison	6836	6	–
Dillonvale			
First National Bank At Dillonvale	14011	–	6
The First National Bank Of Dillonvale	5618	5	5
Dresden			
The Dresden National Bank	6529	6	–
The First National Bank Of Dresden	5144	6	–
Dunkirk			
The First National Bank Of Dunkirk	6628	5	5
The Woodruff National Bank Of Dunkirk	6652	6	–
East Liverpool			
The Citizens National Bank Of East Liverpool	5098	5	–
The First National Bank Of East Liverpool	2146	4	4
The Potters National Bank Of East Liverpool	2544	3	5
East Palestine			
The First National Bank At East Palestine	13850	–	5
The First National Bank Of East Palestine	6593	6	6
Eaton			
The Eaton National Bank	7557	6	5
The First National Bank Of Eaton	530	6	–
The Preble County National Bank Of Eaton	3889	6	6
Edon			
The Farmers National Bank Of Edon	11851	–	–
Elmore			
The First National Bank Of Elmore	6770	6	5
Elmwood Place			
The First National Bank Of Elmwood Place	6314	6	4
Elyria			
First National Bank In Elyria	2863	6	–
The First National Bank Of Elyria	438	6	–
The National Bank Of Elyria	2863	4	–
Fairport Harbor			
The First National Bank Of Fairport Harbor	6068	6	–
Felicity			
The First National Bank Of Felicity	2882	6	–
Findlay			
The American National Bank Of Findlay	3729	4	–
The American-First National Bank Of Findlay	36	4	4
The Buckeye National Bank Of Findlay	3477	4	–
The Farmers National Bank Of Findlay	3477	6	–
The First National Bank And Trust Company Of Findlay	36	–	4
The First National Bank Of Findlay	36	6	–
Flushing			
The Community National Bank Of Flushing	12008	–	–
The First National Bank Of Flushing	3177	6	–
Forest			
The First National Bank Of Forest	7518	5	5
Fostoria			
The First National Bank Of Fostoria	2831	5	5
The Union National Bank Of Fostoria	9192	6	4
Franklin			
The Farmers National Bank Of Franklin	2282	6	–
The First National Bank Of Franklin	738	6	–
The Franklin National Bank	5100	4	2
The Warren National Bank Of Franklin	8000	6	–
Fredericktown			
The First National Bank Of Fredericktown	5640	5	6
Freeport			
The Prairie Depot National Bank Of Freeport	11216	6	6
Fremont			
The First National Bank Of Fremont	5	6	–
The First National Bank Of Fremont	5	3	–
The First National Bank Of Fremont	2703	3	4
The National Bank Of Fremont	13997	–	–
Galion			
The Citizens National Bank Of Galion	1984	3	6
The First National Bank Of Galion	419	4	4
The Galion National Bank	3581	6	–
Gallipolis			
The First National Bank Of Gallipolis	136	5	5
Garrettsville			
The First National Bank Of Garrettsville	2034	5	5
Geneva			
The First National Bank Of Geneva	153	6	–
The First National Bank Of Geneva	153	6	6
The First National Bank Of Geneva	2719	6	6
Georgetown			
The First National Bank Of Georgetown	2705	5	6
The Peoples National Bank Of Georgetown	5996	5	3
Germantown			
The First National Bank Of Germantown	86	6	6
Gettysburg			
The Citizens National Bank Of Gettysburg	10058	6	5
Girard			
The First National Bank Of Girard	4884	6	5
Glouster			
The First National Bank Of Glouster	8423	6	–
Granville			
The First National Bank Of Granville	388	6	–
The First National Bank Of Granville	2496	6	–
Green Spring			
The First National Bank Of Green Spring	2037	5	–
Greenfield			
The First National Bank Of Greenfield	101	6	–
The Peoples National Bank Of Greenfield	10105	5	4
Greenville			
Greenville National Bank	13944	–	–
The Farmers National Bank Of Greenville	1092	5	4
The Greenville National Bank	7130	5	5
The Second National Bank Of Greenville	2992	5	5
Greenwich			
The First National Bank Of Greenwich	7001	5	4
Grove City			
The First National Bank Of Grove City	6827	6	6
Hamilton			
The First National Bank & Trust Company Of Hamilton	56	5	3
The First National Bank Of Hamilton	56	4	–
The Miami Valley National Bank Of Hamilton	3840	4	–
The Second National Bank Of Hamilton	829	4	4
Harrison			
The First National Bank Of Harrison	8228	6	5
Harveysburg			
The Harveysburg National Bank	11617	–	–
Haviland			
The Farmers National Bank Of Haviland	10436	6	6
Hicksville			
The First National Bank Of Hicksville	4867	5	5
The Hicksville National Bank	5802	5	6
Higginsport			
The First National Bank Of Higginsport	9394	6	–
The First National Bank Of Winchester	9394	6	–
Hillsboro			
The Farmers And Traders National Bank Of Hillsboro	9243	6	3
Hillsborough			
The Citizens National Bank Of Hillsborough	2039	5	–
The First National Bank Of Hillsborough	787	6	–
The Hillsborough National Bank	787	6	–
The Merchants National Bank Of Hillsborough	2449	5	5
Hopedale			
The First National Bank Of Hopedale	6938	6	6
Hubbard			
The Hubbard National Bank	2389	6	–
Hudson			
The National Bank Of Hudson	9221	6	6
Huron			
The First National Bank Of Huron	4778	6	–
Ironton			
The Citizens National Bank Of Ironton	4336	5	5
The First National Bank Of Ironton	98	2	4
The Second National Bank Of Ironton	242	5	–
Jackson			
The First National Bank Of Jackson	1903	4	5
Jackson Center			
The First National Bank Of Jackson Center	8536	5	5
Jefferson			
The First National Bank Of Jefferson	427	6	–
The Second National Bank Of Jefferson	2026	6	–
Jewett			
The First National Bank Of Jewett	13150	–	5
Kalida			
The First National Bank Of Kalida	7074	6	–
Kansas			
The First National Bank Of Kansas	11598	6	6
Kent			
The Kent National Bank	652	5	4
Kenton			
The First Commercial National Bank Of Kenton	2500	–	5
The First National Bank Of Kenton	2500	5	5
The Kenton National Bank	3505	5	5
Kingston			
The First National Bank Of Kingston	9536	6	5
Kinsman			
The First National Bank Of Kinsman	13836	–	–
The Kinsman National Bank	3077	6	–
La Rue			
The Campbell National Bank Of La Rue	6675	6	5
Lakewood			
The Peoples National Bank Of Lakewood	13715	–	4
Lancaster			
The Fairfield National Bank Of Lancaster	7517	4	4
The First National Bank Of Lancaster	137	6	–
The Hocking Valley National Bank Of Lancaster	1241	4	6
The Lancaster National Bank	9547	5	3
Lebanon			
Lebanon National Bank And Trust Company, Lebanon	2360	6	–
The Citizens National Bank And Trust Company Of Lebanon	4239	6	–
The Citizens National Bank Of Lebanon	4239	5	–
The Farmers And Merchants National Bank Of Lebanon	8507	6	–
The First National Bank Of Lebanon	1238	6	–
The Lebanon Citizens National Bank & Trust Co., Lebanon	2360	5	4
The Lebanon National Bank	2360	5	–
The Lebanon-Citizens National Bank, Lebanon	2360	–	–
Leetonia			
The First National Bank Of Leetonia	3519	6	–
Leipsic			
The First National Bank Of Leipsic	6565	6	–
Lewisville			
The First National Bank Of Lewisville	8978	5	–
Lima			
The American National Bank Of Lima	5125	6	–
The First National Bank Of Lima	2035	5	–
The Lima National Bank	2859	6	–
The Merchants National Bank Of Lima	2497	6	–
The National Bank Of Lima	13767	–	5
The Ohio National Bank Of Lima	3772	6	–
The Old National Bank Of Lima	8701	6	–
The Old National City Bank Of Lima	8701	6	6
Lockland			
The First National Bank Of Lockland	4133	6	4
Lodi			
The Exchange National Bank Of Lodi	7017	6	–
The First National Bank Of Lodi	53	6	–
The Lodi National Bank	7017	6	–
The Peoples National Bank Of Lodi	10677	5	6
Logan			
First National Bank In Logan	7649	6	6
First-Rempel National Bank On Logan	7649	–	6
The First National Bank Of Logan	92	6	–
The National Bank Of Logan	7649	5	–
The Rempel National Bank Of Logan	9284	6	–
London			
The Central National Bank Of London	10373	5	4
The Madison National Bank Of London	1064	4	4
Lorain			
The First National Bank Of Lorain	2625	6	–
The National Bank Of Commerce Of Lorain	5371	4	4
The National Bank Of Lorain	14290	–	–
Loudonville			
The First National Bank Of Loudonville	6657	6	–
Louisville			
The First National Bank Of Louisville	9630	6	–
Loveland			
The First National Bank Of Loveland	6816	6	–
The Loveland National Bank	6779	5	5
Lowell			
The First National Bank Of Lowell	5329	5	6
Lynchburg			
The First National Bank Of Lynchburg	11772	4	6
Madisonville			
The First National Bank Of Madisonville	8557	6	–
Malta			
The Malta National Bank	2052	5	5
Manchester			
The Farmers National Bank Of Manchester	9091	5	5
The Manchester National Bank	1982	5	–
Mansfield			
The Citizens National Bank & Trust Company Of Mansfield	2577	6	4
The Citizens National Bank Of Mansfield	2577	5	–
The Farmers National Bank Of Mansfield	800	6	–
The First National Bank Of Mansfield	436	5	–
The Mansfield Savings Trust National Bank	13920	–	–
The Richland National Bank Of Mansfield	480	6	–
Mantua			
The First National Bank Of Mantua	5370	6	5
Marietta			
The Central National Bank Of Marietta	5212	5	–
The Citizens National Bank Of Marietta	4164	4	5
The First National Bank Of Marietta	142	3	3
The German National Bank Of Marietta	5212	4	–
The Marietta National Bank	859	6	–
The New First National Bank Of Marietta	13971	–	3
Marion			
The City National Bank Of Marion	5650	5	–
The First National Bank Of Marion	287	6	–
The Marion National Bank	6308	4	6
The National City Bank And Trust Company Of Marion	11831	4	5
Mason			
The First National Bank Of Mason	7403	5	–

City, Bank	Ch. No.	L	S
Massillon			
The First National Bank In Massillon	13687	–	–
The First National Bank Of Massillon	216	4	4
The First National Bank Of Massillon	13687	–	–
The Merchants National Bank Of Massillon	4286	4	–
The Union National Bank Of Massillon	1318	4	4
Mc Connelsville			
The First National Bank Of Mc Connelsville	46	6	–
Mcarthur			
The Vinton County National Bank Of Mcarthur	2036	5	5
Mcconnelsville			
The Citizens National Bank Of Mcconnelsville	5259	4	5
The First National Bank Of Mcconnelsville	46	4	–
The First National Bank Of Mcconnelsville	2712	4	4
Mechanicsburgh			
The Farmers National Bank Of Mechanicsburgh	2325	6	–
Medina			
The First National Bank Of Medina	2053	6	–
The Medina County National Bank Of Medina	5139	5	–
The Old Phoenix National Bank Of Medina	4842	6	5
The Phoenix National Bank Of Medina	2091	6	–
Mendon			
The First National Bank Of Mendon	9274	6	6
Miamisburg			
The Citizens National Bank Of Miamisburg	4822	6	–
The First National Bank Of Miamisburg	3876	5	4
Middleport			
The Citizens National Bank Of Middleport	8441	6	6
The First National Bank Of Middleport	2210	6	–
The Middleport National Bank	4472	6	–
The Mutual National Bank Of Middleport	11614	–	–
Middletown			
The First & Merchants National Bank Of Middletown	2025	5	3
The First National Bank Of Middletown	1545	5	–
The Merchants National Bank Of Middletown	2025	5	–
Milford			
The Citizens National Bank Of Milford	8188	5	–
The Milford National Bank	3234	4	5
Millersburgh			
The First National Bank Of Millersburgh	1923	6	–
Mineral City			
The First National Bank Of Mineral City	11948	–	–
Minerva			
The First National Bank Of Minerva	1930	6	–
The First National Bank Of Minerva	5344	6	–
Mingo Junction			
The First National Bank Of Mingo Junction	5694	6	5
The Mingo National Bank Of Mingo Junction	14183	–	6
Monroe			
The Monroe National Bank	7947	5	3
Monroeville			
The First National Bank Of Monroeville	2438	6	–
Montpelier			
National Bank Of Montpelier	13912	–	5
The First National Bank Of Montpelier	5315	6	–
The Montpelier National Bank	5341	4	5
Morrow			
The First National Bank Of Morrow	8709	5	5
The Morrow National Bank	8741	6	5
Mount Gilead			
The First National Bank Of Mount Gilead	258	6	–
The First National Bank Of Mount Gilead	14323	–	–
The Morrow County National Bank Of Mount Gilead	2459	5	–
The Mt. Gilead National Bank	6620	6	4
The National Bank Of Morrow County At Mount Gilead	5251	4	6
Mount Healthy			
The First National Bank Of Mt. Healthy	7661	6	5
The Mount Healthy National Bank	14192	–	–
Mount Orab			
The Brown County National Bank Of Mt. Orab	10692	6	5
Mount Pleasant			
The First National Bank Of Mount Pleasant	492	6	–
The Mount Pleasant National Bank	6640	6	–
The Peoples National Bank Of Mount Pleasant	6667	5	5
Mount Sterling			
The Citizens National Bank Of Mount Sterling	9095	5	–
The First National Bank Of Mt. Sterling	5382	4	–
The First-citizens National Bank Of Mt. Sterling	5382	6	–
Mount Vernon			
Knox National Bank In Mt. Vernon	7638	6	5
The Farmers And Merchants National Bank Of Mount Vernon	7248	6	–
The First National Bank Of Mount Vernon	908	6	4
The Knox County National Bank Of Mount Vernon	1051	6	–
The Knox National Bank Of Mount Vernon	3328	6	–
The New Knox National Bank Of Mt. Vernon	7638	6	–
Mount Washington			
The First National Bank Of Mount Washington	9761	6	–
Napoleon			
The First National Bank Of Napoleon	1917	5	–
The First National Bank Of Napoleon	5218	4	5
Neffs			
The Neffs National Bank	9799	6	6
New Bremen			
The First National Bank In New Bremen	14294	–	–
The First National Bank Of New Bremen	7851	5	5
New Carlisle			
The First National Bank Of New Carlisle	6594	6	–
The New Carlisle National Bank	6594	–	6
New Concord			
The First National Bank Of New Concord	6976	6	5
New Holland			
The First National Bank Of New Holland	7187	5	4
New Lexington			
The Citizens National Bank Of New Lexington	6505	5	5
The First National Bank Of New Lexington	2056	6	–
The Peoples National Bank Of New Lexington	13596	–	4
New Lisbon			
The First National Bank Of New Lisbon	2203	6	–
New London			
The First National Bank Of New London	1981	6	–
The New London National Bank	4712	6	–
The Third National Bank Of New London	10101	5	5
New Matamoras			
The First National Bank Of New Matamoras	5999	6	6
New Paris			
The First National Bank Of New Paris	9211	6	5
New Philadelphia			
The Citizens National Bank Of New Philadelphia	1999	4	5
New Richmond			
The First National Bank Of New Richmond	1068	6	–
The New Richmond National Bank	7542	6	5
New Vienna			
The First National Bank Of New Vienna	10947	6	–
Newark			
The First National Bank Of Newark	858	2	4
The Franklin National Bank Of Newark	7787	4	–
The Park National Bank Of Newark	9179	4	5
The Peoples National Bank Of Newark	3191	6	–
Newcomerstown			
The First National Bank Of Newcomerstown	5262	5	4
Newton Falls			
The First National Bank Of Newton Falls	7391	6	–
Niles			
The City National Bank Of Niles	4977	6	–
The First National Bank Of Niles	4190	6	–
North Baltimore			
The First National Bank Of North Baltimore	4347	4	4
Norwalk			
The Citizens National Bank Of Norwalk	11275	5	1
The First National Bank Of Norwalk	215	4	–
The Norwalk National Bank	931	6	–
Norwood			
The First National Bank Of Norwood	6322	4	4
The Norwood National Bank	8505	5	–
Oak Harbor			
The First National Bank Of Oak Harbor	6632	6	5
The National Bank Of Oak Harbor	14203	–	–
Oberlin			
The Citizens National Bank Of Oberlin	2718	6	–
The First National Bank Of Oberlin	72	6	–
Okeana			
The First National Bank Of Okeana	9450	6	6
Orrville			
The First National Bank Of Orrville	6379	6	–
The National Bank Of Orrville	13742	–	6
The Orrville National Bank	6362	6	5
Osborn			
The First National Bank Of Osborn	9675	6	5
Ottawa			
The First National Bank Of Ottawa	7006	6	5
Oxford			
The First National Bank Of Oxford	4599	6	–
The Oxford National Bank	6059	5	3
Painesville			
First National Bank In Painesville	14232	–	5
The First National Bank Of Painesville	220	5	–
The Painesville National Bank	2842	6	–
The Painesville National Bank And Trust Company	13318	–	5
Pandora			
The First National Bank Of Pandora	11343	6	6
Paulding			
The First National Bank Of Paulding	5917	6	–
The National Bank Of Paulding	14300	–	–
The Paulding National Bank	5862	5	4
Piketon			
Piketon National Bank	7039	5	6
Piqua			
The Citizens National Bank & Trust Company Of Piqua	1061	5	4
The Citizens National Bank Of Piqua	1061	5	–
The Piqua National Bank	1006	4	–
The Piqua National Bank And Trust Company, Piqua	1006	4	5
The Third National Bank Of Piqua	3750	6	–
Plain City			
The Farmers National Bank Of Plain City	5522	6	5
Plymouth			
The First National Bank Of Plymouth	1904	4	–
The Peoples National Bank Of Plymouth	7035	6	5
Pomeroy			
The First National Bank Of Pomeroy	132	6	–
The Pomeroy National Bank	1980	5	4
Port Clinton			
National Bank Of Port Clinton	6227	6	5
The First National Bank Of Port Clinton	6227	6	–
The First National-Magruder Bank Of Port Clinton	6227	6	–
The Magruder National Bank Of Port Clinton	12365	–	–
The Port Clinton National Bank	13989	–	–
Portsmouth			
The Central National Bank Of Portsmouth	7781	4	6
The Farmers National Bank Of Portsmouth	1088	6	–
The First National Bank Of Portsmouth	68	2	3
The Iron National Bank Of Portsmouth	1948	6	–
The Kinney National Bank Of Portsmouth	1958	6	–
The National Bank Of Portsmouth	13832	–	4
The Portsmouth National Bank	935	5	–
The Security Central National Bank Of Portsmouth	7781	–	5
Powhatan Point			
The First National Bank Of Powhatan Point	7759	5	5
Quaker City			
The Quaker City National Bank	1989	4	5
Racine			
The First National Bank Of Racine	9815	6	6
Ravenna			
The First National Bank Of Ravenna	106	6	–
The Ravenna National Bank	6466	5	–
The Second National Bank Of Ravenna	350	4	4
Richwood			
The First National Bank Of Richwood	9199	5	6
Ripley			
The Citizens National Bank Of Ripley	3291	3	5
The Farmers National Bank Of Ripley	933	6	–
The First National Bank Of Ripley	289	6	–
The Ripley National Bank	2837	4	4
Rock Creek			
The First National Bank Of Rock Creek	7790	6	–
Rockford			
The First National Bank Of Rockford	11803	–	–
The Rockford National Bank	11804	–	–
Rocky River			
The First National Bank Of Rocky River	12347	–	3
Roseville			
The First National Bank Of Roseville	5555	6	–
Sabina			
The First National Bank Of Sabina	8411	6	5
Saint Clairsville			
First National Bank In St. Clairsville	13922	–	4
The First National Bank Of St. Clairsville	315	4	4
The Second National Bank Of St. Clairsville	4993	5	5
Saint Marys			
The First National Bank Of Saint Marys	14132	–	–
The First National Bank Of St. Marys	4219	6	5
Saint Paris			
The Central National Bank Of Saint Paris	8127	5	5
The First Central National Bank Of Saint Paris	2488	–	–
The First National Bank Of Saint Paris	2488	4	5
Salem			
The Farmers National Bank Of Salem	973	4	4
The First National Bank Of Salem	43	6	–
The First National Bank Of Salem	43	4	–
The First National Bank Of Salem	2691	4	3
Sandusky			
The Citizens National Bank Of Sandusky	3141	6	–
The Commercial National Bank Of Sandusky	6455	6	–
The First National Bank Of Sandusky	16	6	–
The Moss National Bank Of Sandusky	2810	6	–
The Second National Bank Of Sandusky	210	5	–
The Third National Bank Of Sandusky	2061	4	–
The Third National Exchange Bank Of Sandusky	4792	5	5
Sardinia			
The Farmers National Bank Of Sardinia	12013	–	–
The First National Bank Of Sardinia	7800	5	6
Sardis			
The First National Bank Of Sardis	7711	6	–
Scio			
The Farmers And Producers National Bank Of Scio	5197	6	–
Senecaville			
The First National Bank Of Senecaville	7399	6	6
Seven Mile			
The Farmers National Bank Of Seven Mile	9518	6	5
Shelby			
The First National Bank Of Shelby	1929	4	5
Sidney			
The Citizens National Bank Of Sidney	7862	4	4
The First National Bank Of Sidney	257	6	–
The First National Exchange Bank Of Sidney	5214	4	4
Smithfield			
First National Bank At Smithfield	13171	6	6
The First National Bank Of Smithfield	501	4	–
Somerset			
The First National Bank Of Somerset	7237	6	–
Somerton			
The First National Bank Of Somerton	7984	6	–
Somerville			
The Somerville National Bank	9859	6	5
South Charleston			
The Farmers National Bank Of South Charleston	2754	6	–
The First National Bank Of South Charleston	171	6	–
Spring Valley			
The Spring Valley National Bank	7896	6	6
Springfield			
Farmers National Bank Of Springfield	9446	5	–
Lagonda National Bank Of Springfield	14105	–	4
Logonda-Citizens National Bank Of Springfield	2098	5	4
The Citizens National Bank Of Springfield	5160	3	–
The First National Bank And Trust Company Of Springfield	238	5	3
The First National Bank Of Springfield	238	3	–
The Lagonda National Bank Of Springfield	2098	4	–
The Mad River National Bank Of Springfield	1146	3	–
The Second National Bank Of Springfield	263	5	–
The Springfield National Bank	2620	4	–
Steubenville			
The Commercial National Bank Of Steubenville	5039	5	–
The First National Bank Of Steubenville	1164	6	–
The Jefferson National Bank Of Steubenville	1062	6	–
The National Exchange Bank & Trust Company Of Steubenville	2160	4	3
The National Exchange Bank Of Steubenville	2160	4	–
The Peoples National Bank Of Steubenville	7688	6	3
The Steubenville National Bank	3310	6	–
Stockport			
The First National Bank Of Stockport	8042	5	5
Summerfield			
The First National Bank Of Summerfield	6662	6	5
Sycamore			
The First National Bank Of Sycamore	11383	5	5
Tiffin			
The City National Bank Of Tiffin	5427	5	5
The Commercial National Bank Of Tiffin	7795	3	3
The First National Bank Of Tiffin	900	6	–
The National Exchange Bank Of Tiffin	907	5	–
The Tiffin National Bank	3315	4	4
Tippecanoe City			
The Citizens National Bank Of Tippecanoe City	8839	6	4
The Tipp National Bank Of Tippecanoe City	3004	5	5
The Tipp-citizens National Bank Of Tippecanoe City	3004	–	–

City, Bank	Ch. No.	L	S
Toledo			
National Bank Of Toledo	14030	–	3
The Commercial National Bank Of Toledo	2296	6	–
The First National Bank Of Toledo	91	3	1
The Holcomb National Bank Of Toledo	4585	6	–
The Ketcham National Bank Of Toledo	3820	6	–
The Merchants National Bank Of Toledo	1895	4	–
The National Bank Of Commerce Of Toledo	3820	4	–
The National Bank Of Toledo	4585	6	–
The Northern National Bank Of Toledo	809	3	–
The Second National Bank Of Toledo	248	4	–
The Toledo National Bank	607	6	–
The West Toledo National Bank Of Toledo	13256	–	–
Toronto			
The First National Bank Of Toronto	8705	6	–
The National Bank Of Toronto	8826	6	5
Troy			
The First National Bank Of Troy	59	6	–
The First National Bank Of Troy	59	4	–
The First National Bank Of Troy	2727	6	–
The First Troy National Bank And Trust Company	3825	5	4
The Troy National Bank	3825	5	–
Uhrichsville			
The Farmers And Merchants National Bank Of Uhrichsville	2582	6	–
Upper Sandusky			
The Commercial National Bank Of Upper Sandusky	5448	6	–
The First National Bank Of Upper Sandusky	90	4	6
Urbana			
The Champaign National Bank Of Urbana	916	3	3
The Citizens National Bank Of Urbana	863	4	5
The National Bank Of Urbana	4805	5	–
The Third National Bank Of Urbana	2071	5	–
Utica			
The First National Bank Of Utica	7596	6	5
Van Wert			
The First National Bank Of Van Wert	422	4	5
The Van Wert National Bank	2628	5	5
The Van Wert National Bank	13797	–	–
Versailles			
The First National Bank Of Versailles	9336	6	5
Wadsworth			
The First National Bank Of Wadsworth	5828	6	4
The Wadsworth National Bank	5870	6	–
Wapakoneta			
The Auglaize National Bank Of Wapakoneta	9961	4	6
The First National Bank Of Wapakoneta	3157	4	3
The Peoples National Bank Of Wapakoneta	3535	4	4
Warren			
The First National Bank Of Warren	74	5	–
The New National Bank Of Warren	6289	6	–
The Second National Bank Of Warren	2479	5	2
The Trumbull National Bank Of Warren	1578	6	–
The Union National Bank Of Warren	6353	6	–
The Western Reserve National Bank Of Warren	3362	4	–
Washington			
The Midland National Bank Of Washington Court House	4763	5	–
Washington C H			
The Fayette County National Bank Of Washington	1972	5	–
The First National Bank Of Washington	284	5	–
Washington Court House			
The First National Bank Of Washington Court House	13490	–	2
Watertown			
The First National Bank Of Watertown	6943	6	6
Wauseon			
The First National Bank Of Wauseon	7091	5	6
Waverly			
The First National Bank Of Waverly	5635	4	4
Waynesville			
The Waynesville National Bank	2220	4	4
Wellington			
The First National Bank In Wellington	12321	–	–
The First National Bank Of Wellington	464	6	–
The First National Bank Of Wellington	2866	6	–
Wellston			
The First National Bank Of Wellston	3565	3	5
Wellsville			
The First National Bank Of Wellsville	1044	6	–
The Peoples National Bank Of Wellsville	6345	4	6
West Alexandria			
The First National Bank Of West Alexandria	11733	–	–
West Liberty			
The Logan National Bank Of West Liberty	2942	6	–
West Milton			
The Citizens National Bank Of West Milton	14264	–	–
The First National Bank Of West Milton	9062	6	6
West Union			
The First National Bank Of West Union	9487	6	–
The National Bank Of Adams County Of West Union	13198	6	5
Westerville			
The First National Bank Of Westerville	7671	6	–
Weston			
The First National Bank Of Weston	6656	6	6
Williamsburg			
The First National Bank Of Williamsburg	9930	6	–
Williamsport			
The Farmers National Bank Of Williamsport	10267	5	5
Willoughby			
The First National Bank Of Willoughby	11994	4	6
Wilmington			
The Citizens National Bank Of Wilmington	8251	5	5
The Clinton County National Bank Of Wilmington	1997	4	–
The Clinton County Natl Bank & Trust Co. Of Wilmington	1997	5	4
The First National Bank Of Wilmington	365	5	5
Woodsfield			
The Citizens National Bank Of Woodsfield	13847	–	–
The First National Bank Of Woodsfield	5414	4	6
Wooster			
The Citizens National Bank Of Wooster	7670	5	3
The National Bank Of Wooster	1912	6	–
The Wayne County National Bank Of Wooster	828	4	4
The Wooster National Bank	4657	6	–
Xenia			
The Citizens National Bank Of Xenia	2575	4	5
The First National Bank Of Xenia	369	6	–
The Second National Bank Of Xenia	277	6	–
The Xenia National Bank	2932	4	4
Youngstown			
The Commercial National Bank Of Youngstown	2482	3	4
The First National Bank Of Youngstown	3	5	–
The First National Bank Of Youngstown	3	2	1
The First National Bank Of Youngstown	2693	3	–
The Mahoning National Bank Of Youngstown	2350	4	3
The Old National Bank Of Youngstown	6147	–	–
The Second National Bank In Youngstown	12332	6	6
The Second National Bank Of Youngstown	2217	5	–
The Union National Bank Of Youngstown	13586	–	3
The Wick National Bank Of Youngstown	4970	6	–
Zanesville			
The Citizens National Bank In Zanesville	5760	–	3
The Citizens National Bank Of Zanesville	2529	5	–
The Commercial National Bank Of Zanesville	5769	6	–
The First National Bank Of Zanesville	164	3	3
The Muskingum National Bank Of Zanesville	1230	6	–
The Old Citizens National Bank Of Zanesville	5760	3	5
The Second National Bank Of Zanesville	131	6	–
The Union National Bank Of Zanesville	4298	6	–

INDIAN TERRITORY

City, Bank	Ch. No.	L	S
Ada			
The Ada National Bank	5633	6	–
The Citizens National Bank Of Ada	7071	6	–
The First National Bank Of Ada	5620	6	–
Afton			
The First National Bank Of Afton	8790	6	–
Antlers			
The Antlers National Bank	7667	6	–
The Citizens National Bank Of Antlers	8082	6	–
Ardmore			
The Ardmore National Bank	5922	6	–
The Bankers National Bank Of Ardmore	8354	6	–
The City National Bank Of Ardmore	4723	6	–
The First National Bank Of Ardmore	4393	6	–
Atoka			
The Atoka National Bank	5791	6	–
The Citizens National Bank Of Atoka	7666	6	–
Bartlesville			
The American National Bank Of Bartlesville	7032	5	–
The Bartlesville National Bank	6258	6	–
The First National Bank Of Bartlesville	5310	6	–
Beggs			
The First National Bank Of Beggs	6868	6	–
Bennington			
The First National Bank Of Bennington	7099	6	–
Berwyn			
The First National Bank Of Berwyn	7209	6	–
Blanchard			
The First National Bank Of Blanchard	8702	6	–
Bokchito			
The Bokchito National Bank	7499	6	–
The First National Bank Of Bokchito	6683	6	–
Boswell			
The Boswell National Bank	8353	6	–
The First National Bank Of Boswell	7651	6	–
Boynton			
The First National Bank Of Boynton	6511	6	–
Bristow			
The First National Bank Of Bristow	6260	6	–
Broken Arrow			
The Arkansas Valley National Bank Of Broken Arrow	7600	6	–
The First National Bank Of Broken Arrow	7115	6	–
Byars			
The First National Bank Of Byars	7389	6	–
Caddo			
The Caddo National Bank	7368	6	–
The Choctaw National Bank Of Caddo	5246	5	–
Calvin			
The Citizens National Bank Of Calvin	7053	5	–
The First National Bank Of Calvin	6980	6	–
Centralia			
The First National Bank Of Centralia	7706	6	–
Checotah			
The First National Bank Of Checotah	5128	6	–
Chelsea			
The First National Bank Of Chelsea	5955	6	–
Chickasha			
The Chickasha National Bank	8203	6	–
The Citizens National Bank Of Chickasha	5547	6	–
The First National Bank Of Chickasha	5431	5	–
Claremore			
The First National Bank Of Claremore	4987	6	–
Coalgate			
The Coalgate National Bank	7321	6	–
The First National Bank Of Coalgate	5647	6	–
Colbert			
The First National Bank Of Colbert	7962	6	–
Collinsville			
The First National Bank Of Collinsville	6138	6	–
Comanche			
The Citizens National Bank Of Comanche	8361	–	–
The Comanche National Bank	8366	6	–
The First National Bank Of Comanche	6299	6	–
Cornish			
The First National Bank Of Cornish	7420	6	–
Coweta			
The First National Bank Of Coweta	6879	6	–
Davis			
The First National Bank Of Davis	5298	6	–
The Merchants & Planters National Bank Of Davis	7442	6	–
Dewey			
The First National Bank Of Dewey	8270	6	–
Duncan			
The City National Bank Of Duncan	8616	6	–
The Duncan National Bank	7289	6	–
The First National Bank Of Duncan	5379	6	–
Durant			
The Choctaw-Chickasaw National Bank Of Durant	6928	6	–
The Durant National Bank	5590	6	–
The Farmers National Bank Of Durant	6928	6	–
The First National Bank Of Durant	5129	5	–
Eufaula			
The Eufaula National Bank	5967	6	–
The First National Bank Of Eufaula	5902	5	–
Fort Gibson			
The Farmers National Bank Of Fort Gibson	8079	6	–
The First National Bank Of Fort Gibson	6539	6	–
Fort Towson			
The First National Bank Of Fort Towson	8078	6	–
Francis			
The First National Bank Of Francis	7185	6	–
Hartshorne			
The First National Bank Of Hartshorne	7050	6	–
Haskell			
The First National Bank Of Haskell	7822	6	–
Henryetta			
The First National Bank Of Henryetta	6867	6	–
Holdenville			
The American National Bank Of Holdenville	7619	6	–
The First National Bank Of Holdenville	5270	6	–
The National Bank Of Commerce, Holdenville	6540	6	–
The National Bank Of Holdenville	5735	6	–
Hugo			
The First National Bank Of Hugo	6130	6	–
The Hugo National Bank	7747	6	–
Idabel			
The First National Bank Of Idabel	8486	6	–
Keota			
The First National Bank Of Keota	8177	6	–
Kiefer			
The First National Bank Of Kiefer	8553	6	–
Kingston			
The First National Bank Of Kingston	7893	6	–
Kiowa			
The First National Bank Of Kiowa	8638	6	–
Konawa			
The First National Bank Of Konawa	7633	6	–
The Konawa National Bank	8213	6	–
Lehigh			
The Lehigh National Bank	5755	6	–
The Merchants National Bank Of Lehigh	8189	6	–
Lindsay			
The Citizens National Bank Of Lindsay	6171	6	–
The First National Bank Of Lindsay	6171	6	–
The Lindsay National Bank	6710	6	–
Madill			
The City National Bank Of Madill	7723	6	–
The First National Bank Of Madill	5404	6	–
The Madill National Bank	6365	6	–
Mannsville			
The First National Bank Of Mannsville	6578	6	–
Marietta			
The Farmers National Bank Of Marietta	8278	6	–
The First National Bank Of Marietta	5345	6	–
The Marietta National Bank	5958	6	–
Marlow			
The First National Bank Of Marlow	5724	5	–
Miami			
The First National Bank Of Miami	5252	6	–
Milburn			
The First National Bank Of Milburn	7842	6	–
Mill Creek			
The First National Bank Of Mill Creek	7197	6	–
The Merchants & Planters National Bank Of Mill Creek	8546	6	–
Minco			
The First National Bank Of Minco	8644	6	–
Morris			
The First National Bank Of Morris	8876	6	–
Mounds			
The First National Bank Of Mounds	6263	6	–
Muldrow			
The First National Bank Of Muldrow	6717	6	–
Muscogee			
The First National Bank Of Muscogee	4385	4	–
Muskogee			
The City National Bank Of Muskogee	6911	6	–
The Commercial National Bank Of Muskogee	5236	5	–
Nowata			
The First National Bank Of Nowata	5401	5	–
The Nowata National Bank	6367	6	–
Oakland			
The Cotton National Bank Of Oakland	5404	6	–
Okemah			
The First National Bank Of Okemah	6477	6	–
The Okemah National Bank	7677	6	–
Okmulgee			
The Citizens National Bank Of Okmulgee	6241	6	–
The First National Bank Of Okmulgee	5418	6	–
The Okmulgee National Bank	6855	6	–
Owasso			
The First National Bank Of Owasso	7964	6	–
Pauls Valley			
The First National Bank Of Pauls Valley	5091	6	–
The National Bank Of Commerce Of Pauls Valley	6639	5	–
The Pauls Valley National Bank	7892	6	–
Porter			
The First National Bank Of Porter	7615	6	–
The Porter National Bank	8676	6	–
Porum			
The First National Bank Of Porum	8479	6	–

City, Bank	Ch. No.	L	S
Poteau			
The First National Bank Of Poteau	7118	6	–
The National Bank Of Poteau	7104	6	–
Pryor Creek			
The First National Bank Of Pryor Creek	5546	6	–
Purcell			
The Chickasaw National Bank Of Purcell	4756	6	–
The Purcell National Bank	4636	6	–
The Union National Bank Of Purcell	7697	6	–
Quinton			
The First National Bank Of Quinton	6517	6	–
Ramona			
The First National Bank Of Ramona	7251	6	–
Ravia			
The First National Bank Of Ravia	7976	6	–
Roff			
The First National Bank Of Roff	5417	6	–
Rush Springs			
The First National Bank Of Rush Springs	8336	6	–
Ryan			
The First National Bank Of Ryan	5800	6	–
Sallisaw			
The First National Bank Of Sallisaw	5596	6	–
The Merchants National Bank Of Sallisaw	7571	6	–
Sapulpa			
The American National Bank Of Sapulpa	7788	6	–
The First National Bank Of Sapulpa	5951	6	–
South Mcalester			
The American National Bank Of South Mcalester	6230	6	–
The City National Bank Of South Mcalester	6406	6	–
The First National Bank Of Mcalester	5052	5	–
The First National Bank Of South Mcalester	5052	6	–
The State National Bank Of South Mcalester	5537	6	–
Spokogee			
The First National Bank Of Dustin	6804	6	–
The First National Bank Of Spokogee	6804	6	–
Sterrett			
The First National Bank Of Sterrett	7950	6	–
Stigler			
The American National Bank Of Stigler	7432	6	–
The First National Bank Of Stigler	7217	6	–
Stonewall			
The First National Bank Of Stonewall	7054	6	–
Stratford			
The First National Bank Of Stratford	8524	6	–
Sulphur			
The First National Bank Of Sulphur	5748	6	–
Tahlequah			
The Cherokee National Bank Of Tahlequah	6414	6	–
The First National Bank Of Tahlequah	5478	6	–
Talihina			
The First National Bank Of Talihina	7780	6	–
Terral			
The First National Bank Of Terral	7996	6	–
Tishomingo			
The American National Bank Of Tishomingo	7042	6	–
The First National Bank Of Tishomingo	5809	6	–
Tulsa			
The Central National Bank Of Tulsa	8552	6	–
The City National Bank Of Tulsa	5732	6	–
The Farmers National Bank Of Tulsa	6669	6	–
The First National Bank Of Tulsa	5171	5	–
Tupelo			
The First National Bank Of Tupelo	8609	6	–
Tuttle			
The First National Bank Of Tuttle	8475	6	–
Vinita			
The Cherokee National Bank Of Vinita	5860	6	–
The Farmers National Bank Of Vinita	6602	6	–
The First National Bank Of Vinita	4704	4	–
The Vinita National Bank	5083	6	–
Wagoner			
The City National Bank Of Wagoner	7628	6	–
The First National Bank Of Wagoner	5016	6	–
The Wagoner National Bank	6048	6	–
Wapanucka			
The Farmers National Bank Of Wapanucka	5950	6	–
The First National Bank Of Wapanucka	5950	6	–
The Peoples National Bank Of Wapanucka	8137	6	–
Warner			
The First National Bank Of Warner	8809	6	–
Webbers Falls			
The First National Bank Of Webbers Falls	8024	6	–
Weleetka			
The First National Bank Of Weleetka	6324	6	–
The Weleetka National Bank	6689	6	–
Wetumka			
The American National Bank Of Wetumka	7724	6	–
Wetumpka			
The First National Bank Of Wetumpka	5935	6	–
Wewoka			
The Farmers National Bank Of Wewoka	8052	6	–
The First National Bank Of Wewoka	6254	6	–
Wilburton			
The First National Bank Of Wilburton	6890	6	–
Woodville			
The First National Bank Of Woodville	7707	6	–
Wynnewood			
The First National Bank Of Wynnewood	5126	6	–
The Southern National Bank Of Wynnewood	5731	6	–

OKLAHOMA TERRITORY

City, Bank	Ch. No.	L	S
Altus			
The City National Bank Of Altus	8775	6	–
Alva			
The Alva National Bank	6490	6	–
The Exchange National Bank Of Alva	5587	6	–
The First National Bank Of Alva	5587	6	–
Anadarko			
The Citizens National Bank Of Anadarko	6307	6	–
The First National Bank Of Anadarko	5905	6	–
The National Bank Of Anadarko	5923	6	–
Apache			
The First National Bank Of Apache	7127	6	–
Arapaho			
The First National Bank Of Arapaho	6257	6	–
Billings			
The Billings National Bank	12045	–	–
The First National Bank Of Billings	5960	5	–
Blackwell			
The Blackwell National Bank	6916	6	–
The First National Bank Of Blackwell	5460	6	–
The State National Bank Of Blackwell	7583	6	–
Buffalo			
The First National Bank Of Buffalo	8896	6	–
Carmen			
The Carmen National Bank	6844	6	–
The First National Bank Of Carmen	6719	6	–
Cashion			
The First National Bank Of Cashion	6161	6	–
Cement			
The First National Bank Of Cement	8144	6	–
Chandler			
The Chandler National Bank	5354	–	–
The Chandler National Bank	6142	6	–
The First National Bank Of Chandler	5354	6	–
The Union National Bank Of Chandler	6269	6	–
Cherokee			
The First National Bank Of Cherokee	6677	6	–
Cleveland			
The Cleveland National Bank	7386	6	–
The First National Bank Of Cleveland	5911	6	–
Clinton			
The Clinton National Bank	6851	6	–
The First National Bank Of Clinton	6940	6	–
Cordell			
The City National Bank Of Cordell	6647	6	–
The First National Bank Of Cordell	6052	6	–
Cushing			
The Farmers National Bank Of Cushing	8730	6	–
The First National Bank Of Cushing	6893	6	–
Custer City			
The First National Bank Of Custer City	8727	6	–
Davenport			
The First National Bank Of Davenport	8668	6	–
Edmond			
The First National Bank Of Edmond	6156	6	–
El Dorado			
The First National Bank Of El Dorado	8126	6	–
El Reno			
The Citizens National Bank Of El Reno	5985	6	–
The First National Bank Of El Reno	4830	6	–
Elk City			
The Elk City National Bank	6164	6	–
The First National Bank Of Elk City	5766	6	–
Enid			
The Enid National Bank	8231	6	–
The First National Bank Of Enid	5335	6	–
Erick			
The First National Bank Of Erick	8010	6	–
Fairfax			
The Fairfax National Bank	8202	6	–
The First National Bank Of Fairfax	7972	6	–
Fairview			
The First National Bank Of Fairview	7117	6	–
Fort Sill			
City National Bank Of Lawton	5753	5	–
The First National Bank Of Fort Sill	5753	6	–
Foss			
The First National Bank Of Foss	6736	6	–
Frederick			
The City National Bank Of Frederick	8206	6	–
The First National Bank Of Frederick	8140	6	–
The Frederick National Bank	8140	–	–
Gage			
The First National Bank Of Gage	8543	6	–
Geary			
The First National Bank Of Geary	6163	6	–
Granite			
The First National Bank Of Granite	8342	6	–
Guthrie			
The Capitol National Bank Of Guthrie	4705	5	–
The Guthrie National Bank	4348	5	–
The National Bank Of Commerce Of Guthrie	7299	6	–
The National Bank Of Guthrie	4383	6	–
Guymon			
The First National Bank Of Guymon	8138	6	–
Harrison			
The First National Bank Of Harrison	6753	6	–
Hastings			
The First National Bank Of Hastings	8209	6	–
The National Bank Of Hastings	8210	6	–
Helena			
The First National Bank Of Helena	8349	6	–
Hennessey			
The First National Bank Of Hennessey	5473	6	–
The Hennessey National Bank	6111	6	–
Hobart			
The City National Bank Of Hobart	6267	6	–
The Farmers & Merchants National Bank Of Hobart	6358	6	–
The First National Bank Of Hobart	5954	6	–
The Hobart National Bank	5915	6	–
Hollis			
The First National Bank Of Hollis	8061	6	–
The Groves National Bank Of Hollis	8825	6	–
The Hollis National Bank	8056	6	–
Hominy			
The First National Bank Of Hominy	7927	6	–
Kaw City			
The First National Bank Of Kaw City	8577	6	–
Kingfisher			
The Farmers National Bank Of Kingfisher	6702	6	–
The First National Bank Of Kingfisher	5328	6	–
The Kingfisher National Bank	5740	6	–
The Peoples National Bank Of Kingfisher	5790	6	–
Lamont			
The First National Bank Of Lamont	7783	6	–
Lawton			
The First National Bank Of Lawton	5914	6	–
The Lawton National Bank	8375	6	–
Leger			
The Altus National Bank Of Leger	7159	6	–
The Altus National Bank, Altus	7159	6	–
The First National Bank Of Altus	6113	6	–
The First National Bank Of Leger	6113	6	–
Lexington			
The Farmers National Bank Of Lexington	7207	6	–
The First National Bank Of Lexington	5462	6	–
The Lexington National Bank	5462	6	–
Luther			
The National Bank Of Luther	8563	6	–
Mangum			
The City National Bank Of Mangum	7328	6	–
The First National Bank Of Mangum	5508	6	–
The Mangum National Bank	5811	6	–
Maud			
The First National Bank Of Maud	8294	6	–
Mcloud			
The First National Bank Of Mcloud	6660	6	–
Medford			
The First National Bank Of Medford	5796	6	–
Mountain View			
The First National Bank Of Mountain View	5656	6	–
Newkirk			
The Farmers National Bank Of Newkirk	8214	6	–
The First National Bank Of Newkirk	5272	6	–
Norman			
The City National Bank Of Norman	6450	6	–
The Cleveland County National Bank Of Norman	5612	6	–
The First National Bank Of Norman	5248	5	–
The National Bank Of Norman	7293	6	–
Okeene			
The First National Bank Of Okeene	5887	6	–
Oklahoma City			
The American National Bank Of Oklahoma City	5716	6	–
The Commercial National Bank Of Oklahoma City	6981	6	–
The First National Bank Of Oklahoma City	4402	6	–
The Oklahoma City National Bank	6678	6	–
The Oklahoma National Bank Of Oklahoma City	4770	6	–
The Security National Bank Of Oklahoma City	8472	5	–
The State National Bank Of Oklahoma City	4862	6	–
The Western National Bank Of Oklahoma City	5159	6	–
Olustee			
The Farmers National Bank Of Olustee	8754	6	–
The First National Bank Of Olustee	8316	6	–
Pawhuska			
The American National Bank Of Pawhuska	8313	6	–
The Citizens National Bank Of Pawhuska	7883	6	–
The First National Bank Of Pawhuska	5961	6	–
Pawnee			
The Arkansas Valley National Bank Of Pawnee	5492	6	–
The First National Bank Of Pawnee	5224	6	–
The Pawnee National Bank	7611	6	–
Perry			
The First National Bank Of Perry	6972	6	–
Ponca City			
The Farmers National Bank Of Ponca City	6061	6	–
The First National Bank Of Ponca City	5474	6	–
Pond Creek			
The First National Bank Of Pond Creek	6655	4	–
The National Bank Of Pond Creek	7103	6	–
Prague			
The First National Bank Of Prague	7177	6	–
The Prague National Bank	8159	6	–
Ralston			
The First National Bank Of Ralston	6232	6	–
Sayre			
The First National Bank Of Sayre	6058	6	–
Seiling			
The First National Bank Of Seiling	8615	6	–
Shattuck			
The First National Bank Of Shattuck	8687	6	–
Shawnee			
The First National Bank Of Shawnee	5095	6	–
The Oklahoma National Bank Of Shawnee	5875	6	–
The Shawnee National Bank	5115	6	–
The State National Bank Of Shawnee	6416	6	–
Stillwater			
The First National Bank Of Stillwater	5206	6	–
The National Bank Of Commerce Of Stillwater	5436	6	–
The Stillwater National Bank	5347	4	–
Stroud			
The First National Bank Of Stroud	6306	6	–
Taloga			
The First National Bank Of Taloga	7019	6	–
Tecumseh			
Farmers National Bank Of Tecumseh	7756	6	–
The First National Bank Of Tecumseh	5378	6	–
Temple			
The Farmers National Bank Of Temple	8310	6	–
The First National Bank Of Temple	6570	6	–
Texhoma			
The First National Bank Of Texhoma	8852	6	–
Thomas			
The First National Bank Of Thomas	7278	6	–
The Thomas National Bank	7771	6	–
Tonkawa			
The First National Bank Of Tonkawa	7444	5	–
The Tonkawa National Bank	8595	6	–

City, Bank	Ch. No.	L	S
Verden			
The First National Bank Of Verden	8759	6	–
The National Bank Of Verden	8859	6	–
Wakita			
The First National Bank Of Wakita	5982	6	–
Walters			
The First National Bank Of Walters	6612	6	–
The Walters National Bank	7811	6	–
Wanette			
The First National Bank Of Wanette	6641	6	–
The State National Bank Of Wanette	8304	6	–
Watonga			
The First National Bank Of Watonga	5804	6	–
Waukomis			
The First National Bank Of Waukomis	7967	6	–
Waurika			
The Citizens National Bank Of Waurika	8715	6	–
The First National Bank Of Waurika	8744	6	–
The Waurika National Bank	8861	6	–
Weatherford			
The First National Bank Of Weatherford	5352	6	–
The German National Bank Of Weatherford	7238	6	–
The National Exchange Bank Of Weatherford	5758	6	–
Woodward			
The First National Bank Of Woodward	5575	6	–
Yukon			
The First National Bank Of Yukon	6159	6	–

OKLAHOMA

City, Bank	Ch. No.	L	S
Achille			
The Farmers And Merchants National Bank Of Achille	10380	6	6
The First National Bank Of Achille	10347	6	–
Ada			
The Ada National Bank	5633	6	–
The Citizens National Bank Of Ada	7071	6	–
The First National Bank In Ada	12591	–	4
The First National Bank Of Ada	5620	4	–
The Merchants And Planters National Bank Of Ada	10513	6	–
The Security National Bank Of Ada	12144	–	–
Addington			
The First National Bank Of Addington	10001	6	–
Afton			
The First National Bank Of Afton	10339	6	–
Alex			
The First National Bank Of Alex	10193	6	5
Aline			
The Clarks National Bank Of Aline	12113	–	–
Allen			
The Allen National Bank	11149	–	–
The First National Bank Of Allen	9620	6	–
Altus			
Altus National Bank	12155	6	5
The City National Bank Of Altus	8775	6	–
The First National Bank Of Altus	6113	6	6
The National Bank Of Commerce Of Altus	13756	–	5
Alva			
The Alva National Bank	6490	6	–
The Central National Bank Of Alva	12152	–	–
The First National Bank Of Alva	5587	5	6
Anadarko			
Anadarko National Bank, Anadarko	5923	6	–
The First National Bank Of Anadarko	5905	6	4
The National Bank Of Anadarko	5923	6	–
Antlers			
The Antlers National Bank	7667	6	–
The Citizens National Bank Of Antlers	8082	6	–
The First National Bank Of Antlers	7667	6	5
The First National Bank Of Antlers	14131	–	–
Apache			
The American National Bank Of Apache	12120	5	5
The First National Bank Of Apache	7127	5	5
Arapaho			
The Farmers National Bank Of Clinton	6257	–	–
The First National Bank Of Arapaho	6257	6	–
Arcadia			
The First National Bank Of Arcadia	10612	–	–
Ardmore			
Exchange National Bank Of Ardmore	11093	5	4
First National Bank At Ardmore	13677	–	5
State National Bank Of Ardmore	10394	5	–
The American National Bank Of Ardmore	12053	–	–
The Ardmore National Bank	5922	5	–
The Bankers National Bank Of Ardmore	8354	6	–
The City National Bank Of Ardmore	4723	6	–
The First National Bank In Ardmore	12472	–	5
The First National Bank Of Ardmore	4393	5	–
Atoka			
The American National Bank Of Atoka	8994	6	–
The Atoka National Bank	5791	6	–
Aylesworth			
The First National Bank Of Aylesworth	10385	6	–
Barnsdall			
The Barnsdall National Bank	12076	–	–
Bartlesville			
First National Bank In Bartlesville	6258	6	4
The American National Bank Of Bartlesville	7032	6	–
The Bartlesville National Bank	6258	6	–
The Central National Bank Of Bartlesville	11837	–	–
The Exchange National Bank Of Bartlesville	11688	–	–
The First National Bank Of Bartlesville	5310	4	–
The Union National Bank Of Bartlesville	9567	5	2
Beaver			
The First National Bank Of Beaver	10804	–	–
Beggs			
The American National Bank Of Beggs	12203	–	–
The Farmers National Bank Of Beggs	10482	6	–
The First National Bank Of Beggs	6868	6	6
Bennington			
The American National Bank Of Bennington	12369	–	–
The Bennington National Bank	10343	6	–
The First National Bank Of Bennington	7099	5	6
Berwyn			
The First National Bank Of Berwyn	7209	6	6

City, Bank	Ch. No.	L	S
Bigheart			
The First National Bank Of Barnsdall	11460	–	–
The First National Bank Of Bigheart	11460	–	–
Billings			
The First National Bank In Billings	12041	–	–
The National Bank Of Billings	11219	–	–
Binger			
The First National Bank Of Binger	12133	–	–
Bixby			
The First National Bank Of Bixby	10467	6	–
Blackwell			
The Blackwell National Bank	6916	6	–
The Blackwell National Bank	12038	–	–
The First National Bank In Blackwell	14278	–	–
The First National Bank Of Blackwell	5460	4	5
The Security National Bank Of Blackwell	12040	–	–
The State National Bank Of Blackwell	7583	6	–
Blair			
First National Bank In Blair	12130	–	3
The First National Bank Of Blair	10368	6	–
Blanchard			
The First National Bank Of Blanchard	8702	6	5
Blue Jacket			
The First National Bank Of Blue Jacket	10627	–	–
Boise City			
The First National Bank Of Boise City	11084	6	–
Bokchito			
The Bokchito National Bank	7499	6	–
The First National Bank In Bokchito	12211	–	–
The First National Bank Of Bokchito	6683	6	–
The First National Bank Of Bokchito	9835	6	–
Boley			
The First National Bank Of Boley	12012	–	–
Boswell			
The Boswell National Bank	8353	6	–
The Citizens National Bank Of Boswell	11940	–	–
The Farmers And Merchants National Bank Of Boswell	11190	–	–
The First National Bank Of Boswell	7651	6	–
The State National Bank Of Boswell	10363	6	–
Boynton			
The American National Bank Of Boynton	12265	–	–
The First National Bank Of Boynton	6511	6	5
Braggs			
The First National Bank Of Braggs	10437	3	–
Braman			
The First National Bank Of Braman	10003	6	5
Brinkman			
The First National Bank Of Brinkman	12131	–	–
Bristow			
The American National Bank Of Bristow	10849	–	–
The Bristow National Bank	10115	6	–
The First National Bank Of Bristow	6260	6	–
Britton			
The First National Bank Of Britton	12223	–	–
Broken Arrow			
The Arkansas Valley National Bank Of Broken Arrow	7600	6	–
The Citizens National Bank Of Broken Arrow	10255	6	–
The First National Bank Of Broken Arrow	7115	5	5
Broken Bow			
The First National Bank Of Broken Bow	10424	6	–
Buffalo			
The First National Bank Of Buffalo	8896	6	–
Butler			
The First National Bank Of Butler	10981	–	–
Byars			
The American National Bank Of Byars	11498	–	–
The First National Bank Of Byars	7389	6	–
Byron			
The First National Bank Of Byron	11419	–	–
Caddo			
The Caddo National Bank	7368	5	–
The Security National Bank Of Caddo	10010	6	–
Calera			
The Calera National Bank	11182	5	–
Calumet			
The First National Bank Of Calumet	12200	–	–
Calvin			
The Calvin National Bank	10226	6	–
The First National Bank Of Calvin	6980	5	6
Canadian			
The First National Bank Of Canadian	9993	6	–
Caney			
The First National Bank Of Caney	11612	–	–
Carmen			
The Carmen National Bank	6844	6	–
The Carmen National Bank	10203	6	–
The First National Bank In Carmen	12498	6	5
Carnegie			
The Farmers National Bank Of Carnegie	12059	–	–
The First National Bank Of Carnegie	11763	6	6
Carney			
The First National Bank Of Carney	12315	–	–
Carter			
The First National Bank Of Carter	12147	–	–
Cashion			
The First National Bank Of Cashion	6161	6	–
Castle			
The First National Bank Of Castle	12310	–	–
Cement			
The First National Bank Of Cement	12335	–	–
Centrahoma			
The First National Bank Of Centrahoma	12116	–	–
Centralia			
The First National Bank Of Centralia	7706	6	–
Chandler			
The Chandler National Bank	6142	6	–
The Farmers National Bank Of Chandler	12060	–	–
The First National Bank Of Chandler	5354	5	3
The Union National Bank Of Chandler	6269	5	4
Chattanooga			
The First National Bank Of Chattanooga	11705	–	–

City, Bank	Ch. No.	L	S
Checotah			
The Commercial National Bank In Checotah	11920	6	–
The Commercial National Bank Of Checotah	10063	5	–
The First National Bank Of Checotah	5128	4	–
The Peoples National Bank Of Checotah	10051	5	5
Chelsea			
The First National Bank Of Chelsea	5955	6	6
Cherokee			
The Alfalfa County National Bank Of Cherokee	9008	6	–
The Cherokee National Bank	12049	–	–
The Farmers National Bank Of Cherokee	9884	5	–
The First National Bank Of Cherokee	6677	6	–
Cheyenne			
The First National Bank Of Cheyenne	12245	–	–
Chickasha			
Oklahoma National Bank Of Chickasha	9938	–	4
The Chickasha National Bank	8203	5	6
The Citizens National Bank Of Chickasha	5547	5	–
The Citizens-Farmers National Bank Of Chickasha	5547	–	5
The Farmers National Bank Of Chickasha	12230	–	–
The First National Bank Of Chickasha	5431	3	4
The Oklahoma National Bank Of Chickasha	9938	5	6
Claremore			
The First National Bank Of Claremore	4987	6	–
The National Bank Of Claremore	10117	5	5
Cleveland			
The Cleveland National Bank	7386	5	4
The First National Bank Of Cleveland	5911	4	4
Clinton			
The Clinton National Bank	6851	6	–
The First National Bank Of Clinton	6940	6	5
The Oklahoma National Bank Of Clinton	9985	–	–
The Oklahoma State National Bank Of Clinton	9985	6	–
The Security National Bank Of Clinton	12050	–	–
Coalgate			
The City National Bank Of Coalgate	11676	–	–
The Coalgate National Bank	7321	6	–
The First National Bank In Coalgate	12529	–	–
The First National Bank Of Coalgate	5647	6	–
Colbert			
The First National Bank Of Colbert	10381	6	6
Collinsville			
The Collinsville National Bank	10280	6	–
The First National Bank Of Collinsville	6138	6	–
The First National Bank Of Collinsville	9965	6	–
Comanche			
The Comanche National Bank	8366	6	–
The First National Bank Of Comanche	6299	6	6
The State National Bank Of Comanche	11771	–	–
Commerce			
The First National Bank Of Commerce	10689	5	5
Cordell			
The Cordell National Bank	9971	6	–
The Cordell National Bank	12302	–	–
The Farmers National Bank Of Cordell	9968	4	5
The First National Bank In Cordell	12299	–	–
The First National Bank Of Cordell	6052	6	–
The State National Bank Of Cordell	9972	6	–
Coweta			
The First National Bank Of Coweta	6879	5	5
The National Bank Of Commerce Of Coweta	10031	6	–
The Security National Bank Of Coweta	12111	–	–
Coyle			
The First National Bank Of Coyle	12148	5	5
Cushing			
The Farmers National Bank Of Cushing	8730	6	–
The Farmers National Bank Of Cushing	10332	6	6
The First National Bank Of Cushing	6893	5	3
The Oklahoma National Bank Of Cushing	12054	–	–
Custer City			
The First National Bank Of Custer City	8727	5	5
The Peoples National Bank Of Custer City	12185	–	–
The Peoples State National Bank Of Custer City	9981	6	–
Davenport			
The First National Bank Of Davenport	8668	6	–
Davidson			
The First National Bank Of Davidson	11654	6	–
Davis			
The City National Bank Of Davis	12149	–	–
The First National Bank Of Davis	5298	5	5
The Merchants And Planters National Bank Of Davis	7442	6	–
Depew			
The Depew National Bank	11661	–	–
The State National Bank Of Depew	12104	–	5
Devol			
The First National Bank Of Devol	11535	6	–
Dewey			
The First National Bank Of Dewey	8270	5	5
The Security National Bank Of Dewey	9986	6	–
Drumright			
The First National Bank Of Drumright	10595	–	–
Duncan			
The City National Bank Of Duncan	8616	6	6
The Duncan National Bank	7289	6	–
The First National Bank In Duncan	12812	–	–
The First National Bank Of Duncan	5379	6	–
The First National Bank Of Duncan	10244	6	–
The Oklahoma National Bank Of Duncan	12051	–	–
The Security National Bank Of Duncan	12065	–	5
Durant			
The American National Bank Of Durant	12126	–	–
The Commercial National Bank Of Durant	11842	–	–
The Durant National Bank	5590	4	–
The Durant National Bank In Durant	13018	–	3
The Farmers National Bank Of Durant	6928	6	–
The First National Bank In Durant	14005	–	6
The First National Bank Of Durant	5129	3	4
The State National Bank Of Durant	10538	6	–
Dustin			
The American National Bank Of Dustin	10563	–	–
The First National Bank Of Dustin	12171	–	–

City, Bank	Ch. No.	L	S
Edmond			
The Citizens National Bank Of Edmond	10151	5	4
The First National Bank Of Edmond	6156	5	4
El Dorado			
The Farmers And Merchants National Bank Of El Dorado	8944	6	–
The First National Bank Of El Dorado	8126	6	–
The First National Bank Of El Dorado	9963	6	6
El Reno			
The Citizens National Bank Of El Reno	5985	4	1
The First National Bank Of El Reno	4830	4	4
Elk City			
The Farmers National Bank Of Elk City	12093	–	–
The First National Bank Of Elk City	5766	6	–
The First National Bank Of Elk City	9952	5	5
Enid			
The American National Bank Of Enid	11584	–	–
The Central National Bank Of Enid	12044	–	–
The Enid National Bank	10202	6	–
The First National Bank Of Enid	5335	6	–
The First National Bank Of Enid	9586	4	3
The Garfield National Bank Of Enid	12039	–	–
The Security National Bank Of Enid	14315	–	–
Erick			
First National Bank Of Erick	10875	6	5
The Farmers National Bank Of Erick	12207	–	–
Eufaula			
The Eufaula National Bank	5967	4	–
The First National Bank Of Eufaula	5902	4	–
The State National Bank Of Eufaula	10388	5	5
Fairfax			
The Fairfax National Bank	8202	5	–
The First National Bank Of Fairfax	7972	6	6
Fairland			
The First National Bank Of Fairland	10487	–	–
Fairview			
The Farmers And Merchants National Bank Of Fairview	9767	6	6
Fletcher			
The First National Bank Of Fletcher	12141	–	–
Foraker			
The First National Bank Of Foraker	10356	5	–
Forgan			
The First National Bank Of Forgan	11232	–	–
Fort Gibson			
First National Bank In Fort Gibson	8079	–	5
The Citizens National Bank Of Fort Gibson	10561	5	–
The Farmers National Bank Of Fort Gibson	8079	6	–
The First National Bank Of Fort Gibson	6539	6	–
Fort Sill			
The City National Bank Of Lawton	5753	5	4
Fort Towson			
The American National Bank Of Fort Towson	11256	–	–
The First National Bank Of Fort Towson	8078	6	–
Francis			
The Francis National Bank	10454	6	–
Frederick			
First National Bank In Frederick	13760	–	5
The City National Bank Of Frederick	8206	6	–
The First National Bank Of Frederick	8140	5	5
The National Bank Of Commerce Of Frederick	10095	6	–
Geary			
The First National Bank Of Geary	6163	6	–
The First National Bank Of Geary	10020	6	5
Goltry			
The First National Bank Of Goltry	11394	–	–
Gotebo			
The First National Bank Of Gotebo	10389	5	–
Gracemont			
The First National Bank Of Gracemont	12318	–	–
Grandfield			
The First National Bank Of Grandfield	10006	6	–
Granite			
The First National Bank Of Granite	12142	–	–
Grove			
The First National Bank Of Grove	10119	6	–
Guthrie			
The First National Bank Of Guthrie	4348	3	4
The Guthrie National Bank	4348	5	–
The National Bank Of Commerce Of Guthrie	7299	6	–
Guymon			
The City National Bank Of Guymon	9964	6	6
The First National Bank Of Guymon	8138	5	5
The Texas County National Bank Of Guymon	12179	–	–
Hammon			
The Farmers National Bank Of Hammon	10521	–	–
The First National Bank Of Hammon	10521	–	–
Hanna			
The First National Bank Of Hanna	11551	–	–
Harrah			
The First National Bank Of Harrah	9980	6	6
Hartshorne			
The First National Bank Of Hartshorne	7050	4	–
The Hartshorne National Bank	11064	5	–
The Hartshorne National Bank	13100	–	–
Haskell			
The First National Bank Of Haskell	7822	5	4
The Haskell National Bank	10160	6	–
Hastings			
First National Bank In Hastings	10094	6	–
The First National Bank Of Hastings	8209	6	–
The National Bank Of Hastings	8210	6	–
The National Bank Of Hastings	10094	6	–
The Oklahoma National Bank Of Hastings	12150	–	–
Haworth			
The First National Bank Of Haworth	10500	–	–
Healdton			
The First National Bank Of Healdton	11018	6	–
Heavener			
The First National Bank Of Heavener	9888	6	6
The State National Bank Of Heavener	10239	6	6
Helena			
The Farmers National Bank Of Helena	12376	–	–
The Helena National Bank	12081	–	5
Hennessey			
The Farmers And Merchants National Bank Of Hennessey	10209	6	2
The First National Bank Of Hennessey	5473	5	4
Henryetta			
The First National Bank Of Henryetta	6867	5	–
The Miners National Bank Of Henryetta	10349	6	–
The Peoples National Bank Of Henryetta	12629	–	–
Hinton			
The First National Bank Of Hinton	12107	–	–
Hitchcock			
The First National Bank Of Hitchcock	12088	–	–
Hobart			
The City National Bank Of Hobart	6267	6	–
The City National Bank Of Hobart	10288	6	–
The Farmers And Merchants National Bank Of Hobart	6358	6	–
The First National Bank Of Hobart	5954	6	–
The Hobart National Bank	5915	6	–
Holdenville			
The American National Bank Of Holdenville	7619	6	–
The American National Bank Of Holdenville	12087	–	–
The Farmers National Bank Of Holdenville	10659	–	–
The First National Bank Of Holdenville	5270	4	5
The State National Bank Of Holdenville	10013	6	–
Hollis			
First National Bank In Hollis	8825	5	–
The City National Bank Of Hollis	8825	6	–
The Farmers National Bank Of Hollis	12237	–	–
The First National Bank Of Hollis	8061	6	–
The Groves National Bank Of Hollis	8825	6	–
The National Bank Of Commerce Of Hollis	10240	6	6
The State National Bank Of Hollis	10249	6	–
Hominy			
The First National Bank Of Hominy	7927	5	5
The Hominy National Bank	12069	–	–
The National Bank Of Commerce Of Hominy	10002	6	4
Hooker			
The Farmers And Merchants National Bank Of Hooker	12128	–	–
The First National Bank Of Hooker	10566	–	–
Hugo			
The City National Bank Of Hugo	12136	–	–
The First National Bank Of Hugo	6130	6	–
The Hugo National Bank	7747	5	–
The National Bank Of Commerce At Hugo	12801	–	6
Hulbert			
The First National Bank Of Hulbert	10520	–	–
Hydro			
The Farmers National Bank Of Hydro	10442	6	–
The First National Bank Of Hydro	9944	6	5
Idabel			
The American National Bank Of Idabel	11246	–	–
The First National Bank Of Idabel	8486	6	–
The Idabel National Bank	11913	–	5
The State National Bank Of Idabel	12106	–	–
Jennings			
The First National Bank Of Jennings	11791	–	–
Jones			
The First National Bank Of Jones	12322	–	–
Kaw City			
First National Bank In Kaw City	10075	6	5
National Bank Of Kaw City	10402	5	5
The Farmers National Bank Of Kaw City	10075	6	–
Kemp City			
The First National Bank Of Kemp City	12161	–	–
Kenefick			
The First National Bank In Kenefick	12102	–	–
Kenefie			
The First National Bank Of Kenefic	10104	6	–
Keota			
The First National Bank Of Keota	8177	6	–
The Keota National Bank	10298	6	–
Kiefer			
The First National Bank Of Kiefer	12239	–	–
Kingfisher			
The Citizens National Bank Of Kingfisher	12068	–	–
The First National Bank Of Kingfisher	5328	5	5
The Peoples National Bank Of Kingfisher	9954	6	4
Kingston			
The First National Bank Of Kingston	9881	6	6
Kiowa			
The First National Bank Of Kiowa	8638	6	–
The Peoples National Bank Of Kiowa	10515	–	–
Konawa			
The First National Bank Of Konawa	7633	6	5
The Konawa National Bank	8213	6	–
Kusa			
The First National Bank Of Kusa	10967	–	–
The First National Bank Of Schulter	10967	–	–
Lahoma			
The First National Bank Of Lahoma	9974	5	–
Lamont			
The First National Bank Of Lamont	7783	6	–
Laverne			
The First National Bank Of Laverne	11891	–	–
Lawton			
The American National Bank Of Lawton	12067	5	4
The First National Bank Of Lawton	5914	5	–
The Lawton National Bank	9962	6	–
The Security National Bank Of Lawton	11680	–	–
Leedey			
The First National Bank Of Leedey	12109	–	–
Leger			
The First National Bank Of Altus	6113	–	–
Lehigh			
The Lehigh National Bank	5755	6	–
The Merchants National Bank Of Lehigh	8189	6	–
Lenapah			
The Citizens National Bank Of Lenapah	11436	–	–
The First National Bank Of Lenapah	11436	–	–
The Lenapah National Bank	9951	6	–
Lexington			
The Farmers National Bank Of Lexington	7207	6	–
Lindsay			
The First National Bank Of Lindsay	6171	5	5
Loco			
The First National Bank Of Loco	12221	–	–
Locust Grove			
The First National Bank Of Locust Grove	12103	–	–
Lone Wolf			
The First National Bank Of Lone Wolf	10096	5	3
Luther			
The First National Bank Of Luther	8563	5	5
Madill			
The City National Bank Of Madill	7723	6	–
The First National Bank In Madill	13021	6	6
The Madill National Bank	6365	6	–
The Madill National Bank	10286	6	6
The Marshall County National Bank Of Madill	11192	–	–
Mangum			
The City National Bank Of Mangum	7328	6	–
The First National Bank Of Mangum	5508	4	3
The Mangum National Bank	5811	5	6
Marietta			
The Farmers National Bank Of Marietta	8278	6	–
The First National Bank Of Marietta	5345	6	5
The Love County National Bank Of Marietta	12330	–	–
The Marietta National Bank	5958	5	6
Marlow			
The First National Bank In Marlow	12129	–	2
The First National Bank Of Marlow	5724	6	–
The National Bank Of Marlow	10205	6	6
The State National Bank Of Marlow	9946	5	5
Maud			
The First National Bank Of Maud	8294	6	6
Maysville			
The Farmers National Bank Of Maysville	10283	6	–
The First National Bank Of Maysville	8999	6	5
Mcalester			
The National Bank Of Mcalester	13770	–	4
Mcloud			
The First National Bank Of Mcloud	6660	6	6
Medford			
The First National Bank Of Medford	5796	5	5
Miami			
The First National Bank Of Miami	5252	3	3
The Ottawa County National Bank Of Miami	10019	3	–
Milburn			
The First National Bank Of Milburn	9920	5	–
Mill Creek			
The First National Bank Of Mill Creek	7197	5	4
The Merchants And Planters National Bank Of Mill Creek	8546	6	–
The Mill Creek National Bank	12188	6	–
Minco			
The First National Bank Of Minco	8644	6	6
Moore			
The First National Bank Of Moore	12035	6	5
Morris			
The First National Bank Of Morris	8876	6	–
The Morris National Bank	11932	6	–
Mounds			
The First National Bank Of Mounds	6263	5	–
Mountain View			
The First National Bank Of Mountain View	5656	5	5
Muldrow			
The First National Bank Of Muldrow	6717	6	–
The First National Bank Of Muldrow	9975	5	–
Mulhall			
The First National Bank Of Mulhall	9032	6	–
Muskogee			
The American National Bank Of Muskogee	9701	6	–
The Citizens National Bank Of Muskogee	12918	–	4
The Commercial National Bank In Muskogee	12890	5	3
The Commercial National Bank Of Muskogee	5236	3	–
The Exchange National Bank Of Muskogee	10321	4	–
The First National Bank And Trust Company Of Muskogee	4385	–	4
The First National Bank Of Muskogee	4385	3	–
The Muskogee National Bank	9023	1	–
The Muskogee-Security National Bank, Muskogee	12277	6	–
The Oklahoma National Bank Of Muskogee	10113	6	–
The Security National Bank Of Muskogee	12277	–	–
Nash			
The First National Bank Of Nash	11306	5	4
New Wilson			
The First National Bank Of New Wilson	10574	6	–
Newkirk			
The Eastman National Bank Of Newkirk	9011	5	4
The Farmers National Bank Of Newkirk	8214	6	–
The First National Bank Of Newkirk	5272	5	6
The Security National Bank Of Newkirk	12206	–	–
Ninnekah			
The First National Bank Of Ninnekah	12173	–	–
Noble			
The First National Bank Of Noble	9937	5	5
Norman			
The City National Bank In Norman	12157	–	6
The City National Bank Of Norman	6450	6	–
The Farmers National Bank Of Norman	7293	6	–
The First National Bank Of Norman	5248	5	4
The National Bank Of Norman	7293	6	–
The Security National Bank Of Norman	12036	–	5
Nowata			
The Commercial National Bank Of Nowata	9949	4	5
The First National Bank Of Nowata	5401	5	5
The Nowata National Bank	6367	6	–
The Producers National Bank Of Nowata	9948	6	–
Oakland			
The First National Bank Of Madill	5404	5	–
Oilton			
The First National Bank Of Oilton	11129	–	–
Okarche			
The First National Bank Of Okarche	11894	–	–

City, Bank	Ch. No.	L	S
Okeene			
First National Bank In Okeene	10913	–	–
The National Bank Of Okeene	10913	–	–
Okemah			
The First National Bank Of Okemah	6477	6	5
The Okemah National Bank	7677	4	4
Oklahoma City			
City National Bank And Trust Company Of Oklahoma City	9564	–	–
First National Bank In Oklahoma City	4862	3	–
Oklahoma National Bank Of Oklahoma City	13276	–	–
The American National Bank Of Oklahoma City	5716	3	–
The American-First National Bank In Oklahoma City	4862	–	–
The Farmers National Bank Of Oklahoma City	9564	4	–
The Fidelity National Bank Of Oklahoma City	12016	–	–
The First National Bank & Trust Company Of Oklahoma City	4862	–	1
The First National Bank Of Capitol Hill, Oklahoma City	9584	6	–
The Liberty National Bank Of Oklahoma City	11230	–	2
The Oklahoma City National Bank	6678	6	–
The Oklahoma National Bank In Oklahoma City	9856	–	–
The Oklahoma Stock Yards National Bank Of Oklahoma City	9856	4	–
The Security National Bank Of Oklahoma City	8472	3	6
The South Oklahoma National Bank Of Oklahoma City	13276	–	–
The Southwest National Bank Of Oklahoma City	11481	–	–
The State National Bank Of Oklahoma City	4862	3	–
The Tradesmens National Bank Of Oklahoma City	11628	–	–
The Western National Bank Of Oklahoma City	5159	5	–
Okmulgee			
The American National Bank Of Okmulgee	12048	6	–
The Central National Bank Of Okmulgee	11001	–	–
The Citizens National Bank In Okmulgee	13751	–	6
The Citizens National Bank Of Okmulgee	6241	5	6
The Exchange National Bank Of Okmulgee	9947	6	–
The Farmers National Bank Of Okmulgee	9696	6	–
The First National Bank Of Okmulgee	5418	5	–
The Okmulgee National Bank	6855	6	–
The Union National Bank Of Okmulgee	11963	–	–
Oktaha			
The First National Bank Of Oktaha	10015	6	–
Olustee			
The Farmers National Bank Of Olustee	8754	6	–
The First National Bank Of Olustee	8316	6	–
The First National Bank Of Olustee	9960	5	–
Owasso			
The First National Bank Of Owasso	7964	6	–
Paden			
The First National Bank Of Paden	11824	–	–
The Paden National Bank	11788	–	–
The State National Bank Of Paden	12312	–	–
Pauls Valley			
The Exchange National Bank Of Pauls Valley	12215	–	–
The First National Bank Of Pauls Valley	5091	5	3
The National Bank Of Commerce Of Pauls Valley	6639	6	–
The Pauls Valley National Bank	7892	6	5
Pawhuska			
National Bank Of Commerce In Pawhuska	14304	–	6
The American National Bank Of Pawhuska	8313	6	6
The Citizens National Bank Of Pawhuska	7883	5	5
The Citizens-First National Bank Of Pawhuska	13527	–	3
The First National Bank Of Pawhuska	5961	4	6
The First National Bank Of Pawhuska	13355	–	–
The Liberty National Bank Of Pawhuska	11314	4	–
The Live Stock National Bank Of Pawhuska	13355	–	–
The National Bank Of Commerce Of Pawhuska	12212	–	–
Pawnee			
The Arkansas Valley National Bank Of Pawnee	5492	6	–
The First National Bank Of Pawnee	5224	5	4
The Pawnee National Bank	7611	5	4
Perry			
First National Bank In Perry	14020	–	5
The First National Bank Of Perry	6972	5	5
Picher			
The First National Bank Of Picher	11194	–	–
The Picher National Bank	11624	–	–
Pocasset			
The First National Bank Of Pocasset	10960	6	6
Ponca City			
First National Bank In Ponca City	9801	5	4
The Farmers National Bank Of Ponca City	6061	6	–
The Farmers National Bank Of Ponca City	9801	6	–
The First National Bank At Ponca City	13891	–	5
The First National Bank Of Ponca City	5474	6	–
The Germania National Bank Of Ponca City	9616	6	–
Pond Creek			
Farmers National Bank Of Pond Creek	10005	6	–
First National Bank In Pond Creek	10005	6	6
The First National Bank Of Pond Creek	6655	6	–
The National Bank Of Pond Creek	7103	6	–
Porter			
The First National Bank Of Porter	7615	6	6
The Merchants And Planters National Bank Of Porter	12394	–	–
Porum			
The First National Bank Of Porum	8479	6	–
The Guaranty National Bank Of Porum	11568	–	–
The National Bank Of Commerce Of Porum	10649	6	–
Poteau			
The Central National Bank Of Poteau	12158	–	–
The First National Bank Of Poteau	7118	6	–
The Le Flore County National Bank Of Poteau	12135	–	–
The National Bank Of Poteau	7104	6	–
Prague			
The First National Bank Of Prague	7177	5	4
The Prague National Bank	8159	5	5
Pryor Creek			
The American National Bank Of Pryor Creek	12117	–	5
The First National Bank Of Pryor Creek	5546	6	5
Purcell			
The Chickasaw National Bank Of Purcell	4756	5	–
The Mcclain County National Bank Of Purcell	12134	–	4
The Union National Bank Of Purcell	7697	6	–
Putnam			
The First National Bank Of Putnam	12086	–	–
Quapaw			
The First National Bank Of Quapaw	11157	–	–
Quinton			
The First National Bank Of Quinton	6517	6	6
Ralston			
The First National Bank Of Ralston	6232	5	6
Ringling			
The First National Bank Of Ringling	10548	4	4
Roff			
The Farmers And Merchants National Bank Of Roff	10172	6	–
The First National Bank Of Roff	5417	6	–
Rosston			
The First National Bank Of Rosston	10737	–	–
Rush Springs			
The First National Bank Of Rush Springs	8336	6	5
Ryan			
The First National Bank Of Ryan	5800	5	–
Salisaw			
First National Bank In Sallisaw	7571	5	–
Sallisaw			
The American National Bank Of Sallisaw	12555	–	–
The Citizens National Bank Of Sallisaw	10474	5	–
The Farmers National Bank Of Sallisaw	9973	6	–
The First National Bank Of Sallisaw	5596	6	–
The Merchants National Bank Of Sallisaw	7571	6	–
Sand Springs			
The First National Bank Of Sand Springs	12079	5	–
Sapulpa			
The American National Bank Of Sapulpa	7788	5	4
The First National Bank Of Sapulpa	5951	5	–
Sasakwa			
The First National Bank Of Sasakwa	10314	6	–
Sayre			
The American National Bank Of Sayre	12486	–	–
The Beckham County National Bank Of Sayre	9976	6	6
The First National Bank Of Sayre	6058	6	–
The First National Bank Of Sayre	9959	5	6
Seiling			
The First National Bank Of Seiling	8615	6	5
Seminole			
The First National Bank Of Seminole	9514	6	4
Sentinel			
The First National Bank Of Sentinel	9995	5	–
The Security National Bank Of Sentinel	12298	–	–
Shattuck			
The First National Bank Of Shattuck	8687	6	–
The Shattuck National Bank	9987	6	5
Shawnee			
The American National Bank Of Shawnee	13930	–	–
The Federal National Bank Of Shawnee	12339	6	4
The National Bank Of Commerce In Shawnee	12441	6	–
The National Bank Of Commerce Of Shawnee	9998	6	–
The Oklahoma National Bank Of Shawnee	5875	6	–
The Shawnee National Bank	5115	5	5
The State National Bank Of Shawnee	6416	4	4
Shidler			
The First National Bank Of Shidler	12165	–	–
The Shidler National Bank	12177	–	–
Skiatook			
The First National Bank Of Skiatook	9969	6	–
The Oklahoma First National Bank Of Skiatook	13361	–	–
The Oklahoma National Bank Of Skiatook	10464	6	–
Slick			
The First National Bank Of Slick	11982	–	–
The Slick National Bank	12388	–	–
Snyder			
The First National Bank Of Snyder	10317	6	–
The Kiowa National Bank Of Snyder	10311	6	–
The Kiowa National Bank Of Snyder	12218	–	–
Soper			
The First National Bank Of Soper	10366	6	–
South Mcalester			
The American National Bank Of Mcalester	6230	4	–
The City National Bank Of Mcalester	6406	5	–
The First National Bank Of Mcalester	5052	4	4
Spiro			
The First National Bank Of Spiro	9275	4	–
Spokogee			
The First National Bank Of Dustin	6804	6	–
Sterrett			
The First National Bank Of Sterrett	7950	5	–
Stigler			
The American National Bank Of Stigler	7432	6	–
The First National Bank Of Stigler	7217	5	6
The Security National Bank Of Stigler	12331	–	–
Stillwater			
First National Bank Of Stillwater	5206	–	4
The American National Bank Of Stillwater	12082	–	–
The American-first National Bank Of Stillwater	5206	–	–
The First National Bank Of Stillwater	5206	6	–
The National Bank Of Commerce Of Stillwater	5436	6	–
The Stillwater National Bank	5347	5	6
Stilwell			
The First National Bank Of Stilwell	9970	5	6
Stonewall			
The First National Bank Of Stonewall	7054	5	–
Stratford			
The First National Bank Of Stratford	8524	4	5
Stroud			
The First National Bank Of Stroud	6306	6	6
The State National Bank Of Stroud	12095	–	–
The Stroud National Bank	10615	–	–
Stuart			
The First National Bank Of Stuart	10007	6	–
The Liberty National Bank Of Stuart	11315	6	–
Sulphur			
Park National Bank Of Sulphur	9046	5	6
The Farmers National Bank Of Sulphur	11016	–	–
The First National Bank Of Sulphur	5748	6	–
Tahlequah			
The Central National Bank Of Tahlequah	10468	6	–
The First National Bank Of Tahlequah	5478	5	4
The Guaranty National Bank Of Tahlequah	11485	6	–
The Liberty National Bank Of Tahlequah	12089	5	–
Talihina			
The First National Bank Of Talihina	7780	6	–
The First National Bank Of Talihina	10672	–	–
Taloga			
The First National Bank Of Taloga	7019	5	–
Tecumseh			
Farmers National Bank Of Tecumseh	7756	6	–
The First National Bank Of Tecumseh	5378	6	–
The Tecumseh National Bank	10304	5	5
Temple			
First National Bank In Temple	11384	–	–
The First National Bank Of Temple	6570	6	–
The Security National Bank Of Temple	11384	–	–
The Temple National Bank	9967	6	–
Terlton			
The First National Bank Of Terlton	9991	6	–
Terral			
The First National Bank Of Terral	7996	6	–
The First National Bank Of Terral	11648	–	–
Texhoma			
The Farmers National Bank Of Texhoma	12125	–	–
The First National Bank Of Texhoma	8852	6	6
Thomas			
The First National Bank Of Thomas	7278	5	5
Tipton			
The First National Bank Of Tipton	11052	6	–
Tishomingo			
The American National Bank Of Tishomingo	7042	6	–
The Farmers National Bank Of Tishomingo	10431	5	–
The First National Bank Of Tishomingo	5809	5	–
The First National Bank Of Tishomingo	12908	–	–
The Tishomingo National Bank	10012	6	–
Tonkawa			
The American National Bank Of Tonkawa	12356	–	–
The Farmers National Bank Of Tonkawa	11397	–	–
The First National Bank In Tonkawa	11397	–	6
The First National Bank Of Tonkawa	7444	6	–
The Tonkawa National Bank	8595	6	–
Tulsa			
National Bank Of Tulsa	13679	–	4
The American National Bank Of Tulsa	10342	5	–
The Central National Bank And Trust Company Of Tulsa	8552	6	–
The Central National Bank Of Tulsa	8552	4	–
The Exchange National Bank Of Tulsa	9658	3	2
The Farmers National Bank Of Tulsa	6669	6	–
The First National Bank & Trust Company Of Tulsa	5171	–	3
The First National Bank Of Tulsa	5171	4	–
The Fourth National Bank Of Tulsa	13480	–	–
The Liberty National Bank Of Tulsa	10262	6	–
The National Bank Of Commerce Of Tulsa	9942	5	6
The Oklahoma National Bank Of Tulsa	9943	6	–
The Planters National Bank Of Tulsa	10904	–	–
The Producers National Bank Of Tulsa	12042	4	5
The Security National Bank Of Tulsa	12043	6	–
The Tulsa National Bank	7085	–	–
The Union National Bank Of Tulsa	10906	5	–
Tulsa National Bank, Tulsa	12043	–	–
Tupelo			
The Farmers National Bank Of Tupelo	10531	6	–
The First National Bank Of Tupelo	8609	6	–
Tuttle			
The First National Bank Of Tuttle	8475	6	–
Tyrone			
The Farmers National Bank Of Tyrone	12163	–	–
The First National Bank Of Tyrone	10032	6	5
Valliant			
The American National Bank Of Valliant	11181	–	–
The Citizens National Bank Of Valliant	11459	–	–
The First National Bank Of Valliant	9992	6	–
Verden			
The First National Bank Of Verden	8759	6	–
The National Bank Of Verden	8859	6	6
Vian			
The First National Bank Of Vian	10573	5	5
Vinita			
The Cherokee National Bank Of Vinita	5860	6	–
The Farmers National Bank Of Vinita	6602	6	–
The First National Bank Of Vinita	4704	4	3
The Vinita National Bank	5083	5	–
Wagoner			
The American National Bank Of Wagoner	12368	–	–
The City National Bank Of Wagoner	7628	6	–
The First National Bank Of Wagoner	5016	5	5
The Wagoner National Bank	6048	6	–
Wakita			
The First National Bank Of Wakita	5982	6	–
Walters			
The American National Bank Of Walters	12118	–	–
The First National Bank Of Walters	6612	6	–
The Walters National Bank	7811	6	6
Walters National Bank	14108	–	6
Wanette			
The First National Bank Of Wanette	6641	6	6
The State National Bank Of Wanette	8304	6	–
Wapanucka			
The First National Bank Of Wapanucka	5950	6	–
The Peoples National Bank Of Wapanucka	8137	6	–
Warner			
The First National Bank Of Warner	8809	6	–
Washington			
The First National Bank Of Washington	10277	6	5
Watonga			
The First National Bank Of Watonga	5804	6	–

City, Bank	Ch. No.	L	S
Waukomis			
The Waukomis National Bank	10227	5	5
Waurika			
The Farmers National Bank Of Waurika	12094	–	–
The First National Bank Of Waurika	8744	6	5
The Waurika National Bank	8861	6	6
Waynoka			
The First National Bank Of Waynoka	9709	6	6
Weatherford			
The First National Bank Of Weatherford	5352	5	–
The German National Bank Of Weatherford	7238	6	–
The Liberty National Bank Of Weatherford	7238	6	5
Webbers Falls			
The First National Bank Of Webbers Falls	8024	6	–
Weleetka			
The First National Bank Of Weleetka	6324	6	–
The State National Bank Of Weleetka	12074	–	–
Wellston			
The First National Bank Of Wellston	9983	6	–
The Wellston National Bank	12078	–	6
Westville			
The First National Bank Of Westville	10158	5	6
Wetumka			
The American National Bank Of Wetumka	7724	6	5
The American National Bank Of Wetumka	14322	–	–
The National Bank Of Commerce Of Wetumka	12099	–	–
Wetumpka			
The First National Bank Of Wetumpka	5935	6	–
Wewoka			
The Farmers National Bank Of Wewoka	8052	6	6
The First National Bank Of Wewoka	6254	6	–
Wheatland			
The First National Bank Of Wheatland	12169	–	–
Wilburton			
The First National Bank Of Wilburton	6890	6	–
The Latimer County National Bank Of Wilburton	10170	6	–
Wilson			
The First National Bank Of Wilson	12827	–	–
Woodville			
The First National Bank Of Woodville	7707	6	–
Woodward			
The First National Bank Of Woodward	5575	5	5
Wynnewood			
The First National Bank Of Wynnewood	5126	4	5
The Southern National Bank Of Wynnewood	5731	5	5
The State National Bank Of Wynnewood	12334	–	–
Wynona			
The First National Bank Of Wynona	11396	–	–
The Wynona National Bank	12052	–	–
Yale			
The Farmers National Bank Of Yale	10722	–	–
The First National Bank Of Yale	10014	6	5
Yukon			
The First National Bank Of Yukon	6159	6	5
The Yukon National Bank	10196	5	5

OREGON

City, Bank	Ch. No.	L	S
Albany			
The First National Bank Of Albany	2928	4	4
The Linn County National Bank Of Albany	4326	6	–
Arlington			
The Arlington National Bank	3918	6	–
The First National Bank Of Arlington	3676	6	–
Ashland			
The First National Bank Of Ashland	5747	5	3
The United States National Bank Of Ashland	9431	6	–
Astoria			
The Astoria National Bank	4403	5	–
The First National Bank Of Astoria	3486	5	5
The National Bank Of Commerce Of Astoria	13354	–	4
Athena			
The First National Bank Of Athena	4516	6	5
Aurora			
The First National Bank Of Aurora	11975	–	–
Baker City			
The Baker City National Bank, Baker City	4206	6	–
The Citizens National Bank Of Baker City	6768	4	5
The First National Bank Of Baker	2865	6	3
The First National Bank Of Baker City	2865	5	–
Bandon			
The First National Bank Of Bandon	9718	6	–
Bend			
The First National Bank Of Bend	9363	6	–
The Lumbermens National Bank Of Bend	13093	–	2
Burns			
The First National Bank Of Burns	6295	3	5
The Harney County National Bank Of Burns	8691	5	5
Canby			
First National Bank In Aurora	10619	–	6
The First National Bank Of Canby	10619	6	6
Canyon City			
The First National Bank Of Grant County At Canyon City	6491	6	–
Clatskanie			
First National Bank In Clatskanie	14001	–	6
The First National Bank Of Clatskanie	11758	–	–
Condon			
The Condon National Bank	8261	6	–
The First National Bank Of Condon	7059	6	3
The First National Bank Of Condon	14241	–	–
Coquille			
The First National Bank Of Coquille	6849	6	6
Corvallis			
First National Bank Of Corvallis	4301	–	4
The Benton County National Bank Of Corvallis	8750	6	–
The First National Bank Of Corvallis	4301	5	–
Cottage Grove			
The First National Bank Of Cottage Grove	5642	6	5
Dallas			
Dallas National Bank	7472	6	3
The First National Bank Of Dallas	7072	6	–
Dalles City			
The Citizens National Bank Of Dalles City	11807	–	–

City, Bank	Ch. No.	L	S
East Portland			
The First National Bank Of East Portland	3025	6	–
Elgin			
The First National Bank Of Elgin	6644	6	5
Enterprise			
The Wallowa National Bank Of Enterprise	3912	6	5
Eugene			
The United States National Bank Of Eugene	10345	6	5
Eugene City			
The Eugene National Bank Of Eugene City	3986	6	–
The First National Bank Of Eugene	3458	4	5
The First National Bank Of Eugene City	3458	6	–
Forest Grove			
The First National Bank Of Forest Grove	8036	5	3
The Forest Grove National Bank	8554	6	5
Gardiner			
The First National Bank Of Gardiner	10676	5	5
Grants Pass			
The First National Bank Of Southern Oregon At Grants Pass	4168	5	4
Halfway			
The First National Bank Of Halfway	11466	–	–
Harrisburg			
The First National Bank Of Harrisburg	9146	6	6
The Harrisburg National Bank	11885	–	–
Heppner			
The Farmers And Stock Growers National Bank Of Heppner	11007	–	–
The First National Bank Of Heppner	3774	6	6
The National Bank Of Heppner	3953	6	–
Hermiston			
The First National Bank Of Hermiston	9281	6	6
Hillsboro			
The American National Bank Of Hillsboro	9923	6	–
The Commercial National Bank Of Hillsboro	9917	–	5
The First National Bank Of Hillsboro	3966	6	–
The Hillsboro National Bank	9917	6	–
Hood River			
The First National Bank Of Hood River	7272	6	3
Independence			
First National Bank Of Independence	3979	6	5
The First National Bank Of Independence	3972	6	–
The Independence National Bank	3979	6	–
Island City			
The First National Bank Of Island City	3313	6	–
Joseph			
The First National Bank Of Joseph	8048	6	–
Junction City			
The First National Bank Of Junction City	10218	5	4
Klamath Falls			
The American National Bank Of Klamath Falls	11801	5	5
The First National Bank Of Klamath Falls	7167	5	3
La Grande			
The Farmers And Traders National Bank Of La Grande	4452	6	–
The First National Bank Of La Grande	13602	–	3
The La Grande National Bank	3655	3	4
The United States National Bank Of La Grande	9314	5	4
Lakeview			
The Commercial National Bank Of Lakeview	11121	6	5
The First National Bank Of Lakeview	7244	5	6
Lebanon			
The First National Bank Of Lebanon	9127	5	6
The Lebanon National Bank	10164	6	6
Linnton			
The First National Bank Of Linnton	10534	6	–
Madras			
The First National Bank Of Madras	11691	–	–
Marshfield			
The Coos Bay National Bank Of Marshfield	12077	–	–
The First National Bank Of Coos Bay At Marshfield	7475	5	5
Mcminnville			
The First National Bank Of Mcminnville	3399	5	5
The Mcminnville National Bank	3857	5	–
The United States National Bank Of Mcminnville	9806	6	–
United States National Bank Of Mcminnville	3857	–	4
Medford			
Medford National Bank	13771	–	5
The First National Bank Of Medford	7701	4	3
The Medford National Bank	8236	5	5
Merrill			
The First National Bank Of Merrill	10056	6	5
Milton			
The First National Bank Of Milton	9201	6	–
The Valley National Bank Of Milton	13633	–	–
Molalla			
The First National Bank Of Molalla	11271	–	6
Monmouth			
The First National Bank Of Monmouth	10071	6	5
Mount Angel			
The First National Bank Of Mount Angel	12193	–	–
Newberg			
The First National Bank Of Newberg	7537	6	6
United States National Bank Of Newburg	9358	6	4
North Bend			
The First National Bank Of North Bend	9328	5	5
The North Bend National Bank	14054	–	–
Ontario			
Ontario National Bank	9348	4	4
Ontario National Bank	9348	–	4
The First National Bank Of Ontario	5822	6	6
Oregon City			
The First National Bank Of Oregon City	8556	6	5
Paisley			
Paisley National Bank	10432	6	6
Pendleton			
The American National Bank Of Pendleton	9228	5	–
The Commercial National Bank Of Pendleton	7301	6	–
The First Inland National Bank Of Pendleton	13576	–	4
The First National Bank Of Pendleton	2630	4	6
The National Bank Of Pendleton	4249	6	–
The Pendleton National Bank	3665	6	–

City, Bank	Ch. No.	L	S
Portland			
Brotherhood Co-Operative National Bank Of Portland	12613	3	–
Brotherhood National Bank Of Portland	12613	–	6
Columbia National Bank Of Portland	12613	–	6
Lumbermens National Bank Of Portland	9180	5	–
The Ainsworth National Bank Of Portland	3402	6	–
The American National Bank Of Portland	12557	–	4
The Central National Bank Of Portland	13294	–	6
The Citizens National Bank Of Portland	13299	–	3
The Commercial National Bank Of Portland	3422	6	–
The First National Bank Of Portland	1553	3	1
The Merchants National Bank Of Portland	3536	5	–
The Northwestern National Bank Of Portland	10300	6	–
The Oregon National Bank Of Portland	3719	6	–
The Portland National Bank	3184	6	–
The Portland National Bank	12557	–	–
The United States National Bank Of Portland	4514	1	1
The West Coast National Bank Of Portland	12470	–	–
Prairie City			
The First National Bank Of Prairie City	9763	6	4
Prineville			
The First National Bank Of Prineville	3851	6	–
The Prineville National Bank	12655	–	–
Redmond			
The First National Bank Of Redmond	11294	6	–
The Redmond National Bank	11302	6	–
Roseburg			
The Douglas National Bank Of Roseburg	9423	5	5
The First National Bank Of Roseburg	4624	6	–
The Roseburg National Bank	8955	6	–
Saint Helens			
The First National Bank Of St. Helens	11200	5	5
Saint Johns			
Peninsula National Bank Of Portland	10103	6	4
The First National Bank Of Saint Johns	9047	6	–
The Peninsula National Bank Of Saint Johns	10103	6	–
Salem			
First National Bank In Salem	3405	5	5
The Capital National Bank Of Salem	3405	5	–
The First National Bank Of Salem	2816	6	–
The United States National Bank Of Salem	9021	6	5
Scappoose			
The First National Bank Of Scappoose	10992	6	6
Sheridan			
The First National Bank Of Sheridan	8721	6	6
Silverton			
The First National Bank Of Silverton	11106	6	6
Springfield			
The First National Bank Of Springfield	8941	6	6
Stayton			
The First National Bank Of Stayton	11917	–	–
Sumpter			
The First National Bank Of Sumpter	6547	6	–
The Dalles			
The Citizens First National Bank Of The Dalles	3441	–	–
The Dalles National Bank, The Dalles	3534	6	–
The First National Bank Of The Dalles	3441	4	4
The First National Bank Of The Dalles	3441	–	–
Tillamook			
The First National Bank Of Tillamook	8574	6	4
The Tillamook National Bank	13192	–	–
Toledo			
The First National Bank Of Toledo	11937	–	–
The National Security Bank Of Toledo	14306	–	–
Union			
The First National Bank Of Union	2947	5	5
The Union National Bank	8387	6	–
Vale			
The First National Bank Of Vale	8528	6	–
The United States National Bank Of Vale	9496	5	–
The Vale National Bank	12262	–	–
Wallowa			
The Stockgrowers And Farmers National Bank Of Wallowa	9002	6	3
Wheeler			
The First National Bank Of Wheeler	12427	6	–
Woodburn			
The First National Bank Of Woodburn	11906	–	–

PENNSYLVANIA

City, Bank	Ch. No.	L	S
Adamsburg			
The First National Bank Of Beaver Springs At Adamsburg	5777	5	–
Addison			
The First National Bank Of Addison	6709	6	6
Akron			
The Akron National Bank	9364	6	5
Albion			
First National Bank At Albion	13871	–	6
The First National Bank Of Albion	9534	5	5
Alexandria			
The First National Bank Of Alexandria	11263	6	4
Aliquippa			
The Aliquippa National Bank	9902	6	–
The First National Bank Of Aliquippa	8590	6	5
Allegheny			
The Enterprise National Bank Of Allegheny	4991	6	–
The First National Bank Of Allegheny	198	5	–
The First National Bank Of Allegheny At Pittsburgh	198	6	–
The German National Bank Of Allegheny	2261	4	–
The National Bank Of America At Pittsburgh	2261	5	4
The Second National Bank Of Allegheny	776	5	–
The Second National Bank Of Allegheny, Pittsburgh	776	6	5
The Second National Bank Of Pittsburgh	776	–	6
The Third National Bank Of Allegheny	2235	6	–
Allentown			
The Allentown National Bank	1322	2	2
The First National Bank Of Allentown	161	5	–
The Merchants National Bank Of Allentown	6645	6	–
The Merchants National Bank Of Allentown	6645	–	6
The Merchants-Citizens Natl Bank & Trust Co Of Allentown	6645	6	4
The Second National Bank Of Allentown	373	5	4

City, Bank	Ch. No.	L	S
Allenwood			
The Allenwood National Bank	11593	6	5
Altoona			
The First National Bank Of Altoona	247	5	4
The Second National Bank Of Altoona	2781	6	5
Ambler			
The Ambler National Bank	14037	–	–
The First National Bank Of Ambler	3220	4	4
Ambridge			
The Ambridge National Bank	10839	5	5
The Economy National Bank Of Ambridge	13087	6	5
The First National Bank Of Ambridge	8459	6	–
Annville			
The Annville National Bank	2384	6	5
Apollo			
The First National Bank Of Apollo	5723	5	5
Ardmore			
The Ardmore National Bank	9905	6	–
The Ardmore National Bank And Trust Company, Ardmore	9905	5	–
Arendtsville			
The National Bank Of Arendtsville	9139	5	4
Arnold			
The Arnold National Bank	11896	5	–
The National Deposit Bank Of Arnold	11896	6	4
Ashland			
The Ashland National Bank	5615	3	3
The Citizens National Bank Of Ashland	2280	4	4
The First National Bank Of Ashland	403	6	–
Ashley			
The First National Bank Of Ashley	8656	6	5
Aspinwall			
The First National Bank Of Aspinwall	8824	6	–
Atglen			
The Atglen National Bank	7056	5	4
Athens			
The Athens National Bank	5202	4	4
The Farmers National Bank Of Athens	4915	4	4
The First National Bank Of Athens	1094	6	–
Auburn			
The First National Bank Of Auburn	9240	5	–
Austin			
The First National Bank Of Austin	12562	6	5
Avella			
The Lincoln National Bank Of Avella	7854	6	6
Avoca			
The First National Bank Of Avoca	8494	5	5
Avondale			
The National Bank Of Avondale	4560	5	4
Avonmore			
The First National Bank Of Avonmore	7594	6	4
Bainbridge			
The First National Bank Of Bainbridge	9264	6	–
Bakerton			
The First National Bank Of Bakerton	11757	5	4
Bala-cynwyd			
The Bala-Cynwyd National Bank	12695	–	–
Bally			
The First National Bank Of Bally	9402	5	3
Bangor			
First National Bank In Bangor	14170	–	4
The First National Bank Of Bangor	2659	4	4
The Merchants National Bank Of Bangor	4513	5	4
Barnesboro			
The First National Bank Of Barnesboro	5818	6	5
Bath			
The First National Bank Of Bath	5444	6	4
Beaver			
The Beaver National Bank	5042	6	–
The First National Bank Of Beaver	3850	6	–
The Fort Mcintosh National Bank Of Beaver	8185	5	5
Beaver Falls			
First National Bank At Beaver Falls	14117	–	5
The Farmers National Bank Of Beaver Falls	4894	5	5
The First National Bank Of Beaver Falls	3356	4	4
Beaver Springs			
The First National Bank Of Beaver Springs	5777	6	5
Beaverdale			
The First National Bank Of Beaverdale	11317	6	5
Bedford			
First National Bank And Trust Company Of Bedford	3089	–	5
The First National Bank Of Bedford	3089	5	6
The First National Bank Of Bedford	14284	–	–
The Hartley National Bank Of Bedford	14239	–	–
Beech Creek			
The Beech Creek National Bank	13205	6	6
Bellafonte			
The Farmers National Bank Of Bellafonte	13118	–	–
Belle Vernon			
The First National Bank Of Belle Vernon	4850	4	5
Bellefonte			
The First National Bank Of Bellefonte	459	5	5
Belleville			
The Belleville National Bank	5306	6	5
The Farmers National Bank Of Belleville	10128	6	6
The Kishacoquillas Valley National Bank Of Belleville	10128	–	6
Bellevue			
The Bellevue National Bank	5509	6	–
The Citizens National Bank Of Bellevue	8761	5	–
Bellwood			
The First National Bank Of Bellwood	7356	6	5
Bendersville			
The Bendersville National Bank	9114	6	4
Benson			
The First National Bank Of Benson	7935	6	–
Bentleyville			
The Bentleyville National Bank	8196	6	–
The Citizens National Bank Of Bentleyville	13663	–	6
The Farmers And Miners National Bank Of Bentleyville	9058	6	5
The First National Bank Of Bentleyville	8196	6	–
Benton			
The Columbia County National Bank Of Benton	6328	6	6
Berlin			
The First National Bank Of Berlin	5823	6	5
The Philson National Bank Of Berlin	6512	6	5
Bernville			
The First National Bank Of Bernville	8913	5	3
Berwick			
The Berwick National Bank	6162	6	4
The First National Bank Of Berwick	568	6	6
Berwyn			
Berwyn National Bank	13999	–	6
The Berwyn National Bank	3945	5	4
Bethlehem			
The Bethlehem National Bank	14007	–	–
The First National Bank And Trust Company Of Bethlehem	138	–	3
The First National Bank Of Bethlehem	138	3	5
The Lehigh Valley National Bank Of Bethlehem	2050	4	4
Big Run			
The Citizens National Bank Of Big Run	5667	6	4
Biglerville			
The Biglerville National Bank	7917	6	5
Birdsboro			
The First National Bank Of Birdsboro	3905	5	4
The First National Bank Of Birdsboro	13917	–	–
Black Lick			
The First National Bank Of Black Lick	8428	6	–
Blairsville			
Blairsville National Bank	13868	–	6
The Blairsville National Bank	4919	6	4
The First National Bank Of Blairsville	867	6	–
Bloomsburg			
The Bloomsburg National Bank	5211	5	–
The Farmers National Bank Of Bloomsburg	4543	6	5
The First National Bank Of Bloomsburg	293	5	4
Blossburg			
The Citizens National Bank And Trust Company Of Blossburg	13381	–	4
The Miners National Bank Of Blossburg	5007	5	–
Blue Ball			
The Blue Ball National Bank	8421	4	3
Blue Ridge Summit			
The First National Bank Of Blue Ridge Summit	12281	6	5
Bolivar			
The Bolivar National Bank	6135	6	5
The Citizens National Bank Of Bolivar	12355	6	5
Boswell			
The First National Bank Of Boswell	6603	6	6
Boyertown			
The Farmers National Bank And Trust Company Of Boyertown	2900	6	3
The Farmers National Bank Of Boyertown	2900	5	–
The National Bank And Trust Company Of Boyertown	2137	–	3
The National Bank Of Boyertown	2137	3	5
Braddock			
First National Bank Of Braddock	13866	–	4
The Braddock National Bank	2828	4	3
The First National Bank Of Braddock	2799	5	–
The Union National Bank Of Braddock	6796	6	–
Bradford			
The Bradford National Bank	2428	4	4
The Commercial National Bank Of Bradford	4199	5	4
The First National Bank Of Bradford	2470	5	–
Bridgeport			
The Bridgeport National Bank	8329	5	4
Bridgeville			
The Bridgeville National Bank	14251	–	–
The First National Bank Of Bridgeville	6636	6	4
Bristol			
The Farmers National Bank Of Bucks County, Bristol	717	3	4
Brockway			
The First National Bank Of Brockway	13566	–	–
Brockwayville			
The First National Bank Of Brockway	5497	–	6
The First National Bank Of Brockwayville	5497	5	–
Brookville			
The First National Bank Of Brookville	897	6	–
The Jefferson County National Bank Of Brookville	2392	4	5
The National Bank Of Brookville	3051	5	4
Brownstown			
The Brownstown National Bank	9026	6	6
Brownsville			
The First National Bank Of Brownsville	135	6	–
The Monongahela National Bank Of Brownsville	648	4	6
The National Deposit Bank Of Brownsville	2457	6	5
The Second National Bank Of Brownsville	2673	5	6
Bruin			
The First National Bank Of Bruin	8919	5	5
Bryn Mawr			
The Bryn Mawr National Bank	3766	5	4
Burgettstown			
The Burgettstown National Bank	2408	6	–
The Peoples National Bank Of Burgettstown	13009	–	–
The Washington National Bank Of Burgettstown	6944	5	5
Burnham			
The First National Bank Of Burnham	11257	6	5
Burnside			
The Burnside National Bank	11902	6	5
Butler			
The Butler County National Bank & Trust Co Of Butler	4374	–	5
The Butler County National Bank Of Butler	4374	3	4
The Farmers National Bank Of Butler	5391	6	–
The First National Bank Of Butler	309	6	–
The Merchants National Bank Of Butler	9814	6	–
The South Side National Bank Of Butler	11760	–	–
The Union National Bank Of Butler	13447	–	–
Cairnbrook			
The First National Bank Of Cairnbrook	10704	6	6
California			
The First National Bank Of California	4622	5	5
Cambridge Springs			
The First National Bank Of Cambridge Springs	6533	6	–
The Springs National Bank Of Cambridge Springs	9430	5	–
The Springs-First National Bank	14029	–	–
The Springs-First National Bank Of Cambridge Springs	9430	6	4
Camp Hill			
The Camp Hill National Bank	12380	5	3
Canonsburg			
The First National Bank At Canonsburg	13813	–	3
The First National Bank Of Canonsburg	4570	6	5
Canton			
The Farmers National Bank Of Canton	9317	5	6
The First National Bank Of Canton	2505	4	5
Carbondale			
The First National Bank Of Carbondale	664	5	5
Carlisle			
The First National Bank Of Carlisle	21	6	–
The Merchants National Bank Of Carlisle	4444	5	–
Carmichaels			
The First National Bank Of Carmichaels	5784	6	5
Carnegie			
The Carnegie National Bank	6174	6	5
The Union National Bank Of Carnegie	12934	6	5
Carrolltown			
The First National Bank Of Carrolltown	5855	6	5
Cassandra			
The First National Bank Of Cassandra	12720	6	5
Castle Shannon			
The First National Bank Of Castle Shannon	9128	6	6
Catasauqua			
The Lehigh National Bank Of Catasauqua	8283	6	4
The National Bank Of Catasauqua	1411	4	4
Catawissa			
The Catawissa National Bank	7448	5	4
The First National Bank Of Catawissa	4548	5	5
Cecil			
First National Bank In Cecil	14094	–	3
The First National Bank Of Cecil	7076	6	4
Center Hall			
The First National Bank Of Centre Hall	12192	6	5
Central City			
The Central City National Bank	11967	6	4
Centralia			
The First National Bank Of Centralia	9568	6	6
Chalfont			
The Chalfont National Bank	12582	–	3
Chambersburg			
The National Bank Of Chambersburg	593	5	3
The Valley National Bank Of Chambersburg	4272	4	3
Charleroi			
First National Bank In Charleroi	14123	–	6
The First National Bank Of Charleroi	4534	5	5
The National Bank Of Charleroi	13585	–	–
The National Bank Of Charleroi And Trust Company	13585	–	2
Chartiers			
The First National Bank Of Carnegie	4762	5	–
The First National Bank Of Chartiers	4762	6	–
Cheltenham			
The Cheltenham National Bank	12526	5	4
Cherry Tree			
The First National Bank Of Cherry Tree	7000	6	3
Chester			
The Chester National Bank	2904	4	5
The Delaware County National Bank Of Chester	355	3	2
The First National Bank Of Chester	332	4	3
The Pennsylvania National Bank Of Chester	6654	4	–
Christiana			
The Christiana National Bank	7078	5	4
The National Bank Of Christiana	2849	6	–
Clairton			
The Clairton National Bank	6495	5	–
Clarion			
The First National Bank Of Clarion	774	4	5
The First National Bank Of Clarion	14043	–	–
The Second National Bank Of Clarion	3044	6	–
Clarks Summit			
The Abington National Bank Of Clarks Summit	10383	6	5
Claysburg			
The First National Bank Of Claysburg	10232	6	4
Claysville			
The Farmers National Bank Of Claysville	9307	5	5
The First National Bank Of Claysville	4273	6	–
The National Bank Of Claysville	4255	5	4
Clearfield			
The Clearfield National Bank	4836	5	5
The County National Bank At Clearfield	13998	–	2
The County National Bank Of Clearfield	855	4	3
The Farmers And Traders National Bank Of Clearfield	8464	6	–
The First National Bank Of Clearfield	768	4	–
Clifton			
The First National Bank Of Clifton Heights	6275	6	5
Clifton Heights			
Clifton Heights National Bank	14122	–	6
Clintonville			
The First National Bank Of Clintonville	6948	6	–
The Peoples National Bank Of Clintonville	9154	6	5
Clymer			
The Clymer National Bank	9898	5	6
Coaldale			
Farmers National Bank And Trust Company Of Bedford	11188	5	4
Farmers National Bank Of Bedford	11188	5	–
The Broad Top National Bank Of Coaldale	11188	6	–
The First National Bank Of Coaldale	9739	5	5
Coalport			
The First National Bank Of Coalport	6887	4	6

City, Bank	Ch. No.	L	S
Glenside			
The Glenside National Bank	9668	6	–
Goldsboro			
The First National Bank Of Goldsboro	9072	6	5
Grantham			
The Grantham National Bank	9727	6	–
Gratz			
The First National Bank Of Gratz	9473	6	5
The Gratz National Bank	14301	–	–
Green Lane			
The First National Bank Of Green Lane	14214	–	3
The Green Lane National Bank	2131	6	–
The Valley National Bank Of Green Lane	9084	5	2
Greencastle			
The Citizens National Bank Of Greencastle	5857	6	6
The First National Bank Of Greencastle	1081	6	4
Greensburg			
First National Bank In Greensburg	14055	–	4
The Farmers National Bank Of Greensburg	1894	6	–
The Fifth National Bank Of Pittsburgh	1894	6	–
The First National Bank & Trust Company Of Greensburg	2558	–	5
The First National Bank Of Greensburg	2558	5	4
The Merchants And Farmers National Bank Of Greensburg	2562	4	6
The Westmoreland National Bank Of Greensburg	4974	5	–
Greenville			
The Greenville National Bank	2251	5	3
Grove City			
The First National Bank Of Grove City	5044	4	3
The Grove City National Bank	5501	5	4
The Peoples National Bank Of Grove City	5501	5	–
Halifax			
The Halifax National Bank	5601	4	4
Hallstead			
The First National Bank Of Hallstead	7702	6	6
Hamburg			
The First National Bank And Trust Company Of Hamburg	9028	6	3
The First National Bank Of Hamburg	9028	4	–
The National Bank Of Hamburg	14250	–	4
Hanover			
The First National Bank Of Hanover	187	4	4
Harleysville			
The Harleysville National Bank	9541	5	3
Harmony			
The Harmony National Bank	2335	6	–
Harrisburg			
The First National Bank Of Harrisburg	201	4	–
The Harrisburg National Bank	580	2	2
The Merchants National Bank Of Harrisburg	3713	5	–
Harrisville			
First National Bank In Harrisville	13812	–	5
The First National Bank Of Harrisville	6859	6	5
Hastings			
The First National Bank Of Hastings	11227	6	5
Hatboro			
The Hatboro National Bank	2253	6	5
Hatfield			
The Hatfield National Bank	13026	–	–
The Hatfield National Bank And Trust Company, Hatfield	13026	–	–
The Hatfield National Bank, Hatfield	13026	–	3
Hawley			
The First National Bank Of Hawley	6445	6	5
Hays			
The Hays National Bank	6507	5	5
Hazelhurst			
The Hazelhurst National Bank	8380	6	–
Hazleton			
The First National Bank Of Hazleton	3893	6	2
The Hazleton National Bank	4204	5	3
Hegins			
First National Bank Of Hegins	13994	–	5
The First National Bank Of Hegins	9107	6	4
Herminie			
The First National Bank Of Herminie	10188	6	5
Herndon			
The First National Bank Of Herndon	6049	6	6
The Herndon National Bank	13982	–	6
Hershey			
The Hershey National Bank	12688	–	3
Hickory			
The Farmers National Bank Of Hickory	7405	6	6
Highland Park			
The State Road National Bank Of Highland Park	13196	–	5
The Upper Darby National Bank, Upper Darby	13196	–	–
Hollidaysburg			
The Citizens National Bank Of Hollidaysburg	6874	6	4
The First National Bank Of Hollidaysburg	57	6	–
The First National Bank Of Hollidaysburg	2744	5	–
Homer City			
The Homer City National Bank	8855	5	4
Homestead			
The First National Bank Of Homestead	3829	5	3
The Homestead National Bank	5365	5	–
Honesdale			
The Honesdale National Bank	644	4	5
Honeybrook			
The First National Bank Of Honeybrook	1676	4	3
Hooversville			
The Citizens National Bank Of Hooversville	11413	6	5
The First National Bank Of Hooversville	6250	6	3
The Hooversville National Bank	14156	–	3
Hop Bottom			
The Hop Bottom National Bank	9647	6	4
Hopewell			
The Hopewell National Bank	9638	6	6
Houston			
The First National Bank Of Houston	5908	5	4
Houtzdale			
The First National Bank Of Houtzdale	6695	6	6
Howard			
The First National Bank Of Howard	9249	6	5
Hughesville			
The First National Bank Of Hughesville	3902	6	5
The Grange National Bank Of Lycoming County, Hughesville	8924	5	5
Hummelstown			
The Hummelstown National Bank	2822	5	4
Huntingdon			
The First National Bank Of Huntingdon	31	5	3
The Standing Stone National Bank Of Huntingdon	6090	4	–
The Union National Bank Of Huntingdon	4965	5	6
Union National Bank And Trust Company Of Huntingdon	4965	–	5
Hyndman			
The Hoblitzell National Bank Of Hyndman	6615	6	5
The National Bank Of South Pennsylvania At Hyndman	4063	6	–
Indian Head			
The First National Bank Of Indian Head	12326	–	–
Indiana			
First National Bank In Indiana	14098	–	3
The Citizens National Bank Of Indiana	7993	6	6
The First National Bank Of Indiana	313	4	4
Intercourse			
The First National Bank Of Intercourse	9216	4	2
Irvona			
The First National Bank Of Irvona	11115	6	6
Irwin			
The Citizens National Bank Of Irwin	5255	5	5
The First National Bank Of Irwin	4698	6	4
Jeannette			
The First National Bank Of Jeannette	4092	6	6
The Jeannette National Bank	5527	6	–
The Peoples National Bank Of Jeannette	7792	6	–
Jefferson			
Codorus National Bank In Jefferson	14071	–	6
The Codorus National Bank Of Jefferson	9660	6	4
The First National Bank Of Jefferson	11370	6	5
Jenkintown			
Citizens National Bank Of Jenkintown	12530	5	6
The Jenkintown National Bank	2249	3	–
Jermyn			
The First National Bank Of Jermyn	6158	6	4
Jerome			
The First National Bank Of Jerome	12029	6	5
Jersey Shore			
The Jersey Shore National Bank	1464	6	–
The National Bank Of Jersey Shore	6155	6	–
The Union National Bank Of Jersey Shore	13197	–	4
The Williamsport National Bank, Williamsport	1464	5	6
Williamsport National Bank, Williamsport	1464	–	6
Jessup			
The First National Bank Of Jessup	9600	6	5
Johnsonburg			
The Johnsonburg National Bank	4544	6	6
Johnstown			
The Cambria National Bank Of Johnstown	5059	6	–
The Citizens National Bank Of Johnstown	4212	6	–
The First National Bank Of Johnstown	51	6	–
The First National Bank Of Johnstown	51	4	–
The First National Bank Of Johnstown	2739	4	3
The Moxham National Bank Of Johnstown	12098	5	4
The National Bank Of Johnstown	10590	6	–
The Union National Bank Of Johnstown	7465	5	–
The United States National Bank Of Johnstown	5913	3	3
United States National Bank In Johnstown	13781	–	6
Juniata			
The First National Bank Of Juniata	8238	6	6
Kane			
The First National Bank Of Kane	5025	6	5
Kennett Square			
National Bank & Trust Company Of Kennett Square	2526	–	4
The National Bank Of Kennett Square	2526	4	6
Kingston			
The First National Bank Of Kingston	12921	–	5
The Kingston National Bank	14023	–	3
Kittaning			
The Kittaning National Bank	1654	–	–
Kittanning			
The Farmers National Bank Of Kittanning	3104	3	4
The First National Bank Of Kittanning	69	6	–
The Merchants National Bank Of Kittanning	5073	4	5
The National Bank Of Kittanning	2654	5	–
The National Kittanning Bank	6127	4	3
Knoxville			
The First National Bank Of Knoxville	9978	6	5
Koppel			
First National Bank At Koppel	14070	–	6
The First National Bank Of Koppel	11938	6	5
Kutztown			
The Keystone National Bank Of Reading	1875	4	–
The Kutztown National Bank	5102	3	3
The National Bank Of Kutztown	1875	6	–
Laceyville			
The Grange National Bank Of Wyoming County At Laceyville	8845	6	5
Lake Ariel			
The First National Bank Of Lake Ariel	9886	5	4
Lancaster			
The Conestoga National Bank Of Lancaster	3987	6	4
The Farmers National Bank Of Lancaster	597	6	–
The First National Bank Of Lancaster	333	4	–
The Fulton National Bank Of Lancaster	2634	4	2
The Lancaster County National Bank Of Lancaster	683	6	3
The Northern National Bank Of Lancaster	3367	6	–
The Peoples National Bank Of Lancaster	3650	6	–
Landisville			
The First National Bank Of Landisville	9312	6	5
Langhorne			
The Peoples National Bank & Trust Company Of Langhorne	3063	6	6
The Peoples National Bank Of Langhorne	3063	5	–
Lansdale			
First National Bank Of Lansdale	430	5	–
The Citizens National Bank Of Lansdale	7735	5	–
The First National Bank Of Lansdale	430	–	2
Lansdowne			
The Lansdowne National Bank	11386	–	–
The National Bank Of Lansdowne	13151	–	4
Lansford			
The Citizens National Bank Of Lansford	7051	5	5
The First National Bank Of Lansford	5234	5	4
Laporte			
The First National Bank Of Laporte	9528	6	5
Latrobe			
First National Bank In Latrobe	13700	–	5
The Citizens National Bank Of Latrobe	3910	6	–
The Commercial National Bank Of Latrobe	14133	–	5
The First National Bank Of Latrobe	3831	6	6
The Peoples National Bank Of Latrobe	5744	5	5
Lawrence Park			
The Lawrence Park National Bank	13371	–	–
Lawrenceville			
The First National Bank Of Lawrenceville	9702	6	5
Le Raysville			
The First National Bank Of Le Raysville	6350	6	6
Lebanon			
Lebanon National Bank, Lebanon	680	–	4
The Farmers National Bank Of Lebanon	4979	6	–
The First National Bank Of Lebanon	240	5	4
The Lebanon National Bank	680	5	6
The Peoples National Bank Of Lebanon	4955	4	5
The Valley National Bank Of Lebanon	655	5	–
Leechburg			
The Farmers National Bank Of Leechburg	9290	6	6
The First National Bank Of Leechburg	5502	5	4
Leesport			
The First National Bank Of Leesport	9495	6	4
Lehighton			
Citizens National Bank And Trust Company Of Lehighton	6531	6	3
The Citizens National Bank Of Lehighton	6531	5	–
The First National Bank Of Lehighton	2308	5	3
Lemasters			
The Lemasters National Bank	8405	6	–
The Peoples National Bank Of Lemasters	10950	5	6
Lemoyne			
West Shore National Bank Of Lemoyne	13494	–	4
Leola			
The Leola National Bank	13186	–	–
Lewisburg			
The Lewisburg National Bank	745	5	4
The Union National Bank Of Lewisburg	784	5	5
Lewiston			
The Mifflin County National Bank Of Lewistown	1579	3	2
Lewistown			
The Citizens National Bank Of Lewistown	5289	5	4
The Russell National Bank Of Lewistown	10506	6	4
Liberty			
The Farmers National Bank Of Liberty	11127	5	5
Ligonier			
Ligonier National Bank	13432	–	5
The First National Bank In Ligonier	13658	–	5
The First National Bank Of Ligonier	6281	5	6
The National Bank Of Ligonier	6832	6	6
Lilly			
The First National Bank Of Lilly	8450	6	4
Lincoln			
The Lincoln National Bank	3198	5	4
Lititz			
Lititz Springs National Bank Of Lititz	9422	6	4
The Farmers National Bank Of Lititz	5773	6	5
The Lititz National Bank	2452	6	–
Littlestown			
The First National Bank Of Littlestown	5531	–	–
The Littlestown National Bank	9207	6	4
Liverpool			
The First National Bank Of Liverpool	8326	6	4
Lock Haven			
The County National Bank Of Lock Haven	11692	6	–
The First National Bank Of Lock Haven	507	5	3
The Lock Haven National Bank	1273	6	–
Loganton			
The Loganton National Bank	9345	6	5
Loysville			
The First National Bank Of Loysville	11524	6	5
Luzerne			
The Luzerne National Bank	8921	6	4
Lykens			
The First National Bank Of Lykens	11062	4	4
Lyndora			
Lyndora National Bank	8576	6	–
Lyndora National Bank	8576	–	5
Madera			
The Madera National Bank	7400	6	5
Mahaffey			
The Mahaffey National Bank	7610	5	5
Mahanoy City			
The First National Bank Of Mahanoy City	567	4	3
The Union National Bank Of Mahanoy City	3997	4	4
Malvern			
The National Bank Of Malvern	3147	6	4
Manheim			
The Keystone National Bank Of Manheim	3635	5	4
The Manheim National Bank	912	4	4
Manor			
The Manor National Bank	6456	4	4
Mansfield			
First National Bank In Mansfield	13618	–	6
The First National Bank Of Mansfield	8810	6	6
The Grange National Bank Of Mansfield	8831	5	–
Mapleton			
The First National Bank Of Mapleton	11244	6	6

City, Bank	Ch. No.	L	S
Marcus Hook			
The Marcus Hook National Bank, Marcus Hook	11505	–	–
Marienville			
The Gold Standard National Bank Of Marienville	5727	4	4
Marietta			
The Exchange National Bank Of Marietta	10707	6	5
The Exchange National Bank Of Marietta	14276	–	–
The First National Bank Of Marietta	25	6	–
The First National Bank Of Marietta	25	4	2
The First National Bank Of Marietta	2710	6	–
Marion Center			
The Marion Center National Bank	7819	6	4
Mars			
The Mars National Bank	5599	5	4
Martinsburg			
The First National Bank Of Martinsburg	7974	6	4
Marysville			
The First National Bank Of Marysville	7353	6	4
Masontown			
The First National Bank Of Masontown	5441	5	5
The Masontown National Bank	6528	5	6
The Second National Bank Of Masontown	14333	–	–
Mauch Chunk			
The First National Bank Of Mauch Chunk	437	6	–
The Linderman National Bank Of Mauch Chunk	2852	6	–
The Mauch Chunk National Bank	6534	4	3
The Second National Bank Of Mauch Chunk	469	4	–
Maytown			
The Maytown National Bank	9461	6	5
Mc Adoo			
The First National Bank Of Mc Adoo	8619	5	5
Mc Alisterville			
The Farmers National Bank Of Mc Alisterville	9526	6	2
Mc Clure			
The First National Bank Of Mc Clure	7769	6	5
Mc Connellsburg			
The First National Bank Of Mc Connellsburg	8083	6	5
Mc Donald			
The First National Bank Of Mc Donald	4752	6	5
The Peoples National Bank Of Mc Donald	5058	6	–
Mc Kees Rocks			
The First National Bank Of Mc Kees Rocks	5142	5	3
Mc Keesport			
The Citizens National Bank Of Mc Keesport	4876	6	–
The First National Bank Of Mc Keesport	2222	4	3
The National Bank Of Mc Keesport	4625	4	4
The Union National Bank Of Mc Keesport	7559	5	5
Mc Veytown			
The Mc Veytown National Bank	8773	6	4
Mcconnellsburg			
The Fulton County National Bank Of Mcconnellsburg	13765	–	6
Mckees Rocks			
The First National Bank Of Mckees Rocks	14107	–	–
Mckeesport			
The Union National Bank At Mckeesport	13967	–	6
Meadville			
First National Bank Of Meadville	4938	–	4
The First National Bank Of Meadville	115	6	–
The Merchants National Bank & Trust Company Of Meadville	871	–	5
The Merchants National Bank Of Meadville	871	6	6
The National Bank Of Crawford County	1124	6	–
The New First National Bank Of Meadville	4938	4	6
Mechanicsburg			
Mechanicsburg National Bank	8969	5	–
The First National Bank Of Mechanicsburg	380	4	–
The Second National Bank Of Mechanicsburg	326	4	2
Media			
The Charter National Bank Of Media	3666	5	–
The First National Bank Of Media	312	3	4
Mercer			
The Farmers And Mechanics National Bank Of Mercer	2256	5	5
The Farmers National Bank Of Mercer	13846	–	6
The First National Bank Of Mercer	392	5	3
The Mercer County National Bank Of Mercer	4909	6	–
Mercersburg			
The First National Bank Of Mercersburg	9330	5	5
Meshoppen			
The First National Bank Of Meshoppen	5429	6	5
Meyersdale			
The Citizens National Bank Of Meyersdale	5833	6	4
The First National Bank Of Meyersdale	2258	6	–
The Second National Bank Of Meyersdale	5801	6	5
Middleburgh			
The First National Bank Of Middleburgh	4156	5	2
Middletown			
The Citizens National Bank Of Middletown	7826	6	–
The National Bank Of Middletown	585	6	–
Midland			
The First National Bank Of Midland	8311	5	5
Midway			
The Midway National Bank	6626	5	4
Mifflinburg			
The First National Bank Of Mifflinburg	174	6	–
Mifflintown			
The First National Bank Of Mifflintown	4039	6	5
The Juniata Valley National Bank Of Mifflintown	5147	5	4
Mildred			
The First National Bank Of Mildred	9552	6	5
Milford			
The First National Bank Of Milford	5496	3	5
Millersburg			
The First National Bank Of Millersburg	2252	5	4
Millerstown			
The First National Bank Of Millerstown	7156	6	4
The German National Bank Of Millerstown	2241	6	–
Millersville			
The Millersville National Bank	9259	6	6

City, Bank	Ch. No.	L	S
Millheim			
The Farmers National Bank And Trust Company Of Millheim	9511	6	4
The Farmers National Bank Of Millheim	9511	6	–
Millsboro			
The First National Bank Of Millsboro	7310	6	6
Millville			
The First National Bank Of Millville	5389	6	6
Milton			
First Milton National Bank, Milton	253	6	4
The First National Bank Of Milton	253	6	–
The Milton National Bank	711	5	–
Minersville			
The First National Bank Of Minersville	423	5	5
The Union National Bank Of Minersville	6131	6	5
Mocanaqua			
The First National Bank Of Mocanaqua	12349	6	4
Mohnton			
The Mohnton National Bank	8968	6	–
Monaca			
The Citizens National Bank Of Monaca	5879	5	5
The Monaca National Bank	5878	6	6
Monessen			
First National Bank And Trust Company Of Monessen	5253	6	5
The Citizens National Bank Of Monessen	11487	6	6
The First National Bank Of Monessen	5253	6	–
The Monessen National Bank	5253	6	–
The National Bank And Trust Company Of Monessen	12994	–	–
The Peoples National Bank And Trust Company Of Monessen	5956	6	5
The Peoples National Bank Of Monessen	5956	5	–
Monongahela City			
The First National Bank Of Monongahela City	5968	5	4
Monroeton			
The First National Bank Of Monroeton	12597	–	–
Montgomery			
Farmers And Citizens National Bank Of Montgomery	8866	6	5
The First National Bank Of Montgomery	5574	5	5
Montoursville			
The First National Bank Of Montoursville	6997	5	4
Montrose			
The Farmers National Bank Of Montrose	6746	6	–
The First And Farmers National Bank & Trust Co. Of Montrose	2223	5	4
The First And Farmers National Bank Of Montrose	2223	–	–
The First National Bank Of Montrose	2223	5	–
Morton			
The Morton National Bank	13015	–	–
Moscow			
The First National Bank Of Moscow	9340	6	3
Mount Carmel			
The First National Bank Of Mount Carmel	3980	4	4
The Union National Bank Of Mount Carmel	8393	4	3
Mount Holly Springs			
The First National Bank Of Mount Holly Springs	8493	6	3
Mount Jewett			
The Mount Jewett National Bank	7473	6	5
Mount Joy			
The First National Bank And Trust Company Of Mount Joy	667	–	4
The First National Bank Of Mount Joy	667	4	–
The Union National Mount Joy Bank	1516	4	4
Mount Morris			
The Farmers And Merchants National Bank Of Mount Morris	6983	5	–
Mount Pleasant			
The Citizens National Bank Of Mount Pleasant	4875	5	–
The Farmers And Merchants National Bank Of Mount Pleasant	4892	6	–
The First National Bank Of Mount Pleasant	386	4	5
The Peoples National Bank Of Mount Pleasant	9198	6	5
Mount Union			
The Central National Bank Of Mount Union	10206	5	4
The First National Bank Of Mount Union	6411	6	5
Mount Wolf			
The Union National Bank Of Mount Wolf	9361	6	4
Union National Bank In Mount Wolf	14121	–	6
Mountville			
The Mountville National Bank	3808	6	2
Muncy			
The Citizens National Bank Of Muncy	3480	6	4
The First National Bank Of Muncy	837	6	–
Munhall			
The First National Bank Of Munhall	8795	6	–
Myerstown			
The Farmers National Bank Of Myerstown	9752	6	–
The Myerstown National Bank	5241	5	4
Nanticoke			
The First National Bank Of Nanticoke	3955	6	4
The Miners National Bank Of Nanticoke	13524	–	4
The Nanticoke National Bank	7406	5	4
Narberth			
The Narberth National Bank	12595	–	–
The National Bank Of Narberth	14139	–	–
Natrona			
The First National Bank Of Natrona	5729	5	5
Nazareth			
The Nazareth National Bank	5077	5	–
The Nazareth National Bank & Trust Company, Nazareth	5077	–	4
The Second National Bank Of Nazareth	5686	4	5
Neffs			
The Neffs National Bank	12471	5	4
Nescopeck			
The Nescopeck National Bank, Nescopeck	12159	–	5
Nesquehoning			
The First National Bank Of Nesquehoning	10251	6	4
New Albany			
The First National Bank Of New Albany	8973	5	5

City, Bank	Ch. No.	L	S
New Alexandria			
The New Alexandria National Bank	6580	6	4
New Berlin			
The First National Bank Of New Berlin	7897	5	5
New Bethlehem			
The Citizens National Bank Of New Bethlehem	5051	6	–
The First National Bank Of New Bethlehem	4978	5	4
New Bloomfield			
The First National Bank Of New Bloomfield	5133	3	2
New Brighton			
The National Bank Of Beaver County, New Brighton	632	5	–
The National Bank Of New Brighton	3259	6	–
The Old National Bank Of New Brighton	7395	4	4
The Union National Bank Of New Brighton	4549	4	3
New Castle			
First National Bank Of Lawrence County At New Castle	562	6	3
The Citizens National Bank Of New Castle	4676	5	4
The First National Bank Of New Castle	562	5	–
The National Bank Of Lawrence County At New Castle	1156	4	–
The Union National Bank Of New Castle	8503	6	6
New Cumberland			
The New Cumberland National Bank	7349	4	4
New Florence			
New Florence National Bank	13907	–	6
The New Florence National Bank	10353	6	6
New Freedom			
First National Bank In New Freedom	13887	–	5
The First National Bank Of New Freedom	6715	4	5
New Haven			
The New Haven National Bank	6408	6	–
The Union National Bank Of Connellsville	6408	6	6
New Holland			
The Farmers National Bank & Trust Company Of New Holland	8499	–	4
The Farmers National Bank Of New Holland	8499	6	6
The New Holland National Bank	2530	5	6
New Hope			
The Solebury National Bank Of New Hope	11015	–	4
New Kensington			
The First National Bank Of New Kensington	4913	5	4
The Logan National Bank Of New Kensington	13571	–	3
The Union National Bank Of New Kensington	13084	5	6
New Milford			
The Grange Naional Bank Of Susquehanna County At New Milford	8960	6	6
New Salem			
The Delmont National Bank Of New Salem	5837	6	–
The First National Bank Of New Salem	6599	6	–
New Tripoli			
The New Tripoli National Bank	9656	6	4
New Wilmington			
The Depositors National Bank Of New Wilmington	13845	–	–
The First National Bank Of New Wilmington	9554	6	6
Newfoundland			
The First National Bank Of Newfoundland	12911	–	5
Newport			
The Citizens National Bank Of Newport	7716	6	5
The First National Bank Of Newport	4917	5	4
The Perry County National Bank Of Newport	5245	6	–
Newtown			
The First National Bank And Trust Company Of Newtown	324	5	4
The First National Bank Of Newtown	324	3	–
Newville			
The Farmers National Bank Of Newville	9588	6	6
The First National Bank Of Newville	60	4	4
Nicholson			
The First National Bank Of Nicholson	7910	5	4
Norristown			
The First National Bank Of Norristown	272	5	–
The Montgomery National Bank Of Norristown	1148	4	3
The Peoples National Bank Of Norristown	2581	3	4
North Belle Vernon			
The Peoples National Bank Of North Belle Vernon	11995	5	6
North East			
The First National Bank Of North East	741	5	–
The First National Bank Of North East	4927	6	6
The National Bank Of North East	9149	6	5
North Girard			
The First National Bank Of North Girard	12363	6	6
North Wales			
The North Wales National Bank	4330	5	4
Northumberland			
The First National Bank Of Northumberland	566	4	–
The Northumberland National Bank	7005	6	4
Numidia			
The Valley National Bank Of Numidia	11981	–	5
Nuremburg			
The First National Bank Of Nuremburg	12563	5	5
Oakdale			
The First National Bank Of Oakdale	5327	4	5
Oakmont			
The First National Bank Of Oakmont	7642	6	4
The Oakmont National Bank	12858	–	–
Oil City			
Oil City National Bank, Oil City	14274	–	4
The First National Bank Of Oil City	173	5	5
The Lamberton National Bank Of Oil City	5565	4	–
The Oil City National Bank	5240	4	3
Oley			
The First National Bank Of Oley	8858	5	3
Olyphant			
First National Bank Of Olyphant	8806	5	–
The National Bank Of Olyphant	14079	–	5
Orangeville			
The Farmers National Bank Of Orangeville	11058	–	–
Orbisonia			
The First National Bank Of Orbisonia	8985	6	–
The Orbisonia National Bank	10335	5	–

City, Bank	Ch. No.	L	S
Orwigsburg			
The First National Bank & Trust Company Of Orwigsburg	4408	5	4
The First National Bank Of Orwigsburg	4408	4	–
Osceola			
The First National Bank Of Osceola	6501	5	4
Osceola Mills			
The Peoples National Bank Of Osceola Mills	11966	5	6
Oxford			
The Farmers National Bank Of Oxford	2906	5	5
The National Bank Of Oxford	728	3	3
Palmerton			
The First National Bank Of Palmerton	8930	4	3
Paoli			
The Paoli National Bank	12358	6	–
Parkers Landing			
The First National Bank Of Parkers Landing	6045	6	5
Parkesburg			
The Parkesburg National Bank	2464	5	–
Parnassus			
The Parnassus National Bank	7363	6	6
The Parnassus National Bank, New Kensington	7363	–	6
Patterson			
The Peoples National Bank Of Mifflin	9678	6	5
The Peoples National Bank Of Patterson	9678	6	–
Patton			
The First National Bank Of Patton	4857	4	3
The First National Bank Of Patton	14263	–	–
The Grange National Bank Of Patton	8233	6	–
Peckville			
The First National Bank Of Peckville	13754	–	–
The Peckville National Bank	7785	6	5
Pen Argyl			
The First National Bank Of Pen Argyl	4352	4	4
The Pen Argyl National Bank	7710	5	4
Penbrook			
The National Bank Of Penbrook	12197	6	5
The Penbrook National Bank	9344	6	–
Pennsburg			
The Farmers National Bank Of Pennsburg	2334	4	3
The Perkiomen National Bank Of Pennsburg	2301	5	–
Perkasie			
The First National Bank Of Perkasie	5736	4	4
Perryopolis			
The First National Bank Of Perryopolis	6344	6	6
Petersburg			
The First National Bank Of Petersburg	10313	6	4
Philadelphia			
Central-Penn National Bank Of Philadelphia	723	–	–
City National Bank Of Philadelphia	13180	–	2
Commercial National Bank & Trust Company Of Philadelphia	3604	–	3
Commercial National Bank Of Philadelphia	3604	–	3
Corn Exchange National Bank & Trust Company, Philadelphia	542	6	2
Mt. Airy National Bank & Trust Company In Philadelphia	13113	6	4
Mt. Airy National Bank In Philadelphia	13113	–	5
National Bank Of Germantown & Trust Company, Philadelphia	546	–	2
Overbrook National Bank Of Philadelphia	12573	5	5
The Bank Of North America, Philadelphia	602	2	–
The Broad Street National Bank Of Philadelphia	11539	3	–
The Centennial National Bank Of Philadelphia	2317	4	–
The Central National Bank Of Philadelphia	723	5	–
The Chestnut Street National Bank Of Philadelphia	3723	6	–
The City National Bank And Trust Company Of Philadelphia	13180	–	–
The City National Bank Of Philadelphia	543	6	–
The Commercial National Bank Of Pennsylvania At Philadelphia	556	4	–
The Commonwealth National Bank Of Philadelphia	623	5	–
The Consolidation National Bank Of Philadelphia	561	4	–
The Corn Exchange National Bank Of Philadelphia	542	2	–
The Drovers And Merchants National Bank Of Philadelphia	11476	–	–
The Eighth National Bank Of Philadelphia	522	2	6
The Erie National Bank Of Philadelphia	13032	–	3
The Farmers And Mechanics National Bank Of Philadelphia	538	2	–
The First National Bank Of Philadelphia	1	4	–
The First National Bank Of Philadelphia	1	2	–
The First National Bank Of Philadelphia	2731	2	1
The Fourth National Bank Of Philadelphia	286	6	–
The Fourth Street National Bank Of Philadelphia	3557	2	–
The Franklin Fourth Street National Bank Of Philadelphia	5459	–	–
The Franklin National Bank Of Philadelphia	5459	4	–
The Girard National Bank Of Philadelphia	592	2	–
The Independence National Bank Of Philadelphia	3085	6	–
The Kensington National Bank Of Philadelphia	544	3	3
The Keystone National Bank Of Philadelphia	2291	5	–
The Lehigh National Bank Of Philadelphia	13341	–	–
The Manayunk National Bank Of Philadelphia	3604	3	–
The Manayunk-Quaker City National Bank Of Philadelphia	3604	4	–
The Manufacturers National Bank Of Philadelphia	557	5	–
The Market Street National Bank Of Philadelphia	3684	2	4
The Mechanics National Bank Of Philadelphia	610	3	–
The Merchants National Bank Of Philadelphia	2462	2	–
The National Bank Of Commerce	11482	–	–
The National Bank Of Commerce Of Philadelphia	547	6	–
The National Bank Of Germantown, Philadelphia	546	2	–
The National Bank Of Mount Airy In Philadelphia	13113	5	–
The National Bank Of North Philadelphia	11908	6	–
The National Bank Of Northern Liberties, Philadelphia	541	5	–
The National Bank Of Olney	14120	–	–
The National Bank Of Olney In Philadelphia	12931	6	3
The National Bank Of The Republic Of Philadelphia	1647	4	–
The National Deposit Bank Of Philadelphia	7929	5	–
The National Exchange Bank Of Philadelphia	755	6	–
The National Security Bank & Trust Co Of Philadelphia	1743	–	5
The National Security Bank Of Philadelphia	1743	2	–
The Ninth National Bank Of Philadelphia	3371	4	–
The North Broad National Bank Of Philadelphia	13325	–	3
The Northeast National Bank & Trust Co In Philadelphia	13175	–	–
The Northeast National Bank Of Holmesburg	13175	–	–
The Northeast National Bank Of Philadelphia	13175	–	2
The Northern National Bank Of Philadelphia	4192	3	–
The Northwestern National Bank & Trust Co Of Philadelphia	3491	–	4
The Northwestern National Bank Of Philadelphia	3491	4	–
The Northwestern National Bank Of Philadelphia	14197	–	–
The Pelham National Bank And Trust Company Of Philadelphia	13185	–	–
The Penn National Bank Of Philadelphia	540	4	6
The Philadelphia National Bank	539	1	1
The Philadelphia-Girard National Bank, Philadelphia	539	–	–
The Produce National Bank Of Philadelphia	3507	6	–
The Quaker City National Bank Of Philadelphia	4050	3	–
The Queen Lane National Bank In Germantown At Philadelphia	12860	4	–
The Second National Bank Of Philadelphia	213	4	2
The Seventh National Bank Of Philadelphia	413	6	–
The Sixth National Bank Of Philadelphia	352	4	4
The South Philadelphia National Bank Of Philadelphia	14171	–	–
The Southwark National Bank Of Philadelphia	560	3	–
The Southwestern National Bank Of Philadelphia	3498	6	4
The Spring Garden National Bank Of Philadelphia	3468	6	–
The Tenth National Bank Of Philadelphia	3423	3	–
The Textile National Bank Of Philadelphia	7522	3	4
The Third National Bank Of Philadelphia	234	3	–
The Tioga National Bank & Trust Company Of Philadelphia	13003	–	3
The Tioga National Bank Of Philadelphia	13003	–	–
The Tradesmens National Bank Of Philadelphia	570	3	–
The Tulpehocken National Bank & Trust Co. Of Philadelphia	13185	–	–
The Union National Bank Of Philadelphia	563	3	–
The Western National Bank Of Philadelphia	656	5	–
Tradesmens National Bank & Trust Company Of Philadelphia	570	4	2
Philipsburg			
The First National Bank Of Philipsburg	4832	4	4
The Moshannon National Bank Of Philipsburg	5066	5	5
The Philipsburg National Bank	4832	6	–
Phoenixville			
Farmers And Mechanics-National Bank Of Phoenixville	1936	–	3
The Farmers And Mechanics National Bank Of Phoenixville	1936	6	6
The National Bank Of Phoenixville	674	5	6
Picture Rocks			
The Picture Rocks National Bank	11643	6	4
Pine Grove			
The Pine Grove National Bank	8151	6	6
The Pine Grove National Bank & Trust Company, Pine Grove	8151	–	5
Pitcairn			
The First National Bank Of Pitcairn	5848	6	6
The Peoples National Bank Of Pitcairn	11892	6	6
Pittsburgh			
First National Bank At Pittsburgh	252	2	1
National Bank Of America In Pittsburgh	14271	–	4
The Allegheny National Bank Of Pittsburgh	722	6	–
The American National Bank Of Pittsburgh	7581	6	–
The Bank Of Pittsburgh, National Association	5225	2	–
The Citizens National Bank Of Pittsburgh	619	6	–
The City National Bank Of Pittsburgh	2195	6	–
The Colonial National Bank Of Pittsburgh	6567	6	–
The Columbia National Bank Of Pittsburgh	4910	4	–
The Commercial National Bank Of Pittsburgh	2711	4	–
The Cosmopolitan National Bank Of Pittsburgh	6216	6	–
The Diamond National Bank Of Pittsburgh	2236	5	4
The Duquesne National Bank Of Pittsburgh	2278	2	4
The Exchange National Bank Of Pittsburgh	1057	2	5
The Farmers Deposit National Bank Of Pittsburgh	685	3	1
The Federal National Bank Of Pittsburgh	6023	3	–
The First National Bank Of Birmingham, Pittsburgh	926	5	6
The First National Bank Of Pittsburgh	48	4	–
The First National Bank Of Pittsburgh	48	5	–
The First National Bank Of Pittsburgh	2745	5	–
The First-Second National Bank Of Pittsburgh	252	3	–
The Forbes National Bank Of Pittsburgh	13153	–	4
The Fort Pitt National Bank Of Pittsburgh	2415	5	–
The Fourth National Bank Of Pittsburgh	432	5	–
The German National Bank Of Pittsburgh	757	3	–
The Highland National Bank Of Pittsburgh	12414	5	4
The Industrial National Bank Of Pittsburg	6806	6	–
The Iron City National Bank Of Pittsburgh	675	5	–
The Keystone National Bank Of Pittsburgh	7560	5	–
The Keystone National Bank Of Pittsburgh	14210	–	–
The Liberty National Bank Of Pittsburgh	4339	5	–
The Lincoln National Bank Of Pittsburgh	4883	4	–
The Marine National Bank Of Pittsburgh	2237	3	–
The Mechanics National Bank Of Pittsburgh	700	6	–
The Mellon National Bank Of Pittsburgh	6301	1	1
The Merchants And Manufacturers National Bank Of Pittsburgh	613	4	–
The Metropolitan National Bank Of Pittsburgh	2279	4	–
The Monongahela National Bank Of Pittsburgh	3874	3	4
The National Bank Of Western Pennsylvania At Pittsburgh	4918	5	–
The Pennsylvania National Bank Of Pittsburgh	4222	4	6
The Peoples National Bank Of Pittsburgh	727	3	–
The Pitt National Bank Of Pittsburgh	13701	–	4
The Pittsburgh National Bank Of Commerce, Pittsburgh	668	4	–
The Republic National Bank Of Pittsburgh	6153	6	–
The Second National Bank Of Pittsburgh	252	4	–
The Smithfield National Bank Of Pittsburgh	2281	6	–
The Third National Bank Of Pittsburgh	291	3	5
The Tradesmens National Bank Of Pittsburgh	678	5	–
The Union National Bank Of Pittsburgh	705	4	4
The United States National Bank Of Pittsburgh	5017	5	–
The Washington National Bank Of Pittsburgh	6725	5	–
Western National Bank Of Pittsburgh	4918	5	–
Pittston			
The First National Bank Of Pittston	478	4	3
The Liberty National Bank Of Pittston	11865	5	4
The Pittston National Bank	1435	–	–
Pleasant Unity			
The Pleasant Unity National Bank	6581	6	5
Plumer			
The First National Bank Of Plumer	854	6	–
Plumville			
The First National Bank Of Plumville	7887	6	6
Plymouth			
The First National Bank Of Plymouth	707	5	4
The Plymouth National Bank	6881	6	4
Point Marion			
The First National Bank Of Point Marion	6114	6	5
The Peoples National Bank Of Point Marion	9503	5	6
Port Allegany			
The Citizens National Bank Of Port Allegany	6066	6	–
Port Allegheny			
The First National Bank Of Port Allegheny	3877	6	5
Port Royal			
The First National Bank Of Port Royal	11369	6	5
The Port Royal National Bank	11373	6	3
Portage			
The First National Bank Of Portage	7367	6	6
Portland			
Portland National Bank	6665	5	5
The Portland National Bank	13606	–	5
Pottstown			
The Citizens National Bank & Trust Company Of Pottstown	4714	5	4
The Citizens National Bank Of Pottstown	4714	4	–
The National Bank Of Pottstown	608	3	3
The National Iron Bank Of Pottstown	3494	4	3
Pottsville			
The City National Bank Of Pottsville	14262	–	–
The Government National Bank Of Pottsville	1152	5	–
The Merchants National Bank Of Pottsville	8964	6	4
The Miners' National Bank Of Pottsville	649	4	4
The Pennsylvania National Bank & Trust Co Of Pottsville	1663	6	4
The Pennsylvania National Bank Of Pottsville	1663	4	–
Providence			
The First National Bank Of Providence	521	6	–
Punxsutawney			
The County National Bank Of Punxsutawney	9863	6	4
The Farmers National Bank Of Punxsutawney	5965	6	–
The First National Bank Of Punxsutawney	3030	6	–
The Punxsutawney National Bank	5702	4	4
Quakertown			
The Merchants National Bank Of Quakertown	6465	4	5
The Quakertown National Bank	2366	3	3
Quarryville			
The Farmers National Bank Of Quarryville	8045	6	6
The Quarryville National Bank	3067	6	4
Ralston			
The First National Bank Of Ralston	9508	6	6
Reading			
Farmers National Bank And Trust Company Of Reading	696	5	2
Penn Natinal Bank And Trust Company Of Reading	2899	–	3
The Commercial National Bank Of Reading	2473	6	–
The Farmers National Bank Of Reading	696	2	–
The First National Bank Of Reading	125	4	–
The National Union Bank Of Reading	693	3	–
The Penn National Bank Of Reading	2899	4	–
The Reading National Bank	4887	3	–
The Reading National Bank And Trust Company	4887	–	2
The Second National Bank Of Reading	2552	2	–
The Union National Bank Of Reading	14277	–	–
Rebersburg			
The Rebersburg National Bank	11789	6	6
Red Lion			
First National Bank And Trust Company Of Red Lion	5184	–	4
The Farmers And Merchants National Bank Of Red Lion	6708	5	4
The Red Lion First National Bank	5184	6	6
Reedsville			
The Reedsville National Bank	4538	5	5
Renova			
The First National Bank Of Renova	3763	6	6
Republic			
The First National Bank Of Republic	10466	6	6
Reynoldsville			
The Citizens National Bank Of Reynoldsville	6263	6	–
The First National Bank Of Reynoldsville	4908	5	4
The Peoples National Bank Of Reynoldsville	7620	5	4
The Peoples National Bank Of Reynoldsville	13957	–	–
Rices Landing			
The Rices Landing National Bank	7090	6	4
Richland			
The Richland National Bank	8344	6	6
Ridgway			
The Elk County National Bank Of Ridgway	5014	4	4
The Ridgway National Bank	5945	3	3

City, Bank	Ch. No.	L	S
Ridley Park			
The Ridley Park National Bank	10847	5	4
Riegelsville			
The First National Bank Of Riegelsville	9202	4	4
Rimersburg			
The First National Bank Of Rimersburg	6676	6	3
The Rimersburg National Bank	6569	6	–
Ringtown			
The First National Bank Of Ringtown	6950	6	5
Roaring Spring			
First National Bank Of Roaring Spring	12304	–	5
Rochester			
The First National Bank Of Rochester	2977	4	4
The Peoples National Bank Of Rochester	7749	6	6
The Rochester National Bank	5170	6	–
Rockwood			
The Farmers And Merchants National Bank Of Rockwood	9769	6	6
The First National Bank Of Rockwood	5340	6	6
The Union National Bank Of Rockwood	14067	–	–
Rome			
The Farmers National Bank Of Rome	10246	6	5
Roscoe			
The First National Bank Of Roscoe	5495	6	4
Roseto			
The First National Bank Of Roseto	13002	–	–
Roslyn			
The Keswick National Bank Of Glenside	13141	–	–
The Roslyn National Bank	13141	–	–
Royersford			
The Home National Bank Of Royersford	4751	6	–
The National Bank Of Royersford	3551	4	3
Rural Valley			
The Peoples National Bank Of Rural Valley	13908	–	6
The Rural Valley National Bank	6083	6	5
Russellton			
The First National Bank Of Russellton	10493	6	6
Saegertown			
The First National Bank Of Saegertown	11910	6	6
Saint Marys			
The Saint Marys National Bank	6589	4	3
Saint Michael			
The Saint Michael National Bank	12588	–	5
Salisbury			
The First National Bank Of Salisbury	6106	6	5
Saltsburg			
The First National Bank Of Saltsburg	2609	5	4
Saxton			
The First National Bank Of Saxton	7229	6	5
Sayre			
The First National Bank Of Sayre	5666	6	4
The Merchants And Mechanics National Bank Of Sayre	5684	6	5
The National Bank Of Sayre	5684	6	–
Scenery Hill			
The First National Bank Of Scenery Hill	7262	5	3
Schaefferstown			
The First National Bank Of Schaefferstown	8962	6	6
Schellburg			
The First National Bank Of Schellburg	10666	5	5
The First National Bank Of Schellsburg	10666	–	6
Schuylkill Haven			
The First National Bank Of Schuylkill Haven	5216	4	–
The First Natl Bank & Trust Co Of Schuylkill Haven	5216	6	4
Schwenksville			
The National Bank & Trust Company Of Schwenksville	2142	–	4
The National Bank Of Schwenksville	2142	5	5
Scottdale			
First National Bank Of Scottdale	13772	–	5
The Broadway National Bank Of Scottdale	5974	5	6
The First National Bank Of Scottdale	4098	6	5
Scranton			
Scranton National Bank	13947	–	5
The County National Bank Of Scranton	13040	–	–
The First National Bank Of Scranton	77	6	–
The First National Bank Of Scranton	77	3	–
The First National Bank Of Scranton	2697	4	1
The Hyde Park National Bank Of Scranton	13225	–	–
The Peoples National Bank Of Scranton	8235	5	–
The Second National Bank Of Scranton	49	6	–
The Third National Bank Of Scranton	1946	3	6
The Traders National Bank Of Scranton	4183	3	6
The Union National Bank Of Scranton	8737	4	4
Third National Bank And Trust Company Of Scranton	1946	–	3
Selins Grove			
The First National Bank Of Selins Grove	357	4	3
Selinsgrove			
The Farmers National Bank Of Selinsgrove	8653	6	5
Sellersville			
The Sellersville National Bank	2667	3	3
Seven Valleys			
The Seven Valleys National Bank	9507	6	5
Seward			
The Citizens National Bank Of Seward	13011	–	–
The First National Bank Of Seward	11899	6	–
Sewickley			
First National Bank In Sewickley	13699	–	5
The First National Bank Of Sewickley	4462	5	5
The Union National Bank Of Sewickley	13496	–	–
Shamokin			
National-Dime Bank Of Shamokin	6942	–	3
The First National Bank Of Shamokin	3045	6	–
The Market Street National Bank Of Shamokin	5625	5	5
The National Bank Of Shamokin	6942	5	5
The Northumberland County National Bank Of Shamokin	689	6	–
The West End National Bank Of Shamokin	12805	6	3
Sharon			
First National Bank In Sharon	13803	–	5
The First National Bank Of Sharon	1685	4	3
The Mc Dowell National Bank Of Sharon	8764	4	4
The Merchants And Manufacturers National Bank Of Sharon	6560	6	5
The Sharon National Bank	2244	6	–
Sharpsville			
The First National Bank Of Sharpsville	6829	6	4
The Sharpsville National Bank	7873	6	–
Sheffield			
The Sheffield National Bank	6193	5	4
Shenandoah			
The Citizens National Bank Of Shenandoah	9247	4	4
The First National Bank Of Shenandoah	3143	6	4
The Merchants National Bank Of Shenandoah	4546	4	4
The Miners National Bank Of Shenandoah	13619	–	2
The Union National Bank Of Shenandoah	14293	–	–
Sheraden			
The First National Bank Of Sheraden	5977	6	–
Shickshinny			
The First National Bank Of Shickshinny	5573	6	4
Shingle House			
The First National Bank Of Shingle House	6799	6	5
Shippensburg			
The First National Bank Of Shippensburg	834	5	4
The Peoples National Bank Of Shippensburg	6946	6	5
Shippenville			
The First National Bank Of Shippenville	7874	6	6
Shoemakersville			
The First National Bank Of Shoemakersville	11841	6	4
Siegfried			
The Cement National Bank Of Siegfried	5227	5	–
The Cement National Bank Of Siegfried At Northampton	5227	4	3
Sipesville			
The First National Bank Of Sipesville	11849	6	6
Slatington			
The Citizens National Bank Of Slatington	6051	4	4
The National Bank Of Slatington	2293	2	4
Sligo			
Sligo National Bank, Sligo	8946	6	5
The Grange National Bank Of Clarion County At Sligo	8946	6	–
Slippery Rock			
The Citizens National Bank Of Slippery Rock	8724	5	–
The First National Bank Of Slippery Rock	6483	6	6
Smethport			
The Grange National Bank Of Mc Kean County At Smethport	8591	5	3
Smithfield			
The First National Bank Of Smithfield	6642	6	5
Smithton			
The First National Bank Of Smithton	5311	5	6
Somerfield			
The First National Bank Of Somerfield	8901	6	6
Somerset			
The Farmers National Bank Of Somerset	5452	5	5
The First National Bank Of Somerset	4100	5	4
The Peoples National Bank Of Somerset	13900	–	6
The Somerset County National Bank Of Somerset	4227	6	–
Souderton			
The Peoples National Bank Of Souderton	13251	–	2
The Union National Bank Of Souderton	2333	4	–
Union National Bank And Trust Company Of Souderton	2333	6	3
South Bethlehem			
The Bethlehem National Bank, Bethlehem	3961	6	5
The South Bethlehem National Bank	3961	6	–
South Fork			
The First National Bank Of South Fork	6573	6	5
Spangler			
The First National Bank Of Spangler	7181	6	4
Spartansburg			
The Grange National Bank Of Spartansburg	9110	6	4
Spring City			
The National Bank And Trust Company Of Spring City	2018	6	3
The National Bank Of Spring City	2018	5	–
Spring Grove			
The First National Bank Of Spring Grove	6536	6	6
The Peoples National Bank Of Spring Grove	8141	6	6
The Spring Grove National Bank, Spring Grove	6536	–	5
Spring Mills			
The First National Bank Of Spring Mills	11213	5	4
Springdale			
The National Bank Of Springdale	8320	–	4
The Springdale National Bank	8320	5	4
Springfield			
The Springfield National Bank	13031	–	–
Springville			
The First National Bank Of Springville	11393	6	6
State College			
The First National Bank Of State College	7511	5	5
The Peoples National Bank Of State College	12261	6	4
Steelton			
The Steelton National Bank	3599	6	–
Stewartstown			
The First National Bank Of Stewartstown	4665	6	5
The Peoples National Bank Of Stewartstown	6444	6	6
Stoneboro			
The First National Bank Of Stoneboro	6638	4	5
Stoystown			
The First National Bank At Stoystown	14089	–	6
The First National Bank Of Stoystown	5682	5	4
Strasburg			
The First National Bank Of Strasburg	42	5	–
The First National Bank Of Strasburg	2700	6	–
The First National Bank Of Strasburg	2700	5	6
Strausstown			
Strausstown National Bank	13863	–	4
The Strausstown National Bank	10452	6	5
Stroudsburg			
The First National Bank Of Stroudsburg	2787	6	5
The First-stroudsburg National Bank, Stroudsburg	3632	–	4
The Stroudsburg National Bank	3632	4	3
Summerville			
The Union National Bank Of Summerville	6739	6	5
Sunbury			
The First National Bank Of Sunbury	1237	3	2
The Sunbury National Bank	6877	6	–
Susquehanna			
The City National Bank Of Susquehanna	3144	5	5
The First National Bank Of Susquehanna	1053	4	5
Susquehanna Depot			
The First National Bank Of Susquehanna Depot	1053	5	–
Sutersville			
The First National Bank Of Sutersville	6270	6	6
Swarthmore			
Swarthmore National Bank & Trust Company, Swarthmore	7193	6	5
The Swarthmore National Bank	7193	5	–
Swineford			
The First National Bank Of Swineford	7003	6	6
Swissvale			
The First National Bank Of Swissvale	6109	5	4
Sykesville			
First National Bank In Sykesville	14169	–	6
The First National Bank Of Sykesville	7488	6	5
Tamaqua			
The First National Bank Of Tamaqua	1219	4	4
The Tamaqua National Bank	7286	4	3
Tarentum			
First National Bank And Trust Company Of Tarentum	4453	6	5
First National Bank In Tarentum	13940	–	4
The First National Bank Of Tarentum	2285	6	–
The National Bank Of Tarentum	4453	6	–
The Peoples National Bank Of Tarentum	5351	4	4
Telford			
The Telford National Bank	9257	5	3
Terre Hill			
The Terre Hill National Bank	9316	6	6
Thompsontown			
The Farmers National Bank Of Thompsontown	10211	6	5
Three Springs			
The First National Bank Of Three Springs	10183	6	–
Timblin			
The First National Bank Of Timblin	11204	6	6
Tioga			
The Grange National Bank Of Tioga	8092	6	6
Tionesta			
The Citizens National Bank Of Tionesta	5040	6	5
The Forest County National Bank Of Tionesta	5038	5	5
Titusville			
The First National Bank Of Titusville	622	6	–
The Hyde National Bank Of Titusville	2466	6	–
The Roberts National Bank Of Titusville	2834	6	–
The Second National Bank Of Titusville	879	3	3
Topton			
The National Bank Of Topton	8223	4	1
The Topton National Bank	3358	6	–
Towanda			
The Citizens National Bank Of Towanda	2337	4	4
The First National Bank Of Towanda	39	4	3
Tower City			
The Tower City National Bank	6117	6	4
Tower City National Bank	14031	–	5
Trafford City			
The First National Bank Of Trafford	6962	–	6
The First National Bank Of Trafford City	6962	6	5
Tremont			
The First National Bank Of Tremont	797	5	–
The Tremont National Bank	6165	6	5
Trevorton			
The First National Bank Of Trevorton	7722	5	5
Troy			
The First National Bank Of Troy	4984	5	4
The Grange National Bank Of Bradford County At Troy	8849	5	5
Tunkhannock			
The Citizens National Bank Of Tunkhannock	6438	6	5
The Wyoming National Bank Of Tunkhannock	835	5	5
Turbotville			
The Turbotville National Bank	9803	5	5
Turtle Creek			
First National Bank Of Turtle Creek	6574	6	4
The National Bank Of Turtle Creek	6568	6	–
Tyrone			
First Blair County National Bank Of Tyrone	4355	–	5
The Blair County National Bank & Trust Company Of Tyrone	6516	6	4
The Blair County National Bank Of Tyrone	6516	5	–
The Farmers And Merchants National Bank Of Tyrone	6499	6	6
The First National Bank Of Tyrone	4355	5	4
Ulster			
The First National Bank Of Ulster	9505	6	6
Ulysses			
The Grange National Bank Of Potter County At Ulysses	8739	6	5
Union City			
National Bank Of Union City	14093	–	4
The First National Bank Of Union Mills, Union City	110	6	–
The Home National Bank Of Union City	8879	5	3
The National Bank Of Union City	5131	6	4

City, Bank	Ch. No.	L	S
Uniontown			
The First National Bank Of Uniontown	270	6	–
The National Bank Of Fayette County, Uniontown	681	4	3
The Second National Bank Of Uniontown	5034	6	3
The Third National Bank Of Uniontown	13485	–	–
The Uniontown National Bank And Trust Company	12500	5	6
Vanderbilt			
The First National Bank Of Vanderbilt	8190	6	6
Vandergrift			
The Citizens National Bank Of Vandergrift	7816	5	6
The First National Bank Of Vandergrift	5080	6	–
Verona			
The First National Bank Of Verona	4877	5	5
Volant			
The First National Bank Of Volant	11834	–	6
Wampum			
First National Bank In Wampum	14112	–	6
The First National Bank Of Wampum	6664	6	6
Warren			
The Citizens National Bank Of Warren	2226	4	5
The First National Bank Of Warren	520	4	5
The Warren National Bank	4879	2	3
Washington			
The Citizens National Bank Of Washington	3383	4	2
The Farmers And Mechanics National Bank Of Washington	4181	6	–
The First National Bank Of Washington	586	4	–
The Old National Bank Of Washington	7263	–	–
The Peoples National Bank Of Washington	9901	6	3
Waterford			
The Ensworth National Bank Of Waterford	10027	6	5
Watsontown			
The Farmers National Bank Of Watsontown	3459	5	5
The Watsontown National Bank	2483	5	5
Wayne			
The Main Line National Bank Of Wayne	12504	5	–
Waynesboro			
Citizens National Bank & Trust Company Of Waynesboro	5832	–	3
First National Bank & Trust Company In Waynesboro	11866	6	3
First National Bank In Waynesboro	11866	5	–
The Citizens National Bank Of Waynesboro	5832	3	–
The First National Bank Of Waynesboro	244	6	–
The National Bank Of Waynesboro	11866	–	–
The Peoples National Bank Of Waynesboro	4445	4	–
The Union National Bank Of Waynesburg	13873	–	5
The Waynesboro National Bank And Trust Company	13005	–	–
Waynesburg			
First National Bank And Trust Company Of Waynesburg	13134	–	4
The American National Bank Of Waynesburg	6105	5	–
The Citizens National Bank Of Waynesburg	4267	4	–
The Farmers And Drovers National Bank Of Waynesburg	839	5	–
The First National Bank Of Waynesburg	305	6	–
The Peoples National Bank Of Waynesburg	5085	4	–
Weatherly			
The First National Bank Of Weatherly	6108	6	4
Webster			
The First National Bank Of Webster	6937	6	–
Wehrum			
The First National Bank Of Wehrum	7112	6	–
The National Bank Of Wehrum	12602	–	–
Weissport			
The Weissport National Bank	10214	6	5
Wellsborough			
The First National Bank Of Wellsborough	328	5	5
The Wellsborough National Bank	3938	6	–
Wellsville			
The Wellsville National Bank	8498	6	5
Wernersville			
The Wernersville National Bank	8131	3	–
The Wernersville National Bank & Trust Co, Wernersville	8131	–	4
West Alexander			
The Citizens National Bank Of West Alexander	11993	6	6
The Peoples National Bank Of West Alexander	8954	5	4
The West Alexander National Bank	5948	5	–
West Chester			
National Bank Of Chester County & Trust Co, West Chester	552	–	3
The Farmers National Bank Of West Chester	2857	–	6
The First National Bank Of West Chester	148	4	3
The National Bank Of Chester County, West Chester	552	4	6
West Conshohocken			
The Peoples National Bank Of West Conshohocken	8890	6	–
West Elizabeth			
The First National Bank Of West Elizabeth	6373	6	–
West Greenville			
The First National Bank Of Greenville	249	6	4
The First National Bank Of West Greenville	249	6	–
West Grove			
The National Bank & Trust Company Of West Grove	2669	6	4
The National Bank Of West Grove	2669	6	–
West Middlesex			
The First National Bank Of West Middlesex	6913	6	4
West Newton			
The First National Bank Of West Newton	5010	5	5
West York			
The Industrial National Bank Of West York	8938	5	4
Westfield			
The Farmers And Traders National Bank Of Westfield	9513	6	5
Wilcox			
Wilcox National Bank	12933	6	6
Wilkes Barre			
The First National Bank Of Wilkes Barre	2736	6	–
The Second National Bank Of Wilkes Barre	104	4	3
Wilkes-barre			
Miners National Bank Of Wilkes-barre	13852	–	3
The First National Bank Of Wilkes-barre	30	4	–
The First National Bank Of Wilkes-barre	2736	4	3
The Hanover National Bank Of Wilkes-barre	14344	–	–
The Luzerne County National Bank Of Wilkes-barre	9235	5	–
The Wyoming National Bank Of Wilkes-barre	732	5	3
Wilkinsburg			
The Central National Bank Of Wilkinsburg	5265	6	6
The First National Bank At Wilkinsburg	13823	–	4
The First National Bank Of Wilkinsburg	4728	5	4
Williamsburg			
First National Bank Of Williamsburg	14182	–	6
The Farmers And Merchants National Bank Of Williamsburg	9392	6	6
The First National Bank Of Williamsburg	6971	5	5
Williamsport			
The City National Bank Of Williamsport	2139	5	–
The First National Bank Of Williamsport	175	4	2
The Lumberman's National Bank Of Williamsport	734	6	–
The Lycoming National Bank Of Williamsport	2227	4	–
The Merchants National Bank Of Williamsport	3705	6	–
The West Branch National Bank Of Williamsport	1505	4	–
Wilmerding			
First National Bank Of Wilmerding	5000	3	1
The East Pittsburgh National Bank Of Wilmerding	5000	6	–
The Wilmerding National Bank Of Wilmerding	6325	6	–
Wilson			
The First National Bank Of Clairton	6794	6	5
The First National Bank Of Wilson	6794	6	–
Winburne			
Bituminous National Bank Of Winburne	7334	–	6
The Bituminous National Bank Of Winburne	7334	5	–
Windber			
Citizens National Bank In Windber	14082	–	6
The Citizens National Bank Of Windber	6848	6	4
The Windber National Bank	5242	6	–
Windsor			
The First National Bank Of Windsor	12063	6	6
Woodlawn			
Aliquippa National Bank, Aliquippa	10951	6	5
The First National Bank Of Woodlawn	10951	5	–
Wrightsville			
The First National Bank Of Wrightsville	246	5	4
Wyalusing			
The First National Bank Of Wyalusing	5339	6	–
The National Bank Of Wyalusing	10606	6	5
Wyoming			
The First National Bank Of Wyoming	8517	5	4
Yardley			
The Yardley National Bank	4207	4	4
Yardley National Bank	13950	–	5
York			
The Central National Bank & Trust Company Of York	9706	–	5
The Central National Bank Of York	9706	6	5
The Drovers And Mechanics National Bank Of York	2958	5	5
The Eastern National Bank Of York	12305	–	–
The Farmers National Bank Of York	2228	5	–
The First National Bank Of York	197	5	3
The Western National Bank Of York	2303	4	5
The York County National Bank, York	694	4	3
The York National Bank	604	5	–
The York National Bank & Trust Company, York	604	6	3
York Springs			
The First National Bank Of York Springs	7856	6	4
Youngsville			
The First National Bank Of Youngsville	8165	6	4
The Youngsville National Bank	14345	–	–
Youngwood			
The First National Bank Of Youngwood	6500	6	5
Yukon			
The First National Bank Of Yukon	12808	–	–
Zelienople			
The First National Bank Of Zelienople	6141	6	5
The Peoples National Bank Of Zelienople	7409	4	2
The Union National Bank Of Zelienople	14215	–	–

PORTO RICO

City, Bank	Ch. No.	L	S
San Juan			
The First National Bank Of Porto Rico At San Juan	6484	3	–

RHODE ISLAND

City, Bank	Ch. No.	L	S
Anthony			
The Coventry National Bank Of Anthony	1161	5	–
Ashaway			
The Ashaway National Bank	1150	4	3
Bristol			
The First National Bank Of Bristol	1292	5	–
The National Eagle Bank Of Bristol	1562	6	–
Centerville			
The Centreville National Bank Of Warwick, West Warwick	1284	–	4
Cumberland			
The Cumberland National Bank	1404	6	–
East Greenwich			
The Greenwich National Bank Of East Greenwich	1405	6	–
Greenville			
The National Exchange Bank Of Greenville	1498	3	–
Hopkinton			
The First National Bank Of Hopkinton	1054	4	–
Kingston			
The National Landholders Bank Of Kingston	1158	5	–
Newport			
The Aquidneck National Bank Of Newport	1546	2	–
The Aquidneck National Bank Of Newport	1546	–	–
The Aquidneck Natl Exchange Bank & Savings Co Of Newport	1546	5	2
The First National Bank Of Newport	1021	5	–
The National Bank Of Rhode Island Of Newport	1532	4	–
The National Exchange Bank Of Newport	1565	3	–
The Newport National Bank	1492	1	3
The Union National Bank Of Newport	2554	3	–
North Providence			
The Pacific National Bank Of North Providence	1616	4	–
The Pacific National Bank Of Pawtucket	1616	6	–
The Slater National Bank Of North Providence	856	3	–
The Slater National Bank Of Pawtucket	856	6	–
Pascoag			
The Pascoag National Bank	1512	5	–
Pawtucket			
The First National Bank Of Pawtucket	843	3	–
Phenix			
The Phenix National Bank	1460	6	–
Providence			
Rhode Island Hospital National Bank Of Providence	13901	–	1
The American National Bank Of Providence	1472	2	–
The Atlantic National Bank Of Providence	2913	6	–
The Blackstone Canal National Bank Of Providence	1328	1	1
The City National Bank Of Providence	1429	6	–
The Columbus National Bank Of Providence	13981	–	3
The Commercial National Bank Of Providence	1319	4	–
The Fifth National Bank Of Providence	1002	4	–
The First National Bank Of Providence	134	2	–
The Fourth National Bank Of Providence	772	4	–
The Globe National Bank Of Providence	1126	4	–
The Lime Rock National Bank Of Providence	1369	6	–
The Manufacturers National Bank Of Providence	1283	3	–
The Mechanics National Bank Of Providence	1007	1	1
The Merchants National Bank Of Providence	1131	1	–
The National Bank Of Commerce & Trust Co Of Providence	1366	–	2
The National Bank Of Commerce Of Providence	1366	2	4
The National Bank Of North America, Providence	1036	3	–
The National Eagle Bank Of Providence	1030	4	–
The National Exchange Bank Of Providence	1339	1	–
The Old National Bank Of Providence	1151	3	–
The Phenix National Bank Of Providence	948	1	1
The Providence National Bank	1302	1	1
The Rhode Island National Bank Of Providence	983	3	–
The Roger Williams National Bank Of Providence	1506	4	–
The Second National Bank Of Providence	565	3	–
The Third National Bank Of Providence	636	5	–
The Traders National Bank Of Providence	1396	6	–
The United National Bank Of Providence	5925	3	–
The Weybosset National Bank Of Providence	1173	4	–
Scituate			
The Scituate National Bank	1552	6	–
Slatersville			
The First National Bank Of Smithfield	1035	4	–
The First National Bank Of Smithfield, Slatersville	1035	4	3
Wakefield			
The National Exchange Bank Of Wakefield	1554	6	–
The Wakefield National Bank	1206	5	–
Warren			
The First National Bank Of Warren	673	4	–
The National Hope Bank Of Warren	1008	4	–
The National Warren Bank Of Warren	1419	4	–
Warwick			
The Centreville National Bank Of Warwick, Centreville	1284	4	–
Westerly			
The National Niantic Bank Of Westerly	823	4	–
The National Phenix Bank Of Westerly	1169	5	–
The Washington National Bank Of Westerly	952	4	–
Wickford			
The Wickford National Bank	1592	5	–
Woonsocket			
The Citizens National Bank Of Woonsocket	970	3	–
The First National Bank Of Woonsocket	1402	6	–
The National Globe Bank Of Woonsocket	1423	4	–
The National Union Bank Of Woonsocket	1409	4	–
The Producers National Bank Of Woonsocket	1421	3	–
The Woonsocket National Bank	1058	4	–

SOUTH CAROLINA

City, Bank	Ch. No.	L	S
Abbeville			
The National Bank Of Abbeville	3421	5	–
Aiken			
The First National Bank Of Aiken	9650	5	–
Allendale			
The First National Bank Of Allendale	11111	6	–
Anderson			
The Carolina National Bank Of Anderson	12175	–	–
The Citizens National Bank Of Anderson	9104	5	–
The National Bank Of Anderson	2072	6	–
Bamberg			
The First National Bank Of Bamberg	11704	–	–
Barnwell			
The First National Bank Of Barnwell	11287	6	–
Batesburg			
The Citizens National Bank Of Batesburg	10815	6	–
The First National Bank Of Batesburg	5595	4	4
Bennettsville			
The Peoples National Bank Of Bennettsville	10743	–	–
The Planters National Bank Of Bennettsville	6385	4	6
Bishopville			
The Bishopville National Bank	10872	–	–
The First National Bank Of Bishopville	10263	5	6
Bowman			
The National Bank Of Bowman	11562	–	–

City, Bank	Ch. No.	L	S
Brunson			
The First National Bank Of Brunson	10832	5	–
Camden			
The First National Bank Of Camden	9083	3	4
Charleston			
Peoples-first National Bank Of Charleston	1621	3	4
The Atlantic National Bank Of Charleston	10708	4	–
The Bank Of Charleston National Banking Association	2044	2	–
The Commercial National Bank Of Charleston	10543	6	–
The Dime National Bank Of Charleston	12273	–	–
The Exchange National Bank Of Charleston	12702	–	–
The First National Bank Of Charleston	1622	3	–
The Germania National Bank Of Charleston	10708	6	–
The Norwood-Carolina National Bank Of Charleston	12865	–	–
The Peoples National Bank Of Charleston	1621	2	–
The South Carolina National Bank Of Charleston	2044	3	2
Cheraw			
The First National Bank Of Cheraw	9342	5	–
Chester			
The Citizens National Bank Of Chester	10699	–	–
The National Bank Of Chester	1804	6	–
The National Exchange Bank Of Chester	8471	3	5
The Peoples National Bank Of Chester	10663	–	2
Clinton			
First National Bank Of Clinton	8041	4	5
Clio			
The First National Bank Of Clio	11153	6	–
Clover			
The First National Bank Of Clover	11439	6	5
Columbia			
The Carolina National Bank Of Columbia	1680	4	–
The Central National Bank Of Columbia	1765	6	–
The Columbia National Bank	12412	3	4
The First National Bank Of Columbia	13720	–	5
The Liberty National Bank Of South Carolina At Columbia	9687	4	–
The National Loan And Exchange Bank Of Columbia	6871	3	3
The National State Bank Of Columbia	10315	4	–
The Palmetto National Bank Of Columbia	8133	2	–
The Peoples National Bank Of Columbia	10597	5	–
The Union National Bank Of Columbia	9687	4	–
Conway			
The Conway National Bank	10536	5	5
The First National Bank Of Conway	9690	6	–
The Peoples National Bank Of Conway	10537	5	5
Darlington			
Carolina National Bank Of Darlington	9999	4	–
The Darlington National Bank	2512	6	–
Dillon			
The First National Bank Of Dillon	10908	6	–
Elloree			
The First National Bank Of Elloree	10679	5	5
Fairfax			
The First National Bank Of Fairfax	10979	6	–
The National Security Bank Of Fairfax	12668	–	–
Florence			
The First National Bank Of Florence	9747	4	–
The First National Bank Of Florence	12799	–	–
Fort Mill			
The First National Bank Of Fort Mill	9941	6	6
Gaffney			
The First National Bank Of Gaffney	5064	5	6
The Merchants And Planters National Bank Of Gaffney	10655	4	3
The National Bank Of Gaffney	5064	6	–
Greenville			
The City National Bank Of Greenville	5004	5	–
The First National Bank Of Greenville	1935	5	3
The Fourth National Bank Of Greenville	9190	6	–
The National Bank Of Greenville	1935	4	–
The Norwood National Bank Of Greenville	8766	3	–
The Peoples National Bank Of Greenville	10635	6	3
The Woodside National Bank Of Greenville	11499	4	6
Greenwood			
National Loan & Exchange Bank Of Greenwood	7027	4	5
The First National Bank Of Greenwood	7027	6	–
Greer			
The First National Bank Of Greer	12025	–	–
Hartsville			
The First National Bank Of Hartsville	10137	6	–
Holly Hill			
The First National Bank Of Holly Hill	10680	6	6
Honea Path			
The National Bank Of Honea Path	12381	6	6
Lake City			
The Farmers And Merchants National Bank Of Lake City	10681	5	–
Lamar			
The Lamar National Bank	11080	6	–
Lancaster			
The First National Bank Of Lancaster	7858	5	–
Laurens			
The Enterprise National Bank Of Laurens	10605	6	–
The Farmers National Bank Of Laurens	10859	–	–
The Laurens National Bank	10652	6	–
The National Bank Of Laurens	3540	6	–
Leesville			
The National Bank Of Leesville	9057	3	5
Lexington			
The Home National Bank Of Lexington	9296	4	6
Manning			
The First National Bank Of Manning	11155	6	–
Marion			
Marion National Bank	10085	4	3
Mullins			
The Davis National Bank Of Mullins	14341	–	–
The First National Bank Of Mullins	9876	5	6
Newberry			
The National Bank Of Newberry	1844	4	–
North			
The First National Bank Of North	11914	–	–
Norway			
The Farmers National Bank Of Norway	11189	6	–
Olanta			
The First National Bank Of Olanta	10748	5	–
Orangeburg			
The Edisto National Bank Of Orangeburg	10650	5	4
The First National Bank In Orangeburg	13918	–	6
The First National Bank Of Orangeburg	5269	6	–
The Orangeburg National Bank, Orangeburg	10674	5	–
The Peoples National Bank Of Orangeburg	10674	6	–
The Southern National Bank Of Orangeburg	14135	–	–
Prosperity			
The Citizens National Bank Of Prosperity	12774	–	–
The Peoples National Bank Of Prosperity	6994	6	–
Rock Hill			
The First National Bank Of Rock Hill	3616	6	–
The National Union Bank Of Rock Hill	5134	3	–
The Peoples National Bank Of Rock Hill	9407	4	3
Saint George			
The First National Bank Of Saint George	12233	–	–
Saint Matthews			
The St. Matthews National Bank	10651	6	–
Saluda			
The First National Bank Of Saluda	10798	–	–
The Planters National Bank Of Saluda	10802	–	–
Sharon			
The First National Bank Of Sharon	9533	4	5
Spartanburg			
The American National Bank Of Spartanburg	6658	4	5
The Carolina National Bank Of Spartanburg	12146	–	–
The Central National Bank Of Spartanburg	4996	3	3
The Commercial National Bank Of Spartanburg	14211	–	1
The First National Bank Of Spartanburg	1848	2	4
The National Bank Of Spartanburg	1848	6	–
Springfield			
The First National Bank Of Springfield	10586	5	6
Sumter			
The City National Bank Of Sumter	10129	4	6
The First National Bank Of Sumter	3809	4	6
The National Bank Of South Carolina Of Sumter	10660	3	2
The National Bank Of Sumter	3082	6	–
The National Bank Of Sumter	10670	4	6
The Simonds National Bank Of Sumter	3809	6	–
Union			
The Citizens National Bank Of Union	9742	5	–
The Merchants And Planters National Bank Of Union	2060	5	–
Wagener			
The First National Bank Of Wagener	10485	6	–
Walterboro			
The First National Bank Of Walterboro	9849	4	–
Whitmire			
The First National Bank Of Whitmire	6102	6	–
Winnsboro			
The Winnsboro National Bank	2087	6	–
Woodruff			
The First National Bank Of Woodruff	10593	6	–
Yorkville			
The First National Bank Of York	6931	6	–
The First National Bank Of Yorkville	6931	6	–

DAKOTA TERRITORY

City, Bank	Ch. No.	L	S
Aberdeen			
The Aberdeen National Bank	3326	6	–
The First National Bank Of Aberdeen	2980	6	–
The Northwestern National Bank Of Aberdeen	3932	6	–
Ashton			
The First National Bank Of Ashton	3437	6	–
Bismarck			
The Bismarck National Bank	2677	6	–
The Capital National Bank Of Bismarck	2986	6	–
The First National Bank Of Bismarck	2434	6	–
The Merchants National Bank Of Bismarck	3169	6	–
Brookings			
The First National Bank Of Brookings	3087	6	–
Canton			
The First National Bank Of Canton	2830	6	–
Casselton			
The First National Bank Of Casselton	2792	6	–
Chamberlain			
The First National Bank Of Chamberlain	2911	6	–
Clark			
The First National Bank Of Clark	3479	6	–
Columbia			
The First National Bank Of Columbia	3352	6	–
De Smet			
The First National Bank Of De Smet	3435	6	–
Deadwood			
The Deadwood National Bank	3552	6	–
The First National Bank Of Deadwood	2391	4	–
The Merchants National Bank Of Deadwood	2461	6	–
Dell Rapids			
The First National Bank Of Dell Rapids	3508	6	–
Devil's Lake			
The First National Bank Of Devil's Lake	3397	6	–
The Merchants National Bank Of Devil's Lake	3714	6	–
Doland			
The First National Bank Of Doland	3522	6	–
Fargo			
The Citizens National Bank Of Fargo	3602	6	–
The First National Bank Of Fargo	2377	6	–
The Red River Valley National Bank Of Fargo	2514	6	–
Grafton			
The First National Bank Of Grafton	2840	6	–
The Grafton National Bank	3096	6	–
Grand Forks			
The Citizens National Bank Of Grand Forks	2570	6	–
The First National Bank Of Grand Forks	2564	6	–
The Grand Forks National Bank	3301	6	–
The Second National Bank Of Grand Forks	3504	6	–
Hillsboro			
The First National Bank Of Hillsboro	3400	6	–
The Hillsboro National Bank	3411	6	–
Huron			
The Beadle County National Bank Of Huron	2989	6	–
The First National Bank Of Huron	2819	6	–
The Huron National Bank	3267	6	–
The National Bank Of Dakota, Huron	3636	6	–
Jamestown			
The First National Bank Of Jamestown	2578	6	–
The James River National Bank Of Jamestown	2580	6	–
The Jamestown National Bank	3331	6	–
Lakota			
The First National Bank Of Lakota	4143	6	–
Larimore			
The First National Bank Of Larimore	2854	6	–
Lisbon			
The First National Bank Of Lisbon	3669	6	–
Madison			
The Citizens National Bank Of Madison	3151	6	–
The First National Bank Of Madison	3149	6	–
The Madison National Bank	3597	6	–
Mandan			
The First National Bank Of Mandan	2585	6	–
Mayville			
The First National Bank Of Mayville	3673	6	–
Minot			
The First National Bank Of Minot	4009	6	–
Mitchell			
The First National Bank Of Mitchell	2645	6	–
The Mitchell National Bank	3578	6	–
Park River			
The First National Bank Of Park River	3436	6	–
Parker			
The First National Bank Of Parker	3675	6	–
Pembina			
The First National Bank Of Pembina	3438	6	–
Pierre			
The First National Bank Of Pierre	2941	6	–
The Pierre National Bank	4104	6	–
Plankinton			
The First National Bank Of Plankinton	3130	6	–
Rapid City			
The Black Hills National Bank Of Rapid City	3401	6	–
The First National Bank Of Rapid City	3237	6	–
Redfield			
The First National Bank Of Redfield	3398	6	–
Sioux Falls			
The Citizens National Bank Of Sioux Falls	3586	6	–
The Dakota National Bank Of Sioux Falls	2843	6	–
The First National Bank Of Sioux Falls	2465	6	–
The Minnehaha National Bank Of Sioux Falls	3393	6	–
The Sioux Falls National Bank	2823	6	–
Sturgis			
The First National Bank Of Sturgis	3739	6	–
Valley City			
The Farmers And Merchants National Bank Of Valley City	2650	6	–
The First National Bank Of Valley City	2548	6	–
Wahpeton			
The First National Bank Of Wahpeton	2624	6	–
The National Bank Of Wahpeton	4106	6	–
Watertown			
The Citizens National Bank Of Watertown	3349	6	–
The First National Bank Of Watertown	2935	6	–
The Watertown National Bank	3414	6	–
Yankton			
The First National Bank Of Yankton	2068	4	–

SOUTH DAKOTA

City, Bank	Ch. No.	L	S
Aberdeen			
First National Bank & Trust Company Of Aberdeen	2980	–	4
First National Bank Of Aberdeen	2980	–	–
The Aberdeen National Bank	3326	3	–
The Dakota National Bank Of Aberdeen	8642	3	–
The First National Bank Of Aberdeen	2980	3	5
The Northwestern National Bank Of Aberdeen	3932	6	–
Alcester			
The Alcester National Bank	10822	–	–
The Farmers And Merchants National Bank Of Alcester	10818	–	–
Alexandria			
The First National Bank In Alexandria	12611	–	–
The First National Bank Of Alexandria	5918	5	–
The Security National Bank Of Alexandria	10187	4	–
Arlington			
The First National Bank In Arlington	13286	–	5
The First National Bank Of Arlington	5916	4	–
Armour			
The First National Bank Of Armour	8012	6	–
Belle Fourche			
The First National Bank Of Belle Fourche	6561	4	6
Beresford			
The First National Bank Of Beresford	10813	4	4
Bison			
The First National Bank Of Bison	13477	–	–
Brandt			
The First National Bank Of Brandt	10893	–	–
Bridgewater			
The Farmers National Bank Of Bridgewater	7426	6	6
The First National Bank Of Bridgewater	6925	6	–
Bristol			
The Citizens National Bank Of Bristol	10868	–	–
The First Naitonal Bank In Bristol	10868	–	–
The First National Bank Of Bristol	8480	6	–
Britton			
First National Bank In Britton	13460	–	3
The First National Bank Of Britton	6073	5	6
Brookings			
Farmers National Bank Of Brookings	6462	4	–
The Brookings National Bank	13181	–	–
The First National Bank Of Brookings	3087	3	–
The Security National Bank Of Brookings	12838	–	–
Bryant			
The First National Bank Of Bryant	10772	–	–

City, Bank	Ch. No.	L	S
Canton			
The First National Bank Of Canton	2830	3	3
The National Bank Of Canton	4637	6	–
Carthage			
First National Bank Of Carthage	10833	5	–
Castlewood			
The First National Bank Of Castlewood	6000	5	–
Centerville			
The First National Bank Of Centerville	5477	4	3
Chamberlain			
The Brule National Bank Of Chamberlain	8550	5	–
The Chamberlain National Bank	4282	6	–
The First National Bank And Trust Company Of Chamberlain	13483	–	3
The First National Bank Of Chamberlain	2911	6	–
The Whitbeck National Bank Of Chamberlain	9301	3	–
Clark			
The Clark County National Bank Of Clark	6409	4	4
The First National Bank Of Clark	3479	6	–
Clear Lake			
The Deuel County National Bank Of Clear Lake	12877	6	3
The First National Bank Of Clear Lake	6357	5	–
Colman			
The First National Bank Of Colman	6688	4	–
Custer			
The First National Bank Of Custer City	4448	6	–
Davis			
The First National Bank Of Davis	11457	6	6
De Smet			
The De Smet National Bank	5355	5	–
The First National Bank Of De Smet	3435	6	–
Deadwood			
The American National Bank Of Deadwood	4983	6	–
The Deadwood National Bank	3552	6	–
The First National Bank Of Deadwood	2391	3	3
The Merchants National Bank Of Deadwood	2461	6	–
Dell Rapids			
New First National Bank In Dell Rapids	12872	–	–
The First National Bank Of Dell Rapids	3508	3	–
The Home National Bank Of Dell Rapids	9693	2	5
Doland			
The First National Bank Of Doland	3522	6	–
The Merchants National Bank Of Redfield	3522	6	–
Eden			
The First National Bank Of Eden	11506	–	–
Egan			
The First National Bank Of Egan	7252	4	4
Elk Point			
The First National Bank Of Elk Point	5901	5	6
Elkton			
The First National Bank Of Elkton	6368	5	–
Emery			
The Security National Bank Of Emery	11812	5	5
Ethan			
The First National Bank Of Ethan	13549	–	6
Eureka			
The First National Bank Of Eureka	11527	–	–
Fairfax			
Farmers National Bank Of Fairfax	12325	4	–
The Farmers National Bank Of Fairfax	13302	–	5
The First National Bank Of Fairfax	8711	6	–
Farmer			
The First National Bank Of Farmer	11456	–	–
Faulkton			
The First National Bank Of Faulkton	10961	–	–
Flandreau			
The First National Bank Of Flandreau	5854	4	4
Florence			
The First National Bank Of Florence	10774	–	–
Fort Pierre			
The First National Bank Of Fort Pierre	4237	6	–
The Fort Pierre National Bank	9587	6	4
Frankfort			
The First National Bank Of Frankfort	10683	–	–
Frederick			
The First National Bank Of Frederick	8624	4	–
Freeman			
The First National Bank Of Freeman	6181	6	4
Garden City			
The Farmers National Bank Of Vienna	11558	5	3
The First National Bank Of Garden City	11558	–	–
Garretson			
The First National Bank Of Garretson	7755	6	–
Gary			
The First National Bank Of Gary	9393	6	4
The National Bank Of Gary	10846	5	5
Gettysburg			
Potter County National Bank Of Gettysburg	8776	–	5
The First National Bank Of Gettysburg	8776	5	5
Goodwin			
The First National Bank Of Goodwin	10797	–	–
Gregory			
The First National Bank Of Gregory	8600	5	–
The Gregory National Bank	9377	5	–
Groton			
The First National Bank Of Groton	7885	4	4
Hayti			
The First National Bank Of Hayti	10800	–	–
Hecla			
The First National Bank Of Hecla	9679	5	4
Henry			
The First National Bank Of Henry	10416	6	–
Highmore			
The First National Bank Of Highmore	7794	5	4
Hot Springs			
The First National Bank Of Hot Springs	4370	6	–
The Hot Springs National Bank	6339	6	–
The Peoples National Bank Of Hot Springs	9166	6	–
Howard			
The First National Bank Of Howard	6585	5	–
The Howard National Bank	10780	–	–
The New First National Bank Of Howard	12920	–	–
Hudson			
The First National Bank Of Hudson	7335	4	4
Huron			
First National Bank In Huron	13466	–	–
The Beadle County National Bank Of Huron	2989	6	–
The City National Bank Of Huron	8781	6	–
The First National Bank Of Huron	2819	5	–
The Huron National Bank	3267	6	–
The National Bank Of Dakota, Huron	3636	6	–
The National Bank Of Huron	8841	4	3
The Security National Bank Of Huron	13466	–	–
Kennebec			
The First National Bank Of Kennebec	10098	5	–
Lake Norden			
The First National Bank & Trust Company Of Lake Norden	13221	–	4
The First National Bank Of Lake Norden	10714	5	–
The Lake Norden National Bank	13221	–	–
Lake Preston			
The Farmers National Bank Of Lake Preston	10773	–	–
The First National Bank Of Lake Preston	10758	5	–
Lead			
The First National Bank Of Lead	4631	4	3
Lemmon			
First National Bank In Lemmon	12857	–	4
New First National Bank In Lemmon	12857	5	–
The First National Bank Of Lemmon	9269	5	–
Leola			
The First National Bank Of Leola	13459	–	–
Letcher			
The First National Bank Of Letcher	9188	5	4
Madison			
The Citizens National Bank Of Madison	3151	6	–
The First National Bank Of Madison	3149	5	–
The Lake County National Bank Of Madison	10636	3	–
The Northwestern National Bank Of Madison	13517	–	–
Mcintosh			
The First National Bank Of Mcintosh	9283	6	–
Menno			
The First National Bank Of Menno	11323	–	–
Midland			
The First National Bank Of Midland	10637	6	4
Milbank			
The Farmers And Merchants National Bank In Milbank	13407	–	3
The Farmers And Merchants National Bank Of Milbank	8698	5	6
The First National Bank Of Milbank	6473	3	–
The Merchants National Bank Of Milbank	8698	4	–
Miller			
The First National Bank Of Miller	6789	4	–
Mitchell			
The First National Bank Of Mitchell	2645	3	–
The Mitchell National Bank	3578	3	3
Western National Bank Of Mitchell	7455	4	–
Mobridge			
First National Bank In Mobridge	13467	–	3
The First National Bank Of Mobridge	10744	4	5
The Security National Bank Of Mobridge	11590	6	6
Morristown			
The First National Bank Of Morristown	9817	5	–
Mount Vernon			
The First National Bank In Mount Vernon	13282	–	–
The First National Bank Of Mount Vernon	7582	5	–
Oldham			
The First National Bank Of Oldham	10256	4	–
The Oldham National Bank	12662	–	3
Onida			
The First National Bank Of Onida	11585	6	–
The Onida National Bank	12777	–	–
Parker			
The First National Bank Of Parker	3675	6	3
Parkston			
The First National Bank Of Parkston	7662	4	3
Philip			
The First National Bank Of Philip	13430	–	–
Pierre			
First National Bank In Pierre	14252	–	4
The First National Bank Of Pierre	2941	3	3
The National Bank Of Commerce Of Pierre	4279	3	–
The Pierre National Bank	4104	3	3
Pollock			
The First National Bank Of Pollock	11237	–	–
Pukwana			
The First National Bank Of Pukwana	9958	4	3
Rapid City			
The Black Hills National Bank Of Rapid City	3401	6	
The First National Bank Of Rapid City	3237	4	4
The Rapid City National Bank	14099	–	3
Redfield			
The American National Bank Of Redfield	8125	5	5
The First National Bank Of Redfield	3398	6	–
The German American National Bank Of Redfield	8125	6	–
The Redfield National Bank	6256	5	4
Ree Heights			
The First National Bank Of Ree Heights	13061	–	–
Saint Lawrence			
The First National Bank Of St. Lawrence	12547	4	5
Salem			
The First National Bank Of Salem	5898	4	–
The Mccook County National Bank Of Salem	12784	–	1
Scotland			
The Corn Belt National Bank Of Scotland	11031	–	–
The First National Bank Of Scotland	7048	6	–
Selby			
The First National Bank Of Selby	9376	4	4
Sherman			
First National Bank In Garretson	12488	–	–
The First National Bank Of Sherman	12488	–	–
Sioux Falls			
Northwest Security National Bank Of Sioux Falls	10592	–	–
Security National Bank And Trust Company Of Sioux Falls	10592	–	2
The American National Bank Of Sioux Falls	9915	6	–
The Citizens National Bank And Trust Company Of Sioux Falls	12881	–	–
The Citizens National Bank In Sioux Falls	12881	–	–
The Dakota National Bank Of Sioux Falls	2843	6	–
The First National Bank And Trust Company In Sioux Falls	3393	–	–
The Minnehaha National Bank Of Sioux Falls	3393	6	–
The Scandinavian-American National Bank Of Sioux Falls	10553	–	–
The Security National Bank Of Sioux Falls	10592	3	–
The Sioux Falls National Bank	2823	6	–
The Union National Bank Of Sioux Falls	4629	6	–
Sisseton			
Citizens Security National Bank Of Sisseton	6395	6	5
The Citizens National Bank Of Sisseton	6395	4	–
The First National Bank Of Sisseton	5428	4	4
The Security National Bank Of Sisseton	11341	–	–
South Shore			
Farmers National Bank Of Estelline	11689	–	5
The Farmers National Bank Of South Shore	11689	–	–
The Farmers National Bank Of Strandburg	11689	–	–
The First National Bank Of South Shore	7686	6	–
Spearfish			
The American National Bank Of Spearfish	8248	6	–
The First National Bank Of Spearfish	4874	6	–
Springfield			
The First National Bank Of Springfield	8942	6	–
Sturgis			
The Commercial National Bank Of Sturgis	6990	6	3
The First National Bank Of Sturgis	3739	6	–
Toronto			
The First National Bank Of Toronto	6381	5	–
Tyndall			
The Citizens National Bank Of Tyndall	11637	–	–
The First National Bank Of Tyndall	6792	3	2
Veblen			
The First National Bank Of Veblen	9858	4	–
Vermilion			
The First National Bank And Trust Company Of Vermilion	13346	–	3
The First National Bank Of Vermilion	4603	5	–
The Vermilion National Bank	7352	5	–
Vermillion			
First National Bank In Vermillion	13346	–	6
Viborg			
The First National Bank Of Viborg	10808	–	–
The Security National Bank Of Viborg	13589	–	4
Vienna			
The First National Bank Of Vienna	7597	6	–
Volga			
The First National Bank Of Volga	6099	5	5
Wakonda			
The First National Bank Of Wakonda	7968	6	–
Watertown			
Security National Bank Of Watertown	7504	4	–
The Citizens National Bank And Trust Company Of Watertown	3349	–	–
The Citizens National Bank Of Watertown	3349	5	4
The First Citizens National Bank Of Watertown	2935	–	6
The First National Bank And Trust Company Of Watertown	2935	–	3
The First National Bank Of Watertown	2935	3	–
The Watertown National Bank	3414	6	–
Waubay			
The First National Bank Of Waubay	6124	6	–
Webster			
The Dakota National Bank Of Webster	12374	–	–
The Farmers And Merchants National Bank Of Webster	8559	4	4
The First National Bank Of Webster	6502	6	–
Wessington			
The Citizens National Bank Of Wessington	12888	–	–
The First National Bank Of Wessington	8325	6	–
Wessington Springs			
The First National Bank Of Wessington Springs	6446	5	–
The National Bank Of Wessington Springs	12620	–	–
Wetonka			
The First National Bank Of Wetonka	11441	4	–
White			
The Farmers National Bank Of White	7134	6	–
The First National Bank Of White	6294	6	4
White Lake			
The First National Bank Of White Lake	8291	5	5
The United States National Bank Of White Lake	8332	6	–
White Rock			
The First National Bank Of White Rock	6185	5	3
The Roberts County National Bank Of Sisseton	6185	–	6
Wilmot			
The First National Bank Of Wilmot	11399	–	4
Winner			
The First National Bank Of Winner	11119	6	–
The Winner National Bank	12024	–	–
Woonsocket			
The Citizens National Bank Of Woonsocket	5946	5	–
The First National Bank Of Woonsocket	5946	6	–
Yankton			
First Dakota National Bank And Trust Company Of Yankton	2068	–	–
The Dakota National Bank Of Yankton	9445	3	4
The First Dakota National Bank & Trust Company Of Yankton	2068	–	6
The First National Bank And Trust Company Of Yankton	2068	–	–
The First National Bank Of Yankton	2068	4	–
The National Bank Of Commerce	11653	–	–
The Yankton National Bank	4613	6	–

TENNESSEE

City, Bank	Ch. No.	L	S
Athens			
The Citizens National Bank Of Athens	10735	5	5
The First National Bank Of Athens	3341	4	4
Big Sandy			
The First National Bank Of Big Sandy	13077	–	–
Bristol			
The First National Bank In Bristol	13640	–	4
The First National Bank Of Bristol	2167	6	–
The First National Bank Of Bristol	2796	3	2
The National Bank Of Bristol	2796	6	–
Brownsville			
The First National Bank Of Brownsville	6042	6	–
Camden			
The First National Bank Of Camden	8506	6	–
Cardiff			
The First National Bank Of Cardiff	4303	6	–
Carthage			
The First National Bank Of Carthage	7928	6	–
Centerville			
The Citizens National Bank Of Centerville	9827	6	–
The First National Bank Of Centerville	3288	6	6
Chattanooga			
Chattanooga National Bank	13654	–	–
Citizens National Bank Of Chattanooga	9176	6	–
The American National Bank Of Chattanooga	7817	6	–
The Chattanooga National Bank	3691	6	–
The City National Bank Of Chattanooga	1746	6	–
The Commercial National Bank Of Chattanooga	13746	–	3
The First National Bank Of Chattanooga	1606	2	2
The Fourth National Bank Of Chattanooga	4060	6	–
The Hamilton National Bank Of Chattanooga	7848	2	1
The Merchants National Bank Of Chattanooga	4456	6	–
The Third National Bank Of Chattanooga	2559	6	–
Clarksville			
The Clarksville National Bank	2720	5	6
The Farmers And Merchants National Bank Of Clarksville	3241	6	–
The First National Bank Of Clarksville	1603	4	3
Cleveland			
The Cleveland National Bank	1666	4	3
Coal Creek			
The First National Bank Of Coal Creek	10028	5	6
Columbia			
The First National Bank Of Columbia	1713	6	–
The Maury National Bank Of Columbia	4849	3	4
The Phoenix National Bank Of Columbia	7870	4	5
The Second National Bank Of Columbia	2568	6	–
Cookeville			
The Cookeville National Bank	9692	6	–
The First National Bank Of Cookeville	9667	5	5
Copperhill			
The First National Bank Of Polk County At Copperhill	9027	5	6
Covington			
The First National Bank Of Covington	10491	5	–
Crossville			
The First National Bank Of Crossville	9809	6	5
Dayton			
The American National Bank Of Dayton	5679	6	6
The First National Bank Of Dayton	4362	6	–
Decherd			
The First National Bank Of Franklin County At Decherd	7397	5	4
Dickson			
The Citizens National Bank Of Dickson	8292	6	5
The Dickson National Bank	10577	6	–
The First National Bank Of Dickson	6930	5	4
Doyle			
The First National Bank Of Doyle	10190	6	5
Ducktown			
The First National Bank Of Ducktown	9565	6	–
Dyersburg			
First-citizens National Bank Of Dyersburg	5263	1	3
The First National Bank Of Dyersburg	5263	4	–
Elizabethton			
The First National Bank Of Elizabethton	9558	5	6
The Holston National Bank Of Elizabethton	10976	4	6
Erwin			
Erwin National Bank	10583	–	5
The First National Bank Of Erwin	9720	6	–
Etowah			
The First National Bank Of Etowah	9162	5	5
Fayetteville			
Elk National Bank Of Fayetteville	8555	4	3
Farmers National Bank Of Fayetteville	10198	6	3
The Elk National Bank Of Fayetteville	3702	6	–
The First National Bank Of Fayetteville	2114	5	4
Union National Bank Of Fayetteville	13948	–	5
Franklin			
The Farmers National Bank Of Franklin	3062	6	–
The Harpeth National Bank Of Franklin	8443	5	5
The National Bank Of Franklin	1834	3	–
Gainesboro			
The First National Bank Of Gainesboro	5536	6	–
Gallatin			
First And Peoples National Bank Of Gallatin	5545	5	4
The First National Bank Of Gallatin	1707	6	–
The First National Bank Of Gallatin	4236	6	–
The Peoples National Bank Of Gallatin	5545	5	–
Greeneville			
The Citizens National Bank Of Greeneville	13482	–	6
The First National Bank Of Greeneville	4177	6	5
Harriman			
First National Bank In Harriman	12031	4	4
The First National Bank Of Harriman	4501	6	–
The Harriman National Bank	11915	5	6
The Manufacturers National Bank Of Harriman	4654	5	–
Hohenwald			
The First National Bank Of Hohenwald	11985	6	5
Huntland			
The First National Bank Of Huntland	8601	6	5
Huntsville			
The First National Bank Of Huntsville	10192	6	6
Jackson			
The First National Bank Of Jackson	2168	2	3
The National Bank Of Commerce Of Jackson	12790	5	4
The Second National Bank Of Jackson	3576	4	5
The Security National Bank Of Jackson	10334	5	4
Jefferson City			
The First National Bank Of Jefferson City	11479	5	5
Jellico			
The First National Bank Of Jellico	7665	6	5
The National Bank Of Jellico	7636	6	–
Johnson City			
The City National Bank Of Johnson City	6236	5	–
The First National Bank Of Johnson City	3951	6	–
The Hamilton National Bank Of Johnson City	13635	–	3
The Tennessee National Bank Of Johnson City	11839	4	4
The Unaka And City National Bank Of Johnson City	6236	3	3
The Unaka National Bank Of Johnson City	5888	4	–
The Washington County National Bank Of Johnson City	12469	–	–
Jonesboro			
The First National Bank Of Jonesboro	4715	6	6
Kenton			
The First National Bank Of Kenton	10404	6	–
Kingsport			
The First National Bank Of Kingsport	10842	6	5
Kingston			
The First National Bank Of Kingston	12319	6	6
Knoxville			
Holston-Union National Bank Of Knoxville	4648	4	5
Park National Bank Of Knoxville	2049	–	5
The American National Bank Of Knoxville	10327	5	–
The City National Bank Of Knoxville	3837	2	4
The East Tennessee National Bank Of Knoxville	2049	2	3
The First National Bank Of Knoxville	391	6	–
The Hamilton National Bank Of Knoxville	13539	–	3
The Holston National Bank Of Knoxville	4648	2	–
The Mechanics National Bank Of Knoxville	2658	4	–
The State National Bank Of Knoxville	4102	6	–
The Third National Bank Of Knoxville	3708	3	–
The Union National Bank Of Knoxville	10401	3	–
La Follette			
The Farmers National Bank Of La Follette	12484	–	–
The First National Bank Of La Follette	7225	6	4
The National Bank Of La Follette	7225	6	–
The Peoples National Bank Of La Follette	12467	–	6
Lawrenceburg			
The First National Bank Of Lawrenceburg	6093	4	5
Lebanon			
The American National Bank Of Lebanon	5754	6	–
The Lebanon National Bank	8714	5	–
The National Bank Of Lebanon	1664	6	–
The Second National Bank Of Lebanon	1708	6	–
Lenoir City			
The First National Bank Of Lenoir City	8673	5	5
Lewisburg			
The First National Bank Of Lewisburg	8934	4	3
Lexington			
The First National Bank Of Lexington	12324	6	5
Linden			
The First National Bank Of Linden	10181	6	6
Loudon			
The First National Bank Of Loudon	12080	6	5
Lynnville			
The First National Bank Of Lynnville	8558	6	–
Manchester			
The First National Bank Of Manchester	5528	5	6
Martin			
The City National Bank Of Martin	9112	5	–
The First National Bank Of Martin	5617	6	–
Maryville			
The Blount National Bank Of Maryville	14279	–	–
The First National Bank Of Maryville	10542	4	5
Mcminnville			
The American National Bank Of Mcminnville	7834	6	–
The First National Bank Of Mcminnville	2221	4	4
The National Bank Of Mcminnville	2221	6	–
The Peoples National Bank Of Mcminnville	2593	4	6
Memphis			
National Bank Of Commerce In Memphis	13681	–	5
Southern National Bank Of Memphis	12348	5	–
The Central-State National Bank Of Memphis	2127	4	–
The Continental National Bank Of Memphis	4307	6	–
The First National Bank Of Memphis	336	2	1
The Fourth National Bank Of Memphis	2096	6	–
The German National Bank Of Memphis	1636	6	–
The Memphis National Bank	3633	6	–
The Mercantile National Bank Of Memphis	10540	5	–
The Merchants National Bank Of Memphis	1407	6	–
The National Bank Of Commerce Of Memphis	5056	4	–
The National City Bank Of Memphis	9184	4	–
The State National Bank Of Memphis	2127	3	–
The Tennessee National Bank Of Memphis	1225	6	–
Union Planters National Bank And Trust Company Of Memphis	13349	–	1
Morristown			
City National Bank Of Morristown	8025	3	5
The First National Bank Of Morristown	3432	4	5
The Hamblen National Bank Of Morristown	8025	–	4
Mount Pleasant			
The First National Bank Of Mount Pleasant	9319	3	4
Murfreesboro			
The First National Bank Of Murfreesboro	1692	3	6
The Stones River National Bank Of Murfreesboro	2000	4	–
Nashville			
Broadway National Bank Of Nashville	9774	4	4
Fourth And First National Bank Of Nashville	150	3	–
Fourth And First National Bank Of Nashville	1669	2	3
Tennessee-Hermitage National Bank Of Nashville	9532	4	6
The American National Bank Of Nashville	3032	2	1
The Central National Bank Of Nashville	12276	–	–
The Commercial National Bank Of Nashville	3228	6	–
The Cumberland Valley National Bank Of Nashville	9659	5	–
The First National Bank Of Nashville	150	4	–
The Fourth National Bank Of Nashville	1669	3	–
The Hermitage National Bank Of Nashville	9532	6	–
The Mechanics National Bank Of Nashville	2200	6	–
The Merchants National Bank Of Nashville	2513	6	–
The Merchants National Bank Of Nashville	6729	6	–
The Second National Bank Of Nashville	771	6	–
The Tennessee National Bank Of Nashville	10622	–	–
The Third National Bank Of Nashville	1296	5	–
Third National Bank In Nashville	13103	–	2
Newport			
The First National Bank Of Newport	9632	4	6
Oliver Springs			
The Tri-County National Bank Of Oliver Springs	11998	6	5
Oneida			
The First National Bank Of Oneida	8039	6	5
The Scott County National Bank Of Oneida	8039	6	–
Paris			
The First National Bank Of Paris	9334	4	–
Petersburg			
The First National Bank Of Petersburg	10306	5	3
Pikeville			
The First National Bank Of Pikeville	10470	6	6
Pulaski			
The Citizens National Bank Of Pulaski	4679	6	–
The Giles National Bank Of Pulaski	1990	6	–
The National Bank Of Pulaski	1727	6	–
The National Peoples Bank Of Pulaski	6076	5	–
The Peoples National Bank Of Pulaski	2635	6	–
Ripley			
The First National Bank Of Ripley	10449	6	6
Rockwood			
The City National Bank Of Rockwood	12264	6	–
The First National Bank Of Rockwood	4169	6	5
The First National Bank Of Rockwood	14231	–	–
The Rockwood National Bank	12257	5	5
Rogersville			
The Rogersville National Bank	4015	6	–
Russellville			
The First National Bank Of Russellville	10508	6	–
Savannah			
The First National Bank Of Savannah	8889	5	3
Selmer			
The First National Bank Of Selmer	8836	6	5
Sevierville			
The First National Bank Of Sevierville	12440	–	–
Shelbyville			
First National Bank Of Shelbyville	10785	–	4
The Farmers National Bank Of Shelbyville	10785	4	5
The National Bank Of Shelbyville	2198	6	–
The Peoples National Bank Of Shelbyville	3530	4	4
Smithville			
The First National Bank Of Smithville	13056	5	5
Smyrna			
The First National Bank Of Smyrna	9807	6	5
South Pittsburg			
The First National Bank Of South Pittsburg	3660	5	4
Sparta			
The American National Bank Of Sparta	7912	6	–
The First National Bank Of Sparta	3614	5	4
Spring City			
The First National Bank Of Spring City	9470	6	–
Springfield			
The First National Bank Of Springfield	12639	6	4
The Peoples National Bank Of Springfield	6189	6	–
The Springfield National Bank	2019	6	–
Sweetwater			
The First National Bank Of Sweetwater	11202	6	6
Tazewell			
The Claiborne National Bank Of Tazewell	7740	6	–
Tracy City			
The First National Bank Of Tracy City	7314	5	5
Trenton			
The Citizens National Bank Of Trenton	12438	5	4
The First National Bank Of Trenton	8406	6	–
Tullahoma			
The First National Bank Of Tullahoma	3107	6	3
The Traders National Bank Of Tullahoma	4020	5	4
Union City			
The Farmers And Merchants National Bank Of Union City	4442	6	–
The First National Bank Of Union City	3919	6	–
The Old National Bank Of Union City	9629	5	4
The Third National Bank Of Union City	9239	6	4
Wartrace			
The First National Bank Of Wartrace	9627	6	–
Waverly			
The Citizens National Bank Of Waverly	9331	6	–
The First National Bank Of Waverly	5963	6	–
Winchester			
The American National Bank Of Winchester	8631	6	–
The Farmers National Bank Of Winchester	8640	5	5
Woodbury			
The First National Bank Of Woodbury	9089	6	–

TEXAS

City, Bank	Ch. No.	L	S
Abilene			
The Abilene National Bank	33336	6	–
The American National Bank Of Abilene	7028	6	–
The Citizens National Bank In Abilene	13727	–	5
The Citizens National Bank Of Abilene	6476	6	5
The Commercial National Bank Of Abilene	7944	6	–
The Farmers And Merchants National Bank Of Abilene	4166	4	4
The First National Bank Of Abilene	3195	6	–
Alba			
The Alba National Bank	6896	6	6
Albany			
The Albany National Bank	5680	6	6
The First National Bank Of Albany	3248	6	5
Allen			
The First National Bank Of Allen	10645	–	–
Alpine			
State National Bank Of Alpine	12289	5	5
The First National Bank Of Alpine	7214	5	5
Alto			
The First National Bank Of Alto	13964	–	–
Alvarado			
The First National Bank Of Alvarado	3644	6	6
Alvin			
The First National Bank In Alvin	12580	–	–
The First National Bank Of Alvin	7070	6	–
Alvord			
The Alvord National Bank	6067	6	–
The Alvord National Bank, Alvord	12671	–	–
The Farmers And Merchants National Bank Of Alvord	8071	6	–
The First National Bank Of Alvord	12664	–	–
Amarillo			
The Amarillo National Bank	4710	5	5
The Amarillo National Bank, Amarillo	14206	–	–
The City National Bank Of Amarillo	11629	–	–
The First National Bank Of Amarillo	4214	4	5
The National Bank Of Commerce, Amarillo	6865	5	5
Amherst			
The First National Bank Of Amherst	12619	–	–
Anderson			
The First National Bank Of Anderson	7337	5	6
Angleton			
The First National Bank Of Angleton	14204	–	5
Anna			
The First National Bank Of Anna	12867	6	6
Annona			
The First National Bank Of Annona	7257	6	3
Anson			
The Farmers And Merchants National Bank Of Anson	8897	6	–
The First National Bank Of Anson	6091	6	6
Aransas Pass			
The First National Bank Of Aransas Pass	10274	6	4
Archer City			
The First National Bank Of Archer City	5711	6	–
Arlington			
The Arlington National Bank	7345	6	–
The Citizens National Bank Of Arlington	5806	6	–
The Farmers National Bank Of Arlington	11931	–	–
The First National Bank Of Arlington	11931	–	–
Aspermont			
The First National Bank Of Aspermont	5786	5	4
Athens			
The Athens National Bank	6400	6	6
The First National Bank Of Athens	4278	5	6
Atlanta			
The Atlanta National Bank	7694	6	6
The First National Bank Of Atlanta	4922	5	6
Aubrey			
The First National Bank Of Aubrey	7495	6	–
Austin			
The American National Bank Of Austin	4322	2	4
The Austin National Bank	4308	3	3
The Capital National Bank In Austin	13926	–	–
The City National Bank Of Austin	3289	6	–
The First National Bank Of Austin	2118	6	–
The State National Bank Of Austin	2617	4	–
Avery			
The First National Bank Of Avery	10638	6	6
Bagwell			
The First National Bank Of Bagwell	10657	6	6
Bailey			
The First National Bank Of Bailey	12741	–	6
Baird			
The First National Bank Of Baird	3286	6	6
The Home National Bank Of Baird	5493	6	–
Ballinger			
The Ballinger National Bank	4193	6	–
The Citizens National Bank Of Ballinger	6757	6	–
The First National Bank Of Ballinger	3533	5	5
Bandera			
The First National Bank Of Bandera	11814	–	–
Bangs			
The First National Bank Of Bangs	11874	–	–
Bardwell			
The First National Bank Of Bardwell	10678	6	6
Barlett			
The Bartlett National Bank	7317	4	6
Bartlett			
The First National Bank Of Bartlett	5422	5	6
Bastrop			
The First National Bank Of Bastrop	4093	6	6
Bay City			
The Bay City National Bank	7753	6	–
The First National Bank Of Bay City	6062	6	5

City, Bank	Ch. No.	L	S
Beaumont			
The American National Bank Of Beaumont	5825	4	–
The Beaumont National Bank	5201	5	–
The Citizens National Bank Of Beaumont	5841	6	–
The City National Bank Of Beaumont	12199	–	–
The Commercial National Bank Of Beaumont	9357	6	–
The First National Bank Of Beaumont	4017	3	5
The Gulf National Bank Of Beaumont	6338	5	–
The Texas National Bank Of Beaumont	12138	–	–
Beeville			
The Commercial National Bank Of Beeville	4866	5	5
The First National Bank Of Beeville	4238	6	5
Bellevue			
The First National Bank Of Bellevue	8672	6	4
Bells			
The First National Bank Of Bells	7524	6	6
Bellville			
The First National Bank Of Bellville	4241	5	5
Belton			
The Belton National Bank	3295	6	–
The Belton National Bank	7509	6	6
The Citizens National Bank Of Belton	4167	6	–
The Farmers National Bank Of Belton	13810	–	6
The First National Bank Of Belton	2735	6	–
The Peoples National Bank Of Belton	8518	6	3
Benjamin			
The First National Bank Of Benjamin	7669	6	–
Bertram			
The First National Bank Of Bertram	11519	6	–
Big Spring			
The First National Bank In Big Spring	13984	–	6
The First National Bank Of Big Spring	4306	5	6
The State National Bank Of Big Spring	12543	6	5
The West Texas National Bank Of Big Spring	6668	6	5
Bishop			
The First National Bank Of Bishop	12612	–	–
Blackwell			
The First National Bank Of Blackwell	12722	–	–
Blanco			
The Blanco National Bank	8134	6	3
Blooming Grove			
The Citizens National Bank Of Blooming Grove	7055	6	6
The First National Bank In Blooming Grove	13555	–	6
The First National Bank Of Blooming Grove	4768	6	–
Blossom			
The Blossom National Bank, Blossom	13052	–	–
The Farmers National Bank Of Blossom	12843	–	–
The First National Bank Of Blossom	5733	6	–
Blum			
The First National Bank Of Blum	6069	6	–
Bogata			
The Bogata National Bank	10639	6	–
The First National Bank Of Bogata	10483	6	6
Bonham			
The Bonham National Bank	1640	6	
The Fannan County National Bank Of Bonham	5146	5	–
The First National Bank Of Bonham	3094	5	–
The State National Bank Of Bonham	12699	–	–
Bonita			
The First National Bank Of Bonita	10163	6	–
Booker			
The Edwards National Bank Of Booker	11408	–	–
The First National Bank Of Booker	11400	–	–
Borger			
The First National Bank Of Borger	13014	–	–
Bowie			
The Bowie National Bank Of Bowie	4231	–	–
The City National Bank Of Bowie	4785	4	6
The First National Bank Of Bowie	4265	4	6
The National Bank Of Bowie	8330	5	–
The Security National Bank Of Bowie	12731	–	–
Brady			
The Brady National Bank	7827	4	5
The Commercial National Bank Of Brady	8573	6	4
The First National Bank Of Brady	4198	6	–
Breckenridge			
First National Bank In Breckenridge	14027	–	6
The First National Bank Of Breckenridge	7422	6	6
Brenham			
The Farmers National Bank In Brenham	13678	–	6
The Farmers National Bank Of Brenham	10860	5	3
The First National Bank Of Brenham	3015	4	3
Bridgeport			
The Bridgeport National Bank, Bridgeport	12409	–	–
The First National Bank Of Bridgeport	8731	6	6
Bronte			
The First National Bank Of Bronte	8641	6	–
The First National Bank Of Bronte	12723	–	–
Brownfield			
The First National Bank Of Brownfield	11415	–	–
Brownsville			
State National Bank Of Brownsville	12236	6	–
State National Bank Of Brownsville	12236	–	4
The First National Bank In Brownsville	12792	5	6
The First National Bank Of Brownsville	4577	4	–
The Merchants National Bank Of Brownsville	7002	4	5
Brownwood			
Citizens National Bank At Brownwood	14273	–	6
First National Bank In Brownwood	4695	5	5
The Brownwood National Bank	4695	4	–
The Citizens National Bank In Brownwood	13588	–	3
The Citizens National Bank Of Brownwood	8312	5	6
The City National Bank Of Brownwood	4344	6	–
The Coggin National Bank Of Brownwood	9812	6	6
The First National Bank Of Brownwood	2937	6	–
The Merchants National Bank Of Brownwood	4344	6	–
Bryan			
The City National Bank Of Bryan	4070	5	4
The First National Bank Of Bryan	3446	5	5
The Merchants And Planters National Bank Of Bryan	4070	6	–
Buda			
The Farmers National Bank Of Buda	12241	6	–

City, Bank	Ch. No.	L	S
Burkburnett			
First National Bank In Burkburnett	13668	–	3
The First National Bank Of Burkburnett	8706	5	5
Burnet			
The Burnet National Bank	6966	5	5
The First National Bank Of Burnet	3007	6	–
Byers			
The First National Bank Of Byers	8787	6	6
Bynum			
The First National Bank Of Bynum	10549	6	–
Caddo			
The First National Bank Of Caddo	11625	–	–
Caddo Mills			
The First National Bank Of Caddo Mills	9637	6	–
The State National Bank Of Caddo Mills	12936	–	–
Caldwell			
The Caldwell National Bank	6607	5	6
The First National Bank Of Caldwell	6614	6	–
Calvert			
The First National Bank Of Calvert	3742	6	–
Cameron			
First National Bank In Cameron	13731	–	6
The Citizens National Bank Of Cameron	5484	4	5
The First National Bank Of Cameron	4086	6	5
Campbell			
The Campbell National Bank	7348	6	–
The Campbell National Exchange Bank	10473	6	–
Canadian			
The First National Bank Of Canadian	6826	6	–
The Southwest National Bank Of Canadian	11722	–	–
Canton			
The First National Bank Of Canton	8891	6	6
Canyon			
The Canyon National Bank	7961	6	–
The First National Bank In Canyon	14090	–	4
The First National Bank Of Canyon	5238	5	6
The Stockmens National Bank Of Canyon	5238	6	–
Carthage			
The First National Bank Of Carthage	6197	6	6
The Merchants And Farmers National Bank Of Carthage	6152	6	–
Celeste			
The First National Bank Of Celeste	5324	5	6
Celina			
The Farmers And Merchants National Bank Of Celina	12783	–	–
The First National Bank Of Celina	6046	6	–
Center			
The Farmers National Bank Of Center	7249	6	–
The First National Bank Of Center	5971	6	–
Center Point			
The First National Bank Of Center Point	6040	6	–
Channing			
The First National Bank Of Channing	10949	–	–
Childress			
The Childress National Bank	6024	6	–
The City National Bank In Childress	12672	–	–
The City National Bank Of Childress	5992	5	–
The First National Bank In Childress	12666	–	5
The First National Bank Of Childress	4571	6	–
Chillicothe			
The First National Bank Of Chillicothe	12513	–	–
Cisco			
The American National Bank Of Cisco	11357	6	–
The Citizens National Bank Of Cisco	6115	6	–
The First National Bank In Cisco	12795	–	–
The First National Bank Of Cisco	4134	6	–
The Merchants And Farmers National Bank Of Cisco	7360	6	–
Clarendon			
The First National Bank Of Clarendon	5463	6	5
Clarksville			
First National Bank In Clarksville	13974	–	4
Red River National Bank In Clarksville	13428	–	3
The City National Bank Of Clarksville	10643	6	–
The First National Bank Of Clarksville	3973	6	6
The Red River National Bank Of Clarksville	4982	5	6
Claude			
The First National Bank Of Claude	7123	6	4
Cleburne			
The Citizens National Bank Of Cleburne	6791	6	–
The City National Bank Of Cleburne	13107	6	4
The Cleburne National Bank, Cleburne	13951	–	–
The Farmers And Merchants National Bank Of Cleburne	4386	4	–
The First National Bank Of Cleburne	2982	6	–
The Home National Bank Of Cleburne	10411	5	–
The National Bank Of Cleburne	4035	5	–
Cleveland			
The First National Bank Of Cleveland	10276	6	6
Clifton			
The Clifton National Bank, Clifton	11930	–	–
The First National Bank In Clifton	12717	–	–
The First National Bank Of Clifton	7245	5	–
Clint			
The First National Bank Of Clint	12677	–	–
Clyde			
The Clyde National Bank	8780	6	1
The First National Bank Of Clyde	8106	6	–
Coleman			
First Coleman National Bank Of Coleman	13595	–	2
The Coleman National Bank	4683	5	–
The First National Bank Of Coleman	3433	5	–
Collinsville			
The Collinsville National Bank, Collinsville	11325	–	–
The First National Bank Of Collinsville	6300	6	–
The Security National Bank Of Collinsville	12738	–	–
Colorado			
Colorado National Bank In Colorado	13562	–	6
The Citizens National Bank Of Colorado	4395	6	–
The City National Bank Of Colorado	5276	6	5
The Colorado National Bank	2801	6	6
The First National Bank Of Colorado	2893	6	–
The Peoples National Bank Of Colorado	4950	6	–

City, Bank	Ch. No.	L	S
Comanche			
State National Bank In Comanche	14227	–	–
The Comanche National Bank	4246	5	5
The Farmers And Merchants National Bank Of Comanche	7105	5	–
The First National Bank Of Comanche	3561	5	–
Commerce			
The Citizens National Bank Of Commerce	12778	–	–
The Commerce National Bank	4021	6	–
The First National Bank Of Commerce	4021	6	–
The Planters And Merchants National Bank Of Commerce	6224	6	–
Como			
The Como National Bank, Como	12681	–	–
The First National Bank Of Como	9931	6	–
Conroe			
First National Bank In Conroe	12809	–	5
The First National Bank Of Conroe	6394	6	–
Coolidge			
The First National Bank Of Coolidge	7231	5	4
Cooper			
The Delta National Bank Of Cooper	5533	5	6
The Farmers National Bank Of Cooper	10626	6	–
The First National Bank In Cooper	13046	–	5
The First National Bank Of Cooper	4500	6	–
Corpus Christi			
State National Bank Of Corpus Christi	12235	–	4
The City National Bank & Trust Company Of Corpus Christi	7668	6	6
The City National Bank Of Corpus Christi	7668	4	–
The Corpus Christi National Bank	4423	5	–
Corrigan			
The Corrigan National Bank, Corrigan	12247	–	–
Corsicana			
The City National Bank Of Corsicana	3915	5	–
The Corsicana National Bank	3645	5	5
The First National Bank Of Corsicana	3506	3	3
The State National Bank Of Corsicana	11022	3	3
Cotulla			
Stockmens National Bank In Cotulla	14302	–	6
The Stockmens National Bank Of Cotulla	7243	5	6
Covington			
The First National Bank Of Covington	7147	6	–
Crandall			
The Citizens National Bank Of Crandall	5938	5	6
The First National Bank Of Crandall	5824	6	6
Crawford			
The First National Bank Of Crawford	10400	6	–
Cresson			
The Cresson National Bank	8965	6	–
Crockett			
The Farmers And Merchants National Bank Of Crockett	5953	6	–
The First National Bank Of Crockett	4684	5	6
Crosbyton			
The First National Bank Of Crosbyton	9989	6	6
Cross Plains			
The Farmers National Bank Of Cross Plains	8583	6	6
Crowell			
The First National Bank Of Crowell	6402	6	–
The Foard County National Bank Of Crowell	9178	6	–
Cuero			
Buchel National Bank In Cuero	14164	–	4
The Buchel National Bank Of Cuero	8562	6	4
The First National Bank Of Cuero	4140	6	–
Cumby			
The First National Bank In Cumby	12719	–	–
The First National Bank Of Cumby	5719	6	–
Cushing			
The First National Bank Of Cushing	13211	–	–
Daingerfield			
The Citizens National Bank Of Daingerfield	7096	6	6
The National Bank Of Daingerfield	4701	6	5
Dalhart			
First National Bank In Dalhart	14199	–	6
The Dalhart National Bank	7977	6	–
The First National Bank Of Dalhart	6762	6	5
Dallas			
Dallas National Bank	11749	3	4
First National Bank In Dallas	3623	–	1
Mercantile National Bank At Dallas	13743	–	4
North Texas National Bank In Dallas	12736	3	4
Republic National Bank & Trust Company Of Dallas	12186	5	1
The American Exchange National Bank Of Dallas	3623	2	4
The American National Bank Of Dallas	3132	5	–
The Bankers And Merchants National Bank Of Dallas	4213	6	–
The Central National Bank In Dallas	12650	–	–
The Central National Bank Of Dallas	4127	6	–
The City National Bank Of Dallas	2455	1	4
The Commonwealth National Bank Of Dallas	8664	4	–
The Dallas National Bank	3008	6	–
The First National Bank Of Dallas	2157	6	–
The Fourth National Bank Of Dallas	3664	6	–
The Gaston National Bank Of Dallas	7113	6	–
The Mercantile National Bank In Dallas	12707	5	–
The Mercantile National Bank Of Dallas	4707	6	–
The Merchants National Bank Of Dallas	10331	6	–
The National Bank Of Commerce Of Dallas	3985	5	6
The National Bank Of Dallas	5078	6	–
The National Exchange Bank Of Dallas	3623	5	–
The Ninth National Bank Of Dallas	4415	6	–
The North Texas National Bank At Dallas	3834	6	–
The Republic National Bank Of Dallas	12186	3	–
The Security National Bank Of Dallas	10564	3	–
The Southwest National Bank Of Dallas	11996	4	–
The State National Bank Of Dallas	3664	6	–
The Tenison National Bank Of Dallas	10965	5	–
The Texas National Bank Of Dallas	7052	6	–
The Trinity National Bank Of Dallas	9341	6	–
The Union National Bank Of Dallas	9245	6	–
Dawson			
The First National Bank Of Dawson	10694	6	4
The Liberty National Bank Of Dawson	11239	5	6
De Kalb			
First National Bank At De Kalb	14312	–	–
The First National Bank In De Kalb	12287	–	–
The First National Bank Of De Kalb	8449	6	–
De Leon			
The Farmers And Merchants National Bank Of De Leon	7553	6	3
The First National Bank Of De Leon	5660	6	–
Decatur			
The City National Bank Of Decatur	5665	5	–
The First National Bank In Decatur	13623	–	3
The First National Bank Of Decatur	2940	5	6
The Wise County National Bank Of Decatur	4116	6	–
Del Rio			
Del Rio National Bank	7433	4	5
First National Bank Of Del Rio	5294	4	–
The First National Bank Of Del Rio	5294	4	6
Denison			
The Citizens National Bank Of Denison	12728	6	4
The First National Bank Of Denison	2099	6	–
The National Bank Of Denison	4447	4	–
The State National Bank Of Denison	3058	3	5
Denton			
The Denton County National Bank Of Denton	4708	5	5
The Exchange National Bank Of Denton	2949	5	–
The First National Bank Of Denton	2812	5	–
Deport			
The First National Bank Of Deport	6430	6	6
Desdemona			
The First National Bank Of Desdemona	11452	–	–
Detroit			
The First National Bank Of Detroit	4682	6	–
The Planters National Bank Of Detroit	13259	–	–
Devine			
The Adams National Bank Of Devine	7212	5	5
Dickens			
The First National Bank Of Dickens	8303	6	–
Dickinson			
The First National Bank Of Dickinson	12855	6	6
Dodd City			
The First National Bank Of Dodd City	5728	6	6
Dublin			
The Citizens National Bank Of Dublin	5836	5	–
The Dublin National Bank	4865	6	6
The Farmers National Bank Of Dublin	12758	–	–
The First National Bank Of Dublin	4062	6	–
Eagle Lake			
The First National Bank Of Eagle Lake	7534	6	4
Eagle Pass			
The Border National Bank Of Eagle Pass	5181	4	–
The First National Bank Of Eagle Pass	4490	5	5
The Simpson National Bank Of Eagle Pass	5060	6	–
Eastland			
The American National Bank Of Eastland	11258	5	–
The Citizens National Bank Of Eastland	11630	–	–
The City National Bank Of Eastland	7183	6	–
The Eastland National Bank	4466	6	–
The Eastland National Bank, Eastland	14299	–	–
The Exchange National Bank Of Eastland	12448	–	–
Eddy			
The First National Bank Of Eddy	10668	–	–
Edgewood			
The First National Bank Of Edgewood	10624	5	6
Edinburg			
The First National Bank In Edinburg	14124	–	–
The First National Bank Of Edinburg	13315	–	2
Edna			
The Allen National Bank Of Edna	8123	6	–
El Campo			
The First National Bank Of El Campo	6112	5	4
El Dorado			
The First National Bank Of El Dorado	8575	6	6
El Paso			
El Paso National Bank	12769	5	4
The American National Bank Of El Paso	7530	6	–
The Border National Bank Of El Paso	10974	4	–
The City National Bank Of El Paso	7514	3	–
The Commercial National Bank Of El Paso	10140	6	–
The El Paso National Bank Of Texas	3608	6	–
The First National Bank Of El Paso	2532	1	4
The Lowdon National Bank Of El Paso	5239	6	–
The National Bank Of Commerce Of El Paso	9155	6	–
The National Border Bank Of El Paso	12487	–	–
The National Exchange Bank Of El Paso	7075	6	–
The State National Bank Of El Paso	2521	3	4
Electra			
The First National Bank In Electra	13284	–	–
The First National Bank Of Electra	10050	6	–
The Security National Bank Of Electra	11928	–	–
Elgin			
The Elgin National Bank	8156	6	6
The First National Bank Of Elgin	4410	6	–
The First National Bank Of Giddings	4410	6	6
Emhouse			
The First National Bank Of Emhouse	12759	–	–
Emma			
The Citizens National Bank Of Crosbyton	8515	6	6
The First National Bank Of Emma	8515	6	–
Emory			
The First National Bank Of Emory	6814	6	6
Enloe			
The First National Bank Of Enloe	6271	6	–
Ennis			
Citizens National Bank In Ennis	13667	–	6
The Citizens National Bank Of Ennis	7331	5	3
The Ennis National Bank	2939	5	–
The First National Bank In Ennis	12110	5	6
The Peoples National Bank Of Ennis	3532	6	–
Evant			
The First National Bank Of Evant	12739	–	–
Fabens			
The First National Bank Of Fabens	11700	–	6
Fairfield			
The First National Bank Of Fairfield	4291	6	–
Falfurrias			
The First National Bank In Falfurrias	14072	–	6
The First National Bank Of Falfurrias	11792	6	6
Falls City			
The Falls City National Bank	8606	5	6
Farmersville			
The Farmers And Merchants National Bank Of Farmersville	6011	5	–
The Farmersville National Bank, Farmersville	13048	–	–
The First National Bank At Farmersville	14212	–	–
The First National Bank In Farmersville	13277	–	–
The First National Bank Of Farmersville	3624	6	–
Farwell			
The Farwell National Bank, Farwell	12005	–	–
The First National Bank Of Farwell	8431	6	–
Fayetteville			
The Farmers National Bank Of Fayetteville	10954	5	6
Ferris			
The Citizens National Bank Of Ferris	6553	6	–
The Ferris National Bank	6376	6	6
Flatonia			
The First National Bank Of Flatonia	4179	6	–
Floresville			
First City National Bank Of Floresville	6320	–	4
The City National Bank Of Floresville	8519	5	6
The First National Bank Of Floresville	6320	4	3
Floydada			
The First National Bank Of Floydada	7045	6	5
The Floyd County National Bank Of Floydada	12692	–	–
Follett			
The Farmers National Bank Of Follett	11158	–	–
The First National Bank Of Darrousett	11158	–	–
The Follett National Bank	12101	6	6
Forney			
The City National Bank Of Forney	6078	6	6
The Farmers National Bank Of Forney	9369	5	5
The National Bank Of Forney	4014	6	–
Fort Stockton			
The First National Bank Of Fort Stockton	9848	6	6
Fort Worth			
Stockyards National Bank Of Fort Worth	6822	4	4
The American National Bank Of Fort Worth	4848	5	–
The City National Bank Of Fort Worth	2359	6	–
The Continental National Bank Of Fort Worth	11997	–	–
The Farmers And Mechanics National Bank Of Fort Worth	4004	4	–
The First National Bank Of Fort Worth	2349	2	–
The Fort Worth National Bank	3131	2	3
The Merchants National Bank Of Fort Worth	3631	6	–
The National Bank Of Commerce Of Fort Worth	11430	–	–
The National Live Stock Bank Of Fort Worth	4946	6	–
The State National Bank Of Fort Worth	3221	5	–
The Texas National Bank Of Fort Worth	12371	3	6
The Traders National Bank Of Fort Worth	2689	5	–
The Western National Bank Of Fort Worth	7165	5	–
Franklin			
The First National Bank Of Franklin	7838	5	4
Frankston			
The First National Bank Of Frankston	7623	6	–
Fredericksburg			
The Fredericksburg National Bank, Fredericksburg	13610	–	–
Freeport			
The Freeport National Bank	10420	5	6
Frisco			
The First National Bank Of Frisco	6346	6	–
Frost			
The First National Bank Of Frost	6968	6	6
The Frost National Bank	13507	–	4
The Frost National Bank, Frost	13507	–	–
Gainesville			
The First National Bank Of Gainesville	2836	4	–
The Gainesville National Bank	2802	6	–
The Gainesville National Bank In Gainesville	13698	–	–
The Lindsay National Bank Of Gainesville	6292	5	–
The Red River National Bank Of Gainesville	3229	6	–
Galveston			
Hutchings-Sealy National Bank Of Galveston	12434	–	–
The American National Bank Of Galveston	4321	4	–
The City National Bank Of Galveston	8899	4	3
The First National Bank Of Galveston	1566	3	4
The Galveston National Bank	4153	5	–
The Merchants National Bank Of Galveston	8068	6	–
The National Bank Of Texas, Galveston	1642	5	–
The Seawall National Bank Of Galveston	8070	–	–
The South Texas National Bank Of Galveston	12434	–	–
The United States National Bank Of Galveston	12475	3	2
Ganado			
The First National Bank Of Ganado	10076	6	–
Garland			
The Citizens National Bank Of Garland	7140	6	–
The First National Bank Of Garland	7140	6	6
The National Bank Of Garland	7989	6	–
The State National Bank Of Garland	7989	6	4
Gatesville			
The Citizens National Bank Of Gatesville	4388	6	–
The City National Bank Of Gatesville	4732	6	–
The Farmers National Bank Of Gatesville	8928	6	–
The First National Bank Of Gatesville	4097	6	5
The Gatesville National Bank	6150	6	6
George West			
The First National Bank In George West	14012	–	–
The First National Bank Of George West	12919	5	6
Georgetown			
The City National Bank Of Georgetown	12680	–	–
The First National Bank Of Georgetown	4294	6	3
Gilmer			
The Farmers And Merchants National Bank Of Gilmer	5741	4	6
The First National Bank Of Gilmer	5288	6	6
Glen Rose			
The First National Bank In Glen Rose	13170	–	–
The First National Bank Of Glen Rose	5795	6	–

City, Bank	Ch. No.	L	S
Godley			
The Citizens National Bank Of Godley	11143	–	–
Goldthwaite			
The First National Bank In Goldthwaite	12589	–	–
The First National Bank Of Goldthwaite	4687	6	–
The Goldthwaite National Bank	6092	4	–
Goliad			
The Commercial National Bank Of Goliad	7548	6	–
The First National Bank Of Goliad	4565	4	5
Gonzales			
The Farmers National Bank Of Gonzales	8392	5	5
The Gonzales National Bank	6277	6	–
Goose Creek			
The First National Bank Of Goose Creek	14101	–	–
Gordon			
The First National Bank Of Gordon	5759	6	6
Goree			
The First National Bank Of Goree	8200	6	6
Gorman			
The First National Bank Of Gorman	7410	6	6
Graford			
The First National Bank Of Graford	12437	–	–
Graham			
First National Bank In Graham	4418	6	5
The Beckham National Bank Of Graham	4418	6	–
The First National Bank Of Graham	4391	6	–
The Graham National Bank	5897	6	6
Granbury			
The City National Bank Of Granbury	5808	5	–
The First National Bank Of Granbury	3727	4	5
Grand Prairie			
The City National Bank Of Grand Prairie	12714	–	–
The First National Bank Of Grand Prairie	11171	–	–
Grand Saline			
The Citizens National Bank Of Grand Saline	8884	6	–
The First National Bank Of Grand Saline	5722	6	–
The National Bank Of Grand Saline	5696	6	–
The State National Bank Of Grand Saline	12745	6	5
Grandview			
The Farmers And Merchants National Bank Of Grandview	7269	5	–
The First National Bank Of Grandview	4389	6	6
Granger			
The First National Bank Of Granger	6361	6	6
The Granger National Bank	11642	6	6
Grapevine			
The Farmers National Bank Of Grapevine	8318	5	–
The Grapevine National Bank	5439	6	–
The Tarrant County National Bank Of Grapevine	12708	–	6
Greenville			
The City National Bank Of Greenville	5035	6	–
The Commercial National Bank Of Greenville	7510	4	–
The First National Bank Of Greenville	2998	5	–
The Greenville National Bank	3646	6	–
The Greenville National Exchange Bank	8581	3	4
The Hunt County National Bank Of Greenville	3016	6	–
Gregory			
The First National Bank Of Gregory	10241	5	6
Groesbeck			
Citizens National Bank In Groesbeck	14126	–	6
The Citizens National Bank Of Groesbeck	6461	6	6
The Groesbeck National Bank	4269	6	–
Groom			
The First National Bank Of Groom	11447	–	–
The State National Bank Of Groom	12742	–	–
Groveton			
First National Bank In Groveton	14104	–	6
The First National Bank Of Groveton	6329	4	6
Gunter			
The First National Bank Of Gunter	6404	6	–
Hale Center			
The First National Bank Of Hale Center	12744	–	–
Hallettsville			
First National Bank Of Hallettsville	4338	5	5
The Lavaca County National Bank Of Hallettsville	4338	6	–
Hamilton			
The Hamilton National Bank	4451	5	5
The Perry National Bank Of Hamilton	11800	–	–
Hamlin			
The Farmers And Merchants National Bank Of Hamlin	12700	–	6
The First National Bank Of Hamlin	8252	5	6
The Hamlin National Bank	8427	6	–
Handley			
The First National Bank Of Handley	12696	–	–
Hansford			
The First National Bank Of Hansford	10871	–	–
The First National Bank Of Spearman	12696	–	–
Harlingen			
The First National Bank Of Harlingen	12219	–	–
The Security National Bank Of Harlingen	12119	–	–
Harrisburg			
The Harrisburg National Bank	12840	–	–
The Harrisburg National Bank Of Houston	12840	–	6
Haskell			
Haskell National Bank	14149	–	3
The Farmers National Bank Of Haskell	7825	6	–
The First National Bank Of Haskell	4333	6	–
The Haskell National Bank	4474	6	6
Hawkins			
The First National Bank Of Hawkins	10728	–	–
Hawley			
The First National Bank Of Hawley	8535	6	–
Hearne			
The First National Bank Of Hearne	4976	6	–
Hebbronville			
The First National Bank Of Hebbronville	12995	–	5
Hemphill			
First National Bank In Hemphill	13526	–	6
The First National Bank Of Hemphill	8526	6	6
Hempstead			
The Farmers National Bank Of Hempstead	4905	6	–
Henderson			
Citizens National Bank Of Henderson	13443	–	2
The Farmers And Merchants National Bank Of Henderson	6780	6	6
The First National Bank Of Henderson	6176	6	5
Henrietta			
The Farmers National Bank Of Henrietta	4068	6	–
The First National Bank Of Henrietta	13815	–	–
The Henrietta National Bank	3022	6	–
Hereford			
The First National Bank Of Hereford	5604	5	6
The Hereford National Bank	5604	6	–
The Western National Bank Of Hereford	6812	6	6
Hico			
The First National Bank Of Hico	4366	6	–
The Hico National Bank, Hico	7157	5	6
Higgins			
First National Bank In Higgins	8249	–	6
The Citizens National Bank Of Higgins	8249	6	–
The First National Bank Of Higgins	8179	6	–
Hillsboro			
The Citizens National Bank Of Hillsboro	4900	4	4
The Farmers National Bank Of Hillsboro	3762	4	6
The Hill County National Bank Of Hillsboro	3046	6	–
The Sturgis National Bank Of Hillsboro	3786	5	–
Holland			
The First National Bank Of Holland	8008	6	6
Hondo			
The First National Bank Of Hondo	5765	5	6
Honey Grove			
First National Bank In Honey Grove	13416	–	4
The American National Bank Of Honey Grove	13019	–	–
The First National Bank Of Honey Grove	2867	5	6
The Planters National Bank Of Honey Grove	4112	6	–
The State National Bank Of Honey Grove	10617	6	–
Houston			
First National Bank In Houston	13683	–	3
Houston National Bank	9353	5	4
San Jacinto National Bank Of Houston	13925	–	4
South Texas Commercial National Bank Of Houston	10152	2	1
The American National Bank Of Houston	9226	6	–
The City National Bank Of Houston	13943	–	5
The Commercial National Bank Of Houston	3517	4	–
The First National Bank Of Houston	1644	1	3
The Guaranty National Bank Of Houston	12062	4	5
The Houston National Bank	4028	6	–
The Houston National Exchange Bank	9353	3	–
The Lumbermans National Bank Of Houston	8645	3	–
The Merchants National Bank Of Houston	5858	4	–
The National Bank Of Commerce Of Houston	10225	3	2
The National City Bank Of Houston	8288	5	–
The National Exchange Bank Of Houston	2092	5	–
The Planters And Mechanics National Bank Of Houston	4463	6	–
The Public National Bank & Trust Company Of Houston	12055	–	3
The Public National Bank Of Houston	12055	4	–
The Seaport National Bank Of Houston	12566	–	–
The Second National Bank Of Houston	8645	6	2
The South Texas National Bank Of Houston	4350	4	–
The State National Bank Of Houston	12070	4	3
The Union National Bank Of Houston	9712	3	1
Howe			
The Farmers National Bank Of Howe	5670	5	6
The First National Bank Of Howe	5681	6	–
Hubbard			
The Farmers National Bank Of Hubbard	7407	6	–
The First National Bank Of Hubbard	5008	5	6
Hughes Springs			
The First National Bank Of Hughes Springs	6922	6	6
Huntsville			
The First National Bank Of Huntsville	4208	6	6
The Gibbs National Bank Of Huntsville	4208	5	–
Hutto			
The First National Bank In Hutto	13475	–	–
The Hutto National Bank	9625	6	6
Iowa Park			
The First National Bank Of Iowa Park	5589	6	6
The State National Bank Of Iowa Park	13614	–	–
Ireland			
The First National Bank Of Ireland	12786	–	–
Irene			
The First National Bank Of Irene	10713	–	–
Italy			
The Citizens National Bank Of Italy	6471	6	–
The Farmers National Bank Of Italy	12701	–	–
The First National Bank Of Italy	5663	4	5
Itasca			
The Citizens National Bank Of Itasca	4924	6	–
The First National Bank Of Itasca	4461	5	6
The Itasca National Bank	5749	4	6
Jacksboro			
The Citizens National Bank Of Jacksboro	5761	6	–
The First National Bank Of Jacksboro	4483	4	4
The Jacksboro National Bank	7814	6	6
Jacksonville			
The Citizens National Bank Of Jacksonville	6883	6	–
The First National Bank Of Jacksonville	5581	4	5
Jakehamon			
The First National Bank Of Jakehamon	11503	–	–
Jasper			
The Citizens National Bank Of Jasper	10478	–	5
The First National Bank Of Jasper	6134	6	–
Jayton			
The First National Bank Of Jayton	9845	6	6
Jefferson			
The Commercial National Bank Of Jefferson	8770	6	6
The Commercial National Bank Of Jefferson	13450	–	–
The National Bank Of Jefferson	1777	6	–
The Rogers National Bank Of Jefferson	7129	–	–
The State National Bank Of Jefferson	4721	6	–
Josephine			
The First National Bank Of Josephine	12724	–	–
Junction			
Junction National Bank, Junction	14330	–	–
The First National Bank Of Junction	10845	–	–
Karnes City			
The City National Bank Of Karnes City	8565	6	–
The Karnes County National Bank Of Karnes City	5614	6	6
The State National Bank Of Karnes City	12689	–	–
Kaufman			
The Citizens National Bank In Kaufman	12763	–	–
The Citizens National Bank Of Kaufman	4492	6	–
The Farmers And Merchants National Bank Of Kaufman	10757	5	6
The First National Bank Of Kaufman	3836	5	6
Kemp			
The First National Bank Of Kemp	5932	5	6
Kenedy			
First Nichols National Bank Of Kenedy	12187	–	5
The First National Bank Of Kenedy	12182	5	6
The Kenedy National Bank	8013	6	–
The Nichols National Bank Of Kenedy	12187	–	–
Kerens			
First National Bank Of Kerens	13656	–	3
The First National Bank Of Kerens	7529	6	6
The Kerens National Bank, Kerens	11411	–	–
Kilgore			
The Kilgore National Bank	12698	6	5
The Kilgore National Bank, Kilgore	12698	–	–
Killeen			
The First National Bank Of Killeen	5750	5	–
Kingsbury			
The First National Bank Of Kingsbury	10266	6	–
Kingsville			
The First National Bank Of Kingsville	12968	5	4
Knox City			
The First National Bank Of Knox City	7953	6	6
Kosse			
The First National Bank Of Kosse	9205	6	–
The Kosse National Bank, Kosse	13279	–	–
Krum			
The First National Bank Of Krum	10418	6	–
Kyle			
The Kyle National Bank, Kyle	7149	–	–
La Coste			
The La Coste National Bank	10189	5	6
La Feria			
The First National Bank Of La Feria	12747	–	6
La Grange			
The First National Bank Of La Grange	3906	4	5
La Porte			
The First National Bank Of La Porte	12421	–	–
Ladonia			
The First National Bank Of Ladonia	4311	4	–
The Ladonia National Bank	5739	6	–
The Weldon National Bank Of Ladonia	4515	6	–
Lakeview			
The First National Bank Of Lakeview	12835	–	6
Lamesa			
The First National Bank Of Lamesa	11163	6	6
The Lamesa National Bank, Lamesa	13111	–	–
The State National Bank Of Lamesa	12767	–	–
Lampasas			
The City National Bank Of Lampasas	7394	–	–
The First National Bank Of Lampasas	3261	6	6
The Lampasas National Bank	5645	6	–
The Peoples National Bank Of Lampasas	7572	6	6
Lancaster			
The First National Bank Of Lancaster	11423	6	5
Laredo			
The First National Bank Of Laredo	2486	5	5
The Laredo National Bank	5001	3	4
The Milmo National Bank Of Laredo	2486	4	–
The Rio Grande National Bank Of Laredo	4146	6	–
Leonard			
The First National Bank Of Leonard	5109	5	6
The Leonard National Bank	12382	6	5
Levelland			
The First National Bank Of Levelland	12798	–	–
Lewisville			
The First National Bank Of Lewisville	7144	5	6
Liberty			
The First-Liberty National Bank Of Liberty	12850	–	–
Lindale			
The First National Bank Of Lindale	7956	6	–
Linden			
The First National Bank Of Linden	10476	–	4
Lipan			
The First National Bank Of Lipan	10598	6	5
Littlefield			
The First National Bank Of Littlefield	12824	–	–
Livingston			
The Citizens National Bank Of Livingston	6169	6	–
The First National Bank Of Livingston	6169	6	6
Llano			
The Citizens National Bank Of Llano	12463	–	–
The First National Bank Of Llano	4316	6	–
The Home National Bank Of Llano	7119	6	–
The Iron City National Bank Of Llano	4371	6	–
The Llano National Bank	5853	6	–
Lockhart			
First-lockhart National Bank, Lockhart	13934	–	4
The First National Bank Of Lockhart	4030	5	6
The Lockhart National Bank	5491	6	6
Lockney			
The First National Bank Of Lockney	9126	6	6
The Lockney National Bank	9193	6	–
Lometa			
The First National Bank Of Lometa	10323	5	6
Lone Oak			
The Citizens National Bank Of Lone Oak	12760	–	–
The Farmers National Bank Of Lone Oak	7657	6	–
The First National Bank Of Lone Oak	6605	6	–

City, Bank	Ch. No.	L	S
Longview			
The Citizens National Bank Of Longview	6043	6	–
The First National Bank Of Longview	4077	6	4
The Rembert National Bank Of Longview	12411	5	5
Lorena			
The First National Bank Of Lorena	8621	6	–
The Lorena National Bank, Lorena	13191	–	–
Lott			
The First National Bank Of Lott	6223	5	5
The First National Bank Of Lott	13647	–	–
The Lott National Bank, Lott	12943	–	–
Lovelady			
The First National Bank Of Lovelady	8742	6	6
The State National Bank Of Lovelady	12803	–	–
Lubbock			
First National Bank At Lubbock	14208	–	–
The Citizens National Bank Of Lubbock	8208	6	5
The Farmers National Bank Of Lubbock	11003	–	–
The First National Bank In Lubbock	12682	–	–
The First National Bank Of Lubbock	6195	6	–
The Lubbock National Bank	12683	–	4
Lufkin			
The Angelina County National Bank Of Lufkin	6009	6	–
The Lufkin National Bank	5797	4	5
Luling			
The First National Bank In Luling	13919	–	5
The First National Bank Of Luling	4266	6	–
Mabank			
The First National Bank Of Mabank	6422	6	6
Madisonville			
The First National Bank Of Madisonville	6356	6	6
Malakoff			
The First National Bank Of Malakoff	10403	6	6
Manor			
The Farmers National Bank Of Manor	7146	6	–
Mansfield			
The First National Bank Of Mansfield	7201	5	–
Marble Falls			
The First National Bank Of Marble Falls	4545	6	–
Marfa			
The Marfa National Bank	8674	5	3
Marlin			
Marlin National Bank, Marlin	14114	–	–
Marlin-Citizens National Bank, Marlin	5606	–	6
The Citizens National Bank Of Marlin	12737	–	–
The First National Bank Of Marlin	4706	5	4
The Marlin National Bank	5606	4	6
Marshall			
The First National Bank Of Marshall	3113	5	5
The Marshall National Bank	4101	5	5
The State National Bank Of Marshall	12703	5	5
Mart			
The Farmers And Merchants National Bank Of Mart	7546	6	3
The First National Bank Of Mart	5850	5	5
Martindale			
The Martindale National Bank, Martindale	10941	–	–
Mason			
The Citizens National Bank Of Mason	4378	6	–
The First National Bank Of Mason	4378	6	–
The German-American National Bank Of Mason	7098	6	–
The Mason National Bank, Mason	7098	5	5
Matador			
The First National Bank Of Matador	11002	–	5
Mathis			
The First National Bank Of Mathis	11838	–	–
Maud			
The Maud National Bank	10182	6	–
May			
The First National Bank Of May	8327	6	6
Mcallen			
The First National Bank In Mcallen	13183	–	–
The First National Bank Of Mcallen	11175	–	–
Mcgregor			
The Citizens National Bank Of Mcgregor	5504	6	–
The First National Bank Of Mcgregor	4076	5	6
The Mcgregor National Bank	7599	6	–
Mckinney			
Central National Bank Of Mckinney	14236	–	5
The Collin County National Bank Of Mckinney	2909	3	5
The First National Bank In Mckinney	13427	–	–
The First National Bank Of Mckinney	2729	5	6
Mclean			
American National Bank In Mclean	14165	–	–
The American National Bank Of Mclean	10957	–	–
The First National Bank Of Mclean	7413	6	–
Meadow			
The First National Bank Of Meadow	12928	–	–
Melissa			
The Melissa National Bank	10008	6	4
Melvin			
The First National Bank Of Melvin	12752	–	–
Memphis			
The First National Bank Of Memphis	6107	5	3
The Hall County National Bank Of Memphis	8005	5	5
Menard			
The Bevans National Bank Of Menard	11414	–	–
The First National Bank Of Menard	10044	6	–
The Menard National Bank, Menard	11406	–	–
Mercedes			
The First National Bank Of Mercedes	11879	5	5
Meridan			
The First National Bank Of Meridan	4016	6	–
Merit			
The First National Bank Of Merit	7378	6	6
Merkel			
The Farmers And Merchants National Bank Of Merkel	7481	6	6
The First National Bank Of Merkel	5661	6	–
The Merkel National Bank	7466	6	–
The Southern National Bank Of Merkel	10052	6	–
Mertzon			
The First National Bank Of Mertzon	9810	6	6

City, Bank	Ch. No.	L	S
Mesquite			
The First National Bank Of Mesquite	6140	6	5
Mexia			
The Citizens National Bank Of Mexia	5697	6	–
The City National Bank Of Mexia	11964	6	5
The First National Bank Of Mexia	3014	6	–
The Prendergast-Smith National Bank Of Mexia	12190	–	4
Midland			
The First National Bank Of Midland	4368	5	6
The Midland National Bank, Midland	6410	5	4
Midlothian			
First National Bank In Midlothian	13670	–	6
The Farmers National Bank Of Midlothian	8568	6	–
The First National Bank Of Midlothian	7775	6	6
Miles			
The Miles National Bank	6935	6	–
The Runnels County National Bank Of Miles	7414	6	–
Milford			
The First National Bank Of Milford	12685	–	–
Millsap			
The First National Bank Of Millsap	12687	6	6
Mineola			
The First National Bank Of Mineola	5127	5	5
The Mineola National Bank	8037	6	–
Mineral Wells			
The City National Bank Of Mineral Wells	12734	6	5
The First National Bank Of Mineral Wells	5511	4	6
The State National Bank Of Mineral Wells	12669	5	5
Mission			
The First National Bank Of Mission	10090	5	6
Montague			
The First National Bank Of Montague	3165	6	–
Moody			
The First National Bank Of Moody	5774	5	5
Moore			
The Moore National Bank	8817	6	6
Moran			
The First National Bank Of Moran	10874	–	–
The Moran National Bank, Moran	12727	–	–
Morgan			
The First National Bank Of Morgan	6247	6	–
Moulton			
The First National Bank Of Moulton	5399	6	–
Mount Calm			
The First National Bank In Mount Calm	13669	–	6
The First National Bank Of Mt. Calm	10297	6	5
Mount Pleasant			
State National Bank Of Mount Pleasant	6139	6	–
The First National Bank In Mount Pleasant	13257	–	–
The First National Bank Of Mount Pleasant	4722	5	–
The Merchants And Planters National Bank Of Mount Pleasant	6139	6	–
Mount Vernon			
The First National Bank Of Mount Vernon	5409	6	6
The Merchants And Planters National Bank Of Mount Vernon	7674	6	6
Munday			
First National Bank In Munday	13593	–	–
The Citizens National Bank Of Munday	8215	6	–
The First National Bank Of Munday	7106	6	6
Nacogdoches			
The Commercial National Bank Of Nacogdoches	5991	6	–
The First National Bank Of Nacogdoches	4405	6	–
The Stone Fort National Bank Of Nacogdoches	6627	6	4
Naples			
The Morris County National Bank Of Naples	7194	6	5
The Naples National Bank	8585	5	–
Navasota			
The Citizens National Bank Of Navasota	5190	5	6
The First National Bank Of Navasota	4253	5	5
Necessity			
The First National Bank Of Necessity	11659	–	–
Nederland			
The First National Bank Of Nederland	6596	6	–
Needville			
The First National Bank Of Needville	12718	–	–
Nevada			
The First National Bank Of Nevada	5721	5	6
New Boston			
The First National Bank Of New Boston	5636	5	6
The New Boston National Bank	8522	6	6
New Braunfels			
The Comal National Bank Of New Braunfels	7924	6	–
The First National Bank Of New Braunfels	4295	5	4
Newcastle			
Farmers National Bank Of Newcastle	14154	–	–
The First National Bank Of Newcastle	10472	6	6
Newsome			
The First National Bank Of Newsome	10661	6	–
Newton			
The First National Bank Of Newton	12898	–	–
Nixon			
The First National Bank Of Nixon	10682	6	–
The Nixon National Bank, Nixon	12782	–	–
Nocona			
The City National Bank Of Nocona	8610	6	–
The Farmers And Merchants National Bank Of Nocona	7617	6	2
The First National Bank Of Nocona	4621	6	–
The National Bank Of Nocona	5338	6	–
The Nocona National Bank, Nocona	5338	5	–
The Peoples National Bank Of Nocona	11959	–	5
Nordheim			
The First National Bank Of Nordheim	12390	–	–
Normangee			
The First National Bank Of Normangee	10275	6	6
North Fort Worth			
The Exchange National Bank Of North Fort Worth	8287	6	–
The Stockyards National Bank Of North Fort Worth	6822	6	–
Norton			
The First National Bank Of Norton	12415	–	–

City, Bank	Ch. No.	L	S
O'donnell			
The First National Bank Of O'donnell	12831	–	–
Oakville			
The First National Bank Of Oakville	8807	6	–
Ochiltree			
The First National Bank Of Ochiltree	8769	6	–
The First National Bank Of Perryton	8769	6	6
The Ochiltree National Bank, Ochiltree	8911	6	–
Odell			
The First National Bank Of Odell	12709	–	–
Odessa			
The Citizens National Bank Of Odessa	8169	6	6
The First National Bank Of Odessa	13608	–	6
The Odessa National Bank	6410	6	–
The Odessa National Bank, Odessa	13238	–	–
The Western National Bank Of Odessa	8925	6	–
Oglesby			
The First National Bank Of Oglesby	12652	–	–
Olney			
The City National Bank Of Olney	12676	–	5
The First National Bank Of Olney	8982	4	5
Omaha			
The First National Bank Of Omaha	10426	6	–
Orange			
First National Bank In Orange	13661	–	6
The First National Bank Of Orange	4118	4	4
The Orange National Bank	6050	6	6
Ozona			
The Ozona National Bank	7748	6	5
Paducah			
The First National Bank Of Paducah	10230	6	6
The Security National Bank Of Paducah	12748	–	–
Paint Rock			
The First National Bank Of Paint Rock	8306	6	–
Palestine			
The East Texas National Bank Of Palestine	12556	–	4
The First National Bank Of Palestine	3694	4	6
The Palestine National Bank	4436	6	–
The Royall National Bank Of Palestine	7170	4	5
Pampa			
First National Bank In Pampa	14207	–	–
The First National Bank Of Pampa	9142	6	6
The Pampa National Bank, Pampa	13291	–	–
Panhandle			
The First National Bank Of Panhandle	13070	–	–
Paradise			
The First National Bank Of Paradise	12416	–	–
Paris			
The American National Bank Of Paris	8542	4	5
The City National Bank Of Paris	4411	4	–
The First National Bank Of Paris	3638	4	4
The Liberty National Bank In Paris	13541	–	–
The Liberty National Bank Of Paris	12651	–	–
The Paris National Bank	5079	6	–
Pearsall			
The Pearsall National Bank	6989	5	3
The Pearsall National Bank In Pearsall	13572	–	3
Pecan Gap			
The Pecan Gap National Bank	13266	–	–
Pecos			
The First National Bank Of Pecos	8771	6	5
Perrin			
The First National Bank Of Perrin	12424	–	–
Perryton			
The Perryton National Bank, Perryton	11595	–	–
Petty			
The Citizens National Bank Of Petty	10647	6	–
The First National Bank Of Petty	5569	6	–
Pharr			
The First National Bank Of Pharr	10169	5	3
Pickton			
The First National Bank Of Pickton	12915	–	–
Pilot Point			
The Pilot Point National Bank	4777	6	6
Pittsburg			
The First National Bank Of Pittsburg	4863	5	6
The Pittsburg National Bank	7376	6	6
Plainview			
The Citizens National Bank Of Plainview	9081	6	–
The City National Bank Of Plainview	14015	–	–
The First National Bank In Plainview	13489	–	–
The First National Bank Of Plainview	5475	6	6
The Plainview National Bank, Plainview	9802	–	–
The Third National Bank Of Plainview	9802	6	–
Plano			
The Farmers And Merchants National Bank Of Plano	5692	6	–
The Farmers National Bank Of Plano	12622	–	–
The First National Bank Of Plano	13511	–	6
The Plano National Bank	3764	5	6
Pleasanton			
First National Bank In Pleasanton	13642	–	–
The First National Bank Of Pleasanton	8103	6	6
Port Arthur			
The First National Bank Of Port Arthur	5485	5	4
The Merchants National Bank Of Port Arthur	12091	–	–
Port Lavaca			
The First National Bank Of Port Lavaca	5367	5	–
Port Neches			
The First National Bank Of Port Neches	11799	6	6
Post			
The Citizens National Bank Of Post	12969	–	–
The First National Bank Of Post	9485	–	6
Post City			
The First National Bank Of Post City	9485	6	5
Poth			
The First National Bank Of Poth	10320	6	6
Princeton			
The First National Bank Of Princeton	8611	6	–
Purdon			
The First National Bank Of Purdon	10927	6	6
Putnam			
The First National Bank Of Putnam	9749	6	–

City, Bank	Ch. No.	L	S
Quanah			
The Citizens National Bank Of Quanah	9906	6	–
The City National Bank Of Quanah	4361	6	–
The First National Bank In Quanah	12307	6	6
The First National Bank Of Quanah	4144	6	–
The Quanah National Bank, Quanah	4571	6	–
The Security National Bank Of Quanah	12308	–	–
The State National Bank Of Quanah	5972	6	–
Quinlan			
The First National Bank Of Quinlan	11970	5	–
The Quinlan National Bank Of Quinlan	12761	–	–
Quitaque			
The First National Bank Of Quitaque	11706	–	–
Quitman			
The First National Bank Of Quitman	10646	6	–
Ralls			
The First National Bank Of Ralls	12927	–	–
Ranger			
The First National Bank Of Ranger	8072	6	–
Raymondville			
The First National Bank Of Raymondville	12789	–	6
Reagan			
The First National Bank Of Reagan	12715	–	–
Refugio			
The First National Bank Of Refugio	12462	–	6
Rhome			
The First National Bank In Rhome	13285	–	–
The First National Bank Of Rhome	10509	–	–
Rice			
The First National Bank Of Rice	11632	–	–
Richland			
The First National Bank Of Richland	12508	–	–
Richmond			
The First National Bank Of Richmond	10350	5	6
The Fort Bend National Bank Of Richmond	12648	–	–
Rio Grande			
The First National Bank Of Rio Grande	11591	6	6
Rising Star			
The First National Bank Of Rising Star	7906	6	6
Robert Lee			
The First National Bank Of Robert Lee	8659	6	–
Robstown			
The First National Bank Of Robstown	12554	–	–
The Gouger National Bank Of Robstown	12753	–	–
The Robstown National Bank, Robstown	14157	–	–
The State National Bank Of Robstown	12729	–	–
Roby			
The First National Bank Of Roby	5865	6	–
Rochelle			
The Rochelle National Bank, Rochelle	12796	–	–
Rockdale			
The First National Bank Of Rockdale	4175	6	6
Rockport			
The First National Bank Of Aransas Pass, Rockport	4438	6	–
The First National Bank Of Rockport	4438	5	6
Rocksprings			
The First National Bank Of Rocksprings	11634	–	–
Rockwall			
The Citizens National Bank Of Rockwall	6679	6	–
The Farmers And Merchants National Bank Of Rockwall	4717	6	–
The Farmers National Bank Of Rockwall	8204	6	6
The First National Bank In Rockwall	13402	–	6
The First National Bank Of Rockwall	3890	6	–
The Rockwall County National Bank Of Rockwall	4911	6	–
The Rockwall National Bank	6703	6	–
Rogers			
The First National Bank Of Rogers	5704	6	5
Roscoe			
The First National Bank Of Roscoe	12899	–	–
Rosebud			
The First National Bank Of Rosebud	5513	6	5
The Planters National Bank Of Rosebud	8066	6	6
Rosenberg			
The First National Bank Of Rosenberg	12756	–	–
Rotan			
The First National Bank Of Rotan	8693	6	6
Rowena			
The First National Bank Of Rowena	12408	–	–
Rowlett			
The First National Bank Of Rowlett	12654	–	–
Roxton			
The First National Bank Of Roxton	5710	5	6
Royse			
The First National Bank Of Royse	6551	6	6
Rule			
The First National Bank Of Rule	8242	6	6
Runge			
The Runge National Bank	6522	6	–
Rusk			
The First National Bank Of Rusk	4346	5	–
Sabinal			
The Sabinal National Bank	7807	5	6
Saint Jo			
Citizens National Bank In Saint Jo	13519	–	–
The Citizens National Bank Of Saint Jo	8402	5	6
The First National Bank Of Saint Jo	5325	5	5
San Angelo			
San Angelo National Bank Of San Angelo	13587	–	–
The Central National Bank Of San Angelo	10664	4	3
The Citizens National Bank Of San Angelo	4659	6	–
The Concho National Bank Of San Angelo	2767	5	–
The First National Bank Of San Angelo	2767	4	5
The Landon National Bank Of San Angelo	6807	6	–
The San Angelo National Bank	3260	5	6
The Western National Bank Of San Angelo	6807	6	–

City, Bank	Ch. No.	L	S
San Antonio			
Bexar County National Bank Of San Antonio	14283	–	4
National Bank Of Commerce Of San Antonio	6956	3	3
The Alamo National Bank Of San Antonio	4525	2	3
The City National Bank Of San Antonio	5217	3	–
The Commercial National Bank Of San Antonio	12162	5	5
The Fifth National Bank Of San Antonio	4748	6	–
The Frost National Bank Of San Antonio	5179	2	3
The Groos National Bank Of San Antonio	10148	4	4
The Lockwood National Bank Of San Antonio	3738	4	–
The National Bank Of Fort Sam Houston At San Antonio	13578	–	3
The San Antonio National Bank	1657	3	5
The South Texas National Bank Of San Antonio	14179	–	–
The State National Bank Of San Antonio	10793	5	–
The Texas National Bank Of San Antonio	3298	6	–
The Traders National Bank Of San Antonio	2883	6	–
Woods National Bank Of San Antonio	7316	5	–
San Augustine			
The First National Bank Of San Augustine	6214	5	6
The San Augustine National Bank	6245	6	–
San Juan			
The First National Bank Of San Juan	11279	–	–
San Marcos			
The First National Bank Of San Marcos	3346	6	6
The Glover National Bank Of San Marcos	3344	6	–
The National Bank Of San Marcos	3344	6	–
The Wood National Bank Of San Marcos	3344	6	–
San Saba			
The City National Bank Of San Saba	10806	–	–
The First National Bank Of San Saba	7700	6	–
The San Saba National Bank	9781	6	–
Sanger			
The First National Bank Of Sanger	7886	5	5
The Sanger National Bank	8690	6	6
Santa Anna			
The First National Bank Of Santa Anna	8109	6	–
The Santa Anna National Bank, Santa Ana	13854	–	–
The State National Bank Of Santa Anna	12768	–	–
Santo			
The First National Bank Of Santo	8176	5	5
Savoy			
The First National Bank Of Savoy	7645	6	–
Schulenburg			
The First National Bank Of Schulenburg	8034	6	6
Schwertner			
The First National Bank Of Schwertner	10956	5	6
Sealy			
The Farmers National Bank Of Sealy	10398	6	–
The Sealy National Bank	6390	6	–
Seminole			
The Seminole National Bank	8465	6	–
Sequin			
The First National Bank Of Sequin	5097	5	4
Seymour			
The Davis National Bank Of Seymour	5904	6	–
The Farmers National Bank Of Seymour	7482	6	6
The First National Bank Of Seymour	4263	5	5
Shamrock			
The First National Bank Of Shamrock	7306	6	–
Sherman			
The Commercial National Bank Of Sherman	5864	5	–
The Commercial National Bank Of Sherman	10607	6	–
The Grayson County National Bank Of Sherman	5192	6	–
The Merchants And Planters National Bank Of Sherman	3159	3	3
Shiner			
The First National Bank Of Shiner	5628	2	5
Silverton			
The First National Bank Of Silverton	8816	6	6
Sipe Springs			
The First National Bank Of Sipe Springs	11525	–	–
Smithville			
The First National Bank Of Smithville	7041	6	6
Snyder			
Snyder National Bank	14270	–	6
The First National Bank Of Snyder	5580	6	–
The Snyder National Bank	7635	6	6
Sonora			
The First National Bank Of Sonora	5466	5	5
Sour Lake			
The Citizens National Bank Of Sour Lake	11021	6	4
The First National Bank Of Sour Lake	6810	6	–
The Sour Lake National Bank, Sour Lake	6856	6	–
Spur			
The City National Bank Of Spur	10703	6	6
The Spur National Bank	9611	5	5
Stamford			
The Citizens National Bank Of Stamford	7640	6	–
The First National Bank In Stamford	13598	–	3
The First National Bank Of Stamford	5560	5	6
Stanton			
The First National Bank Of Stanton	8094	6	5
The Home National Bank Of Stanton	9053	5	6
The Stanton National Bank	8112	6	–
Stephenville			
Farmers-first National Bank Of Stephenville	12730	5	5
The Erath County National Bank Of Stephenville	4081	6	–
The Farmers National Bank Of Stephenville	8054	6	–
The First National Bank Of Stephenville	4095	6	–
Sterling City			
The First National Bank Of Sterling City	9813	6	6
Stratford			
The First National Bank Of Stratford	8018	6	–
The Sherman County National Bank Of Stratford	11223	–	–
The Stratford National Bank	8018	6	–
Strawn			
The First National Bank Of Strawn	10229	6	6
The Strawn National Bank	12775	–	6
Streetman			
The First National Bank Of Streetman	12423	–	–

City, Bank	Ch. No.	L	S
Sudan			
The First National Bank Of Sudan	12725	–	6
Sulphur Springs			
First National Bank In Sulphur Springs	12845	6	5
First National Bank Of Sulphur Springs	13653	–	6
The City National Bank Of Sulphur Springs	3989	5	5
The First National Bank Of Sulphur Springs	3466	6	–
Sweetwater			
The City National Bank Of Sweetwater	11468	6	–
The First National Bank Of Sweetwater	5781	5	–
Swenson			
The Swenson National Bank, Swenson	12266	–	–
Sylvester			
The First National Bank Of Sylvester	12684	–	–
Taft			
The First National Bank Of Taft	12309	6	6
Tahoka			
The First National Bank Of Tahoka	8597	6	6
Taylor			
First Taylor National Bank, Taylor	3027	–	6
The City National Bank Of Taylor	5275	5	4
The First National Bank Of Taylor	3027	5	4
The Taylor National Bank	3859	6	6
Teague			
The First National Bank Of Teague	8195	6	4
The Teague National Bank	13067	4	4
Temple			
First National Bank Of Temple	13778	–	–
The Bell County National Bank Of Temple	4404	6	–
The City National Bank Of Temple	6317	5	6
The First National Bank In Temple	13206	–	–
The First National Bank Of Temple	3227	5	–
The Temple National Bank	3858	6	–
Terrell			
The American National Bank Of Terrell	4990	4	5
The First National Bank Of Terrell	3816	4	6
The Harris National Bank Of Terrell	4990	6	–
The State National Bank In Terrell	13287	–	–
The State National Bank Of Terrell	12733	–	–
Texarkana			
The City National Bank Of Texarkana	7392	6	–
The First National Bank Of Texarkana	3065	6	–
The Interstate National Bank Of Texarkana	3998	6	–
The Texarkana National Bank	3785	4	3
Texas City			
The First National Bank Of Texas City	9936	6	6
The Texas City National Bank	10040	6	3
Texline			
The First National Bank Of Texline	10782	–	–
Thorndale			
The First National Bank Of Thorndale	5882	5	6
Thornton			
The Farmers National Bank Of Thornton	12713	–	–
The First National Bank Of Thornton	8538	5	5
Throckmorton			
The First National Bank Of Throckmorton	6001	4	5
Timpson			
The First National Bank Of Timpson	6177	6	–
Tioga			
The First National Bank Of Tioga	7714	6	–
Tolar			
The First National Bank Of Tolar	8001	6	–
Tom Bean			
The First National Bank Of Tom Bean	11019	6	5
Toyah			
The First National Bank Of Toyah	8355	6	–
Trenton			
The First National Bank Of Trenton	5737	6	6
Trinity			
First National Bank Of Trinity	13706	–	3
The Trinity National Bank	10078	6	4
Troup			
The First National Bank Of Troup	6212	6	4
Tulia			
The First National Bank Of Tulia	6298	5	5
The Tulia National Bank	6298	6	–
Turkey			
The First National Bank Of Turkey	11138	–	–
Turnersville			
The First National Bank Of Turnersville	8843	6	–
Tyler			
The Citizens National Bank Of Tyler	5343	5	4
The City National Bank Of Tyler	4353	6	–
The Farmers And Merchants National Bank Of Tyler	7515	6	–
The First National Bank Of Tyler	3651	6	–
The Jester National Bank Of Tyler	6234	6	–
The Peoples National Bank Of Tyler	13110	4	5
The Tyler National Bank	4747	6	–
Uvalde			
The Commercial National Bank Of Uvalde	6831	5	6
The First National Bank Of Uvalde	4517	6	–
The Uvalde National Bank	5175	6	–
Valley Mills			
First National Bank In Valley Mills	13675	–	–
The First National Bank In Valley Mills	13272	–	–
The First National Bank Of Valley Mills	9148	6	–
Valley View			
The First National Bank Of Valley View	7731	6	5
The Valley View National Bank, Valley View	12711	–	–
Van Alstyne			
The Farmers National Bank Of Van Alstyne	7016	6	–
The First National Bank Of Van Alstyne	4289	6	6
Velasco			
The Velasco National Bank	4662	6	–
Venus			
The Farmers And Merchants National Bank Of Venus	7798	6	–
The First National Bank Of Venus	5549	6	–

City, Bank	Ch. No.	L	S
Vernon			
The First National Bank Of Vernon	4033	6	–
The Herring National Bank Of Vernon	7010	5	3
The State National Bank Of Vernon	4130	6	–
The Vernon National Bank, Vernon	4065	–	–
The Waggoner National Bank Of Vernon	5203	5	5
Victoria			
The First National Bank Of Victoria	4184	4	–
The Peoples National Bank Of Victoria	11291	–	–
The Victoria National Bank	10360	2	3
Waco			
The American National Bank Of Waco	3901	6	–
The Central National Bank Of Waco	10220	6	–
The Central Texas Exchange National Bank Of Waco	10220	5	–
The Central Texas National Bank Of Waco	9828	6	–
The Citizens National Bank Of Waco	3135	4	3
The Exchange National Bank Of Waco	8818	6	–
The Farmers And Merchants National Bank Of Waco	4349	6	–
The First National Bank Of Waco	2189	3	2
The Liberty National Bank Of Waco	11140	5	5
The National City Bank Of Waco	6572	4	3
The Provident National Bank Of Waco	4309	6	–
The Waco National Bank	2189	6	–
Walnut Springs			
The First National Bank Of Walnut Springs	8130	6	–
Waxahachie			
Citizens National Bank In Waxahachie	13516	–	2
The Citizens National Bank Of Waxahachie	3212	4	6
The First National Bank Of Waxahachie	2974	6	–
The Waxahachie National Bank	4379	3	–
Weatherford			
The Citizens National Bank Of Weatherford	2723	5	5
The First National Bank Of Weatherford	2477	5	5
The Merchants And Farmers National Bank Of Weatherford	3975	6	–
The Parker County National Bank Of Weatherford	12762	–	–
Wellington			
The City National Bank In Wellington	12166	–	–
The City National Bank Of Wellington	9805	6	–
The First National Bank In Wellington	13249	–	2
The First National Bank Of Wellington	8102	6	–
Weslaco			
The First National Bank Of Weslaco	12641	5	6
West			
The First National Bank Of West	5543	6	–
The National Bank Of West	8239	6	5
The State National Bank In West	13022	–	–
The State National Bank Of West	12712	–	–
The West National Bank	13935	–	3
West Columbia			
The First National Bank Of West Columbia	11453	–	–
Wharton			
The First National Bank Of Wharton	4903	6	–
The Wharton National Bank	6313	6	–
Wheeler			
The First National Bank Of Wheeler	12627	–	–
White Deer			
The Farmers National Bank Of White Deer	14272	–	–
The First National Bank Of White Deer	11647	–	–
Whitesboro			
The City National Bank Of Whitesboro	10634	6	6
The First National Bank Of Whitesboro	5847	5	6
The Whitesboro National Bank	10634	–	6
Whitewright			
The First National Bank Of Whitewright	4692	5	5
The Planters National Bank Of Whitewright	6915	5	6
Whitney			
First National Bank In Whitney	13649	–	6
The Citizens National Bank Of Whitney	7915	6	–
The First National Bank Of Whitney	7875	6	6
Wichita Falls			
City National Bank In Wichita Falls	13665	–	–
The American National Bank Of Wichita Falls	11301	–	–
The City National Bank Of Commerce Of Wichita Falls	4248	5	–
The City National Bank Of Wichita Falls	4248	5	–
The City National Bank Of Wichita Falls	4248	3	3
The Exchange National Bank Of Wichita Falls	11486	–	–
The First National Bank Of Wichita Falls	3200	4	3
The National Bank Of Commerce Of Wichita Falls	10547	6	–
The Panhandle National Bank Of Wichita Falls	3200	6	–
The Security National Bank Of Wichita Falls	11762	5	6
Wichita National Bank Of Wichita Falls	13676	–	4
Wills Point			
The First National Bank Of Wills Point	5018	6	6
The State National Bank Of Wills Point	12670	–	–
The Van Zandt County National Bank Of Wills Point	6071	6	–
Windom			
The First National Bank Of Windom	12691	–	–
Winfield			
The First National Bank Of Winfield	10488	6	–
The Winfield National Bank, Winfield	12505	–	–
Winnsboro			
The Farmers National Bank Of Winnsboro	6168	6	–
The First National Bank Of Winnsboro	5674	4	6
Winters			
The First National Bank Of Winters	10717	–	–
Wolfe City			
The Citizens National Bank Of Wolfe City	8178	6	–
The Wolfe City National Bank In Wolfe City	13199	–	3
The Wolfe City National Bank, Wolfe City	3984	6	–
Woodsboro			
The First National Bank Of Woodsboro	11379	–	–
Wortham			
The First National Bank Of Wortham	6686	6	5
Wylie			
The First National Bank Of Wylie	5483	6	–
The Wylie National Bank, Wylie	12583	–	–
Yoakum			
The First National Bank Of Yoakum	4363	6	–
The Yoakum National Bank	8694	5	4

City, Bank	Ch. No.	L	S
Yorktown			
The First National Bank Of Yorktown	6987	5	5

UTAH TERRITORY

City, Bank	Ch. No.	L	S
Logan			
The First National Bank Of Logan	4670	6	–
Nephi			
The First National Bank Of Nephi	3537	6	–
Ogden			
The Commercial National Bank Of Ogden	3739	6	–
The First National Bank Of Ogden	2597	6	–
The Utah National Bank Of Ogden	2880	6	–
Park City			
The First National Bank Of Park City	4564	6	–
Provo City			
The First National Bank Of Provo City	2641	6	–
The National Bank Of Commerce, Provo City	4486	6	–
Salt Lake City			
The American National Bank Of Salt Lake City	4432	6	–
The Commercial National Bank Of Salt Lake City	4051	6	–
The Deseret National Bank Of Salt Lake City	2059	2	–
The First National Bank Of Utah	1695	6	–
The Miners National Bank Of Salt Lake City	1646	6	–
The National Bank Of The Republic At Salt Lake City	4310	6	–
The Salt Lake City National Bank Of Utah	1921	5	–
The Union National Bank Of Salt Lake City	3306	6	–
The Utah National Bank Of Salt Lake City	4341	6	–

UTAH

City, Bank	Ch. No.	L	S
Beaver City			
The First National Bank Of Beaver City	9119	6	–
Bingham Canyon			
The First National Bank Of Bingham Canyon	11631	–	–
Brigham City			
The First National Bank Of Brigham City	6036	4	5
Coalville			
The First National Bank Of Coalville	7696	5	3
Delta			
The First National Bank Of Delta	11529	6	–
Gunnison			
The Gunnison City National Bank Of Gunnison	11725	–	–
Layton			
The First National Bank Of Layton	7685	6	4
Logan			
The First National Bank Of Logan	4670	4	3
Magna			
The First National Bank Of Magna	11228	–	–
Moab			
The First National Bank Of Moab	10925	5	3
Monticello			
The First National Bank Of Monticello	11266	–	–
Morgan			
The First National Bank Of Morgan	6958	4	6
Murray			
The First National Bank Of Murray	6558	4	3
Myton			
The First National Bank Of Myton	11702	6	–
Nephi			
The First National Bank Of Nephi	3537	4	–
The Nephi National Bank	8508	4	4
Ogden			
First National Bank Of Ogden	2597	4	1
First Security Bank Of Utah, National Association Ogden	2597	–	4
First Utah National Bank Of Ogden	2597	4	–
The Commercial National Bank Of Ogden	3139	4	–
The First & Utah National Bank Of Ogden	2597	6	–
The First National Bank Of Ogden	2597	3	–
The National Bank Of Commerce Of Ogden	7296	4	4
The Pingree National Bank Of Ogden	7296	5	–
The Utah National Bank Of Ogden	2880	4	–
Park City			
The First National Bank Of Park City	4564	4	–
Price			
The First National Bank Of Price	6012	4	3
Provo City			
The First National Bank Of Provo City	2641	6	–
Salt Lake City			
Security National Bank Of Salt Lake City	9652	–	3
The Commercial National Bank Of Salt Lake City	4051	5	–
The Continental National Bank Of Salt Lake City	9403	3	4
The Continental Nationl Bank & Trust Co Of Salt Lake City	9403	–	1
The Deseret National Bank Of Salt Lake City	2059	1	1
The First National Bank Of Salt Lake City	2059	–	2
The National Bank Of The Republic At Salt Lake City	4310	4	–
The National City Bank Of Salt Lake City	10308	4	–
The National Copper Bank Of Salt Lake City	9652	3	2
The Utah National Bank Of Salt Lake City	4341	4	–
The Utah State National Bank Of Salt Lake City	4341	3	2
Smithfield			
The Commercial National Bank Of Smithfield	10135	5	5
Spanish Fork			
The First National Bank Of Spanish Fork	9111	5	6

VERMONT

City, Bank	Ch. No.	L	S
Barre			
The National Bank Of Barre	2109	4	–
The Peoples National Bank Of Barre	7068	5	4
Barton			
The Barton National Bank	2290	6	–
Bellows Falls			
The National Bank Of Bellows Falls	1653	3	5
The Windham National Bank Of Bellows Falls	13894	–	5
Bennington			
The Bennington County National Bank Of Bennington	2395	3	–
The County National Bank Of Bennington	2395	5	4
The First National Bank Of Bennington	130	3	4
Bethel			
The National White River Bank Of Bethel	962	4	6
The National White River Bank Of Bethel	13755	–	–

City, Bank	Ch. No.	L	S
Bradford			
The Bradford National Bank	7267	6	4
Brandon			
The Brandon National Bank	404	4	5
The Brandon National Bank	13712	–	–
The First National Bank Of Brandon	278	5	4
Brattleboro			
The First National Bank Of Brattleboro	470	6	–
The Peoples National Bank Of Brattleboro	2305	3	–
The Vermont National Bank Of Brattleboro	1430	4	–
Vermont-Peoples National Bank Of Brattleboro	1430	4	4
Bristol			
The First National Bank Of Bristol	6252	6	6
Burlington			
The First National Bank Of Burlington	861	6	–
The Howard National Bank & Trust Company Of Burlington	1698	–	4
The Howard National Bank Of Burlington	1698	3	5
The Merchants National Bank Of Burlington	1197	3	4
Castleton			
The Castleton National Bank	1598	6	–
Chelsea			
The First National Bank Of Chelsea	2120	6	–
The National Bank Of Orange County At Chelsea	4929	5	6
The Orange County National Bank Of Chelsea	1004	6	–
Chester			
The National Bank Of Chester	4380	6	6
Danville			
The Caledonia National Bank Of Danville	1576	4	5
Derby Line			
The National Bank Of Derby Line	1368	4	6
Enosburg Falls			
The Enosburg Falls National Bank	13986	–	6
The First National Bank Of Enosburg Falls	7614	6	6
Factory Point			
The Factory Point National Bank	3080	6	–
Fair Haven			
The Allen National Bank Of Fair Haven	2422	4	5
The First National Bank Of Fair Haven	344	4	5
Hyde Park			
The Lamoille County National Bank Of Hyde Park	1163	5	–
Irasburg			
The Irasburg National Bank Of Orleans At Irasburg	1541	6	–
Island Pond			
The Island Pond National Bank	4275	5	5
Jamaica			
The West River National Bank Of Jamaica	1564	6	–
Lyndon			
The National Bank Of Lyndon	1140	4	–
Lyndonville			
The Lyndonville National Bank	3158	5	–
Manchester			
The Battenkill National Bank Of Manchester	1488	5	–
Manchester Center			
The Factory Point National Bank Of Manchester Center	3080	5	4
Middlebury			
The National Bank Of Middlebury	1195	3	2
Middletown Springs			
The Gray National Bank Of Middletown Springs	3150	6	–
Montpelier			
The First National Bank Of Montpelier	748	4	5
The Montpelier National Bank	857	3	6
The Montpelier National Bank	13915	–	–
Newport			
The National Bank Of Newport	2263	5	5
North Bennington			
The First National Bank Of North Bennington	194	4	2
Northfield			
The Northfield National Bank	1638	5	6
Orwell			
The First National Bank Of Orwell	228	5	3
Poultney			
The Citizens National Bank Of Poultney	9824	5	5
The First National Bank In Poultney	13261	6	6
The First National Bank Of Poultney	2545	4	–
The National Bank Of Poultney	1200	6	–
The Poultney National Bank	14234	–	6
Proctorsville			
The National Black River Bank Of Proctorsville	1383	5	6
Richford			
The Richford National Bank	11615	5	6
Royalton			
The National Bank Of Royalton	1673	6	–
Rutland			
The Baxter National Bank Of Rutland	1700	4	–
The Central National Bank Of Rutland	1700	6	5
The Clement National Bank Of Rutland	2537	–	–
The Clement National Bank Of Rutland	2950	4	5
The Killington National Bank Of Rutland	2905	6	6
The Merchants National Bank Of Rutland	3311	6	–
The National Bank Of Rutland	1450	4	–
The Rutland County National Bank Of Rutland	820	4	5
Saint Albans			
The First National Bank Of Saint Albans	269	6	–
The Vermont National Bank Of Saint Albans	1583	6	–
The Welden National Bank In Saint Albans	13800	–	6
The Welden National Bank Of Saint Albans	3482	4	6
Saint Johnsbury			
The First National Bank Of St. Johnsbury	489	4	4
The Merchants National Bank Of St. Johnsbury	2295	4	5
Springfield			
The First National Bank Of Springfield	122	3	4
Swanton			
The Ferris National Bank Of Swanton	4258	6	–
The National Union Bank Of Swanton	1634	6	–
The Peoples National Bank Of Swanton	4943	6	–

City, Bank	Ch. No.	L	S
Vergennes			
The Farmers National Bank Of Vergennes	2475	5	–
The National Bank Of Vergennes	1364	4	5
Waterbury			
The Waterbury National Bank	1462	6	–
Wells River			
The National Bank Of Newbury At Wells River	1406	3	3
The National Bank Of Newbury, Wells River	1406	4	–
West Randolph			
The Randolph National Bank Of Randolph	2274	6	–
The Randolph National Bank Of West Randolph	2274	6	–
White River Junction			
The First National Bank Of White River Junction	3484	5	4
The Hartford National Bank Of White River Junction	9108	6	–
The National Bank Of White River Junction	3484	4	–
Windsor			
The Ascutney National Bank Of Windsor	816	6	–
The State National Bank Of Windsor	7721	6	–
The Windsor County National Bank Of Windsor	13685	–	–
The Windsor National Bank	3257	6	–
Woodstock			
The Woodstock National Bank	1133	3	5

VIRGINIA

City, Bank	Ch. No.	L	S
Abingdon			
The Citizens National Bank Of Abingdon	11313	–	–
The First National Bank Of Abingdon	5150	3	5
The Peoples National Bank Of Abingdon	8819	5	–
The Washington County National Bank Of Abingdon	14223	–	–
Alexandria			
Alexandria National Bank	7093	4	4
The Citizens National Bank Of Alexandria	1716	4	3
The First National Bank Of Alexandria	651	5	4
Altavista			
The First National Bank Of Altavista	9295	6	5
Appalachia			
The First National Bank Of Appalachia	9379	6	4
Appomattox			
The Farmers National Bank Of Appomattox	11205	6	5
Ashland			
The First National Bank Of Ashland	11978	5	6
The Hanover National Bank Of Ashland	12451	–	–
Bassett			
The First National Bank Of Bassett	11976	6	5
Bedford			
The Citizens National Bank Of Bedford	10621	–	–
The Peoples National Bank Of Bedford	11328	6	6
Bedford City			
The First National Bank Of Bedford City	4257	6	–
Berryville			
The First National Bank Of Berryville	7338	6	6
Big Stone Gap			
The First National Bank Of Big Stone Gap	11765	6	5
Blacksburg			
The National Bank Of Blacksburg	12229	–	–
Blackstone			
The First National Bank Of Blackstone	9224	4	5
Bristol			
The Dominion National Bank Of Bristol	4477	4	4
Broadway			
The First National Bank Of Broadway	6666	6	5
Brookneal			
The First National Bank Of Brookneal	10835	6	–
The Peoples National Bank Of Brookneal	11960	6	–
Buchanan			
The Buchanan National Bank	9375	6	5
The First National Bank Of Buchanan	4460	6	–
Buena Vista			
The First National Bank Of Buena Vista	4314	6	–
The First National Bank Of Buena Vista	9890	6	6
The First National Bank Of Lexington	4314	6	5
Charlottesville			
National Bank And Trust Company At Charlottesville	10618	6	4
The Albemarle National Bank Of Charlottesville	9246	6	–
The Charlottesville National Bank	1468	6	–
The Citizens National Bank Of Charlottesville	1742	6	–
The Commerce National Bank Of Charlottesville	11946	–	–
The Farmers And Merchants National Bank Of Charlottesville	11517	6	–
The Jefferson National Bank Of Charlottesville	6005	6	–
The National Bank Of Charlottesville	10618	4	–
The Peoples National Bank Of Charlottesville	2594	3	3
Chase City			
The First National Bank Of Chase City	9291	6	6
Chatham			
The First National Bank Of Chatham	10821	6	6
Chilhowie			
The National Bank Of Chilhowie	8875	6	5
Christiansburg			
The First National Bank Of Christiansburg	7937	6	4
Clarksville			
The First National Bank Of Clarksville	1658	6	–
Clifton Forge			
The Clifton Forge National Bank	9177	3	3
The First National Bank Of Clifton Forge	6008	3	5
The Mountain National Bank Of Clifton Forge	14180	–	–
Clintwood			
The Citizens National Bank Of Clintwood	8362	6	–
Coeburn			
The First National Bank Of Coeburn	6899	6	4
Covington			
The Citizens National Bank Of Covington	5326	4	5
The Covington National Bank	4503	4	5
Crewe			
The First National Bank Of Crewe	9455	4	4
The National Bank Of Crewe	14052	–	6
Culpeper			
The Culpeper National Bank	5591	5	5
The Farmers National Bank Of Culpeper	3570	6	–
The Second National Bank Of Culpeper	5394	4	4
Danville			
American National Bank And Trust Company Of Danville	9343	6	2
The American National Bank Of Danville	9343	4	–
The First National Bank Of Danville	1609	6	–
The First National Bank Of Danville	1985	5	5
The National Bank Of Danville	9475	5	–
The Planters National Bank Of Danville	1985	6	–
The Virginia National Bank Of Danville	10156	6	–
Dillwyn			
The First National Bank Of Dillwyn	11480	6	–
The Merchants And Planters National Bank Of Dillwyn	11501	–	–
Emporia			
The Citizens National Bank Of Emporia	12240	6	6
The First National Bank Of Emporia	8688	5	5
The Planters National Bank Of Emporia	9732	6	–
Esmont			
The Esmont National Bank	8003	6	6
Fairfax			
The National Bank Of Fairfax	6389	5	5
Farmville			
The First National Bank Of Farmville	5683	5	5
The Peoples National Bank Of Farmville	9222	5	5
Ferrum			
The First National Bank Of Ferrum	12311	6	5
Flint Hill			
The First National Bank Of Flint Hill	11797	6	6
Fredericksburg			
The Conway, Gordon And Garnett Natl Bank Of Fredericksburg	5268	5	–
The National Bank Of Fredericksburg	1582	5	6
The Planters National Bank In Fredericksburg	13603	–	3
The Planters National Bank Of Fredericksburg	10325	4	3
Fries			
The First National Bank Of Fries	12290	6	6
Front Royal			
The Citizens National Bank Of Front Royal	13275	–	–
The Front Royal National Bank	2967	6	–
Galax			
The First National Bank Of Galax	8791	6	6
Gate City			
The First And Peoples National Bank Of Gate City	13502	–	6
The First National Bank Of Gate City	7208	6	6
The Peoples National Bank In Gate City	13502	–	6
The Peoples National Bank Of Gate City	7135	5	6
Gloucester			
The First National Bank Of Gloucester	10658	6	6
Gordonsville			
The National Bank Of Gordonsville	10287	6	6
Graham			
The American National Bank Of Graham	7734	6	–
The First National Bank Of Graham	7782	6	–
The Twin City National Bank Of Bluefield	7782	6	6
Grundy			
The First National Bank Of Grundy	11698	6	6
Hallwood			
The Hallwood National Bank	7659	5	6
Hamilton			
The Farmers And Merchants National Bank Of Hamilton	9861	6	6
Hampton			
The Citizens National Bank Of Hampton	13775	–	5
The First National Bank Of Hampton	6842	6	6
The Merchants National Bank Of Hampton	6778	5	5
Harrisonburg			
The First National Bank Of Harrisonburg	1572	4	4
The National Bank Of Harrisonburg	11694	4	4
The Rockingham National Bank Of Harrisonburg	5261	4	4
Herndon			
The Citizens National Bank Of Herndon	14325	–	–
The National Bank Of Herndon	9635	6	4
Honaker			
The First National Bank In Honaker	13880	–	–
The First National Bank Of Honaker	10252	6	6
Hopewell			
The National Bank Of Hopewell	10866	6	–
Hot Springs			
The Bath County National Bank Of Hot Springs	8722	3	6
Independence			
The Grayson County National Bank Of Independence	10834	6	5
Irvington			
The Lancaster National Bank Of Irvington	5290	6	6
Jonesville			
The Peoples National Bank Of Jonesville	8384	6	–
The Powell Valley National Bank Of Jonesville	9924	6	5
Kenbridge			
The First National Bank Of Kenbridge	12251	6	–
Lawrenceville			
The First National Bank Of Lawrenceville	9433	6	–
Lebanon			
The Citizens National Bank Of Lebanon	6886	6	–
The First National Bank Of Lebanon	6886	6	6
Leesburg			
The Leesburg Upperville National Bank	12204	–	–
The Loudoun National Bank Of Leesburg	1738	5	5
The Peoples National Bank Of Leesburg	3917	5	4
Lexington			
The Peoples National Bank Of Lexington	7173	6	5
The Rockbridge National Bank Of Lexington	10696	–	–
Louisa			
The First National Bank Of Louisa	10968	5	–
Lovingston			
The First National Bank Of Nelson County At Lovingston	11957	5	5
Luray			
The First National Bank Of Luray	6031	5	5
The Page Valley National Bank Of Luray	6206	6	5
Lynchburg			
The American National Bank Of Lynchburg	7308	6	–
The First National Bank Of Lynchburg	1558	5	3
The Lynchburg National Bank	1522	3	–
The Lynchburg National Bank And Trust Company	1522	5	4
The National Exchange Bank Of Lynchburg	2506	4	–
The Peoples National Bank Of Lynchburg	2760	3	4
Manassas			
The National Bank Of Manassas	5032	5	5
The Peoples National Bank Of Manassas	6748	5	6
Manchester			
The Manchester National Bank	9663	6	–
The Manchester National Bank Of Richmond	9663	6	–
Marion			
The Marion National Bank	6839	5	5
The Peoples National Bank Of Marion	11718	6	–
Marshall			
Marshall National Bank And Trust Company	10253	6	5
The Marshall National Bank	10253	6	–
Martinsville			
The First National Bank Of Martinsville	7206	5	5
The Peoples National Bank Of Martinsville	9847	6	6
Middleburg			
The Middleburg National Bank	12539	–	–
Monterey			
The First National Bank Of Highland At Monterey	9043	5	–
Mount Jackson			
The Mount Jackson National Bank	3209	3	5
Narrows			
The First National Bank Of Narrows	11444	6	6
New Castle			
The First National Bank Of New Castle	10993	6	6
New Market			
The Citizens National Bank Of New Market	10524	–	–
The First National Bank Of New Market	10568	6	–
Newport News			
The First National Bank Of Newport News	4635	4	5
The National Mechanics Bank Of Newport News	11364	6	–
The Newport News National Bank	6781	6	–
The Schmelz National Bank Of Newport News	11028	4	5
Norfolk			
National Bank Of Commerce Of Norfolk	9885	–	5
Norfolk National Bank Of Commerce & Trusts	6032	6	3
The City National Bank Of Norfolk	4743	6	–
The Colonial National Bank Of Norfolk	13343	–	–
The Continental National Bank Of Norfolk	12151	–	–
The Exchange National Bank Of Norfolk	1137	6	–
The First National Bank Of Norfolk	271	6	–
The National Bank Of Commerce Of Norfolk	6032	3	–
The Norfolk National Bank	3368	2	–
The Peoples National Bank Of Norfolk	1704	6	–
The Seaboard Citizens National Bank Of Norfolk	10194	2	2
The Seaboard National Bank Of Norfolk	10194	3	–
The Virginia National Bank Of Norfolk	9885	3	3
Norton			
The First National Bank Of Norton	6235	6	5
The National Bank Of Norton	9746	5	4
Onancock			
The First National Bank In Onancock	13878	–	6
The First National Bank Of Onancock	4940	6	5
Onley			
The Farmers And Merchants National Bank In Onley	14190	–	–
The Farmers And Merchants National Bank Of Onley	7258	5	6
Orange			
The American National Bank Of Orange	5532	6	–
The Citizens National Bank Of Orange	7150	4	4
The National Bank Of Orange	5438	5	5
Parksley			
The Parksley National Bank	6246	5	5
Pearisburg			
The First National Bank Of Pearisburg	8091	5	6
Penniman			
The First National Bank Of Penniman	11174	–	–
Pennington Gap			
The First National Bank Of Pennington Gap	11858	–	–
Petersburg			
First National Bank And Trust Company Of Petersburg	3515	–	4
The Citizens National Bank Of Petersburg	13792	–	6
The Commercial National Bank Of Petersburg	1769	6	–
The First National Bank Of Petersburg	1378	6	–
The Merchants National Bank Of Petersburg	1548	6	–
The National Bank Of Petersburg	3515	3	5
The Virginia National Bank Of Petersburg	7709	2	3
Phoebus			
The Old Point National Bank Of Phoebus	12267	6	6
Pocahontas			
The First National Bank Of Pocahontas	7847	6	–
Poquoson			
The First National Bank Of Poquoson	12092	6	6
Portsmouth			
American National Bank Of Portsmouth	11381	3	4
The First National Bank Of Portsmouth	9300	5	–
Pulaski			
The Peoples National Bank Of Pulaski	11387	4	4
The Pulaski National Bank	4071	4	4
Purcellville			
The Purcellville National Bank	6018	5	4
Quantico			
The First National Bank Of Quantico	12477	–	4
Radford			
The Farmers And Merchants National Bank Of Radford	11690	6	6
The First And Merchants National Bank Of Radford	6782	–	6
The First National Bank Of Radford	6782	6	6

City, Bank	Ch. No.	L	S
Reedsville			
The Commonwealth National Bank Of Reedsville	10827	6	–
Richlands			
The First National Bank Of Richlands	10850	6	6
The Richlands National Bank	10857	6	6
Richmond			
National State And City Bank Of Richmond	8666	4	–
National State Bank Of Richmond	8666	6	–
The American National Bank Of Richmond	5229	1	–
The Broadway National Bank Of Richmond	10344	4	–
The Central National Bank Of Richmond	10080	2	2
The Farmers National Bank Of Richmond	1570	6	–
The First And Merchants National Bank Of Richmond	1111	–	–
The First National Bank Of Richmond	1111	2	–
The Merchants National Bank Of Richmond	1754	5	–
The National Bank Of Virginia, Of Richmond	1125	4	–
The National Exchange Bank Of Richmond	1155	6	–
The Planters National Bank Of Richmond	1628	4	–
Roanoke			
The American National Bank Of Roanoke	10532	5	–
The Citizens National Bank Of Roanoke	4531	6	–
The City National Bank Of Roanoke	8152	5	–
The Colonial National Bank Of Roanoke	11817	5	–
The Colonial-American National Bank Of Roanoke	11817	–	3
The Commercial National Bank Of Roanoke	4026	6	–
The First National Bank Of Roanoke	2737	4	–
The First National Exchange Bank Of Roanoke	2737	4	3
The Liberty National Bank Of Roanoke	11191	6	–
The National Exchange Bank Of Roanoke	4027	4	–
The Peoples National Bank Of Roanoke	6798	6	–
The Roanoke National Bank	2907	6	–
Rocky Mount			
The First National Bank Of Rocky Mount	6685	6	–
The Peoples National Bank Of Rocky Mount	8984	4	5
Rosslyn			
The Arlington National Bank Of Rosslyn	8389	6	–
Round Hill			
The Round Hill National Bank	11569	6	5
Rural Retreat			
The First National Bank Of Rural Retreat	10061	5	5
Saint Paul			
St. Paul National Bank	8547	4	5
Salem			
The Farmers National Bank Of Salem	1824	5	5
Saltville			
The First National Bank Of Saltville	11265	6	5
Scottsville			
The Scottsville National Bank	5725	5	4
Shenandoah			
The First National Bank Of Shenandoah	11133	–	–
South Boston			
Planters & Merchants First Natl Bank Of South Boston	8643	6	6
Planters And Merchants National Bank Of South Boston	8643	4	–
The Boston National Bank Of South Boston	8414	3	5
The First National Bank Of South Boston	5872	5	–
Stanley			
The Farmers And Merchants National Bank Of Stanley	10973	6	4
Staunton			
The Augusta National Bank Of Staunton	2269	5	5
The First National Bank Of Staunton	1585	6	–
The National Valley Bank Of Staunton	1620	3	4
The Staunton National Bank	6903	5	–
The Staunton National Bank And Trust Company	6903	6	5
The Staunton National Bank, Staunton	6903	–	–
Strasburg			
The First National Bank Of Strasburg	8746	–	5
The Massanutten National Bank Of Strasburg	8753	6	2
The Peoples National Bank Of Strasburg	8746	6	–
Stuart			
The First National Bank Of Stuart	11901	5	4
Suffolk			
National Bank Of Suffolk	9733	4	4
The First National Bank Of Suffolk	4047	6	–
Tazewell			
Tazewell National Bank	6123	6	5
The Farmers National Bank Of Tazewell	11533	6	6
Troutdale			
The First National Bank Of Troutdale	11990	6	6
Troutville			
The First National Bank Of Troutville	9764	6	6
Victoria			
The First National Bank Of Victoria	12183	6	6
The Peoples National Bank Of Victoria	14337	–	–
Vienna			
The Vienna National Bank	11764	6	–
Vinton			
The First National Bank Of Vinton	11911	6	–
Warrenton			
The Fauquier National Bank Of Warrenton	6126	5	5
The Fauquier National Bank Of Warrenton	12966	–	–
The Peoples National Bank Of Warrenton	9642	5	5
Washington			
The Rappahannock National Bank Of Washington	6443	6	6
Waverly			
The First National Bank Of Waverly	10914	5	–
Waynesboro			
The First National Bank Of Waynesboro	7587	6	4
The Waynesboro National Bank	9261	6	–
Williamsburg			
The First National Bank Of Williamsburg	10882	–	–
Winchester			
Farmers & Merchants Natl Bank & Trust Co Of Winchester	6084	5	5
The Farmers And Merchants National Bank Of Winchester	6084	3	–
The Shenandoah Valley National Bank Of Winchester	1635	3	4
Wise			
The First National Bank Of Wise	10611	6	6
The First National Bank Of Wise	10611	–	–
Woodstock			
The National Bank Of Woodstock	11941	–	–
The Shenandoah National Bank Of Woodstock	5449	6	–
Wytheville			
The First National Bank Of Wytheville	9012	4	5
The First National Farmers Bank Of Wytheville	9012	–	4
Wythe County National Bank Of Wytheville	12599	–	6
Yorktown			
The First National Bank Of Yorktown	11554	5	5

VIRGIN ISLANDS

City, Bank	Ch. No.	L	S
Saint Thomas			
The Virgin Islands National Bank Of Saint Thomas	14335	–	–

WASHINGTON TERR

City, Bank	Ch. No.	L	S
Colfax			
The First National Bank Of Colfax	3076	6	–
The Second National Bank Of Colfax	3119	6	–
Davenport			
The Big Bend National Bank Of Davenport	4002	6	–
Dayton			
The Columbia National Bank Of Dayton	2772	6	–
The First National Bank Of Dayton	2520	6	–
The National Bank Of Dayton	3799	6	–
Ellensburg			
The First National Bank Of Ellensburg	3037	6	–
Ellensburgh			
The Ellensburgh National Bank	3867	6	–
Goldendale			
The First National Bank Of Goldendale	4031	6	–
New Tacoma			
The Tacoma National Bank, New Tacoma	2924	6	–
North Yakima			
The First National Bank Of North Yakima	3355	6	–
The Yakima National Bank Of North Yakima	3862	6	–
Oakesdale			
The First National Bank Of Oakesdale	4122	6	–
Olympia			
The First National Bank Of Olympia	3024	6	–
Pomeroy			
The First National Bank Of Pomeroy	3460	6	–
Port Townsend			
The First National Bank Of Port Townsend	2948	6	–
Seattle			
The Boston National Bank Of Seattle	4124	6	–
The First National Bank Of Seattle	2783	6	–
The Merchants National Bank Of Seattle	2985	6	–
The Puget Sound National Bank Of Seattle	2966	6	–
The Washington National Bank Of Seattle	4059	6	–
Sehome			
The Bellingham Bay National Bank Of Sehome	3976	6	–
Snohomish			
The First National Bank Of Snohomish	3887	6	–
Spokane Falls			
The Browne Natoinal Bank Of Spokane Falls	4025	6	–
The Citizens National Bank Of Spokane Falls	4005	6	–
The Exchange National Bank Of Spokane Falls	4044	6	–
The First National Bank Of Spokane Falls	2805	6	–
The Spokane National Bank Of Spokane Falls	3838	6	–
The Traders National Bank Of Spokane Falls	3409	6	–
Sprague			
The First National Bank Of Sprague	3528	6	–
Tacoma			
The Citizens National Bank Of Tacoma	4069	6	–
The Merchants National Bank Of Tacoma	3172	6	–
The National Bank Of Commerce Of Tacoma	3789	6	–
The Pacific National Bank Of Tacoma	3417	6	–
The Tacoma National Bank, Tacoma	2924	6	–
The Washington National Bank Of Tacoma	4018	6	–
Vancouver			
The First National Bank Of Vancouver	3031	6	–
Walla Walla			
The Baker-boyer National Bank Of Walla Walla	3956	6	–
The First National Bank Of Walla Walla	2380	6	–
Whatcom			
The First National Bank Of Whatcom	4099	6	–
Yakima			
The First National Bank Of Yakima	2876	6	–

WASHINGTON

City, Bank	Ch. No.	L	S
Aberdeen			
First National Bank In Aberdeen	11751	6	5
The Aberdeen National Bank	11751	6	–
The American National Bank Of Aberdeen	13091	4	4
The First National Bank Of Aberdeen	4407	6	–
The Grays Harbor National Bank Of Aberdeen	12704	5	3
The United States National Bank Of Aberdeen	9535	6	–
Anacortes			
The First National Bank Of Anacortes	4458	6	–
Auburn			
The Auburn National Bank	12085	–	–
The Auburn National Bank	14038	–	–
The First National Bank Of Auburn	10585	–	–
Bellingham			
The American National Bank Of Bellingham	12234	–	–
The Bellingham National Bank	7474	4	4
The First National Bank Of Bellingham	7372	5	1
The Northwestern National Bank Of Bellingham	9070	6	6
Blaine			
The Blaine National Bank	4471	6	–
The First National Bank Of Blaine	4470	6	–
Bremerton			
The First National Bank Of Bremerton	9280	6	3
Brewster			
The First National Bank Of Brewster	9170	6	5
Burlington			
The Burlington National Bank	10648	6	–
The First National Bank Of Burlington	9808	6	5
Camas			
Clark County National Bank Of Vancouver	10686	–	6
The First National Bank Of Camas	10686	5	5
Camp Lewis			
Army National Bank Of Ft. Lewis	11805	–	–
The Army National Bank Of Camp Lewis	11805	–	–
Centralia			
First National Bank In Centralia	13099	6	5
The First National Bank Of Centralia	4439	6	–
The United States National Bank Of Centralia	8736	5	–
Chehalis			
First National Bank In Chehalis	9389	6	5
The Chehalis National Bank	9389	6	–
The First National Bank Of Chehalis	4203	6	–
Cheney			
The First National Bank Of Cheney	4542	6	–
The National Bank Of Cheney	9080	4	–
The Security National Bank Of Cheney	9144	6	4
Chewelah			
The First National Bank Of Chewelah	8789	6	4
Clarkston			
The First National Bank Of Clarkston	6742	5	–
Cle Elum			
The First National Bank Of Cle Elum	10469	6	4
Colfax			
The Colfax National Bank	7095	3	4
The Farmers National Bank Of Colfax	10511	–	3
The First National Bank Of Colfax	3076	6	–
The Second National Bank Of Colfax	3119	6	–
Colton			
The First National Bank Of Colton	4788	6	–
Colville			
The Colville Valley National Bank Of Colville	13724	–	–
The First National Bank Of Colville	8104	4	5
Connell			
The Connell National Bank	8958	6	–
Conway			
The First National Bank Of Conway	11984	6	5
Cosmopolis			
The First National Bank Of Cosmopolis	12509	–	–
Davenport			
The Big Bend National Bank Of Davenport	4002	6	–
The Davenport National Bank	7527	6	–
Dayton			
The Broughton National Bank Of Dayton	9443	5	3
The Citizens National Bank Of Dayton	4473	6	–
The Columbia National Bank Of Dayton	2772	5	4
The Dayton National Bank	8090	6	–
East Stanwood			
The National Bank Of East Stanwood	13439	–	5
Ellensburg			
The National Bank Of Ellensburg	11045	5	5
The Washington National Bank Of Ellensburg	9079	5	3
Ellensburgh			
The Ellensburgh National Bank	3867	5	–
The Kittitas Valley National Bank Of Ellensburgh	3867	6	–
Elma			
The First National Bank Of Elma	13233	–	–
Enumclaw			
The Enumclaw National Bank	12143	–	–
The First National Bank Of Enumclaw	12114	–	5
Ephrata			
The First National Bank Of Ephrata	11247	–	–
Everett			
Citizens Security National Bank Of Everett	11693	–	4
Security National Bank Of Everett	11693	–	3
The American National Bank Of Everett	6053	6	–
The Citizens National Bank And Trust Company Of Everett	13290	–	–
The Everett National Bank	4738	6	–
The First National Bank Of Everett	4686	4	3
The Puget Sound National Bank Of Everett	4796	6	–
The Security National Bank Of Everett	11693	5	–
Fairhaven			
The Bennett National Bank Of New Whatcom	4171	6	–
The Citizens National Bank Of Fairhaven	5243	6	–
The Fairhaven National Bank	4387	6	–
The First National Bank Of Fairhaven	4171	6	–
Ferndale			
The First National Bank Of Ferndale	11667	–	4
Garfield			
The Garfield National Bank	9185	5	3
The State National Bank Of Garfield	12231	–	5
Gig Harbor			
The First National Bank Of Gig Harbor	13057	–	6
Goldendale			
The First National Bank Of Goldendale	4031	6	–
The National Bank Of Goldendale	11750	–	–
Grandview			
The First National Bank Of Grandview	11546	–	–
Greenwood			
The First Greenwood National Bank, Greenwood	12851	–	–
The Greenwood National Bank	12851	–	–
Harrington			
The First National Bank Of Harrington	9210	6	–
Hoquiam			
The First National Bank Of Hoquiam	4427	4	3
The Hoquiam National Bank	4390	6	–
The Lumbermens National Bank And Trust Company Of Hoquiam	13201	–	–
Kelso			
The First National Bank Of Kelso	8639	3	6
Kennewick			
The First National Bank Of Kennewick	8948	5	6
Kent			
The First National Bank Of Kent	10174	6	5
The Kent National Bank	12217	–	5
Kirkland			
The First National Bank Of Kirkland	11864	–	–
Lind			
The First National Bank Of Lind	9101	6	5

City, Bank	Ch. No.	L	S
Longview			
The First National Bank Of Longview	12392	–	4
The Longview National Bank	12392	–	–
Lynden			
The First National Bank Of Lynden	11808	5	5
Mabton			
The First National Bank Of Mabton	9757	6	–
Malden			
The First National Bank Of Malden	9351	6	–
Medical Lake			
The First National Bank Of Medical Lake	9030	6	5
Monroe			
The First National Bank Of Monroe	9372	6	5
The Monroe National Bank	9478	6	4
Montesano			
First National Bank In Montesano	5472	–	4
The First National Bank Of Montesano	4779	6	–
The Montesano National Bank	5472	4	5
Mount Vernon			
The First National Bank Of Mount Vernon	4529	4	–
The Mount Vernon National Bank	10602	6	–
The Skagit National Bank Of Mount Vernon	12154	–	4
Newport			
The First National Bank Of Newport	8828	6	–
North Yakima			
First National Bank Of Yakima	3355	6	6
The First National Bank Of North Yakima	3355	6	–
The Yakima National Bank Of North Yakima	3862	6	–
The Yakima National Bank, Yakima	3862	6	6
Yakima First National Bank, Yakima	3355	–	2
Oakesdale			
The First National Bank Of Oakesdale	4122	6	–
The National Bank Of Oakesdale	9150	6	–
Odessa			
The First National Bank In Odessa	12170	–	–
The First National Bank Of Odessa	9052	6	–
Okanogan			
The First National Bank Of Okanogan	9411	5	3
Olympia			
The Capital National Bank Of Olympia	4297	5	3
The First National Bank Of Olympia	3024	6	–
The Olympia National Bank	5652	6	–
The Washington National Bank Of Olympia	13662	–	–
Oroville			
The First National Bank Of Oroville	8279	5	–
Palouse			
The Farmers National Bank Of Palouse	9499	6	–
The National Bank Of Palouse	9499	6	–
The Security National Bank Of Palouse	12184	–	4
Palouse City			
The First National Bank Of Palouse City	4186	6	–
Pasco			
The First National Bank Of Pasco	9265	5	–
Paulsbo			
The First National Bank Of Paulsbo	11285	–	–
Pomeroy			
The Farmers National Bank Of Pomeroy	11416	6	5
The First National Bank Of Pomeroy	3460	6	–
Port Angeles			
First National Bank In Port Angeles	6074	6	4
The Cain National Bank Of Port Angeles	6074	6	–
The Citizens National Bank Of Port Angeles	6074	6	–
The First National Bank Of Port Angeles	4315	6	–
Port Townsend			
The American National Bank Of Port Townsend	13351	–	6
The First American National Bank Of Port Townsend	13351	–	5
The First National Bank Of Port Townsend	2948	5	6
The Port Townsend National Bank	4290	6	–
Prosser			
The Benton County National Bank Of Prosser	9417	6	–
The First National Bank Of Prosser	7489	6	–
Pullman			
The First National Bank Of Pullman	4699	4	3
Puyallup			
The First National Bank Of Puyallup	4224	6	–
Quincy			
The First National Bank Of Quincy	9102	6	–
Raymond			
First Willapa Harbor National Bank Of Raymond	11672	–	–
The First National Bank Of Raymond	11672	6	5
Reardan			
The First National Bank Of Reardan	13444	–	3
Reardon			
The Reardon National Bank	10499	–	–
Redmond			
The First National Bank Of Redmond	12121	–	–
Renton			
The First National Bank Of Renton	12399	–	–
Ritzville			
The First National Bank Of Ritzville	5751	6	3
The Pioneer National Bank Of Ritzville	8743	6	–
Rosalia			
The Whitman County National Bank Of Rosalia	9273	5	4
Saint John			
The First National Bank Of Saint John	11172	–	–
Seattle			
Ballard First National Bank Of Seattle	13581	–	5
First National Bank Of Seattle	11280	–	1
First Seattle Dexter Horton National Bank, Seattle	11280	–	2
The Boston National Bank Of Seattle	4124	6	–
The Central National Bank Of Commerce	13470	–	–
The Citizens National Bank Of Seattle	9662	6	–
The Commercial National Bank Of Seattle	4397	6	–
The Dexter Horton National Bank Of Seattle	9798	6	–
The Dexter Horton National Bank Of Seattle	11280	3	5
The First National Bank Of Seattle	2783	5	6
The Horton National Trust And Savings Bank Of Seattle	12007	–	–
The Marine National Bank Of Seattle	11856	–	–
The Mercantile National Bank Of Seattle	9662	6	–
The Merchants National Bank Of Seattle	2985	6	–
The Metropolitan National Bank Of Seattle	11832	–	–
The National Bank Of Commerce Of Seattle	4375	4	3
The National City Bank Of Seattle	10026	5	–
The Pacific National Bank Of Seattle	13230	4	2
The Puget Sound National Bank Of Seattle	2966	6	–
The Seaboard National Bank Of Seattle	11146	–	–
The Seattle National Bank	4229	2	–
The Union National Bank Of Seattle	11280	5	–
The University National Bank Of Seattle	12153	3	3
The Washington National Bank Of Commerce	13471	–	–
The Washington National Bank Of Seattle	4059	6	–
Sedro-woolley			
The First National Bank Of Sedro-Woolley	7908	6	–
Sehome			
The Bellingham Bay National Bank Of New Whatcom	3976	6	–
The Bellingham Bay National Bank Of Sehome	3976	6	–
The Columbia National Bank Of New Whatcom	4351	6	–
The Columbia National Bank Of Sehome	4351	6	–
Selah			
The First National Bank Of Selah	11674	–	–
Shelton			
The First National Bank Of Shelton	13723	–	–
Slaughter			
The First National Bank Of Slaughter	4457	6	–
Snohomish			
The First National Bank Of Snohomish	3887	5	6
The Snohomish National Bank	4526	6	–
South Bend			
The First National Bank In South Bend	12269	–	–
The First National Bank Of Ilwaco	12269	–	–
The First National Bank Of South Bend	4467	6	–
Spokane			
City National Bank Of Spokane	12418	6	–
First National Bank In Spokane	13331	–	–
The Brotherhoods Co-operative National Bank Of Spokane	12418	4	–
The First National Bank Of Hillyard, Spokane	9182	6	5
The First National Trust And Savings Bank Of Spokane	13331	–	3
The National Bank Of Commerce Of Spokane	9589	5	–
The Old National Bank And Union Trust Company Of Spokane	4668	3	2
The Old National Bank Of Spokane	4668	2	–
Spokane Falls			
The Browne National Bank Of Spokane Falls	4025	6	–
The Citizens National Bank Of Spokane Falls	4005	6	–
The Exchange National Bank Of Spokane	4044	2	–
The Exchange National Bank Of Spokane Falls	4044	6	–
The First National Bank Of Spokane	2805	6	–
The Spokane National Bank Of Spokane Falls	3838	6	–
The Traders National Bank Of Spokane	3409	5	–
The Traders National Bank Of Spokane Falls	3409	6	–
The Washington National Bank Of Spokane Falls	4277	6	–
Sprague			
The Fidelity National Bank Of Spokane	3528	4	
The First National Bank In Sprague	12180	–	–
The First National Bank Of Sprague	3528	6	–
Stanwood			
The First National Bank Of Stanwood	11935	–	4
The Stanwood National Bank	13374	–	–
Sunnyside			
First National Bank Of Sunnyside	8481	5	–
The First National Bank Of Sunnyside	8481	–	4
The Sunnyside National Bank	12181	–	–
Tacoma			
The Brotherhood Co-operative National Bank Of Tacoma	12667	4	4
The Citizens National Bank Of Tacoma	4069	6	–
The Columbia National Bank Of Tacoma	4623	6	–
The Lumbermens National Bank Of Tacoma	6006	6	–
The Merchants National Bank Of Tacoma	3172	6	–
The National Bank Of Commerce Of Tacoma	3789	4	–
The National Bank Of Tacoma	3417	3	2
The National Bank Of The Republic, Tacoma	4426	6	–
The Pacific National Bank Of Tacoma	3417	4	–
The Puget Sound National Bank Of Tacoma	12292	6	3
The Tacoma National Bank, Tacoma	2924	6	–
The Washington National Bank In The City Of Tacoma	12667	–	5
The Washington National Bank Of Tacoma	4018	6	–
Tonasket			
First National Bank In Tonasket	14166	–	6
The First National Bank Of Tonasket	10407	5	6
Toppenish			
The First National Bank Of Toppenish	7767	6	6
Vancouver			
The Citizens National Bank Of Vancouver	8987	6	–
The First National Bank Of Vancouver	3031	6	–
The United States National Bank Of Vancouver	9646	5	4
The Vancouver National Bank	6013	3	3
The Washington National Bank Of Vancouver	13137	–	3
Vancouver National Bank	14186	–	–
Waitsburg			
The First National Bank Of Waitsburg	4681	6	–
The First National Bank Of Waitsburg	8895	5	4
Walla Walla			
The Baker-boyer National Bank Of Walla Walla	3956	5	5
The First National Bank Of Walla Walla	2380	3	–
The Third National Bank Of Walla Walla	9068	6	–
Wapato			
The First National Bank Of Wapato	9129	6	5
Washtucna			
The First National Bank Of Washtucna	9054	6	–
Waterville			
The First National Bank Of Waterville	4532	6	–
Wenatchee			
The First National Bank Of Wenatchee	8064	4	3
Whatcom			
The First National Bank Of Whatcom	4099	6	–
White Salmon			
The First National Bank Of White Salmon	10000	6	–
Yakima			
The West Side National Bank Of Yakima	12246	–	–
Zillah			
The First National Bank Of Zillah	9576	6	6

WEST VIRGINIA

City, Bank	Ch. No.	L	S
Albright			
Albright National Bank Of Kingwood	10480	–	–
The First National Bank Of Albright	10480	6	4
Alderson			
The Alderson National Bank	9523	6	6
The First National Bank Of Alderson	5903	5	5
Anawalt			
The First National Bank Of Anawalt	10392	6	6
Ansted			
The Ansted National Bank	8904	5	6
The National Bank Of Ansted	14318	–	–
Bayard			
The Bayard National Bank	11664	6	6
Beckley			
Beckley National Exchange Bank	10589	–	5
The Beckley National Bank	10589	5	6
The First National Bank Of Beckley	6735	6	–
The Peoples National Bank Of Beckley	9038	6	–
Belington			
The Belington National Bank	6634	6	–
The Citizens National Bank Of Belington	6618	6	–
The First National Bank Of Belington	6619	6	5
Berkeley Springs			
The Citizens National Bank Of Berkeley Springs	14198	–	–
Berwind			
The Berwind National Bank	9909	6	–
Bluefield			
The American National Bank Of Bluefield, West Virginia	7734	6	–
The Bluefield National Bank	11109	6	4
The First National Bank Of Bluefield	4643	5	5
The Flat Top National Bank Of Bluefield	6674	4	5
The Flat Top National Bank Of Bluefield	11109	–	4
Bridgeport			
The First National Bank Of Bridgeport	11877	–	–
Buckhannon			
The Central National Bank Of Buckhannon	13646	–	4
The Traders National Bank Of Buckhannon	4760	5	6
Cameron			
The First National Bank Of Cameron	6020	5	5
Ceredo			
The First National Bank Of Ceredo	4775	5	4
Charles Town			
The National Citizens Bank Of Charles Town	7270	5	5
Charleston			
The Charleston National Bank	3236	2	2
The Citizens National Bank Of Charleston	4412	5	–
The First National Bank Of Charleston	1795	6	–
The First National Bank Of Jefferson At Charlestown	1868	6	–
The Kanawha National Bank Of Charleston	4667	3	5
The National Bank Of Commerce Of Charleston	13509	–	4
The National City Bank Of Charleston	8569	5	–
Chester			
The First National Bank Of Chester	6984	6	6
Clark			
The Clark National Bank	10157	6	6
Clarksburg			
The Empire National Bank Of Clarksburg	7029	2	3
The Merchants National Bank Of West Virginia At Clarksburg	1530	4	4
The Traders National Bank Of Clarksburg	4569	5	–
The Union National Bank Of Clarksburg	7681	2	2
Clendenin			
The First National Bank Of Clendenin	7275	6	6
Cowen			
The First National Bank Of Cowen	10559	–	–
Davis			
The National Bank Of Davis	4828	6	6
East Rainelle			
The First National Bank Of East Rainelle	12565	–	–
Eccles			
The National Exchange Bank Of Beckley	12283	–	–
The National Exchange Bank Of Eccles	12283	–	–
Elkins			
Citizens National Bank Of Elkins	12483	6	5
The Elkins National Bank	4718	6	6
The Peoples National Bank Of Elkins	8376	6	5
The Randolph National Bank Of Elkins	7060	6	–
The Tygarts Valley National Bank Of Elkins	14002	–	3
Elm Grove			
The First National Bank And Trust Company Of Elm Grove	8983	5	4
The First National Bank Of Elm Grove	8983	6	–
Fairmont			
First National Bank In Fairmont	13811	–	4
The First National Bank Of Fairmont	961	3	–
The National Bank Of Fairmont	9462	2	3
The Peoples National Bank Of Fairmont	9645	3	5
The Union National Bank Of Fairmont	9645	–	5
Fairview			
The First National Bank Of Fairview	10219	5	5
Fayetteville			
The Fayette County National Bank Of Fayetteville	8345	6	6
The Fayetteville National Bank	5434	6	–
Friendly			
The First National Bank Of Friendly	5814	6	–
Gary			
Gary National Bank	13505	–	6
The Gary National Bank	8333	6	6
Glenville			
The First National Bank Of Glenville	5939	6	–
Gormania			
The First National Bank Of Gormania	8751	6	5
Grafton			
The First National Bank Of Grafton	2445	4	4
Griffithsville			
The Oil Field National Bank Of Griffithsville	10097	5	5

City, Bank	Ch. No.	L	S
Hamlin			
The Lincoln National Bank Of Hamlin	8171	6	6
Harrisville			
The First National Bank Of Harrisville	6790	5	–
Hendricks			
The First National Bank Of Hendricks	7845	5	6
Hinton			
The Citizens National Bank Of Hinton	10348	6	5
The First National Bank Of Hinton	5562	4	3
The National Bank Of Summers Of Hinton	7998	5	4
Huntington			
The American National Bank Of Huntington	9598	5	–
The Commercial National Bank Of Huntington	4607	6	–
The First Huntington National Bank, Huntington	3106	2	2
The First National Bank Of Huntington	3106	2	–
The Huntington National Bank, Huntington	4607	3	–
The West Virginia National Bank Of Huntington	7359	5	–
Hurricane			
The Hurricane National Bank	11670	6	–
Iaeger			
The First National Bank Of Iaeger	11268	6	6
The Tug River National Bank Of Iaeger	12372	5	–
Kenova			
The First National Bank Of Kenova	9913	6	4
Keyser			
The First National Bank Of Keyser	6205	5	4
The National Bank Of Keyser	13831	–	4
Keystone			
The First National Bank Of Keystone	10369	5	6
Kimball			
The First National Bank Of Kimball	11502	6	6
The Kimball National Bank	13484	–	6
Kingwood			
The Kingwood National Bank	6332	6	–
The National Bank Of Kingwood	1608	6	–
Logan			
The First National Bank Of Logan	8136	5	6
The Logan National Bank	8136	6	–
The National Bank Of Logan	13954	–	6
Madison			
Boone National Bank Of Madison	6510	–	5
The Madison National Bank	6510	5	–
Mannington			
The First National Bank Of Mannington	5012	5	5
Marlinton			
First National Bank In Marlinton	13783	–	6
The First National Bank Of Marlinton	6538	6	5
Martinsburg			
The Citizens National Bank Of Martinsburg	4811	3	4
The National Bank Of Martinsburg	1524	6	–
The Old National Bank Of Martinsburg	6283	5	3
The Peoples National Bank Of Martinsburg	2144	6	–
Matewan			
The Matewan National Bank	10370	6	5
Matoaka			
The First National Bank Of Matoaka	11264	5	–
The Matoaka National Bank	12839	6	5
Middlebourne			
The First National Bank Of Middlebourne	6170	5	6
Milton			
The Milton National Bank	12765	6	–
Monongah			
The First National Bank Of Monongah	7545	6	6
Montgomery			
The Merchants National Bank Of Montgomery	9740	5	4
The Montgomery National Bank	5691	4	4
Moorefield			
The South Branch Valley National Bank Of Moorefield	3029	4	4
Morgantown			
The Citizens National Bank Of Morgantown	5583	5	–
The Merchants National Bank Of West Virginia At Morgantown	1502	6	–
The Second National Bank Of Morgantown	2458	5	5
Moundsville			
First National Bank At Moundsville	14142	–	5
The First National Bank Of Moundsville	5717	4	5
Mount Hope			
The First National Bank Of Mount Hope	11049	6	5
Mullens			
The First National Bank Of Mullens	12270	–	–
New Cumberland			
The First National Bank Of New Cumberland	6582	6	–
New Martinsville			
The First National Bank Of New Martinsville	5266	4	5
Newburg			
The First National Bank Of Newburg	7626	5	6
Northfork			
The First Clark National Bank Of Northfork	8309	–	5
The First National Bank Of Northfork	8309	4	4
Oak Hill			
The First National Bank Of Oak Hill	14034	–	–
The Merchants And Miners National Bank Of Oak Hill	13885	–	–
The Oak Hill National Bank	12075	5	5
Parkersburg			
The Citizens National Bank Of Parkersburg	2649	3	5
The Farmers And Mechanics National Bank Of Parkersburg	5320	5	–
The First National Bank Of Parkersburg	180	2	3
The Parkersburg National Bank	1427	4	3
The Peoples National Bank Of Parkersburg	13621	–	4
The Second National Bank Of Parkersburg	864	4	–
Parsons			
The First National Bank Of Parsons	9610	6	4
Pennsboro			
First Citizens National Bank Of Pennsboro	7191	–	5
The Citizens National Bank Of Pennsboro	7246	6	6
The First National Bank Of Pennsboro	7191	5	6
Peterstown			
The First National Bank Of Peterstown	9721	6	5
Philippi			
First National Bank In Philippi	14053	–	6
The Citizens National Bank Of Philippi	6377	5	5
The First National Bank Of Philippi	6302	5	6
Piedmont			
The Davis National Bank Of Piedmont	4088	5	4
The First National Bank Of Piedmont	3629	5	3
The National Bank Of Piedmont	1883	5	–
Pineville			
The Citizens National Bank Of Pineville	8749	6	–
The First National Bank Of Pineville	7672	6	6
Point Pleasant			
Citizens National Bank Of Point Pleasant	13231	–	4
The Merchants National Bank Of Point Pleasant	1504	4	–
The Merchants Natl Bank Of West Virginia At Point Pleasant	1504	5	–
The Point Pleasant National Bank	5701	5	5
Princeton			
The First National Bank Of Princeton	8219	5	6
Ravenswood			
The First National Bank Of Ravenswood	10759	–	6
Reedy			
The First National Bank Of Reedy	10285	6	3
Richwood			
Cherry River National Bank Of Richwood	13627	–	–
Cherry River National Bank, Richwood	13627	–	4
The First National Bank Of Richwood	8434	5	5
Ripley			
The First National Bank Of Ripley	10762	6	5
Romney			
The First National Bank Of Romney	9766	6	4
Ronceverte			
First National Bank In Ronceverte	13830	–	–
The First National Bank Of Ronceverte	5280	5	5
The Ronceverte National Bank	6226	6	6
Rowlesburg			
The First National Bank Of Rowlesburg	9288	6	–
The Peoples National Bank Of Rowlesburg	10250	4	5
Salem			
First National Bank At Salem	14136	–	–
The First National Bank Of Salem	7250	4	5
Shinnston			
The First National Bank Of Shinnston	9453	6	–
Sistersville			
The Farmers And Producers National Bank Of Sistersville	5028	5	–
The First National Bank Of Sistersville	5027	4	–
The Peoples National Bank Of Sistersville	6548	5	–
The Union National Bank Of Sistersville	5028	4	3
South Charleston			
The First National Bank Of South Charleston	11340	6	4
Spencer			
The First National Bank Of Spencer	10127	5	4
St. Albans			
The First National Bank Of St. Albans	9640	6	3
St. Marys			
The First National Bank Of St. Marys	5226	4	3
Sutton			
The First National Bank Of Sutton	6213	6	–
The Home National Bank Of Sutton	9604	5	4
Terra Alta			
The First National Bank Of Terra Alta	6999	4	3
Thurmond			
National Bank Of Thurmond	8998	5	6
Webster Springs			
The First National Bank Of Webster Springs	8360	6	6
The Webster Springs National Bank	14013	–	6
Welch			
Mcdowell County National Bank In Welch	13512	–	4
Mcdowell County National Bank Of Welch	9071	5	6
The First National Bank Of Welch	9048	5	6
Wellsburg			
The First National Bank Of Wellsburg	1387	6	–
The Wellsburg National Bank	1884	5	5
Wellsburg National Bank	14295	–	6
West Union			
First National Bank In West Union	13881	–	6
The First National Bank Of West Union	6424	6	5
Weston			
The National Exchange Bank Of Weston	1607	4	6
The Weston National Bank	13634	–	4
Wheeling			
The Citizens National Bank Of Wheeling	10455	6	–
The First National Bank Of Wheeling	360	6	–
The Merchants National Bank Of West Virginia, Wheeling	1343	6	–
The National Bank Of West Virginia, Wheeling	1424	3	2
The National Exchange Bank Of Wheeling	5164	2	2
The National Savings Bank Of Wheeling	1594	6	–
Williamson			
The First National Bank Of Williamson	6830	5	4
The National Bank Of Commerce Of Williamson	10067	5	4
Williamstown			
The Farmers And Mechanics National Bank Of Williamstown	11483	6	6
The Williamstown National Bank	6233	6	–
Winona			
The Winona National Bank	9850	6	6
Worthington			
The First National Bank Of Worthington	10450	5	6

WISCONSIN

City, Bank	Ch. No.	L	S
Alma			
The First National Bank Of Alma	8338	5	–
Antigo			
The First National Bank Of Antigo	5143	3	3
The Langlade National Bank Of Antigo	5942	3	4
Appleton			
First National Bank Of Appleton	1749	4	2
The Appleton National Bank Of Appleton	1650	6	–
The Citizens National Bank Of Appleton	4937	3	3
The Commercial National Bank Of Appleton	2565	3	–
The First National Bank Of Appleton	1749	3	–
The Manufacturers National Bank Of Appleton	1820	6	–
Ashland			
The Ashland National Bank	3196	4	4
The First National Bank Of Ashland	3590	5	–
The Northern National Bank Of Ashland	3607	4	4
The Union National Bank Of Ashland	13870	–	5
Baldwin			
The First National Bank Of Baldwin	10106	5	4
Bangor			
The First National Bank Of Bangor	13202	6	4
Baraboo			
First National Bank And Trust Company Of Baraboo	3609	–	5
The First National Bank Of Baraboo	2079	6	–
The First National Bank Of Baraboo	3609	3	4
The First National Bank Of Baraboo	14060	–	–
Barron			
The First National Bank Of Barron	10890	–	–
Bayfield			
The First National Bank Of Bayfield	7158	4	5
Beaver Dam			
The American National Bank Of Beaver Dam	4602	4	3
The First National Bank Of Beaver Dam	3270	6	–
The German National Bank Of Beaver Dam	4602	4	–
The National Bank Of Beaver Dam	851	6	–
The Old National Bank Of Beaver Dam	7462	4	3
Beloit			
The Beloit National Bank	836	6	–
The Citizens National Bank Of Beloit	2407	6	–
The First National Bank Of Beloit	2163	6	–
The Second National Bank Of Beloit	2725	5	5
Berlin			
The Berlin National Bank	4641	6	–
The First National Bank Of Berlin	400	6	–
The First National Bank Of Berlin	4620	2	3
Black River Falls			
The First National Bank Of Black River Falls	3897	4	5
Blair			
The First National Bank Of Blair	10667	5	5
Blanchardville			
The First National Bank Of Blanchardville	11114	5	5
Boscobel			
The First National Bank Of Boscobel	1771	5	–
Boyceville			
The First National Bank Of Boyceville	11128	6	–
Brillion			
The First National Bank Of Brillion	7224	4	3
Brodhead			
The First National Bank Of Brodhead	1710	6	–
Bruce			
The First National Bank Of Bruce	11986	–	–
Burlington			
The Burlington National Bank	11783	4	2
The First National Bank Of Burlington	1933	5	–
Campbellsport			
The First National Bank Of Campbellsport	6222	6	–
Cedarburg			
The First National Bank Of Cedarburg	1415	6	–
Chilton			
The Chilton National Bank	5933	4	4
Chippewa Falls			
The First National Bank Of Chippewa Falls	2125	3	3
The Lumbermen's National Bank Of Chippewa Falls	3778	4	3
Clintonville			
The Clintonville National Bank	14242	–	–
The First National Bank Of Clintonville	6273	3	4
Columbus			
The First National Bank Of Columbus	178	4	3
Crandon			
Crandon National Bank	12814	4	4
The First National Bank Of Crandon	9387	5	–
Cuba City			
The First National Bank Of Cuba City	5632	5	–
Dale			
The First National Bank Of Dale	8118	5	4
Darlington			
First National Bank At Darlington	14184	–	4
The Citizens National Bank Of Darlington	3308	4	4
The First National Bank Of Darlington	3161	3	3
De Pere			
The First National Bank Of De Pere	2133	6	–
The National Bank Of De Pere	6469	3	4
Deerfield			
The First National Bank Of Deerfield	11577	6	–
Delavan			
The National Bank Of Delavan	1248	6	–
Dodgeville			
The First National Bank Of Dodgeville	6698	4	3
Durand			
The First National Bank In Durand	13529	–	4
The First National Bank Of Durand	10791	5	5
The Security National Bank Of Durand	14095	–	4
Eagle River			
The First National Bank Of Eagle River	12124	6	3
Eau Claire			
The American National Bank And Trust Company Of Eau Claire	13645	–	3
The Eau Claire National Bank	2759	2	3
The First National Bank Of Eau Claire	2069	5	–
The Union National Bank Of Eau Claire	8281	2	2
Edgerton			
The First National Bank Of Edgerton	7040	4	3
The National Bank Of Edgerton	13932	–	4
Elkhorn			
The First National Bank Of Elkhorn	873	4	3
Evansville			
The First National Bank Of Evansville	1729	6	–
Fairchild			
The First National Bank Of Fairchild	7264	6	6
Fennimore			
The First National Bank In Fennimore	13599	–	5
The First National Bank Of Fennimore	9522	4	5

City, Bank	Ch. No.	L	S
Fond Du Lac			
First-Fond Du Lac National Bank, Fond Du Lac	555	2	–
The Commercial National Bank Of Fond Du Lac	6015	2	2
The First National Bank Of Fond Du Lac	555	5	–
The First-Fond Du Lac National Bank, Fond Du Lac	555	–	2
The Fond Du Lac National Bank	3685	3	–
The National Exchange Bank Of Fond Du Lac	13879	–	–
Fort Atkinson			
The First National Bank Of Fort Atkinson	157	4	4
Fort Howard			
The Mccartney National Bank Of Fort Howard	4783	4	–
The Mccartney National Bank Of Green Bay	4783	3	4
Fox Lake			
The First National Bank Of Fox Lake	426	5	–
Frederic			
The First National Bank Of Frederic	8491	5	5
Glenwood City			
The Farmers National Bank Of Glenwood City	11083	5	5
Grand Rapids			
The Citizens National Bank Of Grand Rapids	10330	3	–
The Citizens National Bank Of Wisconsin Rapids	10330	5	4
The First National Bank Of Grand Rapids	1998	3	–
The First National Bank Of Wisconsin Rapids	1998	4	2
The Wood County National Bank Of Grand Rapids	4639	2	–
The Wood County National Bank Of Wisconsin Rapids	4639	5	2
Grantsburg			
The First National Bank Of Grantsburg	8444	6	4
Green Bay			
Kellogg-Citizens National Bank Of Green Bay	2132	5	2
The Citizens National Bank Of Green Bay	3884	2	–
The City National Bank Of Green Bay	1009	6	–
The First National Bank Of Green Bay	874	6	–
The Kellogg National Bank Of Green Bay	2132	3	–
The National Bank Of Commerce Of Green Bay	1819	6	–
Hartford			
The First National Bank Of Hartford	8671	3	4
Hayward			
The First National Bank Of Hayward	7831	6	–
The Peoples National Bank Of Hayward	12644	–	–
Highland			
The First National Bank Of Highland	10880	–	–
Horicon			
The First National Bank Of Horicon	11104	–	–
Hudson			
The First National Bank Of Hudson	95	4	4
The National Bank Of Hudson	10510	–	–
Hurley			
The First National Bank Of Hurley	4304	6	–
The Hurley National Bank	11594	5	4
Janesville			
The First National Bank Of Janesville	83	6	–
The First National Bank Of Janesville	2748	4	3
The Rock County National Bank Of Janesville	749	4	4
Jefferson			
The National Bank Of Jefferson	1076	6	–
Kaukauna			
The First National Bank Of Kaukauna	3641	4	5
Kenosha			
The Brown National Bank Of Kenosha	12541	–	–
The First National Bank Of Kenosha	212	4	3
United States National Bank And Trust Company Of Kenosha	12351	6	3
United States National Bank Of Kenosha	12351	4	–
Knapp			
The First National Bank Of Knapp	11245	–	–
La Crosse			
The Batavian National Bank Of La Crosse	7347	3	3
The First National Bank Of La Crosse	1313	6	–
The La Crosse National Bank	2344	1	–
The National Bank Of La Crosse	5047	2	2
The Union National Bank Of La Crosse	3412	6	–
Ladysmith			
The First National Bank Of Ladysmith	5535	6	–
The Ladysmith National Bank	7966	5	–
The Pioneer National Bank Of Ladysmith	11826	5	4
Lake Geneva			
The Farmers National Bank Of Lake Geneva	5592	5	4
The First National Bank Of Lake Geneva	3125	4	4
Lancaster			
The First National Bank Of Lancaster	7007	6	–
Madison			
The Commercial National Bank Of Madison	9153	3	3
The First National Bank Of Madison	144	3	1
The University Avenue National Bank Of Madison	13366	–	–
Maiden Rock			
The First National Bank Of Maiden Rock	11432	–	–
Manawa			
The First National Bank Of Manawa	8710	3	4
Manitowoc			
First National Bank In Manitowoc	4975	3	2
Manitowoc National Bank, Manitowoc	13921	–	–
The First National Bank Of Manitowoc	852	6	–
The Manitowoc National Bank	13921	–	–
The National Bank Of Manitowoc	4975	2	–
Marinette			
The First National Bank Of Marinette	4123	4	4
The Stephenson National Bank Of Marinette	4137	3	3
Marion			
First National Bank In Marion	14130	–	5
The First National Bank Of Marion	12286	5	4
The German-american National Bank Of Marion	8887	–	–
Marshfield			
The American National Bank Of Marshfield	5437	4	3
The Citizens National Bank Of Marshfield	14125	–	4
The First National Bank Of Marshfield	4573	4	4
Mayville			
The First National Bank Of Mayville	10653	5	4
The First National Bank Of Mayville	14059	–	–
Medford			
The First National Bank Of Medford	5695	4	2
Menasha			
The First National Bank Of Menasha	3724	3	3
The National Bank Of Menasha	1714	6	–
Menominie			
The First National Bank Of Menominie	2851	2	2
Merrill			
The Citizens National Bank Of Merrill	10176	3	3
The First National Bank Of Merrill	3704	6	–
The National Bank Of Merrill	4736	4	–
Milwaukee			
Bay View National Bank Of Milwaukee	12816	–	4
First Wisconsin National Bank Of Milwaukee	2715	1	1
Marine National Exchange Bank Of Milwaukee	5458	–	1
Sixth Wisconsin National Bank Of Milwaukee	12628	4	3
The American National Bank Of Milwaukee	12482	–	–
The Central National Bank Of Milwaukee	4816	6	–
The First National Bank Of Milwaukee	64	2	–
The First National Bank Of Milwaukee	64	6	–
The First National Bank Of Milwaukee	2715	1	–
The Germania National Bank Of Milwaukee	6853	3	–
The Grand And Sixth National Bank Of Milwaukee	12628	5	–
The Marine National Bank Of Milwaukee	5458	1	3
The Mechanics National Bank Of Milwaukee	12816	4	5
The Merchants National Bank Of Milwaukee	1438	6	–
The Milwaukee National Bank Of Wisconsin	1017	3	–
The National Bank Of Commerce Of Milwaukee	6853	2	2
The National City Bank Of Milwaukee	1483	6	–
The National Exchange Bank Of Milwaukee	1003	2	2
The Northwestern National Bank Of Milwaukee	12564	3	4
The Second Wisconsin National Bank Of Milwaukee	13184	–	–
The Wisconsin National Bank Of Milwaukee	4817	1	–
Mineral Point			
The First National Bank Of Mineral Point	3203	6	–
Mondovi			
The First National Bank Of Mondovi	5779	5	4
Monroe			
The First National Bank Of Monroe	230	3	2
Neenah			
The First National Bank Of Neenah	1602	6	4
The Manufacturers National Bank Of Neenah	2603	4	–
The National Bank Of Neenah	1602	6	–
The National Manufacturers Bank Of Neenah	6034	3	4
Neillsville			
First National Bank Of Neillsville	9606	–	3
The First National Bank At Neillsville	14200	–	5
The First National Bank Of Neillsville	9606	4	–
Nelson			
The First National Bank Of Nelson	10733	–	–
New London			
The First National Bank Of New London	5013	5	4
New Richmond			
The First National Bank Of New Richmond	11412	5	4
Niagara			
The First National Bank Of Niagara	11051	5	5
Oconomowoc			
The First National Bank Of Oconomowoc	5505	3	4
The Oconomowoc National Bank	13616	–	4
Oconto			
The Citizens National Bank Of Oconto	5521	3	4
The First National Bank Of Oconto	14233	–	–
The Oconto National Bank	3541	4	4
Omro			
The First National Bank Of Omro	5566	6	–
Oregon			
The First National Bank Of Oregon	10620	5	5
Oshkosh			
First National Bank In Oshkosh	6604	4	1
The City National Bank Of Oshkosh	9347	2	3
The Commercial National Bank Of Oshkosh	1568	6	–
The Commercial National Bank Of Oshkosh	5557	3	–
The First National Bank Of Oshkosh	218	6	–
The German National Bank Of Oshkosh	4196	5	–
The National Bank Of Oshkosh	2877	6	–
The National Union Bank Of Oshkosh	4508	4	–
The Old Commercial National Bank Of Oshkosh	6604	3	–
The Old National Bank Of Oshkosh	6604	4	–
The Oshkosh National Bank	13806	–	3
The Union National Bank Of Oshkosh	1787	6	–
Park Falls			
The First National Bank Of Park Falls	10489	5	4
Pepin			
The First National Bank Of Pepin	10725	–	–
Peshtigo			
The Peshtigo National Bank	5658	5	5
Phillips			
First National Bank In Phillips	13487	–	2
The First National Bank Of Phillips	7434	3	5
Platteville			
The First National Bank Of Platteville	4650	4	4
Port Washington			
The First National Bank Of Port Washington	9419	5	3
Portage			
The First National Bank Of Portage	4234	3	4
Prescott			
The First National Bank Of Prescott	10522	6	4
Princeton			
Farmers-Merchants National Bank In Princeton	13904	–	5
The Farmers-Merchants National Bank Of Princeton	12575	–	–
The First National Bank Of Princeton	5978	5	–
Racine			
First National Bank And Trust Company Of Racine	457	–	2
The American National Bank Of Racine	10938	6	–
The First National Bank Of Racine	457	4	–
The Manufacturers National Bank & Trust Company Of Racine	1802	–	–
The Manufacturers National Bank Of Racine	1802	4	–
The Union National Bank Of Racine	2557	6	–
Rhinelander			
The First National Bank Of Rhinelander	4312	4	3
The Oneida National Bank Of Rhinelander	11646	4	4
Rib Lake			
The First National Bank Of Rib Lake	6711	5	4
Rice Lake			
The First National Bank Of Rice Lake	6663	5	2
Richland Center			
The First National Bank Of Richland Center	7901	5	–
Rio			
The First National Bank Of Rio	8632	6	6
Ripon			
The American National Bank Of Ripon	4305	4	5
The First National Bank Of Ripon	425	2	2
The German National Bank Of Ripon	4305	2	–
The Ripon National Bank	3146	6	–
River Falls			
The First National Bank Of River Falls	7087	6	–
Saint Croix Falls			
The First National Bank Of Saint Croix Falls	11526	6	–
Seymour			
The First National Bank Of Seymour	6575	4	3
Shawano			
The First National Bank Of Shawano	5469	3	4
The German-american National Bank Of Shawano	6403	4	–
The Shawano National Bank	14314	–	–
The Wisconsin National Bank Of Shawano	6403	4	5
Sheboygan			
The First National Bank Of Sheboygan	2123	6	–
The Security National Bank Of Sheboygan	11150	–	2
Sheboygan Falls			
The Dairymens National Bank Of Sheboygan Falls	5947	6	–
Shullsburg			
The First National Bank Of Shullsburg	4055	3	4
Soldiers Grove			
The First National Bank Of Soldiers Grove	13308	–	4
South Milwaukee			
The South Milwaukee National Bank	4893	6	–
Sparta			
The Farmers National Bank Of Sparta	11463	4	4
The First National Bank Of Sparta	1115	6	–
Stevens Point			
The Citizens National Bank Of Stevens Point	4912	3	3
The First National Bank Of Stevens Point	3001	3	3
Stone Lake			
The First National Bank Of Stone Lake	10322	5	5
Stoughton			
The Citizens National Bank Of Stoughton	9304	5	5
The First National Bank Of Stoughton	5222	3	5
Superior			
The First National Bank Of Superior	2653	6	–
The National Bank Of Commerce	13165	–	–
The Union National Bank Of Superior	14109	–	–
The United States National Bank Of Superior	9140	5	2
Tigerton			
First National Bank In Tigerton	14150	–	4
The First National Bank Of Tigerton	5446	3	4
Viroqua			
The First National Bank Of Viroqua	8529	5	3
The First National Bank Of Viroqua	14058	–	–
Washburn			
The First National Bank Of Washburn	12534	–	–
Watertown			
The Merchants National Bank Of Watertown	9003	3	2
The Wisconsin National Bank Of Watertown	1010	4	5
The Wisconsin National Bank Of Watertown	14064	–	–
Waukesha			
The Farmers National Bank Of Waukesha	1159	6	–
The National Exchange Bank Of Waukesha	2647	3	3
The Waukesha National Bank	1086	3	3
Waupaca			
First National Bank Of Waupaca	14063	–	5
Old National Bank Of Waupaca	4424	–	5
The First National Bank Of Waupaca	4414	6	–
The National Bank Of Waupaca	4424	4	–
The Old National Bank Of Waupaca	4424	3	–
The Waupaca County National Bank Of Waupaca	4414	6	–
Waupun			
The First National Bank Of Waupun	3391	6	–
The National Bank Of Waupun	7898	4	4
Wausau			
American National Bank Of Wausau	4744	4	3
The First National Bank Of Wausau	2820	2	1
The National German-American Bank Of Wausau	4744	3	–
Wautoma			
The First National Bank Of Wautoma	7136	6	–
Wauwatosa			
First National Bank Of Wauwatosa	8689	3	2
The First National Bank Of Wauwatosa	14336	–	–
West Allis			
The First National Bank Of West Allis	6908	3	3
West Bend			
The First National Bank Of West Bend	11060	4	3
West Superior			
The First National Bank Of The City Of Superior	3926	4	2
The First National Bank Of West Superior	3926	6	–
The Keystone National Bank Of Superior, West Superior	4399	6	–
The Northwestern National Bank Of Superior, West Superior	4878	6	–
The Superior National Bank Of West Superior	4680	6	–
Weyauwega			
The First National Bank Of Weyauwega	7470	3	5
Whitewater			
The Citizens National Bank Of Whitewater	2925	6	–
The First National Bank Of Whitewater	124	3	4

WYOMING TERRITORY

City, Bank	Ch. No.	L	S
Buffalo			
The First National Bank Of Buffalo	3299	6	–

City, Bank	Ch. No.	L	S
Cheyenne			
The Cheyenne National Bank	3416	6	–
The First National Bank Of Cheyenne	1800	5	–
The Stock Growers National Bank Of Cheyenne	2652	5	–
Douglas			
The First National Bank Of Douglas	3556	6	–
Laramie City			
The Albany County National Bank Of Laramie City	3615	6	–
The Laramie National Bank Of Laramie City	2518	6	–
The Wyoming National Bank Of Laramie City	2110	4	–
Rawlins			
The First National Bank Of Rawlins	4320	6	–
Rock Springs			
The First National Bank Of Rock Springs	3920	6	–
Sundance			
The First National Bank Of Sundance	4343	6	–
WYOMING			
Basin			
The First National Bank Of Basin	10858	5	–
Buffalo			
The First National Bank Of Buffalo	3299	4	3
Casper			
The Casper National Bank	6850	3	2
The Citizens National Bank Of Casper	11683	5	–
The National Bank Of Commerce Of Casper	11490	6	–
The Stockmen's National Bank Of Casper	7083	4	–
The Wyoming National Bank Of Casper	10533	3	2
Cheyenne			
The American National Bank Of Cheyenne	11380	3	2
The Cheyenne National Bank	3416	6	–
The Citizens National Bank Of Cheyenne	8089	4	–
The First National Bank Of Cheyenne	1800	3	–
The Stock Growers National Bank Of Cheyenne	2652	2	–
Cody			
The First National Bank Of Cody	7319	3	4
The Shoshone National Bank Of Cody	8020	5	4

City, Bank	Ch. No.	L	S
Douglas			
The Douglas National Bank	8087	4	3
The First National Bank Of Douglas	3556	4	–
Evanston			
The Evanston National Bank	8612	4	3
The First National Bank Of Evanston	8534	6	3
Green River			
First National Bank Of Green River	10698	4	2
Greybull			
The First National Bank Of Greybull	10810	5	4
Guernsey			
The First National Bank Of Guernsey	5295	6	–
Hanna			
The First National Bank Of Hanna	11666	–	–
Kemmerer			
The First National Bank Of Kemmerer	5480	3	2
Lander			
The First National Bank Of Lander	4720	3	3
Laramie			
The First National Bank Of Laramie	4989	3	1
Laramie City			
The Albany County National Bank Of Laramie City	3615	5	–
The Albany National Bank, Laramie	3615	4	1
The Laramie National Bank Of Laramie	2518	6	–
The Laramie National Bank Of Laramie City	2518	6	–
The Wyoming National Bank Of Laramie	2110	6	–
The Wyoming National Bank Of Laramie City	2110	6	–
Lingle			
The First National Bank Of Lingle	11231	–	–
Lovell			
The First National Bank Of Lovell	10844	–	3
Lusk			
The First National Bank Of Lusk	11390	6	–
Manville			
The First National Bank Of Manville	11352	6	–
Meeteetse			
The First National Bank Of Meeteetse	6340	4	5

City, Bank	Ch. No.	L	S
Newcastle			
The First National Bank Of Newcastle	7198	6	–
The Newcastle National Bank	11079	–	–
Parco			
The First National Bank Of Parco	12558	–	–
Powell			
The First National Bank Of Powell	10265	4	3
The Powell National Bank	10565	4	–
Rawlins			
The First National Bank Of Rawlins	4320	3	2
The Rawlins National Bank	5413	3	2
The Stockgrowers National Bank Of Rawlins	9557	4	–
Riverton			
The First National Bank Of Riverton	14103	–	–
Rock River			
The First National Bank Of Rock River	11342	6	–
Rock Springs			
The First National Bank Of Rock Springs	3920	4	–
The Rock Springs National Bank	4755	3	2
Saratoga			
The First National Bank Of Saratoga	8961	5	–
Sheridan			
The First National Bank Of Sheridan	4604	3	1
The Sheridan National Bank	8275	4	–
Shoshoni			
The First National Bank Of Shoshoni	7978	6	–
The Wind River National Bank Of Shoshoni	8232	6	–
Sundance			
The First National Bank Of Sundance	4343	6	–
Thermopolis			
First National Bank In Thermopolis	12638	5	3
The First National Bank Of Thermopolis	5949	5	–
Torrington			
The Citizens National Bank Of Torrington	11132	–	–
The First National Bank Of Torrington	9289	6	–
The Torrington National Bank	11309	–	–
Wheatland			
The First National Bank Of Wheatland	8432	6	–
Worland			
The First National Bank Of Worland	8253	6	–

Pre-Civil War (1812-1861)   United States Treasury Notes

Compiled by Russell Rulau

The first paper money issued by the United States Government was not, as is often thought, the Interest Bearing Treasury Notes of 1861, the so-called "7-30's." Issued as a result of the Civil War, these 1861 notes were actually the last in a long series of Treasury notes that commenced in 1812 as a consequence of the financial condition of the nation in the War of 1812.

The U.S. Treasury issued five separate series of notes between 1812-1815 with denominations ranging from $3 to $1,000. Though originally intended as loans to the government, they soon began to circulate since they were receivable for debts, taxes and duties due the federal government. Neither the 1812-1815 notes nor later Treasury notes until 1861 were ever actually legal tender for all debts, public and private, however — an important distinction between them and the legal tender notes beginning in the Civil War.

The panic and depression of 1837-1843 brought about eight more series of Treasury notes in those years. These notes differed from the earlier issues in that they were signed by the Treasurer of the U.S. (the 1812-1815 issues had been signed by appointed commissioners).

The Mexican War was responsible for the next two series of Treasury notes in 1846-1847. These also were signed by the Treasurer of the U.S.

The severe financial conditions surrounding the panic of 1857 brought about the next series of Treasury notes, issued from December, 1857, through March, 1861. These notes were issued at competitive interest rates rather than predetermined interest rates. Confidence in the government was lacking, though, and of the $10 million in 6% notes offered in December, 1860, only $70,200 was taken up. The remainder of the notes was issued at rates above 6%, with the largest numbers going at 10, 10¾, 11 and 12%. (Bids were received as high as 36% but the Treasury rejected all bids over 12%.)

The final issue of Treasury notes was the Interest Bearing Notes of July, 1861, to 1865. Issued to help finance the Civil War, they were not the first government notes but merely the continuation of a long series begun a half-century earlier.

Most of the pre-Civil War Treasury notes bear the date of the Act which authorized them, and an issue date (in ink) as well. The catalog is arranged by authorization (not issue) dates.

All pre-Civil War Treasury notes are rare and seldom met with. Many are unique or exist only in museum collections, and a number of them exist only as specimens or as proofs. Pricing is really not possible; such prices as are given are mainly auction results. The only series of notes usually met with as issued, signed notes, is the Series of 1815.

The catalog which follows lists the various issues of pre-Civil War Treasury notes. The information herein comes from several sources:

United States Notes, by John Knox, 1888.

An Illustrated History of U.S. Loans 1775-1898, by Gene Hessler, BNR Press, 1985.

Author Sheds Light on 1812 Treasury Notes, by Donald Kagin, in Coin World for July 9, 1980.

Important United States Paper Money (Alexandre Vatte-

mare collection auction), by Christie Manson & Woods International, Sept. 17, 1982.

Paper Money Issued by the U.S. Government prior to the Civil War, by Bruce W. Smith, unpublished manuscript, 1977.

Photos and notes from Larry Stevens, Eric P. Newman, Walter Breen.

There is a very interesting tale regarding the circulation of the July, 1861, series (the "7-30's"). Much of the loot taken in Jesse James' first bank robbery, the Clay County Savings Bank in Liberty, Missouri, on Feb. 13, 1866, consisted of 7-30 notes. A few thousand dollars of the money soon turned up in Ohio, Tennessee and Kentucky, but most of the money is said to have been exchanged in England. To the James boys, at least, Treasury bonds were as good as gold.

U.S. TREASURY NOTES
June 1812 - March 1861

WAR OF 1812 NOTES
ACT OF 30 JUNE 1812
1 year notes at 5 2/5% interest. $5,000,000 authorized and issued.

KL#	Denom.		Fine
P1	$100	Eagle on branch at upper right.	—

KL#	Denom.		Fine
P2	$1,000	Eagle on branch at upper left.	—

ACT OF 25 FEBRUARY 1813

1 year notes at 5 2/5% interest. $5,000,000 authorized
and issued.

KL#	Denom.		Fine
P3	$100	No description available.	—

ACT OF 4 MARCH 1814

1 year notes at 5 2/5% interest. $10,000,000 authorized
and issued.

KL#	Denom.		Fine
P4	$20	No description available.	—
P5	$50	No description available.	—
P6	$100	No description available.	—

ACT OF 26 DECEMBER 1814

1 year notes at 5 2/5% interest. $8,318,400 issued.

KL#	Denom.		Fine
			Rare
P7	$20	Eagle on shield at left. Imprint: MDF	
P8	$50	No description available.	
P9	$100	Eagle on branch at right. Imprint: MDF	Rare

ACT OF 24 FEBRUARY 1815 (Called "Small Treasury Notes)

$3 to $50 notes - no interest. $100 notes - indefinite
at 5 2/5% interest. $3,392,994 issued in $3 to $50 notes;
$4,969,400 issued in $100 notes.

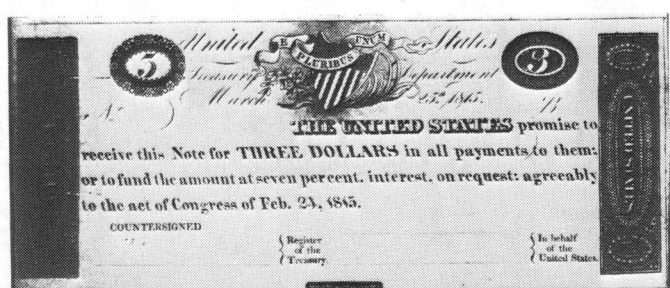

KL#	Denom.		Fine
P10	$3	U.S. shield at center. Imprint: MDF	—

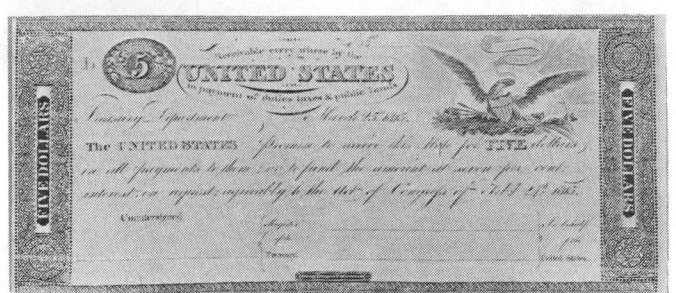

KL#	Denom.		Fine
P11	$5	Eagle on branch at right. Imprint: MDF	—

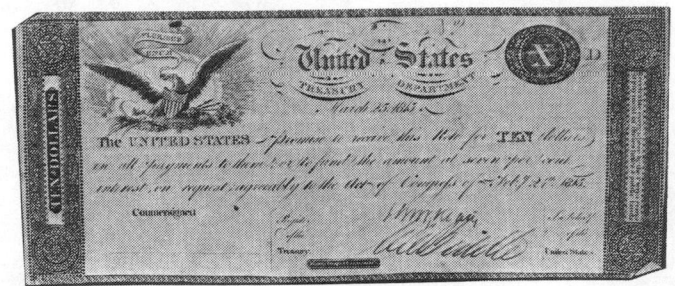

KL#	Denom.		Fine
P12	$10 Type 1	Eagle on branch at left. Text at right. Imprint: MDF	—

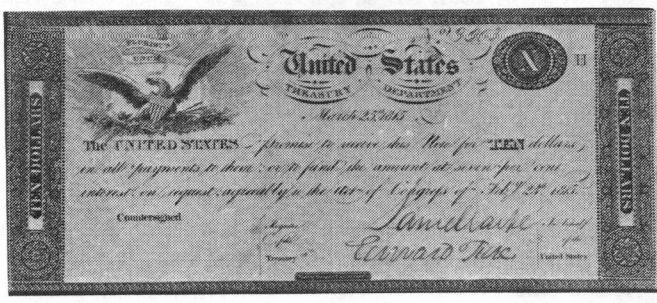

KL#	Denom.		Fine
P13	$10 Type 2	Similar, but TEN DOLLARS at right.	—

KL#	Denom.		Fine
P14	$20	Eagle at left. Imprint: MDF	—

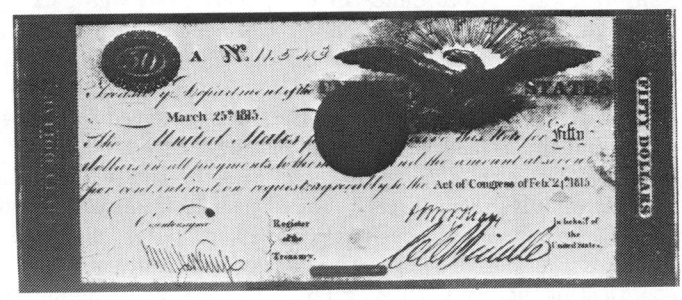

KL#	Denom.		Fine
P15	$50	Eagle on branch at right. Imprint: MDF	—

KL#	Denom.		Fine
P16	$100	Eagle at right, shield at lower center. MDF	—

NOTE: The issue of February, 1815 actually circulated as currency, though not a legal tender for all debts.

PANIC OF 1837 NOTES

ACT OF 12 OCTOBER 1837

1 year notes issued at four different rates of interest
1 mill, 2%, 5% or 6%, the rate written in in ink at
time of issue. The 1-mil rate, which was nominal, was
used on notes intended to circulate as currency.
$10,000,000 authorized and issued (6% notes are rarest)

KL#	Denom.		Fine
P17	$50	No description available	Specimens only
P18	$100	No description available	Specimens only
P19	$500	No description available	Specimens only
P20	$1,000	No description available	Specimens only

ACT OF 21 MAY 1838

1 year notes at 6% interest. $6,888,809 issued.

KL#	Denom.		Fine
P21	$50	No description available	—
P22	$100	No description available	—
P23	$500	No description available	—
P24	$1,000	No description available	—

ACT OF 2 MARCH 1839

1 year notes at 2% or 6% interest. $3,857,276 issued.

KL#	Denom.		Fine
P25	$50	No description available	—
P26	$100	No description available	—
P27	$500	No description available	—
P28	$1,000	No description available	—

ACT OF 31 MARCH 1840

1 year notes at 2%, 5%, 5 2/5% or 6% interest, the
rate written in by ink at time of issuance.

KL#	Denom.		Fine
P29	$50	No description available	Specimens only

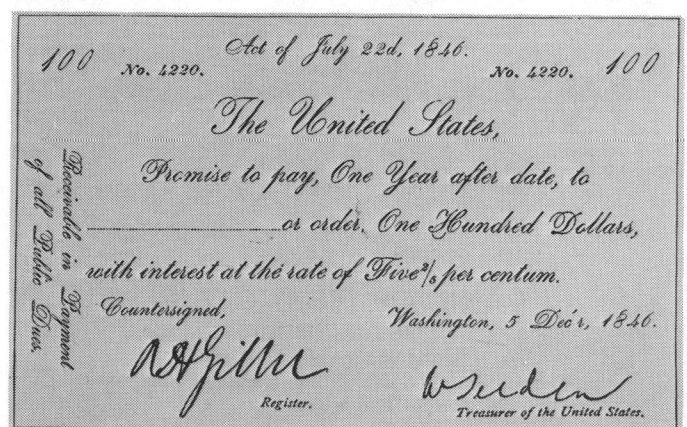

KL#	Denom.		Fine
P30	$100	Knox drawing only available	Specimens only
P31	$500	No description available	Specimens only
P32	$1,000	No description available	Specimens only
P33	$10,000	No description available	Specimens only

ACT OF FEBRUARY 1841

NOTE: Records indicate $7,529,062 was issued in notes
of this issue, but no specimens are known.

ACT OF 31 JANUARY 1842

1 year notes at 2% or 6% interest. $7,959,994 issued
(including reissues).

KL#	Denom.		Fine
P34	$50	No description available	Specimens only
P35	$100	No description available	Specimens only
P36	$500	No description available	Specimens only
P37	$1,000	No description available	Specimens only

ACT OF 31 AUGUST 1842

1 year notes at 2% or 6% interest. $3,025,554 issued.

KL#	Denom.		Fine
P38	$50	Mercury at left, female at right. Imprint: RW&H	—
P39	$100	No description available	Specimens only
P40	$500	No description available	Specimens only
P41	$1,000	No description available	Specimens only

ACT OF 3 MARCH 1843

1 year notes at 1 mill or 4% interest. $1,806,950
issued.

KL#	Denom.		Fine
P42	$50	Female at left, eagle at center, female at right. Imprint: RW&H	—

SPECIAL NOTE: In 1887 there were only $83,425 outstanding in all Treasury notes issued
under acts prior to 1846!

MEXICAN WAR NOTES
ACT OF 22 JULY 1846

1 year notes at 1 mill or 5 2/5% interest. $7,687,800
issued. NOTE: In 1887, only $5,900 was outstanding!

KL#	Denom.		Fine
P43	$50	No description available	Sepcimens only

KL#	Denom.		Fine
P44	$100	Knox drawing only available	Specimens only
P45	$500	No description available	Specimens only
P46	$1,000	No description available	Specimens only

ACT OF 28 JANUARY 1847

60 day or 1 or 2 year notes at 5 2/5% or 6% interest.
$26,122,100 issued (including reissues). NOTE: In
1887, only $950 of 6% notes were still outstanding!

KL#	Denom.		Fine
P47	$50	No description available	Specimens only
P48	$100	Knox drawing only available	Specimens only
P49	$500	No description available	Specimens only
P50	$1,000	No description available	Specimens only

KL#	Denom.		Fine
P51	$5,000	Type 1. Girl at left, eagle at center, lady at right. 2-year notes. Imprint: RWH&E	— Specimens only

KL#	Denom.		Fine
P52	$5,000	Type 2. Female at left, eagle and Washington at center, warrior female at right. Imprint: TC	Specimens only

PANIC OF 1857 NOTES
ACT OF 23 DECEMBER 1857

1 year notes at 3% to 6% interest. $20,000,000
authorized. NOTE: In 1887, only $700 of all these
notes were outstanding!

KL#	Denom.		Fine
P53	$100	Knox drawing only available. Imprint: TC	—
P54	$500	No description available	—
P55	$1,000	No description available	—

ACT OF 17 DECEMBER 1860

1 year notes at 6% to 12% interest. $15,000,000
issued (most at rates of 10 3/4%, 11% or 12%)

KL#	Denom.		Fine
P56	$50	No description available	—
P57	$100	No description available	—
P58	$500	No description available	—
P59	$1,000	No description available	—

ACT OF 2 MARCH 1861

1 or 2 year notes at 6% interest. $35,364,450 issued
($22.4 million in 2-year notes)

KL#	Denom.		Fine
P60	$50	Jackson at left, Webster at right. Black & orange; blue back. Imprint: NBNC	Unique

KL#	Denom.		Fine
P61	$100	Seated female at left, eagle in center. Black & orange; green back.	2500.

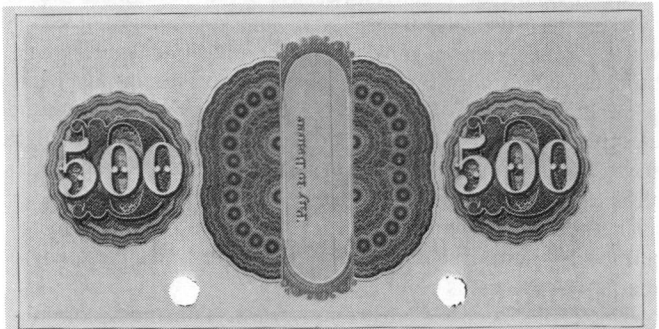

KL#	Denom.		Fine
P62	$500	Type 1. Washington at left, females at center, eagle at right. Black & green; brown back. 60-day note. Imprint: ABNC and RWH&E	Specimens only

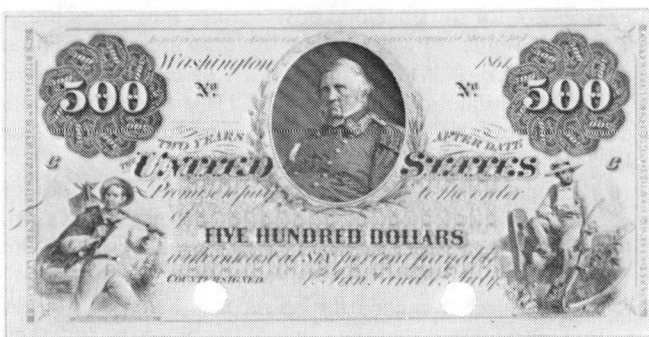

KL#	Denom.		Fine
P63	$500	Type 2. Gen. Winfield Scott at center. 2-year note.	2500.

LIST OF PRINTERS ABBREVIATIONS

ABNC	American Bank Note Company
MDF	Murray Draper Fairman & Co.
NBNC	National Bank Note Co.
RW&H	Rawdon Wright & Hatch
RWH&E	Rawdon Wright Hatch & Edson
TC	Toppan Carpenter & Co.

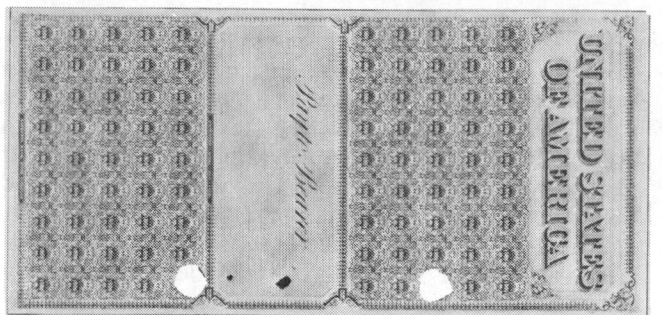

KL#	Denom.		Fine
P64	$1,000	Washington at left, female at center. Black & green, rust back.	5000.
P65	$5,000	No description available	—

CIVIL WAR NOTES
ACTS OF 17 JULY AND 5 AUGUST 1861
3 year notes at 7 3/10%. So-called "7-30s". These are the first Treasury notes widely issued for circulation.
$800,000,000-plus issued.

KL#	Denom.	Fine
P66	$50	
P67	$100	
P68	$500	
P69	$1,000	
P70	$5,000	

ESSAYS FOR ACTS NOT APPROVED
LOAN OF 1848

KL#	Denom.		Fine
P71	$10,000	Rust color. Jackson, female and Washington at top center. Imprint: TC	1500.

ACT OF JUNE 14, 1858

KL#	Denom.		Fine
P72	$5,000	Rust color. Ceres, eagle and Ceres at top center, Franklin at bottom.	750.00

ACT OF JUNE 22, 1860

KL#	Denom.		Fine
P73	$1,000	Eagle on rock at center. Imprint: ABNC	350.00
P74	$5,000	Similar. ABNC	350.00

Postage Stamp Envelopes

By R.B. White

The introduction to these pages gives the background of the financial times preceding the introduction of Fractional Currency. In mid-1862 hard money was fast disappearing from circulation and postage stamps were pressed into service as a means of making small change.

The Postmaster General in his December report of 1862 said: "In the first quarter of the current year, ending September 20th, the number of stamps issued to postmasters was one hundred and four million dollars; there were calls for about two hundred millions, which would have been nearly sufficient to meet the usual demands for the year. This extraordinary demand arose from the temporary use of these stamps as a currency for the public in lieu of the smaller denominations of specie, and ceased with the introduction of the so-called 'postal currency.'"

But stamps were ill-suited for the wear and tear of commerce and at least in the early part of this period, the post office refused to exchange them for new issues. Before Gault produced his encased postage or the die-sinkers had produced their "copperheads" (more commonly now known as Civil War Tokens), a few enterprising printers produced small envelopes, approximately 70 x 35 mm in size, labeled with the value of the stamps contained and usually with an advertising message either for themselves or for some local merchant. This was mainly confined to the larger cities of the east. New York City had by far the most pieces, but Brooklyn, Albany, Cincinnati, Jersey City, and Philadelphia are also represented.

The New York Central Railroad issued a slightly different version. The only example seen being a piece of stiff card with two slots by which the stamp or stamps are captured.

Some of these envelopes have the value of the stamps printed on them, others have blank spaces for hand written values. Occasionally the printed values are changed by hand.

The issues of J. Leach, stationer and printer in New York City, are by far the most common. They have been seen in five distinct types with multiple denominations within the types.

The first listing of Civil War postage stamp envelopes was published by Henry Russell Drowne in the *American Journal of Numismatics* in 1918. That article, primarily based on the Moreau hoard of 77 envelopes, reported that these pieces "were variously printed with black, blue, red and green ink on white, amber, lemon, pink, orange, violet, blue, pale green, buff, manilla and brown paper." Red and blue ink on white paper was the most popular combination. Wood cuts and electrotypes were employed in the manufacture. One single piece bears a picture of Washington. All of the envelopes show evidence of having been hastily made and printed.

In the listings which follow, spaces have been left in the numbering system to accommodate future finds. No claim is made that the list is complete.

These pieces are all extremely rare. The most common probably having no more than half a dozen extant pieces. The pricing thus reflects the rarity of the firm name and the desirability of the design, legend and value. Drowne reported that the 25cts denomination is "by far the most common, about half as many are for 50cts, and a quarter for 10cts and 75cts." All prices are for the envelope only; stamps may be included but there is really no way of knowing that they are original with the envelopes. Any stamps will increase the total value by their own philatelic value. A total of 110 different numbers are listed here; it is doubtful that 500 pieces total of all types still exist.

In the numbering system, a first number is assigned for each firm name or known major design type within that firm. The second number of the system is the stated value of the envelope in cents (blank value shown by 0); "hw" following the second number means the value was hand written. A question mark means that the value of the piece has not been reported. "Vars" means that minor varieties exist.

POSTAGE STAMP ENVELOPES

KL#	Name, address and notations	Value
1-25	H. Armstrong, Hosiery, Laces, etc	
	140 6th Ave, (NYC)	700.
3-?	Arthur, Gregory & Co., Stationer	
	39 Nassau St. NYC	650.
5-25	Bergen & Tripp, Stationer	
	114 Nassau St, NYC	650.
7-25	Berlin & Jones, Stationer	
	134 William St, NYC	650.

KL#	Name, address and notations	Value
9-15	Joseph Bryan, Clothing	
	214 Fulton St, Brooklyn	725.
9-50	Same	650.
11-25	P.D. Braisted, Jr. Billiards	
	14-16 4th Ave, NYC	650.
13-50	G.C. Brown, Tobacco	
	669 Broadway, NYC	650.
15-25	John M. Burnett, Stationer	
	51 William St, NYC	650.
15-25hw50		650.
15-50	Same	650.
17-25	Chas. T. Chickhaus, Tobacco	
	176 Broadway, NYC	725.
19-?	Clarry & Reilley, Stationer	
	12-14 Spruce St, NYC	725.

KL#	Name, address and notations	Value
21-50hw25		
	B.F. Corlies & Macy, Stationer	
	33 Nassau St, NYC	725.
23-30	Crook & Duff, Bar-Lunch-Dining	
	39-40 Park Row, (NYC)	800.
25-?	Cutter Tower & Co, Stationer	
	128 Nassau St, NYC	650.
27-25	Dawley, Stationer & Printer	
	28, 30 & 32 Center St, NYC	650.
28-50	T.R. Dawley, Printer	
	Cor. Reade & Center Streets, NYC	650.
29-0hw25		
	Mad (Ame) A. Doubet, Importer	
	697 & 951 Broadway, NYC	725.
31-25	Francis Duffy, Oysters & Dining	
	239-241 8th Ave, (NYC)	725.
33-25	Embree, Stationer	
	130 Grand St, (NYC)	650.
34-50	Jno. C. Force	
	Brooklyn	800.
35-25	Fox's Old Bowery Theatre	
	(NYC)	800.
37-?	German Opera	
	485 Broadway, NYC	400.

GOULD'S DINING ROOMS,
35 Nassau Street,
Opposite Post Office.   NEW YORK

U. S. POSTAGE
STAMPS.   75 cts.

KL#	Name, address and notations	Value
39-75	Gould's Dining Rooms	
	35 Nassau St, NYC	650.
40-50	Arthur Gregory	
	NYC	800.

KL#	Name, address and notations	Value
41-25	Harlem & NY Navigation Co	
	Sylvan Shore & Sylvan Grove, (NYC)	
	"LEGAL CURRENCY"	850.
43-5	Harpel, Printers	
	Cincinnati	725.
45-10	Irving House, Hotel	
	Broadway & 12th St, NYC	650.
47-25	James, Hatter	
	525 Broadway, (NYC)	650.
49-0	Hamilton Johnston, Stationer	
	545 Broadway, (NYC)	
	with Washington portrait	825.
51-25	C.O. Jones, Stationer	
	76 Cedar St, NYC	650.
53-?	Kaiser & Waters, Stationer	
	104 Fulton St, NYC	650.
55-60	Kavanagh & Freeman, Billards	
	10th & Broadway, NYC	725.
57-25	Lansingh's Gent's Furnishings	
57-50	Albany	650.
59-10	J. Leach, Stationer	
	86 Nassau St, NYC	
	Type I, Value in central diamond, most	
	common type (vars.)	575.
59-15		650.
59-20		575.
59-25		575.
59-30		650.
59-50		575.
59-75		700.

KL#	Name, address and notations	Value
60-15	As Above	700.
60-25	As Above	
	Type II, Eagle between "U" and "S" (vars.)	575.
60-50		575.
61-25	As above	
	Type III, Large central oval with	
	denomination (vars.)	575.
61-50	As above	575.
	Type V, Denomination in oval, flag left,	
	shield right, similar to H. Smith design	575.

KL#	Name, address and notations	Value
62-25	As above	
	Type IV, denomination between flags	575.
63-50	As above	575.
71-75	D.W. Lee, Stationer	
	82 Nassau St, NYC	575.
72-O	R. Letson, Mercantile	
	Dining Room, 256	
	Broadway, NYC	575.
73-25	J.W. Lingard, New	
	Bowery Theatre, (NYC)	650.
74-25	Macoy & Herwig, Stationers	
	112-114 Broadway, (NYC)	650.
75-20	Hy Maillards, Confectionery	
	621 Broadway, (NYC)	650.
75-25	Same	650.
77-25	Frank McElroy, Stationers	
	113 Nassau St, (NYC)	650.
81-10	Metropolitan Hotel	
	NYC	650.
83-25	Miller & Grant, Importers, Laces	
	703 Broadway, NYC	725.

KL#	Name, address and notations	Value
85-50	W.H. Murphy (by D. Murphy's Sons)	
	Stationers, 372 Pearl St, NYC	650.
87-?	Wm. Murphy, Stationer	
	438 Canal St, NYC	650.
89-25	National Express Co.	
	74 Broadway, NYC	800.
93-20	New York Central Railraod (N.Y.C.R.R.)	
	NYC	725.
95-50	N.Y. Consolidated Stage Co.	
	(NYC)	725.

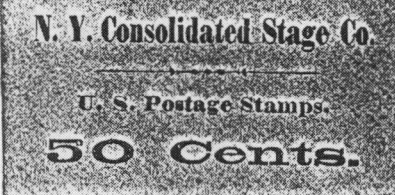

KL#	Name, address and notations	Value
97-25	Niblos Garden - Wm Wheatley	
	(Edwin Forrest) (NYC)	725.
97-50	Same except Ravel Troupe	
	(NYC)	725.
101-10	Nixon's Cremorne Garden,	
	Palace of Music	
	14th and 6th Ave, (NYC)	975.
101-25hw10		725.

NIXON'S CREMORNE GARDEN.
PALACE OF MUSIC.   14th STREET AND 6th AVENUE   EQUESTRIAN SCHOOL.

Postage   25 CTS.   Stamps.

OPERA,   PROMENADE,
BALLET,   EQUESTRIANISM.

ADMISSION TWENTY-FIVE CENTS.

KL#	Name, address and notations	Value
101-25	Postal type hand stamp appears to	
	read "CREMORNE (GARD)EN"	725.

25c.   UNCLE SAM'S   25c.
CHRIS. O'NEILL'S
Wholesale & Retail Liquor Store,
Corner Hudson Av. & Prospect St,
BROOKLYN.
25c.   CHANGE   25c.

KL#	Name, address and notations	Value
103-25	Chris O'Neills, Liquors	
	Hudson Ave, Brooklyn	
	"UNCLE SAM'S CHANGE"	800.
105-?	Oyster Bay House	
	553 Broadway, NYC	650.
107-25	The Oyster House	
	604 Broadway, NYC	650.
109-0	Pettit & Crook's Dining Rooms	
	136 Water St, NYC	
	"UNCLE SAM'S CHANGE"	800.

POMROY'S
699 Broadway, New York.
U. S. POSTAGE STAMPS.
50

KL#	Name, address and notations	Value
111-50	Pomroy's	
	699 Broadway, NYC	650.
113-50	Power, Bogardus & Co., Steamship Line	
	Pier 34, No. River, NYC	700.
115-50	S. Raynor, Envelope Manuf'r	
	118 William St, NYC	650.

KL#	Name, address and notations	Value
117-25	Capt. Tom Reeves, Billards 214 Broadway, NYC	800.

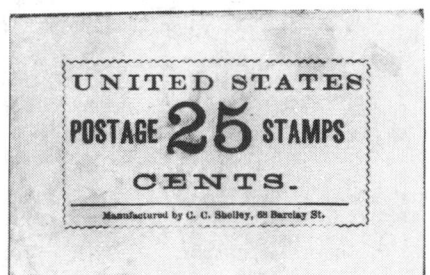

KL#	Name, address and notations	Value
137-25	R.D. Thompson, Stationer 104 Fulton St, NYC (vars.)	650.
139-25	G.W. & S. Turney 77 Chatham St, NYC	650.
140-?	S.C. Upham 403 Chestnut St., Phil.	650.
141-25	James Wiley, Wines & Liquors 307 Broadway, NYC	650.
141-50	Same	650.

KL#	Name, address and notations	Value
159-50	U.S. POSTAGE STAMPS 50 CENTS (vars.)	500.
161-75	U.S. POSTAGE STAMPS 75 CENTS	500.

KL#	Name, address and notations	Value
119-25	Revere House 604-608 Broadway, NYC	650.
121-?	Thomas Richardson, Chop Steak & Oyster House 66 Maiden Lane, NYC	650.
122-50	E.M. Riggin, Sanford House 336 Delaware Ave., Pine St. Wharf, Philadelphia	650.
123-25	Wm Robins, Excelsion Envelope Manufactory 51 Ann St, NYC	575.
125-25	R. Scovel, Stationer 26 Nassau St, (NYC)	650.
126-25	Reuben Scovel "GOVERNMENT CURRENCY" 26 Nassau St, (NYC)	650.
126-50	Same	650.

163-75hw90
U.S. POSTAGE STAMPS 90 CENTS
Hand changed from 75 cents. 650.
Envelopes come with various color ink and paper color combinations. Much of this new information became available through the sale of the Moreau hoard by Bowers & Merena. Photo's on this page courtesy of Bowers & Merena.

A single hoard of these pieces consisting of a "cigar box full" is known to exist but it has not been seen or cataloged. A small group is known to have been lost in a fire some years ago. The author is indebted to Jackson Storm and to the Chase Bank Collection for some of the illustrations, and to Gene Hessler for some of the photography.

PIECES WITH NO COMPANY NAME

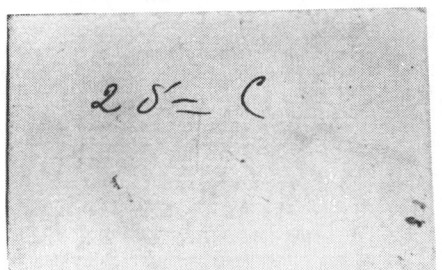

KL#	Name, address and notations	Value
151-25	Blank - marked by hand Envelope perhaps hand made	500.
152-10	U.S. POSTAGE STAMPS 10 CENTS	—
153-20	U.S. POSTAGE STAMPS 20 CENTS	500.
155-25	U.S. POSTAGE STAMPS 25 CENTS (vars.)	500.

KL#	Name, address and notations	Value
156-25	POSTAGE STAMPS 25 CENTS Does not say U.S. postage as others do.	500.
157-25	"UNITED STATES POSTAGE STAMPS" in oval	500.

KL#	Name, address and notations	Value
157-30	U.S. POSTAGE STAMPS 30 CENTS	500.

KL#	Name, address and notations	Value
127-25	C.C. Shelley, Stationer 68 Barclay St, NYC	650.
128-10	H. Smith, Stationer 137 Williams St, NYC Type I, denomination in oval, flag left, shield right (vars.)	575.
128-13	Same	575.
128-25	Same	575.
128-50	Same	575.
129-15hw50	As above Type II, fancy border, no flag, denomination below postage stamps	575.
129-50	Same	575.
130-25	Snow & Hapgood 22 Court St., Boston	650.
131-25	Sonneborn, Stationer 130 Nassau St., NYC (vars.)	650.
133-25	Taylor's Hotel Exchange Place, Jersey City (vars.)	725.
133-50	Same	725.
135-?	Dion Thomas, Stationer 142 Nassau St, NYC	725.

Encased Postage Stamps

By Len Glazer

Encased postage has always been among the most elusive of American numismatic items to collect, and consequently, among the most rewarding. With their natural appeal to numismatists, philatelists, and collectors of antique advertising media, demand has also been strong. This competition for scarce items, especially so in high grades of preservation, has meant a steady upward price progression that also makes Encased Postage Stamps desirable from an investment viewpoint.

While a complete set — by denomination, merchant and major variety — of Encased Postage has never been formed and likely never will be, it is entirely within the grasp of the determined numismatist to assemble a collection that is "complete" within self-set boundries; that is, be denomination, by merchant, by type of merchant (medicinal, dry goods, etc.), by locality of issue, or by any other criteria.

(Encased Postage Stamp photographs in this section are provided through the courtesy of Kagin's.)

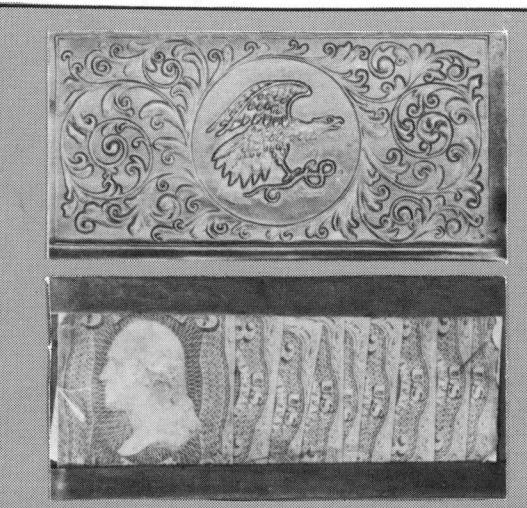

While not generally collected along with the Gault encased postage stamps, the so-called Feuchtwanger rectangular encasement is a contemporary, though unsuccessful, competitor.

Approximately 31x61mm, with a brass frame and no mica cover for the stamps, this item is generally found with a trio of 3-cent postage stamps; a face value of nine cents. The item is also found with other quantities of 3-cent stamps, though the originality of these other denominations is questionable.

Naturally, since the stamps are easily replaced, their condition has little bearing on the value.

KL#	VF
EPS300	395.00

Grading

Three factors must be considered in the grading of Encased Postage Stamps: the case itself, the enclosed stamp and the protective mica.

For the listings which follow, generally accepted standards for coin grading have been used to grade the cases. The accepted standards for grading unused U.S. postage stamps have been considered for that element. For the mica, terminology is that which has been in use since the collecting of Encased Postage Stamps began.

In referring to the price listing that follows, it should be made clear that unlike coins or stamps, which are bought and sold on the basis of generally accepted grading standards, Encased Postage Stamps are sold on the individual merits of the piece involved. This is the result of the many and varied states of preservation of each of the three main elements — case, stamp and mica — of these items.

The valuations quoted refer basically to the condition of the case. If the condition of the stamp and mica are consistent in their own way with that of the case, the valuations can be considered accurate at the time of this catalog's issue. If, however, either the stamp or the mica is significantly better or worse than the case, the value of the item as a whole may be more or less than the figure quoted.

Assume, for example, that a piece with a VF case holds a stamp that is Extremely Fine, protected by a piece of mica which is crazed (see mica grading). The stamp is obviously better than the case, and the crazed mica is also quite nice, though not perfect. The value of such a piece is definitely higher than the quoted VF price, and may be closer to the XF valuation.

Grading of Case

NEW — A condition unknown among Encased Postage Stamps. While there do, indeed, exist specimens which show no wear traces of circulation on the case, the condition of the stamp and/or mica will always contain some imperfection which prevents the accurate description of any Encased Postage Stamp as "New."

ABOUT NEW — The highest grade in which Encased Postage can practically be collected. Just a touch of rubbing on the case, which may or may not still retain some original silvering, if so issued.

EXTREMELY FINE — Higher than average grade, with a bit of noticeable wear on the case; still a very nice piece.

VERY FINE — The average grade for collectible Encased Postage Stamps. The case shows definite wear, but little or no flatness of the embossed lettering. Most catalog values are based on this grade.

FINE — A worn, but acceptable, piece. Generally the lowest undamaged or collectible grade of untampered Encased Postage, since the items did not circulate long enough to attain any greater degree of wear.

Grading of Stamp

In their usage with Encased Postage, stamps are generally described in one of the following degrees of brightness. Since the paper was protected by the mica, the only measurement of the state of preservation of the stamp can be the degree to which it was subjected to the fading effects of sunlight or other causes.

FULLY BRIGHT — A stamp that is 100% as vivid as the day it was issued.

NEAR FULL BRIGHT — Perhaps a spot or two of less than perfect brightness.

BRIGHT — A stamp which has lost some of its original color, but is still sharp and always acceptable.

TONED — A stamp which has darkened with age or exposure to light and other elements.

DULL or FADED — A stamp which has lost much of its color; the lowest generally collectable condition for an undamaged item.

Grading of Mica

Because it is a natural silicate mineral, mica of flawless, perfect quality probably does not exist in connection with its use in Encased Postage Stamps. Collectors are warned that only "perfect" mica generally encountered is acetate which has been used to repair a damaged Encased Postage Stamp. Upon close examination, some flaw can be found on virtually every mica piece used in this manner.

NEARLY PERFECT — The highest degree of preservation for a mica encasement.

CRAZED — Fine cracks in the surface on the surface, or between the thin natural layers of mica. Separation beginning in its early stages. None of the crazing fully breaks the mica, exposing the stamp.

CRACKED — A break in the mica through to the stamp, but with no piece of the mica missing.

CHIPPED — A breaking of only the upper layer or layers of mica, with the chip or chips missing, though the mica beneath remains intact and the stamp protected.

BROKEN — A break in all layers of the mica, with some missing and the stamp exposed. The degree of broken or missing mica should be described.

Other Terms

Two other terms which the collector of Encased Postage will encounter also bear definition.

RIBBED FRAME — Some varieties of Encased Postage are known with cases which have fine parallel lines on the face (stamp side) of the metal case.

SILVERING — Many Encased Postage Stamps were issued with a thin silver wash on the case, to enhance their resemblance to the disappearing silver coinage of the day. More research is needed to determine which issues came with silvering, which came without and which, if any, were issued both ways. Since the silver wore off very quickly, even many high grade pieces have no traces of the original finish. A piece with a high percentage of silvering remaining is worth a premium, but those with just a trace of silver are not; though it is generally mentioned when describing an item for sale.

Rarity Ratings

When dealing with the relative rarity of Encased Postage Stamps, the collector must realize that all are scarce in terms of numismatic collectibles. Even the most common variety "Take Ayer's Pills" may not be easy to locate on the market at any given time.

Following years of study of major collections and auction offerings, and conversations with other specialists, the following table of rarity lists each piece in what we believe to be its correct order, and broken into six categories of rarity. While there may be some disagreement as to order within category, we believe most knowledgeable specialists will agree with the listing.

VERY RARE
1. Arthur M. Claflin
2. B. F. Miles
3. John W. Norris
4. Pearce, Tolle & Holton

RARE
5. White the Hatter
6. Sands' Ale
7. S. Steinfeld
8. Dougan
9. N.G. Taylor & Co.
10. Ellis McAlpin & Co.
11. L.C. Hopkins & Co.
12. Aerated Bread

VERY SCARCE
13. F. Buhl & Co.
14. Weir & Larminie
15. Lord & Taylor
16. H.A. Cook
17. Bailey & Co.

SCARCE
18. Schapker & Bussing
19. G.G. Evans
20. John Shillito & Co.
21. Mendum's Wine Emporium
22. North America Life Insurance Co.

COMMON
23. Tremont House
24. Joseph L. Bates
25. Kirkpatrick & Gault
26. Irving House
27. Brown's Bronchial Troches
28. Burnett's Cocoaine
29. J. Gault
30. Burnett's Cooking Extracts
31. Drake's Plantation Bitters

MOST COMMON
32. Take Ayer's Pills
33. Ayer's Cathartic Pills
34. Ayer's Sarsaparilla

Aerated Bread Co., New York

KL#	Denom.	Fine	VF	XF
EPS1	1¢	800.	1250.	1500.

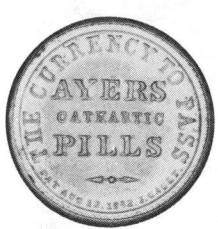

Ayer's Cathartic Pills
(Long arrows variety)

KL#	Denom.	Fine	VF	XF
EPS2	3¢	100.	175.	250.
EPS3	5¢	125.	275.	350.
EPS4	10¢	250.	500.	650.

(Short arrows variety)

KL#	Denom.	Fine	VF	XF ,
EPS5	1¢	150.	225.	300.
EPS6	3¢	100.	175.	250.
EPS7	5¢	125.	275.	350.
EPS8	10¢	200.	350.	500.
EPS9	12¢	300.	550.	1000.
EPS10	24¢	1200.	2000.	3000.
EPS11	30¢	1500.	3000.	4000.

Take Ayer's Pills

KL#	Denom.	Fine	VF	XF
EPS12	1¢	150.	250.	325.
EPS13	3¢	100.	150.	225.
EPS14	5¢	100.	200.	300.
EPS15	10¢	175.	375.	500.
EPS16	12¢	300.	550.	1000.
EPS17	90¢	Two known are both suspect as being counterfeit or altered.		

Ayer's Sarsaparilla
(Small Ayer's)

KL#	Denom.	Fine	VF	XF
EPS18	1¢	300.	625.	925.
EPS19	3¢	350.	550.	750.
EPS20	10¢	300.	625.	925.
EPS21	12¢	700.	1400.	2000.

(Medium Ayer's)

KL#	Denom.	Fine	VF	XF
EPS22	1¢	150.	225.	300.
EPS23	3¢	100.	175.	225.
EPS24	5¢	150.	225.	300.
EPS25	10¢	175.	300.	450.
EPS26	12¢	300.	550.	1000.
EPS27	24¢	1200.	2000.	3000.
EPS28	30¢	1500.	3000.	4000.
EPS29	90¢	2500.	5000.	9000.

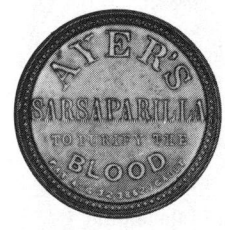

(Large Ayer's)

KL#	Denom.	Fine	VF	XF
EPS30	3¢	275.	400.	750.
EPS31	10¢	450.	700.	1000.

Bailey & Co., Philadelphia

KL#	Denom.	Fine	VF	XF
EPS32	1¢	375.	550.	1000.
EPS33	3¢	375.	550.	1000.
EPS34	5¢	400.	650.	1300.
EPS35	10¢	400.	600.	1250.
EPS36	12¢	1000.	1500.	2500.

Joseph L. Bates "Fancy Goods," Boston
Fancygoods One Word

KL#	Denom.	Fine	VF	XF
EPS41	1¢	150.	225.	300.
EPS42	3¢	300.	450.	650.
EPS43	10¢	200.	375.	600.

Joseph L. Bates Fancy Goods Two Words

KL#	Denom.	Fine	VF	XF
EPS37	1¢	150.	225.	300.
EPS38	3¢	350.	675.	850
EPS39	10¢	200.	375.	600.
EPS40	12¢	300.	550.	1000.

Brown's Bronchial Troches

KL#	Denom.	Fine	VF	XF
EPS44	1¢	225.	375.	550.
EPS45	3¢	175.	300.	400.
EPS46	5¢	175.	300.	400.
EPS47	10¢	250.	375.	500.
EPS48	12¢	600.	1000.	1400.

F. Buhl & Co., Detroit

KL#	Denom.	Fine	VF	XF
EPS49	1¢	400.	650.	1100.
EPS50	3¢	400.	700.	1250.
EPS51	5¢	400.	650.	1100.
EPS52	10¢	750.	1000.	2000.
EPS53	12¢	750.	1500.	2000.

Burnett's Cocoaine Kalliston

KL#	Denom.	Fine	VF	XF
EPS54	1¢	150.	250.	375.
EPS55	3¢	125.	175.	275.
EPS56	5¢	150.	300.	425.
EPS57	10¢	200.	550.	800.
EPS58	12¢	300.	550.	1000.
EPS59	24¢	1500.	2000.	3000.
EPS60	30¢	1750.	3000.	4000.
EPS61	90¢	2500.	5000.	9000.

Burnett's Cooking Extracts
(Plain frame)

KL#	Denom.	Fine	VF	XF
EPS62	1¢	150.	250.	375.
EPS63	3¢	150.	275.	425.
EPS64	5¢	150.	250.	375.
EPS65	10¢	200.	375.	550.
EPS66	12¢	300.	550.	1000.
EPS67	24¢	1500.	2000.	3000.
EPS68	30¢	1750.	3000.	4000.
EPS69	90¢	2500.	5000.	9000.

(Ribbed frame)

KL#	Denom.	Fine	VF	XF
EPS70	10¢	350.	650.	800.

A.M. Claflin, Hopkinton, R.I.

KL#	Denom.	Fine	VF	XF
EPS71	1¢	3000.	6250.	12,750.
EPS72	3¢	3000.	4000.	6000.
EPS73	5¢	3000.	4000.	6000.
EPS74	12¢	3000.	5000.	7500.

H.A. Cook, Evansville, Ind.

KL#	Denom.	Fine	VF	XF
EPS75	5¢	350.	650.	1300.
EPS76	10¢	600.	1200.	2500.

Dougan, New York

KL#	Denom.	Fine	VF	XF
EPS77	1¢	800.	1500.	2500.
EPS78	3¢	800.	1500.	2500.
EPS79	5¢	600.	1000.	2000.
EPS80	10¢	1000.	2000.	3000.

Drake's Plantation Bitters, New York

KL#	Denom.	Fine	VF	XF
EPS81	1¢	175.	225.	300.
EPS82	3¢	125.	275.	400.
EPS83	5¢	200.	300.	400.
EPS84	10¢	225.	375.	550.
EPS85	12¢	300.	550.	1000.
EPS86	24¢	1500.	2500.	3000.
EPS87	30¢	2000.	3000.	4000.
EPS88	90¢	2750.	5500.	9000.

Ellis, McAlpin & Co., Cincinnati

KL#	Denom.	Fine	VF	XF
EPS89	1¢	600.	1250.	1850.
EPS90	3¢	600.	1250.	1750.
EPS91	5¢	800.	1650.	2300.
EPS92	10¢	600.	1250.	1750.
EPS93	12¢	800.	1500.	2250.
EPS94	24¢	1200.	2000.	3000.

G.G. Evans, Philadelphia

KL#	Denom.	Fine	VF	XF
EPS95	1¢	300.	600.	900.
EPS96	3¢	400.	700.	1000.
EPS97	5¢	450.	750.	1250.
EPS98	10¢	450.	750.	1250.

J. Gault
(Plain frame)

KL#	Denom.	Fine	VF	XF
EPS99	1¢	150.	225.	300.
EPS100	2¢	—	12,000.	—
		(Three known)		
EPS101	3¢	150.	250.	350.
EPS102	5¢	150.	250.	375.
EPS103	10¢	200.	300.	500.
EPS104	12¢	300.	550.	1000.
EPS105	24¢	1250.	2000.	3000.
EPS106	30¢	1500.	3000.	4000.
EPS107	90¢	2500.	5000.	9000.

(Ribbed frame)

KL#	Denom.	Fine	VF	XF
EPS108	1¢	400.	700.	1000.
EPS109	3¢	400.	700.	1000.
EPS110	5¢	275.	450.	600.
EPS111	10¢	300.	550.	700.
EPS112	12¢	500.	800.	1500.
EPS113	24¢	1500.	2750.	3500.
EPS114	30¢	1750.	3000.	4000.

L. C. Hopkins & Co., Cincinnati

KL#	Denom.	Fine	VF	XF
EPS115	1¢	700.	1250.	1750.
EPS116	3¢	600.	1150.	1500.
EPS117	5¢	800.	1500.	2250.
EPS118	10¢	700.	1250.	1750.

Irving House, N.Y. (Hunt & Nash)
(Plain frame)

KL#	Denom.	Fine	VF	XF
EPS119	1¢	150.	250.	350.
EPS120	3¢	150.	250.	350.
EPS121	5¢	400.	700.	1000.
EPS122	10¢	200.	300.	450.
EPS123	12¢	300.	550.	1000.
EPS124	24¢	1250.	2000.	3000.
EPS125	30¢	1500.	3000.	4000.

(Ribbed frame)

KL#	Denom.	Fine	VF	XF
EPS126	1¢	400.	700.	1000.
EPS127	3¢	400.	700.	1000.
EPS128	5¢	450.	750.	1500.
EPS129	10¢	350.	550.	750.
EPS130	12¢	500.	800.	1500.
EPS131	24¢	1500.	2750.	3500.

Kirkpatrick & Gault, New York

KL#	Denom.	Fine	VF	XF
EPS132	1¢	150.	225.	300.
EPS133	3¢	125.	200.	275.
EPS134	5¢	175.	350.	500.
EPS135	10¢	200.	300.	500.
EPS136	12¢	300.	550.	1000.
EPS137	24¢	1250.	2000.	3000.
EPS138	30¢	1500.	3000.	4000.
EPS139	90¢	2500.	5000.	9000.

Lord & Taylor, New York

KL#	Denom.	Fine	VF	XF
EPS140	1¢	400.	650.	1250.
EPS141	3¢	400.	650.	1250.
EPS142	5¢	400.	650.	1250.
EPS143	10¢	400.	700.	1500.
EPS144	12¢	800.	1500.	2000.
EPS145	24¢	1500.	2500.	3500.
EPS146	30¢	2000.	4000.	5000.
EPS147	90¢	4000.	7500.	9000.

Mendum's Family Wine Emporium, New York
(Plain frame)

KL#	Denom.	Fine	VF	XF
EPS148	1¢	250.	350.	500.
EPS149	3¢	350.	500.	800.
EPS150	5¢	300.	450.	600.
EPS151	10¢	300.	450.	700.
EPS152	12¢	650.	1250.	1750.

(Ribbed frame)

KL#	Denom.	Fine	VF	XF
EPS153	10¢	400.	700.	1000.

B. F. Miles, Peoria

KL#	Denom.	Fine	VF	XF
EPS154	5¢	3500.	7000.	9000.

John W. Norris, Chicago

KL#	Denom.	Fine	VF	XF
EPS155	1¢	750.	1000.	1700.
EPS156	3¢	1000.	1750.	3000.
EPS157	5¢	1000.	1750.	3000.
EPS158	10¢	1000.	1750.	3000.

North America Life Insurance Co., New York
(Straight "Insurance")

KL#	Denom.	Fine	VF	XF
EPS159	1¢	175.	250.	350.
EPS160	3¢	175.	250.	350.
EPS161	10¢	200.	375.	600.
EPS162	12¢	450.	1000.	1500.

(Curved "Insurance")
(Trial Piece)

KL#	Denom.	Fine	VF	XF
EPS163	1¢	225.	500.	1000.
EPS164	10¢	300.	500.	750.

Pearce, Tolle & Holton, Cincinnati

KL#	Denom.	Fine	VF	XF
EPS165	1¢	1000.	1750.	3000.
EPS166	3¢	800.	1500.	2500.
EPS167	5¢	1000.	1750.	3000.
EPS168	10¢	1100.	2000.	3500.

Sands' Ale

KL#	Denom.	Fine	VF	XF
EPS169	5¢	800.	1500.	2500.
EPS170	10¢	1000.	1750.	2750.
EPS171	30¢	2000.	3500.	5000.

Schapker & Bussing, Evansville, Ind.

KL#	Denom.	Fine	VF	XF
EPS172	1¢	400.	700.	1000.
EPS173	3¢	225.	350.	600.
EPS174	5¢	450.	750.	1250.
EPS175	10¢	450.	800.	1250.
EPS176	12¢	500.	1250.	1750.

John Shillito & Co., Cincinnati

KL#	Denom.	Fine	VF	XF
EPS177	1¢	400.	700.	1000.
EPS178	3¢	250.	350.	600.
EPS179	5¢	250.	450.	900.
EPS180	10¢	275.	425.	750.
EPS181	12¢	500.	1250.	1750.

S. Steinfeld, New York

KL#	Denom.	Fine	VF	XF
EPS182	1¢	1000.	1700.	2500.
EPS183	10¢	1000.	1600.	2500.
EPS184	12¢	1000.	1750.	2750.

N. G. Taylor & Co., Philadelphia

KL#	Denom.	Fine	VF	XF
EPS185	1¢	800.	1250.	1900.
EPS186	3¢	800.	1250.	1750.
EPS187	5¢	800.	1500.	2000.
EPS188	10¢	800.	1250.	1750.

Tremont House (Gage Brothers & Drake), Chicago

KL#	Denom.	Fine	VF	XF
EPS189	1¢	150.	225.	300.
EPS190	5¢	150.	300.	375.
EPS191	10¢	200.	325.	450.
EPS192	12¢	350.	600.	1250.

Weir & Larminie, Montreal

KL#	Denom.	Fine	VF	XF
EPS193	1¢	450.	750.	1250.
EPS194	3¢	400.	700.	1000.
EPS195	5¢	500.	800.	1500.
EPS196	10¢	600.	900.	1700.

White the Hatter, New York

KL#	Denom.	Fine	VF	XF
EPS197	1¢	750.	1000.	1900.
EPS198	3¢	800.	1500.	2500.
EPS199	5¢	900.	1750.	3000.
EPS200	10¢	800.	1500.	2500.

Paper Money Substitutes of the Civil War

The collector's first encounter with U.S. Postage and Fractional Currency invariably provokes two questions: What is it? Why was it?

The first question is easily answered. Postage and Fractional Currency is genuine paper money of the United States issued during the 1862-1875 period in denominations of 3, 5, 10, 15, 25 and 50 cents.

Why paper money in denominations of less than the familiar dollar unit was required in commerce is less easily answered. The causes of this unusual issue of official "paper coins" at a time when people still demanded coins of high intrinsic value can only be found in the jumble of cause and effect that has been the catalyst of numismatic history from time immemorial.

It would be convenient to state, as has frequently been done, that within a few days of the outbreak of the Civil War all of the gold, silver and copper coins in circulation disappeared due to the desire of the timid to save something of universal value from the threatened wreck of the Union, and of the avaricious to hoard something which would possibly increase in value. Undoubtedly, fear and greed acted at once to trigger the hoarding instinct in some individuals, but on the whole, such an observation seems to be overdrawn. Contemporary newspaper accounts make little mention of a serious coin shortage until early in 1862.

There was no pervading fear in the North that the armed forces of the Confederacy would prevail and shatter the Union for all time. If anything, the tendency was to underestimate the power and tenacity of the South.

It would appear that the initial hoarding of hard money was caused by little more than an ingrained distrust of paper money, an attitude more than justified by the nation's experience with non-metallic currency up to that time. The Yankee worker, whose livelihood was completely bound to the money earned tending the lathes and forges of the industrialized North, simply felt more secure when his paper wages had been converted to gold and silver. Consequently, he gave a cool reception to "Greenbacks," which could not be redeemed for either gold or silver and were suspiciously regarded as "faith paper." The reception grew progressively colder as the flood of paper dollars increased.

This practically expressed preference for coins inevitably depreciated Greenbacks in terms of the gold standard. Gold coins commanded a premium of three percent over U.S. and state paper money in January, 1862, the month following the general suspension of specie payment by banks and the Federal Treasury; six percent in June, 1862; 15 percent in July, and 32 percent by the end of 1862. Thereafter the depreciation of Greenbacks accelerated, until at one point in 1864 it required $285 in paper to purchase $100 in gold. The distrust of the Government's fiat paper was also maintained by the snowballing national debt, which reached its high-point of the war — $2.8 billion — in 1865.

A monetary situation whereby gold commanded a substantial premium over a like face value of paper dollars swiftly drove gold coins from commercial channels, effectively removing the United States from a gold standard. It also created a favorable condition for the exporting of silver coins, which disappeared from the marketplace, but at a less precipitous pace than gold.

In 1858 Canada had adopted a decimal system of coinage with a dollar unit similar to that of the United States. In lieu of a sufficient quantity of decimal coinage of British origin, Canada unofficially adopted the coinage of the United States and used it widely in domestic trade. The West Indies and many Latin American countries also imported large quantities of U.S. silver coinage for domestic use. Disappearance of gold from American trade channels and the willingness of foreign users of U.S. silver coins to pay for them with gold combined to produce a legal and highly profitable bullion trade which speculators and bankers found irresistible.

The discounting of Greenbacks in terms of gold enabled the exchange of paper money for silver coins, which were then exchanged for gold in Canada, the West Indies or Latin America. The gold was then returned to the United States, where it was used to purchase more Greenbacks at the metal's high premium rate. A safer round-robin to riches can hardly be imagined. Even in times of national crisis, pragmatic profit taking will attract more adherents than an idealistic consideration for the national good. During the last week of June and the first week of July, 1862, more than $25 million in subsidiary coins vanished from circulation in the North. The shortage of silver coins, particularly in the eastern United States, would not be relieved until the summer of 1876.

Illogically, the Philadelphia Mint continued a small but steady production of silver coins during the 1860s, although they were of no use to the nation's economy. Bullion dealers obtained them directly from the Mint and sped them abroad. In 1863, the entire production of silver coins was exported.

The withdrawal of subsidiary silver coins in the summer of 1862 all but paralyzed the institutions and practice of everyday commerce. The smallest denominations of official money available were discounted $5 Legal Tender Notes and the copper-nickel cents which had been fed into circulation in great quantities to retire demonetized Spanish silver coins and the large copper cents.

When first forced upon the public in 1857, the copper-nickel cent, which was intrinsically worth about 60 percent of face value, had been considered a nuisance; it was regularly discounted three percent and more in large transactions. But with the disappearance of silver coins, the ugly duckling became the belle of the ball. The erstwhile nuisance became the only alternative to walking, or going without a newspaper, or buying a pound of pomegranetes and receiving change in kumquats and quince. Cents were bundled in bags of 25, 50 and 100 in a hopeless attempt to bridge the gap between the 1-cent piece and the $5 bill. By March, 1863, the lowly cent commanded a premium of 20 percent, but few could be found.

The disappearance of nearly all official coinage from trade channels resulted in an outpouring of private emergency monies, some hoary with tradition, others as new and untried as the inspiration which gave them form. State bank notes of $1 and $2 denominations were cut into fractional parts. Other banks issued notes in denominations of $1.25, $1.50 and $1.75. Eastern cities issued their own fractional notes. Merchants, reviving a practice prevalent during the coin shortages of 1837 and 1857, made change in their own promissory notes or "shinplasters," which were notes of small value, redeemable in merchandise at the issuer's place of business. Unscrupulous merchants made change with their own notes even when they had sufficient specie on hand, knowing that the notes were not likely to be presented for redemption by other than their regular neighborhood customers. In like manner, private issues of the eminently collectible Civil War tokens began.

Most novel of the emergency monies called into use was the common postage stamp. The use of postage stamps as a low denomination medium of exchange was not a success, but it led directly to the issuing of the highly successful Postage and Fractional Currency series.

First issued by the Federal Government in 1847, by the time the Civil War began, the adhesive postage stamp had become a well-established part of the public routine. Inasmuch as they were of official origin, had a constant value throughout the country and were easily obtained, consideration of postage stamps as a medium of exchange for coin-deprived people was inevitable. In early July, 1862, Horace Greeley, publisher of the politically influential New York *Tribune*, suggested that stamps pasted on a half sheet of paper, with the other half

folded over the stamps to afford them protection from wear, would make an excellent coin substitute. Other newspapers quickly endorsed the proposal, as did the coin-starved public.

Although there were surely those who attempted to do so, fragile, gummed stamps could not be carried loose in pocket or purse without soon becoming a crumpled, stuck-together, totally useless blob of colored paper.

Methods of affording the stamps a degree of protection were quickly devised. They were pasted on sheets of light vellum paper — with or without a protective flap — which also bore an advertising message and a large numeral indicating the total face value of the stamps. Stamps were also encased in small envelopes, on the outside of which was printed the value of the contents and an advertising message.

It soon became apparent that both methods of preparing stamps for the role of emergency money had as many drawbacks as advantages. Pasting the stamps on sheets of paper did not provide them sufficient protection from wear. Those enclosed in envelopes were better protected, but the method of protection provided an opportunity for petty larceny which wasn't neglected. Few recipients had the time to check the contents of each envelope to determine if it contained the proper denominational total of stamps, or if the stamps were unused, or if rectangles of colored paper had been substituted for the stamps.

The method of stamp packaging which best satisfied the dual requirements of visibility and protection was patented on Aug. 12, 1862, by a New England inventor named John Gault, who encased a single postage stamp in a round brass frame (25 mm in diameter) with a clear mica frontpiece through which the stamp could be viewed. The reverse of this case bore the advertising message of the participating merchant who purchased a quantity of Gault's "encased postage stamps" as a means of giving his customers the precise change required by their purchases.

Stamps encased by Gault were the 1-, 3-, 5-, 10-, 12-, 24-, 30-, and 90-cent denominations of the Series of 1861-1869. That series also contains a 2-cent and a 15-cent stamp, but the 2-cent stamp wasn't issued until July 6, 1863, and the 15-cent value came along on June 17, 1866.

But for the eventual authorization of Postage and Fractional Currency, Gault's encased postage stamps would probably have become the chief means of "spending" postage stamps, although they, too, had their disadvantages. The protective mica shield was easily cracked, and the encased stamps cost the distributing merchant the face value of the stamps, plus about two cents per holder. In view of the 20 percent premium existing on official coins, the additional two cents was of little consequence in the instance of the higher denomination stamps, but in the case of the popular one-cent stamp, it meant an expenditure of three cents for every one-cent encased postage stamp obtained from Gault for monetary use.

The timing of the initiation of Gault's encased stamps also worked against their quantity distribution. At the time of their appearance in midsummer of 1862, the Postmaster General, Montgomery Blair, was still not reconciled to the idea of using postage stamps for money, and was doing his utmost to prevent quantity sales of stamps to anyone desiring them for coinage purposes.

All methods of using stamps for money that had been employed prior to July 17, 1862, suffered the ultimate disadvantage of being illegal, with the consequence that the holder of the stamps could neither redeem them at the post office nor exchange them for Treasury notes.

On that date, however, President Lincoln signed into law a measure proposed in self-defense by Treasury Secretary Salmon P. Chase, providing that "postage and other stamps of the United States" were to be receivable for all dues to the U.S. and were to be redeemable at any "designated depository" in sums less that $5. The law also prohibited the issue by "any private corporation, banking association, firm, or individual" of any note or token for a sum less than $5 — a provision that was widely ignored as the private sector continued its efforts to overcome a coin shortage in the face of which the Government seemed helpless.

The new law was not without its problems of practicality, either. The post office, already facing a stamp shortage before the gummed bits of paper had been declared legal tender, now had the almost impossible task of providing sufficient stamps for postal use as well as "coinage" use.

In addition, there was the problem of who would redeem nearly exhausted specimens of stamps which had been circulating for some time. Blair refused to take them in trade for new stamps and the Treasury would not exchange them for paper money because they hadn't issued them in the first place.

Blair's obstinacy ultimately melted before the heat of public pressure, and he agreed to redeem the masses of soiled and stuck-together stamps, but he continued to insist that the actual intent of the poorly-written law had been for the Treasury Department to print and distribute special stamps that would bear a general resemblance to postage stamps, but would be of a different design. A compromise was finally worked out whereby the Treasury Department would sell and redeem specially marked stamps which the post office would also accept for postage. Blair agreed to print the special stamps for the Treasury.

Before the stamps could be printed, a further decision was made to issue them in a larger, more convenient size, and to print them on a heavier, ungummed paper. Credit for the final form in which Postage Currency appeared is given to Gen. F.E. Spinner, Treasurer of the United States. Spinner pasted unused postage stamps on small sheets of Treasury security paper of uniform size, signed his name to some of them and passed them out to his friends as samples of currency. Congress responded to Spinner's suggestion by authorizing the printing of reproductions of postage stamps on Treasury paper in arrangements patterned after Spinner's models. In this form, the "stamps" ceased to be stamps; they became, in effect, fractional Government promissory notes, a development not authorized by the initial enabling legislation of July 17, 1862. Nonetheless, the notes would be issued without legal authorization until passage of the Act of March 3, 1863, which provided for the issuing of fractional notes by the Federal Government.

Five issues of Postage and Fractional Currency in the total amount of $369 million were printed and released to circulation between Aug. 21, 1862, and Feb. 15, 1876, when a flood of silver from the Comstock Lode drove down silver bullion prices, reducing the intrinsic value of silver coins to a point below face value, thereby insuring that they would remain in circulation. The silver price drop further augmented the supply of circulating silver by triggering a flow back to the United States — where they could be exchanged for their greater face value — of the hundreds of millions of silver coins which had been exported to Canada, the West Indies and Latin America since 1862.

Congressional Acts of Jan. 14, 1875, and April 17, 1876, provided for the redemption of Postage and Fractional Currency in silver coins, and all but about $1.8 million worth was returned to the Treasury for redemption. The outstanding notes remain legal tender and can purchase their face value equivalent in goods and services today.

FIRST ISSUE
August 21, 1862 - May 27, 1863
Denominations: 5¢, 10¢, 25¢, 50¢

The First Issue of U.S. Government stamp money is the only one of the five issues to be identified by name as Postage Currency. The initial printing of the First Issue was released through Army paymasters on Aug. 1, 1862, and was provided for general circulation a few weeks later.

Although it is a moot point, Postage Currency probably constitutes an illegal issue of fractional notes. Rather than being strictly "postage and other stamps of the United States," and despite being "receivable for postage stamps at any U.S. post office," Postage Currency took the form of reproductions of postage stamps printed on paper which carried the promise of the United States to exchange the currency for United States Notes, which gave Postage Currency the attributes of a promissory note, a development beyond the intent of the enabling Act of July 17, 1862.

The stamps reproduced on Postage Currency are the brown (sometimes buff) five-cent stamp of the Series of 1861, bearing the portrait of Thomas Jefferson, and the green ten-cent stamp of the same series, with George Washington's portrait. The 25- and 50-cent denominations bear multiple reproductions of the appropriate stamp. Various colors of paper were used in printing the four notes of the First Issue, but the color does not influence the collector value of the individual note. Faces of the notes are printed in a color approximating the color of the genuine postage stamp, backs are all printed in black.

An interesting feature of the First Issue is the existence of notes with both perforated and straight edges. Apparently, the idea of perforated Postage Currency was a carry-over from the postage stamp printing process and was discarded when the demand for Postage Currency exceeded the capacity of the perforating machines.

Inasmuch as the Bureau of Engraving and Printing had not yet been established, contracts for printing of the First Issue were awarded to private bank note printing companies. The National Bank Note Company printed the face, the American Bank Note Company, the back. The ABNC monogram appears on the backs of some notes.

Total value of Postage Currency issued was more than $20 million.

SECOND ISSUE
October 10, 1863 - February 23, 1867
Denominations: 5¢, 10¢, 25¢, 50¢

The Second Issue of a fractional currency, authorized by Congress on March 3, 1863, all but discarded the concept of postage stamp money. Notes continued to be "receivable for all United States postage stamps," but the identity of the notes was changed from Postage Currency to Fractional Currency, and the notes of the Second Issue did not bear a reproduction of a postage stamp, although the portrait of George Washington on all notes of this issue is the same as that appearing on the 24-cent stamp of the Series of 1861. The Second Issue was made necessary by the ease with which notes of the First Issue had been counterfeited.

All Second Issue notes have a slate-colored face with bronze oval surcharge centered on the portrait of Washington. Back of the 5-cent note is brown; the 10-cent, green; the 25-cent, violet, and the 50-cent note, red or reddish-orange. All backs have a large, bronze numerical outline overprinted.

Some specimen notes of this issue (and of the Third Issue) were printed on paper watermarked "C.S.A." in block letters, for Confederate States of America. The paper, made in England for the printing of Confederate States paper money, was contraband seized from a captured blockade runner.

First Issue notes had been printed by the National Bank Note Company of New York and the American Bank Note Company of New York — which were one concern in all respects but name — at a cost which the Treasury Department thought excessive. The Act of July 11, 1863, instructed the Treasury Department to undertake the printing of its own currency.

Although the primary purpose of Second Issue notes was to retire and replace First Issue notes, they were issued in excess of the requirement, to a total value of $23 million.

THIRD ISSUE
December 5, 1864 - August 16, 1869
Denominations: 3¢, 5¢, 10¢, (15¢ essay), 25¢, 50¢

Authorized by the Act of June 30, 1864, the Third Issue of Fractional Currency was necessitated by an increased demand for the low denomination notes and by the continuing counterfeiting of earlier issues. Counterfeits of the Second Issue were of better quality and even more numerous than those of the First Issue had been.

Third Issue notes provide the greatest number of varieties of any issue of Postage or Fractional Currency. Among these are varieties of paper, different colors of backs, ornamental and numerical value surcharges (or none at all), autographed or printed signatures, no signatures, and multiple designs for a single denomination.

In regard to varieties, the 10-cent note is particularly interesting. Through an oversight, the word CENTS does not appear anywhere on the note. The Third Issue varieties are too extensive to be within the scope of these remarks, but they are indicated and priced in the listing which follows.

The Act of June 30, 1864, contained a provision which, by amending the Act of March 3, 1863, authorized the Secretary of the Treasury to determine the form and denominations of Fractional Currency, the means by which it would be made, and the terms of note redemption. This authority permitted Secretary Chase to issue a 3-cent note to facilitate purchase of the new 3-cent first-class postage stamp. Need for the small note was eventually eliminated by the issue of nickel three-cent coins under the Act of March 3, 1865.

Little events can have lasting repercussions, as exemplified by the story of the 5-cent note of the Third Issue. Without the knowledge or authority of his superiors, Spencer M. Clark, then superintendent of the National Currency Bureau, had his likeness put on the 5-cent note of the Third Issue. Clark's presumptive act so angered Congress that a law was enacted April 7, 1866, prohibiting the placing of the likeness of a living person upon any "bonds, securities, notes, Fractional or Postal Currency of the United States." However, the wording of the law did not prohibit the likeness of a living person if the plate for the intended item had already been prepared. Consequently, Clark's portrait didn't disappear from the nation's currency until the passage of May 17, 1866, legislation which authorized the issue of a nickel 5-cent piece and prohibited the issue of any note with a denomination of less than 10 cents.

Likewise unaffected were the Third Issue 25-cent note bearing the portrait of William Fessenden, and the 50-cent note portraying F.E. Spinner, "The Father of Fractional Currency." The only note affected by the legislation was a proposed 15-cent denomination bearing the portraits of Generals Grant and Sherman, for which the plate had not yet been completed. This note was printed only as an essay, and in uniface form, with face and back being printed on separate pieces of paper.

All of the Third Issue notes were produced by the Treasury Department. Total face value was in excess of $86 million.

POSTAGE AND FRACTIONAL CURRENCY SHIELD

The Postage and Fractional Currency Shield was one of the measures by which the Treasury Department sought to overcome and prevent the wide-spread counterfeiting of Fractional Currency notes.

The shields consisted of a type set of the first three issues of Postage and Fractional Currency mounted on a heavy cardboard shield surmounted by an eagle and 13 stars. Size of the framed unit was 24 by 28 inches. The shields were made available to banks and other commercial institutions in 1866-67 to provide them with a file of genuine notes to use as a reference when checking suspect notes. Those qualified to receive the shield paid face value for the notes ($4.66), plus a presumed transportation charge, for a total cost believed to be $7.50.

The 39 closely-trimmed notes (20 faces and 19 backs) mounted on the shield are specimen notes printed on one side only. They include the scarce 15-cent Sherman/Grant essays and the two faces of the 3-cent note, which are distinguished by dark and light backgrounds to Washington's portrait. The shields upon which the notes were pasted are known in gray, pink and green, with gray being the most common.

Although the shields were produced in a quantity believed to be in excess of 4,500, it is presumed that fewer than 200 remain intact, with many of those folded, faded or water-stained. Apparently demand for the shields was less than the Treasury Department had anticipated and the surplus shields were carelessly stored — by common account in an old shed behind the Treasury Building. The number of intact shields was further reduced by early collectors who obtained them solely to secure the scarcer notes, which they removed from the shield.

FOURTH ISSUE
July 14, 1869 - February 16, 1875
Denominations: 10¢, 15¢, 25¢, 50¢

The Fourth Issue of Fractional Currency continued the refinements evident in the Second and Third Issues, and further diminished the pretense of stamp money with which the five issues of fractional notes were launched. The unaesthetic bronze overprintings were eliminated, and an improved type of paper — containing silk fibers — was used.

Three of the six designs (there are three different 50-cent notes) comprising the Fourth Issue make no mention of "stamps." Allegorical art claimed a greater role in note design than before; the 10-cent note bearing a representation of Liberty, and the 15-cent note, a representation of Columbia. The 25-cent and the trio of 50-cent notes bear definitive male portraits.

The Fourth Issue was produced outside the Treasury Department while the BEP experimented with new dry-printing operations that only succeeded in destroying nearly every hydraulic press the Government owned. Combined with increased demand for Legal Tender notes, the Treasury was forced to job out the production of the Fourth Issue Fractionals to the National and American Bank Note Companies.

The total value of the Fourth Issue was more than $166 million.

FIFTH ISSUE
February 26, 1874 - February 15, 1876
Denominations: 10¢, 25¢, 50¢

The Fifth Issue of Fractional Currency was short and simple, consisting of but three notes, each of a different design. Why a change of design was thought necessary at that time is unclear, but the decision may reflect the Treasury Department's continuing disenchantment with the cost of notes produced by the two New York bank note firms.

Faces of the Fifth Issue were printed by the Bureau of Engraving and Printing, the backs by the Columbian Bank Note Company of Washington, D.C., and Joseph R. Carpenter of Philadelphia. Printing of this issue was terminated when the appropriations for the printing of Fractional Currency were exhausted.

Noteworthy varieties of the Fifth Issue include the green seal 10-cent note and the "long key" and "short key" 10-and 25-cent notes. All notes have faces printed in black, with green backs. All carry printed signatures.

Fifth Issue notes were printed to the total value of nearly $63 million, bringing the total value of all Postage and Fractional Currency issued to about $369 million, of which an estimated $1.8 million remains outstanding.

Fractional Currency Valuations

First Issue "Postage Currency"

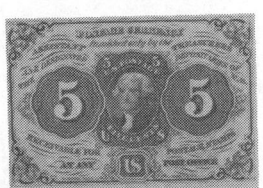 

5 CENTS

KL#	Fr#	Date	Description	VG	VF	Unc
3209	1228	17.7.1862.	Brown. One 5 cent Jefferson stamp at center. Perf. edges; ANBC's monogram on back.	14.00	16.00	155.
3210	1229		Perf. edges; back w/o ANBC's monogram.	15.00	22.00	180.
3211	1230		Straight edges; ABNC's monogram on back.	14.50	16.00	50.00
3212	1231		Straight edges; back w/o ABNC's monogram.	15.00	21.00	150.

10 CENTS

KL#	Fr#	Date	Description	VG	VF	Unc
3213	1240	17.7.1862.	Green. One 10 cent Washington stamp at center. Perf. edges; ABNC's monogram on back.	15.00	18.50	115.
3214	1241		Perf. edges; back w/o ABNC's monogram.	15.50	30.00	130.
3215	1242		Straight edges; ABNC's monogram on back.	11.50	13.00	40.00
3216	1243		Straight edges; back w/o ABNC's monogram.	12.50	40.00	150.

25 CENTS

KL#	Fr#	Date	Description	VG	VF	Unc
3217	1279	17.7.1862.	Brown. Horizontal row of five 5 cent Jefferson stamps. Perf. edges; ABNC's monogram on back.	16.00	25.00	170.
3218	1280		Perf. edges; back w/o ABNC's monogram.	25.00	60.00	275.
3219	1281		Straight edges; ABNC's monogram on back.	11.50	15.00	75.00
3220	1282		Straight edges; back w/o ABNC's monogram.	13.00	60.00	300.

50 CENTS

KL#	Fr#	Date	Description	VG	VF	Unc
3221	1310	17.7.1862.	Green. Horizontal row of five 10 cent Washington stamps. #12 perf. edges; ABNC's monogram on back.	24.00	30.00	290.
3222	1310-A		#14 perf. edges; ABNC's monogram on back.	—	Rare	—
3223	1311		Perf. edges; back w/o ABNC's monogram.	30.00	70.00	300.
3224	1312		Straight edges; ABNC's monogram on back.	17.00	18.50	120.
3225	1313		Straight edges; back w/o ABNC's monogram.	20.00	75.00	300.

Second Issue

5 CENTS

All notes have oval bronze ovpt. on face around head of Washington at center and large bronze outlined denomination numeral(s) on back.

KL#	Fr#	Date	Description	VG	VF	Unc
3226	1232	3.3.1863.	W/o ovpt., on back.	14.00	16.00	45.00
3227	1233		W/ovpt: "18-63" on back.	14.00	16.00	50.00
3228	1234		W/ovpt: "18-63" and "S" on back.	14.00	17.00	75.00
3229	1235		W/ovpt: "18-63" and "R-1" on back. Fiber paper.	17.00	25.00	225.

10 CENTS

KL#	Fr#	Date	Description	VG	VF	Unc
3230	1244		W/o ovpt. on back.	11.00	12.50	45.00
3231	1245		W/ovpt: "18-63" on back.	11.00	15.00	50.00
3232	1246		W/ovpt: "18-63" and "S" on back.	12.00	17.00	65.00
3233	1247		W/ovpt: "18-63" and "1" on back.	20.00	45.00	200.
3234	1248		W/ovpt: "0-63" on upper back.	500.	1200.	2000.
3235	1249		W/ovpt: "18-63" and "T-1" on back. Fiber paper.	16.00	22.00	230.

25 CENTS

KL#	Fr#	Date	Description	VG	VF	Unc
3236	1283	3.3.1863.	W/o ovpt. on back.	11.00	15.00	75.00
3237	1284		W/ovpt: "18-63" on back.	11.00	17.00	85.00
3238	1285		W/ovpt: "18-63" and "A" on back.	11.00	17.00	85.00
3239	1286		W/ovpt: "18-63" and "S" on back.	11.00	17.00	85.00
3240	—		W/ovpt: "18-63" and "1" on back.	—	Rare	—
3241	1288		W/ovpt: "18-63" and "2" on back.	15.00	25.00	120.
3242	1289		W/ovpt: "18-63" and "T-1" on back. Fiber paper.	15.00	19.00	250.
3243	1290		W/ovpt: "18-63" and "T-2" on back. Fiber paper.	15.00	19.00	250.
3244	—		W/ovpt: "18-63" and "S-2" on back.	Reported, not confirmed		

50 CENTS

KL#	Fr#	Date	Description	VG	VF	Unc
3245	1316	3.3.1863.	W/ovpt: "18-63" on back.	20.00	35.00	150.
3246	1317		W/ovpt: "18-63" and "A" on back.	17.00	18.50	150.
3247	1318		W/ovpt: "18-63" and "I" on back.	17.00	18.50	150.
3248	1320		W/ovpt: "18-63" and "0-1" on back. Fiber paper.	20.00	25.00	260.
3249	1321		W/ovpt: "18-63" and "R-2" on back. Fiber paper.	17.00	22.00	275.
3250	1322		W/ovpt: "18-63" and "T-1" on back. Fiber paper.	17.00	22.00	275.

Third Issue

3 CENTS

KL#	Fr#	Date	Description	VG	VF	Unc
3252	1226	3.3.1863.	Portrait of Washington at center with light background.	26.50	30.00	60.00
3253	1227		Portrait with dark background.	26.50	30.00	80.00

5 CENTS

KL#	Fr#	Date	Description	VG	VF	Unc
3254	1236	3.3.1863.	Portrait of Clark at center. Red back.	14.00	18.50	120.
3255	1237		With 'a' on face.	14.00	25.00	140.
3256	1238		Green back.	14.00	16.00	60.00
3257	1239		With 'a' on face.	15.00	18.00	60.00

10 CENTS

KL#	Fr#	Date	Description	VG	VF	Unc
3258	1251	3.3.1863.	Portrait of Washington at center; bronze 10's in each corner. Small sign: Colby-Spinner. Red back.	11.50	14.00	125.
3259	1252		With '1' on face.	13.00	25.00	150.

KL#	Fr#	Date	Description	VG	VF	Unc
3260	1253		Large autographed sign: Colby-Spinner.	16.00	22.00	140.
3261	1254		Large autographed sign: Jeffries-Spinner.	20.00	50.00	250.
3262	1255		Green back w/printed sign: Colby-Spinner.	11.00	14.00	35.00
3263	1255-A		Green back. Large autographed sign: Colby Spinner.	—	Rare	—
3264	1256		With '1' on face. Like 3262.	11.00	20.00	65.00

25 CENTS

KL#	Fr#	Date	Description	VG	VF	Unc
3265	1291	3.3.1863.	Portrait of Fessenden at center. Red back. (No 'a')	11.00	15.00	115.
3266	1292		Small 'a' on face. Red back.	11.00	15.00	150.

KL#	Fr#	Date	Description	VG	VF	Unc
3267	1293		Large 'a' on face. Red back.	11.00	15.00	170.
3268	1294		Green back. (No 'a')	11.00	13.00	80.00
3269	1295		Small 'a' on face. Green back.	11.00	13.00	80.00
3270	1296		Large 'a' on face. Green back.	11.00	13.00	80.00
3270A	—		Like 3270 but 'a' is 7mm to the right and down from normal location. (Very large 'a')	500.	750.	1500.
3271	1297		W/ovpt: "M-2-6-5" on back. Fiber paper.	16.00	25.00	200.
3272	1298		'a' on face; ovpt: "M-2-6-5" on back. Fiber paper.	18.00	50.00	250.
3273	1299		Solid bronze ornamental ovpt. on face. Fiber paper.	250.	450.	1000.
3274	1300		Solid bronze ornamental ovpt. and 'a' on face. Fiber paper.	400.	800.	1500.

50 CENTS

KL#	Fr#	Date	Description	VG	VF	Unc
3275	1324		3.3.1863. Portrait of General Spinner at center; small sign: Colby-Spinner. W/ovpt: 'A-2-6-5' and 50, red back. Printed signature.	38.00	60.00	275.
3276	1325		With '1' and 'a' on face. Printed signature.	100.	150.	750.
3277	1326		With '1' on face. Printed signature.	38.00	70.00	325.
3278	1327		With 'a' on face. Printed signature.	38.00	70.00	325.
3279	1328		Large sign: Colby-Spinner. Autograph signature.	38.00	70.00	275.
3281	1329		Sign: Allison-Spinner. Autograph signature.	38.00	75.00	350.
3282	1330		Sign: Allison-New. Autograph signature.	600.	1250.	2000.

KL#	Fr#	Date	Description	VG	VF	Unc
3283	1331		Multiple 50's in green back.	38.00	70.00	325.
3284	1332		With '1' and 'a' on face.	38.00	80.00	400.
3285	1333		With '1' on face.	38.00	70.00	325.
3286	1334		With 'a' on face.	38.00	75.00	350.
3287	1335		W/ovpt: 'A-2-6-5' on back. Green back.	38.00	75.00	325.
3288	1336		With '1' and 'a' on face. Green back.	150.	400.	1750.
3289	1337		With '1' on face. Green back.	40.00	80.00	325.
3290	1338		With 'a' on face. Green back.	50.00	90.00	350.

KL#	Fr#	Date	Description	VG	VF	Unc
3291	1339		Face similar to #3275. Redesigned green back.	46.00	70.00	350.
3292	1340		With '1' and 'a' on face.	46.00	75.00	350.
3293	1341		With '1' on face.	46.00	80.00	350.
3294	1342		With 'a' on face.	46.00	85.00	350.

KL#	Fr#	Date	Description	VG	VF	Unc
3295	1343		3.3.1863. Red back. Small sign. Printed signature.	44.00	95.00	500.
3296	1344		With '1' and 'a' on face. Printed signature.	75.00	250.	1500.
3297	1345		With '1' on face. Printed signature.	44.00	95.00	500.
3298	1346		With 'a' on face. Printed signature.	44.00	95.00	500.

KL#	Fr#	Date	Description	VG	VF	Unc
3299	1347		W/ovpt: 'A-2-6-5' on back. Red back.	44.00	95.00	500.
3300	1348		With '1' and 'a' on face. Red back.	70.00	350.	1500.
3301	1349		With '1' on face. Red back.	70.00	90.00	475.
3302	1350		With 'a' on face. Red back.	55.00	100.	475.
3303	1351		With small sign. Ovpt: 'S-2-6-4' on back. Fiber paper. Printed signature. Red back.	750.	2000.	4000.
3304	1352		With '1' and 'a' on face. Fiber paper.	—	Rare	
3305	1353		With '1' on face. Fiber paper.	1000.	2750.	5000.
3306	1354		With 'a' on face. Fiber paper.	1250.	3000.	5500.

KL#	Fr#	Date	Description	VG	VF	Unc
3307	1355		Red back. Large autographed sign.	50.00	75.00	475.

KL#	Fr#	Date	Description	VG	VF	Unc
3308	1356		Large autographed sign. w/ovpt: 'A-2-6-5' on back. Red back.	50.00	75.00	475.
3309	1357		Large autographed sign. w/ovpt: 'S-2-6-4' on back. Fiber paper. Red back.	65.00	210.	925.
3310	1358		Green back.	45.00	75.00	425.
3311	1359		With '1' and 'a' on face.	100.	250.	950.
3312	1360		With '1' on face.	45.00	75.00	425.
3313	1361		With 'a' on face.	45.00	75.00	425.
3314	1362		W/ovpt: 'A-2-6-5' on back compactly spaced. (92mm x 30mm). Green back.	45.00	75.00	400.
3315	1363		With '1' and 'a' on face.	100.	225.	850.
3316	1364		With '1' on face.	45.00	75.00	390.
3317	1365		With 'a' on face.	50.00	80.00	485.
3318	1366		W/ovpt: 'A-2-6-5' on back widely spaced. (98mm x 34mm). Green back.	50.00	95.00	500.
3319	1367		With '1' on face.	150.	500.	2000.
3320	1368		W/'1' on face.	55.00	110.	550.
3321	1369		With 'a' on face.	50.00	115.	575.
3322	1370		W/ovpt: 'A-2-6-5' on back. Fiber paper. Green back.	48.00	80.00	600.
3323	1371		With '1' and 'a' on face. Fiber paper. Green back.	100.	500.	1750.
3324	1372		With '1' on face. Fiber paper. Green back.	48.00	80.00	600.
3325	1373		With 'a' on face. Fiber paper. Green back.	60.00	90.00	600.
3326	1373-A		W/ovpt: 'S-2-6-4' on back. Fiber paper. Green back.	1000.	2000.	3000.

Fourth Issue

 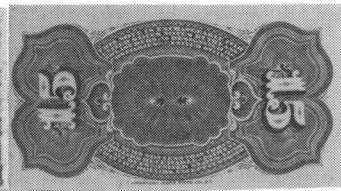

10 CENTS

KL#	Fr#	Date	Description	VG	VF	Unc
3327	1257		3.3.1863. Bust of Liberty at left; 40mm red seal. Wtmkd. paper with pink silk fibers.	11.00	12.50	35.00
3328	1258		Unwtmkd. Paper with pink silk fibers.	11.00	12.50	35.00
3329	1259		Bluish right side of face, paper with violet silk fibers.	12.00	20.00	65.00
3331	1261		38mm red seal; bluish right side of face.	11.00	12.50	35.00

15 CENTS

KL#	Fr#	Date	Description	VG	VF	Unc
3332	1267		3.3.1863. Bust of Columbia at left; 40mm red seal. Wtmk. paper with pink silk fibers.	55.00	60.00	125.
3333	1268		Unwtmkd. paper with pink silk fibers.	55.00	60.00	145.
3334	1269		Bluish right side of face. Paper with violet silk fibers.	55.00	60.00	140.
3336	1271		38mm red seal; bluish right side of face.	55.00	60.00	125.

25 CENTS

KL#	Fr#	Date Description	VG	VF	Unc
3337	1301	3.3.1863. Portrait of Washington at left; 40mm red seal. Wtmkd. paper with pink silk fibers.	12.00	13.00	45.00
3338	1302	Unwtmkd. paper with pink silk fibers.	12.00	13.00	45.00
3340	1303	Bluish right side of face. Paper with violet silk fibers.	13.00	20.00	85.00
3342	1307	38mm red seal; bluish right side of face.	12.00	13.00	45.00

50 CENTS

KL#	Fr#	Date Description	VG	VF	Unc
3343	1374	3.3.1863. Portrait of Lincoln at right. Wtmkd. paper with silk fibers.	28.00	50.00	295.
3344	1375	Unwtmkd. paper with pink silk fibers.	30.00	60.00	300.

KL#	Fr#	Date Description	VG	VF	Unc
3345	1376	3.3.1863. Portrait of Stanton at left; red seal.	17.00	18.00	125.

KL#	Fr#	Date Description	VG	VF	Unc
3347	1379	3.3.1863. Portrait of Dexter at left; green seal.	17.00	18.00	90.00

Fifth Issue, Series of 1874/1875
SHIELD VARIETIES

Long thin solid key

Short thick outlined key

10 CENTS

KL#	Fr#	Date Description	VG	VF	Unc
3348	1264	1874. Portrait of Meredith at left. Green seal with long key.	11.00	12.50	50.00
3349	1265	Red seal with long key.	11.00	12.50	25.00
3350	1266	Red seal with short key.	11.00	12.50	25.00

25 CENTS

KL#	Fr#	Date Description	VG	VF	Unc
3351	1308	1874. Portrait of Walker at left. Red seal with long key.	11.00	12.50	28.00
3352	1309	Red seal with short key.	11.00	12.50	28.00

50 CENTS

KL#	Fr#	Date Description	VG	VF	Unc
3353	1380	Portrait of Crawford at left, pink paper.	17.00	19.00	35.00
3357	1381	Portrait of Crawford at left, white paper.	20.00	27.00	60.00

Proofs and Specimens

All examples are printed uniface with wide or narrow margins. Some notes have 'SPECIMEN' printed in bronze on the blank side. Specimens and proofs of the 4th and 5th issues are extremely rare.

KL#	Fr#	Denomination	Description	VG	VF	Unc
3252SP	—	3 CENTS	Third Issue			
		a. Face with narrow margins, light background.		—	—	95.00
		b. Face with wide margins, light background.		—	Rare	—
		c. Back with narrow margins.		—	—	60.00
		d. Back with wide margins.		—	—	150.
3253SP	—	3 CENTS				
		a. Face with narrow margins, dark background.		—	—	60.00
		b. Face with wide margins, dark background.		—	—	130.
		c. Back with narrow margins.		—	—	60.00
		d. Back with wide margins.		—	—	120.
3212SP	—	5 CENTS	First Issue			
		a. Face with narrow margins.		—	—	55.00
		b. Face with wide margins.		—	—	150.
		c. Back with narrow margins.		—	—	50.00
		d. Back with wide margins.		—	—	140.
3226SP	—	5 CENTS	Second Issue			
		a. Face with narrow margins.		—	—	70.00
		b. Face with wide margins.		—	—	150.
		c. Back with narrow margins.		—	—	55.00
		d. Back with wide margins.		—	—	125.

KL#	Fr#	Denomination	Description	VG	VF	Unc
3254SP	—	5 CENTS	Third Issue.			
		a. Face with narrow margins.		—	—	75.00
		b. Face with wide margins.		—	—	160.
		c. Red back with narrow margins.		—	—	50.00
		d. Red back with wide margins.		—	—	115.
3256SP	—	5 CENTS				
		a. Face with narrow margins.		—	—	55.00
		b. Face with wide margins.		—	—	130.
		c. Green back with narrow margins.		—	—	50.00
		d. Green back with wide margins.		—	—	115.
3216SP	—	10 CENTS	First issue.			
		a. Face with narrow margins.		—	—	65.00
		b. Face with wide margins.		—	—	145.
		c. Back with narrow margins.		—	—	45.00
		d. Back with wide margins.		—	—	125.
3230SP	—	10 CENTS	Second issue.			
		a. Face with narrow margins.		—	—	75.00
		b. Face with wide margins.		—	—	150.
		c. Back with narrow margins.		—	—	50.00
		d. Back with wide margins.		—	—	125.
3258SP	—	10 CENTS	Third issue, small sign: Colby-Spinner.			
		a. Face with narrow margins.		—	—	75.00
		b. Face with wide margins.		—	—	160.
		c. Red back with narrow margins.		—	—	50.00
		d. Red back with wide margins.		—	—	140.
3260SP	—	10 CENTS	Large sign: Colby-Spinner.			
		a. Face with narrow margins.		—	—	75.00
		b. Face with wide margins.		—	—	175.
		c. Red back with narrow margins.		—	—	50.00
		d. Red back with wide margins.		—	—	140.
3261SP	—	10 CENTS	Sign: Jeffries-Spinner.			
		a. Face with narrow margins.		—	—	200.
		b. Face with wide margins.		—	—	4000.
		c. Red back with narrow margins.		—	—	60.00
		d. Red back with wide margins.		—	—	140.
3262SP	—	10 CENTS				
		a. Face with narrow margins.		—	—	155.
		b. Face with wide margins.		—	—	140.
		c. Green back with narrow margins.		—	—	50.00
		d. Green back with wide margins.		—	—	125.
3453SP	—	15 CENTS	Portraits of Grant at right and Sherman at left; small sign: Colby-Spinner.			
		a. Face with narrow margins.		—	—	150.
		b. Face with wide margins.		—	—	225.
		c. Green back with narrow margins.		—	—	100.
		d. Green back with wide margins.		—	—	185.
3454SP	—	15 CENTS	Large sign: Colby-Spinner.			
		a. Face with narrow margins.		—	—	1700.
		b. Face with wide margins.		—	—	5500.
		c. Red back with narrow margins.		—	—	110.
		d. Red back with wide margins.		—	—	190.
3455SP	—	15 CENTS	Sign: Jeffries-Spinner.			
		a. Face with narrow margins.		—	—	175.
		b. Face with wide margins.		—	—	225.
		c. Red back with narrow margins.		—	—	95.00
		d. Red back with wide margins.		—	—	195.
3456SP	—	15 CENTS	Sign: Allison-Spinner.			
		a. Face with narrow margins.		—	—	225.
		b. Face with wide margins.		—	—	300.
		c. Red back with narrow margins.		—	—	95.00
		d. Red back with wide margins.		—	—	195.
3457SP	—	15 CENTS	W/o any signatures.			
		a. Face with narrow margins.		—	Rare	—
		b. Face with wide margins.		—	Rare	—
		c. Red back with narrow margins.		—	—	150.
		d. Red back with wide margins.		—	—	210.
3220SP	—	25 CENTS	First issue.			
		a. Face with narrow margins.		—	—	80.00
		b. Face with wide margins.		—	—	175.
		c. Back with narrow margins.		—	—	70.00
		d. Back with wide margins.		—	—	165.
3236SP	—	25 CENTS	Second issue.			
		a. Face with narrow margins.		—	—	75.00
		b. Face with wide margins.		—	—	195.
		c. Back with narrow margins.		—	—	65.00
		d. Back with wide margins.		—	—	180.
3265SP	—	25 CENTS	Third issue.			
		a. Face with narrow margins.		—	—	60.00
		b. Face with wide margins.		—	—	165.
		c. Red back with narrow margins.		—	—	55.00
		d. Red back with wide margins.		—	—	150.
3268SP	—	25 CENTS				
		a. Face with narrow margins.		—	—	60.00
		b. Face with wide margins.		—	—	165.
		c. Green back with narrow margins.		—	—	55.00
		d. Green back with wide margins.		—	—	155.
3225SP	—	50 CENTS	First issue.			
		a. Face with narrow margins.		—	—	90.00
		b. Face with wide margins.		—	—	220.
		c. Back with narrow margins.		—	—	80.00
		d. Back with wide margins.		—	—	200.
3245SP	—	50 CENTS	Second issue, no surcharge.			
		a. Face with narrow margins.		—	—	80.00
		b. Face with wide margins.		—	—	265.
		c. Back with narrow margins.		—	—	70.00
		d. Back with wide margins.		—	—	280.
3275SP	—	50 CENTS	Third issue, small sign: Colby-Spinner.			
		a. Face with narrow margins.		—	—	85.00
		b. Face with wide margins.		—	—	180.
		c. Red back with narrow margins.		—	—	75.00
		d. Red back with wide margins.		—	—	180.
3279SP	—	50 CENTS	Large sign: Colby-Spinner.			
		a. Face with narrow margins.		—	—	110.
		b. Face with wide margins.		—	—	250.
		c. Red back with narrow margins.		—	—	75.00
		d. Red back with wide margins.		—	—	180.
3281SP	—	50 CENTS	Sign: Allison-Spinner.			
		a. Face with narrow margins.		—	Rare	—
		b. Face with wide margins.		—	Rare	—
		c. Red back with narrow margins.		—	—	75.00
		d. Red back with wide margins.		—	—	150.
3282SP	—	50 CENTS	Sign: Jeffries-Spinner.			
		a. Face with narrow margins.		—	—	150.
		b. Face with wide margins.		—	—	3000.
		c. Red back with narrow margins.		—	—	75.00
		d. Red back with wide margins.		—	—	180.
3283SP	—	50 CENTS	Small sign: Colby-Spinner.			
		a. Face with narrow margins.		—	—	85.00
		b. Face with wide margins.		—	—	180.
		c. Green back with narrow margins.		—	—	75.00
		d. Green back with wide margins.		—	—	185.
3291SP	—	50 CENTS	Small sign: Colby-Spinner.			
		a. Face with narrow margins.		—	—	85.00
		b. Face with wide margins.		—	—	180.
		c. Green back with narrow margins.		—	—	1750.
		d. Green back with wide margins.		—	—	5000.
3295SP	—	50 CENTS	Small sign: Colby-Spinner.			
		a. Face with narrow margins.		—	—	85.00
		b. Face with wide margins.		—	—	220.
		c. Red back with narrow margins.		—	—	75.00
		d. Red back with wide margins.		—	—	180.
3307SP	—	50 CENTS	Large sign: Colby-Spinner.			
		a. Face with narrow margins.		—	—	110.
		b. Face with wide margins.		—	—	250.
		c. Red back with narrow margins.		—	—	75.00
		d. Red back with wide margins.		—	—	180.
3309SP	—	50 CENTS	Sign: Jeffries-Spinner.			
		a. Face with narrow margins.		—	—	125.
		b. Face with wide margins.		—	Rare	—
		c. Red back with narrow margins.		—	—	75.00
		d. Red back with wide margins.		—	—	180.
3310SP	—	50 CENTS	Small sign: Colby-Spinner.			
		a. Face with narrow margins.		—	—	85.00
		b. Face with wide margins.		—	—	220.
		c. Green back with narrow margins.		—	—	75.00
		d. Green back with wide margins.		—	—	185.

Currency Shields

Produced by the Treasury Dept. in 1866-67 for sale to banks to aid in detection of counterfeit notes. These shields consist of 39 specimens of the first, second and third issues. Mounted in a picture frame.

KL#	Fr#	Date	Description	VG	VF	Unc
3354	1382		Gray background.	—	1200.	2200.
3355	1383		Pink background.	—	2500.	6000.
3356	1383-A		Green background.	—	Rare	—

Error Notes

By Alan Herbert, Frederick J. Bart and Harry E. Jones

Considering the more than four billion pieces of U.S. paper money which the Bureau of Engraving and Printing currently produces each year, the miniscule number of error notes which reach the public are a tribute to the BEP's workmanship and quality control — and the reason that U.S. paper money errors enjoy significant popularity (and in many cases, premium value) within the numismatic hobby.

The following listings of major categories of currency errors have been produced to allow the non-specialist to quickly and easily determine the value of any paper money error based on the way it looks. Since, in the final analysis, the value of an error note is usually based on how different it looks from a normal note, no attempt has been made to delve into the technical causes of the errors. While it often requires a familiarity with currency production processes at the Bureau of Engraving and Printing to adequately understand how an error occured or escaped detection, such knowledge is only necessary for the error-variety specialist. These listings will generally answer the most important question in the mind of the non-collector or casual collector who encounters an error note: "What's it worth?"

The listings in this catalog are a simplification of the computerized "Paper Money Cataloging System" developed by consultant Alan Herbert to classify paper money errors and printing varieties.

Error note listings are arranged in the same sequence in which modern U.S. paper money is printed: face printing, back printing, overprinting, cutting.

Wherever possible, valuations for error notes have been provided in up to three grades of preservation. All values quoted are for current, or recent, small size U.S. paper money issues. **Values quoted are in addition to the face value of the note.** As a general rule, paper money errors are most avidly collected in the lower denominations, since few collectors are willing to tie up their money in high-denomination notes. Thus, contrary to expectation, a high denomination or rare note valuable in its own right will not often draw any premium as an error, and may in fact be reduced in value because of a lack of collector demand. It should also be noted that for many types of error notes, there is little demand for notes in circulated condition. In such cases, a dash will be used in the circulated grade columns to indicate little, if any, premium over face value.

Because "star" notes (notes with an open-center 5-pointed star in place of a serial number suffix letter) are printed to replace notes that have been misprinted or damaged in production, they carry a premium value when they are encountered with printing errors. Many collectors also attach special value to error notes which exhibit the red crayon marks (easily faked) or special stickers which Bureau of Engraving and Printing inspectors use to tag unfit notes for destruction.

Some error notes, especially the more spectacular varieties, cannot be evaluated in a catalog listing such as this. Their value must be determined on an individual basis, between buyer and seller. Such listings will be indicated in these pages with a series of dashes in all condition columns.

Multiple Errors

Because of the nature of the note-printing process, one malfunction of the press, one problem with the paper, or one human error will occasionally manifest itself in the form of notes which exhibit two or more distinct types of error. While most such notes are usually caught in the stringent inspection procedure, they are sometimes found in circulation.

The value of such multiple-error notes cannot be computed by simply adding the values of each error represented on the note; rather, it must be determined on an individual basis.

Large-size Note Errors

Paper money errors on large-size U.S. paper money are much scarcer and more valuable than the same type of printing mishap on current-size currency.

Because quantities of notes produced in the period before 1928 were much lower than today, and the printing processes were slower and less mechanical, the chances of errors occuring and escaping undetected were much smaller than is now the case. Additionally, since there were few collectors of paper money, and fewer collectors of error notes in the period when the "saddleblankets" were current, those error notes which did reach circulation were not likely to be saved as collector's items.

The value of large-size currency errors is usually several times the value of the same error on a small-size note. Again, however, specific value must be determined on an individual basis.

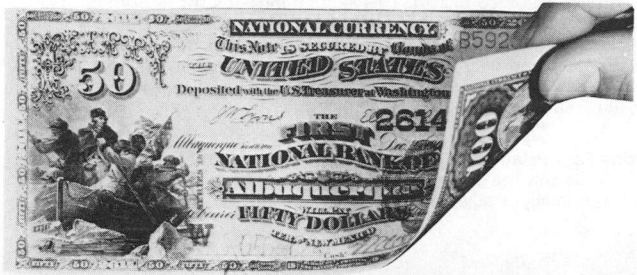

National Currency Errors

While the number of extra printing processes associated with the production of National Bank Notes, such as affixing individual bank names and charter numbers, created extra opportunities for mistakes to be made, all National Currency error notes can be considered extremely rare.

For much of their circulation period, the signatures of the bank officials had to be hand-affixed and the notes were individually cut from the sheets by hand. In effect, they were subject to a second "inspection" at the issuing bank, after they had left the Bureau of Engraving and Printing.

National Currency errors are probably unique in that their value is most often determined by the bank of issue, rather than the type of error. Thus, while all National Bank Note errors are in great demand, those from particularly rare banks or from popularly-collected states will be in greater demand. Naturally, the value of every National Bank Note error is highly individual.

Fake Error Notes

Some types of currency errors naturally lend themselves to fakery. The addition or removal of ink to simulate a genuine printing error is a relatively simple process which the collector must continually bear in mind when confronted with what appears to be an error note.

The collector's best defense against being stuck with a phony error is to either acquire a working knowledge of the printing process and the mishaps which can occur, or to deal with reputable specialists in this area.

Not all apparent error notes which are not genuine can be traced to intentionally deceptive practices. Current U.S. notes are often enocuntered, for example, with backs that are some shade of blue or yellow. Since it can be unequivacably stated that the no modern U.S. paper money has yet been printed with the wrong color of ink — either face or back — all such color variations occurred after the currency reached circulation. The change of the green ink to blue or yellow can usually be traced to the application of bleach or alkali to a note — often when a note mistakenly goes through the washing machine.

First (Back) Printing

This division includes all of the errors that occur during the first printing, the back of current U.S. paper money, including those which result in some or all of the back design being printed on the face of the note.

Missing Back Printing: Any note which has failed to receive the first printing and is completely blank on the back. Usually the result of two sheets going through the press at the same time.

	VG	VF	Unc
Missing Back Printing	75.00	100.	225.

Incomplete Printing, Unprinted: Any note which has had a portion of the back design left unprinted. Often another part of the same currency sheet becomes folded and intercepts the printing. In other cases, a foreign object, such as other paper, marker strips, tape, wrapping material, etc., comes between the printing plate and the paper. Value depends on whether the foreign object is recovered with the note, and on the size and location of the unprinted area. **Note:** Beware of fake errors created by erasing portions of the printing.

	VG	VF	Unc
Incomplete Printing, with foreign object	—	—	500.
Incomplete Printing, without foreign object	10.00	15.00	50.00

Incomplete Printing, Insufficient Ink: A note which displays missing, weak or irregular printing of the back due to a lack of ink or less than the normal amount of ink. May be caused by a "board break" or other defects in the system which presses paper onto the inked printing plate, as well as by problems with the ink or inking operation, itself.

	VG	VF	Unc
Light Printing, Back 25 percent	3.00	5.00	10.00
Light Printing, Back 25-50 percent	4.50	7.50	15.00
Light Printing, Back 50-75 percent	5.00	10.00	20.00
Light Printing, Back 75-95 percent	10.00	15.00	25.00
Light Printing, Back 100 percent	20.00	25.00	35.00

Ink Stain or Smear: Areas of ink of the normal color (though the density may vary) deposited on the back of the note at some point in the printing process, or ink which has been smeared while still wet. Value depends on the size, number and location of the defect. A minimum of one inch in width is necessary for the defect to be considered "large."

	VG	VF	Unc
Ink Stain or Smear, small	2.00	3.00	5.00
Ink Stain or Smear, medium or several small	5.00	8.00	15.00
Ink Stain or Smear, large	8.00	15.00	25.00

Offset Printing, Back to Face: An ink impression of all or part of the back design transferred by some part of the printing press in a mirror-image to the face of the note. Values depend on the percentage of the whole design that is transferred and the darkness (the darker the better) of the ink impression. Values quoted here are for dark offset impressions at or about the percentages indicated.

	VG	VF	Unc
Offset Printing, Back to Face, less than 25 percent	2.00	4.00	5.00
Offset Printing, Back to Face, 25-50 percent	4.50	7.50	10.00
Offset Printing, Back to Face, 50-75 percent	5.00	10.00	15.00
Offset Printing, Back to Face, 75-95 percent	10.00	15.00	20.00
Offset Printing, Back to Face, 100 percent	15.00	30.00	50.00

Double Printing on Back: A note which has been fed through the printing press twice, and shows two complete printed images of the back design.

	VG	VF	Unc
Double Printing on Back	175.	300.	650.

Partial Double Printing on Back: A note which shows doubling of a portion of the back design or partial overlapping image due to a loose plate or other printing press malfunction.

	VG	VF	Unc
Partial Double Printing on Back	50.00	125.	225.

Back Printing Out of Register: Notes which have the back printed out of normal centered position due to faulty feed of the note paper through the printing press or faulty adjustment of press alignment. Front of the note will be properly centered.

	VG	VF	Unc
Back Printing Out of Register, unequal margins	2.00	3.00	10.00

	VG	VF	Unc
Back Printing Out of Register, adjoining note shows	6.00	9.00	35.00

Second (Face) Printing

In the current U.S. currency printing process at the Bureau of Engraving and Printing, 32-note sheets which have received the back printing are then printed with the face design. This section includes those printing varieties and errors which occur during this stage of note production. In recent years, the face design has included the engraved signatures of the Treasurer of the United States and Secretary of the Treasury, but earlier small size U.S. currency, depending on series, had the signatures as part of the overprint, along with the Treasury seal and serial numbers.

Missing Face Printing: Any note which has failed to receive the face printing and exhibits only the overprinting on the front of the note. Usually the result of two sheets going through the press at the same time.

	VG	VF	Unc
Missing Face Printing	200.	350.	650.

Incomplete Printing, Unprinted: Any note which has had a portion of the face design left unprinted. Often another part of the same currency sheet becomes folded and intercepts the printing. In other cases, a foreign object, such as other paper, marker strips, tape, wrapping material (in one case, a Band-Aid), etc., comes between the printing plate and the paper. Value depends on whether the foreign object is recovered with the note, and on the size and location of the unprinted area. **Note:** Beware of fake errors created by erasing portions of the printing.

	VG	VF	Unc
Incomplete Printing, with foreign object	—	—	600.

	VG	VF	Unc
Incomplete Printing, without foreign object	25.00	40.00	125.

Incomplete Printing, Insufficient Ink: A note which displays missing, weak or irregular printing of the face design due to a lack of ink or less than the normal amount of ink. May be caused by a "board break" or other defects of the system which presses paper onto the inked printing plate, as well as by problems with the ink or inking operation, itself.

	VG	VF	Unc
Insufficient Ink, one or more small spots	5.00	10.00	15.00
Insufficient Ink, 25-50 percent of face	10.00	15.00	30.00
Insufficient Ink, 50 percent or more of face	15.00	25.00	40.00
Insufficient Ink, 100 percent of face	20.00	25.00	45.00

Ink Stain or Smear: Areas of ink of the normal color (though the density may vary) deposited on the face of the note at some point in the printing process, or ink that has been smeared while still wet. Value depends on the size, number and location of the defect. A minimum of one inch in width is necessary for the defect to be considered "large."

	VG	VF	Unc
Ink Stain or Smear, small	2.00	4.00	10.00
Ink Stain or Smear, medium or several small	5.00	10.00	20.00
Ink Stain or Smear, large	10.00	20.00	40.00

Offset Printing, Face to Back: An ink impression of all or part of the face design transferred by some part of the printing press in a mirror-image to the back of the note. Values depend on the percentage of the whole design that is transferred and the darkness (the darker the better) of the ink impression. Values quoted here are for dark offset impressions at or about the percentages indicated.

	VG	VF	Unc
Offset Printing, Face to Back, less than 25 percent	2.00	4.00	10.00
Offset Printing, Face to Back, 25-50 percent	4.50	7.50	15.00
Offset Printing, Face to Back, 50-75 percent	5.00	10.00	20.00
Offset Printing, Face to Back, 75-95 percent	10.00	15.00	25.00
Offset Printing, Face to Back, 100 percent	18.00	25.00	50.00

Double Printing on Face: A note which has been fed through the printing press twice, and shows two complete images of the face design.

	VG	VF	Unc
Double Printing on Face	350.	600.	1250.

Partial Double Printing on Face: A note which shows doubling of a portion of the face design or partial overlapping image due to a loose plate or other printing press malfunction.

	VG	VF	Unc
Partial Double Printing on Face	100.	150.	200.

Face Printing Out of Register: A note that has the face printed out of normal centered position due to faulty feed of the note paper through the printing press or faulty adjustment of press alignment. Back of the note will be properly centered.

	VG	VF	Unc
Face Printing Out of Register, unequal margins	2.00	5.00	10.00

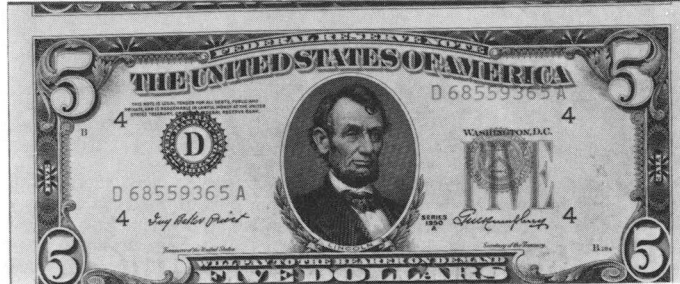

	VG	VF	Unc
Face Printing Out of Register, adjoining note shows	3.00	7.50	20.00

Inverted Face: Since the back is printed first, it is used as a reference to determine an inversion error. Such notes are printed with the face upside down in relation to the back.

	VG	VF	Unc
Inverted Face	200.	300.	600.

Mismatched Denominations: A note printed with one denomination on the back and a different denomination on the face. Often called the "King" of paper money errors.

	VG	VF	Unc
Mismatched Denominations	3500.	5500.	8000.

Third (Overprint) Printing

This section includes all of the errors that occur during the third printing, the application of the overprinting. On current U.S. paper money, that includes the green Treasury seal and serial numbers, and the black Federal Reserve District seal and Federal Reserve District designation numbers in the four corners of the interior of the note's face design. Earlier notes also included the Treasury officials' engraved signatures as part of the overprinting.

Completely Missing Overprint: Any note which failed to receive the complete overprint; i.e., all overprint elements are missing. Usually the result of two sheets going through the overprinting press at the same time.

	VG	VF	Unc
Completely Missing Overprint	40.00	100.	200.

Incomplete Overprint, Unprinted: Any note which has had one or more of the overprint elements left unprinted. Often another part of the same currency sheet becomes folded and intercepts the printing. In other cases a foreign object, such as other paper, marker strips, tape, wrapping material (in one case, a Band-Aid), etc., comes between the printing plate and the paper. Value depends on whether the foreign object is recovered with the note, and how many of the overprint elements are missing. On current notes, because the overprint is applied in a two-color printing process, it is possible for a note to receive only one set of elements (green or black), with the intercepting paper falling off in between.

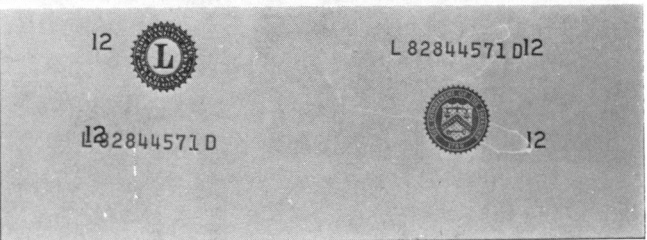

	VG	VF	Unc
Incomplete Overprint, with foreign object	—	—	1500.
Incomplete Overprint, without foreign object	10.00	20.00	50.00

Incomplete Printing, Insufficient Ink: A note which displays missing, weak or irregular printing of the overprint elements due to a lack of ink or less than the normal amount of ink.

	VG	VF	Unc
Incomplete Printing, Insufficient Ink	5.00	10.00	15.00

Ink Stain or Smear: Areas of ink of the normal color (though the density may vary) deposited on the face of the note at some point in the printing process, or ink that has been smeared while still wet. Value depends on the size, number and location of the defect. A minimum of one inch in width is necessary for the defect to be considered "large."

	VG	VF	Unc
Ink Stain or Smear, small	2.00	3.00	5.00
Ink Stain or Smear, medium or several small	4.00	6.00	10.00
Ink Stain or Smear, large	5.00	10.00	25.00

A unique error, attributed to filling one of the ink fonts with green instead of black ink, occurred on a $100 note which has a green district seal, rather than the normal black. As far as is known this is the first instance where this mistake has occurred in more than 130 years.

Offset Printing, Overprint to Back: An ink impression of all or part of the overprint transferred by the overprinting press in a mirror-image to the back of a subsequently-printed note. Value depends on the number of overprint elements thus transferred and the darkness (the darker the better) of the ink impression. Values quoted here are for dark offset impressions at or about the percentages indicated.

	VG	VF	Unc
Offset Printing, Overprint to Back, 25-50 percent	8.00	15.00	40.00
Offset Printing, Overprint to Back, 50-75 percent	12.00	20.00	60.00
Offset Printing, Overprint to Back, 100 percent	35.00	50.00	85.00

Double Printing of Overprint: A note which has been fed through the overprinting press twice, and shows two complete printed images of the overprint elements.

	VG	VF	Unc
Double Printing of Overprint	300.	500.	1000.

Partial Double Printing of Overprint: A note which shows doubling of a portion of the overprint elements, or a partial overlapping image of the overprint design due to a loose plate or other overprinting press malfunction.

	VG	VF	Unc
Partial Double Printing of Overprint	125.	200.	350.

Overprinting Out of Register: A note which has had the third printing out of position on the face of the note, due to faulty sheet feed or faulty adjustment of the press alignment. As a rule, notes have no premium value unless the overprint is far enough out of alignment to overlap some portion of the face design not normally touched. The further out of alignment, the more valuable the error note.

	VG	VF	Unc
Overprint Out of Register Into Design, slightly	5.00	10.00	25.00
Overprint Out of Register Into Design, significantly	10.00	20.00	50.00
Overprint Out of Register, adjoining overprint shows	125.	175.	300.

Inverted Overprint: A note on which the overprinting is upside-down in relation to the face design; the result of a sheet of notes being fed into the overprinting press at a 180-degree rotation from normal.

	VG	VF	Unc
Inverted Overprint	150.	200.	300.

Overprint on Back: A note which has the overprint applied to the back; the result of sheets being fed into the overprinting press with the wrong wide up, or the sheet being folded during the overprinting process.

	VG	VF	Unc
Overprint on Back, normal position	45.00	85.00	225.
Overprint on Back, inverted	200.	400.	700.

Some of the most dramatic paper money errors occur during the printing process when a sheet of bank note paper becomes folded in the printing press at some stage of the operation. This generally causes areas of the notes which would normally be printed to be left blank, and/or other areas to receive ink where it would not normally be found. Similarly, when a malfunction occurs during the cutting of the sheets into individual notes, the results can be spectacular. On all but the most minor and commonly encountered paper, folding and cutting errors, values for such notes is largely dependent on the size and area affected.

	VG	VF	Unc
Overprint on Back, at angle	75.00	100.	250.

Mismatched Serial Numbers: A note on which the serial numbers are not the same; the result of the serial numbering block being incorrectly set, or one or more digits becoming stuck during overprinting.

	VG	VF	Unc
Mismatched Serial Numbers, one digit	35.00	50.00	150.
Mismatched Serial Numbers, two digits	30.00	50.00	175.
Mismatched Serial Numbers, three or more digits	45.00	60.00	300.
Mismatched Serial Numbers, prefix or suffix letter	100.	125.	350.
Two Notes With Identical Serial Numbers	25.00	35.00	100.

Turned Digit: A note which has one or more of digits of the serial number partially visible, the result of the digit being stuck in the numbering block during the overprinting process.

	VG	VF	Unc
Turned Digit	5.00	10.00	20.00

Hawaii, North Africa, "R" & "S" Notes: Because of the popularity of the several World War II era emergency and experimental currency issues, and the relative rarity of error notes among these issues, the values of overprinting errors on these types are highly individual and negotiable.

Paper Errors: Paper in the principal ingredient in a bank note, and defects in the paper itself often result in significant error notes, printed on paper that may be defective, damaged during production or printing, marked or otherwise spoiled. Values are based on the size and prominence of the defect.

	VG	VF	Unc
Printed on *Torn* Paper, small tear	5.00	10.00	25.00

	VG	VF	Unc
Printed on *Torn* Paper, medium or several small tears	15.00	30.00	150.

	VG	VF	Unc
Printed on *Torn* Paper, large tear	25.00	50.00	75.00
Printed on Scrap of Torn Paper	—	—	250.

Interior Fold: A note which shows the result of a folded sheet within the dimensions of a normal note is classed as an interior fold. They are generally smaller and less dramatic than exterior folds.

	VG	VF	Unc
Interior Fold, single	1.00	2.00	5.00
Interior Fold, two	3.00	5.00	10.00

	VG	VF	Unc
Interior Fold, several	5.00	10.00	15.00

Exterior Fold: A fold anywhere on the sheet may affect one or more of the notes and will affect the size and shape of printed and unprinted areas, and where the printing is located if out of normal position. Often when being cut, a portion of the sheet outside the normal margins of the note will remain attached to the note (the piece is sometimes referred to as a "butterfly"). Value depends on the fold and cut, and increases sharply with the size of the affected area.

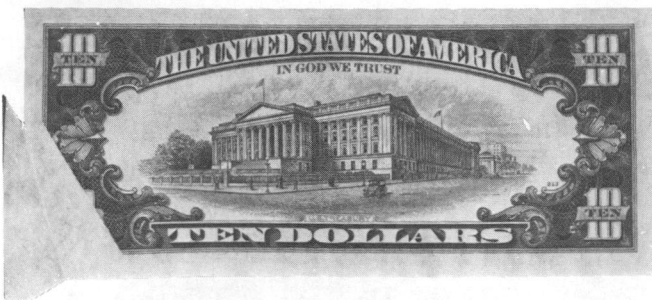

	VG	VF	Unc
Exterior Fold, minor extra paper and corresponding blank area	10.00	20.00	50.00
Exterior Fold, significant extra paper and corresponding blank area	25.00	35.00	200.

	VG	VF	Unc
Exterior Fold, very large extra paper and corresponding blank area	200.	300.	600.

Cutting Errors: Malfunctions in the cutting operating, whereby hundreds or thousands of sheets of bank notes are cut at a time will result in notes which are poorly centered on both sides. Generally, unless part of another note shows, there is little premium value. Notes which exhibit about half of each of two notes are the most valuable.

	VG	VF	Unc
Cut Out of Register, minor	7.50	15.00	65.00
Cut Out of Register, major	75.00	150.	500.
Scrap of Torn or Cut Paper Attached to Note	5.00	10.00	20.00

Fake Cutting Errors

Collectors should be aware of the existence of fake cutting error notes created by unscrupulous persons from the uncut sheets of U.S. paper money now being sold to the public. Any Series 1976 $2 Federal Reserve Note with a star suffix, or any Series 1981 or later $1 FRN with serial number of 99 840 001 or higher that exhibits a cutting error should be viewed with suspicion. At least one advertisement has appeared in a national "gossip" tabloid offering such notes for sale.

Guide to Authentication

Counterfeit paper money has been in existence about as long as paper currency itself. The earliest known Chinese currency, circa 14th century, carries on it a notice that promises death to counterfeiters. Similar warnings were carried on paper money well into the 19th century.

Likewise, for most of the past 500 years, the passing of a counterfeit note, even in ignorance, could doom a person to a long prison term or a short rope dance on the gallows.

In most times and places, even the possession of a counterfeit note has been a felony.

In the United States, the history of counterfeit currency has followed the global pattern closely. With precious metal coinage always a scarce and highly valued commodity in the colonies, North Americans were among the earliest of the world's peoples to adopt paper currency. Many paper money issues were forthcoming from the colonies and other municipal units as early as the 17th century. Counterfeits followed closely on their heels. The techniques by which genuine paper currency was made in the colonial era was crude. Most notes were entirely typeset, or contained just a rough woodcut illustration. It was relatively easy for the dishonest to duplicate the technology.

By the mid-18th century, printers such as Benjamin Franklin were enhancing the security of the notes they printed with elaborate and delicate leafwork designs and other devices aimed at making forgery more difficult. The notes still bore the warning: "Death to Counterfeit."

When the Continental Congress began to issue paper currency to finance its fight for American independence, the paper money authorized quickly became a wartime target. While the usual felons faked the notes for personal profit, the Royalists created nearly-perfect counterfeits in an effort to discredit the currency.

By and large, the efforts of counterfeiters were so vexing to the early issuers of paper money in this country that the general public adopted a mistrust of the medium. With the nation sitting on many productive piles of gold, silver and copper, the production and commercial use of specie remained the norm for the nation's first century. Federally issued paper money was issued only in times of dire economic straits and was quickly retired when the emergency passed.

The fiscal crisis which accompanied the Civil War, and the period of more than a decade before the government totally resumed specie payments, created an atmosphere in which paper money had to be once again accepted as an emergency coinage substitute. The acceptance grew to trust, and by the late 1870s, federally issued paper money circulated freely. Gradually, the convenience factor of paper currency forced the larger gold and silver coins out of everyday commerce. To a large extent, the public acceptance of, and reliance upon, paper money for its daily business needs helped diminish the counterfeiters' opportunities.

Fake currency can only flourish when its victims are unfamiliar with the genuine article. While most money handlers of a century ago could tell by the look, feel and heft whether a gold coin was genuine, based upon years of experience handling many of the pieces, their familiarity with a paper note of the same denomination was not so strong. The fact that there were as many as half a dozen issues of the same denomination circulating side by side — Gold and Silver Certificates, U.S. Notes, Coin Notes, National Bank Notes, etc. — only compounded the problem.

In that situation, counterfeit U.S. currency proliferated. In the days when $5 represented most of a week's wages for the working man, the Main Street money handler, who may have

Counterfeit example of KL 43

seen a bill of a particular type or issue but infrequently, had little experience upon which to base a judgment of authenticity.

It is not coincidental that most surviving counterfeit U.S. notes are issues of the 1880s-1890s. By the end of the 19th century, the government had moved to limit the number of different types of paper money in circulation. Early in the 20th century, some standardization of design began to take place, culminating in the issue of the new small-size paper money in 1929, at which time each denomination appeared with a unique face portrait and back design, regardless of type.

That standardization, along with the elimination of circulating gold coins in 1933 in favor of paper money and an increase in public awareness of currency authentication procedures helped diminish the threat of counterfeit currency to the average American.

Today, most Americans will go through their entire lifetimes without ever encountering a counterfeit note. Most counterfeiting schemes are caught before the notes ever hit circulation in this country. In fact, there are more counterfeit U.S. dollars being made and passed abroad than in this country — a tribute to the international acceptance of the U.S. currency, and proof, once again, that counterfeits flourish where public unfamiliarity can be exploited.

It is not surprising that collecting of counterfeit paper money is a modern phenomenon. For most of history in nations around the world, possession of counterfeit currency represented, at best, a financial loss to a person, and in extreme cases, a possible date with a noose.

In the United States, mere possession of counterfeit currency was not made illegal until well into the 20th century.

Prior to that, in typical cases in which a fraudulent note was discovered by a bank or the Treasury Department, it was "canceled" by having a word such as "Counterfeit," "Worthless" or "Bad," written, stamped or punched onto the note. It was then returned to the person who had deposited it. That person had to fend for himself, as best he could, in returning the note from whence it came. Eventually, the phony note would reach a dead end when the passer could not be found or convinced to make a refund. At that point, the counterfeit was destroyed or stuck in a drawer to be discovered by later generations.

Because these counterfeits could not be spent, in some cases the only examples the hobby has of some colonial-era paper currency issues are the counterfeits; all of the genuine notes having been redeemed, lost or destroyed.

To a lesser extent, a similar situation can be found among U.S. paper money, especially in high denomination early federal notes, and some First Charter National Bank Notes, in which counterfeits outnumber genuine survivors.

It is to address this situation that this section of the *Standard Catalog of United States Paper Money* has been created.

There exists in many collections today, examples of counterfeit notes which have been unknowingly acquired as genuine. It can be generally said that the lower the condition of a surviving note, the greater likelihood of its being counterfeit. The ravages of time and circulation on currency — genuine and counterfeit — soon disguise the details by which the two might have been differentiated earlier in their lives.

Compiled in the following pages are lists of known counterfeit notes. The listings have been modified, for easier use by collectors, from various bank note reporters which were published during the 19th and early 20th centuries to allow banks and merchants to spot counterfeits. The descriptions have been distilled to the points most likely to make a counterfeit identifiable to today's hobbyist. In most cases, the serial number is not a good mark of identification for large-size currency types. While most small-size counterfeits were produced with the same serial number, large-size notes generally had individual serial numbers added by hand after the body of the note had been produced. This often resulted in serial numbers — especially prefix and suffix letters and devices — which today's knowledgeable collector will realize could never have been genuinely issued.

This section is limited to presentation of large-size currency counterfeits.

Persons who discover a note in their holdings to be counterfeit are reminded that current federal law makes illegal the possession of such an item. The letter of the law calls for such notes to be turned in to authorities for destruction.

More pragmatically, while the possession of large-size currency counterfeits is technically illegal, it does not rate highly on the Secret Service's enforcement priority list. There are many in the hobby who would like to see the laws changed to permit legally holding counterfeit large-size notes for their historical interest. Until such time as this might be accomplished, most counterfeits will continue to be held, and to change hands, quietly.

One Dollar
United States Notes

Series 1862
KL 1-4 Chittenden-Spinner. Plate A, B, C, D. Portrait very badly engraved. Mouth crooked, eyes blurred, unnatural expression.

Series 1875
KL 13 Allison-Wyman. Plate D. Engraving coarse, portrait very poor. Attempt to imitate fibers on back.

Silver Certificates

Series 1886
KL 30 Rosecrans-Hyatt. Plate D1768.
KL 32-33 Rosecrans-Huston. Plate B2753. Serial numbers in black, rather than blue.

Series 1891
KL 36 Rosecrans-Nebeker. Plate D. Poor engraving. Scalloped seal.
KL 37 Tillman-Morgan. Plate A16.

Series 1896
KL 39 Bruce-Roberts. Plate C34, D. All fine lines on face lost due to heavy black printing.

Series 1899
KL 40-41 Lyons-Roberts. Plate C. Back of note inverted.
KL 40-41 Lyons-Roberts. Plate C. Crudely photoengraved, lathework and vignettes indistinct.

KL 40-41 Lyons-Roberts. Plate C1661, D1601. Right end has check letter C, left-end check letter resembles upside-down D.
KL 43 Vernon-Treat. No plate letter. Crude woodcut. Names under Lincoln and Grant transposed.
KL 43 Vernon-Treat. Plate B4810, B5147, B7311, B7214. Dangerous counterfeit. Back plate number sometimes added: 2344 or 2844, 3217.
KL 43 Vernon-Treat. Plate C4801. Back plate number 2598. "United' to right of Grant portrait spelled "Usited".
KL 45 Napier-McClung. "Series 1889". Plate B.
KL 45 Napier-McClung. Plate C. 13 stars above eagle are omitted. No back plate number.
KL 45 Napier-McClung. Plate D. No fine lines in scroll work. Poor quality paper. Ink lines imitate fibers.
KL 45 Napier-McClung. Plate D. Serial numbers too large, too heavy, poorly formed. Silk fibers imitated by black ink lines on face, green ink lines on back.
KL 48 Teehee-Burke. Plate B (number indistinct). Red and blue ink lines imitate silk fibers. "Washington D.C." on Treasury seal poorly written.
KL 48 Teehee-Burke. Plate C (number indistinct). Vignettes of Grant and Lincoln especially poor. Three pieces of paper pasted together, with middle piece printed to resemble silk fibers.

Coin Notes

Series 1891
KL 59 Tillman-Morgan. Plate C. Lathework and small lettering poorly executed.
KL 60 Bruce-Roberts. Plate B. Scalloped carmine seal off color. Small words barely readable.
KL 60 Bruce-Roberts. Plate B. Poor counterfeit. pen lines imitate silk fibers. Small seal.

Federal Reserve Bank Notes

Series 1918
KL 71-72 Teehee Burke. Cleveland district. Plate C (no plate number). No attempt to imitate fibers. Poor portrait. Serial numbers out of alignment.

KL 101

Two Dollars
United States Notes

Series 1862
KL 101 Chittenden-Spinner. Plate A, B, C, D. Portrait very badly engraved. Lettering uneven. Imprint of National Bank Note Company almost illegible.

Series 1875
KL 107 Allison-Wyman. Plate D. Printed by photographic process. Has blurred, faded appearance.

Series 1880
KL 112 Bruce-Wyman. Plate D. Portrait of Jefferson has only one eye. Vignette of Capitol only an outline. Many misspelled words. Name under portrait spelled, "Jeffrson." "Legal Tender" on back spelled, "Legal Lender."

Silver Certificates

No Series
KL-? No resemblance to any genuine Silver Certificate. Crudely executed woodcut counterfeit. Has spread eagle vignette on right end; two Indians on left end. Square green back with word "SILVER" at center.

Series 1886
KL 121 Rosecrans-Jordan. Plate A1865. Fair counterfeit. Portrait course. Seal pink, rather than red. Paper has harsh feel.
KL 121 Rosecrans-Jordan. Plate A1870. Face of note a good counterfeit. Back is poorly printed. Lathework broken, blurred and indistinct. Green shading across face of small letters on back missing. BEP imprint at bottom broken and indistinct.
KL 121 Rosecrans-Jordan. Plate C1853. Dangerous counterfeit.
KL 122 Rosecrans-Hyatt. Plate C1857. Poorly executed portrait. Check letter "C" missing at right end. BEP imprint on back barely decipherable.
KL 122-123 Rosecrans-Hyatt. Plate B2235. A very dangerous counterfeit which was re-issued at least four times to correct defects and to keep up with changes in the Treasury seal on genuine notes. The top of the upper loop in the "J" of "James W. Hyatt" is directly under the letter "D" of "D.C." On genuine note, the loop of "J" falls between the "D" and "C."

KL 123

KL 123 Rosecrans-Hyatt. Plate B1863. Seal is bright red instead of dark red. Serial numbers printed in too-dark blue. No cross-hatching on jacket of portrait, just parallel lines.
KL 125 Rosecrans-Huston. Plate D. Poor photographic counterfeit.

Series 1891
KL 126 Rosecrans-Nebeker. Plate B14. Dangerous counterfeit, but on poor quality paper. Upper lip on portrait appears swollen.
KL 126 Rosecrans—Nebeker. Plate C13. Coarsely engraved woodcut. Name "Rosecrans" misspelled "Roscerans." Many other misspellings.
KL 127 Tillman-Morgan. Plate C19. Dangerous counterfeit. White circles around pupils of portrait's eyes are absent. Treasury seal is pink, rather than carmine, and is blurred.
KL 127 Tillman-Morgan. Plate C41. Portrait lacks natural expression. Back printed in much lighter green than genuine note.

Series 1896
KL 128 Tillman-Morgan. Plate B. Note has overall blurred appearance. Serial numbers poor. Portraits on back indistinct.
KL 128 Tillman-Morgan. Plate D. Printed from crudely executed etched plates. Poor paper with no attempt to imitate silk fibers. Back of early version printed in blue, later corrected to green.
KL 129 Bruce-Roberts. Plate B27, C29. Face of notes has blurred, scratchy look. Serial numbers in light blue.

Series 1899
KL 130-139 No check letter. Poorly executed woodcut. Register of the Treasury and Treasurer designations omitted.
KL 130 Lyons-Roberts. Plate A240. Poorly executed on zinc-etched plates.
KL 130 Lyons-Roberts. Plate A578. Poorly done on flimsy paper. No color in Treasury seal and serial numbers.
KL 130 Lyons-Roberts. Plate A568. Two pieces of paper with silk threads pasted between.
KL 130 Lyons-Roberts. Plate C. Very crudely done by photographic process. Blue color at "2," seal and serial number poorly applied.
KL 130 Lyons-Roberts. Plate C117, D174. Deceptive counterfeit. Small letters on face of note poorly done. On back, word "Public" is misspelled, "Purlic."
KL 130 Lyons-Roberts. Plate C177. Portrait poor. Paper is too thick. Back of note has many misspelled words.
KL 132 Vernon-Treat. No check letter. Pale photographic reproduction.
KL 132 Vernon-Treat. No check letter. Printed from crude woodcut plates. Treasury seal and figure "2" at right are purple, instead of blue.
KL 132 Vernon-Treat. Plate A1110. Fair workmanship of etched plates on good bond paper. Portrait of Washington lacks lifelike quality. Green ink on back is too dark.
KL 132 Vernon-Treat. Plate B884 or B984. Poor photo-mechanical reproduction. Portrait very scratchy. Face of note blurred and dark. Green color on back too light.
KL 132 Vernon-Treat. Plate C1044. Printed from poor photo-mechanical plates. Portrait, lettering and scrollwork amateurish. Serial numbers of irregular size and out of alignment.

Coin Notes

Series 1890
KL 141 Rosecrans-Nebeker. Plate A. Head too broad and eyes too large on portrait. Serial numbers poorly formed and faded red color.

series 1891
KL 143 Rosecrans-Nebeker. Plate B. Poorly printed from zinc-etched plates.
KL 143 Rosecrans-Nebeker. Plate C. Portrait blurred. Beard does not extend down far enough to cover part of coat collar. Serial numbers too heavy and too dark blue color.
KL 144 Tillman-Morgan. Plate A. Poor counterfeit with bad portrait. Two pieces of paper pasted together with threads beteen.
KL 144 Tillman-Morgan. Plate B4. D38. Word "Bearer" on front, under "America" spelled "Beurer." Silk fiber imitated by red ink scratches.
KL 144 Tillman-Morgan. Plate B5. Excellent counterfeit. Serial numbers more red-brown than true carmine red. Beard on portrait does not extend down far enough to cover part of white collar.
KL 144 Tillman-Morgan. Plate B28, D27. Poor paper. Portrait lacks lifelike appearance. Many white spots on face.
KL 144 Tillman-Morgan. Plate B33. Portrait too dark, with white streak across iris of each eye. Seal too dark red color. Serial numbers were photographically reproduced and inked over in red.

KL 144 Tillman-Morgan. Plate C32-34. Poor counterfeit on soft, fibrous paper. Silk threads pressed into surface of paper. Portrait has black ink spot obscuring right side of nose. Hair and beard do not appear combed.
KL 145 Bruce-Roberts. Plate D4. Portrait appears flat, not life-like. Eyes appear to be staring. Seal dark red instead of carmine red. Paper much too thin. Silk fibers imitated with red and blue ink.

KL 191
Five Dollars
United States Notes

Series 1862
KL 190 Chittenden-Spinner. Plate A. Series 90. First Obligation back. Best of the counterfeit 1862-1863 USNs. Lathework around figure "5" in upper right corner defective. Lathework on back faulty.
KL 190 Chittenden-Spinner. Plate A. Series 114. Dated March 10, 1863, instead of correct 1862.

Series 1863
KL 191-193 Chittenden-Spinner. Plate A, D. New Series and New Series 70. Has incorrect date of March 10, 1863. Coarse engraving of Liberty vignette looks like woodcut. Chittenden signature made with no attempt to copy actual signature.
KL 191-193 Chittenden-Spinner. Plate A, D. New Series 77. Has incorrect date of March 10, 1863. Passable counterfeit. Liberty vignette lacks cross-hatching in shading. Lathework lines do not flow through green counter on back.
KL 191-193 Chittenden-Spinner. Plate A, D. New Series and New Series 77. Has incorrect date of March 10, 1863. Portrait good, details of Liberty vignette imperfect or missing.

Series 1875
KL 198 Allison-Wyman. Plate A. Photographic counterfeit on coarse, heavy paper. Counters on front and lathework on back blurred.
KL 198 Allison-Wyman. Plate A, D. Photographic counterfeit, somewhat dark and blurred. Numbering good, seal poor.
KL 198 Allison-Wyman. Plate C, C18. No flourishes enclose "Series of 1875" at top left corner.
KL 198 Allison-Wyman. Plate D. Photographed on two thin pieces of paper, pasted together with fibers between. Only color on face is hand-tinted serial numbers.
KL 198 Allison-Wyman. Plate D. Photographic counterfeit as above. Seal and serial numbers badly hand-tinted, black shows through.

Series 1880
KL 200-212. Plate B. Signature of many Treasurer/Register combinations counterfeited. Word "Treasury" under left signature misspelled "Trastay." Many other words misspelled in small lettering on border and elsewhere.
KL 205 Rosecrans-Hyatt. Plate B. Poor woodcut. "Bureau of Engraving and Printing" is reversed, beginning at lower right instead of upper left.
KL 206 Rosecrans-Huston. Plate D. Poorly executed portrait and vignette. Serial numbers defective and off-color.
KL 207 Rosecrans-Huston. Plate B. Many details omitted: titles under signatures, BEP imprint, shield at lower right.
KL 210 Tillman-Morgan. Plate A. Portrait appears cross-eyed. Curved line omitted between "Series of" and "1880." Floral design at end of BEP imprint omitted.
KL 210 Tillman-Morgan. Plate B. Poor photograhic counterfeit on plain paper, lacking silk fibers.
KL 210 Tillman-Morgan. Plate C. Fair lithographic counterfeit. Central vignette too black and coarse. Made of three sheets of paper pasted together with fibers between.
KL 210 Tillman-Morgan. Plate C5. Photo-wood engraving. Poor detail of lathework. Serial numbers too heavy and darker blue than on genuine. Two pieces of paper with fibers between.
KL 210 Tillman-Morgan. Plate D52. Poor photographic counterfeit. Treasury seal and serial numbers painted over with brush.

Series 1907
KL 213-222. Plate B312. Deceptive photo-mechanical counterfeit. Two pieces of paper, fibers imitated by ink marks. Large "V" and Treasury seal brick red instead of bright carmine.
KL 213 Vernon-Treat. Plate B217(?). Poor photo-mechanical counterfeit. All lathework blurred. Plate number may appear to be 210, 227, 230, 233, 237.
KL 213 Vernon-Treat. Plate D. Photographic counterfeit. Large "V" and Treasury seal painted over with color. Back painted muddy green.
KL 215 Napier-McClung. Plate D. Photographic counterfeit on decent paper. Treasury seal lightly tinted with pink. Attempt made to add green color on back.

KL 217 Parker-Burke. Plate B. Crudely etched counterfeit. Two pieces of paper pasted together with fibers between.

Silver Certificates

Series 1886

KL 230 Rosecrans-Hyatt. Plate A2023. Portrait has scratchy, soiled look. Two white patches appear on lower lip near left corner of mouth. Paper lighter than genuine.

KL 230 Rosecrans-Hyatt. Plate D2011. Stud on shirt front missing. "1" in "Pluribus' on coin on back missing.

KL 232-233 Rosecrans-Huston. Plate C. Lines behind upper-right serial number are wavy, not parallel as on genuine. Portrait poor.

KL 233-234 Rosecrans-Huston, Rosecrans-Nebeker. Plate A2733, C2733, C3265, C2736. Serial numbers poor, and parallel lines behind SN are broken. Color of chocolate seal too dark.

KL 235 Rosecrans-Nebeker. Portrait poor with moth-eaten appearance. Color of serial number good, but numerals irregular.

Series 1891

KL 236 Rosecrans-Nebeker. No check letter. Poor woodcut counterfeit. Treasury officials' titles omitted beneath signatures.

KL 236 Rosecrans-Nebeker. Plate A14, D15. Photo-lithographic counterfeit. Poor portrait.

KL 236 Rosecrans-Nebeker. Plate B. Portrait poor. Serial numbers too heavy, irregular.

KL 236 Rosecrans-Nebeker. Plate B7. Portrait very poor. No open front on shirt. Serial numbers too heavy, much darker than genuine.

KL 236 Rosecrans-Nebeker. Plate C. Poor woodcut. Treasury officials' titles omitted beneath signatures. Also missing, "Act of August 4, 1886," "Series of 1891."

KL 236 Rosecrans-Nebeker. Plate C8. Portrait poor; nose too broad and flat. Poorly executed back design.

KL 237 Tillman-Morgan. Plate A. Poor photographic counterfeit. No attempt to color seal, serial numbers or back.

KL 237 Tillman-Morgan. Plate A59. Portrait very poor with lathework broken up. Treasury seal reddish brown instead of carmine.

KL 237 Tillman-Morgan. Plate B. Poor woodcut. Small border lettering omitted. "Dollars" in border at left end misspelled "Dddlars."

KL 237 Tillman-Morgan. Plate B. Portrait, lathework and small lettering very poor. Poor paper.

KL 237 Tillman-Morgan. Plate C5. Lithographic counterfeit. Poor portrait.

KL 237 Tillman-Morgan. Plate D. Good counterfeit. Portrait flat. Treasury numbers too small and badly formed. Silk threads imitated by red ink.

KL 237 Tillman-Morgan. Plate D57. Right side of face on note appears to be a mass of scars. Seal brownish instead of carmine.

Series 1896

KL 238 Tillman-Morgan. Plate B. Photographic counterfeit. General blurred appearance of winged figure of America. Lamp she holds only partly visible. Seal maroon instead of carmine. Back color green is too light.

KL 238 Tillman-Morgan. Plate C. Photographic counterfeit. Back upside down.

KL 238 Tillman-Morgan. Plate C. Photographic counterfeit. Front grayish-brown instead of black. Seal tinted red and serial numbers tinted blue. Back blue-gray, hand-tinted to green.

KL 238 Tillman-Morgan. Plate C22. Silk threads pasted between two thin pieces of paper are too coarse. Serial numbers much too small. Much of shadowing on face made up of solid black, rather than cross-hatching. Seal darker red than genuine.

KL 239 Bruce-Roberts. Plate A. Photo-lithographic counterfeit. Red seal poorly hand-colored. Winged figure of America crudely executed. Back of note has washed appearance. Blue ink imitates silk fibers.

KL 239 Bruce-Roberts. Plate B30. Blurred appearance of winged figure America, lamp only partially visible in her hand.

KL 248

Series 1899

KL 241-251. Signatures indecipherable. No check letter. Serial number Y1832076.

KL 241 Lyons-Roberts. Check letter not visible. Photographic counterfeit. Overall washed out appearance. No attempt to imitate fibers in paper.

KL 241 Lyons-Roberts. Plate A. Poor photographic counterfeit. Seal, "V" and serial number crudely colored.

KL 241 Lyons-Roberts. Plate A32, B20. Good counterfeit, but portrait appears dark and unlifelike. Blue elements are too light a shade. Horizontal stroke in

---

serial number suffix symbol is shaped like an elongated diamond, rather than the genuine teardrop shape.

KL 241 Lyons-Roberts. Plate A161. Portrait coarse and blotchy. Lathework lines on back broken into series of white dots and dashes. Red ink lines imitate silk fibers.

KL 241 Lyons-Roberts. Plate A389. Poor zinc-etched counterfeit. Seal and serial number off-color.

KL 241 Lyons-Roberts. Plate A652. Back plate 493. Dangerous counterfeit. Fine cross-hatching in background of portrait only suggested in counterfeit. Small wording on back poorly formed, lines broken.

KL 241 Lyons-Roberts. Plate B. Back plate 375. Many misspelled words: "v" missing in "Silver" at right end of face, "i" missing in "Washington." "Payable" at left end of face misspelled "Payalle."

KL 241 Lyons-Roberts. Plate B. Poorly lithographed counterfeit on heavy paper. Ink lines imitate silk threads.

KL 241 Lyons-Roberts. Plate B37. "Series of 1899" too large, dark, prominent. Indian's headdress made up of mass of dots, rather than attempting to reproduce delicate feather details. On back, green ink too light, all lathework broken up.

KL 241 Lyons-Roberts. Plate B48, B484. Overall washed appearance with poor portrait of Indian. Colors good, paper fair. Ink marks imitate silk fibers.

KL 241 Lyons-Roberts. Plate B102. Portrait darker than genuine, lathework and lettering broken up. Blue coloring too light.

KL 241 Lyons-Roberts. Plate C. Crude photographic counterfeit on two pieces of paper pasted together with threads between.

KL 241 Lyons-Roberts. Plate C. Photographic counterfeit. Fair paper, good portrait, poor back. Blue coloring too light.

KL 241 Lyons-Roberts. Plate C (number indecipherable). Back plate No. 14 or 143. Faded blue-tone photograph, with details inked over in black. Very poor.

KL 241 Lyons-Roberts. Plate C. Crude photographic counterfeit on two pieces of paper pasted together with too-long silk threads between. Colored ink tints crudely applied to face and back.

KL 241 Lyons-Roberts. Plate C602. Dangerous counterfeit. Seal does not contain oval spaces in outer loops. Serial numbers poor, blue coloring too light.

KL 241 Lyons-Roberts. Plate D. Poor conterfeit. Lathework and small lettering poorly formed. No imitation of fibers.

KL 241 Lyons-Roberts. Plate D209, D239. Poor counterfeit. Lathework and lettering badly done.

KL 242 Lyons-Treat. No check letter. Deceptive pen and ink counterfeit. Several design elements missing including titles under Treasury officials' signatures, and wording above "United States," "This certifies . . . Treasury of the."

KL 242 Lyons-Treat. Check letter not visible. Paper soft and thin. Treasury seal slightly off-color, out of alignment and very poorly executed. Treasury officials' titles poorly executed.

KL 242 Lyons-Teat. Plate A289 (?). Blurred counterfeit. Ink lines imitate silk fibers.

KL 242 Lyons-Treat. Plate A289, A389. Poor counterfeit on two pieces of paper with fibers pasted between. Lathework poor. Serial numbers and seal off-color.

KL 242 Lyons-Treat. Plate A609, B636, C806, M687, N338, S867. Counterfeits B636, C806, possible others have back check number 553. Face on portrait too stout, also feminine looking. Eyes and feather headdress poorly executed. "Series of 1889" rather than "Series of 1899" printed under upper-right serial number. "1889" error corrected on counterfeit with plate number M687.

KL 242 Lyons-Treat. Plate C. Deceptive counterfeit on two pieces of paper with threads pasted between. Back is bluish in color, rather than green.

KL 242 Lyons-Treat. Plate C190 or C790. Lathework on face poor and broken, especially on portrait. Face has washed out appearance. Little attempt made on back to imitate fine lines and scrollwork.

KL 242 Lyons-Treat. plate D930. Half-tone reproduction. Separate face and back papers. May have been caught prior to circulation.

KL 243 Vernon-Treat. Plate A. Check letter very faint in upper-left, missing in lower-right. Washed out appearance. Lathework and ruling broken and disconnected.

KL 243 Vernon-Treat. Plate A1041, A1044. Back plate numbers 682 and 701. Printing heavy and blotchy. Blue on face is darker than genuine, green on back lighter than genuine.

KL 243 Vernon-Treat. Plate B1072. Photo-mechanical counterfeit on single piece of heavy paper. Portrait scratchy. Ornamental work in borders broken up.

KL 243 Vernon-Treat. Plate 1242. Back plate No. 862. Dangerous counterfeit. White spot or patch on left end of Indian's upper lip. Black spot between "a" and "r" of word "Dollars" at right end.

KL 243 Vernon-Treat. Plate C1401. both sides appear faded. Printing on back shorter than on genuine. Blue color on face too light. Serial numbers too large.

KL 243 Vernon-Treat. Plate D. Face plate number eliminated. Back plate number 684. Lathework and small lettering on face is poor, better on back.

KL 243 Vernon-Treat. Plate D. Very dangerous photographic counterfeit. Face and back plate numbers indecipherable or missing. Printed on genuine paper obtained by bleaching the ink off a smaller denomination. Some lettering appears hand-inked, such as the last three letters of "bearer," the word "on" and the first two letters of "demand" on right face of note. Blue color of face is too dark, particularly bad on seal.

KL 243 Vernon-Treat. Plate D2. Dangerous photo-mechanical counterfeit on good bond paper. Portrait excellent, though appears slightly cross-eyed. Seal poorly printed, serial numbers too thick, expecially at lower-left. Back exceptionally good counterfeit.

KL 243 Vernon-Treat. Plate D64. Back plate number possibly 567. Almost all fine lines in letters missing, as are details of headdress; space between dark tops and bottoms of feathers is simply left blank. Back color too blue-green.

KL 243 Vernon-Treat. Plate D1164. Back plate number 782. Face of note is very heavy black. Top of large figure "5" on upper-left end of back is convex, rather than concave.

KL 244 Vernon-McClung. Plate A. Poor photographic counterfeit. Back colored with green watercolor paint. Poor attempt made to color seal and serial numbers on front.

KL 244 Vernon-McClung. Plate A. Pen and brush countereit. "Register of the Treasury" title missing under Vernon's signature.

KL 245 Napier-McClung. Plate B. Poorly executed zinc-etched counterfeit. No attempt to imitate fibers.

KL 245 Napier-McClung. Plate C1509, C1568, C1709, C1791. Very dangerous counterfeits, printed on genuine paper obtained by bleaching smaller denomination notes. Notes are 5/16-inch longer than genuine.

KL 245 Napier-McClung. Plate C1648. Back plate number 688, first "8" broken. Portrait blurred and dark. Scrollwork poor. Treasury officials' title not clear.

KL 245 Napier-McClung. Plate D. Crudely etched zinc-plate counterfeit. Serial number at lower-left one-third larger than that at upper-right.

KL 246 Napier-Thompson. Plate D1728. Right side of Indian's face appears swollen and lumpy. Green ink applied to back heavily to cover defects.

KL 247 Parker-Burke. Plate A39. Poor uncolored photographic counterfeit, except large "V" "Five" and seal colored in light blue. Printed on onion skin paper.

KL 247 Parker-Burke. Plate C15. Back plate 797. Portrait appears flat. Serial numbers smaller than genuine. Register's signature poor.

KL 247 Parker-Burke. Plate C99. "V" and serial numbers purplish rather than blue, Treasury seal too light a shade of blue. Poor lathework.

KL 247 Parker-Burke. Plate D207 or D807. Printed from poorly etched plates. Silk threads imitated by black ink on face, green on back. Serial numbers too large and poorly formed.

KL 248 Teehee-Burke. Plate A— (three numerals indistinct). Headdress feathers and large script letters on face are broken, as is most lathework. Off-color seal and serial numbers. Silk threads imitated by green ink marks.

Coin Notes

Series 1891

KL 256 Rosecrans-Nebeker. Plate A, D. Poor counterfeit, badly engraved portrait.

KL 257 Tillman-Morgan. Plate A, D. Poor counterfeit, badly engraved portrait. Silk fibers imitated by red and blue inked lines.

KL 257 Tillman-Morgan. Plate A12. Terrible portrait. Poor lettering and lathework.

KL 257 Tillman-Morgan. Plate D. Photographic counterfeit touched up with pen and ink. Gray background remains. Red and blue ink lines imitate silk fibers.

KL 257 Tillman-Morgan. Plate D20. Poor lithographic counterfeit on heavy paper. Fibers imitated by ink marks.

Federal Reserve Notes

Series 1914

KL 261 or 276 McAdoo-Burke. New York. Plate A. Poor lithograph. Heavy printing obscures fine engraving lines.

KL 261 or 276 McAdoo-Burke. New York. Plate A (number indistinct). Poor portrait. Entire side of Lincoln's face covered in black. Serial numbers very well done.

KL 261 or 276 McAdoo-Burke. New York. Plate B25 (?). Quite deceptive. Red and blue ink lines imitate silk fibers. Most printing too heavy, obscuring fine lines of engraving.

KL 261 or 276 McAdoo-Burke. New York. Plate D5. Deceptive counterfeit on good bond paper. Red and blue ink lines imitate silk fibers.

KL 263 or 284 McAdoo-Burke. Cleveland. Plate C51. Poor lithograph on cheap, heavy paper with no imitation of silk threads.

KL 266 or 296 McAdoo-Burke. Chicago. Plate A. Poor counterfeit with total lack of detail on face of note. No serial number. Seal has been cut off genuine note and pasted on. Back printed upside down.

KL 266 or 296 McAdoo-Burke. Chicago. Plate A. Deceptive photographic counterfeit on two pieces of paper with threads pasted between.

KL 266 or 296 McAdoo-Burke. Chicago. Plate C. Serial number at upper-right G11754217A, serial number at lower-left is G12839924A.

KL 266 or 296 McAdoo-Burke. Chicago. Plate C58 or C68. Dangerous counterfeit printed from photo-etched plates on single piece of paper. Fibers imitated by ink line. Hair and coat on portrait are much too dark, beard is blurred, not as finely executed as on genuine. Serial numbers out of alignment.

KL 269 or 308 McAdoo-Burke. Kansas City. Plate B. Poor counterfeit from etched plates. Cheap paper, no attempt to imitate fibers.

KL 270 or 312 McAdoo-Burke. Dallas. Plate D. Poor counterfeit. Two pieces of paper pasted together with threads between. Paper quarter-inch shorter than genuine.

KL 271 or 316 McAdoo-Burke. San Francisco. Plate C4. Poor counterfeit. More than quarter-inch longer and somewhat wider than genuine. Portrait and lathework poor.

Ten Dollars
United States Notes

Series 1862

KL 359-360 Chittenden-Skinner. Plate B,C. New Series. Portrait lacks fine, clear lifelike expression. Eagle scratchy. Green ink trifle darker than genuine. Lathework defective, shading of letters coarse. In green medallion counters, right and left of eagle, four green dots seen on genuine, left of figure 1 in "10"; on counterfeits only three dots.

KL 360

KL 359-360 Chittenden-Skinner. Plate B,C. Series 19. Treasury numbers imperfect, ink a brick red color. Portrait poor, unlike genuine, eyes having wild, staring expression. On genuine, line on upper side, under Treasury number, if extended, would be below letter "N" in words "New Series"; on counterfeit, would be near center of the "N." There are eight or ten different counterfeits of this denomination, act and date, some almost equal to the genuine.

KL 359-360 Chittenden-Skinner. Plate B,C,D. New Series 23. Red figures slightly smaller than on genuine. Red ink blurred. Fine line under Treasury number, on genuine, if extended, would be directly under the words "New Series." On counterfeits, it would be near center of "N." Check letter D of counterfeit is of "Act of March 3, 1863," dated "March 10, 1863," otherwise plate is the same. On genuine, under wing of eagle in vignette center are four, clean cut feathers. On counterfeit the feathers are blurred and indistinct.

KL 359-360 Chittenden-Spinner. Plate B,C,D. Series 52. At top of genuine there are 15 small X's on each side of imprint of American Bank Note Co. On counterfeit 15 on left and 16 on right. A second issue has 14 X's on right and 16 on left.

KL (361)? Chittenden-(John C. New) Plate A,B,C,D. New Series 58. (Incorrect Treasurer.) Dated March 10, 1863. A dangerous fake. Lathework around 10's in green medallions slightly blurred. There are nine counterfeits of this issue.

Series 1875

KL 363 Allison-New. Plate C. Fiber imitated by printed lines on back. Portrait and numbering poor. Inscription reads "alegal" and "forten." W and D.C. smaller in "Washington, D.C." On right back "this" is spelled "tnis."

Series 1878

KL (365)? Allison-(A.U. Wyman). Plate D. (Incorrect Treasurer.) Poor photograph and pen and ink. Titles below signatures omitted. Treasury numbers poor, as are portrait and vignette at end.

Series 1880

KL 367 Bruce-Gilfillan. Plate L. No genuine notes with this plate letter, but L is easily altered to D. Imprint at top, "Series of" over 1880 and titles below signatures omitted. Fiber imitated by horizontal printed blue and red lines.

KL 368 Bruce-Wyman. Plate D. Same defects as KL 367 above. Some with plate letter altered to A or L, and Gilfillan changed to Wyman.

KL 371 Rosecrans-Hyatt. Plate B2250. Near normal Treasury numbers and seal. Portrait poor, looks unnatural. Curved line between "Series of" and 1880 omitted. Numerous errors in penalty statement on back.

KL 371 Rosecrans-Hyatt. Plate C. Treasury numbers unequal in size and irregular. Fair color which fades rapidly. No silk threads.

KL 373-374 Rosecrans-Huston. Plate C. Apparent combination of photo and wood engraving. Face of note is heavy, spotted and blotchy. Numbers poor, lines in number panels scratchy.

KL 376 Rosecrans-Nebeker. Plate B5. Fair, lifeless portrait. Poor vignette at lower right. Silk threads imitated by blue lines. On back "This" appears as "Tnis."

KL 377 Tillman-Morgan. Plate B. Poor photo. Color of numbers and seal poor.

KL 377 Tillman-Morgan. Plate C8. Color of Treasury numbers, seal and lower right vignette poor, numbers darker blue and irregular in formation. Columbus vignette blurred. Silk fiber between two sheets of paper, thin enough to feel fiber by rubbing with finger.

KL 379 Lyons-Roberts. Plate B10-16. Portrait, back and lathework poor, nose flat. Two pieces of paper with silk threads between.

Series 1901

KL 380 Lyons-Roberts. Plate A48. Very poor work on thin paper.

KL 380 Lyons-Roberts. Plate A249. Good counterfeit printed on two sheets of paper with coarse silk fibers between, some without fibers. Paper stiff from paste. Seal slightly off color. Quite large red X. Delicate lines too heavy. Letters in two lines above X heavy, broken and crooked. Cross lines missing below "United States of America" and in background of portrait. Different numbers on different notes.

KL 380 Lyons-Roberts. Plate A252. Photo mechanical on poor paper. Pen marks to imitate fiber. Portraits scratchy and indistinct. Pale green back. Seals and numbers lighter than genuine.

KL-380 Lyons-Roberts. Plate A272. Buffalo looks like pen work, but is not. Lewis portrait unnatural. Two pieces of paper with coarse silk fibers. Period rather than comma before "D.C."

KL-380 Lyons-Roberts. Plate B52, C52, C57, C105, (C205?). Treasury number and seal off color, numbers larger. Two pieces of paper with silk threads between. Poor lathework, portrait scratchy. Back off color, but generally better work than face.

KL 380 Lyons-Roberts. Plate B202. Dangerous. Fair, broken lathework. Portraits not lifelike. Navel on female at right shows, does not on genuine. Treasury numbers brown-red, not carmine-red and not as heavy. Buffalo head appears flat. Faded, off color tinge to back. Note waxy or shiny.

KL 380 Lyons-Roberts. Plate B251. Poor portraits and vignette of buffalo. Broken lathework. Treasury numbers and seal darker red, and back darker green. Two pieces of paper with fibers between, 3/8 inch too long.

KL 380 Lyons-Roberts. Plate C. Good photo on fair paper, with silk fibers scattered front and back. Portraits not too lifelike. Buffalo appears to be shedding.

KL 380 Lyons-Roberts. Plate C3. Printed from touched up, zinc-etched plates. Three layers of paper with silk threads between. Very bad portraits and buffalo. Seal and large numeral on face much too light. Green ink on back smeared over white lettering.

KL 380 Lyons-Roberts. Plate C86. A dangerous photo mechanical. Good paper, but no silk threads, or imitations. Bottom of large red X has dark or blurred look. Portraits not lifelike. Shading under large "United States of America" more solid than line work. Back less well done, darker green, with left arm of female not well outlined.

KL 380 Lyons-Roberts. Plate C195. Good work on bond paper. Fiber poorly imitated by green streaks. Defective lathework. Portraits and buffalo deceptive. Back a light yellowish green.

KL 380 Lyons-Roberts. Plate D. Buffalo and portraits coarse and not lifelike. Treasury numbers very bad and too large. Plate number blurred. Back much too dark green. On two pieces of paper with a few red silk fibers.

KL 380 Lyons-Roberts. Plate D. Crude photo touched with water colors on seals, numbers and back. On two pieces of paper with a few silk threads.

KL 380 Lyons-Roberts. Plate D174. Buffalo and portraits not lifelike. Thin paper with coarse silk fibers. Period rather than a comma before "D.C."

KL 380 Lyons-Roberts. Plate D213. Photo mechanical. Good paper with silk threads between, but poorly distributed, in wads or lumps. Portraits poor, buffalo scratchy. Treasury number too large and different style.

KL 381 Lyons-Treat. Plate B. Poorly printed from crude zinc-etched plates on fair paper, with blue ink lines at upper right and black at lower left.

KL 381 Lyons-Treat. Plate B. Good lithograph. Silk thread imitating fiber. Ink is grey-black instead of brilliant black. Portraits and buffalo scratchy and do not stand out. Back of buffalo appears as if sun were shining brightly on it.

KL 381 Lyons-Treat. Plate C376. Crudely executed.

KL 382 Vernon-Treat. Plate A461. Photo mechanical on two pieces of stiff paper with red and blue silk fibers between. Buffalo and portraits defective with loss of detail in shadows. Denominational design, seal and numbering darker red. Back dark blue-green.

KL 382 Vernon-Treat. Plate C454. Two pieces of paper with long very fine silk threads. Lathework and ruling broken and crude on both front and back. Treasury numbers very heavy and lighter color.

KL 382 Vernon-Treat. Plate C501. Deceptive photo mechanical on two pieces of paper, some with silk threads between. Plate engraving of equal depth, giving design flat appearance with no light or shade. Shade lines as heavy as outline. Broken lines in lathework. Treasury numbers poorly formed. Female on back appears to have dark bandage across forehead. Back plate 251.

KL 382 Vernon-Treat. Plate D521. Deceptive photo engraving on good paper. Some have imitation of silk fiber. Large X is 1/8 inch too large and seal slightly larger. Lines of large X and "TEN" broken and irregular. Treasury numbers heaver. Lettering of seal rough and broken, with dots indistinct. Lathework on both sides blurred. Face looks washed out. Back of buffalo lighter. Outline of lapel and collar on Lewis portrait doesn't show and two buttons are missing. Back plate number faint, looks like 251, 253, 851 or 853.

KL 383 Vernon-McClung. Plate C541. Photo mechanical on two thin pieces of bond paper some with silk threads between. Seal and large denominational character are deep pink color with color even rather than shaded. Face has brownish tinge, back is blue-green. Workmanship similar to $10 Anglo and London Paris National Bank of San Francisco.

KL 383 Vernon-McClung. Plate C, C578. Photographic on excellent paper. No attempt to color seal, number or large numeral on face. Back reddish-brown. Another note (C578) also differs in color.

KL 384 Napier-McClung. Plate C633. Photo mechanical on two pieces of paper, with pen and ink marks imitating fiber.

KL 384 Napier-McClung. Plate C634. Deceptive photo mechanical on fairly good paper. Seal and numbers brick red. Small lettering under signatures poor, broken and indistinct. Poor scroll work. Fibers imitated by red and blue ink.

KL 385 Parker-Burke. Plate A13, A19. Photo mechanical on two sheets of paper with imitation silk threads between. Lathework poor in counters at left end of face and entire back. Back plate number 282 on some notes. On female on back of note draping just above feet and feet are white.

KL 385 Parker-Burke. Plate D2. Deceptive, but with poor lathework especially on back, losing most detail. Figures and Treasury numbers too heavy and too large. Photo mechanical on three pieces of cheap, thin paper with silk threads between.

Compound Interest Treasury Notes
Series 1864
KL 392 Colby-Spinner. Serial Number 198380. Photographic reproduction in typical fading brown.

Silver Certificates
Series 1880
KL 412 Scofield-Gilfillan. Plate D. Photographic pen and ink. Poor, very thin paper. Parallel lines imitate fiber. Large red seal (Incorrect).

KL-412 Scofield-Gilfillan. Plate D. Photographic pen and ink. Pink characters photographed black and hand colored, with black showing clearly. Slightly shorter than normal. Large red seal (Incorrect).

KL 412 Scofield-Gilfillan. Plate D. Very poor wood-cut. 1/4 inch shorter. On back reads "whenso." Treasury numbers uneven. Large red seal (Incorrect).

KL 415 Bruce-Wyman. Plate A. Poor photographic pen and ink on poor paper that lacks fibers and parallel silk threads.

KL 415 Bruce-Wyman. Plate C. Poor photographic pen and ink on poor, thin, yellowish paper, missing fibers and silk threads. Titles under signatures, "Robert Morris" and script lettering under "United States" on back missing.

KL 415 Bruce-Wyman. Plate C. Very dangerous photographic pen and ink with fiber imitated with red and blue pen and ink lengthwise on back. Deceptive if held to light looking at face. "Robert Morris" left of portrait omitted.

Series 1886
KL 417 Rosecrans-Hyatt. Plate A. Poorly executed photo wood engraving. Background of portrait represented with dots rather than lines. Treasury numbers not as heavy. Green on back much too dark. Lathework poor.

KL 418 Rosecrans-Hyatt. Plate — (321?) Photographic pen and ink. Omitted are "This certifies that there have been deposited in the Treasury" and titles under signatures. Fiber imitated by drawing fine blue lines and creasing note over lines.

Series 1891
KL 422 Rosecrans-Nebeker. Plate A. "Bureau of Engraving and Printing" omitted, "Register" abbreviated as "Regist." Treasury numbers faded blue, almost green and too heavy. Distinctive paper not imitated.

KL 424 Tillman-Morgan. Plate A17. Well done photo with seals and numbers colored. Back a blue print.

KL 424 Tillman-Morgan. Plate A72. Fair reproduction on two pieces of paper with silk threads between. Silver-gray rather than black ink. Seal a lighter red. "Bureau of Engraving and Printing" omitted. Comma before "D.C." and period after D missing. Face of portrait not as full and nose larger. Treasury numbers not quite as heavy.

KL 424 Tillman-Morgan. Plate A, D. Both face and back printed light brown. Plate A has blue print of back, crudely colored green with brush.

KL 424 Tillman-Morgan. Plate B. "Bureau of Engraving and Printing" missing. At right border, 7 in 1878 is reversed.

KL 424 Tillman-Morgan. Plate B 58. Seal salmon color. Treasury numbers printed black, recolored blue. Very poor lathework.

KL 424 Tillman-Morgan. Plate B14, B74. Dangerous with well engraved portrait. Printed on two pieces of soft, fibrous tissue with silk fibers between. Will not stand rubbing. Seal dark red. Ruling under Treasury number broken and indistinct. Lathework at 10 and X in upper corner very poor.

KL 424 Tillman-Morgan. Plate B, C, D. Good photo, with grey background, especially seal showing through. Color applied with brush. Ink lines imitate fibers.

KL 424 Tillman-Morgan. Plate C47. Good work on two pieces of paper with silk threads between. Portrait does not stand out and right eye barely visible. Imprint under signatures blurred and crowded together. Shading of letters on face heavier.

KL 424 Tillman-Morgan. Plate D. Very poor wood-cut. Portrait unnatural.

KL (424?) Tillman-Morgan. Plate D. "Series of 1901" (Incorrect). Lithograph without lifelike appearance. Pale seal, Treasury numbers blurred. On fair paper with silk fibers.

KL 424 Tillman-Morgan. Plate D3. Portrait has surly expression of mouth. Lower lip very thick and protruding. Treasury numbers maroon. Lathework does not resemble continuous network of lines. Titles under signatures poor, letters crowded. Printed on two pieces of paper with silk fibers between.

KL 424 Tillman-Morgan. Plate D21. Good work on fair paper. Seal decidedly pink. Green ink on back darker.

KL 425 Bruce-Roberts. Plate A16. Poor photo. Brick red seal. Colored with brush.

KL 425 Bruce-Roberts. Plate B14. Lithograph on two sheets of tissue paper with very course red and blue silk fibers between. Lathework crude. Border lettering and "Bureau of Engraving and Printing" illegible. Ornamental work blurred.

Series 1908
KL 429 Parker-Burke. Plate A79. Photo process on two pieces of stiff, brittle paper with ink lines to imitate fibers. Number, large X and "TEN" appear as if made by hand. Face of note has a reddish tint.

Coin Notes
Series 1890
KL 430 Rosecrans-Huston. Plate B. Poor quality. Face has moth-eaten appearance. Lathework very poor. Four pointed star on epaulette.

Series 1891
KL 433 Rosecrans-Nebeker. Plate B2. Pen and ink. Mustache and chin whiskers appear smoothly brushed. "Bureau of Engraving and Printing" missing from both face and back. "This note is legal tender....." on back missing, replaced with X.

KL 434 Tillman-Morgan. Plate A2. Poor, crude woodcut. On two pieces of paper with silk threads between.

KL 434 Tillman-Morgan. Plate B. Photographic, with right eye and mustache hardly visible. Treasury numbers and seal maroon.

KL 434 Tillman-Morgan. Plate C. Poor photograph, with no attempt to color Treasury numbers, seal or back.

KL 434 Tillman-Morgan. Plate C. Extremely poor, from photo-etched plate on two pieces of paper with silk threads between.

KL 434 Tillman-Morgan. Plate C18. Portrait does not stand out. Right end of forehead and right cheek a mass of white patches. Lathework around 10 in upper right corner broken and indistinct. Two pieces of paper with silk threads between.

Gold Certificates

Series 1907

KL 436 Vernon-Treat. Plate D. Poor photo mechanical plates on genuine paper from bleached $1 notes. Faint portions of dollar design show in upper corners of face. Portrait and lathework especially poor. Back better than face.

KL 436 Vernon-Treat. Plate D7. Photo mechanical on two pieces of paper with red and blue silk fibers. Color of seal, denomination X and back too dark. Arcs in scrolls in upper border design appear to be pen and ink, blurred and scratched.

KL 436 Vernon-Treat. Plate D45. Well executed photographic reproduction on good quality paper with no silk threads. Red ink lines as imitations. Check letter and other small letters very small and indistinct. Radiating lines of "sunburst" effect missing except close to center.

KL 437 Vernon-McClung. Plate B. Poor effort with pen and brush on good paper. Back combination of pink and yellow ink.

KL 437 Vernon-McClung. Plate C186. Good photographic work on good paper, with no silk threads. Red ink lines to imitate silk. Radiating lines of "sunburst" effect missing except close to center.

KL 437 Vernon-McClung. Plate D150. Straight photo on bond paper. Denominational device, seal, serial numbers and back colored with brownish-red waterproof drawing ink. On some notes the fibers are imitated with red and blue ink marks. On some notes "United States of America," signatures, portions of "Washington, D.C. and various other parts have been retraced with ink. Poor lathework detail.

KL 438 Napier-McClung. Plate A253. Fair photo mechanical on good paper, without silk threads. Imitated with red and blue ink. Large X and seal on face pale brown. Seal faint and ragged. Lathework poor, back almost devoid of fine lines.

KL 438 Napier-McClung. Plate C265. Photo mechanical with silk fibers imitated with ink. Lathework poor, back flat and lacking fine lines. Face of note stained lemon or yellow.

KL 438 Napier-McClung. Plate D223. Photo mechanical on three pieces of paper with heavy silk thread between. Portrait and ground work poor. Check letter missing from lower right corner.

KL 440 Parker-Burke. Plate A. Photo printed on two pieces of paper, without silk threads or imitations. Yellow coloring applied to seal and large numeral on face of bill and over printed portion of back.

KL 440 Parker-Burke. Plate A9. Photo mechanical, poorly printed on two pieces of paper with silk threads between. On some, seal and large number printed light yellow, on others almost brown. Back not as good as face.

KL 440 Parker-Burke. Plate A19. Dangerous photo etching on two pieces of paper. Silk threads give note a stiff, thick feel. 1/4 inch longer. On back lathework broken and disconnected.

KL 440 Parker-Burke. Plate D. Crude photo mechanical plates. Some about 1/4 inch short. Back very well done. No silk thread or imitation.

KL 441 Teehee-Burke. Plate A234. Very dangerous, from photo process plates on two pieces of paper with silk threads between. Paper heavy and harsh. Hair of portrait blurred. Treasury numbers somewhat irregular, as though hand stamped. Back plate 165.

Federal Reserve Notes

Series 1914

KL 443 McAdoo-Burke. Plate A. Boston. Poor printing from photo mechanical plates on two pieces of paper with red silk threads between. Treasury numbers made by hand, too large, poorly formed and too widely separated. Seal very poor. Back of note blurred in printing. 1/8 inch short.

KL 444 McAdoo-Burke. Plate A21. New York. Fairly good photo mechanical on two pieces of paper with silk threads between. Slightly small, paper too thick and stiff. Figures too large, too heavy and too far apart. Appears like a blurred print. Later issues improved printing, lightened figures, moved closer together.

KL 444 McAdoo-Burke. Plate B4. New York. Poor, from etched plates on one piece of paper, with red and blue ink lines. Lathework particularly poor.

KL 444 McAdoo-Burke. Plate C. New York. Poor job from zinc-etched plates, with red and blue ink line imitations.

KL 444 McAdoo-Burke. Plate C. New York. Poor lithographic copy on single paper without fiber or imitation. Plate number blurred or indistinct.

KL 444 McAdoo-Burke. Plate C47. New York. Deceptive photo mechanical print on single paper with red and blue ink lines. Face is 3/8 inch too large. Portrait doesn't stand out and lacks some detail. Lathework and numbering poor. Digits too large and irregularly spaced. Back too dark, but better lathework than face.

KL 444 McAdoo-Burke. Plate D. New York. Lithographic plates on two sheets of paper with silk threads between. Portrait merges into background, not clearly defined. Numbering heavier and out of alignment. Lathework poor. 1/8 inch small.

KL 444 McAdoo-Burke. Plate D32. New York. Poor photo mechanical on two pieces of paper with red and blue ink lines. Face is 1/4 inch too long. Portrait poor with missing light and shadow, especially in hair. Eyes barely distinguishable. Lathework and numbering poor. Digits larger and not as heavy. Back much darker than normal.

KL 449 McAdoo-Burke. Plate A114, A174. Chicago. Dangerous print from photographic plates on two pieces of paper with silk threads between and some ink line imitations. Portrait lacks detail. Blue seal color slightly off. Small white lines in border lathework indistinct. Numbers off color and irregular. Front and back about 1/4 inch short.

KL 449 McAdoo-Burke. Plate C. Chicago. Very poor photographic plates on two pieces of paper with a few silk threads between. Back blue.

KL 451 McAdoo-Burke. Plate B3. Minneapolis. Very dangerous engraved plates, paper almost identical to genuine. Jackson's face and hair too dark, missing light and shadow effect. Digits in number at upper right end are very irregular. Back print about 1/16th inch long.

KL 453 McAdoo-Burke. Plate D. Dallas. Poor etched plates on cheap paper with red and blue ink lines. 1/8th inch or more smaller than normal.

KL 523

Twenty Dollars
United States Notes

Series 1862

KL 523-524 Chittenden-Spinner. Plate A, B, B2, C. Series 6. Convertible Series. On large green "20" small lines of dots across top and bottom very indistinct. Treasury numbers larger. Lathework poor, lines cannot be traced. Imprint of printer on lower border irregular.

KL 523-524 Chittenden-Spinner. Plate A, B, B2, C, D. New Series. Poor. Lathework in counters very irregular. Center vignette coarse. Treasury numbers poor, bad color. Imprint of printer irregular and defective.

KL 523-524 Chittenden-Spinner. Plate A, B, B2, C. Series 24. Fair. Lathework on counters poor. Center vignette coarse. Letters in imprint of printer crooked and poorly formed. Description matches Series 6 above.

Series 1863

KL 525 Chittenden-Spinner. Plate A, B2. Series 15. Fair engraving and lathework. Convertible back (Not used on this Series).

KL 525 Chittenden-Spinner. Plate A, B2. New Series. Poor engraving, with printing and numbers very imperfect. Lathework on back poor.

KL 525 Chittenden-Spinner. Plate A, B2. New Series. Poor, with center vignette coarsely engraved. Lathework in counters irregular, lines cannot be traced. Imprint of printer poorly done, imperfect lettering.

Series 1875

KL 526 Allison-New. Plate A, B, C, D. Pen and ink. No attempt to imitate lathework. Portrait excellent, but lacks fine lines in background, shaded with brush. Fiber back imitated by pasting tissue paper over fibers in right panel. Other check letters.

KL (526?) Allison-(Gilfillan) (Incorrect Treasurer). Plate B. "Printed by Bureau of Engraving and Printing" omitted. Photographic pen and ink. Lathework and parallel lines scratchy.

Series 1878

KL 528 Allison-Gilfillan. Plate A, B, C, D. Same description as KL (526?) note described above.

Series 1880

KL 531-532 Bruce-Wyman. Plate A, B, C, D. Excellent, but same description as KL (526?), KL 528 above, and KL 540 below. Varieties of this note come with large round seal, large spiked seal and scalloped seal. Others come with same check letters and signatures of Rosecrans as Register, and Jordan, Huston, Hyatt and Nebeker as Treasurer. Some have 1880 changed to 1889 or 1890, but no genuine notes of the latter series bear Hamilton portrait.

KL 539 Rosecrans-Nebeker. Plate D3. Woodcut, with poor portrait. Seal pale pink. Treasury number upper right and titles under signatures omitted. Fibers imitated by ink lines. A second issue has the omissions corrected.

KL 540 Tillman-Morgan. Plate A7. Very dangerous, from engraved plates. Hamilton's nose comes to a sharp point, chin is square. Head, from back of hair to tip of nose at level of ear is a fraction of an inch too wide. Work on coat gives flat effect, merging into background at bottom. In border small figures "20" omitted between X X. Eight point star in octagonal ornament under "Washington" so blurred that it does not stand out in relief. Very deceptive paper with fibers. (See notations above for KL (526?), 528, 531-532.)

Gold Certificates

Series 1882

KL 551-552 — —Gilfillan. Plate A. Dangerous photograph of genuine note. Shows photo grey in counters with figures "20" and in portrait. Seal has reddish tinge applied with brush. Numbering very pronounced and heavier. Note 1/2 inch short and 1/8 inch narrow. Has two parallel silk threads through it. Back light brown.

KL 555 Lyons-Roberts. Plate A51. Poor photo, crudely executed. Coloring applied to seal and numbers.

KL 555 Lyons-Roberts. Plate C. Untinted photo with fair portrait. A second issue has red and yellow poorly applied. Paper has silk threads.

KL (556?) Lyons-Roberts. Plate D. "Series of 1906" (Incorrect). Crude photo on two thin sheets of paper with silk threads between. Colored inks and water colors roughly applied to seals, numbers and back.

Series 1906

KL 558 Vernon-Treat. Plate A106? Lithograph on cheap bond paper, with threads imitated on some notes with pen and ink. Portrait shoulders are not well defined. Coat merges with background. Plate number indistinct. Back better than face.

KL 558 Vernon-Treat. Plate B. Photo-etched plates on two pieces of paper with silk threads between. "XX," seal and numbers more of a lemon color. Letters in "Act of July 12, 1882" heavy and irregular, titles under signatures broken and indistinct. Lathework on back not attempted.

KL 558 Vernon-Treat. Plate B, O. Photo-etched plates on two pieces of paper with silk threads between. Seal and Treasury numbers are red. Yellow XX at left end omitted, replaced by blurred digits, apparently "20." Face lathework poor. "Act of July 12, 1882" and "Series of 1906" in both places heavy and irregular. Titles under signatures broken and indistinct. No attempt to imitate lathework on back.

KL 558 Vernon-Treat. Plate D. Photo on poor paper, silk fibers are photo lines, black on face, reddish brown on back. No attempt to color seal, Treasury number or large XX on face.

KL 558 Vernon-Treat. Plate D1, D7. Poor, crude photo mechanical plates on two pieces of paper with short pieces of heavy blue silk massed to show in the white spaces. Portrait very poor, easily detected.

KL 559 Vernon-McClung. Plate C203. Poor photo mechanical on two pieces of paper with silk threads between. Same plates as KL 560 below. Portrait of Washington bad, background solid black.

KL 559 Vernon-McClung. Plate B91, B111, C132, D40, D125. Photo mechanical on two pieces of paper, with silk threads between on some notes. Center of note is coarse and scratchy. Background of vignette too black, making portrait flat. Numbering, seal and large XX slightly blurred and brownish bronze. "Act of July 12, 1882," "Series of 1906" and titles under signatures all heavier than normal. All are from same plates.

KL 560 Napier-McClung. Plate C200. Poor photo mechanical plates on two pieces of paper with silk threads between. Portrait especially bad, with solid background. (See KL 559, same plates, above).

Silver Certificates

Series 1880

KL 578 Scofield-Gilfillan. Plate A, B, D. Poor photographic pen and ink on poor thin paper, payable at Washington, D.C. Parallel silk threads imitated with ink lines. Also signed Bruce-Gilfillan or Bruce-Wyman. Letters in "Register" and "Treasurer" only partly formed, spelled "Troosurer." On back "Engraved" is spelled "Engroved," with rest of sentence misspelled.

KL 578 Scofield-Gilfillan. Plate B. Photo, with shallow detail, back off color. Large seal and XX surface printed in color.

KL 578 Scofield-Gilfillan. Plate C. Payable at Washington, D.C. Poor photographic pen and ink.

KL 580 Bruce-Gilfillan. Plate C. Paper thick, greasy and stiff, 1/8th inch short, without fibers or parallel threads. In left panel Letters "R", "T" and "E" in "Certificate" are upside down. On back "taxes" spelled "tares" and "Engraved" is "Engravod." Seal is brick red.

KL 581 Parker-Burke. Plate A4. Dangerous photo mechanical on two pieces of paper with silk threads between. Portrait too light, missing many small lines. Hair over ear is white. Lathework on back poor.

Series 1891

KL 588 Tillman-Morgan. Plate A. Poor etching on good paper with blue ink lines imitating fibers.

KL 588 Tillman-Morgan. Plate A27. Photo, detected by grey background.

KL 588 Tillman-Morgan. Plate B. Red and blue ink lines on back imitating fibers. Hair at top of head blends into background. Nose sharp and pointed. Treasury number heavier and lighter shade of red. Back a close copy.

KL 588 Tillman-Morgan. Plate B. Very poor, on two pieces of paper with silk fibers between. Poor resemblance.

KL 588 Tillman-Morgan. Plate B6. Dangerous, with a good portrait, but left side of face presses into background. Fibers imitated with ink lines. Seal lighter than normal red.

KL 588 Tillman-Morgan. Plate C. Well executed on good paper with silk fibers. A white line separating left side of face from background gives appearance of being sunk into background instead of standing out in bold relief. Has large eight scallop seal instead of small twelve scallop seal.

KL 588 Tillman-Morgan. Plate C5. Good, on good paper with silk fibers. Flat portrait. Ends of mustache not curled.

Coin Notes

Series 1890

KL 595 Rosecrans-Nebeker. Plate A. Excellent photo pen and ink. Portrait appears broader. "Series of 1890," "Bureau of Engraving and Printing" omitted. Parallel silk threads imitated by creasing and drawing ink lines. Check letter and seal may differ.

Federal Reserve Notes

Series 1914

KL 598 McAdoo-Burke. Plate C10. Boston. Very deceptive print from photo-etched plates on two pieces of paper with silk fibers between. Portrait is too dark, except in back of neck where fine lines are missing. Detail missing in hair, mustache. Heavy shading under lip makes chin prominent, but absence of fullness under chin. On back airplane and Statue of Liberty barely visible. Back is 1/8th inch long. Notes seen with SN A 1530203 A, but other numbers may be used.

KL 598 McAdoo-Burke. Plate C16, C18. Boston. Crude, hand engraved plates on single paper, with red lines imitiating fibers. Portrait bad. "Secretary of the Treasury" missing under signature.

KL 599 McAdoo-Burke. Plate D51. New York. Dangerous print from lithographic plates on single paper, fibers imitated by pen marks. Portrait too dark. Lathework in borders front and back very poor. Almost no fine lines.

KL 600 McAdoo-Burke. Plate B. Philadelphia. Poor, from etched plates on fair paper, with ink lines imitating fibers. Portrait particularly poor. Lathework broken and disconnected.

KL 609-654 McAdoo-Burke. Plate H. San Francisco. Photograph on two pieces of paper with silk fibers between. No effort to color seal or serial numbers, back touched up, blue-green.

KL 615 Glass-Burke. Plate G100, G109. New York. Photographic plate on two pieces of paper with silk threads between. Border on face of note, background of portrait black rather than fine lines. Treasury numbers black. Some attempt to color seal. Back very dark green, but better than face.

KL 669

Fifty Dollars
United States Notes

Series 1862

KL 668-669 Chittenden-Spinner. Plate C. Series 1. Inferior, engraving badly executed, portrait defective. Nose runs to an unnatural point, and a peculiar "dish" to face. Numbering imperfect. One of Convertible Series.

KL 668-669 Chittenden-Spinner. Plate C. New Series 1. Dangerous, with very good portrait. Buttons on coat not as distinct. White line that crosses lower digit "0" in "50" in large counters at each end of note is missing. On lower left back two of octagonal lines overlap in border.

KL 668-669. Chittenden-Spinner. Plate A, B, C, D. Series 1. Vignette of Hamilton cut from $2 notes and pasted over counterfeit notes.

Series 1863

KL 670 Chittenden-Spinner. Plate A, B, C, D. New Series 1. Dangerous, with portrait equal to genuine. White line that crosses lower portion of "0" in large "50" at each end is missing. Buttons on coat are indistinct. (See description of next note.)

KL 670 Chittenden-Spinner. Plate A, C, D. New Series 2. One of the most dangerous counterfeits ever issued. Engraving excellent, numbering good, lathework fair. On back borders small digits "50" surrounded by circles instead of octagons. Two of these at lower left run together, making number read "550." Balance of description of previous note applies.

Series 1869

KL 671 Allison-Spinner. Plate B. A superior, dangerous note with good engraving, excellent general appearance on plain paper. Lathework nearly perfect. Flourish between "Series of" and "1869" at upper left omitted, or added with pen. On back star at top of large 5 has six points, star at top of 0 and bottoms of 50 have five points. Genuine has five pointed stars at tops, four pointed at bottoms.

Series 1875

KL 673 Allison-Spinner. Plate A, B, C, D. Photographic pen and ink note.

Series 1880

KL 680 Tillman-Morgan. Plate C17. Dangerous. Portrait of Franklin very clear, except line of mouth and opening of ear, more pronounced. "Act of March 3, 1863" over portrait, "Benjamin Franklin," "Engraved and Printed Bureau of

KL 680-681 Tillman-Morgan. Plate A, B, C, D. Excellent pen and ink work. "Act of March 3, 1863" over portrait, "Series" over "United" and "Printed at the Bureau of Engraving and Printing" left of portrait omitted.

Engraving and Printing," "Series" over "United," and on back "Penalty for Counterfeiting," "Series of 1880" and "Bureau Engraving and Printing, Washington, D.C." all omitted.

Compound Interest Treasury Notes
Series 1864
KL 686 Chittenden-Spinner. Plate C. Dated July 15, 1864, Act of June 30, 1864. Poor portrait and vignette, poor numbering. Plates captured in July, 1866.
KL 687 Colby-Spinner. Plate D. Dated December, 1864, Act of June 30, 1864. Poor work.

Interest Bearing Notes
Series 1865
KL 692 Colby-Spinner. Plate C. Dated May 15, 1865, Act of June 30, 1864.
KL 692 Colby-Spinner. Plate D. Dated July 15, 1865, Act of March 3, 1865. Interest 7-30, and notes convertible after three years into 5-20 bonds. Plates captured July, 1866.

Gold Certificates
Series 1882
KL 702 Napier-McClung. Plate A. Pen and ink used in Treasury number and imitating the silk fibers. Color of word "Gold" unlike genuine. Back poor. Printed on single sheet of glazed paper. Back plate number omitted, face plate number indistinct.

Silver Certificates
Series 1891
KL 717 Parker-Burke. Plate A11. Deceptive photo mechanical on two pieces of paper with silk threads between. Portions of photographic number can be seen between blue ink applied with brush. On back lathework is poor, lines broken and disconnected.

Federal Reserve Notes
Series 1914
KL 735 McAdoo-Burke. Plate D1. Very dangerous photo mechanical on two pieces of thin paper with silk threads between. Seal and numbering fair, but too dark a blue. Lathework broken. Back very deceptive, but many fine lines in figure of Panama missing, as is flag on ship at left, and radio antennas.

One Hundred Dollars
United States Notes
Series 1862
KL 784-785 Chittenden-Spinner. Plate A, B, C, D. Dangerous, but defective counterfeit. Coarse engraving. Eagle vignette badly done, scratchy. Stems of feathers in tail near left claw almost invisible. Digits in numbers much longer or "deeper," imperfect, and off color. On back in the scroll work on both sides of the circle, repeated figures are reversed, with 100 on left and 001 on right.

Series 1880
KL 796-797 Rosecrans-Huston. Plate A, B, C, D. Dangerous photo pen and ink. "Engraved and Printed at Bureau of Engraving and Printing" on face and on back "Bureau of Engraving and Printing" omitted. Lathework and parallel ruling indistinct. On back small lettering in penalty irregular.

Interest Bearing Notes
Series 1865
KL 809 Colby-Spinner. Plate B. Dated May 15, 1865, Act of June 30, 1864. Plate engraved by Charles H. Smith, portrait and vignette good. Back is a genuine impression or from an electrotype of a stolen impression of a genuine plate.

Red numbers are off color and figures are uneven. The "U" in "United" just touches outside line of medallion in upper left corner. The last "S" in "States" is less than 1/16th inch from outside line of right corner medallion.

Gold Certificates
Series 1882
KL 818 Lyons-Roberts Plate A. Deceptive photo mechanical on two pieces of paper with silk threads between. Note looks like a washed or bleached genuine note. Seal is crimson, instead of carmine. Lathework very poor. Lyons' title reads "Terasurer."
KL 818 Lyons-Roberts. Plate B5. Notes carry SN C 424363 and C 324369, and possibly others. Number color good, but not bright ultramarine. Portrait does not stand out in bold relief or as lifelike as genuine. Lathework surrounding "100" flat, broken and blurred. Color of word "Gold" abnormal. Back is light salmon. Some have silk fibers imitated with ink lines. Letter "I" in "Deposit" lacks the dot.
KL 820 Vernon-Treat Plate B11. Dangerous lithographic print on genuine paper from bleached smaller denomination. Portrait is flat. Lines "There have been deposited in" and "payable to the bearer on demand" are too heavy and appear to be pen work, or retouching of the plate.

Silver Certificates
Series 1891
KL 842 Tillman-Morgan Plate D1. Very dangerous. On portrait left cheekbone is missing, face appearing narrower than genuine, changing expression. Hair hides top of ear and is not brushed upward. In "James" letters "Ja" are not uniform with rest of letters and J has more of an upward loop. Parallel lines somewhat broken in lower left border. Digit "5" in Treasury number is different, with lower loop an upright oblong, and space below top bar is narrow. Top button of waistcoat has only vertical lines, cross lines missing. Back plate 2.

Federal Reserve Notes
Series 1914
KL 897 McAdoo-Burke Plate C. Dallas. Photo mechanical plates, retouched with sharp instrument by unskilled workman on single piece of paper. Printed lines on back imitate fibers. Lines forming background of portrait look like pen work, or were cut into plate with a knife. Small lettering in "Series of 1914" and "Secretary of Treasury" hand done. Check letter missing from upper left corner. Seal is reddish brown instead of blue. Back is much too light green.

Five Hundred Dollars
United States Notes
Series 1869
KL 907 Allison-Spinner. Plate B, C, D. One of the most dangerous counterfeits, with engraving and workmanship nearly equal to genuine. Star on right of Treasury number blurred. Portrait excellent, but lobe of ear indistinct. Button on coat, nearest lapel is nearly square. In Vignette of Justice, upright holding beam of scale is crooked and too large, shows only from second finger to base. White curve in arm is not a perfect oval. Extended left foot appears clubbed. with short toes. Printed on fiber paper. Must be compared with genuine note to positively identify it.

One Thousand Dollars
United States Notes
Series 1863
KL 968 Chittenden-Spinner Plate A, B, C, D. Very dangerous, nearly equal to genuine. As with genuine, notes carry dates of either March 10, 1862 or March 10, 1863. Lathework in border and on corners much inferior. "Act of March 3, 1863" much coarser. Circles of "1,000" surrounding portrait much more irregular. Face of Morris is more of a front view, and eyes do not cast as far left. Imprint of printer is much narrower. On back the four points at each end are much more pointed.

National Bank Notes

Alabama

Twenty Dollars
Talladega - Isbell National - Check letter A, Series of 1882, Charter No. 4838. Photographic print, touched up with colors. Bank No. 7917

Arizona

Ten Dollars
Phoenix - Phoenix National - Check letter C, Series of 1882, Charter No. 4729. Poor photo, colored with a brush. Bank No. 1973.

Yuma - First National - Check letter E, Series of 1902-1908, Charter No. 7951. Face printed from photograph on two sheets of paper. Back photo etched and crude. Some have silk threads imitating fibers. J.W. Lyons, Register; Ellis H. Roberts, Treasurer. Bank No. 230. Blue seal, numbers and geographic letter "P" are separate prints instead of being colored. Parallel ruling in panel containing bank number at lower left end patched to cover original bank number.

California

Five Dollars
San Francisco - Nevada National - Check Letter D, Series of 1882, Charter No. 5105. Photograph. Portrait, seal, etc. cleverly colored by brush. Paper has fiber between sheets. Treasury number dark colored blue.

Los Angeles - First National - Check letter E, Series of 1908, Charter No. 2491. Poor photograph on bond paper of good quality with red and blue lines to imitate fibers on some notes. J.W. Lyons, Register; Ellis H. Roberts, Treasurer. Bank No. 12661. Numbering, seal and back of note smeared with coloring matter.

Tulare - National Bank of Tulare - Check letter D, Series of 1902-1908, Charter No. 10201. Printed from photograpic plates on two pieces of paper with silk threads between. Most noticeable defect is seal, which is very dark blue, almost black. Back of note blue instead of green.

Ten Dollars
El Centro - El Centro National - Check letter C, Series of 1902, Charter No. 9349. Matches the description of the $10 Pasadena National Bank notes below, except on some the defect in the portrait background does not appear.

Los Angeles - Farmers and Merchants National - Check letter H, Series of 1902, Charter No. 6617. Poorly printed from photo mechanical plates of fair workmanship on two sheets of paper with silk threads distributed between. Figures in Treasury and bank numbers poor and out of alignment. Lathework good. Back too dark a shade of green. Paper thick and harsh, perhaps from pasting sheets together.

Los Angeles - Los Angeles National - Check letter A, Series of 1882, Charter No. 2938. Poor photo, colored with a brush. Bank No. 6958. Brown color of photo shows through red numbers.

Orange - First National - Check letter F, Series of 1902-1908, Charter No. 8181. J.W. Lyons, Register; Chas. H. Treat, Treasurer. Bank No. 84. Same back plate and description as First National Bank of Yuma, Arizona.

Pasadena - Pasadena National - Check letter F, Series 1902-1908, Charter No. 8568. Deceptive, especially face. Photo etching, well printed on two sheets of thin paper with particles of silk distributed between. Seal and serial numbers a trifle darker than normal. Most noticeable defects on back, the back plate number 129, with a blue green tint. Back etching badly done and rough work is noticeable. Some fine lines in script on face have been entirely lost in the etching, giving face a pale appearance. A bad break in crosshatching in background of portrait over McKinley's left shoulder (viewer's right), because a piece of silk was photographed into the background, and an attempt made to eliminate this defect. Outline of bank's original number in panel under portrait, apparently 3335, shows under counterfeit number. Notes from same plates counterfeited on several other banks.

Riverside - National Bank - Check letter D, Series of 1902-1908, Charter No. 8377. W.T. Vernon, Register; Chas. H. Treat, Treasurer. Bank No. 1760. Same back plate and description as First National Bank of Yuma, Arizona.

San Francisco - Anglo and London Paris National - Check letter B, Charter No. 9174. Dangerous. W.T. Vernon, Register; Chas. H. Treat, Treasurer. Bank No. 22644. Printed from photo etched plates of good workmanship on two pieces of paper, some with silk threads between. Figures in Treasury and bank numbers slightly smaller and too widely separated. Not enough parallel ruled lines in scroll containing bank number on lower left face. Lines that do appear are broken and patched to conceal number of reproduced genuine note. Seal trifle too large. Back has bluish tint.

San Francisco - Crocker National - Check letter F, Series of 1902-1908, Charter No. 3555. W.T. Vernon, Register; Chas. H. Treat, Treasurer. Bank No. 3672. Fair photo etching on two sheets of paper with red and blue silk threads between on some notes. Bank number in black ink. Charter and Treasury numbers a very heavy blue. Treasury numbers irregular. Back of note blotchy.

San Francisco - Crocker National - Check letter ?, Series of 1902-1908, Charter No. 3555. Poor. W.T. Vernon, Register; Chas. H. Treat, Treasurer. A second edition of counterfeit described above, check letter not discernible. Printed from etched plates. Treasury number, bank number, charter number and seal printed with dark green on some notes instead of blue on genuine. Back of note printed pale green.

San Francisco - Germania National - Check letter B, Series of 1902, Charter No. 6592, Straight photo on two sheets of paper with no attempt to imitate fibers. Bank out of existence. J.W. Lyons, Register; Ellis H. Roberts, Treasurer.

Bank No. 1922, dated Jan. 16, 1903. Geographical letter "T," charter number and treasury number put on with rubber stamp. Seal tinted, but shows photography black imprint underneath. Back a photographic print in dark blue.

San Francisco - Wells Fargo Nevada National - Check letter G, Series of 1882, Charter No. 5105. Poor photo on heavy bond paper, no silk fiber. Bank No. 6945. Treasury numbers traced over with red ink. Back better than face, a fair imitation, except coloring around charter number, which is a muddy green.

Twenty Dollars
Los Angeles - U.S. National - Check letter B, Series 1902-1908, Charter No. 7632. A raised note, from a one dollar note, with pen and ink reproduction. Parts of host note still intact, especially lathework. Portrait of McCulloch very poor. Many mistakes in lettering, over portrait, "National" misspelling of "National." At bottom of face, "Casher" misspelling of "Cashier."

Colorado

Ten Dollars
Denver - Denver National - Check letter E, Series of 1882, Charter No. 3269. A crude photograph. Bank No. 13503.

Twenty Dollars
Grand Junction - Mesa County National - Check letter ?, Series of ?, Charter No. 7766. A very crude reproduction, printed from poor woodcut plates. Series number missing. Portrait of Washington. J.W. Lyons, Register of the Treasury; Ellis H. Roberts, Treasurer of the United States. Should not deceive easily.

Connecticut

Five Dollars
Jewett City - Jewett City National - Check Letter B, Series of Sept. 1, 1865, Charter No. 1478. Very poor. Bank has gone out of existence.

Norwalk - Central National - Check Letter A, Series of 1882, Charter No. 2342. Woodcut. Counterfeits have Charter No. 404, genuine is 2342.

Suffield - First National - Check Letter C, Series of 1882, Charter No. 497. Photograph, untinted. Bank No. 8675.

Waterbury - Citizens National - Check Letter D, Series of 1902, Charter No. 791. J.W. Lyons, Register; Ellis H. Roberts, Treasurer. Bank No. 3415. Printed from photo mechanical plates on fair paper, some notes without silk threads. Harrison's portrait poorly executed. Back has good color, deceptive.

Twenty Dollars
Portland - First National - Check letter A, Series of May 10, 1865, Charter No. 1013. In vignette at left, "1715" misprint for "1775." Shield on back has six imperfect stars, genuine has seventeen perfect stars.

Idaho

Five Dollars
Wallace - Wallace National - Check Letter ?, Series of 1902-1908, Charter No. 9134. Portrait of Harrison. Bank No. 1757. Very poorly printed from poorly executed zinc-etched plates on two sheets of paper with silk threads distributed between.

Illinois

Five Dollars
Aurora - First National - Check Letter A, Series of Nov. 2, 1863, Charter No. 38. None genuine signed "S.B. Colby, Register of the Treasury."

Canton - First National - Check Letter A, Series of May 21, 1864, Charter No. 415. None genuine signed "S.B. Colby, Register of the Treasury."

Cecil - First National - No such bank, all fraudulent.

Chicago - Central National - Check Letter A, Series of May 10, 1865, Charter No. 2047. None genuine signed "S.B. Colby, Register of the Treasury."

Chicago - First National - Check Letter A, Series of May 10, 1865, Charter No. 3. None genuine signed "S.B. Colby, Register of the Treasury."

Chicago - Fort Dearborn National - Check Letter C, Series of 1882, Charter No. 3698. Photograph, poorly colored. Bank No. 6197. Front is grayish brown-black. Green panel on back containing Charter No. 3698 is blue-green.

Chicago - Fort Dearborn National - Check Letter K, Series of 1882, Charter No. 3698. Photograph on fair paper. W.S. Rosencrans, Register; C.N. Jordan, Treasurer. Portrait of Garfield. Bank No. 40452. Red and blue coloring matter has been applied to original photographic numbers and an attempt has been made to color seals.

Chicago - German National - Check Letter A, Series of Mar. 10, 1865, Charter No. 1734. None genuine signed "S.B. Colby, Register of the Treasury."

Chicago - Merchants National - Check Letter A, Series of May 10, 1865, Charter No. 642. Same plate as Traders National, below.

Chicago - Traders National - Check Letter A, Series of May 10, 1865, Charter No. 966. On the genuine note, on back, at lower right corner the perpendicular line, if extended would strike figure five and border of note. On counterfeit it would strike between the figures.

Chicago - Union National - Check Letter A, Series of May 10, 1865, Charter No. 698. None genuine with date "May 10, 1865."

Galena - First National - No such bank, all fraudulent.

Omaha - First National - Check Letter A, Series of 1902-1908, Charter No. 10291. J.C. Napier, Register; Lee McClung, Treasurer, portrait of Harrison. Printed from crudely etched plates on two pieces of paper with silk threads distributed between. Very poor.

Paxton - First National - Check Letter A, Series of Oct. 20, 1871, Charter No. 1876. None genuine signed "S.B. Colby, Register of the Treasury."

Peru - First National - Check Letter A, Series of June 2, 1864, Charter No. 441. None genuine signed "S.B. Colby, Register of the Treasury," and dated May 10, 1865.

Quincy - National Bank of Quincy - Check letter A, Series ?, Charter No. ? Poor photograph. Bank No. 1633.

Virginia - Farmers National - Check letter A, Series of May 10, 1865, Charter No. 1472. All dated "May 10, 1865" are fraudulent.

Ten Dollars

Chicago - First National - Check letter K, Series of 1902, Charter No. 2670. Poorly printed from photo mechanical plates of fair workmanship, on two sheets of paper with silk threads distributed between. Figures in Treasury and bank numbers poor and out of alignment. Lathework poor. Back of note darker green than genuine. Paper thick and harsh, perhaps from pasting sheets together.

Rockford - Third National - Check letter B, Series of 1902, Charter No. 479. Photograph. Back badly faded. Treasury and bank numbers printed in red instead of blue. Back brown rather than green.

Springfield - Illinois National - Check letter F, Series of 1902-1908, Charter No. 3548. W.T. Vernon, Register; Chas. H. Treat, Treasurer. Bank No. 4965. Work is same as on counterfeit $10 note of Anglo and London Paris National Bank of San Francisco.

Twenty Dollars

Metropolis - National State - Check letter A, Series of 1882, Charter No. 5234. Photograph, poor. Bank No. 1198.

Indian Territory

Twenty Dollars

Marietta - Marietta National - Check letter A, Series of 1882, Charter No. 5958. Very poor photo, on two sheets of paper with a few silk threads between, with green color poorly applied.

Indiana

Ten Dollars

Lafayette - Lafayette National - Check letter A, Series of Dec. 22, 1874, Charter No. 2213. All with bank number 1496 are counterfeits. Treasury number 165167.

Muncie - Muncie National - Check letter A, Series of Feb. 14, 1865, Charter No. 793. All with bank number 1496 are counterfeits. Treasury number 165167, both as on Lafayette National above.

Richmond - Richmond National - Check letter A, Series of March 15, 1873, Charter No. 1102 and 2090. All with bank number 1496 are counterfeits. Treasury number 165167 as on notes above.

Vevay - First National - Check letter A, Old Series, Charter No. 346. All with bank number 1496 and Treasury number 165167 (as above), and bank number 1048, Treasury number 810516 are counterfeits.

Twenty Dollars

Indianapolis - First National - Check letter A, Series of Nov. 2, 1863, Charter No. 55. On lower left corner, butt of gun touches border, on genuine note it does not.

South Bend - South Bend National - Check letter A, Series of 1882, Charter No. 1739. Poor photo on two sheets of paper with red and blue silk between. Bank No. 1777.

Kansas

Five Dollars

Beloit - German National - Check letter ?, Series of 1908, Charter No. 6701. Combination of crude zinc etching and job press work. J.W. Lyons, Register; Ellis H. Roberts, Treasurer. Bank No. 394. Portrait of Harrison.

Ten Dollars

Emporia - Emporia National - Check letter A, Series of 1902-1908, Charter No. 1985. Poor photo mechanical print on three sheets of paper with silk threads between. Seal and numbering fair, on some notes too light, on others too dark. McKinley portrait poor. Back too light green. Figure of Liberty only an outline, lacking detail work.

Wichita - National Bank of Commerce - Check letter F, Series of 1882-1908, Charter No. 5169. Exceedingly dangerous photo mechanical reproduction, plates touched up with graver, on two sheets of paper, with some notes showing distributed silk threads between. Threads are too thick and too long. J.W. Lyons, Register; Ellis H. Roberts, Treasurer. Numbering, seal and geographical letter "W" well executed and of good color. In vignette at right end of face, hand of female figure grasping lightning bolt appears maimed. On genuine, fingers are well defined. Back darker than genuine. Lathework excellent.

Kentucky

Five Dollars

Lebanon - Marion National - Check letter D, Series of 1882, Charter No. 2150. Poor photograph. Bank No. 1578. Threads between sheets of paper.

Lexington - Fayette National - Check letter D, Series of 1882, Charter No. 1720. Photograph. Bank No. 2032.

Lexington - National Exchange - Check letter D, Series of 1875, Charter No. 2393. Poor counterfeit, with colors poorly applied with a brush.

Owensboro - United States National - Check letter B, Series of 1902-1908, Charter No. 9456. W.T. Vernon, Register; Charles H. Treat, Treasurer. Poor woodcut production on two sheets of paper, with silk threads distributed between. Portrait of Harrison scratchy. Lettering and lathework poor and light. Seal, numbering, charter number and geographical letter "S" all poorly done and too light a blue. Back of note poor and too light.

Ten Dollars

Louisville - American National - Check letter H, Series 1882-1908, Charter No. 4956. Plain uncolored photo on two sheets of paper with silk threads between on some notes. J. Fount Tillman Register; D.N. Morgan, Treasurer. Bank No. 15397.

Twenty Dollars

Mayfield - First National - Check letter A, Series of 1882, Charter No. 2245. Uncolored photograph. Bank No. 5211.

Louisiana

Five Dollars

New Orleans - Union National - Check letter C, Series of 1882, Charter No. 1796. Good photo, but color put on with a brush. Bank No. 5470. Panel on back blotchy green.

Ten Dollars

New Orleans - Germania National - Check letter C, Series of 1882, Charter No. 1591. Printed on fair paper, without silk threads, on a few notes imitated by ink lines. Vignettes coarse and scratchy. First lot had no scroll lines on right end of face of note above eagle's wing. Later plate was changed, adding these lines. Back well executed. In center panel, in charter number 1591, light brown shading on right and bottom of 9 omitted. Bank and Treasury numbers poor color and larger than genuine.

New Orleans - Hibernia National - Check letter B, Series of 1882, Charter No. 2086. Number, seal and panel on back poorly colored. No threads in paper. Bank No. 524.

Opelousas - Planters National - Check letter C, Series of 1902-1908, Charter No. 9872. Poor photo. W.T. Vernon, Register; Lee McClung, Treasurer. Bank No. 86. Seal, numbers and geographical letter "S" on face of note green. Back blue instead of green.

Maryland

Ten Dollars

Baltimore - National Union Bank of Maryland - Check letter C, Series of 1875, Charter No. 1489. John Allison, Register; John C. New, Treasurer. Bank No. 1837. Pen and brush reproduction of fair workmanship on parts of note. Poorest are title of bank, color and formation of seal and numbering, while lathework and fine border work is untraceable. Back of note, lettering at top and bottom of vignette barely readable. Fair paper with no fiber or imitations.

Twenty Dollars

Baltimore - Second National - Check letter B, Series of 1902, Charter No. 414. Lithographic reproduction on glazed paper, with silk threads imitated with pen and ink.

One Hundred Dollars

Baltimore - National Exchange - Check letter A, Series of July 1, 1865, Charter No. 1109. The description of the counterfeit $100 note on the National Revere Bank of Boston applies to this note.

Massachusetts

One Dollar

Boston - National Eagle - Check letter A, Series of 1875, Charter No. 993, Bank No. 9640. Photograph. The only counterfeit known (up to that time) of a National Bank one dollar note. On good paper, black work fairly reproduced, red numbering poor.

Five Dollars

Boston - Boylston National - Check letter C, Series of 1875, Charter No. 545. Photograph. Poor counterfeit, easily detected.

Boston - Fourth National - Check letter A, Series of 1882, Charter No. 2277. Photograph, with numbers colored with a brush and fiber imitated with ink.

Boston - Globe National - Check letter C, Series of 1875, Charter No. 936. Photograph, with green tinting on back poor, and entirely omitted in space at top where words "National Currency" appear.

Boston - Pacific National - Check letter B, Series of 1875, Charter No. 2373. Photograph. Bank out of existence.

Dedham - Dedham National - Check letter B, Series of 1875, Charter No. 669. Photograph. Green tinting on back poor and omitted in space at top where words "National Currency" appear.

Fall River - Pocasset National - Check letter C, Series of 1875, Charter No. 679. Photograph. Bank No. 762.

Harwich - Cape Cod National - Check letter A, Series of 1882, Charter No. 712. Photo, colored, with red lines for silk fibers. Green missing from panel on back containing charter number.

Holyoke - Home National - Check letter H, Series of 1908, Charter No. 3128. Poor photographic blueprint on bond paper. No attempt made to color Treasury or bank numbers.

Leicester - Leicester National - Check letter C, Series of 1875, Charter No. 918. Photograph. Poor counterfeit.

Lynn - First National - Check letter A, Series of 1882, Charter No. 638. Photo, colored, on two sheets with fiber between.

New Bedford - First National - Check letter B, Series of 1875, Charter No. 261. Photo. The green in border on the back of the note is printed and not put on with a brush.

New Bedford - Merchants National - Check letter C, Series of Feb. 14, 1865, Charter No. 799. Good counterfeit. In words "Five Dollars," lower center face of note, letter "S" appears above line of other letters. On back of genuine note, right thigh of Columbus perfectly formed, on counterfeit it has a clubbed or swollen appearance.

Northhampton - First National - Check letter C, Series of May 2, 1864, Charter No. 383. None genuine signed "S.B. Colby, Register of the Treasury."

Southbridge - Southbridge National - Check letter B, Series of 1875, Charter No. 934. Poor photograph. Bank No. 409.

Waltham - Waltham National - Check letter B, Series of 1882, Charter No. 688. Photo. Seal and Treasury number are a blue tint. Panel on back should be green. Bank No. 6149.

Westfield - Hampden National - Check letters C and D, Series of Aug. 1, 1865, Charter No. 1367. Fair. Connection of upward standard with rail in bulwark of ship plain on genuine note. Not seen on the counterfeit.

Ten Dollars

Athol - Millers River National - Check letter B, Series of 1882, Charter No. 708. Poorly colored photo on two sheets of paper with silk fiber between. Panel on back of genuine containing charter number 708 is green, on counterfeit it is not.

Boston - Eliot National - Check letter C, Series of 1882, Charter No. 536. Poorly colored photo with ink lines for threads. Bank No. 4235.

Boston - Second National - Check letter G, Series of 1902, Charter No. 322. Poor photo on two sheets of paper, some with silk threads between.

New Bedford - Mechanics National - Check letter B, Series of 1882, Charter No. 743. Photograph with fibers imitated. Bank No. 11793. Charter, bank and Treasury numbers brown instead of carmine. Panel on back containing charter number 743 should be green.

Roxbury - Peoples National - Check letter A, Series of 1882, Charter No. 595. Photo, with seal, etc. tinted and fibers imitated with ink lines. Bank No. 8201.

Worcester - Mechanics National - Check letter N, Series of 1902-1908, Charter No. 1135. J.W. Lyons, Register; Ellis H. Roberts, Treasurer. Printed from photo etched plates on rather thick paper with silk fibers imitated by printed lines, those on face black and on back green.

Twenty Dollars

Boston - Fourth National - Check letter A, Series of 1882, Charter No. 2277. Photo, poorly colored, on two sheets of paper with threads between. Bank No. 42431.

Boston - National Security - Check letter B, Series of 1902-1908, Charter No. 1675. Printed from etched plates on poor quality paper with no attempt to imitate silk threads. Bank numbers printed black. Wrong charter number (891) appears in blue on face of note, but correct number (1675) appears several times on border. W.T. Vernon, Register; Charles H. Treat, Treasurer.

One Hundred Dollars

Boston - First National - Check letter A, Series of Feb. 2, 1864, Charter No. 200. On genuine vignette at left end, water drops from both sides of bow oar. On counterfeit from only one side. Crossbar of "T" omitted in "Maintain" at right end. This defect is often corrected by reprint, pen or pencil, but will not deceive if closely examined. On genuine, the sailor standing in bow of boat has a medium sized head and face, with partially open mouth. On counterfeit, the head and face is large and broad, with broad, full forehead and closed mouth. On the genuine notes the lettering on back in correctly punctuated. On the counterfeits, in lower panel, second line, after the word "it," a comma is omitted, and again after "printed" on the fourth line in the same panel. The plates for this note were used for several other banks, as listed.

Boston - National Revere - Check letter A, Series of July 20, 1865, Charter No. 1295. The genuine note has a 1/16th inch space between edge of wing of Liberty and shading of letter "O" in upper right corner. On counterfeits, the space is about 1/32nd inch. On genuine in left vignette, water drops from both sides of bow oar, on counterfeit from but one side. On genuine distance between wing of Liberty and check letter A is over 3/16ths of an inch, on counterfeit barely 1/8th inch. On genuine a line drawn sharply under words "with the U.S. Treasurer at Washington," if extended strikes the lower lip of Liberty. On counterfeit it would strike the chin. Face of sailor in bow of boat resembles a skeleton or death's head. On back of genuine notes in the upper lettered panel, on the third line, right, the words "other debts" are properly spaced. On the counterfeit, the "R" in "other" joins the "D" in "debts.," and the "D" is raised above the preceeding letters. The plates for this note were used for several other banks, as listed.

New Bedford - Merchant's National - Check letter A, Series of Feb. 14, 1865, Charter No. 799. The description of the counterfeit $100 note on the National Revere Bank of Boston applies to this note.

Pittsfield - Pittsfield National - Check letter A, Series of July 20, 1865, Charter No. 1260. The description of the counterfeit $100 note on the National Revere Bank of Boston applies to this note.

Michigan

Five Dollars

Bay City - First National - Check letter B, Series of 1882, Charter No. 2853. Photo. Color of Treasury numbers and seal very poor. Bank No. 22.

Flint - Flint National - Check letter C, Series of 1882, Charter No. 3361. Photograph. Bank No. 11464. Large scalloped seal. Parallel threads.

Grand Rapids - Old National - Check letter F, Series of 1882, Charter No. 2890. Fair counterfeit. Ink on back more purple than brown. Bank No. 10819.

Jackson - Peoples National - Check letter D, Series of Oct. 2, 1865, Charter No. 1533. Poor lithograph, with numerous defects.

Niles - Citizens National - Check letter B, Series of 1882, Charter No. 1886. Poor photo. Chocolate scalloped seal has washed appearance. Fiber imitated with pen and ink on good quality paper.

Ten Dollars

Detroit - First National - Check letter C, Series of 1882, Charter No. 2707. Photo with parallel silk threads in paper. Bank No. 5612. Color put on with a brush.

Detroit - Union National - Check letter B, Series of 1882, Charter No. 3487. Photographic note, with colors applied with a brush.

Monroe - First National - Check letter D, Series of 1902, Charter No. 1587. Very poor photo, colored with a brush. Portrait of McKinley very poor. Lathework cannot be traced. Numbering bad, no silk threads.

Minnesota

Five Dollars

Albert Lea - Citizens National - Check letter G, Series of 1902-1908, Charter No. 6128. J.W. Lyons, Register; Ellis H. Roberts, Treasurer. Poor photo mechanical on poor paper. Charter, Treasury and bank numbers well formed but too light a blue. Seal is off color. Black printing on whole face of note and also green on back too light, giving complete note a faded appearance. Some notes have ink lines to imitate silk fibers.

Brainerd - First National - Check letter C, Series 1882-1908, Charter No. 2590. Bank No. 2513. Printed from zinc-etched plates on two sheets of paper with red ink lines between to imitate fibers.

Mississippi

Ten Dollars

Jackson - First National - Check letter C, Series of 1882, Charter No. 3332. Photographic print, on two sheets of paper with silk fiber between. Seal, etc. touched up with color. Bank No. 1292. Seal yellowish brown instead of chocolate.

Missouri

Five Dollars

Joplin - First National - Check letter C, Series of 1882, Charter No. 3841. Photograph. Bank No. 3834. Fiber imitated with pen and ink.

Plattsburg - First National - Check letter C, Series of 1882, Charter No. 4215. Printed from photo etched plates on fair paper. No effort to imitate silk threads. Correct charter number (4215) appears on the border of the face of note. Wrong charter number (10231) is printed in two places on face. Bank No. 16247. All blue numbers are too widely separated and not as heavy. Harrison's portrait poor. Lathework, especially on back, not well defined.

Springfield - National Exchange - Check letter C, Series of 1882, Charter No. 5082. J. Fount Tillman, Register; Ellis H. Roberts, Treasurer. Bank No. 5825. Direct photo with coloring matter applied to numbers and geographical letter "M." Original charter number can be seen under coloring. Bears the back impression of the State National Bank of St. Louis, as charter number of that bank, 5172, appears in center of note. Back is a photo. No silk or imitation.

St. Louis - National Bank of Commerce - Check letter U, Series of 1902-1908, Charter No. 4178. Very poor photo reproduction, with coloring matter applied to charter number and back of note.

St. Louis - State National - Check letter C, Series of 1882, Charter No. 5172. J.W. Lyons, Register; Ellis H. Roberts, Treasurer. Poor photo with coloring applied to numbers and geographical letter "M." No silk fiber or imitations.

Ten Dollars

Columbia - Exchange National - Check letter D, Series of 1902-1908, Charter No. 1467. J.W. Lyons, Register; Ellis H. Roberts, Treasurer. Bank No. 387. Printed from crude photo mechanical plates on genuine paper, probably from bleaching a smaller demonination note. Seal, numbering and geographical letter "M" are printed in purple ink. Back is brown instead of green.

Montana

Ten Dollars

Butte - Silver Bow National - Check letter B, Series of 1902, Charter No. 4283. Poor photo. Bears charter number 4256, which is wrong. All numbers and geographical letter "W" printed in purple ink. W.T. Vernon, Register: Lee McClung, Treasurer.

Nebraska

Ten Dollars

Omaha - United States National - Check letter E, Series of 1902, Charter No. 2973. Very crude photo mechanical reproduction on one sheet of paper. Some notes have ink lines to imitate fibers. Back of specimen seen printed upside down. J.W. Lyons, Register; Ellis H. Roberts, Treasurer. Bank No. 1078.

New Hampshire

Five Dollars

Derry - Derry National - Check letter C, Series of 1882, Charter No. 499. Good photo. Note a purple color, with other colors added for numbers. Seal reddish-brown instead of chocolate color. Paper thick with one long silk thread but no distributed fibers.

New Jersey

Five Dollars

Morristown - National Iron - Check letter A, Series of 1882, Charter No. 1113. Deceptive. Portrait of Garfield flat. "Cash" misspelling for "Cash'r." "Treasurg" misspelling in "Register of the Treasury." On lower back in penalty clause the words "engraving," "this" and "paper" have letters transposed.

Ten Dollars

Trenton - First National - Check letter I, Series of 1902, Charter No. 281. Printed from photo mechanical plates on one piece of heavy paper with no attempt to imitate fibers. J.W. Lyons, Register; Ellis H. Roberts, Treasurer. At lower center of face the word "Trenton" and date "February 25, 1903" omitted.

Fifty Dollars

Bridgeton - Bridgeton National - Check letter A, Series of 1882, Charter No. 2999. Poor photograph. Seal, numbers and back colored with brush. Bank No. 142.

New Mexico

Five Dollars

Alamogordo - Citizens National - Check letter ?, Series of 1902, Charter No. 8315. Badly printed photo etched note. Detailed description unnecessary.

Ten Dollars

Carlsbad - Carlsbad National - Check letter B, Series of 1902, Charter No. 6884. Poor, photo etched on two sheets of paper. Bank No. 82. Bank out of existance.

New York

Two Dollars

Kinderhook - National Union - Check letter A, Series of July 1, 1865, Charter No. 929. On genuine note, check letter A at left of note near vignette has one flourish under it. Counterfeit has two flourishes.

Linderpark - National Union - No such bank, all fraudulent.

New York City - Market National - Check Letter A, Series of July 1, 1865, Charter No. 964. On genuine note, over letters "ar" in "market" are three flourishes. Counterfeit has only one.

New York City - Marine National - Check Letter A, Series of July 1, 1865, Charter No. 1215. Genuine title reads Marine National Bank of the City of New York. Counterfeit omits words, "the City of."

New York City - Ninth National - Check Letter A, Series of July 1, 1865, Charter No. 387. Genuine title reads Ninth National Bank of the City of New York. Counterfeit omits "the."

New York City - St. Nicholas National - Check Letter A, Series of July 1, 1865, Charter No. 972. On genuine note, "New York" over date of July 1, 1865 is in italic letters, sometimes called stump letters. On the counterfeit the "New York" is in script letters.

Peekskill - Westchester County National - Check Letter A, Series of Aug. 15, 1865. Note has one flourish under left check letter A. Counterfeit has two flourishes.

Five Dollars

Amsterdam - Manufacturers National - Check letter B, Series of Apr. 15, 1875, Charter No. 2239. General appearance deceptive. Engraving coarse, especially on back. Shading under "Manufacturers" done in straight lines, spaces broken out roughly. No shading inside first A in word and only two shading lines inside second A.

Castleton - National Bank of Castleton - Check letter D, Series of Mar. 10, 1865, Charter No. 942. Good counterfeit, but color of Treasury numbers and seal poor.

Friendship - Citizens National - Check letter C, Series of 1882, Charter No. 2632. Uncolored photo on single sheet of paper without silk threads. J.W. Lyons, Register; Ellis H. Roberts, Treasurer. Bank No. 2235.

New York City - American Exchange National - Check letter F, Series of 1882, Charter No. 1394. Photograph. Bank No. 101798.

New York City - American Exchange National - Check letter B, Series of 1902, Charter No. 1394. Bank No. 24739. Photo mechanical on poor paper, printed in black instead of blue, with ink marks to imitate fibers. Back of note too light.

New York City - Citizens International - No such bank. Not the right seal - appears to be of some secret society. From wood cut plates. Charter No. 196 on face, 127 on back.

New York City - Irving National - Check letter ?, Series of 1902, Charter No. 345. Poor counterfeit, with no check letter. Ink lines imitate fibers. No attempt to imitate fine lines of scroll work. Printed on poor quality paper.

New York City - Mechanics and Metals National - Check letter C, Series of 1902-1908, Charter No. 1250. Printed from engraved plates on good bond paper, with red and blue lines imitating fibers. "Treasnrg" misspelling in "Register of the Treasury." On lower back, "diports" misspelling for "imports." Parallel lines in panel containing bank number at lower left of face on genuine notes are wavy lines. Counterfeit has straight ruled lines. Shade lines in words "National Currency" in border at upper center of face are oblique on genuine notes, horizontal on the counterfeits. Many other mistakes.

New York City - National Bank of Commerce - Check letter G, Series of 1882, Charter No. 733. Photograph. Bank No. 78763.

New York City - National City Bank - Check letter U, Series of 1882, Charter No. 1461. Photo. Partly and poorly colored. Bank No. 29089.

New York City - National Park Bank - Check letter R, Series of 1902-1908, Charter No. 891. W.T. Vernon, Register; Lee McClung, Treasurer. Very poor counterfeit, printed from zinc-etched plates on fair paper. No silk threads or imitations.

Pawling - National Bank of Pawling - Check letter A, Series of Jul 20, 1865, Charter No. 1269. On genuine, check letter A in upper left corner is nearly in center of space between yard-arm and border. On counterfeit it touches or nearly touches the yard-arm.

Rome - Fort Stanwix National - Check letter B, Series of Sept. 1, 1865, Charter No. 1410. Poor counterfeit with scratchy vignette. Shading of large letters on face poor.

Troy - National State Bank - Check letter A, Series of May 10, 1865, Charter No. 991. None genuine signed "Jno. C. New, Treasurer of the United States" and bearing at the same time the old pointed Treasury seal. "Treusury" misspelling under Register's name.

Troy - Fifth National - Check letter A, Series of 1882, Charter No. 991. Apparently no such bank, although not noted. Charter number duplicates National State Bank above. Poor photograph on glazed paper. Seals, etc. not colored. Bank No. 7244.

Ten Dollars

Albany - Albany City National - Check letter A, Series of July 20, 1865, Charter No. 1291. Fair counterfeit. Seal and numbers poor. Lathework on back poor.

Auburn - Auburn City National - Check letter A, Series of July 20, 1865, Charter No. 1285. In vignette on lower left face, Franklin's kite string is broken, or hidden by clouds. On genuine it is wholly visible. Seal and numbers poor. Lathework on back poor.

Buffalo - Farmers and Manufacturers National - Check letter A, Old Series, Charter No. ? No such bank. From altered counterfeit plate of Farmers and Manufacturers National Bank, Poughkeepsie, N.Y.

Buffalo - Marine National - Check letter F, Series of 1902, Charter No. 6184. Crude photo mechanical on fair quality paper, without silk threads. Seal and numbering colored with brush. Original photographic impression visible beneath color.

Ithaca - Tompkins County National - Check letter B, Series of 1882, Charter No. 1561. Photo. Seal, etc. touched up. Fiber between sheets. Bank No. 3894.

Kingston - National Ulster County - Check letter B, Series of 1882, Charter No. 1050. Very poor photo, with colors of numbers, etc. poorly applied. Black and olive colored fibers between two sheets of paper.

Lockport - First National - Check letter A, Series of Feb. 20, 1865, Charter No. 211. None genuine signed "S.B. Colby, Register of the Treasury."

Newburgh - Highland National - Check letter A, Series of July 1, 1865, Charter No. 1106. Fair counterfeit. Numbering, seal and lathework imperfect.

New York - American National - Check letter A, Series of July 1, 1865, Charter No. 50. All with date "July 1st, 1865" are counterfeit.

New York - American Exchange National - Check letter I, Series of 1902, Charter No. 1394. Photograph on good paper. J.W. Lyons, Register; Chas. A. Treat, Treasurer. Entire face of note a sepia tint. Back of note yellow instead of green.

New York - Bank of New York, N.B.A. - Check letter F, Series of 1902, Charter No. 1393. Face of note looks like a tracing through black carbon, filled in with blue indelible pencil.

New York - Citizens Central - Check letter G, Series of 1902, Charter No. 1290. Printed from lithograph plates on two sheets of paper with silk threads between. J.W. Lyons, Register; Ellis H. Roberts, Treasurer. Pink seal is good in color and workmanship. Numbering poor, figures irregular in size and alignment. Lathework poor, especially on back, blurred and indistinct.

New York - Croton National - Check letter A, Old Series, Charter No. 1556. Bank failed. Few genuine notes in circulation.

New York - First National - Check letter A, Series of July 1, 1865, Charter No. 29. None genuine signed "S.B. Colby, Register of the Treasury."

New York - First National - Check letter E, Series of 1882, Charter No. 29. Photographic reproduction on fair paper with no imitation of silk threads. Attempt made to color (brown) Treasury and bank numbers, also panel on back of note.

New York - First National - Check letter M, Series of 1902, Charter No. 29. Issue of Feb. 25, 1903. Poor photo mechanical reproduction on three sheets of paper with a few silk threads between face and middle sheet. J.W. Lyons, Register; Ellis H. Roberts, Treasurer. Bank No. 29842. Title under portrait reads "Willam" instead of "William." On scroll panel, left back of note, "Pavement" misspelling of "Payment." On scroll panel, right back, "Excptd" misspelling of "Except." Lathework very scratchy. Charter number and seal light pink instead of carmine.

New York - Marine National - Check letter A, Series of July 1, 1865, Charter No. 1215. Words "City of" in title, "Marine National Bank of the City of New York" omitted.

New York - Market National - Check letter A, Series of July 1, 1865, Charter No. 964. All dated "July 1, 1865" are counterfeits.

New York - Mechanics National - Check letter A, Series of July 1, 1865, Charter No. 1250. Words "City of" in title, "Mechanics National Bank of the City of New York" omitted.

New York - Merchants National - Check letter A, Old Series, Charter No. 1370. Signatures are printed instead of written. Numbering poor.

New York - National Bank of Commerce - Check letter A, Series of July 1, 1865, Charter No. 733. All dated "July 1, 1865" are counterfeits.

New York - National Bank of Commerce - Check letter R, Series of 1882, Charter No. 733. Poorly executed photograph. Bank No. 29968.

New York - National Bank of the State of New York - Check letter A, Series of July 1, 1865, Charter No. 1476. All dated "July 1, 1865" are counterfeit.

New York - National City - Check letter L, Series of ?, Charter No. 1461. Bank No. 34454. Poorly etched and badly printed on two sheets of paper with silk fibers distributed between. Face of note very dark and blotchy. Portrait of McKinley especially poor. Back of note too light a green.

New York - National Park - Check letter F, Series of 1902-1908, Charter No. 891. Photographic on two sheets of glazed paper. Some have coarse silk threads between. Portrait and title lettering fair. Seal and numbering too light and poorly done. All lathework poor.

New York - Union National - Check letter A, Series of July 1, 1865, Charter No. 1278. All dated "July 1, 1865" are counterfeit.

Poughkeepsie - City National - Check letter A, Series of July 5, 1864, Charter No. 1305. Seal and numbers poor. Lathework on back poor.

Poughkeepsie - Farmers and Manufacturers National - Check letter A, Series of Aug. 1, 1865, Charter No. 1312. "P" and "O" in "Poughkeepsie" are joined, but not on genuine.

Poughkeepsie - First National - Check letter A, Series of July 5, 1864, Charter No. 465. None genuine signed "S.B. Colby, Register of the Treasury."

Red Hook - First National - Check letter A, Series of Feb. 20, 1865, Charter No. 752. All dated "February 26, 1865" are counterfeit.

Rochester - Flour City National - Check letter A, Series of July 1, 1865, Charter No. 1362. All dated "July 1, 1865" are counterfeit.

Rome - Central National - Check letter A, Series of May 12, 1865, Charter No. 1376. All dated "May 12, 1865" are counterfeit.

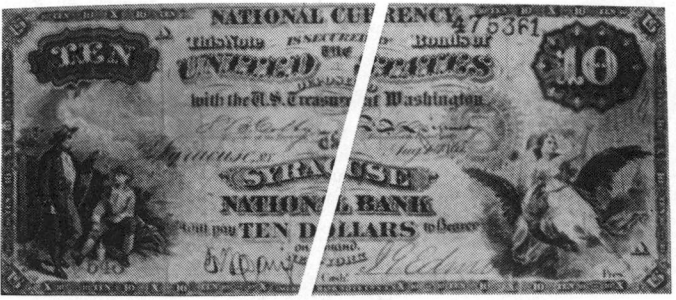

Syracuse - Syracuse National - Check Letter A, Series of Aug. 1, 1865, Charter No. 1341. A dangerous counterfeit when well printed. Lathework was retouched and plate improved to produce these notes. On first lot, numbering, seal and back poorly executed.

Troy - Mutual National - Check letter A, Series of May 10, 1865, Charter No. 992. On counterfeit eagle's wing touches 65, but does not on genuine.

Waterford - Saratoga County National Bank - Check letter A, Series of July 1, 1865, Charter No. 1229. All carrying bank number 1048 are counterfeit.

Watkins - Watkins National - Check letter A, Series of July 1, 1865, Charter No. (456). All dated "August 1, 1865" are counterfeit. Bank out of existence.

Twenty Dollars

Mohawk - National Mohawk Valley - Check letter A, Series of 1882, Charter No. 1130. Photograph, but few in circulation and glass plate captured.

New York - First National - Check letter B, Series of July 10, 1865, Charter No. 29. All dated "July 19, 1865" are counterfeits.

New York - Fourth National - Check letter A, Series of March 1, 1864, Charter No. 290. The heads of figures in the baptismal scene on back and in battle scene on face are almost wholly devoid of expression and the eyes appear as black spots.

New York - Market National - Check letter B, Series of Jan. 19, 1865, Charter No. 964. None genuine with "L.E. Chittenden, Register of the Treasury."

New York - Merchants National - Check letter B, Series of July 19, 1865, Charter No. 1370. None genuine with "L.E. Chittenden, Register of the Treasury."

New York - National Bank of Commerce - Check letter B, Series of Jan. 19, 1865, Charter No. 733. None genuine with "L.E. Chittenden, Register of the Treasury."

New York - National Shoe and Leather - Check letter B, Series of July 19, 1865, Charter No. 917. None genuine with "L.E. Chittenden, Register of the Treasury."

New York - Tradesmens National - Check letter B, Series of July 19, 1865, Charter No. 905. None genuine with "L.E. Chittenden, Register of the Treasury."

Utica - City National - No such bank. The genuine notes have Utica City National Bank, Utica.

Utica - Oneida National - Check letter B, Series of August 19, 1865, Charter No. 1392. None genuine with "L.E. Chittenden, Register of the Treasury."

Fifty Dollars

Buffalo - Third National - Check letter A, Series of March 10, 1865, Charter No. 850. On genuine, above and below words "with the" in line "Deposited with the U.S. Treasurer at Washington," is a flourish. On the counterfeit these are omitted. On vignette of Victory at upper right end, hand is minus thumb or fingers, distinct on genuine. On the left end of back, bandage covers eyes of Justice in coat of arms on genuine, on counterfeit it does not. All counterfeits of $50 National Bank Notes on banks in New York State were printed from these plates, with the names changed, so this description applies to those listed below.

New York - Central National - Check letter A, Series of April 15, 1864, Charter No. 376. None genuine bearing any other charter number than 376. The description of the $50 note of the Third National Bank of Buffalo, N.Y. above, applies to this note.

New York - Mechanics National - Check letter A, Series of April 20, 1865, Charter No. 1250. The description of the $50 note of the Third National Bank of Buffalo, N.Y. above, applies to this note.

New York - Metropolitan National - Check letter A and C, Series of Jan. 10, 1865, Charter No. 1121. The description of the $50 note of the Third National Bank of Buffalo, N.Y. above, applies to this note.

New York - National Bank of Commerce - Check letter A and C, Series of Jan. 10, 1865, Charter No. 733. The description of the $50 note of the Third National Bank of Buffalo, N.Y. above, applies to this note.

New York - National Broadway - Check letter A and C, Series of Jan. 10, 1865, Charter No. 687. Genuine notes of this bank only bear check letter A. The description of the $50 note of the Third National Bank of Buffalo, N.Y. above, applies to this note.

New York - Tradesmens National - Check letter A and C, Series of April 20, 1865, Charter No. 905. Genuine notes of this bank only bear check letter A. The description of the $50 note of the Third National Bank of Buffalo, N.Y. above, applies to this note.

New York - Union National - Check letter A, Series of April 15, 1864, Charter No. 1278. The description of the $50 note of the Third National Bank of Buffalo, N.Y. above, applies to this note.

One Hundred Dollars

New York - Central National - Check letter A, Series of April 15, 1864, Charter No. 376. The description of the counterfeit $100 note on the First National Bank of Boston applies to this note.

Ohio

Five Dollars

Cincinnati - National State Bank - Check letter A, Series of 1882, Charter No. 2798. Photograph. Color of numbers and seal fair but put on with a brush. Back poor. Bank No. 2269.

Springfield - Lagonda National - Check letter B, Series of 1875, Charter No. 2098. Photo. Bank No. 2334. Seal, etc. colored with brush. Back printed upside down. No imitations of fibers.

Ten Dollars

Cincinnati - Third National - Check letter C, Series of 1882, Charter No. 2730. Paper greasy and stiff, no distributed fibers or parallel threads. Vignette is coarse and scratchy. Lathework counters poor. "N" in "Printed" is inverted. Back good.

One Hundred Dollars

Cincinnati - Ohio National - Check letter A, Series of Dec. 22, 1864, Charter No. 630. The description of the counterfeit $100 note on the First National Bank of Boston applies to this note.

Oklahoma

Ten Dollars

Chandler - Union National - Check letter F, Series of 1902-1908, Charter No. 6269. From poorly etched plates on two or more sheets of thin paper with silk threads distributed between. Threads show on surface. Portrait of McKinley poor, bears little resemblance. Back better than face, but poor lathework.

Edmond - First National - Check letter D, Series of 1902-1908, Charter No. 6156. W.T. Vernon, Register; Charles H. Treat, Treasurer. Printed from photo mechanical plates on two sheets of paper with silk fiber distributed between. Dangerous, but back not as good as face, off color, lathework coarse, lines broken in places.

Lone Wolf - First National - Check letter A, Series of 1902, Charter No. 10096. J.C. Napier, Register; Lee McClung, Treasurer. Dangerous photo mechanical on two sheets of thin paper with silk threads distributed between. Under portrait, in panel containing bank number, parallel rules have been patched to cover number of genuine note, which shows behind blue numbers. Signatures of bank officers printed instead of written. Back off color.

Walters - Walters National - Check letter F, Series of 1902-1908, Charter No. 7811. Face of note deceptive. Combination of photographing and etching. Printed on two sheets of paper with silk fibers distributed between. Paper feels stiff and harsh due to pasting. Green on back of note off color.

Oregon

Ten Dollars

Portland - First National - Check letter D, Series of 1902-1908, Charter No. 1553. Same as the description of the Pasadena National Bank, Pasadena, Calif. Made by the same persons. On some, defect in portrait background of the Pasadena note is absent.

Pennsylvania

Two Dollars

Philadelphia - Sixth National - Check Letter A, Series of July 1, 1865, Charter No. 352. No bills from this (confiscated) plate found in circulation.

Five Dollars

Hanover - First National - Check letter D, Series of Feb. 20, 1864, Charter No. 187. Under "Continental Bank Note Co., New York" on lower center border, genuine has "Act approved Feb. 25th, 1863." On counterfeit, "Act approved June 3d, 1864."

Tamaqua - First National - Check letter B, Series of July 1, 1865, Charter No. 1219. Counterfeits seen have wrong charter number. On upper right back, "Ownig" misspelling for "Owing." At lower right back, "Thousaud" misspelling for "Thousand."

Ten Dollars

Ashley - First National - Check letter F, Series of 1902-1908, Charter No. (8656). W.T. Vernon, Register; Chas. A. Treat, Treasurer. Photo mechanical reproduction on fair quality paper with red and blue ink lines imitating fibers. Face of note poorly printed, McKinley's portrait appears smeared. Lathework on both sides very poor, back blotchy and printed with dark green ink.

Philadelphia - First National - Check letter B, Series of Feb. 20, 1864, Charter No. ? All dated "February 20, 1864" are counterfeit.

Philadelphia - Fourth Street National - Check letter ?, Series of 1882, Charter No. 3557. Straight photographic. Geographical letter, charter number, Treasury number, bank serial number and seal touched up with brownish red ink. Some blue ink applied to the charter number on the panel on back of note.

Philadelphia - Fourth Street National - Check letter E, Series of 1902, Charter No. 3557. Face of note appears to be tracing through black carbon, filled in with blue indelible pencil.

Philadelphia - Third National - Check letter B, Series of Feb. 20, 1864, Charter No. 234. "Curreny" misspelling of "Currency" at upper right hand end of border.

Tyrone - Blair County National - Check letter E, Series of 1902-1908, Charter No. 6516. J.W. Lyons, Register; Ellis H. Roberts, Treasurer. Bank No. 4428. Plate number on back indistinct, apparently 227. Dangerous photo mechanical reproduction on two sheets of paper of fair quality with silk threads between on some notes. Portrait of McKinley fair, but specimen seen is printed too black on lower right of chin and neck. Hair too coarse and thick and shading around eyes poor. Seal, Treasury, bank numbers poor and too light a blue. Lathework fair. Parallel ruling under bank number at lower left of note broken. Titles "Register of the Treasury" and "Treasurer of the United States" irregular. Back of note not as good work as face, also too light a green, verging on a bluish green.

Williamsport - First National - Check letter E, Series of 1902-1908, Charter No. 175. Same description as the $10 Pasadena National Bank, Pasadena, Calif. notes, made by the same persons. On some notes defect in portrait background of Pasadena notes is absent.

Twenty Dollars

Philadelphia - Fourth National - Check letter A, Series of Mar. 7, 1864, Charter No. 286. Engraving of title line defective; "A" in "Philadelphia" not crossed. Letter "W" in "Twenty" lower right end of border on face of note shorter than rest of letters. Lettering in end margins of back scarcely legible. In vignette at lower left, "1715" misprint for "1775."

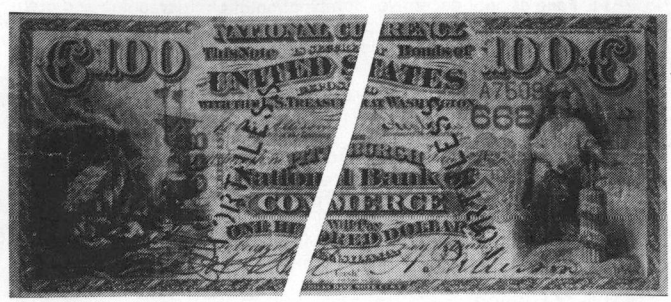

One Hundred Dollars

Pittsburgh - Pittsburgh National Bank of Commerce - Check letter A, Series of 1875, Charter No. 668. The description of the counterfeit $100 note on the National Revere Bank of Boston applies to this note. This is the most dangerous of the $100 National Bank Notes, as it is the only one printed on fiber paper and bearing the scalloped seal.

Wilkesbarre - Second National - Check letter A, Series of Nov. 2, 1863, Charter No. 104. The description of the counterfeit $100 note on the First National Bank of Boston applies to this note.

Rhode Island

Two Dollars

Newport - National Bank of Rhode Island - Check Letter A, Series of Nov. 1, 1865, Charter No. 1532. Lithograph. "National Bank Note Co., New York" and other small lettering is hardly legible because the letters are so poorly formed.

Five Dollars

Providence - Commercial National - Check letter A, Series of 1882, Charter No. 1319. Photograph, with numbers and seal colored with brush, poorly done. Bank No. 20650.

Providence - Blackstone Canal National - Check letter B, Series of 1882, Charter No. 1328. Counterfeits bear wrong (1311) charter number. Signatures "R.C. Taft, Prest." and "J.W. Vernon, Cashier" wrong. These signatures belong to Merchants National Bank of Providence.

Ten Dollars

Providence - Merchants National - Check letter B, Series of 1902, Charter No. 1131. Poor, made from crude woodcut plates. J.W. Lyons, Register; Ellis H. Roberts, Treasurer. Bank No. 15995.

South Dakota

Twenty Dollars

Wessington - First National - Check letter A, Series of 1902, Charter No. 8335. Printed on paper from bleached one dollar note. Under magnification portions of dollar note design can be seen. Poor pen and brush reproduction. Portrait very poor, rough and scratchy. W.T. Vernon, Register; Chas. H. Treat, Treasurer. Bank No. 246.

Tennessee

Five Dollars

Knoxville - Holston National - Check letter ?, Series of 1908, Charter No. 4648. Poor photo counterfeit. Check letter, Treasury and bank numbers cannot be determined. W.S. Rosecrans, Register of the Treasury; E.H. Nebeker, Treasurer of the United States. The back is printed upside down on at least some specimens. So poor work that a detailed description is unnecessary.

Nashville - Wisconsin National - Check letter F, Series of 1902, Charter No. 3032. Plain, uncolored photo reproduction. No attempt to imitate silk thread.

Texas

Five Dollars

Cleburne - Home National - Check letter B, Series of 1902-1908, Charter No. 10041. Crude, etched plates on poor paper with no attempt to imitate silk threads. Both bank and Treasury number printed black. J.C.Npier, Register; John Burke, Treasurer.

Hillsboro - Hill County National - Charter No. 3046. Photo. Bank No. 2135. Whole note photographic color.

Ten Dollars

Atlanta - First National - Check letter ?, Series of 1902, Charter No. 3520. Poor, printed from photographic plates, with silk threads distributed between two sheets of paper.

Beaumont - Gulf National - Check letter C, Series of 1902, Charter No. 6338. Crude photograph printed on two sheets of paper with a few long silk threads distributed between. Colored inks roughly applied to seal, numbers and back.

Breckenridge - First National - Check letter E, Series of 1902, Charter No. 7422. Crude and badly printed on two sheets of paper with silk fibers between. J.W. Lyons, Register; Ellis H. Roberts, Treasurer. Back plate No.312.

Fort Stockton - First National - Check letter A, Series of 1902, Charter No. 9848. W.T. Vernon, Register of the Treasury; Lee McClung, Treasurer of the United States. Similar in workmanship to the $20 counterfeit of the Western National Bank, Fort Worth, Texas.

Fort Worth - National Bank of Fort Worth, Check letter C, Series of 1882, Charter No. 3131. Poor photo. Large scolloped seal gray-blue-black instead of chocolate. Face same color.

Stanton - Home National - Check letter D, Series of 1902-1908, Charter No. 9053. Poorly executed photo etched reproduction on two sheets of paper. In some notes a few pieces of silk thread are distributed. Note is poorly printed.

Weatherford - Merchants and Farmers National - Check letter A, Series of 1882, Charter No. 3975. Photographic print, on two sheets of paper with red and blue silk between, touched up with colors. Bank No. 5005.

Twenty Dollars

Bowie - First National - Check letter A, Series of 1882, Charter No. 4265. Photograph, with no silk threads in paper.

Fort Worth - Western National - Check letter C, Series of 1902, Charter No. 7165. Very poor, printed from zinc-etched plates on poor paper, with no silk threads or imitations.

Hereford - First National - Check letter A, Series of 1882, Charter No. 5604. Poor photo on poor paper, with no silk threads. Incorrect charter number (5607) on face of note, correct charter number (5604) in panel on back.

Vermont

Five Dollars

Montpelier - Montpelier National - Check letter A, Series of 1875, Charter No. 957. Photograph. Bank No. 1166.

St. Johnsbury - First National - Check letter C, Series of 1875, Charter No. 489. Poor counterfeit with color work surface printed.

Ten Dollars

Vergennes - National Bank of Vergennes - Check letter B, Series of 1882, Charter No. 1364. Bank No. 2181. Colors for red seal, etc. put on with brush. No silk threads.

Twenty Dollars

Barre - National Bank, Barre - Check letter A, Old Series, Charter No. 2109. Pen and brush work poorly done. Bank No. 1980.

Virginia

Ten Dollars

Pearlsburg - First National - Check letter F, Series of 1902-1908, Charter No. 8091. Plain uncolored photograph on good quality paper. J.W. Lyons, Register; Chas. H. Treat, Treasurer. Bank No. 1163. Face of note is a sepia tint, back is yellowish brown rather than green.

Washington

Ten Dollars

Bellingham - First National - Check letter ?, Series of 1902, Charter No. 7372. Photo, very poor. Face of note appears faded. Light blue water color applied to seal and numbers.

Burlington - First National - Check letter ?, Series of 1902, Charter No. 9808. Same as Bellingham description above.

Kent - First National - Check letter ?, Series of 1902, Charter No. 10174. Same as Bellingham description above.

Wisconsin

Five Dollars

Milwaukee - First National - Check letter B, Series of 1882, Charter No. 2715. Photo, with very bad color, seal almost gray. Bank No. 269.

Twenty Dollars

Milwaukee - Wisconsin National - Check letter B, Series of 1882, Charter No. 4817. Photographic. Brown coloring matter applied to seal and numbering. No attempt to imitate silk thread.

Military Payment Certificates (MPC) were special currency issued by the U.S. Armed Forces between the end of World War II and 1973.

Their issue to and use by military and certain civilian personnel in lieu of regular U.S. currency was designed to minimize black market trafficking in occupied areas and around U.S. military installations. The various series of MPC replaced each other with no advance warning, and the scrip, exchangeable only by those to whom its issue was authorized, could become worthless overnight. This discouraged its acceptance by unauthorized local civilians.

Given the low rate of military pay during most of this period and the fact the no MPC retains any redemption value, it is no wonder that high denomination notes in uncirculated condition are rare in many of the series.

MPC replacement notes, analogous to star notes in regular U.S. currency, are designated by the lack of a suffix letter in the serial number. They are especially sought-after by collectors.

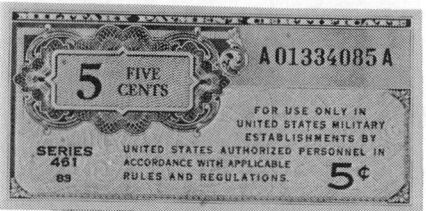

SERIES 461

Issued: European Theater, Sept. 16, 1946; Pacific Theater, Sept. 30, 1946
Withdrawn: March 10, 1947
Areas of Use: Austria, Belgium, England, France, Germany, Greece, Hungary, Iceland, Italy, Japan, Korea, Morocco, Philippines, Ryukyus, Scotland, Trieste, Yugoslavia

KL#	Denomination	Fine	VF	XF	Unc
M1	5 CENTS	2.00	6.00	18.00	60.00
	r. Replacement A-	95.00	250.	450.	600.
M2	10 CENTS	3.00	6.00	18.00	60.00
	r. Replacement A-	90.00	225.	400.	600.
M3	25 CENTS	6.00	15.00	30.00	125.
	r. Replacement A-	550.	650.	—	—
M4	50 CENTS	10.00	18.00	30.00	160.
	r. Replacement A-	550.	650.	—	—
M5	1 DOLLAR	5.00	7.00	15.00	125.
	r. Replacement A-	110.	275.	500.	750.
M6	5 DOLLARS	18.00	30.00	70.00	275.
	r. Replacement A-	650.	1000.	—	—
M7	10 DOLLARS	16.00	25.00	50.00	250.
	r. Replacement A-	200.	600.	900.	—

SERIES 471

Issued: March 10, 1947
Withdrawn: March 22, 1948
Areas of Use: Austria, Belgium, England, France, Germany, Greece, Hungary, Iceland,

Italy, Japan, Korea, Morocco, Philippines, Ryukyus, Scotland, Trieste, Yugoslavia

KL#	Denomination	Fine	VF	XF	Unc
M8	5 CENTS	6.00	15.00	25.00	90.00
	r. Replacement B-	750.	950.	2000.	—
M9	10 CENTS	4.00	12.00	30.00	90.00
	r. Replacement B-	800.	1000.	1800.	—
M10	25 CENTS	10.00	20.00	60.00	225.
	r. Replacement B-	750.	950.	—	—
M11	50 CENTS	15.00	20.00	70.00	325.
	r. Replacement B-	—	Rare	—	—
M12	1 DOLLAR	12.00	25.00	75.00	225.
	r. Replacement B-	700.	750.	1000.	—
M13	5 DOLLARS	550.	1000.	3500.	5500.
	r. Replacement B-	—	Rare	—	—
M14	10 DOLLARS	150.	350.	800.	2100.
	r. Replacement B-	—	Rare	—	—

SERIES 472

Issued: March 22, 1948
Withdrawn: June 20, 1951
Areas of Use: Austria, Belgium, England, France, Germany, Greece, Hungary, Iceland, Italy, Japan, Korea, Morocco, Philippines, Ryukyus, Scotland, Trieste, Yugoslavia

#M15-M21 blue unpt. and seal of the United States at ctr.

KL#	Denomination	Fine	VF	XF	Unc
M15	5 CENTS	.40	.75	1.75	6.00
	r. Replacement C-	35.00	50.00	200.	500.
M16	10 CENTS	2.00	5.00	12.00	60.00
	r. Replacement C-	75.00	125.	250.	450.
M17	25 CENTS	5.00	15.00	30.00	175.
	r. Replacement C-	—	Rare	—	—
M18	50 CENTS	9.00	18.00	55.00	200.
	r. Replacement C-	400.	600.	—	—
M19	1 DOLLAR	9.00	15.00	60.00	250.
	r. Replacement C-	150.	275.	500.	1600.
M20	5 DOLLARS	100.	180.	500.	2500.
	r. Replacement C-	—	Rare	—	—
M21	10 DOLLARS	30.00	160.	300.	1500.
	r. Replacement C-	—	Rare	—	—

SERIES 481

Issued: June 20, 1951
Withdrawn: May 25, 1954
Areas of Use: Austria, Belgium, England,

France, Germany, Greece, Hungary, Iceland, Italy, Japan, Korea, Morocco, Philippines, Ryukyus, Scotland, Trieste, Yugoslavia

KL#	Denomination	Fine	VF	XF	Unc
M22	5 CENTS	2.00	4.00	7.00	25.00
	r. Replacement D-	75.00	125.	300.	600.
M23	10 CENTS	2.00	3.00	8.00	35.00
	r. Replacement D-	85.00	150.	300.	450.
M24	25 CENTS	10.00	18.00	25.00	60.00
	r. Replacement D-	225.	400.	450.	800.
M25	50 CENTS	12.00	22.00	50.00	140.
	r. Replacement D-	—	Rare	—	—
M26	1 DOLLAR	18.00	55.00	75.00	220.
	r. Replacement D-	450.	475.	600.	1000.

NOTE: #M26 exists with the position # at r. or l; the l. variety is worth 10 percent more.

M27	5 DOLLARS	65.00	140.	400.	1500.
	r. Replacement D-	—	Rare	—	—
M28	10 DOLLARS	20.00	60.00	300.	1250.
	r. Replacement D-	900.	Rare	—	—

SERIES 521

Issued: May 25, 1954
Withdrawn: May 27, 1958
Areas of Use: Austria, Belgium, England, France, Germany, Greece, Hungary, Iceland, Italy, Japan, Korea, Morocco, Philippines, Ryukyus, Scotland, Trieste, Yugoslavia

KL#	Denomination	Fine	VF	XF	Unc
M29	5 CENTS	2.00	6.00	12.00	25.00
	r. Replacement E-	150.	250.	450.	750.
M30	10 CENTS	2.00	6.00	12.00	30.00
	r. Replacement E-	150.	250.	—	—
M31	25 CENTS	7.00	15.00	25.00	70.00
	r. Replacement E-	250.	500.	750.	1100.
M32	50 CENTS	10.00	25.00	40.00	125.
	r. Replacement E-	300.	400.	800.	1200.
M33	1 DOLLAR	9.00	18.00	30.00	110.
	r. Replacement E-	150.	250.	600.	1100.
M34	5 DOLLARS	200.	400.	800.	2500.
	r. Replacement E-	800.	1100.	—	—
M35	10 DOLLARS	100.	275.	450.	1900.
	r. Replacement E-	950.	1500.	1800.	—

SERIES 541

Issued: May 27, 1958
Withdrawn: May 26, 1961
Areas of Use: Cyprus, England, France, Germany, Iceland, Northern Ireland, Italy, Japan, Korea, Morocco, Philippines, Ryukyus, Scotland

KL#	Denomination	Fine	VF	XF	Unc
M36	5 CENTS	1.00	1.50	3.00	6.00
	r. Replacement F-	50.00	75.00	175.	350.
M37	10 CENTS	2.00	3.00	4.00	15.00
	r. Replacement F-	50.00	75.00	175.	350.
M38	25 CENTS	3.00	6.00	15.00	35.00
	r. Replacement F-	75.00	125.	225.	600.
M39	50 CENTS	4.00	10.00	22.00	80.00
	r. Replacement F-	40.00	50.00	150.	300.
M40	1 DOLLAR	10.00	28.00	50.00	200.
	r. Replacement F-	100.	150.	400.	600.
M41	5 DOLLARS	550.	900.	2000.	4500.
	r. Replacement F-	—	Rare	—	—
M42	10 DOLLARS	225.	400.	850.	2500.
	r. Replacement F-	950.	1500.	—	—

SERIES 591

Issued: May 26, 1961
Withdrawn: Pacific, Jan. 6, 1964; Europe, Jan. 13, 1946
Areas of Use: Cyprus, Iceland, Japan, Korea, Philippines

KL#	Denomination	Fine	VF	XF	Unc
M43	5 CENTS	2.00	6.00	13.00	55.00
	r. Replacement G-	110.	200.	400.	650.
M44	10 CENTS	3.00	7.00	15.00	65.00
	r. Replacement G-	600.	700.	800.	1200.
M45	25 CENTS	15.00	28.00	50.00	135.
	r. Replacement G-	—	Rare	—	—
M46	50 CENTS	22.00	40.00	85.00	235.
	r. Replacement G--	600.	700.	800.	1200.
M47	1 DOLLAR	15.00	40.00	85.00	275.
	r. Replacement G-	400.	500.	800.	1200.
M48	5 DOLLARS	450.	550.	1500.	4000.
	r. Replacement G-	—	Rare	—	—
M49	10 DOLLARS	125.	200.	325.	2000.
	r. Replacement G-	450.	800.	1100.	—

SERIES 611

Issued: Jan. 6, 1964
Withdrawn: April 28, 1969
Areas of Use: Cyprus, Japan, Korea, Libya

KL#	Denomination	Fine	VF	XF	Unc
M50	5 CENTS	1.00	2.00	3.00	10.00
	r. Replacement H-	30.00	40.00	60.00	75.00
M51	10 CENTS	1.50	3.00	6.00	17.00
	r. Replacement H-	30.00	40.00	60.00	75.00
M52	25 CENTS	3.00	5.00	8.00	25.00
	r. Replacement H--	700.	800.	—	—
M53	50 CENTS	4.00	6.00	15.00	55.00
	r. Replacement H-	—	Rare	—	—
M54	1 DOLLAR	4.00	6.00	15.00	85.00
	r. Replacement H-	40.00	60.00	90.00	160.
M55	5 DOLLARS	70.00	100.	175.	600.
	r. Replacement H-	600.	800.	1250.	2000.
M56	10 DOLLARS	65.00	130.	200.	550.
	r. Replacement H-	500.	700.	850.	1400.

SERIES 641

Issued: Aug. 31, 1965
Withdrawn: Oct. 21, 1968
Areas of Use: Vietnam

KL#	Denomination	Fine	VF	XF	Unc
M57	5 CENTS	.50	1.00	2.00	5.00
	r. Replacement J-	50.00	75.00	125.	200.
M58	10 CENTS	.50	1.00	3.00	6.00
	r. Replacement J-	55.00	80.00	140.	300.

KL#	Denomination	Fine	VF	XF	Unc
M59	25 CENTS	1.00	2.00	4.00	12.00
	r. Replacement J-	55.00	80.00	140.	300.
M60	50 CENTS	1.00	3.00	6.00	18.00
	r. Replacement J-	80.00	140.	300.	500.
M61	1 DOLLAR	2.00	3.50	8.00	30.00
	r. Replacement J-	300.	500.	650.	800.
M62	5 DOLLARS	25.00	35.00	75.00	250.
	r. Replacement J-	600.	950.	1750.	2500.
M63	10 DOLLARS	12.00	30.00	60.00	200.
	r. Replacement J-	325.	425.	600.	1500.

SERIES 661

Issued: Oct. 21, 1968
Withdrawn: Aug. 11, 1969
Areas of Use: Vietnam

KL#	Denomination	Fine	VF	XF	Unc
M64	5 CENTS	.25	.50	2.00	6.00
	r. Replacement B-	200.	250.	300.	400.
M65	10 CENTS	.25	1.00	2.00	7.00
	r. Replacement B-	55.00	80.00	140.	250.
M66	25 CENTS	1.00	2.00	4.00	15.00
	r. Replacement B-	55.00	80.00	140.	300.
M67	50 CENTS	2.00	3.00	6.00	18.00
	r. Replacement B-	1500.	1750.	1900.	2100.
M68	1 DOLLAR	2.00	3.00	6.00	15.00
	r. Replacement B-	85.00	150.	300.	500.
M69	5 DOLLARS	2.00	3.00	6.00	16.00
	r. Replacement B-	300.	500.	600.	800.

KL#	Denomination	Fine	VF	XF	Unc
M70	10 DOLLARS	150.	250.	450.	1250.
	r. Replacement B-	400.	600.	1750.	2500.
M71	20 DOLLARS	90.00	200.	300.	800.
	r. Replacement B-	325.	500.	800.	1500.

SERIES 651
Issued: April 28, 1969
Withdrawn: Japan, May 19, 1969;
   Libya, June 11, 1969; Korea, Nov. 19, 1973
Areas of Use: Japan, Korea, Libya
NOTE: Similar to Series 641 except for colors
   and the addition of a "Minuteman" at left on
   face.

KL#	Denomination	Fine	VF	XF	Unc
M72A	5 CENTS	—	—	—	2800.
M72B	10 CENTS	—	—	—	2800.

KL#	Denomination	Fine	VF	XF	Unc
M72C	25 CENTS	—	—	—	2800.
M72D	50 CENTS	1000.	1250.	1500.	2500.
M72E	1 DOLLAR	2.00	3.00	8.00	30.00
	r. Replacement A-		Rare		—
M73	5 DOLLARS	25.00	35.00	75.00	150.
	r. Replacement A-		Rare		—
M74	10 DOLLARS	25.00	35.00	80.00	200.
	r. Replacement A-	2000.	2500.		—

SERIES 681
Issued: Aug. 11, 1969
Withdrawn: Oct. 7, 1970
Areas of Use: Vietnam

KL#	Denomination	Fine	VF	XF	Unc
M75	5 CENTS	.50	1.00	2.00	6.00
	r. Replacement C-	35.00	50.00	75.00	125.
M76	10 CENTS	.50	1.00	2.00	8.00
	r. Replacement C-	40.00	60.00	90.00	175.
M77	25 CENTS	.50	2.00	5.00	15.00
	r. Replacement C-	600.	900.	1000.	1250.
M78	50 CENTS	1.00	3.00	6.00	18.00
	r. Replacement C-	60.00	100.	200.	300.
M79	1 DOLLAR	1.00	2.00	4.00	12.00
	r. Replacement C-	50.00	85.00	190.	275.
M80	5 DOLLARS	3.00	5.00	12.00	35.00
	r. Replacement C-	325.	500.	800.	1500.
M81	10 DOLLARS	15.00	20.00	35.00	160.
	r. Replacement C-	325.	500.	600.	1500.
M82	20 DOLLARS	15.00	20.00	45.00	160.
	r. Replacement C-	200.	400.	500.	1500.

SERIES 692
Issued: Oct. 7, 1970
Withdrawn: Fractional denominations, June 1,
   1971; dollar denominations, March 15, 1973
Areas of Use: Vietnam

KL#	Denomination	Fine	VF	XF	Unc
M83	5 CENTS	.75	1.00	2.00	7.00
	r. Replacement E-	35.00	50.00	75.00	125.
M84	10 CENTS	1.00	1.50	2.50	9.00
	r. Replacement E-	40.00	60.00	90.00	175.
M85	25 CENTS	2.00	3.00	4.50	15.00
	r. Replacement E-	150.	200.	300.	500.
M86	50 CENTS	3.00	4.00	6.00	22.00
	r. Replacement E-	150.	200.	300.	500.
M87	1 DOLLAR	5.00	8.00	12.00	30.00
	r. Replacement E-	55.00	80.00	140.	300.
M88	5 DOLLARS	45.00	75.00	150.	250.
	r. Replacement E-	—	Rare	—	—
M89	10 DOLLARS	75.00	130.	250.	550.
	r. Replacement E-	—	Rare	—	—
M90	20 DOLLARS	75.00	100.	220.	450.
	r. Replacement E-	325.	600.	1000.	1800.

Philippine Islands

The Western world discovered the Philippine Islands in 1521 when Ferdinand Magellan claimed them for Spain. After nearly four centuries of Spanish colonialism, the Philippines were ceded to the United States in 1898 as part of the settlement extracted from Spain ending the Spanish-American War. In 1935, the Islands became a self-governing commonwealth of the United States. The country was occupied by the Japanese during World War II from 1941-1944. On July 4, 1946, the nation attained independence as a republic.

By Act of Congress on March 2, 1903, the issue of coinage and paper money in the Philippines was authorized, and distribution of silver certificates — produced by the U.S. Bureau of Engraving and Printing in Washington, D.C. — began, withe series dated between 1903-1916.

In 1918, Treasury Certificates were issued, "payable in silver pesos or in gold coin of the United States," with series designations through 1941 and a special 1944 "Victory" issue.

In 1904, a series of notes in denominations of 5-200 pesos was issued by El Banco Espanol Filipino. A second series of bank notes was issued in 1908 produced by the BEP. In 1912, the bank changed its name to The Bank of the Philippine Islands, under which banner it continued to circulate currency with issues dated through 1933. The Philippine National Bank began circulation in 1916, and continued until Series 1937.

UNITED STATES ADMINISTRATION

BANCO ESPANOL FILIPINO

1904 ISSUE

Printer: Barclay & Fry, Ltd., England

KL#	Denom.	Date	Description	Good	Fine	XF
PI-A31	5 Pesos	1.1.1904. Black on pink paper.		—	Rare	—

KL#	Denom.	Date	Description	Good	Fine	XF
PI-A32	10 Pesos	1.1.1904. Black. Green paper.		—	Rare	—
PI-A33	25 Pesos	1.1.1904. Black. Lt. purple paper.		—	Rare	—
PI-A34	50 Pesos	1.1.1904. Black. Green paper.		—	Rare	—
PI-A35	100 Pesos	1.1.1904. Black. Yellowish-brown paper.		—	Rare	—
PI-A36	200 Pesos	1.1.1904. Black. Yellowish-brown paper. Back m/c.		—	Rare	—

Notes Printed in the United States
1908 ISSUE

#1-6 printer: USBEP (w/o imprint).
#1-3 have 1 stamped sign. (at l.) and 2 printed sign.

KL#	Denom.	Date	Description	Good	Fine	XF
PI1	5 Pesos	1.1.1908. Black on red unpt. Woman seated at l. Back red. Sign. *J. Serrano* at l.	25.00	125.	325.
PI2	10 Pesos	1.1.1908. Black on brown unpt. Woman w/flowers at ctr. Back brown.			
		a. Sign. *Julian Serrano* at l.	—	Rare	—
		b. Sign. *J. Serrano* at l.	75.00	225.	—

KL#	Denom.	Date	Description	Good	Fine	XF
PI3	20 Pesos	1.1.1908. Black on lilac unpt. Woman at l. Back tan.			
		a. Sign. *Julian Serrano* at l.	—	Rare	—
		b. Sign. *J. Serrano* at l.	200.	550.	—

#4-6 have only 2 printed sign.

KL#	Denom.	Date	Description	Good	Fine	XF
PI4	50 Pesos	1.1.1908. Black on blue unpt. Woman standing w/flower at l. Back red.	200.	600.	—

KL#	Denom.	Date	Description	Good	Fine	XF
PI5	100 Pesos	1.1.1908. Black on green unpt. Woman seated w/scroll and globe at l. Back olive.	250.	675.	—
PI6	200 Pesos	1.1.1908. Black on tan unpt. Justice w/scales and shield at ctr. Back orange.	—	—	—

BANK OF THE PHILIPPINE ISLANDS

A name change in English for the Banco Espanol Filipino.

1912 ISSUE

#7-12 printer. USBEP (w/o imprint). Designs like previous issue.

KL#	Denom.	Date	Description	Good	Fine	XF
PI7	5 Pesos	1.1.1912. Black on red unpt. Similar to #1.				
		a. Sign. D. Garcia and Jno. S. Hord.		2.00	15.00	60.00
		b. Sign. D. Garcia and E. Sendres.		2.00	15.00	60.00
PI8	10 Pesos	1.1.1912. Black on brown unpt. Similar to #2.				
		a. Sign. D. Garcia and Jno. S. Hord.		5.00	18.00	80.00
		b. Sign. D. Garcia and E. Sendres.		5.00	18.00	80.00

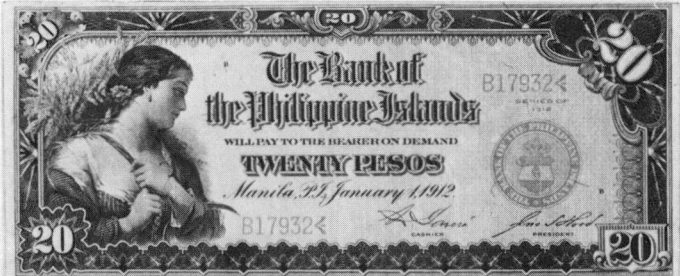

KL#	Denom.	Date	Description	Good	Fine	XF
PI9	20 Pesos	1.1.1912. Black on lilac unpt. Similar to #3.				
		a. Sign. D. Garcia and Jno. S. Hord.		6.00	25.00	95.00
		b. Sign. D. Garcia and E. Sendres.		6.00	25.00	95.00

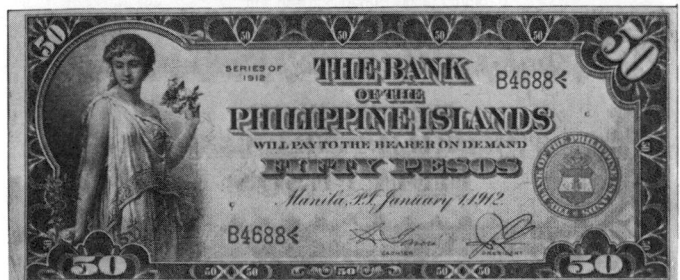

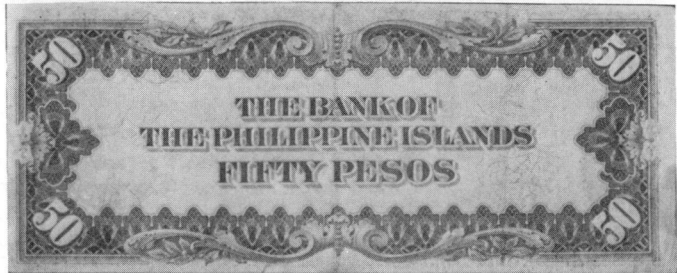

KL#	Denom.	Date	Description	Good	Fine	XF
PI10	50 Pesos	1.1.1912. Black on blue unpt. Similar to #4.				
		a. Sign. D. Garcia and Jno. S. Hord.		17.50	95.00	350.
		b. Sign. D. Garcia and E. Sendres.		15.00	80.00	325.

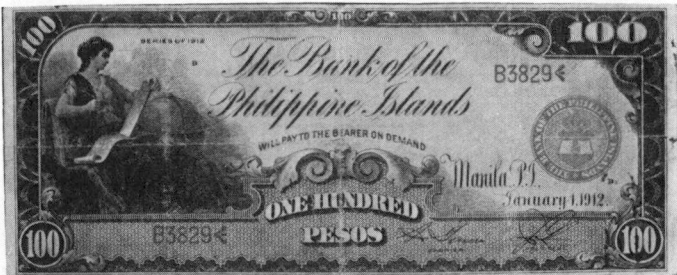

KL#	Denom.	Date	Description	Good	Fine	XF
PI11	100 Pesos	1.1.1912. Black on green unpt. Similar to #5.				
		a. Sign. D. Garcia and Jno. S. Hord.		50.00	170.	550.
		b. Sign. D. Garcia and E. Sendres.		50.00	170.	550.
PI12	200 Pesos	1.1.1912. Black on tan unpt. Similar to #6.				
		Sign. D. Garcia and Jno. S. Hord.		175.	600.	—

1920 ISSUE

#13-15 like #7b-9b except for date and serial # prefix-suffix.
Sign. D. Garcia and E. Sendres.
Printer: USBEP (w/o imprint).

KL#	Denom.	Date	Description	Good	Fine	XF
PI13	5 Pesos	1.1.1920. Black on red unpt. Like #7b.		2.00	10.00	50.00
PI14	10 Pesos	1.1.1920. Black on brown unpt. Like #8b.		3.00	12.50	65.00
PI15	20 Pesos	1.1.1920. Black on lilac unpt. Like #9b.		4.00	25.00	100.

1928 ISSUE

#16-21 designs like #7-12 but w/o unpt. Sign. D. Garcia and Fulg. Borromeo.
Printer: USBEP (w/o imprint).

KL#	Denom.	Date	Description	Good	Fine	XF
PI16	5 Pesos	1.1.1928. Black. Like #7.		2.00	10.00	45.00
PI17	10 Pesos	1.1.1928. Black. Like #8.		3.00	12.00	50.00
PI18	20 Pesos	1.1.1928. Black. Like #9.		4.00	20.00	75.00
PI19	50 Pesos	1.1.1928. Black. Like #10.		10.00	50.00	200.
PI20	100 Pesos	1.1.1928. Black. Like #11.		40.00	150.	425.

KL#	Denom.	Date	Description	Good	Fine	XF
PI21	200 Pesos	1.1.1928. Black. Like #12.		85.00	250.	600.

1933 ISSUE

#22-24 like #16-18 except for date and serial # prefix-suffix. Sign. D.
Garcia and P. J. Campos. Printer: USBEP (w/o imprint).

KL#	Denom.	Date	Description	Good	Fine	XF
PI22	5 Pesos	1.1.1933. Black. Like #16.		2.00	10.00	45.00
PI23	10 Pesos	1.1.1933. Black. Like #17.		2.50	12.00	55.00
PI24	20 Pesos	1.1.1933. Black. Like #18.		3.50	20.00	80.00

PHILIPPINE ISLANDS
SILVER CERTIFICATES

#25-38 printer: USBEP (w/o imprint).

1903 ISSUE

KL#	Denom.	Date Description	Good	Fine	XF
PI25	2 Pesos	1903. Black on blue unpt. J. Rizal at l. Back blue.			
		a. Sign. Wm. H. Taft and Frank A. Branagan.	90.00	300.	850.
		b. Sign. Luke E. Wright and Frank A. Branagan.	100.	375.	950.

KL#	Denom.	Date Description	Good	Fine	XF
PI26	5 Pesos	1903. Black on red unpt. Pres. McKinley at l. Back red.			
		a. Sign. Wm. H. Taft and Frank A. Branagan.	100.	350.	950.
		b. Sign. Luke E. Wright and Frank A. Branagan.	125.	475.	1150.
PI27	10 Pesos	1903. Black on brown unpt. Washington at ctr. Back brown.			
		a. Sign. Wm. H. Taft and Frank A. Branagan.	185.	650.	1350.
		b. Sign. Luke E. Wright and Frank A. Branagan.	225.	750.	—

KL#	Denom.	Date Description	Good	Fine	XF
PI27A	10 Pesos	1903. Like #27 but black vertical ovpt. *Subject to the provisions of the/Act of Congress approved/ June 23, 1906* on face. Sign. Henry C. Ide as *Governor General*, and Frank A. Branagan.	—	—	—

NOTE: The chief executive's title before 1905 was *Civil Governor*.

1905 ISSUE

#28-31 issued w/ovpt. like #27A. Sign. Luke E. Wright as *Governor General*, and Frank A. Branagan.

KL#	Denom.	Date Description	Good	Fine	XF
PI28	20 Pesos	1905. Black on yellow unpt. Mt. Mayon at ctr. Back tan.	—	Rare	—
PI29	50 Pesos	1905. Black on red unpt. Gen. H. W. Lawton at l. Back red.	—	Rare	—
PI30	100 Pesos	1905. Black on green unpt. F. Magellan at ctr. Back olive.	—	Rare	—
PI31	500 Pesos	1905. Black. M. Lopez de Legazpi at ctr. Back purple.	—	Rare	.

1906 ISSUE

KL#	Denom.	Date Description	Good	Fine	XF
PI32	2 Pesos	1906. Black on blue unpt. Similar to #25 but new authorization date, and payable in silver or gold.			
		a. Sign. James F. Smith and Frank A. Branagan.	50.00	185.	650.
		b. Sign. W. Cameron Forbes and J. L. Barrett.	70.00	235.	950.
		c. Sign. W. Cameron Forbes and J.L. Manning.	70.00	235.	900.
		d. Sign. Francis Burton Harrison and J. L. Manning.	60.00	200.	675.
		e. Sign. Francis Burton Harrison and A. P. Fitzsimmons.	50.00	185.	650.
PI33	500 Pesos	1906. Black. Similar to #31.	—	Rare	

1908 ISSUE

KL#	Denom.	Date Description	Good	Fine	XF
PI34	20 Pesos	1908. Black on yellow unpt. Similar to #28.			
		a. Sign. James F. Smith and Frank A. Branagan.	75.00	300.	800.
		b. Sign. W. Cameron Forbes and J. L. Barrett.	100.	350.	—
		c. Sign. W. Cameron Forbes and J. L. Manning.	125.	475.	—
		d. Sign. Francis Burton Harrison and J. L. Manning.	100.	350.	—
		e. Sign. Francis Burton Harrison and A. P. Fitzsimmons.	65.00	280.	750.

1910 ISSUE

KL#	Denom.	Date Description	Good	Fine	XF
PI35	5 Pesos	1910. Black on red unpt. Similar to #26.			
		a. Sign. W. Cameron Forbes and J. L. Barrett.	50.00	180.	
		b. Sign. W. Cameron Forbes and J. L. Manning.	45.00	160.	
		c. Sign. Francis Burton Harrison and J. L. Manning.	60.00	220.	—
		d. Sign. Francis Burton Harrison and A. P. Fitzsimmons.	40.00	135.	385.

1912 ISSUE

KL#	Denom.	Date Description	Good	Fine	XF
PI36	10 Pesos	1912. Black on brown unpt. Similar to #27.			
		a. Sign. W. Cameron Forbes and J. L. Barrett.	75.00	300.	—
		b. Sign. W. Cameron Forbes and J. L. Manning.	75.00	300.	—
		c. Sign. Francis Burton Harrison and J. L. Manning.	75.00	300.	—
		d. Sign. Francis Burton Harrison and A. P. Fitzsimmons.	40.00	200.	550.

1916 ISSUE

KL#	Denom.	Date Description	Good	Fine	XF
Pl37	50 Pesos	1916. Black on red unpt. Similar to #29.	—	Rare	—
Pl38	100 Pesos	1916. Black on green unpt. Similar to #30.	—	Rare	—

PHILIPPINE NATIONAL BANK
EMERGENCY ISSUES

#39-42 eagle on back, locally printed.

KL#	Denom.	Date Description	VG	VF	Unc
Pl39	10 Centavos	20.11.1917. Gold on yellow unpt. Back yellow.	5.00	15.00	60.00

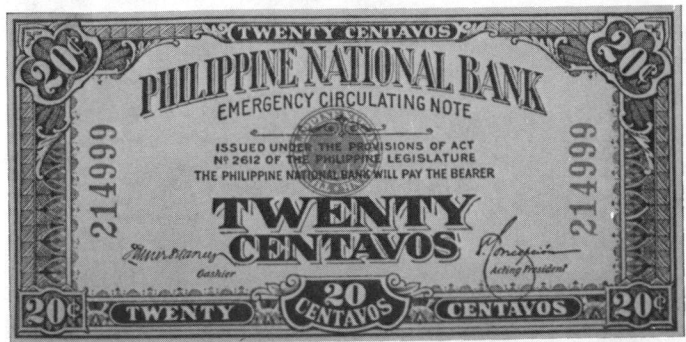

KL#	Denom.	Date Description	VG	VF	Unc
Pl40	20 Centavos	20.11.1917. Blue on yellow unpt. Back blue.	5.00	15.00	60.00
Pl41	50 Centavos	22.9.1917. Black on green unpt. Back green.	4.00	10.00	45.00
Pl42	1 Peso	22.9.1917. Black on red unpt. Back red.	6.00	25.00	75.00

#43-45 new bank name, seal and sign. ovpt. on Bank of the Philippine Islands notes.

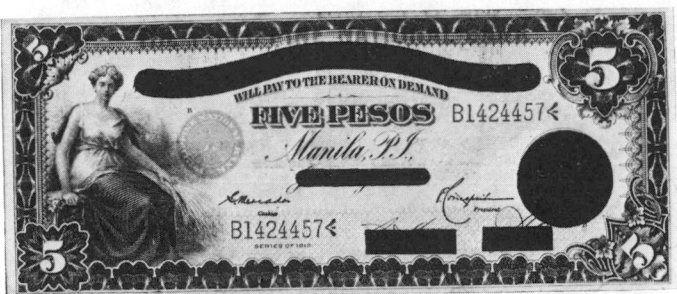

KL#	Denom.	Date Description	VG	VF	Unc
Pl43	5 Pesos	ND (old date 1912). Ovpt. on #7.	—	Rare	—
Pl43A	10 Pesos	ND (old date 1912). Ovpt. on #8.	—	Rare	—
Pl43B	20 Pesos	ND (old date 1912). Ovpt. on #9.	—	Rare	—

REGULAR ISSUES

#44-56 Printer: USBEP (w/o imprint).

1916 ISSUE

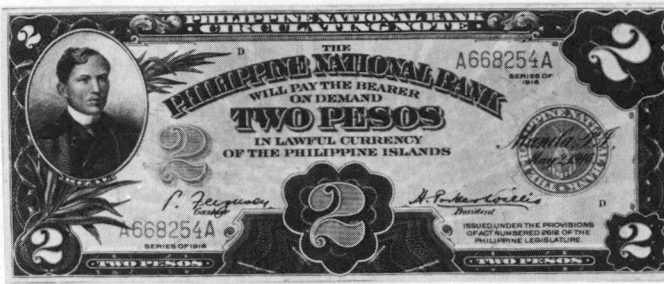

KL#	Denom.	Date Description	Good	Fine	XF
Pl44	2 Pesos	1916. Black on blue unpt. J. Rizal at l. (similar to Silver and Treasury Certificates). Back blue.	65.00	250.	—
Pl45	5 Pesos	1916. Black on red unpt. Pres. Wm. McKinley at l. (similar to Silver and Treasury Certificates). Back red-orange.			
		a. Sign. S. Ferguson and H. Parker Willis.	100.	350.	—
		b. Sign. S. Mercado and V. Concepcion.	1.50	4.00	15.00
Pl46	10 Pesos	1916. Black on brown unpt. Washington at ctr. (similar to Silver and Treasury Certificates). Back brown.			
		a. Sign. S. Ferguson and H. Parker Willis.	100.	385.	—
		b. Sign. S. Mercado and V. Concepcion.	4.00	20.00	85.00

1918 ISSUE

KL#	Denom.	Date Description	Good	Fine	XF
Pl47	1 Peso	1918. Black on orange unpt. Charles A. Conant at l. Back green.	45.00	150.	450.

1919 ISSUE

KL#	Denom.	Date Description	Good	Fine	XF
Pl48	20 Pesos	1919. Black on yellow unpt. William A. Jones at ctr. Back tan.	75.00	350.	—

1920 ISSUE

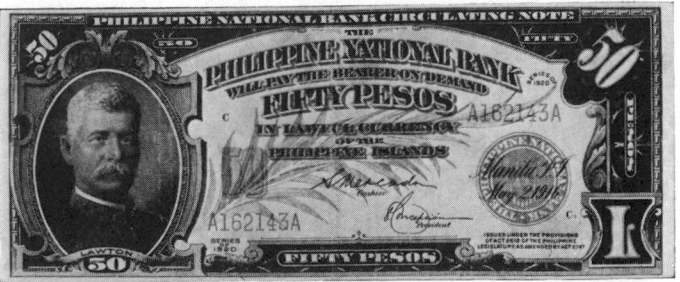

KL#	Denom.	Date Description	Good	Fine	XF
Pl49	50 Pesos	1920. Black on green unpt. Gen. Lawton at l. Back red.	6.00	25.00	85.00

KL#	Denom.	Date	Description	Good	Fine	XF
PI50	100 Pesos		1920. Green on red unpt. Magellan at ctr. Back olive.	—	Rare	—

1921 ISSUE

#51-55 designs like previous issue but notes w/o unpt.

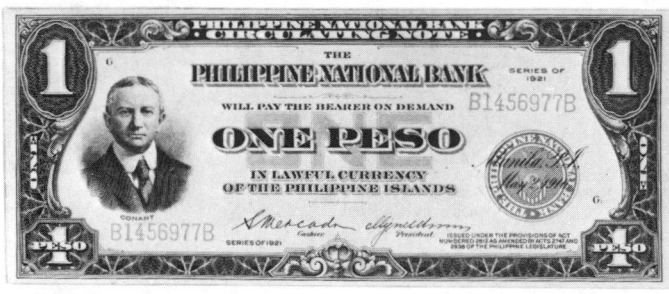

KL#	Denom.	Date	Description	Good	Fine	XF
PI51	1 Peso	1921. Like #47.		25.00	85.00	225.
PI52	2 Pesos	1921. Like #44.		30.00	100.	325.
PI53	5 Pesos	1921. Like #45.		1.50	5.00	12.50
PI54	10 Pesos	1921. Like #46.		3.00	20.00	65.00

KL#	Denom.	Date	Description	Good	Fine	XF
PI55	20 Pesos	1921. Like #48.		7.50	50.00	185.

1924 ISSUE

KL#	Denom.	Date	Description	Good	Fine	XF
PI56	1 Peso	1924. Like #51.		10.00	50.00	135.

1937 ISSUE

#57-59 printer: USBEP w/imprint on back. Text reads *PHILIPPINES* instead of *PHILIPPINE ISLANDS*.

KL#	Denom.	Date	Description	VG	VF	Unc
PI57	5 Pesos	1937. Similar to #53.		5.00	20.00	50.00

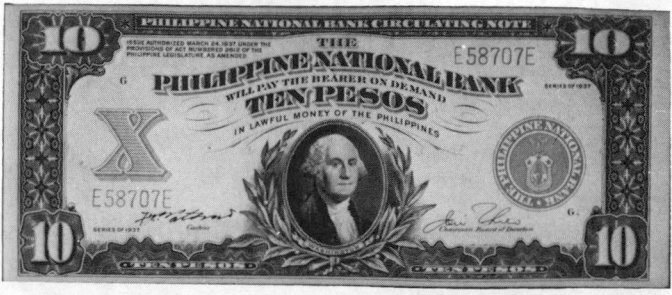

KL#	Denom.	Date	Description	VG	VF	Unc
PI58	10 Pesos	1937. Similar to #54.		10.00	35.00	125.
PI59	20 Pesos	1937. Similar to #55.		15.00	75.00	275.

PHILIPPINE ISLANDS

TREASURY CERTIFICATES

1918 ISSUE

#60-101 printer: USBEP (w/o imprint).

KL#	Denom.	Date	Description	Good	Fine	XF
PI60	1 Peso	1918. Black on green unpt. A. Mabini at l. Back green.				
		a. Sign. Francis Burton Harrison and A. P. Fitzsimmons.		7.50	45.00	150.
		b. Sign. Francis Burton Harrison and V. Carmona.		10.00	60.00	200.
PI61	2 Pesos	1918. Black on blue unpt. J. Rizal at l. Back blue.		25.00	150.	400.
PI62	5 Pesos	1918. Black on lt. red unpt. Wm. McKinley at l. Back red-orange.		40.00	200.	—

KL#	Denom.	Date	Description	Good	Fine	XF
PI63	10 Pesos	1918. Black on brown unpt. G. Washington at ctr. Back brown.		150.	750.	—

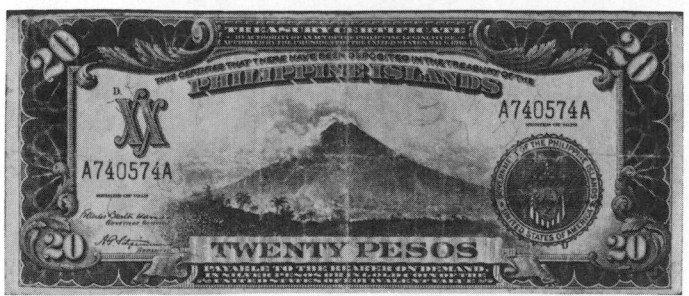

KL#	Denom.	Date	Description	Good	Fine	XF
PI63A	20 Pesos	1918. Black on yellow unpt. Mayon volcano at ctr. Blue ornate *XX* at upper l. Back tan. Sign. Harrison-Fitzsimmons.	40.00	200.	550.

KL#	Denom.	Date	Description	Good	Fine	XF
PI64	20 Pesos	1918. Like #63A but w/o ornate *XX* at l. Sign. Harrison-Carmona.	50.00	225.	600.
PI65	50 Pesos	1918. Black on green unpt. Gen. Lawton at l. Back red.			
		a. Sign. Francis Burton Harrison and A. P. Fitzsimmons.	100.	450.	—
		b. Sign. Francis Burton Harrison and V. Carmona.	100.	450.	—
PI66	100 Pesos	1918. Black on green unpt. Magellan at ctr. Back olive.			
		a. Sign. Francis Burton Harrison and A. P. Fitzsimmons.	—	Rare	—
		b. Sign. Francis Burton Harrison and V. Carmona.	—	Rare	—
PI67	500 Pesos	1918. Black on orange unpt. Legazpi at ctr. Back purple.	—	Rare	—

1924 ISSUE

#68-72 w/o unpt., otherwise designs like previous issue.

KL#	Denom.	Date	Description	Good	Fine	XF
PI68	1 Peso	1924. Like #60.			
		a. Sign. Leonard Wood and Salv. Lagdameo w/title: *Acting Treasurer.*	7.50	35.00	125.
		b. Sign. Leonard Wood and Salv. Lagdameo w/title: *Treasurer.*	10.00	40.00	150.
		c. Sign. Henry L. Stimson and Salv. Lagdameo.	7.50	35.00	125.
PI69	2 Pesos	1924. Like #61, but large denomination numeral added in red at lower l. ctr.			
		a. Sign. Leonard Wood and Salv. Lagdameo w/title: *Acting Treasurer.*	12.50	75.00	225.
		b. Sign. Leonard Wood and Salv. Lagdameo w/title: *Treasurer.*	10.00	60.00	180.
		c. Sign. Henry L. Stimson and Salv. Lagdameo.	8.00	50.00	170.

KL#	Denom.	Date	Description	Good	Fine	XF
PI70	5 Pesos	1924. Black. Like #62.	20.00	100.	275.
PI71	10 Pesos	1924. Black. Like #63.	8.00	45.00	300.

KL#	Denom.	Date	Description	Good	Fine	XF
PI72	500 Pesos	1924. Blue unpt. and numeral. Like #67.	750.	2000.	—

1929 ISSUE

Because of the changeover from large to small size currency in the U.S.A., many changes were effected on U.S.A.-Philippine currency beginning with the 1929 issue. Significant design alterations were introduced as well as some color change.

KL#	Denom.	Date	Description	Good	Fine	XF
PI73	1 Peso	1929. Black on orange unpt. A. Mabini at l. Design similar to #60 but several minor alterations in plate. Back orange.			
		a. Sign. Dwight F. Davis and Salv. Lagdameo.	5.00	25.00	85.00
		b. Sign. Theodore Roosevelt and Salv. Lagdameo.	6.00	45.00	175.
		c. Sign. Frank Murphy and Salv. Lagdameo.	3.00	15.00	75.00
PI74	2 Pesos	1929. Black on blue unpt. J. Rizal at l. Similar to #61 but several minor alterations in plate. Back blue.			
		a. Sign. Theodore Roosevelt and Salv. Lagdameo.	6.00	45.00	150.
		b. Sign. Frank Murphy and Salv. Lagdameo.	3.00	15.00	80.00

KL#	Denom.	Date	Description	Good	Fine	XF
PI75	5 Pesos	1929. Black on yellow unpt. Wm. McKinley at l., Adm. Dewey at r. Back yellow.	7.50	40.00	195.

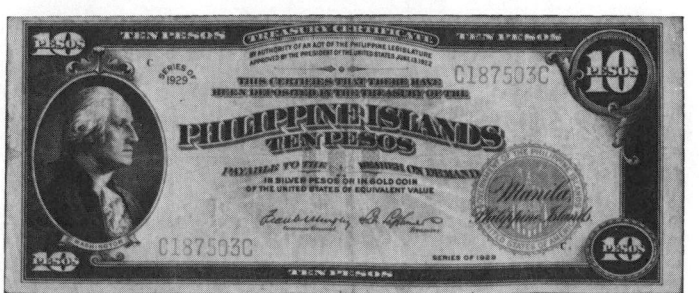

KL#	Denom.	Date	Description	Good	Fine	XF
PI76	10 Pesos	1929. Black on brown unpt. G. Washington at l.	12.50	50.00	250.
PI77	20 Pesos	1929. Black on yellow unpt. Mayon volcano at ctr. Similar to #64 but several minor alterations in plate. Back tan.	25.00	75.00	350.

KL#	Denom.	Date Description	Good	Fine	XF
PI78	50 Pesos	1929. Black on green unpt. Gen. Lawton at l.	65.00	285.	—

KL#	Denom.	Date Description	Good	Fine	XF
PI79	100 Pesos	1929. Black on green unpt. Magellan at l.	—	Rare	—

KL#	Denom.	Date Description	Good	Fine	XF
PI80	500 Pesos	1929. Black on orange unpt. Legazpi at l.	—	Rare	—

PHILIPPINES (COMMONWEALTH)
TREASURY CERTIFICATES
1936 ISSUE

#81-88 new red Commonwealth seal. Sign. Manuel Quezon and Antonio Ramos.

Notes read *PHILIPPINES* instead of *PHILIPPINE ISLANDS*.

KL#	Denom.	Date Description	VG	VF	Unc
PI81	1 Peso	1936. Similar to #73.	2.00	5.00	15.00
PI82	2 Pesos	1936. Similar to #74.	3.00	7.00	30.00
PI83	5 Pesos	Similar to #75.			
		a. Regular issue. Serial #D1D to D3 244 000D.	2.50	6.00	17.50
		b. US War Dept. issue (1944). #D3 244 001D to D3 544 000D.	30.00	100.	250.
PI84	10 Pesos	1936. Similar to #76.			
		a. Regular issue. Serial #D1D to D2 024 000D.	4.00	15.00	55.00
		b. US War Dept. issue (1944). #D2 024 001D to D2 174 000D.	50.00	150.	350.
PI85	20 Pesos	1936. Similar to #77.			
		a. Regular issue. Serial #D1D to D1 664 000D.	10.00	75.00	325.
		b. US War Dept. issue (1944). #D1 664 001D to D1 739 000D.	50.00	150.	400.
PI86	50 Pesos	1936. Similar to #78.	75.00	225.	—
PI87	100 Pesos	1936. Similar to #79.			
		a. Regular issue. Serial #D1D to D41 000D.	150.	350.	—
		b. US War Dept. issue (1944). #D41 001D to D56 000D.	—	Rare	—
PI88	500 Pesos	1936. Similar to #80.	—	Rare	—

1941 ISSUE

#89-93 like previous issue. Sign. Manuel Quezon and A.S. de Leon.

KL#	Denom.	Date Description	Good	Fine	XF
PI89	1 Peso	1941. Like #81.			
		a. Regular issue. Serial #E1E to E6 000 000E.	1.50	4.00	9.00
		b. Processed to simulate used currency at Bureau of Standards (1943). #E6 008 001E to E6 056 000E; E6 061 001E to E6 072 000E; E6 080 001E to E6 324 000E. Total 300,000 notes.			Fine 175.

KL#	Denom.	Date Description	VG	VF	Unc
		c. Naval Aviators' Emergency Money Packet notes (1944). #E6 324 001E to E6 524 000E.	5.00	15.00	50.00
PI90	2 Pesos	1941. Like #82.	3.50	15.00	60.00
PI91	5 Pesos	1941. Like #83.			
		a. Regular issue. Serial #E1E to E1 188 000E.	5.00	20.00	65.00

KL#	Denom.	Date Description	VG	VF	Unc
		b. Processed like #89b (1943). #E1 208 001E to E1 328 000E.			Fine 300.
		c. Packet notes like #89c (1944). #E1 328 001E to E1 348 000E.	15.00	50.00	130.

KL#	Denom.	Date Description	VG	VF	Unc
PI92	10 Pesos	1941. Like #84.			
		a. Regular issue. Serial #E1E to E800 000E.	5.00	20.00	65.00
		b. Processed like #89b (1943). #E810 001E to E870 000E.			Fine 350.
		c. Packet notes like #89c (1944). #E870 001E to E890 000E.	20.00	70.00	200.
PI93	20 Pesos	1941. Like #85.	60.00	250.	—

NOTE: 50, 100 and 500 Pesos notes Series of 1941 were printed but never shipped because of the outbreak of World War II. All were destroyed in 1949, leaving extant only proof impressions and specimen sheets.

VICTORY ISSUE

#94-101 "VICTORY Series No. 66" twice on face instead of date, black *VICTORY* ovpt. in large letters on back. Blue seal.

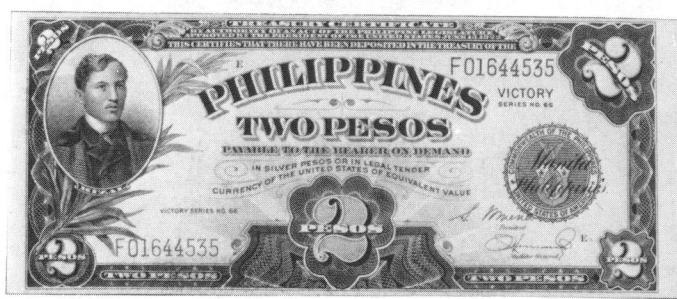

KL#	Denom.	Date Description	VG	VF	Unc
PI94	1 Peso	ND (1944). Like #89. Sign. Osmena and Hernandez.	.75	1.50	6.00
PI95	2 Pesos	ND (1944). Like #90.			
		a. Sign. Osmena and Hernandez w/title: *Auditor General*.	1.00	2.00	12.50
		b. Sign. Roxas and Guevara w/title: *Treasurer*.	3.00	12.00	50.00
PI96	5 Pesos	ND (1944). Like #91. Sign. Osmena and Hernandez.	2.50	7.50	40.00
PI97	10 Pesos	ND (1944). Like #92. Sign. Osmena and Hernandez.	3.00	12.50	75.00
PI98	20 Pesos	ND (1944). Like #93.			
		a. Sign. Osmena and Hernandez w/title: *Auditor General*.	5.00	25.00	100.
		b. Sign. Roxas and Guevara w/title: *Treasurer*.	12.50	50.00	250.
PI99	50 Pesos	ND (1944). Like #86.			
		a. Sign. Osmena and Hernandez w/title: *Auditor General*.	30.00	100.	300.
		b. Sign. Roxas and Guevara w/title: *Treasurer*.	40.00	150.	—
PI100	100 Pesos	ND (1944). Like #87.			
		a. Sign. Osmena and Hernandez w/title: *Auditor General*.	60.00	200.	—
		b. Sign. Osmena and Guevara w/title: *Treasurer*.	75.00	275.	—
		c. Sign. Roxas and Guevara.	60.00	200.	—
PI101	500 Pesos	ND (1944). Like #88.			
		a. Sign. Osmena and Hernandez w/title: *Auditor General*.	300.	—	—
		b. Sign. Osmena and Guevara w/title: *Treasurer*.	300.	—	—
		c. Sign. Roxas and Guevara.	300.	—	—

Signers of U.S. Paper Money

Register of the Treasury	Treasurer of the U.S.	Terms of Office Began	Terms of Office Ended
Lucius E. Chittenden	F.E. Spinner	4-17-1861	8-10-1864
S.B. Colby	F.E. Spinner	8-11-1864	9-21-1867
Noah L. Jeffries	F.E. Spinner	10-5-1867	3-15-1869
John Allison	F.E. Spinner	4-3-1869	6-30-1875
John Allison	John C. New	6-30-1875	7-1-1876
John Allison	A.U. Wyman	7-1-1876	6-30-1877
John Allison	James Gilfillan	7-1-1877	3-23-1878
Glenni W. Scofield	James Gilfillan	4-1-1878	5-20-1881
Blanche K. Bruce	James Gilfillan	5-21-1881	3-31-1883
Blanche K. Bruce	A.U. Wyman	4-1-1883	4-30-1885
Blanche K. Bruce	Conrad N. Jordan	5-1-1885	6-5-1885
William S. Rosecrans	Conrad N. Jordan	6-8-1885	5-23-1887
William S. Rosecrans	James W. Hyatt	5-24-1887	5-10-1889
William S. Rosecrans	J.N. Huston	5-11-1889	4-21-1891
William S. Rosecrans	Enos H. Nebeker	4-24-1891	5-31-1893
William S. Rosecrans	Daniel N. Morgan	6-1-1893	6-19-1893
James F. Tillman	Daniel N. Morgan	7-1-1893	6-30-1897
James F. Tillman	Ellis H. Roberts	7-1-1897	12-2-1897
Blanche K. Bruce	Ellis H. Roberts	12-3-1897	3-17-1898
Judson W. Lyons	Ellis H. Roberts	4-7-1898	6-30-1905
Judson W. Lyons	Charles H. Treat	7-1-1905	4-1-1906
William T. Vernon	Charles H. Treat	6-12-1906	10-30-1909
William T. Vernon	Lee McClung	11-1-1909	3-14-1911
James C. Napier	Lee McClung	3-15-1911	11-21-1912
James C. Napier	Carmi A. Thompson	11-22-1912	3-31-1913
James C. Napier	John Burke	4-1-1913	9-30-1913
Gabe E. Parker	John Burke	10-1-1913	12-31-1914
Houston B. Teehee	John Burke	3-24-1915	11-20-1919
William S. Elliott	John Burke	11-21-1919	1-5-1921
William S. Elliott	Frank White	5-2-1921	1-24-1922
Harley V. Speelman	Frank White	1-25-1922	9-30-1927
Walter O. Woods	Frank White	10-1-1927	5-1-1928
Walter O. Woods	H.T. Tate	5-31-1928	1-17-1929
Edward E. Jones	Walter O. Woods	1-22-1929	5-31-1933

Secretary of the Treasury	Treasurer of the U.S.	Began	Ended
William G. McAdoo	John Burke	4-1-1913	12-15-1918
Carter Glass	John Burke	12-16-1918	2-1-1920
D.F. Houston	John Burke	2-2-1920	1-5-1921
Andrew W. Mellon	Frank White	5-2-1921	5-1-1928
Andrew W. Mellon	H.T. Tate	4-30-1928	1-17-1929
Andrew W. Mellon	Walter O. Woods	1-18-1929	2-12-1932
Ogden L. Mills	Walter O. Woods	2-13-1932	3-3-1933
William H. Woodin	Walter O. Woods	3-4-1933	5-31-1933
William H. Woodin	W.A. Julian	6-1-1933	12-31-1933
Henry Morgenthau, Jr.	W.A. Julian	1-1-1934	7-22-1945
Fred M. Vinson	W.A. Julian	7-23-1945	7-23-1946
John W. Snyder	W.A. Julian	7-25-1946	5-29-1949
John W. Snyder	Georgia Neese Clark	6-21-1949	1-20-1953
George M. Humphrey	Ivy Baker Priest	1-28-1953	7-28-1957
Robert B. Anderson	Ivy Baker Priest	7-29-1957	1-20-1961
C. Douglas Dillon	Elizabeth Rudel Smith	1-30-1961	4-13-1962
C. Douglas Dillon	Kathryn O'Hay Granahan	1-3-1963	3-31-1965
Henry H. Fowler	Kathryn O'Hay Granahan	4-1-1965	10-13-1966
Joseph W. Barr	Kathryn O'Hay Granahan	12-21-1968	1-20-1969
David M. Kennedy	Dorothy Andrews Elston*	5-8-1969	9-16-1970
David M. Kennedy	Dorothy Andrews Kabis	9-17-1970	2-1-1971
John B. Connally	Dorothy Andrews Kabis	2-11-1971	7-3-1971
John B. Connally	Romana Banuelos	12-17-1971	5-16-1972
George B. Shultz	Romana Banuelos	6-12-1972	5-8-1974
William E. Simon	Francine I. Neff	6-21-1974	1-19-1977
W. Michael Blumenthal	Azie Taylor Morton	9-12-1977	8-4-1979
G. William Miller	Azie Taylor Morton	8-6-1979	1-4-1981
Donald T. Regan	Angela M. Buchanan	3-7-1981	7-1-1983
Donald T. Regan	Katherine Davalos Ortega	9-23-1983	1-29-1985
James A. Baker III	Katherine Davalos Ortega	1-29-1985	8-17-1988
Nicholas F. Brady	Katherine Davalos Ortega	9-15-1988	6-30-1989
Nicholas F. Brady	Catalina Vasquez Villalpando	12-11-1989	1-20-1993
Lloyd Bentsen	Mary Ellen Withrow	3-1-1994	12-22-1994
Robert E. Rubin	Mary Ellen Withrow	1-10-1995	—

*During her term of office, Mrs. Elston married Walter L. Kabis; the first time the signature of a United States Treasurer had been changed during the term of office.